Business Studies

Second Edition

Ian Marcousé

Andrew Gillespie   Barry Martin

Malcolm Surridge   Nancy Wall

Marie Brewer   Andrew Hammond

Ian Swift   Nigel Watson

Edited by

Ian Marcousé

Hodder Arnold

A MEMBER OF THE HODDER HEADLINE GROUP

This Second Edition is dedicated to the
memory of Tim Gregson-Williams. He
will be sorely missed.

The *Business Studies Teacher's Book, Second Edition*
(ISBN: 0340-81111-0, publishing August 2003)
provides comprehensive and detailed answers to all the
questions and exercises in *Business Studies, Second
Edition*.

Also available are *Business Studies for AS, Second
Edition* (ISBN: 0340-81112-9, publishing July 2003)
and *Business Studies for AS Teacher's Book, Second
Edition* (ISBN: 0340-81113-7, publishing August 2003).

Orders: please contact Bookpoint Ltd, 130 Milton Park, Abingdon,
Oxon OX14 4SB. Telephone: (44) 01235 827720, Fax: (44) 01235
400454. Lines are open from 9.00 – 6.00, Monday to Saturday, with a 24
hour message answering service. You can also order through our
website: www.hoddereducation.co.uk

British Library Cataloguing in Publication Data
A catalogue record for this title is available from The British Library

ISBN-10: 0 340 81110 2
ISBN-13: 978 0 340 81110 8

First published 1999
Second edition published 2003
Impression number   10 9 8 7 6
Year   2007 2006

Copyright © 1999, 2003 Ian Marcousé, Andrew Gillespie, Barry Martin,
Malcolm Surridge, Nancy Wall, Marie Brewer, Andrew Hammond,
Ian Swift, Nigel Watson (© 1999 Clive Ruscoe)

Cover illustration from Jon H. Hamilton
Typeset by GreenGate Publishing Services, Tonbridge, Kent
Printed in Dubai for Hodder Arnold, an imprint of Hodder Education,
a division of Hodder Headline, 338 Euston Road, London NW1 3BH

CONTENTS

PEOPLE IN ORGANISATIONS

OPERATIONS MANAGEMENT

EXTERNAL INFLUENCES ON BUSINESS

OBJECTIVES AND STRATEGY

BUSINESS SKILLS AND EXAM TECHNIQUES

INTRODUCTION

How to use this book

This book is written for students of AS and Advanced Level Business Studies. It is also suited to first year undergraduates and to those studying a wide range of professional courses. The 95 units of the book are organised into several main sections:

Units 1–13	Marketing
Units 14–29	Finance
Units 30–45	People in Organisations
Units 46–59	Operations Management
Units 60–74	External Influences on Business
Units 75–87	Objectives and Strategy
Units 88–95	Business Skills and Exam Techniques

Each unit is self contained. Therefore it is not necessary to read the units in the sequence in which they appear. Nevertheless references are made to other units, so that the reader can see where to find related topics.

The units have a common style. They start by defining key terms, move on to explain the key issues within the topic, then identify 'Issues for Analysis' and conclude with 'An evaluation'. Within the text are a number of 'In Business' up-to-date mini case studies, each selected to show how the textbook theory applies in the real world. At the end of each unit is a 'Workbook' section with revision questions and exercises. The book also has an exceptionally detailed index, to enable readers to quickly find what they need.

Business Studies is written by a team of experienced teachers and examiners in the subject. It is up to date and full of real case material. Even so, the students who will get the most out of the book are those who are regularly reading extra business stories in newspapers or magazines. Business television programmes are also very useful. In every case, the chances of exam success are maximised by thinking, while watching or reading, about the textbook concepts implied by the material. A television programme on Japan might refer to the huge size of the market; the student should then think: 'economies and diseconomies of scale' or 'market segmentation'. Practising business concepts in this way is a valuable aid to memory and understanding.

Note to students

What is a textbook for? It provides a useful reference book, of course, for when you need to know more about a topic to answer a case study question. It also provides a huge number of questions and exercises to enable you to test yourself in preparation for a test or exam. This book attempts to provide something more, however. It is written to be read. The text is intended to be a lively, relatively easy read. It contains plenty of real business examples and is always focused upon a key area of Business Studies. The book can be used, therefore, as a prime source of the wider reading that is at the heart of every student success.

Other valuable reading matter includes:

The Complete A–Z Handbook of Business Studies, Lines, Marcousé and Martin, Hodder & Stoughton 2003
Business Review – a quarterly business magazine published by Philip Allan, Market Place, Deddington, OX15 0SE
Sunday newspapers such as *The Sunday Times*, the *Observer* and the *Mail on Sunday*.

Note to teachers

This book sets out to help develop a student's skills from GCSE standard up through AS level to full A level. No textbook can 'produce' A grades, but this one does aspire to help achieve high grades by combining an accessible style of writing with more demanding sections outlining the 'Issues for Analysis' and 'An evaluation'. The 'Workbook' sections also move up the skill levels from knowledge through application and analysis to demanding, evaluative questions.

Business Studies is packed with questions. They broadly fall into three categories:

1. REVISION QUESTIONS

These are designed to be answered after reading a unit. They represent a moderately challenging way of getting the students to reflect on the key terms and themes within the text. It is envisaged that this will be an effective way to introduce a topic (releasing teaching time for activities rather than chalk and talk). It will also, in extremis, be a way to achieve reasonable coverage of syllabus areas if timetable pressures mean that not everything can be taught.

The revision questions are written at AS or at A level standard, depending on the subject content. In some cases both standards are provided. The AS questions require recall and explanation, with some minor elements of application. The A level questions are more analytic.

2. DATA RESPONSE QUESTIONS

Although not all syllabuses use data response as a form of assessment, it remains an excellent way of providing a challenging, but not too long, exercise for home or classwork. Most of the data response questions are written at AS standard. In other words they are primarily testing application and analysis rather than evaluation. The authors believe that there is no better data response question than one based upon today's newspaper. Nevertheless these exercises will provide a useful fallback position for when current news is not as helpful as it might be.

3. CASE STUDIES

Business Studies contains more than 90 new case studies. Most are tailored specifically to the syllabus material within a unit. For example, the Market Research unit contains a study on research at Braebourne Water. The focused nature of the cases should make them much easier to use than the broader, integrated cases supplied in case study books or photocopiable packs. Only the cases in the integrated units at the end of each section of the book have clear synoptic elements.

The *Business Studies Teacher's Book Second Edition* is also available (ISBN: 0340–81111–0). It provides answers and mark schemes to the Workbook questions and also a reading list for every unit in the book. It is an invaluable resource.

Acknowledgements

Many people have contributed hugely to this book. Other than the authors, few put in as much work as the person responsible for the cover design: Pauline Stacey. This remarkable A level student put in hundreds of hours perfecting the design of the cover, the back cover and the spine. Professional designers then took over, but Pauline's energy and creativity was an example to anyone who doubts Herzberg's theory of motivation.

Other students have been helpful at various stages with the text itself. Taking pride of place are Vivien Wilson and Richard Thorburn. Intelligent and constructive criticism was also received from Chris Thompson, Melanie Coutinho, Hoshil Popat and Daniel Martyn. My thanks to them all.

The idea for the book emerged from many lunchtime sessions at the Hodder and Stoughton canteen between Tim Gregson-Williams and Ian Marcousé. Both knew there was a need for a new, more appropriate textbook for modern Business Studies courses. Finding the time was the hardest bit! After that problem was overcome, Ian designed the chapter structure and key features and put the writing team together. At GreenGate Publishing, David Mackin and Katie Chester performed miracles.

From the point of view of the authors, every family member has been inconvenienced and therefore deserves our gratitude and apologies. Probably Ian's family and dog suffered most, so a particular apology to Maureen, Claire, Jonny and Jumble.

It is also important to acknowledge that books such as this can only be written because of the wonderful resources of libraries such as the City Business Library, the Birkbeck Library and Senate House Library. The Financial Times Annual Reports service also deserves a special mention. The Internet is a wonder, but serious research cannot yet ignore the quality of the resources available on paper.

Ian Marcousé

The authors and publisher would like to thank the following for permission to reproduce copyright text material:

The Associated Examining Board for granting permission to reproduce Paper 2 (0650/2), Summer 1997 and Paper 3 (A/BUS/3), Summer 1998 on pages 610–613. Also, for permission to reproduce brief extracts from the following mark schemes plus additional AEB material as detailed in text: Mark Scheme, Paper 3, Summer 1998 (A/BUS/3) and Mark Scheme, Paper 7, Summer 1998 (0650N).

Any answers or hints on answers are the sole responsibility of the author and have not been provided or approved by the AEB.

AQA pages 624, 628; The Association of the British Pharmaceutical Industry, page 380; Bank of England, page 458; The Benchmarking Exchange, page 363; *The Birmingham Post*, page 325; *British Airways Reports and*

Accounts, 1997–1998, page 259; Butterworth Heinemann Publishers, a division of Reed Educational & Professional Publishing Ltd., page 255; Capstone Publishing (extracts from *The Ultimate Book of Business Quotations*, Stuart Crainer, 1997), pages 2, 68, 226, 236, 250, 358, 386; *Caterer and Hotelkeeper*, page 542; Century Business Books, page 263; Coca-Cola, page 256; Consumers' Association, *The Which? Hotel Guide 2002*, page 445; Elsevier Science, page 573; *The Engineer*, page 394; *The Express on Sunday*, page 277; *Growing Business*, page 139; *Financial Times*, pages 16, 41, 236, 239, 241, 251, 287, 325, 340, 370, 401, 404, 438, 446, 480, 490, 494, 519, 525, 554; Frederick Herzberg, page 221; HarperCollins, pages 231–232; Inland Revenue website, page 476; Institute of Business Ethics website, page 497; Kogan Page Ltd., page 597; KPMG Consulting, page 397; Macmillan Publishers Ltd. (extract from *Mastering Accounting*, 1983), page 316; National Institute of Economic and Social Research, pages 445, 453, 456, 464, 465, 524; Office for National Statistics, pages 426, 433, 435, 436, 439, 440, 450, 451, 457; Ohmae, K, *The Mind of the Strategist*, Penguin, 1983, page 592; *Personnel Today*, page 300; Pizza Express PLC, page 164; © 1996 by James Womack and Daniel Jones, Pocket Books, a division of Simon & Schuster, page 358; Regester Larkin Ltd, page 603; *The Scotsman*, page 395; Texas Instruments website, pages 495, 496; *The Birmingham Post*, page 325; *The Economist*, pages 299, 442, 523; The European Commission, pages 442, 447, 466; *The Grocer*, pages 15, 53, 55–56, 71–72, 209-210, 539; *The Guardian*, pages 151 296–297, 509; *The Independent*, pages 412, 438, 504, 508; *The Sunday Times*, pages 17, 275, 454; *The Times*, pages 44 (© Times Newspapers Limited, 2002), 49 (© Times Newspapers Limited, 1998), 55–56, 134 (© Times Newspapers Limited, 1998), 72 (© Times Newspapers Limited, 1998), 80 (© Times Newspapers Limited, 1998), 81 (© Times Newspapers Limited, 1998), 138, 275 (© Times Newspapers Limited, 2002); Unilever, page 262; The World Bank, pages 424, 462; West Yorkshire Trading Standards Service, page 488.

The authors and publisher would also like to thank the following for permission to reproduce copyright illustrative material:

© Amet Jean Pierre/Corbis Sygma, page 79; Associated Press, pages 467, 469, 497; Castrol International, page 599; © W. Cody/Corbis, page 430; © Darama/Corbis, page 238; © Dave G Houser/Corbis, page 74; Corbis-Bettman, pages 37, 219, 345, 344, 535; Dell Computer Corporation, page 70; Dyson, page 377; © Shamim Ferdaus/Corbis Sygma, page 68; Format Partners, pages 298, 450; Jennifer Bates/Friends of the Earth, page 510; © Gillette, page 385; © Getty Images/AFP, page 156; Greenpeace, page 513; © The Image Bank/Getty Images, page 427; © Zen Icknow/Corbis, page 425; © Bob Krist/Corbis, page 199; the Kent and Sussex Courier, page 267; Life File, pages 74, 260; Mars, page 581; Microsoft Corporation, page 535 (Corbis/Wolfgang Kaehler); © Bruce Peebles/Corbis, page 344; © Jose Luis Pelaez/Corbis, page 298; © Steve Prezant/Corbis, page 298; Richmond Foods, page 213, 345; Safeway, page 409; Sign UK/Faversham House Group Ltd, page 18; © Greg Smith/Corbis Saba, page 546; Sony, page 378; www.wembleystadium.com, page 343; © Ian Walton/Getty Images, page 68.

Every effort has been made to trace copyright holders but this has not been possible in all cases; any omissions brought to our attention will be corrected in future printings.

MARKETING – INTRODUCTION AND OVERVIEW

DEFINITION
Marketing is the process of learning about your customers and competitors, so that you can provide the right products at the right price in the right place, promoted in the right way to achieve your business objectives.

1.1 Where do you start?

The starting point is to gather accurate market knowledge. A successful business needs to understand its customers' needs, wants, habits and attitudes. For a small firm, this may be easy. The baker who bakes bread and cakes by night and serves customers by day will learn exactly how crusty and how airy the bread should be, how jammy the doughnuts and so on. Larger firms cannot reproduce this closeness between the decision makers and the customers. They require other approaches.

For the large firm, market knowledge consists of five main elements:

- knowing the size of the market (the value of purchases made by all the customers)
- knowing the competitors' market shares, their brand images and their strengths and weaknesses
- understanding your existing customers' habits, likes, dislikes and their image of your product compared with rivals; how loyal are they?
- understanding the image and attitudes buyers of rival products have towards yours; why are they not buying yours?
- knowing the key distribution methods and outlets.

Gaining this knowledge requires time, money and expertise. A great deal can be found through secondary and primary research (see Unit 4). Facts and figures can be gathered easily, though perhaps expensively. Much harder is to gain a full understanding of the psychology of the consumer. For example, when smokers of Benson & Hedges King Size are asked why they buy that brand, they usually suggest product quality and/or taste. In other words, they give an answer that sounds sensible. Yet in blind product tests (a taste test with the brand name removed), Benson & Hedges smokers cannot tell their brand from any other. Therefore the sensible answer is not the real one. Psychology-based research such as a group discussion is needed to reveal that image-based reasons are the key in this case.

Business IN

THE MIGHTY RED

Red Bull is a marketing phenomenon. Launched in 1995 to a baffled audience, its slogan 'Red Bull gives you wings' meant nothing until clubbers discovered its huge jolt of caffeine. Achieving shop distribution was difficult at first, despite providing retailers with far higher profit margins than on other drinks. Word of mouth and TV advertising helped push sales to £90 million by 2000. Then the Austrian owners found a way to boost sales further, by getting motorway service stations to sell it as a stimulant to help keep drivers from getting drowsy. Sales in 2001 ballooned to £150 million in Britain alone – a sales figure higher than the worldwide revenues generated by Manchester United plc. The Mighty Reds beaten by Mighty Red Bull.

Having acquired strong market knowledge, firms use it to analyse the marketplace. The main method is segmentation analysis. This means identifying the key characteristics within the market. This can reveal important sub-sectors within the market, such as super-premium lagers (extra strong lagers such as Carlsberg Special Brew). If sales within this sector are growing faster than the beer market as a whole, breweries will analyse the different needs of consumers within the sub-groups. This may lead to a new product aimed at a particular type of customer within the sector.

1.2 How do you decide what to do?

The key to all decision making is clear objectives. In other words, you must know exactly what you are trying to achieve. This sounds obvious, but the business reality is harder. A firm with a 17% market share wants to grow. It is tempted to set a target of 25% share within four years. Yet is it realistic? If it proves impossible to achieve, the consequences may be serious. After all, a **marketing** objective of growth may trigger increases in production capacity. In other words, extra machinery may be bought or even a new factory opened to cope with the expected increases in demand and therefore output. If the extra demand never comes, the firm will be left with expensive, under-used equipment.

Objectives must be set with sufficient optimism to make the targets challenging – but should never become unrealistic.

With objectives clarified, the next step is to identify the right strategy. Firms usually identify two or three alternative approaches. Then use market research to help make a choice. For example, sales growth may come from a new product launch, or a revamp of an existing product. Research will help forecast the effect on sales of each option. Unit 2 shows in more detail how firms make marketing decisions.

MARKETING OBJECTIVES	POSSIBLE MARKETING STRATEGIES
Increase market share from 17% to 25% within 3 years	Reposition our Brand XYZ in the mass-market sector by cutting its price; launch new upmarket, high-price brands in each of the next 3 years
Within 2 years, to increase to 30% the proportion of our sales coming from new products	Increase the new product development budget by 50% and the market research budget by 30%
Reduce the proportion of over-60s among our market from 40% to 25% over the next 2 years	Relaunch our product with livelier, younger packaging and advertising; use direct mail to offer free samples to those who have just qualified to vote

1.3 Are there any keys to marketing success?

Many markets change continually, as consumer tastes change, the ferocity of competition changes, or as a result of changing technology. Yet there are some marketing principles which always prove valuable.

JUMP BEFORE YOU'RE PUSHED

Apple was the first provider of user-friendly personal computers. It enjoyed a cult status and huge brand loyalty, even in the face of fierce competition from the suppliers of IBM-compatible PCs. Even as Windows

EXPERTS SAY:

'*Marketing is not a function, it is the whole business seen from the customer's point of view.*'
Peter Drucker, the ultimate management guru

'*Marketing is too important to be left to the marketing department.*'
David Packard, computer company founder

'*Marketing strategy is a series of integrated actions leading to a sustainable competitive advantage.*'
John Sculley, Pepsi chief

'*Every company should work hard to obsolete its own product line ... before its competitors do.*'
Philip Kotler, marketing expert

'*The railroads collapsed because they thought they were in the railroad business, when really they were in the transportation business ... they were product oriented instead of customer oriented.*'
Theodore Levitt, Harvard Business School marketing guru

'*While great devices are invented in the laboratory, great products are invented in the marketing department.*'
William Davidor, author

Source: The *Ultimate Book of Business Quotations*, Stuart Crainer, Capstone Publishing, 1997

software made PCs increasingly easy to use, Apple continued to assume its products were the best. Accordingly, it priced them high; typically they cost 25% more than PCs. Only when sales slid dramatically in 1996/97 did the company start to rethink. But too late. It only acted when pushed.

Contrast Apple's approach with that of Philip Morris, producer of the world's biggest selling brand – Marlboro cigarettes. Philip Morris boldly jumped to destroy the threat to its brand posed by price-cutting, discount brands – even at the short-term cost of a profit reduction of over $1 billion.

The lesson taught by these examples is that successful marketing is about anticipating change, not just reacting to it. Firms should not wait until established brands are slipping before devising a strategy for giving them a new lease of life.

EXPLOIT YOUR ASSETS

Anyone can analyse a market to obtain market knowledge (given sufficient time and money). Therefore any firm can find out what customers want – and supply it. This means competition is fierce, so profit is hard to come by. For example, if a producer of fridges spotted an opportunity for red, instead of white, doors – a few months' of sales advantage would soon disappear when rivals copied the idea.

The answer is asset-led marketing. This means making decisions based not only on consumer needs, but also on the business's strengths. BMW researchers might find that its customers want a smaller, less powerful BMW for their 17–20-year-old sons and daughters. This opportunity may exist, but the firm may decide that a smaller, low cost BMW would make little or no use of the company's strengths. In this case it would have no advantages over Ford or Renault, and BMW would not want to compete.

Companies analyse the market, then see which opportunities allow them to draw on their strengths. A good example was when Mars investigated the ice-cream market in 1989. The company identified an opportunity for an adult-oriented, high quality, premium priced choc ice. The long-established Mars bar enabled a move into the ice-cream market from a position of strength (see Figure 1.1).

Some firms hold onto neither a market oriented nor an asset-led approach. They are still rooted in product orientation. This means that business decisions are

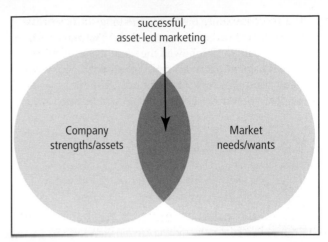

Figure 1.1

based upon the convenience and attitudes of the production staff, rather than the customer. This approach may work in certain situations. Where market change is constant, however, the firm will soon get left behind.

Of the three possibilities (product oriented, market oriented and asset-led), companies following the latter course are the most likely to succeed in the long term.

KEEP AWARE OF CONSUMER PSYCHOLOGY

When sales are falling, firms often respond by cutting prices. This was Sainsbury's reaction to Tesco's achievement of market leadership in the mid-1990s. It is the reaction seen in every high street to a bad period of trading. The result is likely to be a sales increase. If prices are cut sufficiently, sales may leap ahead. Yet what is the point of a sales increase, unless profit is boosted too? As its chief executive explained in 1997, Sainsbury's '… panicked. Instead of reinforcing its leadership credentials – quality and choice – it competed on price … which led to lower profit margins.'

The problem with cutting prices is the effect on consumer image. A strong brand with a prestigious image may become an 'also-ran' if promoted regularly at hefty discounts. And once lost, a good image is hard to regain.

Consumer psychology is also affected by other messages, such as promotional offers. '25% extra FREE!' is attractive to everyone, but when offered too often, may devalue the key to long-term success – the strength of the brand name.

BOB, BARNEY AND THOMAS

In 2002, HIT Entertainment made profits of nearly £25 million on sales of just over £100 million. Yet just a few years before it was losing money heavily. Why the turnaround? At the heart of it was one man, *Bob the Builder*. HIT is the animation company behind *Bob the Builder* and *Barney the Dinosaur*. In 2001 Bob became a global phenomenon, propelling HIT to become the fourth largest children's video distributor in the massive American market. In 2002 Bob and Barney were joined by another star, as HIT bought the company with the rights to *Thomas the Tank Engine* for £130 million. Hit believes it now has the marketing strength to boost distribution and therefore sales of its products worldwide. If so, its brand new programme Rubbadubbers should clean up.

Business IN

Characteristics of three types of firm

MARKET ORIENTED	ASSET-LED MARKETERS	PRODUCT ORIENTED
Monitors and responds to changing fashions	Monitors changing tastes; responds to long-term opportunities	Assumes changing fashions will return to square one – to the company's benefit
Wide range of product lines, pack sizes, colours and styles ('The customer's always right')	A few main product lines; wide range of options, but only supplies to order	One or two product lines with few options ('Trust us, we know best')
Promotional activity based upon special offers, competitions and eye-catching display	Promotional activity based on long-term, image-building advertising	Little promotional spending; focus on providing information through brochures

Certain companies have achieved long-term, world-wide marketing success, for instance Levi's, Coca-Cola and McDonald's. All followed the same strategy: consistent, heavy spending on advertising campaigns to develop a strong consumer image of the brand. Unit 7 shows in more detail how a marketing strategy can be developed.

1.4 Integrated marketing

Whenever a marketing decision is to be made, three questions must be asked:

- can we afford it?
- can we produce it?
- what knock-on effects may it have?

CAN WE AFFORD IT?

Large firms have huge marketing budgets. Unilever, for example, spends over £3,000 million (yes, £3 billion) every year on advertising and promotions worldwide. A typical national TV advertising campaign costs in excess of £1 million. So firms have to work out the cost of achieving the marketing objectives they set themselves, and then make sure they can afford that level of expenditure. Often the strategy marketing managers want to adopt costs more than their budget allows. In which case they might – on occasion – request a budget increase. More often, though, they will trim their plans back to stay within their resources. Trimming back may leave them in too weak a position to compete effectively. If Coca-Cola is spending £8 million on TV, Pepsi may be wasting its money spending £3 million on the same medium.

CAN WE PRODUCE IT?

Every marketing decision affects the operations of the business. A major advertising campaign may boost short-term demand by 40%. Have the extra units been produced in advance and stockpiled or is the factory prepared to increase production as soon as the extra demand arrives? Even major companies such as Nestlé

have been caught out by a level of demand they could not meet, causing empty shelves, dissatisfied customers and furious shopkeepers.

Long before a marketing strategy is put into action, therefore, it must be discussed with operations management – those responsible for meeting customer demand.

WHAT ARE THE KNOCK-ON EFFECTS?

Large companies are complex organisations. Decisions made in one department or one country may have knock-on effects elsewhere. The decision by Carlsberg-Tetley in 1996 to market an alcoholic soft drink called 'Thickhead' brought a storm of complaint. It was said to taste of sherbet lemons, and therefore be particularly appealing to young children. Carlsberg-Tetley, like every large company, has many important dealings with government. Attracting howls of consumer and pressure group protest might make future dealings difficult or might start a consumer boycott. The company withdrew the brand.

ISSUES FOR **analysis**

When analysing why a firm pursues a particular marketing approach, or what strategy it might pursue in the future, it is useful to consider the following points:

- Successful marketing must be tailored to the market needs, wants and conditions; therefore no single approach will succeed in all markets at all times.
- Large, established firms have huge advantages over small, new firms; the latter can overcome these, though, if they listen to their customers and respond quickly, flexibly and innovatively to changing tastes.
- Large firms want to make decisions on the basis of quantified, 'scientific' evidence; the most brilliant marketing moves, however, are those requiring judgement or hunch (brilliant leaps into the unknown include Sony's development of PlayStation and Nokia's move from making car tyres to mobile phones!).
- Marketing strategies must change over time, as brands develop from their launch (birth) stage through growth towards maturity (see Unit 5).
- Long-term success comes from knowing your strengths and being consistent about exploiting and publicising them; the most important strength in marketing is a strong brand name.

1.5 Marketing
an evaluation

Marketing lies at the heart of every successful business. Even firms with no marketing department have to be focused upon their customers if they are to succeed. It would be wrong to see marketing as purely passive, though. Marketing managers know they must respond to consumer tastes, but take exceptional delight in persuading people to buy what they do not need, or even want. Sunday colour supplements are full of advertisements for absurdly overpriced 'collectors' items' – and have been for 20 years. *Someone* must be buying! In a wealthy country such as Britain, the ethics of this matter little. Far more controversial is the success of firms such as Nestlé and Coca-Cola in persuading people in developing countries to spend scarce income on highly priced Western products. The power of advertising to persuade can give rise to fierce criticism of the role of marketing.

For most consumers, the great benefit of marketing is its effectiveness at finding out what they want – and then providing it. The huge choice of products in the modern supermarket is a tribute to the success of modern marketing.

KEY terms

marketing – the all-embracing function that links the company with customer tastes to get the right product to the right place at the right time. Marketing decisions are made through the marketing model, based on the findings of market research, and carried out through the marketing mix.

product awareness – the proportion of all those within a target market who are aware of a particular brand/product. Brand leaders such as Coca-Cola may have almost 100% awareness, whereas only 60% of soft drink buyers are aware of 7-Up.

AS Level Exercises

A. REVISION QUESTIONS

(40 marks; 80 minutes)

Read the unit, then answer:

1 Explain the need for 'accurate market knowledge'. *(4)*
2 Distinguish between primary and secondary research. *(4)*
3 How might segmentation analysis help:
  a Tesco Stores decide on their future marketing strategy *(4)*
  b Heinz decide on the marketing of their salad cream. *(4)*
4 Suggest a suitable strategy to meet the following marketing objectives:
  a building up sales of Werther's Original through non-traditional outlets such as cinemas *(4)*
  b shifting the image of Marks and Spencer to make it younger and trendier. *(4)*
5 Identify two strengths and two weaknesses of product orientation. *(4)*
6 What is meant by the term 'consumer psychology'? *(3)*
7 Identify three problems that might arise from a failure to integrate marketing decisions into decisions made elsewhere in a business. *(3)*
8 What would you judge to be the most useful piece of marketing advice given in this unit? Explain and justify your answer. *(6)*

B. REVISION EXERCISES

B1 Case Study

After a fruitless job hunt, Juan Olaria returned to college to start up a driving school business on-site.

He rented a small office opposite the student social area and set up a computer system for monitoring bookings and cash flow. Obtaining the cars was no problem, as his parents ran a second-hand car business. The arrangement was that Juan rented the cars for £30 per day, as and when he needed them.

Before opening, Juan had to decide on his marketing strategy. His primary target market was college students and his service would be based on second-hand cars. It was not hard to decide, therefore, that his prices should be relatively low. But how low? And did he need to promote his business, or could he rely solely on word of mouth?

Telephoning round the driving schools listed in *Yellow Pages* revealed prices of between £14 and £18 per hour. Some offered starter packages at £50 for five lessons, but there was little other evidence of promotional pricing. There were no driving advertisements in the local newspaper, so it seemed that directories such as *Yellow Pages* were the only form of advertising used by competitors.

Juan considered relying solely on word of mouth, but eventually decided to advertise on local radio. £300 bought him five spots but, more importantly, made it easier to write a more exciting press release for the local newspaper and radio journalists. The story of the student's bold move into business featured strongly over the following weeks. It achieved exactly what Juan had hoped for – several enquiries from students at other schools and colleges in the district. Juan's business was motoring.

Questions *(40 marks; 50 minutes)*

1 Outline Juan's marketing objectives and strategy. *(8)*

2 How well suited was his strategy to his objectives? *(6)*

3 a Explain the meaning of 'market segmentation'. *(3)*

3 b How effectively did Juan apply this approach? *(6)*

4 Why might driving schools use only directories rather than other forms of media advertising? *(7)*

5 To build his business in the medium term, Juan may need to attract a wider market than just students. What problems may he face if he attempts to broaden his customer-base in this way? *(10)*

B2 Case Study

Pizza the Action

In January 1998, David Di Mello left his job as marketing manager of Pizza Foods to start up his own pizza business. He had noticed the shift in consumer demand away from cheap frozen pizza slices and own-label pizzas. He believed the time was ripe for American-style super-premium pizzas. Made with fresh dough which rises in the oven, smells superb and tastes special. Selling at a 20% price premium, these had already swept through the American retail market.

David's target was partly the major retail brands such as McCain's and Goodfellas, and partly the buoyant take-away and delivery markets. His first year sales target was to take 1% of the £400 million take-away market and 2% of the main-meal pizza market.

David had already signed an exclusive UK distribution deal with a major American supplier of Mama Frescha pizzas. To achieve effective sales and distribution, he made an arrangement with Nestlé. The marketing he would handle himself.

He decided his target market was 25–30-year-olds without kids. His budget allowed for £100,000 to be spent on advertising in the first year, but how should it be spent? On image-building colour magazine advertising or on door-to-door leaflets and special offers? Now was the time to decide.

The UK pizza market: actual and forecast sales

	1996	1999 (est)
Retail – main-meal pizzas	£177m	£210m
Retail – other	£73m	£70m
Restaurant	£540m	£590m
Take-away	£310m	£400m
Other	£88m	£100m
Total	£1,188m	£1,370m

Questions *(20 marks; 25 minutes)*

1 What value of sales does David expect for the first year of his business? *(3)*

2 From the figures in the table, does David seem to have targeted the right segments of the market? *(3)*

3 The three main producers in the retail sector of the pizza market have a market share of over 40% between them. What problems might that pose for David's business? *(5)*

4 David's objective is to set up a business which will be successful for at least 10 years. In the light of this, consider which of the two promotional options he should choose. *(9)*

MARKETING OBJECTIVES AND DECISION MAKING

DEFINITION

Marketing objectives are the marketing targets that must be achieved for the company to achieve its overall goals. Examples include 'Boosting sales from 600,000 to 1 million in two years' or 'Repositioning our product to make it appeal more to the under-25s'.

The link between marketing objectives and decision making is that decisions have to be based upon a clear sense of direction. That direction is provided by clear objectives.

2.1 How are marketing objectives set?

AT A VERY SENIOR LEVEL IN THE COMPANY

In most firms, marketing is central to board-level strategic decisions. Not marketing in the sense of price cuts and promotions, but marketing in the sense of analysing growth trends and the competitive struggle within the firm's existing markets. And decisions about which markets the firm wishes to develop in future. For example, in early 1997, the business giant Unilever (Walls, Persil, Birds Eye, CK One and much else) set its sights on obtaining one-third of its world-wide sales from Asian markets by the year 2001. This company objective was based upon observation of the rapid growth rates in economies such as Singapore, Taiwan and China.

This company objective of growth in Asia enabled the directors to decide the marketing objectives. So, did this company objective of one-third of sales coming from the Far East mean the *marketing* objectives were exactly the same? Not quite, because there were other options. Unilever had the financial strength to buy Asian businesses and therefore 'buy' sales. It may not have been necessary to increase sales in Asia on existing product lines. In fact they chose a combination of buying local firms and boosting the marketing on existing brands. The target was met by 2002.

ROOTED IN THE COMPANY'S VISION OF ITS FUTURE (ITS MISSION)

A **vision** is a company's projection of what it wants to achieve in the future. It should be ambitious, relevant, easy to communicate and capable of motivating staff. Or even inspiring them. Bill Gates' 1980s vision for Microsoft was 'A computer on every desk and in every home'. Today, that seems uninspiring, even obvious. In the 1980s it seemed extraordinary.

A firm's marketing objectives need to reflect the firm's long-term aims/mission. The American car company Chrysler's mission statement says 'Our purpose is to produce cars and trucks that people will want to buy, will enjoy driving, and will want to buy again'. This sets the background for marketing objectives that focus on developing new, probably niche market, exciting rather than ordinary cars.

In his book *Even More Offensive Marketing*, Hugh Davidson suggests there are six requirements for a successful company vision. See the table on the following page.

BY STRIKING A BALANCE BETWEEN WHAT IS ACHIEVABLE AND WHAT IS CHALLENGING

Objectives work best when they are clear, achievable, challenging and – above all else – when staff believe in them. To fit all these criteria, the firm must root the objectives in market realities.

In 1999 the Chairman of Iceland frozen food stores set a new objective. He wanted to reposition the stores to appeal to wealthier, middle class customers. All Iceland foods would be organic and GM-free. There would be no more Buy One Get One Free offers. By early 2000 the plan had flopped and the Chairman resigned. The company had attempted an objective that was out of line with marketplace reality. It was too ambitious.

Marketing objectives should not be set until the decision makers have a clear view of current customer behaviour and attitudes. This will probably require a lot of market research into customer usage and attitudes to the different products they buy and don't buy.

REQUIREMENT	COMMENT
1 Provides future direction	As shown in the above examples of Microsoft and Chrysler
2 Expresses a consumer benefit	e.g. Prêt à Manger: 'Our mission is to sell handmade extremely fresh food …'
3 Realistic	Realistic? Conservative Party 1997: 'Our mission is to create the greatest volunteer party in the Western democratic world.' Within five years party membership and morale collapsed.
4 Motivating	The Body Shop: 'Tirelessly work to narrow the gap between principle and practice, whilst making fun, passion and care part of our daily lives.'
5 Fully communicated	Easy to achieve if it's as simple as Kwik Fit's 'To get customers back on the road speedily, achieving 100% customer delight.'
6 Consistently followed in practice	A company might claim to be at the leading edge of technology; it will lose all credibility if it reacts to the next recession by cutting spending on research and development

Another key aspect is the marketing budget. How much can the business afford to spend on marketing? There is no point in setting a bold objective unless the resources are available to enable it to be met.

Once the marketplace and financial factors have been considered, objectives can be decided which stretch people, but do not make them snap. Cadbury's has had a 30% share of the UK chocolate market for decades. Setting a target of 35% for two years' time would be implausible. After all, will Mars or Nestlé just sit and watch? A wise marketing director might accept the challenge of 32% in two years' time – but would warn everyone that it might be very difficult to achieve this. (Note: each 1% of the chocolate market represents over £20 million of sales, so these matters are not trivial.)

2.2 Types of marketing objective

There are four main types of marketing objective:

- increasing product differentiation
- growth
- continuity
- innovation.

ZARA

One day in 1998 saw an unusual event. The deputy editor of Vogue queued outside a new shop in London's Regent Street, waiting for it to open for the first time. Furthermore, this was a shop famed in Europe for its low prices, not for its designer labels. It was Zara, a retailer that never advertises and is run by a man who never gives interviews. He is also one of the richest men in Europe, with a £6,000 million fortune.

Amancio Ortega set up in business in 1963, with 5,000 pesetas (about £18). In 1975 he opened his first Zara store in Spain. Ortega built the business around the insight that modern women want fashionable, good quality clothes – and that being fashionable requires a production system that quickly translates catwalk fashions into new clothes on the shop rails. When a new look hits the fashion pages or the front pages of newspapers, Zara's versions are usually in its shops within two weeks.

Zara's progress throughout Spain, then continental Europe, then Britain, has been as rapid as that of Gap and H&M. Yet Zara is the most profitable by far. Its October 2002 opening of its largest store ever, in Oxford Street, London, saw a scrum of shoppers. For Zara, word of mouth has been enough to build a retail empire.

IN Business

INCREASING PRODUCT DIFFERENTIATION

Product differentiation is the extent to which consumers see your product as different from the rest. It is the key to ensuring that customers buy you because they want you – not because you're the cheapest. It is a major influence on the value added and therefore profit margins achieved by the product.

To increase product differentiation requires a fully integrated marketing programme. Objectives must be set which separate your product from its rivals. These include:

- distinctive design and display
- unusual distribution channels – avoiding supermarkets, perhaps
- advertising based on image building, not sales boosting, e.g. television and cinema advertising rather than blockbuster sales promotions or competitions
- an integrated marketing programme focused solely upon the relevant age group or type of person.

GROWTH

Some firms see growth as their main purpose and their main security blanket. They may reason that once they are Number 1, no-one else will be able to catch them. So they set sales or market share targets which encourage staff to push hard for greater success.

This is understandable but may prove self-defeating. A school or college pushing hard for rapid growth in student numbers would risk damaging its reputation. Class sizes would rise, hastily recruited new staff may be ineffective, middle management would be overstretched and quality standards would be at risk.

Just these things – and worse – happened during the 1980s and 1990s boom in private pensions. Giant companies such as Prudential were later condemned for mis-selling, as sales staff persuaded millions of people to abandon good, safe pension schemes. The sales staff were earning huge commissions on every sale, and the private pension companies were delighted by the sales growth. But in 1997 the new Labour government started naming and shaming the companies responsible for persuading people to buy an inferior pension. Years of building up the good name of a brand such as Prudential was being threatened. And the companies were forced to spend billions of pounds compensating those who had been sold an inappropriate pension.

Of course, the pursuit of growth does not have to lead to disaster. The rapid growth of Prêt à Manger in recent years was in response to buoyant consumer demand. If Prêt had not rushed to satisfy this demand for high quality sandwiches, other companies would have done so. Therefore the company's objective of rapid growth was very sensible. Too slow would have become too late.

CONTINUITY FOR THE LONG TERM

The companies which own major brands such as Levi's, Bacardi or Cadbury's know that true success comes from taking a very long-term view. Unilever even tells its brand managers that their key role is to hand over a stronger brand to their successor. In other words they must think ahead 10 years or so.

Doubtless Bacardi could boost sales and profits this year by running price promotions with the major supermarkets and off-licences. Or next year by launching Bacardi iced lollies or bubble gum. But where would the brand's reputation be in a few years' time? Would it still be a classy drink to ask for at a bar?

Large firms think a great deal about their corporate image and the image of the brands they produce. They may try to stretch their brands a little, to attract new customers. Yet Cadbury's must always mean chocolate, not just snack products. Levi's must always mean jeans, not just clothes. Only in this way can the brands continue to add value in the long term.

INNOVATION

In certain, major sectors of the economy, a key to long-term competitive success is innovation. In other words bringing new product or service ideas to the marketplace. There are two main categories of business where innovation is likely to be crucial: fashion-related and technology-related, as shown in the following table.

JD WETHERSPOON

JD Wetherspoon's growth has been astonishingly rapid within the mature, saturated pub market. From sales of less than £5 million in 1990, turnover rose to £89 million by 1997. To push sales and profits further, managing director John Hutson set the objective of boosting food sales in order to boost revenue per customer. The strategy was to hire food guru Egon Ronay to recommend how to improve food quality and consistency. He brought in new menus and a new staff training programme. The pay-off came quickly, with a sharp increase in food sales. By early 1998 food sales accounted for over 20% of sales, compared with 16% before the new strategy. This element in the company's growth plan helped drive sales forward to £484 million in 2001. With 522 outlets, JD Wetherspoon is now Britain's biggest pub chain.

Business Category	Business Sector
Fashion-related	• The music business • Clothing and footwear • Entertainment, e.g. eating out
Technology-related	• Consumer electronics and IT • Cars and aircraft • Medicines and cosmetics

Timescale	Target (% of sales from products launched in past 5 years)	Strategy for Meeting Target
First year	32	One national new product launch plus another in test market
Second year	35	One national new product launch and two others in test market
Third year	40	Two national new product launches

There are two key elements to innovation: get it right and get in first. Which is the more important? This is not possible to answer, as past cases have given contradictory results. The originator of the filled ice-cream cone was Lyons Maid (now Nestlé) with a product called King Cone. Walls came into the market second with Cornetto. In this case, getting it right proved more important than getting in first. In many other cases, though, the firm in first proved dominant for ever. The Boeing 747; the Sony Walkman; even the humble Findus Crispy Pancake (with its 80% market share); all have built long-term success on the back of getting in first.

The purpose of objectives is to set out exactly what the business wants to achieve. To ensure success, it is helpful to set more limited targets – staging posts en route to the destination. For example, a firm pursuing the objective of innovation may want at least 40% of sales to come from products launched within the past five years. If, at present, only 30% of sales come from this source, a jump to 40% will not be easy. The following targets may help, especially if – as in the table below – they are linked with the strategy for achieving them. Targets such as these:

- ensure that all the marketing staff know what to aim for
- provide a sound basis for cooperation with other departments (such as R&D and operations management)
- provide an early warning of when the strategy is failing to meet the objectives – should it be rethought? Or backed with more resources?
- help psychologically; just as an end-of-year exam can concentrate the mind of a student, so a target can motivate managers to give of their best.

These benefits hinge on a key issue: have the targets been communicated effectively to the staff? This is an obvious point, but vital nonetheless. If the entire marketing department is based in one large office, it would be astonishing if anyone was unaware of new objectives. But what if it is a retail business and there are 400 branches around the country? Then a head office initiative can fall down at the local level, when a local manager thinks he or she knows best. Expertly considered **marketing targets** may fail unless they are communicated effectively to all the relevant staff.

2.4 Marketing objectives and the small firm

Do small firms set aside time to consider, set and write down objectives and targets? Very, very rarely. If you interviewed a dozen small-business proprietors, you might find none who found the time, and several who would regard such time as wasted.

There are two issues here:

1 In a very small firm, with all business decisions taken by the proprietor, the marketing objectives may be clear in the mind of the boss, even though they are not written down. That may work satisfactorily. When the firm gets 15 or more staff, it may have to change.
2 The bosses of small firms often find themselves swamped by day-to-day detail. Customers expect to speak to them personally, staff check every decision and may wait around for their next 'orders'. Only if they learn to delegate will they find the time to think carefully about future objectives and strategy.

There are some bright, young entrepreneurs, however, who apply a more thoughtful approach. Julian Richer identified a gap in the hi-fi market for high quality equipment sold by music enthusiasts at discount prices. This was intended to appeal to younger, more street-wise buyers. The target image was 'fun'. In the summer, customers receive free iced lollies; at Christmas, mince pies. The public face of Richer Sounds was that 'We have a laugh. We don't take ourselves seriously, but we do take our customers seriously'. Behind the scenes, though, careful target setting for stores and sales staff helped Richer Sounds achieve a *Guinness Book of Records* entry for the highest sales per square foot of any store in the UK.

2.5 Constraints on meeting marketing objectives

However well conceived, objectives do not lead automatically to success. Various factors may occur which restrict the chances of the objectives succeeding. These are known as **constraints**. They may occur within the firm (internal constraints) or may be outside its control (external constraints).

INTERNAL CONSTRAINTS

1 Financial constraints affect virtually every aspect of every organisation. Even Manchester United has a budget for players, which the manager must keep within. A marketing objective might be set which is unrealistic, given the firm's limited resources. That is an error of judgement. Or the firm may have the finance in place at the start, but setbacks to the firm may cause budget cuts which make the objectives impossible to reach.
2 Personnel constraints may be important. The objective of diversifying may be appealing, but the firm may lack expertise in the new market. A recruitment campaign may fail to find the right person at a salary the business can afford. This may result in the project being delayed, scrapped or – worst of all – carried on by second rate staff.
3 Market standing. The marketing objectives may be constrained most severely by the firm's own market

position. The big growth sector in food retailing has been in chilled, prepared meals. So why no activity from the food giant Heinz? The answer lies in its success at establishing itself as *the* producer of canned soup and bottled salad cream and ketchup. The Heinz market image (its key marketing asset) is so narrowly focused that customer attitudes constrain it from competing effectively in chilled foods.

EXTERNAL CONSTRAINTS

1   Competition is usually the main constraint outside the firm's control. It is the factor which prevents *The Sun* from charging 50p a copy. It is also the factor which makes it so hard to plan ahead in business. You may set the objective of gaining an extra 1% market share only to be hit by a price war launched by a rival.
2   Consumer taste is also important. If fashion moves against you, there may be little or nothing you can do to stop it. A logical approach is to anticipate the problem by never seeking fashionability. Reebok made the mistake of following Nike down the road of ever-more-trendy trainers. But being permanently trendy required huge promotional spending. Reebok's loss of market share forced it to pull back from the young end of the US trainer market.
3   The economy can also cause huge problems when setting medium-to-long-term objectives. This year's economic boom becomes next year's recession. Sales targets have to be discarded and a move upmarket comes to seem very foolish.

2.6 Marketing decision making – the marketing model

Successful marketing is not just about thinking. It is about decisions and action. Marketing decisions are particularly hard to make, because there are so many uncertainties. The following procedure, shown in Figure 2.1, is one of the most effective ways of ensuring the decision is well thought through.

Figure 2.1

The intention is to ensure that the strategy decided upon is the most effective at achieving the marketing objectives. In this process, market research is likely to be very important. It is crucial for finding out the background data and again for testing the hypotheses. Test marketing may also be used. This is a way of checking whether the market research results are accurate, before finally committing the firm to an expensive national marketing campaign.

The **marketing model** is the way to decide how to turn a marketing objective into a strategy.

ISSUES FOR **analysis**

Marketing objectives are the basis for all marketing strategy. Therefore they will be central to almost every substantial exam question on marketing. For example, pricing decisions will depend upon the objectives. A firm pursuing growth might price a new product relatively cheaply, to ensure high market penetration and to discourage competition. Objectives will also affect the advertising approach: aimed at encouraging loyalty from existing users, or developing a new image/customer base.

To understand objectives fully, it is vital to be able to distinguish them from strategy. It is also important to remember that the setting of objectives cannot be done in isolation. The managers have to bear in mind the market situation, findings from market research and the financial resources and personnel the firm has available. Levi's objective of diversification foundered when it launched a range of two- and three-piece suits. On paper the objective may have looked fine; but in practice it became a classic marketing failure.

2.7 Marketing objectives
an evaluation

What career are you aiming for? If you have a definite answer to that question, you probably have a clear idea how to achieve it. You are also likely to be very well motivated towards the qualifications you need. Most A level students have little idea of what they want to do. In other words they have no objectives. As a result, they have no plan and may struggle to find the motivation to succeed.

Marketing objectives are just as important. They allow a clear strategy to be devised, a plan to be set and give the motivation to succeed. Therefore they are the most important element of marketing.

> **KEY terms**
>
> **constraints** – factors which limit a firm's ability to achieve its objectives.
>
> **marketing model** – a procedure for making marketing decisions in a scientific manner.
>
> **marketing targets** – specific, measurable goals to be achieved within a relatively limited timescale.
>
> **vision** – conceiving where the business wants to be in the future; the term implies something ambitious.

AS Level Exercises

A. REVISION QUESTIONS

(45 marks; 70 minutes)

Read the unit, then answer:

1 Explain why it is important for a business to have clear marketing objectives. (3)
2 What do businesses mean by the term 'vision'? (3)
3 Why is it important that marketing objectives should be rooted in thorough market research? (4)
4 **a** State the four main types of marketing objective. (4)
  b Decide which one is most likely to be important for:
    i Coca-Cola
    ii Yorkie Bars
    iii Dyson Appliances (3)
5 Why might a firm seek to increase the product differentiation of one of its brands? (3)
6 What problems might a firm face if it focuses solely upon short-term objectives? (5)
7 Is it essential that marketing objectives should be written down in detail? Explain your answer. (4)
8 Explain the meaning of the terms:
  a internal constraints (3)
  b external constraints (3)
9 Outline two external constraints that might affect car sales over the coming months. (4)
10 Identify and explain two problems a firm might face if it makes marketing decisions without using a decision making framework such as the marketing model. (6)

B. REVISION EXERCISES

B1 Data Response

Bzheanz Mzheanz Heinz

In Spring 1997 Heinz made its first move into the Russian food market. Although the economy was growing at that time, average wage levels were still very low – typically under £25 per week. Yet Heinz chose to price its baked beans at around 50p per can – the equivalent of charging £5 in Britain.

Heinz had set its sights on the long-term objective of building a prestigious brand name. When the famous beans first came to Britain in 1901 they were sold by Fortnum and Mason for £1.50 per can. Now Heinz was aiming to pull off the same trick again – nearly 100 years later.

Its target sales figure for year 1 was 12 million cans in Russia. This compares with 450 million cans in the UK each year. If the company's strategy is successful, Heinz beans may become the fashionable food to serve at Moscow dinner parties. Even before the move by Heinz, its products were available on the black market. It gained the status accorded to other Western products such as Coca-Cola and Levi's.

The company hoped that Russia would become one of the top five bean-eating countries in the world. This was

before the August 1998 meltdown of the Russian economy that cut living standards sharply. Will Beanz still Mean Roubles? That remainz to be seen.

Questions *(30 marks; 40 minutes)*

1 Identify the company's marketing objective for its beans in Russia. (3)
2 State the target Heinz set as the test of whether its objective was met. (3)
3 **a** Explain the strategy Heinz chose to meet its objectives. (4)
  b Suggest and explain an alternative strategy it might have adopted. (6)
4 **a** Outline the external constraints faced by Heinz. (5)
  b Discuss how a business might react to changed external constraints, if it was determined to achieve its marketing objectives. (9)

B2 Case Study

Hoshil and Sunil's business started in rather dubious circumstances. While students they built up their capital by trading in 'second-hand' mobile phones. Their great friend Jayesh came up with the bright idea. They would open a night club aimed at young Asians. It would have two dance floors, one for Indian music and one for Western pop music. One of the bars would be alcohol-free, have pool tables and music soft enough to chat. It would be a night club, but with some of the benefits of a pub. The vision was clear: to provide a thriving social facility for young Asian men and women.

The investment outlay would be £150,000. Hoshil and Sunil put in £25,000 each and were fortunate that Hoshil's wealthy brother Satyam was able to put in the other £100,000. They would soon be ready to start.

Sunil and Jayesh planned their marketing strategy. The objective was clear: to maximise takings from day 1. They needed to pay back their borrowings as soon as possible. After carrying out market research at their local community centre, the boys decided to focus on better-off 16–24-year-olds. Prices would be kept relatively high, as there was no competition in the area. The location would be in the centre of Croydon, as the new Tramlink service would bring people by public transport from a long way away.

Despite the agreement to focus on the better off, when there was only a week until the opening night, Sunil panicked. Would there be enough people to create a good atmosphere? He printed 2,000 leaflets saying 'Half Price Drinks For All The First Week!' and distributed them through the local newsagents. The opening night went very well and on the following

Saturday it was impossible to move. By the second week, though, the numbers were dropping away. When research was carried out it showed that customers thought the drinks were expensive.

It took about six months to establish a really strong reputation as a top club. Large profits were being made and Hoshil's skills as a host were becoming well known. The national paper The Daily Jang ran a whole feature on him. He was very happy, while Sunil and Satyam were enjoying the large dividends on their investments. Jayesh congratulated them on their achievements, but was focused on his own, new computer business. It was bound to be a success.

Questions *(50 marks; 60 minutes)*

1 Outline the business importance of the following terms:
  a marketing strategy *(5)*
  b market research *(5)*
2 How important to the success of the club were the clear vision and objectives? Explain your answer. *(10)*
3 Discuss which of the four types of marketing objective were involved in this business success. *(8)*
4 How serious a risk did Sunil take by carrying out a marketing campaign that was at odds with the overall strategy? *(10)*
5 What do you consider to be the most important aspects of marketing for a small business? *(12)*

ANALYSING THE MARKET

DEFINITION

A market is a place where buyers and sellers meet. This may be in the street, a giant shopping centre or on the trading floor of a stock exchange. In marketing, though, there is a slightly different meaning for the phrase 'the market'. When businesses refer to the market for their products, they mean the customers. How many there are, whether the number is rising or falling, what their purchasing habits are and much else. Successful marketing relies on a complete understanding of the market.

3.1 What market are we in?

This sounds a daft question, but the marketing guru Theodore Levitt considers it vital. Is Liverpool FC in the football business, the sports business or the leisure business? Tottenham Hotspur nearly went into liquidation in the 1980s because of an unsuccessful diversification towards leisure clothing. Today Chelsea has its own hotel and restaurant complex. Barcelona FC runs an ice hockey team and a basketball side.

When looking at the size and growth of a market, it is essential to be clear on the market under consideration. As the above example shows, it can be difficult to decide on where the market's boundaries are. Even when that is settled, the market can probably be broken down into many sub-sectors. The car market, for example, can be broken down into luxury, executive, large family, small and sports vehicles. The issue of market segmentation is dealt with in more detail in Unit 6.

3.2 Market size and trends

Market size is the measurement of all the sales by all the companies within a marketplace. It can be measured in two ways: by volume and by value. Volume measures the quantity of goods purchased, perhaps in tonnes, in packs or in units. Market size by value is the amount spent by customers on the volume sold. So the difference between volume and value is the price paid per unit.

Take, for example, these figures for the UK yogurt market:

2001 market by value	*£710 million*
2001 market by volume	*2,730 million servings*
Average price per serving	*26.0 pence (£710m/2,730m)*

Source: Key Note Market Report 2002

Market size matters because it is the basis for calculating market share, i.e. the proportion of the total market held by one company or brand. This, in turn, is essential for evaluating the success or failure of a firm's marketing activities. Market size is also the reference point for calculating trends. Is the market size growing or declining? A growth market is far more likely to provide the opportunities for new products to be launched or new distribution initiatives to be successful.

In business, the most worrying markets are where volume is rising but value is falling. This means the average price paid is falling quite rapidly. Computer manufacturers have grown used to this situation. For most firms, though, it is very hard to cope with the combination of extra output/costs with lower value/revenue.

The table at the top of the next page gives an example of some different market sizes (by value), together with their most recent sales trends. The huge differences in market size give a good indication of the sales potential for a new company or a new product. The massive size of the soft drinks market means that the annual increase of 4.9% represents £117 million of extra sales. Plenty of room for new brands of the size of Lilt or Lucozade, which have sales of £20–30 million per annum.

Individual firms can do little to influence the overall growth of a market. Many factors are involved, mostly stemming from broader economic and social changes. The main factors affecting market growth are:

- economic growth, in other words the growth of real incomes throughout the economy; luxury markets will grow rapidly when people feel better off
- social changes, for example the move away from family meals at home has led to above average growth rates for markets such as fast-food, confectionery and prepared sandwiches
- changes in fashion, most obviously in the market for trainers; when fashion was an important influence, young people bought new trainers more often

MARKET	2001 UK MARKET SIZE	TREND (CHANGE SINCE 2000)	
Soft drinks	£2,481,544,000	+4.9%	+£117 million
Bagged crisps & snacks	£1,836,016,000	+2.1%	+£38 million
Hot drinks (tea, coffee, chocolate)	£1,049,619,000	−4.0%	−£44 million
Soup	£373,328,000	+2.5%	+£9 million
Ice-cream	£769,569,000	+3.0%	+£23 million

Source: *The Grocer*, 17/12/01 (quoting data from IRI InfoScan)

(increasing market size by volume) and were prepared to pay higher prices (increasing market value)

- the ability of the suppliers to identify and meet consumer requirements; the cinema market seemed in terminal decline until multi-screen, modern cinemas revitalised the market.

3.3 Market share

Market share is the proportion of the total market held by one company or product. It can be measured by volume, but is more often looked at by value. Among major companies in mature markets such as soft drinks or confectionery, market share is usually the focus of a great deal of attention. Famously, Coca-Cola's biggest marketing mistake was in response to a decline in its US market share from just 22.5% to 21.8% during the 1980s. Deciding that the taste of the product was less popular than Pepsi's, Coca-Cola changed its product formula and relaunched as New Improved Coca-Cola. The American population, brought up on *the original* Coke rejected the new product, forcing the company to reintroduce the old formula. The embarrassment was huge, as Pepsi gloated publicly about the better taste of Pepsi. All because of a slip of 0.7% in market share.

Market share is taken by most firms as the key test of their marketing strategy. Total sales are affected by factors such as economic growth, but market share only measures a firm's ability to win or lose against its competitors. As shown in the table below, rising market share can also lead to the producer's ideal of market leadership or market dominance. Kit-Kat has

market leadership among confectionery brands. Walkers has market dominance among crisps and snacks. Nestlé's position with Nescafé is stronger still, as the 'nearest competitor' is Nescafé Gold Blend.

There are many advantages to a business in having the top-selling brand (the **brand leader**). Obviously, sales are higher than anyone else's, but also:

- The brand leader will get the highest distribution level, often without needing to make much effort to achieve it. Even a tiny corner shop will stock Heinz. Success breeds success.
- Brand leaders will be able to offer lower discount terms to retailers than the Number 2 or Number 3 brands in a market. This means higher revenues and profit margins per unit sold. For example Nescafé may offer only an 8% margin to the retailer, whereas Maxwell House may need to offer 14%.
- The strength of a brand leading name such as Walls Magnum makes it much easier to obtain distribution and consumer trial for new products based on that brand name.

FIGHTING FOR MARKET SHARE

Large firms operating in consumer markets focus a great deal on market share. Usually, every brand is looked after by a brand manager. He or she will have agreed targets for market share that must be met or beaten by the year-end.

At the start of the year, the brand manager will divide up his or her budget between above-the-line activity (media advertising), below-the-line promotions and market research. He or she will probably be

LEADING BRAND IN ITS MARKET	SALES OF LEADING BRAND	MARKET SIZE (BY VALUE)	MARKET SHARE	SHARE OF NEAREST COMPETITOR
Walkers crisps	£488 million	£1,836 million	26.6%	7.4%
Nescafé	£153 million	£435 million*	35.2%	15.2%
Kit-Kat	£179 million	£2,553 million	7.0%	4.9%
Heinz soup	£133 million	£373 million	35.7%	11.4%
Wall's Magnum	£72 million	£770 million	9.4%	5.4%

Source: *The Grocer*, 17/12/01 (quoting from IRI Infoscan)

*Market for instant coffee

trying to strike a balance between this year's market share targets and the needs of future years. Media advertising boosts short-term sales but also strengthens brand awareness and image for years to come. Below-the-line activity merely strengthens short-term demand. A balanced approach might consist of two bursts of TV advertising during the year supported by trade promotions (to boost distribution), consumer price promotions, a consumer competition and an on-pack special offer. During the year, the market research budget will be used to check that the TV commercials achieve their objectives and to monitor customer attitudes to the brand (and its competitors).

If the marketing plan proves unsuccessful, with market share sliding by the mid-year, a rethink may be needed. The Autumn advertising budget may be cut back to provide more money for a big consumer promotion. Or on-pack special offer pricing may be needed to boost sales and market share. The risk with these actions is that rival firms may feel forced to respond, causing a flurry of promotional activity which cancels itself out.

TRAINER WARS

In 1987, Reebok was the dominant supplier of sports footwear to America. It had a 30% share – far in excess of the Number 2, Nike. Then, as the market size exploded in the early 1990s, Reebok found it increasingly difficult to compete. Nike kept hitting home with the smarter moves. With Michael Jordan and Tiger Woods, it was Nike who tied up the biggest star names. And Nike who proved one step ahead in new product development. By 1996 Nike was spending almost $1,000 million a year on marketing. Reebok could afford $400 million, but this was insufficient to prevent a slide in market share. By 2001, Reebok's market share fell to under 15% of the US market. By now Nike was the clear brand leader.

In early 1998 Reebok announced a change in strategy. No longer would it attempt to compete in the fashion-oriented youth market dominated by Nike marketing. Reebok would aim more at the adult market, accepting that lower market share would not matter as long as costs fell sharply enough.

Reebok was raising the white flag in the trainer wars. In Europe, it would be Adidas that would keep Nike on its toes, as shown in the Nike and Adidas TV advertising battle during the 2002 World Cup.

Source: Adapted from *The Financial Times*

Business IN

3.4 Consumer usage and attitudes

Market analysis is rooted in a deep understanding of customers. Why do they buy Walkers crisps, not Golden Wonder? And who are the key decision makers? Purchasers (perhaps parents buying a multipack in Tesco) or the users (perhaps young teenage children slumped in front of the television)? Is the brand decision a result of child **pester-power**, or parental belief in the product's superiority? Knowledge of such subtleties is essential. Only then can the firm know whether to focus marketing effort on the parent or the child.

To acquire the necessary knowledge about usage and attitudes, firms adopt several approaches. The starting point is usually qualitative research such as group discussions. Run by psychologists, these informal discussions help pinpoint consumers' underlying motives and behaviour. For example, it is important to learn whether Kit-Kat buyers enjoy nibbling the chocolate before eating the wafer biscuit. In other words, to discover whether playing with confectionery is an important part of the enjoyment. This type of information can influence future product development.

The huge multinational Unilever has appointed a head of knowledge management and development (David Smith), to ensure that insights such as this can be spread around the business. As he says, 'The company's collective knowledge is potentially a great competitive advantage'. By encouraging improved communication and networking, Unilever believes it is benefiting from:

- improved decision making
- fewer mistakes
- reduced duplication
- converting new knowledge more quickly into added value to the business.

Among the other ways to gather information on customer usage and attitudes are quantitative research and obtaining feedback from staff who deal directly with customers. An example of the latter would be bank staff whose task is to sell services such as insurance. Customer doubts about a brochure or a product feature, if fed back to head office, might lead to important improvements.

Quantitative research is a common way to monitor customer usage and attitudes. Many firms conduct surveys every month, to track any changes over time in brand awareness or image. This procedure may reveal that a TV commercial has had an unintended side-effect in making the brand image rather too upmarket. Or that customers within a market are becoming more concerned about whether packaging can be recycled.

3.5 Consumer profiles

Marketing decisions are very hard to make without a clear picture of your customers. Who are they? Young? Outgoing? Affluent? Or not. From product and packaging design, through pricing, promotion and distribution – all these aspects of marketing hinge on knowing your **target market**.

A consumer profile is a statistical breakdown of the people who buy a particular product or brand, e.g. what percentage of consumers are women aged 16–25? The main categories analysed within a consumer profile are the customers' age, gender, social class, income level and region. Main uses of profile information are:

- for setting quotas for research surveys
- for segmenting a market
- for deciding in which media to advertise (*Vogue* or the *Sun*?).

A large consumer goods firm will make sure to obtain a profile of consumers throughout the market as well as for its own brand(s). This may be very revealing. It may show that the age profile of its own customers is becoming older than for the market as a whole. This may force a complete rethink of the marketing strategy. The company may have been trying to give the brand a classier image, but end up attracting older customers.

3.6 Market mapping

Having analysed consumer attitudes and consumer profiles, it is possible to create a market map. This is done by selecting the key variables that differentiate the brands within a market. Then plotting the position of each one. Usually this is done on a two-dimensional diagram as below. Here, the image of shoe shops has been plotted against the key criteria of price (premium–budget) and purpose (aspirational–commodity). For example, Bally shoes are expensive and are bought to impress others. Church's are expensive but bought because their buyers believe they are a top quality product.

Market mapping enables a firm to identify any gaps or niches in the market that are unfilled. It also helps monitor existing brands. Is the firm's image becoming too young and trendy? If so, booming sales in the short term might be followed by longer term disappointment. By monitoring the position of their brands on the market map, firms can see more easily when a repositioning exercise is required. This may involve a relaunch with a slightly different product, a new pack design and a new advertising campaign.

Figure 3.1

Source: author's estimates

Business IN

THE TOAST OF LONDON

Founded in 1945, Dualit built up a reputation for its toasters and kettles. Fierce competition from multinational electrical goods firms in the 1960s and 1970s forced it out of the consumer market. Instead of giving up, the company redesigned its products to aim for the catering trade. Dualit stainless steel, extra-durable toasters became the norm in cafes and hotel kitchens. Dualit's founder has explained that: 'I spotted a gap in the market and started to cater for the smaller demand in what was a niche area'. Remarkably, the elegant and robust design of the Dualit toaster made it fashionable in the 1990s. Despite costing more than £100, the Dualit made a comeback in a small segment of the consumer market. The company now employs 75 skilled workers in South London and makes more than £1.5 million profit on £10 million of sales.

Source: Adapted from *The Sunday Times*

3.7 Industrial versus consumer markets

Analysing **industrial markets** requires a slightly different approach. When selling to other firms, image is less of an issue. Traditionally, all that mattered was the right product at the right price at the right time. Today this will not always do. Firms are looking for more from their suppliers. They want complete solutions to problems or requirements. This may require the design of a brand new, tailor-made product. Or organising a series of suppliers to work together to supply a complete unit of production. For instance, a car manufacturer might want matching car seats, carpets and interior trim to be delivered to the right part of a production line at precise times.

To find out exactly what is needed, direct contact with potential and existing customers is essential. Fortunately it is also possible, as industrial markets are unlikely to have more than a hundred or so customers. Each may have slightly different requirements, so flexibility will be a key requirement. Visits to **trade exhibitions** should generate some contacts. Sales representatives should then follow these up by visiting the customer to discuss requirements.

Market analysis is therefore largely based on information gained from individual customers, rather than from general sources such as secondary research. The industrial supplier that waits for the phone to ring is likely to lose out in the short term. It will also fail to gather the market knowledge needed to keep improving the products in line with changing customer demand.

Trade exhibitions are important for generating contacts and raising a company's profile (© SignUK/Faversham House Group Ltd)

ISSUES FOR **analysis**

Among the main issues raised by this unit are:

- The importance to a firm of constantly measuring and rethinking its position in the market. This is why expenditure on market research needs to be regular; not just related to the latest new project.
- Given the importance of market knowledge, how can new firms break into a market? The answer is: with difficulty. Mars did remarkably well to break into the ice-cream market in 1990. But it has probably not yet made a profit on ice-cream in the UK market.
- If all companies follow similar techniques for market analysis, why don't they all come up with the same answers? Fortunately, there remains huge scope for initiative and intuition. Two different managers reading the same market research report may come up with quite different conclusions. The launch of the low cost airline easyJet in 1996 was one man's vision, Stelios Haja-Iaannou. At the time, British Airways predicted that easyJet would flop.

3.8 Market analysis
an evaluation

Market analysis is at the heart of successful marketing. All the great marketing decisions are rooted in a deep understanding of what customers really want. From the marketing of The Spice Girls through to the 2001 launch of Sony PlayStation 2. These successes were rooted in an understanding of the consumer. The clever market stall trader acquires this understanding through daily contact with customers. Large companies need the help of market research to provide a comparable feel. Techniques such as market mapping then help clarify the picture.

Successful marketing strategies rely upon the firm's ability to target the real requirements of the customers. How it goes about this task (through the marketing mix) is a less important consideration.

KEY terms

brand leader – the brand with the highest market share. In fragmented markets such as chocolate, the brand leader may have no more than Kit-Kat's 7.0%.

industrial markets – those where products are sold only to other companies, e.g. heavy lorries.

pester-power – the ability of children to pester their parents into buying the products they want.

product positioning – deciding on the image and target market you want for your own product or brand.

target market – the type of customer your product or service is aimed at. For example the target market for Cherry Coke is 10–16-year-olds from both sexes.

trade exhibitions – annual events where suppliers display their products and services to the buyers who come to see what is new or improved.

AS Level Exercises

A. REVISION QUESTIONS
(35 marks; 70 minutes)

Read the unit, then answer:

1 What market would you consider each of the following businesses to be in?
 a Müller Fruit Corner
 b Rolls Royce Motors
 c Virgin Trains *(3)*

2 What is the difference between market size by volume and market size by value? *(3)*

3 In 1998, sales of Pringles rose 39% to achieve sales of £121 million. What share did this give it of the market for bagged crisps and snacks (see page 15)? *(2)*

4 Identify three factors outside the control of a business that can influence its rate of growth. *(3)*

5 Why does the text suggest that whereas Kit-Kat has market leadership, Walker's has market *dominance*? *(3)*

6 Why is it important to find out the way consumers use the products they buy? *(3)*

7 Identify four benefits a business may gain from effective knowledge management. *(4)*

8 **a** Explain the meaning of the term 'consumer profile'. *(3)*

 b Why might the manager in charge of Sunny Delight find it useful to know the brand's consumer profile? *(4)*

9 Read the In Business on the Dualit toaster. Briefly explain how the company benefited from analysing its market. *(4)*

10 Explain how an industrial market differs from a consumer market. *(3)*

All outlets (grocery and impulse)

			52 w/e 02 Nov '97 Value Sales (£)	52 w/e 01 Nov '98 Value Sales (£)	% chg
1	(1)	Nestlé Kit-Kat	162,459k	163,151k	0.4
2	(2)	Mars bar	128,376k	132,343k	3.1
3	(3)	Cadbury's Dairy Milk	99,131k	96,584k	−2.6
4	(6)	Mars Maltesers	81,242k	89,382k	10.0
5	(5)	Mars Twix	86,714k	88,268k	1.8
6	(4)	Cadbury's Roses	88,843k	86,244k	−2.9
7	(7)	Mars Snickers	75,216k	75,074k	−0.2
8	(8)	Nestlé Quality Street	65,511k	68,415k	4.4
9	(9)	Mars Galaxy	62,242k	59,075k	−5.1
10	(10)	Nestlé Aero	58,471k	58,995k	0.9
11	(11)	Cadbury's Milk Tray	43,922k	45,379k	3.3
12	(13)	Cadbury's Fruit & Nut	43,507k	43,726k	0.5
13	(15)	Nestlé Polo	42,329k	42,630k	0.7
14	(−)	Mars Celebrations	12,830k	42,478k	231.1
15	(14)	Mars Bounty	42,475k	41,800k	−1.6
16	(16)	Cadbury's Crunchie	40,401k	37,299k	−7.7
17	(19)	Cadbury's Whole Nut	37,075k	37,118k	0.1
18	(−)	Cadbury's Creme Egg	32,590k	36,863k	13.1
19	(18)	Nestlé Smarties	38,594k	36,467k	−5.5
20	(17)	Cadbury's Time Out	39,078k	35,918k	−8.1
Total market value			**3,189,707k**	**3,354,418k**	**5.2**

Sugar confectionery

		52 w/e 02 Nov '97 Value Sales (£)	52 w/e 01 Nov '98 Value Sales (£)	% chg
1	Nestlé Polo	42,329k	42,630k	0.7
2	Mars Opal Fruits	29,804k	35,475k	19.0
3	Trebor Softmints	35,971k	34,381k	−4.4
4	Trebor Extra Strong Mint	33,487k	32,702k	−2.3
5	Nestlé Rowntree Fruit Pastilles	34,181k	32,460k	−5.0

Source: IRI InfoScan

B. REVISION EXERCISES

B1 Data Response
Look at the table of data on the previous page.

Questions *(25 marks; 25 minutes)*

1 Explain the meaning of the term 'market value'. (2)
2 The outstanding new confectionery product success in 1998 was the launch of Mars Celebrations. It was designed to compete with Cadbury's Roses and Nestlé Quality Street. What reasons might explain why these products suffered little from this new competitor? (5)
3 Nestlé Smarties had a poor sales year. Outline two factors that might explain this. (4)
4 A new product success in 1998 was the launch of the Polo Supermint. Nestlé launched it at the younger end of the market than the traditional Polo buyer. What benefits might this have for Nestlé? (5)
5 Only two of the brands in the confectionery Top 20 have been launched in the past 10 years. Most are more than 50 years old. Consider why brand loyalties may be so stable in markets such as confectionery. (9)

B2 Case Study
Graham Smith winked at Raya Farmer as the first guest signed in. She smiled cheesily. It had taken 10 months and £340,000 to get the Lakeside Coaching Inn open. Graham had found it hard to cope at times, but Raya's cool head helped to see it through. Now, with the lounge bar taking good business and the restaurant fully booked for tonight – opening night – the booking of a hotel room rounded off a very good start.

The idea had come about in a strategy meeting at Swallow Hotels, where Graham and Raya both used to work. Graham was operations manager and Raya the marketing manager. Raya had just completed a £50,000 market research programme to produce a market mapping exercise which no-one seemed interested in. Graham, though, had a quiet word with Raya afterwards. He said: 'Don't you think there's a market for a chain of reasonably priced hotels with character? At the moment you wouldn't know if you're in Torquay or Tokyo. They're identically dull.' She nodded keenly, making it clear that she had hoped the meeting would come to exactly that conclusion. Instead, over the following weeks, Graham and Raya talked it through together.

Having looked at market trends, Raya was convinced an opportunity existed. Graham had always yearned to be his own boss, so this seemed like the time to start.

Both he and Raya could find £40,000 of share capital. After discussions with NatWest Bank, the pair were offered a loan of £200,000, secured against hotel premises. Helped by £60,000 put into the business by Raya's uncle, they set out to buy their first outlet. It would be the first of perhaps a hundred 'traditional inns' they intended to link within their chain. Raya believed that would be enough to achieve a 4% share of the billion pound market for business travel.

Market mapping – hotel chains in the UK

The intention was to guarantee certain service standards, such as all rooms have a bathroom, a TV and a telephone. Apart from that, though, the more original the inn the better. For example, one might be an old pub serving a wide range of real ales. Another might specialise in good local food. The travellers would be able to choose the one to suit their needs and tastes.

From the start the idea showed promise. The key, though, would be forming a national chain. While Graham looked after the business, Raya went to visit other pubs and inns to try to persuade their owners to join a marketing syndicate. Raya would organise the links with companies and business travel agents to ensure a regular stream of customers. Three months of hard, expensive travelling led finally to a breakthrough when a group of eight hotels in Somerset and Devon agreed to join. After that it became much easier to sell the concept and within six months she had signed up 100 traditional inns nationally.

Press release – launch of Britain's newest hotel chain

The Traditional Inns Group

Business travellers are tired of dull hotels with formula food. Finance directors despair of the excessive prices charged by expense account hotels. The Traditional Inns Group will change all that. We are a national chain of a hundred hotels with character, warm hospitality, great beer and great food. Near Bath we have a seventeenth century coaching inn. Just outside Newcastle is a nineteenth century converted water mill. The Traditional Inns Group guarantees the service consistency business travellers demand, but in truly original settings. For further details phone …

At last there was a really strong story to send out as a press release to the travel trade magazines and in a direct mailing to businesses throughout Britain. The Traditional Inns Group had arrived. Marks & Spencer agreed to put the chain on its list of approved hotel groups for business travelling. The future seemed assured.

Questions   *(40 marks; 70 minutes)*

1 Why was it important that Raya:
  a had conducted a £50,000 market research programme   *(5)*
  b had a clear market share target?   *(5)*

2 Consider why Swallow Hotels may have been uninterested in Raya's market mapping exercise.   *(10)*

3 In the long term, the success of the Traditional Inns Group will depend upon satisfied customers, repeat purchase and good word of mouth. How might Graham and Raya set about achieving this?   *(10)*

4 Discuss the importance of market mapping in the process of analysing a market.   *(10)*

MARKET RESEARCH

DEFINITION

Market research gathers information about consumers, competitors and distributors within a firm's target market. It is a way of identifying consumers' buying habits and attitudes to current and future products. Market research data can be numerical (such as what proportion of 16–24-year-olds buy *The Sun* every day?) or psychological (why do they buy *The Sun*?).

4.1 Researching into a new market

Where do you start? What do you need to know first? And how do you find it out?

The starting point is to discover the marketing fundamentals: market size, market potential and market shares.

Market size means the value of the sales made annually by all the firms within a market. For example, in 2001 the UK yoghurt market was worth £710 million. Market potential can be measured by the annual rate of growth. In the case of yoghurt, this has been at a rate of 6% per year, by value. This implies that, by the year 2005, the potential market size will be nearly £900 million.

When looking at a completely new market, these statistics will not be available. So research may be needed into other indicators. For example, the producer of an innovative new fishing rod would find out the number of people who go fishing regularly.

Market shares are also of crucial importance when investigating a market, as they indicate the relative strength of the firms within the market. In 2001, 28% of the yoghurt market was held by Müller, making it the leading brand by far. A benefit it received for its strong market share was a distribution level of almost 100% – nearly every grocery store stocked Müller. If one firm dominates, it may be very difficult to break the market.

So how can firms find out this type of information? The starting point is secondary research: unearthing data which already exists.

4.2 Secondary research

Trade press: All the above data about the yoghurt market came from an article in *The Grocer* magazine. Every major market is served by one or more magazines written for people who work within that trade. A subscription to *Caterer and Hotelkeeper* or to *The Grocer* soon provides a wealth of statistical and other information. The name and contact details of relevant magazines can be found in BRAD (British Rate And Data) – available at many public libraries.

Trade associations: These associations represent the interests of member companies within a market. For example, the Society of Motor Manufacturers and Traders collects production and sales statistics for the UK car market. It also speaks on behalf of the whole industry, perhaps when the Government is considering car tax increases. Trade associations represent a huge potential source of useful information on market size and trends. Most public libraries have their details listed in a directory called *Trade Associations and Professional Bodies of the United Kingdom* (published by Gale Research, 13th ed, 1997).

Market intelligence reports: These include data on market size by volume and value, market shares, sales trends, sales forecasts, market segmentation, details of advertising spending and distribution channels. They are hugely useful, but also hugely expensive. Fortunately, larger – business oriented – libraries often hold the reports produced by the big three: Keynotes, Mintel and Retail Business (EIU).

Other important sources of secondary data include:

- Government publications produced by the Office of National Statistics, such as the *Annual Abstract of Statistics*, *Social Trends* and *Economic Trends*. These provide data on population trends and forecasts (e.g. for a cosmetics producer to find how many 16–20-year-old women there will be in the year 2008); and on the amount consumers spend on different categories of product.
- Newspaper articles and special reports; for example, the *Financial Times* produces an eight-page report on information technology every three months. It gives the latest trends and ideas.

Once a firm has the necessary data on the market as a whole, a strategy can be developed for penetrating it. For example, if secondary data revealed that the average age of Bacardi drinkers was rising year on year, a rival company might decide an opportunity exists for a new white rum.

Having obtained background data, further research is likely to be tailored specifically to the company's needs, such as carrying out a survey among 18–25-year-old drinkers of spirits. This type of first-hand research gathers primary data.

	SECONDARY RESEARCH	PRIMARY RESEARCH
Pros	• often obtained without cost • good overview of a market • usually based on actual sales figures, or research on large samples	• can aim questions directly at your research objectives • latest information from the marketplace • can assess the psychology of the customer
Cons	• data may not be updated regularly • not tailored to your own needs • expensive, but reports on many different marketplaces	• expensive, £5,000+ per survey • risk of questionnaire and interviewer bias • research findings may only be usable if comparable backdata exists

4.3 Primary research

The process of gathering information directly from people within your target market is known as primary (or field) research. When carried out by market research companies it is expensive, but there is much that firms can do for themselves.

For a company that is up and running, a regular survey of customer satisfaction is an important way of measuring the quality of customer service. When investigating a new market, there are various measures that can be taken by a small firm with a limited budget:

• Retailer research – the people closest to a market are those who serve customers directly – the retailers. They are likely to know the up-and-coming brands, the degree of brand loyalty, the importance of price and packaging – all crucial information.
• Observation – when starting up a service business in which location is an all-important factor, it is invaluable to measure the rate of pedestrian (and possibly traffic) flow past your potential site compared with that of rivals. A sweet shop or a dry-cleaners near a busy bus stop may generate twice the sales of a rival 50 metres down the road.
• In-depth interviews – even if only with a few consumers, these can lead to ideas that would not otherwise have emerged, such as the importance of

a psychological price barrier ('Oh, I'd never pay over a tenner for a book.').

For a large company, primary research will be used extensively in new product development. For example, if a company were considering the possibility of launching Orange Chocolate Buttons, the development stages – plus research – would probably be those shown in the table below.

4.4 Qualitative research

Qualitative research is in-depth research into the motivations behind the attitudes and buying habits of consumers. It does not produce statistics such as '52% of chocolate buyers like orange chocolate'; instead it gives clues as to why they like it (is it really because it's orange, or because it's different/a change?). Qualitative research is usually conducted by psychologists, who learn to interpret the way people say things as well as what they say.

Qualitative research takes two main forms:

1 Group discussions: Also known as focus groups, these are free-ranging discussions led by psychologists among groups of 6–8 consumers. The group leader will have a list of topics that need discussion, but will be free to follow up any point made by a group member. Among the advantages of group discussions are:

	DEVELOPMENT STAGE		PRIMARY RESEARCH
1	The product idea (probably one of several)	1	Group discussions among regular chocolate buyers – some young, some old
2	Product test (testing different recipes – different sweetness, orangeyness, etc.)	2	A taste test on 200+ chocolate buyers (on street corners, or in a hall)
3	Brand name research (testing several different names and perhaps logos)	3	Quantitative research using a questionnaire on a sample of 200+
4	Packaging research	4	As 3.
5	Advertising research	5	Group discussions run by psychologists to discover which advertisement has the strongest effect on product image and recall
6	Total proposition test: testing the level of purchase interest, to help make sales forecasts	6	Quantitative research using a questionnaire and product samples on at least 200+ consumers

- may reveal a problem or opportunity the company had not anticipated
- reveals consumer psychology, such as the importance of image and peer pressure
- a good way of shortlisting options from a number of possibilities; for example whittling six different pack designs down to two, which will then be researched quantitatively (see section 4.5).

RESEARCHING HÄAGEN DAZS

IN Business

Group discussions were used prior to the UK launch of Häagen Dazs. Groups of men and women were each given a half-litre tub of Häagen Dazs and asked questions about when, how and with whom they would like to eat it. Respondents spoke about sharing a spoon with their partner, feeding each other and 'mellowing out' in front of a video. This led to a breakthrough in food advertising: Häagen Dazs was advertised as a sensual pleasure to be shared. Its huge success when launched has become recognised as a success for qualitative research.

2 In-depth interviews: Informal, in-depth interviews between a psychologist and a consumer. They have the same function as group discussions, but avoid the risk that the group opinion will be swayed by one influential person.

Typical research questions to be answered by:

Qualitative research	Quantitative research
• *Why do people really buy Levi's?*	• *Which pack design do you prefer?*
• *Who in the household really decides which brand of shampoo is bought?*	• *Have you heard of any of the following brands? (Ariel, Daz, Persil, etc.)*
• *What mood makes you feel like buying Haagen Dazs ice-cream?*	• *How likely are you to buy this product regularly?*
• *When you buy your children Frosties, how do you feel?*	• *How many newspapers have you bought in the past seven days?*

4.5 Quantitative research

Quantitative research asks pre-set questions on a large enough sample of people to provide statistically valid data. Questionnaires can answer factual questions

such as 'How many 16–20-year-olds have heard of Chanel No 5?' There are three key aspects to quantitative research:

- sampling, i.e. ensuring that the research results are typical of the whole population, though only a sample of the population has been interviewed
- writing a questionnaire that is unbiased and meets the research objectives
- assessing the validity of the results.

SAMPLING

The two main concerns in sampling are how to choose the right people for interview (sampling method) and deciding how large a number to interview (sample size). There are four main sampling methods:

Random sample: Selecting respondents to ensure that everyone in the population has an equal chance of being interviewed. This sounds easy, but is not. If an interviewer goes to a street corner one morning and asks passers-by for an interview, the resulting sample will be biased towards those who are not in work, who do not own a car and have time on their hands (the busy ones will refuse to be interviewed). As a result the sample will not be representative. So achieving a truly random sample requires careful thought.

Research companies use the following method:

- pick names at random from the electoral register, e.g. every 50th name
- send an interviewer to the address given in the register
- if the person is out, visit up to twice more before giving up (this is to maximise the chances of catching those who lead busy social lives and are therefore rarely at home).

This method is effective, but slow and expensive.

Quota sample: Selecting interviewees in proportion to the consumer profile within your target market, for example:

	ADULT CHOCOLATE BUYERS	RESPONDENT QUOTA (SAMPLE: 200)
Men	40%	80
Women	60%	120
16–24	38%	76
25–34	21%	42
35–44	16%	32
45+	25%	50

This method allows interviewers to head for busy street corners, interviewing whoever comes along. As long as they end up achieving the correct quota, they can interview when and where they want to. As this is a relatively cheap and effective way of sampling, it is the one used most commonly by market research companies.

Stratified sample: Only interviewing those with a key characteristic required for the sample. For example, the producers of Oil of Olay might decide to interview only women aged 30–45, the potential buyers of the future. Within this stratum/section of the population, individuals could be found at random (hence stratified random sample) or by setting quotas based on factors such as social class and region.

Cluster sample: Sampling only within a specified area/areas. For example, in selected university towns (perhaps for bank accounts) or in seaside resorts (for swimwear). This is not a common form of sampling, though valuable for student projects.

Having decided which sampling method should be used, the next consideration is how many interviews should be conducted? 10? 100? 1,000? The most high-profile surveys conducted in Britain are the opinion polls – asking people how they will vote in a general election. These quota samples of between 1,000 and 1,500 respondents are considered large enough to reflect the opinions of the electorate of 44 million. How is this possible?

Of course, if you only interviewed 10 people, the chances are slim that the views of this sample will match those of the whole population. Of these 10, seven may say they would definitely buy Chocolate Orange Buttons. If you asked another 10, however, only three may say the same. A sample of 10 is so small that chance variations make the results meaningless. In other words, a researcher can have no statistical confidence in the findings from a sample of 10.

A sample of 100 is far more meaningful. It is not enough to feel confident about marginal decisions (e.g. 53% like the red pack design, 47% like the blue one), but is quite enough if the result is clear cut (e.g. 65% like the name 'Spark'; 35% prefer 'Valencia'). Many major product launches have proceeded following research on as low a sample as 100.

With a sample of 1,000 a high level of confidence is possible. Even small differences would be statistically significant with such a large sample. A further benefit of large sample sizes is that they allow sub-groups to be analysed. For example, research into the sales prospects for a new product shows that 59% say they will definitely buy. But who exactly are the keen ones? Breaking the results down by age group may show that 71% of 16–20-year-old men will buy, but only 32% of 45–60-year-olds. In which case the advertising can be directed at the younger group. If the sample size is 100, each sub-group may contain fewer than 10 people, giving the findings no validity. A sample size of 1,000 provides large enough sub-groups to allow valid conclusions.

So why doesn't everyone use samples of 1,000? The answer is money. Hiring a market research agency to undertake a survey of 100 people would cost approximately £5,000. A sample of 1,000 people would cost three times that amount – good value if you can afford it, but not everyone can. As shown in the earlier example of launching Orange Chocolate Buttons, a company might require six surveys before launching a new product. So the spending on research alone might reach £90,000, if samples of 1,000 were used.

Market researchers know that no result from a sample can be relied upon 100%. You can only be 100% sure of the population's opinion if you ask all of them – but that would be impractical. Researchers have come to accept that 95% reliability is good enough, in other words they are willing to accept a finding that should be right 19 times out of 20 (95%). This is known as a 95% confidence level.

For example, a researcher may present the following findings to a client:

	PREFER		PREFER
Advertisement A	48%	Brand name X	31%
Advertisement B	52%	Brand name Y	32%
		Brand name Z	37%

The researcher might say that, given the large sample size used for the advertising research, one can have 95% confidence in the preference for B, i.e. the result is statistically reliable. The apparent preference for brand name Z may not be reliable, however, if the sample size were relatively small. Therefore the researcher would recommend that the client should regard names X, Y and Z as liked equally. So the client should choose between them on other criteria, such as image.

Quantitative research is expensive and its results may influence major decisions such as whether to launch a new product. So a mistake in writing the questionnaire may prove very costly. For instance, the wording may influence respondents to sound more positive about a new product than they really feel. What are the key features of a good questionnaire?

- Clearly defined research objectives. What exactly do you need to find out?
- Ensure that questions do not point towards a particular answer.
- Ensure that the meaning of each question is clear, perhaps by testing (piloting) questions before putting them into fieldwork.

- Use mainly closed questions, i.e. ones with a limited number of pre-set answers that the respondent must tick; only in this way can you ensure quantifiable results.
- It is useful, though, to include a few open questions, to allow respondents to write a sentence or two, providing more depth of understanding.
- Ensure that the questionnaire finishes by asking full demographic and usership details, i.e. respondents' sex, age, occupation (and therefore social class) and buying habits. This allows more detailed analysis of sub-groups within the sample.

Having written a questionnaire in draft form, research companies trial it by getting experienced interviewers to try it out. Experienced researchers know that questionnaires are unlikely to be right first time. A question that seems clear to the writer may be interpreted in different ways by different people.

4.6 Other important considerations in primary research

Response rate: If a company sends out 2,000 questionnaires and only 200 people send back a response, the question must be asked: are those who respond typical of those who do not respond? Or is there a bias built into the findings as a consequence of the low response rate?

Face-to-face versus self-completion: In the past, most surveys were conducted by interviewers who asked the questions face-to-face. This had drawbacks such as cost and the risk of bias (a bubbly young interviewer may generate more positive responses). Clear benefits, however, included a high response rate and the assurance that the interviewer could help to explain an unclear question. Today, self-completion questionnaires are increasingly common.

4.7 Market research in the twenty-first century

Market research is increasingly influenced by technology. Instead of standing on windy street corners, interviewers are more likely to be sitting in a telephone booth in an office. There they can interview people over the phone, keying their answers directly into a computer. This provides results at the touch of a button at the end of a day's work. It is a cheaper and much quicker way to conduct quantitative research. Already most opinion polls are carried out this way.

An even stronger trend is towards database-driven research. Instead of finding the right people by trial and error, client firms supply research companies with database information on current or ex-customers.

Retailers such as Tesco and Sainsbury have millions of customer names on their databases, all grouped into categories such as regular/irregular shoppers, petrol buyers, disposable nappy buyers and so on. If Tesco wants to survey customer satisfaction with their baby products section, it knows exactly who should be contacted.

Manufacturers have learned from this and are rapidly developing the same database information. One of the major cigarette companies has developed a database of millions of its customers by logging every entry for a promotion or special offer. The same company has used this information to plot, by postcode, brand buying habits throughout the country. So instead of running poster advertising campaigns nationally, different brands are advertised on posters in different parts of the country.

The future of market research is clearly bound up in computers, the Internet, TV observation cameras and – quite soon – interactive cable TV. The basics will remain crucial, however: the avoidance of bias in the wording of questions, large enough sample sizes to provide valid data and intelligent analysis of the research findings.

ISSUES FOR **analysis**

When developing an argument in answer to a case study or essay question, market research offers the following main lines of analysis:

- The key role of market research in market orientation, i.e. basing decisions upon the consumer, rather than the producer's needs or opinions.
- The need for a questioning approach to data. When presented with a research finding one needs to know: Was the sample size large enough? Who paid for the research? Business people learn to ask questions about every 'fact' shown by research.
- The importance of market knowledge: large, established firms have a huge advantage over newer, smaller firms because of their knowledge of consumer attitudes and behaviour, built up from years of market research surveys.

4.8 Market research
an evaluation

In large firms, it is rare for any significant marketing decision to be made without market research. Even an apparently minor change to a pack design will only be carried out after testing in research. Is this overkill? Surely marketing executives are employed to make judgements, not merely do what surveys tell them?

The first issue here is the strong desire to make business decisions as scientifically as possible. This dates back to the work of FW Taylor and is kept alive today through the concept of the marketing model (see Unit 2.6). Quantitative research, especially, fits in with the desire to act on science not hunch. Yet this can be criticised, such as by John Scully, former head of Apple Computers, who once said: 'No great marketing decision has ever been made on the basis of quantitative data.' He was pointing out that true innovations such as the Sony Walkman and great advertisements such as Levi's 'launderette' commercial were the product of creativity and hunch, not science.

The second issue concerns the management cul-ture. In some firms, mistakes lead to inquests, blame and even dismissal. This makes managers keen to find a let-out. When the new product flops, the manager can point an accusing finger at the positive research results: 'It wasn't my fault. We need a new research agency.' In other firms, mistakes are seen as an inevitable part of learning. For every Sinclair C5 (unresearched flop) there may be a Sony Walkman (unresearched moneyspinner). In firms with a positive, risk-taking approach to business, qualitative insights are likely to be preferred to quantitative data.

AS Level Exercises

A. REVISION QUESTIONS

(30 marks; 60 minutes)

Read the unit, then answer:

1 State three ways in which a cosmetics firm could use market research. *(3)*
2 Outline three reasons why market research information may prove inaccurate. *(6)*
3 Distinguish between primary and secondary research. *(3)*
4 What advantages are there in using secondary research rather than primary? *(3)*
5 Which is the most commonly used sampling method? Why may it be the most commonly used? *(4)*
6 State three key factors to take into account when writing a questionnaire. *(3)*
7 Outline the pros and cons of using a large sample size. *(4)*
8 Why may street interviewing become less common in the future? *(4)*

B. REVISION EXERCISES

B1 Market Research Assignment

Hampton is a medium-sized producer of health foods. Its new company strategy is to break into the £400 million market for breakfast cereals. It has thought up three new product ideas that it wishes to test in research before further development takes place. They are:

- Cracker: an extra-crunchy mix of oats and almonds
- Fizzz: crunchy oats which fizz in milk
- St James: a luxury mix of oats, cashews and pecan nuts

The research objectives are to identify the most popular of the three, in terms of product trial and regular usage; to identify price expectations for each; to find what people like and dislike about each idea and each brand name; and to be able to analyse the findings in relation to consumers' demographic profile and current usage patterns.

Questions *(30 marks; 35 minutes)*

1 Write a questionnaire based upon the above details, bearing in mind the advice given in section 4.5. *(12)*
2 Explain which sampling method you would use and why. *(6)*
3 Interview 6–8 people using your questionnaire, then write a 200 word commentary on its strengths and weaknesses. *(12)*

B2 Case Study

Braebourne Ltd supplies water coolers and mineral water to business customers. Started by a 22-year-old fresh from university in 1990, by 1997 its turnover was over £3 million and profit in excess of £400,000. The business has thrived from the 35% annual growth of the market as a whole, and from its excellent customer service. Braebourne only takes on customers who are within an hour's drive of one of their depots. Also, the delivery drivers are hired and trained for their customer-friendly approach.

When the business was small, the managing director had regular contact with all the customers and could therefore monitor customer satisfaction. Now he relies on regular surveys of customer opinion. Last month, 350 of Braebourne's 7,000 customers replied to the questionnaire. Here is an extract from the findings:

WATER:	Awful	Poor	Fair	Good	V. Good	Excellent
Please rate the following:						
taste:	0%	0%	3%	8%	32%	57%
clarity:	0%	1%	6%	9%	41%	43%
presentation of bottles:	0%	3%	7%	9%	62%	19%

DELIVERY:	Awful	Poor	Fair	Good	V. Good	Excellent

Please rate your driver on the following:

	Awful	Poor	Fair	Good	V. Good	Excellent
courtesy:	0%	3%	11%	24%	33%	29%
helpfulness:	1%	3%	15%	28%	34%	19%
timekeeping:	3%	2%	9%	21%	27%	38%

Questions *(15 marks; 30 minutes)*

1 How may the long term prospects of Braebourne be helped by effective use of market research? *(4)*
2 For what reasons may the reliability of this survey be called into question? *(4)*
3 What conclusions might the company draw from the above results? *(7)*

A Level Exercises

A. REVISION QUESTIONS
(20 marks; 45 minutes)

Read the unit, then answer:

1 Distinguish between qualitative and quantitative research. *(3)*
2 Explain two aspects of marketing in which consumer psychology is important. *(4)*
3 In the future it is likely that all interviewers will have laptop computers to key in answers immediately. Then a modem link can be used to send results instantly to head office. Outline two possible benefits of this. *(4)*
4 'Respondents preferred the green to the blue label, though this was not significant at the 95% confidence level.' Explain this statement in your own words. *(3)*
5 Distinguish between quota and stratified sampling methods. *(3)*
6 Identify three possible sources of bias in primary market research. *(3)*

B. REVISION EXERCISES

B1 Case Study
The Peckham Pet Shop has suffered a sales downturn. The 58-year-old proprietor, Anne Smith, has asked Jim – a Business Studies student at the local college – to look into the problem. He found the sales figures for the last five years and comparable figures for the whole petcare industry. By indexing both sets of figures to a base period of 100, he was able to draw direct sales comparisons.

	5 yrs ago	4 yrs ago	3 yrs ago	2 yrs ago	Last year	This year
Peckham	100	106	107	101	95	98
Industry	100	104	109	115	121	127

Having completed this, Jim's next move was to write a customer questionnaire. He asked about people's likes and dislikes of the store, attitudes to its range of stock and range of prices and where else they buy their petcare products. He then placed the questionnaires on the counter, next to the cash till, and asked Anne to get customers to fill them in.

After two weeks, Jim was disappointed to hear that only 12 questionnaires had been completed. Anne explained that she had only asked those who she knew well. Two weeks later, a total of 30 were filled in, so Jim started his analysis of the findings. Within a couple of days he went to see Anne to present his conclusions. The main ones were that:

- the great majority of the customers are over 50
- they like the service, stock and quality at Peckham far more than elsewhere
- they do go to other shops for petcare products, not just Peckham
- the disappointing sales performance recently may just be temporary; cost reductions such as cutting back on the Saturday sales staff may be enough to restore the shop's profitability.

Questions *(25 marks; 45 minutes)*

1 Distinguish between primary and secondary research, using examples from the case. *(5)*
2 Assess the primary research method used by Jim. Why may the findings lack reliability? *(6)*
3 Evaluate Jim's recommendations in the light of the evidence provided in the case. *(8)*
4 Explain and justify your own recommendations as to what Anne should do. *(6)*

C. ESSAY QUESTIONS

1 'Market research is like an insurance policy. You pay a premium to reduce your marketing risks.' To what extent do you believe this statement to be true?
2 After 10 years of rising sales, demand for Campex Tents has stabilised. How might Campex make use of market research to analyse why this has happened and help decide what strategy to adopt to return to sales growth.
3 The Sony chairman once said that market research predicted the Walkman would be a flop. His conclusion was that research is useful in relation to existing products, but does not work with innovative new products.
   a Why may this be?
   b How could research be used to best effect for assessing new innovations?

PRODUCT LIFE CYCLE AND PORTFOLIO ANALYSIS

DEFINITION
The product life cycle shows the sales of a product over time.

5.1 What is the product life cycle?

The product life cycle shows the sales of a product over time. When a new product is first launched sales will usually be slow. If the product succeeds sales will then grow, until at some point they begin to stabilise. This might be because competitors have introduced similar products or because the market has now become saturated. Once most households have bought a dishwasher, for example, sales are likely to be relatively slow. This is because new purchases will mainly involve people who are updating their machine rather than new buyers. At some point sales are actually likely to decline. Perhaps because new technology means the product has become outdated. Or because competitors have launched a more successful model. The five key stages of a product's life cycle are known as: introduction, growth, maturity and decline and can be illustrated on a product life cycle diagram.

The typical stages in a product's life are shown in Figure 5.1 below.

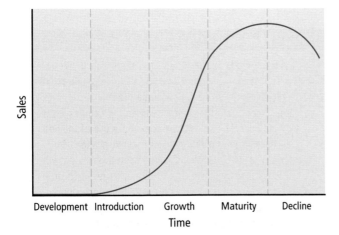

Figure 5.1 Product life cycle

MARKETING

STAGE OF PRODUCT LIFE CYCLE	EXAMPLE OF A TYPE OF PRODUCT	EXAMPLE OF A PARTICULAR BRAND OF PRODUCT
Introduction	Digital TV; 3G mobile phones; self cleaning glass	Wrigley's Extra Thin Ice (dissolving gum); Nestlé's Café Hazelnut, Café Caramel and Café Vanilla (speciality coffees); vanilla Coca-Cola; Nokia 6650
Growth	Broadband internet access; digital cameras; MP3; organic chocolate; premium ice cream; laptops; coloured contact lenses; electric cars; supermini cars; videoconferencing; white chocolate cosmetic surgery	Harry Potter books; Sony PlayStation 2; Lego Mindstorm; Friends Reunited; BMW Mini
Maturity and saturation	washing machines; sliced white bread; tea; toothbrushes; brown chocolate	Coca-Cola; Cadbury's Dairy Milk; Typhoo; Tetley; Monopoly
Decline	Board games; 35mm cameras; high fat foods; artifical sweeteners; cigarettes	National Lottery (Lotto); Pokémon; Furby; Microsoft 2000; ONDigital (now shut down!)

Business IN

NEW PRODUCTS: NOKIA

Few companies in business history have ridden a product life cycle as brilliantly (and profit ably) as Nokia did with 2G (2nd Generation) mobile phones between 1997 and 2002. So Nokia was desperately keen to be first to the market with Europe's first 3G handset. It managed this in 2002 with the 6650 model. It has a large colour screen and dual mode, meaning it can switch between the old 2G and the new 3G networks. It also has an in-built camera: users can take photos with their phones and send these to their friends. This is called photo messaging.

Despite the attractions of the 6650, sales were not expected to be particularly high in the short term. The company estimated it would have to wait until 2004 before 3G phones accounted for over 10% of its total sales. Partly this was due to technical problems; for example 3G requires large amounts of power which reduce the phone's battery life. Another issue was the price: in 2002 Nokia's 3G phone was priced at 800 euros (£480).

In 2002, 2G mobile phones were in their maturity phase, with sales flagging slightly. The birth of 3G was coming just in time for Nokia.

5.2 What use is the product life cycle?

The concept of a product life cycle is useful because it highlights the need for a firm to alter its marketing policies at different stages of a product's life. In the growth phase the firm may be trying to increase its access to distribution channels. In the maturity phase it might develop new varieties of the product to maintain sales. In the decline phase it may have to reduce price to try to regain market share.

The product life cycle helps managers plan their marketing strategies. However, managers should realise that the duration of the life cycle will vary from one product to another. If, for example, the product is a fad (such as Pokémon) the overall life of the product will be quite short. Other products have very long life cycles. The first manufactured cigarettes went on sale in Britain in 1873. By chance, sales hit their peak (120,000 million!) exactly 100 years later. Since 1973 sales have gently declined.

It is also important to distinguish between the life cycle of a product category and the life cycle of a particular brand. Sales of wine are growing, but a brand that was once the biggest seller (Hirondelle) has virtually disappeared as wine buyers have become more sophisticated. Similarly, chocolate is a mature market but particular brands are at different stages in their life cycles: Mars bars are in maturity while Dream bars are in their growth stage.

Managers must also be aware that the pattern of sales from growth to maturity to decline is not inevitable. If they make the right decisions they can often keep sales growing. Just because sales begin to fall they must not assume that the product is entering a decline phase. It may well be a temporary or seasonal drop in sales. If managers believe their product is declining they may reduce their marketing efforts when in fact sales were about to increase! The life cycle model therefore needs to be treated with caution. It is a useful to tool to examine what has happened to sales and consider what might happen in the future. But managers must relate it to their own experiences, their own markets and any other information they have about future sales.

Features and implications of the different stages of the life cycle

	INTRODUCTION	GROWTH	MATURITY	DECLINE
Sales	Low	Growing rapidly	At their highest	Falling
Costs per unit	High; no economies of scale	Falling; economies of scale	Low	Low
Competitors	Few	Growing	High	Falling
Product	One basic model	Product modifications and improvements	Diversify; new models	Remove weaker items
Promotion	Build awareness; high levels of promotion	Aim to generate interest; target new market segments	Stress differences with competitors	Lower budgets to keep costs down
Distribution	Limited	Growing number of outlets	High level of distribution	Reduce unprofitable channels
Price	May be skimming or penetration strategy	May keep penetrating the market or push prices up	May use competitive pricing	May increase prices, exploiting the loyalty of regular customers

5.3 Cash flow and the product life cycle

In the development phase before a product is launched, cash flow will be negative. The firm will be spending money on research and development, market research and production planning, but no revenue is yet being generated. It may also decide to test market the product, which again costs money.

Once the product is on sale cash should begin to come in. However at this stage sales are likely to be low and the firm will still be heavily promoting the product to generate awareness. Overall cash flow is likely to continue to be negative. In many cases the cash flow will not become a positive figure until the growth stage of the life cycle. By then sales will be increasing and promotional costs can be spread over more units. This reduces costs per unit, making them

easier to cover. Cash flow should then continue to improve until the decline stage when the volume of sales and the amount of cash coming in begins to fall.

The changes in cash flow are related to the capacity utilisation of the firm. A large factory producing small quantities will be a drain on cash flow and profitability. In the early stages of a product's life the capacity utilisation is likely to be quite low. Therefore the cost per unit will be high. The combination of a high unit cost and low sales leads to negative cashflow. As sales grow, capacity utilisation increases and unit costs start to fall.

It is important, therefore, for firms to manage their cash flow effectively during the life cycle. Although a product may prove successful in the long term it may also cause the firm severe liquidity problems in the short term unless its finances are properly managed.

5.4 Extension strategies

The aim of an **extension strategy** is to prevent a decline in the product's sales. There are various means by which this can be achieved:

- By changing elements of the **marketing mix**; for example, new promotional techniques such as special offers can be used.
- By targeting a new segment of the market; when sales of Johnson and Johnson's baby products started to fall the company repositioned the product and aimed it at adults.
- By developing new uses for the product; the basic technology in hot-air paint strippers, for example, is no different from that of a hairdryer.

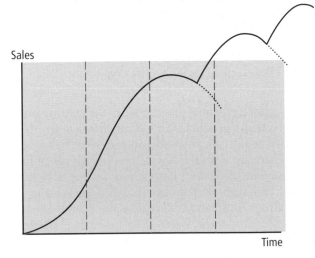

Figure 5.3 The effect of extension strategies

The continued success of products such as Coca-Cola and Kellogg's cornflakes is not just due to luck. It is due to sophisticated marketing techniques which have managed to maintain their sales over many years despite fierce competition. The Kellogg's logo is regularly updated, new pack sizes are often introduced and various competitions and offers are used on a regular

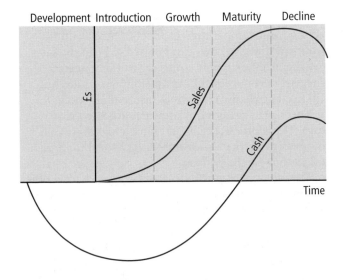

Figure 5.2 Product life cycle and cash flow

basis to keep sales high. The company has also tried to increase the number of students and adults eating its products. It has run advertising campaigns to encourage people to eat the product throughout the day as well as in the morning.

5.5 Is a decline in sales inevitable?

In the standard product life cycle model it seems as if decline is inevitable. This may be true in some situations. For example, developments in technology may make some products obsolete. On the other hand the decline in sales may be the result of poor marketing. Effective extension strategies may ensure that a product's sales are maintained. The long term success of products and services such as Monopoly and Kit-Kat shows that sales can be maintained over a very long period of time. Creative marketing can avoid the decline phase for a substantial period of time – but only if the product is good enough to keep buyers coming back for more. In 2002 Yorkie chocolate bars were relaunched with a tongue-in-cheek 'For Men Only' advertising campaign. Sales, which had been slipping for years, rose 27% and held their higher sales level into 2003.

One of the reasons for sales decline may be that some managers assume the product will fail at some point and so do not make enough effort to save it. This is known as 'determinism': managers think sales will decline and so sales do fall because of inadequate marketing support. Instead of adapting their **marketing strategy** to find new ways of selling the product they let it decline because they assume it cannot be saved.

It is important to remember that a life cycle graph only shows what has happened. It is not a prediction of the future. Top marketing managers try to influence the future, not just let it happen.

5.6 The product portfolio

Product **portfolio analysis** examines the existing position of a firm's products. This allows the firm to consider its existing position and plan what to do next. There are several different methods of portfolio analysis. One of the best known was developed by a firm of management consultants called the Boston Consulting Group and is known as the Boston Matrix.

The Boston Matrix shows the market share of each of the firm's products and the rate of growth of the markets in which they operate. By highlighting the position of each product in terms of market share and market growth the firm can analyse its existing situation and decide what to do next.

In Figure 5.4, product A has a high market share of a low growth market. The size of the circle depends on the turnover of the product. This type of product is known as a **cash cow**. An example of a cash cow might be Heinz baked beans. The overall market for baked

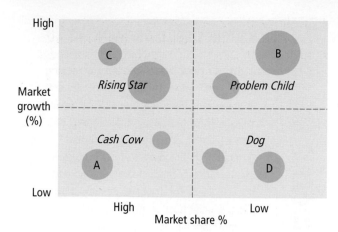

Figure 5.4 Product portfolio: the Boston Matrix

beans is mature and therefore slow growing. Within this market the Heinz brand has a market share of about 50%. This type of product generates high profits and cash for the company because sales are relatively high whilst the promotional cost per unit is quite low. Consumers are already aware of the brand, which reduces some of the need for promotion. High and stable sales keep the cost per unit relatively low. Heinz can therefore 'milk' cash from baked beans to invest in newer products such as Heinz organic ketchup.

Product B, by comparison, is in a high growth market but has a low market share. This type of product is known as a **problem child**. It may well provide high profits in the future; the market itself is attractive because it is growing fast and the product could provide high returns if it manages to gain a greater market share. These products usually need a relatively high level of investment to keep them going. They may need relaunches to help find a profitable position in the market. Heinz organic baby food is in this position. Heinz hopes to persuade mothers to buy pre-prepared baby food rather than make their own but may not succeed.

A third type of product is known as a **star** or 'rising star'. These products (like C) have a high market share and are selling in a fast growing market. These products are obviously attractive – they are doing well in a successful market. However, they may well need protecting from competitors' products. Once again the profits of the cash cows can be used to keep the sales growing. Heinz organic soups are in this category. They are very successful with fast growing sales but still need heavy promotion to ensure their success.

The fourth category of products are known as **dogs**. These products (like D) have a low share of a low growth market. They hold little appeal for a firm unless they can be revived.

The purpose of portfolio analysis is to examine the existing position of the firm's products. Once this has been done the managers can plan what to do next. Typically this will involve four strategies:

- building – this involves investment in promotion and distribution to boost sales; this is often used with question marks

- holding – this involves marketing spending to maintain sales; this is used with star products
- milking – this means taking whatever profits you can without much more new investment; this is often used with cash cow products
- divesting – this involves selling off the product and is common with 'dogs'.

When analysing the importance of the product life cycle and portfolio model it might be useful to consider:

- product life cycle and portfolio analysis are used to examine the existing position of a firm's product or products in the market and plan what to do next
- the models do not in themselves tell the firm what to do; managers must interpret their findings and decide on the most effective course of action
- managers must avoid letting these models become self fulfilling e.g. deciding the product is in decline and so letting its sales fall
- product life cycles are generally becoming shorter due to the rapid developments in technology and the increasing levels of competition in most markets
- as well as the life cycle for a particular product we can also consider the life cycle of a category of products; for example, we might examine the life of Flora margarine and the life cycle for the whole margarine market.

Business IN — THE SWATCH PORTFOLIO

The Swatch Group Ltd in Biel (Switzerland) is the largest manufacturer and distributor of watches in the world. It has a 25% share of the world market and produces over 114 million watches a year. It has 160 production centres situated mainly in Switzerland, but also in France, Germany, Italy, USA, Virgin Islands, Thailand, Malaysia and China. It produces over 18 brand names offering watches in all price and market categories:

- Breguet, Léon Hatot, Omega, Longines and Rado in the luxury, prestige and the top range segment, where watches can be priced at £200 to £10,000+
- Tissot, Calvin Klein, Certina, Mido, Hamilton and Pierre Balmain in the middle segment, at prices between £50 and £200
- Swatch and Flik Flak in the basic segment of £10–£50.

5.7 Product life cycle
an evaluation

Product life cycle and portfolio analysis are important in assessing the firm's current position within the market. This is known as a marketing audit. It is an essential step in the planning process. However, simply gathering data does not in itself guarantee success. A manager has to interpret the information effectively and then make the right decision.

Of the two approaches, product portfolio analysis is the more widely used. It helps a manager look critically at the firm's product range. Then decisions can be made on how the firm's marketing budget should be divided up. By contrast, product life cycle is found more often in textbooks than in the boardroom. It is a way of analysing what *has happened* to a product or brand. History can be useful or interesting, but it does not necessarily help you anticipate the future.

Think of all the fashions which died out, but then made a comeback. Then you realise anything is possible! There are no fixed rules in marketing. A product can start to grow and then sales suddenly fall. Alternatively sales may grow and grow for many years. A marketing manager needs to be flexible and use past data in connection with forecasts and even intuition.

The various strategies which are chosen will depend on the firm's portfolio of products. If most of the firm's products are cash cows, for example, it needs to be developing new products for future growth. If, however, the majority are problem children then it is in quite a high risk situation. It needs to try to ensure some products do become stars. If it has too many dogs then it needs to be investing in product development or acquiring new brands.

Both the product life cycle and product portfolio analysis are tools to help firms with their marketing planning. By analysing their existing situation they can identify what needs to be done to fulfil their objectives. However, like all planning tools, simply being able to examine the present position does not in itself guarantee success. Firms still have to be able to select the right strategy and implement it successfully.

portfolio analysis – an analysis of the market position of the firm's existing products; it is used as part of the marketing planning process.

cash cow – a product with a high share of a low growth market.

dogs – products which have a low share of a low growth market.

star – a product which has a high share of a fast growing market.

problem child – a product with a small share of a fast growing market.

marketing mix – the combination of variables through which the firm carries out its marketing strategy; for example, the product, the price, the place and the promotional mix.

marketing strategy – the way in which a firm aims to fulfil its objective, for example a firm may pursue a niche market or mass market strategy.

extension strategy – a strategy to prevent sales from declining.

AS Level Exercises

A. REVISION QUESTIONS

(35 marks; 60 minutes)

Read the unit, then answer:

1 Identify the different stages of the product life cycle. Give an example of one product or service you consider to be at each stage of the life cycle. *(4)*
2 Explain what is meant by 'extension strategies'. *(4)*
3 Outline the likely relationship between cash flow and the different stages of the life cycle. *(4)*
4 How is it possible for products such as Barbie to apparently defy the decline phase of the product cycle? *(6)*
5 What is meant by 'product portfolio analysis'? *(3)*
6 Distinguish between a cash cow and a star product in the Boston Matrix. *(4)*
7 Explain the likely relationship between capacity utilisation and the different stages of the life cycle. *(4)*
8 Firms should never take decline (or growth) for granted. Therefore they should never take success (or failure) for granted. Explain why this advice is important if firms are to make the best use of product life cycle theory. *(6)*

B. REVISION EXERCISES

B1 Data Response
Golden Wonder

Golden Wonder crisps was founded more than 50 years ago and grew to become the market leader. However, by the time Clive Sharpe led a management buyout from Dalgety in 1995 its sales were going backwards even though the market was still growing. Three years later, after a thorough shake up of the company, sales were back on the upward path. 'It's a great brand with a great reputation and we want to exploit it and take it into new territories', says Mr Sharpe.

Golden Wonder is best known for its crisps which are competing in a tough and mature market. Its main competitor is Pepsico, which has half the UK market with Walkers. Mr Sharpe claims Golden Wonder crisps beat Walkers 2:1 in blind tastings. But the group has a market share of just 19% including own-label brands for supermarkets – which Walkers does not make. Golden Wonder also makes branded snacks in which its best-known product is Wotsits. Pepsico has about a third of the snacks market, also under the Walkers brand. United Biscuits has a similar share with KP. This developing sector is where Golden Wonder is seeking most of its growth.

Questions *(30 marks; 35 minutes)*

1 What is meant by 'market share'? *(3)*
2 How can the company exploit the Golden Wonder brand name to keep its sales up? *(6)*
3 If Golden Wonder beats Walkers in taste tests, as Mr Sharpe claims, analyse the possible reasons why Walkers has a bigger market share. *(9)*
4 The market size for bagged crisps and snacks in 1998 was £1,702 million. If Golden Wonder achieved its claimed market share, what level of sales revenue would that represent? *(4)*
5 In 1995 the sales of Golden Wonder were falling; afterwards they increased. Discuss whether this means the product life cycle model is wrong. *(8)*

B2 Data Response
Persil Tablets

In 1998 Lever Brothers launched Persil Tablets – a new way to do your washing. All you have to do is put two tablets in the bag, put them in your wash and turn the machine on. The launch was Lever's latest attempt to get ahead of Procter and Gamble's Ariel in the washing powder wars that have been going on for many years. Four years earlier the launch of Persil Power with a patented 'accelerator' ingredient turned into a disaster when it was discovered that it weakened fabrics and left the colours faded. Procter and Gamble delighted in showing clothes ruined by Persil Power and the product was quickly withdrawn.

After the Persil Power fiasco consumers are rather distrustful of innovative products in this market and so Lever played down the 'newness' of the tablets. Instead it stressed that the tablets reduce wastage because most people put too much powder or liquid into their wash. Less wastage means less sales as the product does not have to be bought as often. Lever, however, believes the fact people change their clothes more often means the market has underlying growth. Over time the tablets are expected to take 20% of the billion pound washing powder market. As Persil tablets were being launched, Procter and Gamble were busy test marketing their own Ariel Discs in Grimsby.

Questions *(30 marks; 35 minutes)*

1 Distinguish between market share and market growth. *(3)*
2 Outline the factors that might determine the success of Persil Tablets in the market. *(6)*
3 Examine how the promotion of Persil Tablets might vary at different stages in its life cycle. *(6)*
4 Consider whether new product development is essential for success in the washing powder market. *(6)*
5 In the early 1980s the brand-leading detergent was Daz. By 1998 it was still fourth in the £750 million market for detergents, but with sales declining at a rate of 8% per year.
  a Where would this place Daz on the Boston Matrix? *(3)*
  b Given this placing, what factors should its owners, Procter and Gamble, take into account for the future marketing of Daz? *(6)*

B3 Case Study

Freedom Publishing produces a range of magazines aimed at different segments of the market. For example it produces:

- *Shout it Out*, aimed at young men between the ages of 15 and 20
- *Cool It*, for 20 to 24-year-olds into the latest fashions, clubs, music
- *Active Living*, aimed at 30 to 35-year-olds interested in outdoor activities
- *Out and About*, aimed at pensioners who want to travel, go to exhibitions and have weekend breaks.

Another of its publications is *Girl Power*. This is aimed at teenage girls and focuses on fashion tips, the latest music, new bands, etc. The magazine was a best-seller for many years and became the cash cow of the company. It was one of the very first magazines it produced and helped finance the start-up of many others. However in recent months sales have been disappointing and some of the senior managers think it has had its day. The marketing manager of *Girl Power*, Sindy Beal, is considering what to do next. For example, should she get rid of it? Or try and boost sales?

Year	Girl Power Sales (000s)
Four years ago	190
Three years ago	240
Two years ago	260
Last year	265
This year to date	262

Questions *(30 marks; 40 minutes)*

1 Draw a diagram of the product life cycle and highlight at which stage you think is *Girl Power*. State and justify your choice. *(10)*
2 What factors could influence what Sindy does next? *(10)*
3 If Sindy does decide to try and revive sales of *Girl Power*, suggest and explain an extension strategy she could try to adopt. *(10)*

A Level Exercises

A. REVISION QUESTIONS
(25 marks; 50 minutes)

Read the unit, then answer:

1 Outline three possible factors which can influence the shape of the product life cycle. *(6)*
2 Explain how the marketing of a product might vary at different stages in its life cycle. *(5)*
3 Explain the possible value of product portfolio analysis for a firm. *(4)*
4 A firm discovers that most of its products are becoming 'cash cows'. How might it react? *(4)*
5 Games n' Things believes that its latest computer software sports game is a star product. What implications might this have for the marketing of the product? *(6)*

B REVISION EXERCISES

B1 Case Study

Fenters

Fenters is a manufacturer of kitchen electrical products such as kettles, toasters and hobs. The firm has recently diversified into the microwave market and has launched its first microwave called Fast Friend. The product took three years to develop as this was a completely new market and technology for Fenters. Product development proved costly and had been more difficult than the company thought. The product launch was delayed on two occasions because of problems with the design. Despite anxiety before the launch the product was well received by both the trade press and retailers. Initial sales looked promising and led to a large number of advance orders. The company congratulated itself on its success and felt confident that sales would continue to grow. If the trend continued the firm would even have to consider extending its capacity. 'When you have a great product, sales tend to look after themselves', said Tom Gardiner, the managing director. Ambreen Gill, the marketing director, felt this did not show much real understanding of marketing but decided it was probably best not to tell the boss he was wrong!

Questions *(40 marks; 50 minutes)*

1 Analyse the factors Fenters might take into account when deciding how much to spend promoting the launch of the new product. *(10)*
2 Examine the factors which may influence the sales of the new product. *(10)*
3 To meet the increased orders Fenters may need to increase its capacity. Consider the difficulties this might pose to the company. *(10)*
4 According to the managing director, 'When you have a great product, sales tend to look after themselves'. Critically assess this statement. *(10)*

C. ESSAY QUESTIONS

1 Consider the view that the decline stage of the product life cycle is inevitable.
2 To what extent can portfolio planning guarantee a firm's success?
3 'The actual life cycles of products are all different. This makes the model of the product life cycle useless as a planning tool.' Do you agree with this view? Explain your answer.

NICHE VERSUS MASS MARKETING

DEFINITION

Mass marketing means devising products with mass appeal and promoting them to all types of customer. Niche marketing is tailoring a product to a particular type of customer. This limits the sales potential but makes the product more attractive to those in the target group.

6.1 Mass marketing

Mass marketing is the attempt to create products or services that have universal appeal. Rather than targeting a specific type of customer, mass marketing aims the product at the whole market. The intention is that everyone should be a consumer of the product. Coca-Cola is a good example of a firm that uses mass marketing techniques. The company aims its product at young and old alike. Its goal has always been to be the market leader, and it still is today. The ultimate goal of mass marketing is to achieve market domination. The ultimate prize of mass marketing is the creation of generic brands. These are brands that are so closely associated with the product that customers treat the brand name as if it were a product category. Examples include Hoover (vacuum cleaner) and Bacardi (white rum).

THE ORIGINS OF MASS MARKETING

Mass marketing started alongside mass production at the turn of the twentieth century. The architect was Henry Ford and the product was the Model T. Before the Model T, cars were too expensive to be owned by more than a handful of rich Americans. Ford decided that he wanted to see every American family owning a

Ford car. To do this profitably Ford had to revolutionise the way that cars were produced. By producing a standardised product from standardised parts Ford was able to reduce his costs. Ford did not even offer a choice of colour. Ford famously joked that you could have a Model T in 'any colour, so long as it's black'.

As costs fell Ford cut his prices. This brought the car within the budget of more American families. So demand grew further. Ford cut his prices continuously between 1909 and 1916. As a consequence sales rose by an astonishing 4,594% during the same period.

By the early 1920s Ford's mass marketing and mass production strategies had given the company over 50% of the US car market. Ford managed to create a virtuous reinforcing circle (see Figure 6.1). If mass marketing is carried out successfully it can be highly profitable. Even today many firms still set out

Low costs

Which created

Increased sales

Low prices

Which in turn created

Figure 6.1

to be high volume, low margin operators and achieve handsome profits. However, it is important to note that mass marketing does not have to go hand in hand with low prices. For example, Calvin Klein, producer of CK One, took the decision to target its latest fragrance at the mass market. First, by taking the unusual step of aiming its latest fragrance at both men

Push assembly line, 1913: dropping the Ford engine into the Model T chassis (© Corbis-Bettman)

and women the target market was doubled at a stroke. The decision to attract the mass market was also evident in terms of distribution policy. Calvin Klein decided to sell the fragrance through record shops as well as the more traditional distribution outlets of boutiques and department stores. By doing this Calvin Klein increased the chance of trial purchase from those who might not have considered buying fragrances before. The company's mass marketing strategy was vindicated by phenomenal sales and profitability. A highly effective advertising campaign featuring the supermodel Kate Moss provided the necessary **product differentiation** to sell high sales volumes without the need to cut prices.

PAN EUROPEAN AND GLOBAL MARKETING

Many firms have looked to exploit the fact that the world is shrinking. Modern communications and travel have created a situation where consumers of all nationalities are developing common habits and wants. Brands such as Levi's, Sony, McDonald's and Coca-Cola are available everywhere. The result is a global mass market for standardised consumer products. The **global marketing** approach involves selling the same product with the same marketing strategy the world over. McDonald's aims to create the same brand identity for its products the world over. Individual elements of the marketing mix may be adjusted slightly to suit local conditions but the general thrust of the marketing strategy does not vary from region to region. For example, the price of a Big Mac in Budapest is considerably lower than in London, but this is just a reflection of the differences in living standards between the two cities rather than anything more significant. Global marketing is therefore just an example of mass marketing but on a larger scale than even Henry Ford could have imagined.

THE BENEFITS OF GLOBAL MARKETING

- A global approach to marketing will increase the potential size of the target market. If the marketing strategy proves to be successful the rewards are massive in terms of sales volumes and profits. Western businesses such as Volkswagen and Tesco

have targeted the undeveloped markets of Eastern Europe for this very reason.

- In markets where product differentiation is low, survival against international competitors may require cost-reducing economies of scale. Most domestic markets are not large enough to create the output level required to generate these vital economies of scale. Global competition has also created severe pricing pressures. One way of coping with these pressures is to market your products on the largest possible stage, spreading costs and creating revenues across the globe. So therefore firms need to export. Firms selling a mass market product need to think globally just to survive.

- Standardising a marketing strategy can help to cut costs. First, a global strategy can be implemented more rapidly. Second, by selling the same product in the same manner everywhere, advertising and packaging costs need not be duplicated. Recently Mars the confectionery manufacturer renamed their famous Opal Fruit brand 'Starburst' for this very reason. The cost savings created by this type of strategy can be translated into lower worldwide prices giving the firm yet another source of competitive advantage.

- Due to rapidly advancing technology, product life cycles in many markets are getting shorter. If firms are not to be left behind they must attempt to develop more new products. However, new products are still very expensive to develop. Today, new products must repay their development costs more quickly if the firm is to make a profit on its new product launches. The extra sales generated by a global marketing strategy are important in terms of shortening the payback times on new products.

6.2 Niche marketing

INTRODUCTION

A market niche is a small segment of a larger market. Niche marketing is the process by which firms attempt to, first, find and then exploit new or under-served market sectors. It involves aiming at a relatively small target market with a specialised product designed to

The potential problems of going global

DIFFICULTY	KEY QUESTION	EXAMPLE
Cultural problems	Does the product fit the lifestyle and values of every nationality?	McDonald's struggled at first in France, as the French took meals too seriously for fast-food
Brand names	Does the name translate effectively?	Vauxhall were forced to change their Nova brand name in Spain. 'No va' in Spanish means 'no go'. Not a helpful brand name for a new car!
Consumer preference for local producers	Is the brand seen as 'foreign', or is it given the image of a local product?	Ford is widely seen as British, even though it is an American firm which imports many of its cars into Britain

meet the specific needs of that niche. A simple example is the holiday firm Saga, which aims only at the over-50s.

Firms adopting a niche market strategy must make their profits from a relatively small sales volume. This presents a problem as overheads cannot be spread over a high output level. So fixed costs per unit are high. Firms using niche marketing need high prices to compensate. Therefore the product must be highly differentiated and highly valued by the niche it is aimed at.

NICHE MARKETING IN THE MOTOR INDUSTRY

There are many reasons why firms in the motor industry have chosen to adopt niche marketing strategies.

- Niche markets can act as safe havens for small firms. In the mass market the small firm will always struggle against the economies of scale of larger firms. To survive, small firms often operate in niches that are too small for large firms to be interested. A small car manufacturer using this strategy is Morgan Cars. This England-based company makes hand-built sports cars aimed firmly at the nostalgic enthusiast. Morgan's sales of 500 cars per year give it a market share of below 0.05%. This niche is profitable for Morgan, but companies like Ford feel they can use their resources more effectively elsewhere. This is particularly true when the larger firms are making good profits in their mass markets. Why develop a new product for a tiny niche market when one aimed at the mass market will have far more sales potential?
- Large firms may switch to a niche marketing approach when a market has stopped growing. In a mature market the only way to gain further sales is to take market share from competitors. One way of achieving this is by using niche marketing tactics. Ten years ago Ford would have rejected the idea of developing a car aimed at a niche capable of sales of only 5,000 units per year. However this is exactly what Ford is doing today. It has a separate new product development division (called the Special Vehicle Team). It specialises in niche market vehicles with projected sales of less than 5,000 cars per year. By producing cars that tap into unmet needs, Ford has a better chance of tempting customers from their rivals. Niche products are being used by Ford in order to break existing brand loyalties.

- Niche marketing can also be used to help improve the sales of mass market products sold by the same manufacturer. Jaguar launched the high performance XJ220 partly to provide additional glamour to the family brand name. Niche market products can be highly profitable in their own right. However their effect on overall company profits can be even more substantial. The XJ220 created a 'halo effect' that added value and sales volume to the more established Jaguar models.

HOT STUFF IN A NICHE MARKET

In 1985, Andrew Palmer spotted a gap in the food market. Heinz dominated soup sales, but the market was slowly declining. He decided to market a range of fresh, chilled 'home-made' soups which would be expensive but with a distinctly better taste than from cans or packets. Prices would be three times those of canned soup, but the quality of the soups would add the value required to justify the price. Palmer found the necessary capital and the 'New Covent Garden Soup Company' was born.

It started in London, but spread nationwide by 1990. Quickly, Marks & Spencer and Sainsbury's copied the style of packaging and product, but the company kept introducing new flavours and survived the competition. In the year to June 1997, sales of £16 million yielded operating profits of over £2.4 million. Then a medium-sized food group called S Daniels offered £22 million to buy the business. Andrew Palmer became a millionaire.

Business
IN

NICHE RADIO

In August 2002 the BBC launched a new niche market digital radio station called 1Xtra. According to Wilber Wilberforce, the station's programme editor 1Xtra is aimed at urban 16 to 25 year olds who enjoy a combination of hip-hop, raga, drum 'n' bass and UK garage that is collectively known as 'Black Music'. Unfortunately for the BBC, research conducted just prior to the station's launch revealed that ownership of digital radios is very low amongst urban 16 to 25 year olds. Consequently, despite the undoubted popularity of 'Black Music', 1Xtra is likely to remain a tiny niche market radio station until cheap digital radios become available.

Business
IN

HOW DO FIRMS GO ABOUT IDENTIFYING NEW MARKET NICHES?

The approach used to identify niche markets varies from company to company. However there are some general lessons to be learned.

If possible be close to your own market: Small firms may have an advantage over larger firms in terms of identifying market niches. This is because smaller firms are said to be closer to their consumers. But what exactly does this mean?

- Many ideas for niche market products come from direct customer feedback at the point of sale. 'Off the cuff' comments on likes and dislikes about the present product range can provide valuable insights and ideas for new niche products. In small firms the manager is more likely to pick up these ideas. They are in more regular contact with customers and their front-line staff. A customer complaint or request may spark an idea for a totally new product or service.
- Small specialist firms are often run by enthusiasts. Indeed, the idea to set the business up in the first place may have come from the experiences of the owner as a consumer. An example of this was James Dyson who decided to design a bagless vacuum cleaner that would not suffer from suction problems.

AIMING HIGH

The world market for wristwatches is exceptionally fragmented. Most people choose their watch largely on the basis of design and price. Brand names count for little in the mass market. An exception is Swatch – the Swiss brand which has sold over 250 million watches since its 1983 launch.

At the top end of the market, most of the prestige brands such as Cartier sell in very small volume. Only Rolex combines high price with relatively high volume (rumoured, says the Financial Times, to be 700,000 units per year). Citizen of Japan has tried to break away from general competition by designing watches to meet specific market niches. This allows it to charge £100+ instead of its more usual £50. An example is the Altichron. This watch gives a climber the height above sea level as he or she ascends a mountain. A useless feature for most people, but real added value to a climber. And a nice way for a Japanese firm to break into the Swiss home market.

Utilise modern secondary market research information: Both manufacturers and retailers have always been keen to swop sales figures in order to gain valuable **market intelligence** information. The fact that many shoppers use retail loyalty cards has added even more value to this data. Databases can now be merged and cross-referenced so that retailers and manufacturers know not only what has been sold but also the identity of the buyer. Knowing the identity of a potential buyer is vital for targeting promotion. If a firm knows the names and addresses of potential consumers they can be contacted via direct mail. Advances in technology now make it possible to target with a precision that was once inconceivable. Precision reduces direct mail costs substantially because it reduces wastage. It avoids the huge expense of a mass medium such as television advertising. Secondary market research information held on complex databases can also be used to conduct market mapping exercises. This process is described in detail in Unit 3.

ISSUES FOR **analysis**

- It is useful to analyse niche marketing in relation to price elasticity. Niche market products are invariably designed to meet the needs of customers looking for something different. This means that buyers of niche market goods are likely to be less price sensitive than consumers of mass market brands. This is especially true for the first brand to open up a niche market. Consumers may regard the originator of the market segment as 'the real thing'. An example would be Haagen Dazs in the super-premium ice-cream sector. On average, niche products are less price elastic than mass market products. Therefore higher prices can be charged.
- Fundamentally there are two approaches to making profit. The first is to be a high volume, low margin operator. The second is to charge higher prices and be a low volume, high margin operator. This is the route taken by those who adopt niche marketing tactics.
- In developed economies there is a trend away from mass to niche marketing. It will be difficult for large firms to be profitable in niche markets unless they can find a way to produce efficiently in small batches. Niche marketing implies a move away from mass production.

6.3 Niche versus mass marketing
an evaluation

Which is better? Mass or niche marketing? The answer is that it depends. In the bulk ice-cream market, large packs of vanilla ice-cream have become so cheap that little profit can be made. Better by far, then, to be in a separate niche, whether regional (Mackie's Scottish ice-cream) or upmarket such as Rocombe Farm or Haagen Dazs. The latter can charge 10 times as much per litre as the mass market own-label bulk packs.

Yet, if one looks at the marketing of films or books, would a firm rather be selling a critic's favourite or a blockbuster smash hit? The latter, of course. Film-makers such as Steven Spielberg have shown not only mastery over the technical side of film production and direction but also a sure marketing touch. They can tell whether a story will appeal to a mass audience. Conventional businesses such as Heinz, Kellogg's and even Chanel show that mass marketing does not have to mean devaluing a brand name.

Business IN

global marketing – marketing throughout the world as if it is one market, for instance using the same brand name and brand advertising.

market intelligence – useful information about consumers, distributors or competitors.

pan-European marketing – marketing throughout Europe as if it is a single market, i.e. same brand name and advertising.

price elasticity – the responsiveness of demand to a change in price.

product differentiation – the extent to which consumers perceive your brand as being different from others.

AS Level Exercises

A. REVISION QUESTIONS
(30 marks; 60 minutes)

Read the unit, then answer:

1 Identify three advantages of niche marketing over mass marketing. *(3)*
2 Give three reasons why a large firm may wish to enter a niche market. *(3)*
3 Why do small firms frequently appear better at spotting and then reacting to new niche market opportunities? *(4)*
4 Give two reasons why average prices in niche markets tend to be higher than those charged in most mass markets. *(2)*
5 Many firms have developed global marketing strategies during the 1990s. Outline three of the motivations for such a move. *(6)*
6 Outline two factors a firm should consider before embarking on a global marketing strategy. *(4)*
7 State three reasons why information technology has made niche marketing a more viable option for large firms. *(3)*
8 Explain why it is important for a large firm to be flexible if it is to operate successfully in niche markets. *(5)*

B. REVISION EXERCISES

B1 Data Response

The New Beetle

Volkswagen is drawing up contingency plans to build its new Beetle model in Europe as a result of soaring demand for the Mexican-built car in North America and a global queue of more than 2,000 would-be buyers.

A decision on whether to proceed, and at which of the group's plants that should be, will be made by May, Ferdinand Piech, chairman, told the Financial Times at the European launch of the car. VW will start selling the new VW in Europe on November 27 at prices starting from DM34,950 (£12,650).

The original Beetle, launched in 1945, has sold more than 21 million units and is still produced at Puebla in Mexico, mainly for developing world markets. Although production of the new Beetle is still climbing from the start-up phase, more than 40,000 have been delivered to North American buyers. A decision was taken several months ago to lift capacity at Puebla from 121,500 to 162,000 a year.

With VW's executives in the US indicating that North American markets alone could absorb most of the Mexican output, only around 80,000 new Beetles will be allocated for sale in Europe next year, 45,000 of them for Germany.

The UK market will not receive right-hand drive versions of the new Beetle until the end of 1999, although VW will offer 1,000 left-hand drives in the Spring to customers who have already ordered.

Source: Adapted from *The Financial Times*, 9/11/98

Questions *(25 marks; 30 minutes)*
1 Explain the meaning of the terms:
  a contingency plan *(2)*
  b capacity. *(2)*
2 Volkswagen planned the Beetle as a niche market product aimed at trendy young drivers. It was to sell at a price premium over cars such as the Golf (approx £10,000) and the Seat (approx £9,000).
  a Given that approach, how might Volkswagen promote the Beetle when it is launched in Britain in late 1999? *(6)*
  b How might the company's marketing strategy change if the Beetle's sales success persuades Volkswagen to mass market the product in Britain? *(8)*
3 Discuss the business consequences of a continued failure by Volkswagen to produce enough cars to meet the demand for this new Beetle. *(7)*

B2 Case Study

A Niche Interest in Computers

The IT revolution has created opportunities for both large and small firms. When Mike Penfield and Dianne Tomkinson met during their last year at university they discussed the idea of setting up their own business together. They felt that many large studios had overlooked a potentially profitable niche within the design market. Mike and Dianne shared a background in design and IT. Their idea was to offer affordable access to high quality computer facilities, backed up by advice and help. They planned to cater for the needs of small firms who wanted to hire the technology required to produce their own distinctive posters and brochures rather than having to buy it or sub-contract the work out. In other words they planned to benefit from being small.

The couple provided most of the necessary start-up capital to set up Desire Design Ltd. With the aid of a bank loan the business opened its first outlet in Croydon in 1998 with seven Apple Macs, two printers and a scanner being available for hire. Fortunately for the couple, the business proved to be a roaring success. The concept of hiring proved popular for two reasons. First, entrepreneurs appreciated the cost savings that came from doing design work in house rather than having to pay expensive design studio fees. Second, hiring was also a more viable option than outright purchase for the majority of small firms as clients only paid for what they used.

Dianne was keen to pursue growth. So a decision was made to reinvest most of the firm's profits in new equipment. Today, Desire has more than 50 fully equipped workstations to hire out and the couple are looking to diversify. One of their current ideas is to offer a budget website design service targeted specifically at small firms.

Questions   (30 marks; 60 minutes)

1 Describe the niche Mike and Dianne identified.   (4)
2 Explain why the profit margins in niche markets are frequently higher than in the mass market.   (5)
3 Outline three key criteria for successful operation in a niche market.   (6)
4 Consider the problems Desire may run in to as a result of Dianne's policy of growth.   (7)
5 Discuss whether a small operator such as Desire Design can only survive by competing in niche markets.   (8)

B3 Case Study

The Niche Marketing of BMW's New Mini

In the summer of 2001 BMW launched the new Mini. The new car was designed so that it resembled the original Mini, the best selling car that was a design icon of the 1960s and 70s. However, the new model was bigger, safer and more luxurious than its predecessor. These improvements were intended to create a car that was right up to date but without losing the character, fun and excitement of the original Mini.

The new Mini was a strategically important new product for BMW. The aim being that this new car would enable BMW to capitalise on the growing small car segment of the car market. By diversifying in this way the company would no longer be so dependent upon sales of its luxury cars for the bulk of its profits.

The car was aimed at creating a new market niche by appealing to twenty and thirty-somethings with high disposable incomes who want a funky, more stylish alternative to mass-market small cars. According to BMW promotional material the new Mini was 'for individuals who were not interested in following the crowd'.

BMW's marketing department used persuasive advertising to promote the brand. The 'Mini Adventures' TV advertising campaign was based around a series of humorous story lines featuring good looking young people having fun and adventure in their new Mini. In addition to the above-the-line activity, BMW used a variety of innovative below-the-line tactics. For example, part of Gatwick South's departure lounge was transformed into a shrine devoted to the new Mini. Passengers waiting for their flights were given access to a colourful and stylish Mini lounge area equipped with terminals offering free Internet access to www.mini.co.uk. Tactics like this helped to create exactly the sort of trendy image that BMW wanted for the brand.

The new Mini had a very successful first year in terms of sales: 30,000 cars were sold in the UK alone and in America the car was so popular that waiting lists developed. To address the supply and demand mismatch, BMW plan to increase the annual production of the new Mini by 15 to 20% in order to cope with demand levels that have clearly caught the company by surprise.

Questions   (30 marks; 35 minutes)

1 Explain how BMW might have gone about identifying whether a niche market opportunity existed for the new Mini.   (6)
2 How can large firms like BMW benefit from selling niche market products like the new Mini?   (8)
3 The new Mini was priced at £11,000 in the UK when it was launched in 2001. Discuss whether BMW should consider increasing the price of the car in the future.   (10)
4 To be successful, niche market products must be differentiated. Explain how BMW went about creating the product differentiation needed to ensure the new Mini's success.   (6)

MARKETING STRATEGY

DEFINITION

Marketing strategy is a carefully evaluated plan for future marketing activity that balances company objectives, available resources and market opportunities.

7.1 What is strategy?

Strategy is the plan of the medium- to long-term actions required to achieve the company goals or targets. Marketing strategy is the marketing contribution. The term strategy implies that the plan has been carefully thought out. Successful marketing requires careful planning. This requires an understanding of the nature, possibilities and potential of the business and the environment in which it is operating. Marketing strategy is finding a fit between the company objectives, customer requirements and the activities of competitors.

WHY HAVE STRATEGY?

The aim of this planning is to shape the company's activities and products to generate the best returns for the business. It ensures that marketing activity makes the best possible contribution to the success of the business. Marketing strategy is about *adding value*. It takes advantage of any unique selling points. It helps the business to identify the right mix of design, function, image or service.

STRATEGY IS ABOUT THE FUTURE

The term 'strategy' implies looking to the future. It is important not to look at what is working well now but at what future prospects are. The Ford Motor Company recognised that rising petrol prices meant large cars were likely to go out of fashion. It started to invest in the production of small cars. If it had continued to invest in the most profitable part of the business it would have continued to expand production of large cars.

STRATEGY MUST BE ACHIEVABLE

Strategy is concerned with what is possible not just desirable. It must take into account market potential and company resources. The company needs to recognise its own limitations and potential. It also needs to consider economic and social circumstances. Many UK firms held back from developing new export markets when the pound was strong between 1997 and 2002. In America, the popularity of products such as

Bacardi Breezer and Smirnoff Ice is leading to calls for advertising bans, as they are said to encourage underage drinking.

STRATEGY IS COMPANY SPECIFIC

Each company will have a different marketing strategy. This will reflect its individual circumstances. Different companies within the same industry may be pursuing different goals. They will develop different strategies. Within the same industry, one company may be aiming to increase market share whilst another looks for cost reductions in order to compete on price. The tyre industry is a good example of this. The market leaders were faced with increasing price competition from developing countries. They had to develop new marketing strategies. Their responses differed. Goodyear reduced costs. Michelin put its effort into innovation and widened its product range. Pirelli decided to concentrate on the market for luxury and speed.

Marketing strategy is the marketing plan of action which:

- *contributes to the achievement of company objectives*
- *finds the best fit between company objectives, available resources and market possibilities*
- *looks to the future*
- *is carefully thought out*
- *is realistic*

7.2 Strategy versus tactics

Strategy is not the same as tactics. Strategy is an overall plan for the medium to long term. Tactics are individual responses to opportunities or threats. They tend to be short term. The marketing strategy may be to increase sales by developing a new market segment. One of the tactics used may be to undercut a competitor on price in a price sensitive segment of the market.

Defining strategy:	
Business review	● *Where are we now?*
Objectives	● *Where do we want to be?*
Strategy	● *How shall we get there?*
Plans	● *Ways and means of carrying out strategy*

7.3 Developing a marketing strategy

The strategic planning process is at the heart of marketing. It involves laying down clear plans for marketing activities. If the strategy is to work it requires an excellent knowledge of the business, its markets and its customers.

To develop a marketing strategy it is necessary to:

1 define overall company objectives
2 analyse the existing business
3 understand the market
4 analyse available resources.

Company objectives identify priorities for the organisation. They take account of the external climate and the state of the business. Marketing strategy should contribute to the achievement of these objectives. The marketing element will not be independent. To be effective it needs to work with the other business functions. Doubling market share may require an increase in production. This involves operations, finance and personnel.

If the strategy is to work there must be a clear understanding of the existing business and the market in which it is operating. The two are interlinked. Sales may be increasing. This may be due to better products. It could be poor performance by a competitor. The analysis will include the whole business but concentrate on marketing. There are several tools that can be used. These include:

1 Statistical analysis: A good starting point is to look at past performance. Figures need to be gathered for sales, market share and contribution, ideally broken down by product. The trends can be analysed. This analysis should help to explain the patterns. This will be useful for estimating future sales.

2 Market research: The statistical analysis should be supported by market research. An understanding of customer buying behaviour will help explain sales patterns. It will indicate future buying patterns. Market research will also provide information about the state of the total market and the behaviour of competitors.

3 SWOT analysis: This is a tool used to audit the internal and external business environments. SWOT stands for Strengths, Weaknesses, Opportunities and Threats.

Business IN

TOO MANY SEATS?

2002 was a record year for cinemas. Audience figures reached 174 million matching the previous record set in 1971. This success, partly due to the release of successful films such as *The Lord of the Rings* and *Star Wars Episode 2*, masks an underlying problem in the industry.

After years of audience decline customers started returning during the early 1990s. This led to an expectation of even further growth, leading to huge investment into new multiplex complexes. The result is that in spite of record attendance, most big cities such as Manchester and Birmingham have too many cinema screens. In 2000 the number of screens rose by 200 or 6% while seat sales only grew by 2.8%. This growth is expected to slow and analysts are suggesting that there will be some consolidation in the market. There have already been signs of this. In 2001 ABC cinemas bought the Odeon chain resulting in the closure of 36 cinemas. In spite of these closures the feeling of industry experts is that 'it is a question of being selective about locations and getting the right size of cinema'. Cinema owners are also looking at new developments such as the screening of live events, e.g. music and sport.

Source: *The Times*, 24/8/02

Internal review

The internal audit looks at what the business is doing well (strengths) and what it could do better (weaknesses).The emphasis is on marketing but other aspects are important. A company with inefficient production processes will have high costs. It will find it difficult to compete on price. Each business will have its own problems and areas of excellence. Key areas include:

● Company reputation – what is the reputation of the business? Marks and Spencer has a reputation for quality. Microsoft has a reputation for innovation. But Skoda? Or Iceland? What reputations have they?
● Market representation – is the business strong or weak in any particular market or market segment?
● Brands – does the company have any strong brands?
● New products – does the business have any new products ready for the market?
● Distribution – are the products widely available in the market?

External review

The external review looks at the business environment.

The opportunities and threats audit will look at issues such as:

- **State of the economy** – is the economy growing or in recession? Are any sectors of the economy performing differently? A period of recession may be a threat to a company supplying luxury goods but an opportunity for a manufacturer supplying own label goods to supermarkets.
- **Market** – are there any gaps in the market? Are new markets available? What are competitors doing? An aggressive marketing campaign by a competitor will be a threat. The failure of a competitor will be an opportunity.
- **Technology** – how may technological change affect the business? Are products keeping pace with change? Is technology opening up new markets? Video conferencing is an opportunity for telecommunications firms. It could be seen as a threat to the business travel industry.
- **Demography** – how will changes in population structure affect the market and the business? The growth in the number of old people has provided opportunities for businesses providing goods and services required by the elderly. The falling number of young people coming into the job market may be a threat to industries that rely on young people for their workforce.

ANALYSIS OF AVAILABLE RESOURCES

The marketing strategy cannot be finalised without considering available resources. The strategy must be realistic and achievable. Company resources will include products, finance and human resources. A strategy to expand into overseas markets will fail unless the company can commit the resources needed to penetrate that market. When certain skills are not available it may be possible to purchase them from external specialists. The growth of advertising agencies is a reflection of this.

7.4 Marketing strategy – the final piece of the jigsaw

Finding the best marketing strategy is like finding the last piece of the jigsaw. All of the other pieces are now in place. The company objectives, available resources and an understanding of the business and the environment in which it is operating. The final piece to deliver business success is the strategy. The strategy should flow naturally from the situation that the company is in and the prospects for the future. It should take advantage of the company strengths and the available market opportunities. It cannot try to do

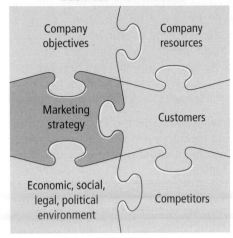

Business Environment

Company objectives — Company resources — Marketing strategy — Customers — Economic, social, legal, political environment — Competitors

Market Environment

Figure 7.1

everything but should pick out priorities according to the circumstances. A good strategy will link together analysis of customer preferences to the company's strengths. This is known as *asset-led marketing*.

Marketing strategy should:

- *be part of the overall business strategy*
- *add value*
- *be asset led – use the company's strengths*
- *take advantage of market opportunities*
- *address the company's weaknesses*
- *be prepared to react to any threats*

7.5 Types of strategy

There are many possible strategies for any one business. The strategy may be specific to a particular product. It may focus on the whole product range, or be focused on new products or new markets. At any one time the business could be pursuing several different strategies. A business may have one strategy for one product and another for a different product.

Among the main marketing strategies are the following:

Market penetration: This is about increasing market share. It is the most common and safest strategy. It concentrates on existing markets and products. The business should have good knowledge of these. The strategy will involve finding ways of increasing sales. This may be by:

- Finding new customers – perhaps by widening the product's appeal to attract additional buyers.

- Taking customers from competitors – this may be achieved by aggressive pricing or by offering additional incentives to the customer.
- Persuading existing customers to increase usage – many food companies give recipes with their products to suggest additional ways of using the product. Shampoo manufacturers introduced a frequent wash shampoo to boost product usage.

Market development: This is about finding new markets for existing products. It is a more risky strategy as it involves dealing with new customers and markets. It may be done by:

- **Repositioning** the product – this will target a different market segment. This could be by broadening the product's appeal to a new customer base. Rover's traditional market for Land Rovers was farming and military use. It has now repositioned the product to appeal to town dwellers.
- **Moving into new markets** – many British retailers have opened up outlets abroad. Some, such as Tesco and Laura Ashley, have opened up their own outlets. Others have entered into joint ventures or have taken over a similar operation in another country.

Business IN

REPOSITIONING HOVIS

By 2001, the Hovis brand name was becoming tired. It was still much-loved and trusted, yet market research showed it to be seen as old fashioned. Unsurprisingly, sales were slipping. The brand owner, British Bakeries, called in a specialist packaging design company to re-position the brand. Out went the traditional wheat sheaves and 'warm', brown colours. In came a dramatic new look, with bright packaging covered in pictures of baked beans, cucumber, and other foods that people eat with bread. It gave the brand a much younger feel, and beat rival brands hands-down for visual display and appeal in-store. Since then, Hovis brown and white bread have become the brand leaders for the first time in the company's 115 year history, boosting sales by a value of 31% since the relaunch.

Product development: Most companies continually develop their products. In some industries, such as electronics or pharmaceuticals, innovation is essential. In highly competitive markets companies use product development to differentiate their product from the competitor's product. Strategies may include:

- Changing an existing product – this may be to keep the products attractive. Washing powders and

shampoos are good examples of this. The manufacturers are continually repackaging or offering some 'essential' new ingredient.
- Developing new products – Mars ice-cream bar is a classic example of a new and successful product development.

7.6 Marketing strategy in different markets

INDUSTRIAL VERSUS CONSUMER MARKETS

Although exams tend to focus on consumer products and services, there are sometimes questions on firms which sell to industrial and business customers. Examples include firms producing heavy lorries, metal components or services such as security or cleaning. There are some differences between consumer and industrial marketing. Often because the number of potential buyers may be far fewer. A supplier of metal components may have only 12 potential customers in the country.

Developing strategies will, however, be a very similar process. It will still need an excellent understanding of the product and the market. To a great extent the differences will depend on how competitive the market is. In some industrial markets there may be only one customer or one product. This will clearly result in different strategies. It may require working directly with the buyer to develop the product. Where customers are limited the industrial business may have no alternative but to look to overseas markets if it wishes to expand. If the market for its products is stagnant or saturated the business may need to develop new products.

For many industrial products there will be little difference to the consumer market. There will still be a need for **competitive differentiation** and correct positioning of the product.

7.7 Marketing strategy – a risky business?

Making changes in any business carries a certain amount of risk. Careful evaluation of the business and market situation will reduce the risk involved. Some strategies are more risky than others. The closer the business stays to its existing market and products the lower the risk. As it moves away from these known areas so the risk increases. Ansoff shows this in his matrix (see Figure 7.2).

As Ansoff's matrix shows, the least risky strategy is market penetration. Both the market and products are known to the business. With both product development and market development the risk is increased as the business moves into new areas. **Diversification** is the most risky strategy. Here both products and the market are new to the business.

Existing   New

PRODUCTS

Figure 7.2 Ansoff's matrix

7.8 Marketing strategy – a continual process

Once the strategy has been developed it needs to be constantly reviewed. An idea that looks good on paper will not necessarily work in action. There may need to be some testing of strategies, especially if they are risky. Market research and monitoring are necessary to ensure that the actions are producing the desired results. Evaluation of results will feed back into the system and in turn contribute to the development of revised objectives and strategies. This ongoing cycle is known as the **strategic cycle**.

Figure 7.3 The strategic cycle

STRATEGY NEEDS TO BE RESPONSIVE

A company's marketing strategy does not exist in a vacuum. It may provoke responses from competitors. Market opportunities will be changing constantly. If the company is to be successful it needs to be responsive and to adjust the strategy to cope with any changes in the environment or within the company. For example, the giant Heinz company found that its approach to global marketing was ineffective – it shifted strategy to become more local. Only in Britain were baked beans an important seller, so the baked bean pizza was developed for the UK alone. In Korea, people love to pour ketchup on pizza, so a deal with Pizza Hut put a Heinz bottle on every table.

IN Business

BRITISH AIRWAYS THREATS AND STRATEGIES

British Airways has had more than its fair share of threats. During the 1990s, airline deregulation in Europe led to a growth in cut-price airlines. The huge success of these cheap, no-frills operations led British Airways to set up its own cut-price operation called 'Go'. Go was successful and BA sold it in 2001 to a management buyout team for £110 million saying that it was impractical for one company to run two businesses. (It was resold to easyJet for £400 million in 2002).

It wasn't long before BA was faced with a more substantial threat to its existence. The terrorist attacks in September 2001 had a devastating impact on the airline industry. BA was reported to be losing £2 million a day and many analysts feared that the airline would go bankrupt. Then, in 2003, BA was hit again by the war in Iraq plus the SARS virus in the Far East. However, although bruised, it has survived. The key to survival has been to cut costs and for the first time in its history to offer low priced, short-haul fares that compete with prices offered by the low cost airlines.

The low cost airlines still remain a threat; the scale of which can be seen in the number of orders for new planes. At the same time as British Airways has 20 planes mothballed in the Mojave Desert, Ryanair and easyJet have both placed orders for new aircraft. Analysts expect the discounters' share of the market to rise to 12–15% by 2010. If it is to survive, British Airways will need an imaginative and successful marketing strategy.

ISSUES FOR **analysis**

Issues that may need to be considered in response to case study or essay questions are:

- The relative importance of strategic market planning in different types of businesses. Can small firms possibly devote the time, thought and resources to strategy that would be spent by firms such as Heinz?
- The extent to which it is possible to develop clear strategies in a constantly changing marketplace.

- The influence of individuals may be important. The degree of risk in a firm's strategy may depend partly on the personality of the key decision maker. An entrepreneurial marketing director may achieve breakthroughs (or disasters) which a more cautious person would avoid.
- How do businesses find a balance between what is desirable and what is achievable? In some firms, the balance is determined at the top (by directors who may not understand fully the market conditions). Others adopt a more participative style, in which directors consult junior executives to get a clear idea of what can be achieved.

the only business objective may be survival. Strategy may then be reduced to crisis management. The other reality is that the business environment is not always clear and logical so it may be very difficult to generate realistic and effective strategies.

7.9 Marketing strategy
an evaluation

It would be nice to think that businesses carefully evaluate the marketing environment and then devise a strategy that fits in with overall company objectives. In reality the strategy may be imposed by management, shareholders or even circumstances. In some instances

KEY terms

competitive differentiation – making your product or buying experience different from that of your competitors.

demography – the study of populations.

diversification – when a company expands its activities outside its normal range. This may be done to reduce risk or to expand possible markets.

repositioning – changing the product or its promotion to appeal to a different market segment.

AS Level Exercises

A. REVISION QUESTIONS
(30 marks; 70 minutes)

Read the unit, then answer:

1 What is marketing strategy? (3)
2 What is the difference between marketing strategy and marketing tactics? (3)
3 What is a unique selling point? Give two examples. (4)
4 What is meant by product differentiation? (3)
5 What are the four steps in developing a marketing strategy? (4)
6 What is a SWOT analysis? (3)
7 Why is it important for a firm to examine its internal resources before deciding on a strategy? (3)
8 What is meant by 'market penetration'? (3)
9 What is the difference between market development and product development? (4)

B. REVISION EXERCISES

B1 Activities
This can be a group or individual exercise.
Select a current advertisement from the TV or from a magazine or newspaper.

Questions
1 Analyse the advertisement in detail. You will want to look at issues such as:
   a What is the advertisement about? A product, a service, an improvement to an existing product, a special offer?
   b What is the message in the advertisement? Identify the key features such as price, quality, comparisons with rivals, etc.
   c Who is it aimed at? What is the target group or groups?
   d Is it a new or existing product?
   e Does the product have any rivals? If so, is the company trying to differentiate its product? How?
2 Research the market for this product. You might attempt to do this via the Internet, or visit a good business library. (A full list of available resources and libraries is given in the *A–Z Coursework Handbook* 3rd edition, Marcouse I, Hodder and Stoughton, 2003.) Visit the appropriate retail outlet and carry out a comparison of the shelf space, prices and display strengths of this product in relation to its competitors.
3 Decide what you believe the marketing strategy is for this company or product. Try to determine how this advertisement will fit into an overall marketing strategy.
4 Prepare your conclusions and analysis as a marketing presentation.

B2 Data Response

Shoppers Are Going Upmarket

According to research done by the British Retail Consortium shoppers are switching away from discount products to more upmarket goods. This trend towards quality rather than quantity is most evident in the electrical goods sector with shoppers opting for more expensive household gadgets. Of the 1,000 adults surveyed, 71% of those who said they were spending more on electrical goods said the extra had gone on better quality goods.

The food sector has also seen a change from traditional foods to exotic foreign and health foods. About half of those who said they were spending more on food said they were buying more upmarket products.

Source: *The Times*, 21/8/98

Questions *(30 marks; 35 minutes)*

1 What is meant by discount goods? *(3)*
2 a What do customers seem to want from electrical goods? *(3)*
  b How might an electrical goods retailer react to these findings? *(6)*
3 What changes might a food manufacturer make to its marketing strategy, as a result of the information in the article? *(8)*
4 As a food manufacturer, what other information would you like to have before deciding on a new marketing strategy? Explain your answer. *(10)*

A Level Exercises

A. REVISION QUESTIONS

(25 marks; 50 minutes)

Read the unit, then answer:

1 How does marketing strategy relate to the objectives of a business? *(5)*
2 Why is market research an important part of marketing strategy? *(6)*
3 What is meant by the strategic cycle? *(3)*
4 What is the difference between industrial and consumer markets? *(3)*
5 Why is market development more risky than market penetration? *(4)*
6 Why might a business use retrenchment as part of its marketing strategy? *(4)*

B. REVISION EXERCISES

B1 Data Response

Perfect Partners produces ready-made meals. These are reheated in either the microwave or the oven. The products are fresh and sold from the chilled counter. They are only sold in single portion sizes and the company has concentrated solely on the one-person meals market. It has not attempted to compete on price, as the market is very competitive. Strong advertising, aimed at young single people, has supported the product. The emphasis has been on quality and convenience. The company hopes to establish a strong reputation for quality that will ensure repeat sales.

The company has aimed at steady growth to enable expansion of production facilities to take place without disruption. The new production facilities will also provide flexibility so that they can respond to market opportunities.

The company objective is to double turnover in 10 years with a view to floating on the stock market. Sales have increased each year, slightly above the growth in the total market. This has pleased the firm as the market is highly competitive and has had many new entrants, including supermarket own-brands. There is also considerable competition from manufacturers of similar frozen products. Market research indicates that the company has developed a strong brand image.

A recent market survey has produced some interesting results for the company's marketing department to consider. The following graph shows past and expected sales of one-person meals in the UK.

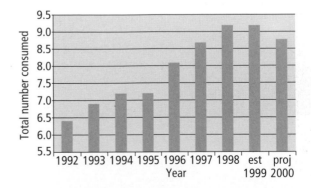

The total market has been growing steadily each year. However it would seem that the sales for this year will be around the same level as last year. The survey also predicts that:

- Future sales will fall. This is partly a result of the expected recession but there is also evidence that this market has peaked.
- Consumption of one-person meals is heaviest in large families. This would seem to contradict the idea that lone dining is concentrated in single households.
- The survey also revealed that the total market for ready-prepared meals should continue to grow in the medium term.

Questions *(40 marks; 60 minutes)*

1 Use the graph to calculate the percentage growth in the market from 1994 to 1998. Show your workings clearly. *(6)*

2 Outline briefly the firm's current marketing strategy. *(4)*

3 In note form, conduct a SWOT analysis for the business based on the information given in the case study. *(8)*

4 In the light of the new research, a change might be necessary to the firm's current marketing strategy. How should the firm decide whether the strategy needs to be changed? *(10)*

5 Identify two new marketing strategies the firm might follow in response to the information in the case study. Outline the advantages and disadvantages of each. *(12)*

B2 Case Study

Abbey Sees No Future in Mortgages

Abbey National is the UK's second biggest mortgage lender. It has around 14% of the mortgage market based on outstanding loans. It is second only to the Halifax, which has about 20% of the market.

In 1989 it became the first building society to convert to a bank and float on the Stock Exchange. Mortgage lending was its core business, but this has plunged in recent years. In the first quarter of 1998, net new loans hit zero. There are several reasons for this:

1 New entrants into the mortgage market have undercut the established providers who are tied into a network of expensive high street branches.

2 The remaining mutual building societies such as Nationwide have embarked on a discounting campaign.

3 The great British mortgage has become a commodity item. Traditionally, borrowers stayed with the same lender for 25 years. Now the average life of a mortgage is 7 years.

Analysts see the mortgage market polarising. One group of customers chooses their lender solely on the headline interest rate. These customers tend to move around, as more attractive deals become available. The second group is prepared to pay higher rates for more flexible products and better service. Abbey National's strategy to meet these challenges is to produce products to attract the second group of customers and to try to keep existing customers for longer. Another part of Abbey's strategy is to continue diversifying into more profitable areas of financial services. Currently, almost 50% of profits come from this area. The chief executive has set a target of obtaining 65% of profit from non-mortgage business within the next five years. He expects new lending to claim about 5% of the total market. He believes that Abbey has to continue to diversify into markets with stronger rates of growth and in which competition is weaker. As an example, he cites the life assurance and pensions markets, which Abbey entered in 1991 with the acquisition of Scottish Mutual.

Questions *(45 marks; 70 minutes)*

1 What is meant by the expression 'become a commodity item'? *(4)*

2 a Why has Abbey National decided not to compete in the mortgage market? *(8)*

   b Do you consider that Abbey is right to make this strategic decision? Explain your answer. *(8)*

3 How is the marketing strategy followed by a bank likely to differ from that of another business? *(5)*

4 How should Abbey National decide on the future marketing strategy for the business? *(10)*

5 Comment on the diversification strategy being suggested by Abbey's chief executive. *(10)*

C. ESSAY QUESTIONS

1 How useful is Ansoff's matrix in evaluating the risk involved in new marketing strategies?

2 Only large companies need and can afford to have a marketing strategy. Discuss this statement.

3 Marketing strategy can only be successful if a firm has set the right objectives. Discuss.

4 Marketing strategy is the key to business success. Discuss.

MARKETING PLANS AND MARKETING BUDGETS

DEFINITION

A marketing plan is a detailed statement of the company's marketing strategy. It explains how the strategy has been determined and how it will be carried out. Marketing budgets are planning and control tools used by the marketing department. They ensure that spending is kept under constant review.

8.1 The marketing plan

The marketing plan puts the company's marketing strategy into action. It explains the background to the planned marketing activity. It describes the marketing strategy and explains how it contributes to the overall corporate objectives. The marketing strategy is broken down into action plans. These are the individual activities that put the strategy into practice. The mix of activities is known as the strategic mix. The marketing plan details the individual marketing activities that make up this *strategic mix*. And how the marketing budget is to be spent.

The purpose of the marketing plan is to ensure that staff understand the actions that will be taken, the reasons behind the actions and the timing of the actions. For example, the production department may want to know when the annual advertising campaign will be run. Then it can ensure stocks are high enough to cover the boost to demand.

WHAT DOES A MARKETING PLAN LOOK LIKE?

For smaller businesses the marketing plan may be an informal document. Larger companies will formalise the plans in report format. Typically it will have the contents shown in the table below:

WHY IS MARKETING PLANNING IMPORTANT?

'If I had eight hours to chop down a tree I'd spend six sharpening my axe'

Abraham Lincoln

A properly developed marketing plan is important because:

- it helps to ensure that marketing activity is properly focused and integrated
- it enables everyone in the organisation to know exactly what will happen, and when
- it enables the business to take advantage of market opportunities
- it helps to ensure that the business remains healthy by preparing for possible problems
- it puts the business in a better position to react to unexpected events.

Contents of a marketing plan

Introduction	• *Gives an overview of the plan and the background to it*
Corporate and marketing objectives	• *States the overall business aims and the relevant marketing objectives*
Marketing strategy	• *Outlines the strategy that will be used to achieve the objectives*
Action plans	• *Details the individual marketing activities used to carry out the strategy, including above- and below-the-line activities plus detailed timings*
Detailed budgets	• *Breakdown of expected revenue and costs by product or department or marketing activity*
Control tools	• *Details of how the budgets and plans will be monitored*

FOR	AGAINST
• Allows firms to anticipate changing conditions	• Changes occur so fast that planning is a waste of time, especially long-term planning
• Provides clear objectives and direction	• Strategies are often vague and general • They do not allow managers to be responsive to opportunities • They stifle initiative
• The process of analysis helps managers to understand the market	• Managers do not use the information and it is often out of date
• Businesses that plan are more effective	• There are many reasons for business success

8.2 Marketing planning
an evaluation

It is generally accepted that **strategic planning** is good for businesses. However, there are critics. The table above outlines some of the arguments.

— RONALDO

Paying $44.5 million dollars for a player may seem an expensive way to kick-start a new marketing strategy, but this is what Real Madrid did. In September 2002 they signed Ronaldo, the Brazilian footballer whose goals helped Brazil to win the 2002 World Cup. This signing is part of a plan to maximise the Spanish club's future earnings and to catch up with Manchester United's worldwide appeal.

Ronaldo has agreed to cede any new image rights to the club and Real are hopeful that his presence will allow them to penetrate new markets in the Far East. Certainly the 300 journalists from every continent who were there when the deal was announced gave an indication of the worldwide appeal of the star. The club's president Florentino Perez said 'One of the most important things for Real is its image. We all know that Ronaldo is one of the best players in the world but he is also one of the most universal images. We will begin selling shirts bearing the player's name immediately and we are sure there will be massive demand. In five years we want to be in every country of the world.'

Adapted from a Reuters story by Simon Basket in YAHOO!SPORT
http://uk.sports.yahoo.com

8.3 What is a marketing budget?

In everyday language a budget is the amount available for spending. In business a budget is a target. It is not only an expenditure target but also a target for achievement. The marketing budget is the quantified plan for the marketing department. It shows the marketing objectives in numerical terms such as market share or distribution targets. It is usually produced as an annual budget, but for the purpose of control will often be broken down into monthly figures.

For example, the marketing objective may be to increase sales by 10%. The budget will give monthly sales targets which will deliver that annual figure. Alongside the sales figures, targets for expenditure will be given. So if the additional sales are to be generated by a new advertising campaign, the budget will include expenditure targets for that advertising.

SETTING BUDGETS

The way in which budgets are determined will vary from business to business. The budget should result from the planning process. First, the marketing strategy should be set. This will follow from the corporate objectives. Then the business can decide on the budget needed to carry out the strategy. If it is too expensive, a cheaper approach may be needed. Or it may be necessary to rethink the objectives. Nestlé *could* set the objective of Yorkie outselling Cadbury's Dairy Milk. But it would be prohibitively expensive to actually achieve it.

Having decided on the overall strategy and budget, sales targets and spending budgets can be allocated to each cost centre. This process is helped by analysing carefully the firm's product portfolio. The Boston Matrix can be used to identify which brands are worth heavy investment. And which ones should be milked by allocating a minimal marketing budget.

METHODS OF SETTING BUDGETS

There are several different ways that budgets are set:

Business IN

- **Incremental budgeting** – also known as 'last year plus a bit'. This is the most common method. The advantage is that it is easy to understand. Everyone involved is aware of what happened last year. The problem is that it is inflexible. It does not allow for unexpected events. This may mean that market opportunities can be missed. It may also result in departments unnecessarily spending to ensure that they use up their allocated expenditure. Managers may fear that if budgeted expenditure is not used, a lower budget will be allocated next time.

- **Sales-related budgeting** – using this method, expenditure is allocated in proportion to sales. This means that if sales increase by a certain percentage, the department will be allowed to increase expenditure by the same or a related percentage. This is often used to determine promotional expenditure. The most common way is to allocate spending using a percentage of the level of sales.

- **Task-based costing** is a method used by some businesses. This involves deciding on the marketing activities required to achieve the marketing objectives. These activities are costed out and the amount agreed becomes the budget.

- **Competitor parity budgeting** – expenditure is allocated in line with competitors' spending. The arguments for using this method are that it avoids competitive wars and uses the knowledge that other firms have of the market. This is difficult to justify. First, it is difficult to know exactly what and how competitors are spending. Second, it is inefficient. Competitor spending may not be efficient and may be totally inappropriate for the business's particular needs. There is also little evidence that it avoids competitive wars.

- For many smaller businesses the only feasible way of allocating expenditure to marketing may be by asking the question, **'What can we afford?'**

BUDGET ALLOCATION – HOW IS IT TO BE SPENT?

One of the most difficult questions facing the marketing manager is how to spend the available resources. The level of expenditure will depend on many factors. These include:

- The amount available – the marketing department will have to work within the constraints of the allocated finance.
- The likely return from the expenditure – any marketing expenditure should produce a return. It should be evaluated in the same way as any investment in the business.
- Type of product – some products are supported by very high levels of spending whilst others are not. The level of spending will be related to product differentiation and value added. In markets where there is little difference between competing products, businesses will want to use marketing to give their product a competitive edge. It is only possible

to afford high marketing budgets, though, if value added is high. Cosmetics, cars and washing powder are examples of this. Each is supported by high levels of promotional spending.

- Product life cycle – for most products the highest levels of expenditure will be in the launch and growth stages. From time to time the product may need to be supported with additional spending, perhaps due to an extension strategy.
- Type of customer – companies selling consumer goods and services will tend to have higher levels of marketing expenditure than those supplying industrial customers.

MARKETING EXPENDITURE

It is a common error to equate marketing expenditure with the cost of advertising. Many other costs are associated with marketing the product. Among the most important are the design and development of the packaging, thorough and independent market research and the achievement of good distribution. The costs of promoting the product can be divided into above and below the line. Above the line comes the budget for main media advertising, such as television. Below the line covers all other promotional spending.

ABOVE-THE-LINE	BELOW-THE-LINE
Television	Point-of-sale (POS) advertising
Newspapers & magazines	Competitions
Radio	Special offers
Cinema	Direct mailshots

8.4 How are budgets used?

Budgets set estimated levels of sales and expenditure. The actual levels can be recorded and the difference observed. The difference is known as **variance**. It may be a positive variance or a negative variance. If sales are higher this will be a positive variance. If expenditure is higher this will be a negative variance. If variances occur they can be analysed. This is important. The business needs to know why variances have happened. This is just as important for positive variances as it is for negative variances. Positive variances will show that something is going well or doing better than expected. Negative variances mean that targets are not being achieved and may be a warning sign. A higher than expected level of sales may mean a shift in buying patterns or just an increase in business. If it is a shift in buying patterns the business needs to understand why, so that it can react. Budgets may need to be adjusted to take account of the reasons for the variances. The review and setting of budgets is a continuous cycle.

MEASURING PERFORMANCE AGAINST BUDGET

If performance is to be measured effectively then it is important that there is a range of indices that can be used. The management accounting system will produce some figures such as sales and costs. It may need to be developed to produce other information to measure marketing effectiveness. Competitive information will be important. Car manufacturers look at market share figures based on new car registrations as a key measure of performance. If Ford's market share figures are slipping behind the targets, the company will step up its marketing effort (including price cutting) to regain its intended levels.

The budgetary cycle

- *State goals*
- *Measure performance*
- *Analyse performance*
- *Correct/adjust activities if necessary*
- *Revise budgets*
- *If necessary adjust strategy*

MARKETING AUDIT

It is essential that businesses review the effectiveness of their marketing activity. The *marketing audit* is a periodic check. Many companies use this in addition to the normal budgeting activity. It is additional to the normal budgetary checks. It enables the business to ensure that it is responding to changes in the market environment. It takes a wider view of marketing activity.

ISSUES FOR **analysis**

There are several issues that are likely to be important when looking at marketing plans and budgets, either in an examination context or as a part of coursework.

- Consideration should be given to the usefulness or otherwise of the plans or budget. Do they really help the business to manage its marketing effort or does the process constrain real marketing initiatives? Quite often this will depend on other factors in the business such as management style. Are staff encouraged to stick rigidly to the plan or is initiative rewarded? Is the budget used as a carrot or a stick?
- Another issue is to be able to analyse variances, the difference between the budgeted and actual results. Take care that you understand whether the variance is positive or negative. Remember higher costs is bad (negative) but higher sales is good (positive).
- When analysing the variances you should consider all the information available. Sales may be lower than expected but in a recession or a highly competitive situation the figures may not be as bad as they seem. They may even be good if they compare favourably with the overall growth of the market. The business will make decisions after analysing the variances, but only after considering all the external and internal factors that may have influenced the results.
- It is also important to understand that variances can occur because of problems with setting the budgeted figures. If sales are lower it may be for no other reason than that the expected sales were overestimated.

8.5 Marketing budgets
an evaluation

Not everyone agrees that the use of budgeting is a good idea. There are arguments both for and against its use.

Arguments for the use of budgets:

- They set targets which give staff guidelines for action.
- Targets motivate staff as they try to achieve them.
- Having budgets enables measurement.
- The process of setting budgets means that thought has gone into plans.
- Control expenditure.
- Monitoring of performance against targets means that changes can be seen.

Arguments against the use of budgets:

- Budgets can be inflexible.
- Opportunities may be missed as managers apply budget limits strictly.
- Some **budget holders** may feel that they must use all available spending. This is particularly true if the budget for the next year is set on the basis of today's level. Managers may be concerned that if they under spend they will not be able to argue for a higher spending level next year. This may lead to unnecessary or inefficient expenditure.
- The process of preparing budgets is time consuming.
- Managers may see financial allocations as a reflection of their own status rather than basing expenditure on market needs.

Nevertheless, most businesses find that using some sort of budgetary system is an essential part of management. It enables planning to be focused and it is a very useful control tool. To work effectively it needs to be flexible enough to take advantage of any market opportunities and to respond quickly to any threats. As with many management tools, budgeting works well if the people using the system understand that it is an aid to planning and control rather than a rigid system.

KEY terms

budget holder – a person who is responsible for a particular budget area.

strategic planning – developing a plan of action which sets out to achieve objectives taking account of the business and market environment in which the business is operating.

variance – the difference between expected and actual figures.

A Level Exercises

A. REVISION QUESTIONS
(30 marks; 60 minutes)

Read the unit, then answer:

1 What is a marketing plan? (2)
2 List four topics that you would expect to be included in a marketing plan. (4)
3 Outline two reasons why firms prepare marketing plans. (4)
4 What is a marketing budget? (2)
5 What does incremental budgeting mean? (3)
6 What is the difference between task-based costing and competitor parity budgeting? (3)
7 List five factors that might influence the level of marketing expenditure. (5)
8 What is meant by 'below-the-line promotion'? (2)
9 What is variance analysis? (2)
10 How do budgets help the business to control its activities? (3)

B. REVISION EXERCISES

B1 Data Response

Golden Wonder

> The total crisp and snack market in the UK is estimated to be worth about £1.4 billion. The three market leaders are Walkers, KP Foods and Golden Wonder. In October 1998 Golden Wonder celebrated the 3rd anniversary of its £59 million management buyout

led by Clive Sharpe. Despite the company being in a precarious state when the buyout occurred, the snack food maker has been giving its two main competitors, KP Foods and Walkers Crisps, a run for their money.

When Sharpe took over, the company had just suffered an eight-month strike, its distribution was patchy and its manufacturing ill-focused. The management team paid off the £47 million of debt that came with the business. It could have sold the business at this stage but instead decided to return to its backers to ask them to provide £30 million to invest in new manufacturing facilities and to back an annual marketing expenditure of £25 million. £11 milion on sales promotion and £14 million on 'above-the-line' spending – television advertising and the like.

The results have been staggering. Turnover at Golden Wonder has risen by more than 25%. This at the same time that Walkers' market position has been stagnant, despite the efforts of Gary Lineker and the Spice Girls.

Sharpe has decided that the way forward is to be innovative. One thing that he has done is to reorganise the business. The business is now split into the following functions:

- Planning – where should the company be going and what should it sell?
- Development – turning those ideas into products.
- Demand creation – marketing those products.
- Fulfilment – making and getting the products into the shops.

In the past year Golden Wonder has spent more than £1million on trend analysis to see what new products could be brought to the market. According to the development manager, Paul Boothman, there has been hardly any innovation in snack foods for the last five years. 'You have to segment the market and see where there are needs', he says. 'Take teenagers, which we define as those between 14 and 18. If you look at how they are in the mornings; their physical status is that they need nutrition; their mental status is that they are rushed and disorientated. They need something that is familiar and which will set them up for the day. As the morning goes on, tiredness becomes peckishness and then real hunger.'

Golden Wonder clearly sees morning snacks as an area it should be exploiting. Boothman is concerned that the savoury snack makers are missing out on potential sales that go largely to confectionery groups. 'One of the ways of winning this battle is by delivering healthy products that taste like snacks. After all, no-one believes that chocolate or crisps are healthy, even if they do have packaging that proclaims lower fat content. People tend to sacrifice health and nutrition because they can buy something tasty and immediate. But they are changing to want something healthy as well. Soft drinks companies have adapted – snack food manufacturers have to do likewise.'

Sources: *The Times*, 15/9/98; *The Grocer*, 13/6/98

Questions   (30 marks; 40 minutes)

1 What is meant by' impulse sales' and what are the marketing implications for these products? (6)
2 What is the difference between above - and below-the-line marketing expenditure? (3)
3 With an annual marketing budget of £25 million how would Golden Wonder try to ensure it gets a good return from this investment? (6)
4 Why was it important for Golden Wonder to sort out its problems and to invest in manufacturing before investing in marketing? (6)
5 Consider how Golden Wonder could justify spending £1 million on analyses of sales and market trends. (9)

B2 Case Study

Ewans Motor Company is a car dealer based in the Midlands. It has two outlets. One has the franchise for a range of small family cars. The other offers larger luxury cars.

Business has been steady over the last few years but has seen no real growth in total sales or profitability. The business is facing increased local competition from another garage offering a similar range of family cars. There is also the threat of an economic downturn in the area as one of the largest employers is threatening to cut staff as a result of lower export sales due to the stronger pound.

The owner, Peter Ewans, has brought in a new marketing manager with the hope that the business can cope with these challenges and hopefully increase profitability. The new marketing manager, Don Fore, agreed to join the business providing the marketing budget was increased from its current 1% of turnover. He feels that in the more competitive climate, especially in the small car business, that the budget needs to be slightly more than doubled. He is sure that he can justify this additional expenditure by raising profitability. He also introduced the concept of a marketing budget that he feels is long overdue. Previously, expenditure has been on a rather ad hoc basis and there have been no targets set for sales or profitability. There has also been little or no monitoring of the results.

After analysing both the market situation and the figures for the business for the last few years, Don Fore produced the following marketing budget figures:

	Last Year	Budget This Year
Sales: small cars	1,600	2,000
Sales: luxury cars	800	950
Average selling price: small cars	£12,000	£11,900
Average selling price: luxury cars	£25,000	£25,000
Average contribution per small car	£840	£740
Average contribution per luxury car	£3,000	£3,000
Total marketing expenditure	£392,000	£800,000
Breakdown of marketing expenditure		
Price discounting	0	£200,000
Direct mailing	£100,000	£200,000
Advertising	£150,000	£250,000
Promotional offers	£92,000	£100,000
Sponsorship	£50,000	£50,000

He felt that there was going to be a need to use some price discounting on the smaller cars to combat the increased competition in the area. His plan was to allow the salespeople to discount the price by as much as they felt was necessary to ensure the sale. He allowed an average of £100 for each small car for this. To support the salespeople he planned to double the mail shots. These would inform customers of special offers and also invite them to special family days. These days would be very child oriented, offering family entertainment and gifts for children. All of the slightly increased promotional budget would be spent on this. He also planned to support the family days with additional advertising in the local press. The sponsorship of sporting activities in local schools fitted into his plan so this would also be continued.

Industry reports suggested that the luxury car business would grow at about 6% in this year so he decided to do very little except for mail shots to support this sector of the market.

At the end of the year the actual figures were:

	Actual
Sales: small cars	1,800
Sales: luxury cars	800
Average selling price: small cars	£11,800
Average selling price: luxury cars	£25,000
Average contribution per small car	£640
Average contribution per luxury car	£3,000
Total marketing expenditure	£960,000

Breakdown of marketing expenditure:

Price discounting	£360,000
Direct mailing	£180,000
Advertising	£250,000
Promotional offers	£120,000
Sponsorship	£50,000

After analysing the results, Don Fore feels that both the marketing plan and the budgeting exercise have been successful.

Questions *(50 marks; 70 minutes)*

1 Do you think that the marketing plan was appropriate for the business in its present circumstances?
(10)

2 Why did Don Fore feel that a marketing budget was long overdue? *(4)*

3 What advantages and disadvantages might there be for the business in introducing a marketing budgeting system? *(8)*

4 Calculate the variances between the budgeted and actual figures. *(8)*

5 Why do you think the more significant variances might have occurred? *(8)*

6 Using the figures and other information in the case study, comment on Don Fore's assertion that the marketing plan and the budgeting exercise were successful. *(12)*

C. ESSAY QUESTIONS

1 Some businesses do not have formalised marketing plans. Discuss the arguments for and against a formal marketing planning system.

2 Discuss the advantages and disadvantages of a formalised budget for marketing.

3 Many firms are moving away from the 'last year plus a bit' approach to producing marketing budgets. Discuss two alternative approaches and explain why the firm might use these methods.

4 Marketing budgets are the key to management and control of marketing activity. Discuss.

ELASTICITY OF DEMAND

DEFINITION
Elasticity measures how the demand for a product changes in response to a change in a variable such as price or income.

9.1 Introduction

The demand for goods and services is determined by a wide variety of factors. The demand for a new Rover 200 car, for example, will be influenced by its price, the price of similar small cars, the amount spent on advertising, seasonality and many other factors. Elasticity measures the degree to which one of these variables affects demand.

Each variable that affects demand has its own relevant elasticity. A price rise is almost certain to cut demand and an increase in advertising spending is likely to increase it. So the price and advertising elasticities of demand can be calculated. The elasticities most commonly used in business are price and income.

9.2 Price elasticity of demand

In the short term, the most important factor affecting demand is price. If Coca-Cola raised the price of Coke, sales would almost certainly fall. Some consumers would switch to a cheaper brand. Others would purchase Coke less frequently. If a 10% price increase caused demand to fall by only 1%, Coca-Cola could benefit hugely by increasing the price.

So the crucial question is *how much* will demand fall when the price increases? This question can be answered by calculating the price elasticity of demand for Coca-Cola. Price elasticity is not about whether demand changes when price changes, it is about the *degree* of change. Consequently, price elasticity is a unit of measurement rather than being a thing in itself. A price cut will not cause price elasticity to fall. Instead the price elasticity figure explains the effect the price cut is likely to have on demand. Will demand rise by 1%, 5% or 25% following the price cut? The answer can only be known by referring to the product's price elasticity of demand. Price elasticity measures the *responsiveness* of demand to a change in price.

Some products are far more price sensitive than others. Following a 5% increase in price the demand for some products may fall greatly, say by more than

20%. The demand for another type of product may fall by less than 1%.

Price elasticity can be calculated by using the following formula:

$$\text{price elasticity} = \frac{\text{\% change in quantity demanded}}{\text{\% change in price}}$$

Price elasticity measures the percentage effect on demand of each 1% change in price. So if a 10% increase in price led demand to fall by 20%, the price elasticity would be 2. Strictly speaking, price elasticities are always negative, because price up pushes demand down, and price down pushes demand up. For example:

$$\frac{-20\%}{+10\%} = -2$$

The figure of −2 indicates that for every 1% change in price, demand is likely to change by 2%. All price elasticities are negative. This is because there is a negative **correlation** between price and quantity demanded. In the short term, a price cut will always boost sales and a price rise will always cut sales. The only exception to this is when a price rise on a luxury good helps to boost its long-term status to a potential buyer.

9.3 Using price elasticity information

Price elasticity of demand information can be used for two purposes:

1 SALES FORECASTING

A firm considering a price rise will want to know the effect the price change is likely to have on demand. Producing a sales forecast will make accurate production, personnel and purchasing decisions possible. For example, when News International cut the cover price of *The Sun* by 25% from 25p to 20p, sales rose 16% to more than 4 million copies per day. The price elasticity of *The Sun* proved to be:

$$\frac{+16\%}{-20\%} = -0.8$$

This information could be used by News International to predict the likely impact of future price changes. A price cut of 10% could lead to a rise in circulation of 8% ($-10\% \times -0.8 = +8\%$). This is valuable information to know. Before implementing the price cut the company would check the current production capacity. It would be foolish to cut price only to find that the new higher demand level cannot be met.

2 PRICING STRATEGY

There are many external factors beyond a firm's control that determine a product's demand and therefore profitability. For example, a soft drinks manufacturer can do nothing about a wet summer that hammers sales and profits. However, the price the firm decides to charge *is* within its control. And it can be a crucial factor in determining demand and profitability. Price elasticity information can be used in conjunction with internal cost data to forecast the implications of a price change on profit.

Example:

A second-hand car dealer currently sells 60 cars each year. On average each car costs him £2,000 to buy. Annual overheads are £18,000. Currently he charges his customers £2,500 per car. This means the business makes a profit of:

total revenue = £2,500 × 60 = £150,000
total cost = £18,000 + (2,000 × 60)
= £138,000
total profit = £150,000 − £138,000
= £12,000

From past experience the salesman believes the price elasticity of his cars is approximately 0.75. The dealer is thinking about increasing his prices to £3,000 per car. An increase of 20%. Using the price elasticity information, a quick calculation would reveal the impact on profit:

percentage change in demand = +20% × −0.75
= −15%

A 15% fall in demand on the existing sales volume of 60 cars per year will produce a fall in demand of 9 cars per year:

$$\frac{60}{100} \times 15 = 9 \text{ cars per year}$$

So demand will fall to 51 cars per year after the price increase. On the basis of these figures the new annual profit would be:

total revenue = new price × new sales volume
= £3,000 × 51 cars
= £153,000
total cost = £18,000 + (51 × £2,000)
= £120,000
new profit = £33,000

So following the 20% increase in price, profits should increase by:

$$\frac{£33,000 - £12,000}{£12,000} \times 100 = 175\%$$

Obviously in this case the car dealer should change his pricing strategy. However, this is all based on two assumptions:

1 that the price elasticity of the cars actually proves to be −0.75
2 other factors that could also affect demand remain unchanged following the price increase.

9.4 Classifying price elasticity

PRICE ELASTIC PRODUCTS

A **price elastic** product has a price elasticity of above one. This means that the percentage change in demand is greater than the percentage change in price that created it. For example, if a firm increased prices by 5% and as a result demand fell by 15%, price elasticity would be:

$$\frac{-15\%}{+5\%} \times 100 = -3$$

The figure indicates that for every 1% change in price there will be a 3% change in demand. The higher the price elasticity figure the more price elastic the product is. Cutting price on a price elastic product will boost total revenue. This is because the extra revenue gained from the increased sales volume more than offsets the revenue lost from the price cut. On the other

IN Business

INELASTIC NEWSPAPERS?

In September 2002 *The Daily Telegraph* raised its cover price from 50p to 55p. In the same month the price of a copy of *The Sunday Times* went up by 20p. These price increases were in sharp contrast to the price-cutting strategies used by the broadsheet dailies during the 1990s. Ivan Fallon, the Chief Executive of the *Independent*, claimed that his newspaper lost £1 billion in the previous decade as a result of price cuts. This change in pricing strategy reflects the fact that newspaper owners now believe that their broadsheets are price inelastic rather than price elastic. The strong brand loyalties that exist within the market mean that price increases, rather than price decreases are the route to higher revenues and profits. This point was backed up by the fact that following the *Telegraph*'s decision to increase price by 10%, circulation fell by only 1.77%.

hand, a price increase on a price elastic product will lead to a fall in total revenue.

Although a price cut on a price elastic product will increase revenue, it might not boost profits. Total revenue will increase. However, a price cut that increases sales volume will also increase costs as more of the product now has to be produced. To predict the impact on profits one must also have access to cost information. It is also important to note that price cutting can damage brand image. First, customers often associate high prices with high quality. Second, a price cutting decision is usually difficult to reverse due to consumer resistance to price increases. Finally, the actions of the competition must also be taken into account. If your price cut prompts a price war, the much needed gains in sales volume might not arise.

PRICE INELASTIC PRODUCTS

Price inelastic products have price elasticities below one. This means the percentage change in demand is less than the percentage change in price. In other words, price changes have hardly any effect on demand. Perhaps because consumers feel they *must* have the product or brand in question. The stunning dress, the trendiest designer label, or – less interestingly – gas for central heating. Customers feel they must have it, either because it really is a necessity, or because it is fashionable. Firms with price inelastic products will be tempted to push the prices up. A price increase will boost revenue because the price rise creates a relatively small fall in sales volume. This means the majority of customers will continue to purchase the brand but at a higher, revenue-boosting price.

9.5 Strategies to reduce price elasticity

All businesses prefer to sell price inelastic products. Charging more for a price inelastic product guarantees an increase in short-term profit. Cutting price on a price elastic product, however, increases total revenue in the very short term but may hit profit. A sharp rise in sales will probably be at the expense of competitors. They will have little choice but to respond. A price war may result.

It is important to realise the price elasticity of a brand is not set in stone. Price elasticity is not an external constraint. Firms use a variety of strategies to try to reduce the price elasticity of their products. The most important influence on a brand's price elasticity is substitutability. If consumers have other brands available that they think deliver the same benefits, price elasticity will be high. So to make a brand price inelastic the firm has to find ways of reducing the number of substitutes available (or acceptable). How can this be done?

INCREASING PRODUCT DIFFERENTIATION

Product differentiation is the degree to which consumers perceive that a product is different (and preferably better) than its rivals. Some products are truly different, such as a Jaguar car. Others are differentiated mainly by image, such as Coca-Cola. The purchasers of highly differentiated products like Coke often remain brand loyal despite price rises.

HORIZONTAL INTEGRATION

This occurs when two firms in the same industry and at the same stage of production decide to merge or when one decides to take the other over. In 2003 low-cost airline Ryanair bought the rival Buzz. Horizontal integration decreases rivalry and consumer choice. Many analysts predicted that this decrease in competition would lead to an increase in air fares.

PRICE FIXING

Some markets are less competitive than they first appear. This is because firms in the same industry decide to form a **cartel**. Instead of competing against each other, the cartel members behave as if they were one large monopolist. Consumers might have a theoretical choice of who to purchase from. But the suppliers may have agreed to charge very similar prices. By reducing genuine choice and competition, cartels can successfully reduce price elasticity.

9.6 Techniques used to estimate price elasticity of demand

There are two main techniques that can be used to estimate a brand's price elasticity of demand.

Year	Price Change (%)	Demand Change (%)	Estimated Price Elasticity of Demand
1999	+2	−2.4	$\dfrac{-2.4\%}{+2\%} = -1.2$
2001	+2.5	−2.9	$\dfrac{-2.9\%}{+2.5\%} = -1.16$
2002	−4	+5	$\dfrac{+5\%}{-4\%} = -1.25$

PAST SALES FIGURES

A simple way to estimate price elasticity is to consider what happened to sales the last time the firm changed its prices.

Example:

A firm manufacturing washing machines has changed the price of its leading model three times in recent years. Sales responded in the manner shown in the table at the foot of page 60.

By taking the average value of the price elasticities over the period, the firm could get an idea of the overall price elasticity for the product. In this case it would be:

$$\frac{-2 + -1.16 + -1.25}{3} = -1.20$$

The danger of this approach is that it ignores the other factors affecting demand besides price. For example, when the firm cut its prices in 2002 demand increased. The critical question, though, is whether the price cut created *all 5%* of the demand increase that followed. Were other factors at work? Maybe some of the increase in demand would have happened anyway even if prices had not been cut? Some of the increase in demand may have been created by competitors cutting back on advertising support or by cuts in UK interest rates.

PRIMARY QUANTITATIVE MARKET RESEARCH

Before launching a new product firms use representative matched samples. Each sample of potential consumers is then asked how much they would be prepared to purchase at a given price level. The price levels quoted will vary between samples. By identifying the differences in the quantities the samples intend to purchase, the price elasticity can be estimated.

9.7 Income elasticity of demand

Income elasticity of demand measures the responsiveness of demand to a change in the overall spending power of consumers. This is measured by comparing income increases with inflation. If incomes rise 6% while inflation is 4%, spending power has risen 2%. This measurement of spending power is known as *real income*. A 2% rise in real incomes might lead consumers to spend 10% more on eating out. If so, eating out would be considered a highly income elastic activity.

Income elasticity is calculated as follows:

$$\text{income elasticity} = \frac{\%\ \text{change in quantity demanded}}{\%\ \text{change in real income}}$$

Economic growth tends to fluctuate due to the effects of the trade cycle. Economic booms are followed by downturns which can become recessions. Income levels follow this pattern, with profound effects on the demand for most goods and services. These effects can vary greatly from product to product. During booms, when incomes grow rapidly, the demand for some types of good will increase greatly, whilst the demand for other types of good may actually fall.

9.8 Classifying income elasticity

Products and services can be grouped into three categories of income elasticity. Unlike price elasticity, income elasticity figures are not always negative.

NORMAL GOODS

As real incomes increase the demand for normal goods will also increase. This means that a normal good will have a positive income elasticity that is below one. A typical example of a normal good is petrol. As real incomes increase, many people may feel that they can now afford more weekend trips out in the car. So following a 2% increase in real income the demand for petrol might rise by 0.5%. On the basis of these figures the income elasticity of petrol would appear to be:

$$\frac{+0.5\%}{+2\%} = +0.25$$

This figure of +0.25 indicates that a 1% increase in real income will create an increase in demand of 0.25%. So when real incomes rise the demand for normal goods will also rise, but at a slower rate.

LUXURY GOODS

Luxury goods also have a positive income elasticity. However, unlike a normal good the income elasticity

Business IN

SALES OF LUXURIES RECOVER IN SOUTH KOREA.

The economy of South Korea was hit badly by the Asian crisis of 1997, which led to a high unemployment rate and falling consumer income levels throughout the country. Since the beginning of 2000 the economy of South Korea has recovered. In 2001 real incomes increased by 3.3% and were forecast to increase by as much as 5.8% in 2002.

This recovery had a profound effect upon the sales of premium branded goods in South Korea. For example sales of imported Gucci clothes increased by over 44% during 2001. According to the company, sales rose because the disposable incomes of South Korea's middle class population increased. It appears from this information that the income elasticity of Gucci clothes may be even higher than +10.

figure will be above one. The demand for luxury goods will grow at a faster rate than the increase in real income that created the change in demand. This responsiveness will also apply in reverse. During recessions, when real incomes fall, the demand for luxury goods will fall sharply. By a far bigger percentage than the initial fall in real income. As a result the demand for luxury goods tends to be more volatile than that of normal goods during a typical trade cycle.

INFERIOR GOODS

Inferior goods have a negative income elasticity. So people buy less of these products or services when they are better off. And more of them when they hit hard times. They are cheap substitutes for products they prefer to buy when they can afford to. Such as 'no frills' baked beans.

For example, If real incomes grew by 2% the demand for a budget own-label tin of baked beans might actually drop by 10%. In this case the own label would have an income elasticity of:

$$\frac{+10\%}{+2\%} = -5$$

ISSUES FOR **analysis**

In examinations, elasticity of demand is a key discriminator between good and weak candidates. Really weak candidates never bring the concept into their answers at all. Better candidates apply it, but imprecisely. Top grade students see where it is relevant and show a clear understanding of the concept and its implications. Here are some of the ways elasticity can be used for business analysis:

- When answering a question about pricing, elasticity is a vital factor. Even if a firm faces severe cost increases, a price rise will be very risky if its products have a high price elasticity. Pricing decisions must always start with careful consideration of price elasticity.

- People naturally assume that marketing (especially advertising) is always about trying to increase sales. In fact, most firms are far more interested in their image. A glance at any commercial break will confirm this. Companies focus upon their image because that is the way to differentiate themselves from others. That, in turn, is the way to reduce price elasticity and therefore give the company stronger control over its pricing.

- Good students rarely refer to 'elasticity'. They refer to price elasticity or income elasticity. This is because it is quite wrong to assume that products have the same level of price and income elasticities. A luxury car such as a Rolls Royce has a very low price elasticity, but its income elasticity is very high. In the 1991 recession, Rolls Royce sales fell by more than 30% when real incomes fell by less than 3%!

- When considering any question about business strategy, income elasticity is an important issue. A firm selling luxury products may be very vulnerable to recessions, as the income elasticity of its products is likely to be high. Therefore it should ensure that its financial position (its balance sheet) is always strong – because recessions are not easy to predict. The business could also consider diversifying.

9.9 Elasticity of demand
an evaluation

For examiners, elasticity is a convenient concept. It is hard to understand, but very easy to write exam questions on! But how useful is it in the real world? Would the average marketing director know the price elasticities of his or her products?

In many cases the answer is no. Examiners and textbooks exaggerate the precision that is possible with such a concept. The fact that the income elasticity of Rolls Royce cars appeared to be around +10 in 1991 does not mean it is always that high. Price elasticities change over time as competition changes and consumer tastes change. Income elasticities may vary as products come to seem more or less of a necessity.

Even though elasticities can vary over time, certain features tend to remain constant. Strong brands such as Levi's and Coca-Cola have relatively low price elasticity. This gives them the power over market pricing that ensures strong profitability year after year. For less established firms, these brands are the role model. Everyone wants to be the Coca-Cola of their own market or market niche.

KEY terms

cartel – an agreement by producers to limit supply to keep prices high.

correlation – the relationship between one variable and another.

income elasticity – the effect on demand of changes in consumer spending power.

price elastic – a product which is highly price sensitive, so price elasticity is above 1.

price inelastic – a product which is not very price sensitive, so price elasticty is below 1.

AS Level Exercises

A. REVISION QUESTIONS
(40 marks; 80 minutes)

Read the unit, then answer:

1 a If a product's sales have fallen by 21% since a price rise from £2 to £2.07, what is its price elasticity? *(4)*
 b Is the product price elastic or price inelastic? *(1)*

2 State two methods Nestlé might take to reduce the price elasticity of KitKat chocolate bars. *(2)*

3 A firm selling 20,000 units at £8 is considering a 4% price increase. It believes its price elasticity is –0.5.
 a What will be the effect upon revenue? *(4)*
 b Give two reasons why the revenue may prove to be different from the firm's expectations. *(2)*

4 Explain three ways a firm could make use of information about the price elasticity of its brands. *(6)*

5 Identify three external factors that could increase the price elasticity of a brand of chocolate. *(3)*

6 A firm has a sales target of 60,000 units per month. Current sales are 50,000 per month at a price of £1.50. If its products have a price elasticity of –2, what price should the firm charge to meet the target sales volume? *(4)*

7 Why is price elasticity always negative? *(2)*

8 Why may the manager of a product with a price elasticity of –2 be reluctant to cut the price? *(3)*

9 When the recession hit, a 3% fall in consumers' real incomes caused sales of a firm's product to rise from 40,000 to 44,800.
 a Calculate the product's income elasticity. *(4)*
 b Suggest the type of product it is. *(1)*

10 Suggest two brands that:
 a have low price elasticity but high income elasticity *(2)*
 b have low income elasticity but high price elasticity. *(2)*

B. REVISION EXERCISES

B1 Data Response
(20 marks; 30 minutes.)

A firm selling Manchester United pillowcases for £10 currently generates an annual turnover of £500,000. Variable costs average at £4 per unit and total annual fixed costs are £100,000. The marketing director is considering a price increase of 10%. Given that the price elasticity of the product is believed to be –0.4, calculate:

1 the old and the new sales volume *(3)*
2 the new revenue *(3)*
3 the expected change in profit following the price increase *(6)*

4 if the firm started producing mass-market white pillowcases, would their price elasticity be higher or lower than the Manchester United ones? Why is that? *(8)*

B2 Case Study

A firm producing ice-cream has recently cut the price of two of its leading brands by 10%. One of its brands, Spice Spangle, is a budget mass-market product which is targeted at children. Finesse is sold in a totally different market segment. Its premium price creates far higher margins from a relatively low sales volume. The table below shows the impact the price cuts have had on the two brands.

Questions *(40 marks; 70 minutes)*

1 Complete the gaps in the table. *(8)*
2 From the data above, calculate the price elasticity of the two brands. *(6)*
3 Discuss the wisdom of the two respective price cuts. *(10)*
4 What additional sales would be needed on the Finesse brand to pay for the 10% price cut? *(6)*
5 Should pricing decisions always be based upon the impact they have on short-term profits? *(10)*

	Spice Spangle Pre-price cut	Post-price cut	Finesse Pre-price cut	Post-price cut
Sales volume (000) units	5,000	7,000	1,000	1,050
Sales value (£000)	2,000	2,520	1,500	1,418
Variable cost of goods sold (£000)	1,000	1,200	750	788
Gross profit (£000)	1,000		750	
Advertising, administration and distribution expenses (£000)	600	750		90
Net profit	400	570	650	540

C. ESSAY QUESTIONS

1 'Reducing price elasticity should be the number one goal of any firm's marketing strategy.' Discuss the validity of this statement.

2 As marketing director of a successful company, explain how you would go about reducing the price elasticity of one of your leading confectionery brands. What external and internal constraints are you likely to encounter along the way?

3 Outline and evaluate the factors that might affect the price elasticity of demand for a fitness centre. Why might managers wish to change the price elasticity of the centre?

MARKETING MIX

DEFINITION
The marketing mix is a marketing tool. It is a checklist. It focuses attention on the various elements of marketing needed to carry out the marketing strategy. It consists of four factors (product, price, promotion and place) cemented together by effective market research.

10.1 How is it used?

Marketing managers look at each of the ingredients in the mix. They decide what marketing actions need to be taken under each of the headings. If marketing activity is to be effective each ingredient needs to be considered. It will be constrained by the budget available for marketing activity. For each market situation there will be an optimum combination of the ingredients. This will give a balance between cost and effectiveness. The ingredients need to work with each other. A good product poorly priced may fail. If the product is not available following an advertising campaign the expenditure is wasted.

A successful *mix* will produce customer satisfaction. It will achieve the marketing objectives.

10.2 For each market situation there will be a different mix

The mix will ensure that the marketing effort is correctly targeted. There are different markets. Industrial markets are different from consumer markets.

INDUSTRIAL MARKETS

In industrial markets, one business is supplying another. The products will be:

- materials and parts, including raw materials, part-finished goods, component parts, supplies such as packaging, office supplies
- capital goods, including machinery, vehicles, buildings, office equipment
- services such as banking, insurance, distribution.

Businesses purchase these products in order to produce their own products for the market. They will have concerns about cost, reliability, quality and availability. In industrial markets the product may have exact specifications agreed with the customer. There will be less scope for modifying the product.

CONSUMER MARKETS

The consumer market supplies the final consumer (the 'end-user'). It is a much larger and more complex market. In order to understand this market businesses look at:

Buying habits: Most purchases fall into two categories:

- Convenience goods – these are bought frequently. They include most non-durable goods. They are consumed when used. They can be:
  - regular purchases
  - impulse purchases
  - emergency purchases.
- Shopping goods – the customer will take longer to choose. They include durable goods such as cars and household goods. They are used over and over again.

The type of consumer: Customers can be categorised in several ways. Such as by:

- Spending power – customer expectations and buying patterns vary with spending ability. Lower income households will look for less expensive hotels with family sized rooms. Higher income families will look for more exclusive locations and better facilities.
- Age – there are some products such as toys or sheltered housing that are age specific. Businesses sometimes modify the product to make it appeal to other groups. Johnson and Johnson repositioned its baby products. It changed its promotion to encourage women to buy.
- Gender – many products are gender specific. If the product is sold as 'unisex' there will be a larger market. Calvin Klein sells perfumes for men and women. The marketing however suggests some of them can be used by males or females. Some products can be modified slightly and marketed to appeal to a different gender group. Cosmetics companies have developed cosmetics for men. These are similar products to those sold to women. The packaging and market support have been changed to appeal to men.

WITHIN EACH MARKET THERE MAY BE MANY DIFFERENT SEGMENTS

The differences in customers and buying habits result in many 'markets within markets'. These are known as market segments. Each segment will require its own marketing mix. The fashion industry is an example. At one end, cheap, cheerful with mass availability is the key. At the other end exclusivity and quality workmanship are important.

10.3 The ingredients are not equally important

In most cases the product is the vital ingredient. No amount of marketing effort will make a poor product succeed. However a good product without good support may also fail. The balance will vary. In a price-sensitive market, pricing will be important. This is seen in the petrol market. If one company reduces its price the others follow rapidly. In industrial markets reliability and quality may be the overriding considerations.

10.4 Product

A product is something that is offered to the market. Businesses need to understand what the product is and what it means to the consumer.

A product can be:
- a good such as a washing machine or shampoo
- a service such as accountancy or hairdressing
- a place such as a tourist destination
- a person such as a football player or pop star.

Understanding the type of product is important. Businesses will need a different marketing strategy to sell a chocolate bar than a washing machine. For the chocolate bar the location and the wrapping may be important features. For the washing machine, design and performance are more likely to be significant to the customer.

WHAT THE PRODUCT MEANS TO THE CUSTOMER

Products are not just physical things. They *do* something for the customer. Mobile phones are not just communication devices. They are also fashion accessories. Look at Nokia's range of interchangeable mobile phone covers.

Products provide both *tangible* and *intangible* benefits. Tangible benefits are those that can be measured. Cars have different performance levels. A Ford Focus will not give the same speed performance as a Porsche 811. Intangible benefits cannot be measured. They include things such as pleasure, satisfaction or peace of mind. Haagen Dazs ice-cream advertising does not emphasise the nutritional value of the ice-cream. It concentrates on building an image for the brand. Building society advertisements emphasise security (an intangible benefit) above convenience (a tangible benefit).

BRAND VALUES

On 2 October 2002 EMI proudly announced 'the biggest record deal in British history'. Robbie Williams had agreed to record his next six albums with EMI in return for a payment of between £50 and £80 million. The media loved the deal and so did the stock market. The name Robbie Williams was enough to push up the share price of EMI. Few noticed, though, the announcement just two days later that Guy Chambers would no longer be writing songs with or for Williams. Chambers' songs such as 'Millennium' and 'Rock DJ' were a vital part of Williams' success. EMI said 'there are plenty of good songwriters who Robbie could work with', but it raised the question of whether Robbie Williams – the brand name – is more important than the Robbie Williams music.

MAKING THE PRODUCT FIT THE MARKET

Good marketing means developing products that 'fit' the market. They need to be designed correctly and then developed to keep pace with market changes. Businesses use market and product research to tailor products to customer requirements. *Market research* is essential. It will help to understand the customer and the product. It will tell the business:

- who the customer is
- how the customer makes their purchasing decisions
- what the customer wants from the product
- if there are gaps in the market
- what rival products are in the market
- what competitors are doing.

Product research concentrates on the product in order to:

- produce new products
- modify existing products.

THE ROLE OF NEW PRODUCTS

New products are important to businesses. They give competitive advantage. They bring new customers. New products may come from product research. They may have been developed to fill a gap in the market. When a new product is developed it should take account of market and customer requirements. Test marketing is useful. The product may be launched in a small area to test customer reactions. Modifications can then be made before the final launch.

MANAGING EXISTING PRODUCTS

Once a product is in the market the business needs to monitor customer and competitor reaction regularly.

It is essential that the product is developed as necessary. This will maintain the life of the product. It will ensure that it does not get overtaken by rival products. Car manufacturers introduce new models on a regular basis. They also modify their existing models continually. These modifications keep the product 'fresh' in the eyes of the customer.

In a highly competitive market it is essential to make the product stand out from its rivals. In order to attract customer attention businesses try to differentiate their product from other products. Some are easier to differentiate than others. The secret is to find the modification that will have the most customer appeal. Understanding what customers want helps to ensure that the modifications are effective. When video recorders were first introduced manufacturers kept adding more complex features. This differentiated their products in a highly competitive situation. Some manufacturers realised that customers wanted a machine that was easy to use. This has now become a standard product feature.

Modifications can be made to:

- the design, such as shape or colour
- the performance, such as adding extra features or making the product easier to use
- service levels, such as improving after-sales care or the guarantee period.

Businesses may also modify existing products to make them attractive to a different market segment. This may be just repackaging. Products sold to overseas markets will often require repackaging. In other cases the product may be altered. Heinz introduced a range of tinned products with lower sugar content to appeal to the health conscious customer. These are sold alongside its normal products.

10.5 Price

(Pricing is dealt with more fully in Unit 11.)

Price plays a critical part in marketing activity. Incorrect pricing policy could:

- Lose customers – if the price is not '*right*' customers will buy rival products. Consumers have a fair idea of what is the correct price for a product.
- Lose revenue – obviously lost customers mean lost revenue. Revenue can also be lost if the price is too low. There needs to be a balance between sales and revenue. An understanding of **price elasticity of demand** will help businesses to make correct pricing decisions.

Pricing involves a balance between being competitive and being profitable.

PRICING STRATEGIES

Pricing strategies will depend on the product and the market. There are different strategies for new and existing products.

Strategies for new products include:

- Skimming – setting a high price when the product is introduced. This maximises initial returns.
- Penetration – setting a low price to guarantee entry into the market.

For existing products there are other strategies:

- Price leader – the business will set the market price.
- Price taker – the business will match the market price.
- Predator – the business will undercut the market price.

Once the strategy has been determined there are many different pricing *tactics* that can be used. These include:

- Loss leaders – prices are set deliberately low, possibly below cost. This encourages buyers, who then purchase related products. This in turn generates profits. Supermarkets often offer some products at below cost in order to attract customers into the store. These customers will hopefully then fill their baskets with these and other goods. Similarly, car manufacturers make most of their profits on parts sales rather than the initial sale of the car.

BATTLE OF THE CONSOLES

In August 2002 Sony and Microsoft announced price cuts on their games consoles, as part of the war for dominance of this £20 billion world market. The two companies, together with Nintendo, vie with each other to produce ever more sophisticated machines. The current winner is the Sony PlayStation 2, which has sold more than 33 million machines since its launch in March 2000. This is eight times more than its rivals the Microsoft Xbox and Nintendo's GameCube.

Once the battle of technology has been fought, the companies keep the product alive by cutting prices and the battle moves to level 2. Microsoft had to reduce the price of its Xbox very soon after its launch because Sony reduced its price. In this latest move Sony is in a strong position. It has already covered its development costs and can afford to reduce prices to maintain its domination. Microsoft clearly feels that it cannot allow Sony any more competitive advantage at this stage in the product life cycle of Xbox and so is matching the price reduction.

The battle looks likely to continue well into the future. Sony is expected to have its new generation game machine on the market by 2005 and the press has reported that Microsoft is looking to launch Xbox2 in 2004.

Business IN

- Psychological pricing – prices are set just below psychological price barriers such as £10. A price of £9.99 seems lower than £10.00.
- Special-offer pricing – this includes offers such as 'three for the price of two'.

10.6 Promotion

This is about communication. It is about telling potential consumers about a product. The aim is to persuade customers to buy the product. The extent to which this ingredient is important will depend on:

- The competitiveness of the market – where no alternatives are available the consumer will have less choice. There will be less need to persuade the customer to buy.
- Availability – if the product is in short supply there will be little need to promote it. In Russia, toilet paper is scarce. Russian customers are less concerned about the thickness, softness or number of sheets in the roll than people in the West, where several products are competing for customer approval in crowded markets.
- How easily the product can be differentiated in the market – if the differences are obvious to the customer there may be less need for promotion.
- The stage of the product life cycle – a new product will usually need promotional support. Promotion will tell customers that the product is available. It will persuade them to try the new product. If the product has been altered, promotion will tell customers of the changes.

Promotion should be:

- informative
- persuasive
- reassuring.

There are many forms of promotion. It is not just advertising!
Promotion includes:

- Advertising – this includes direct advertising such as through the TV, radio and newspapers. It also includes indirect advertising such as product placement.

> *'I know half the money I spend on advertising is wasted, but I can never find out which half.'*
>
> *Lord Leverhume, British industrialist*

Source: *The Ultimate Book of Business Quotations*, Stuart Crainer, Capstone Publishing, 1997

- Direct selling – customers are approached directly. This may be by direct contact. Telesales is a growing business.
- Direct marketing – this will include mailshots, perhaps supported by sales catalogues.

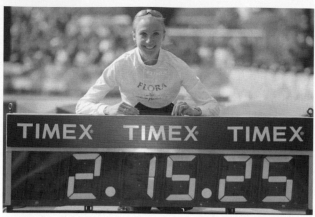

The London Marathon: sponsorship as a promotional and PR exercise (© Ian Walton/Getty Images)

- Point-of-sale – promotional material is often used where the product is being sold. It may include displays, free samples or special offers.
- Incentives – these include loyalty cards, bonus points and sometimes price incentives.
- Public relations – this is not direct marketing but involves ensuring that the company or product name is known and is well thought of by customers. This will include activities such as sponsorship of sport or arts.

Promotion is often talked about as being above- or below-the-line. Above-the-line is direct advertising through consumer media such as press, TV, cinema and radio. All other forms of promotion are considered below-the-line activity. This would include direct selling and promotional activities such as incentives. Businesses will not just use one method of promotion. They will have a mixture of activities. This is known as the promotional mix. The mix will need to be balanced to be as effective as possible. The mix of promotional activities will depend on:

- the size of the market
- the type of product
- the cost.

Promotion needs to be effective. Being effective means getting a balance between coverage and cost. TV advertising is expensive but has huge coverage. There is no point in advertising table tennis equipment on TV at peak viewing times. It is more effective to use a specialist magazine for table tennis players. If players belong to clubs they could also be targeted by direct mail.

10.7 Place

This is about availability. It includes the physical place, availability and timing.
The key questions facing firms are:

- What are the best outlets for reaching potential customers?
- How can I convince those outlets to stock my products?

- What is the most effective way to get my products to those outlets?

Compare, for a moment, McVitie's Jaffa Cakes and Burton's Jammie Dodgers. Both are well-known biscuit brands, but the former is distributed in 90% of retail outlets whereas the latter is in only 64%. Clearly this restricts sales of Jammie Dodgers, because few customers would make a special journey to find them. Both companies have a similar view of the right outlets for their products (supermarkets, corner shops, garages, canteens and cafés). So why may Burton's be losing out to McVitie's in this particular race? Possible reasons include:

- Jaffa Cakes have higher consumer demand, therefore retail outlets are more willing to stock the product
- Jammie Dodgers may have more direct competitors; high product differentiation may make Jaffa Cakes more of a 'must stock' line
- If Jaffa Cakes have more advertising support, retailers know customers will ask for the product by name while the advertising campaign is running
- McVitie's have a much larger market share, therefore the company is in a stronger position to cross-sell (i.e. persuade a shopkeeper to buy a range of McVitie brands).

In this case, both firms were clear about the target outlets for their product. This is not always the case – there may be important decisions to be made. If you are launching the world's first robotic lawnmower, would you want it in every garden centre, DIY outlet, department store and Argos catalogue? That would depend on

Figure 10.1 Channels of distribution

your overall strategy. Perhaps you feel that, while the only supplier, you should price high to enjoy high profit margins to recoup your investment (skimming the market). In which case you should perhaps only distribute through department stores. Later, you could bring the price down and strike a deal with B&Q. Persuading retailers to stock your product is never easy. For the retailer, the key issues are opportunity cost and risk. As shelf space is limited, stocking your chocolate bar probably means scrapping another. Which one? What revenue will be lost? Will one or two customers be upset? ('What! No Coffee Walnut Whips any more!') These factors represent the opportunity cost of stocking your product. The other consideration is risk. A brand new chocolate bar endorsed by a supermodel may be a slimmer's delight, but high initial sales may then flop, leaving the shopkeeper with boxes of slow-moving stock.

The remaining issue to consider is the distribution channel. In other words, how the product passes from producer to the consumer. Sold directly, as with pick-your-own strawberries? Or via a wholesaler, then a retailer, as with newspapers bought from your local shop? There are three main channels of distribution:

1 Traditional – in the days before hypermarkets and superstores, shops bought their stock from wholesalers, who in turn bought from producers. The profit mark-up applied by the 'middle man' added to the final retail price, but wholesalers had many other advantages. They 'broke bulk', meaning that they might buy a container load of Andrex, but be happy to sell in boxes of 48 packs to shopkeepers. This ensured that small shops did not need to hold high stock levels.
2 Modern – Sainsbury's, B&Q and WH Smith do not buy from a wholesaler. They buy direct from producers and then organise their own distribution to their outlets. Their huge selling power gives them huge buying power. Therefore they are able to negotiate the highest discounts from the producers.
3 Direct – years ago, door-to-door selling was an important distribution method. Today this has given way to many other approaches. Retailers of home computers in Britain and America are being hit hard by fierce competition from direct sales companies such as Dell. By cutting out the wholesaler and the retailer, Dell is able to offer low prices for up-to-date machines. Already very successful at

THE DISTRIBUTION OF CK ONE

The hugely successful launch of the fragrance CK One had many unusual features. In an era of niche marketing, Unilever targeted a multi-racial, multi-ethnic, ageless, genderless audience. Yet it applied this apparently mass market approach through completely unorthodox distribution channels. A fragrance on sale in a record shop? Or in a night club? Why not? In this way CK One acquired an image of being young and different – yet it sold to both sexes and many age groups. And having established a general brand name in the fragrance market, young consumers who like experimenting can choose from a range of CK products.

Source: Adapted from *Unilever Magazine*, no. 106

Business IN

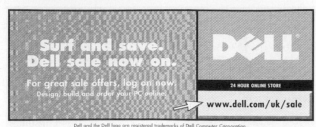

Dell Computers advertised on the Internet (© Dell Computer Corporation)

attracting customers through its media advertising, Dell now gets a quarter of its orders via the Internet. This low-cost form of promotion gives Dell a major competitive edge. Dixons and Computer World have huge overheads to pay; Dell has very few.

10.8 Where does the marketing mix fit into marketing planning?

The marketing mix should follow on from the marketing strategy. Managers need an excellent understanding of the market if they are to *mix* the ingredients effectively.

- Statistical analysis should highlight trends. Investigation will reveal the reasons for them.
- Market research should provide:
  - an understanding of the product's place in the market, the market segments and target customers
  - customers' views on the product
  - reasons for the success or failure of the product
  - an understanding of competitive activity.
- **SWOT analysis** will identify internal strengths and weaknesses. It will highlight external opportunities and threats.
- The marketing strategy should follow from this analysis. The marketing mix will put the strategy into practice (see the table at the bottom of the page).

EVALUATING THE MARKETING PLAN

The marketing mix can also be used to evaluate the marketing plan. Marketing activities can be reviewed

using the marketing mix to ensure that the marketing objectives will be achieved (see Figure 10.2).

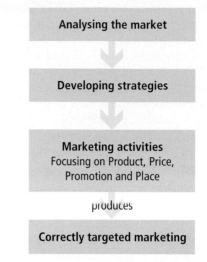

Figure 10.2 Where do the four Ps fit into marketing planning?

When answering questions on the marketing mix consideration should be given to the following:

- How well the mix is matched to the strategy; only if every aspect of the mix is coordinated and focused will it be effective. The giant Unilever (Wall's) flopped with their UK launch of Ranieri luxury Italian ice-cream because the product was distributed through mass market outlets such as Tesco before it had built its prestige through smaller, more exclusive outlets.
- The relative importance of the ingredients in the marketing mix. Although the product is likely to be the most important element of the mix, every case is different. Taste tests show Coca-Cola to be no better than Pepsi. Yet Coke outsells its rival by up to 20 times – in nearly every country in the world.
- How each of the mix ingredients can be used to achieve effective marketing. The mix elements must be tailored to each case. One product may require (and afford) national television advertising. In another case, small-scale local advertising might be supported by below-the-line activity to increase distribution. There is never a single answer to a question about the marketing mix. The best approach depends on the product, its competitive situation, the objectives and the marketing budget

MARKET ANALYSIS	STRATEGIC RESPONSE THROUGH MARKETING MIX
• Statistical analysis shows sales are falling; research identifies the cause as competitors' pricing	• Redesign products to have lower costs, then reposition at a lower price level
• The SWOT analysis identifies an advanced product feature as the reason current buyers are purchasing our product	• Focus heavily upon this in advertising and at the point of sale
• Criticism is made of the lack of availability of our product	• Switch resources from advertising to improving incentives to retailers to stock our product

The concept of marketing mix has remained unchanged since it was first introduced in the 1950s. It has proved to be a useful marketing tool. It still serves the useful purpose of focusing marketing activity. However many believe that there are strong arguments for adding a fifth ingredient – people. Many also feel that it should not be presented as a list of equally important parts but that the mix should be seen with the product at the core, supported by the other ingredients.

With the growing importance of customer service and of good sales staff, it is legitimate to extend the marketing mix to include people. Businesses can support and differentiate their product by the people they employ. Any business based on day-to-day contact with customers cannot ignore the importance of its employees. Retail outlets rely on their salesforce to enhance the shopping experience. A customer who feels the salesperson is rude or lacks knowledge will go elsewhere.

Asda supermarkets use one of the staff as a greeter. They stand at the entrance of the store to 'greet' customers. The type of people employed and their attitude can be used to support corporate identity. Disney employees have to be smart, without facial hair, and be 'upbeat'. The leading accountancy firms insist that their employees dress smartly. Well-trained salespeople ensure that the customer has a satisfactory buying experience. A customer buying a computer wants reassurance that the salesperson knows about the product. This gives them confidence to buy.

Although the four Ps are presented as a list there is no doubt that in almost every case the product is the most important ingredient. A successful marketing mix should be matched to the marketing strategy. And that strategy is rooted in how well the product is matched to the segment of the market being targeted.

In the future, it is likely that the marketing mix will be product plus marketing support. Marketing support will be a mix of price, promotion, place and people.

KEY terms

marketing planning – producing a schedule of marketing activities based upon decisions about the marketing mix. This will show the when, what and how much of a product's advertising, promotions and distribution drives over the coming year.

price elasticity of demand – a measure of how sensitive demand is to changes in price.

SWOT analysis – analysing the Strengths, Weaknesses, Opportunities and Threats facing a business or a product.

10.10 Workbook

AS Level Exercises

A. REVISION QUESTIONS
(30 marks; 60 minutes)

Read the unit, then answer:

1 What are the four ingredients of the marketing mix? *(4)*
2 What is the difference between industrial and consumer markets? *(2)*
3 What is the difference between shopping and convenience goods? *(2)*
4 List three ways in which businesses categorise customers. *(3)*
5 What is meant by a market segment? *(3)*
6 List three ways, with examples, of how a business can differentiate the product. *(3)*
7 Why are new products important to a business? *(4)*
8 List three different ways of promoting the product. *(3)*
9 What is meant by the promotional mix? *(3)*
10 What are the three main channels of distribution? *(3)*

B. REVISION EXERCISES

B1 Data Response

Milk Tray Revamped as Competition Intensifies

Cadbury spent 18 months planning a relaunch of Milk Tray – its boxed chocolate brand. This was the first major change to the product in over four years. The chocolates are now presented in a box with a patented curve to one side and updated graphics. The same design is also used for another brand, Darkness, that was launched in 1996. The new packaging is said to provide 'a more sophisticated and desirable gift for the modern consumer' and is expected to add 10% growth to sales.

The marketing director, Alan Palmer, said that the activity was to fight off increasing competition from other sectors. 'Milk Tray is mostly bought as a gift. In recent years chocolate has been losing out to other gifts such as wine and flowers. The brand must be seen to be as relevant and contemporary as those products.'

The market for boxed chocolate assortments grew by 8% in value in 1996. 3% was due to volume growth and the remainder was a result of higher raw material costs. This is in spite of heavy competition from 'twist wraps' such as Roses and Quality Street. Alan Palmer feels that the traditional presentation of the twist wraps may be their downfall. He believes consumers want a fresh approach.

The price of the newly packaged chocolates was about 5% higher than previously. The range was also widened to include larger sized boxes and special limited editions at Christmas time. The relaunch was supported by a £3 million campaign. This promotional spending was almost double the amount spent in the previous year.

Source: *The Grocer*, 26/4/97

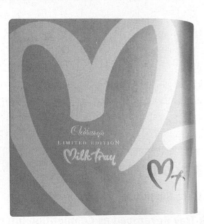

Milk Tray – rebranding to compete against the competition

Questions *(25 marks; 30 minutes)*

1 Why did Cadbury feel it was necessary to relaunch Milk Tray? *(4)*
2 Explain, using a numerical example, the statement 'The market for boxed chocolate assortments grew by 8% in value in 1996. 3% was due to volume growth and the remainder was a result of higher raw material costs.' *(5)*
3 Why might the firm have decided to relaunch the product rather than launch a new product? *(5)*
4 Why has the advertising budget been doubled? *(2)*
5 Evaluate the actions taken by Cadbury using the marketing mix as a guide. *(9)*

B2 Data Response

Cellnet

BT's Cellnet mobile phone network has over 3 million subscribers. Early in 1998 it launched its largest advertising campaign since it was formed in 1985. Cellnet has been troubled by a high level of lapsed customers. This 'churn', as it is known in the industry, runs at about 20–30% a year for the whole market. Cellnet's loss of customers has been at the higher end of the range. The marketing team estimates that the campaign will pay for itself easily in the first year if the new initiative brings this disconnection rate down to nearer the 20% level.

The £20 million advertising and direct mail campaign was planned to draw attention to a range of new initiatives. These include:

- a discount programme similar to BT's 'Friends and Family'
- ending minimum contract periods
- compensating customers if they sign up to an inappropriate plan
- a new scheme called 'First for Firms' which gives discounted call rates to businesses when calling 10 selected numbers
- additional discounts for business customers choosing longer term contracts
- tariff cuts
- introduction of a new pre-pay package.

The managing director explained that the new 'First' programmes had been developed in the USA so that rivals would not get to hear about the scheme before it was launched. He said that the aim of the scheme was to end confusion in the market.

Cellnet hopes that the new initiatives backed by the promotional spending will reduce the loss of customers to rivals and increase their subscriber base.

Source: Adapted from *The Times*, 28/5/98

Questions *(25 marks; 30 minutes)*

1 What might be the reasons for the high level of 'churn' in the mobile phone market? *(4)*
2 Why did Cellnet develop the 'First' programme in the USA? *(2)*
3 Use the marketing mix to review Cellnet's campaign. *(8)*
4 State and explain Cellnet's marketing objective. *(4)*
5 How important do you think the £20 million advertising campaign will be to the success of the whole campaign? *(7)*

A Level Exercises

A. REVISION QUESTIONS
(30 marks; 60 minutes)

Read the unit, then answer:

1 How does the marketing mix help to ensure that marketing effort is effective? *(4)*

2 Why might overseas markets require a different marketing mix from home markets? *(4)*

3 What is the difference between tangible and intangible benefits given by a product? *(3)*

4 What is the relationship between market research and the marketing mix? *(4)*

5 Explain how a firm might modify its product to widen the customer-base, using examples. *(4)*

6 How do large businesses such as supermarkets take advantage of a shorter distribution chain? *(3)*

7 How does the marketing mix fit into marketing planning? *(4)*

8 To what extent can the marketing mix be used to evaluate the marketing plan? *(4)*

B. REVISION EXERCISES

B1 Case Study

The Battle for Customers

A leading UK supermarket chain is considering expanding into India. It sees this as a relatively untapped market. The home market is saturated and price wars and loyalty cards have reduced profit margins. In the UK the supermarkets have been blamed for the disappearance of the corner shop. In India the situation is very different. A recent survey by an Indian market research firm, ORG-Marg, has concluded that small grocery shops will continue to dominate the food retailing market for the foreseeable future. Several firms who have been lured to India by its rapid economic growth and over 1 billion mouths to feed have not been successful in their attempts to establish supermarkets in India's largest cities. Neither of the two main contenders have managed to break even since opening in the early 1990s. They are continuing to expand and hoping that eventually economies of scale will permit lower prices and hopefully improve their standing and their profitability.

These new supermarkets have faced several problems:

- Not least of these is that customers like their local stores. Although they are cramped busy places they give an old-fashioned level of service.
- The local stores do not stock as many brands as the supermarkets but they will stock an item if a customer wants it. If they do not have what the customer wants they will get it.
- The local stores offer a free delivery service and allow customers credit.
- The supermarkets cannot match the cost base of the local store. The poor infrastructure makes operational costs very expensive.
- Government laws limiting urban development mean that property prices are high. The smaller stores have often been in the family for generations and so the initial cost of the site has long since been forgotten.

To try to gain customers, one of the supermarket chains has introduced promotions such as coupons and advertised in local newspapers. Another has teamed up with local manufacturers. They obtain staples such as lentils and rice locally. These are then packaged and branded by local manufacturers. This has helped to lower prices for customers and improve margins. A recent entrant into the market is trying to stay ahead of the competition. It has invested in air-conditioning and additional telephone lines to ensure that customers do not have to wait when they call.

The UK chain has looked at the existing market in India and feels it can succeed. However the managers know they will only do this after a struggle to change customer attitudes.

Questions *(30 marks; 45 minutes)*

1 What is meant by 'the home market is saturated'? *(2)*

2 What are the marketing implications for a business in a saturated market? *(6)*

3 Why might expansion allow economies of scale? *(4)*

4 What problems might a British retailer have in marketing its product in India? *(6)*

5 Using the marketing mix, analyse the existing market and evaluate the UK firm's chances of success. *(12)*

C. ESSAY QUESTIONS

1 How important is the marketing mix in developing a firm's marketing strategy?

2 'The product is the most important part of the marketing mix.' Discuss.

3 Some analysts argue that advertising in the media is a waste of time and money. They suggest that below-the-line promotion is much more cost effective. To what extent do you agree with this?

PRICING

DEFINITION
Price is the amount paid by the customer for a good or service.

11.1 How important is price?

Price is important. It is one of the main links between the customer (demand) and the producer (supply). It is the focus of marketing activity to add value to the product. And is fundamental to a firm's revenues and gross profit margins.

As part of the marketing mix it plays a strong role in marketing the product. It is fundamental to most consumer buying decisions. The importance of price to the customer will depend on several factors:

- customer sensitivity to price
- the level of competitive activity
- the availability of the product.

CUSTOMER SENSITIVITY TO PRICE

Consumers have an idea of the correct price for a product (see Figure 11.1). They balance price with other considerations. These include:

- The features of the product such as its design and performance – customers will pay more for a car with a larger engine or better comfort.
- The quality of the product – products seen as having higher quality can carry a price premium. This may be real or perceived quality.
- How much they want it – all purchases are personal. Customers will pay more for goods they need or want.
- Their income – customers buy products within their income range. Consumers with more disposable income are less concerned about price. Uncertainty about future income will have the same effect as lower income. In a recession even those who are working will be more sensitive to price. They are aware of the possibility of losing their income.

Figure 11.1 The 'right' price

Pound Stop Ltd: an example of low pricing (© Life File/Emma Lee)

Chanel: an example of the high quality designer market
(© Corbis/Dave G Houser)

THE LEVEL OF COMPETITIVE ACTIVITY

In a competitive market price is important. Customers have more choice in a competitive market. Price is one element in that choice. Businesses may use price to differentiate their product. They may also use price as part of their promotional activity. For some products such as **branded goods** the price is kept higher to reinforce the brand's value. In a **monopoly** the business is able to charge higher prices.

THE AVAILABILITY OF THE PRODUCT

If the product is readily available consumers are more price conscious. They know they can go elsewhere and find the same product – perhaps cheaper. Scarcity removes some of the barriers to price. This can be seen in the art world where huge prices are paid for paintings. Shortage of the product forces the price up.

11.2 Price determines business revenue

Pricing is important to the business. Unlike the other ingredients in the marketing mix it generates revenue. Sales revenue is arrived at using a simple formula:

sales revenue = price per unit × number sold

Getting the price right is therefore vital. Price is important in persuading customers to buy. Price determines demand. If the price is not right the business could:

- Lose customers – lost customers mean lost revenue. Demand is directly related to price (see Unit 9). If the price is too high, sales and therefore revenue will be lost. If goods remain unsold costs of production will not be recovered.
- Lose revenue – revenue can also be lost if the price is too low. The business will not be maximising its revenue. There needs to be a balance between sales and revenue. If lower prices mean higher sales the business may be able to take advantage of **economies of scale**. This will generate additional profit. Understanding the relationship between demand and price is fundamental.

Pricing involves a balance between being competitive and being profitable.

11.3 How do businesses decide what price to charge?

At certain times during a product's life cycle pricing is especially important. Incorrect pricing when the product is launched could cause the product to fail. At other stages in the product's life pricing may be used to regenerate interest. It may also be used to avoid the product being overtaken by rivals.

THE RISK OF UNDERPRICING

Chris and Becky Barnard risked everything on opening a restaurant in the country. Their sales projections convinced their bank to provide a £40,000 overdraft (on top of a £110,000 mortgage on the property). They decided on the upmarket name Avins Bridge Restaurant and set their price at £17 a head for a three-course meal. The restaurant opened in the summer 1997.

Although evening trade proved reasonable, lunchtimes were dead. By February 1998 the situation was very worrying. With an average of just 16 meals a day (perhaps one table of four at lunch and three in the evening) the business was operating well below break-even. Drastic action was needed. A failed special offer of a free dessert proved that their relatively elderly, affluent customers were not price sensitive. So the Barnards decided to push prices up – and to cut costs by running the restaurant without any outside staff.

Although things are still a struggle, the higher prices are helping to keep the restaurant going while the Barnards wait for word-of-mouth to bring in new customers.

There are two basic pricing decisions:

- pricing a new product
- managing prices throughout the product life.

Both decisions require a good understanding of the market – consumers and competitors.

Businesses need to know what competitors are charging and how customers feel about price. For price changes they need to know how their customers and competitors will react. They need to understand how other market factors, such as changes to the economy, affect purchasing.

There are several ways that businesses obtain market information:

- market research can provide consumer reactions to possible price changes
- competitive research tells the company about other products and prices
- analysis of sales patterns shows how the market reacts to price and economic changes
- sales staff can report on customer reactions to prices.

Pricing decisions also require an understanding of costs. These costs must include purchasing, manufacturing, distribution, administration and marketing.

Cost information should be available from the company's management accounting systems.

The lowest price a firm can consider charging is set by costs. Except as a temporary promotional tactic (a loss leader), businesses must charge more for the product than the variable cost. This ensures that every product sold contributes towards the fixed costs of the business.

The market determines the highest price that can be charged. The price that is charged will need to take account of the company objectives. The right price will be the one that achieves the objectives.

Figure 11.2 Determining the price

When making changes to product prices the business needs to understand the relationship between price changes and demand. Demand for some products is more sensitive to price changes than others. Price elasticity of demand measures how sensitive demand is to price changes (see Unit 9). If demand for a product is sensitive to price changes an increase in price could cut total revenue.

11.4 Pricing methods

There are several different pricing methods.

COST-PLUS

This is the most commonly used method. The average cost is calculated. This is total cost divided by the number of units. Total cost will include both fixed and variable costs. A mark-up is then added to give the selling price. The level of mark-up should take into account market circumstances. Businesses often set target mark-ups. These may need to be reduced if the price is too high for the market. They can also be increased if there is an opportunity to raise prices.

Example:
A business is manufacturing educational CDs. The overheads or fixed costs are £40,000. The variable costs for each CD amount to £5. The business is producing 20,000 units.
The total costs will be:

£40,000 + (20,000 × £5) = £140,000.

The average cost for each CD will be:

$$\frac{£140,000}{20,000} = £7$$

This is the minimum price that could be charged if the company is to break even.
In this case the company adds a 200% mark-up.
The selling price will be £7 + (7 × 200%) = £21.

The mark-up that is used varies from product to product. Grocers add an average of about 25%. Clothes shops look for a 100% mark-up. For cosmetics the mark-up can be as high as 2000%!

This method ensures that some profit is made. It is sometimes known as *absorption pricing*. This is because all costs are accounted for in the price.

CONTRIBUTION PRICING

The price is calculated using variable costs plus a contribution. It is also known as *marginal pricing*.

Example:
In the example above the variable costs are £5. The minimum price has to be above £5.

Any price over £5 will make a contribution to overheads. When sufficient units have been sold to pay for the overheads any further sales will contribute to profit.

If the business charges £6 for the product the contribution will be £1.

The fixed costs are £40,000. The first 40,000 units will pay for fixed costs. Any sales above this will provide profit.

If the price were £10 the contribution would be £5. The first 8,000 units would contribute to fixed costs.

Profit is only ensured if there are sufficient sales to cover fixed costs. The level of mark-up over variable costs needs to take market conditions into account. This method is often used for special order pricing. If the business already has sufficient sales to cover fixed costs, special orders can be sold at a lower price. Care needs to be taken that the lower price does not harm the existing market. (Covered in detail on page 117.)

COMPETITIVE

This method sets the price in relation to competitors' prices. This approach is used on products which have little or no market power. In other words they lack the reputation or brand loyalty to allow them to set their own price.

There are two main types of competitive pricing:

- Pricing at the prevailing market price – for example, if every local petrol station is charging 79.9p per litre of petrol, you have little alternative but to adopt that price. If you price higher your sales volume will be very low. If you price lower, you may start a price war.

- Pricing at a discount to the market leader. How do Lee or Wrangler price their jeans? How do Crosse and Blackwell or Sainsbury's price their salad cream? All price at a discount to the market leader. If Levi's price 501s at £49.99, Wrangler will price their equivalent at £39.99.

PRICE DISCRIMINATION

All markets can be broken down into different segments. In some cases, these segments can be identified and separated from the mass market. Then it may be possible to use price discrimination to charge different prices to different people for the same product.

Rail travel is a good example. Business travellers have little choice but to travel in peak times. Prices are therefore kept high. At other times of the day the train operators want to attract customers. They therefore offer cheaper prices for off-peak travel. This approach will only be successful if the segments can be clearly defined and are separate. If customers from one segment can buy from a cheaper segment, they will surely do so. That is why price discrimination is only effective with services which must be used by an individual. Goods such as Mars bars are inappropriate. If you charge more for Mars bars in London than in Middlesborough, a trader will buy up the northern supplies and sell them down south.

11.5 Flexibility is the best method

Although it helps to explain each method separately, many businesses use a combination of methods. They may start with cost-plus. In the long term revenue must be greater than costs. However there are risks in using this rigidly, ignoring competition. Businesses need to be flexible when setting prices. The core of the business may be based on cost-plus pricing but there may be opportunities to make additional profit using other methods. One-off deals may be made at lower than normal prices. These sales generate additional

profit, providing the core business covers fixed costs. Businesses also need to have the flexibility to deal with changes in market circumstances. Pricing should also ensure that there is sufficient margin to enable the company to cope with unexpected events. Sudden cost increases or competitive pressure could tip the balance between profit and loss.

11.6 Pricing strategies

Pricing strategies will depend on the product and the market. Different strategies will be needed for new and existing products.

STRATEGIES FOR NEW PRODUCTS

There are two main pricing strategies: skimming and penetration.

Skimming is used when the product is innovative. As the product is new there will be no competition. The

Advantages and disadvantages of different pricing methods

METHOD	ADVANTAGES	DISADVANTAGES
Cost-plus	• Ensures all costs are covered • Effective way to set own price for products with market power	• Only works if all output is sold • Inflexible; may miss opportunities to price higher
Contribution	• Ensures variable costs are covered • Flexible; especially useful with special-order pricing	• Must be careful to ensure fixed costs are covered • Flexibility may upset regular customers
Competitive	• Sensitive to the market • Little alternative for unbranded products	• May not cover costs • Undesirable to be at the mercy of competitors
Discrimination	• Good way to maximise revenue and profit • A way of rationing a scarce resource such as peak-time rail tickets	• Difficulties with customer leakage • Those paying full price may resent being discriminated against, and look for a different supplier

price can therefore be set at a high level. Customers interested in the new product will pay this high price. The business can recoup some of the development costs. It will also be able to gauge market reaction. If sales become stagnant the price can be lowered to attract customers who were unwilling to pay the initial price. The price can also be lowered if competitors enter the market.

Penetration pricing is used when launching a product into a market where there are similar products. The price is set lower to gain market share. Once the product is established the price can be increased. Hopefully, high levels of initial sales will recover development costs.

STRATEGIES FOR EXISTING PRODUCTS

For existing products there are several pricing strategies. These are:
- Price leader – the price is set above the market level. This is possible when the company has strong brands or there is little effective competition.
- Price taker – the price is set at the market level. This happens in highly competitive markets. Businesses want to avoid a price war that will reduce profits.
- Predatory (or destroyer) pricing – this involves undercutting the market price with the specific intention of driving weaker producers out of the market. It is an aggressive strategy aimed at taking market share. Short-term profit is sacrificed to strengthen the firm's long-term position. Stronger firms set prices at a level that the other company cannot match without getting into financial difficulties. They use their financial security to underwrite the price reduction. It is also used to prevent new entrants gaining market share. In the 1990s British Airways was accused by Richard Branson of adopting this approach to hurt Virgin Atlantic.

The choice of pricing strategy will depend on the competitive environment. The grid in Figure 11.3 shows how the choice of pricing strategy will vary according to the level of competition.

Figure 11.3 Pricing strategy and level of competition

11.7 Pricing tactics

Once the strategy has been determined there are many different pricing tactics that can be used. They can be part of normal pricing or used as promotional tactics.

They include:
- Loss leaders – prices are set deliberately low. This may be below costs. The idea is to encourage customers to buy other products or **complementary goods** that generate profit. Supermarkets commonly use this tactic. Baked beans have been sold as low as 5p per can to attract custom. Children's sticker albums may be offered very cheaply – but the packs of stickers to go inside are often expensive.
- Psychological pricing – prices are set at a level that seems lower to the customer. A price of £19.99 seems more than 1p less than £20.
- Special-offer pricing – buy one get one free. Or offers made for a period of time or to clear stocks.
- Discounting – discounts are offered in a variety of ways. They may be for:
  - early payment
  - quantity purchased
  - seasonal offers
  - trade business.

PRICING MAKES HITS

Record companies use a range of marketing tactics to turn a newly released single into a hit. The company wants to sell albums as they are very profitable. Hits increase the popularity of the artist. The record companies lose money on singles but they are a way of marketing albums. The record companies use pricing to get singles to the Number 1 spot. They offer special deals to the retailers. For example one company gives its dealers a free single for every one they buy. This enables the dealers to offer huge discounts to the customer and still make good profits. One problem is that cheap singles now threaten to undermine the album market. If singles with 4 tracks are sold for £1.99 why should customers pay £12.99 for an album with 12 tracks?

ISSUES FOR **analysis**

When answering a question on pricing it is important to understand:

- The relationship between price and demand.
- The role of pricing as one part of an overall marketing strategy.
- The influence of price upon profitability. Many products have profit margins of only 20%. Therefore a 10% price cut will halve profit per unit. It would take a huge increase in demand to compensate.

- The factors influencing pricing such as cost, customer psychology and competitors.
- The role of pricing in achieving company objectives.
- How to choose the most appropriate pricing policies and tactics for different market situations.

11.8 Pricing
an evaluation

Economists think of price as a neutral factor within a marketplace. Its impact upon demand can be measured, predicted and captured in the concept of price elasticity. Many businesses would disagree – especially those selling consumer goods and services. The reason is that consumer psychology can be heavily influenced by price. A '3p off' flash makes people reach for the Mars bars. But if they are half price people wonder whether they are old stock or have suffered in the sun. They are *too* cheap.

When deciding on the price of a brand new product, marketing managers have many options. Pricing high might generate too few sales to keep retailers happy to stock the product. Yet pricing too low carries even more dangers. Large companies know there are no safe livings to be made selling cheap jeans, cheap cosmetics or perfumes.

If there is a key to successful pricing, it is to keep it in line with the overall marketing strategy. When Häagen Dazs launched in the UK at prices more than double those of its competitors, many predicted failure. In fact the pricing was in line with the image of adult, luxury indulgence and Häagen Dazs soon outsold all other premium ice-creams. The worst pricing

approach would be to develop an attractively packaged, well made product and then sell it at a discount to the leading brands. In research people would welcome it, but deep down they would not trust the product quality. Because psychology is so important to successful pricing, many firms use qualitative research rather than quantitative – to obtain the necessary psychological insights.

Häagen-Dazs – priced to match the luxury image
(© Amet Jean Pierre/Corbis Sygma)

KEY terms

branded goods – goods with a brand name or identity. This may be a business name such as Mars or a product name such as Ariel.

complementary goods – products bought in conjunction with each other, such as bacon and eggs or Gillette shavers and Gillette razors.

economies of scale – reductions in unit costs made possible by increased scale of production.

monopoly – a market dominated by one supplier.

Business Objective	Pricing Strategy	Explanation
Profit maximisation	Price discrimination	Maximising takings from every segment of the market
Long-term profit growth	Penetration pricing	Building market share to strengthen long-term profit potential
Diversification	Cost-plus	Imposing quite a high mark-up to generate the profits to finance diversification
Survival	Contribution	When a recession or a price war threatens survival, pricing may have to be below average costs (variable plus fixed) for a while

AS Level Exercises

A. REVISION QUESTIONS
(25 marks; 50 minutes)

Read the unit, then answer:

1 How can price be used to differentiate a product? *(3)*
2 How does the availability of the product affect pricing? *(3)*
3 Why might businesses lose revenue if the price is not set correctly? *(4)*
4 List two problems caused by setting the price too low. *(2)*
5 What determines the highest price and lowest price that can be charged for a product? *(4)*
6 What is meant by cost-plus pricing? *(3)*
7 What is a discount? *(2)*
8 What is meant by a 'complementary product'? Give two examples. *(4)*

B. REVISION EXERCISES

B1 Data Response – Filling the Train

British Airways has been hit by the introduction of Eurostar. BA estimate that it has lost 61% of its Paris market and 52% of the Brussels traffic. In spite of this apparent success, Eurostar lost £180 million in 1997 and is not expected to make a profit until at least 2001. The major problem is that the trains are running half empty. The average load on the Paris run is 50% and only 35% on the trips to Brussels. Only Friday night and Sunday night trains are full. After the initial impact on the airlines the situation now seems to have stabilised and the airlines are again seeing growth in their market.

Analysts feel that the only way forward for Eurostar is to attract more customers, and that will probably involve reducing prices. This is a problem for Eurostar whose main marketing thrust has been to attract business customers. It has recently introduced Premium First. This service offers improved service and increased flexibility. Customers can, for example, switch to a different train or even to a British Midlands flight if necessary. The fare for this service of £399 is below the £422 that BA charges for its fully flexible return air ticket to Paris. The normal first class fare compares well with the cost of air travel. £319 compared to an average price of £358 for the airlines operating on the London to Paris route.

This new pricing structure has increased Eurostar's profit per passenger from 40% last year to 55% this year.

Questions
(30 marks; 35 minutes)

1 On the Premium First ticket, what is the average profit per passenger? *(3)*
2 How can Eurostar make a profit of 55% per passenger but make an overall loss of £180 million? *(5)*
3 Why do analysts say that Eurostar needs to increase passenger numbers? *(6)*
4 How might Eurostar set about attracting more passengers? *(6)*
5 Discuss the possible consequences of Eurostar deciding to reduce its prices in order to attract more customers onto the trains. *(10)*

B2 Data Response

Supermarket Price Wars

1999 is expected to see strong competition between supermarkets. During 1998 the supermarkets were subjected to strong criticism in the press when a survey showed that food prices in the UK were generally higher than in other parts of Europe and the USA. The supermarket chains reacted by saying the comparisons were unfair. Nevertheless it is expected that future marketing will concentrate on price. Any price war will be damaging. It is likely that the two largest supermarket chains, Sainsbury and Tesco, will begin the price cutting. Sainsbury has already started its preparation by cutting out £100 million in costs by reorganising regional management.

If a full-blown price war begins there are likely to be casualties. Asda's unique selling point of low prices will be hard to sustain. Safeway is considered vulnerable and unlikely to cope with a prolonged reduction in prices. Another casualty could be the discounters such as Aldi and Netto. Their margins are already low and it is difficult to see what they could do to re-establish the pricing gap. They may be forced to change tactics. Kwik Save and Somerfield have moved upmarket following their recent merger. They have increased prices and are offering a better quality range of products together with improved service.

Source: Adapted from *The Times*, 7/12/98

Questions *(30 marks; 35 minutes)*
1 How will the cost cutting undertaken by Sainsbury help if there is a price war? *(5)*
2 Why might Safeway be unable to sustain a long period of price cutting? *(5)*
3 What is meant by Asda's 'unique selling point' and why might this be lost? *(6)*

4 What do the actions of Somerfield and Kwik Save following their merger tell you about the role of price in marketing? *(6)*
5 The American retail giant Walmart is considering entering the British grocery market with a strategy of penetration pricing. What does this mean and what are the implications of this for the other grocery chains? *(8)*

A Level Exercises

A. REVISION QUESTIONS
(30 marks, 30 minutes)

Read the unit, then answer.

1 In what sort of market will a firm adopt a 'market taker' approach to pricing? *(3)*
2 How does pricing differ from the other marketing mix ingredients? *(3)*
3 What does 'skimming' mean and when is it used by a business? *(4)*
4 If a business is interested in long-term profit growth, what sort of pricing strategy might it use and why? *(4)*
5 Why are branded goods usually sold at a higher price than similar unbranded goods? *(5)*
6 What sort of market research is most useful when measuring customer attitudes to pricing? *(2)*
7 How can pricing be used to extend a product's life cycle? *(5)*
8 When might a firm use loss leaders as a pricing tactic? *(4)*

B. REVISION EXERCISES

B1 Data Response

UK Drivers Benefit From the Introduction of the Euro

The introduction of the Euro is expected to reduce the huge gaps in prices of new cars throughout Europe. The gap in prices from one European country to another is currently as much as 35%. Analysts are predicting that this will be reduced in Euro participating countries to 5% in five years' time. Prices in mainland Europe are also expected to fall as a result of the introduction of the Euro.

In the meantime, British car buyers will find it easier to purchase their new car at mainland European prices as French dealers turn their attention to the UK market. French car salesmen are predicting a boom in cross-Channel business. At the end of 1998 a London dealer quoted a price of £13,400 for a new Honda Civic 1.4 and a

Paris dealer £10,433 for the same car. If the French prices do fall further it will clearly make cross channel buying very enticing.

Source: Adapted from The Times, 26/11/98

Questions *(30 marks; 35 minutes)*
1 Give two possible explanations for the gap in car prices between European countries. *(6)*
2 Why is the introduction of the Euro expected to result in closer price harmonisation between European countries? *(6)*
3 Why will French car dealers turn their attention to the British market? *(5)*
4 How do you think British car dealers should react to this situation? *(7)*
5 Car manufacturers such as Honda have been using price discrimination in Europe. Explain how this may have benefited the companies concerned. *(6)*

B2 Case Study

Prices for Ices
Success in its Central London ice-cream parlours made Helden Djaz decide to launch its products nationally. The marketing director was convinced that the key product was a chocolate ice-cream bar, with its fresh cream ice-cream and thick Swiss chocolate. He knew it was only a couple of years since £1 had seemed an excessive price for a choc ice, yet the success of Magnum ice-cream had burst through that price barrier. His plan was to distribute the bars through prestigious outlets only, and to set a retail price of £1.80.

The Helden Djaz marketing director believed this high price was necessary as retailers would be offered a 50% profit margin on sales, production costs per unit would be 30p and fixed costs of £400,000 had to be covered.

He still had to convince the managing director, though. She believed it would be more profitable to price the product at £1.44p, as research had indicated that sales volume would be 30% higher at that price. The production director, meanwhile, suggested that 'I've always favoured cost-plus pricing. If we work on cost plus 60% and a sales forecast of 2 million bars a year, the retail price should be £1.60.'

A meeting was to be held that afternoon to finally agree the price.

Questions *(50 marks; 60 minutes)*

1 The marketing director's pricing policy could be considered an example of 'market skimming'. What does this mean and why might a firm use such an approach? *(8)*

2 a From the managing director's figures, what appears to be the price elasticity of the product? *(4)*

b How and why might the company try to reduce this level of price elasticity? *(8)*

3 a The Helden Djaz directors are arguing over which single price to set for their product. Outline the implications of using price discrimination in setting their prices. *(8)*

b What might be the problems in succeeding with this approach? *(6)*

4 a Prove that the production director's calculations are right. *(6)*

b Discuss whether a cost-plus approach is right for this product. *(10)*

C. ESSAY QUESTIONS

1 Discuss the main factors influencing the price a firm sets for its product.

2 How should the pricing strategy for an innovative new product differ from an established product?

3 'Competitive pricing is the only way to ensure that your product is correctly priced in its market.' Analyse this statement.

4 'Pricing is the most important part of the marketing mix.' To what extent do you believe this statement to be true?

MARKETING MATHS

DEFINITION
Statistical methods used by marketing managers to help understand their markets and customers.

12.1 Simple ways of describing sample results

MEASURES OF CENTRAL TENDENCY

Marketing managers like simple and clear information, provided it is accurate. A good way of describing a survey sample result is by giving an average. 'On average 52% of customers said they preferred X to Y' means that a number of samples were taken and on average 52% in each sample gave this answer. Averages are also quick ways of understanding whole distributions. To say that 35% of the nation buys a newspaper daily tells you about the population, but not about any particular individual in detail. So we need to understand averages, also called measures of central tendency.

The most common form of average is the arithmetic mean, but there are other averages, in particular the median and the mode (see the table below).

USING MEASURES OF CENTRAL TENDENCY IN MARKETING AND PLANNING SALES

Two sellers of hot-dogs from stalls outside London stations recently recorded their daily sales on 100 weekdays (see the table at the top of the next page).

It is very useful for seller A to know the average number of sales each day, but really only because the range of sales, 35 to 39, is quite small. If the seller brought in the number of hot-dogs nearest to the mean, 37, to sell each day, he would not lose out too much in terms of dissatisfied customers or unsold stock.

However, for seller B, whose sales fluctuate greatly, the mean is not so useful. With B there are some extreme observations, when sales are very low. This drags the mean down and complicates the picture.

It is more useful for seller B to know that he sells 35 hot-dogs on more days than any other. This, the mode, is more useful than the mean in helping to plan. If he brought the mean number (27) of hot-dogs, he would have many dissatisfied customers. The modal number (35), satisfies customers nearly all the time.

Any business selling products sold in sizes, for example clothes or shoes, would find the mode more useful than the mean. A shoe manufacturer would not know how many of the various sizes of shoes to make simply by knowing that the average foot size was 6.783! A car maker also needs to know the most popular car in a range, e.g. LX or GLX.

The median for seller A is 37 and for seller B it is 30. Note that for seller B the mode is nearly 35. The median is not especially useful here. However, as shown below, the median is particularly useful in diagrams of distributions.

12.2 Useful diagrams to explain distributions

The sales of the hot-dogs can be presented diagrammatically in a frequency distribution, as shown below.

AVERAGE	DEFINITION	ADVANTAGES	LIMITATIONS
Arithmetic mean	The usual arithmetic average – the sum of frequencies times values, divided by sum of frequencies	Well known and easy to understand; can be used in further analysis	Not necessarily a whole number or an actual value in the distribution; distorted by extreme values
Mode	The most common or frequently occurring value	Useful for sellers of goods in sizes, e.g. shoes	May be more than one modal value; not based on all values
Median	The middle value when the data are listed in size order	The value which divides the distribution in two	If there is an even number of items in the distribution, it needs to be estimated, not based on all values

SELLER A			SELLER B		
Sales of Hot-dogs	Number of Days	Sales × Days	Sales of Hot-dogs	Number of Days	Sales × Days
35	18	630	5	15	75
36	21	756	25	20	500
37	22	814	30	21	630
38	24	912	35	42	1470
39	15	585	38	2	76
Totals:	100	3697	Totals:	100	2751
mean is 36.97			mean is 27.51		

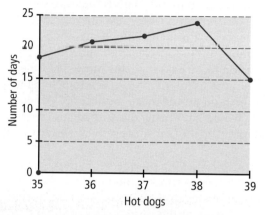

Figure 12.1 Seller A: daily sales of hot-dogs

Figure 12.2 Seller B: daily sales of hot-dogs

The mean, median and mode are useful in analysing such diagrams. The mode will be at the top, being the most frequent value. The median divides the area of the distribution in two. The median will always lie between the mean and mode.

12.3 Range of a distribution

As we learned from comparing the two hot-dog sellers, it is useful to know the range of a distribution. While the averages give us an indication of a distribution by describing its middle, it is also essential to have an indication of width or range. We could pick the two ends of the distribution and choose the extreme values. But this view of the range could be distorted if

there were one extreme value at one end. It is therefore useful to pick the values which lie 25% below the top and 25% above the bottom. This indicates the range where the middle 50% lie. This is covered for seller A in the table below.

25th value from bottom	*36 hot-dogs*
25th value from top	*38 hot-dogs*
interquartile range	*2 hot-dogs*

This shows a distribution with little variation between the top 25% (upper quartile) and bottom 25% (lower quartile). In other words, demand for hot-dogs is quite consistent and predictable.

12.4 Correlation

Businesses are always keen to learn about the effect on sales of marketing strategies such as TV advertising, sales promotion or direct mailshots. Often researchers will compare sales volume and advertising expenditure. A good way to do this is on a graph. In Figure 12.3 there is clearly a strong relationship, or **correlation**, between the two. The correlation is positive – as one increases so does the other. It is important to realise that each point correlating the two variables represents one observation covering a period of time.

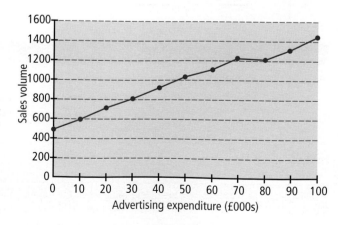

Figure 12.3 Strong positive correlation between advertising expenditure and sales

In Figure 12.4, however, there is little link, as the diagram is more or less a collection of randomly dispersed points. There is no apparent correlation between advertising expenditure and sales.

Figure 12.4 Little correlation between advertising expenditure and sales

What the researcher is looking for is cause and effect, namely evidence that the advertising has caused the increase in sales. Correlation by itself does not indicate cause and effect. The rising of the sun in the morning may be strongly correlated with the delivery time of newspapers to letterboxes but it does not *cause* them to be delivered. A strong correlation is evidence that cause and effect *may* be present. Further evidence is needed to know how the variables are affecting each other. Clearly, the purpose of advertising is to generate sales, so it is highly likely that cause and effect may be at work. But managers know there are many variables at work all the time in markets. The sales of a product could rise because of cheaper borrowing, the disappearance of a competitor, or even unusual weather, and not just advertising. In cases like that shown in Figure 12.5, where there is weak correlation, researchers clearly should be considering other variables as well as advertising.

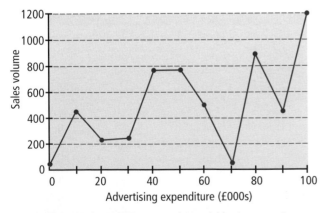

Figure 12.5 Loose correlation: are other variables important?

12.5 Sales forecasting

Businesses are always trying to predict the future. This helps with planning and beating competitors. One

CORRELATION

The Met Office's Weather Initiative is a business which charges a fee for predicting the sales of products ranging from lemonade to cat food. It uses correlation analysis to predict how demand will vary according to the time of year and the prevailing weather. It has found that lemonade sales rise in the summer, but tail away if the weather is very hot (presumably consumers switch to non-fizzy drinks or to iced-lollies). More surprisingly, cat food is weather-affected. Rainy days boost demand (perhaps the cats don't go out?) while if it's hot, sales decline, possibly because the cats eat less.

More than 600 companies use the Met Office's service, generating a fee income of over £1 million a year. Correlation is becoming big business.

IN **Business**

simple way of predicting the future is to assume that it will be just like the past. For the immediate future this may be very realistic. Forecasting often relies on *extrapolation*, as in Figure 12.6. Extrapolation simply means predicting future **trends** based on what has happened in the past. Assuming that little changes. Drawing a forecast by eye on a graph can be just as reliable as and easier than using a complex mathematical technique.

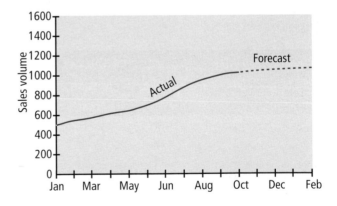

Figure 12.6 Extrapolating a trend

Here a very steady upwards **trend** over a long period may well continue, and be predicted to continue.

However, such stability and predictability are rare. The values of data plotted over time, called time-series analysis, can vary because of seasonal influences and also because of genuinely new or random factors, which can never be predicted. While researchers expect more new cars to be sold in August each year because of the new registration letter, there is little point in comparing August sales with sales the previous

January. It is important to identify the trend over a longer period to see whether sales are rising or falling, ignoring the seasonal or cyclical factors.

MOVING AVERAGES

A common way of identifying the trend is by using moving averages. In the table below, sales of soft drinks are shown each quarter. More are sold in the summer (quarter 3) because of the seasonal factor of hotter weather. There are four seasons or quarters in a year so the researcher decides to find the 4-period moving average of the sales in order to find the trend. The average of sales each quarter with the **seasonal variation** ironed out will show the trend. So each successive group of 4 quarters is added up to produce the 4-quarter moving annual total. Each of these totals could be divided by 4 to give an average. However that gives rise to the problem of deciding which quarter the average should be associated with. Because there is an even number of observations, the average would not line up with any of the quarters.

A statistical device called centring is used. Each successive pair of 4-quarter totals is added up to produce an 8-period total. The total actually contains information from 5 quarters, 3 of them added in twice. As there are 5 quarters, the middle one can be identified and compared with the trend figure. Incidentally, this helps to smooth out the seasonal variations even more. This figure, when divided by 8, then gives a moving average which can be placed alongside an actual quarter. This moving quarterly average is the **trend**. On the graph this can now be extrapolated by eye.

Forecasting the trend may be useful. But it does not tell the business how many it is likely to sell in a particular quarter. To estimate this the seasonal variation needs to be added back. This can be done by taking the seasonal variations for each quarter and finding the average seasonal variation for quarter 1 etc. This is then added to each of the trend figures for quarter 1 to get the actual forecast.

Figure 12.7

To forecast the sales for 1998 quarter 2, we need to extrapolate the trend line by eye and then add on the average seasonal variation. This gives the predicted actual value. The forecast trend here is about £147,000. The average seasonal variation for a quarter 2 is minus £7,060. So the forecast actual value would be about £139,040, below trend. Businesses need the forecast actual value: the trend may be useful but it is not the actual number sold.

The moving averages technique of forecasting has some limitations. The points calculated for the trend will always be less than the number of points in the

Soft drinks sales (£000s)

YEAR	QUARTER No.	SALES REVENUE	4-QUARTER MOVING TOTAL	8-QUARTER MOVING TOTAL	QUARTERLY MOVING AV. TREND	SEASONAL VARIATION	AVERAGE SEASONAL VARIATION	RANDOM VARIATION
1995	1	116						
	2	122						
	3	145			126.88	18.13	29.04	−10.92
	4	126	509		126.75	−0.75	−6.75	6.00
1996	1	113	506	1015	129.25	−16.25	−14.75	−1.50
	2	124	508	1014	131.00	−7.00	−7.06	0.06
	3	163	526	1034	132.00	31.00	29.04	1.96
	4	122	522	1048	134.75	−12.75	−6.75	−6.00
1997	1	125	534	1056	138.25	−13.25	−14.75	1.50
	2	134	544	1078	141.13	−7.13	−7.06	−0.06
	3	181	562	1106	143.00	38.00	29.04	8.96
	4	127	567	1129				
1998	1	135	577	1144				
	2							
	3							
	4							

actual raw data. This technique is most appropriate in stable circumstances when elements of the business environment, such as competition, are not expected to change very much. It is less useful in periods of change or instability.

When developing an argument in answer to a numerical question, case study or data response question, 'marketing maths' will help in the following ways:

- understanding the key role of sampling theory, i.e. how to get useful and reliable information cheaply and quickly
- quickly understanding a whole set of data, a population or a distribution
- knowing how confident to be in information
- telling the difference between correlation and causation to avoid costly mistakes
- forecasting the near future in a meaningful way
- understanding and using tables and graphs.

12.6 Marketing maths
an evaluation

As someone once said, 'there are lies, damn lies and statistics'. Quantitative information is extremely important but it is only one type of information and is nearly always historical, describing what has already happened rather than what is about to happen. Quantitative information should always be used in conjunction with other types of information. If only quantative information were used, many products would never reach production, particularly new or innovative products, because there is no historical data to support them.

Quantitative skills can help the manager not only to present part of the support needed his or her own proposals, but also to analyse ideas put forward by others. Such skills are needed throughout marketing analysis, especially market research. However, good business decisions may sometimes be taken irrespective of statistics. Statistics, though, can always be used to show whether or not a decision was the right one after the event!

KEY terms

correlation – the extent to which change in the value of one variable is related to change in that of another. Correlation does not necessarily imply a causal relationship.

cyclical variation – a repetitive pattern of change in the value of a variable, e.g. sales.

sales forecasting – predicting future sales using statistical methods.

seasonal variation – change in the value of a variable, e.g. sales, that is related to the seasons.

trend – the general path a series of values, e.g. sales, follows over time, disregarding variations or random fluctuations.

A Level Exercises

A. REVISION QUESTIONS
(25 marks; 30 minutes)

Read the unit, then answer:

1 Explain the difference between correlation and causation. (4)
2 How can you isolate the trend in a series of data? (5)
3 Distinguish between 'seasonal' and 'cyclical'. (4)
4 Explain how you would choose the number of periods in a moving total or average? (3)
5 What is centring a moving average and why is it done? (3)
6 What do you understanding by the term 'extrapolation'? How is it used to make a sales forecast? (6)

B. REVISION EXERCISES

B1 Examining Understanding *(20 marks; 30 minutes)*

1 Which of the three would be the most useful for measuring:
   a weekly earnings of the typical adult
   b dress size
   c average weekly consumption of beer?
   Briefly explain your reasoning. (9)
2 Two firms repairing washing machines in different cities record weekly usage of a key spare part over five weeks as follows:

	Firm A	Firm B
Week 1	40	10
Week 2	45	20
Week 3	50	50
Week 4	55	80
Week 5	60	90

   a What is the mean weekly usage of the spare part for each firm? (4)
   b Is this arithmetic mean useful for planning stockholding of the spare part? (3)
   c What else is it important to know about the distributions and why? (4)

B2 Data Response

Twice in recent years a leading Knightsbridge department store has been embarrassed by running out of ice-cream during hot weather. Its new foods manager wants to avoid this happening again, but without tying up capital in ice-cream stocks throughout the summer months. Her solution is to correlate past daily sales with the temperature on that day. This was easy to do as the sales data was already on her computer, and she could download the weather data from the Met Office website. Here is some of the data:

Sales of individual ice-cream portions per day

Temperature at Noon (°C)	Occasion			
	1st	2nd	3rd	4th
<16	22	16	24	
17–18	28	31		
19–20	34	39	41	
21–22	44	57	43	54
23–24	68	73	67	69
25–26	88	81	94	
27–28	103	121	117	
29–30	142	70*		
31–32	188	206		
33–34	229			
35–36	80*			
37+	–			

*Days on which stock was sold out

1 Draw a graph to show the correlation more clearly. (8)
2 Add a line of best fit. How close a correlation does there seem to be? (8)
3 The store's fridges can only hold a maximum of 150 portions at any one time, so daily sales above that level can only be achieved if a delivery comes during the day. How might the foods manager use the information provided by the correlation graph? (9)

B3 Data Response

Lanes Ltd runs a cafeteria for its employees, where all fixed overheads are paid by the company. At present 50 cold meals are served at each lunchhour, for which £1.20 is charged and the gross profit is 50p. Cold lunches can be kept chilled and there is no wastage. The management has decided to introduce an alternative hot lunch at £2.40 earning a gross profit of 80p. However, any hot lunches prepared but not sold are wasted.

For an experimental period of 20 days, 25 hot lunches are prepared each day, and the demand for these is as follows:

No. of lunches	15	16	17	18	19	20	21	22	23	24
No. of days required	1	1	3	2	3	4	2	2	1	1

Questions *(40 marks; 60 minutes)*

1 a Draw a frequency histogram of the data, and calculate the arithmetic mean, median and mode for the number of hot lunches required. Which might be the most useful in this context? (15)
   b The demand for hot and cold lunches remains as above over the next 20 days. Lanes Ltd prepares 20 hot lunches a day. Calculate its total gross profit over this period. Calculate the extra profit over 20 days of serving both hot and cold lunches instead of just cold lunches. (25)

B4 Data Response

Three furniture manufacturers, X, Y and Z, are all currently profitable. Y and Z concentrate largely on the manufacture and distribution of fitted kitchen furniture in the EU, Y within a particular country and Z throughout the EU. X makes a range of high-priced reproduction furniture. Figure 1 shows the distributions of the sizes of the orders placed by furniture retailers and wholesalers with X, Y and Z.

Questions
(30 marks; 40 minutes)

1 Describe the distributions and compare and contrast them. (6)
2 What cost advantages may Z have over Y? (6)
3 Outline the usefulness of the mean, median and mode to these firms. (6)
4 Explain briefly the terms job, batch and flow production. How might they be relevant to each of X, Y and Z? (6)
5 How might a deep recession affect X? (6)

B5 Data Response

Trading Company Ltd is concerned about an uncertain economic background and wishes to forecast sales revenue for the second half of 1999. Recent sales figures are shown in the table below.

Year		Sales Revenue (£000s)	Moving Average Trend	Seasonal Variation	Average Seasonal Variation
1996	Q1	230			
	Q2	240			
	Q3	288	249.25	38.75	59.08
	Q4	242	248.75	−6.75	−15.25
1997	Q1	224	253.25	−29.25	−28.75
	Q2	242	257.25	−15.25	−15.63
	Q3	322	259.25	62.75	59.08
	Q4	240	263.75	−23.75	−15.25
1998	Q1	242	270.25	−28.25	−28.75
	Q2	260	276.00	−16.00	−15.63
	Q3	356	280.25	75.75	59.08
	Q4	252			
1999	Q1	264			

Questions
(25 marks; 30 minutes)

1 How was the trend figure of 263.75 derived for 1997 quarter 4? (8)
2 Attempt a forecast for the last two quarters of 1999 and comment on the usefulness of your forecast. (17)

C. ESSAY QUESTIONS

1 'Since we can never know the future, it is pointless trying to forecast it.' Discuss.
2 'Quantitative sales forecasting techniques have only limited use. Qualitative judgements are needed in a constantly changing world.' Evaluate this statement.

INTEGRATED MARKETING

13.1 Marketing – an overview

INTRODUCTION

Which is more important to a firm – revenue or costs? You might say that they are equally important. Or you might say that a firm must have revenue – therefore revenue is the key. Yet students revise costs (finance and accounting) far more thoroughly than revenue (marketing). This is partly because they feel weaker at finance and wish to improve; also, they underestimate the analytic demands (and importance) of marketing.

Firms can have many different objectives, but profit making is clearly a vital aspect of business activity. The most important formula in this subject is the one for profit.

profit = **total revenue – total costs**

or, to use the expanded form:

profit = (**price** × **quantity**) – ([**variable cost** × **quantity**] + **fixed costs**)

Marketing decisions have a direct influence upon:

- the price and quantity of goods sold
- the variable cost per unit (as bulk-buying discounts are affected by sales volume)
- fixed costs, as they include marketing expenditures such as advertising and promotions.

In other words, marketing influences every aspect of the profit formula.

WHAT IS MARKETING?

- Is it about responding to consumers or persuading them?
- Is it about creating competition or attempting to avoid it?
- Is it ethical or unethical?

Every textbook has its own definition. A definition such as 'to fulfil consumer needs, profitably' suggests that marketing is about identifying and meeting needs, and is therefore serving the consumer's best interests. Is this true? Always? Do consumers need Snickers chocolate or Apple Hooch?

Marketing today is seen as the all-embracing function that acts as the focal point of business activity. Top business consultant Richard Schonberger describes the best modern firms as those that 'build a chain of customers'. In other words marketing forms the link between the firm and its customers. It therefore determines the type and quantity of goods to be designed and produced.

'A' GRADE MARKETING

Marketing consists of a series of concepts and themes (such as the marketing mix). All good students know these; better ones can group them together and relate them to one another. They can be grouped as follows:

- An understanding of markets – the price mechanism, price elasticity, market segmentation, and competitive tactics.
- An understanding of consumer behaviour – psychological factors in product pricing and image, brand loyalty, consumer resistance.
- Product portfolio analysis – product life cycle, Boston Matrix.
- Marketing decision making – the marketing model, market and sales research and analysis, the need to anticipate, not just reflect, consumer taste.
- Marketing strategy – both in theory and in practice through the marketing mix/four Ps.

'A' grade marketing requires a grasp of big underlying issues such as those that follow. These are areas of discussion for conclusions to answers or case studies. They represent ways of evaluating the wider significance of concepts such as the product life cycle.

ISSUE 1   Is marketing an art or a science?

Is marketing about judgement and creativity, or scientific decision making? If it is a science, the numerate information provided by market research would lead to a 100% success rate with new products. The reality, of course, is different. Kellogg's researched Pop Tarts heavily – and spent millions advertising a flop – while Bailey's Irish Cream became a worldwide best-seller even though research said women would not buy a whisky-based liqueur.

Marketing relies upon anticipating consumer behaviour. Research can help enormously, but the final decision on strategy is a judgement. Therefore individual flair and luck play an important part.

ISSUE 2   Does marketing respond to needs or create wants?

It is easy to see the importance of marketing to the firm. But what are its effects upon the consumer/general public? Is it just a way of encouraging people to want things they do not need?

Health issues are important in this debate. McDonald's may make your day, but is it what your stomach needs? And is it right that children should pester their parents for Potato Waffles, when potatoes are cheaper and more nutritious? You must form some views on these questions. You may feel that the marketeers' pursuit of new products, flavours, trends and glitz makes life fun. Or you may feel that marketing can manipulate people, and that its most persuasive arm (TV advertising) needs to be controlled. The Government's recent decision to ban cigarette advertising implies that they favour control.

ISSUE 3   Has market orientation gone too far in Britain?

The trend towards a market-led approach was good for companies which produced the same products in the same way, year after year. Market orientation brought in new ideas and more attractive product design.

However, it also encouraged Ford to focus too much on the styling and imagery of their cars while BMW and Honda concentrated upon their production quality and reliability. Money that had once been spent on research and development was now spent on market research. The number of engineering graduates declined as the numbers on marketing and accounting courses ballooned. Manufacturing industry depends upon high quality engineers and a skilled workforce. Marketing is not enough.

Marketing

A. SHORT-ANSWER QUESTIONS

1 Why is a reduction in price unlikely to benefit a firm whose products are price inelastic? (2)
2 Distinguish between primary and secondary research. (2)
3 Why might a firm's long-term pricing policy differ from its short-term one? (3)
4 Explain the term 'product differentiation'. (2)
5 Give two reasons why a firm may sell, for a limited period of time, part of its product range for a loss. (2)
6 List three factors a firm should consider when determining the price of a new product. (3)
7 Give two ways in which decisions made within the marketing department might affect activities in the personnel department. (2)
8 Distinguish between marketing objectives and marketing strategy. (3)
9 Identify three factors that are likely to influence the choice of distribution channel for a product. (3)
10 Give two examples of ethical dilemmas a marketing manager might face. (2)
11 Distinguish between product orientation and market orientation. (3)
12 A business decides to reduce the price elasticity of its product from £3.00 to £2.75. As a result, sales rise from 2,500 to 3,000 units. Calculate the price elasticity of demand for its product. (3)
13 Explain what is meant by 'negative income elasticity'. (2)

14 State two business objectives, other than profit maximisation, that will influence a firm's marketing strategies. (2)
15 The price of a good is 100p of which 40p is the contribution. If the price is cut by 30%, how much extra must be sold to maintain the same total contribution? (3)
16 Only one in five new product launches are successful. Why? Give three reasons. (3)
17 State three ways of segmenting a market. (3)
18 What is a marketing budget? (2)
19 Suggest three possible extension strategies for a brand of bottled lager for which sales have levelled out. (3)
20 State two strategies a firm might adopt to defend itself if a price war broke out. (2)

B. DATA RESPONSE

1 A manufacturer of footballs has sales of 100,000 units a month and fixed costs of £240,000 a month. Raw materials are £3.00 per unit and the pricing method is a 100% mark-up on variable costs. When it last increased its prices, price elasticity proved to be about 0.6. Now it is thinking of a further 10% price rise.
   a Calculate the effect on profit of this 10% rise. State your assumptions.
   b What factors may have caused the price elasticity to have changed since the time it was measured at 0.6?

13.2 Revision questions

UNIT 13 | INTEGRATED MARKETING

2　You are product development manager of a new tinned catfood called Leno. Its consumer USP (unique selling point) is 'a low-fat, high-fibre food for superfit cats'. Market research has convinced you that demand will be sizeable. Your marketing director wants to be satisfied on four key issues before giving the go-ahead to launch…

a　That you have considered three pricing methods, and can now make a recommendation on a suitable pricing policy.

b　That you can explain the research you conducted and how it has helped you make your sales forecast.

c　That you can explain the method you will use to set an advertising budget.

d　That you have considered carefully three of the most likely responses by existing competitors to the launch of Leno.

Write a report to the marketing director covering these points.　　　　*(20)*

ROLE PLAYS AND SIMULATIONS

Should Schweppes launch this new product?

Appendix A – Briefing document

> Sparkler is a brand new, sparkling, exotic fruit drink. It is aimed at the mass market, and will sell at the same price as Coca-Cola (35p). Schweppes has developed the product, registered the trademark and is about to hold a meeting to decide whether or not to launch it.

As joint marketing directors:

1　Decide what you recommend and why.
2　Prepare an OHP presentation to explain your views.

Appendix B – Market research findings

Regular drinkers of:

	Pepsi	Coke	Sparkling orange	Other fruit flavours	TOTAL
Sample size	80	340	170	50	640
Will definitely try	24%	21%	32%	39%	26%
Will probably try	36%	37%	39%	38%	37.5%
Following product trial:					
Will definitely buy regularly	21%	17%	35%	47%	27%
Will probably buy regularly	37%	31%	32%	36%	32%

Source: Adapted from Gallup Poll Research Company

Appendix C – Cost data

	Production of cans per week		
	Up to 99,000	100,000–499,000	500,000+
Sparkler production cost per can	3.3p	3.0p	2.8p
Sparkler delivery cost per can	2.7p	2.0p	1.2p

Weekly fixed costs:

Salaries and administration	£20,000
Marketing costs	£40,000
Other expenses	£10,000

Appendix D – Market size and share data

	Market size	Coca-Cola	Pepsi	Orange	Other fruit
3 years ago	£2.5 bn	23.4%	8.9%	7.4%	4.6%
2 years ago	£2.7 bn	23.9%	8.7%	7.7%	4.9%
Last year	£3.1 bn	24.1%	8.6%	7.9%	5.3%

Appendix E – Sales information

Forecast sales volume	If research is positive	If research is negative
Year 1	400,000 pw	200,000 pw
Year 2	600,000 pw	300,000 pw
Year 3	700,000 pw	280,000 pw
Year 4	750,000 pw	200,000 pw

INTEGRATED CASE STUDY

14 January 1999 was a red letter day for Chris and Charlie. After several months of struggle, the deal was signed. They were the new owners of Orchard Soft Drinks Ltd. The terms of the management buyout gave them a 30% shareholding each, with the remaining 40% held by a venture capital company.

Their success at raising the £1.4 million purchase price was partly due to an astute analysis of the market for soft drinks and a clear strategy for the future. Both were the result of Charlie's deep understanding of the UK market for soft drinks. Her nine years as marketing director had not been wasted.

Charlie's analysis began with data on the UK market size. This was backed up by a forecast of the future demand for soft drinks, based on extrapolation of the trend. See Table 1 and the accompanying graph.

This huge volume of soft drinks resulted in a UK market size of over £6,700 million in 1997. Market intelligence

reports suggested an even brighter future. Charlie found forecasts of future consumption which led her to produce a useful piece of analysis. She calculated that 84% of the sales growth between 1997 and 2002 would be enjoyed by just two sectors: fizzy drinks and bottled water. Others, such as fruit drinks and juices, would continue to sell well but not produce much growth.

Charlie then looked at buying behaviour by age. She found that adults represent under 20% of the sales of soft drinks. Might there be room for a fizzy drink aimed at adults?

To investigate further, Charlie commissioned six group discussions. They revealed many interesting points:

- fizzy drinks were seen as unhealthy and unappetising
- adults were reluctant to pay much for soft drinks
- adults liked fruit juices and bottled waters, but drank alcoholic drinks socially
- they didn't feel there was a soft drink for them – the ones they liked were aimed at children.

	1988	1989	1990	1991	1992	1993	1994	1995	1996	1997
Million litres	7,290	8,330	8,685	8,340	8,550	8,765	9,235	10,035	9,895	10,345
% change	+5.8	+14.3	+4.3	−4.0	+2.5	+2.5	+5.4	+8.7	−1.4	+4.5

Source: Zenith International in the 1998 Sucralose Soft Drinks Report

Forecast of future demand for soft drinks

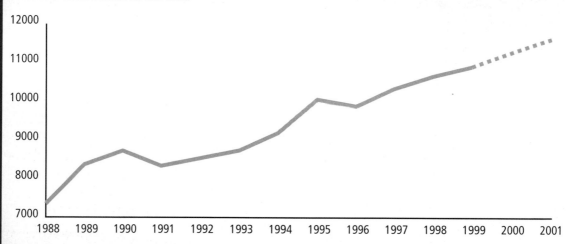

After she had observed the first discussion, Charlie prepared some product concept statements to show in the other five groups. The most popular proved to be:

'Aimé – refreshing mandarin and passion fruit juice with sparkling mineral water'

This would be priced at 95p and come in a 600cl bottle. This would price it at the top end of the market, but Chris and Charlie were confident that it would succeed. So too were the financiers, who were sufficiently impressed to lend over £1 million.

The next step was to develop a product that would be really exceptional – lively, fruity, original and refreshing. This took two months. Meanwhile designers were working on an innovative packaging and pack design. By the end of April Aimé was ready for its British launch. With an advertising budget of only £600,000 for the first six months, little could be afforded beyond cinema advertising. Charlie was confident, however, in the effectiveness of sampling and selling products at the Derby, Wimbledon, Ascot and at department stores. The free samples would generate awareness. The product image would be enhanced, she hoped, by free publicity in the glossy women's magazines.

She organised a huge charity party for London's fashion business. Then followed it up by bombarding the magazines and photographers with free cases of Aimé.

Chris and Charlie had budgeted for sales of 20,000 units in month one, rising to 70,000 by month six. Although this was not achieved, they both felt there were grounds for optimism. Now they had to decide on the budget for the next six months.

Sales of Aimé – Budget and actual

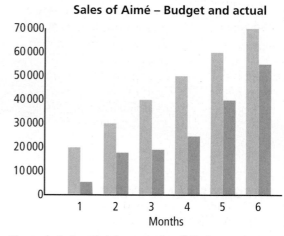

Figure 1 Budgeted and actual sales of Aimé

Questions *(45 marks; 60 minutes)*

1 Why may forecasts based on extrapolation prove inaccurate? *(4)*
2 a Outline Charlie's marketing strategy for Orchard Soft Drinks. *(6)*
  b Analyse the Strengths, Weaknesses, Opportunities and Threats of this strategy. *(16)*
3 How effectively has the business made use of market research? *(9)*
4 What sales budgets would you set for the next six months? Explain your reasoning. *(10)*

INTRODUCTION TO FINANCE AND ACCOUNTS

14.1 Why do businesses need accounts?

Kelly Thomson left college determined to set up her own business. Her brother, James, an engineer, had designed a revolutionary new lawnmower. At the flick of a switch, it could dig out weeds whilst cutting grass. Between them they had £5,000 saved. That was enough to cover the cost of building a working prototype. By September the prototype was ready, so Kelly and James arranged an appointment with their bank manager. Kelly had calculated that they would need £15,000 to rent a small workshop and hire another person to help manufacture the mower. The bank manager insisted on seeing a business plan before lending them the money.

Two weeks later, they returned with a business plan including a projected profit and loss account, balance sheet and cash flow forecast. Having seen these, the bank manager granted the £15,000 loan. Production began immediately and by the start of November they were ready to sell their unique new product.

The problem they now faced was that no-one wanted to buy a lawnmower in November. They continued producing 50 mowers a week in anticipation of a demand surge in the spring. Just after Christmas a supplier demanded payment for the debt they had built up with him. Sadly, the £15,000 was gone and the trickle of revenue was just enough to cover the interest on the loan. When the bank manager refused to grant them an overdraft, they were forced to close down the business, having sold fewer than 100 lawnmowers. James managed to sell the patent for the mower to a large garden tools manufacturer for £15,000, just

enough to repay the loan. However, £5,000 of savings was lost as a result of poor financial planning. A proper approach to accounting could have saved their business.

Kelly's tale illustrates the importance of careful financial planning. Without a clear idea of when, and how much, cash is going to enter or leave a business, failure is likely. In order to run any business it is vital to make sure the firm has enough cash to pay its bills and buy-in stock. Without stock firms have nothing to sell. Unpaid bills may mean no electricity or telephone.

Management accounting ensures that firms keep a careful check on their cash flows. Careful monitoring means firms are able to plan ahead, perhaps arranging an overdraft or discussing a delay in payments to their suppliers.

In addition to keeping a check on a firm's day-to-day finance – its **working capital** – managers can use accounting to:

- identify the costs involved in making a product – this can be the first step in deciding the selling price
- work out how many products they need to sell to make a profit
- measure how well their staff have performed
- keep tight control over the way in which the firm's money is spent.

Along with these uses of management accounting, the role of financial accounting is also important. Kelly's story shows how hard it can be to raise finance. This is true for existing as well as new firms.

Barclays Bank lends over £1 billion a year to small businesses. Any existing business looking for a loan from Barclays will need to submit previous years' profit and loss accounts and balance sheets.

Graham Howie, an experienced business banker at Barclays, says: 'I would not lend to an existing business which is unable to supply copies of previous years' audited accounts.'

Financial accounts have one key advantage over management accounts for external users. Published accounts have to be audited by an independent accountant. This means they are checked to see that they show a true and fair view of the company's financial position. In addition, management accounts are rarely seen by any external users, so it is clear that financial accounts play a key role in business.

MANAGEMENT ACCOUNTING	FINANCIAL ACCOUNTING
Focuses on the present and the future	Reports what happened in the past
Is for internal users	Is for external users
Needs to be easy to use, relevant and up to date	Needs to be reliable, accurate and consistent
Is ruled by managers' requirements	Is ruled by accounting conventions and legal requirements
Covers departments and divisions	Covers the whole firm

14.2 Major accounting documents

The following units explain in detail all the main accounting documents. To provide an overview, here is a brief explanation of each.

FINANCIAL ACCOUNTING

Balance sheet: This is a snapshot of a firm's assets, liabilities and sources of capital at any moment in time. It helps answer questions such as:

- What is the business worth?
- Can it afford to expand?
- Is it a safe investment?

Profit and loss account: This shows the level of profit made in the most recent trading period (usually the financial year). Profit is calculated by subtracting costs and expenses from revenue. This helps answer questions such as:

- Is the firm trading successfully?
- Are the senior managers proving effective?
- Is it likely to be a profitable investment?

Cash flow statement: This is required in the published financial accounts of public limited companies only. It shows where cash has come from and where cash has been used over the course of the past year. It answers these questions:

- How easily was the firm able to find the cash to finance its recent activities?
- Was the finance generated from within the business, or was outside finance needed?

LOSING ON AND OFF THE PITCH

Leeds United announced an annual loss of £34 million for the 2001–2002 season. No business can continue operating in the long term without doing something to address such losses. Along with the announcement of these figures, Chairman Peter Ridsdale made it clear that the club would be seeking to reduce its running costs and provide one-off revenues by selling more of its star players. August of 2002 saw Leeds sell Rio Ferdinand to Manchester United and Robbie Keane to Tottenham Hotspur in deals which generated a combined figure of £37 million – too late to offset the 2001–2002 loss but helping the club in its next financial year.

In addition to cutting costs by shedding the substantial salaries commanded by these 2 stars, Leeds also plan to trim the squad by 6 players, in order to reduce the wage bill by at least £1 million per year. The long term future of the club, as with many other football clubs, is dependent upon being able to halt their losses and cover their costs.

MANAGEMENT ACCOUNTING

Cash flow forecasts: These estimate what the firm's bank account will look like in each month of the coming year. If a serious overdraft is predicted, it can be discussed with bankers to ensure that the deficit is financed.

Budgets: These are financial plans which can be set for costs and/or revenues. They are a way of coordinating, motivating and controlling the key activities of the business over the coming year.

Contribution statements: These set out the contribution to overheads made by each division or department of a firm. This helps in making decisions about allocating resources between the different parts of the business, e.g. providing more capital to finance expansion of the most profitable product area.

Investment appraisal: These calculations help decide whether a prospective investment project is financially attractive. Investment decisions from buying new machinery to building a new factory are made using the techniques of investment appraisal.

Break-even charts: These indicate revenues and costs and therefore profit at all possible levels of output. They enable the break-even point, where neither a profit nor a loss is made, to be identified. They can be useful in decision making on issues such as pricing, cost cutting or expansion.

Figure 14.1 shows the main strands of both financial and management accounting.

Figure 14.1 Financial and management accounting

Figure 14.2 shows the categories of users.

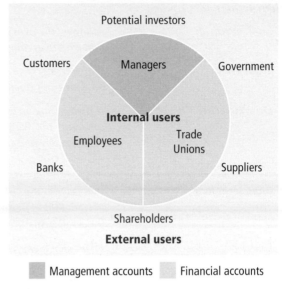

Figure 14.2 Users of accounts

14.3 Users of published accounts

There are three main groups of users of published accounts. Each may be looking for different information, but all hope to find it in the same set of documents: largely the profit and loss account and the balance sheet.

- Internal management – uses published information largely as a matter of record. Possibly as public recognition for its own achievements. The actual contents (such as the profit made and any successes at cutting stock or debt levels) would have been known internally for some months before the figures are published.
- Other internal users – perhaps employees or trade unions who can check a firm's published accounts if threatened with redundancy or when putting in a pay claim. Only the most open, self-confident managements share current management accounting data with staff. So most have to wait until the published figures to be sure of the firm's financial performance.
- External users – also have access to the published accounts of limited companies. Groups such as suppliers, customers, banks or potential investors can use the accounts to gain an overall picture of the firm's efficiency and stability.

ENRON – AN ACCOUNTING FIASCO

The years 2001 and 2002 saw a number of huge accounting scandals. The collapse of Enron, the American energy provider, sent shock waves throughout the world's financial markets and raised a number of questions about the accounting and financial reporting practices of the firm. The fundamental cause of the problem was that Enron had been 'hiding' its debts in the accounts of other companies – companies that had been set up by Enron but whose accounts were kept separate. Sooner or later these debts had to come out and, as they did, the whole firm came tumbling down.

Job losses ran into the thousands, not just Enron employees but employees at Enron's suppliers whose debts were never met by the American giant. A further consequence was that shareholders in Enron, many of whom were staff who had invested their life savings in the company they believed in, lost everything. The case of Enron led to much examination of accounting regulations, both in the US and the UK and pressure to ensure that such a scandal could not be allowed to occur again. This will require a tightening of the rules and regulations covering how firms compile and present their accounts.

In Business

Short-term (under 1 year):

- *Bank overdraft* — *Allowing the firm's bank account to go into the red up to an agreed limit. Flexible and easy to arrange but interest charges are high.*

- *Trade credit* — *Suppliers agree to accept cash payment at a given date in the future. Failure to pay on time can present problems on future orders.*

- *Debt factoring* — *A firm selling on credit 'sells' its debt to a factor. The factor is responsible for collecting the debt. The firm receives 80% of the debt in cash from the factor immediately and the balance, minus the factor's fee, when the debt is collected.*

Medium-term (2–4 years):

- *Bank term loan* — *Banks lend sums of capital, often at a fixed rate of interest, to be repaid over a fixed period. Makes financial planning easy but interest rates can be high, particularly for small firms.*

- *Leasing* — *Firms sign a contract to pay a rental fee to the owner of an asset in return for the use of that asset over a period of 2–4 years (usually). Expensive, but avoids large cash outflows when buying new assets.*

Long-term (5+ years):

- *Owners' savings* — *Most small businesses are set up with the owners' savings. They are 'interest free' but will be lost if the business fails. Banks will not provide a loan or overdraft unless the owners are sharing the financial risk.*

- *Sale of shares* — *Private and public limited companies can sell shares in the ownership of the company. In return, shareholders gain a say in how the firm is run and are entitled to a share of profits.*

- *Reinvested profits* — *Profits are the most important source of long-term finance. This form of finance is good because there are no interest payments to be made.*

- *Venture capital loans* — *These specialist providers of risk capital can provide large sums. The finance is usually partly loan capital and partly share capital.*

- *Government loans* — *Although much paperwork is involved and only some firms are eligible, national government and the EU do offer grants and loans for firms. Less than 3% of business finance stems from this source.*

- *Debenture loans* — *Long-term loans repayable on a certain date are called debenture loans. These are secured on specific assets and carry fixed interest payments.*

14.4 Raising finance

The story at the beginning of this unit illustrated another key issue in accounting – how to raise finance. The finance may be used for a variety of purposes. A firm may seek long-term finance for building a factory or buying out another business. Short-term finance may be used to buy extra stock or get through periods where cash flow is poor due to seasonal factors. The above table shows the sources of finance available to firms.

14.5 Accounting in the twenty-first century

Computers have taken much of the number crunching out of accounting. A vast array of specialist accounting software packages exist, simplifying the process of accounting for managers of small and large businesses alike. Furthermore, sophisticated information recording systems, such as EDI (**electronic data interchange**) enable firms to compile statements of costs and revenues, daily, just hours after the day's trading is over.

This process is becoming even cheaper and easier through the use of **intranets**. These advances mean that management accounting has become more complex, yet more useful. The forecasts involved in producing sales or cost budgets gain in accuracy as the quality of past information improves. The time has already arrived when most large firms have completely computerised accounting systems. The first decade of the twenty-first century is likely to see most small businesses follow suit. The good news is that as IT advances, accounting packages become easier to use for those with little accounting experience. However, the theory behind accounting is unlikely to change significantly for a long time to come. IT can make accounting easier, but it is still vital to understand what accounts actually show.

A further development in recent years, which is set to continue, is the growing use of social **auditing**. Pioneered in the UK by firms such as The Body Shop, a social audit attempts to include non-financial factors in a firm's accounts. Conventional accounts judge a firm's performance purely on measures such as profit and revenues. Social accounting includes measures such as pollution emissions and labour turnover to try to show a fuller picture of a firm's performance. Recently, major multinationals such as Shell and BP have begun to publish social audits. The accounting profession is working on a set of common social accounting standards. Nevertheless, the practice is unlikely to become widespread until a change in the law forces firms to include social measures in their annual published accounts.

ISSUES FOR analysis

Key issues for analysis include:

- The difference between cash and profit can lead to excellent analytical comment. Firms which sell on credit record a profit on items for which no cash has yet been received. The importance of cash was made clear earlier in this unit. Without cash, bills go unpaid and stocks are not bought. So it is possible for profitable firms to run out of cash and go out of business. In examinations, many students treat cash flow and profit as if they are the same thing. Distinguishing clearly between the two is a helpful starting point for strong analysis of a financial issue.

- Also important is to have a broad range of accounting information. With more information, a clearer picture can be built up. Several years' of figures are needed to identify trends in revenues, costs or profits. If similar information about competitors is also available, the accounts you are analysing can really be put into context.

- A third key form of analysis is to place any accounting question firmly in the context of the business. Is it small or large? Is it largely dependent on just one product or customer? Is its marketplace fast-moving, with short product life cycles and fierce competition? Are the managers experienced, prudent and looking towards the long-term future?

14.6 Finance and accounts
an evaluation

Reliability is a key issue when looking at any accounts. Management accounts, such as cash flow forecasts and investment appraisals, are predictions. In other words, they are not statements of fact but educated guesses. This means that they should be used only as a guideline. Questions need to be asked, such as who drew up

'The accounts are a snapshot of the business at a moment in time. Take a picture the following day and the scene may look very different. As with many of us, companies try to look their best when they are photographed and sometimes dress for the occasion'.

MA Pitcher (quoted in Pocket Accounting, *C Nobes, Penguin Books, 1995)*

the accounts? Do they have an interest in making the accounts point in a particular direction? Budgets are also open to a certain degree of bias based upon personal interest. Financial accounts are supposed to present a true and fair view of a firm's financial position. They are checked by an independent auditor. However, creative accounting techniques exist which can be used, legally, to muddy the waters.

A second key point to remember is how accounts fit into the big picture of Business Studies. Feel the weight of this book. There are several units dedicated to accounting, but a great number of units cover other areas of business activity. Accounts are good at dealing with financial, quantitative information. They are, however, notoriously poor at dealing with qualitative issues. How should you value the experience of managers in a firm's accounts? How much is a brand name like Guinness worth? The growing awareness of qualitative issues in accounting has led to the growth in the use of social audits, but accounts are limited in terms of what they can say.

Look at the accounts, but don't forget the people behind them.

KEY terms

auditing – an independent check on the methods and procedures used to draw up a company's accounts.

Companies' House – where the Registrar of Companies holds the records for all the limited liability companies in the country. These include the latest financial statement.

electronic data interchange – computers linked by a permanently open telephone line which enables them to swop data. This system, for example, enables Dixon's to know the sales total from all their stores within minutes of closing time on a Saturday.

intranets – an internal, closed version of the Internet. Companies can set up their own intranet which can only be accessed by company staff. This enables quick, cheap electronic communication of data such as sales figures.

working capital – the finance available for the day-to-day running of the business.

AS Level Exercises

A. REVISION QUESTIONS

30 marks; 60 minutes

Read the unit, then answer:

1 Give two examples of situations in which firms would use:
 a short-term
 b medium-term
 c long-term
 sources of finance (6)
2 Explain what is meant by 'working capital'. (3)
3 Give three functions of management accounting. (3)
4 State how each of the following groups might use a firm's accounts:
 a trade unions
 b shareholders
 c suppliers
 d potential investors
 e rival companies. (5)
5 Briefly explain the purpose of auditing accounts. (3)
6 What are the main problems involved in preparing a social audit? (3)
7 State three benefits that the use of information technology has brought to accounting. (3)
8 Explain one advantage and one disadvantage to a firm of having large sums of cash for a long period of time. (4)

B. REVISION EXERCISES

B1 Data Response

Khilna and Co manufacture women's fashionwear in a large factory in South London. It employs 1,000 local semi-skilled staff in a run-down area in the borough of Lambeth. The managing director has expressed her desire to retire soon and has been experiencing growing problems in her dealings with union representatives at the factory. Before passing the leadership of the firm on to her successor, Khilna plans to borrow £4 million to invest in new machinery, costing a total of £6 million – to be paid over three years.

This investment is possible given the current favourable trading conditions. These have led to record profits over the past three years – profits which, rumour has it, have made the firm an attractive takeover target for various larger clothing firms.

Questions *(25 marks; 30 minutes)*
1 State four groups or individuals who may be interested in seeing the financial accounts of Khilna and Co. (4)
2 For the four users identified in your answer to question 1, explain why each one would be interested in seeing the accounts. (12)
3 Why might those considering a takeover bid be interested in seeing the management accounts as well? (9)

B2 Case Study

Barakat Ltd needs to borrow £10,000 to finance the purchase of a new machine. The managers hope that the machine will make enough money to pay for itself after 12 months. If there are problems, however, it could take as long as 18 months.

The finance director is considering two options:

● Arrange an overdraft facility with the bank for £10,000. In return, the bank will charge interest at 15% per annum on the overdraft. This is charged at 1.25% per month on the sum outstanding at the start of the month.
● Arranging a loan with the bank for the £10,000. The money will be paid back in 18 equal instalments of £587 over a year and a half.

Questions *(25 marks; 30 minutes)*
1 How much interest will the firm pay in total if the loan option is taken? (2)
2 In the end, the firm decided to use the overdraft. The new machine boosted profits by £1,000 per month. The firm used these extra profits to pay off the overdraft, so the amount owed gradually fell.
 a How long did the machine take to pay for itself? (2)
 b Complete the following table, indicating the amount of interest paid on the overdraft: (10)

Month	Overdraft Outstanding at End of Month	Interest Paid on Overdraft this Month
Jan	£9,000	£125
Feb	£8,000	
Mar		
Apr		
May		
Jun		
Jul		
Aug		
Sep		
Oct		

3 How much did the firm pay in interest, in total? (2)
4 Was it better to use the overdraft or the loan? (2)
5 If the machine had not operated as effectively as hoped, and it had taken 18 months to pay back the £10,000 cost – which option would have been the more attractive? (7)

REVENUE, COSTS AND PROFIT

DEFINITION

Revenue is the value of total sales made by a business within a period, usually one year. Costs are the expenses incurred by a firm in producing and selling its products. These include expenditure upon wages and raw materials.

There are a number of types of profit but, in broad terms, profit can be defined as the difference which arises when a firm's sales revenue exceeds its total costs.

15.1 Business revenues

The revenue or income received by a firm as a result of trading activities is a critical factor in its success. When commencing trading or introducing a new product, businesses may expect relatively low revenues for several reasons:

- their product is not well known
- they are unlikely to be able to produce large quantities of output
- it is difficult to charge a high price for a product which is not established in the market.

At the start of each year, most firms plan the management of their finances. The starting point is an assessment of the income or revenue they are likely to receive during the coming financial year. Businesses calculate their revenue through use of the following formula:

sales revenue =
    volume of goods sold × average selling price

You can see that there are two key elements which comprise sales revenue: the quantity of goods that are sold and the prices at which they are sold. A firm seeking to increase its revenue can plan to sell more or aim to sell at a higher price. Similarly, firms often maintain high prices, even though this policy may reduce sales. Such companies, often selling fashion and high technology products, believe that this approach results in higher revenue and profits.

To sustain a high revenue from relatively few sales a company has to be confident that consumers will be willing to pay a high price for their product. And that direct competition will not appear – at least in the short term. This is a strategy employed by major pharmaceutical companies. They spend huge amounts on researching and developing new products and then protect them with patents. This then allows them to earn high profits by accepting relatively low sales but at high prices. A high price/low output strategy offers the additional benefit of keeping down the cost of producing the goods.

BRITISH AIRWAYS EXPECTS REVENUES TO FALL WHILE PROFITS RISE

British Airways has announced that it expects its revenues to fall during the 2002–2003 financial period. The company said that revenue had fallen by 10% during the last quarter of the previous year and they could not forecast when it would rise again. British Airways has suffered declining demand for its flights due to increasing competition from low cost airlines such as Ryanair and easyJet. A further factor depressing sales has been the gloom in the international travel market following terrorist attacks in the United States and Bali. British Airways has, however, managed to increase its profitability as a consequence of a tough cost cutting programme.

IN Business

The alternative way of boosting revenue is to charge a low price in an attempt to sell as many products as possible. In some markets this may lead to high revenues and profits. Firms following this approach are likely to be operating in markets where the goods are fairly similar and consumers do not exhibit strong preferences for any brand. This is true of the overseas holiday market where competition is fierce and businesses seek to maximise their sales and revenue.

Businesses adopt a **revenue oriented** approach for different reasons. If the company has few costs which vary with the level of its output, then it will seek to maximise revenue. Because its costs are not sensitive to the level of its sales, then maximising sales will result in maximum profits. This is the position for companies operating the Government's rail franchises. A full train has few extra costs than a half empty one, so the franchise holders seek high revenues.

The new venture

Paul Merrills has achieved his lifetime ambition of opening a restaurant specialising in French cuisine in south London. Paul is a highly regarded and experienced restaurateur and wants to create a unique atmosphere in his new venture. How would you advise him to maximise his revenue in these circumstances? What factors influenced your advice?

You will have realised from the analysis so far that price, cost and volume are all important elements of a firm's planning and success. Each of these factors affect each other and all of them together determine the profitability of a business.

If a business cannot control its costs then it will be unable to sell its products at a low price. In turn, this will mean a low sales volume. This will mean that overhead costs such as the rent of a factory will be spread over a low output, causing further pressure on costs of production.

It is to the costs of production that we now turn our attention.

15.2 The costs of production

There are many definitions of the term 'costs'. Economists often assess the cost of something in terms of the foregone alternative, the **opportunity cost**. For example, the cost of new computer-aided design technology may be the retraining programme which had to be postponed as a result of the decision to purchase the CAD equipment. An accountant is more likely to consider the **accounting costs**. He or she would talk in terms of the value of the resources involved. Thus the cost of the new CAD equipment might be £50,000. Throughout this unit we will be referring to accounting costs.

Costs are a critical element of the information necessary to manage a business successfully. Managers need to be aware of the costs of all aspects of their business for a number of reasons:

- They need to know the cost of production to assess whether it is profitable to supply the market at the current price.
- They need to know actual costs to allow comparisons with their forecasted (or budgeted) costs of production. This will allow them to make judgements concerning the cost efficiency of various parts of their enterprise.
- They also need to know if they have sufficient finance to afford the expected costs.

15.3 Fixed and variable costs

This is an important classification of the costs encountered by businesses. This classification has a number of uses. For example, it is the basis of calculating break-even, which is covered in a later unit.

FIXED COSTS

Fixed costs are any costs which do not vary directly with the level of output. These costs are linked to time rather than to the level of business activity. Fixed costs exist even if a business is not producing any goods or services. An example of a fixed cost is rent, which can be calculated monthly or annually. It will not vary, whether the office or factory is used intensively to produce goods or services or is hardly utilised at all.

If a manufacturer can double output and still use the same factory (but more intensively) the amount of rent will not alter – thus it is a fixed cost. In the same way, a factory's rent will be unchanged during the period when the factory is closed for the annual summer holiday. As these costs stay high even when business is slack, it is important for firms to use their facilities (especially their premises) intensively. This is true because the firm's fixed costs do not alter as facilities are used more intensively, yet it is likely that revenue will as it sells its increased output of goods or services.

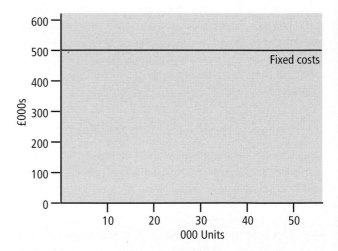

Figure 15.1 Fixed costs of £500,000

In Figure 15.1, you can see that the firm faces fixed costs of £500,000 irrespective of the level of output. Contrast two levels of annual output. How much would the fixed cost of production be for each unit if production were (a) 10,000 units a year and (b) 50,000 units a year? What might be the implications of this distinction for the managers of the firm?

Other examples of fixed costs include the uniform business rate, management salaries, interest charges and depreciation.

In the long term, fixed costs can alter. The manufacturer referred to earlier may decide to increase output significantly. This may entail the renting of additional factory space and the negotiation of loans for additional capital equipment. Thus rent will rise, as may interest payments. We can see that in the long term fixed costs may alter, but that in the short term they are – as their name suggests – fixed!

VARIABLE COSTS

Variable costs are those costs that vary directly with the level of output. They represent payments made for the use of inputs such as labour, fuel and raw materials. If our manufacturer doubled output then these costs would rise significantly. There would be extra costs for the additional raw materials and fuel which would be required. Also more labour would most probably be required, incurring extra costs in the form of wages.

Figure 15.2 Variable costs of 80p per unit

The graph in Figure 15.2 shows a firm with variable costs of 80p per unit. This means variable costs rise steadily with, and proportionately to, the level of output. Thus a 10% rise in output will increase variable costs by the same percentage.

SEMI-VARIABLE COSTS

The classification of costs into fixed and variable is simple and very convenient. In businesses, however, not all costs can be classified so simply. Take the case of a delivery vehicle operated by a local bakery. Many of the operating costs of this vehicle are fixed. These include the costs of insurance and the road fund licence. However, if demand rises sharply, transport costs will rise as the business increases its deliveries. More fuel will be needed, servicing will be required more regularly as its mileage increases and wear and tear will be greater. In these circumstances we should say that this vehicle's cost is semi-variable, i.e. part fixed and part variable.

15.4 Total costs

When added together, fixed and variable costs (plus any semi-variable costs) give the total costs for a business. This is, of course, a very important element in the calculation of the profits earned by a business.

The relationship between fixed, variable and total costs is straightforward to calculate but has important implications for a business. If a business has relatively high fixed costs as a proportion of total costs, then it is likely to seek to maximise its sales to ensure that the fixed costs are spread across as many units of output as possible. In this way the impact of high fixed costs is lessened. Similarly, if variable costs rise less than proportionately with output, due to, say, the benefits of bulk-buying raw materials and fuel, then a business will seek to produce the highest level of output possible.

The table below shows the costs incurred by the The Norfolk Brewery Ltd in producing a single brand of beer – Yarmouth Ale. Can you explain why the average cost of producing a gallon of Yarmouth Ale alters according to the level of output? What is the significance of this for the management team of the Norfolk Brewery?

LEVEL OF OUTPUT (GALLONS)	FIXED COSTS (£000)	VARIABLE COSTS (£000)	TOTAL COSTS (£000)	COST PER GALLON (£)
5,000	100,000	10,000	110,000	22.0
10,000	100,000	20,000	120,000	12.0
15,000	100,000	30,000	130,000	8.7
20,000	100,000	40,000	140,000	7.0
25,000	100,000	50,000	150,000	6.0
30,000	100,000	60,000	160,000	5.3
35,000	100,000	70,000	170,000	4.9
40,000	100,000	80,000	180,000	4.5

15.5 Direct and indirect costs of production

Direct costs are those which can be directly attributed to the production of a particular product or service and allocated to a particular cost centre. Raw materials and piece-rate wages are examples of direct costs.

Indirect costs are the opposite of direct costs. They are those costs which cannot be directly attributed to a particular production line or cost centre. These costs can sometimes be difficult to control and managers have to be aware of this and not allow indirect costs to become disproportionately high. Examples of indirect costs include depreciation, management, administration, marketing and some expenses such as rent, business rates and telephone charges.

Thus, fixed costs are normally the same as indirect costs but variable costs can be direct or indirect.

Another term for indirect costs is 'overheads'. Overheads are costs that are not generated directly by the production process. The term can be used interchangeably with indirect costs. Overheads are not always fixed costs, though they are usually.

Examples of fixed overheads include administrative costs, lighting and heating, whilst the commission payments to a salesforce or the postage costs incurred by a mail order company are examples of variable overheads.

DESCRIPTION	TYPE	£000
Gross profit: the revenue earned by a firm less the cost of achieving the sales. These costs are essentially direct costs such as wages and raw materials	Sales revenue	760
	– Cost of sales	510
	= Gross profit	250
Operating profit: this is the firm's gross profit minus the overheads associated with production, for example rent and rates	– Overheads	75
	= Operating profit	175
Pre-tax profits: the business's operating profit plus one-off items such as the costs of staff restructuring, including redundancy payments	+ One-off items	(25)
	= Pre-tax profits	150
Profit after tax: not surprisingly this is simply pre-tax profits less tax which is levied on company profits (called corporation tax)	– Tax	40
	= Profit after tax	110

15.6 Profits

Having considered revenues and costs, it is now appropriate to focus upon a prime motive for business activity – profit. Profit is a *comparison* of revenues and costs. This comparison determines whether or not an enterprise makes any profit. As we saw at the beginning of this unit the key formula is:

profit = total revenue – total costs

THE TYPES OF PROFIT

Although profit is always revenue – costs, there are different types of cost which can be allowed for. This leads to different types of profit. These are set out in the table below.

Perhaps the most important of these various types of profit is profit after tax, since this is the profit which the business can decide how to allocate. The most important uses to which this profit can be put are:

- payments to shareholders in the form of dividends
- reinvestment into the business to purchase capital items such as property and machinery.

BIRDS EYE WALL'S CUT COSTS

Birds Eye Wall's has announced that it plans to cut 320 jobs from its factory in Gloucester during 2003. The job losses will be part of a 'restructuring programme' aimed at lowering the company's costs. The changes (part of a plan to cut costs by up to £12 million a year) involve making fewer ice cream products and moving from a 7-day to a 5-day working week. The changes are expected to reduce significantly the company's variable costs in the long-term, though there are likely to be additional costs in the short-term.

About 770 people are currently employed at the firm's ice cream manufacturing business at Gloucester. In line with its commitments to trade unions, Birds Eye Wall's vowed there would be no compulsory redundancies before September 2003, except by agreement.

Birds Eye Wall's Chairman, Mr James Hill, said that any employees made redundant would receive a generous settlement package, well in excess of the legal minimum.

Business IN

THE IMPORTANCE OF PROFIT

Undeniably, profits are important to the majority of businesses. Profits are usually assessed in relation to some yardstick, for example the capital invested or sales revenue. They are important for the following reasons:

- they provide a measure of the success of a business
- they provide funds for investment in further fixed assets
- they act as a magnet to attract further funds from shareholders enticed by the possibility of high returns on their investment
- profit is the source of more than 60% of all the finance used to help companies grow; without profit, firms would stand still.

MIXED MESSAGES ON PROFITS FROM THE HIGH STREET

High street fashion clothing retailer Next has announced a substantial rise in its profits for the six months to July 2002. The company reported a 24% rise in profits to £93 million; during the same period sales revenue rose by 26%. The company enjoyed rising sales in its catalogue business as well.

However, over the same six months the John Lewis Partnership saw its profits fall from £44 million to £34 million. John Lewis runs 26 department stores as well as the Waitrose food shops. Despite a 5% growth in sales the group's profits fell because of increased costs.

The group's store refurbishment scheme pushed up costs and made a severe dent in the level of profits.

A profitable, thriving business community will attract other, new businesses who seek to benefit from the commercial vitality of the region. The new businesses may in turn create more prosperity. A virtuous, upward spiral of prosperity can result.

15.7 Profit quality and the utilisation of profit

PROFIT QUALITY

Profit quality refers to the likelihood of a source of profit continuing into the future. If a profit has arisen as a result of a one-off source (such as selling assets for more than their expected value), its quality is said to be low since it is unlikely to continue. A good example is profits from foreign exchange transactions. One year, a firm might make 20% of all its profit from this source. The following year it is just as likely to make losses from the exact same source.

High quality profit is trading profit which can be expected to be sustained into future years. Clearly, high quality profit is more attractive to managers and particularly to potential investors who may be seeking high returns into the future.

PROFIT UTILISATION

The profits generated by a business can be put to two broad uses:

- paid to shareholders in the form of dividends
- retained within the company for future (or immediate) investment.

Profit paid to shareholders in the form of dividends is termed 'distributed profit'. It is important that a company pays shareholders a sufficient dividend in order to be able to attract share capital into the company. Many shareholders are interested in short-term returns and not the long-term benefits which they may derive from the company reinvesting profits.

Companies retain profits they do not pay to shareholders (undistributed profits) in their reserves. These reserves may be used in a number of ways. They could be used to finance new business activities such as the building of a new factory or a major programme of research and development. Alternatively, they may be held as a precaution against less profitable years. In these circumstances the reserves may be utilised to pay shareholders dividends.

ISSUES FOR **analysis**

When analysing costs, revenues and profit, there are some key issues to consider:

- Is the information based upon the firm's actual experience, or is it being estimated as part of a business plan? Many new businesses underestimate operating costs and are all too optimistic about potential revenues. No answer can impress unless it shows a clear grasp of whether the figures are actual or forecast.
- A key element with respect to the revenues earned by a business is the relationship between the price charged and the volume of sales achieved. This relates to many marketing issues, but it is worth noting that choosing a price is an exercise requiring considerable judgement. Simply raising price will not necessarily provide more revenue for a firm. This statement is true because as a firm raises its price it can reasonably expect to lose some sales as customers switch to cheaper brands. Factors influencing consumers' decisions will include the quality of the products in question and the availability of competitors' products.
- Calculations of revenues or profits are always based upon a series of assumptions, such as ignoring the possible effect of bulk buying on variable costs per unit. These assumptions should always be stated as part of a good exam answer.

15.8 Revenue, costs and profit
an evaluation

A key evaluative theme from this unit relates to profits. It may be true to say that the higher the profit, the better. However, this could be regarded as simplistic. First, the type of profit mut be defined. A realistic and meaningful assessment of profit is likely to involve some sort of comparison. It is instructive to compare the level of profits earned with one of the following:

- the profits earned by other, similar businesses
- the profits earned in previous years
- the profits which were anticipated
- the capital invested in the business.

An assessment of the true worth of a business's performance as measured by its profits should also take account of the general state of the economy – are businesses in general prospering, or is it a time of recession? It should also take into account any unusual circumstances such as, for example, the business being subject to direct action by a pressure group. Or suffering from a price war.

It is wrong, therefore, to simply assume that high profits = success and low profits = failure. A house builder would need to be doing brilliantly to break even during a recession. Equally, an ice-cream supplier deserves no credit for high profits in a heatwave.

KEY terms

accounting costs – expressing costs in terms of the resources involved.

one-off profit – profit from a source other than trading, which cannot be expected to recur regularly, such as winning a major court case.

opportunity costs – an economist's approach to costs whereby the cost of a decision is measured in terms of the foregone alternative.

profit margin – this is profit expressed as a proportion of revenue. Thus, if a business produces tables at a cost of £160 each and sells them for £200 then the profit margin = £40/£200 × 100 = 20%.

profit utilisation – how a firm uses its profit after taxation.

revenue oriented – some firms focus upon maximising their revenues because the structure of their costs means that extra sales can be achieved whilst incurring few additional costs.

AS Level Exercises

A. REVISION QUESTIONS
(35 marks; 70 minutes)

Read the unit, then answer:

1 Why might a business initially receive low revenues from a product newly introduced to the market? *(3)*
2 In what circumstances might a company be able to charge high prices for a new product? *(3)*
3 For what reasons might a firm seek to maximise its sales revenue? *(3)*
4 State two reasons why firms have to know the costs they incur in production. *(2)*
5 Distinguish, with the aid of examples, between fixed and variable costs. *(4)*
6 Give two examples of costs which might be semi-variable. *(2)*
7 What is meant by the term 'direct costs'? *(3)*
8 Explain the difference between gross profit and operating profit. *(3)*
9 Give two reasons why profits are important to businesses. *(2)*
10 What is meant by the term 'profit quality'? *(4)*

11 Outline one advantage and one disadvantage to a company of deciding to lower the proportion of profits it distributes to its shareholders. *(4)*
12 State two purposes for which a firm's profit might be used. *(2)*

B. REVISION EXERCISES

B1 Data Response
1 What are the missing words from this passage of text?
Revenue is the value of _____ made within a time period (such as a financial year). It is calculated by the formula:
Revenue = _____ × Price
2 a If a firm sells 200 units of widgets at £3.20 and 40 units of squidgets at £4, what is its total revenue?
  b The following month, the firm cuts its prices by 10%. This causes demand to rise 20%. What is its new revenue level?
  c In the above example, each widget costs £1.30 to make, while each squidget costs £1.50. Based upon production of 200 and 40 units respectively, what are the total variable costs?

3 Elliott and Gabble Ltd had the following costs last month:

materials	£200
salaries	£400
rent	£220
interest	£100

a What is the firm's fixed costs total?

b What is the percentage effect upon fixed costs of the firm's interest charges going up by £36?

4 a Explain how total costs are calculated.

b Calculate Elliott and Gabble's total costs for next month, assuming sales are double the level of last month.

5 a State the formula for calculating profit.

b A firm sells 500 units at £2.50. Each costs £1.10 to make. Fixed costs are £420. What is the profit?

B2 Stimulus Questions

Berry's Mowers Ltd

Mike Berry opened a small lawnmower manufacturing business in Cumbria in the late 1970s. Twenty years later his business had prospered into a major regional supplier of mowers. The company benefited from steadily rising profits as it became better known in the north-west of England.

Mike's company faced strong competition from larger businesses and suffered from relatively high fixed costs in relation to its scale of output. However, the mowers had a good reputation for reliability. The company produced three different lawnmowers – the Lawn Glyde, the Lawnrider and the Lawnraker – priced at £129, £150 and £99 respectively.

The company had recently established a system of cost centres within the business. This was to improve its financial controls. Mike's finance director had calculated the following annual costs of production for the company's premier mower – the Lawnrider:

Output	Fixed Costs (£000s)	Variable Costs (£000s)	Total Costs (£000s)
0	150	0	150
500	150	10	160
1,000	150	19	169
2,000	150	34	184
3,000	150	49	199
4,000	200	67	267

Questions *(30 marks; 35 minutes)*

1 What is meant by the term 'cost centre'? *(3)*

2 Explain the implications for a business of facing relatively high fixed costs. *(5)*

3 The finance director has found that variable costs do not rise steadily with output. Consider the possible reasons for this. *(6)*

4 Calculate the sales level that generates the most profit for the company. *(7)*

5 To what extent are 'steadily rising profits' an indication that a company is prospering? *(9)*

B3 Case Study

Loch Garron Distillery looks to the future

Loch Garron Distillery has taken the decision to cease production of Highland Dew and to concentrate on production of the increasingly popular Caledonian Spirit. Caledonian Spirit is sold throughout the world and sales have been buoyant in North America and Japan over recent years. The whisky is renowned for its quality and for the long period over which it is allowed to mature.

The company is seeking to expand and utilise its capacity at its distillery in Perthshire more fully. It believes that by reducing its costs it will be able to price Caledonian Spirit more competitively, increasing its revenue and profits. This will allow it to operate more effectively in a market that is becoming increasingly competitive.

The managers at Loch Garron Distillery forecast that each bottle of Caledonian Spirit that is sold will generate £15 in revenue. Variable costs, including taxes and excise duties, will amount to £9 per bottle. The fixed costs of operating the distillery are substantial and expected to be £300,000 per year. Sales forecasts are more difficult to make, but they range between 35,000 bottles and 60,000 bottles per year.

Questions *(25 marks, 30 minutes)*

1 What is meant by the following terms:
a 'revenue'
b 'fixed costs'? *(4 marks)*

2 Explain two benefits the company might receive as a result of increasing the output of its distillery. *(6 marks)*

3 Calculate the level of profit or loss that will be made from the sale of Caledonian Spirit if sales are:
(i) 35,000 bottles per year or
(ii) 60,000 bottles per year. *(6 marks)*

4 Discuss the case for and against reducing the price of Caledonian Spirit. *(9 marks)*

BREAK-EVEN ANALYSIS

Break-even analysis compares a firm's revenue with its fixed and variable costs to identify the minimum sales level needed to make a profit. This can be shown in a graph known as a break-even chart.

16.1 Introduction

The starting point for all financial management is to know how much goods or services cost to produce. This was covered in detail in the previous unit. Businesses also benefit from knowing how many products they have to sell in order to cover their costs. This is particularly important for new businesses with limited experience of their products or their markets. It is also of value for established businesses which are planning to produce a new product.

Look at the following revenue and cost figures for Burns and Morris Ltd, manufacturers of silk ties:

OUTPUT OF TIES (PER WEEK)	SALES INCOME (£ PER WEEK)	TOTAL COSTS (£ PER WEEK)
0	0	10,000
100	4,000	11,500
200	8,000	13,000
300	12,000	14,500
400	16,000	16,000
500	20,000	17,500
600	24,000	19,000

You can easily identify that Burns and Morris Ltd has to sell 400 ties each week to break even. Note what happens to its profits if sales are lower – or higher.

To calculate the **break-even point** we need information on both costs and prices. A change in costs or in the firm's pricing policy will change the level of output at which the firm breaks even.

Break-even analysis is simple to understand, and useful – especially in small firms. Businesses can use break-even to:

- estimate the future level of output they will need to produce and sell in order to meet given objectives in terms of profits
- assess the impact of planned price changes upon profit and the level of output needed to break even
- assess how changes in fixed and/or **variable costs** may affect profits, and the level of output necessary to break even

- take decisions on whether to produce their own products or components or whether to purchase from external sources
- support applications for loans from banks and other financial institutions – the use of the technique may indicate good business sense as well as forecast profitability.

Break-even can be calculated or shown on a graph. The calculation of break-even is simpler and quicker than drawing **break-even charts**.

16.2 Calculating break-even

Calculating the break-even point for a product requires:

- the selling price of the product
- its **fixed costs**
- its variable costs per unit.

Fixed costs are expenses which do not change in response to changing demand or output. Fixed costs have to be paid whether or not the business is trading. Examples include rent, business rates and interest charges. On the other hand, variable costs will alter as demand and output adjust. An increase in output will require greater supplies of materials, for example. A doubling of demand will increase variable costs.

The break-even output level can be calculated by the formula:

$$\frac{\text{fixed costs}}{\text{selling price per unit} - \text{variable cost per unit}}$$

The following example shows how to use this formula to calculate break-even.

Example: Sue's guided tours

Sue Pittman operates an open-top bus in London during the summer months to take tourists on sightseeing tours of the capital. The bus conducts four trips each day and Sue estimates that the cost of each trip is £200 in fuel, depreciation and wage costs for the driver and courier. The trip includes a snack and soft drinks for all the passengers as well as a London guidebook. These items cost £5 for each passenger on the bus. The maximum number of passengers Sue is allowed to take on each trip is 40. Sue has priced the trips at £15 per passenger.

T-ONLINE FORECASTS BREAK-EVEN FOR 2003

T-Online is Europe's biggest Internet Service Provider (ISP). The German-owned group supplies over 9 million customers in Austria, Spain and France as well as Germany itself. The T-Online group of companies has announced that its German operations should break even by the end of 2003. T-Online has launched a cost-cutting drive in an attempt to ensure that costs are no more than revenues. In addition, T-Online is increasingly charging its customers on a metered basis, allowing it to charge higher prices and increase revenue.

However, T-Online's overseas operations in Austria, France and Spain currently account for the bulk of the group's overall losses. It is expected that these will take another 2 years to turn around, a T-Online spokesperson announced. Break-even for the entire group is unlikely to be achieved before 2005.

The first thing we should note is that the fixed cost of each tour is £200. Sue has to pay for the fuel, wages and depreciation irrespective of how many passengers she has. So it is easy to fill in the top of the formula we set out above. Fixed costs per tour are £200.

Calculating the bottom half of the formula is only a little more difficult. We know that she charges each passenger £15 per tour and that the variable costs associated with each passenger are £5. This pays for the snacks and drinks and the guidebook given to each passenger. The amount left (the **contribution**) is £10 for each customer. So the formula will look like this:

Sue's break-even output

$$= \frac{\text{fixed costs}}{\text{selling price per unit} - \text{variable cost per unit}}$$

$$= \frac{£200}{£15 - £5}$$

$$= \frac{£200}{£10}$$

$$= 20 \text{ passengers}$$

In other words, Sue will need 20 passengers on each of her tours to break even.

As we have seen, the break-even level of output can be calculated using the simple equation above. More understanding of the sensitivity of the relationships between costs, sales revenue and production can be achieved through the use of break-even charts.

16.3 Break-even charts

A break-even chart is a graph showing a company's revenues and costs at all possible levels of demand/output. The break-even chart is constructed by first drawing the horizontal axis to represent the output of goods or services for the business in question – from zero units to maximum output. The horizontal axis shows output per time period – usually output per month or year. The vertical axis represents costs and revenues in pounds.

Example: Berry & Hall Ltd

Berry & Hall Ltd are manufacturers of confectionery. One popular line is Aromatics – a distinctive sweet with a strong fragrance. These sweets are priced at £1 a kilogram. The variable (or original) cost of production per kilogram is 60 pence and the fixed costs associated with this product are estimated at £50,000 a year. The company's maximum output of Aromatics is 250,000 kilograms per year.

First, put scales on the axes. The output scale goes from zero to the company's maximum annual output; this will be 250,000 kilograms. The vertical axis records values of costs and revenues. It goes from £0 to maximum output multiplied by the selling price. In this case it will have a maximum value on the axis of £250,000 (£1 × 250,000).

Having drawn the axes and placed scales upon them, the first line to draw is fixed costs. Since this value does not change with output it is a horizontal line placed at £50,000.

Figure 16.1 Fixed costs for Aromatics

These costs cover rent and rates for the factory and also interest paid on loans taken out by Berry & Hall Ltd.

Next, add on variable costs to arrive at total costs. The difference between total costs and fixed costs is variable costs. Total costs start at the fixed costs line and then rise diagonally. To see where they rise to, calculate total costs at the maximum output level. In the case of Aromatics, this is 250,000 kilograms per year. The total cost is fixed costs (£50,000) plus variable costs of producing 250,000 kilograms (£0.60 × 250,000 = £150,000). So total cost at this level of output is £50,000 + £150,000 = £200,000.

This point can now be marked on the chart, i.e. £200,000 at an output level of 250,000 kilograms. This can be joined to the total costs at zero output: £50,000. This is illustrated in Figure 16.2.

Finally, sales revenue must be added. This is drawn in a similar way to total costs. For the maximum level of output calculate the sales revenue and mark this on the chart. In the case of Aromatics, maximum output of 250,000 kilograms multiplied by selling price gives £250,000 each year. If Berry & Hall does not produce and sell any Aromatics it will not have any sales revenue. Thus zero output results in zero income. A straight, diagonal line from zero to £250,000 therefore represents the sales revenue for Aromatics (see Figure 16.3).

This brings together costs and revenues for Aromatics. A line drawn down from the point where total costs and sales revenue cross shows break-even output. For Aromatics, it is 125,000 kilograms per year. This can be checked using the formula method explained above.

Figure 16.2 Fixed, variable and total costs for Aromatics

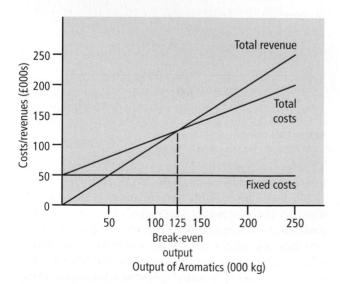

Figure 16.3 Break-even output for Aromatics

16.4 Using break-even charts

Various pieces of information can be taken from a break-even chart such as Figure 16.3. As well as the break-even output it also shows the level of profits earned, or losses incurred, by Aromatics at every possible level of output. Many conclusions can be reached, such as:

- Any level of output lower than 125,000 kilograms per year will mean the product is making a loss. The amount of the loss is indicated by the vertical distance between the total cost and the total revenue line. For example, at an output level of 90,000 units per year, Aromatics would make a loss of £14,000. This is because sales are worth £90,000 but costs are £104,000 (£54,000 + £50,000).
- Sales in excess of 125,000 kilograms of Aromatics per year will earn the company a profit. If the company produces and sells 150,000 kilograms of Aromatics annually it will earn a profit of £20,000. At this level of output total revenue is £150,000 and total costs are £130,000. This is shown on the chart by the vertical distance between total revenue and total costs at 150,000 units of output.
- The **margin of safety**. One feature of a break-even chart is that it can show the safety margin. This is the amount by which demand can fall before the firm starts making losses. It is the difference between sales and the break-even point. If sales of Aromatics were 175,000, with a break-even output of 125,000, the margin of safety would be 50,000 units.

margin of safety = 175,000 − 125,000
= 50,000 kilograms

That is, output could fall by 50,000 units before losses are made. The higher the margin of safety the less likely it is that a loss-making situation will develop. The margin of safety is illustrated in Figure 16.4.

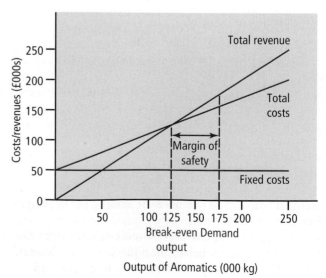

Figure 16.4 Margin of safety

16.5 Break-even analysis in a changing environment

The application of break-even analysis to the production of Aromatics showed how the technique operates. But it assumed a very stable (and therefore unrealistic) business environment. Competitors may have reacted to the introduction of Aromatics by producing similar products. This competition may have forced Berry & Hall to reduce the price of Aromatics. Alternatively, more advertising may have been needed, raising Berry & Hall's costs. In either case the break-even point and the break-even chart would change.

Suppose that Berry & Hall chose to carry out additional advertising for Aromatics and that this advertising cost £25,000 over the first year. What impact would this have upon the break-even point and the break-even chart? The extra costs would require a higher output (and income) to break even. The rise in marketing costs can be regarded as a fixed cost because this cost must be borne whatever the level of output. This is shown in Figure 16.5.

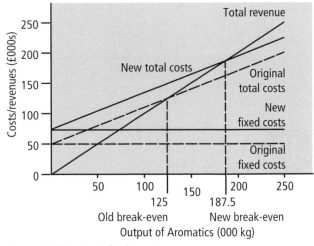

Figure 16.5 A rise in fixed costs

The break-even chart shows the increased fixed cost and total cost lines which create a higher break-even output. This also has the effect of reducing the level of profit (or increasing the loss) made at any level of output. Any factor leading to a fall in fixed costs will have the opposite effects. Other external factors can impact upon the break-even level of output and associated profits. If the cost of labour declines, due perhaps to improving productivity, then the variable cost and total cost lines will rise less steeply. Falling costs of raw materials would have a similar effect.

If costs remain unchanged and prices fall then this will result in a higher break-even level of production. Lower prices mean that more has to be produced and sold before a profit-making position can be reached. Conversely, a rise in price will result in a lower level of production necessary for break-even to be attained. Figure 16.6 illustrates the impact of a fall in the market price of a product.

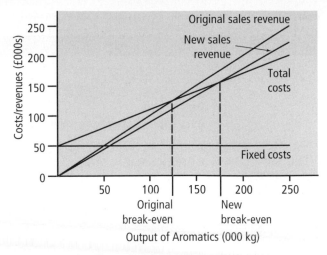

Figure 16.6 The effects of a fall in price

The previous chart shows the effects of a fall in prices. When using break-even analysis, a business may draw several charts using different prices to assess the impact of price changes. This approach is particularly useful in markets where prices may be volatile.

ISSUES FOR **analysis**

Analytical issues in relation to break-even centre upon the effective use of break-even charts. It is important to appreciate how changes in the business environment might affect the break-even position of a business. Any analysis of break-even should recognise that changes in revenues or costs will impact upon the level of break-even output.

As an example, you should be able to state whether, in the following circumstances, break-even output will rise or fall:

- wage negotiations result in a 4% pay rise
- the business rate levied upon a firm's premises is increased
- the market price for the business's product increases
- a change in the value of the pound means that raw materials fall in price by 5%.

A break-even chart shows the level of profit or loss at any level of output. If the firm's circumstances change it is important to be able to quantify the extent to which profitability changes at any level of output.

16.6 Break-even analysis
an evaluation

As with most techniques of financial control, break-even analysis has advantages and disadvantages.

Break-even analysis is simple to conduct and understand. Also it is cheap and can be carried out quickly. It shows profit and loss at various levels of output, particularly when it is presented in the form of a chart. This may be of particular value when a business is first established. Indeed it may be that financial institutions will require this sort of financial information before lending any money to someone aspiring to run a business.

	CAUSE	EFFECT
Internal factors	• Employing extra sales staff • Price increase • Automation replaces direct labour	• Fixed costs rise, so total costs rise and break-even point rises • Revenue rises more steeply; break-even point falls • Fixed costs rise while variable costs fall; uncertain effect on break-even point
External factors	• Recession cuts demand • Price war forces price cut • Inflation pushes up variable costs	• Break-even point unaffected, though safety margin is reduced • Revenue rises less steeply; break-even point rises • Variable and total cost lines rise more steeply; break-even point rises

Although it is a rudimentary technique, break-even analysis can cope with changing circumstances. We have seen that the technique can allow for changing revenues and costs and gives a valuable rule-of-thumb guide to potential profitability.

However, break-even does have some drawbacks. It pays little attention to the realities of the marketplace. A major flaw is that it assumes all output is sold. This may well be untrue and, if so, would result in an inaccurate break-even estimate. If a firm sells less than it produces it incurs costs without earning the corresponding revenue. This will substantially reduce profits. In times of recession, a firm may have difficulty in selling all that it produces.

Although break-even can cope with changes in prices and costs, in the real world such factors change regularly making it difficult to use as a forecasting technique. Changes in tastes and fashions, exchange rates and technology are all examples of factors which could invalidate break-even forecasts.

The model assumes that costs increase constantly and that firms do not benefit from economies of scale. If, for example, a firm negotiates lower prices for purchasing larger quantities of raw materials then its total cost line will no longer be straight. It will, in fact, level out at higher outputs. Similarly, break-even analysis assumes the firm sells all its output at a single price. In reality firms frequently offer discounts for bulk purchases. Finally, break-even analysis is only as good as the data on which it is based: poor quality data can result in inaccurate conclusions being drawn.

In Business

CHANNEL TUNNEL FAILS TO BREAK EVEN AFTER SEVEN YEARS

Eurotunnel, the firm that operates the Channel Tunnel, once again recorded a loss in 2001–2002. The company, which recorded a loss of £132 million, believes that it will break even during 2003.

Eurotunnel has suffered several setbacks in its attempts to bring the Channel Tunnel to profitability. The activities of asylum seekers attempting to break into Eurotunnel's property in France have imposed additional security costs on the company. Their activities have also disrupted services, reducing the company's revenue. The number of freight trains running through the tunnel fell by 50% in the first half of 2002.

However, freight services are increasing once again and even though passenger numbers on Le Shuttle have fallen, price rises have boosted revenues.

KEY terms

break-even chart – a line graph showing total revenues and total costs at all possible levels of output or demand from zero to maximum capacity.

break-even point – the level of output at which total revenue equals total costs. At this level of output the business makes neither a profit nor a loss.

contribution – total revenue less variable costs. The calculation of contribution is useful for businesses which are responsible for a range of products.

fixed costs – any costs which do not vary directly with the level of output, for example rent and rates.

margin of safety – the amount by which current output exceeds the level of output necessary to break even.

variable costs – those costs which vary directly with the level of output. They represent payments made for the use of inputs such as labour, fuel and raw materials.

AS Level Exercises

A. REVISION QUESTIONS
(30 marks; 60 minutes)

Read the unit, then answer:

1 What is meant by the term 'break-even point'? *(3)*
2 State three reasons why a business might conduct a break-even analysis. *(3)*
3 List four items of information necessary to construct a break-even chart. *(4)*
4 How would you calculate the contribution made by each unit of production? *(2)*
5 Describe the relationship on a break-even chart between fixed costs and total costs. *(3)*
6 Explain why the variable cost and total revenue lines commence at the origin of a break-even chart *(3)*
7 What point on a break-even chart actually illustrates break-even output? *(2)*
8 Explain how, using a break-even chart, you would illustrate the amount of profit or loss made at any given level of output. *(3)*
9 Why might a business wish to calculate its margin of safety? *(5)*
10 A business is currently producing 200,000 units of output annually, and its break-even output is 120,000 units. What is its margin of safety? *(2)*

B. REVISION EXERCISES

B1 Data Response
(50 marks; 60 minutes)

1 a Draw a break-even chart to show the position of a firm with:
   ● maximum capacity of 5,000 units
   ● fixed costs of £6,000
   ● selling price of £4
   ● variable costs of £2 per unit. *(9)*
  b Show on the graph, and state, the profit or loss made at sales of 4,000 units. *(4)*
  c Indicate on the graph, and state, the safety margin at that level of output. *(4)*
2 A firm has the capacity to produce 20,000 units. Current demand is 50% of that level. Fixed costs are £120,000 and the variable cost is £8 per unit. The product's price is £18.

a Calculate the current level of profit. *(5)*
b Calculate the break-even point. *(4)*
c Calculate profit and safety margin if demand rose to 14,000 units. *(6)*
3 At an output level of 24,000 units, a firm's costs are:
   salaries: £48,000
   rent and rates: £24,000
   raw materials: £12,000
   piece-rate labour   £36,000
   a What are the firm's total costs at 20,000 units? *(7)*
   b If the product's selling price is £6, what is its break-even point? *(3)*
4 Explain two strengths and two weaknesses of break-even analysis. *(8)*

B2 Case Study

The Successful T-shirt Company
The Successful T-shirt Company sells fashion T-shirts throughout the European Union. The shirts are available in a range of colours and all contain the prized Successful logo.

The shirts are sold to retailers for £15 each. They cost £5 to manufacture and the salesperson receives £0.60 commission for each item sold to retailers. The distribution cost for each shirt is £0.40. The fixed costs of production are £10,000 per month.

The company is considering expanding production and has approached its bank for a loan. The bank has asked the company to draw up a business plan including a cash flow forecast and break-even chart.

Questions *(30 marks; 35 minutes)*
1 What is a break-even chart? *(4)*
2 Calculate the following:
   a the variable cost of producing 1,000 T-shirts
   b the contribution earned through the sale of one T-shirt. *(6)*
3 Construct a break-even chart to show:
   a the monthly level of output necessary for the Successful T-shirt Company to break even
   b the safety margin, if sales are 1,500 units. *(10)*
4 To what extent is break-even analysis a useful technique for a small company selling fashion products? *(10)*

A Level Exercises

A. REVISION EXERCISES

A1 Data Response

Break-even analysis: an essential tool

It is essential that each business owner carries out a break-even analysis of his or her current or proposed enterprise. A break-even analysis examines the interaction amongst fixed costs, variable costs, prices and unit volume to determine the point at which revenues and total costs are equal.

The following example shows how break-even analysis can help the manager of a business.

When Melanie Howe started up her hair-dressing business, she estimated monthly fixed costs of £10,000 and variable costs of £15 per customer. Her market research had suggested 1,500 customers per month at an average spend of £25.

In fact after the opening period, trade settled down at just 800 customers per month. When talking to her clients, Melanie gained the impression that price was not much of an issue to them, so she wondered whether to put her prices up to help her profitability. It was fortunate for her that her fixed costs proved to be just £5,000 rather than the forecast figure of £10,000.

Questions *(40 marks; 50 minutes)*

1 What is meant by the term 'unit volume'? *(3)*

2 Outline two reasons why a business might use break-even analysis. *(6)*

3 a Draw Melanie's forecast break-even chart. *(8)*

b Mark and state the forecast level of monthly sales revenue and profit. *(6)*

c Illustrate the change in fixed costs on the graph and identify and state the actual level of profits earned each month, given that 800 customers paid an average of £25 each. *(8)*

d Consider whether break-even analysis is an appropriate technique to analyse the impact of an increase in price. *(9)*

B. ESSAY QUESTIONS

1 Comment on the view that break-even analysis is only of relevance to small businesses.

2 'Break-even analysis is of limited value to businesses because it ignores the market.' To what extent do you agree with this statement?

B3 Case Study

Tourists' Delight

The Farne Islands lie close to the coast of Northumberland and are amongst Britain's most important seabird sanctuaries. They are home to many different species, including puffins and eider ducks; there is also a large colony of seals. St Cuthbert died on Inner Farne in 687 and the chapel built in his memory is a popular attraction.

Tourists cross from the Northumberland port of Seahouses in small cruisers. The only boat is called *The Grace Darling* and makes two trips each day. Jim Marshall, the owner of *The Grace Darling*, estimates that the cost of each trip is £90 including fuel, harbour dues, depreciation and wages for the crew. These costs remain the same no matter how many passengers he takes. The price of the trip includes a tea or coffee for all the passengers and the landing fee charged by the National Trust who own the islands. These items cost an additional £2 for each passenger on the boat. Jim is allowed to take a maximum of 50 passengers on each trip. Jim has priced the day trips at £5 per passenger to ensure a positive contribution from every tourist.

The trips are popular in the summer months, but few passengers want to make the crossing between November and March when the weather can be stormy and the sea rough. However, on a fine day, a dozen or two tourists might want to make the trip.

Questions *(25 marks, 30 minutes)*

1 What is meant by the term 'contribution'? *(2)*

2 a Calculate the level of variable costs incurred when *The Grace Darling* has just sufficient passengers to break even on a trip to the Farne Isles. *(4)*

b Calculate the profit or loss earned if *The Grace Darling* carries 40 passengers on a crossing to the Farne Islands. *(3)*

3 The National Trust has informed Jim that landing fees will increase from next summer. Jim is considering raising his prices to compensate for this. Examine the possible effects of these actions on the break-even point of *The Grace Darling*. *(7)*

4 Evaluate the usefulness of break-even analysis to Jim in these circumstances. *(9)*

CONTRIBUTION

DEFINITION

Contribution is the difference between sales revenue and variable cost. It is the difference between the income generated from sales and the variable costs of producing the goods to generate those sales. Contribution is used to pay the company's fixed overheads. Once these have been covered, additional contribution generates profit. The concept of contribution is important to many businesses. Particularly those that produce a number of products.

17.1 Contribution per unit

Mars bars cost 30p each from the wholesalers. Every time a shop sells one for 40p, it has generated 10p of **contribution**. This 10p is not profit, because no account has been taken of the shop's overheads. Only if enough 10 pences are received will the overheads be covered. Beyond that number, all further contribution becomes pure profit.

Contribution per unit is determined by:

- the variable costs, which can be reduced by shrewd buying, by reducing wastage or by redesigning the product/service to simplify it and reduce costs
- the selling price, which can be increased if the customer is being offered something unique, but may need to be cut if competition becomes stronger.

Increasing contribution per unit will increase the chances of making profits overall. This can be done either by boosting the price or by cutting the variable costs. Note the effect on contribution and profit of increasing the price. If a shop charges 42p instead of 40p for a Mars (a 5% price rise), contribution per unit rises from 10p to 12p. This 20% increase in contribution per unit is likely to boost profit considerably. Profit will increase unless the 5% price rise causes demand to drop by 20% or more.

Variable costs	• *Costs such as raw materials and labour actually used in making the product itself. Variable costs therefore fluctuate directly in relation to output.*
Fixed costs	• *These costs of the business are fixed overheads such as rent, rates or administration. They do not vary with the level of output but remain unchanged in the short term.*
Profit	• *The difference which arises when the sales revenue gained from a product is greater than the total costs (fixed and vari able) involved in supplying the products.*

17.2 Total contribution

Total contribution is found by multiplying contribution per unit by quantity. If 200 Mars bars are sold per week at 40p, the total contribution from Mars bars is £20. If the price rise pushes demand down to 180 units, total contribution will be 180 × 12p = £21.60.

The revenue earned by every product comprises three distinct elements (see table below). The sum of the component sections for an individual product will always equal the product's selling price. For a business's total output these components represent the sales revenue it generates. If the product's selling price rises or falls, then the level of profit associated with the sales will rise or fall accordingly.

Business IN

FOSTER'S SEES GREATER CONTRIBUTION FROM WINE

Foster's, one of Australia's largest brewers of beer, has seen sales of wine make an increasing contribution to the company's profits over recent years. In 2000 Foster's bought the Californian wine producers Beringer and as a result in 2001 the company's wine sales exceeded those of beer for the first time. This trend is expected to continue into the future.

The company's contribution to profits from wine grew by 30% in the year 2000–2001 compared to a more modest 5.4% growth in contribution from beer. As a result Foster's profits rose by over 20% to £203.6 million. Australian wine exports have risen dramatically over recent years. In Britain they now rival France for the top spot.

Contribution first goes towards paying for the fixed costs of the company. After these have been paid, further contributions go towards profit. From this you can see that if contributions are only sufficient to cover fixed costs then the business will break even. That is, it will neither make a profit nor a loss.

Contribution calculations do not have to be carried out on single products. Indeed, it can be argued that contribution is a particularly useful concept when a business produces a range of products.

17.3 Calculating profit using contribution

Among the uses of the contribution concept is that it provides a quick way of calculating profit. This is important because most examinations involve tight timing. So speed of work can help generate more marks.

Example:
Simpson Ltd produces a range of fruit juices for supermarkets in Wales and the south of England.

production	= 100,000 units
total sales revenue (SR)	= £150,000
total variable costs (VC)	= £85,000
fixed costs (FC)	= £40,000
total contribution	= SR – VC
	= £150,000 – £85,000
	= £65,000

From these figures we can also determine Simpson's overall level of profit:

profit = contribution – fixed costs
= £65,000 – £40,000
= £25,000

Why bother to use contribution to calculate profit? Surely a simpler approach is the one outlined below:

sales revenue – total costs = profit

where total costs = fixed costs + variable costs

which would give us exactly the same answer.

SR – FC – VC = profit
£150,000 – £40,000 – £85,000 = £25,000

This works well with companies which provide only one product or service. Most companies (including Simpson) have several products, however. In which case the contribution approach is more helpful. The contribution statement below provides a breakdown of the company's products. It shows how much each contributes towards covering Simpson's fixed costs and profit.

This statement provides a lot of useful information. It shows that:

- each product is making a positive contribution
- orange juice is the key product
- tropical juice is very profitable (contribution is 60% of revenue, compared with 23% for apple juice).

Contribution statement for Simpson Ltd

	ORANGE JUICE	APPLE JUICE	TROPICAL JUICE	COMPANY TOTAL
Revenue	£80,000	£30,000	£40,000	£150,000
Ingredients	£30,000	£17,000	£7,000	£54,000
Other variable costs	£16,000	£6,000	£9,000	£31,000
Contribution	£34,000	£7,000	£24,000	£65,000
Fixed overheads				£40,000
Profit				**£25,000**

Unit 28 explains how firms attempt to allocate the company's fixed overheads to different products or departments. This is to try to work out the profit generated by each product, rather than just the contribution.

DOWN ON THE FARM

In 1998 British farming was suffering from an awful year. The effect of BSE on cattle prices was compounded by falling consumer interest in meat, plus the impact of a strong pound on import prices. Pork, milk and wheat could be imported at lower prices than for many years.

One Northumberland farmer explained her difficulties. Her mixed farm produced vegetables and cereal crops, but the main cash earner for the past few years had been pigs. She bred and raised young weaners and then sold them on. Her direct costs were £26 per pig and in the past she had been able to sell them at auction for up to £60. Now, in October 1998, she had just sold 100 piglets for £1,000. Just £10 per pig. Instead of the usual positive contribution, she had lost heavily on every pig sold. And that was before taking the overhead costs of the farm into account. She could only hope that cereal prices rose before selling her crop later in the month.

Business IN

17.4 Contribution costing

Using contribution costing we place fixed costs to one side. Using this technique requires managers to focus upon whether or not an individual product makes a positive contribution. So long as the sales revenue from a particular product exceeds the associated variable cost then the product's contribution will be positive. This could be helpful to Simpson Ltd if it were considering a new line – for example, peach juice.

We have already seen that calculating variable costs is relatively easy. If a product is making a positive contribution, the company knows it is helping towards paying for the fixed costs. If fixed costs are already covered, as in the case of Simpson Ltd, extra contribution from peach juice will add to profit. Any launch or other overhead costs associated with the new product must, though, be taken into account (see the table below).

Possible output and contribution for peach juice

OUTPUT	PER UNIT	5,000 UNITS	10,000 UNITS
Selling price	£1.50	£7,500	£15,000
Variable costs			
Materials	£0.10	£500	£1,000
Labour	£0.09	£450	£900
Other	£0.06	£300	£600
Total	£0.25	£1,250	£2,500
Contribution	£1.25	£6,250	£12,500
One-off design costs		£10,000	£10,000
Profit or Loss (1st year)		£3,750 loss	£2,500 profit

The table shows contribution rising along with output and eventually exceeding fixed overheads. At 5,000 units of output the company makes a loss of £3,750. Producing and selling 10,000 units of output makes a £2,500 profit. It follows that somewhere between these two points lies the place where the company breaks even. That point will be where there are enough individual contributions of £1.25 to cover the fixed costs.

This is given by:

$$\frac{\text{fixed costs}}{\text{contribution (per unit)}} = \textbf{break-even point}$$

For peach juice:

$$\frac{\text{£10,000}}{\text{£1.25}} = 8{,}000 \text{ units}$$

Therefore the new product would break even at 8,000 units of production manufactured and sold. Break-even analysis is covered more fully in Unit 16.

17.5 Contribution pricing

Contribution allows a company to analyse whether each of its products covers its own variable costs. Prices can be set in relation to the direct cost of producing that good rather than an inflated figure including fixed costs.

The principle of setting prices at a level above the variable cost of production is straightforward.

Example:
Bridge Street Enterprises manufactures a number of products, including a popular range of garden gnomes. The company sells 6,000 gnomes annually at £20 each. Its fixed costs are £24,000 and its variable cost per gnome is £15. The manager of the company knows that each sale of a gnome will contribute £5 towards the fixed overheads of the business. If all prices are set this way it is likely that the company will make a profit as long as sufficient sales are achieved.

By ignoring fixed costs, businesses can enjoy much more flexibility in their pricing decisions. Successful products can be priced to make a high level of contribution. Less successful or maturing products can be priced to make a lower contribution, yet still help toward the company's fixed costs. Maintaining a large product range may make it hard for competitors to find gaps in the market.

The approach encourages new products to be introduced and tested. All the company needs is to show it can cover its own direct costs of production, and make a positive contribution towards the fixed costs.

Contribution pricing may lead to companies adopting price discrimination whereby they charge different prices to different groups of consumers for the same product. Anglia Railways can charge a customer £20 for a weekend return ticket from Norwich to London that would cost nearer £100 at weekday peak times. If it charged all its customers the same price, it would make little profit. However, the company is aware that it can charge weekday business users a higher price for weekday travel. Sales of tickets to business users provide a large contribution and enhance the company's profits. Contribution pricing allows a company to operate price discrimination with greater confidence.

Alternatively, a company may make a deliberate decision to price its product below variable cost. In these circumstances the product will be sold at a loss. Firms operate loss leaders in order to attract customers to purchase other products on which they make a profit.

17.6 Special-order decisions

Contribution also helps managers make decisions regarding additional customer orders at reduced prices. These are termed special-order decisions. Questions based on this concept are very popular with examiners as they illustrate the principle of contribution pricing very effectively.

For example, Simpson Ltd sells cartons of fruit juice for £1.50. How might the company respond if a customer offers a different price from the standard one? Two situations may occur:

1 The customer offers a price over and above the usual selling price – the natural reaction would be to jump at this chance to increase profits. However, this scenario is most likely to occur in circumstances in which the customer has special requirements. Examples could include a quick delivery time or slightly different product specifications. Either case could cause problems for the company. It may be that meeting such an order results in increased costs, for example overtime payments, meaning that profits are lower than initially expected. Such orders therefore require careful deliberation.

2 The customer offers a price below the usual selling price – the acceptability of such an order depends on the price being offered and production capacity available to the company. Assume a customer contacts Simpson and offers a price of £1.10 per carton for 10,000 cartons. This represents a fairly large order. How should Simpson decide whether or not to accept this order? The company calculates that its variable costs per carton are currently 80p. So contribution per unit is £1.10 – £0.80 = 30p.

Simpson Ltd – special-order decision

	FOR A SINGLE PRODUCT	FOR 10,000 UNITS ORDER
Sales revenue	£1.10	£11,000
Variable cost	£0.80	£8,000
Contribution	£0.30	£3,000

Accepting the order will make a positive contribution of £3,000. This would indicate that Simpsons should accept the order. But this is subject to the proviso that Simpsons possesses **spare capacity** (i.e. production capacity which is currently idle). Unless Simpsons has spare capacity, the company could incur additional fixed costs as a result of renting or purchasing machinery, property or other fixed assets. There is also the possibility that the company may have to pay overtime to employees, resulting in a higher variable cost per unit of production. These factors may reduce the company's profitability. When taking this type of order it is important to make sure that the customer you are selling to is unable to resell your own products, to your usual customers, at a cheaper price than you would normally charge them.

17.7 Benefits and drawbacks of contribution techniques

Contribution pricing and costing offer companies a number of advantages and disadvantages. The benefits are:

- contribution costing avoids arbitrary allocation of fixed overheads
- contribution costing and pricing are simple to operate
- the contribution approach looks at the business as a whole rather than individual product lines
- contribution pricing and costing can be adjusted to allow for changes as they happen.

But, of course, contribution techniques have a number of drawbacks as well:

- it is often difficult to classify costs into which are variable and which are fixed
- contribution can easily be confused with profit – remember contribution only becomes profit when all fixed costs are paid
- contribution can only really be used over short-run situations when fixed overheads do not alter and the scale of output is fixed.

ISSUES FOR **analysis**

When answering questions in response to a case study or other examination question requiring analysis, contribution offers a number of lines of argument:

- Contribution assists companies in their decision making. It provides additional information which can result in better quality decisions by managers. This is true especially when deciding whether or not to continue production or whether to accept or reject particular orders. Contribution can also assist managers taking pricing decisions. Contribution techniques can assist companies in price discrimination or determining the selling prices of loss leaders.
- A key underlying principle of contribution is to isolate the issues involved in a decision from the rest of the business. It encourages firms to consider what happens at the margin. A firm looking only at its average costs might not realise that profit can be boosted by selling extra output at below average cost (as long as variable costs are covered). The same logic applies in other types of business analysis such as investment appraisal and decision trees.

17.8 Contribution
an evaluation

The use of contribution is a valuable way of assessing the value to a firm of a product or department. However, there is a danger of attaching too much importance to what is a short-term indicator. The prices and costs of the firm in question can change quite rapidly, often altering the situation dramatically. Any assessment should take this into account.

Considering the contribution of a product may also require a wider assessment of the firm's activities and circumstances. The competitive position of the company, the state of the market and the product's stage in the product life cycle may all have relevance to any judgement. Similarly, government and EU policies may affect the potential earnings and costs of a product.

KEY terms

break-even point – the level of output at which total revenue equals total costs. At this level of output the business makes neither a profit nor loss.

contribution – contribution is total revenue minus total variable costs. Therefore contribution minus fixed costs equals profit.

spare capacity – the extent to which production capability exceeds the current level of orders.

AS Level Exercises

A. REVISION QUESTIONS
(35 marks; 70 minutes)

Read the unit, then answer:

1. Define the term 'contribution per unit'. *(3)*
2. Give three examples of fixed costs. *(3)*
3. Explain the difference between contribution and profit. *(4)*
4. Distinguish between fixed and variable costs. *(3)*
5. Outline one advantage to companies of using contribution costing. *(4)*
6. What is a 'multi-product line'? *(3)*
7. Why might companies engage in price discrimination? *(4)*
8. Explain what is meant by a special-order decision. *(4)*
9. What is the main use to which contribution statements are put? *(5)*
10. State two disadvantages of using contribution costing. *(2)*

B. REVISION EXERCISES

B1 Case Study
The Bakery de Bologna had been a fixture in Cardiff for more than 30 years. Two years ago, Zino Mancini handed the bakery over to his daughter Serena and her husband. Serena worked tirelessly to build the business up, but there seemed a relentless customer trend towards one-stop shopping at the huge Tesco, Sainsbury and Asda stores nearby. Her introduction of innovations such as freshly baked pizzas helped to build up her lunchtime trade, but the steady decline in bread sales continued. She tried cutting the price of bread by 20% on Monday to Wednesday, but despite a 25% rise in sales, she noticed that profits seemed worse than ever.

Serena decided to set out exactly what she knew about the costs of baking each product, to compare them with the prices she charged. This is set out on the following page.

The picture confirmed Serena's impression that the business was making enough for them to live on, but nothing like enough to build the capital to finance expansion. And if bread sales kept sliding, the profitability of the business would fall away dramatically.

Then came a phone call. A hugely successful South Wales restaurant chain needed a new supplier of bread rolls. Their previous supplier's quality had slipped and they had been sacked. The sales volumes would be huge. 400 rolls per restaurant per day, times 5 outlets times 6 days would mean 12,000 rolls per week! The contract price would be 6p per roll, delivered to each restaurant.

Serena's first thought was that it was hopeless. With a total contribution of only £120 per week, the delivery overhead costs would make the contract a loss maker. Serena's husband was not so sure, though. He phoned the supplier of the flour they used for rolls to see whether a bulk discount could be offered if they pushed their order up by 1,200%! Unsurprisingly, the supplier offered a much cheaper price. Prompted by

	Bread	Rolls	Filled Rolls	Speciality Bread	Pizzas	Cakes	Total
Price	90p	20p	£1.00	£1.25	£3.50	80p	
Direct costs	40p	5p	£0.30p	£0.50p	£1.10	30p	
Contribution p.u.	50p	15p	70p	75p	£2.40	50p	
Sales per week	800	1000	500	400	250	400	
Total contribution	£400	£150	£350	£300	£600	£200	£2,000
Weekly overheads							£1,600
Weekly profit							£400

this, Serena phoned her bakery equipment suppliers and found out about a super-fast machine for mixing and shaping bread rolls. This automation would enable her to cut the direct labour cost per roll. After much pressing of calculator keys, both were convinced they could cut the direct cost per roll to 3p and hold the addition to overheads to £160 per week.

The following morning Serena drove to the restaurant's head office with a basket full of freshly baked rolls. She handed them over confidently and was given an appointment straightaway. Thirty minutes and two cappucinos later, Serena headed home with a signed contract in her hand.

Questions *(50 marks; 70 minutes)*

1 Outline three other pieces of information it would be useful to have to assess the bakery's financial position. *(6)*

2 a Calculate the price elasticity of the Bakery de Bologna's bread. *(5)*

  b Calculate the effect of the price cut on the profitability of the bread, as measured by its total contribution. *(6)*

  c Explain why the price cut might still have been worthwhile for the business as a whole. *(6)*

3 Calculate the effect on the bakery's overall weekly profits of accepting the restaurant's order. *(6)*

4 a Taking into account the information in the text and the data table, consider two other strategies Serena might adopt in future, to build up the profitability of her business. *(12)*

  b Then decide and explain which one of the two you would recommend and why. *(9)*

B2 Case Study

Goodfellow's Holiday Village

Brian Goodfellow is the owner and manager of Goodfellow's Holiday Village. The Holiday Village is based on a former farm in Cumbria and provides accommodation for tourists spending time in the Lake District. Some of the farm buildings have been converted to provide high quality accommodation and fields close to the farm have caravans permanently

sited in them. The Village is located close to a number of the Lake District's most famous attractions and is very popular with tourists. Many return year after year.

Brian has developed three types of accommodation that he offers to his customers.

● **Bed & Breakfast.** Walkers who are only staying for a day or two favour this type of accommodation.

● **Caravans.** A cheaper form of accommodation for tourists who are staying for a week or two and who want to cater for themselves.

● **Converted Farm Buildings.** Tourists choosing this option receive the benefits of luxury accommodation.

	Bed and Breakfast	Caravans	Farm Buildings
Selling price (per week)	£245	£350	£550
Variable costs (per unit)	£165	£260	£440
Annual sales (in weeks)	300	420	160

The table above shows the selling prices, variable costs and sales for the three options over the previous year. Presenting financial information in this way assists Brian in managing his business. For example, this approach allows Brian to calculate total contribution from each of the three options as well as contribution per unit.

The Village's fixed costs are £60,000 per annum. The fixed costs paid by Brian include business rates and interest charges.

Questions *(25 marks, 30 minutes)*

1 Distinguish between 'total contribution' and 'contribution per unit'. *(4)*

2 a Calculate the contribution per unit made by the Bed & Breakfast option. *(2)*

  b How much profit did Goodfellow's Holiday Village make last year? *(5)*

3 Examine one difficulty that Brian might face in classifying all the Village's costs as fixed or variable. *(5)*

4 'Presenting financial information in this way assists Brian in managing his business.' To what extent do you agree with this statement? *(9)*

A Level Exercises

A. REVISION EXERCISES

A1 Data Response

JC Croft Ltd is a small manufacturing company producing electronic components for sale to larger car manufacturers. Although it also accepts specialised 'one-off' contracts it relies mainly on three products. The fixed overheads of the company total £1.8 million per annum. The company provides the following information regarding the three products:

Product	Gizmos	Widgets	Gadgets
Selling price/unit	£40	£60	£80
Variable costs:			
Labour	£20	£38	£54
Materials	£22	£12	£14
Sales (units)	240,000	160,000	80,000

Questions *(30 marks; 35 minutes)*

1 a Calculate the contribution per unit of each product.

(5)

b Calculate the total contribution made by each production line. *(5)*

c Calculate the profit made by the JC Croft Ltd. *(3)*

2 JC Croft Ltd has received an order from an Austrian firm for 20,000 Gadgets at a price of £70 (converted from 100 Euros). Analyse the factors the company should consider before reaching a decision on whether or not to accept the order. *(9)*

3 Evaluate the case for JC Croft Ltd using contribution costing. *(8)*

A2 Data Response

Standex plc designs and sells computer software for banks and investment companies. The software can process thousands of foreign exchange transactions per second. Therefore it has been in high demand in the City of London. Despite the fact that its price tag of £8,750 is £2,000 more than the nearest competitor product, the Standex product has sold well. This has ensured that the £115,000 development costs have been recovered.

Every system sold by Standex costs only £1,550 in variable costs (including installation). The annual fixed overheads of the business are £252,000. In the last 12 months, 105 banks have bought the Standex software. This has generated nearly enough profit to finance the new, improved version the company wants to launch at the end of next year.

Now a Japanese bank has faxed through a request for 15 copies of the software for £75,000. The marketing manager is delighted, but the managing director of Standex responded by saying: 'What a cheek! They're asking for a discount of over 40%! We'll never make any money if we give our product away.' Should the order be accepted or not?

Questions *(30 marks; 35 minutes)*

1 Explain the business importance of the term 'safety margin'. *(5)*

2 Calculate Standex's break-even point and safety margin. *(7)*

3 With sales of 105 units, what was the company's:
a total contribution *(4)*
b profit? *(2)*

4 Consider whether the company should accept the special order from Japan. Evaluate the situation using numerical and qualitative analysis. *(12)*

CASH FLOW MANAGEMENT

Cash flow is the flow of money into and out of a business in a given time period.

18.1 Importance of cash flow management

Managing cash flow is one of the most important aspects of financial management. Without adequate availability of cash from day to day, even the most successful company could fail. As bills become due it is essential that there are sufficient funds to pay them. If a company delays paying its suppliers they may be reluctant to deliver further supplies. Workers will be very unlikely to tolerate not being paid. If bills remain unpaid then the **creditors** of the business may take the company to court. This could result in the company being made insolvent. A sole trader could be made bankrupt.

Cash flow problems are the most common reason for business failure. This is particularly true for new businesses. It is estimated that 70% of businesses that collapse in their first year fail because of cash flow problems.

Cash flow is not the same as profit. Profit is the difference between revenue and costs. It is available:

- to the owners as the return on their investment, or
- can be retained in the business for development of the business.

Cash flow is the movement of money through the business. It is possible for a company to be cash rich but unprofitable. A company may also be profitable but unable to pay its suppliers (creditors). Figure 18.1 shows how a small firm might suffer cash flow difficulties when receiving a large order. It will eventually make £10,000 profit on the order, but in the short term goes £40,000 into the red.

In the short term, cash flow plays a vital role. Businesses can survive without making profit for some time. For long-term survival and – especially – growth, profit is essential.

MANAGING CASH FLOW

To manage cash flow, businesses need to continually review their current and future cash position. They can review their future position by forecasting future cash flows. This will enable them to:

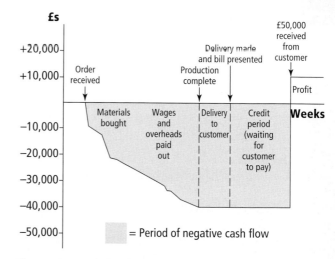

Figure 18.1 Cash flow for small firm accepting a profitable £50,000 order

- anticipate the timing and amounts of any cash shortages
- arrange financial cover for any anticipated shortages of cash
- review the timings and amounts of receipts and payments.

They can review their current cash flow position by:

- comparing the actual situation with the forecast
- analysing when their **debtors** are due to pay
- taking any necessary measures to correct cash shortfalls.

18.2 Cash flow forecasts

A cash flow forecast sets out the anticipated cash inflows and cash outflows over the coming months. Each column shows money coming into and out of the business in that month. The forecast then shows the effect of each month's cash flows upon the firm's cash balance/total. It is like a mini bank statement. One essential rule when constructing a cash flow forecast is that money is shown when it is received or paid. The cash flow forecast will show if there is sufficient cash available each month. A negative cash flow in any time period will indicate that the company has insufficient funds. If the firm has an overdraft facility, this may be sufficient to cope with the period of negative cash flow. If not, preventative action must be taken quickly.

Banks always request a cash flow forecast when considering an application for a loan from a new or an existing business. They do this in order to ensure that the business:

- has enough cash to enable it to survive
- is able to pay the interest on the loan
- will be able to repay the loan
- is aware of the need for cash flow management.

LATE PAYMENT WOES

Surveys repeatedly show that late payment is the number one concern for small businesses. One in four small firms say this is their biggest problem. They are right to be worried. It is estimated that 10,000 small firms collapse each year because customers fail to pay their bills.

The Government has recognised the problem and has been trying to help. In August 2002 the final stage of the Late Payment of Commercial Debts Act 1998 came into force. This law makes it easier for firms to claim interest on late payments and to recover up to £100 of the costs of chasing the debt. Business organisations will also be able to challenge 'grossly unfair' contractual terms on behalf of small firms.

It remains to be seen if this proves helpful. Many consider that in order to get business small firms have to be flexible on payment. Some are worried that large firms will use the new law against smaller ones thus making it even harder for them to survive.

SOLVING CASH FLOW PROBLEMS

If the cash flow forecast predicts a cash shortage the business can take actions to avoid the problem. It can do this in several ways:

1 Speeding up cash inflows: This can be done by:

- Negotiating shorter credit for customers – the average producer in the UK has to wait 75 days to be paid. If customers agree to pay for the goods earlier, cash is received earlier. In a very competitive market the length of credit may be a competitive issue. Large companies often insist on longer credit. Some companies offer discounts to encourage early payment of bills.
- Credit management – businesses can improve cash flow by ensuring that payment is received on time.

This is likely to involve writing reminder letters and making phone calls to persuade customers to pay promptly.

- Factoring – it may be possible to factor the debt. By factoring the company is able to receive 80% of the amount due within 24 hours of an invoice being presented. The factor then collects the money from the customer when the credit period is over. And pays the seller the remaining 20% less the factoring fees. These depend on the length of time before the payment is due, the credit rating of the creditor and current rates of interest. The fees are usually no more than 5% of the total value of the sale.

THE FACTORING BUSINESS

Alex Lawrie is the UK's largest factoring company. It is part of the Lloyds TSB group and is based in Banbury. It offers a complete payment collection service. It will send out invoices to customers and undertake to collect the payments. Typically it will pass 85% of the invoice value to the company within 24 hours of the invoice being sent out. The rest of the money is sent when payment is received.

The advantage to the business is to ease cash flow by delivering money from the sale much earlier than can normally be expected. It handles the invoicing and relieves the company from the burden of credit control.

The cost of the service is around 1% of annual turnover. In addition, the business will pay interest on the money that it receives until Alex Lawrie gets it in from customers. This is roughly equivalent to the cost of an overdraft. The factoring company would normally only take the company on if it has a turnover of more than £50,000 a year.

2 Delaying cash outflows: This can be done by:

- Negotiating longer credit for supplies – this postpones cash outflows, which can help the firm get through a difficult period. The length of credit will often depend on the stability of the company. New companies often have difficulty in negotiating credit.
- Leasing rather than buying equipment – expenditure on fixed assets is a substantial drain on cash, especially for new businesses. By leasing rather than buying, the cash can remain in the business.
- Renting rather than buying buildings – this also allows capital to remain in the business.

3 Cutting or delaying expenditure: Ways of decreasing expenditure include:

- decreasing levels of stock
- cutting costs
- postponing expenditure, e.g. on new company cars.

4 Finding additional funding to cover cash shortages: This can be done by:

- Using an overdraft – an overdraft is arranged with a bank. It allows the business to overdraw up to an agreed limit negotiated in advance. Overdrafts usually incur high rates of interest. As much as 6% over **base rate**. As Figure 18.2 shows, however, an overdraft ensures the firm only borrows money on the days it really needs it. It is a very flexible form of borrowing. This makes it suitable for small or short-term shortages of cash. Although it should only be used to fund short-term problems, a recent study of firms in Bristol found that 70% of small firms had a permanent overdraft. A risky aspect of an overdraft is that the bank can withdraw the facility at any time and demand instant repayment. So, when a firm needs it most, such as in a recession, it may find the bank has withdrawn it.

Figure 18.2 Daily cash balances for a firm with a £25,000 overdraft

- Taking out a short-term loan – this incurs a lower rate of interest than an overdraft. Although less flexible than an overdraft, short-term loans offer more security and are cheaper.

- Taking out a long-term loan – this is more appropriate when the financial need is for a longer term, for example a three-year loan to help fund a new computer network.
- Sale and leaseback of assets – if a business has fixed assets it may be possible to negotiate a sale and lease-back arrangement. This will release capital and give an immediate inflow of cash. The equipment will be paid for through a leasing arrangement. This will be a regular and ongoing cost that must be budgeted for.

Whatever measure is chosen it needs to be effective in the short term. The action chosen will depend on the firm's circumstances at the time.

10.3 How reliable are cash flow forecasts?

Although they are useful, cash flow forecasts are only as good as the estimates they are based on. Businesses need to be aware that the figures are estimates and to build in some safety margins.

Companies should ask themselves what would happen if:

- sales were lower
- the customer did not pay up on time
- prices of materials were higher than expected.

Using spreadsheets enables companies to look at some of these possibilities. With the use of spreadsheets it is possible to adjust both the timings and amounts. This enables a business to evaluate the most likely and the worst case situations.

As well as being useful for ensuring successful start-ups, cash flow forecasts can also be used to provide an ongoing check on future cash flow. They can also be used to evaluate the effect of accepting a special order.

Example:

Treasured Memories produces commemorative pottery. It has been approached by a London store to supply a limited edition of 1,000 plates for a royal wedding. The plates will sell to the store for £35 each. The cost of materials is £9 per plate and labour costs

Cash flow forecast for Treasured Memories

	SEPT.	OCT.	NOV.	DEC.	JAN.	FEB.	MARCH
Cash in							£35,000
Cash out							
Wages	£2,000	£2,000	£2,000	£2,000			
Materials		£2,250	£2,250	£2,250	£2,250		
Other costs	£750	£750	£750	£750			
Total outflow	£2,750	£5,000	£5,000	£5,000	£2,250		
Opening balance	0	(£2,750)	(£7,750)	(£12,750)	(£17,750)	(£20,000)	(£20,000)
Closing balance	(£2,750)	(£7,750)	(£12,750)	(£17,750)	(£20,000)	(£20,000)	£15,000

are £8 each. Additional costs will be £3 per plate. The store wants to have the plates available for sale from next January. The store will pay for the goods next March. The plates will take four months to produce so production needs to start this September. Production will be spread evenly over four months. Suppliers will give one month's credit for the materials. The order seems too good to refuse but the finance manager is worried. He has produced the cash flow forecast shown at the bottom of page 124.

The cash flow forecast shows that although the order is profitable it could cause serious cash flow problems. If the company is to accept the order, the bank manager needs to be asked to provide an overdraft facility of at least £20,000. It also needs to include any interest costs in the decision making.

Overtrading is when firms try to expand without having sufficient financial backing. Many firms try to finance growth by using working capital. This is a risky strategy that may result in cash flow problems. In some cases it is possible to expand the business using cash available topped up with overdrafts, but this could put the business at risk. Any delay in payment or unexpected problem may result in severe cash flow problems. It is generally considered better for firms to finance growth by using long term capital such as retained profit or business loans.

ISSUES FOR **analysis**

When answering a question on cash flow management, it is important to understand that the figures are only the starting point for analysis and decision making. Consideration needs to be given to:

- The validity of the figures – who constructed the forecast? Is he or she unbiased? Reliable?
- What the figures show.
- The possible solutions to any problems.
- The advantages and disadvantages of the possible solutions.
- The need to take full account of the circumstances of the business. If sales are to a foreign country such as Russia, payment may not be certain and even if it arrives, changes in currency values may make cash inflows worth fewer pounds than forecast.
- The differences between cash flow and profitability.

18.4 Cash flow management
an evaluation

There is no doubt that cash flow management is a vital ingredient in the success of any small business. For a new business, cash flow forecasting helps to answer key questions. Is the venture viable? How

Business

IN

— **SMALL FIRMS AND CASH FLOW**

Girobank asked a sample of 200 businesses with turnover of between £1 million and £100 million if they would consider loans secured against the assets of their business to expand their operations.

31% said overdrafts are their preferred way of financing growth. 9% dislike debt so much that they will not undertake any kind of borrowing. 11% have no idea how they would fund expansion. 49% did say they would use loans when expanding:

- 28% like it because payments are structured and it aids financial planning.
- 16% would use loans because they never have sufficient capital.
- 5% would use it to protect their existing capital.

One significant finding was that smaller companies prefer to use overdrafts when expanding. Amongst firms with 1–10 employees, 48% prefer overdrafts to loans.

Gareth Williams, head of marketing at Girobank, said: 'An overdraft is flexible and a useful source of working capital – it helps many businesses cope with the ebbs and flows of day-to-day trading.Companies should be wary of using it to fund long-term expansion. Overdrafts can be repayable on demand, which may severely disrupt cash flow.'

much capital is needed? Which are the most dangerous months? For an existing business the cash flow forecast identifies the amount and timing of any cash flow problems in the future. It is also useful for evaluating new orders or ventures.

Nevertheless, completing a cash flow forecast does not ensure survival. Consideration needs to be given to its usefulness and limitations. It must be remembered that cash flow forecasts are based on estimates. These estimates are not just amounts but also timings. The firm must be aware that actual figures can differ wildly from estimates – especially for a new, inexperienced firm. When preparing cash flow forecasts managers need to ask themselves 'what if?'. A huge mistake is to only look at one central forecast. Far better to look at best case and worst case scenarios. Spreadsheets allow for easy manipulation of data. It is easy to see the impact of single and multiple changes to the forecast figures. This should help to reduce the risks. It does not guarantee results. Continual awareness of the economic and market climate is just as important as number crunching.

bankruptcy – applies to individuals. If a sole trader or partnership is unable to pay its bills the creditors can take the debtor to court and have the individual declared bankrupt.

base rate – the interest rate set by the Bank of England which high street banks use to set their savings and loan interest rates.

credit control – the management of debtors. It includes vetting potential customers for creditworthiness, following up on late payment and pursuing bad debts.

creditors – individuals or other businesses that are owed money by the business.

debtors – individuals or companies who owe money to the business.

insolvency – applies to companies. When unpaid creditors take a debtor to court the company is declared insolvent. It may be closed down, which is known as liquidation. It could be put into receivership.

AS Level Exercises

A. REVISION QUESTIONS
(35 marks; 70 minutes)

Read the unit, then answer:

1 What is meant by 'cash flow'?   *(4)*
2 Why is it important to manage cash flow?   *(5)*
3 What is a cash flow forecast?   *(3)*
4 What benefit might a firm get from reviewing its current cash position?   *(4)*
5 Explain two limitations of cash flow forecasts.   *(4)*
6 Give two reasons why a bank manager might want to see a cash flow forecast before giving a loan to a new business.   *(2)*
7 Identify three ways a business might benefit from factoring its debts.   *(3)*
8 How might a firm benefit from delaying its cash outflows?   *(3)*
9 What problems might a firm face if its cash flow forecast proved unreliable?   *(3)*
10 How might a firm benefit from constructing its cash flow forecasts on a computer spreadsheet?   *(4)*

B REVISION EXERCISES

B1 Data Response

Kerri's soft drinks
Kerri has been helping a friend to refill drinks machines. She now has the opportunity to take on the franchise as the friend is going to college. The franchise is fairly simple. She must purchase a minimum quantity of juice each month. The minimum is £150. This has to be paid immediately, as the supplier does not allow any credit. With this amount of stock her friend has been making sales of £450 per month. This, however, is not received until two months later.

Other expenses include van rental of £100 per month and other costs which total £100 each month.
Kerri has £50 cash in the bank. Her father has offered her a loan of £400.

Questions   *(30 marks; 35 minutes)*
1 Assuming that Kerri starts the business in January, construct a cash flow forecast for the first six months.   *(10)*
2 Comment on the cash flow.   *(5)*
3 Suggest and discuss possible solutions to any problems you can see.   *(9)*
4 Do you think she should take on the franchise?   *(6)*

B2 Data Response

Merlin Construction

Merlin Construction has planning permission to convert an old office block into four flats. The directors managed to borrow £130,000 from the bank in January. They used £100,000 to buy the building that month. The work will start in January and take nine months to complete. The plan is to build and sell the two upstairs flats in June and then complete the ground floor flats. These will be sold in September. The flats should sell for £60,000 each. Materials are estimated to cost about £10,000 a month with one month's credit. Wages and salaries will be £4,000 a month. Interest charges will be £1,000 a month. Other expenses will be £1,000 a month.

Questions   *(30 marks; 35 minutes)*

1 Construct a cash flow forecast for the business for January to September.   *(10)*
2 What does this cash flow forecast show?   *(4)*
3 Suggest and discuss three possible courses of action. *(12)*
4 Outline two ways in which the cash flow forecast might be unreliable.   *(4)*

B3 Data Response

Statutory Interest for Late Payments

The Labour government has announced that it is planning to help small businesses by introducing legislation to control late payment by debtors. Large companies are accused of delaying payment of bills. This puts pressure on the cash flow of small firms. One idea that has been suggested is to make compulsory interest payments due on overdue debts.

Industry views are divided. While many think that this will be helpful to small firms there is concern about how it would be enforced and the size of company that would be affected. Others are worried that as small firms tend to be net debtors they could face interest charges if they are late with payments. Another problem is that if the bill only covered small firms this would put them at a disadvantage compared to larger firms when negotiating sales.

Questions   *(30 marks; 35 minutes)*

1 Explain how late payment affects businesses.   *(6)*
2 Why is the government trying to help small businesses? *(6)*
3 Why is it necessary to introduce legislation to encourage businesses to pay their bills promptly?   *(4)*
4 What is meant by the suggestion that small firms tend to be 'net debtors'?   *(4)*
5 Do you agree that small firms would be at a competitive disadvantage if the bill were introduced? Explain your answer.   *(10)*

A Level Exercises

A. REVISION QUESTIONS
(30 marks; 60 minutes)

Read the unit, then answer:

1 Why is cash flow management a vital business activity? *(4)*
2 What are the limitations of a cash flow forecast? *(4)*
3 Examine Figure 18.1. Explain how the firm's cash flows would be affected if it used a debt factor. *(4)*

4 Outline three actions managers might take to correct a cash shortage.   *(6)*
5 Examine Figure 18.2. Outline two ways the firm might cope with a decision by the bank to reduce the overdraft facility to £15,000.   *(4)*
6 How might a cash flow forecast be useful in evaluating whether or not to accept a large customer order? *(5)*
7 Why might a cash flow forecast give a false sense of security?   *(3)*

B. REVISION EXERCISES

B1 Case Study

East to West

Shushma and Arif are cousins. On a recent visit to India they were impressed by the beautiful silk and embroidered fabrics being produced in their uncle's village. They have decided to set up a business that they will call East to West, to import and sell the fabrics. They have joint savings of £6,000.

This will pay for a trip to India and the purchase of their first lot of material for £4,000. Half of the fabric will be sold to a local garment manufacturer. He will pay £4,000 for it in four monthly instalments. They plan to sell the remainder on market stalls two days a week. They hope to get a higher price for these sales. They will need to buy a van in March. They estimate that £3,000 should buy a reliable one. The running costs for the van are estimated to be £600 a year for insurance, £150 for road tax and £150 a month for petrol and maintenance. The insurance and road tax will have to be paid when they purchase the van. They plan to visit India in March to purchase the fabric and

to start selling in April. They will visit India again in July to purchase another £4,000 of fabric. They will pay themselves £200 a month each.

They realise that their savings are not going to be sufficient to start the business. They have made an appointment to see a bank manager and have produced the cash flow forecast shown below.

Questions (30 marks, 35 minutes)

1 On the basis of the cash flow shown, how much money do you think they need to borrow from the bank? Explain the figure you recommend. (6)

2 If you were the bank manager, what else would you want to know before granting the loan? (4)

3 Would you give them a loan? Explain your reasons. (6)

4 The bank manager is unwilling to give them more than a £2,000 loan. Discuss two alternative courses of action they could take. (6)

5 Consider the ways in which the cash flow forecast may help Shushma and Arif make a success of their business start-up. (8)

Cash flow forecast, East to West (£s)

	March	April	May	June	July	Aug.	Sept.
Sales to garment manufacturer		1,000	1,000	1,000	1,000	1,000	1,000
Market sales		1,500	1,500	1,500	1,500	1,500	1,500
Total income		2,500	2,500	2,500	2,500	2,500	2,500
Fabric	4,000				4,000		
Van	3,000						
Road tax	150						
Insurance	600						
Petrol/maintenance	150	150	150	150	150	150	150
Travel	1600				1600		
Wages	400	400	400	400	400	400	400
Market stalls		300	300	300	300	300	300
Total expenditure	9900	850	850	850	6450	850	850
Monthly balance	(9900)	1650	1650	1650	(3950)	1650	1650
Opening balance	6000	(3900)	(2250)	(600)	1050	(2900)	(1250)
Closing balance	(3900)	(2250)	(600)	1050	(2900)	(1250)	400

C. ESSAY QUESTIONS

1 'Cash flow management is more important than profit.' To what extent do you believe this to be true?

2 Analyse the importance of cash flow forecasting for a new business venture.

3 'Cash flow management is important for small companies but not for large companies.' Discuss this statement.

CONTROL OF WORKING CAPITAL

Working capital is the finance available for the day-to-day running of the business.

19.1 What is working capital?

All businesses need money. It is required by the business to buy machinery and equipment. This expenditure on **fixed assets** is known as *capital expenditure*. The business also needs money to buy materials or stock and to pay wages and the day-to-day bills such as electricity and telephone bills. This money is known as *working capital*.

Managing working capital is about ensuring that cash available is sufficient to meet the cash requirements at any one time. This is also known as having enough *liquidity*. If the bills cannot be paid on time there are serious consequences. In the worst situation the business may fail. Insufficient working capital is the commonest cause of business failure. Managing working capital is therefore a vital business activity.

19.2 The liquidity cycle

Managing working capital is a continuous process. When a business starts up it takes time to generate income. Money to pay for stock and the running costs will need to be found from the initial capital invested in the business. As the business cycle gets going, income from customers will be available to pay for expenditure. The firm needs to ensure that there is always sufficient cash to meet daily requirements. If the business is expanding or takes on a special order, extra care needs to be taken. Sufficient funds are needed to pay for the additional expenditure until the revenue arrives. This continuous process is known as the liquidity cycle. This is shown in Figure 19.1, which also shows why working capital is sometimes referred to as circulating capital.

As can be seen from Figure 19.1, managing working capital is about two things:

- ensuring the business has enough finance to meet its needs
- keeping cash moving rapidly through the cycle, so there is enough to meet future orders.

Each business will have its own distinct cycle.

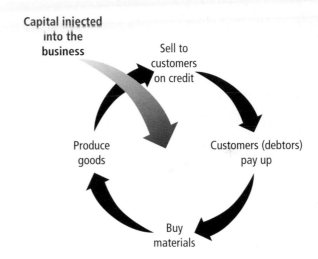

Figure 19.1 The liquidity cycle

Businesses will also be subject to unexpected events and need to be able to cope with these. Therefore it is helpful to have a generous overdraft limit, which can be drawn upon when needed.

19.3 Problems caused by insufficient working capital

- With suppliers – a firm with too little working capital will struggle to pay its bills on time. It has no spare cash. It may resort to delaying payments. It may need to borrow more money. Delaying payment means that suppliers are not paid on time. They may reduce the **credit period** or refuse credit for a future order.
- With banks – if the business is resorting to borrowing it will have the additional cost of interest charges. If the bank is concerned about the liquidity situation it may impose higher charges. The business will find it more difficult to get loans. Any lender will want to be assured that the company is managing its working capital.
- Opportunities may be missed – the business may not be able to buy supplies in bulk. This removes the advantage of lower bulk-buying prices. Even more importantly it may have to refuse a large

order because it cannot finance the extra working capital requirement.

In the longer term, shortage of cash means that no funds are available for development. The business will not be able to grow. In extreme cases creditors may ask for the business to be declared insolvent. A sole trader or partnership will be declared bankrupt. Most creditors will only take this action if they feel that there is little hope of being paid. They will look at the future prospects and past performance of the business.

19.4 How much working capital do businesses need?

The working capital requirement varies from business to business. It depends on:

- The length of the business process. There are huge variations in the length of the liquidity cycle for different businesses. A fruit stall market trader buys supplies for cash from a wholesaler in the morning and sells everything (for cash) by late afternoon. The cycle takes less than a day. By contrast, a small construction firm building four houses may take a year between starting the project and having cash paid by a new homeowner.
    The length of the business cycle is a combination of:
    - The length of the production process. This depends on the product. A service industry such as a restaurant has a very short production time. To construct a road bridge takes a little longer.
    - The time taken to get the product to the market. Overseas markets have a longer distribution process. Seasonal products may be manufactured but not delivered for many months.
- The credit given to purchasers. This depends on market conditions. As a general rule business customers expect longer credit than private customers. A retail business receives payments sooner than a manufacturer or wholesaler. The relationship between firms also affects the credit period. A large, important customer may demand longer credit. A sole supplier can insist on early payment.
- The credit given for purchases of materials or stock. Most businesses obtain credit for their purchases. The length of time allowed before payment depends on:
    - how established the firm is (an established firm can negotiate longer credit than a new firm)
    - its credit record (a firm with a good record of paying can negotiate longer credit)
    - its credit worthiness (a firm that appears solvent can obtain longer credit than a firm that is struggling)
    - market conditions (the credit period varies from industry to industry; credit is often used as part of the sales package)
    - the size of the order (larger orders may get longer credit)
    - regular orders (regular customers expect longer credit than occasional customers).

The business needs to take into account both the timing and the amounts involved when working out its working capital requirements. It also needs to include an allowance for uncertainty. An extra 10% on top of the expected cash requirement would usually be sufficient. For a new small firm such as a new restaurant, though, a bigger safety net can be wise. It can take months for word to spread sufficiently to push the business above its break-even point.

19.5 Can a business have too much working capital?

In America and Britain it is thought important that a business should not have too much working capital. The term 'too much' implies that the capital would be wasted. In some ways this is true. There is no point in having too much capital tied up in stock or giving too much credit to customers. There is a problem, though, in defining what 'too much' actually means.

Japanese and German firms have always tended to adopt a very cautious approach to their finances. In the early 1990s many were criticised by English analysts. They questioned why firms such as Honda and Sony had billions of dollars of cash lying idle on their **balance sheets**. Why so much working capital? Fortunately for companies in both countries, their caution helped them enormously when severe recessions hit them (especially Japan) in the mid-1990s.

It should always be remembered that whereas you can have too much stock or too many debtors, you can never have too much cash!

19.6 How can a business manage its working capital?

Maintaining good liquidity in a business is about managing the elements of the liquidity cycle. There are several ways that the business can minimise its working capital needs. These are centered on:

- Controlling cash.
- Obtaining maximum possible credit for purchases – delaying payment of bills will allow time for receipt of income from customers.
- Getting goods to the market in shortest possible time – the sooner goods reach the customer the sooner payment is received. Production and distribution should be as efficient as possible.
- Collecting payments efficiently – the business should aim to collect payment as soon as possible.

It can do this by increasing the proportion of cash customers.

i   If cash payment is not possible because of market conditions the firm should give the shortest possible credit period. Early payment should be encouraged by offering incentives such as discounts for early payment.

ii If credit is granted the business should control its debtors – confusingly this is known as credit control. Credit control involves:

- ensuring the debtor is creditworthy before granting credit (by getting a bank reference)
- constantly reviewing the credit position of existing customers
- following up on non-payment.

● Minimising spending on fixed assets – this keeps cash in the business. The business must balance its need for cash and its need for fixed assets. A compromise is to lease rather than buy equipment. This increases expenses but conserves capital.

● Controlling costs – this can be done by keeping administrative and production costs to a minimum. Efficient production reduces costs. Savings may be possible by upgrading machinery to replace labour. This has an impact on short-term capital availability but reduces the working capital requirements over the longer term.

● Stock management (see Unit 56) – stocks, whether raw material or finished goods, tie up money. If the business minimises its stock levels, working capital requirements will be lower. Stock management includes:

- ensuring an efficient production process, minimising work in progress
- ensuring goods are delivered promptly, minimising stocks of finished goods
- minimising stock losses, for example by efficient stock rotation.

Longer term improvements can stem from a move to just-in-time production (see Unit 50). This should reduce stocks of raw materials, work in progress and finished goods. The firm must balance the cost of stockholding with incentives to buy in bulk. Together with JIT purchasing, this helps to minimise stock losses from obsolescence. Good warehousing and security reduces other losses.

19.7 Causes of liquidity problems

Many liquidity problems are a result of the firm not setting aside sufficient money for working capital. This results in a hand-to-mouth existence. If short-term funds are used for purchasing fixed assets this could cause working capital problems. There will be constant pressure to find the money to repay the borrowing.

Good management of liquidity and an awareness of external events will be all that is necessary for most businesses to avoid liquidity problems. However, there is always a need to be prudent. Businesses can experience

DELL ON LINE

Dell Computer Corporation is the world's no. 1 personal computer manufacturer with an estimated 14% of the global market. It has an enviable record of success. One factor in this success is the careful management of stock. Computers are made to the customer specification. At the assembly plant they do not keep stocks of finished machines, only component parts. After an order is received the computer is constructed. It is then shipped to a distribution centre. Here it meets up with its various peripherals. These items such as monitors and keyboards are not held in stock but are delivered to the distribution centres directly from the suppliers.

Minimising its investment in working capital in this way has helped Dell to finance and maintain its incredible growth. It has also helped the company to avoid the problems of holding stocks of computers when a change in technology makes yesterday's models obsolete and slashes their value.

unexpected problems. A firm may feel confident in its liquidity position until a major customer goes into liquidation. Suddenly the debtors payment expected next week becomes a bad debt. Often when one firm goes under, others are dragged down with it.

Internal causes of liquidity problems can include:

● Production problems – interruptions to production delay the product reaching the market. Prolonged delays such as strikes are a major problem.
● Marketing problems – if demand for a product is slow, sales staff may offer longer credit terms to try to shift unsold stocks.
● Management problems – poor stock or production management can result in additional costs.

External causes of liquidity problems include:

● Changes to the economic climate – this may include inflation, recession or changes to taxation.
● Lower demand – this may be caused by recession, changes in fashion or seasonal factors.
● Unexpected non-payment by customers – this may be a payment delay or may become a bad debt if the customer goes out of business.

19.8 Dealing with liquidity problems

Any business may be faced from time to time with a liquidity emergency. In this situation there are several measures that can be taken. The following table shows the measures, the result of them and possible pitfalls.

Dealing with working capital shortages

MEASURE	RESULT	DRAWBACKS
Discounting prices	• Increases sales • Reduces stock • Generates cash	• May undermine pricing structure • May leave low stocks for future activity
Reduce purchases	• Cuts down expenditure	• May leave business without means to continue
Negotiate more credit	• Allows time to pay	• May tarnish credit reputation
Delay payment of bills	• Retains cash	• Will tarnish credit reputation
Credit control – chase debtors	• Gets payments in and sooner	• May upset customers
Negotiate additional finance	• Provides cash	• Interest payments add to expenditure • Has to be repaid
Factor debts	• Generates cash • A proportion of the income is guaranteed	• Reduces income from sales • Costs can be high
Selling assets	• Releases cash	• Assets are no longer available
Sale and leaseback	• Releases cash • Asset is still available for use	• Increases costs – lease has to be paid • Company no longer owns asset

19.9 Working capital in the balance sheet

One of the ways a firm can monitor its working capital is by use of its **balance sheet**. On the balance sheet working capital is **current assets** minus current liabilities. It is also known as *net current assets*.

current assets
=
stock (raw materials, part-produced goods and finished goods)
+
debtors (money owed to the business)
+
cash (cash held in the business or in bank accounts)

current liabilities
=
creditors
(money owed by the business for goods or services)
+
short-term loans/overdrafts
(to be repaid within one year)

Example:
P Perfect Ltd manufactures scientific instruments. The assets section of its balance sheet for last year showed:

Fixed assets		£750,000
Stock	£95,000	
Debtors	£65,000	
Cash	£10,000	
Current assets		£170,000
Creditors	£80,000	
Overdraft	£20,000	
Current liabilities		£100,000
Working capital		£70,000
Assets employed		£820,000

This shows the business has £70,000 of working capital. In other words, of the £820,000 invested in the business, £750,000 is tied up in fixed assets. Only £70,000 is available for the day-to-day running of the firm. Despite having only £70,000 available, the firm has managed to obtain £170,000 of current assets. This is because it has obtained £100,000 of short-term finance from credit given by suppliers (creditors) and a bank overdraft.

If a rush order required the purchase of £100,000 more stock, where could the money come from? P Perfect has only £10,000 of cash. Perhaps the creditors or the overdraft levels could be increased? If not, the firm would need to increase its working capital.

WAYS OF INCREASING WORKING CAPITAL

• sell some fixed assets for cash, i.e. switch resources from fixed capital to working capital
• raise a long-term loan to increase the assets employed, but leave the extra cash in current assets
• raise more share capital – this will also increase assets employed and current assets
• over the coming months, ensure that trading profits are retained in the business to build up the cash total.

19.10 How useful is the balance sheet?

Basing working capital management on balance sheet ratios has its limitations. The balance sheet gives only a snapshot view. It does not give any indication of timing. Perhaps the money owed has to be paid tomorrow, but the debtor payments are not due for three months. If working capital is to be well managed it needs to be considered continually. What bills are due next week? What cash is available and how much do we expect to receive?

The balance sheet is also historic. It is a record of what has happened in the past. Good management of working capital is about looking at the future. It has been known for firms to boost their working capital position just before the balance sheet is prepared. This window dressing will make the liquidity situation seem better.

A more useful tool for managing working capital is the cash flow forecast. It gives the business an indication of the expected flow of cash in and out of the business. It will highlight any danger times when there appears to be a cash shortfall (see Unit 18).

ISSUES FOR analysis

To analyse working capital management in a business case study or data response question it is important to remember:

- For small firms especially, the liquidity cycle is the equivalent of blood circulating round the body. If the cash dries up, the firm dies.
- The problems caused by too little or too much working capital.
- How businesses can cope with poor working capital situations and the pitfalls of any actions.
- Business requirements for working capital will depend on the nature of the business. It is also necessary to understand that managing working capital is not just about cash management. It goes far deeper and involves most aspects of the business. As in most Business Studies situations, care should be taken to relate the answer to the circumstances of the particular business.

It would be nice if there were a perfect, 'right' level of working capital. But there is not. Sainsbury's has operated very successfully for decades with a hugely negative working capital. This is because it sells its stock quickly, yet gets a long credit period from suppliers. So the creditors' item (a liability) is huge, but stocks (an asset) are low. As it is a cash-rich business, it is always confident that enough cash will come through today's tills to pay yesterday's bills. So the tell-tale sign about working capital is not whether it is high or low, positive or negative. The key issues are: can the firm fund the short-term actions it would like to take, and is the working capital position improving or worsening?

19.11 Control of working capital
an evaluation

Managing working capital is very important for every business. As in many other areas of business it is about getting the balance right. Too much liquidity is wasteful – too little can be disastrous. Businesses need to consider working capital requirements right from the outset. Most new businesses underestimate their working capital needs. Typically, firms only allow £20 of working capital for every £100 of fixed capital (assets). Accountants usually advise a £50:£50 ratio.

Managing working capital is not just about managing cash flow. The timing and amounts of cash flow are important, but working capital management goes beyond that. It is about managing the whole business. In this respect it is an integrated activity. It involves each aspect of the company. Efficient production keeps costs to a minimum and turns raw inputs into finished goods in the shortest possible time. Effective management of stock can have considerable impact on working capital requirements. Effective marketing ensures that the goods are sold and that demand is correctly estimated. This avoids wasted production. Cash then flows in from sales. Efficient distribution gets the goods to the customer quickly. The accounting department can help to control costs. Effective credit control improves cash flow. Each of these can reduce the need for cash and/or ensure that sufficient cash is available for the business to meet its objectives.

KEY terms

bad debts – payments that are long overdue and cannot be expected to be received.

balance sheet – a statement of the assets and liabilities of the business at a point in time (usually the end of the financial year). It shows where the money is in the business and where it came from.

bankruptcy – applies to individuals. If a sole trader or partnership is unable to pay its bills the creditors can take the debtor to court and have the individual declared bankrupt.

credit period – the length of time allowed for payment.

current assets – cash or assets that can be turned into cash. This includes stock and money owed to the company.

factoring – obtaining part-payment of the amount owed from a factoring company. The factoring company will then collect the debt and pass over the balance of the payment.

fixed assets – items that are used over and over again by the business. They include buildings, equipment and vehicles.

insolvency – applies to companies. When unpaid creditors take a debtor to court the company may be declared insolvent.

AS Level Exercises

A. REVISION QUESTIONS
(40 marks; 70 minutes)

Read the unit, then answer:

1 What is working capital? *(3)*
2 What is capital expenditure? *(3)*
3 What does it mean when it is said that a firm has enough liquidity? *(3)*
4 What is working capital used for? Give two examples. *(5)*
5 What problems might arise if a firm is operating with very low working capital? *(4)*
6 Why might a business be unable to get a loan or overdraft if it has working capital difficulties? *(4)*
7 Explain two factors that influence the amount of working capital required by a firm. *(4)*
8 Outline three ways in which a business can improve its working capital situation. *(6)*
9 How does better stock management help a firm to control its working capital requirements? *(5)*
10 List three ways in which stock levels can be reduced. *(3)*

B. REVISION EXERCISES

B1 Data Response

Small Businesses Hit by Economic Downturn

It is normally expected that small businesses are the hardest hit by any economic downturn. However, Barclays Bank has reported that the number of small firms closing down in the third quarter of 1998 was less than the previous quarter despite the slow-down in economic growth. There was, in fact, a net gain in the number of businesses. The number of new business start-ups was 118,000 in the period from July to September whilst the number of closures was 110,000. Barclays' conclusion was that the economic downturn was having more impact on larger businesses and that smaller businesses might not feel the impact until the following year.

A different survey by a firm specialising in factoring showed a slightly different picture. Its research indicated that the hardest hit firms were those with turnover above £50 million or below £2.5 million. They highlighted several problems faced by businesses:

- In order to combat fierce competition, firms were having to discount prices. This caused a reduction in profitability.

- Firms have reduced their stock levels, including raw materials, work in progress and finished goods.
- There was a high level of cancelled orders.
- Payments were being received on average 23 days after their due date. This situation was unchanged from the previous year except in the clothing industry where payments had slipped a further 10 days.
- Exporters were having a difficult time. They were hard hit by the strong pound and were experiencing the longest payment delays since the last recession.

Source: Adapted from *The Times*, 10/11/98

Questions *(30 marks; 35 minutes)*
1 Explain the meaning of the term 'factoring'. *(3)*
2 Barclays feels that small firms would be hit by the economic downturn in the following year (1999). What changes might firms need to make to their working capital management to prepare for a period of falling demand? *(6)*
3 How do increased payment delays affect a firm's working capital? *(8)*
4 On average, customers pay their bills 23 days late. In fact, some will pay early, others on time and some very late indeed. How might factoring be of use to a firm in this situation of uncertainty? *(5)*
5 What are the advantages and disadvantages of firms reducing stocks in times of economic downturn? *(8)*

B2 Case Study

Hatta Lighting

Hatta Lighting plc makes component parts for the car industry. It started out making bulbs but now also supply a range of electrical and electronic components. The company started as a family-run business but expansion has meant that five years ago it became a public limited company. During the last two years its performance has been mediocre and dividends paid to shareholders have been falling. The share price has also fallen. One of the largest shareholders has decided that change was necessary and has managed to exert enough pressure to replace the established chairman. The new chairman has a strong financial background but has been involved in the retailing industry for many years. He has asked the management team to produce some information. The team has come up with the following:

	Last year	This year	Industry average
Stock turnover materials	44 days	48 days	40 days
Stock of finished goods	£780,000	£910,000	£700,000
Average days before payment	38	54	42
Working capital at year end	£560,000	£380,000	Not available

After examining these figures the new chairman is very concerned about the liquidity situation of the company. Several large debts totalling £500,000 are due to be paid short. The firm does not have sufficient cash available to pay these. He sees this as being the most urgent issue facing the company and he has arranged an urgent meeting of all the managers. He has asked each of the three department heads (marketing, finance and production) to come up with ideas to solve the problem.

Questions *(45 marks; 60 minutes)*

1 What might be the reasons for the increase in the stock of finished goods and materials? *(6)*
2 Consider what suggestions the production director might make? Explain your reasoning. *(10)*
3 The finance director sees slow payment as his major problem. Examine the ways in which the firm might tackle this problem. *(10)*
4 Outline the contribution the marketing department might make to help improve the liquidity situation. *(9)*
5 Apart from tackling the issue of slow payment, consider what other short-term measures the firm might take to overcome the immediate liquidity crisis. *(10)*

A Level Exercises

A. REVISION QUESTIONS

(30 marks; 60 minutes)

Read the unit then answer:

1 What is meant by the 'liquidity cycle'? *(4)*
2 Why might a shortage of working capital prevent a firm from growing? *(4)*
3 What determines the length of the business process? *(3)*
4 Why is it thought advisable for a firm not to have too much working capital? *(3)*
5 What impact does the length of the business process have on working capital? *(4)*
6 Getting money in from customers is a vital part of working capital management. List two things a firm can do to ensure that cash is collected efficiently. *(2)*
7 What internal factors could affect a firm's liquidity? *(4)*
8 List two measures that a firm can take to deal with a liquidity problem. Outline the problems that this might cause. *(6)*

B. REVISION EXERCISES

B1 Data Response

Pakistan's Cement Industry Faces Collapse

The cement industry in Pakistan is facing a serious cash flow crisis. The industry which has an annual production capacity of 15 million tonnes is facing bankruptcy. If it collapses it will take with it many small banks who have acted as guarantors. The slowdown in industrial and infrastructure development and the reduction in house building is a direct reflection of the slump in economic activity. This has meant reduced demand for cement products. Current production levels are running at 8 million tonnes annually. This has had a serious impact on the cash coming into the business.

The producers recognise that at current levels of demand the industry cannot be profitable. They blame the present government for raising taxes. The latest increase means that tax now accounts for 74% of the price of the product. This has also contributed to the reduction in demand, as the product is now too expensive for smaller purchasers. An increase in prices would produce very little return for the producers and could reduce demand even further.

The problems in the industry, however, go further back. In the early 1990s the industry appeared very profitable and attracted investors. The result was an increase in capacity that was not matched by an increase in demand. At that time the profitability of the industry was helped by a favourable tax regime. The industry was exempt from sales tax and other duties and taxes. These exemptions were subsequently withdrawn in response to pressure on the Pakistani government from the World Bank and the IMF.

One of the largest investors in the industry is Army Welfare Trust, a huge private sector conglomerate with an interest in at least 34 different industrial concerns. Because of its size and diversity it should be able to withstand the cash flow problems in its cement division. Other cement producers without a similar cushion are unlikely to survive.

Source: Adapted from *Khaleej Times UAE*, 12/11/98

Questions
(30 marks; 35 minutes)

1 What percentage level of total capacity is the cement industry now running at? (3)

2 Outline two external factors that have caused the cash flow crisis affecting the cement industry. (4)

3 Explain how the expansion of the industry in the early 1990s contributed to the problems now faced by the industry. (6)

4 Discuss the validity of the view that a conglomerate is more likely to withstand a cash flow problem than a smaller firm. (9)

5 The cash flow problems within this industry have been caused by both internal and external problems. What do you think is the most important factor in maintaining a healthy liquidity situation? (8)

B2 Case Study

Kachins Garments

Kachins is a clothing manufacturer in the Midlands. It is run by a husband and wife team, Chris and Georgina. Georgina's father started the business 35 years ago as a tailor's shop making suits for individual customers. However, there was far too much competition from ready-to-wear high street retailers. Gradually the emphasis was shifted to standardised production of clothes for small independent shops. Over the last 10 years the business has moved to mass producing goods for a large High Street retail chain. By the end of last year 80% of production was for this retailer.

Although working for the retail chain has not been easy – it demands very high standards – both Chris and Georgina feel the firm has benefited from the association. The quality of the finished product has improved significantly. The retailer included high penalty clauses for poor quality goods. The large regular orders meant that money has been available to invest in better equipment. This has enabled the company to reduce costs and so keep prices at a competitive level.

Chris and Georgina became worried towards the end of last year. Unfortunately the retailer has been faced with difficulties as its fashionable image slipped in the high street. Chris and Georgina also suspected that the retailer had been importing more goods from overseas. These have become much cheaper because of the strength of the pound.

In November their worst fears were realised when the retailer cancelled an order for £60,000 worth of goods. This is obviously going to seriously affect their cash flow situation. Chris and Georgina realise that if they are to survive they need to take action. Their accountant has drawn up balance sheets for the previous year and for this financial year. This is shown on the next page.

Balance sheet for year ended 31 December

	Last Year (£s)	This Year (£s)
Fixed assets	670	690
Stock	240	300
Debtors	90	84
Cash	4	2
Total current assets	**334**	**386**
Overdraft	0	27
Creditors	115	140
Total current liabilities	**115**	**167**
Working capital	219	219
Assets employed	**889**	**909**
Loans	300	300
Shareholders' funds	589	609
Total capital employed	**889**	**909**

Questions
(40 marks; 60 minutes)

1 What are the advantages and disadvantages of having one major customer? *(8)*
2 Consider the effect on working capital management of mass producing clothing instead of producing one-off garments to meet specific customer orders. *(8)*
3 From the figures given in the balance sheet, comment on the effect that the cancelled order has had on the liquidity of the business. *(12)*
4 Suggest and evaluate ways in which Chris and Georgina might react to this situation. *(12)*

C. ESSAY QUESTIONS

1 Managing working capital is vital for the future of any business. Discuss.
2 In periods of economic downturn it is even more important to control working capital in the business. Do you agree with this statement?
3 To what extent do you agree with the following statement? 'Managing working capital is not just the business of the finance department. It is the responsibility of everyone in the business.'

SOURCES OF FINANCE

20.1 The need for finance

Whether a business is starting out or developing, it needs money. Businesses starting up need money to invest in fixed assets such as buildings and equipment. This is known as *capital expenditure*. They also need money to purchase materials or to buy in finished goods. The money used to purchase stock and to pay the bills is known as **working capital**. Both the working capital and money for capital expenditure has to be found before the business starts to generate any income.

Once the business is established the income from customers should provide sufficient working capital plus some profit. This profit can be returned to the investors in the business or it could be reinvested in the business. If the business wants to expand it will probably need to find additional finance. Sometimes businesses have problems. They may have a cash problem caused by changes in market conditions. They will need to find additional funding to enable them to continue.

20.2 Sources of finance

The type and amount of finance that is available will depend on several factors. These are:

- **The type of business** – a sole trader will be limited to the capital the owner can put into the business plus any money he or she is able to borrow. A partnership will have the resources of all the partners. A limited company will be able to raise share capital. In order to become a plc it will need to be of a certain size and have a track record of success. This will make borrowing easier.
- **The stage of development of the business** – a new business will find it much harder to raise finance than an established firm. As the business develops it is easier to persuade outsiders to invest in the business. It is also easier to obtain loans as the firm has assets to offer as security.
- **How successful the firm is** – a track record of success will encourage both lenders and investors. Lenders will have more confidence that their loan will be returned. Investors will be keen to invest so they can share in the rising profits.

- **The state of the economy** – when the economy is booming business confidence will be high. It will be easy to raise finance both from borrowing and from investors. In a recession the opposite will be true. It will also be more difficult for businesses to find investors when interest rates are high. They will invest their money in more secure accounts such as building societies. Higher interest rates will also put up the cost of borrowing. This will make it more expensive for the business to borrow.

Finance for business comes from two main sources:

1 inside the business – known as internal finance
2 outside the business – known as external finance.

INTERNAL FINANCE

Retained profit

Once the business starts to generate sales it will hopefully make some profit. This provides a return on the investment in the business. However it is also a source of finance. Research shows that over 60% of business investment comes from reinvested, retained profit.

Squeezed out of working capital

By cutting stocks, chasing up debtors or delaying payments to creditors, cash can be generated from a firm's working capital. This is an internal source of finance. However, when cash is taken from working capital for a purpose such as buying fixed assets, the liquidity position worsens.

Sale of assets

An established business has assets. These can be sold to raise cash. The business loses the asset but has the use of the cash. It makes good business sense for businesses to dispose of redundant assets. They can finance development without extra borrowing. If the asset is needed, it may be possible to sell it, but imme-

> *Reuters, the media company, is looking at releasing £100 million of capital from the sale and leaseback of its London offices. It has appointed NM Rothschild to investigate the options available. Rothschild recently advised the BBC on a £1 billion deal which allowed the broadcaster to raise funds to develop the White City studios at no cost to the licence fee payer.*
>
> *(The Times, 16 August 2002)*

diately lease it back. In this way the business has use of the money and the asset. This is known as sale and leaseback. Recently Marks & Spencer, Safeway and the BBC have used their property to release cash in this way.

EXTERNAL FINANCING

Few firms are able to operate without some external finance, i.e. finance from outside their own resources.

External finance for day-to-day working capital:

Trade credit

This is the simplest form of external financing. The business obtains goods or services from another business. It does not pay for these immediately. The average credit period is two months.

Bank overdrafts

This is the commonest form of borrowing for businesses. It is an effective short-term source of finance. The bank allows the firm to overdraw up to an agreed level. This has the advantages of:

- flexibility
- the firm only needs to borrow what it needs.

It is, however, an expensive way of borrowing, and can be withdrawn instantly by the lender.

Factoring

A factoring company might provide a firm with 80% of its invoiced sales within 24 hours. It then provides the other 20% (minus a fee) after collecting the debt from the firm's customer. This is a common way to finance small, rapidly growing firms with high profit margins.

External finance for growth and expansion:

Leasing

This is a common way to finance the acquisition of new fixed assets. Instead of buying a new fleet of company cars for cash, for example, they are leased. A contract is signed committing the firm to pay a monthly sum for the next three years. The cars never become the firm's property. The business has use of the asset without the capital expenditure.

Loan capital, such as a bank loan

Banks offer a range of loans. They may be medium term or long term with variable or fixed interest rates. Banks will only lend if they are confident the loan will be repaid. They will insist on a well thought out business plan. They are also likely to ask for collateral, i.e. some form of security. For a sole trader this is a personal asset such as a house, which can be sold to repay the debt if the business fails. For other businesses the assets of the business may suffice. The bank may call in the loan if it fears that the business is in trouble.

If the business is unable to get a loan because it is unable to provide security it may be able to take

advantage of the Department of Trade and Industry (DTI) guaranteed loan scheme. Loans from £5,000 to £250,000 are available for periods of between two and ten years. The DTI will guarantee 70% of the loan (85% if the business has been trading for more than two years). The borrower negotiates the terms of the loan with the lender. They pay a premium to the DTI of 1.5% of the outstanding balance. This facility has several exclusions. It is, for example, only available to businesses with an annual turnover below £1.5 million (£3 million for a manufacturer) or 200 employees.

Debentures or corporate bonds

These are loans to the business by individuals or financial organisations. They are for a specified length of time, typically 25 years, and secured against a specific asset (usually property) and carry a fixed rate of interest. They are the business equivalent of a mortgage.

Owners equity (also known as share capital)

This is the money put into the business by the owner or owners. For new businesses this is the most likely source of finance. Many businesses are started with individual savings. This money has the advantage that it has no interest charges. The money is also at risk. If the business fails the money is likely to be lost.

Venture capital

This is a way of getting outside investment for businesses that are unable to raise finance through the stock markets. Venture capitalists invest in smaller, riskier companies. They may make a loan or become part-owners. It is a much riskier form of investment.

Grants

There are many different grants available to businesses. These are sponsored by the Government, the EU and other agencies such as The Prince's Trust. Growth Resourcing Associates offer an Internet advisory service for obtaining grants. They estimate that there are over 1,000 different grants available. Research shows, however, that fewer than 3% of all new firms are financed by grants.

20.3 Finance should be adequate and appropriate

Having adequate funding means ensuring the business has sufficient access to finance to meet its capital and working capital requirements. When a business starts up it needs sufficient funds to enable it to survive until it starts to generate enough income. Expansion also requires the purchase of additional equipment and additional working capital needs.

Appropriate financing means matching the type of finance to its use. A distinction is made in company financing between short- and long-term finance (see Figure 20.1). Short-term finance is usually considered to be for less than one year. Medium-term is one to five years. Long-term finance is longer than five years. Short-term finance should not be used to finance long-term projects. Using short-term finance such as overdrafts puts continual pressure on the company's working capital.

Figure 20.1 Short- and long-term sources of finance

It is appropriate to use an overdraft to cope with irregularities in working capital. If the overdraft becomes permanent then it is effectively funding the provision of assets. A machine should not be purchased with the aid of a short-term loan. The machine will generate income over its lifetime, and this should provide sufficient return to repay the loan and any interest payments plus some contribution to its replacement.

When a business expands without a solid financial foundation it is known as **overtrading**.

SOURCES OF FINANCE IN THE BALANCE SHEET

The **balance sheet** is a financial statement at a particular point in time. Usually this will be at the end of the company's accounting period. It shows where the money is in the business and where the money came from. The balance sheet shows the sources of finance for any particular firm.

Example:

Balance sheet for Advance Ltd

	£
Fixed assets	57,000
Current assets	
Stock	21,000
Debtors	25,000
Bank	2,000
Total current assets	48,000
Current liabilities	
Creditors	19,000
Overdraft/short-term loan	0
Total current liabilities	19,000
Working capital	29,000
Total assets	86,000
Financed by:	
Loans	40,000
Share capital	46,000
Total capital employed	86,000

This business has trade credit of £19,000, a long-term loan of £40,000 and the owners have invested £46,000. The business has a good working capital situation.

Acid test ratio:
= (current assets – stock):current liabilities
= £27,000:£19,000
= 1.4:1

Gearing:
= loans ÷ capital employed × 100
= £40,000 ÷ £86,000 × 100
= 46%

Both the gearing and the acid test ratio indicate that the company is well financed. It is not relying on too much external funding. Its working capital position is very healthy.

20.4 Financing growth

Growth is often seen as a natural development for a business, but it can be risky. If it is not managed well it can destroy a successful business. There are a number of reasons why growth should take place:

- a business may need to expand to take advantage of economies of scale, to keep pace with competitors or to supply a market where demand is not satisfied
- a larger business will find it easier to ride out fluctuations in economic activity, to cope with setbacks, to compete and to raise finance
- a business with a mixture of activities will have a spread of risk
- a business may be below break-even level.

Whatever the motive for growth it requires financial back-up. Ideally the growth should generate additional profit. But before profit comes the cash investment in the assets and personnel needed to succeed.

GROWTH REQUIRES ADEQUATE FINANCING

Cash flow planning is just as important when a business is looking for growth as at any other stage of its life. Not only is capital required for the purchase of new assets but the firm must ensure that there is adequate working capital. This is required to fund the additional raw materials, labour costs and general overheads until the increased business activity generates sufficient income. A promising long-term growth opportunity could, if the funding is inadequate, cause the business to fail in the short term. Such failures are usually due to overtrading.

Overtrading means growing faster than can be sustained by a firm's capital base. A small firm may have been producing goods for years when, suddenly, demand starts to surge ahead. This happened to Doc Martens shoes in the 1980s and again in the 1990s. It happened to the toy importer Kids' Biz in the yo-yo boom of 1998–1999. Step by step, overtrading happens as follows:

1. a demand upsurge hits a firm with small stocks and a small production capacity
2. it uses its overdraft to fund the extra sales and soon reaches 100% capacity
3. as sales shoot ahead, today's costs are rising rapidly, but cash inflows from customers lag behind
4. excess demand means capacity must be increased, causing a huge cash requirement
5. and so on.

GROWTH REQUIRES APPROPRIATE FINANCING

By its very nature, growth is a long-term activity, so appropriate long-term finance should be sought to fund it.

Example:

Advance Ltd (see balance sheet on facing page) wants to expand. The company is in a saturated market but the owners have identified a growth opportunity supplying another range of components. There is a growing market for these components and hardly any

competition. It needs a machine costing £25,000. Advance Ltd needs external finance to fund the growth. The balance sheet shows it has only £2,000 in cash. The fixed assets cannot be turned into cash. It does not wish to bring in additional investors, as this would mean losing some control of the company.

If the company takes on a short-term loan of £25,000 it would put a great deal of strain on working capital. The current liabilities would increase from £19,000 to £44,000. This would leave it with working capital of £4,000. Although this is positive, the acid test ratio gives a clearer picture. The acid test will go from 1.4:1 to 0.6:1 (27,000:44,000). This is uncomfortably poor liquidity. It may make suppliers, customers and investors wary about the business. Using long-term borrowing will avoid these problems.

If Advance took out a long-term loan the balance sheet would look like this:

Balance sheet if Advance Ltd took out a long-term loan

	£
Fixed assets	82,000
Current assets	
Stock	21,000
Debtors	25,000
Bank	2,000
Total current assets	48,000
Current liabilities	
Creditors	19,000
Overdraft/short-term loan	0
Total current liabilities	19,000
Working capital	29,000
Total assets	111,000
Financed by:	
Loans	65,000
Capital	46,000
Total capital employed	111,000

The working capital situation remains healthy. However this move has affected the gearing. This was 46%. It is now 59% (65,000 ÷ 111,000 × 100). This higher level of gearing will make it more difficult for Advance to obtain any more loan capital. The relationship between borrowed funds and the owner's investment is less favourable and will make the company seem less stable and creditworthy.

MAKING GROWTH WORK

Although growth can significantly improve a company's fortunes, growth for growth's sake is not desirable. Many companies that expanded in the past are now looking to return to their 'core business' activity. Many successful companies have collapsed in the process of expansion. For most businesses, growth can have significant advantages. It is essential that the financial aspects be managed carefully. Any new

FINANCING GROWTH

How do rapidly growing small firms finance their growth? By venture capital? By loans? To find an answer to this question, Hamish Stevenson from Templeton College, Oxford, looked at 100 of the fastest growing firms of the 1990s. One of these is R Frazier, a firm which recycles computers. Its sales grew from £294,000 to £7,400,000 in just three years. An increase of more than 2,400%! In common with the majority of the firms, R Frazier's early growth was self-funded, in other words from reinvested profits, over-drafts and trade credit. 'These are the real entrepreneurs,' says Stevenson. 'They grab money where they can. It is fly-by-the-seat-of-their-pants finance.' The 54 firms which used this method were doing so 'through default not by design', according to the research.

Twenty-one of the firms were helped by equity finance; 15 from venture capital houses and 6 from business angels. Just 10 used long-term bank debt.

Having survived, even thrived, through these hectic early years, as many as 40 of the firms are looking at, or in the process of, floating their firms on the London Stock Market. This would secure the finance for the next stage of growth.

venture carries an element of risk. So, too, does rapid growth in existing markets. The firm needs to evaluate this to minimise the impact of the risk.

Ideally, businesses should look to grow steadily. Each step should be established with secure funding. This careful approach will minimise risk. It spreads the need for funding and makes finance easier to obtain.

Any business that is keen to grow needs to recognise that it is not always beneficial. It needs to:

- estimate the timing and value of additional sales
- estimate timing and amounts of all additional costs
- do a cash flow forecast to ensure that it has the necessary working capital
- perform an investment appraisal to ensure that the return from the project is acceptable.

If it still feels that the development is worthwhile then it needs to ensure that:

- the amount of any funding covers both capital and working capital needs
- that the funding is available for long enough to enable it to repay the loan from profits generated by the expansion.

It also needs to ensure that it has looked at other aspects of the business such as marketing, distribution and staffing.

When analysing or suggesting appropriate sources of finance, the key issues are:

- Whether the business itself is risky or stable. If risky (such as a low cost airline), the form of financing should be as safe as possible. The collapse of the world's first major, low cost airline (Laker Airways) was due to high capital gearing for a business caught in a price war.
- Whether the founding family of the business is determined to hold onto power. If so, it will be very reluctant to sell more than 49% of the shares. This may force it to finance growth by borrowings rather than safer share capital. Rupert Murdoch's media empire grew in this way, and was fortunate to survive the early 1990s' recession.
- For what reason is the business seeking finance? The key here is to ensure that the finance is adequate and appropriate. The type of finance should be matched to the capital need. For example, long-term asset purchases might be financed by a long-term bank loan.
- What effect will extra financing have on the balance sheet? Analysis of ratios such as the acid test and gearing helps reveal the degree of risk involved.

20.5 Sources of finance
an evaluation

Finding finance may involve balancing conflicting interests. Internal sources of finance may be too limited to provide opportunities for business development. If retained profit is used, shareholders wanting a return on their investment may not be satisfied.

Obtaining external financing increases the money that is available. However, it has its downsides. Borrowing increases gearing and risk. Raising extra share capital dilutes the control held by existing shareholders.

The cost of finance will also reduce the company's net profit and, in the case of limited companies, reduce dividends paid to shareholders. The cost of borrowing, if not offset by additional profit from sales, will reduce the net profit ratio and the return on capital employed. If the growth is successful this may prove nothing worse than a short-term problem. The problem comes if costly growth leads to costly failure. This happened to Carlton and Granada TV companies when they flopped with ITV Digital in 2002.

Having adequate and appropriate finance at each stage in the firm's development will ensure it stays healthy. Decisions about where to obtain the finance will be a matter of balancing the business objectives, the reasons for the funding and the balance sheet implications.

KEY terms

balance sheet – a financial statement showing the assets and liabilities of the business at a point in time.

core business – the basic business activity. The core business is the major activity of the business.

overtrading – when a firm expands without obtaining appropriate funding.

private limited company – a business with limited liability whose shares are not available to the public.

public limited company (plc) – a company with limited liability and shares which are available to the public. Its shares can be quoted on the Stock Exchange.

Stock Exchange – a market for stocks and shares. It supervises the issuing of shares by companies. It is also a second-hand market for stocks and shares.

working capital – the money needed to finance the day-to-day running of the business. It allows stock to be bought and wages and bills to be paid.

AS Level Exercises

A. REVISION QUESTIONS

(25 marks; 30 minutes)

Read the unit, then answer:

1 What is meant by 'capital expenditure'? *(2)*
2 What is the importance to firms of working capital? *(3)*
3 What is meant by 'retained profit'? *(2)*
4 Outline two ways in which businesses can raise money from internal sources. *(4)*
5 Explain the term 'factoring'. *(3)*
6 Outline two sources of finance that can be used for long-term business development. *(4)*
7 Why might a new business find it difficult to get external funding for its development? *(3)*
8 What are the advantages and disadvantages of raising capital by selling shares? *(4)*

B. REVISION EXERCISES

B1 Activity

EBS: A Business for Our Times

> Executive Business Services is a modern day business success story. It was started by Val Hood in 1990. She had been made redundant from her job when she was two months pregnant. She did not qualify for redundancy payments. Working from a bedroom at home using a PC and a printer she built up a client base by offering to take on their excess typing work. Her main selling point was that she would do the work within 24 hours. Inevitably this meant working very long days. Although at times she had too much work she could not afford to pay staff.
>
> This changed in 1995 when she tendered for work from an insurance company that wanted to close down its typing pool. Winning the contract allowed her to expand. She took on three more staff, all mothers who worked from home. In 1998 the business made a profit of £50,000. It now operates from offices in South London, employs 26 home-based workers and has a client list of 60 firms.
>
> Mrs Hood believes that this type of work will grow in the future. As businesses seek to reduce costs they will increasingly outsource routine work such as typing. This is now made easier with the use of computer-based technology. As the business has grown, she has ensured that both the equipment and the skills have developed. The firm uses e-mail and has software that is compatible with that used by the clients. In addition to typing, the firm will take shorthand, translate and transcribe. It collects and delivers work but also has work dictated over the telephone.
>
> Mrs Hood's next venture is to launch a recruitment agency providing security-cleared temps to those firms who do not wish to have work leaving the office.
>
> (**Source:** Adapted from *The Times*, 15/12/98)

This business is typical of the way in which many businesses start and grow. At each stage in the development of the business it will have needed money to finance the development.

Questions *(30 marks; 35 minutes)*
1 Identify the stages in the development of the business. *(4)*
2 For each stage in the development identify the financial needs. *(4)*
3 Investigate possible sources of funding for each stage. *(8)*
4 Consider the pros and cons of these sources. *(8)*
5 Finally identify and justify the best way of financing the latest expansion plans. *(6)*

B2 Data Response

Mayday Printers

Mayday Printers specialises in last minute printing for firms. Its major selling point is that it will turn a job around within 24 hours providing the artwork is ready. Mayday is able to charge a premium for this service and is seldom short of work. The firm does, however, need to be extremely flexible. This means having a flexible work force and very reliable machines. It has had to turn away several large jobs lately because of a lack of machinery and now the managers are considering buying an additional large printer. Although they know that this will not be used at full capacity they are worried that turning away business will damage their reputation and lead to a loss of business in future. The company is in good financial health with a strong cash flow, though the cash position can be strained sometimes when there is a rush of work. To complete an order Mayday might have to pay bonus wages to staff, often before payment is received.

The finance director has come up with two proposals that he will present to the next Board meeting. The first is to buy a new printer and to fund the purchase with a bank loan. The printer will cost £100,000 so he suggests taking out a loan for that amount. The loan will be at bank rate plus 8% and will be for 10 years. The bank rate is currently 4%.

The alternative proposal is to rent this new machine. He has found a company who will do this. The cost of the rental including a maintenance contract would be £1,500 per month. The marketing department expects to pick up at least 5 additional contracts during the first year. These should generate at least £20,000 of revenue, but just as importantly will protect the company's reputation and existing business.

Questions *(20 marks; 30 minutes)*
Prepare a report for the Board outlining the advantages and disadvantages of each proposal. End your report with a clear recommendation.

A Level Exercises

B1 Data Response

Empire Building in the Car Sales Market

Reg Vardy plc is the third largest car retailer in the UK. It is challenging to become Number 2. This year the company is planning to use £35 million to buy some smaller rival dealerships and expand its empire. It currently has almost 70 dealerships out of a total of 6,000 in the UK. It is seeking to buy businesses that will fill its geographical gaps.

Last year Vardy bought 16 dealerships that were strong in the second-hand market. This was a sector where the company wanted to strengthen its position. The move clearly worked. Pre-tax profits rose to £12.3 million, up from £8.4 million the previous year. This jump in profits was in the context of an over-all 9% reduction in the volume of sales for the industry as a whole. It also took place in a market where prices for new cars were falling.

Analysts attribute this success to Vardy's excellent stock management systems. It manages to move the cars within 30 days. Moving the cars quickly puts it in a better position to react to falling prices. It is not holding stocks of cars bought when prices were higher. This has enabled it to react to falling prices without having to cut into profits. Turnover has also been supported by its strength in the second-hand market. When new car sales fall, used car sales often pick up.

Va dy s planning to fund the acquisitions by borrowing the required £35 million. This would bring their total borrowing to £77 million. Gearing, which is currently 40%, would increase to 75%.

Source: Adapted from *The Times*, 8/1/99

Questions *(30 marks; 35 minutes)*

1 By what percentage did the profit grow following the £35 million investment? *(3)*
2 What is meant by 'gearing will be 75%'? *(3)*
3 Why might a firm such as Vardy wish to expand? *(6)*
4 How does the efficient stock management system help the profitability of the business? *(6)*
5 Discuss whether it would be advisable for the company to raise the extra £35 million by a share issue? *(12)*

B2 Case Study

Odd Jobs Ltd

Jeff Hale was made redundant from his job in the printing industry at the age of 51. Having worked with the firm since he was 15 he received a small pension which would be paid straightaway and a lump sum redundancy payment of £30,000.

He decided to set up a business called Odd Jobs Ltd. The idea was to fill the gap in the market between the DIY enthusiast and general builders. He knew from experience that it was often very difficult to get a builder to come and do the smaller jobs.

He set up the business as a limited company with a friend, Malcolm Baines, who had also been made redundant. They each invested £20,000 of their redundancy money. The remainder they used to reduce their mortgages to take some financial pressure off them whilst the business was becoming established. They rented a small office and a van and bought tools and office equipment. After making their purchases they were confident that they had sufficient working capital to finance the business until it became profitable. Their policy was to charge a reasonable rate for the job. They had a fixed scale of charges for the run-of-the-mill jobs and gave a detailed estimate for any more complicated work.

They soon got a reputation for good quality work and after six months they found that they no longer needed to advertise. They resisted the temptation to do larger jobs preferring to keep to their original idea. Most jobs took less than half a day to complete. Seven years later they now employ two office staff and a team of four other workers. They have bought three vans with the help of a £40,000 bank loan. Each van is equipped with a full set of tools. The business is prospering and they can look back with satisfaction. Even during a period of recession they were mostly unaffected.

Jeff and Malcolm feel that there is no more room for expansion in their home town. They have been looking at setting up another branch in another town 35 km away. They feel that this is near enough to keep control of both businesses and to gain some advantage from the good reputation of the business.

They have prepared a business plan and feel that to make the venture work they will need to get a loan or some other external funding. They estimate that they will need around £40,000. £10,000 of this will be spent on office equipment and tools and £15,000 on the purchase of a new van. The remainder will be used as working capital to fund office rental and wages.

Their balance sheet for last year was as follows:

Odd Jobs Ltd: Balance sheet for the year ending December 1998

Fixed assets:		
Office equipment & tools	£63,000	
Vehicles	£40,000	
Total fixed assets		£103,000
Current assets:		
Stock	£2,000	
Debtors	£9,000	
Cash	£4,000	
Total current assets	£15,000	
Short-term liabilities:		
Creditors	£9,000	
Working capital		£6,000
Assets employed		£109,000
Financed by:		
Capital	£69,000	
Bank loan	£40,000	
Capital employed		£109,000

Questions *(35 marks; 45 minutes)*

1 If the bank will not provide the loan, consider how else the business could obtain the £40,000 needed for the expansion. *(8)*
2 Assuming that Jeff and Malcolm obtain the bank loan, prepare a balance sheet for the following year. Assume that stock, debtors, creditors and capital remain unchanged. *(7)*
3 Calculate and comment on the gearing ratio before and after the loan. *(8)*
4 Write a report advising Jeff and Malcolm on the expansion. *(12)*

PROFIT AND LOSS ACCOUNTS

A profit and loss account is an accounting statement showing a firm's sales revenue over a trading period and all the relevant costs generated to earn that revenue.

21.1 Introduction

The function of accounting is to provide information to various stakeholder groups (for example shareholders, managers and creditors) on how a particular business has performed during a given period. The period in question is usually one year. The key financial documents from which this information can be drawn are balance sheets and profit and loss accounts. This unit focuses on the profit and loss account. The balance sheet is covered in Unit 22.

The profit and loss account is a statement that records all a business's costs within a given trading period. Profit and loss accounts constitute a vital piece of evidence for those with interests in a company. For many stakeholders profit is a major criterion by which to judge the success of a business:

- shareholders are an obvious example of those assessing profitability
- government agencies such as the Inland Revenue require data on profits or losses to be able to calculate the tax liability of an organisation
- suppliers to a business also need to know the financial position of companies they trade with in order to establish their reliability, stability and creditworthiness
- potential shareholders and bankers will also want to assess the financial position of the company before committing their funds to the business.

For all of these groups the profit and loss account provides important information.

Making a profit is one of the most significant objectives for business organisations. It is common for businesses to aim to make the maximum possible profit, especially in the long term. It is this profit motive which motivates many people to establish their own business. Without the potential for making a profit, why should individuals and companies commit time and resources to what may be a risky venture?

In spite of the importance of the profit motive, a number of organisations exist which pursue objectives other than profits. Charities seek to assist those who are in need; their task is to redistribute resources rather than make profits. Other organisations such as the Co-op, building societies and many social clubs exist to provide the best possible service to their members. Because of this they reinvest all the 'profits' they earn. But even charities must seek to generate revenues to at least match their expenditure.

21.2 The uses of profit and loss accounts

The information yielded by a profit and loss account can be used for a number of purposes:

- it can measure the success of a business compared with previous years or other businesses
- the calculation of profit can assess the actual performance of the business compared with expectations
- it can help in obtaining loans or finance from banks or other lending institutions (creditors would want some proof that the business was capable of repaying any loans)
- it enables the owners and managers of a business to plan ahead, for example for future investment in the company.

21.3 Measuring profit

Profit is what remains from revenue once costs have been deducted. However, the word 'profit' on its own means little to an accountant. Profit is such an important objective and such a good indicator of company performance that it is broken down into different types. This enables more detailed comparisons and analyses to be made.

The main types of profit are:

- **Gross profit**

This is the measure of the difference between turnover and the cost of manufacturing or purchasing the products which have been sold. It measures the amount of profit made on trading activities alone, i.e the amount of profit made on buying and selling activities.

gross profit = turnover – cost of goods sold

Gross profit is calculated *without* taking costs which could be classified as expenses (administration, advertising) or overheads (rent, rates) into account.

This is a useful measure as, if a company is making a lower level of gross profit than a competitor, it is clear that the company must look very closely at its trading position. It may be that the business should attempt to find a cheaper supplier.

- **Net profit**

This is found by subtracting expenses and overheads from gross profit. It is often termed operating profit.

net profit = gross profit – (expenses + overheads)

Net (operating) profit is a very useful measure. A business may find itself making a healthy gross profit but a very small net profit in comparison to competitors. The business may not be controlling costs such as salaries and distribution as effectively as it might.

The calculation of both gross and net profit allows owners, managers and other interested parties to make a more detailed and informed assessment of a business's performance.

PROFIT QUALITY

It is not just the amount of profit that a business makes which is important, but also the likelihood of this profit source continuing for some time. If a profit has arisen as a result of a one-off circumstance (such as selling assets for more than their expected value), its quality is said to be low because it is unlikely to continue into the future. On the other hand, high quality profit is trading profit that is expected to last for a number of years.

21.4 Determining profit

Businesses calculate their profit or loss at regular intervals during a trading period. This supplies managers with important information to assist in the running of the business. At the end of the trading period the final calculation is made which will form a major element of the published accounts.

Figure 21.1 sets out the basic structure of a profit and loss account. Although this is the format adopted by a large number of firms, there is some variation according to the type of business.

The profit and loss account itself is actually divided up into three sections:

1 **The trading account** calculates the gross profit made on trading activities.

2 **The profit and loss account** calculates the overall level of profit made by a business. Gross profit + any income other than from sales – expenses = operating (net) profit.

3 **The appropriation account** shows how any profits made by the business have been distributed (i.e. where the profits have gone to).

		£m
	Revenue	26.0
less	Cost of sales	17.0
gives	**Gross profit**	**9.0**
less	Overheads	4.0
gives	**Operating (or Trading) Profit**	**5.0**
plus	One-off items	1.5
gives	**Pre-tax Profits**	**6.5**
less	Tax	2.0
gives	**Profit after Tax**	**4.5**
less	Dividends	2.0
gives	**Retained Profit**	**2.5**

Figure 21.1 The basic structure of a profit and loss account

THE TRADING ACCOUNT

The trading account shows how much revenue has been earned from sales less the cost of goods sold. In other words it calculates gross profit.

turnover (sales revenue) – cost of goods sold = gross profit

When calculating turnover, taxes on sales such as VAT are also excluded. Although customers pay taxes to the business as part of the purchase price, the business has to pass it on to Customs and Excise. The business does not, therefore, receive any part of this revenue and so it is excluded from the sales figure.

The next stage in calculating gross profit requires businesses to deduct cost of sales from their turnover figure.

cost of goods sold = opening stock + purchases – closing stock

Cost of goods sold simply records the expenses incurred in making or buying the products that have been sold in the current financial period.

In most cases companies will actually start a financial period selling stock that was made or bought in the previous financial period (opening stock). The cost of making this stock is therefore brought into this period as this is when it is going to be sold. To this is added the cost of any purchases of stock made over the period.

Lastly in the calculation of cost of sales, closing stock is deducted. This is a similar concept to opening stock. It follows that if, at the beginning of a period, stock is being sold that was left over from the last period, at the end of this current period there may well be stocks left that were not yet sold. These leftover stocks (closing stock) need to be subtracted from the cost of goods sold, as they have not been sold. They will probably be sold in the next financial period and the costs of their production will be included in the account for that period.

A key point here is that closing stock at the end of the current financial period becomes opening stock for the next period.

These calculations provide a value for the total cost of goods that we have actually *sold* during the period in question. An example of a trading account is shown below.

H Baker Ltd: Trading account for the period ended 30 May

	£	£
Sales turnover		47,800
Less cost of goods sold		
Opening stock	4,700	
add Purchases	24,000	
less Closing stock	6,000	22,700
Gross profit		**25,100**

If cost of goods sold exceeds turnover, a loss is made.

THE PROFIT AND LOSS ACCOUNT

The profit and loss account sets out the net profit, or net loss, made by the business. The gross profit figure is necessary to calculate net profit so the profit and loss account naturally follows on from the trading account.

An important relationship to remember is that net profit equals gross profit (plus any income other than from sales) less expenses.

Other income: Businesses can receive other income in a variety of forms and from a range of activities. Examples might include:

- rent received from property owned, but not used, by the business
- commissions received for selling other firms' products
- dividends from shares held in other companies or interests on deposits.

However, do not be surprised if you don't see this on all profit and loss accounts, as not all businesses (particularly small ones) receive income from areas other than trading.

Expenses: Expenses are payments for something which is of immediate use to the business. These payments include cash expenditures on labour and fuel as well as non-cash items such as depreciation.

Examples of expenses include:

- wages and salaries
- rent and rates

- insurance costs
- heating and lighting
- distribution costs
- depreciation.

Operating profit: Deducting expenses from gross profit leads to operating profit. Most firms regard this as the key test of their trading performance for the year. At the very least a firm would want operating profit to be:

- up by at least the rate of inflation compared with the previous year
- a higher percentage of the capital employed in the business than the cost of that capital (e.g. the interest rate)
- high enough to ensure that shareholders can be paid a satisfactory dividend but still have money left to reinvest in the future of the business.

APPROPRIATION ACCOUNT

Net profit can be used in two main ways. It can be either *distributed* or *retained*. Usually businesses retain some profits and distribute the remainder. The balance between these two uses is influenced by a number of factors.

- Distributed profit – various people are going to want to take their share of the net profit. For example, the company's shareholders receive their allocation of net profit through dividends.
- Retained profit – any prudent owner or manager of a business will use some of the profit made by the business to reinvest in the business for the future.

The profit retained by the business could be 'earmarked' against expected future expenses, or for investment in some new assets to replace old ones, or even for expansion.

A complete profit and loss account for a private limited company is shown in the following table.

H Baker Ltd: Profit and loss account for the period ended 30 May

	£	£
Sales turnover		47,800
Less cost of goods sold		
Opening stock	4,700	
add Purchases	24,000	
less Closing stock	6,000	22,700
Gross profit		**25,100**
Less expenses		
Wages and salaries	8,100	
Distribution	1,850	
Advertising	2,300	
Rent and other bills	3,550	
Depreciation	1,200	17,000
Operating profit		**8,100**
Taxation		2,025
Profit after tax		**6,075**
Dividends		4,000
Retained profit		**2,075**

From the appropriation account it can be seen exactly how much profit has been shared out as dividends and how much has been kept by the company for reinvestment. This lets all those concerned know exactly what has happened to the profit made in the year.

21.5 Examining profit and loss accounts

The first thing to do when looking at a profit and loss account is to look at the title. The title will always read:

Business name
Profit and loss account for the year ended
DD/MM/YY

The title provides some important information. First, the business name shows whether the firm has unlimited or limited liability. If the latter, it shows whether it is a small private company (Ltd) or a large public limited company (plc).

The year-end date is also an important factor to take into consideration when comparing company accounts. Many types of businesses and markets suffer from trends and fashions as well as seasonal fluctuations in demand.

The dates of the financial year can affect what the accounts will show. If the profit and loss account covers a period of less than one year's trading it is worth noting whether it covers key selling periods such as December.

Most profit and loss accounts record the appropriate information for at least two years' trading. This

assists stakeholders in identifying trends. For example, it is possible to look at the increase, if any, in turnover, expenses or net profit. This helps to make a judgement about the financial well-being of the business.

21.6 Public limited companies

Public limited companies are required by law to publish their accounts. This means that they are available for scrutiny not only by the owners (shareholders), potential investors and bankers, but also by competitors.

When a company draws up its profit and loss account purely for internal use, it will look similar to the account of H Baker Ltd. However, when the accounts are drawn up for external publication companies include as little information as possible. They usually supply no more detail than is required by law. This format is illustrated on the following page. It can be seen that the account for external use does not provide as much information as the one for internal use. This minimises the information competitors might be able to use to gain an advantage.

CONSOLIDATED ACCOUNTS

During the last 25 years many companies have been taken over by other companies to form groups.

Each company within such a group retains its separate legal identity, but the group is also legally obliged to produce a consolidated profit and loss account (and balance sheet). A **consolidated account** simply records the aggregated position of the group as a whole.

Examples of organisations producing consolidated accounts include The Body Shop International and Tesco. It is quite likely that the accounts of any large organisations you examine will be consolidated accounts.

21.7 Profit and loss accounts and the law

The legal requirements relating to the profit and loss account are set out in the Companies Act 1985 and amended by the Companies Act of 1989. This legislation demands the production of financial statements including a profit and loss account. It also specifies the information to be included in these accounts.

The profit and loss account does not have to detail every expense incurred by the firm, but summarises the main items under standard headings. In spite of this, some items must be recorded either in the profit and loss account itself, or in separate notes. The Acts set out acceptable formats for presentation of the relevant data. One of these is illustrated in the Chesterton profit and loss account.

Chesterton plc: Profit and loss account for external use for the period ending 31 March

	£
Turnover	1,530,000
Cost of goods sold	858,000
Gross profit	672,000
Overheads	420,000
Profit on ordinary activities before tax	**252,000**
Tax on ordinary activities	70,000
Profit on ordinary activities after tax	182,000
Dividends	90,000
Retained profit	**92,000**

The notes to the profit and loss accounts must disclose details of:

- auditor's fees
- depreciation amounts
- the total of directors' emoluments (earnings)
- the average number of employees, together with details of cost of wages and salaries together with national insurance and pensions.

Limited company profit and loss accounts are also required to show the financial results of any changes to the structure of the company. This requirement includes the purchase or the sale of a part of the business. Companies must disclose the following:

- Exceptional items – these are large (usually one-off) financial transactions arising from ordinary trading activities. However, they are so large as to risk distorting the company's trading account. An example of exceptional items took place when the high street banks incurred unusually large bad debt charges.
- Extraordinary items – these are large transactions outside the normal trading activities of a company. As a result they are not expected to recur. A typical example is the closure of a factory or division of a business. These items have only been included in the profit and loss account over recent years.

ISSUES FOR **analysis**

The profit and loss account is an important piece of information for anyone with an interest in business. Analysis of profit and loss accounts can provide an insight into the performance of a business. Identifying trends in turnover can provide evidence about the success of a company within the marketplace. Is turnover rising after allowing for inflation? If so, this could be a healthy sign.

The profit and loss account also gives details of how well the company is controlling its costs. Analysing the trends in gross and net (or operating) profits can be of value. For example, a rising figure for gross profits alongside a falling net profit figure could suggest that a promising business is not controlling its overheads. Alternatively, it might mean that the business has incurred exceptional costs – maybe due to restructuring.

The key to analysing a profit and loss account is to look at the performance of the business over a number of years. This may involve comparing various elements of the profit and loss account to gain a further insight into the business. This approach is followed up in Unit 23.

RECORD LOSS FOR BRITISH NUCLEAR FUELS

British Nuclear Fuels (BNFL) has reported a £2.3 billion loss for the 2001–2002 financial year, the worst result in the company's history. Despite this the company claims that its financial performance is, in fact, getting better.

Chairman Hugh Collum said it had been an important year for the company, which had achieved an underlying profit before tax and exceptional items of £22 million. The record losses are thought to reflect the cost of cleaning up Britain's radioactive sites as well as the cost of closing down some reactors. These are recorded as exceptional items in the company's accounts.

However, help is on the way. The government has presented proposals to create a separate agency to take on these clean-up costs. This will mean that BNFL no longer has to pay them – in effect the costs will be passed on to the taxpayer.

Business IN

21.8 Profit and loss accounts
an evaluation

Two evaluative themes can be considered in relation to profit and loss accounts. It is easy to make the assumption that a rising level of net or operating profit is evidence of a company that is performing well. There are a number of factors that need to be considered when making such a judgement. Has a new management pushed up prices, boosting profit for a year or so, but at the cost of damaged market share in the future? Is a company which pollutes the environment, uses materials from unsustainable sources, but makes a large profit, a successful business? Is profit necessarily the best measure of the performance of a business?

Even if we assume current profits are a good indication of how a company is performing, a number of other factors need to be taken into account. Is the market growing or declining? Are new competitors coming onto the scene? To what extent is the business achieving its corporate objectives? Is the profit earned likely to be sustained into the future – that is, is the profit of good quality? Information such as this is vital if a meaningful judgement is to be made about the performance of a business.

KEY terms

consolidated account – this is the sum of the accounting data for all the divisions of a business – a holding company and its subsidiaries.

cost of goods sold – calculation of the direct costs involved in making the goods actually sold in that period.

gross profit – turnover less cost of goods sold. Profit made on trading activities.

net profit – gross profit + any other income less expenses. Profit on ordinary activities; sometimes called operating profit.

turnover – sales revenue, i.e. the value of sales made.

A Level Exercises

A. REVISION QUESTIONS
(35 marks, 70 minutes)

Read the unit, then answer:

1 Give two reasons why a firm's bank would want to see its profit and loss account. (2)
2 For what reasons should sales taxes such as VAT be excluded from a business's turnover figure? (3)
3 List the elements necessary to calculate cost of sales. (4)
4 Distinguish between gross and net profit. (4)
5 Explain the term 'profit quality'. (3)
6 What are bad debts? How do they differ from provision for bad debts? (5)
7 State the function of the appropriation account. Is it equally important to all businesses? (4)
8 Give examples of exceptional and extraordinary items which might appear in the profit and loss account of a business. (4)
9 What is a consolidated profit and loss account? (3)
10 Give three examples of items that might appear in the notes to a profit and loss accounts. (3)

B. REVISION EXERCISES

B1 Data Response

> The chairman of the Dantex Corporation has come under some pressure lately. Shareholders have complained about the firm's lacklustre performance. Today, though, he is creating favourable headlines. The Sunday Press has announced that 'Dantex Drives Forward'. In the Financial

> Guardian the chairman is quoted as saying: 'This is a great day for Dantex. Pre-tax profit is up by more than 50% and we have been able to double our dividends to shareholders. I am confident we will be able to maintain or increase this dividend next year.'
>
> Source: The *Guardian*

Profit and loss account for Dantex Corporation plc

	This Year (£m)	Last Year (£m)
Turnover	24.5	25.8
Cost of sales	10.0	9.6
Operating expenses	12.4	11.1
Operating profit		
Extraordinary items	4.5	1.0
Pre-tax profit	6.6	4.1
Taxation	1.6	1.2
Profit after tax	5.0	2.9
Dividends	3.0	1.5
Retained profit		

Questions *(20 marks; 30 minutes)*

1 Calculate the Dantex Corporation's operating profit and retained profit for this year and last. (4)
2 Analyse the Dantex profit performance this year, by comparing it with last year. Within your answer, consider the quality of the profit made by Dantex this year. (8)
3 Use your analysis to comment on the accuracy of the chairman's statement. (8)

B2 Data Response

JJB Sports plc: consolidated profit and loss account (simplified)

	6 Months to 31/7/98 (£000s)	6 Months to 31/7/97 (£000s)
Turnover	115,610	88,566
Gross profit	56,063	43,622
Operating expenses	(40,012)	(29,584)
Operating profit	**16,051**	**14,038**
Interest	496	188
Taxation	(5,232)	(4,730)
Profit after tax	11,315	9,496
Dividends	(3,501)	(2,025)
Retained profit	**7,814**	**7,471**

Questions   (35 marks; 40 minutes)

1 a Calculate JJB's cost of sales for both periods.   (5)
  b Calculate each figure as a percentage of the company's sales turnover for the corresponding period. (4)
  c Comment on your findings.   (6)
2 a Calculate the percentage increase JJB Sports achieved in 1998 compared with 1997 in
  i sales turnover   (3)
  ii operating profit.   (3)
  b Analyse the data to suggest why the increase in operating profit was not as great as the increase in turnover. (8)
3 Why may it be unfair to judge a firm such as JJB Sports on its profit performance over a six month period?   (6)

B3 Data Response

The profit and loss account below is adapted from Reuters 1997 annual report and accounts. Reuters is a London-based worldwide news agency.

Consolidated profit and loss account for the year ended 31 December

	1997 (£m)	1996 (£m)	1995 (£m)
Revenue	**2,882**	2,914	2,703
Operating costs	**(2,290)**	(2,273)	(2,152)
Operating profit	**592**	641	551
Goodwill amortisation	**(51)**	(49)	(41)
	541	592	510
Loss from associates	**(1)**	(7)	(12)
Income from investments plus net interest receivable	**86**	67	60
Profit before taxation	**626**	652	558
Taxation	**(236)**	(210)	(185)
Profit after taxation	**390**	442	373
Dividends	**(190)**	(190)	(158)
Retained profit	**200**	252	215

Questions   (30 marks; 35 minutes)

1 Explain the meaning of the following terms:
   goodwill
   consolidated profit and loss account
   retained profit.   (6)
2 Outline two uses to which the data above might be put   (4)
3 a Identify three key trends in the data.   (3)
  b Analyse the possible causes of the trends you have identified.   (8)
4 Evaluate the usefulness of this data to an investor considering purchasing shares in Reuters.   (9)

BALANCE SHEETS

DEFINITION

The balance sheet is an accounting statement that shows an organisation's assets and liabilities at a precise point in time, usually the last day of the accounting year.

Assets are resources owned by the organisation which have a monetary value. Liabilities are debts owed by the organisation to other parties. Liabilities are sources of finance.

Capital is money or resources invested by the owner(s) in the organisation. It is a source of finance used by the business to acquire assets.

22.1 Introduction

As stated in Unit 21, accounting provides information to stakeholders on how a particular business has performed over a given period of time. Profit and loss accounts form the basis by which much of this information is obtained. Balance sheets provide the means whereby owners, managers, financiers and other stakeholders can obtain information about an organisation which is not available on the profit and loss account. This unit focuses on the balance sheet.

The balance sheet shows where a business has obtained its finances – its *liabilities*. It also lists the assets purchased with these funds. Therefore the balance sheet shows what the business owns and what it owes. For many financiers this is of vital importance when deciding whether or not to:

- invest in a business
- lend it some money
- buy the organisation outright.

A balance sheet enables the various stakeholders to make decisions as to that company's stability, its ability to pay debts and its ability to expand. A balance sheet therefore shows how secure a business is and what the potential for profit may be. It shows the asset strength built up in a business over all its years of trading. Whereas a profit and loss account shows profits made from trading during the previous year.

How a business is financed and the resources it owns are of vital importance when making business plans and decisions. For example, if an organisation wanted to buy an expensive piece of equipment, how should it do it?

- Buy it outright using cash from its bank account. Yes, if there are sufficient funds to do so. But may the business be left short of money to meet future needs like paying bills, wages or buying new stock?
- Get a loan from the bank. Again, this is a reasonable method of finance provided the business does not already have a lot of loans. Existing debt levels are shown on the balance sheet and can be examined to avoid the firm becoming dangerously indebted.
- Attract new investors. An organisation can take a partner or attract new shareholders. With the new funds invested it can purchase the equipment outright, therefore incurring no monthly payments or interest. The extra funds invested mean that the bank account and cash flow will not be disrupted. However, new investors will receive a share of company profits and may want some say in the running of the business as well.

There is no single correct answer to the above. It depends on many factors including the individual company's current circumstances. Some organisations may have a very healthy bank balance whereas others may be struggling. It is the balance sheet that shows the current circumstances of the business. By analysing this information, decisions can be made to match the source of finance to the business needs.

22.2 The composition of the balance sheet

The balance sheet of a business is a 'snapshot' showing the position of a company at a given point in time. It only shows what the business owns and owes on the date the balance sheet was compiled. In other words, the balance sheet is a picture of an organisation's assets and liabilities at that date.

Despite the fact that there are two different formats, assets and liabilities are classified in exactly the same manner on both. It is just the way the balance sheet is drawn that differs. The classifications that are used are:

ASSETS

- Fixed assets – those items of a monetary value which have a long-term function and can be used repeatedly such as vehicles or machinery. These are assets the business plans to hold for a year or more and are not intended for immediate resale.
- Current assets – these are items of a monetary value which are likely to be turned into cash before

the next balance sheet date. These include stocks, debtors and cash.
- Other assets – assets which do not fall into either of the above categories, e.g. investments in other businesses.

LIABILITIES

- Shareholders' funds – money or resources invested by the owners; called 'capital' for sole traders or partnerships and 'share capital' for limited companies.
- Long-term liabilities – money owed by the business that has to paid in more than one year's time.
- Current liabilities – money owed by the business that has to paid in less than one year's time.

22.3 The vertical balance sheet

The vertical balance sheet is the one most widely used in business today. By law, all public limited companies must publish their accounts in this form. Therefore it is the format focused upon in this unit.

The foundations of the vertical balance sheet (at the bottom) consist of the firm's capital. This may have come from shareholders, bankers or from reinvested profit. If Spark Ltd has £400,000 of capital invested, it follows that it must have £400,000 of assets. The top section shows the type of assets bought. The table below shows a summarised and simplified version of this position.

Spark Ltd: Simplified vertical balance sheet

	£
Long-term (fixed) assets	300,000
Short-term (current) assets	100,000
Total assets	400,000
Total capital	400,000

ASSETS ON THE VERTICAL BALANCE SHEET

Fixed assets are long-term assets, including:

Tangible assets:

- Land and buildings – property owned by the business, either freehold or leasehold.
- Plant/machinery/equipment – anything from specialised machinery used in manufacturing to computers or even furniture.
- Vehicles – all types.

Intangible assets:

- Goodwill – the prestige a business enjoys which adds value over and above the value of its physical assets.
- Patents/copyright – exclusive rights to make or sell a particular invention.

Current assets include stock, debtors and cash. In balance sheets, these assets are treated differently from fixed assets. This is because they change on a daily basis as bills come in, stock is sold and cash comes into the shop tills. The sudden arrival of £20,000 of stock from a supplier adds to current assets. But if the company now owes £20,000 to that supplier, it is clearly no better off. So current liabilities such as this are deducted from current assets to give a total called net current assets (or **working capital**).

Spark Ltd: Fuller version of the firm's balance sheet

	£	£
Property	180,000	
Machinery and vehicles	120,000	300,000
Stock	80,000	
Debtors and cash	60,000	
Current liabilities	(40,000)	
Net current assets		100,000
Assets employed		400,000
Total capital		400,000

Notes

- The two-column format allows individual items to be shown on the left, leaving the 'big picture' totals to be seen clearly on the right.
- Current liabilities of £40,000 have been deducted from the £140,000 of current assets to show net current assets of £100,000.
- Assets employed of £400,000 still balances with the capital employed (total capital).

CAPITAL ON THE VERTICAL BALANCE SHEET

Companies have three main sources of long-term capital: shareholders (share capital), banks (loan capital) and reinvested profits (reserves). Loan capital carries interest charges which must be repaid, as must the loan itself. Share capital and reserves are both owed to the shareholders, but do not have to be repaid. Therefore they are treated separately. Share capital and reserves are known as shareholders' funds and are kept separate from loan capital.

Assuming Spark Ltd's capital came from £50,000 of share capital, £250,000 of loan capital and £100,000 of accumulated, retained profits, the final version of the vertical balance sheet would look like this:

Spark Ltd: Balance sheet for 31 December last year

	£	£
Property	180,000	
Machinery and vehicles	120,000	300,000
Stock	80,000	
Debtors and cash	60,000	
Current liabilities	(40,000)	
Net current assets		100,000
Assets employed		**400,000**
Loan capital	250,000	250,000
Share capital	50,000	
Reserves	100,000	150,000
Total capital employed		**400,000**

THE CONCEPT OF CAPITAL AS A LIABILITY

It is hard to see why money invested by the owners should be treated as a **liability**. This is due to a concept in accounting called 'business entity'. This states that a business and its owners are two separate legal entities. From the point of view of the business, therefore, any money paid to it by the owners is a liability because the firm owes it to the shareholders. In reality, capital invested by the owners is only likely to be paid back in the event of the business ceasing to trade.

22.4 More detail on balance sheet calculations

WORKING CAPITAL

Current liabilities need to be repaid in the near future, hopefully using current assets. Taking the former away from the latter gives a figure termed *working capital*. This shows an organisation's ability or inability to pay its short-term debts.

If current assets exceed current liabilities the business has enough short-term assets to pay short-term debts. It has positive working capital and should therefore have enough money for its day-by-day needs.

If current assets are less than current liabilities the business does not have enough short-term assets to pay short-term debts. Working capital is negative, e.g. current assets are £50,000 but current liabilities are £70,000, so working capital is –£20,000. This may mean a day-to-day struggle to pay the bills.

The balance between current assets and liabilities is a very important figure. Suppliers and banks expect to be paid when debts are due. At the least, the failure to pay on time will mean a worsening in relations. At worst, it may result in court action.

THE EFFECT OF MAKING A NET LOSS ON THE BALANCE SHEET

In the event that a business makes a net loss rather than a net profit over a financial year, then the layout of the balance sheet remains completely unchanged. The only effect is that instead of the net profit being added to the reserves, thus increasing the shareholders' funds invested, a net loss is inserted and deducted from the capital account. Thus decreasing the reserves and therefore the capital employed.

This reflects that if a business has made a loss over the financial period, expenses have exceeded revenues received. Therefore the overall value of the business will have fallen and so must the value of the owners' funds invested.

22.5 The published accounts of limited companies

The Companies Act of 1985 sets out minimum standards for the format and contents of balance sheets for external publication. Extra details will often be included in the notes which accompany these accounts.

The main differences between published company accounts and the standard vertical format for balance sheets are:

- Current liabilities are termed '**creditors** due within one year'.
- Assets employed are termed 'total assets less current liabilities'.
- Long-term liabilities are termed 'creditors due after one year'.
- Most important of the differences is that whereas private limited company accounts balance assets employed with capital employed, published plc accounts balance net assets with shareholders' funds. This is done by deducting long-term liabilities from the assets employed (to give 'net assets'). So these long-term loans are taken away from assets instead of being included as capital. The advantage of this is to enable shareholders to see at a glance what the balance sheet suggests the business is 'worth'. That is, the bottom line of the balance sheet (the shareholders' funds).

Below is a recent balance sheet for external publication for JD Wetherspoon. Note that two years are shown side by side. This is to help financial interpretation of the accounts and the analysis of trends. This helps stakeholders to use ratio analysis on the accounts. Key conclusions to be drawn from JD Wetherspoon's balance sheets over the two years include:

- the business is growing rapidly as a result of investing heavily in fixed assets
- increasingly, current liabilities are outweighing current assets, causing net current assets to be negative

	2002 £000	2001 £000
Fixed assets	745,041	625,093
Stock	8,594	7,503
Debtors	15,919	13,750
Investments & cash	13,812	10,032
Creditors due within one year	122,919	81,965
Net current assets	(84,594)	(50,680)
Total assets less current liabilities	660,447	575,223
Creditors due after one year	350,314	301,384
Total net assets	**310,133**	**273,839**
Share capital	129,111	120,613
Reserves	181,022	153,226
Shareholders' funds	**310,133**	**273,839**

Source: Annual Accounts for JD Wetherspoon, 2002

- reserves jumped in 2002 suggesting that the company had a profitable year – in fact operating profits exceeded £28 million.

In summary, JD Wetherspoon is expanding rapidly and generating healthy levels of profits. However, the worsening of its short-term (working capital) position may cause stakeholders some concern.

22.6 Window dressing accounts

Window dressing means presenting company accounts in such a manner as to flatter the financial position of the company.

Window dressing is a form of creative accounting which is concerned with making modest adjustments to sales, debtors and stock items when preparing end-of-year financial reports. There is a fine dividing line between flattery and fraud.

In many cases window dressing is simply a matter of tidying up the accounts and is not misleading. Two important methods of window dressing are:

1 Massaging profit figures – surprisingly, it is possible to 'adjust' a business's cost and revenue figures. At the end of a poor year, managers may be asked to bring forward as many invoices and deliveries as possible. The intention is to inflate, as much as possible, the revenue earned by the business in the final month of trading.
2 Hiding a deteriorating **liquidity** position – this allows businesses to present balance sheets which look sound to potential investors. A business may execute a sale and leaseback deal just prior to

accounts being published. This increases the amount of cash within the business and makes it look a more attractive proposition.

It is important to remember that although window dressing happens, the overwhelming majority of companies present their accounts as fairly and straightforwardly as possible.

FORD LOOKS LESS ATTRACTIVE TO INVESTORS

Ford, the world's second largest car maker, is struggling because of the large amount of debt on its balance sheet. The debt recorded on the company's balance sheet is over £100 billion, a figure which analysts consider to be too high. The company's financial woes are worsened by fears that the company is committed to paying substantial pensions to its former employees. This could add to the company's debt burden.

The company, under its new Chief Executive Bill Ford Junior (great-grandson of the company's founder) is also experiencing a period of low profitability. In particular its luxury car division (which includes Jaguar) is thought to be losing the company money.

The company's poor profitability and debt-laden balance sheet are likely to make it more difficult for the company to raise further capital.

Are the new products making money?
© Getty Images/AFP

The balance sheet is an important statement full of information for anyone with an interest in a business. Analysis of the balance sheet can provide the reader with an insight into the strengths and weaknesses of a business, its potential for growth, its stability and how it is financed.

The balance sheet gives details as to where and how an organisation has obtained its finance alongside information as to what this finance has been spent on. This allows judgements to be made about the financial performance of the business in question.

Examining individual balance sheets can be interesting and provides the reader with a great deal of information. However, it must be remembered that a balance sheet is only a 'snapshot' of a business on one day out of 365, and that for a meaningful analysis to take place it must be compared with previous balance sheets, to see what changes or trends can be identified. The primary method of balance sheet analysis is through accounting ratios. These are explained in Unit 23.

22.7 Balance sheets
an evaluation

Several key areas can be considered with regard to balance sheets. The first is the assumption that just because a company possesses thousands or millions of pounds' worth of assets it is doing well. It is how the company has financed these assets that counts. A company could look in quite a stable position, but what would be the effect of a rise in interest rates if most of the company is financed by debt?

Similarly equal importance must be placed on the short-term asset structure of the company. Many prof-

itable companies close down or go into liquidation, not through lack of sales or customers but through poor short-term asset management, i.e. management of working capital.

As with all financial data and decisions, it is not sufficient just to consider the numerical information. External considerations such as the state of the market or economy must be taken into account. Also the quality of management and skills of the workforce should be considered. Comparisons with similar sized organisations in the same industry must be used. Also an investigation into the non-financial aspects of the business. A company could have millions of pounds of assets, a healthy bank account, a good profit record and be financed mainly by share capital. However, all of this means little if the workforce is about to go on strike for three months or its products are becoming obsolete.

KEY terms

creditors – those a firm owes money to, e.g. suppliers or bankers.

debts – sums owed to a firm by customers who have bought goods on credit.

liability – a debt, i.e. a bill that has not been paid or a loan which has not been repaid.

liquidity – a measurement of a firm's ability to pay its short-term bills.

working capital – day-to-day finance for running the business (current assets – current liabilities).

A Level Exercises

A. REVISION QUESTIONS

(30 marks; 60 minutes)

Read the unit, then answer:

1 Define the term 'balance sheet'. (3)
2 Distinguish between fixed and current assets. (3)
3 Explain why it is that the two parts of a balance sheet will always balance. (2)
4 What are the main reasons for presenting a balance sheet in vertical format? (3)
5 How would you calculate working capital? (2)
6 What are the differences between debentures and ordinary bank loans? (3)
7 Explain what is meant by the term 'window dressing' (4)
8 Describe two types of shares issued by limited companies. (4)
9 What is the difference between an intangible and a tangible fixed asset? (3)
10 State two items other than share capital you might find in the 'financed by' section of a plc. (3)

B. REVISION EXERCISES

B1 Data Response

D Parton Ltd: Year ending 31 December 1999

		£000
	Property	600
	Stock	120
	Machinery (at cost)*	240
	Creditors	100
	Cash	170
	Reserves	350
less	Debtors	280
	Tax due	140
	Assets employed	(200)
	Net current assets	760
	Overdraft	200
	Share capital	500
	Capital employed	760

*Book value £120,000

Questions *(20 marks; 25 minutes)*

1 a Identify 10 mistakes in the balance sheet above. (10)
   b Draw up the balance sheet correctly. (10)

B2 Stimulus Question

The balance sheet shown below is taken from Waterford Wedgwood's 1998 annual report and accounts. Waterford Wedgwood is a major exporter of very high quality china and glassware.. In 1998 its sales turnover rose to £730.5 million from £529.7 million in 1997.

Waterford Wedgwood Consolidated balance sheet as at 31 December 1998

	1998 £m	1997 £m
Intangible assets	16.8	–
Tangible assets	226.6	212.7
Financial assets	6.7	7.3
Stocks	203.9	213.3
Debtors	132.9	118.2
Cash	68.2	58.4
Creditors	171.6	197.0
Net current assets	233.4	192.9
Assets employed	**483.5**	**412.9**
Long-term liabilities	295.1	201.7
Share capital	232.1	230.9
Reserves	(47.5)	(29.4)
Minority interests	3.8	9.7
Capital employed	**483.5**	**412.9**

Questions *(30 marks; 40 minutes)*

1 Explain the meaning of the following terms:
   a consolidated balance sheet
   b assets employed (4)
2 Describe two external users of financial information and explain why they might analyse a balance sheet. (6)
3 a Identify **three** key trends in this data. (3)
   b Analyse the possible causes and implications of the trends you have identified. (6)
4 Evaluate the usefulness of this data to an investor considering purchasing shares in Waterford Wedgwood. (11)

B3 Case Study

T & J Speedpart Ltd are a family-owned limited company which specialises in making and supplying parts for old Volkswagens. The business was started as a partnership in 1982 by two mechanics who were finding it difficult to get replacement parts for their old VW Beetles. In 1991 Terry Whitlow bought out his partner by raising money from his family and the company became private limited. Since then, Terry's son and daughter have both entered the firm, Andrew to manage the ever increasing mail order side of the business and Laura to try to develop the current range of parts they have on offer.

The figures on the following page are available from their balance sheet.

Reserves	£30,000
Share capital	£230,000
Debtors	£13,000
Creditors	£44,000
Machinery	£90,000
Proposed dividends	£25,000
Cash	£3,500
Bank	£6,500
Loan (3+ years)	£100,000
Stock	£43,000
Vehicles	£36,000
Land and buildings	£237,000

Their accountant has advised that they can cut staffing costs by installing a new computerised system to handle the mail order enquiries and maintain stock records. The cost of such a system has been quoted at £26,000. He suggests that they can use £5,000 from their liquid assets and easily add to their existing loan commitment to purchase this system.

Questions *(30 marks; 35 minutes)*

1 What is meant by the term 'liquid assets'? *(3)*
2 Calculate the following:
  a total current assets
  b total current liabilities
  c working capital *(6)*
3 Construct a vertical balance sheet showing the new position of T & J Speedpart Ltd if the accountant's plans are put into practice. *(9)*
4 Comment on the strengths and weaknesses of T & J Speedpart Ltd's balance sheet, now that the accountant's plans have been carried out. *(12)*

B4 Case Study

MFI continues to grow

Furniture group MFI continued its recent growth and enjoyed another profitable year according to its Annual Report and Accounts, published in June 2002. The balance sheet for the company is shown below.

John Hancock, Chief Executive, said: 'I am pleased to report that we have achieved another half-year of healthy growth'.

He commented that the company had looked at all the Group's strategic development opportunities and identified its main priorities, as being:

- to continue the roll-out of refurbished MFI stores
- to continue to broaden its product ranges into bathrooms and sofas
- to complete the redevelopment of the Hygena Cuisines chain in France.

These are the areas offering the best future growth and returns for shareholders.

Balance sheet for MFI Furniture Group as at 15 June 2002

	2002	2001
	£m	£m
Fixed assets	355.1	299.2
Stock	138.4	?
Debtors	123.2	91.8
Investments & cash	98.0	97.4
Creditors due within one year	297.5	237.9
Net current assets/(liabilities)	?	76.6
Total assets less current liabilities	417.2	375.8
Creditors due after one year	15.6	7.8
Total net assets	**401.6**	**368.0**
Share capital	110.6	103.4
Reserves	291.0	?
Shareholders' funds	**401.6**	**368.0**

Questions *(25 marks, 30 minutes)*

1 Distinguish between creditors and debtors. *(3)*
2 a Complete MFI's balance sheet by inserting the missing figures. *(3)*
  b Explain one way in which MFI might have window dressed its accounts to make them look as favourable as possible. *(4)*
3 MFI is investing heavily in refurbishing its stores. Explain whether the balance sheet would encourage financial institutions to lend it further capital to finance its plans. *(6)*
4 To what extent can you judge the performance of MFI over the period 2001–2002 from the information included in the company's balance sheets? *(9)*

C. ESSAY QUESTIONS

1 'Balance sheets can only measure the financial worth of a business. The real worth depends upon far more.' Discuss how important a balance sheet is, then, in judging whether a firm is well managed.
2 Consider whether a balance sheet is more useful than a cash flow forecast, or vice versa.
3 'Balance sheet evaluation is the key to making successful long-term investment decisions.' To what extent do you believe this statement to be true?

RATIO ANALYSIS

DEFINITION

Ratio analysis is an examination of accounting data by relating one figure to another. This allows more meaningful interpretation of the data and the identification of trends.

23.1 Introduction

The function of accounting is to provide information to stakeholders on how a business has performed over a given period. But how is performance to be judged? Is an annual profit of £1 million good or bad? Very good if the firm is a small family business. Woeful if the business is JD Wetherspoon and annual sales are more than £700 million. What is needed is comparative information. A way of judging a firm's financial performance in relation to its size and in relation to the performance of its competitors. The method used for this is called ratio analysis.

Financial accounts, such as the profit and loss account and the balance sheet, are used for three main purposes:

- financial control
- planning
- accountability.

Ratio analysis can assist in achieving these objectives. It can help the different users of financial information to answer some of the questions they are interested in. And may raise several new questions such as:

- Is this company/my job safe?
- Should I stop selling goods to this firm on credit?
- Should I invest in this business?

23.2 Interpreting final accounts: the investigation process

To analyse company accounts, a well-ordered and structured process needs to be followed. This should ensure that the analysis is relevant to the question being looked at. The seven-point approach shown at the top of the next column is helpful:

23.3 Types of ratio

The main classifications of ratios are as follows:

- **Profitability ratios**

    Measure the relationship between gross/net profit and sales, assets and capital employed. These are sometimes referred to as performance ratios.

The investigation process

Step 1 Reason	The starting point for interpreting financial accounts is establishing why you are doing so. If you are considering supplying a company with a large order of goods, you want to try to establish its financial stability and ability to pay.
Step 2 Identification	Identify the relevant figures from the financial accounts.
Step 3 Process	Decide what method(s) of analysis will provide you with the most useful and meaningful results. (See Figure 23.2.)
Step 4 Calculation	Make a comparison between data by calculating one figure as a ratio of another. Such as profit as a percentage of sales revenue or borrowings as a proportion of total capital.
Step 5 Comparison	Compare the figures from this period with the results from the last period, those of your competitors or other companies under investigation.
Step 6 Interpretation	Look at the results obtained and interpret them in relation to values that would be considered poor, average or good.
Step 7 Action	If certain results are worrying, initiate further investigation (maybe into areas which are not covered in the financial accounts), or take corrective action.

- **Activity ratios**

    These measure how efficiently an organisation uses its resources such as stocks or total assets.

- **Liquidity ratios**

    These investigate the short-term and long-term financial stability of a firm by examining the relationships between assets and liabilities. These are sometimes called **solvency** ratios.

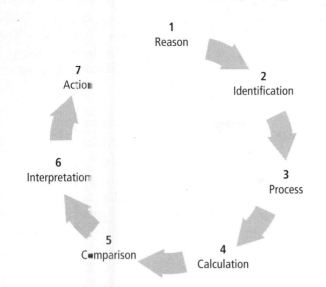

Figure 23.1 Seven-point approach to ratio analysis

- **Gearing**

  Examines the extent to which the business is dependent upon borrowed money. It is concerned with the long-term financial position of the company.

- **Shareholder ratios**

  This group of ratios is concerned with analysing the returns for shareholders. These examine the relationship between the number of shares issued, dividend paid, value of the shares, and company profits.

The following sections look at each classification of ratios in more detail.

23.4 Profitability ratios

For private businesses, a key objective is to make a profit. But how much profit? Consider the following example.

Example:
Companies A and B operate in the same market. At the end of the year they report profits as follows:

	COMPANY A	COMPANY B
Profit	£100,000	£1 million

Which is the more successful company? Company B, surely. However, if additional information is taken into account:

	COMPANY A	COMPANY B
Profit	£100,000	£1 million
Capital invested	£200,000	£10 million

This shows that company A has done very well compared with the capital invested in the business. Much better, in fact, than company B. Profitability ratios allow comparisons such as this to be made in detail. The figures can be compared in percentage terms. This makes comparison easier.

	COMPANY A	COMPANY B
Profit	£100,000	£1 million
Divided by Capital invested	£200,000	£10 million
× 100 (to get a percentage)	50%	10%

Company A's success can now be seen much more clearly.

Unit 21 distinguished between various types of profit. Because of the different types of profit, there are a number of different profit ratios. These are detailed below.

GROSS PROFIT MARGIN

This ratio examines the relationship between the profit made before allowing for overhead costs (gross profit) and the level of turnover/sales made. It is given by the formula:

$$\text{gross profit margin} = \frac{\text{gross profit}}{\text{turnover (sales)}} \times 100\%$$

For example, a furniture shop buys sofas for £200 and sells them for £500 each, making a gross profit of £300 per sofa. In a week it sells 10, so its gross profit is £3,000 and sales are £5,000. The gross profit margin is therefore:

$$\frac{\text{gross profit}}{\text{turnover}} = \frac{£3,000}{£5,000} \times 100 = 60\%$$

Note that although this sounds a terrific profit margin, no allowance has yet been made for all the overhead costs of the business, such as rent, rates, staff costs, advertising and much more.

Interpretation:
Obviously, the higher the profit margin a business makes the better. However, the level of gross profit margin will vary considerably between different markets. For example, the amount of gross profit percentage on clothes (especially fashion items) is far higher than on food. Any result gained must be looked at in the context of the industry in which the firm operates. It will always be possible to make comparisons with previous years' figures. This will establish whether or not the firm's trading position has become more or less profitable.

Altering the ratio:

The gross profit margin can be improved by:

- raising sales revenue whilst keeping the cost of sales static, or
- reducing the cost of sales made whilst maintaining the same level of sales revenue.

Business IN

PROFIT MARGINS BOOSTED BY COMMITTED EMPLOYEES

A report published by International Survey Research shows that British employees are significantly less committed than workers in other advanced economies. The report also shows that organisations with highly committed employees achieve higher levels of profits.

The report, based on the views of 360,000 employees from the top ten economies in the world, showed that only 59% of employees in Britain viewed their employers favourably. Over the three years of the study, the net profit margin rose by 2.06% in businesses with committed employees. In comparison, companies viewed less favourably by their employees, suffered a 1.38% fall in net profit margins.

NET PROFIT MARGIN

This ratio measures the relationship between the net profit (profit made after all overhead expenses have been deducted) and the level of turnover or sales made. It is given by the formula:

$$\text{net profit margin} = \frac{\text{net profit}}{\text{turnover (sales)}} \times 100\%$$

The furniture shop with its £5,000 sales and £3,000 gross profit has overheads of £2,500 per week. So its weekly net profit is £3,000 *minus* £2,500, i.e. £500. The net profit margin is:

$$\frac{\text{net profit}}{\text{turnover}} = \frac{£500}{£5,000} \times 100 = 10\%$$

Interpretation:

As with gross profit, a higher percentage result is preferred. The net profit margin establishes whether the firm has been efficient in controlling its expenses. It should be compared with previous years' results and with other companies in the same industry to judge relative efficiency. The net profit margin should also be compared with the gross profit margin. The gross profit margin may have improved while the net profit margin declined. This would show that profits made

on trading are rising, but overhead expenses are increasing at an even faster rate. Thus efficiency is declining. This can be investigated further by comparing each category of expenses with sales to determine where the problems are occurring.

For example:

$$\text{expenses:sales ratio} = \frac{\text{administration}}{\text{turnover (sales)}} \times 100\%$$

The firm may have managed to push its sales and gross profits up by hiring more sales staff. The staff may have added £1,000 a week to sales and £600 a week to gross profit. But if these staff cost the firm £1,200 a week the extra overhead cost will hit the net profit margin – hard.

Altering the ratio:

The net profit margin can be improved by:

- raising sales revenue whilst keeping expenses low, or
- reducing expenses whilst maintaining the same level of sales revenue.

RETURN ON CAPITAL EMPLOYED (ROCE)

This is sometimes referred to as being the primary efficiency ratio and is perhaps the most important ratio of all. It measures the efficiency with which the firm generates profit from the funds invested in the business. It answers the key question anyone would ask before investing or saving: What annual percentage return will I get on my capital?

$$\text{ROCE} = \frac{\text{operating profit}}{\text{capital employed}} \times 100\%$$

Operating profit is profit after all operating costs and overheads have been deducted. It can also be called trading (or net) profit. It is also acceptable to calculate return on capital employed using pre-tax profit.

Capital employed is long-term loans plus shareholders' funds. When looking at published accounts, it is helpful to remember that capital employed = assets employed. This helps because assets employed is always shown (though called *total assets less current liabilities*) whereas the figure for capital employed is rarely given.

Interpretation:

The higher the value of the ratio the better. ROCE measures profitability, and no shareholder will complain at huge returns. The figure needs to be compared with previous years and other companies to determine whether this year's result is satisfactory or not.

A firm's ROCE can also be compared with the percentage return offered by interest-bearing accounts at banks and building societies. If bank interest rates are 8%, what is the point of a sole trader investing money in his or her business, working very hard all year and making a return on capital employed of 6%? They would be better off investing their money and staying at home.

So what is the right level of ROCE? There is no clear answer, but most companies would regard a 20% ROCE as very satisfactory. The returns achieved by a selection of public companies in 2002 are shown in the table below.

Altering the ratio:
The return on capital employed can be improved by:

- increasing the level of profit generated by the same level of capital invested, or
- maintaining the level of profits generated but decreasing the amount of capital it takes to do so.

23.5 | Activity ratios

Activity ratios or asset utilisation ratios are concerned with how well an organisation manages its resources. Primarily they investigate how well the management controls the *current* situation of the firm. They consider stock, debtors and creditors. This area of ratios is linked, therefore, with the management of *working capital*.

STOCK TURNOVER

This ratio measures the number of times a year a business sells and replaces its stock. For example, if a market stall trader bought stock from wholesalers every morning and sold all the stock by the end of the afternoon, replacing the stock daily would mean a stock turnover of 365 times per year. The formula for stock turnover is:

$$\text{stock turnover} = \frac{\text{cost of goods sold}}{\text{stock}}$$

expressed as *times per year*.

Interpretation:
This ratio can only really be interpreted with knowledge of the industry in which the firm operates. For example, we would expect a greengrocer to turn over stock virtually every day, as the goods have to be fresh. Therefore, we would expect to see a result for stock turnover of approximately 250 to 300 times per year. This allows for closures and holidays and the fact that some produce will last longer than one day. A second-hand car sales business might take an average of a month to sell the cars; therefore the stock turnover would be 12 times.

It is possible to convert this ratio from showing the number of times an organisation turns over stock to showing the average number of days stock is held. It is given by the formula:

$$\text{stock turnover} = \frac{365}{\text{number of times}}$$

expressed as *days*.

It is also possible to express stock turnover in terms of weeks or months.

Altering the ratio:
The stock turnover ratio can be improved by

- reducing the average level of stocks held, without losing sales, or
- increasing the rate of sales without raising the level of stocks.

Note that the stock turnover ratio has little meaning for service industries as they do not buy or sell stocks of goods.

DEBTORS' COLLECTION PERIOD

This particular ratio is designed to show how long, on average, it takes the company to collect debts owed by customers. Customers who are granted credit are called debtors. The formula for this ratio is:

$$\text{debtors' collection period} = \frac{\text{debtors}}{\text{sales turnover}} \times 365$$

expressed as *days*.

Interpretation:
Debtors' collection period (usually called debtor days) shows how long a firm is having to wait for the money owed to it. Therefore the shorter the debt collection period the better. A low debtor days figure means cash flow is boosted by early inflows. Generally, then, a low figure is a good thing. It should be remembered,

The Return on Capital Employed (ROCE) achieved by a selection of public companies, 2002

COMPANY	ANNUAL OPERATING PROFIT	CAPITAL EMPLOYED	ROCE
Pizza Express (restaurants)	£38,200,000	£147,600,000	25.88%
Cadbury Schweppes (confectionery & soft drinks)	£774,000,000*	£3,341,000,000	23.17%
The Body Shop International (cosmetics, retailing)	£20,200,000	£124,000,000	16.29%
JD Wetherspoon (pubs)	£44,300,000	£660,440,000	6.70%

* Based on interim year results.

though, that offering long credit terms is a viable marketing strategy. Different companies allow different amounts of time for debtors to settle invoices. Standard credit terms are usually for 30, 60 or 90 days. The debtor days figure should ideally be compared with the official number of days the organisation allows for settlement. In other words, company X may have a higher debtor days figure than company Y, not through incompetence but due to a deliberate management strategy.

Altering the ratio:

The debtors' collection period can be improved by reducing the amount of time for which credit is offered, e.g. from 90 to 60 days. Offering incentives for clients to pay on time, e.g. cash discounts or stepping up the efficiency of the credit control department. A common approach is **aged debtors analysis**. This means sorting debtors into the age of their debts to you – oldest first. This helps focus upon collecting debts from the slowest payers. It also may encourage a firm to refuse to supply a persistent slow payer in future.

ASSET TURNOVER RATIO

The asset turnover ratio measures how many pounds worth of sales a company can generate from its asset base. Company directors often use the phrase 'make the assets sweat'. In other words, make the assets work hard. If there is a period in the year when the factory is quiet, an active company director might want to find a source of extra business. In this way the company could keep generating sales from its existing assets. This would push up the asset turnover.

$$\text{asset turnover} = \frac{\text{sales turnover}}{\text{assets employed}}$$

expressed as *times per year*.

The restaurant chain Pizza Express had the following asset turnover figures in 2001 and 2002:

	SALES TURNOVER	ASSETS EMPLOYED	ASSET TURNOVER
2001	£185,100,000	£126,400,000	1.46 times
2002	£212,000,000	£147,600,000	1.44 times

Source 2002 Annual Report and Accounts, Pizza Express plc

In 2002 the asset turnover ratio for Pizza Express fell compared with the previous year. This figure represented a substantial decline on the asset turnover figures achieved by the company a few years earlier. This trend suggests that the company's efficiency is declining as its size increases.

Interpretation:

Some companies pursue a policy of high profit margins, perhaps at the cost of high sales. An antiques shop in an expensive part of town may be beautifully laid out, but never seem to have any customers. Its asset turnover will be low because it generates low sales from its high asset base. Fortunately for the firm, its profit margins may be so high that the occasional sale generates enough profit to keep the business going.

Other companies may follow a low price, high sales approach. Tesco used to call this 'pile them high, sell them cheap'. Here profit margins may be low, but the asset turnover so high that lots and lots of small profits add up to a healthy profit total. Asset turnover, then, should be looked at in relation to (net) profit margins.

In the case of Pizza Express, the figures below show how asset turnover affects return on capital employed. If net profit margins are multiplied by asset turnover, the result is the company's ROCE. So boosting asset turnover is as helpful to a firm as boosting its profit margins.

	net profit margin	×	asset turnover	=	ROCE
2001	21.4%	×	1.46	=	31.2%
2002	18.0%	×	1.44	=	25.9%

Source 2002 Annual Report and Accounts, Pizza Express plc

Altering the ratio:

To increase asset turnover there are two options. Either work at increasing sales from the existing asset base (making the assets sweat). Or sell off under-utilised assets, so that the sales figure is divided by a lower asset total. Either approach would then have the effect of boosting a company's ROCE.

23.6 Liquidity ratios

These ratios are concerned with the short-term financial health of a business. They are concerned with the organisation's working capital and whether or not it is being managed effectively. Too little working capital and the company may not be able to pay all its debts. Too much and it may not be making the most efficient use of its financial resources.

CURRENT RATIO

This ratio looks at the relationship between current assets and current liabilities. It is often referred to as the working capital ratio and examines the **liquidity** position of the firm. It is given by the formula:

current ratio = current assets:current liabilities

This is expressed as a ratio, for example 2:1 or 3:1.

Example:

Bannam Ltd has current assets of £30,000 and current liabilities of £10,000.

current ratio = current assets : current liabilities
= 30,000 : 10,000
= 3 : 1

current ratio = 3:1

Interpretation:

From the above worked example the result shows that Bannam Ltd has three times as many current assets as current liabilities. This means that for every £1 of short-term debts owed they have £3 of assets to pay them. This is a comfortable position.

Accountants suggest the 'ideal' current ratio should be approximately 1.5:1, i.e. £1.50 of assets for every £1 of debt. Any higher than this and the organisation has too many resources tied up in unproductive assets; these should really be invested more profitably. A low current ratio means a business may not be able to pay its debts. It is possible that the result may well be something like 0.8:1. This shows the firm has only 80p of current assets to pay every £1 it owes.

The current ratios of a selection of public companies in 2002 are shown in the table at the bottom of the page.

As this table shows, it would be wrong to panic about a liquidity ratio of less than 1. Very successful firms such as Sainsbury and JD Wetherspoon have often had spells when their liquidity levels were less than 1.

Altering the ratio:

If the ratio is so low that it is becoming hard to pay the bills, the company will have to try to bring more cash into the balance sheet. This could be done by:

- selling under-used fixed assets
- raising more share capital
- increasing long-term borrowings
- postponing planned investments.

THE ACID TEST

This ratio is sometimes also called the quick ratio or even the liquid ratio. It examines the business's liquidity position by comparing current assets and liabilities, but it omits stock from the total of current assets. The reason for this is stock is the most illiquid current asset, i.e. it is the hardest to turn into cash without a loss in its value. It can take a long time to convert stock into cash. Furthermore, stock may be old or obsolete and thus unsellable.

By omitting stock the ratio directly relates cash and near cash (cash, bank and debtors) to short-term debts. This provides a tighter measure of a firm's liquidity. It is given by the formula:

acid test = (current assets − stock) : current liabilities

Again, it is expressed in the form of a ratio such as 2:1.

Interpretation:

Accountants recommend that an 'ideal' result for this ratio should be approximately 1:1. Thus showing that the organisation has £1 of short-term assets for every £1 of short-term debt. A result below this, e.g. 0.8:1, indicates that the firm may well have difficulties meeting short-term payments. However, some businesses are able to operate with a very low level of liquidity; supermarkets, for example, who have much of their current assets tied up in stock.

The acid test ratios of a selection of public companies in 2002 are shown in the table at the top of the following page.

23.7 Gearing

Gearing is sometimes included in the classification of liquidity ratios. But this ratio focuses on the long-term financial stability of an organisation. It measures long-term loans as a proportion of a firm's capital employed. It shows how reliant the firm is upon borrowed money. In turn, that indicates how vulnerable the firm is to financial setbacks. Highly geared companies can suffer badly in recessions, because even when times are hard they still have to keep paying high interest payments to the bank.

The formula for gearing is:

$$\text{gearing} = \frac{\text{long-term loans}}{\text{capital employed}} \times 100\%$$

Once again this is expressed as a percentage.

long-term loans = bank loans + debentures

capital employed = loans + share capital + reserves

Interpretation:

The gearing ratio shows how risky an investment a company is. If loans represent more than 50% of capital employed, the company is said to be highly geared. Such a company has to pay interest on its borrowings before it can pay dividends to shareholders or retain profits for reinvestment. The higher the gearing the

Current ratios of a selection of public companies, 2002

COMPANY	BALANCE SHEET DATE	CURRENT ASSETS	CURRENT LIABILITIES	CURRENT RATIO
Smiths Group	31/7/02	£1,352,700,000	£931,800,000	1.45:1
John Lewis	26/1/02	£693,700,000	£593,000,000	1.17:1
Cadbury Schweppes	16/6/02	£1,640,000,000	£1,630,000,000	1.01:1
J Sainsbury	30/3/02	£3,728,000,000	£4,708,000,000	0.79:1
JD Wetherspoon	28/7/02	£38,325,000	£122,919,000	0.31:1

Acid test ratios of a selection of public companies, 2002

Company	Balance Sheet Date	Current Assets – Stock	Current Liabilities	Acid Test Ratio
Smiths Group	31/7/02	£878,200,000	£931,800,000	0.94:1
John Lewis	26/1/02	£391,700,000	£593,000,000	0.66:1
Cadbury Schweppes	16/6/02	£1,066,000,000	£1,630,000,000	0.65:1
J Sainsbury	30/3/02	£2,977,000,000	£4,708,000,000	0.63:1
JD Wetherspoon	28/7/02	£29,731,000	£122,919,000	0.24:1

Gearing of a selection of public companies, 2002

Company	Balance Sheet Date	Long-term Loans	Capital Employed	Gearing
Smiths Group	31/7/02	£967,600,000	£1,977,000,000	48.94%
John Lewis	26/1/02	£479,600,000	£1,920,000,000	24.98%
Cadbury Schweppes	16/6/02	£2,384,000,000	£5,725,000,000	41.64%
J Sainsbury	30/3/02	£1,454,000,000	£6,363,000,000	22.85%
JD Wetherspoon	28/7/02	£292,915,000	£660,417,000	44.35%

higher the degree of risk. Low geared companies provide a lower risk investment. Therefore they can negotiate loans more easily and at lower cost than a highly geared company.

Banks would be especially reluctant to lend to a firm with poor liquidity and high gearing. It is useful, therefore, to look at the gearing for the same firms whose liquidity was investigated earlier. This is shown in the table above.

Smiths Group (an engineering company), Cadbury Schweppes and JD Wetherspoon all have quite high gearing levels. These businesses might experience difficulties if interest rates rose, or if they encountered a really poor period of trading. However, if their markets have growth potential, these companies probably have the resources to benefit from it.

In contrast John Lewis and J Sainsbury have fairly low gearing levels. This could be a weakness if the economy was expanding rapidly. Their management teams could be judged as timid as the companies are not in a position to benefit from rapid growth. An investment in a firm with a low gearing could be regarded as safe, but dull.

HIGH GEARING WEAKENS ARCADIA'S COMPETITIVE POSITION

Arcadia, the retail group that owns shoppers' favourites including Burtons and Top Shop, is nervous about a forecast fall in spending on the high street. In autumn 2002 the company expressed its concern that the British economy could be heading for a decline in consumer spending in 2003.

A spokesperson for Arcadia said that the company operated in the highly competitive fashion clothing sector which is highly vulnerable to changes in the state of the economy, and particularly consumer spending. Arcadia is judged to be more vulnerable than many of its competitors because of the high level of its gearing (64.12% in its latest balance sheet). Because the company is committed to substantial interest payments, any decline in spending hits profits hard. At the same time the company is less able to cut prices and offer other promotions.

However, the 2002 takeover of Arcadia by entrepreneur Philip Green (the owner of the BHS chain) may mean that Arcadia can reduce its gearing level in early 2003.

Business

IN

Altering the ratio:
The gearing ratio can be altered in several ways depending on whether the organisation wishes to raise or lower its gearing figure.

RAISING GEARING	REDUCING GEARING
Buy back ordinary shares	Issue more ordinary shares
Issue more preference shares	Buy back debentures (redeeming)
Issue more debentures	Retain more profits (increase reserves)
Obtain more loans	Repay loans

23.8 Shareholder ratios

Investing in shares provides two potential sources of financial return. The share price might rise, providing a capital gain. In addition, firms pay annual dividends to shareholders. The size of the dividends depends upon the level of profits made in the year. Shareholder ratios provide a way of judging whether the shares are expensive or inexpensive, and whether the dividends are high enough. They do, however, put some pressure on companies to achieve short-term profits and to pay out high dividends. This may damage the interests of the company's stakeholders in the long term.

EARNINGS PER SHARE (EPS)

This ratio measures the company's **earnings** (profit after tax) divided by the number of ordinary shares. This can be used to measure a company's profit performance over time. It also shows the potential for paying out a dividend to shareholders. It is given by the formula:

$$\text{earnings per share} = \frac{\text{net profit after tax}}{\text{no. of ordinary shares}}$$

usually expressed in pence.

Interpretation:
Earnings per share is relatively meaningless if analysed on its own, although the higher the result the better for shareholders. Meaning can only be established by comparisons with previous years' results.

Altering the ratio:
This ratio can only really be improved by increasing the level of profits made. This may cause the pressure for short-term profits mentioned earlier.

PRICE : EARNINGS RATIO (PE RATIO)

This is a more useful ratio than earnings per share as it analyses the relationship between the earnings of the individual share and its current market price. The market prices for shares are not listed in the annual report as they are subject to frequent fluctuations.

However, the values for shares can be easily obtained from quality daily papers or from the Internet. The PE ratio is given by the formula:

$$\text{PE ratio} = \frac{\text{market price (pence)}}{\text{earnings per share (pence)}}$$

Interpretation:
The reason this ratio is not expressed in units is that it shows the relationship between the market share price and the last reported earnings for that share. If a share's current market value is £2.50 and the last earnings per share result was 50p, the price earnings ratio shows that the price of the share is five times that of its earnings. Investors use this ratio to help them determine the relative value of shares. If shares on the London stock market generally have PE ratios of around 15, a PE ratio of 5 would suggest that this company is rated only one-third as highly as the average share/company. In general, the higher the PE result the better. A high PE ratio reflects confidence in the future of the business. A high result may be due to high future expectations and an anticipation that earnings in the future may increase.

Altering the ratio:
Many things can affect the price:earnings ratio. As it is based upon the market value of the share, anything which could affect this value has an effect on the ratio. Thus the state of the economy, government policy, actions of competitors, actions of the company or speculation and rumour can all cause this ratio to alter.

DIVIDEND YIELD

This ratio directly relates the amount of dividend actually received to the market value of the share. It shows the shareholders' annual dividends as a percentage of the sum invested. It is given by the formula:

$$\text{dividend yield} = \frac{\text{ordinary share dividend}}{\text{market price (pence)}} \times 100\%$$

Interpretation:
Again, the higher the result the better. However, it would once more need to be compared against previous years and the results of competitors.

Altering the ratio:
As this ratio is based partly on the market price of ordinary shares, anything which affects this value will impact on the ratio. A higher result can be obtained by either making greater profits or making a greater proportion of profit available for distribution as dividend.

ISSUES FOR **analysis**

There are many more areas of ratio analysis than those outlined within this unit. Specialist ratios exist for all types of organisations, especially those in the public or voluntary sector where profits and capital are not so readily determined.

Another aspect that needs discussion is that the analysis and interpretation of financial statements is really only the first step in a lengthy process. The data gathered from this exercise must be presented to and understood by those who will then go on to make decisions based upon it. Also consider the validity of making long-term decisions based upon findings from a profit and loss account and balance sheet that may be several months out of date. As well as conducting ratio analysis, other information contained within the annual reports should also be used, such as the chairman's report.

As a final point for further investigation, the accuracy of ratio analysis itself is often called into question. Factors such as the effect of inflation on accounts from one year to the next, differences in accounting policies and the effect of economic change may have a significant effect on the ratios.

23.9 Ratio analysis
an evaluation

Ratio analysis is a powerful tool in the interpretation of financial accounts. It can allow for **inter-firm comparisons**, appraisal of financial performance and the identification of trends. It can therefore be of great help in financial planning and decision making.

However, because of its usefulness and the range of possible applications, there is a tendency to attach too much importance to the results gained from this analysis. Other types of analysis exist and there are sometimes more important issues at stake than just financial performance.

Many financial analysts are now using the concept of 'added value' to see if shareholder value has been increased. Consideration must also be given to the fact that often stakeholders are not fluent in financial and business terminology and that the use of ratio analysis may be a case of 'blinding them with science'. Also a changing society has seen a change in focus away from pure financial performance, towards consideration of social and ethical factors. Although ratio analysis is useful, it is limited in the area it investigates.

KEY terms

aged debtors analysis – listing debtors in age order, to identify the slowest payers.

earnings – for a company, earnings means profit after tax.

inter-firm comparisons – comparisons of financial performance between firms. To be valuable, these comparisons should be with a firm of similar size within the same market.

liquidity – the ability of a firm to meet its short-term debts. Liquidity can also be understood as being the availability of cash or assets that can easily be converted into cash.

solvency – when an organisation's assets exceed its external debts. If external debts are greater than the value of assets, then a state of insolvency exists.

A Level Exercises

A. REVISION QUESTIONS

(40 marks; 70 minutes)

Read the unit, then answer:

1 List four groups of people who may be interested in the results of ratio analysis. *(4)*

2 State the key stages in conducting an analysis of company accounts using ratios. *(7)*

3 Briefly explain the difference between activity ratios and profitability ratios. *(4)*

4 Explain why the return on capital employed (ROCE) is regarded as one of the most important ratios. *(3)*

5 Why might the managers of a company be pleased if its stock turnover ratio was falling? *(4)*

6 What might the debtor collection period tell you about the way in which a business controls its finances? *(4)*

7 Outline the difference between the current ratio and the acid test ratio. *(2)*

8 Why might a small investor be particularly interested in the dividend yield ratio? *(4)*

9 Outline two problems a company might experience if its gearing ratio rose significantly. *(4)*

10 Explain one reason why investors might treat the results of ratio analysis with caution. *(4)*

B. REVISION EXERCISES

B1 Practice Exercises

1 J Orr Ltd makes garden gnomes. When analysing J Orr's annual accounts, state and explain which three ratios you think would be of most use to:

a a firm wondering whether to supply J Orr with materials on credit *(6)*

b the trade union representative of J Orr's workforce *(6)*

c a pensioner, wondering whether J Orr will be a good investment *(6)*

d the management of J Orr's main rival, Gnometastic Ltd *(6)*

e J Orr's main customer, Blooms of Broadway garden centre. *(6)*

2 a Construct a vertical balance sheet from the following information. Make sure to include net current assets, assets employed and capital employed. *(8)*

Fixed assets	£80,000	Dividends due	£10,000
Trade creditors	£24,000	Reserves	£84,000
Share capital	£40,000	Overdraft	£14,000
Stock	£36,000	Trade debtors	£28,000
Cash	£28,000		

b Assess the short-term and long-term financial health of the business. *(12)*

3 A garden furniture producer wants to buy a garden centre. It has identified two possible businesses and conducted some ratio analysis to help it decide which

one to focus on. Look at the ratios for each business and decide which one you would recommend and why. *(10)*

	Blooms of Broadway	Cotswold Carnations
Gross margin	60%	45%
Return on capital	15.2%	14.6%
Stock turnover	18 times	24 times
Gearing	52%	35%
Sales growth (last 3 years)	+3.5% per year	+4.8% per year

4 Balance sheet for GrowMax Co as at 31 December

	£000
Fixed assets	860
Stock	85
Debtors	180
Cash	15
Current liabilities	200
Loans	360
Share capital	160
Reserves	420

a Calculate the firm's net current assets and capital employed. *(4)*

b Last year's revenue was £1,460,000 and operating margin was 10%. Comment on the firm's profitability. *(7)*

c GrowMax's main rival offers its customers 30 days' credit.

i How does this compare with GrowMax? *(4)*

ii Outline two further questions the GrowMax management should want answered before deciding whether their customer credit policy should be revised. *(6)*

d Outline three difficulties with drawing firm conclusions from comparisons between the ratios of two rival companies. *(9)*

B2 Data Response

Since the beginning of the year, Velux has enjoyed rapid growth as a result of booming exports to America. Financing the increased production has required an extra £80,000 of working capital, and now the production manager has put in an urgent request for £240,000 of new capital investment.

The firm's managing director doubts that he can find the extra capital without giving up control of the business (he currently holds 54% of the shares). The finance director is more optimistic. He suggests that: 'Our balance sheet is in pretty good shape and the mobile phone business is booming. I'm confident we can get and afford a loan.' So it came as a huge blow to hear that Barclays had turned the company down. It wondered what it had done wrong.

Velux balance sheet as at 31 December

	£000	£000
Fixed assets[1]		420
Stock	250	
Debtors[2]	140	
Cash	130	520
Current liabilities		380
Assets employed		560
Loans	200	
Share capital	50	
Reserves	310	
Capital employed		560

[1] Depreciated straight line over 10 years
[2] Including a £15,000 debtors item 12 months overdue

Questions *(30 marks; 35 minutes)*

1 Why might the bank manager have turned the request down? *(10)*
2 Recommend how the expansion might be financed, showing the effect of your plan upon key indicators of the firm's financial health. *(12)*
3 Given your answers to 1 and 2, discuss whether the firm should proceed with its expansion plan *(8)*

B3 Data Response
Look carefully at the extract below, then answer the questions. It will help to know that Harry Ramsden's is a famous chain of fish and chip restaurants.

Harry Ramsden's plc: Extract from annual report & accounts

P&L account	1997 £000	1996 £000
Turnover	6,833	4,888
Gross profit	5,273	4,280
Operating profit	1,838	1,528
Interest	318	192
Pre-tax profit	1,520	1,336
Corporation tax	474	402
Profit after tax	1,046	934
Dividends	495	441
Transfer to reserves	551	493

Balance Sheet, 30 Sept.	1997 £000	1996 £000
Fixed assets	13,706	8,964
Stock	252	113
Debtors	3,229	2,388
Cash	103	75
Creditors	5,911	3,873
Net current assets	(2,327)	(1,297)
Assets employed	11,380	7,667
Loans	2,055	258
Shareholders' funds	9,325	7,409
Capital employed	11,380	7,667

Questions *(40 marks; 50 minutes)*

1 State Harry Ramsden's:
  a 1997 earnings *(1)*
  b 1997 working capital. *(1)*
2 Calculate Harry Ramsden's:
  a 1997 cost of sales *(2)*
  b 1996 and 1997 gearing. *(4)*
3 a Assess the company's profitability in 1997 compared with 1996. *(8)*
  b What further information would be needed in order to make a full assessment of the effectiveness of the company's management at generating profit in 1997? *(6)*
4 Restaurant chains such as Pizza Express have an asset turnover ratio of around 2.
  a What is Harry Ramsden's 1997 asset turnover? *(2)*
  b Briefly explain the possible causes and effects of this figure compared with Pizza Express *(6)*
5 Grimsby Fish Co is considering whether to invest in Harry Ramsden's. Consider the main weaknesses for outsiders of using a company's accounts to decide on such a major decision. *(10)*

C. ESSAY QUESTIONS

1 'Ratios are of little to no use to a person intending to make a small investment.' Comment on the accuracy of this statement.
2 'The ability to assess the long- and short-term financial stability of an organisation is vital to every stakeholder.' To what extent do you agree with this statement?
3 With the economy entering a recession, an investor wants to reassess her share portfolio. Examine which ratios she should focus upon, given the economic circumstances.

USES AND LIMITATIONS OF ACCOUNTS

DEFINITION

Accounting information is drawn up according to a set of principles and conventions. It is largely financial and numerical although many judgements and opinions are involved. Accounting analysis ignores other information which may be equally important, such as the company's market share. Accounting data should be used with caution as part of an overall picture of the business.

24.1 Nature of accounts

The main accounting statements are set out in the table below.

The main accounting statements:

Balance sheet	*A statement of assets and liabilities of a business at a point in time. Assets are valued at historic cost which can lead to distortions. A balance sheet is drawn up on one day in the year, which gives scope for manipulating the values of assets and liabilities.*
Profit and loss account	*The firm's revenues and expenses over a period, usually a year. This links two balance sheets. Calculating profit depends on a series of assumptions and conventions. So profit is an accounting opinion, while cash is a matter of fact.*
Cash flow statement	*This is the story of how cash flowed in and out of a business during the previous financial year. This shows where the firm's funds have come from and how they have been used.*

24.2 Uses and users of accounts

There are two types of accounting information: financial accounts and management accounts.

- Financial accounts are those which companies publish and are therefore available to anyone. The 1985 Companies Act insists that large companies have to publish a balance sheet, a profit and loss account and a cash flow statement. Smaller companies have lesser requirements and unlimited firms have no requirement to publish any financial details.

- Management accounts are drawn up for internal use. They are designed to help managers make decisions. Accounts may be drawn up for a particular department, factory or product known as a profit or cost centre. The use of profit or cost centres provides managers with detailed information to help with management decision making.

The main users of published accounts and the reasons why they need accounting information are shown in the table at the top of the next page.

24.3 What accounts do not cover

Accounts cover accounting, financial and numerical information only. Published annual accounts contain further information in the chairman's report and the directors' report. But what is *not* covered may be more important that what *is*.

For example, accounts are historical and so do not reflect a changing business environment. The more volatile the environment, the less useful accounts are. Accounts do not reflect the arrival of a new competitor, or the loss of a valued supplier. Either may affect business prospects much more than the accounts would suggest.

Accounts say nothing about human resource matters except statistics about the pay of senior staff. The quality of the workforce, changes in senior personnel, and training to meet new technology are not covered. Nor is there discussion of the quality of the business's technology, its marketing, or the impact of the macroeconomic environment.

Indeed, accounts cannot do the work we ask them to do. Accounting information is but one source on which to base analysis and decision making. Marketing measures such as market share and new product success may be more important in the long term.

	The main users of published accounts:
Competitors	Businesses want to see how well they are doing compared with similar firms. They will look at profit margins, purchases of new machinery, trends in sales, etc.
Customers	Customers are interested in profits to find out if prices are too high. Also, if they have a long-term relationship, they will want to see signs of financial stability, e.g. good liquidity and moderate gearing.
Employees	Employees look for long-term stability, healthy trends in sales, sound liquidity to pay wages, and profitability to see if higher wages could be claimed.
Lenders	Lenders want to see adequate fixed assets as collateral for the loan and strong cash flow to pay the interest and repay the loan, leaving sufficient for normal operations. Lenders will also want to know what other loans the business has and how highly geared it is. Namely how risky the loan is.
Managers	Managers are concerned that published financial accounts show the business in a good light, as this will give confidence both inside and outside the business. They are more interested in management accounts which show what is happening now and in the near future. These are highly confidential.
Shareholders	Shareholders want to see a rising trend of sales revenue and profits and with costs under control. This should ensure dividends rising each year and keeping ahead of inflation.
Stakeholders	This modern term includes all those who have any kind of interest in the organisation, including owners, employees, managers, lenders, suppliers, customers, the general public, environmental groups and trade unions. For example, environmentalists would study annual reports and accounts to check on 'green' policies.
Suppliers	Suppliers will be especially keen to check that the company is liquid enough to pay its bills and to take credit from its suppliers. Otherwise they will want to supply only for cash.

24.4 Problems in handling accounts

LIQUIDITY AND PROFITABILITY

There is often confusion about the way the terms 'cash' and 'funds' are used. Strictly, 'cash' should only be used when actual money is received or paid. So cash received from sales is not the same as sales revenue. Someone who buys from you may buy on credit and so become a 'debtor', the asset which matches the sales revenue. But when will you actually receive the cash?

This distinction may not matter greatly for firms with a wide variety of customers, most of whom pay up within a month or two. What about a construction firm, though? It may be working on a two-year tunnel-building project. It might account for the revenue being generated by the work being done, but the cash may not come for six or more months. The profit and loss account may look good while the firm is running out of cash.

PROFIT QUALITY

The profits a firm makes from its ongoing operations can be regarded as high quality profit because they are likely to recur year after year. By contrast, one-off profits from extraordinary items should be considered low quality. Today's windfall profit on foreign exchange dealings may turn into 'unlucky' losses next year. So it is important to check that the reported profit of a business is actually generated from its normal trading activities.

A company may sell a piece of surplus land to another business. There may be a surplus on disposal of these assets, where the sale value exceeds the book (balance sheet) value. The accounts should separate this one-off profit from operating or trading profits. When analysing accounts, it is important to consider whether the profit is high or low quality. The example below shows two equally sized rival firms. Firm A declares pre-tax profits of £80,000. Firm B has made £60,000. Notice the difference in the quality, however.

	FIRM A (LOW QUALITY PROFIT)	FIRM B (HIGH QUALITY PROFIT)
Sales turnover	£420,000	£480,000
Cost of sales	£290,000	£340,000
Overheads	£110,000	£80,000
Operating profits	£20,000	£60,000
Extraordinary items	£60,000	–
Pre-tax profit	£80,000	£60,000

ASSET VALUATION

Debtors and bad debts: Debtors are those who owe the business money because they have bought goods on credit. Most businesses will be happy to sell on credit to valued and long-term customers. However, even these can delay payment or go into liquidation. The value of debtors in current assets can overstate assets in the balance sheet and will influence the liquidity ratio. The debtors figure itself does not tell you who owes the money: are the debtors stable, long-term customers? Or are they new customers with little credit history? Have sales staff sold goods in hope, without carrying out proper credit checks? How 'old' are the debtors? Are any amounts long overdue and therefore unlikely to be paid? Is there an **aged debtors analysis**? Is a large part of debtors owed by one business, possibly in difficulty? Are any debtors likely to go 'bad'?

Taking an over-optimistic view that some doubtful debtors will pay up is a way of **window dressing** the year-end accounts. The prudent approach is to create a provision for bad debts. This would be deducted from revenue in the profit and loss account and from current assets in the balance sheet. This reduces the apparent size, profitability and liquidity of the business. The debtors position is well worth investigating in any serious financial review.

Depreciation: Depreciation of a fixed asset is regarded as a source of funds. It is charged to revenue each year to allocate the historic cost of the asset to the years of its predicted useful life. But it is not a movement of cash. The only time cash moves is when the fixed asset is bought and if any cash is raised from selling it at the end of its useful life to the business. It is a common mistake to regard depreciation as building up a pile of cash to replace the asset when it wears out.

Depreciation reduces reported profit and potentially taxable profit. There are various methods of depreciation, some of which write off expense more in the early years. On the other hand reduced depreciation helps boost reported profit. This, however, may be harmful in the long run as under-accounting for the cost of a fixed asset overstates the balance sheet: the accounts show a machine worth more than it is.

Land and buildings: Because of the convention of valuing at historic cost, land and buildings are likely to be shown at less than current market value. These are generally appreciating assets. A significant undervaluation can be of great concern. First, if balance sheet values are well below market value, the business may be open to hostile takeover. The assets can be broken up and sold to give the purchaser a surplus. Second, undervaluing fixed assets means the business does not have the **collateral** for loans that it should, possibly restricting sensible borrowing and investment.

Intangible assets: Intangible fixed assets include patents, copyrights, brand names, licences and goodwill. They are fixed assets, just like machinery, helping the business to produce and sell.

Intangible assets, or intellectual property, are very difficult to value. The value of a trademark or brand name builds up over time as the related products gain sales and consumer loyalty. The most reliable valuation for an intangible asset is when it is sold, which happens rarely.

However, businesses with significant brand names run the risk that their balance sheets will severely understate the value of the business. In this sense their accounts do not give a true and fair view. It also makes them vulnerable to takeover bids as they look cheap. Recently it has been possible to show an estimate for the value of brand names as a fixed asset and businesses such as Guinness have done this. However, businesses might use this as a way of inflating asset values and also their reserves.

Goodwill can only arise when a business is bought. Let us say company A buys B for £10,000,000 when the book value of B's assets is £8,000,000. This means that A has paid £2,000,000 for the goodwill in B. The goodwill represents B's good name, its ready-made products and its customer-base. B was worth more to A as a **going concern** than the value of its parts. Acquiring businesses often attempt to write off goodwill because of the difficulty of valuing it properly. The existence of goodwill in a balance sheet should always raise questions: did the acquiring company pay too much, and thereby now overstate its own worth? Has the acquiring company used the good name of B successfully and is its value still there? If the acquisition was unsuccessful, then there is much goodwill to be written off against future profits.

Stock valuation: At the end of every trading period, businesses must undertake stock checks. This process is crucial to the establishment of final accounts. The closing stock valuation appears in both the balance sheet and the profit and loss account and can have a significant effect on reported profit. Stock is the least liquid of the current assets. The stock check must be done fairly and not overstate the quantities. Also, unsaleable or slow-selling items of stock will need to be properly valued. This will apply particularly in the case of fast-moving consumer goods or items in markets where fashion and taste change quickly. Stock which will not sell has possibly only scrap value or no value. Closing stock must be valued at historic cost or net realisable value, whichever the lower.

UNIT 24 I USES AND LIMITATIONS OF ACCOUNTS

KEY terms

aged debtors analysis – listing unpaid customer bills in age order, with the most overdue account at the top of the list. This enables the credit controller to focus on late payers.

collateral – the security offered to back up a request for a loan. Usually the only acceptable form of collateral to a bank is property, since that tends to appreciate in value, whereas other business assets depreciate.

24.5 Problems with ratio analysis

Ratio analysis is dealt with fully in Unit 23 and is an essential part of financial analysis. It is important to treat ratios cautiously as they are based on published accounting information and are therefore subject to all the reservations expressed in this unit. Ratio analysis can only be as good as the figures on which it is based.

Ratio analysis is often based upon comparisons within one business across time. For example, stock turnover ratios could be measured over five years. This would show whether the turnover was speeding up, which implies more efficient management. However, if the faster stock turnover has been at the expense of empty shelves and dissatisfied customers, this conclusion is not so clear. It is often, and rightly, said that ratios raise questions, they do not answer them.

It is also common to make comparisons between businesses in the same industry. It is sensible to try to establish standard ratios for, say, the chocolate industry. Cadbury's might have yardsticks for judging itself. The problem is finding a comparable firm. Mars might seem a natural, but in fact Mars has two main businesses in Britain – chocolate and pet food (Whiskas and Chum are made by Mars). So an apparently sensible comparison becomes redundant.

There is also a temptation to rely too heavily on rule-of-thumb ratios. For example, it is sometimes said that an engineering firm should have a particular value for its current ratio, whereas for a baker a different figure would apply. Again, these 'rules' should be used carefully and in the light of individual circumstances.

24.6 Window dressing

Window dressing means dressing up the accounts to make them look as flattering as possible on the balance sheet date. This can be misleading to users of published accounts, such as shareholders. It can be argued, however, that it is no more than tidying up before being seen in public, just as you might do before the family arrives on Christmas Day.

Where window dressing strays towards fraud is when there is a deliberate intention to mislead. This happens rarely within public companies. Nevertheless it is a possibility, which means accounts must never be treated with 100% confidence.

The bank balance and cash holdings, like all other assets in the balance sheet, will be shown at their value on that day only. These figures can be window dressed. Firms can delay placing orders or paying bills until after the balance sheet date.

Have any fixed assets been sold, with the proceeds swelling the bank account? If so, has this type of cash flow manipulation put the business in a dangerous

position? It may be that the business will be replacing the machinery with high cash outflow in the near future.

Business in AUDITS

One result of the 2002 collapse of Enron, the giant energy company, was a desire to tighten the scrutiny of auditors. Government ministers saw that Enron's directors, accountants and auditors had too cosy a relationship. So they asked an independent committee to look at changing UK procedures so that audit committees would report directly to shareholders, rather than just to management. It is hoped that this will now force auditors to be more independent, and to scrutinise company accounts more rigorously.

ISSUES FOR analysis

When interpreting accounting information, there are several key lines of analysis:

- Look to see if any trends are emerging. Is liquidity worsening or gearing rising over the years? Is the company implementing a credible strategy for dealing with the situation?
- Look for comparable data. A net profit margin of 7% may sound low, but Sainsbury's is around that level so any supermarket chain should be quite pleased to match it.
- Consider the context. If the recent summer has been superb, of course Wall's will have made good profits, have relatively low stocks and have a high acid test ratio. If a deep recession has taken place, of course Barratt's Homes will have been struggling, may have high stocks and poor cash flow.
- Make sure to examine the age and type of information. Is it already six months old? In which case, what may have happened since? Also consider whether it is audited, whether it is actual information or merely a forecast.

24.7 Uses and limitations of accounts
an evaluation

Accounts and financial information are essential but they are only one source of information which managers should use. In the short run, cash flow is more important than profit. Yet unprofitable activities cannot last in the long run. Accounting myopia must not exclude other considerations such as investment in technology, marketing or human resources, nor must it prevent strategic thinking and visions for the future. Non-financial motives must be considered. It is doubtful whether on purely accounting and financial analysis Concorde would have been built, the Channel Tunnel excavated or a man put on the moon. Nor would any business logically finance 'blue-skies' or totally open-ended research, with the possibility of no financial return. Over-reliance on crude accounting rules of thumb can cost businesses and the economy dear.

going concern – the accounting assumption that unless there is evidence to the contrary, the organisation will continue its usual operations into the foreseeable future.

window dressing – presenting the company accounts in such a manner as to flatter the financial position of the firm. This is a form of creative accounting in which there is a fine dividing line between flattery and fraud.

WORKBOOK | 24.8

A Level Exercises

A. REVISION QUESTIONS
(30 marks; 60 minutes)

Read the unit then answer:

1 Explain why firms keep accounting records. (3)
2 Why should an 'extra-ordinary' item generating profit not be included in a company's trading profit? (3)
3 When should a business treat 'debtors' as bad? (2)
4 Why are businesses sometimes tempted to be optimistic about their debtors' capacity to pay? (3)
5 Why is land seen as a non-depreciating asset? (3)
6 What is goodwill and why do users of accounts treat it with caution? (5)
7 **a** How should a business value its stock-holdings? (2)
  b Why is this method appropriate? (3)
8 Give three strengths and three weaknesses of ratio analysis. (6)

B. REVISION EXERCISES

Case Study

The Takeover

Francis plc was founded 20 years ago and is a well-known company which makes precision components bought by manufacturers of consumer durables. Francis has grown through retained profit and has always been wary of borrowing. Sales have always been steady and the value of its land and buildings is considerably understated in its balance sheet. Three years ago it acquired a smaller rival company.

Most of Francis' shares are owned by institutions, the largest being a major pension fund. The managers of this fund have just reported to the directors of Francis that there are rumours in the City that Neale plc, a relatively new company in the same line of business, may be carrying out a feasibility study for a possible takeover bid. Neale's directors are being advised by a major investment bank which would also arrange the financing of any bid.

Alarmed, the directors of Francis compared their latest balance sheet with that of Neale. These balance sheets are in Table 1 below. 'We have nothing to fear here,' said the managing director of Francis to his major shareholder. 'Neale is heavily borrowed already and we have no loans.'

Two weeks later, a takeover bid was launched offering the shareholders in Francis plc a 25% premium on the present share value by means of a package of 20% cash and 80% shares in Neale plc.

Latest annual accounts of Francis plc and Neale plc

Table 1 Balance sheet (as at 31 December)

	Francis plc £m	Neale plc £m
Land and buildings	50	50
Machinery	125	100
Vehicles	50	30
Goodwill	50	0
Stock	150	100
Debtors	200	150
Cash	10	100
Creditors	130	100
Overdraft	0	150
Assets employed	**505**	**280**
Long-term liabilities	0	112
Share capital	350	50
Reserves	155	118
Capital employed	**505**	**280**

Table 2 Profit and loss account (year ending 31 December)

	Francis plc £m	Neale plc £m
Sales revenue	900	900
Cost of sales	550	500
Gross profit	350	400
Overheads	270	300
Operating profit	80	100
Surplus on extraordinary item	60	0
Pre-tax profit	140	100

Questions *(30 marks; 50 minutes)*

1 Carry out a full analysis of the available accounts of Francis plc and Neale plc, using appropriate techniques including accounting ratios. *(14)*
2 If you were a shareholder in Francis plc, what other information would you seek before deciding whether to accept Neale's offer? *(6)*
3 On the basis of the information available, advise the major shareholder whether to accept the offer. *(10)*

C. ESSAY QUESTIONS

1 'Sales are vanity. Profit is sanity.' 'Profit equals guesswork. Cash is a fact.' Discuss.
2 'Window dressing financial accounts at the year-end is fraud.' 'All businesses can be expected to show their best side to the world and this is merely all that so-called window dressing usually amounts to.' Discuss.

REVENUE AND CAPITAL SPENDING

DEFINITION

Revenue spending is expenditure on current assets and expenses, that is things that are used once. Examples are stock, electricity bills or rent.

Capital spending is expenditure on fixed assets, or things that are used repeatedly. Examples are premises, machinery or vehicles.

Depreciation is the accounting process concerned with the fall in the value of a fixed asset over time. To maintain a true and fair view of the state of the business in the accounts, this fall in value should be reflected in the book value of the assets.

25.1 Revenue spending

Revenue spending, or expenditure, is concerned with the money spent by a business on its day-to-day running. Normally, there are three categories of revenue spending:

- items which will be used only once, such as office consumables (paper, printer toner and so on)
- items that will be used up in the very near future, such as the stock of components for an assembly line
- items that have been used before they are paid for, such as rates or advertising.

Although these items only have a short-term impact on a firm, they have a direct influence on a firm's profits. The cost of stock bought for resale and the money spent on advertising is taken from the firm's revenue to calculate the profits of the firm.

25.2 Capital spending

Capital spending, or expenditure, is concerned with the money spent by a business on its long-term operations. Any item that a business owns that will be used over a long period of time is paid for through capital spending. It is normal accounting practice to think of one year as the difference between the short and long-term. Buying fixed assets therefore counts as capital spending. These assets such as vehicles or machinery are bought by a firm with the intention of their being used for several years.

Capital spending does not have a direct influence on a firm's profits. It is still important to the business since the items bought will be used to produce the output that contributes to a firm's profits.

In the following table are some examples of spending by firms and how they are classified.

SPENDING	CAPITAL/ REVENUE	EXPLANATION
Buying property	Capital	A long-term asset for the business
Extending premises	Capital	For the long-term use of the business
Repairs to premises	Revenue	A one-off payment to maintain the business and its premises in a usable state
Wages and salaries	Revenue	A one-off payment for work done in the previous week/month
Buying a delivery van	Capital	For repeated use by the business
Petrol for the van	Revenue	Petrol can only be used once then more must be bought
Goods bought for resale	Revenue	They will be sold on to customers once

25.3 The effect of capital and revenue spending on the final accounts

Both capital and revenue spending will affect the final accounts of a business. However, they will affect the accounts in different ways. Revenue spending on short-term items only affects one accounting period. Capital spending is accounted for over the years of the expected lifetime of the asset. The profit and loss account shows the performance of a business over a period of time such as a year. The balance sheet looks at the state of the business at a specific moment.

Items which have been paid for and used up only affect one accounting period. So they appear only on the profit and loss account for the relevant trading period. Revenue spending of £50,000 on staff salaries, then, will be charged in full to the year's profit and loss account.

Items which the business intends to keep and use repeatedly over a long period of time, its fixed assets, will appear on the balance sheet. Apart from depreciation, dealt with below, they have no direct impact on the business's profits for a particular period. Even when they are first purchased they do not appear on the profit and loss account. This is because of their long-term nature, which means they affect more than just one single accounting period. Therefore spending £50,000 on new shop premises will not show up as a cost to the year's profit and loss account. It will be accounted for solely on the balance sheet.

For example, if a firm buys a new factory and machinery to use alongside its existing plant, its accounting profit for the year will not be affected. The capital spending of the firm has increased, and this will be shown on a balance sheet as an increase in the firm's fixed assets. Of course, this will have to have been financed, so there will be an equal change in owners' capital or long-term liabilities, depending on how the deal was financed.

Once the new plant is being used, there will be expenses to be paid, such as the power needed to run the machines, the raw materials to be processed and the wages of any new staff employed. These items will all appear as expenses on the profit and loss account. As such they will reduce the firm's net profit. It would be expected that the extra output from the new plant would bring in sufficient extra revenue to increase profits overall. Any profit made will be recorded on the balance sheet as a source of funds, and could be used to fund future capital spending.

For managers, it is important to achieve the right balance between revenue and capital spending. Too much capital spending could lead to a lack of funds to pay for the revenue items needed to generate income and profits for the business. Too little capital spending may cause a firm to have revenue items that cannot be processed as the plant required is not available. Achieving a balance between the two is essential if firms are to maximise their profitability potential.

25.4 Depreciation

When a business buys a **fixed asset**, it will intend to keep it and use it for a period of several years. It is extremely unlikely that these assets will retain their original value throughout their lives. Whilst it is possible for assets to appreciate, in other words to increase their value, as often happens with property, it is more usual for the value to fall, or depreciate, over time.

SSAP 12 gives a precise definition of depreciation. It says depreciation is:

> ... *a measure of the wearing out, consumption or other reduction in the useful economic life of a fixed asset whether arising from use, effluxion of time or obsolescence through technological or market changes.*

Assets depreciate for several reasons:

- They are subject to wear and tear – as assets are used, they will inevitably get damaged or worn, which will reduce their level of performance and their worth to the firm.
- They may not be looked after correctly – repairs carried out by non-experts or using sub-standard parts, or repairs that are left for some time, can reduce the **useful life** of the asset.
- They become obsolete – as technology develops, someone will eventually produce a new, updated version that is quicker or more efficient than the asset currently in use.
- The products they produce become obsolete – machines are often highly specialised, but as demand changes, the product being made will have to change, possibly leading to a change in a firm's fixed assets.

A central objective of accounting is to produce statements that give a 'true and fair view' of the state of the business. If a year-old car is valued in the accounts at the price when new, it will mean the accounts are misleading.

Depreciation is the accountant's way of showing the fall in the value of an asset over time. The aim is to make sure that, when an asset reaches the end of its useful life, the value shown in the accounts books is a close reflection of its likely value when resold or scrapped. Depreciation is not used to provide a pot of money to pay for a replacement at the end of an asset's life. There is no movement of cash into a special account. Depreciation is an entry in the books of account, but one for which there is no corresponding physical action.

25.5 Methods of depreciation

All methods of calculating depreciation are based on the same basic information:

- The original cost of the asset, called the **historic cost**.
- The estimated length of life of the asset.
- An estimate of the value the asset will have when it comes to the end of its useful life. This is referred to as the **residual value**. Depending on the asset, this may be either the resale value of the asset or its scrap value

Using this information, it is possible to calculate the amount of money to be charged as depreciation each year over the useful life of the asset so that the historic cost is reduced sufficiently to match the residual value. The depreciation charge for a single year is an expense for the business, and appears on the profit and loss account like any other expense. This causes a reduction in the level of pre-tax profit.

The total of all the depreciation charges made on an asset throughout its life is shown on the balance sheet, reducing the book value of the asset. This causes a fall in the net assets of the business.

Of course, having used estimates, it is highly unlikely that the residual value achieved at the end of the asset's useful life will match exactly the true value that can be realised by the sale or scrapping of the asset. Any difference will be recorded as a deficit or surplus on disposal, and added or subtracted from profits as necessary.

There are two commonly used methods of calculating the annual depreciation charge – the straight line method and the declining balance method.

STRAIGHT LINE METHOD

The straight line depreciation method is the simplest to use. It assumes that the depreciation charge is constant throughout the life of the asset, implying that the

fall in value of the asset is the same whether in the first year of the asset's use or the last.

To calculate straight line depreciation, the following formula is used:

$$\frac{\text{historic cost} - \text{residual value}}{\text{useful life}}$$

The amount to be depreciated is divided equally between each year of the useful life of the asset.

For example, a firm of accountants buys a new computer for £3,500. Past experience has told them that in three years they will need to update their system. They believe that at the end of three years the second-hand value of the machine will be £500.

Using straight line depreciation, the annual depreciation charge will be:

$$\frac{£3,500 - £500}{3} = \frac{£3,000}{3} = £1,000$$

For each of the three years of this asset's useful life, a depreciation charge of £1,000 will be made.

On the profit and loss account, there will be an expense of £1,000 in each of the three years, reducing the firm's net profit.

On the balance sheet, the value of the computer will be reduced by £1,000 each year, so that at the end of the three years, the computer is valued at the estimated £500, as shown in the following table:

YEAR	DEPRECIATION CHARGE	BOOK VALUE OF COMPUTER
Now	–	£3,500
1	£1,000	£2,500
2	£1,000	£1,500
3	£1,000	£500

At the end of the third year, the firm's accounts show that the asset has a value of £500. The same as the residual value estimated at the start of its life. It may be that the computer could now actually be sold for £750, giving the firm a surplus of £250 on disposal. Equally, the computer may now be so obsolete that it can only be sold for scrap and spare parts, and will

ADVANTAGES OF THE STRAIGHT LINE METHOD	DISADVANTAGES OF THE STRAIGHT LINE METHOD
• The most widely used in Britain, by far	• Does not depreciate assets such as cars and machinery realistically; therefore leaves assets over-valued on the balance sheet
• Approved for tax calculations by Inland Revenue	• Relies heavily on guesstimates of an asset's future useful life and future residual value
• Encourages long-term thinking, because it does not cut profits too much in the first year of investment	• If an asset such as a computer becomes obsolete earlier than expected, the under-provision for depreciation will require a large write-down of the asset's book value

only raise £200, thereby showing a deficit on disposal of £300.

The method is criticised because most assets do not in reality lose the same amount each year. It is said that driving a new £15,000 car away from the dealers reduces it value by up to £3,000 immediately. Some makes of car that are five or six years old will lose little more value for being another year older.

DECLINING BALANCE METHOD

This method is sometimes also called the reducing balance method.

The declining balance method of calculating depreciation makes the assumption that a constant percentage of the asset's value will be lost each year. For example, a £100 asset may lose 50% of its value in Year 1, cutting its balance sheet value to £50; and 50% in Year 2, cutting its value to £25. It is more complicated to work out than the straight line method. Yet it reflects more accurately the way assets such as cars lose value. The heaviest depreciation in money terms is in the first year of the asset's life.

To calculate the depreciation charge using the declining balance method, a percentage figure must be found that will reduce the historic cost to the estimated residual value over the asset's estimated life. In exam situations, this percentage figure will be provided, perhaps 40% per year.

Commonly accepted lengths of life of assets

Asset	Length of Life (years)
Buildings	40
Machinery	10
Furniture and fittings	5
Vehicles	4

Using the computer example given above, where the purchase price was £3,500, the residual value £500 and the estimated life three years, the percentage to be used is slightly less than 48%. As this figure has been rounded up, the final value will be slightly different from the estimated residual value.

The percentage is used to calculate the depreciation to be charged each year. The amount of depreciation is then subtracted from the value shown on the accounts to find the new balance sheet value of the asset (the book value).

The depreciation charges will be as shown in the table at the top of the next page.

The straight line method depreciated the computer by £1,000 per year. The declining balance method charges the same total amount, but loads it heavily onto the early part of the asset's life.

The depreciation charge shown on the profit and loss account for the computer is different each year, as

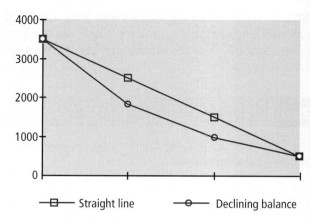

Figure 25.1 Comparison of depreciation methods

shown in the table above. As time passes, the asset loses less of its value. The value of the asset shown on the balance sheet is given in the 'closing book value' column.

With most fixed assets, as the asset grows older, the costs of maintenance and repair tend to increase. By using the declining balance method of calculating depreciation, these costs can be balanced against the falling depreciation charge, giving a relatively constant charge to the profit and loss account. Using the straight line method, the total annual cost of the asset, found by adding the depreciation charge and maintenance costs, will increase year by year.

Business IN

DEPRECIATION

On 22 July 2002 Manchester United signed Rio Ferdinand in a deal worth £33 million. The view among fans and in the sports pages of the papers was that it was the right move by manager Alex Ferguson. Yet stock market analysts hated it and Manchester United shares fell 8.5%.

One seller of the shares explained that Ferdinand will be paid wages of around £3.5 million a year and that his 5 year contract will cause a depreciation charge of £33m/5 = £6.6 million. So Ferdinand will cost the club £10 million per year. As the club makes an annual profit before tax of around £30 million, Rio Ferdinand could single-handedly cost the shareholders one third of the annual profit.

25.6 The effect of depreciation on accounts

Accounts are intended to provide a 'true and fair view' of the financial state of a business. The user of accounts wants to know that the company's assets

Year	Opening Book Value (£)	Depreciation (%)	Depreciation Charge (£)	Closing Book Value (£)
Now	0	–	–	3,500.00
1	3,500.00	48%	1,680.00	1,820.00
2	1,820.00	48%	873.60	946.40
3	946.40	48%	454.27	492.13

Advantages of the declining balance method	Disadvantages of the declining balance method
• Heavy depreciation provision in the first year matches second-hand value of assets	• Heavy first year depreciation may discourage investment in assets (hits short-term profits)
• More accurate fixed asset valuations on balance sheet	• Usually not acceptable to Inland Revenue for charging company (corporation) tax

really are worth the amount stated on the balance sheet. Or that the company really is profitable. Yet both the figure for profit and that for the value of assets rely upon accurate rates of depreciation.

- Too little depreciation might be charged by overestimating the useful life of the asset or overestimating the residual value. This will mean expenses are underestimated. This will cause profits during the life of the asset to be artificially high. The assets will be over-valued on the balance sheet. Directors might choose to do this as a form of window dressing.
- Charging too much depreciation will have the opposite effect. Expenses will be higher than they

should be, so a lower profit is recorded for several years. At the end of its useful life, an over-depreciated asset would be worth more than expected, so a surplus is recorded on disposal.

As depreciation affects the value of both the profit and loss account and balance sheet, accountants should always try to be prudent when calculating depreciation charges. This means making cautious assumptions, such as that a computer will only prove useful for three years, not four.

DVD CAUSES RED FACES

One area of business that has suffered from inappropriate rates of depreciation has been rental televisions and videos. The standard policy, up to a few years ago, was to depreciate sets over 80 months (6 years and 8 months). The long time period helped the firms' balance sheets look very healthy with a high stock valuation.

However, the pace of technological change has meant that televisions and videos can no longer be rented out for such long periods of time. Customers want the latest feature like wide-screen sets and DVD players. This leaves firms with unrentable sets and a loss on disposal of the asset.

While some money can be recouped from 'ex-rental' sales, the affair makes it important for firms to look more closely at realistic depreciation periods.

ISSUES FOR **analysis**

Careful understanding of revenue spending, capital spending and depreciation can offer the following lines of analysis:

- Profit is not the same as cash. A high depreciation charge cuts a firm's stated profit, but has no effect on its cash flow. Be careful to distinguish cash from profit.
- Capital spending is not charged in full to the current year's profit. It is spread over the lifetime of the asset through depreciation. This means investment in fixed assets does not hurt a firm's short-term profit. What a pity, then, that accountants treat investment in R&D as revenue spending. It is therefore charged in full against current profit, which discourages this type of long-term investment.
- Neither the profit and loss account nor the balance sheet should be regarded as facts. They are accounts drawn up on the basis of various estimates and assumptions. Depreciation is a good example. An optimist might assume a computer will last for four years and therefore depreciate it lightly. A pessimist might anticipate quick obsolescence and depreciate over two years. In year one, who could know which view was correct? Therefore either set of accounts could be right. The only definite accounting fact is a firm's current cash position.

When BMW bought Rover Cars it was said that Rover's annual profit was about £100 million. BMW sent in their own accountants and within a few months they had 'restated' the results to show an annual *loss* of £100 million. German accounting standards are tougher, especially in relation to depreciation. A British firm might depreciate machinery over a 10-year period. A German rival might decide from the start to replace the equipment after four years. This would make the German's rate of depreciation more than twice as high.

In the long term, which business is more likely to succeed? The British firm which declares high profits and pays shareholders large dividends? Or the German which declares lower profits, pays lower dividends, but has much more up-to-date equipment?

If accounts are to give a true and fair view of the state of the business, then depreciation must be accounted for. To ignore it would be to present a false picture. However, the calculations are based on estimates of the future, so any depreciation figure must be used with caution.

fixed asset – Any item owned by a firm that will last for more than one year.

historic cost – the initial price paid for an asset.

preventative maintenance – checking and cleaning machinery before it needs it or goes wrong. In other words preventing the need for maintenance.

residual value – the value of an asset at the end of its useful life.

SSAP – Statement of Standard Accounting Practice. The principles that govern all accounting.

useful life – the length of time an asset will be used by a business.

A Level Exercises

A. REVISION QUESTIONS
(30 marks; 60 minutes)

Read the unit, then answer:

1 Distinguish between revenue spending and capital spending. *(4)*
2 Say whether each of the following is revenue or capital spending:
   a purchasing stock for resale
   b building a factory extension
   c repairing the roof of a factory
   d paying the wages of shop-floor workers. *(4)*
3 Explain the key differences between straight line and declining balance depreciation. *(5)*
4 True or false: straight line depreciation charges more for depreciation in the early years of an asset's life than the later years. *(1)*
5 An airline depreciates its aircraft over 25 years. It believes that an aircraft bought for £65 million can be sold at the end of its life for £15 million.
   a What will the annual depreciation charge be, using the straight line method? *(3)*
   b What would be the book value of the aircraft after 10 years? *(3)*
6 Will increasing the depreciation charge for a year increase or decrease the reported profit for that year? *(1)*

7 When they buy a fixed asset, firms have to decide the number of years over which they will depreciate it: 4 years? 5 years? 10 years? What factors might influence this decision? *(4)*
8 Why may it cause a problem if a firm underestimates the depreciation that should be charged to its accounts? *(5)*

B. REVISION EXERCISES

B1 Data Response
A machine costs £10,000, and is expected to have a useful life of four years. It is estimated that at the end of its life it will have a residual value of £2,000.

Questions *(25 marks; 30 minutes)*
1 Explain the term 'depreciation'. *(2)*
2 Calculate the depreciation charge and net book value for each year using:
   a the straight line method *(2)*
   b the declining balance method (use a depreciation rate of 33%). *(4)*
3 Compare the figures for both methods obtained in question 2. *(6)*
4 State three factors that could influence the useful life of an asset. *(3)*
5 Analyse the effect that the differing methods would have on a firm's profits. *(8)*

B2 Data Response

Look at this extract from last year's annual accounts for MK Conroy Ltd. Then answer the questions below.

Profit and loss account		End-of-year balance sheet	
	£000		£000
Turnover	4,200	Fixed assets	1,050
Cost of sales	2,800	Stock	700
Gross profit	1,400	Debtors	420
Overheads	920	Cash	70
Depreciation	100	Current liabilities	1,040
Interest	80	Net current assets	150
Pre-tax profit	300	**Assets employed**	**1,200**
Corporation tax	100	Loans	600
Dividends	150	Shareholders' funds	600
Retained profit	50	**Capital employed**	**1,200**

Questions
(30 marks; 35 minutes)

1 MK Conroy's capital spending last year amounted to £150,000.
  a What was the value of the firm's fixed assets at the start of last year? *(4)*
  b What was the firm's revenue expenditure last year? Explain your answer. *(6)*

2 If, this year, the firm spends £500,000 on new machinery with an effective life of five years, explain the effect this will have on MK Conroy's profit and loss account. *(6)*

3 MK Conroy has £1,050,000 of fixed assets, of which £650,000 is in the form of freehold property.
  a What is likely to be the rate of depreciation on the property? *(2)*
  b If technological change made it necessary to write off the firm's remaining fixed assets this year (i.e. write them down to zero), explain the effect that would have on the company's accounts. *(12)*

B3 Case Study

Time and 'The Place'

It had always been Wai-Yee's ambition to open a dance club. She had spent some great nights in Manchester clubs, but wished there was a really good club in her home town of Altrincham. When she met Tony, it soon became the subject of conversation. And within three months it became a reality.

The Place opened in a blaze of publicity. Tony had been to school with Noel Gallagher, whose presence at the opening party ensured a huge turnout. The *Manchester Evening News* focused its article on the huge cost of The Place. There were huge leather sofas for people to flop down on, three massive mahogany bars and a £50,000 lighting system. The capital expenditure totalled £320,000.

Throughout the first year, The Place did marvellous business. The takings of £32,000 per week generated gross profit of £20,000 – easily enough to cover the £15,000 of weekly overheads. Wai-Yee was in heaven. She had not only become a local celebrity – she was

also feeling rich for the first time. At the end of the first year, a big dividend payout allowed her to spend £50,000 on a Mercedes sports convertible.

When Stringfellows Dance opened up in central Manchester at the start of the second year, Tony and Wai-Yee assumed it would have little effect on them. But steadily business started to slide away. A 'half price' night did well, but seemed to highlight the problems of The Place, causing business to slide still further. With takings of only £16,000 per week, the gross profit could not cover the overheads. At the end of its second year, The Place closed down. The lease could be sold off for £30,000, but the rest of the assets could only be disposed of at their residual values.

Financial details for The Place

Item	Capital Spending	Depreciation Period (straight line)	Residual Value
5-year lease	£50,000	5 years	zero
Fixtures & fittings	£140,000	4 years	zero
Sound & lighting	£80,000	5 years	£20,000
Computers & other items	£50,000	5 years	£5,000

Questions
(40 marks; 60 minutes)

1 Explain the meaning of the term 'capital expenditure', distinguishing it clearly from revenue expenditure. *(5)*

2 Prove that year 1 depreciation for The Place was £66,000. Show your workings. *(6)*

3 Calculate the annual profit made by The Place in its first year, stating your assumptions clearly. *(8)*

4 Tony and Wai-Yee paid themselves huge dividends at the end of their excellent first year. Why should they have been more cautious? *(6)*

5 Over the second year as a whole, the operating profit of The Place was £12,000 before depreciation.
  a What would the net profit (after depreciation) have been if the business had continued trading? *(2)*
  b Calculate the actual net profit of The Place in its second year, given that it closed down. *(6)*
  c If Wai-Yee and Tony had known from the start that their club would have only two years of trading, how would that have affected the depreciation charges and therefore the profit for year 1? *(7)*

C. ESSAY QUESTIONS

1 'Depreciation is based on estimates at best, and guesses at worst.' Does this invalidate their use in accounting?

2 Research and development spending is charged to revenue, whereas spending on fixed assets is treated as capital expenditure. Yet both are forms of investment in a firm's future. Discuss the possible implications of this.

3 Assess the relative importance of capital and revenue expenditure to a manufacturing firm.

INVESTMENT APPRAISAL

DEFINITION

Investment appraisal is how a business decides if a capital investment project is worthwhile. Or, where alternatives exist, which option is likely to be the best. Investment appraisal involves several numerical techniques, but also takes into account qualitative factors.

26.1 Capital investment

Capital investments are vital for any firm. They are usually expensive, often long term and, given the limited nature of a firm's resources, likely to be irreversible. These three factors alone demonstrate how important it is for a firm to do everything it possibly can to make the right decision when faced with potential investments.

There will be a vast range of capital investments throughout the life of the firm. Consider, for example, a firm of accountants. A selection of capital investment decisions that may have to be made are:

- premises
- office furniture
- fixtures and fittings
- computer hardware
- fax and telephone links
- photocopier
- company cars
- expansion of premises.

Once a business is set up, the need for capital investments continues. The equipment initially purchased could need replacing due to the inevitable wear and tear, or in response to developing technology. An increase in demand may cause the firm to expand its productive capacity. Any general growth in the firm or diversification into other areas will lead to further investments being made.

Capital investment hinges on three main factors:

- the firm's objectives
- the opportunities it faces
- the constraints it works within.

26.2 Qualitative issues

Although capital investment deals with the **cash flows** and expected profitability for the firm, there are also many qualitative issues surrounding investment decisions. The main qualitative considerations will be:

- The objectives of the firm – a profit-maximising firm, for example, will take a different view of a potential investment than will one attempting to improve its market position. The first will choose the project with the largest returns. The second could be more inclined to invest in machines that produce a better quality product, even if this is more expensive or is estimated to bring in smaller returns.
- External costs and benefits – the impact on the environment, or perhaps more cynically, the effect on a firm's reputation of not satisfying the 'green'

INVESTMENT APPRAISAL IN THE UK

A recent survey for the magazine *Management Decisions* found widespread misuse of investment appraisal techniques within the UK. The study, covering 866 UK manufacturers, averaging a sales turnover in excess of £10 million, found that smaller firms were less likely to use discounted cash flow (DCF) methods – they preferred to rely on a 'knowledge of the business' and intuitive managerial judgement. Although larger firms tended to use both net present value and internal rate of return techniques, their techniques were often flawed.

The most notable problems identified were a failure to take proper account of inflation and the use of excessively high discount rates. Inflation will push up the quantity of future cash flows without increasing their value, and so ought to be eliminated from DCF calculations. Using too high a discount rate will affect the present value of future cash flows, causing firms to err on the side of caution and lose valuable investment opportunities.

Business IN

movement, are increasingly being set against financial rewards in capital decisions.
- The current, and expected, state of the economy – the 'feel-good' factor amongst consumers and businesses has a direct effect on whether businesses make an investment now, delay it for the future or even drop it altogether.
- Past experience – a firm may have always bought its machines from a particular supplier and always received excellent service. It will be strongly tempted to continue buying from this supplier, even if a new supplier offers a deal that looks better.

26.3 Cash flows

To make a financial assessment of a capital investment, the first step is to estimate the expected cash flows associated with it. The cost of the investment is calculated, and set against the expected returns. This shows the profit over the lifetime of the investment.

It is usual to label the time at which the investment is made as year 0 (or 'now'). Year 1 shows the cash flows that have taken place by the end of the first year of the investment, and so on. The table below shows an investment of £50,000 which will bring in net cash flows of £80,000 over the following years. The figure in the bottom right of the table shows the overall net cash flow from this investment. That figure of £30,000 can also be called the profit over the lifetime of the investment. The graph shown in Figure 26.1 uses the same data to show the effect of the investment on the company's bank balance over the four years (these figures are the same as the **cumulative cash flow**).

Year	Cash In	Cash Out	Net Cash Flow	Cumulative Cash Flow
0	0	£50,000	(£50,000)	(£50,000)
1	£30,000	£20,000	£10,000	(£40,000)
2	£50,000	£30,000	£20,000	(£20,000)
3	£40,000	£20,000	£20,000	–
4	£40,000	£10,000	£30,000	£30,000

Whilst being a simple numerical procedure, the calculation of the net cash flow for a real investment decision is extremely difficult. Businesses operate in a dynamic environment that can change on a day-to-day basis.

Predictions are made several years into the future against the uncertain backdrop of such factors as:
- the performance of the asset
- the reaction of competitors
- the taste of consumers
- the economy
- technological developments.

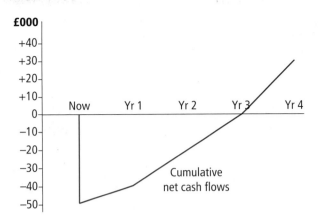

Figure 26.1 Investment cash flow graph

This makes the accuracy of predictions uncertain at best, and widely inaccurate at worst.

Before a manager can place any reliance on the projected figures for the investment, several important questions must be asked:

- What is the source of the predictions? Are the performance figures for a new piece of machinery based on the manufacturers' claims, or have they been tested by the buyer, or independent experts? Whatever the source, managers must feel able to

SIEMENS

While many firms take into account the financial aspects of investment appraisal, a failure to look at the qualitative factors can lead to very costly mistakes. Since capital investment decisions are usually large scale and long term, a firm can find itself committed even though external circumstances change around it.

This is clearly illustrated by the experience of Siemens. In the mid-1990s, the UK attracted large amounts of inward investment. One such company was Siemens, who opened a semi-conductor plant on Tyneside. And then promptly had to shut it again at a massive cost to the firm.

In between the decision to locate the plant in the north-east and its opening many months later, the state of the market for semi-conductors, especially in the Far East, collapsed, and Siemens was left with the wrong plant producing the wrong sort of chip in the wrong place. It was no comfort to the workers on Tyneside that Siemens immediately invested another huge sum in a different plant to make different chips. They chose to do it in France.

IN Business

trust the information before it is used as the basis for such an important decision.

- How good is the information? The source may be reliable, but that in itself says little about the actual quality of the information. Are there sales forecasts based on market research? If so, was the sample size large enough to be confident of its reliability? And what variables have been taken into account in finding the figures? As a simple rule, the better the quality of information passed to a manager, the better the decisions will be.

- What risks are associated with the figures? With the uncertain nature of the environment surrounding the business, it will be impossible for predictions to be 100% accurate, but do they carry a 95% confidence level? The greater the potential inaccuracy in the figures, the more of a gamble being taken by managers.

All these factors combine to make any business forecasting risky. While the risks can never be removed completely, good managers reduce the risks as much as possible before making a decision.

26.4 Quantitative techniques

There are several quantitative techniques to analyse a potential investment. All are based on the expected cash flows associated with the project. Each one considers a different aspect of the proposal. No one method can be said to be better than another, and it is usual for several to be used in making a decision.

PAYBACK

This refers to the time it takes for an investment to repay the initial outlay. For example, if a £6,000 investment yielded net cash flows of £1,000 per month, the payback period would be six months. In calculating the payback period, it is usual to work to the nearest month. In the example below, a £100,000 investment brings in £30,000 in year 1 and £40,000 in year 2.

YEAR	NET CASH FLOW	CUMULATIVE CASH FLOW
0	(£100,000)	(£100,000)
1	+£30,000	(£70,000)
2	+£40,000	(£30,000)
3	+£60,000	+£30,000
4	+£35,000	+£65,000

By the end of year 2, therefore, the company is still £30,000 down. In year 3 +£60,000 is expected, so the anticipated payback is half way through the year.

Overall payback is 2.5 years. Note that this assumes the £60,000 received in year 3 is spread evenly throughout the year. If the company sells a gift product, the Christmas seasonal peak may mean that payback only really occurs in November or December.

In this case, the month of payback is clearly month 6 (half way through the year). In other cases it can be hard to see the payback month. It may need to be calculated. This can be done using the following formula:

$$\text{month of payback} = \frac{\text{income required}}{\text{contribution per month}}$$

In the above case, the income needed in the third year is £30,000. The total income, or contribution, for year 3 is £60,000, so the monthly contribution is £60,000 ÷ 12 = £5,000. Using the formula, we get:

$$\frac{£30,000}{£5,000} = 6 \text{ months}$$

The payback period, then, is two years and 6 months. When a payback calculation is made, it is important that the final answer is considered carefully. It is easy to put the wrong year down, even when the answer has been calculated accurately.

For a business, payback is a simple calculation to make. It gives some indication of the level of risk associated with a potential investment. The longer the payback period, the longer your money is at risk. And the greater the likelihood that something unexpected may spoil your plans. However, payback fails to take into account the overall profitability of the potential project, as it ignores cash flows that occur after payback is achieved. As a result, it will often be used in business as a minimum, or screening, criterion. Projects with a long payback period will be discarded, but payback will rarely be used by itself in making an investment decision.

AVERAGE RATE OF RETURN

This method compares the average annual profit generated by an investment with the amount of money invested in it. In this way, two or more potential projects can be considered to find out which has the 'best' return for the amount of money being put into it in the first place.

ADVANTAGES OF PAYBACK	DISADVANTAGES OF PAYBACK
• Easy to calculate	• Not a measure of profitability
• Focuses upon the short term	• Ignores what happens after the payback period
• Takes into account the timing of cash flows	• May encourage a short-termist attitude

Average rate of return (ARR) is calculated by the formula:

$$\frac{\text{average annual return}}{\text{initial outlay}} \times 100$$

There are three steps in calculating ARR:

1 Calculate the total profit over the lifetime of the investment (net cash inflows minus the investment outlay).
2 Divide by the number of years of the investment project (this gives the average annual profit).
3 Apply the formula:

$$\frac{\text{average annual profit}}{\text{initial outlay}} \times 100$$

For example, BJ Carpets is considering whether to invest £20,000 in a labour-saving wrapping machine. The company policy is to invest in projects only if they deliver a profit of 15%+ a year (see the cash flow table below).

Here, the £20,000 investment generates £36,000 of positive cash flows in the four years. That represents a lifetime profit of £16,000 (see bottom right-hand corner of the table).

BJ Carpets: cash flow

YEAR	NET CASH FLOW	CUMULATIVE CASH FLOW
0	(£20,000)	(£20,000)
1	+£5,000	(£15,000)
2	+£11,000	(£4,000)
3	+£10,000	+£6,000
4	+£10,000	+£16,000

To apply the three steps, then:

Step 1 *Identify lifetime profit*	**£16,000**
Step 2 *Divide by no. of years (4)*	**£4,000**
Step 3 *Calculate annual profit as a % of initial outlay*	**£4,000/£20,000 × 100 = 20%**

BJ Carpets can therefore proceed with this investment, as the ARR of 20% is comfortably above its criterion rate of 15%.

The average rate of return method takes account of all the cash flows throughout the life of a project. And focuses on the key decision making factor: profitability. However, it ignores *when* the cash flows occur, which can have a large bearing on the risks of a project. Look at this example of the *average* rate of return on two investments, both of £10,000.

YEAR	NET CASH FLOW	
	INVESTMENT A	INVESTMENT B
0	(£10,000)	(£10,000)
1	+£10,000	+£3,000
2	+£6,000	+£6,000
3	+£3,000	+£10,000
ARR	30%	30%

Investments A and B come out with the same average profitability. Yet investment A's quick, one year payback makes it greatly preferable to investment B. After all, it is much easier to forecast one year ahead than three years. So investment B's crucial year 3 might prove much worse than expected. Meaning the ARR proves much lower in reality than the 30% expected at the start.

DISCOUNTED CASH FLOWS

When considering predicted cash flows in the future, it is worth remembering that money has a 'time value'. This means that having money in the hand now is worth more to a business than the same quantity of money in the future. In the same way, asking a student if they would prefer to receive £100 now or £100 in five years' time will almost always be answered by taking the money now. The reasons for this are clear:

- Future cash flows are subject to risk – there can be no guarantee that a promise of money in five years, however sincerely made, will be fulfilled. Bankruptcy, death or just forgetfulness may prevent the promise being carried out.
- Opportunity costs come into play – the money, if received now, could be used profitably, whether invested in a business venture or put into a bank or building society account. £100 put into a savings account today could earn a lot of interest in five years.

ADVANTAGES OF AVERAGE RATE OF RETURN	DISADVANTAGES OF AVERAGE RATE OF RETURN
• Uses all the cash flows over the project's life ...	• ... but, because later years are included, the results will not prove as accurate as payback
• Focuses upon profitability	• Ignores the timing of the cash flows
• Easy to compare % returns on different investments, to help make a decision	• Ignores the time value (opportunity cost) of the money invested

In short, it is always preferable to have money now than the promise of the same quantity of money in the future. This is because money held at the present time has a greater value than the same quantity of money received in the future. In other words, £100 received in a year's time is worth less to a firm than £100 in the bank today. How much less? Well, if interest rates were 10%, £100 in the bank for a year would become £110. So £100 in a year's time would be worth about 10% less than £100 today.

When considering potential capital investments on the basis of predicted future cash flows, it makes sense to ask: 'What will the money we receive in the future really be worth in today's terms?' These **present values** are calculated using a method called *discounting*.

To discount a future cash flow, it is necessary to know:

- how many years into the future we are looking, since the greater the length of time involved, the smaller the present or discounted value of money will be
- what the prevailing rate of interest will be.

Once these have been determined, the relevant discount factor can be found. This can be done by calculation or looked up in discount tables. An extract from a discount table is given below.

Years Ahead	6%	8%	10%	12%	15%
0	1.00	1.00	1.00	1.00	1.00
1	0.94	0.93	0.91	0.89	0.87
2	0.89	0.86	0.83	0.80	0.76
3	0.84	0.79	0.75	0.71	0.66
4	0.79	0.74	0.68	0.64	0.57
5	0.75	0.68	0.62	0.57	0.50

The future cash flows are then multiplied by the appropriate discount factor to find the present value. For example, the present value of £100 received in five years' time, if the expected rate of interest is 10%, would be:

£100 × 0.621 = £62.10

The higher the rate of interest expected, and the longer the time to wait for the money to come in, the less that money is actually worth in today's terms.

So how does a firm decide which discount factor to choose? There are two main ways:

1 the discount factor can be based on the current rate of interest, or the rate expected over the coming years
2 a firm may base the factor on its own criteria, such as that it wants every investment to make at least 15%; therefore it expects future returns to be positive even with a 15% discount rate.

There are two ways businesses use this technique of discounting future cash flows to find their present value. These are the net present value method and the internal rate of return.

Net present value (NPV): This method calculates the present values of all the money coming in from the project in the future. Then sets these against the money being spent on the project today. The result is known as the net present value of the project. It can be compared with other projects to find which has the highest return in real terms, and should therefore be chosen.

The technique can also be used to see if *any* of the projects are worth undertaking. All the investments might have a negative net present value. In other words, the present value of the money being spent is greater than the present value of the money being received. If so, the firm would be better off putting the money in the bank and earning the current rate of interest. Projects are only worth carrying out if the net present value is positive.

For example, a firm is faced with two alternative proposals for investment. Both cost £250,000, but have different patterns of future cash flows over their projected lives. The rate of interest over the period is anticipated to average around 10%. The calculation is shown in the table at the bottom of the page.

Despite the fact that both these projects have the same initial cost, and they bring in the same quantity of money over their lives, there is a large difference in their present values. Project Y, with most of its income coming in the early years, gives a much greater present value than project Z, whose most profitable years come later in its life.

	Project Z			Project Y		
Year	Cash Flow	Discount Factor	Present Value	Cash Flow	Discount Factor	Present Value
0	(£250,000)	1.00	(£250,000)	(£250,000)	1.00	(£250,000)
1	+£50,000	0.91	£45,500	+£200,000	0.91	+£182,000
2	+£100,000	0.83	£83,000	+£100,000	0.83	+£83,000
3	+£200,000	0.75	£150,000	+£50,000	0.75	+£37,500
NPV =			+£28,500			+£52,500

ADVANTAGES OF NPV	DISADVANTAGES OF NPV
• Takes the opportunity cost of money into account	• Complex to calculate and communicate
• A single measure which takes the amount and timing of cash flows into account	• The meaning of the result is often misunderstood
• Can consider different scenarios	• Only comparable between projects if the initial investment is the same

This method of appraising investment opportunities has an in-built advantage over the previous techniques. It pays close attention to the timing of cash flows and their values in relation to the value of money today. It is also relatively simple to use the technique as a form of 'what if?' scenario planning. Different calculations can be made to see what returns will be obtained at different interest rates or with different cash flows to reflect different expectations. The results, however, are not directly comparable between different projects when the initial investments differ.

The advantages and disadvantages of NPV are shown at the top of the page.

Internal rate of return (IRR): This is the second appraisal method that makes use of discounted cash flows. Unlike net present value, IRR makes it possible to compare projects with different initial values. Like NPV it involves the calculation of the net present value of a potential project. But instead of attempting to predict what the prevailing interest rate will be, it allows the interest rate to vary until a rate is found at which the net present value equals zero. This rate is then compared with either a pre-set criterion rate internal to the firm to decide if the project passes that criterion, or with the prevailing rate of interest to see if the project is financially viable.

In order to find the discount rate that achieves a net present value of zero, a process of trial and error is normally used. A discount rate is chosen, and the net present value calculated. If this is positive, a higher discount rate is tried, or if negative, a lower one. This process continues until a rate is found that gives a net present value of zero. This rate is the internal rate of return.

Computer software is available which carries out the IRR trial and error calculations in an instant. Without this software, the process of trial and error can be made easier by plotting the first few attempts on a graph. Drawing the curve formed by the plotted points shows the discount rate where the net present value is zero. For example, the earlier example of Project Z can be used. Its forecast cash flows have been calculated using 10%, 15% and 20% discount factors. The net present values have then been plotted on the graph shown in Figure 26.2.

The internal rate of return for this project is just over 15%, since this is the discount rate at which the net present value equals zero. Reading it off the graph you can see that the figure is about 15.5%. Since it is looking at returns relative to discount rates, rather than in terms of their absolute value, projects with different levels of investment can be directly compared. Although it requires a more complex series of calculations, modern computer software (such as Excel) is able to calculate the internal rate of return instantly.

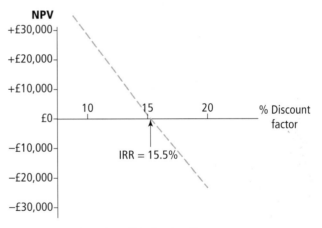

Figure 26.2 Graph to show IRR of project Z

Project Z's net cash flows discounted at different rates

YEAR	FORECAST NET CASH FLOWS	10% DISCOUNT FACTOR	PRESENT VALUE (AT 10%)	15% DISCOUNT FACTOR	PRESENT VALUE (AT 15%)	20% DISCOUNT FACTOR	PRESENT VALUE (AT 20%)
0	(£250,000)	1.00	(£250,000)	1.00	(£250,000)	1.00	(£250,000)
1	+£50,000	0.91	£45,500	0.87	+£43,500	0.83	+£41,500
2	−£100,000	0.83	£83,000	0.76	+£76,000	0.69	+£69,000
3	−£200,000	0.75	£150,000	0.66	+£132,000	0.58	+£116,000
NPV =			+£28,500		+£1,500		−£23,500

When developing an argument in answer to a case study or essay question, investment appraisal can offer the following main lines of analysis:

- Decision making against a background of uncertainty, such as predicting cash flows or the future level of interest rates in the economy.
- Balancing risks against potential rewards.
- Questioning the reliability of given data – who provided the information? How was it gathered? What variables were taken into account?
- Basing decisions on a mixture of quantitative and qualitative data. In particular, not placing too great an emphasis on numbers on the basis that they are somehow more concrete and therefore more reliable than, for example, environmental considerations or the interests of stakeholders.
- For each of the quantitative techniques, it is likely that firms will set minimum criteria which projects must meet before they can be accepted. These criterion rates will help a firm analyse and evaluate their investment options, or even reject all available alternatives.

26.5 Investment appraisal
an evaluation

Investment appraisal methods will often give conflicting advice to managers, who must be willing to make decisions based on a trade-off between risks and profit. This must be taken alongside the objectives of the business, which could well dictate which of the criteria involved is of most importance to the firm.

The size of the firm will also have an impact. Small firms will often have neither the time nor the resources to undertake a scientific approach to investment appraisal. They will often rely on past experience or the owner's hunches in making decisions such as these. In larger firms, however, the issue of accountability will often lead managers to rely heavily on the projected figures. In this way, should anything go wrong, they can prove they were making the best decision possible at the time, given the information available.

The techniques of investment appraisal will continue to benefit from the improvements in computers and information technology. Even the more complicated techniques can be made simple by the use of computer programs. The range of 'what if?' scenarios can be multiplied many times over. However, the usefulness of the techniques is still dependent on the accuracy of the predictions on which the calculations are based. More detailed and comprehensive information should enable firms to be more precise in their forecasting. But predicting the future has always been, and will continue to be, an inexact science. Managers must still be wary of cash flow predictions, and be able to measure risk against potential benefits.

In many respects, it is the qualitative side of investment appraisal which is becoming increasingly important. Concern for the environment and other social responsibilities may play a greater role in a firm's considerations of potential investments.

KEY terms

cash flow – the movement of cash into and out of a firm. In terms of investment appraisal, these are directly associated with the project under consideration.

cumulative cash flow – the build up of cash over several time periods, for example if cash flow is +£20,000 for three years in a row, cumulative cash in year 3 is +£60,000.

present values – the calculation of future cash flows in terms of their current purchasing power. It is derived from the notion of money having a time value.

qualitative factors – issues surrounding a decision that are based on wider concerns than an accounting profit or financial returns, such as the environment or human rights.

quantitative factors – the results of calculations on potential investments. The results may look precise, but managers should question their validity and ask how they were prepared.

A Level Exercises

A. REVISION QUESTIONS
(40 marks; 70 minutes)

Read the unit, then answer:

1 Distinguish between qualitative and quantitative investment appraisal. *(4)*
2 Why should forecast cash flow figures be treated with caution? *(4)*
3 How useful is payback period as the sole method for making an investment decision? *(4)*
4 Briefly outline the circumstances in which:
   a payback period might be the most important appraisal method for a firm. *(4)*
   b average rate of return might be more important than payback for a firm. *(4)*
5 How are criterion levels applied to investment appraisal? *(3)*
6 Explain the purpose of discounting cash flows. *(4)*
7 Using only quantitative analysis, would you prefer £100 now, or £105 in one year's time, at an interest rate of 10%? *(3)*
8 Using the same data as in question 5, which option would you prefer using just qualitative analysis? *(3)*
9 What qualitative issues might a firm take into account when deciding whether to invest in a new fleet of lorries? *(4)*
10 Why is it important to ask for the source before accepting investment appraisal data? *(3)*

B. REVISION EXERCISES

B1 Data Response *(30 marks; 40 minutes)*
1 Net annual cash flows on an investment are forecast to be:

	£000
Now	(600)
End of year 1	100
End of year 2	400
End of year 3	400
End of year 4	180

Calculate the payback and the average rate of return. *(8)*

2 The Board of Burford Ltd is meeting to decide whether to invest £500,000 in an automated packing machine or into a new customer service centre. The production manager has estimated the cash flows from the two investments to calculate the following table:

	Packing Machine	Service Centre
Payback	1.75 years	3.5 years
NPV	+£28,500	+£25,600

a On purely quantitative grounds, which would you choose and why? *(6)*
b Which four other factors should the Board consider before making a final decision? *(4)*

3 The cash flows on two alternative projects are estimated to be:

	Project A		Project B	
	Cash In	Cash Out	Cash In	Cash Out
Year 0	–	£50,000	–	£50,000
Year 1	£60,000	£30,000	£10,000	£10,000
Year 2	£80,000	£40,000	£40,000	£20,000
Year 3	£40,000	£24,000	£60,000	£30,000
Year 4	£20,000	£20,000	£84,000	£40,000

Discount factors (at 8%) are:

Year 1: 0.93; Year 2: 0.86; Year 3: 0.79; Year 4: 0.735.

Carry out a full investment appraisal to decide which (if either) of the projects should be undertaken. Interest rates are currently 8%. *(12)*

B2 Data Response
Dowton's new finance director has decided that capital investments will only be approved if they meet the following criteria:

Payback	30 months
Average rate of return	18%
Net present value	10% of the investment outlay

The assembly department has proposed the purchase of a £600,000 machine that will be more productive and produce to a higher quality finish. The department estimates that the output gains should yield the following cash flow benefits during the expected four-year life of the machine:

Year 0	−£600,000
Year 1	+£130,000
Year 2	+£260,000
Year 3	+£360,000
Year 4	+£230,000

In addition:

- the machine should have a resale value of £100,000 at the end of its life
- the relevant discount factors are:
  End year 1: 0.91; Year 2: 0.83; Year 3: 0.75; Year 4: 0.68.

Questions *(30 marks; 35 minutes)*
1 Conduct a full investment appraisal then consider whether Dowton's should go ahead with the investment on the basis of the quantitative information provided. *(16)*
2 Outline any other information it might be useful to obtain before making a final decision. *(8)*
3 Explain two sources of finance that might be appropriate for an investment such as this. *(6)*

B3 Case Study

The beef crisis of 1996 caused by the outbreak of BSE was a major problem for many farmers, but for some it proved to be a golden opportunity. Harry Peters, who for many years had reared poultry on his farm in Lancashire, realised that people were looking for alternative foods. He thought he could take the opportunity to farm ostriches, initially to supply to local restaurants, and then to butchers and supermarkets as the taste caught on.

His son had recently completed a business course at a local college, and knew the importance of market research before undertaking a new project such as this. He therefore set up a research programme based on sending questionnaires to several local restaurants and butchers. He also found national sales figures for ostrich meat as a proportion of total meat consumption.

From his research results, Harry's son was able to make the following estimates:

Initial purchase cost of the birds: £75,000
Annual cash outflows: £15,000
Annual cash inflows: £17,000 for the first year, £30,000 for the next two years, and £42,000 for the final three years.

Alternatively, Harry could invest the money in a building society at a fixed annual rate of 6%.

Questions *(50 marks; 60 minutes)*

1 Assess the reliability of the cash inflow figure given in the case study. *(8)*
2 Using the data given, calculate the following:
   a the net and cumulative cash flows for this project for its projected life of six years *(8)*
   b the time taken for the project to pay back the initial investment *(6)*
   c the average rate of return *(6)*
   d the net present value of the project. *(7)*
3 Based on your calculations, should Harry go ahead with the investment? Explain your reasoning. *(5)*
4 Discuss what other factors should be taken into account in making this decision. *(10)*

B4 Case Study

Hungry Jims is a supplier of frozen pies and savoury products to wholesalers throughout the south-east of England. The Chief Executive, Jim Allday, has noticed that his sales have been declining slowly over the last few years.

Jim is now looking at selling direct to retailers via the Internet. The marketing department has researched the proposal. It is anticipated that the project would require an initial investment of £2 million, which includes a £500,000 marketing budget.

Over the first three years, the annual expected sales via the Internet are:

Year 1: £2.5 million; Year 2: £3.5 million; Year 3: £4 million.

The finance department has calculated that the contribution from Internet sales is likely to be 50%, with an annual overhead cost of £500,000. The company's average cost of capital is approximately 10% a year.

Questions *(30 marks; 35 minutes)*

1 Calculate the payback period for this project. *(4)*
2 Calculate the average rate of return. *(6)*
3 Calculate the net present value for this project *(6)*
4 From your calculations, would you suggest this project is worthwhile? *(4)*
5 Assess the other factors Jim would be likely to take into account in making this decision. *(10)*

C. ESSAY QUESTIONS

1 'Quantitative investment appraisal is based on nothing more than educated guesses.' Does this, then, invalidate its use in business?
2 Evaluate the relative importance of qualitative and quantitative information in investment appraisal decisions.
3 Assess the implications for a business of getting an investment appraisal decision wrong.

27.1 Introduction

Budgeting is the process of setting targets covering all aspects of costs and revenues. Budgeting is a method for turning a firm's strategy into reality. A budgeting system should allocate and monitor costs and revenues. Most firms use a system of budgetary control as a means of supervision.

The process starts with an assessment of likely sales revenues for the coming year. Then a cost ceiling is set that allows for an acceptable level of profit. This budget for the whole company's costs is then broken down by division, department or by cost centre. The budget may then be broken down further so that each manager has a budget and therefore some spending power.

27.2 What is budgeting for?

- To ensure that no department or individual spends more than the company expects, thereby preventing unpleasant surprises.
- To provide a yardstick against which a manager's success or failure can be measured (and rewarded). For example, a store manager may have to meet a sales budget of £450,000 at a maximum operating cost of £320,000. As long as the budget holder believes this target is possible, the attempt to achieve it will be motivating. The company can then provide bonuses for achieving or beating the profit target.
- To enable spending power to be **delegated** to local managers who are in a better position to know how best to use the firm's money. This should improve and speed up the decision making process – and help motivate the local budget holders. The management expert Peter Drucker refers to 'management by self-control'. He regards this as the ideal approach. Managers should have clear targets, clear budgets and the power to decide how to achieve them. Then they will try everything they can to succeed.

27.3 Setting budgets

Setting budgets is not an easy job. How do you decide exactly what level of sales are likely next year? Furthermore, how can you plan for costs if the cost of your raw materials tends to fluctuate? Most firms treat last year's budget figures as the main determinant of this year's budget. Minor adjustments will be made for inflation and other foreseeable changes. It is very unlikely that budgets will fall if this method is being used. The great advantage of this method is that very little time needs to be spent on the budget setting task.

An alternative approach is **zero budgeting**. This approach sets each department's budget at zero and demands that budget holders, in setting their budget, justify every pound they ask for. This helps to avoid the common phenomenon of budgets creeping upwards each year. The advantages and disadvantages of this method are set out below.

Advantages of zero budgeting:

- Helps to identify those departments that no longer need as large a budget. This can release funds for growth areas elsewhere within the organisation.
- Can work effectively as a way of cutting the entire cost base of the organisation. This may be necessary in times of recession.

Disadvantages of zero budgeting:

- In order to justify every pound of every budget, a great amount of management time is spent on the budget setting process. This time could be used, perhaps more effectively, elsewhere.
- Fails to overcome the age-old problem that some managers are more devious than others in trying to justify a larger budget than is really needed.

The best criteria for setting budgets are:

- To be clear about the firm's objectives and the strategy for achieving them. Departments with a key role to play in achieving objectives might expect an increase in the year's budget. Departments where no extra activity is required can expect their budget to be frozen, or perhaps cut back a little to release funds.
- To involve as many people as possible in the process. People will be more committed to reaching the targets if they have had a say in how the budget was set.
- To make the process as transparent as possible, so that everyone knows how decisions are reached. In a school or college, for example, an allowance of £20 per student per subject is far clearer than encouraging every department head to go and haggle with the Principal.

27.4 Advantages and disadvantages of budgeting

ADVANTAGES

Budgets are a way to control and monitor costs. Senior managers will approve each department's budget and can then allow the budget holders to run their departments day by day. Only departments which are over budget need attract the regular attention of senior management.

A company-wide system of departmental budgets can be drawn together to give an overall picture for the firm. This is a vital tool in coordinating a firm's diverse activities. This is easy to achieve on modern computer networks or intranets. Every departmental budget spreadsheet can be linked with the company's master budget. The chief executive can therefore find out at the touch of a button what's going well or badly, and who is responsible.

Budgets are often said to have a motivational effect on staff. Budget holders who have the authority to decide how the budget is spent will feel valued and trusted. Meanwhile, the budget can be used as a target for departments, whether they are attempting to exceed budgeted sales or keep costs under the budgeted figure. Success gives a sense of achievement to those who have met their targets.

DISADVANTAGES

Budgeting is not an exact tool because it is based on assumptions and predictions which are subject to error. If a budget is set incorrectly, it can be very demoralising for a manager who is attempting to achieve the impossible.

Clever (or powerful) managers may be able to convince their bosses to provide a higher budget than is really necessary. The incentive is clear; if you are given plenty of spending power it becomes easier to do well at your job. For example, a brand manager with a large advertising budget should be in a strong position to achieve the sales target. Unfortunately, managers with influence in the boardroom may achieve generous budgets at the cost of insufficient budgets for products or departments with higher growth prospects.

Managers may take short-term decisions that help meet current budgets at the cost of damaging future customer goodwill. For example, costs could be trimmed back to meet the budget by using materials of a slightly lower quality. This kind of short-termism may be particularly likely if managers are offered large bonuses for meeting or beating their budgets.

27.5 Other types of budgeting

FLEXIBLE BUDGETING

Flexible budgeting adjusts the budgeted figures in line with the actual sales volume achieved. This ensures that variances show changes in costs rather than a mixture of costs and sales volumes. In the example below, how can a manager identify the cause of the cost overrun?

	Budget	Actual	Variance
Factory cost	£120,000	£132,000	£12,000 Adverse

Costs are £12,000 higher than forecast, but that would be understandable if demand were up 10%. But if demand was as expected, the extra £12,000 costs must be due to paying more for the materials or for labour. Flexible budgets get round this problem. They automatically adjust all variable items to allow for changes in sales volume. For example, if this company had enjoyed a 10% rise in sales in the month, the flexed budget would adjust the budgeted figure by +10% and show:

	Budget	Actual	Variance
Factory cost	£132,000	£132,000	£0

27.6 Budgetary variances

Variance is the amount by which the actual result differs from the budgeted figure. It is usually measured each month, by comparing the actual outcome with the budgeted one. It is important to note that variances are referred to as adverse or favourable – not positive and negative. A **favourable variance** is one which leads to higher than expected profit (revenue up or costs down). An **adverse variance** is one which reduces profit, such as costs being higher than the budgeted level.

The following table shows when variances are adverse or favourable:

VARIABLE	BUDGET	ACTUAL	VARIANCE	
Sales of X	150	160	10	Favourable
Sales of Y	150	145	5	Adverse
Material costs	100	90	10	Favourable
Labour costs	100	105	5	Adverse

The value of regular variance statements is that they provide an early warning. If a product's sales are slipping below budget, managers can respond by increasing marketing support, or by cutting back on production plans. In an ideal world, slippage could be noted in March, a new strategy put into place by May and a recovery in sales achieved by September. Clearly, no firm wishes to wait until the end-of-year profit and loss account to find out that things went badly. An early warning can lead to an early solution.

MANAGEMENT BY EXCEPTION

In a large company, with many separate cost centres, senior managers will have hundreds of budget statements to review each month. In order to avoid information overload, most budgeting systems work on the basis of management by exception. Senior managers will only concern themselves with departmental budgets which show large variances (probably adverse). In large companies management authority is usually delegated down through the organisation. Senior managers only get involved with problem areas or areas of great success.

ISSUES FOR **analysis**

- Variances are the key to analysing budgets. Once a variance between budgeted and actual figures has been identified, the analysis can begin. The important step is to ask why that variance occurred. Does the person responsible know the reason? Is it a one-off or does this same person offer a different excuse each month for poor performance?
- Variance analysis is a means of identifying symptoms. It is down to the user of the variance figures to make a diagnosis as to the exact nature of any problem, and then to suggest the most appropriate cure.
- Although budgets and variances sound very focused upon numbers, they are rooted in everyday actions by people. Sales budgets will only be achieved if the salesforce is enthusiastic and well managed. Production costs will only be kept down if wastage is low and commitment is high. When analysing budgetary problems, therefore, managers soon find themselves looking at the quality of management in departments such as marketing and production.

27.7 Budgeting
an evaluation

Budgets are a management tool. The way in which they are used can tell you a lot about a firm's **culture**. Firms with a strict autocratic culture will tend to use a tightly controlled budgetary system. Managers will have budgets imposed upon them and variances will be watched closely by supervisors. Organisations with a more open culture will use budgeting as an aid to discussion and empowerment.

Whatever the culture, if a manager is to be held accountable for meeting a budget, he or she must be given influence over setting it and control over reaching it.

Although budgets are set for future time periods, analysis of actual against budgeted performance can only take place after the event. This is true of all financial monitoring and this leads to doubts as to its effectiveness as a planning tool. Other measures may be far more reliable in predicting future performance – market research indicating growing levels of customer complaints may well be more useful in predicting future performance.

From an even broader perspective, it could be argued that budgets and other financial measures are unhelpful in some circumstances. Perhaps firms should look at their objectives before deciding on the most useful measure of performance. Financial measures are fine for firms attempting to maximise their profits, but sales figures will be more relevant for firms pursuing an objective of growth, whilst customer complaint levels will be particularly relevant to firms aiming for excellence in their levels of service.

KEY terms

adverse variance – when the variance between actual and budgeted figures results in lower profit.

culture – the attitudes and approaches that typify the way staff carry out their tasks.

delegate – pass authority down the hierarchy.

favourable variance – when the variance between actual and budgeted figures results in higher profits.

variance analysis – studies variances between actual and budgeted figures, looking for causes of those variances with a view to suggesting solutions.

zero budgeting – a system of setting budgets to zero every year and expecting budget holders to justify every pound of their budget.

AS Level Exercises

A. REVISION QUESTIONS
(30 marks; 60 minutes)

Read the unit, then answer:

1 Explain the meaning of the term 'budgeting'. (2)
2 List three advantages that a budgeting system brings to a company. (3)
3 Why is it valuable to have a yardstick against which performance can be measured? (3)
4 Explain what Peter Drucker means by calling budgeting 'management by self-control'. (4)
5 What are the disadvantages of a zero-based budgeting system? (3)
6 How might a firm respond to an increasingly adverse variance in labour costs? (4)
7 Explain what is meant by a 'favourable cost variance'. (2)
8 Why is management by exception a useful time-saving measure for management? (3)
9 Briefly explain how most companies actually set next year's budgets. (3)
10 Why should budget holders have a say in the setting of their budgets? (3)

B. REVISION EXERCISES

B1 Data Analysis

	January			February		
	B	A	V	B	A	V
Sales revenue	140*	150	10	180	175	?
Materials	70	80	(10)	90	95	?
Other direct costs	30	35	(5)	40	40	0
Overheads	20	20	0	25	22	?
Profit	20	15	(5)	?	18	?

*All figures in £000s

Questions *(20 marks; 20 minutes)*
1 What are the five missing numbers from the variance analysis above? (10)
2 Outline one financial strength and two weaknesses in this data, from the company's viewpoint. (6)
3 How might a manager set about improving the accuracy of a sales budget? (4)

B2 Data Response

Budget Data for Clinton and Collins Ltd. (£000s)

	January		February		March		April	
	B	A	B	A	B	A	B	A
Sales revenue	160	144	180	156	208	168	240	188
Materials	40	38	48	44	52	48	58	54
Other direct costs	52	48	60	54	66	62	72	68
Overheads	76	76	76	78	76	80	76	80
Profit	(8)	(18)	(4)	(20)	14	(22)	34	(14)

Questions *(25 marks; 30 minutes)*
1 Use the data to explain why February's profits were worse than expected. (5)
2 Why might Clinton and Collins Ltd have chosen to set monthly budgets? (5)
3 Explain how the firm might have set these budgets. (6)
4 The directors of Clinton and Collins Ltd knew that the recession was causing problems for the firm but were unsure as to whether things were improving or worsening. To what extent does the data suggest an improvement? (9)

B3 Case Study

Foxbury Ltd is a manufacturer of bicycle parts, set up by three old friends in Oxfordshire:

- Russ Day is trained as an accountant and therefore fills the role of finance director
- Nigel Pearce is marketing director
- Nick Johns handles production and fulfils the role of managing director.

When they set up the business, two years ago, Russ convinced the others of the need for a budgetary system. They were won over by his arguments and a system was established whereby the three directors were given control of a budget – one for marketing, one for production and one for finance and administration. Russ monitored performance closely and was disappointed to see Nigel's marketing department overspending its budget. By the end of the first year's trading, Russ complained several times to Nigel that he was spending too much, but Nigel insisted that the frequent trips he made to Holland and Hong Kong were vital to building up a good relationship with customers. Before the start of the next financial year, the three directors met to try to agree next year's budget. Nigel insisted that the previous year's budget had been set too low. Russ again suggested that Nigel had failed to control his expenditure effectively.

Nick intervened, suggesting that as sales were buoyant, they could afford to increase all three budgets by the 20% that Nigel wanted. Nick felt that this was appropriate since labour and material costs had both increased substantially since last year. Russ was also happy with the suggestion, because although he didn't need any extra money this year, he would be happy to drive a larger company car and spend a little more on decorating his office. The directors agreed and the budget was set. At the end of that year, profits fell by 75% despite a healthy increase in sales.

Questions *(25 marks; 50 minutes)*

1 Explain the arguments Russ might have used to convince his colleagues of the need for a budgeting system. *(6)*
2 What problems does the case study indicate may arise from such a system? *(5)*
3 How might Foxbury Ltd's management seek to overcome these problems? *(8)*
4 Explain why profits fell so dramatically despite an increase in sales. *(6)*

A Level Exercises

A. REVISION QUESTIONS
(40 marks; 40 minutes)

1 Fill in the missing figures in the table below: *(5)*

	Budgeted	Actual	Variance
Sales (units)	1,000	900	?
Selling price (£s)	?	120	?
Revenue (£s)	100,000	?	?

2 Explain why variances are labelled adverse or favourable, rather than positive or negative. *(4)*
3 State three possible problems with budgeting systems. *(3)*
4 Outline two advantages and two disadvantages of zero-based budgeting. *(8)*
5 The table below shows November's budgeted and actual figures for Redden Roofracks Ltd:

	Budgeted	Actual
Sales (units)	12,000	10,500
Price	£40	£50
Sales revenue	?	?
Variable cost per unit	?	£25
Total variable cost	£240,000	?
Fixed costs	£160,000	£170,000
Profit	?	?

a Replace all the question marks. *(6)*
b Identify the variance for each variable and state whether it is adverse or favourable. *(14)*

B. REVISION EXERCISES
B1 Data Response

In the board meeting, things have turned nasty: 'Our 8p price cut has been a huge success. Sales rose 20% to 60,000 at £1.12. What a pity we've been let down by Finance!' said the marketing director.

The finance director replied: 'But profits collapsed from £8,000 to just £3,800! I know overheads moved up £1,000 to £13,000, but the rest of the profit collapse is due to that stupid marketing decision!'

Questions *(25 marks; 30 minutes)*

1 Identify the following variances:
  a price *(2)*
  b sales *(2)*
  c revenue *(2)*
  d overheads *(2)*
  e variable cost per unit *(4)*
  f profit. *(2)*
2 Analyse the variances to try to settle the argument *(11)*

B2 Case Study

Petts plc had seen 12 continuous years of profit growth until the recession hit. As a music publishing and retail company, Petts had borrowed heavily during the last year to finance expansion. This borrowing was now a big problem as sales from the retail outlets were tumbling, with customers reducing expenditure on luxuries such as music.

At the latest board meeting, things came to a head. The finance director complained bitterly about over-staffing at the retail outlets and criticised the promotional budget of £1.5 million spent promoting new bands. The response from the director in charge of recording was straightforward: 'All we're doing is spending the budget we were allocated!'. The boss, Charlotte Petts, attempted to soothe the meeting by suggesting that cutting back on various employee perks could reduce indirect costs by 25%. She also suggested that head office staff could be reduced from 120 to 90.

The board spent some more time studying the budgets and variances before agreeing to make changes at their next meeting.

Questions   (30 marks; 45 minutes)

1 Explain the causes of the profit variances for Petts plc.   (8)
2 Using information from the text, explain the changes in Petts plc's interest payments during the year.   (4)
3 Discuss the advantages and disadvantages of reducing the number of head office staff from 120 to 90.   (10)
4 Why should the size of departmental budgets be regularly reviewed?   (8)

Budget and variance analysis for Petts plc, 2002 (£m)

	Quarter 1			Quarter 2			Quarter 3			Quarter 4
	B	A	V	B	A	V	B	A	V	B
Revenue	12.2	11.8	(0.4)	13.2	12.6	(0.6)	12.8	12.4	(0.4)	13.6
Head office costs	1.8	2.0	(0.2)	1.8	2.0	(0.2)	1.8	2.0	(0.2)	1.8
Indirect costs	1.9	1.9	–	1.9	1.9	–	1.9	1.9	–	1.9
Interest	2.5	2.7	(0.2)	2.5	2.7	(0.2)	2.5	2.7	(0.2)	2.5
Retail costs	3.2	3.5	(0.3)	3.3	3.5	(0.2)	3.0	3.3	(0.3)	1.5
Cost of supplies	3.2	3.1	0.1	3.3	3.2	0.1	3.1	3.1	–	1.0
Profit	−0.4	−1.4	(1.0)	0.4	−0.7	(1.1)	0.5	−0.6	(1.1)	0.9

C. ESSAY QUESTIONS

1 'Budgeting systems can often be demotivating to middle and lower managers.' Explain why this may be so.
2 'The success of a budgeting system depends on the prevailing leadership style of an organisation.' Is this true?
3 To what extent is it true to suggest that budgets are the most important financial documents for most managers?

COST CENTRES AND OVERHEAD ALLOCATION

DEFINITION

A cost centre is a section, product or department of a business that can be held accountable for some of the costs of the business.

A profit centre is a part of the business for which a separate profit and loss account can be drawn up.

Overhead allocation refers to the way in which a business divides its indirect costs between its cost centres.

28.1 The purpose of cost centres and profit centres

Cost centres, like **profit centres**, are sections of a business than can be seen as being distinct from other operations of the firm. In a school, each subject department can be seen as a cost centre. The Business Studies department has its own salary, stationery and textbook costs. By dividing a large organisation into cost centres, it is possible to hold individual managers to account for the costs incurred in their departments.

The total costs of the business can be divided up among each of these cost centres. Similarly, part of the firm's revenues can be seen to be due to the operations of each profit centre. Cost centres can be the basis for deciding the price to charge for a product. Or even which products to continue producing, and which to kill off. The idea of using separate centres, instead of just looking at the firm as a whole, has several purposes:

- Accounting – management accounting depends on the availability of accurate information to be able to monitor the activities in all the areas of a business. By using cost centres for separate products or areas, individual performances can be more easily

The Max Factor cosmetics counter at the Daimaru department store in Kyoto (© Bob Krist/Corbis)

analysed. This allows firms to take corrective action wherever necessary.

- Organisational – the use of cost centres allows managers to see which areas of the business are working well, and which are underperforming. This helps senior managers make the right decisions to improve the overall running of the firm.
- Motivational – theorists argue that giving middle managers control over a distinct area of the firm's operations motivates them more strongly to fulfil their responsibility. They will be spurred on to make their area the most profitable in the business.

ADVANTAGES OF COST AND PROFIT CENTRES	PROBLEMS OF COST AND PROFIT CENTRES
• Some control of operations is delegated to the local level, which can be motivating	• Parts of the firm can put themselves before the business as a whole
• The successes and failures of individual departments can be identified clearly	• The reason for good or bad performances may be external to the cost centre, and not under its control
• Problems can be traced more easily	• Not all costs and revenues can be associated directly with a particular part of the firm
• Decision making is aided, for example on setting prices	• They can create extra pressure on more junior managers

Note that cost centres and profit centres are largely the same thing. The only difference is that cost centres only incur costs. Profit centres also generate revenues, therefore their profit can be calculated. For instance the Heinz market research department generates no sales and is therefore a cost centre. The soups division generates costs and revenues and can therefore be a profit centre.

28.2 Establishing cost and profit centres

The way in which a business divides itself up into cost centres will vary according to the circumstances of the firm. Some of the more common bases for cost centres are:

- A product – where a firm has several products that can be easily differentiated from each other, then the different products can each form a cost centre. .
- A group of machines – a particular work area for which the inputs and outputs can be observed.
- A department – an area of activity within the business that performs a specific function.
- A location – if the firm is geographically spread, each separate location can be used as a cost centre.
- A person – some individuals may have responsibility for a specific area of operation and spending, and could be accountable themselves for the costs involved.

If a firm wishes to use cost centres, it will choose a basis that is appropriate for its own situation. A firm with several factories spread around the country may use location as the basis for its cost centres. One which produces a range of different products may be more interested in how each of its products are doing. So it will use the products as individual cost centres.

The aim of using cost centres is to provide managers with information to monitor the performance of the individual parts of the company. The choice of cost centre must be appropriate to the situation of the firm.

28.3 Types of cost

For the purpose of allocating costs to the various cost centres of the business, it is necessary to know which costs are direct, and which are indirect.

Direct costs are those costs which are linked completely to a specific product or area of operation.

For example, a car manufacturer will have clear direct costs when it buys components from an outside firm, such as headlights or tyres. These costs can be attributed directly to the specific make and model of car being produced. This will provide managers with a precise breakdown of the money spent on this product.

Alongside the direct costs of producing a car, the firm will also have costs that are not linked directly to the production of a particular item. These costs are often referred to as overheads. They cover a range of the firm's activities. For example, building a new factory that will produce a range of different models will be a cost the firm must pay, even though the money paid is not associated clearly with any one model.

Indirect costs are costs that are general to some or all areas of the business.

Note that the distinction is not always a clear one – costs such as wages, depreciation and so on can be either direct or indirect, depending on individual circumstances.

Some common direct costs:

- *Wages of factory labour*
- *Materials*
- *Components*
- *Depreciation of specialised machinery*
- *Marketing specific to one product/cost centre*

Some common indirect costs:

- *Supervisors'/managers' wages/salaries*
- *Running service departments such as personnel*
- *Heating and lighting*
- *Depreciation of general machinery*
- *Administration costs*
- *General marketing*
- *Running expenses, such as telephone bills, rent*

28.4 Methods of allocating overheads

The way a firm allocates its overheads or **indirect costs** between its products will have a significant effect on the performance of each of its cost/profit centres.

Example:

In a year, a firm produces two products called ABC and XYZ. They produce 100 ABCs and 200 XYZs. ABCs sell for £5 each, whilst XYZs sell for £8 each. Apart from marketing, it is known that the total cost of producing ABCs is £200, and of XYZs £800. The total spent on marketing is £600.

The way in which the marketing overhead is allocated between the two products will affect how each has performed, as shown by the profits made over the year.

If the marketing overheads are split evenly between the two products, the profit and loss accounts for each are as shown in the table at the top of the next page.

PROFIT AND LOSS ACCOUNT ABC		PROFIT AND LOSS ACCOUNT XYZ	
	£		£
Sales revenue	500	Sales revenue	1,600
Direct costs	(200)	Direct costs	(800)
Allocated marketing cost	(300)	Allocated marketing cost	(300)
Profit for product	0	Profit for product	500

Looking at these figures, a manager may conclude that the resources being used to produce ABCs at no profit may be better invested in a new product or in producing extra XYZs.

If, on the other hand, overheads are split on the basis of the quantity produced, then twice as much of the marketing costs will be allocated to XYZ, since twice as many are produced. The profit and loss accounts would now be:

PROFIT AND LOSS ACCOUNT ABC		PROFIT AND LOSS ACCOUNT XYZ	
	£		£
Sales revenue	500	Sales revenue	1,600
Direct costs	(200)	Direct costs	(800)
Allocated marketing cost	(200)	Allocated marketing cost	(400)
Profit for product	100	Profit for product	400

From this second example, a manager may conclude that it is worthwhile continuing with the now profitable ABC product.

Clearly, the method used to allocate costs between different centres will have an effect on how the performance of each centre looks. It is very important that the method used is fully appreciated by anyone reviewing the performance of the business and its various cost/profit centres. If not, it could lead to inappropriate decisions being made with regard to the allocation of resources for future production.

The most common method of allocating overhead costs are:

- full **costing**
- absorption costing
- marginal costing.

FULL COSTING

Full costing is the simplest method of allocating indirect overheads between the various cost centres of a firm. As such, it may also be the least accurate.

When using full costing, an arbitrary method is used to decide what proportion of all the firm's over-

head costs are to be allocated to each cost centre. For example, a firm has two departments, A and B. Department A produces 25% of the firm's output by volume, and department B 75%. If output by volume is the chosen method for allocating all the overheads, department A will be charged with 25% of all the overhead costs incurred by the business, whilst department B will account for the remaining 75%.

If the **direct costs** for department A are £300,000, and for department B £650,000, and overheads are £400,000, the calculation of the full or total cost will be:

Department A:

Direct cost		*£300,000*
Overhead allocation	= 25% of £400,000	*£100,000*
Full cost		*£400,000*

Department B:

Direct cost		*£650,000*
Overhead allocation	= 75% of £400,000	*£300,000*
Full cost		*£950,000*

Advantages of using full costing:

- Relatively simple to use and therefore inexpensive to administer.
- All costs are recovered by the costs allocated to each centre.
- As will be seen, even the more complex methods of allocating overheads can not guarantee accuracy, so using such a simple system can be seen as being fair. All departments or areas are being treated equally.

Disadvantages of using full costing:

- The arbitrary nature of the allocation method can lead to overheads being unfairly distributed between the different cost centres. The system might lead to clear absurdities, such as a one-person department being charged the same for canteen facilities as one with a hundred staff.
- Decisions made on the basis of full costing could be incorrect. The information generated by this system could be misleading.

ABSORPTION COSTING

Absorption costing is a refinement of the full costing method. Instead of using an all-inclusive approach and allocating total overheads proportionately, each aspect of the overheads is absorbed separately by cost centres on an appropriate basis.

The way overheads are allocated to each cost centre varies depending on the cost involved. Some possible bases for allocation overhead costs are shown in the table at the top of the next page.

For example, if we look at the firm mentioned in the full costing section, the overheads of £400,000 might be made up of three elements:

- Rent   £90,000
- Canteen costs   £210,000
- Insurance   £100,000

OVERHEAD	BASIS FOR ALLOCATION
Rent & rates	• Physical area taken up by the cost centre
Heating	• Physical area taken up by the cost centre
Canteen costs	• Number of employees in the cost centre
Health & safety costs	• Number of employees in the cost centre
Personnel administration	• Number of employees in the cost centre
Depreciation	• Value of capital used by the cost centre
Insurance	• Value of capital used by the cost centre

Using absorption costing, the 75:25 split used earlier is not appropriate. Instead, we need more information on each department, as below:

	A	B
Percentage of the physical area used	66%	33%
Percentage of total employees	33%	66%
Percentage of total capital used	25%	75%

The overhead costs can now be apportioned to the two cost centres in relation to these different proportions.

Advantages of using absorption costing:

- It is fair, as the different rates of usage of each aspect are taken into account.
- It ought to give the firm an accurate basis on which to cost each unit of output. This ought to allow accurate pricing policies, especially if a cost-plus pricing system is used.

Disadvantages of using absorption costing:

- Not all costs can be divided accurately in this way – some workers or areas of the factory may be used by more than one cost centre. This is particularly a problem when a firm makes a wide range of products.
- This approach is more expensive to run than full costing, as it requires careful measurement of factors like the capital invested into each department.

MARGINAL OR CONTRIBUTION COSTING

Under this approach, the valuation of a centre's costs rests solely on the basis of direct costs. Overheads are excluded from each centre's cost total. They are only included when producing the whole firm's profit and loss account.

Financial decisions about a product or a department depend largely upon contribution. Contribution is the amount of money from the sale of a product that is available for the firm to pay off its fixed costs. It is found by the calculation:

$$\text{contribution per unit} = \text{selling price} - \text{marginal (direct) costs}$$

For example, if a product has direct costs of £20 per unit, and is sold for £25, then for each sale the firm has £5 which it can put towards paying off its overheads, i.e. each sale contributes £5 to fixed costs.

Using this approach, it does not matter how much of the overhead costs each of the firm's products use up. As long as a product can be sold for more than its direct costs, it helps the firm pay off its fixed costs. Once these have all been paid for, it helps increase the firm's profit.

However, while this method allows the firm to make direct comparisons between its different cost or profit centres, it does nothing to make sure that each is treated fairly. A cost centre that uses a large proportion of a particular overhead can be seen to be making a positive contribution if this overhead is ignored. The firm must take care in deciding which costs are direct and which are indirect if this method is going to be used.

ISSUES FOR analysis

The worked example given above shows that great care must be taken in interpreting the results obtained from any analysis made on the basis of overhead allocation. There will seldom be a case where there is a clear distinction between which product each employee works on, or how much area a cost centre uses. It is extremely unlikely that any system of allocating overheads could ever be completely fair and unbiased.

Even the use of marginal, or contribution, costing is not as clear cut as it may appear. A positive contribution is a good sign, but could the resources bring in a better contribution if switched to boost the output of another product or to develop a completely new one? In other words, what is the opportunity cost of keeping resources in their present use?

There may, of course, be other reasons for continuing to make a product, even if it does not make a positive contribution to overheads, such as:

- Is it part of a product range, which helps to keep total sales up?
- Does the product help to symbolise the firm in some way?
- Does the product have sentimental value to the owner or to a group of customers?

28.5 Cost centres
an evaluation

The use of cost centres and the various methods for allocating overheads needs to be used with care. It ought not to be taken in isolation from all the other aspects of the firm. Determining the full cost of a product is difficult. Therefore it is vital to allow for other factors such as the marketing, human and social implications of a decision.

It is perhaps better to think of the costing methods as ways of finding out which questions to ask, rather than actually providing answers. If one product has a large share of the physical area of the business, does it use this space effectively? Are the large numbers of workers in a cost centre efficient, or would the product, and the firm as a whole, benefit from some capital investment? Only when such matters are considered can valid judgements about products or other cost centres be made.

KEY terms

cost centre – a department or section of an organisation to which specific costs can be allocated.

costing – dividing up production and selling costs into direct and indirect components.

direct costs – costs that can be attributed directly to a cost centre.

indirect costs – overheads such as rent which cannot be attributed to a specific cost centre.

profit centre – a department which generates costs and revenues, allowing a profit and loss account to be drawn up.

AS Level Exercises

A. REVISION QUESTIONS
(25 marks; 30 minutes)

Read sections 28.1 to 28.3, then answer the following.

1 State two benefits of dividing an organisation into profit centres. *(2)*
2 What is the difference between a cost centre and a profit centre? *(2)*
3 Why may the use of cost and profit centres help staff motivation? *(2)*
4 Cost centres help identify the cost per unit of each product made by a firm. Outline two possible benefits to the firm of having this data. *(4)*
5 Section 28.2 suggests five ways in which a firm can split itself up into cost or profit centres. Which would you think is the most appropriate for:
   a WHSmith retail division
   b Cadbury's chocolate products
   c a large department store, such as Harrod's?
   Briefly state your reasoning. *(6)*
6 Explain the difference between direct and indirect costs. *(2)*
7 Decide whether each of these costs are direct or indirect:
   a a corporate advertising campaign
   b the salaries of the personnel department
   c the ingredients to make a product
   d the interest charges on the firm's loans
   e the electricity used to make the product. *(5)*
8 Broadly, the concept of direct and indirect costs can be said to be similar to the division between fixed and variable costs. Which is the best match?
   a Direct costs are similar to _____ costs. *(1)*
   b Indirect costs are similar to _____ costs. *(1)*

B. REVISION EXERCISE

B1 Data Response
Charli Beale started up beauty.com with just £2,000 while studying for her A Levels. The website started by offering cosmetics imported from Paris and Milan, although six months ago Charli started offering an own label range called C.B. From the start she made C.B. a separate profit centre and appointed an enthusiastic young executive to manage the brand. His first target was to achieve a break-even level by month six, which he has just managed (see figures for the latest month in the table below).

	Imported	C.B.	Total
Revenue	£47,000	£25,000	£72,000
Materials	£11,500	£5,500	£17,000
Direct labour	£18,500	£10,500	£29,000
Other direct costs	£8,000	£6,000	£14,000
Total direct costs	£38,000	£22,000	£60,000
Fixed costs	£5,500	£3,000	£8,500
Profit	£3,500	£0	£3,500

Questions *(30 marks; 35 minutes)*
1 Explain what is meant by the term profit centre. *(2)*
2 Outline two reasons why a small business start-up may benefit especially from the use of profit centres. *(6)*
3 Examine how the 'enthusiastic young executive' might use the profit centre figures for the C.B. range? *(6)*
4 Using profit centres has allowed Charli to delegate authority.
   a What does this mean? *(2)*
   b Outline two possible disadvantages to Charli of delegating authority to her profit centre managers. *(6)*
5 Discuss whether traditional methods, such as profit centres, are really needed in the modern world of 'dot.com' businesses. *(8)*

A Level Exercises

A. REVISION QUESTIONS

(35 marks; 60 minutes)

Read the unit, then answer:

1 What is meant by a 'cost centre'? *(3)*
2 What is the difference between a direct and an indirect cost? *(4)*
3 Give three examples of:
  a direct costs
  b indirect costs
  for a newsagents. *(6)*
4 Explain two reasons why Manchester United plc might want to divide the business up into profit centres. *(4)*
5 State two possible disadvantages to a firm of establishing cost centres. *(2)*
6 Outline two ways of allocating overheads. *(4)*
7 Why is the method of allocating overheads important to a firm producing several products? *(3)*
8 Suggest one suitable way of allocating each of the following overheads. Explain your answers.
  a marketing *(3)*
  b power *(3)*
  c recruitment. *(3)*

B. REVISION EXERCISES

B1 Data Response

O'Connor Cycles produces three standard models of bikes. Overheads are allocated on an even basis between the three products. The figures for the previous year's trading were:

	Dynamo	Shark	Avenger
Selling price	£75	£50	£100
Quantity	100	150	75
Total direct cost	£5,000	£3,000	£6,000
Allocated overhead	£2,000	£2,000	£2,000

Questions *(30 marks; 35 minutes)*

1 Calculate the profit/loss made by each of the three types of bike using this overhead allocation. *(6)*
2 Explain why contribution theory would suggest that the firm continues to produce all three models. *(5)*
3 **a** Suggest a more appropriate way to allocate overheads. *(3)*
  b Calculate the new profit/loss figures on this basis. *(8)*
4 If you were the manager of this firm, explain what areas of the firm's performance you would wish to question after examining these figures. *(8)*

B2 Case Study

Meredith Fabrications is a small manufacturer of specialist material for outdoor clothing such as fellwalking and rock climbing. A typical garment is made up of three types of material: lining, stuffing and waterproof covering. For a normal month's production of 1,000 garments, the costs are:

	Lining	Stuffing	Water-proofing
Direct labour	£5,000	£4,000	£3,000
Direct materials	£4,000	£2,000	£6,000
Other direct costs	£6,000	£5,000	£4,000

The cost of assembling 1,000 items is £3,000. At present the firm is averaging a profit per 1,000 items of £2,500.

The firm has just been approached by a supplier of similar materials, which has offered to supply the firm with lining at a cost of £7,000 per 1,000 garments. The other direct costs, such as zips and labelling, would still be paid by Meredith Fabrications. By concentrating only on producing the stuffing and waterproofing and the assembling of the clothing, Meredith Fabrications believes it can double its output of finished items.

Questions *(40 marks; 50 minutes)*

1 Calculate the cost of manufacturing a normal month's 1,000 garments. *(5)*
2 Calculate the firm's total costs if the linings were bought-in. *(7)*
3 Examine the advantages of treating each item as a separate cost centre. *(8)*
4 Discuss the other factors the firm should consider before accepting or rejecting the new supplier. *(12)*
5 Advise the firm on whether it should accept the new supplier's offer. Justify your recommendations. *(8)*

PRODUCTIVITY AND PERFORMANCE

30.1 Productivity – what is it?

The productivity of a firm is a measurement of its efficiency. It measures output in relation to inputs. A firm can increase its efficiency by producing more with the same inputs or producing the same amount with fewer inputs.

The most common measure is **labour productivity**. This measures the amount a worker produces over a given time. For example, an employee might make 10 pairs of jeans in an hour. Measuring productivity is relatively easy in manufacturing where the number of goods can be counted. In the service sector it is not always possible to measure anything tangible. Productivity in services can be measured in some cases (the number of customers served, number of patients seen, the sales per employee). But how can the productivity of a receptionist be measured?

When considering a firm's efficiency it is important to distinguish between productivity and total output. By hiring more employees the firm may increase the total output, but this does not necessarily mean that the output per employee has gone up. Similarly, it is possible to have less total output with higher productivity because of a fall in the number of workers. Imagine, for example, 20 employees producing 40 tables a week in a furniture company. Their productivity on average is 2 tables per week. If 5 employees make 15 tables the overall output has fallen, but the output *per worker* has risen. This situation of falling output but rising productivity happened in many manufacturing companies in the UK in the early 1990s. Faced with high interest rates, high exchange rates and a recession, many companies were forced to rationalise their organisations. This led to high levels of redundancies and extra work for those who still had a job. The result was that there were fewer people working but at the same time there was often higher output per person.

Business IN

PRODUCTIVITY

In 2002 for the sixth year in succession Nissan's Sunderland factory was acknowledged as the most productive in Europe. Its productivity level of 95 cars per worker per year was more than double the rates achieved by European rivals such as Rover, Volkswagen and Peugeot. However, even the Sunderland plant achieves only half the productivity of the world's best – operated by Mitsubishi Motors of Japan. Of the top 10 plants in the world, the first 9 are in Japan. The tenth is in South Korea. Each worker at Mitsubishi's best plant produces almost 180 cars per year. The most efficient plant in North America – Honda's Marysville factory in Ohio – is similarly behind its Asian rivals, producing 96 cars per employee.

What might explain the productivity differences? The age of the factories provides a part-explanation, with those at the top tending to be the newest plants. The type of car is also important. There is more work in producing a Jaguar than a Fiat. Researchers usually conclude, though, that the main explanation is the quality of management.

30.2 Why does productivity matter?

The output per employee is a very important measure of a firm's performance. It has a direct impact on the cost of producing a unit. If productivity increases, then, assuming wages are unchanged, the labour cost per unit will fall. Imagine that in one factory employees make 5 pairs of shoes a day but in another one they make 10 pairs a day. Assuming the wage rate is the same this means the labour cost of a pair of shoes

	DAILY WAGE RATE	PRODUCTIVITY RATE (PER DAY)	WAGE COST (PER PAIR)
Factory 1	£50	5	£10
Factory 2	£50	10	£5

will be halved in the second factory (see the table above). With lower labour costs this firm is likely to be in a better competitive position.

By increasing productivity a firm can improve its competitiveness. It can either sell its products at a lower price or keep the price as it was and enjoy a higher profit margin. This is why firms continually monitor their productivity relative to their competitors and, where possible, try to increase it. However, they need to make sure that quality does not suffer in the rush to produce more. It may be necessary to set both productivity and quality targets.

30.3 How to increase productivity

INCREASE INVESTMENT IN MODERN EQUIPMENT

With more modern or more sophisticated machines and better production processes, output per worker should improve. Many modern factories have relatively few production workers. Mechanisation and automation are everywhere. However, firms face financial constraints and should be cautious about assuming that mechanisation guarantees higher profits. In the 1980s the American car giant General Motors invested billions of dollars in robotic production lines. Breakdowns meant they never proved as efficient as intended. More importantly, when customer buying habits switched to smaller cars, the machines proved much less flexible than humans. The investment proved unprofitable and by the early 1990s the company was close to financial failure.

It is also true to say that many people call for new technology when in fact more output can be squeezed out of the existing equipment. It may prove more efficient to run the machines for longer, spend more on careful maintenance to prevent breakdowns and discuss how to improve working practices. Firms can often achieve significant productivity gains without new equipment. This is the reason for the success of the **kaizen** approach taken in many firms. Important benefits can be achieved from what seem like relatively small changes to the way the firm operates rather than large-scale investment in technology.

IMPROVE THE ABILITY LEVEL OF THOSE AT WORK

To increase productivity a firm may need to introduce more training for its employees. A skilled and well-trained workforce is likely to produce more and make fewer mistakes. Employees should be able to complete the task more quickly and not need as much supervision or advice. They should be able to solve their own work-related problems and may be in a better position to contribute ideas on how to increase productivity further.

However, firms are often reluctant to invest in training because employees may leave and work for another firm once they have gained more skills. Training also involves higher costs in the short run, which the business may not be able to afford, and the actual training period may cause disruptions to the normal flow of work. There is also a danger that the training will not provide sufficient gains to justify the initial investment. So any spending in this area needs to be properly costed and researched. Simply training people for the sake of it is obviously of limited value. However, in general, UK firms do not have a particularly good record in training. More investment here could probably have a significant effect on the UK's productivity levels.

It should also be remembered that elaborate training may not be necessary for a firm which recruits the right people. Great care must be taken in the selection process to find staff with the right skills and attitudes. A firm with a good reputation locally will find it much easier to pick the best people. This is why many firms take great care over their relations with the local community.

IMPROVE EMPLOYEE MOTIVATION

Professor Herzberg once said that most people's idea of a fair day's work was less than half what they could give. If they wanted to. The key to success, he felt, was to create the circumstances in which people wanted to give all they could to the job. His suggestions on how to provide job enrichment are detailed in Unit 31.

There is no doubt that motivation matters. A motivated salesforce may achieve twice the sales level of an unmotivated one. A motivated computer technician may correct twice the computer faults of an unmotivated one. And, in both cases, overall business performance will be affected.

THE ROLE OF MANAGEMENT

The management's style and ability can have a significant impact on motivation and on how effectively resources are used. Good managers can bring about substantial productivity gains through well-organised work, the effective management of people and the coordination of resources. Bad managers can lead to wastage, inefficiency and low productivity.

Perhaps the key management role is to identify increasing productivity as a permanent objective. For example, the Japanese bulldozer company Komatsu set a target of a 10% productivity increase every year, until the world-leading American producer Caterpillar had been overhauled. In many firms, productivity is not a direct target. The focus, day by day, is on production, not productivity. After all, it is production which ensures customer orders are fulfilled. An operations manager, faced with a 10% increase in orders, may simply ask the workforce to do overtime. The work gets done; the workforce is happy to earn extra money; and it's all rather easy to do. Harder by far to reorganise the workplace to make production more effective. Managers whose main focus is on the short term, therefore, think of production not productivity.

Problems increasing productivity

Firms often struggle to increase their productivity. In some cases this is because managers are failing to use their resources effectively. In other cases there are genuine obstacles. The firm's equipment and the quality of its workforce, for example, can limit the maximum output per worker. In the long run the firm can invest in training and more modern technology (assuming it has the necessary funds) but in the short run it may well be constrained.

Managers may also face resistance from the workers. This is because productivity gains may be at the expense of jobs. If new working practices enable employees to produce 10% more but the overall number of orders has not increased, the firm may have to make some employees redundant. By increasing productivity, therefore, the employees may in effect be working themselves out of a job. Consequently, when management talk of the need to increase productivity, employees are often quite suspicious. On the other hand, if productivity is not increased, the firm may struggle to compete and *everyone's* job may be under threat.

The need to be competitive seems to be increasingly clear to employees, possibly because of much greater international competition than in the past. As a result, negotiations between management and workers over productivity have tended to become more cooperative. Both sides now appear to appreciate the need to improve the firm's performance and to realise that this requires greater productivity. This may not lead to unemployment provided the firm can increase its overall number of orders – and to do this it must increase competitiveness! Greater productivity may, therefore, increase long-term job opportunities rather than destroy them. It is certainly true that a firm which fails to boost productivity as much as its rivals will find it harder to compete.

If greater productivity does lower the unit cost and lead to a higher profit margin, workers are naturally eager to share in these gains. This is why pay and productivity are often linked in pay negotiations. Employees may accept the need to boost productivity but in return negotiate a pay increase.

The end of a production line © Richmond Foods

When answering a case study or essay it might be useful to consider the following points:

- Productivity is an important determinant of a firm's international competitiveness because it can have a significant impact on unit costs.
- High productivity does not in itself guarantee that a firm is competitive – it also depends on other factors such as the cost of materials, product quality, product design, good marketing and external factors such as the exchange rate.
- The productivity within an industry will depend on a combination of factors such as training, capital equipment and production techniques. The productivity of UK firms is typically quite low compared with American, German or Japanese competitors.

The importance of productivity to a firm depends primarily on the level of value added involved. Top-price perfumes such as Chanel have huge profit margins. Production costs are a tiny proportion of the selling price. Therefore a 10% productivity increase might have only a marginal effect on profit and virtually none on the competitiveness of the brand. For mass market products in competitive markets, high productivity is likely to be essential for survival. A 5% cost advantage might make all the difference. Therefore, when judging an appropriate recommendation for solving a business problem, a judgement is required as to whether boosting productivity is a top priority for the business concerned.

30.5 Productivity and performance
an evaluation

Greater labour productivity can lead to greater efficiency and higher profitability. This is because, other things being equal, it lowers the labour cost per unit. However, productivity is only one factor which contributes to a firm's success. A firm must also ensure it produces a good quality product, that it is marketed effectively and that costs are controlled. There is little point increasing productivity by 20% if at the same time you pay your staff 30% more. Similarly, there is no point producing more if there is no actual demand. Higher productivity, therefore, contributes to better performance but needs to be accompanied by effective decision making throughout the firm.

KEY terms

capacity – total output which could be produced with existing resources.

capital intensive – high level of capital equipment compared to labour.

kaizen – a Japanese term meaning 'continuous improvement'. Regular, small increases in productivity may achieve more (and be less disruptive) than major changes to working methods.

labour intensive – high level of labour input compared to the amount of capital equipment.

labour productivity – output per worker.

AS Level Exercises

A. REVISION QUESTIONS
(40 marks; 70 minutes)

Read the unit, then answer:

1 What is meant by the term 'productivity'? *(3)*
2 Why may it be hard to measure the productivity of staff who work in service industries? *(4)*
3 How does productivity relate to labour costs per unit? *(4)*
4 Explain how a firm might be able to increase its employees' productivity. *(4)*
5 How can increased investment in machinery help to boost productivity? *(3)*
6 Identify two factors which help and two factors which constrain your productivity as a student. *(4)*
7 Outline the likely effect of increased motivation on the productivity of a teacher. *(5)*
8 Calculate the change in productivity at BDQ Co since last year: *(4)*

	Output	Number of Staff
Last year	32,000	50
This year	30,000	40

9 Explain how motivation and productivity might be linked. *(4)*
10 Explain how productivity can be linked to unit labour costs. *(5)*

B. REVISION EXERCISES

B1 Data Response

Productivity

In 1997 Europe's most efficient car plant was the Nissan factory in Sunderland. Its productivity level of 98 cars per worker was three times higher than Rover's Longbridge plant. The implications of this difference are enormous. Assuming workers at both plants are paid £25,000 a year, the labour costs per car are as follows:

	Labour Cost per Worker	Cars per Worker*	Labour Cost per Car
Nissan, Sunderland	£25,000	98	£255
Rover, Longbridge	£25,000	33	£758

*Source: Economist Intelligence Unit, 1998

Clearly, having labour costs which are treble the Nissan figures makes it much harder for Rover to compete effectively in the mass market.

Among the explanations offered for this big difference in productivity are:

- better design – Japanese cars are designed with fewer components than British ones

- more reliable plant – Nissan's Sunderland plant has an exceptionally low rate of stoppage, partly because it is quite new and partly because of careful maintenance
- excellent workforce management and motivation at Nissan.

Questions *(30 marks; 35 minutes)*

1 Explain how productivity affects labour costs per unit. *(4)*
2 Outline how each of the three 'explanations offered for this big difference' could affect productivity. *(12)*
3 Explain two other possible reasons why the Sunderland plant has higher productivity than Rover. *(6)*
4 Analyse the benefits Nissan can derive from being able to compete more effectively in the market than Rover. *(8)*

B2 Case Study

Going Potty

Fabienne de Bruges was trying to explain the need to boost productivity to the employees at her ceramics factory, FB Ltd. Relations between Fabienne and her staff had not been good in recent years. The company was not doing well and she blamed the workers. 'On average you work 8 hours a day at £5 an hour and produce around 160 pots each. Meanwhile at Frandon I am told they produce 280 pots a day. Can't you see that this makes it cheaper for them and if things go on like this we'll be out of business? You need to work much harder to get our unit costs down! I know you are expecting to get a pay rise this year but I cannot afford it until you produce more; then we'll think about it.'

Jeff Battersby, the spokesperson for the employees, was clearly annoyed by Fabienne's tone. 'Firstly, Ms de Bruges, have you ever considered that if you paid us more we might produce more for you? I'm not surprised productivity is higher at Frandon – they get about £56 a day. There's no point demanding more work from us if you are not willing to pay for it – we're not slaves you know. If you paid us £7 an hour like Frandon I reckon we could increase productivity by 50%. However, that's not the only issue: they've got better equipment. It's not our fault if the kilns don't work half the time and take an age to heat up. Sort out the equipment and our pay and you'll soon see productivity improve. Why not *ask* us next time instead of jumping to conclusions?'

Questions *(60 marks; 75 minutes)*

1 a FB Ltd employs 50 pot makers whilst Frandon Ltd employs 30 people in production. Calculate the total output for each of the two companies. *(4)*
  b With reference to FB Ltd and Frandon Ltd, explain the difference between 'total output' and 'productivity'. *(6)*

2 a Calculate the average labour cost per pot at FB Ltd if employees are paid £5 an hour and their daily output is 160 pots each. *(4)*

b What is the wage cost per pot at Frandon? (Assume an 8-hour day.) *(3)*

c Analyse the short- and long-term benefits to Frandon of its lower labour costs per unit. *(12)*

d Jeff Battersby claims that if the employees at FB Ltd were paid £7 an hour their productivity would increase 50%. What would the unit wage cost be then? *(5)*

3 Would you recommend Fabienne increases the pay of her employees to £7 an hour? Justify your answer. *(12)*

4 Discuss the possible gains from involving employees in discussions about how to improve productivity. *(14)*

A Level Exercises

A. REVISION QUESTIONS
(60 marks; 90 minutes)

Read the unit, then answer:

1 What problems might a firm face when trying to increase its productivity? *(4)*

2 Why is it important for a firm to increase its productivity? *(4)*

3 How can productivity increase if the total output is falling? *(4)*

4 a Vartex Ltd employs 120 production staff. Their average earnings are £17,500 per year. This year's output is expected to be 42,000 units.

   i Calculate labour productivity at Vartex. *(4)*

   ii Calculate the labour cost per unit. *(4)*

b A benchmarking exercise has shown that Vartex's most efficient competitor pays £21,000 per year to its 80 staff. The staff produce a total annual output of 48,000 units.

   i Calculate the competitor's labour productivity. *(4)*

   ii Calculate the labour cost per unit for the competitor. *(4)*

   iii Both firms price their goods at £59.00. Assuming there are no other costs, what profit per unit is made by each business? *(6)*

5 Identify three factors other than productivity which affect a firm's competitiveness. *(3)*

6 Why is productivity likely to be especially important for a product with low value added? *(4)*

7 'Increasing production is easy. Increasing productivity is hard.' Explain the meaning of this statement. *(5)*

8 Why might unions resist management's attempts to increase productivity? *(6)*

9 Why might unions welcome management's attempts to increase productivity? *(4)*

10 Explain how productivity can fall even if total output is increasing. *(4)*

B. REVISION EXERCISES

B1 Data Response

Productivity and Competitiveness

In a recent study on competitiveness, Japanese car component manufacturers outperformed UK firms by a 2:1 margin in productivity and 100:1 in quality. Productivity was measured in terms of annual units of output divided by labour hours and quality by the number of supplied parts per million claimed by vehicle manufacturers to have been defective. The study identified the key features of 'world class' plants: substantially higher volumes of finished parts compared with similar sized concerns; high capacity utilisation; more automated assembly processes; integrated and tightly controlled processes.

Questions *(30 marks; 35 minutes)*

1 What is meant by 'competitiveness'? *(4)*

2 Why might the productivity of UK firms be so much lower than Japanese companies? *(8)*

3 Consider the possible implications of UK suppliers having much lower productivity and quality than Japanese companies. *(9)*

4 What problems might UK firms face when trying to increase productivity? *(9)*

B2 Case study

Semmings Ltd

The mood at Semmings Ltd was gloomy. The unions and management had recently met to discuss targets for next year and had been unable to reach any agreement. According to management it was vital for employees to increase their productivity by at least 3% if the firm was to be able to compete successfully against its fierce competitors, Frentons and GTR. Whilst the unions accepted that more productivity was desirable there were two main sticking points:

- How could it possibly be achieved? The workers were working their hardest already.
- Why should they bother when management was only offering them a 1% pay increase when inflation was predicted to be 3%?

Negotiations had gone on for nearly two weeks but neither side would budge. The management said greater productivity must happen. It was prepared to discuss *how* it could be achieved and would welcome ideas from the unions. After all, the survival of the firm depended on it. It certainly could not afford more than 1%. The unions felt the management offer was unacceptable and were being pressed by some of the workforce to ballot for industrial action. As one worker put it: 'They always blame us for poor productivity, but look at the 20-year-old machinery we have to work with, and those second-rate components they buy in!'

Questions *(40 marks; 60 minutes)*

1 Analyse the possible ways in which Semmings Ltd might be able to increase its productivity. *(8)*
2 Examine the possible reasons why the unions at Semmings might be reluctant to accept the management's plan to increase productivity. *(8)*
3 Semmings Ltd needs to improve its performance. To what extent is an increase in productivity essential to increase a firm's performance? *(8)*
4 Discuss the problems a firm might face in attempting to increase its productivity every year. *(10)*
5 How might Semmings benefit from discussing issues such as productivity with its staff? *(6)*

C. ESSAY QUESTIONS

1 'Greater productivity is the real key to a firm's success.' Discuss this statement.
2 'In modern, wealthy economies, increasingly quality matters more than productivity.' Critically assess this view.
3 Some managers believe the most effective means of increasing productivity is to pay more. Discuss this view.

B3 Case study

Productivity and performance

Martin Faruq was explaining the need for greater productivity to employee representatives at the Glasgow plant of the US computer giant, IXT. 'As you know there is significant overcapacity at the moment in the worldwide PC market. Whilst IXT maintains a good market position it is very likely the company will look to reduce capacity in the coming few years. It is looking to get rid of its most inefficient factories. We may be on the Head Office list of closures unless we can improve productivity. The UK is not a cheap place to produce and our productivity last year was 8% below the company average. Add to that the strong pound and we are looking very vulnerable indeed. We need to change and we need to change quickly.' Some of the employee representatives immediately started to explain how much had been achieved at the Glasgow plant in the 3 years since Martin had taken over. 'You cannot push the staff any harder; we are already working 110%!' Some staff suspected Martin was simply looking for a way of getting even more out of them than he had already and that he was blaming them for factors completely out of their control. 'You can't hold us responsible for the strong pound or the lack of demand in the market' said one, 'we're doing the best we can'.

Martin listened carefully and replied: 'Look, I'm not blaming anyone but we need to look for ways of improving productivity or we will all be in trouble. Let's look at the data and start thinking. Jack Shilvekio is coming out from the Dallas Head Office next month and I want something to show him. He's already hinted that he thinks there's no point being here if Britain's not in the Euro. We need a plan to convince him we are worth holding on to.'

	Glasgow plant	Average of all company factories
Index of Productivity	92	100
Capital investment levels last year	+12%	+5%
Average age of machines	8 years	5 years
Participation of staff in quality circles	25%	50%
Number of models produced	10	6
Basic working week	35 hours	37 hours

Questions *(30 marks; 45 minutes)*

1 Consider the ways in which productivity might be improved at IXT's Glasgow factory. *(15)*
2 Discuss whether an increase in productivity is certain to improve the competitiveness of products produced by the Glasgow factory. *(15)*

MOTIVATION IN THEORY

DEFINITION

One key theorist (Professor Herzberg) believes motivation occurs when people do something because they want to do it. Others think of motivation as the desire to achieve a result. The difference between these two definitions is important and should become clear during this unit.

31.1 Introduction

In February 1996 Fulham Football Club was placed 95th in the League, one place away from relegation to the Vauxhall Conference. When the club's centre forward was booked in a home game, the home fans shouted off, off, off! The club's manager was shuffled to one side and a new one appointed, Micky Adams.

One year later Fulham sat on top of the 3rd division and the centre forward was the fans' hero – one of the Football League's top goal scorers. What had happened?

The new manager had made a few free transfer signings, but the team was largely the same. Their pay had not risen, nor had a new bonus scheme been introduced. The key difference was in the players' motivation. They had found a new spirit, a new confidence, a new will to win. The transformation was purely psychological.

Later, Micky Adams did the same again at Brighton and at Leicester City. In football, so in business. Motivation matters. This is why it merits a unit to itself – and why many consider motivation theory to be the most important topic within Business Studies.

31.2 FW Taylor and scientific management

Although there were earlier pioneers, the starting point for the study of motivation is FW Taylor (1856–1917). As with most of the other influential writers on this subject, Taylor was American. His influence over the twentieth century world has been massive. Much business practice in America, Europe, Japan and the former Communist countries is still rooted in his writing and work.

A recent biography of Taylor is titled *The One Best Way*. This sums up neatly Taylor's approach to management. He saw it as management's task to decide exactly how every task should be completed. Then to devise the tools needed to enable the worker to achieve the task as efficiently as possible. This method is evident today in every McDonald's in the world. Fries are cooked at 175 degrees for exactly three minutes, then a buzzer tells employees to take them out and salt them. Throughout every McDonald's are a series of dedicated, purpose-built machines for producing milkshakes, toasting buns, squirting chocolate sauce and much else. Today, one hundred years after his most active period working in industry, FW Taylor would feel very much at home ordering a Big Mac.

So, what was Taylor's view of the underlying motivations of people at work? How did he make sure that the employees worked effectively at following 'the one best way' laid down by managers?

Taylor believed that people work for only one reason – money. He saw it as the task of the manager to devise a system which would maximise efficiency. This would generate the profit to enable the worker to be paid a higher wage. Taylor's view of human nature was that of 'economic man'. In other words people were motivated only by the economic motives of self-interest. Therefore a manager could best motivate a worker by offering an incentive (a 'carrot') or a threat (the 'stick'). One can view Taylor as a manipulator or even a bully. But he believed his methods were in the best interests of the employees themselves.

Taylor's influence stemmed less from his theories than his activities. He was a trained engineer who acted as a very early management consultant. His methods were as follows:

- Observe workers at work, recording and timing what they do, when they do it and how long they take over it (this became known as time and motion study).
- Identify the most efficient workers and see how they achieve greater efficiency.
- Break the task down into small component parts which can be done quickly and repeatedly.
- Devise equipment specifically to speed up tasks.
- Set out exactly how the work should be done in future; 'each employee', Taylor wrote, 'should receive every day clear-cut, definite instructions as to what

he is to do and how he is to do it, and these instructions should be exactly carried out, whether they are right or wrong.'

- Devise a pay scheme to reward those who complete or beat tough output targets, but penalises those who cannot or will not achieve the productivity Taylor believed was possible.

As an engineer, Taylor was interested in practical outcomes, not in psychology. There is no reason to suppose he thought greatly about the issue of motivation. The effect of his ideas was profound, though. Long before the publication of his 1911 book *The Principles of Scientific Management*, Taylor had spread widely his managerial practices of careful measurement, monitoring and – above all else – control. Before Taylor, skilled workers chose their own ways of working and had varied, demanding jobs. After Taylor, workers were far more likely to have limited, repetitive tasks; forced to work at the pace set by a manager or consultant engineer.

To maximise the efforts put in by workers, Taylor devised an incentive system known as differential **piece-rate**. This offered a meagre payment per unit produced. Beyond a threshold, though, the payment became generous. For example:

- 2p per unit for the first 500 per day
- 5p per unit all those above 500 per day.

The threshold was set at a level at which those producing 500 received barely a living wage. Those unable to keep up even that pace would have no alternative but to find another job. The incentive to achieve 700 or so

per day was massive. It would mean earning double the rate earned by those on 500 per day. Despite Taylor's enthusiasm for this approach, it was resented so bitterly by workers that it usually had to be abandoned soon after introduction. Piece-rate itself, of course, lives on today.

Among those influenced by Taylor was Henry Ford. His Model T was the world's first mass produced motor car. By 1911 the Ford factory in Detroit, USA was already applying Taylor's principles of high **division of labour**, purpose-built machinery and rigid management control. When Ford introduced the conveyor belt in 1913, he achieved the ultimate Taylorite idea – men's pace of work dictated by a mechanical conveyor belt, the speed of which was set by management.

Beyond America, Mussolini was an admirer of Ford. So was Stalin. Communist factories in Eastern Europe, Russia and China imitated Taylor's methods. In every case the result was a huge improvement in productivity for several years. Though it was also commonly the case that workers eventually rebelled against being treated like machines. **Trade union** membership thrived in factories run on Taylorite lines, as workers wanted to organise against the suffocating lives they were leading at work. Fortunately, in many Western countries further developments in motivation theory pointed to new, more people-friendly approaches.

Business IN

TAYLOR LIVES ON

In June 2002 Websense announced a boom in sales of their software for monitoring and blocking staff access to web sites. Apparently the software is bought by human resource managers to check up on staff. What do sales of 'web spies' say about modern business? Nearly 100 years ago the Ford Motor factories employed 'spotters' to monitor the number of breaks taken by each worker, and to check on workers' interest in, or membership of, trade unions. Ford had followed FW Taylor's insistence upon controlling every aspect of the workplace. If staff are so bored that surfing the web seems fun, perhaps human resource departments should consider enriching the job rather than putting tougher control systems in place.

Early days of mass production at Ford: the assembly line
(© Corbis–Bettman/UPI)

31.3 Elton Mayo and the human relations approach

Elton Mayo (1880–1949) was a medical student who became an academic with a particular interest in people in organisations. An Australian, he moved to

America in 1923. His methods were heavily influenced by FW Taylor. An early investigation of a spinning mill in Pennsylvania identified one department with labour turnover of 250% compared with 6% elsewhere in the factory. His Taylorite solution was to prescribe work breaks. These had the desired effect.

Mayo moved on to work at the Hawthorne plant of Western Electric Company in Chicago. His investigations there are known as the Hawthorne Experiments.

He was called in to Hawthorne to try to explain the findings of a previous test into the effects of lighting upon productivity levels. The lighting conditions for one work group had been varied while those for another had been held constant. The surprise was that whatever was done to the lighting, production rose in *both* groups. This proved that there was more to motivation and efficiency than purely economic motives.

Between 1927 and 1932 Mayo conducted a series of experiments at Hawthorne. The first is known as the Relay Assembly Test. Six volunteer female assembly staff were separated from their workmates. A series of experiments was carried out. The results were recorded and discussed with the women. Every 12 weeks a new working method was tried. The alternatives included:

- different bonus methods, such as individual versus group bonuses
- different rest periods
- different refreshments
- different work layout.

Before every change, the researchers discussed the new method fully with the operators. Almost without exception productivity increased with every change. At the end, the group returned to the original method (48-hour, 6-day week with no breaks) and output went up to the highest yet! Not only that, but the women claimed they felt less tired than they had at the start.

The experiments had started rather slowly, with some resistance from the operatives. Progress became much more marked when one member of the group retired. She was replaced by a younger woman who quickly became the unofficial leader of the group.

MAYO'S CONCLUSIONS

- The women gained satisfaction from their freedom and control over their working environment.
- 'What actually happened was that six individuals became a team and the team gave itself wholeheartedly and spontaneously to cooperation in the experiment' (E. Mayo, 1949).
- Group norms (expectations of one another) are crucial and may be influenced more by informal than official group leaders.
- Communication between workers and managers and worker-to-worker influences morale and output.
- Workers are affected by the degree of interest shown in them by their managers; the influence of this upon motivation is known as 'the Hawthorne effect'.

The consequences of Mayo's work were enormous. He influenced many researchers and writers, effectively opening up the fields of industrial psychology and industrial sociology. Many academics followed Mayo's approach in what became known as the human relations school of management.

Businesses also responded to the implications of Mayo's work for company profitability and success. If teamwork, communications and managerial involvement were that important, firms reasoned that they needed an organisational structure to cope. In Taylor's era, the key person was the engineer. The winners from Mayo's work were personnel departments. They grew throughout America and Britain in the 1930s, 40s and 50s as companies tried to achieve the Hawthorne effect.

31.4 Maslow and the Hierarchy of Needs

Abraham Maslow (1908–1970) was an American psychologist whose great contribution to motivation theory was the 'Hierarchy of Needs'. Maslow believed everyone has the same needs – all of which can be organised as a hierarchy. At the base of the hierarchy are physical needs such as food, shelter and warmth.

MASLOW'S LEVELS OF HUMAN NEED	BUSINESS IMPLICATIONS
• Physical needs, e.g. food, shelter and warmth	• Pay levels and working conditions
• Safety needs, e.g. security, a safe structured environment, stability, freedom from anxiety	• Job security, a clear job role/description, clear lines of accountability (only one boss)
• Social needs, e.g. belonging, friendship, contact	• Teamworking, communications, social facilities
• Esteem needs, e.g. strength, self-respect, confidence, status and recognition	• Status, recognition for achievement, power, trust
• Self-actualisation, e.g. self-fulfilment; 'to become everything that one is capable of becoming', wrote Maslow	• Scope to develop new skills and meet new challenges and to develop one's full potential

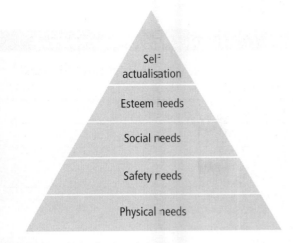

Figure 31.1 Maslow's Hierarchy of Needs

When unsatisfied, these are the individual's primary motivations. When employees earn enough to satisfy these needs, however, their motivating power withers away. Maslow said that 'It is quite true that humans live by bread alone – when there is no bread. But what happens to their desires when there is bread?' Instead of physical needs, people become motivated to achieve needs such as security and stability – which Maslow called the safety needs. In full, Maslow's hierarchy consisted of needs as shown by the diagram above.

Ever since Maslow first put his theory forward (in 1940) writers have argued about its implications. Among the key issues raised by Maslow are:

- Do all humans have the same set of needs? Or are there some people who need no more from a job than money?
- Do different people have different degrees of need, for example are some highly motivated by the need for power, while others are satisfied by social factors? If so, the successful manager would be one who can understand and attempt to meet the differing needs of his or her staff.
- Can anyone's needs ever be said to be fully satisfied? Perhaps the hierarchy diagram (see Figure 31.1) should have an open top to suggest that the human desire for achievement is limitless.

Maslow's work had a huge influence on the writers who followed him, especially McGregor and Herzberg. The Hierarchy of Needs is also used by academics in many subjects beyond Business, notably Psychology and Sociology.

31.5 Herzberg's two factor theory

The key test of a theory is its analytic usefulness. On this criterion, Herzberg's theory is the strongest by far.

The theory stems from research conducted in the 1950s into factors affecting workers' **job satisfaction** and dissatisfaction. It was carried out on 200 accountants and engineers in Pennsylvania, USA. Despite the

limited nature of this sample, Herzberg's conclusions remain influential to this day.

Key quotes from Professor Herzberg:	
On the two factor theory	*'Motivators and hygiene factors are equally important, but for different reasons'*
On movement	*'If you do something because you want a house or a Jaguar, that's movement. It's not motivation'*
The risks of giving bonuses	*'A reward once given becomes a right'*
The importance of training	*'The more a person can do, the more you can motivate them'*
The importance of always treating staff fairly	*'A remembered pain can lead to revenge psychology … They'll get back at you some day when you need them'*
On communication	*'In industry, there's too much communication. And of course it's passive … But if people are doing idiot jobs they really don't give a damn'*
On participation	*'When participation is suggested in terms of control over overall goals, it is usually a sham'*

Herzberg asked employees to describe recent events which had given rise to exceptionally good feelings about their jobs. Then probed for the reasons why. 'Five factors stand out as strong determiners of job satisfaction', Herzberg wrote in 1966, 'achievement, recognition for achievement, the work itself, responsi-

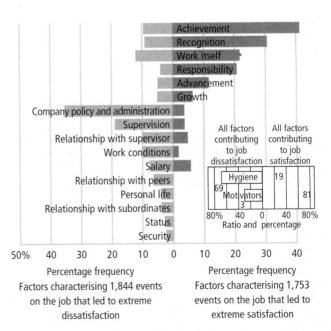

Figure 31.2 Comparison of satisfiers and dissatisfiers

Motivators (can create positive satisfaction)	Hygiene Factors (can create job dissatisfaction)
• Achievement	• Company policy and administration (the rules, paperwork and red tape)
• Recognition for achievement	• Supervision (especially being over-supervised)
• Meaningful, interesting work	• Pay
• Responsibility	• Interpersonal relations (with supervisor, peers, or even customers)
• Advancement (psychological, not just a promotion)	• Working conditions

bility and advancement – the last three being of greater importance for a lasting change of attitudes.' He pointed out that each of these factors concerned the job itself, rather than issues such as pay or status. Herzberg called these five factors 'the motivators'. The researchers went on to ask about events giving rise to exceptionally bad feelings about their jobs. This revealed a separate set of five causes. Herzberg stated that 'the major dissatisfiers were company policy and administration, supervision, salary, interpersonal relations and working conditions.' He concluded that the common theme was factors which 'surround the job', rather than the job itself. The name he gave these dissatisfiers was '**hygiene factors**'. This was because fulfilling them would prevent dissatisfaction, rather than causing positive motivation. Careful hygiene prevents disease; care to fulfil hygiene factors prevents job dissatisfaction.

THANK HEAVEN IT'S MONDAY!

Poor Jason Fitzgerald. Every Friday evening he has to drag himself away from work to get back to reality – a bit of cooking, seeing friends and so on. But on Monday morning he's up early to get back to his job as Communications and Development Executive on Sony PlayStation 2. He spends his days playing games, to make sure that he is in touch with any new trends or innovations. As video games take 2 years and £2–£3 million to develop, he organises consumer trials of games in development, to make sure that the moves are fun and challenging. At present his main focus is on multi-player games.

As Herzberg would say, he is motivated by the challenging, interesting work. He enjoys the teamworking and financial aspects of the job, but they are not the motivators. His motivations are intrinsic, in other words they come from his love of the job.

Business

IN

SUMMARY

Motivators have the power to create positive job satisfaction, but little downward potential. Hygiene factors will cause job dissatisfaction unless they are provided for, but do not motivate. Importantly, Herzberg saw pay as a hygiene factor, not a motivator. So a feeling of being underpaid could lead to a grievance; but high pay would soon be taken for granted. This motivator/hygiene factor theory is known as the *two factor theory*.

MOVEMENT AND MOTIVATION

Herzberg was keen to distinguish between movement and motivation. Movement occurs when somebody does something; motivation is when they *want* to do something. This distinction is essential to a full understanding of Herzberg's theory. He did not doubt that financial incentives could be used to boost productivity: 'If you bully or bribe people, they'll give you better than average performance.' His worries about bribes ('carrots') were that they would never stimulate people to give of their best; people would do just enough to achieve the bonus. Furthermore, bribing people to work harder at a task they find unsatisfying would build up resentments which might backfire on the employer.

Herzberg advised against payment methods such as piece-rate. They would achieve movement, but by reinforcing worker behaviour, making them inflexible and resistant to change. The salaried, motivated employee would work hard, care about quality and think about – even welcome – improved working methods.

JOB ENRICHMENT

The reason why Herzberg's work has had such impact on businesses is because he not only analyses motivation, he also has a method for improving it. The method is job enrichment, which he defined as 'giving people the opportunity to use their ability'. He suggested that, for a job to be considered enriched, it would have to contain:

• A complete unit of work – not just a small repetitive fragment of a job, but a full challenging task;

Herzberg heaped scorn upon the 'idiot jobs' that resulted from Taylor's views on the merits of high division of labour.

- Direct feedback – wherever possible, a job should enable the worker to judge immediately the quality of what they have done; direct feedback gives the painter or the actor (or the teacher) the satisfaction of knowing exactly how well they have performed. Herzberg disliked systems which pass quality inspection off onto a supervisor: 'a man must always be held responsible for his own quality'. Worst of all, he felt, was annual appraisal – in which feedback is too long delayed.

- Direct communication – for people to feel committed, in control and to gain direct feedback, they should communicate directly – avoiding the delays of communicating via a supervisor or a 'contact person'. For a Business student, this leads to an important conclusion: that communications and motivation are interrelated.

CONCLUSION

Herzberg's original research has been followed up in many different countries, including Japan, Africa and Russia. An article he wrote on the subject in the *Harvard Business Review* in 1968 (called 'Just One More Time, How Do You Motivate Employees') has sold more than one million reprinted copies. His main insight was to show that unless the job itself was interesting, there was no way to make working life satisfying. This led companies such as Volvo in Sweden and Toyota in Japan to rethink their factory layouts. Instead of individual workers doing simple repetitive tasks, the drive was to provide more complete units of work. Workers were grouped into teams, focusing on significant parts of the manufacturing process, such as

assembling and fitting the gearbox. And then checking the quality of their work. Job enrichment indeed.

31.6 Motivation
an evaluation

Most managers assume they understand human motivation. But they have never studied it. As a result they may underestimate the potential within their own staff. Or unthinkingly cause resentments that fester.

The process of managing people takes place in every part of every organisation. By contrast, few would need to know the financial concept of gearing in their working lives. So lack of knowledge of motivation theory is particularly unfortunate – and has exceptionally widespread effects. In some cases, ignorance leads managers to ignore motivation altogether. They tell themselves that control and organisation (i.e. paperwork!) are their only concerns. Other managers may see motivation as important, but fail to understand its subtleties.

For these reasons, there is a case for saying that the concepts within this unit are the most important in the whole subject.

BIBLIOGRAPHY

E Mayo, *The Social Problems of Industrial Civilisation*, Routledge 1975 (1st edition 1949).
AH Maslow, *Motivation and Personality*, Harper Collins 1987 (1st edition 1954).
F Herzberg, *The Motivation To Work*, Wiley International 1959.

ISSUES FOR analysis

In an exam context, the starting point is usually to select the most appropriate theory to answer a question. If a case study context suggested poor relations between management and workforce, Elton Mayo's would be very suitable. If motivation was weak, Herzberg's theory provides a comprehensive analysis.

When applying a theory, the analysis is strengthened by using a questioning approach. Herzberg's theory is admirable, but it is not perfect. It provides insights, but not necessarily answers. And certainly not blueprints. A job enrichment programme might be highly effective in one situation, but a disappointment in another.

This leads on to another key factor. The success of any new policies will depend hugely on the history of trust – or the lack of it – in the workplace. Successful change in the factors involved in motivation may be very difficult and slow to achieve. There are no magic solutions.

Accordingly, when a firm faces a crisis, changes in factors relating to motivation will rarely provide an answer. A crisis must be solved in the short term, but human motivation requires long-term strategies.

KEY terms

division of labour – subdivision of a task into a number of activities, enabling workers to specialise and therefore become very efficient at completing what may be a small, repetitive task.

hygiene factors – 'everything that surrounds what you do in the job' such as pay, working conditions and social status. All potential causes of dissatisfaction, according to Herzberg.

job satisfaction – the sense of well-being and achievement gained from doing a satisfying job.

piece-rate – the rate of payment for piecework.

piecework – work that is paid per 'piece' produced. Workers' pay is therefore directly related to the amount they produce.

trade union – an organisation that represents the interests of the workforce in a particular trade or profession.

AS Level Exercises

A. REVISION QUESTIONS
(50 marks; 75 minutes)

Read the unit, then answer:

1 Which features of the organisation of a McDonald's could be described as Taylorite? **(3)**
2 Explain the meaning of the term 'economic man'. **(3)**
3 What is meant by 'time and motion study'? How did Taylor make use of this method? **(5)**
4 Explain the difference between piece-rate and differential piece-rate. **(3)**
5 Identify three main consequences of Taylor's work. **(3)**
6 Give a brief outline of Mayo's research methods at the Hawthorne plant. **(5)**
7 How may 'group norms' affect productivity at a workplace? **(3)**
8 Explain the meaning of the term 'the Hawthorne effect'. **(2)**
9 Explain two effects upon firms of Mayo's work on human relations. **(4)**
10 Which two levels of Maslow's hierarchy could be called 'the lower order needs'? **(2)**
11 Describe in your own words why Maslow organised the needs into a hierarchy. **(4)**
12 State three business implications of Maslow's work on human needs. **(3)**
13 Herzberg believes pay does not motivate, but it is important. Why? **(3)**
14 How do motivators differ from hygiene factors? **(3)**
15 What is job enrichment? How is it achieved? **(4)**

B. REVISION EXERCISES

B1 Data Response
Study Figure 31.2. It shows the results of Herzberg's research into the factors which cause positive job satisfaction and those which cause job dissatisfaction. The length of the bars shows the percentage of responses. Their width indicates how likely the respondent was to say that the effect was long term.

Questions   *(20 marks; 25 minutes)*
1 Which of the factors had the least effect on satisfaction or dissatisfaction? **(1)**
2 One of Herzberg's objectives was to question whether good human relations were as important in job satisfaction as claimed by Elton Mayo. Do you think he succeeded? **(6)**
3 Responsibility had the longest lasting effects on job satisfaction. Why may this be the case? **(5)**
4 Discuss which of the factors is the most important motivator. **(8)**

B2 Case Study
Tania was delighted to get the bakery job and looked forward to her first shift. It would be tiring after a day at college, but £32 for 8 hours on a Friday would guarantee good Saturday nights in future.

On arrival, she was surprised to be put straight to work, with no more than a mumbled 'you'll be working packing machine B'. Fortunately she was able to watch the previous shiftworker before clocking-off time, and could get the hang of what was clearly a very simple task. As the 18.00 bell rang, the workers streamed out, but not many had yet turned up from Tania's shift. The conveyor belt started to roll again at 18.16.

As the evening wore on, machinery breakdowns provided the only, welcome relief from the tedium and discomfort of Tania's job. Each time a breakdown occurred, a ringing alarm bell was drowned out by a huge cheer from the staff. A few joyful moments followed, with dough fights breaking out. Tania started to feel quite old as she looked at some of her workmates.

At the 22.00 mealbreak, Tania was made to feel welcome. She enjoyed hearing the sharp, funny comments made about the shift managers. One was dubbed 'Noman' because he was fat, wore a white coat and never agreed to anything. Another was called 'Turkey' because he strutted around, but if anything went wrong, went into a flap. It was clear that both saw themselves as bosses. They were not there to help or to encourage, only to blame.

Was the bakery always like this, Tania wondered? Or was it simply that these two managers were poor?

Questions   *(25 marks; 30 minutes)*
1 Analyse the working lives of the shiftworkers at the bakery, using Herzberg's two factor theory. **(8)**
2 If a managerial follower of Taylor's methods came into the factory, how might he or she try to improve the productivity level? **(7)**
3 Later on in this (true) story, Tania read in the local paper that the factory was closing. The reason given was 'lower labour productivity than at our other bakeries'. The newspaper grumbled about the poor attitudes of local workers. Consider the extent to which there is some justification in this view. **(10)**

MOTIVATION IN PRACTICE

DEFINITION

Assessing how firms try to motivate their staff and how successful these actions appear to be. In this context, companies take 'motivation' to mean enthusiastic pursuit of the objectives or tasks set out by the firm.

There are three main variables which influence the motivation of staff in practice:

- the company culture
- its approach to managing its people
- the financial reward systems.

All three will be analysed using the theories outlined in Unit 31.

32.1 Company culture

Company culture means the accepted set of attitudes, values and habits within an organisation – its ethos. Every business has its own culture, as does every college and every classroom. Within an hour of joining a new class, its culture becomes apparent. Is it purposeful? Cooperative? Open? Challenging? Self-disciplined? Or just disciplined? In most workplaces, the culture emerges quite quickly. In some retail businesses, young part-timers get their enjoyment from pranks and sarcasm; in others the satisfaction comes from doing the job well.

HOW DOES CULTURE RELATE TO MOTIVATION?

Company culture can be positive or negative in many ways. Most affect motivation, either directly or indirectly. For example, the traditional police force culture was often sexist and racist. This may have boosted the team spirit of the white males involved. Yet their motivation may have been towards 'solving' crime in a manner determined by their prejudices rather than by police procedure. For instance, stopping and searching young blacks rather than solving burglaries.

The most obvious direct impact of culture upon motivation is through what Elton Mayo called **group norms** (see Unit 31). FW Taylor conceived the notion of 'a fair day's work for a fair day's pay', but Mayo was the theorist who analysed the social factors affecting what staff regard as fair. The work culture in one office may be so weak that idle chatting, social phone calls, tea breaks and computer game playing may halve the productivity compared with a similar office in another firm. Where the culture is strong, a slack period of the year is treated as the opportunity to improve systems or to carry out research into new customer needs. Where the culture is weak, a slack period means still slacker behaviour. Mayo pointed out that the difference in attitude was often to do with the unofficial leader or leaders of the staff concerned. It is also to do with tradition and – of course – the company or departmental culture.

HOW CAN A FIRM ACHIEVE THE CULTURE IT DESIRES?

If a new managing director wanted to shift a company's culture from being 'safety first, risk free, nine-to-five' to a more entrepreneurial, flexible one, where would he or she start? It should be accepted at the start that this will not be easy. A dull, safe company will have been recruiting dull, safe people for years. They will have become used to a culture in which failure means blame (even though, as fewer than one in four new products succeed in the marketplace, three failures in a row may not be unreasonable). They will probably be used to checking every decision with their boss; and spending much of their day looking forward to five o'clock.

Changing the culture will require four key factors:

1 clear communication to all staff about why and how change is to be achieved

2 a new organisational structure, with fewer layers of supervisory management and therefore more delegation of authority to more junior staff

3 identifying staff training needs and meeting them – both now and regularly in the future

4 a genuine change in attitude at the top, the effects of which will eventually spread throughout the business. Key indicators will be the types of managers who are promoted and demoted in the reorganisation and how the first major mistake is treated.

> 'The worst mistake a boss can make is not to say well done.'
>
> John Ashcroft, British executive

> 'Motivation is everything. You can do the work of two people, but you can't be two people. Instead, you have to inspire the next guy down the line and get him to inspire his people.'
>
> Lee Iacocca, successful boss of Chrysler Motors

> 'I have never found anybody yet who went to work happily on a Monday that had not been paid on a Friday.'
>
> Tom Farmer, Kwik-Fit founder

> 'Motivating people over a short period is not very difficult. A crisis will often do just that, or a carefully planned special event. Motivating people over a longer period of time, however, is far more difficult. It is also far more important in today's business environment.'
>
> John Kotter, management thinker

> 'People become motivated when you guide them to the source of their own power and when you make heroes out of employees who personify what you want to see in the organisation.'
>
> Anita Roddick, Body Shop founder

> 'My best friend is the one who brings out the best in me.'
>
> Henry Ford, legendary car maker

Source: *The Ultimate Book of Business Quotations*, Stuart Crainer, Capstone Publishing, 1997

32.2 Effective management of people

Good management can mean different things in different circumstances. Sometimes decisive leadership is called for. At other times careful planning and good organisation are the key factors. Effective management of people comes from a boss who has the experience, the foresight and the skills to ensure that staff feel confident and prove competent or better in their day-to-day tasks.

JOB ENRICHMENT

Professor Herzberg defines job enrichment as 'giving people the opportunity to use their ability'. A full explanation of his theory is outlined in Unit 31.

How can job enrichment be put into practice? The key is to realise the enormity of the task. It is not cheap, quick or easy to enrich the job of the production line worker or the supermarket checkout operator. The first thought might be to provide more variety to the work. The supermarket worker might

switch between the checkout, shelf stacking and working in the warehouse Known as job rotation, this approach reduces repetition but still provides the employee with little challenge. Herzberg's definition of job enrichment implies giving people 'a range of responsibilities and activities'. Job rotation only provides a range of activities. To provide job enrichment, workers must have a complete unit of work (not a repetitive fragment), responsibility for quality and for self-checking and be given the opportunity to show their abilities.

Full job enrichment requires a radical approach. Take a conventional car assembly line, for example (see Figure 32.1). Workers each have a single task they carry out on their own. One fits the left-hand front door to a car shell which is slowly moving past on a conveyor belt – one car every 22 seconds. Another worker fits right-hand front doors and so on. Job enrichment can only be achieved by rethinking the production line completely.

Figure 32.1 Traditional production line

Figure 32.2 shows how a car assembly line could be reorganised to provide more enriched jobs. Instead of working in isolation, people work in groups on a significant part of the assembly process. An empty car shell comes along the conveyor belt and arrives at the Interior Group Area. Six workers fit carpets, gloveboxes, the dashboard and much else. They check the quality of their own work, then put the vehicle, now looking significantly more like the finished product, back on the conveyor belt. Not only does the teamwork element help meet the social needs of the workforce, but there are also knock-on effects. The workers can be given a time slot to discuss their work and how to improve it. When new equipment is needed, they can be given a budget and told to meet potential suppliers. In other words, they can become managers of their own work area.

Figure 32.2 Enriched groupworking line

Such a major step would be expensive. Rebuilding a production line might cost millions of pounds and be highly disruptive in the short term. There would also be the worry that teamworking might make the job more satisfying, yet still be less productive than the boring but practical system of high **division of labour**.

JOB ENLARGEMENT

Job enlargement is a general term for anything that increases the scope of a job. There are three ways it comes about:

1 Job rotation – increasing a worker's activities by switching between tasks of a similar level of difficulty. This does not increase the challenge, but may reduce the boredom, of a job.
2 Job loading – increasing workload, often as a result of redundancies. It may mean having to do more of the same, but often entails one or two extra activities that have to be taken on.
3 Job enrichment – this enlargement of the scope of the job involves extra responsibilities and challenges as well as extra activities/workload.

Of these, only job enrichment is likely to provide long-term job satisfaction. Employers may like to use the term 'job enrichment', but often they are really carrying out job rotation or job loading.

EMPOWERMENT

Empowerment is a modern term for delegation. There is only one difference between the two. The empowered worker not only has the authority to manage a task, but also some scope to decide what that task should be. An Ikea store manager has power delegated to him or her. But head office rules may be so rigid that the manager has little scope for individual judgement. An empowered store manager would be one who could choose a range of stock suited to local customers, or a staffing policy different from the national store policy.

Empowerment means having more power and control over your working life. Having the scope to make significant decisions about how to allocate your time and how to move forward. It is a practical application of the theories of Herzberg and McGregor. It may lead to greater risks being taken, but can also lead to opportunities being identified and exploited. Above all else, it should aid motivation.

One major worry about empowerment in recent years has come from the financial services industry. A trader called Nick Leeson carried out a series of reckless trades which lost hundreds of millions of pounds and brought about the collapse of Barings Bank. In the stock market shake-out of 2001/2002 a series of other speculative failures emerged. In most cases, a fundamental problem was that the company bosses did not understand fully the risks that were being taken. Empowerment is highly dangerous in a situation of ignorance.

TEAMWORKING

Teamworking is the attempt to maximise staff satisfaction and involvement by organising employees into relatively small teams. These teams may be functional (the 'drive-thru crew' at a McDonald's) or geographic. The key features of such teams are that they should be:

- multi-skilled, so that everyone can do everyone else's job
- working together to meet shared objectives, such as to serve every customer within a minute or produce a gearbox with zero defects
- encouraged to think of the future as well as the present, in a spirit of kaizen (**continuous improvement**).

From a theoretical point of view, teamworking fits in well with Mayo's findings on the importance of group working and group norms. It can also be traced back to Maslow's emphasis on social needs. In practical terms, modern managers like teamworking because of the flexibility it implies. If worker A is absent, there are plenty of others used to dealing with the job. Therefore there is no disruption. Teamworking also gives scope for motivating influences such as job enrichment and quality circles.

GENBA-SHUGI

Genba-shugi is a Japanese phrase meaning 'respectable shop floor'. It points out that, even though Japanese managers are very status-conscious, working on the shop floor is a dignified and necessary part of building a career. Toyota recruits graduates and puts them on the production line so that they learn exactly what it is like to make a car. For 2 or 3 years staff may be switched from department to department to gain a full understanding of the shop floor aspects of the whole business. The British approach of occasionally putting a boss 'Back to the Floor' for a week makes good television (it's a BBC series) but is no substitute for learning the hard way.

Above all else, genba-shugi means staff know that managers really understand their problems. A hotel manager who has spent three months in the kitchens knows the importance of air conditioning and top quality equipment. A Toyota boss who has spent a year on the production line knows the value of cell production and empowerment. For effective management of people, genba-shugi is a term worth remembering.

Business IN

Professor Charles Handy suggests in his book *Inside Organisations* (BBC Books, 1990) that 'a good team is a great place to be, exciting, stimulating, supportive, successful. A bad team is horrible, a sort of human prison'. It is true that the business will not benefit if the group norms within the team discourage effort. Nevertheless, teamworking has proved successful in many companies in recent years. Companies such as Rolls Royce, Trebor, Rover and Komatsu have reported large improvements in absenteeism and labour turnover, and significant shifts in workforce attitudes.

32.3 Financial reward systems

PIECEWORK

Piecework means working in return for a payment per unit produced. The payment itself is known as piecerate. Pieceworkers receive no basic or shift pay, so there is no sick pay, holiday pay or company pension.

Piecework is used extensively in small-scale manufacturing, for example of jeans or jewellery. Its attraction for managers is that it makes supervision virtually unnecessary. All the manager need do is operate a quality control system which ensures the finished product is worth paying for. Day by day, the workers can be relied upon to work fast enough to earn a living (or a good) wage.

Piecework has several disadvantages to firms, however:

- Scrap levels may be high, if workers are focused entirely on speed of output.
- There is an incentive to provide acceptable quality, but not the best possible quality.
- Workers will work hardest when they want higher earnings (probably before Christmas and before their summer holiday). This may not coincide at all with seasonal patterns of customer demand.
- Worst of all is the problem of change. Herzberg pointed out that 'the worst way to people is piecerate … it reinforces behaviour'. Focusing people on maximising their earnings by repeating a task makes them very reluctant to produce something different or in a different way (they worry that they will lose out financially).

PERFORMANCE-RELATED PAY (PRP)

Performance-related pay is a financial reward to staff whose work is considered above average. It is used for employees whose work achievements cannot be assessed simply through numerical measures (such as units produced or sold). PRP awards are usually made after an appraisal process has evaluated the performance of staff during the year.

A 1991 survey found that 56% of private sector firms used PRP for clerical and managerial staff. Merit pay was the 'big idea' of the 1980s. The use of PRP has grown slightly since then (to 60%), but the method is increasingly being questioned. In 1996, for example, Scottish Amicable loosened its link between pay and performance.

On the face of it, PRP is a highly attractive system for encouraging staff to work towards the organisation's objectives. The usual method is:

1 establish targets for each member of staff/management at an appraisal interview
2 at the end of the year, discuss the individual's achievements against those targets
3 those with outstanding achievements are given a Merit 1 pay rise or bonus worth perhaps 6% of salary; others receive between 0% and 6%.

Despite the enthusiasm they have shown for it, employers have rarely been able to provide evidence of the benefits of PRP. Indeed, the Institute of Personnel Management concluded in a report that:

> *'It was not unusual to find that organisations which had introduced merit pay some years ago were less certain now of its continued value … it was time to move on to something more closely reflecting team achievement and how the organisation as a whole was faring.'*

This pointed to a fundamental problem with PRP. Rewarding individuals does nothing to promote teamwork. Furthermore, it might create unhealthy rivalry between managers – each going for the same Merit 1 spot.

Among other problems for PRP systems are:

- Whether the incentives are large enough to motivate – to keep costs down, firms usually allow no more than 2–3% of the wage bill for merit pay. The HSBC Bank system, for instance, provides between 0% and 6% as a performance-related reward.
- Perceived fairness/unfairness – staff often suspect that those awarded the maximum are being rewarded not for performance but out of favouritism. This may damage working relations and team spirit.
- Whether they have a sound basis in human psychology – without question, Professor Herzberg would be very critical of any attempt to influence work behaviour by financial incentives. A London School of Economics' study of Inland Revenue staff found that only 12% believed that PRP had raised motivation at work, while 76% said it had not. Herzberg would approve of the researchers' conclusion that 'the current system has not succeeded in motivating staff to any significant degree, and may well have done the reverse'.

As the last point illustrates, a key assumption behind PRP is that the chance to be paid a bit more than other employees will result in a change in individual behaviour, in increased motivation to work. A survey for the Government publication *Employment in*

PRP AND HSBC BANK

HSBC Bank uses a performance-related pay system for its 40,000 clerical staff. It is based on appraisal linked to customer service. It gives each employee one of the following ratings:

- unacceptable (U)
- improvement required (I)
- good (G)
- high achievement (H)
- outstanding (O).

Oustanding achievers receive an extra 6% per year on their salary whereas category I staff receive no performance bonus. Those in category U receive no pay increase at all, not even a rise to keep up with inflation.

HSBC's head of compensation, Pam Wood, believes the system 'focuses people's attention on performance on the job, rather than just turning up and being paid'. The bank's trade union takes a different view. It believes every employee has a right to an annual pay rise. It also suspects the proposals give an unhealthy amount of power to the managers of the clerical staff.

Britain found that 'pay incentives were thought important for hard work by less than one in five and for quality standards by less than one in ten'.

So why do firms continue to pursue PRP systems? There are three possible reasons:

- to make it easier for managers to manage/control their staff (using a carrot instead of a stick)
- an underlying Theory X view on the part of senior managers – a 1996 survey found that two-thirds of personnel managers saw monetary incentives as a good way to motivate employees
- to reduce the influence of collective bargaining and therefore trade unions.

PROFIT SHARING

A different approach to financial incentives is to provide staff with a share of the firm's annual profit. This puts staff in the same position as shareholders as, in effect, they are paid an annual dividend. This offers clear psychological benefits:

- Staff can come to see profit positively – before they may have regarded it as an unfair way of diverting pay from their own pockets to those of shareholders.
- Herzberg and other theorists warn that financial incentives distort behaviour. For example, if you pay a striker £500 per goal, wave goodbye to passing in the penalty area. Profit sharing, however, is more of a financial reward than an incentive. It may encourage people to work harder or smarter, but should not stop them working as a team.
- If paid to staff in the form of free shares, the employees may develop a strong sense of identity with the company and its fortunes.

Profit sharing can represent a substantial bonus on top of regular earnings. For instance, the John Lewis Partnership pays an annual bonus which is usually worth over 20% of an employee's earnings. In 2002 the John Lewis Partnership shared nearly £250 million among its 37,500 employees! In other cases, such as Tesco, the profit share is well below 5%. At such a low level it is clearly more of a thank you than a serious incentive.

SHARE OWNERSHIP

On the face of it, this is a far more radical approach to financial reward. It has the potential to achieve the business ideal: workers, managers, directors and shareholders thinking as one. Without question it has a pedigree. In his book *The Way Ahead*, Bill Gates suggests that employee share ownership has been fundamental to the success of Microsoft. The promise of a shareholding helps Microsoft attract the brightest graduates to work for it – and helps keep them focused on the company's success.

There are two main ways of providing employee share ownership:

1 Save as you earn – this is usually a five-year scheme in which staff save perhaps £50 per month. At the end of the five years they can convert their cash savings into shares at the price the shares were at the start of the five-year period. Often this will pro-

Pros and cons of profit sharing

Pros	Cons
Encourages staff to think about the whole business, not just their own job	If the employee share is only a small proportion of annual profit, the payouts may be meaninglessly small
Encourages thinking about cost saving as well as revenue raising	Large payouts, though, may either hit shareholder dividends or reduce the investment capital for long-term expansion
Focus on profit may make it easier for staff to accept changes in working practices, i.e. it may lessen resistance to change	Because no single individual can have much impact on overall profits, there may be no incentive effect

vide a substantial, immediate profit. Most employees hold onto the shares, hoping they will prove a sound long-term investment.

2   Share options – senior managers are often given the option to buy a substantial number of the company's shares at a discounted price at some agreed date in the future. For example, today's share price is 100p. A manager is given the option to buy 50,000 shares at 80p in 3 years' time. Three years later, a boom in share prices has taken the price to 280p. The manager buys the 50,000 shares at 80p and sells them for 280p. Profit: $50,000 \times £2 = £100,000$. Very nice for the manager, but very annoying for others in the department who may feel they work harder than their boss – and should also be allowed to enjoy this substantial perk. In 2002 the massive corporate collapses of Enron and Worldcom were blamed, in part, on the greed of senior executives with huge share options.

FRINGE BENEFITS

These are forms of reward other than income. Some managers have generous expense accounts. Many have company cars. Usually all maintenance and running costs are paid by the company. In some cases, even petrol for private mileage can be charged to the employer. Other fringe benefits include:

- membership of clubs or leisure centres
- low interest rate loans or mortgages
- discounts on the company's products, such as the British Airways' perk of air fares at 90% off!

In all cases, fringe benefits are offered to encourage staff loyalty and to improve human relations.

ISSUES FOR analysis

The key ways to analyse motivation in practice are:

- To select and apply the relevant motivation theory to the method being considered. Often modern methods appear to be based upon an understanding of human psychology, but careful scrutiny reveals they are not. Good analysis of methods such as performance-related pay or job rotation would require a critical eye.
- To question the publicly stated motives of the organisation or manager concerned. Businesses can be very loose in their use of words such as 'motivation' or 'empowerment'. They can be euphemisms for tougher targets and greater pressure. If the recent history of a firm makes employees sceptical of the goodwill of managers, students should be equally questioning.
- As John Kotter has said, 'Motivating people over a short period is not very difficult.' The key test of a new approach to motivation is over a 2–5 year period, not the early months of a new initiative. So always consider the timescale.

32.4 Motivation in practice
an evaluation

There are many aspects of business studies which point solely towards money. How profitable is this price or that? What is the forecast net cash flow for April? And so on. In such circumstances it is understandable that human implications may be forgotten. A high price for an AIDS cure may be profitable, but life-threatening to those who cannot afford the medicine. April's positive cash flow might be achieved only by sacking temporary staff.

When covering motivation in practice, there is little excuse for ignoring the implications for people. Exaggerated commissions or performance-related pay can lead sales staff to oversell goods or services which may cause customers huge difficulties later on, such as cosmetic surgery or questionable investments. Also within the workplace, serious problems can arise. Bullying to 'motivate' staff into working harder, or creating a culture of overwork which leads to stress.

Fortunately there are many businesses in which the management of motivation is treated with respect. Companies which know that quick fixes are not the answer. Successful motivation in the long term is a result of careful job design, employee training and development, honesty and trust. It may be possible to supplement this with an attractive financial reward scheme. But money will never be a substitute for motivation.

KEY terms

continuous improvement (kaizen) – moving productivity and product quality forward in regular, small steps.

division of labour – subdividing a job into small, repetitive fragments of work.

group norms – the types of behaviour and attitude seen as normal within a group.

AS Level Exercises

A. REVISION QUESTIONS
(40 marks; 70 minutes)

Read the unit, then answer:

1 Explain the business meaning of the term 'culture'. *(3)*
2 Outline the culture in any company you have worked for. *(5)*
3 How should a manager deal with a mistake made by a junior employee? *(4)*
4 State three reasons why job enrichment should improve staff motivation. *(3)*
5 Distinguish between job rotation and job enrichment. *(4)*
6 How does 'empowerment' differ from 'delegation'? *(4)*
7 Identify three advantages to an employee of working in a team. *(3)*
8 State two advantages and two disadvantages of offering staff performance-related pay. *(4)*
9 What might be the implications of providing share options to senior managers but not to the workforce generally? *(5)*
10 What problems might result from a manager bullying staff to 'motivate' them? *(5)*

B. REVISION EXERCISES

B1 Data Response
In 1998, Britain's most successful car factory was Nissan UK's plant in Sunderland. Its productivity level of nearly 100 cars per worker per year was three times higher than rivals such as Rover. So, how was this achieved? Of course, there were many operational factors, such as high investment and effective lean production. Also important, though, has been the effective management and motivation of personnel.

From the time it opened in 1986, Nissan took care to establish a positive staff culture. Young, enthusiastic staff were recruited who had no preconceptions about making cars. Heavy emphasis was placed on training and continued education for staff. When production started, the views and suggestions of staff were welcomed. Each production department had a kaizen (continuous improvement) unit, manned by dedicated staff. Supervisors were empowered to interview, select and organise their staff. This encouraged a sense of responsibility and commitment. The result has been the acceptance by staff that Nissan's success is not only the company objective but also their own. 'Everybody takes a defect personally', says Craig Douglas, a supervisor in the plant's engine shop.

Mr Cushnaghan, the plant's deputy managing director, is clear that Nissan's success would have been much harder to achieve if trying to change practices in an older factory, because of 'cultural hangover'. 'That culture is an immense drag on a company's ability to make progress,' he says, 'Here, because we created the culture from day one, that drag doesn't exist. This place is full of change.'

Questions
(30 marks; 35 minutes)

1 Outline the workplace culture at Nissan, as suggested by the text. *(4)*
2 How well has the approach adopted by Nissan fitted Herzberg's model of job enrichment? *(6)*
3 Consider the advantages to a business of empowering supervisors to interview and select their staff rather than leaving this task to the personnel department. *(8)*
4 Nissan staff are well paid, but receive only a salary. There are no financial reward systems that encourage them to work harder. How, then, can they be the most productive workforce in the British car industry? *(6)*
5 Consider how managers might attempt to tackle a 'cultural hangover' from an earlier period. *(6)*

B2 Data Response

Gambling on People

Procter and Gamble is the world's biggest advertiser and one of America's most respected companies. It is the company behind such brands as Fairy Liquid, Ariel, Crest, Max Factor, Head & Shoulders, Vidal Sasoon, Pringles, Sunny Delight and hundreds more. Behind its marketing success lies an exceptionally strong company culture and an advanced approach to the management of its people.

Procter and Gamble (P&G) was an early advocate of motivating staff by empowerment and job enrichment. Dave Swanson was the principal architect of the organisational design of the system. Swanson joined P&G in the early 1950s after studying at the Manchester Institute of Technology (MIT). While at MIT he had been inspired by the lectures of Professor Douglas McGregor. McGregor attacked the theory of command-and-control management, advocating empowerment. When Swanson had the opportunity to design a new detergent plant in Atlanta, Georgia, he enlisted McGregor's help.

Processes were put in place to make communications and control flow up, down and sideways in a very easy, uninhibited way. They emphasised knowledge of the business and learning new skills for all employees of the plant. The objective was to push the Augusta plant to be as unstructured as possible.. 'We were trying to take away the rule book and substitute principle for mandate … We wanted people to reach for responsibility,' Swanson said. They did. Factory productivity went up 30% and the system was expanded to other P&G plants.

In his book *What America Does Right*, Robert Waterman describes P&G as a pioneer in pushing leadership, responsibility and decision making down to the plant floor.

Source: *P&G99*, Decker C, HarperCollins 1998

Questions   (30 marks; 35 minutes)

1 How might motivation be affected by 'taking away the rule book'?   (6)
2 Explain the importance to staff motivation of freely flowing, accurate communication.   (6)
3 Explain how the views of McGregor given in the text compare with his Theories X and Y.   (8)
4 In this case, high motivation boosted productivity by 30%. Discuss whether increased motivation need always result in increased productivity.   (10)

B3 Activity

Write a questionnaire for self-completion by full-time employees. Your research objectives are to discover:

- whether there are any policies in place for encouraging workplace involvement/consultation
- whether job enrichment or job rotation measures exist (and what is their effect)
- how your respondents would describe the workplace culture
- whether there are any financial bonuses available, such as piece-rate or performance-related pay, and what is their effect on motivation
- how highly motivated the employees feel themselves to be
- how highly motivated they believe their colleagues to be..

This questionnaire should be conducted on at least 10 respondents. It is preferable for them to be face-to-face, but if that is not possible, self-completion is acceptable.

When the research is completed, analyse the results carefully and write a summary of them in report form.

A Level Exercises

A. REVISION QUESTIONS

(35 marks; 50 minutes)

Read the unit, then answer:

1 Why is it hard to change the culture of a business?   (4)
2 What kind of workplace culture do you think a Theory X manager would like to establish?   (4)
3 The text suggests that changing a business culture requires four key factors. State and explain one other factor that might be important.   (4)

4 What problems might be faced when trying to enrich the job of a bus driver?   (5)
5 Discuss the advantages and disadvantages of being required to tackle every homework assignment in a team.   (8)
6 How would performance-related pay be regarded by:
  a FW Taylor   (5)
  b Abraham Maslow.   (5)

B. REVISION EXERCISES

B1 Case Study – McJobs or McMillions?

Louise Todd started Call Correct six years ago. She had worked in the computer industry and spotted the potential for writing software that would guide and control telesales staff. Untrained operators would be able to follow clear instructions in big type on the computer screen in front of them. All they would need to do would be to type moderately quickly and to have a clear – preferably warm – speaking voice. Just as McDonald's hires untrained staff and can put them to work straightaway, so could Call Correct.

Louise's first client was a double glazing firm in Burnley. She visited the firm to agree a sales script and a payment structure: £200 set-up fee and £15 per customer appointment. She hired a couple of university students at £5 per hour, who worked Monday–Friday, 4.00 to 8.00 p.m. The results were excellent. The students averaged two successful appointments per hour.

Business mushroomed from there. Clients came thick and fast and Louise had to repeatedly expand the size of her call centre. After four years of operation she employed 120 students every evening and 50 during the day. Call Correct made £280,000 profit that year. Louise was heading to become a millionaire.

That same year, however, the business started to hit severe problems of absenteeism and labour turnover. This forced Louise to employ more people to recruit and select staff which in turn was beginning to cost a significant amount in recruitment advertising in the local press.

Louise decided that she needed a new financial reward structure. Instead of paying an hourly rate, she would pay an attendance fee and then commission per successful call. Typically, it might be a £15 attendance fee and £5 per successful call. So, in a four-hour shift students could earn £35. But if they tried especially hard, they might make more successful calls, bringing their earnings up to perhaps £50.

This immediately had a positive impact, pushing up staff earnings – and the company's. Flushed with success, Louise opened up a second centre close to Manchester Metropolitan University. She was determined to build up the business to reach an annual profit level of £1 million. Unfortunately, just as she was spending time and money on this new centre, things went drastically wrong at the original site. Absentee levels had risen sharply, as staff stress levels rose under the pressure to sell at all costs. Worse still, four clients cancelled their contract with her, blaming an unacceptable level of wasted customer calls. Appointments booked for sales staff proved worthless, with customers claiming that they had not agreed to the appointment, or that they had just said yes to get rid of pushy telephone callers.

Louise was telling her tale of woe to the careers officer at Manchester Metropolitan. He arranged for her to see the University's professor of human resources. A lengthy chat pointed Louise towards a different approach. She hired a conference centre for a day and paid for all her workers to attend. They spent the day talking through the problems of telesales and the needs of the clients. They agreed that an over-incentivised sweatshop approach to telephone selling could not be right in the twenty-first century. A fortnightly meeting between Louise and staff was agreed, as was a return to hourly pay. But in future, all staff would receive a profit share based on the previous month's profit.

Just six months ago Louise opened her third centre, this time in Belfast. Her profit for this year looks likely to exceed £1 million, even after the profit-share payments. Louise managed successfully to switch from McJobs to McMillions.

Questions (50 marks; 60 minutes)

1 What may be the implications for motivation of hiring untrained staff and 'putting them to work straightaway'? (6)

2 Louise's chosen financial reward structure caused problems.
 a Explain why it did so. (8)
 b Outline how a performance-related pay package might have been structured to achieve Louise's objectives. (8)

3 Consider how Elton Mayo might have viewed Louise's management of her staff. (10)

4 Why may it have been more successful to pay an hourly rate plus a profit share than an attendance fee plus commission? (8)

5 Soon, Louise will need to establish a new layer of middle management at each of her call centres. What advice would you give her about the qualities she should look for when recruiting these managers? (10)

C. ESSAY QUESTIONS

1 Discuss the importance of financial reward systems in the motivation of young, part-time staff.

2 Five million workers say they have been bullied in the workplace. This might be by fellow workers but is more usually by a supervisor or manager. Discuss why a manager might bully a worker and what the effects might be on the organisation and the individuals. (The TUC's free leaflet *Bullied At Work* is available by sending an A5 stamped, addressed envelope to TUC Publications, Congress House, Great Russell Street, London WC1B 3LS.)

3 Discuss the view that there is no one ideal method to motivate staff, because everyone is different.

LEADERSHIP AND MANAGEMENT STYLES

DEFINITION
Management involves getting things done through other people. Leadership, at its best, means inspiring staff to achieve demanding goals. According to Peter Drucker, a manager does things right; a leader does the right thing.

33.1 Introduction

The way in which managers deal with their employees is known as their management style. For example, some managers are strict with workers. They always expect deadlines to be met and targets to be hit. Others are more relaxed and understanding. If there is a good reason why a particular task has not been completed by the deadline, they will be willing to accept this and give the employee more time. Although the way in which everyone manages will vary slightly from individual to individual, their styles can be categorised under three headings: **autocratic**, **democratic** and **paternalistic**.

Autocratic managers are authoritarian; they tell employees what to do and do not listen much to what workers themselves have to say. Autocratic managers know what they want doing and how they want it done. They tend to use one-way, top-down communication. They give orders to workers and do not want much feedback. Democratic managers, by comparison, like to involve their workers in decisions. They tend to listen to employees' ideas and ensure people contribute to the discussion. Communication by democratic managers tends to be two-way. Managers put forward an idea and employees give their opinion. A democratic manager would regularly delegate decision making power to junior staff.

The delegation of authority which is at the heart of democratic leadership can be approached in one of two main ways:

1 Management by objectives – the leader agrees clear goals with staff, provides the necessary resources, and allows day-to-day decisions to be made by the staff in question; this approach is advocated by Peter Drucker (see Unit 36) and by Douglas McGregor (see below) in his support for what he called the Theory Y approach to management.
2 Laissez-faire, meaning 'let it be' – this occurs when managers are so busy or so lazy that they do not take the time to ensure that junior staff know what to do or how to do it. Some people might respond very well to the freedom to decide on how to spend their working lives; others may become frustrated.

It is said that Bill Gates, in the early days of Microsoft, hired brilliant students and told them no more than to create brilliant software. Was this a laissez-faire style or management by objectives? Clearly the dividing line can be narrow.

A paternalistic manager thinks and acts like a father. He or she tries to do what is best for the staff/children. There may be consultation to find out the views of the employees, but decisions are made by the head of the 'family'. This type of manager believes employees need direction but think it is important that they are supported and cared for properly. Paternalistic managers are interested in the security

Assumptions and approaches of the three types of leader

	DEMOCRATIC	PATERNALISTIC	AUTOCRATIC
Style derived from	Belief in Maslow's higher order needs or in Herzberg's motivators	Mayo's work on human relations and Maslow's lower and middle order needs	A Taylorite view of staff
Approach to staff	Delegation of authority	Consultation with staff	Orders must be obeyed
Approach to staff remuneration	Salary, perhaps plus employee shareholdings	Salary plus extensive fringe benefits	Payment by results, e.g. piece-rate
Approach to human resource management	Recruitment and training based on attitudes and teamwork	Emphasis on training and appraisal for personal development	Recruitment and training based on skills; appraisal linked to pay

and social needs of the staff. They are interested in how workers feel and whether they are happy in their work. Nevertheless it is quite an autocratic approach.

33.2 McGregor's Theory X and Y

In the 1950s Douglas McGregor undertook a survey of managers in the USA and identified two styles of management, which he called Theory X and Theory Y. Theory X managers tend to distrust their subordinates; they believe employees do not really enjoy their work and that they need to be controlled. In McGregor's own words, many managers believe 'The average human being has an inherent dislike of work and will avoid it if he can.' Note that McGregor is not putting it forward as a theory about workers, but about managers. In other words, Theory X is about the view managers have of their workforce. Theory Y managers, by comparison, believe that employees do enjoy work and that they want to contribute ideas and effort . A Theory Y manager is, therefore, more likely to involve employees in decisions and give them greater responsibility. The managerial assumptions identified by McGregor as Theory Y included:

- 'Commitment to objectives is a function of the rewards associated with their achievement.'
- 'The average human being learns, under proper conditions, not only to accept but to seek responsibility.'
- 'The capacity to exercise a relatively high degree of imagination, ingenuity and creativity in the solution of organisational problems is widely, not narrowly, distributed in the population.'

Source: *The Human Side of Enterprise*, D McGregor, Penguin Books 1987 (first published 1960)

It is clear that Theory Y managers would be inclined to adopt a democratic leadership style. Their natural approach would be to delegate authority to meet specific objectives.

The Theory X approach is likely to be self-fulfilling. If you believe people are lazy, they will probably stop trying. Similarly if you believe workers dislike responsibility and fail to give them a chance to develop, they will probably stop showing interest in their work. They end up focusing purely on their wage packet because of the way you treat them.

In his book *The Human Side of Enterprise*, McGregor drew upon the work of Maslow and Herzberg. It need be no surprise that there are common features to the theories of these three writers. McGregor's unique contribution was to set issues of industrial psychology firmly in the context of the management of organisations. So whereas Herzberg's was a theory of motivation, McGregor's concerned styles of management (and thereby leadership).

So, which is the 'right' approach? Clearly a Theory Y manager would be more pleasant and probably

Theory X managers believe:	*Theory Y managers believe:*
• *Employees dislike work and will avoid it if they can*	• *Putting some effort into work is as natural as play or rest; employees want to work*
• *Employees prefer to be directed, want to avoid responsibility and have little ambition*	• *Employees want responsibility provided there are appropriate rewards*
• *Employees need to be controlled and coerced*	• *Employees are generally quite creative*

more interesting to work for. As outlined in the 'In Business' on Harold Geneen, however, a Theory X approach can work. It is especially likely to succeed in a business employing many part-time, perhaps student, workers, or in a situation where a business faces crisis.

HAROLD GENEEN

Harold Geneen, who died aged 87 in 1998, was the man who made ITT one of America's most powerful multinational corporations.

When Geneen became President of ITT in 1959, the company was a loose-knit empire with modest profits. By the time he left he had bought 350 companies in 80 countries and created America's 11th biggest firm with sales of $17 billion. Geneen introduced a system of incredibly strict accountability. His system involved monthly meetings at which executives had to explain their results and achievements to Geneen. The ordeal of being cross-questioned in these meetings made some managers physically ill. According to Geneen the skill of management lay in being able to 'smell' the truth. He liked complete control, relied only on 'unshakeable facts' to make logical decisions and insisted, 'I want no surprises'.

33.3 Team-based management

The role of managers is changing in many firms, which are now encouraging employees to work in teams. In this system managers are increasingly seen as a support to employees rather than as a supervisor. In the words of Tom Peters (see Unit 44), they are 'coaches and facilitators' not 'policemen'; they are there to help employees fulfil their potential. This approach relies on a high degree of trust between employees and managers and a common sense of purpose.

To gain this trust managers must show that they want employees to contribute and take greater responsibility for decision making. They must show they value the workers' input. In companies such as Rover and Unipart, for example, employees are encouraged to take control over their own work and develop ways of improving the process for themselves. In such organisations there is a conscious effort to remove the distinction between managers and workers (or 'them and us'). At Rover, for example, everyone is called an associate; at Unipart everyone is a 'team member'.

Although a simple change of name could in itself be a gimmick, it reflects a move away from the traditional company hierarchy. All Unipart employees are salaried (rather than being paid wages or piece-rate) and have the same terms and conditions as managers. Salaries differ according to different skills and responsibilities, but everyone is treated in the same way, i.e there is **single status**. In the past, people would eat in different canteens according to their rank within the organisation. They would have different car parking areas and would have different sickness benefits. In many companies such obvious distinctions no longer exist.

Strangely, though, this progressive move has coincided with a rapid increase in share options and other financial incentives for directors and senior managers. Huge payouts for those at the top of an organisation must undermine the desire to build team spirit.

LEADER OF THE PACK

In December 2002 Judy Gibbons took her executive team at MSN, Microsoft's Internet business, to spend a week in the South African bush. It was the high point of a leadership programme developed by Judy from Jim Collins' book *Good To Great*. Collins believes great leadership is not based on personal charisma, but on a blend of personal humility and professional determination.

Judy's job as Head of the Europe, Middle East and Africa regions of MSN means leading a staff of 350 in 16 countries. Knowing that she cannot personally 'lead' all these people, her concern is to encourage best practice in her senior team.

The first two days were spent on a leadership course based in the South African bush. The most inspiring part was instruction on an African tribal custom called 'indaba'. When the tribal leaders meet with the chief on a specific concern, each person speaks, and this continues round with each person having an opportunity to speak in turn, again and again. Gradually people shift their position and a consensus emerges.

After this, several days in the Kruger National Park kept up the feeling of shared experiences and teamwork. Judy's approach shows that skilled leadership need not be based on power, or on 'establishing who's boss'. It can succeed through a combination of democratic and paternalistic styles.

Adapted from *The Financial Times*, 19/12/02

33.4 What is the best style of management?

Each style of management can work well in different situations. If there is a crisis, for example, people often look for a strong leader to tell them what to do. Imagine that sales have unexpectedly fallen by 50%, causing uncertainty, even panic, within the organisation. The management needs to take control quickly and put a plan into action. An autocratic style might work well at this moment. In a stable situation where employees are trained and able to do their work successfully a more democractic leadership style might be

---

'*When the effective leader is finished with his work, the people say it happened naturally.*'
Lao-Tzu (604–531BC), Chinese philosopher

'*The quality of a leader is reflected in the standards they set for themselves.*'
Ray Kroc (1902–1984), the man behind McDonald's

'*Leadership is practiced not so much in words as in attitude and in actions.*'
Harold Geneen (b. 1910) famous chief executive of the huge American corporation ITT

'*A leader shapes and shares a vision, which gives point to the work of others.*'
Charles Handy (b. 1932), management thinker

'*The leader's job is to help everyone see that the platform is burning, whether the flames are apparent or not.*'
Larry Bossidy (b. 1935), chief executive of Allied Signal Corporation

Source: *The Ultimate Book of Business Quotations*, Stuart Crainer, Capstone Publishing, 1998

Business

IN

more appropriate. It is often said that countries elect very different types of leaders when there is a threat of war or economic instability than when the country is doing well. Similarly, think about how people react when they are learning to drive. For the first few lessons they are uncertain what to do and are grateful to be told. Once they have passed their test and have driven for several years they will no doubt resent anyone telling them how to drive better!

The best style of management at any moment will depend on an enormous range of factors such as the personalities and abilities of the manager and the workers, and the nature of the task (see Figure 33.1). Imagine a confident manager who knows his or her job well but is faced with an unusually difficult problem. If the staff are well trained and capable, the manager would probably ask for ideas on what to do next. If, however, the manager was faced with a fairly routine problem he or she would probably just tell the employees what to do because there would be no need for discussion.

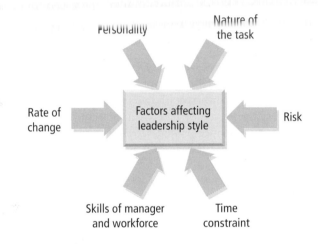

Figure 33.1 Factors affecting leadership style

A manager's style should, therefore, change according to the particular situation and the people involved. It will also vary with the time and degree of risk involved. If a decision has to be made urgently and involves a high degree of risk, the manager is likely to be quite autocratic. If there is plenty of time to discuss matters and only a low chance of it going wrong the style may well be more democratic.

33.5 Does the style of management matter?

The way in which a manager deals with his or her colleagues can have a real impact on their motivation and how effectively they work. An experienced workforce which is used to being involved in decisions may resent a manager who always tries to tell them what to do. This might lead to a reduction in the quality of their work, a fall in productivity and an increase in

labour turnover. If, however, these employees were involved in decision making, the firm could gain from better ideas and a more highly motivated workforce. This does not mean that everyone wants to be involved or indeed that it is appropriate. Employees may lack the necessary training or experience. Therefore a democratic approach might simply mean taking longer for management to reach the decision it was going to make anyway.

33.6 What is the most common style of management?

The style of management which people adopt depends on many factors such as their personality, the particular circumstances at the time and the culture of the organisation. Although we have discussed three main styles the actual approach of most managers is usually a combination of all of them, depending on the task or the nature of the situation. If an order has to be completed by tomorrow and time is short, for example, most managers are likely to be autocratic to make sure it gets done. If, however, there is plenty of time available the manager may be more democratic. No-one is completely autocratic or completely democratic, it is simply a question of degree. However, some managers do tend to be more autocratic than others. This often depends on their own experiences (What was their boss like? What worked well when they were being trained?) and their personality (Do they like to

ARE YOU BORN A GOOD LEADER?

According to management writer Warren Bennis, the most important ingredient of a business leader is the ability to provide a vision. He or she must also show passion, integrity, curiosity and daring. The question is, can such qualities be taught or are you born with them? Ruth Tait, head of a recruitment company, interviewed a series of business leaders for her book Roads To The Top. She found it difficult to identify any common attributes although many of the executives had some childhood adversity that seemed to give them their drive. She also found that while management education was regarded as helpful it was stressed far less than the learning they achieved from experience.

Although there is always argument about whether leaders are born or made, the idea that leadership is acquired through experience seems to be gaining favour.

Business IN

be in control of everything? Are they willing to delegate? Do they value the opinions of others?).

In general the move has been towards a more democratic style of management in the UK in recent years. This is probably because employees expect more from work than they did in the past. They are better educated, have a higher basic standard of living and want more than just money in return for their efforts. Having satisfied their lower level needs they are now looking to satisfy their higher level needs. The growth of **democratic management** and greater participation has also increased with the move towards lean production and the emphasis on techniques such as total quality management. These methods of production require much more involvement by the employees than in the past. Employees are given control over their own quality, given the authority to make decisions over the scheduling of work and are expected to contribute ideas on how to improve the way they are working. This approach requires much more trust in employees than was common many years ago. It has to be matched with a more democratic leadership style.

Just one style of management
(© Darama/Corbis)

ISSUES FOR **analysis**

Among the main lines of analysis are:

- Management style can have a significant impact on the way people work. By adopting the right approach employees are likely to be more motivated and show greater commitment. Therefore effective analysis of leadership should be rooted in the theories of writers such as Mayo and Herzberg.
- The 'correct' management style will depend on factors such as the task, the people involved and the amount of risk. There is no one style which is always appropriate. Therefore the context of the business case is always relevant.
- It may not be easy for managers to change their style. There may be situations in which managers should be more democratic; this does not necessarily mean they will be. Effective management training could be a useful way to persuade managers to be flexible.
- There is some debate about the extent to which you can train people to become effective managers or leaders. One extreme

view is that good managers and leaders are born that way – if this is true companies have to put their resources into finding the right sort of person. It is more likely that a good leader is a combination of training and personal characteristics.

33.7 Management styles
an evaluation

All firms are seeking effective managers. Good managers make effective use of the firm's resources and motivate the staff. They provide vision and direction and are therefore a key element of business success. Look at any successful company and you will usually find a strong management team. The problem is knowing what it is that makes a good manager and what is the 'best' management style. Even if we thought we knew the best style, can we train anyone to adopt this approach or does it depend on their personality? There are, of course, no easy answers to these questions. The 'right' style of management will depend on the particular circumstances and the nature of the task and while it is possible to help someone develop a particular style it will also depend on the individual's personality. As employees have benefited from a higher standard of living in the UK and have higher expectations of work, managers have generally had to adopt a more democratic style to motivate people. However, there are plenty of autocratic managers who also succeed.

KEY terms

autocratic management – autocratic managers keep most of the authority to themselves; they do not delegate much or share information with employees. Autocratic or authoritarian managers tend to tell employees what to do.

democratic management – democratic managers take the views of their subordinates into account when making decisions.

paternalistic management – a paternalistic manager believes he or she knows what is best for the employees. Paternalistic managers tend to tell employees what to do but will often explain their decision. They are also concerned about the social needs of employees.

single status – occurs when all employees are given the same rights and conditions, e.g. the same rights to pension and sickness benefits.

team-based management – decisions are made by teams rather than workers being told what to do by a supervisor.

AS Level Exercises

A. REVISION QUESTIONS

(30 marks; 60 minutes)

Read the unit, then answer:

1 Distinguish between autocratic and paternalistic management. *(4)*
2 Identify two features of democratic management. *(2)*
3 Identify one advantage and one disadvantage of an autocratic management approach. *(4)*
4 Distinguish between McGregor's Theory X and Theory Y. *(4)*
5 Why is it 'clear that Theory Y managers would be inclined to adopt a democratic leadership style'? *(4)*
6 Why is trust so important for successful teamworking? *(4)*
7 Why have many firms introduced teamworking in recent years? *(4)*
8 Explain a circumstance in which an authoritarian approach to leadership may be desirable. *(4)*

B. REVISION EXERCISES

B1 Data Response

Unipart

When John Neill shows you around Unipart's headquarters be prepared for some rather unusual features – the lecture theatre, the technical library, the in-house TV studio, the squash courts and fitness centre. Not forgetting the aromatherapy and reflexology suites and the shower rooms. The company was bought off Rover by a management buy-out group led by Neill (managing director) in 1987. It remains an unquoted company which means it does not have to focus simply on short-term shareholder value but can think and plan long term.

Neill is a champion of lean production techniques and his Japanese enthusiasm extends to employee relationships In the past he cannot recall any forced redundancies at Unipart. And when he hires consultants to help reorganise the firm, he guarantees employment of those whose jobs vanish. However, Neill is no soft touch for the workers. Back in the 1970s when labour relations in the UK car industry were poor he routinely fired workers for going on strike. In 1987, at the time of the buyout, he cut the workforce sharply to eliminate overstaffing. Finally, in 1992, he ended union recognition altogether.

In some respects Neill's approach is old-style paternalism. Hence his insistence on making shares available to workers. For those who hold shares over the long haul the gains are a reward for loyal service. 'I'm a very strong believer in the free enterprise system. The way we're trying to do it is the capitalist sytem on the moral ground. If a warehouseman can retire and buy a cottage or put his kids through higher education, that's what we're trying to do'.

Source: Adapted from *The Financial Times*, 6/2/98

Questions *(30 marks; 35 minutes)*

1 Explain the meaning of the following terms:
   a union recognition *(3)*
   b old-style paternalism. *(3)*
2 Outline the evidence that John Neill is a paternalistic manager. *(8)*
3 Consider the possible effects of a switch by John Neill to a more democratic leadership style. *(10)*
4 What do you think influences the way in which someone manages? *(6)*

B2 Assignment

An Investigation into a Leader

1 Arrange to interview an employee. Preferably this person should be a full-timer who has worked for at least a year. The employee could be a manager but should not be a director.
2 Your objective is to gain a full understanding of the leadership style prevailing at the employee's workplace, and the style employed by the individual's own manager.
3 Devise your own series of questions in advance, but make sure to include the following themes:
   a How open are communications within the business?
   b Are staff encouraged to apply a questioning or critical approach?
   c Are there any forums for discussion or debate on important policy issues affecting staff?
   d What does the organisational hierarchy look like? Where is your employee on that diagram? How powerful or powerless does he or she feel?
   e How exactly does the employee's boss treat him or her? Is there delegation? Consultation? How effective is communication between the two of them?

Write at least 600 words summarising your findings and drawing conclusions about how well the experience conforms to the leadership theory dealt with in this unit.

B3 Case Study

'If you take your eyes off them for one minute they'll probably walk off with half the shop,' said Brian Brimpton to Frank Shore. Frank was a business colleague of Brian who found it difficult to hide his surprise that Brian was talking about his own workforce! 'I pay them well to make sure they get out of bed in the morning but I watch them all the time. I've had too much money taken out of the tills and stolen from the shops in the past to be able to relax for one minute,' continued Brian. 'I've got security cameras in all my shops and they're focused on the tills not the shoppers! I make them empty their pockets in the morning and put everything in their lockers so if I ever catch them with money on them I know they've stolen it. I do random checks every day and not surprisingly I'm catching more and more of them doing it.'

Frank pointed out that he did not have any of these policies but that theft in his stores was much lower than in Brian's. 'You're either lucky and have managed to find some honest employees or more likely you haven't discovered how much is being stolen yet!' said

Brian. 'You know, Brian, I used to think like you,' continued Frank, 'but a few years ago I changed my approach. I started listening to my staff and found that much of what they said was valuable. I've now decided that you should always try to involve your employees more in making decisions. It's worked for me.' 'So far, may be,' said Brian, 'but just you wait and see. Trust me, Frank, I know. They always bite the hand that feeds them.'

Questions   (30 marks; 45 minutes)

1 In what ways could Brian be described as a Theory X manager?   (4)
2 Outline the problems that might result from a Theory X approach.   (6)
3 Is Frank right when he says 'you should always try to involve your employees more in making decisions'?   (8)
4 Consider whether Frank would be able to cure the security problems if he took over as manager at Brian's business.   (12)

A Level Exercises

A. REVISION QUESTIONS

(30 marks; 60 minutes)

Read the unit, then answer:

1 How might an attempt at democratic leadership slip into a laissez-faire style?   (4)
2 What might be the effects of a prime minister running the government in a laissez-faire leadership style?   (4)
3 Why might a Theory X approach be self-fulfilling?   (4)
4 Outline the possible benefits of a Theory Y approach.   (4)
5 Do you think you can train someone to change their management style?   (4)
6 Many managers claim to have a democratic style of leadership. Often their subordinates disagree. Outline two ways of checking the actual leadership style of a particular manager.   (4)
7 Analyse the leadership style adopted by your teacher/tutor.   (6)

B. REVISION EXERCISES

B1 Data Response

The Importance of Single Status

A revolution has been occurring in local government in recent years with the elimination of occupational inequalities between manual and white-collar workers. The change is a cultural change as much as a change in conditions and is typical of developments throughout British industry. Raising the status of manual workers to that of white-collar colleagues is becoming a vital part of the modernisation of British employment relations. British managers finally seem to have realised that it is time to stop treating manual workers as inferiors. Many companies are now negotiating to give manual workers monthly rather than weekly pay, longer holiday entitlements and the same sick pay terms and pension rights as office staff. In return, managers hope to achieve greater employee flexibility and be able to adopt a more team-based approach. Amongst the numerous firms introducing single status deals are British Steel, Anglian Water, Royal Ordnance and Castle Cement. The single status approach is very common in new firms or on greenfield sites. It is less common in older plants with established practices based on a more divisive culture.

Questions   (20 marks; 25 minutes)

1 What is meant by 'single status' ?   (3)
2 Examine the view that single status is 'a vital part' of modern, team-based management.   (8)
3 Consider the possible problems of introducing single status into an organisation.   (9)

B2 Case Study

Toshiba Changing Course

Few UK factories are required within a year to switch over completely to making radically different products. This was the experience of Toshiba's microwave oven factory in Plymouth. The company decided it should change to industrial air-conditioners. These are more complex products selling to businesses rather than consumers – and costing up to 20 times more. Six years and £20 million of investment later, Yoshitomo Ninomiya, the Japanese manager in charge of the transformation, feels confident of its future.

Turning out microwaves was a largely unskilled assembly job. Air-conditioners involve more complex and varied manufacturing, as many systems are tailor-made to fit a particular building. Therefore education was vital. Forty British staff went to Toshiba's main Japanese air-conditioner factory in Fuji for three to nine months for training. The same number of Japanese experts spent three months in Britain to help set up the new production process.

Neil Lancaster, head of manufacturing when the plant made ovens, recalls: 'We were treated like babies with no knowledge. At the time the regime seemed highly prescriptive and difficult to come to terms with.' The main change involved looking at options for improvement, then sticking to the best one to ensure all the items were made to the same high quality. At the start, all the products were 'clones' of Japanese air-conditioners.

Now the factory makes 60 product 'families' with sales of over £30 million per year. A British design team of seven ensures that products are customised to meet client requirements.

During the changes, Mr Ninomiya has learned that British workers are less attuned to working in teams than their Japanese counterparts. He believes this lack of 'team thinking' means the average UK manager needs to be tougher than his Japanese equivalent to get people to do what's required. Happily, individual British engineers can be more innovative than the team-oriented Japanese. Mr Ninomiya praises some 'super' ideas for improving production.

Source: *The Financial Times*, 19/11/97

Questions *(40 marks; 60 minutes)*

1 Outline the key factors in making this transformation a success. *(6)*
2 Discuss Mr Ninomiya's leadership style. *(10)*
3 Why might British people be less used to working in teams than those in Japan? *(6)*
4 In Toshiba's case, what might have been the benefits and drawbacks to teamworking? *(10)*
5 Experts suggest that there will be less mass production and more customised production in future. What implications does this have for leadership styles? *(8)*

C. ESSAY QUESTIONS

1 'A good leader can always turn an ineffective business into a successful one.' To what extent can good management make a difference to the success of a firm?
2 'Management is no longer about leading others; it is about working with them.' Critically assess this view.
3 Consider the view that autocratic management has no place in today's business world.
4 'Good managers are born and not made.' Discuss this view.

COMMUNICATION

DEFINITION

Communication is the process by which information is exchanged between one group or person and another.

34.1 The importance of good communications

Effective communication is essential for organisations. Without it employees do not know what they are supposed to do, why they are supposed to do it, how to do it or when to do it by. Similarly, managers have little idea of how the business is performing, what people are actually doing or what their customers think.

Communication links the activities of all the various parts of the organisation. It ensures that everyone is working towards a common goal and enables feedback on performance. Imagine studying for an exam if you were not told by the teacher what you were supposed to do and had no idea of the standard of your work. Then you can appreciate how important good communication is. By communicating effectively the management is able to explain the objectives of the organisation, and employees can have an input into the decisions which are made (see Figure 34.1).

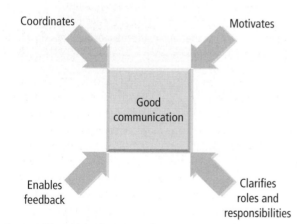

Figure 34.1 Communication

Effective communication is also vital for successful decision making. To make good decisions managers need high quality information. If they do not know what is happening in the market, for example, they are less likely to be successful. If, however, their market knowledge is good they are more likely to develop an appropriate marketing plan. Effective communication provides managers with the information they need, in a form they can use, when they need it.

Good communication is also extremely important to motivate employees. People need to know how they

Good quality information should be:

- *easily accessible*
- *up to date*
- *cost effective*

are getting on, what they are doing right and in which areas they could improve. Working on your own without any kind of feedback at all is extremely difficult. It is much easier if someone is taking an interest and providing support. Interestingly, nearly all staff surveys reveal that employees do not feel that management communicates with them very effectively. There is clearly a general need for managers to improve in this area.

To ensure that communication is motivating, managers need to ensure that employees:

- understand the objectives of the organisation as a whole
- understand why their job is important and how it contributes to the overall success of the firm
- know how the job should be completed
- know how they are doing in their work (obtain quick, effective feedback).

By communicating effectively management is likely to have a much more focused and committed workforce. Recognising staff achievements meets their ego needs, whilst simply showing an interest helps in meeting their social needs. Mayo's study of the Hawthorne plant in Chicago (see Unit 31) highlighted the importance of social needs at work. These findings still seem valid today. Communication with employees also includes target setting. People usually respond well to having goals set out for them (provided these are agreed between the manager and subordinate rather than imposed on them). By establishing targets people have something to measure their performance against and can see how they are getting on.

As well as communicating internally, it is also important for organisations to communicate effectively with external groups such as suppliers, customers, the media and investors. These groups will only be able to fully understand the management's actions if they know the reasons behind them. By communicating on a regular basis with external groups the firm is able to monitor its success and learn how to improve the quality of its operations. By listening to customer comments, for example, a firm can find out what can be done to improve service levels. This willingness to listen and a desire to actively encourage input from a wide variety of groups lies behind the kaizen approach of continuous improvement.

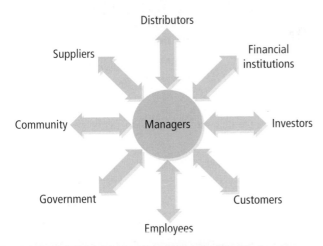

Figure 34.2 Managers must communicate with other groups

COMMUNICATIONS AT SHELL

In 2002 the executive chairman of Shell, pledged to 'redouble' efforts to communicate with shareholders after coming under heavy criticism. Investors were unusually strong in attacking the chairman's 'brusque' manner, poor ability to communicate strategy and defensiveness when dealing with critical questions. One of Shell's top five shareholders said: 'He seems to show a complete disdain for communication with the City.' Shareholders said there had continued to be difficulty in gaining meetings with Mr Watts and the firm's strategic goals had been badly explained. Shell's leading shareholders include Legal & General, Barclays Global Investors, Scottish Widows and Standard Life.

While all firms would agree that good communication is needed, this does not mean that it is easy to achieve. Firms often have communication problems which can undermine their performance. In many cases these problems occur because messages are passed on in an inappropriate way. There are, of course, several ways of passing information on to others:

- speak to them directly
- fax them
- telephone them
- send them a memo
- put a note on the noticeboard.

The most appropriate method depends on what exactly it is you are communicating. If, for example, you want to send someone a detailed market research report it would probably be inappropriate to read it out to them on the telephone. It might be better to send them a printed copy and to discuss the key points face to face. Managers must, therefore, consider the most suitable means of communicating a specific message. Anything which is particularly sensitive or confidential such as an employee's appraisal, for example, should be done face to face. A general announcement about the menu in the canteen, by comparison, could easily be put on a noticeboard.

One of the main problems facing managers is that they do not have the time or resources needed to communicate effectively. In a large company of several thousand people, for example, it is impossible for the senior management to meet and discuss progress with each employee individually. Obviously this task can be delegated but at the cost of creating a gap between the senior managers and other staff. Even when it is delegated there rarely seems enough time for people to meet. Imagine if your teacher met with every student he or she teaches for one hour a week to go over homework individually. This may be desirable but would leave very little time for actual teaching! As a result managers are often forced to use other methods of communication (e.g. notes, noticeboards, memos), even if they know these are not necessarily the most effective means of passing on messages.

34.2 Information technology and communication

The ongoing developments in **information technology** create enormous opportunities for improvements in communication. The use of technology such as e-mail, faxes, mobile phones and network systems speeds up communication. The Internet, for example, provides a tremendous resource allowing employees quick access to a very wide range of data. Some firms now use computerised management information systems (MIS) which provide managers with the information they need, such as the latest sales figures, when they need it.

Developments in IT are certainly making it easier, quicker and cheaper to keep in touch. However, this does not mean that more investment in IT automatically proves beneficial. Systems can become outdated rapidly or employees may lack the appropriate training, for example. There is also the issue of cost. There are many communications tools now available but a firm cannot afford all of them. Even if it could, it would not actually need them all. The introduction of IT must therefore be carefully managed. The potential gains must be weighed up against the costs, and its impact on other areas of the organisation properly assessed. The firm should also be aware that the latest technology does not always lead to better communication. It may just lead to more communication and consequently communication overload.

34.3 Communication and size

As a firm grows it tends to introduce more layers of hierarchy. This makes communication more difficult as messages from the top of the organisation to the bottom have to go through more people. This slows down decision making. It also introduces a greater risk that the message will get distorted. Instead of communicating directly to the person you want to talk to, you have to contact someone else who then gets in touch with another person and so on. In the end your message can become rather confused. Another problem is that as the number of people involved in an organisation increases, the use of written communication rises even faster. Instead of a quick conversation to sort something out you can end up passing numerous messages backwards and forwards. This can lead to a tremendous amount of paperwork and is often far less effective than face-to-face communication. When you are actually talking to someone you can get immediate feedback and can see if they do not fully understand something. You can then talk it through until you are happy they have understood what you mean. When you send them a written message, however, you are never quite sure how they will interpret it. What you think you have said and what they think you have said can be very different.

The amount of written information which is generated in a large organisation can lead to communication overload. So much information is gathered to keep control that it gets in the way of making decisions. Take a look at the average manager's desk and you will see the problem. It is covered in letters, reports and memos and consequently people can become swamped by the amount of information they are dealing with. This overload can lead to inefficiencies. For example, managers may not be able to find the information they want when they need it. Or they may have so much data that they cannot easily decide what is really important.

Communication is also becoming more difficult with the changes occurring in employment patterns. With more people working part time, working from home and with more outsourcing, managing communication is becoming an increasingly more complex process.

34.4 Methods of communication

The traditional methods of communication within organisations – such as **team briefings** and newsletters – remain the most popular, even though they are not

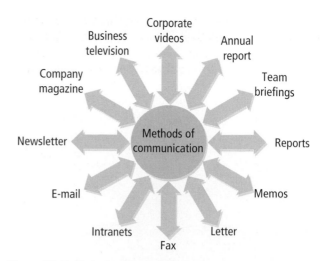

Figure 34. 3 Methods of communication

necessarily the most effective. Other more modern methods of communication include video, e-mail, **intranets** (private Internet sites) and business television.

COMMUNICATION ON THE FACTORY FLOOR

Throughout the factory and warehouse at Unipart are rooms filled with computers. These are called 'Faculties on the Floor' and are training centres used by Unipart to help increase employee skills. John Neill, the company's chief executive, says that increasing productivity 'is a never-ending crusade' and believes it must be a priority of the business. His 'Faculty on the Floor' makes it quicker and easier for employees to access information and thereby make better decisions.

Inside the shop-floor faculties, small groups drawn from Unipart's 9,500 employees meet to share ideas and experience. They discuss how to improve work methods, whether they involve making parts such as exhaust systems or the distribution of products ranging from tents to mobile telephones. The computers also link the workers via the Internet with employees in other Unipart locations. Mr Neill's zeal for training is rooted firmly in its practical benefits to the company. 'Within a company it is vital to link the education and training effort to what people are doing in their work,' he says. 'Our philosophy is to encourage employees to learn something in the morning and put it into practice in the afternoon.' The Faculty on the Floor approach improves communication throughout the business at a level where it can really make a difference.

Business IN

Communication will also occur through meetings with staff representatives. EU legislation is trying to ensure that more communication of this type occurs. Under present EU law, for example, companies with more than 1,000 employees in the EU and at least 250 staff in two or more countries must set up European works councils (EWCs) to consult with their employees. In Germany these types of employee works councils have worked well for many years. Employees have the right to be consulted on issues such as new working procedures and organisational change. They are also entitled to general information on the economic and financial position of the organisation and the company's investment plans.

Formal communication within a firm occurs via the established channels such as works councils. Information communication occurs when employees develop their own channels. This is often known as the 'grapevine'. Messages often pass around the organisation more quickly on the grapevine than through the established channels (just think how quickly you find out if someone is in trouble at school!) but the information is not always accurate. Sometimes managers use the grapevine to try out a new idea and see how workers react. If the proposal is disliked the managers can always deny it was their idea later.

ISSUES FOR analysis

When analysing the role and importance of communications within a firm it may be useful to consider the following points:

- Effective communication can improve motivation and lead to better decision making internally; it can also provide better links and feedback with external groups such as suppliers and consumers.
- Effective two-way communication is a vital element of democratic management and the kaizen approach.
- Information technology can help communications but needs to be managed carefully.
- Communication often becomes more difficult as organisations grow; poor communication can lead to diseconomies of scale because of motivation, coordination and control difficulties.

34.5 Communication
an evaluation

Good communications lie at the heart of effective management. To plan, coordinate and control a business requires high quality, **two-way communication**. However, communication needs to be managed if it is to be effective. Managers need to think carefully about the best way of communicating a message – and the best timing. The most effective channel of communication will vary according to the information you are trying to pass on. You may want to talk through a particular plan face to face; large amounts of quantifiable data may be best communicated in a report. In many cases managers may not be able to use the most effective channel of communication because it is too expensive or people are too far apart.

Generally, firms have to be careful of communication overload. More and more data is now available – this does not mean it is always useful. However, a firm which communicates effectively is likely to be more in touch with consumers, have a more motivated and committed workforce and find it easier to bring about change. The management of information is, therefore, a means of gaining a competitive advantage. Information technology can help improve communications but has to be used effectively.

A Level Exercises

A. REVISION QUESTIONS
(40 marks; 70 minutes)

Read the unit, then answer:

1 Identify four groups with whom managers need to communicate regularly. (4)
2 Identify two methods of communication used within a firm. Outline one advantage and one disadvantage of each one. (6)
3 Explain why good communications within a firm are important. (3)
4 Given that noticeboards are known to be a rather poor way of communicating, why do so many firms use them? (3)
5 How have improvements in information technology helped to improve communication? (3)
6 State three actions a firm could take in order to improve the effectiveness of communication. (3)
7 Outline three reasons why communications within a firm are sometimes poor. (6)
8 Identify three reasons why communications may be poorer in large firms than in small ones. (3)
9 Explain why good communication is an important part of motivating employees. (4)
10 Some people claim that the developments in information technology have made communications worse not better. Do you agree with this view? Why? (5)

B REVISION EXERCISES

B1 Data Response

Employee Communication
Faced with intensifying competition and an accelerating pace of change, companies are seeing effective communication with employees as an ever more important part of organisational efficiency. It is also a constructive way to harness employees' commitment, enthusiasm and ideas. However, companies tend to place considerable emphasis on communicating big but vague messages about change and company performance. It is highly debatable whether such messages are relevant to employees or easily understood by them. Employee attitude surveys consistently highlight communication as a major source of staff dissatisfaction.

While managers tend to use communication channels which send general messages downwards, employees place more importance on mechanisms which communicate immediate and applicable information. For example, around 40% of staff found one-to-one meetings with their manager very useful while less than 5% gave business television the same rating. Another problem is considerable 'noise' in organisations and a great temptation to equate communication simply with the provision of information.

Questions *(30 marks; 35 minutes)*

1 Explain the business meaning of the following terms:
 a communication channels (2)
 b noise. (2)
2 What might be the value to staff of a 'one-to-one' meeting with their manager? (5)
3 Explain why communication is more than just 'the provision of information'. (5)
4 Examine the importance of good communication within either a McDonald's restaurant or a supermarket. (7)
5 Discuss the problems which can occur when employees are dissatisfied. (9)

B2 Case Study

Communications Problems at Globex
'I couldn't really tell you,' said Frank Delaney to one of his friends who had asked how his new job was going. 'I don't want to criticise my boss but she's never there when I need to see her. Every day I get a series of e-mails from her, most of which don't make any sense to me at all. What's a ZF300 anyway? And whenever you try to speak to her about it she's in a rush and hasn't got time to talk. After the first day when she introduced me to everyone I don't suppose I've talked to her for more than 15 minutes at a time. When I got the job here at Globex, I thought it would be so different.'

'The trouble is I've got important decisions to make and wouldn't mind some advice. "E-mail me" she says, which is fine except she never seems to answer them. To be honest, though, I'm not sure I'm using this new system properly. In my opinion you can't beat actually talking to someone. You can usually sort things out much more quickly. I waited outside her office for nearly an hour yesterday to try and catch a few minutes with her. What makes it worse is last week she e-mailed me and told me what a wonderful job I'm doing. How the hell does she know? I'm surprised she even remembered my name.'

'Whenever I do get through to ask her opinion she tells me to use my initiative, so that's what I do. I make up the rules as I go along and hope it works out okay. In my last place everyone saw everyone else each day; the business was small enough to talk. And you always knew they'd be in the canteen at lunch time. At this place we are much more spread out and I can never find people when I want them. It's a bit lonely I can tell you. The way I'm feeling at the moment I'll just do my job and see if she notices if I get it wrong.'

Questions   (50 marks; 60 minutes)

1 Analyse how effectively information technology is being used in communications at Globex. (10)
2 Consider the communication problems which can occur within a large organisation such as Globex. (12)
3 With reference to the case study, discuss the relationship between communication and motivation. (10)
4 Write a report to Frank's boss (the office manager) outlining the problems Frank is having with her approach to communications, some possible solutions to those problems and your recommendations to her on what she should do. Make sure to explain your recommendations fully. (18)

B3 Case Study

Extraordinary Communication

Geeta Bandhari started Extraordinary Fashions 10 years ago. When she began it was one small shop on the outskirts of Oxford targeting 'taller and larger ladies' and offering a range of modern fashions. The shop had been remarkably successful, catering for a market niche that was not served well by other stores. She now owns 6 shops in the south-east.

Geeta tried to keep a firm control over the day to day affairs of the business and liked to be out and about visiting the stores as much as she could. However, with the success of the business came more paperwork and more form filling. This not only irritated her but also kept her out of circulation quite a lot of the time. If she wasn't dealing with administration she was meeting and negotiating with suppliers. This also involved a lot of travel. Geeta admitted she was reluctant to let go of the business and kept most of the decision making to herself: 'It's my business. I built it up and I know what makes it work. If it goes wrong my employees can always go and get another job; I can't suddenly rebuild what I've achieved.'

Whilst staff generally admired Geeta there was a growing sense that she needed to let go a bit more. 'We can't do much without her say-so, but she's not always easy to get hold of', said Sinead Fellows. Sinead had run the Newbury shop for 3 years but was now considering leaving. A new Next store had opened up nearby and Sinead had already been for a first interview. At Extraordinary Fashions, the shop managers felt they were only able to grab a word with Geeta in passing and never had a chance to talk things through properly. Sinead had wanted to discuss her future at the company with Geeta but there never seemed to be time. At least at Next there were more career opportunities and someone would listen to her. When she was at Extraordinary Fashions, new items would simply appear for her to sell without any discussion about the needs of her particular customers. Requests for particu-

lar types of clothes or suggestions of how to improve the business were rarely acknowledged and Sinead was not even sure that Geeta bothered to read them. The only thing Geeta seemed interested in was the sales figures. If these ever dipped Sinead soon got a phone call asking to know why. Yet even then the conversations were rather brief and Geeta seemed to spend most of the time telling her to try harder. Apparently the business as a whole was doing well but Sinead never really had any sense of this. In fact she hardly knew any of the other store managers.

In a last attempt to speak to her boss, Sinead made a special visit to Oxford only to find Geeta was late because she had overrun at a meeting with the bank. Geeta was shocked to hear that Sinead was leaving; she had assumed Sinead was enjoying the work at Newbury. In an attempt to keep her, Geeta offered Sinead more pay but by this time Sinead was clearly determined to leave. Once she realised this, Geeta tried to hurry the conversation up – she'd just seen the latest figures on store performance and wanted to think about them without interruptions.

	Sales per employee (Oxford store = base 100)	Absenteeism rates (Oxford store = base 100)
Newbury	90	102
Oxford	100	100
Southampton	75	110
Winchester	70	125
London	105	90
Bristol	120	75
Bath	102	100
Cambridge	95	99

Questions   (30 marks; 45 minutes)

1 Discuss the ways in which communication might be improved at Extraordinary Fashions. (15)
2 Consider the possible benefits of improved communication at Extraordinary Fashions. (15)

C. ESSAY QUESTIONS

1 'Good communications make the difference between business success and business failure.' Critically assess this view.
2 Consider the view that the effect of the increasing use of information technology simply provides more information rather than better information.
3 Consider the view that effective communications is at the heart of successful operations management.

ORGANISATIONAL STRUCTURE

Organisational structure is the formal and systematic way the management of a business is organised. When presented as a diagram, it shows the departmental functions and who is answerable to whom.

35.1 Introduction

Soon after the start of the industrial age, organisations became larger and more complex. Early management thinkers, such as FW Taylor and H Fayol, began to consider how best to design the structure of an organisation. Both these writers had production and engineering backgrounds. They saw the function of organisations as converting inputs, such as money, materials, machines and people, into output. Therefore designing an organisation was like designing a machine, the objective being to maximise efficiency. Their thinking was mechanistic; the principles of good management were like the principles of physics. Their approach was prescriptive. Early managers wanted to be told the best way to manage. And the organisational structure which would be the most effective.

35.2 The formal organisation: a hierarchy

The first significant attempt at organisational structure is the classical or formal hierarchy, as in Figure 35.1. Such a diagram looks familiar today and is very much part of the way we now think about organisations. It is probably the first way many people would think of describing the structure of the organisation in which they work. The diagram has many advantages. It gives a quick and simple way of gaining a mental map of an organisation. It is based on the main managerial functions and is controlled from the top layer of senior management. It suggests how all the parts and people fit together and defines each person's place and role.

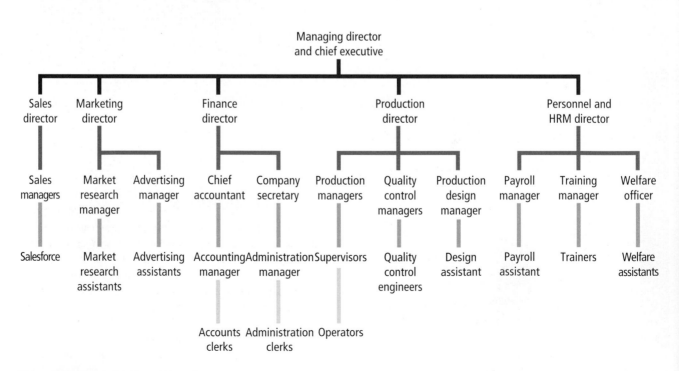

Figure 35.1 Classical or formal hierarchy

35.3 Principles of management and organisational structure

Figure 35.1 also gives a good insight into many of the fundamental characteristics of the theory and principles of management and organisation structure. These are set out below.

SOME PRINCIPLES AND CHARACTERISTICS OF MANAGEMENT AND ORGANISATIONAL STRUCTURE

Managerial functions: Management is an activity which can be divided neatly into functions: production, marketing, sales, accounting and finance, human resources and so on. The job of the managing director, and the other directors, sitting at the top of the 'pillars', is to ensure that all these functions are coordinated. So if each function, or department, plays its part properly, the whole organisation will succeed.

Chain of command: In a hierarchy, the vertical chain of command can be seen. The salesforce reports to the sales manager and the directors report to the managing director. Information is communicated up the hierarchy through the layers and orders are communicated down.

Authority: Authority flows from position in the hierarchy and is a source of power. The production manager has formal authority over the supervisors, who have authority over the operators below them.

Accountability and responsibility: A hierarchy and defined lines of authority lead to clear accountability and responsibility. A subordinate is accountable to a manager who must be responsible for him or her. Whereas authority can be delegated to a junior manager, responsibility rests at the top.

The clearer and more tightly defined the organisation chart and the organisation's rules and procedures, the more likely are accountability and responsibility to rest with named individuals. This can be positive as personal accountability can lead to high motivation. However, in an atmosphere of mistrust or in difficult times, such accountability can be a threat and reduce morale.

Span of control: The number of subordinates reporting to a manager. Fayol thought the span should never exceed five. A narrow span of control means tight supervision, less discretion and therefore less chance of mistakes. This may be suitable where tasks are straightforward, relatively unchanging and easily checked and measured. For instance, production of components to given tolerances, or the checking of standardised application forms and paperwork. A narrow span may mean more levels in the hierarchy or ranks, and therefore greater promotion prospects. A wide span of control reduces supervision and leads to greater **delegation** and job enrichment.

Levels of hierarchy: The number of layers in a hierarchy will reflect the number of supervisory and managerial levels, ranks or grades. The more there are and the taller the organisation structure, the greater the opportunities for miscommunication, or distorted or deliberately filtered communication. Also the more remote the top and bottom of the hierarchy are from each other.

De-layering: The removal of one or more layers from a hierarchy as organisations attempt to become leaner and fitter. This can assist communication, cut out bureaucracy and overhead costs, and motivate staff by increasing individual authority and responsibility. However, it can widen the span of control, reducing supervision and lead to overwork and perhaps stress. De-layering is sometimes a convenient term for redundancies.

Centralisation: Centralisation means that only the top levels of the hierarchy have the authority to take decisions. In an organisation which is spread geographically, for example, it implies that all key decisions will be taken at head office. This can ensure tight financial control since targets will be set for the whole organisation from the centre. It can lead to coherent strategies in marketing and production and sharing of resources. Also it can simplify and speed up decision making. However, centralisation reduces the opportunities for input from the lower levels of the hierarchy or the more distant parts of the organisation. This can lead to poor communication and demotivation.

Decentralisation: This implies widespread **delegation** and the passing of power down to lower levels in the hierarchy for decision making. This can motivate and empower junior managers and supervisors and can lead to greater innovation and enthusiasm. It also reduces the need for tight control and communication. However, it can lead to loss of control by senior managers and head office. It can also lead to lack of direction or less consistency (which may damage the corporate identity).

Bureaucracy: A bureaucracy is where the work of the organisation closely follows rules and procedures. Precedent is important in making decisions. Anything unusual will be referred up the hierarchy. Job descriptions will be tightly and narrowly defined. Individuals will have little discretion. Work will probably be broken into small tasks which are measured and checked. Paperwork and forms will be common. Overt respect for authority will be high. The strongest source of power will be position power in the hierarchy. Conformists are likely to be successful, ensuring a stable corporate culture.

35.4 Organisational behaviour

Do people in organisations actually behave as the formal hierarchy suggests?

In reality, businesses, or the people in them, do not always behave in the way the organisation chart would suggest. Communication may not always be upwards but sideways; employees in different functions find it better to talk direct rather than 'through the proper channels', i.e. via their boss.

The objectives of staff in different parts of a business may not always match the corporate objectives because of personal interests or rivalries:

- sales staff may believe they do all the hard work while marketing executives merely dream up fanciful campaigns
- production managers may pursue product quality for its own sake rather than that required by the customers
- accountants will see budgets as an objective which others see as constraints
- position power, for example that held by the chief executive's personal assistant, may be used to filter communication. Informal groups may influence individual behaviour away from formal objectives.

Organisational success relies upon bringing staff together in a shared vision of what needs to be done and everyone's role in achieving it. Diagrams of organisation hierarchies may give little clue about the reality of who is contributing most to business success.

'Hierarchies just get in the way of business, cutting off managers from their customers, insulating them from the market and creating slow bureaucracies.'
Percy Barnevik, former chief of the industrial giant ABB (Asea Brown Boveri)

'In a hierarchy, every employee tends to rise to his own level of incompetence.'
Lawrence Peter, creator of The Peter Principle

'There has to be some degree of hierarchy, because decisions actually have to be taken.'
George Bull, chief executive

'Middle managers, as we have known them, are cooked geese.'
Tom Peters, management guru

'If you look at General Motors today versus yesterday, they've slimmed a little bit. They had 29 layers. Which means that nobody could really be considered for a top management job before the age 211.'
Peter Drucker, management guru

Source: *The Ultimate Book of Business Quotations*, Stuart Crainer, Capstone Publishing, 1997

35.5 Factors influencing optimal organisational structure

Modern management thinking has moved away from the view that there is one organisational structure which will suit all organisations at all times. What is the best structure for one organisation will depend on many factors. Organisations have vastly different environments in which they operate. Some are reasonably stable while others are constantly changing.

Organisations also differ greatly in size and in objectives. As Charles Handy explained in *Understanding Organizations*, within all large organisations, a culture develops which greatly influences the type of structure which is appropriate. This culture can be thought of as an organisational ideology, a set of norms or a way of life, which is pervasive. The culture of a sixth form college is very different from that of an army officer training school. Similarly, working in the research department of a giant pharmaceutical company is likely to be very different from working as a foreign exchange dealer in a city bank. Indeed, within large organisations, there will be different cultures – the bank's foreign exchange dealing room will work quite differently from the mortgage lending department where a financial adviser patiently explains complex matters to a first-time house buyer.

Some organisations have a culture which is very formal, where there is a strict dress code, where punctuality is all-important or staying late is normal. In some organisations everything operates through committees; rules and procedures are very important. In other, more informal, organisations, individuals rather than committees make decisions. Initiative rather than conformity or obedience is usual. People are judged on results rather than adherence to precedent or established practice. All organisations have signs of power – do people seek expense accounts, a large office, a bigger company car, or share options? Answers to these types of question tell much of the culture of an organisation.

35.6 Organisational structures for different organisational cultures

Following Handy, we can identify four different sets of circumstances or 'cultures', as set out in the table at the top of the next page. Each requires a different organisational structure.

THE FORMAL HIERARCHY

When is this the best structure? The formal hierarchy (see Figure 35.1) is best suited to the role culture. In this culture the role, or job description, is often more

CULTURE	STRUCTURE
Role culture	Formal hierarchy
Task culture	Matrix
Power culture	Web
Person culture	Cluster

important than the individual who fills it. Performance over and above the job description is not required. Tasks are clearly defined, as are accountability and responsibility. There is a clear chain of command. Position power is the major source of power in this culture.

Other features of the role culture are:

- Individual departments or functions can be very strong and self-contained, guarding their own power.
- Roles will be precisely defined using clear job descriptions and definitions of authority.

IKEA

Ikea's huge success in Europe comes from a high degree of central control. Maintenance, internationally, of consistency of the Ikea brand name and image is all-important. This often causes tension between the satellite stores in the UK and head office in Sweden. Local stores want to follow local market trends but this conflicts with the central objective of a consistent brand image everywhere. A good example is store design and product development, which are both run from Sweden. This policy of tight central control has worked so far and no doubt has enabled growth. The policy may well be severely tested if there is a major change in the business environment, such as new competition or a widespread recession.

Source: Adapted from *The Financial Times*

- There are set ways of communicating, such as standard memos with defined circulation lists and 'usual channels', e.g. subordinate to superior and no-one else. There may also be accepted ways of addressing others, such as calling the boss 'Mr' or 'Mrs' instead of using Christian names.
- Decision making will be based largely on precedent.
- There are likely to be many layers of hierarchy in a bureaucratic structure in which there is a narrow span of control.

Managerial functions will need to be strongly coordinated at the top by senior management. Then, if the departments do their job, as laid down by the rules and procedures, the results should be as planned.

THE TASK CULTURE: MATRIX STRUCTURE

The task culture is job or project oriented. Its accompanying structure can be best seen as a matrix. So the matrix organisation, as shown in Figure 35.2, is a common structure for organisations with a task culture.

This attempts to avoid the major disadvantage of the formal hierarchy in which only senior levels of management communicate and work together. In a matrix the functional departments still exist. But people from those departments have the flexibility to work on projects with or for other departments. The development of a new product would require product research and design, consumer and market research, as well as production and management accounting. So a researcher whose **line manager** is the head of research may spend half their time working on a project run by the head of new products. Those who favour formal hierarchies would worry about an employee having two bosses. Japanese firms such as Toyota have proved, however, that working together on projects saves time and therefore allows new products to be brought to the market more quickly.

Matrix management is likely to work best in a business with a relatively wide span of control and relatively few layers of management hierarchy. The structure aims to bring people and resources together and let them get on with particular tasks. Individual capability rather than age or formal status determines people's standing in the task culture. Rules, procedure

	Finance department	Marketing department	Research and development department	Production department
	Finance specialist	Marketing specialist	Research and development specialists	Production specialist
Project manager A				
Project manager B				
Project manager C				
Project manager D				

Figure 35.2 Matrix or net structure

and precedent are less important. Authority flows more from competence on the task rather than place in the hierarchy.

IF YOU CAN'T STAND THE HEAT …

Business **IN**

By 9.00 p.m. the kitchen at Heathcote's is a blur of moving bodies, pans and plates. 'Give me one foie gras, one lobster, one brioche, two signature. Let's go, let's go!' shouts chef/proprietor Paul Heathcote. With the meat and fish sections of the kitchen in a frenzy of activity, even the pastry chefs help out when needed. Later the pressure will be on them. In half an hour the pastry chefs will be masterminding the preparation of the elaborate desserts at this famous restaurant. Now they are willing to take orders from others. Matrix management at its best and simplest means true teamwork.

Advantages:

- Task culture is appropriate where flexibility, creativity and teamwork are important qualities. This would be where the market is volatile or product life cycles are short. Being job or project oriented, the task culture is based on the expertise of a well-trained professional staff and its strength lies in its adaptability.
- Different teams across the functions can be combined as appropriate to meet the needs of different projects. This adds interest and variety to working life and can therefore act as a motivator.

Disadvantages:

- Much of the power and influence in a matrix system lies at quite low levels in the management hierarchy. This gives rise to power groups at lower levels with specialised knowledge and expertise. Senior managers no longer know everything.
- Control may be difficult in the task culture. Dilution of power and control are the price paid by senior managers for fast response and more teamwork.

POWER CULTURE AND THE ENTREPRENEURIAL OR WEB STRUCTURE

A power culture or web is often found in small businesses or entrepreneurial organisations and in some property and trading and finance companies. A power culture is usually dominated by a strong central figure, typically the founder or chairman. Its structure is best pictured as a web (see Figure 35.3). Alan Sugar's company Amstrad was run in this way. Sugar's speed of decision making was the key to success in the early

Figure 35.3 Power culture and the web

stages of the markets for personal computers and satellite dishes.

This culture depends on a central power source radiating power and influence. It may also depend on a few key individuals trusted by the leader. Few decisions are taken collectively or in a committee. This organisation works on precedent, and on anticipating the wishes and decisions of the central power sources. As the views of middle managers carry little or no weight, few of them will be employed. Therefore there are likely to be few layers of hierarchy and a relatively wide span of control. Usually this kind of structure encourages delegation or **empowerment**. Here, though, the control exerted by the leader means that decision making power remains firmly at the top.

THE PERSON CULTURE

The fourth culture is an unusual one. It will not be found pervading many organisations. Its structure is as minimal as possible; a cluster is the best word for it – or perhaps a galaxy of individual stars (see Figure 35.4).

The person culture may be seen where any kind of formal structure seems largely absent. The organisation exists simply to assist as administrative back-up for 'star-performer' individuals. Handy gives barristers' chambers, architects' practices, and some management consultancy firms as examples. Possibly one might include hospitals and universities where cutting-edge research is undertaken, or the creative departments of advertising agencies.

Advantages: The person culture thrives where rules, procedures and precedent are virtually non-existent as new ground is being broken all the time. Creativity is the watchword. The cluster will be successful where

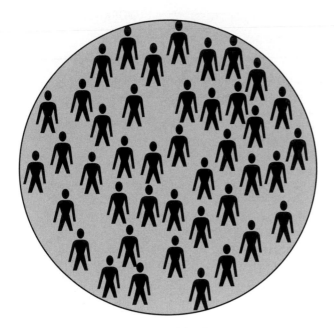

Figure 35.4 The person culture and the cluster

work is often very specialised, with each case unique. And where quick reactions to ever-changing and new events are needed, together with rapid risk taking and decision making.

Disadvantages: Specialised departments of large organisations which operate as unstructured person cultures can become divorced from the main business and become self-running. It may be difficult to set targets or keep them in line with organisational objectives. The department's spending may be difficult to control and its end results may not be apparent. This culture is not often found in manufacturing companies, or large-scale organisations generally.

The choice of the appropriate organisational structure will depend on many factors, especially culture, but also history and ownership, size of organisation, technology, goals and objectives, the business environment and the people.

Structure can be extremely important and must be chosen very carefully. In situations which are subject to rapid change, the rigid procedures of a formal hierarchy may well frustrate competent people who will want to see proper change and development. Too many levels of management may also demotivate good ambitious young managers who feel that red tape and 'dead wood' are blocking their way. However, a person culture with the free-wheeling deregulated structure of the cluster organisation would hardly suit the armed forces with their responsibility for highly powerful and potentially dangerous equipment and armaments. Nor would air passengers feel secure if air traffic controllers and airline pilots did not follow the rules and procedures of a relatively formal organisation.

Handy should have the last word. Perhaps, as he suggests, large firms should contain the various cultures within themselves. So a formal structure and hierarchy could deal with routine and mundane procedures such as processing orders or paying invoices. These make up the majority of any organisation's activity. However, some parts of the organisation, such as the policy or strategic planning section, product design or research and development, or creative marketing, should be organised as a matrix or even cluster. So the best organisation will have different structures to meet its ongoing needs.

253

ISSUES FOR analysis

Work experience, part-time work or project coursework provide good opportunities to examine the structure of an organisation. This applies whether commercial or non-profit making, for example a school or college. The formal structure is often recorded and published in a chart. It will be revealing to analyse the chart to see if the organisation really does work along the lines set out in the chart. How do the people at the top attempt to set objectives and keep the organisation on course? What controls are in place? Is the organisation hierarchical, with rules and procedures, or does it just seem to happen?

All organisations have a culture. A useful exercise would be to classify it and to analyse whether it matches the structure which has been chosen.

Finally, in your organisation or organisations under review, are there powerful groups or individuals not appearing in the formal structure. One good question is this: if you want something done, who do you go to?

KEY terms

delegation – passing power and authority down the hierarchy. It involves giving junior managers greater trust and authority, and requires the superior to release control.

empowerment – a more advanced form of delegation whereby subordinates have more wide-ranging control over their work.

line manager – a manager with specified authority for meeting key operational objectives. Subordinates will be specifically accountable to him or her.

staff manager – manager that does not have line responsibility, but is likely to perform research, advisory or problem-solving functions, such as work study or consultancy services, for line managers.

AS Level Exercises

A. REVISION QUESTIONS
(30 marks; 70 minutes)

Read the unit, then answer:

1 Give three ways in which an organisation chart might be useful. *(3)*
2 Identify two observers outside an organisation who might want to see its organisation chart. Suggest reasons why they might want to see it. *(5)*
3 Distinguish between accountability and responsibility. *(4)*
4 Is there an ideal span of control? Explain your answer. *(5)*
5 Explain in your own words the term 'bureaucracy'. *(3)*
6 What is organisational culture? Is an organisation's culture really 'the way things are done round here' by the most powerful group? *(6)*
7 What organisational structure is most suited for an organisation in a stable environment? *(2)*
8 What organisational structure is most suited for an organisation facing a rapidly changing or unpredictable environment? *(2)*

B. REVISION EXERCISES

B1 Data Response
Deeton & Co has three directors answerable to the chief executive.

- One director is in charge of two accountants.
- The second has five managers answerable to her, each of whom has four subordinates.
- The third has four managers, each with two subordinates.
- One of the managers is answerable to both the second and third directors.

Questions *(15 marks; 20 minutes)*
1 Draw the organisational hierarchy. *(5)*
2 What is the second director's span of control? *(1)*
3 Explain any weaknesses you can identify in this hierarchy. *(9)*

B2 Activity
Consider an organisation you know well. This could be your school or college. Draw an organisation chart to describe in the form a classical hierarchy.

Explain to the rest of your group how realistic a description this chart is of the organisation.

You may find it useful to consider:

- How stable is its environment?
- Have there been new targets, constraints, competition?
- How much internal change has there been in the last two years?
- Has there been a change of leadership?
- How do you get things done in the organisation?
- Is there a powerful informal group?
- Is there a group with power based on knowledge, experience or expertise?
- Is tradition important – 'we've always done it this way'?

- Is promotion usually internal or external or a mix?
- How does communication take place?
- Is it effective?
- Do the departments or sections communicate much with each other?

B3 Case Study
A light engineering business, making plastic components, employs you as a management consultant. Its organisation chart, drawn by the personnel officer, is shown below. The business has been in a stable environment for many years and sells most of its output to a major consumer goods manufacturer. Your friend has just started as a management accountant and tells you that profitability is falling and that administrative overheads seem to be rising as a percentage of sales revenue.

Questions *(30 marks; 45 minutes)*
Write a report on the suitability of the organisational structure. Your terms of reference are to include any recommendations for change.

Within your report, indicate what assumptions you make and any other information you would like. Ensure that your recommendations include suggested amendments to the organisation chart.

You should consider at least the following: the number of departments, clarity of lines of accountability and responsibility, suitability of lines of accountability and responsibility, span of control, fit between structure and actual and potential business environment. Bring in any other relevant points or arguments. *(25)*

Your report should have at least the following headings: 'To/from', 'Date', 'Subject', 'Terms of reference', 'Conclusions', 'Recommendations'. *(5)*

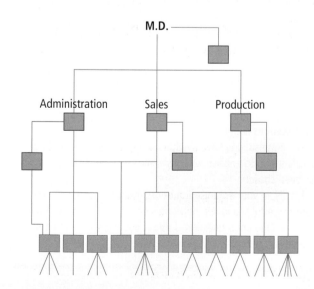

MANAGEMENT BY OBJECTIVES (MBO)

36.1 What is management by objectives?

Every large organisation has problems coordinating the activities of all of its employees. Senior managers may have a clear idea of what they want to achieve. Others within the organisation may not be so sure. If you ask employees in most organisations what they think the overall **objective** of the business is, you are likely to get very different answers. Senior managers may have tried to explain the corporate objectives, but many staff will still be unclear. They may wonder what they are supposed to be doing or how their work helps the business fulfil its overall target. Even if people do understand their role there is a danger that they will be more interested in their own targets rather than those of the firm as a whole. By increasing the size of their own department, for example, individual managers may well gain more power, even if this is not necessarily in the interest of the business. Such problems often increase with the size of the firm. It becomes more difficult to keep in constant and personal contact with people and to check on what they are doing.

The originator of much modern thinking on management by objectives was Peter Drucker. In his 1973 book *Management: Tasks, Responsibilities and Practices* (© Butterworth Heineman Publishers) he wrote that:

'A manager, in the first place, sets objectives. He determines what the objectives should be. He determines what the goals in each area of the business should be. He decides what has to be done to reach these objectives. He makes the objectives effective by communicating them to the people whose performance is needed to attain them.'

Drucker went on to stress that managers must also establish yardsticks to enable staff to focus 'on the performance of the whole organisation and which, at the

BRITISH AIRWAYS' MISSION

British Airways recently produced a new statement of mission, values and goals to drive the business forward for the next 10 years. The mission and values set the company's long-term course and define how it should behave. The goals are the individual steps which will turn the mission into tangible operational and financial targets.

THE NEW MISSION:
- To be the undisputed leader in world travel

THE NEW VALUES:
- Safe and secure
- Honest and responsible
- Innovative and team-spirited
- Global and caring
- A good neighbour

THE NEW GOALS:
- Customers' Choice – Airline of first choice in key markets
- Strong Profitability – Meeting investors' expectations and securing the future
- Truly Global – Global network, global outlook: recognised everywhere for superior value in world travel
- Inspiring People – Building on success and delighting customers.

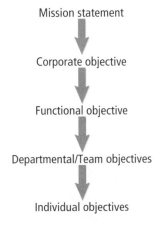

Figure 36.1 Management by objectives

same time, focus on the work of the individual and help him to do it.' In other words, it is not enough to establish objectives. At the same time a system must be established to let people see for themselves how they are performing against the targets set. By delegating power in this way, bosses no longer need to check regularly on what each employee is doing.

36.2 From mission to MBO

The overall reason for the firm's existence is known as its corporate aim or mission. This is often written out in a **mission statement**. For example, the firm might set out to be 'the lowest cost producer in Europe', 'the world's favourite car hire firm' or simply 'to be the best in the industry'. The mission is usually a fairly general target. It sets out the overall purpose of the firm without much detail. Remember Star Trek's 'To boldly go where no man has been before'? This is a typical mission statement – it is meant to inspire and define the underlying purpose of the organisation.

Whilst a mission statement may be motivating, it lacks the specific information needed for planning. What does being the 'best in the industry' mean? The most profitable? The biggest? The fastest growing? To plan properly the firm needs to turn the mission into a corporate objective. This will specify exactly what the firm wants to measure, how much of an increase it wants and when it wants to achieve the target. For example, the firm might set out to 'increase profits by 20% over a five-year period'.

The firm then has to turn this overall objective into more detailed targets for individual departments and managers. To achieve the corporate objective all the different functional managers (such as marketing, finance, operations and human resources) must have their own targets. For example, the marketing objective might be to increase sales, whilst the operations department might try to reduce costs. These func-

Coca-Cola in China

tional objectives then lead to further targets within each business area. To increase sales, for example, the marketing managers might decide to increase the level of promotional activities; to reduce costs the operations manager might aim to reduce the number of reject products. Every time an objective is set, the next level of managers must decide how this is to be fulfilled. If everyone meets their targets successfully then the firm will achieve its overall objective. If the number of defects is reduced, for example, this will decrease costs which in turn will help the firm increase its profitability.

Once managers have agreed their objectives it is possible to develop appropriate strategies. The **strategy** is the plan which shows how to fulfil the objective. If, for example, the objective is to generate 25% of sales from new products, the strategy might be to invest more heavily in research and development.

36.3 How does MBO work?

The MBO system is based on mutually agreed objectives. A manager will discuss with subordinates what needs to be achieved in their particular section of the firm. Between them they will agree specific targets for each subordinate. For the MBO system to work effectively it is important that the objectives are agreed by the subordinates and not simply imposed on them. This is because a target means nothing unless the individual feels committed to achieving it. It is good practice, therefore, to allow staff to set objectives for themselves subject to the superior's approval. They are likely to be much more committed to them because they will feel that they 'own' these targets for themselves. The parent who sets a struggling A level student the objective of 2As and a B is unlikely to generate a positive response.

36.4 Advantages of MBO

- By adopting a system of management by objectives, each manager knows exactly what he or she has to do. Everyone has a clear set of targets which will

---

COCA-COLA EVERYWHERE

Coca-Cola's mission is to ensure its products are within 'an arm's length of desire'. Its advertising may push the need 'To think Coca-Cola – always' but the underlying desire is to get you to think 'Coca-Cola everywhere'. So far, it is not doing badly with sales of over one billion servings a day, but it still wants more and is building a worldwide network of bottlers to increase distribution further. In particular, it has targeted Eastern and Central Europe in recent years to achieve further growth. Before the fall of communism, Pepsi dominated in these areas; Coca-Cola now outsells Pepsi 2 to 1.

Business
IN

help them decide on their own priorities and allocate their resources effectively. This is crucial. A busy executive starts every day with mail, e-mail, voicemail, faxes and scribbled notes left on the desk. Many get bogged down in responding to the requests and problems involved. The stars are the ones who prioritise effectively. They concentrate on the issues which matter most in achieving their – and the company's – objectives.

- The MBO system also acts as a motivator. Individuals are able to track their own performance and measure it against the agreed targets. Theorists such as Herzberg made clear their belief that responsibility is a vital motivator. Peter Drucker believed that the most effective way to give people a sense of responsibility for their working lives was to enable them to decide for themselves how to achieve their objectives.
- At the same time, the targets act as a control mechanism for the organisation. Everyone's performance can be judged against the targets. The potential impact of any variance from these can be identified or anticipated.
- The MBO system should also ensure that employees in every department are all working towards common goals. Without this their efforts may be well intentioned but actually conflict with each other. Attempts by marketing to promote an exclusive image might contradict the attempts of the production department to cut costs by using cheaper packaging. MBO allows delegation to be achieved in a coordinated way.

36.5 Problems of MBO

While the MBO system sounds appealing in theory, in practice it can become bureaucratic and time consuming. Managers and subordinates can spend hours in meetings trying to agree targets which may be unrealistic anyway. There is no point in setting Ryan Giggs the objective of a goal every two games. There are too many factors outside his control to enable him to believe in such a target. Setting targets does not guarantee that they are achieved. In some cases, companies introduce MBO but individual managers are unwilling to delegate fully to their subordinates. This results in frustration as the executive feels they will be held responsible for something they do not fully control.

Another problem is that the objectives can become out of date and inappropriate very quickly. This is especially true if the environment in which the firm operates is changing rapidly. With new competitors, new product offerings, new technology and new legislation the world in which a firm operates can be very dynamic. Targets may soon become irrelevant. Consequently some managers think it is more important to set out the general direction the firm wants to move in. Not try to be too specific about the exact

route. Tying managers down to specific objectives may mean they end up pursuing a target which is inappropriate in a changed environment. Much better, some say, to let managers react for themselves to the situation in which they operate.

TOO MANY TARGETS

In 2002 the National Health Service (NHS) Confederation asked the Government to cut the number of targets it had been set and give managers and doctors the space to deliver its aims. In the same year it was revealed that parts of the NHS had been manipulating waiting lists in order to achieve targets and cut waiting times. The National Audit Office, a government watchdog, found 'pressure to reduce waiting lists has led a significant number of consultants to treat some patients before others with higher clinical priority'. Nine NHS trusts had 'inappropriately adjusted' their waiting lists – 3 of them for 3 years or more – affecting 6,000 patient records. The adjustments varied in seriousness from junior staff following 'established but incorrect' procedures to 'deliberate manipulation or mis-statement' of figures. While in some cases there was little or no impact on patient care, in other cases patients with a serious illness were forced to wait longer for treatment.

36.6 The features of a good objective

A good objective has five main features. It should be:

- Specific – this means it must be clear what the firm is trying to achieve. For example, managers may want to increase sales, increase profit or increase customer satisfaction.
- Measurable – this means that all objectives should include a quantifiable element. For example, the firm might aim to increase profit by 30%. This means that the managers can easily check whether the target has been achieved.
- Agreed – targets need to be agreed by the different people who are involved in the process. There is no point imposing a target on someone. For example, if you were simply told to work harder it is unlikely to have any effect unless you can see the point of it and have a chance to discuss how much additional work you can realistically do.

- Realistic – a target should always be achievable. If you set an objective which cannot be achieved people will not be motivated by it. It may even discourage them because they know the target can never be reached anyway. To work well employees must believe that their efforts can be successful.
- Time specific – all objectives should state quite clearly when they should be achieved. Managers need to know exactly how long they have so that they can plan accordingly.

Imagine you were set an objective of 'increasing sales'. This is a very poor objective. You do not know how long you have to do it or by how much you have to increase sales.

UNILEVER: PATH TO GROWTH

In February 2000 Unilever announced a 5 year strategic plan called 'Path to Growth'. The plan focused on a series of initiatives concentrating on fewer stronger brands to accelerate growth. By 2004 the company is committed to delivering:

- Revenue growth of 5-6% per annum
- Operating profit margins of more than 16% (compared to 11% before the start of Path to Growth)
- Double digit growth of earnings per share

The company has set out to achieve these targets by focusing on its leading brands such as Lipton tea, Dove soap and Hellmann's mayonnaise, and supporting them with an increased marketing budget. At the same time it is selling off its under-performing businesses. For example it has already put up for sale brands such as Elizabeth Arden, Calvin Klein and Karl Lagerfeld, Nautica, Vera Wang, Valentino and Cerruti.

Business IN

ISSUES FOR analysis

- Management by objectives provides a valuable means of coordinating the firm's activities and improving decision making. It is therefore an invaluable way of combatting the diseconomies of scale which can harm the economic performance of large businesses.
- Management by objectives provides a system for managers to review their progress to date and consider how they can contribute to the overall success of the organisation. It can therefore be seen as fundamental to McGregor's ideas on Theory Y leadership, and as a way of implementing Herzberg's desire for job enrichment.
- To work effectively, the targets must be mutually agreed and used as part of a regular appraisal system.

- Management by objectives may restrict managers' efforts; they may focus on the particular targets and not use their initiative.
- Objectives may become out of date quite rapidly in a fast-changing environment. Therefore the business context is an important consideration. For instance, when tackling a business case study you would be most inclined to recommend the use of MBO for a large firm in a relatively stable market.

36.7 Management by objectives
an evaluation

The aim of management by objectives is to coordinate the decisions of all the different parts of the firm. This is needed to bring about a consistent approach and ensure that a workforce of perhaps 50,000 people are all heading in the same direction. It can also form part of a regular appraisal system in which managers and workers meet to review performance and set new targets. However, in recent years MBO has been rejected in many organisations because it can act as a constraint on management thinking. Once certain targets have been set managers may only focus on these areas of their job and may neglect other business opportunities which present themselves. Given the increasing pace of change targets can quickly become out of date, which limits the value of the system.

An even more important issue is that MBO may cause problems to a business with a weak corporate culture. In the 1980s and 1990s, many large financial businesses such as Prudential found severe problems with sales staff. In the pursuit of their sales objectives, the staff had been mis-selling private pension plans to people who would have been better off staying in the state pension scheme. The employees' short-term pursuit of their objectives led the companies into years of bad publicity and very expensive refunds to customers. Management by objectives can give the green light to **short-termist** decision making unless a positive long-term vision is clearly in place.

KEY terms

mission statement – a statement of the firm's overall reason for its existence.

objective – a quantifiable target which helps to coordinate activities.

short-termist – pursuing an objective without considering the longer term impact.

strategy – a plan which shows how to achieve an objective.

AS Level Exercises

A. REVISION QUESTIONS
(30 marks; 50 minutes)

Read the unit, then answer:

1 Explain what is meant by 'management by objectives'. *(3)*
2 Why is it 'not enough to establish objectives'? *(4)*
3 What are the possible advantages of using a management by objectives approach? *(4)*
4 What are the possible disadvantages of using a management by objectives approach? *(4)*
5 Outline three features of an effective objective. *(6)*
6 What is meant by the term 'delegation'. *(3)*
7 Why is delegation an important part of MBO? *(3)*
8 Distinguish between an objective and a mission. *(3)*

B. REVISION EXERCISES

B1 Data Response: British Airways

> Our aim is to provide … customers, whoever they are with the finest service to be found anywhere. We want to offer them the widest choice of fares, of routes and of times of their flights. And because air travel has now become a truly global industry we are determined to forge ever closer links with airlines of like mind throughout the world to deliver together the service our customers desire …
>
> We are a British airline, and proud of it. But that alone is not enough. We have global obligations – to our customers, to our staff in 85 countries, to our shareholders, and to the world itself.
>
> British Airways will fulfil its mission to be the undisputed leader in world travel. We cannot, however, achieve that alone. While boundaries exist on the ground we must join other airlines in other parts of the world in bringing the highest possible standards of safety, style, comfort and service to the people of every nation around the globe.
>
> Source: *British Airways Report and Accounts, 1997–8*

Questions *(30 marks; 35 minutes)*

1 British Airways' mission is 'to be the undisputed leader in world travel'. Why do some firms have mission statements? *(5)*
2 Distinguish between a firm's mission and its objectives. *(3)*
3 Examine two possible influences on a firm's objectives. *(6)*
4 A firm's strategy aims to fulfil its objectives. Outline British Airways' strategy. *(9)*
5 Could British Airways' commitment to its shareholders conflict with its commitment to its staff? Explain your answer. *(7)*

B2 Case Study: George McGarry

George McGarry works as a sales representative for Magnox Computers, a local computer specialist which sells computer networks to companies in Oxford. George has been working there for nearly a year now and is very eager to succeed. Although he enjoys his work he finds that it is not always clear exactly what he should be doing. Obviously his job is to sell the computer systems, but which areas should he be concentrating on? Should he focus on selling more to his existing customers or finding new business? Should he try and sell one or two big orders or try and find more smaller contracts?

Although his boss seems very pleased with him, George is not entirely certain what he is doing! Take last week, for example. George did very few deals, but did manage to make a number of new contacts. His boss was delighted and said that this was good 'for long-term growth'. Only a few months ago, however, George had been criticised for spending too much time on the future and not enough on increasing his weekly sales total. To make matters worse, in his six monthly appraisal he had been given a 20% bonus but he had no idea how this had been calculated.

He had, of course, asked his boss what his targets should be at any given moment. 'It's not as simple as that, George. The messages come down to me from on high and I never know what they're going to be. One month we may want to push a particular product, next month we have hit our overall target and can concentrate on generating new business. Just carry on what you're doing; if there are any problems I'll let you know. There's really no point us sitting down and agreeing long-term targets because they'll only change week to week.'

Questions *(30 marks; 45 minutes)*

1 Analyse the possible gains from introducing management by objectives at Magnox Computers. *(10)*
2 What problems might occur if management by objectives were introduced at Magnox Computers? *(10)*
3 To what extent should firms concentrate on the future rather than the present? *(10)*

C. ESSAY QUESTIONS

1 Bantron plc is a conglomerate which operates in several countries. Despite its rapid growth, Bantron's profitability has been falling. Consider the possible advantages of introducing management by objectives at this time.
2 'In a bureaucratic organisation, management by objectives becomes a checklist. Just another form to be filled in.' How might a business leader make sure that management by objectives becomes a way of driving the business forward?
3 Discuss whether management by objectives is a means of controlling or a means of empowering employees.
4 To what extent is it likely that employees will welcome or resist the introduction of management by objectives within a business?

EMPLOYEE PARTICIPATION AND TEAMWORKING

DEFINITION
Employee participation refers to the extent to which employees are involved in the decision making process. Teamworking means working in a group rather than in isolation, switching tasks as necessary and discussing ways of working more effectively.

37.1 Participation in practice

Before the scientific management revolution, brought in largely by FW Taylor (see Unit 31), most workers set their own pace and method of working. Taylor recommended a top-down approach in which managers would break jobs down into small, repetitive units. Managers would then decide how each job should be done and at what pace. By the 1960s, more and more workers were rebelling against such an imprisoning system. Often by taking industrial action. Far-sighted managements looked for a way to involve staff more in the decision making of the business. This led to interest in ways of achieving employee participation, possibly through **industrial democracy**.

Since then, many managers have come to realise that workers have a tremendous amount to offer in terms of ideas and insight into solving problems. Involving the people who do the work on a daily basis enables managers to learn how the job could be done more effectively. This reveals specific problems faced by the employees in a particular work area.

The importance of managers actually listening to their employees and paying attention to their social needs was highlighted in Mayo's study of the Hawthorne works (see Unit 31). When employees were asked for their opinions their productivity rose, simply because managers were paying them attention and showing that they were valued. Greater participation has been shown to have tangible results in many companies, such as higher motivation, more innovation and lower labour turnover.

There are, of course, problems involved in participation. Involving more people may slow up decisions, although even this can be a good thing. It forces managers to discuss their ideas and listen to employees' comments. This may help to avoid hasty decisions which are then regretted. However, there are some situations, such as a crisis, where a quick decision is important and where any delay may prove damaging. In this situation too much discussion could cause problems.

Participation can also prove frustrating. When people attend a meeting, for example, they often have very different ideas of what they are trying to get out of it. They may well hope to achieve one thing but become irritated when it becomes clear that others are trying to achieve something else. Managers may resent the

PARTNERSHIP

Everyone who works at John Lewis is an owner of the organisation and is called a 'partner'. The fact that partners have a stake in the business means that they have the right to expect managers to explain their decisions to them.

At a store level local managers meet with partners on a regular basis. They provide information on how their part of the business is doing and brief staff on issues concerning the organisation as a whole. Partners have the right to question any decision and receive an explanation. Managers in John Lewis are, therefore, far more accountable to staff than in most other organisations.

At the end of each financial year a percentage of the profits are paid out to each partner. It is often as high as 20% of a partner's annual salary. John Lewis and its sister company Waitrose supermarkets have been successful, growing businesses for many years. This demonstrates that industrial democracy has the potential to be a successful, profitable approach.

Business IN

fact that their ideas are being challenged by workers in meetings and may wish they did not have to discuss things at all. Employees may also be unhappy because they may expect more power than they are actually given. Having become involved in decision making they may well want more information or more control over issues than management is willing to allow.

Participation can also prove costly. Not only are there the costs of actually setting up the consultation, there is also the cost of the work lost while workers are involved in discussions. This does not mean participation should not occur but that managers should weigh up the advantages and disadvantages.

37.2 How do employees participate in decisions?

There are numerous mechanisms to increase the amount of employee participation within a firm. These occur at different levels within the organisation and deal with different types of issues. They include:

- **Quality circles**

  These were originally popular in Japan but were adopted by several UK companies in the 1980s, such as Wedgwood and Unipart. A quality circle is a voluntary group of employees who meet to discuss work-related issues. For example, workers might meet to solve problems of high wastage levels in one part of the factory. Employees are usually paid for their time in meetings and are expected to present their findings to management.

- **Worker directors**

  This form of participation occurs at a very senior level in the organisation. One or two employee representatives are elected by employees to represent them on the company's board of directors. These representatives are allowed to take part in board dicussions and put forward the employees' views. Although this method of representation is quite common in Germany, it is unusual in the UK. Although employees gain an insight into management decision making at a senior level the representatives do not usually have the power to change any decisions.

- **Works councils**

  A **works council** is a committee of employer and employee representatives which meets to discuss companywide issues. Although works councils have worked well in some countries such as Germany they have not been so popular in the UK. However, under European Union legislation larger companies which operate in two or more EU countries must now set up a European works council (covered in more detail in section 37.3). A works council will usually discuss issues such as training, investment

and working practices. It will not cover issues such as pay, which are generally dealt with in discussions with trade union representatives.

- **Autonomous work groups**

  An autonomous work group consists of a team of people who are given a high level of responsibility for their own work. These responsibilities might include the scheduling of the work, decisions over the allocation of their tasks and even the recruitment of new members.

- **Employee shareholders**

  An increasingly common way to develop a common sense of purpose is to give employees shares in the business. For example, employees in Asda have the opportunity to buy a share of the company. This should mean they become more interested in the overall performance of the firm as well their own personal performance.

Other methods of encouraging employee participation include company newsletters, suggestions schemes and a more democratic style of management.

37.3 European works councils

In most European Countries the works council (which consists of elected representatives) is an integral part of employee participation within the firm. It is consulted whenever management plans to do anything which is likely to affect employees, such as changing employment terms and conditions or staffing levels. Up until recently works councils have been very rare in the UK. However, under the EU's Information and Consultation Directive, all employers with more than 50 employees will have to have a works council, whether or not they recognise trade unions. Many UK firms will therefore have to change their approach to employee participation and will have to introduce works councils.

These works councils will have information and consultation rights in relation to company performance and strategic planning. In effect, there must be consultation on any proposed actions by the employer that could affect employees' jobs. Consultation has to be genuine: it must take place in such a way that the works council can influence management's decision. This means employers are going to have to be far more transparent with their workforce when decision-making. The directive also requires employers to 'consult with a view to reaching agreement' on changes in terms and conditions of employment and work organisation – in practice, they are likely to have to negotiate on these matters.

The directive will be introduced in the UK in phases: employers with 150-plus employees will be covered from early 2005, employers with 100-plus employees from early 2007 and employers with 50-plus employees from early 2008. However, given that this approach is so different for most UK companies than their approach at present, it may well be in their interests to start preparing the way now. Some big UK companies have already set up staff consultative committees that meet some of the requirements of the directive. These companies are likely to enjoy a smoother transition when the time comes than those that leave it until the last minute. Employers who act now on a voluntary basis may also be more successful than those who hesitate, because it will show a commitment to consultation.

A road repair gang working successfully as a team (© Life File/Lionel Moss)

EMPLOYEE PARTICIPATION: UNILEVER

Promoting effective dialogue with employees is essential at all times. Our companies use many channels to achieve this. Employees regularly receive workplace briefings, newsletters and electronic bulletins while surveys systematically feed back the views and concerns of employees.

Consultation is widespread and takes many forms. In Canada, the Netherlands and Ghana, for example, formal consultative bodies of a works council type enable employee representatives to meet jointly with management. In 1996 Unilever was one of the first companies to set up a Europe-wide works council. The council provides a framework for the effective exchange of information and consultation of transnational issues in all EU states and Switzerland. Unilever fully respects the right of employees to join trade unions where they wish, and works with unions when they are formed and normally recognised as negotiation partners.

Source: www.unilever.com

37.4 Teamwork

Many organisations now expect employees to undertake their work in teams. This is because they believe that **teamwork** leads to more efficient and effective production. People often respond positively to working with others because this satisfies their social needs. The fact that managers are willing to delegate responsibility to teams also meets employees' ego and self-actualisation needs. Teams also allow individuals to gain from the strengths of others. There may be some areas in which you are relatively weak but someone else is strong, and vice versa. Imagine you are trying to solve a crossword, for example. It is usually much quicker and more fun sharing the task with others. Working in teams also allows individuals to change jobs which can provide some variety at work.

However, some people do not particularly enjoy working in teams. This may be because of their personality. Or because they think their own performance would be better than the other members of the team. They are worried about being dragged down. Teamwork can also bring with it various problems: decision making can be slow and there may be serious disagreements between the members of the group.

In the 1990s the DIY retailer Do It All piloted 'self-managed teamworking' in its Bromsgrove store. Its approach was adapted from the book *Participative Design for Participative Democracy* by Fred and Merrelyn Emery. This book suggested six basic requirements required in a job for people to be productive:

- elbow room for decision making
- opportunity to learn on the job and to go on learning
- variety
- mutual support and respect
- meaningfulness
- a desirable future.

The framework was used by Do It All employees to redesign their jobs in line with the needs they considered of most importance to them. According to the company, staff proved very enthusiastic, so the new approach was rolled out to other stores. Practical examples of the benefits include:

- One employee, who had worked for the previous 15 years as a part-time cashier, had a real interest in plumbing. With the agreement of her colleagues, she switched to working six hours as a cashier and six hours as a maintenance plumber.
- One cashier came up with an idea about how to prevent running out of carrier bags at the till. She was given the budget and additional responsibility for ensuring a smooth supply.

It may never be possible to measure the effect of this programme on the bottom-line profit. A staff attitude survey conducted before and after the changes showed a marked increase in every measure of satisfaction. Labour turnover also fell by 10% over the period. No wonder the company is now introducing self-managed teams into its head office.

SEMCO

Richard Semler is world famous for his belief that people and companies perform best when they are left to themselves without management interference. Semler took over the family business, Semco, from his father and immediately started to dismantle the old structure. Employees were no longer searched when they left the factory; clocking in was ended and then all controls on working hours were removed. Employees wear what they want. One-third of them even set their own salaries. The rest are discussed within business units according to performance. All meetings are open to everyone. There are no receptionists and no secretaries. Managers are elected by their subordinates and their performance is reviewed by subordinates every six months. Those who have not performed satisfactorily will be moved to another position. Management decisions are taken by a 'committee of counsellors'. Even though Semler owns 90% of the company his ideas are often rejected.

Richard Semler recognises that this approach may not be an easy one to imitate (indeed he called his book about the company *Maverick*!). Yet he stresses the need to involve people in decision making to a much greater extent than in the past. According to him, genuine participative management is only possible when managers give up decision making and let employees govern themselves. While other managers watch the Semco approach with interest few have been willing to imitate Semler's ideas. Many are still sceptical about its impact on performance in the long run.

Maverick, by S Semler, Random House, London 2001, and *The End of the Weekend*, Century, 2003

ISSUES FOR analysis

When analysing employee participation within an organisation you might find it useful to consider the following points:

- Approaches to participation, as at Do It All, are all rooted in the theories of Mayo, Maslow and Herzberg. Analysis can be enriched by making and explaining the connections between theory and practice.
- Greater participation by employees may provide the firm with a competitive advantage. It may provide more ideas, greater motivation, greater efficiency and greater commitment from the workforce. This makes change easier, and – in the service sector – has a direct effect upon customer image.
- There is every reason to suppose that employees today need more opportunities for participation; employees are generally better educated and have a higher standard of living and therefore want to be involved to a greater extent.
- Despite this, many researchers argue that since the 1980s many managers have become more authoritarian. Consequently participation may have reduced in many organisations. This is especially true in the public sector, where staff in professions such as medicine or teaching find themselves less involved and less often consulted than in the past.

37.5 Teamworking
an evaluation

Managed effectively, employees can provide better quality and more innovative work at a lower cost and at a faster rate. To achieve such improvements in performance employees must be involved. They must have the ability to contribute and feel they are listened to. Greater participation can help a firm to gain a competitive advantage. This is why managers in all kinds of successful organisations claim that their success is due to their people. However, despite the potential gains from participation this does not mean every manager has embraced the idea. After all, the more that employees participate in decisions, the more that managers have to explain their actions to them. Some managers find this change difficult to cope with.

Participation can also slow up the decision making process and, if handled incorrectly, lead to conflict. Greater participation must be part of a general movement involving greater trust and mutual respect between managers and workers. Employees cannot be expected to participate positively if, at the same time, their conditions and rewards are poor. Successful participation is part of an overall approach in which employees are given responsibility and treated fairly.

Managers must also consider the most effective method and the most appropriate degree of participation for their organisation. This will depend on the culture of the organisation, the pace of change and the attitude and training of both managers and workers. Despite the growth of participation in the UK employee representation is still relatively low. Especially when compared with countries such as Germany where employees are often represented at a senior level. However, although this system appears to work well in Germany this does not necessarily mean it will work as effectively in the UK.

industrial democracy – an industrial democracy occurs when employees have the opportunity to be involved in decision making. In its most extreme form each employee would have a vote.

teamwork – individuals work in groups rather than being given highly specialised, individual jobs.

worker director – an employee representative who is elected to the board of directors.

works council – a committee of management and workers to discuss companywide issues such as training, investment or expansion.

A Level Exercises

A. REVISION QUESTIONS
(40 marks; 70 minutes)

Read the unit, then answer:

1 Explain the possible benefits to a firm of greater employee participation. *(5)*
2 Why do some managers resist greater participation? *(4)*
3 Why do some workers resist greater participation? *(4)*
4 Outline two possible problems of involving employees more in decision making. *(4)*
5 Outline two ways in which employees can be involved in decision making. *(4)*
6 Consider the advantages and disadvantages to a Europe-wide business such as Coca-Cola of the requirement to have a European works council. *(6)*
7 What is meant by an autonomous work group? *(3)*
8 How would teamworking be viewed by:
  a FW Taylor *(5)*
  b Elton Mayo? *(5)*

B. REVISION EXERCISES

B1 Data Response

British Steel's Works Council

> British Steel has decided to set up a consultative works council for its 52,700 employees. British Steel said it wanted to 'build on its strong tradition of consultation' with all its workers.
>
> British Steel has operations in 14 European countries, including the UK. It employs more than 4,000 workers in its Swedish operations, 2,000 in Germany, 700 in Holland and 313 in France. It has a labour force of 44,890 in the UK. The company is proposing a 29-strong works council with 16 representatives from its UK plants, three from Sweden, two from Germany and one each from Holland, France, Finland, Denmark, Ireland, Belgium, Norway and Italy. It will include places for six full-time national trade union officials with five of them from the UK and the others in rotation from recognised unions in the other European countries involved.
>
> The council will meet twice a year to discuss issues such as broad strategy, employment, business reorganisation, health and safety and the environment where these issues have a 'transnational impact'. 'Under no circumstances' will the council become involved in or discuss 'any issues relating to collective bargaining or negotiations within the group undertakings,' said the company.

Questions *(30 marks; 35 minutes)*

1 Distinguish between consultation and negotiation. *(4)*
2 Explain the role of a works council. *(4)*
3 How may British Steel have organised its 'strong tradition of consultation' in the past? *(4)*
4 Analyse the possible gains to British Steel from establishing a works council. *(8)*
5 Consider some of the problems the British Steel works council may face when discussing the issues set out by the management. *(10)*

B2 Exercise

Research into European Works Councils

Use a key word search for 'European works councils' on a web browser such as Yahoo! or on a CD-ROM of *The Financial Times*, *The Guardian* or *The Times*. Identify two articles/case studies that seem interesting. Try to find one that is critical, perhaps written by or about a trade union.

Then write a half-page summary of both articles, followed by a one-page discussion of the value of European works councils to the firms reported on in the articles you read.

B3 Case Study

The Old Hen

'I don't know why I bother,' said Nina Burke, the manageress of the Old Hen pub in Oxford. She had just had one of the weekly staff meetings and all she had heard was one complaint after another. 'They want more money, they want shorter working hours, they want free food, they don't like the T-shirts they have to wear, they don't like the shift arrangements. Honestly, I don't know why any of them even turn up to work, the amount they complain. They even seem to resent being asked for their ideas,' said Nina to her husband.

Nina began to wonder whether she was running these meetings effectively. The previous landlord had never really held staff meetings and had certainly not asked employees for their opinions. When she took over, he had said: 'Half of them will be moving on to new jobs anyway within a few weeks or are just doing this as a part-time job, so what's the point? Tell them what to do and then make sure they get on with it.' Nina began to think he may be right although she had been very enthusiastic when she first had the idea.

She had noticed that staff in this pub seemed to leave very frequently and were generally pretty miserable. They seemed much less motivated than at her previous pub (where she was deputy manager). The money was not good but no worse than anywhere else. She decided it must be because they were not involved in decision making at all. In her last job everyone had felt able to give an opinion (even if their ideas were then ignored!) and were often asked what they thought about how the pub was run. It was a good atmosphere and Nina had enjoyed working there. She hoped she could recreate the same feeling here but was losing confidence that it would ever be possible.

Questions *(40 marks; 60 minutes)*

1 How might Nina's experience at the Old Hen be explained by:
   a a Theory X manager
   b a Theory Y manager. *(10)*
2 Consider whether Nina is right to try and introduce greater employee participation at the Old Hen. *(10)*
3 According to many motivational theorists, employees should respond positively to greater participation. Discuss the possible reasons why Nina's schemes seem ineffective. *(10)*
4 An increasing number of managers claim to be encouraging employee participation. Consider why greater participation might be regarded as particularly valuable today. *(10)*

C. ESSAY QUESTIONS

1 'Greater competitiveness and higher profits in the future will depend upon much more employee participation than in the past.' Critically assess this statement.
2 'Managers are appointed to make decisions. Workers are hired to do the job they are told. Employee participation simply wastes time and money.' Critically assess this view.
3 'Teamwork brings with it more problems than benefits.' Discuss.
4 The European Works Council Directive will force reluctant firms to start works councils for the first time. Discuss the likelihood of success in these circumstances.

TRADE UNIONS

DEFINITION

A trade union is an organisation which employees join to gain greater power and security at work. Union membership can provide greater influence collectively in relations with employers than workers have as separate individuals.

Trade unions have a long history. Their size and influence have declined in the last 20 years but they are still important. Their role has perhaps developed away from confrontation towards cooperation with managers and conflict resolution.

38.1 Introduction

Many people today assume that trade unions belong to the past. In fact they are the biggest membership organisations in the country, and fulfil an important role in protecting the interests of staff against poor employers. The main types of trade union which have developed are shown in the table below.

White-collar unions have shown the greatest growth recently. With new technology, there are fewer semi-skilled production workers to join general unions. The white-collar unions have grown as more and more jobs have been created in services such as healthcare, social work and financial services. The new pattern of union membership reflects the changes in the economy as a whole. See the box below.

Trade unions in the news

A search on the ft.com website produced the following cross-section of headlines about trade unions, during autumn 2002. They demonstrate that unions are involved in a wide variety of different issues.

'*TGWU leader steps in to avert crippling airports strike.*'

'*Unions support fire strike with cash donations.*'

'*Firefighters and employers likely to meet face to face next week.*'

'*Collision prompts fresh look at safety.*'

'*Union protest at "pension robbery".*'

38.2 Functions of trade unions

Unionism grew up to enable employees to counterbalance the economic, social and political power of large and influential employers. Traditionally, unions concerned themselves solely with obtaining satisfactory rates of pay for a fair amount of work in reasonable and safe working conditions. Today the most important aspect of the work of a trade union is protecting workers' rights under the law. Far more time is spent on health and safety, on discrimination and bullying, on unfair dismissal and other legal matters than on pay negotiations.

Types of trade union

TYPE OF UNION	MEMBERS	EXAMPLE
Craft or skill unions	Set up to represent skilled employees. The oldest unions, with origins in the skilled crafts of the middle ages, for example stonemasons	National Union of Journalists (NUJ)
Industrial unions	These represent the members of one particular industry. Often, not necessarily, this includes different skills	Fire Brigades Union (FBU)
General unions	These unions recruit members from all industries and types of employer, and across the whole range of skills and types of work	The General Municipal Boilermakers and Allied Trade Union (GMB)
White-collar unions	These unions attract members who tend to be office rather than direct manufacturing production workers, hence 'white-collar' rather than the 'blue-collar' of the traditional stereotype of the factory worker	The National Union of Teachers (NUT); Banking Insurance and Finance Union (BIFU)

38.3 Types of industrial action by trade unions

Trade unions very rarely call on their members to vote for industrial action. This is because most members have no wish to take action that will cut their own pay, and may jeopardise their job security. In the past 10 years, far fewer working days have been lost to industrial action than to absenteeism or stress. It is important to bear in mind, therefore, that although unions have the following powers, they only tend to use them if the workforce has a substantial grievance. Furthermore such actions are only lawful if they have been put to a secret ballot of the membership, and a majority have said yes. The various types of industrial action taken by trade unions are as follows:

- **Go slow**

  The workforce keeps on working but at the absolute minimum pace to avoid being subject to legitimate disciplinary action.

- **Picketing**

  Workers taking industrial action might stand at the entrance to the venue of the dispute and demonstrate by means of banners or words to other workers not to cross the picket line, i.e. go to work. The 1980s' legislation restricted a picket line to six workers.

- **Strike**

  The workforce simply fails to report for work.

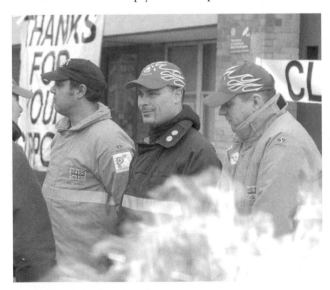

The Fire Service's pay strikes of 2003
Courtesy of the Kent and Sussex Courier

- **Work to rule**

  The workforce applies the employer's own rules and procedures 'to the letter'. An example would be a train driver who insisted on following the checking procedure in the driver's manual before taking the train out of the station. The driver could not be criticised but would inevitably delay or cancel the train.

38.4 Decline in union influence

The election of a new Conservative administration in 1979 heralded a period of dramatic decline in trade union power and influence. The Conservatives were committed to reducing trade union power as part of a process of liberalising the economy. Barriers and restrictions in the labour market were to be broken down, and employers given a freer hand. They aimed for low inflation, abandoning the target of full employment. Thus indirectly weakening the unions' position.

38.5 Union legislation

During the 1980s and 1990s the Conservative government sought to reduce union influence. There were six major acts of parliament, each progressively restraining union ability to take action. The 'closed shop' was abolished so that a union could no longer require an organisation to employ only members of one union, or require individuals to join that union. The legal immunity of a trade union was removed. This meant that a business suffering losses from illegal strike action could sue the union. The huge financial costs soon put a stop to secondary picketing. It became more difficult to organise a strike in such a way as to be legally protected. The management of trade unions became more open and subject to members' influence and control. The main elements of trade union reform are shown in the table at the top of the next page.

38.6 Trade unions today

By the end of the 1980s trade unions had changed dramatically. Trade union membership had fallen from 13 million in 1979 to 7 million in 2002. Of these 7 million, women made up an increasing proportion, in 2002 just over half. Government forecasts suggest the labour force will expand by 1.2 million by 2006. Of these about 900,000 will be women. However, trade unions are finding it hard to recruit both women and the young in the job areas likely to expand such as business services, hotels and catering. Furthermore the Labour administration elected in May 1997 has so far given little indication that it intends to repeal recent union legislation or involve trade unions in policy in the manner of previous Labour governments.

Trade unions have therefore changed substantially. There are many possible reasons for this, in addition to the anti-union legislation in the 1980s. Some of these are given below.

POSSIBLE REASONS FOR UNION CHANGE

- The lack of government commitment to full employment and the reliance on market forces have meant that the full economic cost of union activity has fallen more directly on employers and their

Union legislation in the 1980s and 1990s

Employment Act 1980	• *Employers no longer obliged to recognise or negotiate with a particular trade union or unions* • *Picketing restricted to own place of work and illegal if elsewhere, so that the employer could take civil legal action against secondary picketing* • *Secondary action limited to a direct supplier or customer* • *New 'closed shops' permitted only if 80% of workforce voted in favour in a secret ballot*
Employment Act 1982	• *'Closed shops' could now exist only if there was an 85% secret ballot in favour* • *Removal of trade union immunity from civil action for damages by employer if trade union authorises an unlawful industrial action*
Trade Union Act 1984	• *Trade union now liable if it authorises industrial action without a secret ballot and can be sued by employer*
Employment Act 1988	• *Trade unions must now elect voting members of their governing executive every 5 years* • *Protects union members against being disciplined by the union if they ignore a strike call or refuse to picket, even after a ballot in favour of industrial action*
Employment Act 1990	• *Now unlawful for an employer to refuse to employ a non-union member, putting an end to the 'closed shop'* • *All remaining forms of secondary picketing unlawful* • *Trade unions now liable for virtually any industrial action by members* • *Employers can now dismiss any worker taking part in an unofficial strike without the employee having the right to complain to an industrial tribunal for unfair dismissal*
Trade Union Reform and Employment Rights Act 1993	• *Trade unions to give employers 7 days' notice of official action* • *Creates a new 'citizen's right' to restrain unlawfully organised industrial action, making unofficial strikes harder to undertake* • *Abolishes the remaining wages councils and their statutory minimum pay rates*
Employment Relations Act 1999	• *Provides a legal right to trade union recognition at the workplace, where there is clear support among the workforce; if 50% or more of the workforce belong to a union, recognition must be given by the employer* • *Provided the legal right to 3 months' leave for mothers and fathers when a baby is born*
Human Rights Act 2000	• *This forces all courts in Britain to take into account European Law on Human Rights. Unions have been able to use this to press the case for the ending of age discrimination at work.*

employees. Employers have been keener to resist union pressure and ultimately more willing to shed labour if necessary.

• The UK's membership of the European Union and free trade globally – freer movement of labour, goods, services and business investment – has meant UK businesses have had to resist cost-push pressures. Competition is too powerful to allow firms to agree to uneconomic pay rises.

• The increasing importance of inward investment from European, American and Asian businesses has meant a new management attitude towards unions and the establishment of single-union and no-strike arrangements. Unions such as the electricians (EEPTU) led the way in adopting these. The unions know they have been necessary to bring investment and jobs to this country. Bidding for inward investment has helped bring about a new understanding between employers, unions and government; a sense of shared interest and a common goal.

• The realisation that international competitiveness in cost and quality are the key to future success and jobs – unions have been more willing to embrace change and the new technology and training which go with it. The new workforce needs to be educated and trained. Unions have realised this issue has become important for their members, as pay differentials once were. Without retraining, workers become unemployable when circumstances change. The trade unions have realised the need to reinvent themselves and to be more active in recruitment.

38.7 Union recognition

'Recognition' is fundamental to the legal position of a trade union. In other words, management must recognise a union's right to bargain on behalf of its members. Without management recognition, any actions taken by a union are illegal. This would leave the union open to being sued. For most of the 1990s, even if all staff joined a union, the management did not have to recognise it. Why, then, would any company bother to recognise a union?

- Generally it can be helpful for managers to have a small representative group to consult and negotiate with. **Collective bargaining** removes the need to bargain with every employee individually. Doubtless, every Premiership football manager would prefer that system.

BLUE CIRCLE MOTIVATES UNIONISTS

Recently Blue Circle Cement took a decisive step towards the long-term motivation of its workforce. It struck a deal with its three trade unions ensuring job security and guaranteed pay rises in exchange for increased efficiency and flexibility. The deal covered more than 1,800 staff. The company's lorry drivers would be trained to carry out routine vehicle maintenance. Forklift truck drivers would help out on the cement production line. The details of the agreement were:

What's in it for the company?
- Flexible working
- New technology brought in
- Modest pay increases
- Employees to minimise costs
- Security should help build self-motivation

What's in it for the employees?
- No compulsory redundancies
- NVQ-based training programme
- End to clocking on – all staff to be salaried
- Pay rises agreed to cover next 2 to 5 years
- Drivers' working week cut by an hour

John Gibbons, Blue Circle's human resources manager, said: 'We want the commitment and motivation without the fear. No-one is going to buy into flexible working, increased productivity or training if they think we are just going to cut the head count.'

Business IN

- It may ease cases of possible difficulty, such as relocation, retraining for new technology, downsizing and redundancy, renegotiation of employment conditions and contracts. Trade union officials can be consulted at an early stage about causes, procedure and objectives. This at least may give the workforce the confidence that management are acting properly and thoughtfully. It also gives the opportunity for the trade union to offer advice or objection at an early stage. It promotes consultation, not conflict.
- Trade unions provide a channel of upward communication which has not been filtered by middle managers. Senior managers can expect straight talking about worker opinions or grievances.

The industrial relations climate has changed from militancy and conflict towards an awareness of mutual interest, as recognised in the **TUC's** own words 'an employment charter for a world class Britain'. Therefore employers have become more ready to recognise a trade union at the workplace for positive management reasons.

One reason is to get away from the old multi-union problem where recognition of too many unions at one plant led to confusion, poor communication, rivalry and mistrust between unions competing with each other. An immediate example is the setting up of a new plant, particularly by a company new to an area, perhaps a multinational making a major investment. Here, the company may wish to sign an agreement with one union, perhaps trading a 'no-strike' agreement for single-union status and guarantees as to involvement and consultation.

38.8 Resolving disputes and the role of ACAS

'ACAS' stands for Advisory, Conciliation and Arbitration Service. Founded in 1975, the mission statement of ACAS is:

> *To improve the performance and effectiveness of organisations by providing an independent and impartial service to prevent and resolve disputes and to build harmonious relationships at work.*

ACAS seeks to:

- prevent and resolve employment disputes
- conciliate in actual or potential complaints to industrial tribunals
- provide information and advice
- promote good practice.

ACAS can be used by employers and employees to help them work together to resolve industrial relations disputes before they develop into confrontation. Where there is a collective dispute between management and workforce, either or both may contact ACAS. Before acting, ACAS will want to see that union officials are involved and that the organisation's disputes procedure has been followed. ACAS can also be used to offer conciliation to the parties in a dispute, assuming their own procedures have been exhausted, to avoid damaging industrial action. Such conciliation is entirely voluntary and ACAS has no powers to impose a settlement.

If conciliation is unsuccessful, ACAS can offer arbitration, by providing an independent arbitrator who can examine the case for each side and then judge the right outcome to the dispute. If both sides agree in advance, the arbitrator's decision can be legally binding on both sides. Occasionally, ACAS is asked to provide a mediator who can act as an intermediary suggesting the basis for further discussion.

ACAS is also a great source of advice and operates a number of information centres which can deal with queries on virtually all employment law matters. This service is free of charge.

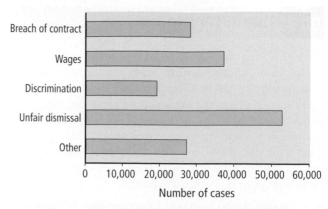

Figure 38.1 Tribunal cases received by ACAS 2002

REBUILDING THE UNIONS

Recently, trade unions embarked on a new initiative to build membership. Over 1,000 young people applied to be the first students at the Trade Union Congress 'Organising Academy'. Under 40 were selected for training to become a new, dynamic force to help rebuild the union movement after 20 years of decline. The key skills are those needed for face-to-face recruitment and building trade union self-sufficiency and confidence at work.

Two-thirds of the trainees in the TUC's academy are women and most are aged 20–30. Most training is on the job. Seven weeks are spent in the classroom at the TUC's National Education Centre.

After six months the trainees are let loose on more ground-breaking work. Six (including three women) are working with the ISTC (iron and steel union) to recruit workers in an anti-union company with a large female workforce. Other projects include low paid shop and hotel workers, research scientists and technicians, and staff working for temping agencies or subcontracting companies.

The injection of new blood and a new organising spirit is what the TUC and its unions are after. To win the arguments they want people who look and sound like the generation they are in danger of losing.

Source: Adapted from the *Guardian*

Business IN

38.9 Unionism: shifting emphasis from collective to individual

Trade unions are now training specialists to recruit for them, often women as they feel that women have better listening skills. People no longer join simply because it is the thing to do. Trade unions now emphasise that they are interested in solving the problems of individual members. For example, individual employment disputes about equal opportunity, redundancy, promotion or training opportunities.

ISSUES FOR **analysis**

Trade unions are no longer a political force and it seems unlikely that they will regain great influence. Consideration of the role of trade unions is likely to arise in individual circumstances such as in case studies or essays about individual businesses. Where a business is contemplating development, for example, investment or change of working practices, trade unions are likely to have a significant role. Key issues are likely to be:

- The net advantages to the employer of union recognition.
- Can consultation and negotiation with a trade union be used to mutual advantage to prevent or solve conflict?
- The extent to which the role and power of unions within a specific workplace is a function of management attitudes and traditions. McGregor's Theories X and Y provide a useful model to analyse why conflict may be normal in one workplace, but unusual in another.
- How can successful and creative management turn the potential threat of trade union representation to a positive opportunity to the business in achieving its objectives in the collective interest?

38.10 Trade unions
an evaluation

Trade unions have evolved considerably in the last 200 years and have probably changed more in the last 20 years than ever before. Their long-term existence has been questioned. They are nothing if not adaptable and have set out to change their image, attracting new members from the newly educated and skilled workforce, particularly its increasing part-time and female sections. Trade unions have to strive to make themselves relevant and appeal to potential members. As with other parts of the business world, unions must work to create healthy demand for the service they provide (and charge for). Undoubtedly they will survive. They certainly have roles to play:

- in maintaining power at work to counterbalance the ownership, economic and legal power of the employers
- to provide individuals with the means to take action when they feel unfairly treated, and
- as the lone voice for the many less skilled workers who might be open to unfair treatment in low paid, part-time and casual occupations in the newly fragmented labour market.

KEY terms

collective bargaining – the process whereby trade unions gain strength through combining. A trade union or unions might represent all the workforce at one plant and negotiate with management on their behalf. Collective bargaining usually focuses on wage rates and terms and conditions of employment.

legal immunities – if acting in furtherance of a trade dispute, a trade union's own funds and property were immune against legal action by an employer who might have suffered loss because of a strike. This was abolished in the early 1980s.

TUC (Trades Union Congress) – the holding organisation to which most British unions belong. It represents unions in discussions with government, employers' organisations and the European Union.

38.11 Workbook

A Level Exercises

A. REVISION QUESTIONS
(45 marks; 80 minutes)

Read the unit, then answer:

1 Why might trade unions be seen as necessary in a modern economy? *(4)*
2 Explain the main functions of trade unions in industrial relations and the economy today. Which functions are the most important today and why? *(8)*
3 Outline three important sources of trade union power. *(6)*
4 Which of the changes in trade union law set out in the table would you consider the most important, and why? *(6)*
5 Explain the ways in which union membership differs today from 1979. *(5)*
6 Why is it so important to a union to gain recognition from employers? *(4)*
7 Outline the role of ACAS. Is ACAS a successful institution? *(7)*
8 How has the growth in international competition affected trade unionism in the UK? *(5)*

B. REVISION EXERCISES

B1 Data Response

Research Evidence on Union Activity and Attitudes
The 1998 Workplace Employee Relations Survey revealed a great deal about the status of trade unions today. Look at the table of data at the top of the next page, then answer the questions.

Questions *(30 marks; 35 minutes)*
1 Explain the meaning of the term 'union recognition'. *(3)*
2 Why may a higher proportion of workers in large organisations be trade union members? *(6)*
3 Where managers are not in favour of unions, only 7% of workers are members.
  a Why may this be the case? *(3)*
  b What might a union representative do to encourage managers to favour trade unions? *(6)*
4 Union recognition has been granted in 45% of workplaces. What benefits would management hope to gain by granting union recognition? *(6)*
5 In 47% of workplaces there are no union members at all – a substantial change from 36% in 1990. Outline three possible reasons for this change over time. *(6)*

	Union Density	Any Union Members	Union Recognition
	% of employees who are members	% of workplaces	% of workplaces
Workplace size			
25 to 49 employees	23	46	39
50 to 99 employees	27	52	41
100 to 199 employees	32	66	57
200 to 499 employees	38	77	67
500 or more employees	48	86	78
Management views on union membership			
In favour	62	98	94
Neutral/not an issue	23	40	29
Not in favour	7	16	9
All workplaces	36	53	45

Base· all workplaces with 25 or more employees.
Figures are weighted and based on responses from 1,889 managers

B2 Case Study

Trade Union Membership and Recruitment

The TUC has launched a £1.5 million 'new unionism' project to revive flagging union recruitment. The 'Organising Academy', set up to train union organisers, is the flagship of the project.

'Organising' is the watchword for the unions at the moment and organisers are what all union officials must become in the twenty-first century if unions are to survive. While recognising that getting people to join unions now is not easy, the TUC is very happy with the high quality of the new recruits. The skills needed by the new organisers are those of face-to face recruitment and building trade union self-sufficiency and confidence.

Most trainees on similar USA and Australian courses are graduates. Two-thirds of the UK trainee organisers are women and most are in their 20s. Most training is on-the-job although seven weeks are spent at the TUC National Education Centre. The recruiting in the UK is done in a more friendly environment than in the union-busting atmosphere of the USA. In many UK companies, however, even where unions are recognised, union activity has been low and workplace representation has suffered after years of neglect.

After six months of training, the 'organisers' are let loose. Six trainees, including three women, are sent to work with the ISTC, the iron and steel union, to work in an anti-union company with a large female workforce, to boost recruitment. Other projects will include low-paid shop workers and hotel workers, research scientists and technicians in pharmaceuticals, dispersed workers in the non-profit and voluntary sectors, and staff working for agencies or subcontracting companies.

The new trainees feel that many young people do not know the functions of trade unions. Not all the trainees have experience of unions, though they are all enthusiastic. It remains to be seen how the new organisers will fit alongside traditional unionism.

Source: Adapted from the *Guardian*, 24/1/98

Questions (30 marks; 40 minutes)

1 Why do you think trade union officials have got to become 'organisers' if unions are to survive? (8)
2 How does the case study demonstrate how union membership has changed since 1979? (6)
3 How has the role and type of trade union official evolved and why? (6)
4 Explain the case you would put to a steel worker to persuade him or her to join a union. (10)

B3 Case Study

Unrest at Rover

Walter Hasselkus, the chairman of Rover, resigned in 1998, taking responsibility for the poor performance of Rover, now owned by BMW. The huge losses at Rover caused rifts on the BMW board and depressed BMW's share price. Productivity at Rover plants in the UK was reckoned to be 30% below that in BMW plants in Germany. This led to the negotiation with British trade unions of a new agreement aimed at saving £150 million per year.

The agreement meant a new pay and working time agreement involving a 4-day, 35-hour, working week and a voluntary redundancy programme to reduce employment by 2,500 jobs. The redundancies were expected to cost £70 or £80 million, depending on the take-up. Quickly 3,000 enquiries were received from Rover workers.

Tony Woodley, negotiator for the TGWU, hailed the deal as the best chance to save 14,000 jobs at Longbridge and 50,000 in and around the West Midlands. Larry Brooke of the MSF union said that serious thought had been given to closing Longbridge and that there was the chance of government aid.

The Longbridge plant would benefit from a £400 million investment in the new Mini, part of a £2 billion overall investment by BMW in the Rover business. The BMW chairman would not reveal plans for the new medium-range Rover car, expected to be built at Longbridge. Analysts felt that BMW was dangling the carrot of new investment hoping to attract government aid.

Rover bosses were booed and heckled by the workforce when they explained details of the rescue package for Longbridge by BMW. They were condemned for letting Rover get into its present parlous state of near-bankruptcy, with 50,000 jobs at stake. Tony Woodley of the TGWU urged workers to support the agreement between the union leaders and BMW, aimed at saving £150 million per year at a cost of 2,500 jobs. He told them that a vote against would give power to those directors on the BMW board who were hostile to Rover. He thought that a 'no' vote would lead to the closure of Longbridge and the end of Rover. Woodley supported the current chairman of BMW, Bernd Pischetsrieder, who was in favour of supporting Rover and taking the longer term view. Despite having their backs to the wall, some of the workers said that they might vote against purely to register their protest.

Source: Adapted from *The Times*, 3, 4 and 11/12/98

Questions *(40 marks; 60 minutes)*

1 Consider the evidence of weaknesses in the unions' negotiating position in dealing with BMW and Rover. *(10)*
2 Evaluate the role of Tony Woodley in these negotiations. *(10)*
3 What might the union have done in the years leading up to these events, to attempt to prevent them occurring in the first place? *(8)*
4 What might be the key elements in the 'longer term view' for both the trade unions involved and BMW/Rover? *(12)*

C. ESSAY QUESTIONS

1 'Strikes or industrial action should be avoided at all costs as they ultimately do nothing to help the workforce.' Discuss
2 'Anti-union legislation removed barriers to the free market and led directly to improved economic performance.' To what extent do you agree with this statement?
3 'Good managers welcome trade unions as a way of improving workplace performance.' Discuss.

FLEXIBILITY AND INSECURITY

DEFINITION
Flexibility is the ability and the willingness of a firm to change its operations in response to changing circumstances. Desirable though this is, it can lead to workforce insecurity: feelings of uncertainty resulting from working in continuously changing circumstances.

39.1 Flexibility

Flexibility is a common aim in modern business. It is seen as important for three main reasons:

- the modern marketplace is changing constantly, and businesses must be in a position to respond quickly to these changes if they are to remain competitive
- consumers are more likely to demand personal attention and customised products, so firms must be able to change their operations to meet the differences in demand
- competitive pressures have forced firms to look for flexibility in seasonal production; modern car workers are expected to work longer hours in the early summer and in mid-winter than at other times to respond to the September and March sales peaks.

Many of the businesses that have achieved major success over the last decade have shown the ability to transform themselves and take advantage of new opportunities. Examples include:

- *Direct Line – easy-to-use telephone insurance*
- *Microsoft – at the forefront of developments in home computing*
- *CNN – satellite television*
- *Nintendo – electronic games.*

In order to meet these demands, firms aim to achieve **flexible specialisation**. This is a situation where firms are able to produce specialised products flexibly. The key factors allowing a firm to achieve flexible specialisation are:

- rapid reprogramming of machinery
- production of batches of similar items
- a multi-skilled workforce that can adapt quickly to changing demands.

The adoption of flexible specialisation by British firms has meant that firms and workers have had to undergo a change of culture. The dominant feelings up to the 1990s were that:

- workers' tasks were clearly demarcated, so that they did only their job, and nothing else
- products were mass produced in an identical fashion
- customers bought the products that were available, rather than dictated what manufacturers should produce.

It is the process of changing to the less familiar flexible specialisation that has led to some of the problems of insecurity associated with modern businesses.

39.2 How firms achieve flexibility

Firms aiming to achieve flexible specialisation have to adopt new ways of working. These new methods include:

- flexible working – creating a workforce that can adapt to changing circumstances
- flexible structures – adopting a structure for the business which allows the firm to change rapidly to a differing environment
- flexible operations – taking decisions as to how the business will run so that new demands can be met rapidly.

FLEXIBLE WORKING

Flexible working means that workers are flexible in their attitudes and abilities at work, and are able to change quickly from one task to another.

In the past, British firms were often characterised by a lack of flexibility. The main causes of this inflexibility were that:

- mass production required low cost, semi-skilled labour to be able to work quickly at the same repetitive task; switching jobs would slow people down
- workers had been trained in only one task or area, and could undertake only one set of tasks for the firm

- managers employed staff to do just one task and workers found this a useful source of job security. No-one else was as efficient as themselves at that one task.

More recently, businesses have attempted to overcome the problems of inflexibility by producing a workforce that is both willing and able to undertake a variety of tasks at work. This allows the firm to respond quickly to changes in the working environment and remain competitive both at home and abroad. Changing staff attitudes has often been difficult, however. Anything that threatens an employee's job security is likely to be treated with hostility. Rover Cars overcame this problem by signing an agreement with staff and trade unions promising that, in return for flexible working, the company would give staff a lifetime job guarantee.

Flexible working has been achieved by British firms using a combination of three ideas:

- Flexible work patterns – it is fairly common for firms to use a system of 'flexitime' by which workers have some element of control over when they work. There will normally be a **core** time, when all workers must be present, but around this there will be a degree of flexibility. When deadlines are pressing, or large orders are building up, workers can put in extra flexitime to cope with the work, and then in return put in fewer hours when work is more slack. Leyland Trucks have taken the idea one step further, and use 'additional vacation days' which operate as extra holidays, to repay its workers who have had to put in extra hours to meet pressing deadlines.

- Training the workforce in a variety of skills – this allows the firm as a whole to be more responsive to changes in demand from consumers. Workers can cover for absent colleagues when necessary to keep production going. They are able to adapt to new tools or new technology quickly, allowing the firm to change its products more easily.

- Changing work cultures – one consequence of the additional training is that workers often feel more loyalty and a greater sense of belonging to the firm. Job enrichment itself is often a motivator to workers, and the reorganisation of work to empower workers and to give them greater responsibility at work will also have a strong motivational effect. Taken together, these factors can produce a workforce committed to the aims of the firm, and therefore willing to adapt to changing circumstances.

FLEXIBLE BUSINESS STRUCTURES

The flexible firm is able to change its own structure in response to changing needs. This means creating a structure that allows quick changes to take place. In order to achieve this, firms have tended to identify a core, which forms the basis for all its operations, and a **periphery**, which consists of all the other tasks needed to run the firm, but which are not central to the business.

For a firm producing household goods such as washing machines, core workers might comprise designers, the market research team and workers on the production line, amongst others. The canteen and cleaning staff, and even advertising campaign staff, may be seen as being less central to the firm, and so may be employed on a part-time basis, or even brought in at specific times to undertake a specific task.

CORE WORKERS	PERIPHERY WORKERS
Full-time employees	Part-time, temporary or self-employed
Do tasks central to the business	Perform less critical, or less permanent tasks
Secure jobs	Insecure jobs
Committed to the firm's goals	Committed to self-interest

The benefit of being a flexible firm, of course, is that the periphery can be increased quickly when needed to meet a particular change in the market-place.

In his book *The Age Of Unreason*, Professor Charles Handy (see Unit 44) suggested that instead of firms comprising two elements, the core and periphery, there were actually three parts to modern firms. He called this idea 'the **shamrock organisation**', as illustrated in Figure 39.1. The first leaf of the shamrock represents the professional core made up of qualified professionals, technicians and managers. The second leaf, called the contractual fringe, is for the work that has been contracted out to someone else because it is not central to the firm. Professor Handy notes that many firms that used to be manufacturers now do little more than assemble parts bought in from suppliers. As much as 80% of a firm's work may be done outside the business itself. The third and final leaf is the flexible labour force, made up of temporary and part-time workers. In effect, Handy has split the periphery into an internal periphery (the flexible labour force) and an external periphery (the contractual fringe).

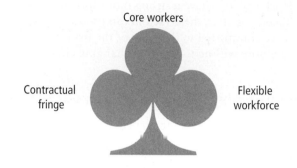

Figure 39.1 Handy's shamrock organisation

FLEXIBLE OPERATIONS

A flexible approach to operations would allow a firm to respond rapidly to changes in its environment. The 1980s and early 1990s saw a range of ideas being adopted by firms, following perceived good practice from abroad.

The key idea being followed was to reduce the size of the business's core, and increase the use of flexible, temporary contract workers, as in Figure 39.2. One way to achieve this is to **contract out** work, often called outsourcing. Outsourcing is when a firm uses sources outside the business to undertake functions that used to be done internally by a section of the business itself. Tasks such as designing new products or undertaking market research can be bought in by the firm as and when it is needed.

Linked to this very closely is the American idea of **downsizing**. This means reducing the size of the firm in an effort to make it more responsive to the marketplace. Theorists who support the idea of downsizing

suggest the benefits of growing larger (economies of scale) are outweighed by the problems large size cause for the control and management of the business, and its communications.

Downsizing is aimed particularly at reducing many of the administrative tasks and office functions traditionally carried out by employees of the business. Instead, these tasks can be contracted out to agencies, and can in theory be increased or decreased in size at very short notice without the need for expensive recruitment processes. This can often be done on a short-term basis if necessary. This ought to make the firm more able to respond quickly to changes in the opportunities available to it, or the threats it faces.

An important debate surrounding the ideas of downsizing and outsourcing concerns a firm's needs for focus. 'Focus' is used to remind managers that their business will have particular strengths and competitive advantages, and that they should concentrate on these areas. The strength of Richard Branson's Virgin Group, for example, was its youthful, enterprising outlook. This started to look more like greedy empire-building when Virgin launched itself into the vodka, the cola, the financial services and the railway businesses.

Outsourcing is seen as a means to achieving focus, as the firm itself undertakes the tasks at which it has a particular specialism. The other functions are bought in from other businesses or individuals who have the skills required by the business.

The flexible firm

Advantages:
- *Quicker response to market changes*
- *More efficient use of resources*
- *Cheaper operations*
- *More use of specialists*

Problems:
- *Requires culture changes*
- *Reliant on factors outside direct control*
- *Possible lack of motivation*
- *Lack of expansion possibilities*
- *Effect on the existing workforce*

39.3 Insecurity

A growing concern with the policies used to achieve flexibility is the effect it has on the workforce. Change is often instinctively resisted by people. It carries with it uncertainty and the unknown. However, the changes being brought by flexible business practices are seen as having a wide-ranging effect on people's working lives, and can carry with them particular threats. However, they will also give individuals new opportunities if they are willing and able to take advantage of them.

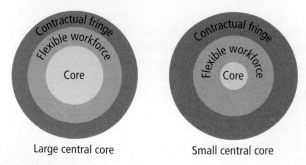

Figure 39.2 The shrinking core

Flexible working

The problems caused to workers are:
- *Redundancy*
- *Constant training*
- *Lack of job security*

The opportunities for workers are:
- *New challenges*
- *Increased self-reliance*
- *Diverse career paths*
- *Learning new skills*

JOB INSECURITY

A TUC report has found that job insecurity in the UK was second only to South Korea. A massive 41% of UK workers were reported to be concerned about the security of their jobs.

The TUC identified domestic factors such as the economic cycle and employment legislation as key factors in determining insecurity. In particular, the stronger employment laws elsewhere in Europe made British job insecurity more understandable.

There were large differences between comparable countries. Other countries with large rates of insecurity, like South Korea and Japan, have been experiencing economic problems while the UK has been relatively prosperous.

The report concludes that the level of insecurity can only be due to a combination of the differences in employment rights, culture and comparative economic performance.

Source: *Express on Sunday*, 23/6/02

THREATS

Human beings instinctively fear change. People are creatures of habit, who feel most at ease when faced with a comfortable routine. The workplace was felt by many to be an area where consistency could be achieved. A career was interrupted only occasionally by change in the form of a promotion or a move to a different firm. One of the features of a good job was generally thought to be a 'job for life'.

As industry has changed, and particularly with the recent drive towards flexible firms, these accepted ideas have been greatly challenged. In fact, it could be said that change will be the only constant in a worker's career.

This constant change brings with it several consequences:

Redundancy: Motivational theories from Mayo's Hawthorne experiments to Maslow's hierarchy (see Unit 31) have stressed the need for workers to feel valued and needed. With many businesses following the path of downsizing, there is a greater chance of workers being made redundant. Indeed, if the trend were to continue, workers may face the prospect of being out of work several times during their working life.

Lack of job security: A lack of job security can be crippling to workers who have been brought up to see the traditional pattern of a job for life with a particular company. How can a worker plan to buy a house, for example, with a 25-year mortgage if he or she can only rely on two or three years' work at a time? What about family life, if one partner needs to move to a different location in search of new job opportunities, or the schooling of children?

Constant training: In order to find employment in a changing industrial scene, workers will have to be constantly upgrading their skills or learning new ones. Traditionally, training and education has been seen as being for young people only. Training later in life can be seen as losing valuable time, or will often be approached in a cynical way, especially if the training has no obvious direct application in the workplace. In response, the Government has appointed a minister for **lifelong learning**. Education and training will no longer end at 16 or 18.

OPPORTUNITIES

New challenges: Constant change within industry means there will always be new openings and new challenges for workers willing to move with the times. Some people thrive on the constant challenge of facing the unknown. They will be willing to adapt to the changing needs of society in order to take advantage of the opportunities to improve themselves and their position in society.

Increased self-reliance: In order to operate effectively within a flexible workforce, workers need to develop skills in a range of areas. The onus for putting together such a **portfolio** rests with the individual. By diversifying their skills in this way, workers will be able to sell themselves to potential employers more effectively. They can start to take charge of their own future.

Diverse career paths: The new patterns of work may enable workers to follow career paths that previously were almost impossible. They may be able to use their portfolio of skills to follow career paths that twist and turn according to the opportunities available and the interests of the worker at any given time. It may become almost impossible for a worker to become trapped in a rut, undertaking the same tasks day after day for many years.

Learning new skills: Increased flexibility means a much greater possibility that workers will have to update

IN **Business**

their own skills at regular intervals. If workers can exercise more self-control over the direction of their career, wherever possible, they will follow paths they find particularly beneficial and interesting. In Maslow's terms, this will allow them to move closer towards self-actualisation, as they have the opportunity to explore the areas that hold meaning to them.

ISSUES FOR analysis

Some commentators have argued that the move by businesses towards flexibility may not be the result of a planned strategy at all. Instead, the pressures brought about by the prolonged recession during the early 1990s may have forced many firms to look for ways to cut their costs whilst remaining profitable. A major attraction of downsizing and outsourcing is that they attack one of the largest costs for most businesses – labour.

Critics of the notion of flexibility have attacked it as being rather short-sighted. They argue that a firm too reliant on outside sources cannot be fully in charge of its own destiny. Similarly, there is an obvious limit to how far a firm can downsize itself. When minimum costs and operations have been reached, what then for the future development of the business?

As a strategy to cope with an adverse economic climate, downsizing has its attractions. So too, however, does the idea of diversifying to spread risks and build a platform on which to develop in the future.

39.4 Flexibility and insecurity
an evaluation

The flexible firm has many attractions for businesses, especially in times of economic hardship. It is unlikely, however, that the full benefits could be felt unless society as a whole undergoes some major shifts. The country needs to cope with, and to accept, regular periods of unemployment and retraining. Actors have always accepted the idea of 'resting between jobs'. There is no shame in it. People need to accept that there is no shame in unemployment, in going back to college, or in starting a new business which doesn't succeed. The consolation is that although the ups and downs of insecurity can be stressful, the boredom of 100% security may be little better.

Firms must question, however, whether the move to flexibility has gone too far. Recently an airline looking for cost savings put one-fifth of the cabin staff on a new, flexible contract with 30% less pay. What is the likely effect on absence, staff turnover and motivation? In the long term, a move back to secure career paths may be the best way to ensure a top quality workforce.

contract out – to switch jobs formerly done within the organisation to outside contractors. This increases flexibility and may cut costs in the short term.

core – the key aspects of the work done at the heart of an organisation.

downsizing – cutting the production capacity of a business, by cutting staff and/or cutting back physical capacity such as factory space or the number of retail outlets.

flexible specialisation – production of limited quantities of a wide range of products to meet the needs of different market niches.

periphery – tasks which are not central to the business and therefore do not have to be done by full-time staff.

portfolio – in this context, a worker's range of skills and experiences. A wide portfolio would make it easier for an employee to switch jobs.

privatised – a business which was once in the public sector (government owned) but now operates in the private sector, and may therefore face more direct competition.

shamrock organisation – Charles Handy's idea that modern firms have three parts: the core, the flexible labour force and the contractual fringe.

UNIT 39 I FLEXIBILITY AND INSECURITY

AS Level Exercises

A. REVISION QUESTIONS
(30 marks; 70 minutes)

Read the unit, then answer:

1 State three features of flexible specialisation. *(3)*
2 Outline three ways in which flexibility may be achieved within a firm. *(6)*
3 What is the difference between a firm's core workers and its periphery? *(4)*
4 What is meant by 'outsourcing'? *(4)*
5 Give three examples of operations in a manufacturing firm that may be considered for outsourcing. *(3)*
6 What do you understand by the phrase 'sticking to the knitting'? *(3)*
7 Give three ways in which flexibility may threaten the workforce. *(3)*
8 Give two reasons for and two reasons against a job for life. *(4)*

B. REVISION EXERCISES

B1 Data Response
Haseldens Ltd is a medium sized firm making components for the motor trade. In response to increasing competition from other suppliers, it has had to find ways to reduce both the costs of its products and the time it takes to meet orders.

The managing director of the firm, Ian Haselden, is keen to develop a more flexible culture within the 20 strong workforce. He feels that "if we are to survive as an independent firm, we must be able to adapt quickly to changing circumstances. Flexible specialisation is the key to achieving this."

Questions *(30 marks; 35 minutes)*
1 What do you understand by the term 'flexible specialisation'? *(3)*
2 Outline three ways in which Haseldens could implement the proposed changes. *(6)*
3 What is meant by the phrase 'flexible culture'? *(3)*
4 Assess the effect these changes could have on Haseldens' competitive position. *(8)*
5 Evaluate the impact the size of the firm may have on the plans to introduce flexible specialisation. *(10)*

B2 Data Response

Flexible Figures

A government-sponsored 1998 survey of British managers found clear evidence of an increase in flexible working (see the chart below). The form of flexibility shown in the bar chart is known as numerical flexibility. It allows managers to adjust their staff numbers quite quickly and cheaply.

The survey also asked about functional flexibility, i.e. the number of staff trained to switch to other job functions. Only one-quarter of staff were multi-skilled in this way. These people tended to be at the firms which used a high proportion of full-time staff. In other words, functional flexibility tends to be at odds with numerical flexibility.

Questions *(30 marks; 35 minutes)*
1 Identify and explain three important conclusions from the bar chart. *(9)*
2 What might be the benefit to a business of increasing the proportion of part-time employees? *(5)*
3 Analyse the possible reasons why 'functional flexibility tends to be at odds with numerical flexibility'. *(8)*
4 Discuss whether it would be beneficial to have more teachers who were part-time or on fixed-term contracts. *(8)*

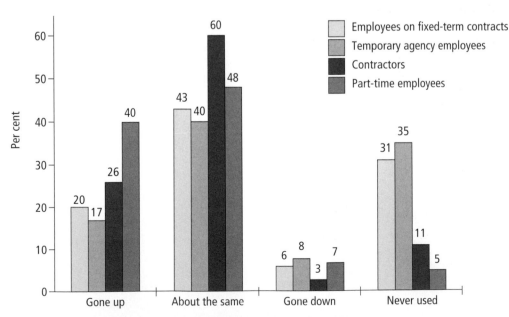

Legend:
- Employees on fixed-term contracts
- Temporary agency employees
- Contractors
- Part-time employees

Gone up: 20, 17, 26, 40
About the same: 43, 40, 60, 48
Gone down: 6, 8, 3, 7
Never used: 31, 35, 11, 5

Source: *The 1998 Workplace Employment Relations Survey,* DTI, October 1998

B3 Case Study

Perry Products has been a successful manufacturer of farming machinery for over 50 years. The founder of the firm, Gordon Perry Snr, began as a farmhand in Northern Ireland in the 1940s, but proved his value by innovating new ideas for farm machinery. Eventually, he set up a business modifying existing machinery for local farmers and then developing and producing his own designs. In the 1960s he moved the business to the UK mainland, setting up his works in the central Lancashire town of Bamber Bridge.

When Gordon Snr retired in 1987, his son, Gordon Jnr, moved from the pharmaceutical company where he worked to take over the family firm. Having a business degree and experience in a large multinational firm, Gordon Jnr set about modernising the firm in an attempt to 'prepare us thoroughly for the challenges of the twenty-first century'.

The key changes made since 1987 have been:

- outsourcing several aspects of the firm's operations, most noticeably the design and development function to a specialist firm
- combining the three existing plants to a purpose-built single factory site
- acquiring state-of-the-art production equipment
- inviting all staff to design and product development conferences every six months.

Questions *(40 marks; 60 minutes)*

1 What might be the benefits and drawbacks of control of this firm passing from father to son when the son had not been involved in the company previously? *(8)*
2 Outline the advantages and disadvantages of outsourcing the design and development function. *(10)*
3 How might the workforce have responded to the changes since 1987? *(10)*
4 Evaluate the firm's strategy in view of the aim to prepare the company for the challenges of the twenty-first century. *(12)*

B4 Case Study

Croft and Co. is a well-established clothing manufacturer. For many years it has successfully supplied many leading retailers with high quality own-brand clothing for both men and women. More recent times have seen competition increase dramatically, but by outsourcing much of its manufacturing abroad to third world countries, Croft has been able to defend its market position successfully.

Recently, there has been a change in top personnel at Croft. Sir Charles Croft has retired and passed the business to his granddaughter, Emily. After reviewing the firm's operations, Emily was shocked to find that the firm has only been able to compete with foreign producers because the labour costs have been reduced substantially with the outsourcing programme. She determined to make it the first area of business to review.

Questions *(25 marks; 30 minutes)*

1 Outline the problems the firm may have faced at first, after adopting its outsourcing policy. *(5)*
2 Examine the potential long-term benefits and drawbacks of having production take place in a foreign country. *(8)*
3 Discuss the ethical arguments for AND against the firm paying wages to third world workers at a level substantially below those in the UK. *(12)*

C. ESSAY QUESTIONS

1 Assess the impact growing flexibility may have upon a manufacturing firm.
2 Analyse the effects that flexible working practices may have on worker motivation in a firm.
3 'Downsizing as a strategy is inherently risky.' What might those risks be, and how might a firm minimise them?

HUMAN RESOURCE MANAGEMENT

DEFINITION

The purpose of human resource management (HRM) is to recruit, develop and utilise an organisation's personnel in the way which is most appropriate to the achievement of that firm's objectives.

40.1 Introduction

Research regularly shows that the most successful organisations are those that make the best use of their staff. So the management of human resources (staff) should be one of the highest profile, highest status jobs in the business world. In reality this is not the case. Twenty years ago 'personnel managers' began a campaign to increase their influence within companies by emphasising that 'human resources' were at least as important as financial resources. Therefore 'human resource directors' were needed in the boardroom to help make and implement important strategic decisions.

This renaming of the personnel function has been implemented in many firms. It remains very questionable, though, as to whether it has any greater significance. Many UK firms remain dominated by accountants and – less often – marketing experts. Therefore the need to get the best out of staff is more a feature of foreign-owned firms, such as those from Japan, Germany and America.

In theory, HRM is about strategic decisions based upon the skills of the workforce. Day by day, however, it concerns recruitment, training, performance appraisal and the attempt to manage staff performance, plus occasional issues of redundancy, dismissal and industrial relations.

40.2 Recruitment and selection

The purpose of the recruitment and selection process is to acquire a suitable number of employees with appropriate skills, in order to meet the manpower requirements of the organisation. It is in the interests of the firm to achieve this goal at a minimum cost in terms of both time and resources.

There are three stages to this process:

1 determining the human resource requirements of the organisation
2 attracting suitable candidates for the vacancy
3 selecting the most appropriate candidate.

1 DETERMINING THE HUMAN RESOURCE REQUIREMENTS OF THE ORGANISATION

Recruitment and selection procedures need to fit in with the overall workforce plan. Workforce planning starts by auditing the current staff. How old are they (how many will be retiring over the next 18 months?)? What are their skills? And how many are prepared to take on new tasks or challenges? This information must be compared with an estimate of the future workforce needs, based on the firm's overall strategy for the next year or two. A sales push into Europe might require more French speakers; planned factory closures may require redundancies and redeployments. The workforce plan must then show how the business can push staff from where they are now, to where they need to be later on.

Efficient workforce planning requires managers to question the existing employment structure at every opportunity. This can occur when:

● an individual leaves the firm because of retirement or finding alternative employment
● an employee is promoted within the business, creating a vacancy
● an increase in workload occurs
● the development of a new product, or an emerging technology, which means that the organisation requires employees with additional skills.

Many businesses fill vacancies automatically with no analysis of alternative actions. However, it may be more effective to consider reorganisation of job responsibilities. Now that Jim has retired we can consider whether his job should be rather different today. A good human resource manager will look ahead to the future needs of a department before just advertising for a replacement. Should Jim's successor be able to speak French? Indeed, is a full-time employee needed? Should the business opt for increased flexibility by shifting to the use of part-time employees? Or contract Jim's tasks out to a specialist firm?

2 ATTRACTING SUITABLE CANDIDATES FOR A VACANCY

Once the firm's human resource provision has been considered and the need for a new recruit established,

WORKFORCE PLANNING AT TESCO

Britain's largest private sector employer is Tesco, with more than 200,000 employees. In October 2002 it announced headline details of its workforce plan for the coming 6 months. It would be hiring 17,000 extra staff before Christmas, 5,000 of whom would be kept on permanently to work in 62 new stores. Tesco's retail director, David Potts, said this came on top of 9,000 jobs created to cope with busier trading conditions at existing stores.

it is necessary to find a method of attracting suitable candidates.

The first step in this process is to develop a *job description*. This will usually consist of:

- a job title
- a statement outlining how the job fits into the overall structure of the organisation
- details of the job's content, such as the tasks which must be performed and the responsibilities involved
- an indication of the working conditions the post holder can expect. This includes details of pay, hours of work and holiday entitlement.

Many firms will then choose to produce a *person specification*. This details the qualities of the ideal candidate, such as 'highly numerate'. This should help to identify the criteria to use to shortlist and then select the best candidates from those who apply.

At this point the business must decide if the post will be filled from within the company or from outside it. Internal recruitment ensures that the abilities of candidates will be known. In addition, other employees will be motivated by the evidence of promotion prospects within the firm. However, external recruitment will provide a wider pool of applicants from which to select. It can also introduce new thinking to the organisation.

The recruitment process can be expensive. It includes not only the cost of the advertising, but also the administration of, perhaps, hundreds of applications. Then there is the management time spent in the shortlisting and interviewing phases. The insurance giant Standard Life spends over £500,000 a year to recruit 50 management trainees. That is over £10,000 each!

The successful management of human resources demands that the effectiveness of recruitment advertising should be monitored. The most common method adopted is to calculate the cost of attracting each new employee. The appropriateness of recruits is also a concern. This can be judged by keeping a record of the proportion of candidates recruited by the firm who remain in employment six months later. Standard Life is rightly proud that 99% of the graduate trainees they employ are still with them two years later.

3 SELECTING THE RIGHT PERSON FOR THE JOB

The selection process involves assessing candidates against the criteria set out in the person specification. The most frequently employed selection process is to:

- shortlist a small number of applicants based on their application forms
- ask for a reference from their previous employers/teachers
- call for interview the individuals whose references are favourable.

The choice of who will be offered the job is made by the interview panel, based on which candidate they feel most closely matches the person specification for the post. Research suggests that the use of interviews is not a very reliable indicator of how well an individual will perform in a job. This is largely because interviewers are too easily swayed by appearance, personal charm and the interview technique of applicants. A number of other selection techniques have therefore been developed to complement, or replace, the use of this selection procedure.

The interview is a common form of selection

Testing: There are two types of test. *Aptitude tests* measure how good the applicant is at a particular skill, such as typing or arithmetic. *Psychometric tests* measure the personality, attitudes and character of an applicant. They can give an indication of whether the applicant will be a team player or a loner, passive or assertive, questioning or accepting, and so on. The firm can make a selection judgement on the appropriate type of person from experience, and from the specific requirements of the job. This approach is particularly common in management and graduate recruitment.

Many doubts have been raised about the accuracy and validity of psychometric tests. Do they give an unfair advantage to certain people? Certainly the questions must be checked to remove social, sex or racial bias. There is also concern about whether firms are

SHELL SEEKS THE RIGHT QUALITIES

The Dutch-owned oil giant Shell believes it knows the qualities required for management success. It has researched carefully among its own high-flyers and come up with a list. When recruiting management trainees it uses a variety of tests to see which applicant best matches the required qualities. These include the ability to explore problems about which they had little previous knowledge, to see long-term implications and to cope better with the unknown. The specific attributes Shell looks for include: problem analysis; creativity and judgement; drive, resilience and empathy (seeing other people's point of view); and the action qualities of organising and implementing.

right to want all their managers to have similar characteristics. A wide range of personalities may lead to a more interesting, sparky atmosphere with livelier debates and better decisions.

Assessment centres: Assessment centres are a means of establishing the performance of job candidates in a range of circumstances. A group of similar applicants are invited to a centre, often for a number of days, for an in-depth assessment. They will be asked to perform tasks under scrutiny, such as role playing crisis situations. This is a good way to assess leadership qualities.

Research suggests this approach is the most effective selection technique for predicting successful job performance. Although the use of these centres is growing they are expensive and time consuming. Only large firms can afford to use this recruitment strategy and it is only appropriate for individuals who will potentially fill senior positions within a firm in the future.

Whichever selection procedure is adopted, a growing number of organisations are encouraging line managers to become involved in the recruitment decision. The role of the human resource department is increasingly one of providing support to functional departments rather than driving the recruitment process itself. Line managers are more aware of the key requirements of a post because they see it being carried out from day to day.

40.3 | Training and development

Training is the process of instructing an individual about how to carry out tasks directly related to his or her current job.

Development involves helping an individual to realise his or her full potential. This concerns general growth, and is not related specifically to the employee's existing post.

An organisation which introduces a training and development programme does so in order to ensure the best possible return on its investment in people.

The four key objectives of training and development are:

1 To help a new employee reach the level of performance expected from an experienced worker. This initial preparation upon first taking up a post is known as 'induction' training. It often contains information dealing with the layout of the firm's operating facility, health and safety measures and security systems. An attempt may also be made to introduce the individual to key employees and give an impression of the culture of the organisation. The firm's induction training should aim to drive each employee along their own personal learning curve as quickly as possible (see Figure 40.1).

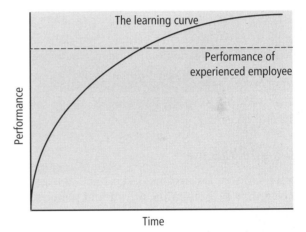

Figure 40.1 Objective of induction training

2 To provide a wide pool of skills available to the organisation, both at present and in the future (see Figure 40.2).

Actual performance → Desired performance

Current level of skill → Required level of skill
Current level of knowledge → Required level of knowledge

Training is aimed at bridging the skills gap

Figure 40.2 The training gap

3 To develop a knowledgeable and committed workforce.
4 To deliver high quality products or services.

TYPES OF TRAINING

On-the-job training involves instructing employees at their place of work on how a particular task should be carried out. This may be done by an experienced worker demonstrating the correct way of performing a task, or by a supervisor coaching an employee by talking them through the job stage by stage. Job rotation involves switching an employee around a range of tasks in order to develop their skills in more than one area.

Off-the-job training is any form of instruction which takes place away from the immediate workplace. The firm itself may organise an internal programme based within on-site facilities, or send employees to a local college or university for an external development scheme. This approach to training is more likely to include more general skills and knowledge useful at work, rather than job-specific content.

THE COST OF NOT TRAINING

If an organisation chooses not to train its workforce it will be faced with additional recruitment costs. This is because when new skills are required existing employees will have to be made redundant and new people employed with the right skills or experience.

Untrained staff will not be as productive, or as well motivated, as those who are trained. They will be unable to deal with change because their skills are specific to the present situation. There may be more accidents in the workplace if the workforce is unskilled. In addition, employees are less likely to know, and work towards, achieving the organisation's aims and objectives.

TRAINING IN PRACTICE

A wide range of research has indicated that organisations in the UK, both in the private and public sector, fail to invest appropriately in training and development. Many organisations view training only as a cost and therefore fail to consider the long-term benefits it can bring.

Rather than planning for the future by anticipating the firm's knowledge and skill requirements, many businesses only develop training programmes as an answer to existing problems. The Government has responded to the reactive nature of UK training by launching the Investors In People (IIP) campaign. This encourages firms to develop a more strategic view of training and development. An organisation can gain IIP accredited status if it analyses its training and development needs, plans and implements a programme in response, and evaluates the effectiveness of its provision.

TRAINING AND MARKET FAILURE

Business people and economists like to emphasise the efficiency of 'the market'. This is the mechanism that ensures that consumer demand for eggs or Smarties is met by the right amount of supplies by the producers. In other words, 'the market' is the matching of supply and demand. Economists believe that the market

INVESTORS IN PEOPLE

Ten years ago, business at the 62-bedroom Park Hotel in Liverpool was poor. Profit had fallen to £60,000 and the occupancy was only 30%. Ron Jones, general manager, decided that the fundamental problem was lack of repeat and recommended (word-of-mouth) business. The cause of this seemed to be the lukewarm efforts of staff.

He responded by bringing in an expert to retrain staff and build morale. And then went for the Investors In People (IIP) award. The first step was to devise a SWOT analysis in conjunction with staff. Then heads of department explained their objectives and the staff skills required to achieve it. Every member of staff had a personal development plan drawn up and was given the training they required.

By the time of receiving the IIP award in 1997, the hotel had already gained in many ways. Labour turnover fell to 5% (compared with 35% for the industry nationally). Occupancy rose to 72% and in 1997 profit was in excess of £500,000 on turnover which had doubled to £1.4 million.

The hotel's general manager, June Matthews, is certain that Investors In People stimulated higher participation and more positive attitudes among staff: 'Without a shadow of doubt it was worth it.'

Business IN

works best when the government allows it to operate freely, without intervention.

The labour market is the supply and demand for labour. This is also allowed to operate quite freely. There are some laws to regulate the ability of employers to hire and fire or to discriminate against certain types of people. Broadly, though, the government allows firms a great deal of freedom.

The free market has served Britain very well in many ways. It can be at its weakest, however, when requiring firms to make long-term investments, such as in top quality staff training. The problem is that it may be cheaper for an individual firm to train no-one, merely hiring in new, experienced staff. In this way, the firm suffers none of the short-term costs and disruption involved in training staff who may leave once their training is complete. However, if several firms adopt this approach, companies offering good training will find that their young staff are 'poached' as soon as they become experienced. This becomes a major disincentive for firms in general to provide high quality training.

In a case such as this, the market can lead to inefficiency rather than efficiency. So it may be desirable for the government to intervene, perhaps by offering tax incentives for firms to train their own staff.

40.4 Appraisal of performance

Appraisal is a formal assessment of the performance of a member of staff. It involves establishing clear objectives for each employee and evaluating actual performance in the light of these goals. The most important element of an appraisal system is usually a one-to-one discussion between an individual and his or her manager. This can be held frequently, but is usually once a year. The discussion may consider specific performance measures such as individual output. Or involve a more general review of the contribution the employee makes to the smooth running of the business.

The main objectives of an appraisal system are:

- to improve the performance of the employee
- to provide feedback to the individual about his or her performance
- to recognise the future training needs of the individual
- to consider the development of the individual's career
- to identify employees in the organisation who have potential for advancement.

An appraisal system provides information which allows the business to plan and develop its human resource provision.

APPRAISAL IN PRACTICE

Research suggests that approximately 80% of UK organisations have some form of appraisal system. The current trend is to extend schemes beyond managers and supervisors to clerical and shop-floor workers. This is being partly driven by the Investors In People initiative. This demands that all employees must be involved in, or have the option of joining, an appraisal system if it is to be recognised by the project.

Use of appraisal does not seem to be limited to large firms. Evidence suggests that the majority of firms employing less than 500 people have in place some form of appraisal system. There is some evidence, however, that linking appraisal with pay can cause disharmony in the workplace.

40.5 Reward systems

FINANCIAL REWARD PROCESS

A reward system consists of financial rewards and employee benefits. Together these two elements make up an individual's total **remuneration**.

- Base pay – the level of wage or salary which represents the rate for the job. It will be based on internal comparisons which reflect the importance of the job within the organisation. Also external comparisons will reflect the market rate for the equivalent post in other firms.
- Additions to base pay – these are influenced by variables such as skill, performance and experience. For example, merit pay reflects an assessment of the individual's level of performance.
- Employee benefits – these include holiday entitlement, pension schemes, sick pay, insurance cover and company cars.

NON-FINANCIAL REWARD PROCESS

Non-financial rewards are the benefits the employee receives in addition to total remuneration. These can include a feeling of achievement, recognition, personal influence and increased responsibility.

The key objectives of a reward system are:

- to ensure individuals with the appropriate levels of skill and motivation are available to the organisation when they are needed
- to communicate to employees what qualities and actions the organisation values
- to encourage and support planned changes within the firm
- to provide value for money.

In order to achieve these goals a reward system must be regarded by employees as 'internally fair' and 'externally competitive'.

PAYMENT SYSTEMS IN PRACTICE

Research suggests that the reward systems employed by UK organisations in the 1970s and 1980s failed to recognise the role of pay as a strategic tool. Emphasis was placed on the need to attract and retain employees, rather than on any wider strategic implications. During the 1990s, performance-related pay became popular. This approach involves the payment of a bonus, or salary increase, which is awarded in line with an employee's achievements over a range of indicators. Today, more emphasis is placed on rewarding the individual's skills, knowledge and competence, while at the same time placing greater significance on non-financial rewards.

ISSUES FOR **analysis**

When analysing a firm's existing approach to managing human resources, or the strategy it might choose to adopt in the future, it is useful to consider the following points :

- Is the business planning ahead to identify its future workforce requirements, or is it responding to short-term events and allowing these to shape human resource policy?

- Is the organisation preparing job descriptions and person specifications in order to ensure the recruitment process selects individuals with the most appropriate skills for the vacant post?
- Have a range of selection techniques been employed by the firm, or is a single method being used? Is an effort made to match the process adopted to the requirements of the job?
- Does the organisation have an employee appraisal system in place? If it does, is the main objective of the process to develop individuals, or to link performance to reward?
- Has the organisation's reward system been designed in a way which motivates employees to help achieve the firm's aims and objectives?
- Does the reward system use non-financial rewards in addition to pay?

40.6 Human resource management
an evaluation

Managing people effectively is the single most common factor that links successful organisations. Is that the same thing as effective human resource management? Some observers consider that once managers start to think of people as 'human resources', they are on a slippery slope towards hiring and firing staff as casually as they might buy or sell raw materials or shares. In many organisations the staff feel that 'H.R.' are 'them', not 'us'. This is because human resource managers may have been responsible for contracting work to outside suppliers, causing redundancies. Or they may have set up performance-related pay systems that force staff to do tasks they do not wish to do, or even disapprove of.

HRM can be used as a tool of a Theory X management, to impose a control system on an unwilling workforce. Or it can be a way to ensure that staff needs and talents become a fundamental part of decision-making in a Theory Y organisation. Clearly, when going for job interviews, the wise applicant judges a firm not by whether the interviewer is a HR manager, but whether the attitudes to staff seem open, positive and participative.

KEY terms

off-the-job training – any form of training not immediately linked to a specific task. It may take place within the firm, perhaps in conference facilities, or away from it, for example at a local technical college.

on-the-job training – the process of instructing employees at their place of work on how a particular job should be carried out. This usually involves watching an experienced operative carry out a task, or actually undertaking the activity and being guided as to appropriate technique.

remuneration – the whole package of rewards offered by an organisation to an employee. This will include additional benefits, such as a pension scheme, share options, company car and so on, as well as basic pay.

selection methods – the process by which organisations choose to differentiate between the applicants for a specific job in order to pick out the most appropriate candidate. The most commonly used technique is interview, but a range of different approaches (e.g. personality testing) are being used more frequently in order to complement traditional methods.

workforce planning – the process of anticipating in advance the human resource requirements of the organisation, both in terms of the number of individuals required, and the appropriate skill mix. Recruitment and training policies are devised with a long-term focus, in order to ensure the firm is able to operate without being limited by a shortage of appropriate labour.

AS Level Exercises

A. REVISION QUESTIONS
(35 marks: 70 minutes)

Read the unit, then answer:

1 Why is it important that an organisation challenges its existing employment structure each time an opportunity to do so emerges? *(4)*

2 Why do 'job descriptions' and 'person specifications' play an important part in the selection of appropriate personnel? *(4)*

3 What advantages does the process of internal recruitment offer to the business over the appointment of individuals from outside the organisation? *(4)*

4 Identify three benefits to a firm of using assessment centres in selecting key staff. *(3)*

5 What might be the costs of not training:
  a new supermarket checkout operators *(4)*
  b crowd stewards at Manchester United. *(4)*

6 How can a form of 'market failure' result when a firm is considering training its employees? *(4)*

7 What is the main purpose of 'induction' training? *(4)*

8 What benefits might a firm derive from achieving an Investors In People award? *(4)*

B. REVISION EXERCISES

B1 Data Response

Recruited by Bill Gates

The richest man in the world, feted by presidents and prime ministers, Bill Gates sees no activity as more important than meeting superior candidates to convince them they should join Microsoft. He even targets the graduate trainees, inviting all 600 in groups to his $60 million home. Mingling with the young guests, he answers questions, gives advice and reinforces the excitement of a career with Microsoft.

Recruitment at Microsoft has two main strands. The first is picking the best of the year's 25,000 computer science graduates. Microsoft creates a shortlist of 8,000 CVs which are reviewed to identify the 2,600 targeted for campus interviews. 800 of these are invited to Microsoft's head office at Seattle.

Each candidate is then interviewed by between three and ten 'Microsoftees'. This lengthy and expensive process provides about 400 graduates each year who join Microsoft.

But this accounts for only 20% of Microsoft's annual recruitment. Most of the remaining 2,000 staff hired each year are the best and brightest people working elsewhere. To identify and track these potential assets, Microsoft maintains a full-time team of 200 recruiting experts. Their job is to head hunt the industry's most talented people and then build and maintain a relationship with them.

The pursuit is relentless, if subtle. Regular telephone calls at discreet intervals, invitations to informal dinners – anything to keep open the lines of communication with the potential candidate. Mike Murray, Microsoft's head of human resources, says 'One day he will be ticked off with his current organisation. That day, he'll call us.'

Mike Murray also makes sure to monitor the performance of the 200 recruiters. When it comes to human resources, Microsoft leaves nothing to chance.

Source: *The Financial Times*, 28/7/98

Questions *(30 marks; 35 minutes)*

1 Many firms state that 'Our most important asset is our people'. What evidence is there that Microsoft actually believes it? *(6)*

2 a Apart from interviewing the candidates for the management trainee posts, how else might Microsoft have selected the right person for the job? *(4)*

  b Which of these methods might have been most suitable for a large computer software company such as Microsoft? Explain your answer. *(8)*

3 Microsoft head hunts staff from other firms using a method known as 'poaching'.
  a What benefits might Microsoft derive from poaching staff from other firms? *(4)*
  b Why might poaching lead to a reduction in the level of training generally in an industry? *(4)*

4 Outline two ways in which Mike Murray might evaluate the performance of the 200 recruiters. *(4)*

B2 Case Study

Human Resource Development at Prest Ltd

In the early 1990s Prest Ltd, manufacturer of electronic components, closed three factories and concentrated its operations on a single site. At the same time it reorganised the remaining plant to cut costs and improve product quality. Before modernisation, 50% of the machinery being used at the site had been over 15 years old. This was replaced with the latest equipment. The new production line was designed to run continuously with operators being expected to take 'first level' decisions at the point of production to keep it functioning. As a result, tasks such as fault finding and machine maintenance became an important part of the job of each worker.

The modernisation of the plant signalled a shift to teamworking, in order to encourage employee flexibility. Multi-skilled operators were needed with a deeper understanding of the production system. The employees needed to know how the new machinery could best be used to ensure consistently high levels of production quality. These changes had clear implications for the human resource department at Prest. Recruitment would have to focus on a new type of employee, and existing employees would need to be retrained.

The human resource manager conducted a feasibility analysis in order to review the strengths and weaknesses of the company's existing workforce and its ability to handle the new situation. This concluded that both shop-floor supervision and the engineering section needed strengthening. In response, 15 new engineers were recruited and 5 staff redeployed to improve production supervision.

As an answer to the immediate need for greater skill levels, a comprehensive training programme in quality control was introduced for all staff. Machine operators were encouraged to mix with engineers during this exercise, helping to break down barriers between the two groups. For many individuals this was the first formal company training they had ever received. The development initiative was successful enough to stimulate requests for further learning opportunities. As a result, Prest created a link with a local technical college to provide more extensive instruction for those who wished to learn more about modern production techniques.

Although the benefits of the training were clear, three problems emerged which Prest had not anticipated. The greater knowledge of the operators made them anxious to put their acquired skills into practice. After nine months the new production line had only reached 80% efficiency. Senior managers believed employees were losing interest when machinery was functioning normally. In addition, some workers felt the extensive training they had received was not reflected in enough increased responsibility. Their expectations of a more interesting job had been raised, but the reality seemed little different than before. Finally, 12 newly trained staff left the company because they could now apply for more highly paid posts at other firms in the area.

Prest also considered the long-term human resource implications of the move to a more sophisticated form of production. The workforce knew little about new production technology, so the firm's training school ran a course on robotics. The decision was also taken to provide a sponsorship scheme to encourage new recruits to study on an engineering degree course at university. The firm wished to ensure it did not face a shortage of talent in the long term.

Questions
(40 marks; 60 minutes)

1 Analyse the significance for each of the four stages of the human resource cycle created by the introduction of new technology and different working practices at Prest Ltd. (10)
2 What human resource issues might emerge as a result of the feasibility study conducted at Prest Ltd? (8)
3 Evaluate the development programme introduced by Prest Ltd in the light of the problems identified by the feasibility study. (6)
4 Consider whether the difficulties experienced after staff training at Prest Ltd suggest that employees can receive too much training. (10)
5 Has the HR Department at Prest Ltd created a 'horizontal fit' between each of the four elements of the human resource cycle in the programme which has been introduced? (6)

A Level Exercises

A. REVISION QUESTIONS

(30 marks; 45 minutes)

Read the unit, then answer:

1 **a** Outline how an appraisal might be conducted. *(4)*
   b Explain the likely goals of an appraisal system. *(4)*
2 Analyse how the process of performance appraisal might be viewed by:
   a a Theory X manager *(4)*
   b Professor Herzberg. *(4)*
3 Explain the difference between a 'payment system' and a 'reward system'. *(4)*
4 How might the reward of an organisation's employees be linked to achieving its aims and objectives? *(5)*

B. REVISION EXERCISES

B1 Case Study

Human Resource Management at Creative Designs

Gemma was starting to lose her temper. She looked around the table at her three colleagues and wondered why they could not see how serious their current problems were. Karen, the marketing manager at 'Creative Designs', was making the same point Gemma had heard a number of times before. 'The project team responsible for swimwear for the new season sees no need to launch a new design. Our present range is still selling well.' The other two managers nodded agreement.

Gemma held her breath, calmed down and tried again: 'But surely the market is changing rapidly. I was chatting to a designer the other day who mentioned some great new swimwear fabrics from Italy. Shouldn't we look at redesigns now to keep us ahead of the competition?'

David from purchasing smiled condescendingly at Gemma: 'I was on the project team. Of course we looked at alternative fabrics, but we have maintained market share with the existing designs and it is not worth the risk of changing at this point.' Gemma knew what was coming next; the production manager Heather was instant in her support for David: 'It is not worth the extra time and expense of setting up a new design run if we don't need to. What is the point in having the project teams to look into this kind of issue if we are not going to accept their advice?' Gemma slumped back in her chair and thought to herself, 'how on earth are we going to break out of this culture?'

When Gemma got home that evening she decided it was time to write down an analysis of Creative Designs' human resource problems and take them to Laura, the company's managing director. Gemma had been running the human resources department for seven months now and could no longer contain her frustration at the lack of progress.

'The people in this organisation are risk averse. If a change is suggested it is resisted, even by senior managers. We make no attempt to anticipate changes in our markets just in case we get it wrong. The reason is obvious, we do not tolerate any form of failure.'

'Our reward, appraisal and promotion system are at the heart of the problem. It is no secret that nobody wants to be in the new project teams that deal with the markets where a new collection is required each year, like designer dresses. You might be persuaded to recommend a line which doesn't sell. Everyone knows there is nothing worse at their annual appraisal meeting than being associated with a project team which made a mistake. You can kiss goodbye to any pay increase for the next year.'

'But performance-related pay need not be linked only to results. We have to look at how difficult the task was in the first place. We must not penalise failure. We are discouraging risk taking, but how can a fashion business succeed in the long term without taking chances?'

'The problem doesn't end there though, our selection process makes things worse. It is a good idea to encourage internal promotion. The policy of advertising new posts to our own staff first is a real motivator. The difficulty is, time and again we end up appointing the person who has not made a mistake. We don't look at an individual's record on project teams and consider the quality of their ideas, we ask have they been associated with a failure? This is just reinforcing the "safety first" culture of the organisation.'

'If our product markets didn't change very much we might get away with all of this, but the fashion industry is a dynamic competitive environment. As our mission statement says: we should be looking to introduce "leading edge, creative designs". The firm will not last unless we move with the market and we cannot do that with the human resource policies we have at present.'

Gemma sat back from the kitchen table. 'Well, I feel better for having written it all down,' she thought. 'On the other hand my own appraisal is in two months and I wonder if I should be quite as outspoken just at the moment. There is no point in making enemies. Perhaps a meeting with Laura is a bad idea … I could try to encourage internal interview panels to be a bit more adventurous in their appointments. At least that would be a start.' Gemma screwed up the piece of paper and took careful aim at the bin.

Questions *(60 marks; 70 minutes)*

1 To what extent does the human resource policy of Creative Designs 'match' the needs of its competitive environment? *(10)*

2 a Analyse the role of performance related pay in this case. *(6)*

b Discuss the types of organisation in which its use may be most appropriate. *(8)*

3 Use this case as a starting point to assess the strengths and weaknesses for firms of organising employees into project teams. *(10)*

4 Evaluate the benefits and costs to Creative Designs of selecting candidates for new posts internally wherever possible. *(12)*

5 Consider the advice you would give Gemma if she was asked to redesign the human resource policies at Creative Designs. *(14)*

C. ESSAY QUESTIONS

1 Johnson Engineering plc are suffering from a lack of skilled engineers. Consider how the human resource department might set about solving this problem.

2 In order to establish a competitive advantage, a business must make sure its selection, appraisal, development and reward of employees each 'fit' together in order to form a single human resource policy approach. Discuss how this might be achieved and the difficulties which may be encountered.

HUMAN RESOURCE STRATEGY

Human resource strategy demands that an organisation should manage its employees in a way which is consistent with the objectives of the whole business. Its purpose is to establish a competitive advantage.

41.1 Workforce planning

The starting point for a human resource strategy is the organisation's strategic plan. A workforce must be put in place which provides departments such as Operations and Marketing with the correct number of appropriately skilled employees to accomplish their targets. In order to achieve this, a long-term focus is required. The likely demand for products or services must be anticipated and the future implications for recruitment and training considered.

Effective communication between departments is vital if this approach is to succeed. The marketing department can supply estimates of future demand. Operations management can detail the number and skill level of shop-floor workers needed to produce the goods. The human resource department will then have to recruit additional staff (or reduce numbers) in line with the approximate requirements identified. If the skill mix of existing employees is inappropriate, a training programme will need to be devised.

Workforce planning is therefore an integrated process. It requires an overview of the whole operation of the business. In order to use human resources successfully to create a competitive advantage, the future position of the firm must be considered. A workforce must be put in place which will allow the strategic plan of the business to be put into effect.

41.2 Creating a human resource strategy

Big firms tend to integrate workforce planning into their overall business plan, rather than develop a 'stand-alone' human resource strategy. Small businesses are much less likely to plan their provision of human resources formally. Where explicit planning does take place the timescale most widely adopted is to attempt to anticipate future personnel requirements over a two- to five-year period.

The main benefits of creating a human resource strategy are:

- to put in place the appropriate employee mix to allow the organisation to achieve its aims and objectives
- to communicate the culture of the business to the workforce
- to develop employees in a way which brings benefits both to the individual and to the organisation
- to provide targets by which the actions of the human resource function can be assessed.

The main problems faced when creating a human resource strategy are:

- Developing an effective human resource strategy will be very difficult if the future direction of the business is not well defined. Any formal planning must therefore be put in place after the overall strategic policy of the organisation has been decided. If this changes over time, then human resource strategy must be adapted in response.
- It is inevitable that estimates of future demand will be used in devising a strategy. These will be subject to changing economic and competitive conditions. Creating a human resource strategy will be more difficult if the business operates in rapidly changing markets.
- Increasingly, **line managers** are asked to play a greater role in implementing human resource strategy. For example, appraisal interviews are more likely to be carried out by these individuals rather than by personnel specialists. In some organisations it is difficult to convince line managers to take employee-related issues seriously. As a result the policy is not executed as intended.

41.3 The link between human resource strategy and competitive advantage

Human resource strategy can provide an organisation with competitive advantage in two ways:

- **Human capital advantage** – this involves selecting appropriate employees, appraising their performance, then rewarding them in a way which fosters commitment. The human resource cycle can be used to shape employees to the needs of the organisation (see Figure 41.1).

- **Human process advantage** – this involves developing the ability of people within the organisation to learn from past experiences. For example, implementing the firm's strategy, working together and developing innovative ideas.

> *human resource advantage*
> *=*
> *human capital advantage*
> *+*
> *human process advantage*

A competitive advantage based on **organisational learning** may last longer than one based on human capital. This is because competitors can also select or develop individuals with appropriate talent. However, the collective experiences and knowledge of an organisation, which has been developed over time, is not easy to copy. For 20 years reporters asked Liverpool managers for the secret of the club's amazing success. There was no secret. It rested in the accumulated wisdom of all the managerial and 'boot room' staff at the club.

41.4 How to develop a competitive advantage based on human capital

The human resource cycle identifies four functions performed within all organisations with respect to

employees. These are selection, appraisal, reward and development. Human resource strategy demands that the organisation should undertake these activities in a planned and systematic way (see Figure 41.2).

Figure 41.2 The link between a strategic approach to managing the HR cycle and competitive success

THE STRATEGIC SELECTION OF HUMAN RESOURCES

Managers are selected to carry out the strategic objectives of an organisation. These should be based upon the requirements of the competitive environment within which the firm operates. One theory is that the selection of employees should reflect the qualities appropriate to the different stages of the product life cycle.

Figure 41.1 Human resource strategy: building a human resource advantage

When selecting a manager to develop a product in a growing market, the firm should seek an individual who is highly competitive by nature and willing to take risks. A young and ambitious recruit who has strong development potential.

The management of a product in the mature phase of the life cycle demands a person tolerant of risk, but who does not seek it.

When a product is in decline, an experienced manager, willing to stress efficiency, is required. The individual must be prepared to accept the product's market position and place emphasis on results now, rather than planning for returns in the future (see Figure 41.3).

Process by which selection is under taken

Life cycle stages

Qualities of the ideal appointment
Knowledge, skills and experience

Figure 41.3 The strategic selection of human resources

A strategic approach to the selection of human resources is made more difficult by the weaknesses of existing selection techniques. For example, interviews are often used to compare candidates with each other. Psychometric tests are employed to identify a person's individual strengths. When firms use these methods they often focus on the applicants for the post, rather than on the needs of the business. In his football management days, TV commentator Ron Atkinson was like that. He would go off to find a strong defender, but come back with another skillful, pacey winger.

Selecting employees in a strategic way is a complex task. It is easy to choose the best of those candidates who offer themselves for a position. Human resource strategy involves appointing an individual on the basis of the extent to which their personal skills and knowledge fit the firm's requirements. This may mean the most highly qualified or experienced candidate is not selected.

THE STRATEGIC APPRAISAL OF HUMAN RESOURCES

Appraisal is the process of gathering and sharing information about an individual in the workplace in order to assess his or her effectiveness and improve performance. The objective is to increase the efficiency of the organisation by trying to get the best out of each individual working in it.

The process used to deliver appraisal should reflect the firm's market environment. The manager of a new product might be appraised by a colleague from another expanding part of the organisation. This would encourage a competitive approach. In contrast,

a manager dealing with a product in decline might be regularly appraised by a superior in order to place emphasis on short-term performance (see Figure 41.4).

Process by which appraisal is under taken

Life cycle stages

Performance targets established
Time frame, information collected

Figure 41.4 The strategic appraisal of human resources

In many firms the focus of appraisal is on the personal development or reward of the individual, rather than the organisation's goals. As a result, appraisal systems often fail to consider how the performance of an employee relates to the wider strategic position of the organisation. Those companies who adopt a more strategic approach to appraisal can gain an advantage over their competitors.

THE STRATEGIC DEVELOPMENT OF HUMAN RESOURCES

The strategic purpose of a development programme is to anticipate the skills and knowledge that will be needed by employees in future. This should enable the business to meet its objectives. This means that internal and external factors facing the firm must be considered when designing a scheme. If a firm anticipates that Britain will join the single currency within a year, individual development programmes may include intensive training on foreign language skills.

A firm plans the training of its employees so that the right number of individuals are in place, with the appropriate skills, to compete successfully in the marketplace. In order to achieve this, the selection and development of the workforce must be integrated. Where it is not possible to recruit individuals with a particular ability then the training programme must be used to fill this gap.

REWARD SYSTEMS – A DEBATE OVER HUMAN RESOURCE STRATEGY

The reward system of an organisation is its method of remunerating employees. Both financial and non-financial benefits must be considered. Most human resource managers believe the reward system should reflect the contribution of individuals to the firm's operation, their level of skill and market worth. This may seem reasonable, even obvious. It can lead to controversy, however. Successive governments have wanted to change the way teachers are paid. Maths teachers paid more than French teachers, 'good' teachers paid more than 'bad' ones. Or might head teachers pay their favourites more than the

IMPROVING UK PERFORMANCE

A 2002 study by McKinsey, management consultants, found a statistical link between good management practices and high productivity. UK factories owned by US and Japanese firms had over 50% higher productivity than UK-owned plants. Some of the explanations were operational, such as the take-up of lean production techniques by fewer than 40% of UK-owned firms. Even more important, said McKinsey, was good use of staff, by involvement, motivation and two-way communication. There was no doubt that effective management of staff was all-important, though the issues McKinsey raised tend not to be high on the agenda of most human resource departments.

ones who argue and criticise? Forty years ago, Professor Herzberg demonstrated that pay has great potential to cause dissatisfaction at work. Modern human resource managers often seem to forget Herzberg's statement that 'the best way to pay people is a monthly salary – period'.

A strategic approach to devising a reward system requires that the objectives of the business be considered. Managers should identify the performance required from an employee in order to help the company to meet its goals. Human resource managers then devise a reward package to attempt to motivate the individual to achieve the desired outcome. This, of course, contradicts the finding of motivation theorists that money is not a motivator. In effect, the approach taken by human resource professionals would be categorised by McGregor as Theory X.

The human resource approach is that the reward system should mirror market conditions. The different competitive climates created by each stage of the product life cycle could form the basis for developing employee compensation packages.

- The manager of a product in a growing market might be paid a basic salary with few fringe benefits. This would be complemented by a substantial incentive element based on market share. Payments in lump sums would be made as particular targets were achieved.
- A reward package for a manager working within a mature market would have a greater stable element in his or her basic salary, with a number of incremental steps based on time served in the post. Bonus payments might reflect the profit earned on the product concerned. Fringe benefits, such as a pension scheme or company car, would form a large element of the scheme.

- A manager dealing with a product in decline would not expect to be rewarded on the basis of market performance. Basic salary would therefore be high, with no incentive element.

The process of designing reward systems in a strategic way would appear to be relatively simple. Despite this there is limited evidence that packages of this type are successful in producing measurable improvements in business performance.

The hope is that reward systems, used strategically, should encourage action consistent with corporate strategy. And therefore form the basis of a human capital advantage for the business. The weakness is that controlling staff behaviour through pay may be based upon fundamental misunderstandings of human psychology. Offering a successful band £5 million for a new recording contract does not guarantee a great album.

MARKS & SPENCER'S FIGHTBACK

After 2 years of falling profits and reputation, Marks & Spencer started to turn itself around in 2001. As part of this process, the HR function was restructured to bring head office and store HR under one management team. This was to give HR a more strategic role, rather than purely serving the day-to-day needs of individual managers.

According to Naomi Stanford of Marks & Spencer, the result was that HR executives were able to:

- form 'business involvement groups' to encourage two-way communication between staff and management
- work with the stores to forge an M&S culture recognisable to our customers
- support the recruitment and departure of staff.

Without question, the long-term success of Marks & Spencer depends upon effective management and motivation of staff. It remains to be seen whether this new approach is the answer.

41.5 Developing a competitive advantage

THE LEARNING ORGANISATION

Over a period of time organisations learn how to compete in a particular market. They develop valuable resources and capabilities which form the basis of an advantage over other companies. This knowledge and experience lies within individuals. Yet no one person may know enough to be effective alone. The collective learning of employees, and the processes used by the organisation to compete, forms a vital weapon within a market. Rival firms are unlikely to possess this organisational learning, because their employees have not shared the same experiences.

In order to be of real value to a business the knowledge and processes developed must be appropriate to a large customer base, or be transferable into other markets. For example, the deep understanding of its customers and staff enabled Sony to diversify successfully into the computer games market. The capacity of an organisation to adapt and learn from experience is therefore a highly valuable asset.

Human resource strategy involves not only building competitive advantage based on human capital. Even more important may be the development of a learning organisation capable of creating and sustaining a competitive advantage.

Human resource strategy aims to build a long-term advantage over competitors based upon human capital and process. In so doing, human resource policies must reflect the firm's competitive environment.

Human resource professionals worry that a strategic approach to human resources may be restricted by trade unions. The ability of the business to shape individual, reward, appraisal or development programmes may be limited by pressure upon a firm to maintain an existing organisation, or industry-wide, scheme. Far more important, however, may be that the attempt to 'shape' individuals flies in the face of convincing research evidence on human psychology. The long-term strategic purpose of HRM may need to incorporate motivation theory for it to be fully effective.

An approach that places organisational objectives before the needs of individual employees may also be questioned ethically. For example, human resource strategy implies that training programmes should focus on company requirements rather than on personal development. This runs counter to movements such as Investors In People which emphasise that personal development should be encouraged by an employer, whether or not there is any direct payback for the firm.

ISSUES FOR analysis

When considering the way in which an organisation manages human resources a number of key questions can be asked in order to analyse the extent to which a strategic approach is being adopted.

- Is there a clear indication that the organisation is planning its future workforce requirements in advance? If so, how far in advance? If declining numbers of physics students means a teacher must be retrained for Business Studies, it will take at least a year.
- To what extent does the planning which is taking place consider the integrated needs of the firm's different departments?
- Does the selection policy of the organisation recruit individuals with the appropriate skills, knowledge and attitudes to deliver the strategic policy? Or does it merely recruit safe, familiar types of people who may be suitable to today's needs, but unable to adapt to change tomorrow?
- Does the appraisal programme of the organisation encourage employees to achieve a level of performance in line with strategic policy? Or has it become a bureaucratic routine?
- Does the approach to training help to develop employees better able to implement company strategy successfully?
- Does the organisation's reward system encourage actions consistent with strategic policy? Or does it cause disharmony due to perceived unfairness between different staff?
- What attempts are made by the organisation to capture the benefits of existing organisation learning and use it to guide the firm's future strategic direction?
- What measures are being employed in order to evaluate the impact of any human resource strategy adopted?

KEY terms

human capital advantage – creating a workforce with knowledge and skills more appropriate to the firm's environment than that of competitors. This can be achieved by selecting suitable employees, appraising their performance, rewarding them in a way which fosters commitment and developing them.

human process advantage – creating a culture within the organisation which helps employees to learn from past experiences and thus outperform the competition.

labour turnover – a measure of the rate at which individuals leave the organisation. When high the figure may reflect an ineffective human resource strategy.

line managers – are responsible for meeting key operational targets. Authority is passed 'down the line' to them.

organisational learning – the build-up of knowledge within a workforce which helps in recognising potential problems and may make it easier to work together to achieve change.

A Level Exercises

A. REVISION QUESTIONS
(40 marks; 70 minutes)

Read the unit, then answer:

1 What is the main function of workforce planning? *(3)*
2 Why must workforce planning be an integrated process? *(3)*
3 What might be the main benefits of creating a human resource strategy for:
   a fast-expanding chain of pubs *(4)*
   b a school suffering from falling numbers? *(4)*
4 Outline two benefits that might result from giving line managers an increasing role in implementing human resource strategy. *(6)*
5 Why is a human process advantage likely to be of greater long-term significance to a business than a human capital advantage? *(3)*
6 What is organisational learning and how might it form the basis of a competitive advantage for a business? *(5)*
7 Explain the meaning of the phrase 'strategic appraisal of human resources' *(4)*
8 The section in the text on the debate over human resource strategy argues the case for and against financially based reward systems. Explain which side of the argument you favour. *(8)*

B. REVISION EXERCISES

B1 Data Response

The Strategic Use of Human Resources
A recent survey by the Industrial Society of 460 companies showed that 40% still use the term 'personnel' manager (or director) to describe the individual in charge of the organisation's employees. In contrast, only 30% have adopted the term 'human resource' manager (or director). In 42% of the organisations questioned, the 'people' function had some form of representation on the board of directors. It is clear from this that in the majority of firms there is none.

The research also considered which individuals within the firm would have primary responsibility for dealing with key human resource issues. The table below summarises the response of organisations (the figures show the percentage of firms surveyed).

	Chief Executive	Personnel/ HRM	Line Manager
Recruitment	2%	73%	25%
Workforce growth/cuts	43%	31%	22%
Appraisal	1%	41%	55%
Training	1%	75%	22%
Reward	15%	76%	6%
Organisation culture	70%	26%	4%
Health & safety	6%	39%	23%

Questions *(30 marks; 35 minutes)*

1 Does the fact that many firms still use the term personnel manager, rather than human resource manager, have any significance for the way in which UK industry approaches the strategic use of human resources? *(3)*
2 Does the lack of representation of the human resource function on 58% of company boards have any significance for the way in which UK industry approaches the strategic use of human resources? *(5)*
3 On the basis of the evidence provided, which areas of the human resource cycle do HR/personnel managers have most influence over? *(4)*
4 a Which areas of human resource policy most frequently interest chief executive officers? *(3)*
   b Why may they be particularly interested in these? *(6)*
5 Evaluate the extent to which the evidence presented suggests that human resources are being managed in a strategic way by UK industry. What further information would help you to examine this issue in greater detail? *(9)*

B2 Case Study
Cutbacks at Merrill Lynch
In the summer and early Autumn of 1998 a series of economic and financial crises hit banks and investment houses alike. Few are bigger than Merrill Lynch, America's biggest securities firm. For this giant, the consequence was giant losses, as a $500 million profit in 1997 became a loss of $164 million in 1998.

In October, the chairman of Merrill Lynch took swift action. He announced a 3,400 worldwide staff cutback – including 400 in London. As the *Guardian* put it: 'Merrill is having to adapt to a more treacherous environment'. The newspapers were struck by the contrast with the chairman's confident strategy statement when he took over in 1996. Then he had mapped out an aggressive thrust into foreign markets to secure Merrill's place as the top global investment bank. The chairman's goal had been to push overseas revenues from 30% to 50% of the total by 2000. That meant expanding the firm's operations through recruitment drives in London, Tokyo and Latin America. Now his worldwide staff cutbacks acknowledged that this target would not be achieved.

The big test for Merrill's senior management would be maintaining staff morale. Throughout its 75-year history, Merrill Lynch has emphasised teamwork instead of cultivating a star system. Would the team spirit be harmed by the cutbacks? The initial response of staff seemed favourable. One executive said of the chairman: 'He is a leader and I have always been impressed by him.' A former Merrill boss said: 'There was something unusual about his ability to work with subordinates. He accomplished our goals and seemed to do it effortlessly.'

Source: The *Guardian*, 17/10/98

Questions   (40 marks; 60 minutes)

1 a What were the Merrill chairman's original business objectives?   (4)

  b Did the human resource strategy match the objective?   (4)

2 Figure 41.2 shows how a successful strategic approach needs to be rooted in the business environment within which the firm works. How well did Merrill Lynch's experience fit that model?   (6)

3 The business had been built up to its top spot through successful teamworking and delegation. What benefits would such an approach offer a service business such as Merrill Lynch?   (10)

4 Discuss why cutbacks may be accepted by some staff, but cause great hostility in other workplaces?   (8)

5 Merrill Lynch has been a hugely profitable business for many years. Is it morally acceptable that one year's losses should lead to redundancies among staff who were not responsible for the strategic mistakes which led to the cutbacks?   (8)

C. ESSAY QUESTIONS

1 Shortly after being appointed, the new chief executive officer announced her determination to 'develop a human resource strategy for the organisation'. Discuss what form this initiative might take.

2 Discuss the benefits to a firm of a strategy to become a 'learning organisation'.

3 Human resource strategy can only have impact within a business if it plays a central role in boardroom decisions. Why may so many human resource departments find it so difficult to obtain full representation at director level?

PERFORMANCE MEASUREMENT

DEFINITION
The process of monitoring employee performance in an objective way. This measures the success or failure of initiatives such as new working or payment methods.

42.1 The need to measure performance

Managers require an objective, unbiased way to measure the performance of personnel. The firm needs to know several things:

- Is the workforce fully motivated?
- Is the workforce as productive as it could be?
- Are the personnel policies of the business helping the business to meet its goals?

A busy, motivated and productive workforce
© Getty Images

It is not possible to measure these things directly. How, for example, can the level of motivation of workers be measured accurately? Instead, a series of indicators are used which, when analysed, can show the firm if its personnel policies are contributing as much to the firm as they should.

There are four key performance indicators used to measure the effectiveness of a personnel department. They are:

- labour productivity
- absenteeism
- labour turnover
- waste levels

Coffee time in the office – valuable communication or poor productivity? (© Steve Prezant/Corbis)

42.2 Labour productivity

CALCULATING LABOUR PRODUCTIVITY

Labour productivity is often seen as the single most important measure of how well a firm's workers are doing. It compares the number of workers with the output that they are producing. It is expressed through the formula:

$$\text{labour productivity} = \frac{\text{output per period}}{\text{no. of employees per period}}$$

For example, if a window cleaner employs 10 people and in a day will normally clean the windows of 150 houses, then the productivity is:

$$\frac{150}{10} = 15 \text{ houses per worker per day}$$

At its simplest, the higher the productivity of the workforce, the better it is performing. Any increase in the productivity figure suggests an improvement in efficiency. Lean production systems look for the greatest outputs from the least inputs. Seeking ways in which output (production) can be increased despite using the same or fewer resources (labour).

The importance of productivity lies in its impact on labour costs per unit. For example, the productivity of AES Cleaning is 15 houses per worker per day; MS Cleaning achieves only 10. Assuming a daily rate of pay of £45, the labour cost per house is £3 for AES but £4.50 for MS Cleaning. Higher productivity leads to lower labour costs per unit. And therefore greater competitiveness both here and against international rivals.

Other issues concerning productivity are dealt with in Unit 30.

PRODUCTIVITY IN THE NHS

The Government has made the funding of the NHS a major strand of its public spending. In the last 4 years, its budget has increased by a third in real terms, and it has been promised a 7.4% increase each year for the next 5 years. Is this money being well spent?

Most of the increases seem to be spent on wages – pay increases above the rate of inflation have been given to some groups of NHS workers, and the number of staff has also increased. None of this seems to have been matched by increases in productivity. The number of admissions has not changed significantly, and other, more complex measures of productivity also fail to give any sign of improvement. In fact, some measures, such as those used by the London School of Economics and the Office for National Statistics, suggest that productivity has declined sharply in the last 2 years.

Source: *The Economist,* 22/6/02

LABOUR PRODUCTIVITY AND COMPETITIVENESS

Labour productivity is a key factor in a firm's level of competitiveness. If a firm is able to produce more from the same, or fewer, number of workers, then there will be definite cost advantages to be gained. This will be particularly true where labour forms a large part of a firm's total costs.

Since the mid 1990s, British car factories have begun to lead the way in productivity in Europe, making British produced cars much more competitive in the marketplace, and hence improving the position of both the individual businesses and the British economy. Interestingly, most of these successful factories are Japanese owned, such as Nissan, Honda and Toyota.

42.3 Absenteeism

CALCULATING ABSENTEEISM

Absenteeism measures how many workers miss work as a percentage of the total number of workers. It is expressed by the formula:

$$\text{absenteeism} = \frac{\text{no. of staff absent}}{\text{total no. of staff}} \times 100$$

If a firm employs 50 people, and on one day 4 are absent, then the absentee rate for that day would be:

$$\frac{4}{50} \times 100 = 8\%$$

To calculate the absentee rate for a year, we need to know the total number of absences for the year as a percentage of the total number of days that should have been worked. For example, if the firm works 5 days a week for 50 weeks a year, then the total number of days each employee could work in a year would be $5 \times 50 = 250$ days. For 50 members of staff, this would give a total number of possible days to be worked of 12,500 days. If the total number of absences for the year were 750 days, the absentee rate for the year would be:

$$\frac{750}{12,500} \times 100 = 6\%$$

CAUSES OF ABSENTEEISM

Aside from genuine illness, the main causes of absenteeism are linked to failures in the firm's human relations system. Often, these can be linked to Herzberg's '**hygiene factors**', such as:

- poor working conditions, making workers uncomfortable or even causing injury
- a failure to respect individuals and to be concerned with their needs
- a failure of teamworking, leading to feelings of alienation, or even bullying
- over-supervision, causing **stress** or the feeling of not being trusted at work
- inappropriate tasks, leading to stress due to workers being unable to complete their tasks satisfactorily
- pay rates that workers believe are too low for the quality or standard of work expected by the job.

THE COSTS OF ABSENTEEISM

For a firm, the costs of absenteeism can be very high.

- Lost production – a direct consequence of absence is that work will not be done. In some cases there may be an opportunity to catch up on the missed work when the absent worker returns. Often, though, the work is lost for ever, as with an absent ambulance driver or production line worker.
- Extra overtime – if deadlines are pressing for the completion of work, it may be necessary for managers to ask other workers to undertake some extra work to meet deadlines. This will involve an extra cost for the firm in the form of overtime payments, as well as possibly the extra costs involved in keeping the plant open to complete the pressing order.
- Increased levels of absenteeism – if workers sense a culture of absenteeism spreading within the firm,

they are more likely to find reasons for absence themselves, leading to a snowballing problem.

MEASURES TO REDUCE ABSENTEEISM

When a firm is faced with the problem of high levels of absenteeism, it will normally look to its human relations system for remedies, such as:

- Flexitime – allows workers some degree of control over the hours they are at work. This allows workers to arrange times that are more convenient to themselves. It can help relieve the pressures caused by such things as childcare or transport problems, which could otherwise lead to workers taking time off as though they were sick.
- Job enrichment – a satisfying, challenging job will ensure that people want to come to work in the morning.
- Improved working conditions – better conditions will make work a more attractive place to be, and cause less dissatisfaction.
- Improved human relations – making workers feel more valued at work will allow them to feel more committed to their workplace. People who feel part of a team do not want to let others down.
- More controversially, the firm could institute extra pay for staff who attend regularly in the form of attendance bonuses. A recent study by the Industrial Society found that the 15% of employers who have introduced such a system actually face *higher* absence rates than those that do not. It is

DTI'S WORK-LIFE BALANCE CAMPAIGN

The Government has urged businesses to try to balance the demands on their workers after a study showed that stress-related absenteeism costs business £7.1 million every week. Many employers seem unaware of how much absenteeism affects profits.

Although the study stresses the benefits of 'work-life balance policies' it found that most businesses had never even considered introducing methods such as flexible working, job shares or employee benefit packages.

The survey found that UK employers are 5 times more likely to offer stress counselling than preventative policies. It seems that, as yet, British businesses have failed to realise that prevention of stress would be better, and cheaper, than attempting to give a cure after problems have arisen.

Source: *Personnel Today*, 2/04/02

likely that this is because the attempted solution, extra pay, does not actually address the problems that cause the absenteeism in the first place.

42.4 Labour turnover

MEASURING LABOUR TURNOVER

This is a measure of the rate of change of a firm's workforce. It is measured by the formula:

$$\text{labour turnover} = \frac{\text{no. of staff leaving per year}}{\text{average no. of staff}} \times 100$$

So a firm which has seen 5 people leave out of its staff of 50 has a labour turnover of:

$$\frac{5}{50} \times 100 = 10\%$$

As with all of these figures, it would be a mistake to take one figure in isolation. It would be better to look at how the figure has changed over a number of years. And to look for the reasons why the turnover rate is as it is.

CAUSES OF LABOUR TURNOVER

If the rate of labour turnover is increasing, it may be a sign of dissatisfaction within the workforce. If so, the possible causes could be either internal to the firm or external.

Internal causes of an increasing rate of labour turnover could be:

- A poor recruitment and selection procedure, which may appoint the wrong person to the wrong post. If this happens, then eventually the misplaced workers will wish to leave to find a post more suited to their particular interests or talents.
- Ineffective motivation or leadership, leading to workers lacking commitment to the firm. They will feel no sense of loyalty or ownership to the business, and will tend to look outside the firm for promotions or new career opportunities. They will not be interested in looking for new ways in which they could contribute to the firm.
- Wage levels that are lower than those being earned by similar workers in other local firms. If wage rates are not competitive, workers will feel dissatisfied by their position. They may look elsewhere to find a better reward for doing a similar job.

External causes of an increasing rate of labour turnover could be:

- More local vacancies arising, perhaps due to the setting up or expansion of other firms in the area.
- Better transport links, making a wider geographical area accessible to workers. New public transport systems such as Manchester's network of trams or Newcastle's Metro rail links enable workers to take employment that was previously out of their reach.

Business

IN

CONSEQUENCES OF HIGH LABOUR TURNOVER

A high rate of labour turnover can have both negative and positive effects on a firm. The negative aspects would be:

- the cost of recruitment of replacements
- the cost of retraining replacements
- the time taken for new recruits to settle into the business and adopt the firm's culture
- the loss of productivity while the new workers adjust.

On the positive side, labour turnover can benefit the business in several ways:

- new workers can bring new ideas and enthusiasm to the firm
- workers with specific skills can be employed rather than having to train up existing workers from scratch
- new ways of solving problems can be seen by workers with a different perspective, whereas existing workers may rely on tried and trusted techniques that have worked in the past.

On balance, then, there is a need for firms to achieve the *right* level of labour turnover, rather than aiming for the lowest possible level.

42.5 Waste levels

CALCULATING WASTE LEVELS

The level of waste produced by the firm is a clear indication of its efficiency. The notion of **zero defects** as an **organisational goal**, and lean production minimising the inputs in relation to the outputs of the firm, both suggest that a firm should minimise its waste.

An indicator of waste levels is found by using the formula:

$$\frac{\text{quantity of waste materials}}{\text{total production}} \times 100$$

If a firm that produces 10,000 items in a year has to scrap the equivalent of 600 items per year, it will have a waste level of:

$$\frac{600}{10,000} \times 100 = 6\%$$

THE COST OF WASTE MATERIALS

Having waste materials is clearly a cost to the business, and reducing waste will reduce these costs and increase efficiency. The main costs associated with waste are:

- the actual cost of the unused or scrapped materials
- the cost of reworking damaged goods
- the loss of reputation caused by faulty products being sold or delivery dates being missed.

REASONS FOR FIRMS PRODUCING WASTE

If a firm wishes to minimise its waste levels, it will need to know why such waste is happening. Likely causes of waste are:

- inadequate training – workers who have not been fully trained in production techniques are more likely to make mistakes
- poor layout of the factory – if products are moved too often whilst under production there is a greater possibility of damage to the work in progress
- a lack of commitment from workers – workers who do not take a pride in their work or who do not feel involved in the success or otherwise of the business will take less care in their work and be more likely to make mistakes.

The solution to these problems lies partly with the personnel function but also with the operations management. The personnel department will have the responsibility to ensure that workers are properly trained. The factory layout is the job of operations managers. Staff motivation is the responsibility of all managers.

42.6 Evaluating a personnel strategy

The measures listed in the table below tell the firm something about its performance. On their own,

Summary of personnel performance indicators	
Labour productivity	$\dfrac{\textit{output per period}}{\textit{no. of employees per period}}$
Absenteeism	$\dfrac{\textit{no. of staff absent}}{\textit{total no. of staff}} \times 100$
Labour turnover	$\dfrac{\textit{no. of staff leaving the firm per year}}{\textit{average no. of staff}} \times 100$
Waste levels	$\dfrac{\textit{quantity of waste materials}}{\textit{total production}}$

though, the figures produced say very little. Comparisons are necessary:

- over time (this year versus last)
- with other similar firms (benchmarking, see Unit 52)
- with targets, such as a 20% improvement on last year.

Each of these comparisons will tell the firm how it is performing in relation to a yardstick. This will indicate to the firm where it is performing well and where it may have a problem. The firm must then investigate carefully the reasons for its performance before it can judge how well its personnel function is operating.

For example, labour productivity may have fallen since 12 months ago. Closer investigation may show that the fall was due to the time taken to train staff on new machinery installed at the start of the year. Figures may show that productivity in the last six months was actually higher than at any time in the past, and the firm could be confident that future productivity will continue to increase. An apparent problem was actually masking an improvement for the firm.

There are several important business issues relating to personnel performance indicators:

- Business success comes from being the best and staying the best. This is always hard but is the only way to be sure of staying at the top. Football managers might say all that counts is what happens on the pitch, but lateness or absence from training is often a good indicator of problems to come. Every manager should be alert to early warning signs, find out the reasons and tackle them straight away.
- All personnel issues are considered 'soft' by some employers. Who cares about labour turnover or health issues, they say, as long as the job gets done and profits are high? This may be true in the short term. For firms pursuing long-term growth, however, the quality and involvement of staff is crucial. So stress matters. So does absence, lateness or low morale.
- In America fewer than one in ten workers belongs to a trade union. In Britain more than one-third are union members. For employers who want to operate without a union, it is clear that good personnel practices are the best way to avoid workforce pressure for union representation. Careful monitoring of performance indicators can enable problems to be spotted and sorted. Trade union officials can fulfil that role, but not all employers want them to.

Performance **ratios** such as labour turnover raise questions. They do not supply answers. Follow-up staff surveys or chats may be needed to discover the underlying problems. Ratios give the firm an indication of what issues need addressing if the firm is to improve its position in the future, but this must be taken within the context of the business as a whole. A high labour turnover figure may have been the result of a deliberate policy to bring in younger members of staff who may be more adaptable to a changing situation at the factory.

Measures of personnel effectiveness are merely indicators for a firm to see where it may be facing problems. The measures may indicate poor performance, or reflect the short-term effect of a change in business strategy.

It must be remembered that these figures are all looking to the past. They tell the firm what has happened to its workforce. Although this has a strong element of objectivity, it is not as valuable as an indication of how the indicators may look in the future.

Most importantly, the figures must be looked at in relation to the objectives of the organisation. A profit-maximising firm will take a completely different view of performance indicators than a family firm which wants to build its long-term market standing.

KEY terms

hygiene factors – elements of working life that have the potential to cause dissatisfaction, such as salary, working conditions, status and over-supervision.

organisational goal – the objectives of the whole enterprise, such as to be the world Number 1 by 2010.

ratio – relating one figure to another to identify relative performance.

stress – the mental and physical wear and tear caused by the feeling that your life is out of your control. This can be caused by severe overwork, but is more often associated with alienating, repetitive jobs.

zero defects – the desire to cut waste to zero. The British Standards Institute has a standard for processes which achieve zero emissions, i.e. no pollution at all.

A Level Exercises

A. REVISION QUESTIONS
(25 marks; 40 minutes)

Read the unit, then answer:

1 Define the following terms:
   a labour productivity
   b labour turnover
   c waste levels. *(9)*
2 Why might an increase in labour productivity not reflect an improvement in performance? *(4)*
3 Give three ways in which a firm could attempt to reduce its level of absenteeism. *(3)*
4 In what ways might labour turnover benefit the firm? *(4)*
5 How might a firm know if its personnel strategy was working effectively? *(5)*

B. REVISION EXERCISES

B1 Data Response
A firm has the following data on its personnel function:

	Year 1	Year 2
Output	50,000	55,000
Quantity of waste material	600	350
Average no. of workers	250	220
No. of staff leaving the firm	12	8
Working days per worker (possible)	230	230
Working days lost for health reasons	1,725	1,012
Average no. of staff absent	4	3

Questions *(30 marks; 35 minutes)*
1 Calculate the following ratios for both years:
   a labour productivity
   b absenteeism
   c labour turnover
   d waste levels
2 Explain what questions these figures might raise in the minds of the firm's management. *(15)*

B2 Data Response

Monitoring Personnel Performance at Best Motors
James West, the new personnel officer at Best Motors, manufacturer of the world-famous handmade sports cars of the same name, sat down at his desk and considered the figures in front of him (see the table below). He would need to report on the existing position of the business to Elizabeth Best, the chief executive, on Friday.

James knew the company operated for 50 weeks of the year (only closing down for the annual works holiday) and that all employees worked full-time, five days each week. He opened his briefcase and got out a calculator. 'The first thing to do is determine the key human resource indicators,' he thought to himself as he started to work.

Questions *(30 marks; 35 minutes)*
1 Calculate labour turnover, absenteeism and labour productivity at Best Motors for all five years. *(8)*
2 Using your results and the data for 'shop-floor accidents', evaluate the effectiveness of Best Motors' human resource strategy. *(9)*
3 What additional information would you seek to help James gain a better understanding of the human resource strategy at Best's? *(5)*
4 Suggest a policy approach to deal with Best's human resource difficulties which James might recommend to Elizabeth when he makes his report at the Friday meeting *(8)*

Personnel Performance – Best Motors

	4 years ago	3 years ago	2 years ago	Last year	This year
No. of leavers	3	2	4	6	7
Working days lost due to absence	124	102	145	169	204
Total annual output	780	803	805	790	811
No. of shop-floor accidents	5	3	7	2	4
Average no. of employees	23	25	25	24	26

B3 Case Study

Turner's Butchers is a chain of three shops in a large town in the North of England. The shops are all supplied with prepared and packaged produce from Turner's Farm, owned by the same family.

The management is particularly concerned at present by the differing performance of the three shops. In particular, it feels there may be a problem with the personnel management in the chain. The concerns were highlighted recently in a report looking at various indicators of personnel effectiveness.

The key section of the report is shown below.

Workforce performance data per shop

	Grayton Road	St. John's Precinct	Lark Hill
Staff (full-time)	8	6	7
Labour turnover	25%	150%	0
Absence rate	5%	12%	1%
Sales per employee	£14,000	£15,000	£18,000

Questions *(30 marks; 45 minutes)*

1 Briefly outline your observations on each of the three shops in terms of their personnel management. *(12)*
2 Give possible reasons for the factors you described in question 1. *(9)*
3 Taking the business as a whole, make justified recommendations as to how any problems could be tackled by the management. *(9)*

B4 Case Study

Steve Fitzhugh and Sonia Oates were arguing – again. The co-founders and owners of Economic Solutions found themselves disagreeing on many aspects of running their business. Established 4 years ago, the firm specialised in offering ergonomic solutions to organisations who wished to improve their general productivity. This time, Sonia was concerned that their own productivity was slipping. She also had concerns with several other aspects of their personnel performance. For example, in the first few years it was almost unheard of for staff to be off work, yet now the staff absence list seemed to be growing on a weekly basis. The firm had also seen a moderate increase in the number of staff leaving, some of whom went on to set up their own businesses offering a similar service.

Steve, on the other hand, felt that these issues were an inevitable part of the life cycle of a new firm.

Questions *(25 marks; 30 minutes)*

1 Outline two ways to measure the productivity of a service firm such as Economic Solutions. *(4)*
2 To what extent should Sonia be concerned about 'a moderate increase in the number of staff leaving' the firm? *(9)*
3 How far do you agree with Steve when he says 'these issues are an inevitable part of the life cycle of a new firm'? *(12)*

C. ESSAY QUESTIONS

1 'Personnel ratios raise questions. Good managers make sure they answer them.' Evaluate this statement.
2 Analyse the ways in which a firm can improve the productivity of its workforce.
3 Assess the ways in which a firm may respond to an increasing rate of labour turnover.

CHANGE MANAGEMENT

DEFINITION

The management of change is the process of planning, implementing, controlling and reviewing the movement of an organisation from its current state to a new position which is believed to be more desirable.

The most extreme change would involve abolishing the existing way of doing things and starting again. More often, adjustments are made to the present approach in order to fit a new position. For example, many companies did this in reorganising their management structure in response to recession in the early 1990s.

All change, from introducing a new piece of machinery to restructuring the organisation, has implications for employees. The management of people is the largest problem which faces those who are trying to move the business successfully to a new position.

43.1 Change

The rate of change in organisations has increased rapidly in the last 15 years. For example, the development of information technology is so great that for many employees their house will soon also be their place of work. The computer firm Digital already has in excess of 1,000 of its 4,000 workforce operating from home.

Today, change is a permanent characteristic of business activity. In some cases it can be anticipated and therefore planned for, in others it is unexpected. For example, a rapid growth in sales may demand extensive change. If it can be foreseen, this will allow the process of expansion to be managed more effectively. Even when a business cannot control the change, anticipating it will allow plans to be made. This is why Nike has always employed an army of young people it calls 'coolbunters'. Their job is to keep in touch with the opinions and attitudes of American youth, and then keep Nike up to date.

In contrast, some changes may be impossible to forecast. For example, the impact of the Foot and Mouth crisis on UK farmers. The effect will be heightened when the factors driving change fall beyond the control of the business, as was true in this case. Shifts in the external business environment are often the most difficult changes which face firms. New consumer tastes, the rise of competitors, reform of legislation, or economic fluctuations are examples of these movements. A firm's managers can try to influence these changes through actions such as advertising or pressure group activity, but their attempts may fail.

The arrow in Figure 43.1 illustrates the direction of growing uncertainty (low to high), and therefore risk, to the organisation associated with different types of change.

	Anticipated change	Unanticipated change
Within business control	**Example** Introduction of new production technology	**Example** Sudden increase in demand requiring expansion
Outside business control	**Example** Change in pattern of demand due to demographic shift	**Example** Collapse of a key supplier

Figure 43.1 Types of change

43.2 Managing a change programme

Figure 43.2 illustrates the four phases involved in managing change.

PLANNING

The first step when organising a change programme is the recognition that a new approach to a given prob-

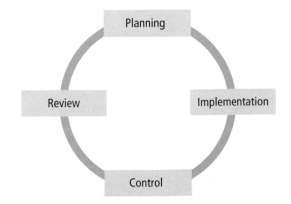

Figure 43.2 Managing change

lem is required. It is then necessary to find a solution which matches the policy to be adopted, to changed circumstances.

For example, consider an organisation which manufactures plastic moulded products, such as the cases for CDs and video games. The company has greater production costs than its immediate competitors and is experiencing difficulties with high absenteeism amongst its shop-floor employees.

The three key questions when planning change management are:

- **Where are we now?**
  e.g. high costs and high absenteeism
- **Where do we want to be?**
  e.g. reduced costs and lower absenteeism
- **How do we get there?**
  e.g. introduce teams producing in work 'cells'.

A change of this kind has many implications:

- jobs would have to be redesigned
- the shop-floor layout changed
- workers trained in new skills
- the recruitment policy adjusted to employ workers with greater potential for moving flexibly between tasks within the cell.

The process of implementing these changes will be made much easier if the people affected by them are involved in identifying the initial problem and evaluating the proposed solution.

IMPLEMENTATION

People implement change, but they are also the most important barrier to its success. Resistance to change may occur in the process of putting the planned developments into action.

Individuals may resist the implementation of change:

- To preserve existing routine.
- To protect pay and employment – if payment is based on output produced, workers may find themselves earning less after the change. This is because it will take time to get used to the new way of doing things.
- To avoid threat to security and status – change can endanger a person's position of authority. As a result they may try to preserve their area of power and influence by resisting the development.
- To maintain group membership – workers may resist change because they are worried about what others may think if they do not. The 'norms', or accepted views, established by a group of employees who work together can be very strong. If some people see a change of production as threatening they may influence the attitudes of the other people around them.

Overcoming resistance to change: There are two key ways in which managers can help individuals overcome their natural resistance to change (see Figure 43.3).

Figure 43.3 Individuals resist the implementation of change

TAXING TIMES AT THE INLAND REVENUE

The Inland Revenue is a government department which organises the collection of tax in the UK. When it introduced a reorganisation of its offices and functions, there seemed to be a positive impact on customer satisfaction.

However, the changes introduced made its employees very unhappy. Two successive surveys of staff attitudes showed widespread hostility on the part of employees to the developments introduced. MORI, the opinion polling company, commissioned by the Board of Inland Revenue, found that 56% of staff 'feel change is happening too rapidly' and only one member of staff in 50 agreed that change had been 'well managed'. A second survey of employee feeling was undertaken by the Industrial Society, again at the request of department officials. It reported 'there is a tremendous thirst for information from senior management ... this leads to a widespread belief that information is being deliberately withheld'.

One workforce representative described staff as experiencing a 'deep-seated crisis in morale', because they are 'starting to feel they are losing sight of their core activity'. He suggested that in the future large numbers of inspectors would leave the department, unable to cope with the change.

IN *Business*

1 Involve those affected by change at every stage of the decision making process. So they understand why a new approach is necessary. Acting in this way develops the commitment of individuals to a decision. If they are involved in the development of the idea from an early stage they have a personal stake in its success.

This approach is used extensively in Japanese companies and is known as 'ringi'. When a decision is to be made, a proposal passes between all the employees who will be affected by it. They are asked to comment on the idea or even suggest a different approach. Gradually agreement about the best way forward emerges and a final plan is developed. Of course, management by consensus is much less useful if rapid change is needed in response to a crisis.

2 Keep all those people affected by a change informed of what is happening at each stage of the process. Make sure everyone is aware of the options available. Many of the difficulties caused by a new situation are the result of a fear of the unknown. By informing those involved some of the uncertainty can be removed.

CONTROL

When a change is introduced the process must be controlled. The final outcome of the programme should be the situation which was identified as 'where we want to be' at the end of the planning phase. Targets should be set for each step of the implementation phase in order that progress is focused and does not lose momentum.

It is important that each target is measurable. It must be possible to say with certainty that it has been achieved. An example of a suitable target is: 'By 31 December this year, 40% of the CD cases produced in this factory should be made by employees working in teams'. This is a measurable target, which can be communicated clearly, understood and therefore used for control purposes. If the outcome of each stage is clearly defined, action can be taken quickly if the process shows any sign of moving out of control.

REVIEW

When the change programme has been implemented the new situation must be analysed. What should be the next phase of the organisation's development? For example, the CD case manufacturer must consider if the movement to cell production has reduced both costs and absenteeism. What new initiatives are required to improve further the competitive position of the company?

A process of constant review is essential because a business which stands still risks moving backwards in the marketplace. New technology, more sophisticated customer requirements and increasing competition may threaten established competitive advantage.

CHANGE FOR THE BETTER

Catomance Technologies, a 60-year-old chemicals manufacturer, nearly hit the buffers in 1999 with a loss of £300,000 on its £4 million turnover. The staff level had halved to 72 employees yet the business still had 6 directors and 4 layers of management. After the managing director led a management buy-out in May 2000, he set about a process of change. The hierarchy was flattened, first to 3 layers, then to 2. New people were brought in who were able to make changes without any 'emotional baggage' caused by long experience of the business and its staff. The sales force was given more authority, enabling the business to act more flexibly when facing competition from major European chemical manufacturers. The changes are working and the business is now profitable.

43.3 Change and the organisation

Businesses consist of individual people who relate to each other within a framework of established customs and practices. These may sometimes be written rules, but are often simply 'the accepted way of doing things'. These traditional approaches can also act as barriers to change, because the organisation shows collective resistance to new developments. This may result in a failure both to recognise the need for change and to implement it effectively (see Figure 43.4).

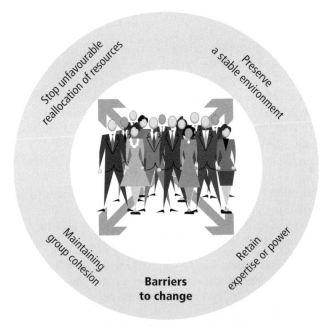

Figure 43.4 Organisations resist the implementation of change

OVERCOMING ORGANISATIONAL RESISTANCE TO CHANGE

In order to overcome resistance to change within an organisation it is necessary to develop a **change management programme** which creates an atmosphere of trust amongst employees. It would help managers to bear in mind Maslow's insights into human psychology. Resistance to change is inevitable if basic human needs are threatened such as security, social ties and personal esteem. It is therefore necessary for managers to consider the human implications of change. If these are understood, they can be planned for, and actions taken to make implementation of the programme as trouble free as possible.

Initially a business must identify the process which is to be altered by the change programme. This may be a particular operating activity, such as production of a given product. Or it may be an organisational issue, for example the way in which communication takes place within the firm.

The 'diamond change management' model shown in Figure 43.5 illustrates the four key elements which should be considered in order to develop an effective programme aimed at overcoming organisational resistance to change.

Figure 43.5 The diamond change management model

Management systems: The objectives of any change introduced should be clearly defined and communicated to employees. The means of informing employees of the goals of a development should be considered carefully. If the purpose of innovation is not clear, individuals will attribute aims which may be false. Rumours about the impact of change will emerge and these will be hard to overcome at a later point once they have gained some acceptance. Planning is also necessary to decide on the extent to which the pay and reward system will be used. For example, staff who must acquire new skills may be encouraged to do so by a pay increase.

Culture and values: Leadership style will have a key impact on the success of a change programme. McGregor's Theory Y manager, who believes that indi-

viduals can be stimulated by their work and will be interested by new developments, will try to encourage employees to get involved in planning change and foster their commitment to its objectives. In contrast, the Theory X manager will consider what steps must be imposed upon employees to ensure the change is adopted with as little resistance as possible. This approach is more likely to use the reward system to facilitate innovation and may resort to coercion or threat. (For example, the possibility of redundancies if change is not accepted).

The organisation's culture will also have to be considered. There may be a long tradition of working in a particular way. It will be important to recognise this and make the need for change very clear.

Technology: The introduction of new technology will often accompany change and at times it will be its main purpose. A change management programme must investigate carefully the potential for introducing supporting information technology. Then ensure continuing research and development to keep one step ahead of the competition.

Skills and organisation: Significant human resource planning issues will often result from major change. The correct number of employees, with appropriate skills, must be in place to implement a change programme successfully. This has important implications for both recruitment and training within the business.

A wide-ranging programme of change may demand a major restructuring of the organisation. For example, the introduction of project teams taking members from different functional departments. In order for such an approach to prove effective employees must be provided with the support required to adjust to changing responsibilities and work practices.

MANAGING THE EXISTING BUSINESS DURING CHANGE

When developing a change management programme it is vital to ensure that existing operations continue to function efficiently. In their enthusiasm to introduce new business processes managers may lose sight of the present position of the firm. Any single change may involve only 10% of the staff. Yet more than 50% of senior management time may be devoted to it. Managers may lose sight of the basics of business life such as customer service. This could be more costly than any resistance to change.

Figure 43.6 illustrates the way in which 'managing the existing business' must be combined with 'managing change' through the three key phases of a change management programme.

By showing a commitment to existing operations, any perceived threat to employee security will be reduced and the introduction of new ideas is therefore more likely to be accepted throughout the organisation.

Source: Marcousé (November 1997)

Figure 43.6 Managing the business during change

43.4 Radical change

BUSINESS PROCESS RE-ENGINEERING

Business process re-engineering (BPR) is an approach to totally rethinking the operation of the organisation.

It starts by asking every individual to map out what they do in their work and how it impacts on the customer experience. It is common to display these around the walls of a room and to encourage employees to circulate and discuss each activity and the extent to which it adds value. BPR concentrates on the processes which are undertaken within the organisation and not on its structure. Once a clear idea has been obtained of what employees do and how this relates to the customer, the company is completely redesigned from scratch. It is a 'fundamental' approach to change because nothing is taken for granted. It is 'radical' because it goes to the root of the process by which the firm adds value, and 'dramatic' in that it is not about small, gradual change, but one major upheaval.

As an approach BPR ensures the efficiency of the organisation as a whole is considered, rather than individual parts. However, it is a technique which has, for the most part, been adopted by organisations facing crisis. This is because successful firms have little incentive to 'reinvent themselves'. Many of the companies which have used BPR have not been saved by the approach. It is therefore difficult to measure its validity. The method has also gained a reputation among staff as little more than a euphemism for large-scale redundancy programmes.

Although businesses may turn to BPR as a way of achieving radical change, most prefer the Japanese approach of continuous improvement (kaizen).

IN Business

MANAGING ORGANISATIONAL CHANGE AT HEWLETT PACKARD

Lew Platt is chief executive of Hewlett Packard, a major North American firm in the computer industry. Although the company is experiencing increasing profits and is in 'fundamentally good shape' he is always looking to guard against complacency.

Platt comments that 'People ask: "What do you think about when you're in the shower or shaving?" Well, I think about how easy it is to just keep doing what you are doing today for a little bit too long. General Motors, Sears, International Business Machines were the greatest companies in their industries, the best of the best in the world. These companies did not make gigantic mistakes. They were not led by stupid, inept people. The only real mistake they made was to keep doing whatever it was that had made them successful for a little too long.'

He believes that 'the real secret is to build an organisation that isn't afraid to make changes while it is still successful, before change becomes imperative for survival.' Platt adopts a leadership style which encourages his managers to be 'always looking over your shoulder at the competition, always thinking about the next move'. He believes that a policy which makes the company successful today, might work for a year, or at the most two, but beyond this to stick to it will 'kill' the company. His approach to management signals to employees that resistance to change and failure to constantly adapt to new market conditions is why large companies fall from their position of market dominance.

ISSUES FOR **analysis**

When analysing a firm's approach to managing change it is useful to consider the following points:

- On implementation of a change programme what signs of individual resistance to change are evident?
- Has the organisation made sure that those directly affected by a change are involved in its planning?
- Have employees been kept informed about the change throughout its implementation and are they aware of all the options open to the organisation?

- Have targets been set to control the change? Are the outcomes measurable?
- Has the organisation reviewed the policy for change after implementation and moved forward to further development, i.e. is the change programme evolving?
- Has the change programme met with resistance from the organisation as a whole?
- Is there evidence that 'management systems', 'business culture and values', 'technology' and 'skills and organisation' have been considered in designing the change programme?
- Has sufficient attention been paid to managing the existing business during the change?
- Is the organisation in need of radical change? Would business process re-engineering (BPR) be an appropriate approach?

43.5 Change management
an evaluation

All organisations must manage change. In order to do so successfully it is necessary to analyse the impact on people. Without employee support no innovation will succeed. The single most important issue is therefore the extent to which trust can be developed between a workforce and the organisation. This will demand a long-term approach, in which individuals are both consulted and kept informed about developments within the business. Resistance to change will emerge if the basic needs of security, social ties, and self-esteem are threatened.

A firm may choose to move towards a programme of gradual change, which Japanese managers call 'kaizen'. An approach of this kind involves every employee being willing to review their role in the business in order to suggest potential improvements to the processes they are directly involved with. Individuals must adjust to a series of continuous improvements, which means that the working environment is one of constant change. In contrast, some firms employ 'step' change. This means trying to establish periods of stability, interspersed by a small number of major innovations. Business process re-engineering is an extreme form of this approach. The most appropriate method of change management will depend on the nature of the business environment the firm operates within.

To remain competitive over time any business must be prepared to change. The ability of employees to manage this process therefore holds the key to the future success (or failure) of all organisations.

KEY terms

anticipated change – when organisations can foresee future developments, either within or outside the business, they can plan their response in advance. This will reduce the risks associated with change and make it more likely that any resistance by individuals, or the organisation as a whole, can be overcome successfully.

business process re-engineering – a new, radical approach to changing the organisation, in which it is completely redesigned based on the processes which are undertaken in order to meet customer needs.

change management programme – a series of steps designed to move the organisation forward to a new operating position. Four key phases are involved in developing an initiative of this type. These are planning, implementation, control and review.

individual resistance to change – pressure from individuals who attempt to oppose the implementation of new developments within the organisation, and maintain the existing situation.

organisational resistance to change – pressure from groups of people within the business, or even the whole workforce, which attempts to resist the implementation of new developments within the organisation, and maintain the existing situation.

unanticipated change – many future developments, particularly in the firm's external environment, cannot be foreseen. For example, changes in consumer tastes, interest rate movements or exchange rate fluctuations are all factors which it will be hard for the business to influence and which may not behave in the manner expected. Planning and implementing change in response to developments of this type will be more difficult and there is therefore a much greater risk of failure.

A Level Exercises

A. REVISION QUESTIONS

(40 marks; 70 minutes)

Read the unit, then answer:

1 Outline why unanticipated change causes organisations difficulty in planning. *(4)*

2 What are the three key questions managers should ask when planning change? *(3)*

3 **a** If a new Head decided that all staff and students should wear the same blue overalls as the school/college 'uniform', how do you think staff would react? *(4)*

   b How might the Head overcome any resistance to the change? *(4)*

4 Distinguish between a measurable target and one which would be ineffective in the process of monitoring change. *(3)*

5 **a** Suggest four ways in which organisations create barriers to introducing change. *(4)*

   b To what extent are these more difficult to overcome than those erected by individuals? *(5)*

6 Why is organisational culture an important factor in change management? *(3)*

7 Outline how the 'diamond change management' model might be used to design a change management programme. *(5)*

8 Explain what activities are involved in undertaking business process re-engineering and consider the implications for its employees of an organisation adopting this radical approach to managing change. *(5)*

B. REVISION EXERCISES

B1 Case Study

Major Changes

Sarah bit her lip to stop herself. She wanted to reply to Nilesh but knew it wouldn't help. He had spent 40 minutes moaning about his colleagues and customers. She excused herself and left.

As she left her office that evening, Sarah thought back over her first fortnight at Cartright's. Being appointed chief executive at 34 was a huge thrill, but already it was wearing off. She had been warned that Cartright's was dull, bureaucratic and inward-looking, but the reality was still a shock. She had been round every department, talking one-to-one to over 100 staff. Most were cautious, bored and focused only on paperwork, not on creating something new or better. The temptation was to leave things be. After all, the business was highly profitable, thanks to a huge 10-year contract supplying the Saudi Arabian government. Why shake things up?

Sarah slept on it, and by the morning had decided. People like Nilesh would be scared of change, they would fight against it and therefore her, but they must be forced to accept it. In the long term, all would benefit. Their working lives would become more interesting and they would have a better chance of keeping their jobs when the Saudi Arabian contract ran out in four years' time.

Having convinced the chairman that her approach was right, she called a board meeting. She announced a new corporate objective: 'to develop new products and customers so that the Saudi Arabian contract provides only 50% of turnover within three years'. To achieve this, there would need to be a complete reorganisation of the board and senior management to reflect the reduced importance of those involved in the Saudi contract. Every manager in the business would have to reapply for his or her job, to prove their commitment to the new approach. Sarah's final presentation slide said 'The culture must change or the business will die'.

Many of the directors were furious at the implied criticism. And worried about their own future. Major Chris Thompson, the finance director, said: 'Cartright's has been successful for 40 years. It may need sharpening up; it doesn't need a revolution. Our staff will never be go-getters. This plan risks everything.'

By the end of the day, rumours had spread throughout the building. There were stories of mass redundancies and a widespread belief that Sarah would be bringing in her own management team. Sarah's response was to call together all 600 staff and tell them her concerns about the future and her plans for change.

Within a few weeks the plan was underway. The interview panel quizzed managers on their strengths and weaknesses, their ideas for the future and on the management style they would like to employ in the future. Only a quarter met the standards set by Sarah. These were given important positions and the other managers were given 12 months to try to change their approach.

The short-term impact of the upheaval was awful. Close contacts with the Saudi government encouraged a very hostile reaction from Cartright's biggest client. Staff sick leave rose dramatically and three long-standing clients were lost.

Ten months later, however, things looked rather better. Nilesh, of all people, had become a key figure. He developed a completely new product that would offer a high service level at a sharply lower cost than before. His team of six were buzzing with ideas. Another star was Vivien, who developed an internal Internet (an 'intranet') which provided all staff with full access to all the sales and production data for the business. This helped staff make better-informed decisions, and emphasised the change from the secretive approach of the old management team.

Twelve months from the start of the programme, half the directors and one-third of the old management team had left. But Cartright's was on course to meet its sales objective. There had been times when Sarah had suffered from terrible stress. Now she felt proud of her enthusiastic team – and very proud of herself.

Questions   *(60 marks; 80 minutes)*

1 Explain the meaning of the terms:
  a bureaucratic
  b culture.   *(6)*
2 a How may organisations become as bureaucratic as Cartright's?   *(7)*
  b Analyse why Sarah was so concerned to change this culture of bureaucracy.   *(10)*
3 Consider how well the process of change at Cartright's fits the diamond change management model (Figure 43.5).   *(15)*

4 Discuss why many directors and staff at Cartright's resisted Sarah's plan for change.   *(10)*
5 Sarah made radical changes to Cartright's. Consider whether she would have been wiser to have made changes more gradually.   *(12)*

C. ESSAY QUESTIONS

1 'Changing a marketing strategy or a production method is quite easy. The problem of change is people.' Discuss.
2 'One of the key differences between a leader and a manager is that a leader stimulates change whereas a manager only responds to it.' Discuss this statement.
3 'People always ask, "Is the change over? Can we stop now?" You've got to tell them, "No, it's just begun." Leaders must create an atmosphere where people understand that change is a continuing process, not an event.' (Jack Welch, chief executive, General Electric Company.) How might a leader set about this task?
4 Research has concluded that 'implementing a new organisation culture and values was a major problem in introducing change'. In the light of this conclusion, consider the most appropriate management action for dealing with resistance to change.

PEOPLE AND ORGANISATIONS – MANAGEMENT GURUS

44.1 | Modern management gurus

IGOR ANSOFF

Born:	1918
Area of study:	Objectives and strategy
Key text:	Corporate Strategy, McGraw-Hill, 1965

EDWARD DEMING

Born:	1900
Died:	1993
Area of study:	Operations management
Key text:	Out of the Crisis, Cambridge University Press,1986

Major contribution to the study of business:

Ansoff was the first writer to develop an understanding of the role of strategic planning in business. He argued that a firm is a 'resource converter'. Human, physical and financial resources are translated into products or services as efficiently as possible. In order to do this managers must develop a formal strategy which matches the strengths of the organisation to its competitive environment.

This decision making process takes place under conditions of 'partial ignorance' because the future of the firm and its environment cannot be anticipated completely. So shaping strategic policy is a high risk process which involves making unique, non-repetitive choices. As such it is quite different from other management decision making problems of an operational nature.

Ansoff's early work provides a series of checklists which managers can employ when developing a strategic position. However, critics suggested this approach is too rigid. It ignores the fact that many organisations develop a competitive advantage based on strategies which emerge over time, rather than being formally planned. Ansoff responded by emphasising the need for strategy to be adapted on a real-time (near immediate) basis to deal with changing competitive environments. This recognised the dynamic nature of strategic decision making. In business, today's correct decision can look foolish tomorrow.

Ansoff now accepts that formal strategic planning is a complex issue which cannot be dealt with by providing a series of rules for managers to follow. Nevertheless he still defends his original contribution to the subject, that formal strategic planning is vital for long-term business success.

Major contribution to the study of business:

Deming is regarded by many people as the originator of the idea of total quality management. He recognised that reducing variability in a process is the key to improving both quality and productivity. This can be achieved by the application of statistical process control, which involves using simple numerate analysis to ensure that a process is proceeding efficiently and at high quality standards. The approach can be applied not just in production, but to service and administrative activities as well.

The principles of Deming's ideas were summarised in his 14 points for management (see the table on the following page). Aimed at senior decision makers, they ranged widely over operations and people management.

He continually stressed the need for an organisation to be customer driven, claiming 'the customer is the most important part of the production line'.

These concepts were far more influential in postwar Japan than in his own country until the late 1970s. Deming visited the Far East on a lecture tour in 1950 and his ideas provided the basis for Japanese industrial success. He challenged the Western idea that quality adds to costs; that quality and productivity must be traded off against each other. When Japanese products such as cameras, cars and copiers began to penetrate North American markets in substantial quantities, Western managers realised the potential of his contribution to business thinking. Almost too late for some firms such as the giant General Motors, which almost went under in the 1980s as car buyers switched to Japanese and German cars. Since then quality has become one of the most significant issues facing modern organisations.

Deming's 14 points for management:

1 *Encourage continual improvement in the work-place.*

2 *Adopt Japanese management techniques where appropriate.*

3 *Stop making defects by ensuring products are made 'right first time' and therefore reduce the need for quality inspection.*

4 *Consider quality as well as price when deciding upon suppliers.*

5 *Do not see the goal of improvement as reaching a desirable finishing point, change should continue forever.*

6 *Use modern training techniques for all employees, including management.*

7 *The role of a leader is to enable others to do their job better.*

8 *Eliminate fear by keeping employees informed through a process of two-way communication.*

9 *Encourage line and staff employees to work together by breaking down barriers between the two.*

10 *Do not constantly warn the workforce about the need for increased effort, only demotivation results.*

11 *Do not use numerical performance targets, instead provide help and guidance.*

12 *Do not employ appraisal systems, or management by objectives; these reduce the pride of employees in their own work.*

13 *Encourage employees to improve themselves through a process of continuous education.*

14 *Show clear senior management support for the principles outlined above.*

PETER DRUCKER

Born:	1909
Area of study:	Objectives and strategy/people
Key text:	The Practice of Management, Heinemann, 1955

Major contribution to the study of business:

Peter Drucker was one of the first writers to give the study of business intellectual respectability. His work has been at the forefront of business thinking over many years. He has influenced developments in a wide range of subject areas. His early working life included a period in a merchant bank and employment as a journalist. Then he spent 18 months studying the internal workings of what was then the largest organisation in the world, General Motors. This experience set a pattern for his later writing which often draws on the case histories of large organisations such as General Electric and IBM.

The management of organisations by a hierarchy of objectives (MBO) is one of Drucker's most influential ideas. He suggests these targets should fall into five key groups dealing with market standing, innovative performance, productivity, liquidity and profitability. It is his view that large firms can only be managed effectively by setting clear goals for subordinates and then delegating tasks to them. With this approach in mind, Drucker was also one of the first writers to develop the principle of using a mission statement to inspire employees to take appropriate action.

Setting clear objectives is the first of five key roles which a manager must undertake identified by Drucker. The other four are to organise, motivate, measure performance and develop people. To motivate, he stressed the need to create 'responsible workers'. The aim of this approach is to help employees develop knowledge, because this represents the possibility for the organisation to improve productivity, quality and performance in parallel. In this sense Drucker's concept of the 'knowledge worker' can be seen as the forerunner of the 'learning organisation' principle which is popular in management theory today.

Drucker has also made contributions to the understanding of the key role which marketing plays in an organisation's success. For example, he identifies the purpose of business as 'the creation of customers and their subsequent satisfaction'. As a result he argues that concern and responsibility for marketing lies with all employees.

One theme connects the wide range of ideas which Peter Drucker has developed about business. It is that human resources must be used effectively to create and sustain a successful organisation. His influence on other writers and practising managers, over a 40-year period, has been wide ranging and significant.

CHARLES HANDY

Born:	1932
Area of study:	People
Key text:	Understanding Organisations, Penguin, 1976

Major contribution to the study of business:

Charles Handy is a leading authority on *organisation culture*. He has written extensively about the future of business and the nature of work. He has industrial experience as an executive at BP. More recently he has worked as an academic, a writer and a broadcaster.

In the late 1980s Handy suggested that organisations will increasingly contract out work and require employees to work flexibly. This proved an accurate forecast of exactly what happened in the 1990s in Britain and America. He described the 'shamrock' organisation of the future as consisting of three employee types:

- Core workers – these are likely to be qualified professionals, technicians or managers, providing the source of organisational knowledge which is key to the functioning of the business. These individuals will be expected to have a long-term commitment to the firm.
- Contract workers – these are contracted to the organisation to complete a specific task; they will not be employed on a long-term basis.
- Peripheral workers – a flexible labour force employed on a part-time or temporary basis in order to meet the organisation's short-term needs.

Handy suggested that this type of organisation will grow as firms seek ever greater flexibility to changes in demand or competition. If he is right, it will mean a steady reduction in the number of people with secure, full-time, salaried employment. (See Unit 39 for a more detailed analysis of the shamrock organisation structure.)

The four types of organisation culture defined by Handy have also had an important impact on academic thinking in this area of business theory. His view is that either 'power', 'role', 'task' or 'person' cultures can be identified in all firms. This approach is reflected in the work of other writers dealing with relationships between employees. (For a more detailed explanation of each type of culture, see Unit 35.)

Charles Handy is currently Britain's leading management guru. Recently he has turned his attention to the need for companies to adopt a 'broader social responsibility' with respect to its employees. To consider the impact of its actions, particularly in the case of the large number of redundancies associated with the trend for firms to downsize. Time will tell if his work in this area will show the foresight evident in his earlier writing.

SIR JOHN HARVEY JONES

Born:	1924
Area of study:	People
Key text:	Making it Happen, *Collins, 1984*

Major contribution to the study of business:

Sir John Harvey Jones is a practising manager, rather than an academic. He became chairman of the chemicals giant ICI in 1982, when the firm was suffering from the impact of a severe recession. He was chairman until 1987. During this time he was responsible for restructuring the company. He created three customer-based divisions rather than a much more complex, product oriented framework, which existed previously. The success of this strategy led to subsequent opportunities for him to outline his views on management, both as an author and TV presenter.

The ideas which Harvey Jones presents are often outspoken, but generate a good deal of interest among fellow managers. He suggests that 'management is an art', in which no one unique solution exists which can be applied to every company. The manager's role is to understand existing business theory and select those elements most appropriate to the organisation's specific position. The aim must be to encourage constant change, at the greatest pace which the firm, and the people within it, can deal with. In order to achieve this, the smallest possible number of levels of hierarchy should be adopted within the organisation structure. Each layer must be clearly seen to be adding value and doing only their own job, and not those of individuals at other levels. In this way, from top to bottom of the organisation, individuals will be stretched in their jobs, resulting in high motivation to achieve.

The advice which Sir John offers is that the 'aim of the business leader must be to be the best'. He argues this will take time because people will not change rapidly. Three to five years is needed for a manager to have a radical impact on an organisation. Despite this, his suggestions, both in books and the BBC TV series *Troubleshooter*, provided practising managers with a clear understanding of what it takes to achieve such an ambitious target.

ROSABETH MOSS KANTER

Born:	1943
Area of study:	People
Key text:	The Change Masters, *Allen and Unwin, 1984*

Major contribution to the study of business:

Kanter is a leading academic authority on the subject of managing change within organisations. She developed the idea that large organisations should have few layers of hierarchy, and contain 'new ventures' which operate as small companies in their own right. This makes the firm more flexible, allowing it to respond to change more quickly. Making success more likely in competitive global markets.

The managers of these organisations play the key role of team leaders. They must *empower* employees who represent a source of knowledge and value to the business. This process implies a degree of self-regulation; giving individuals the freedom to decide what to do and how to do it. In so doing people are motivated and become catalysts for change. Kanter identifies individuals she describes as 'change masters'. They have the ability to move beyond the organisation's established practices and drive the process of innovation. This does not necessarily involve just new products or services. It may equally concern the introduction of technology, or work practices, which are radically different to those being currently employed by the firm. These managers are capable of building teams of employees to put these visions in place and shape the organisation's future.

Kanter has promoted her vision of the role of manager in the twenty-first century, both as a former editor of the influential *Harvard Business Review* and as a Professor of Business Administration at Harvard University. Her ideas about the importance of empowering people have had an important impact on current business theory. Large companies are showing a great deal of interest in empowerment. Whether this really makes a difference in the workplace remains to be seen.

HENRY MINTZBERG

Born:	1939
Area of study:	Objectives and strategy
Key text:	Mintzberg on Management, Macmillan, 1989

Major contribution to the study of business:

Henry Mintzberg is a Canadian academic best known for his work dealing with the structure and culture of organisations, and the styles employed by their managers. He is an outspoken critic of the idea that the strategic direction of a business can be planned formally over a long period of time. It is his view that strategy 'emerges' as a pattern in management action over time. Not as a series of 'designed' steps. This belief led to a public disagreement between Mintzberg and Ansoff.

Mintzberg's early work involved the study of what managers actually do. He rejected the traditional view that their role consisted of defined tasks such as planning, organising, coordinating and controlling. He concluded that they spend very little time thinking ahead. Half the activities they were involved with each day were small tasks which required less than nine minutes of their time and dealt with existing problems. Thus managers in reality are 'fire-fighters', coping with short-term emergencies. He identified three types of managerial role on the basis of his observations, these were 'interpersonal' (e.g. acting as leader), 'informational' (e.g. acting as spokesman) and 'decisional' (e.g. deciding upon resource allocation). His writing places emphasis on the need for greater managerial training to deal with these different functions.

The most influential of Mintzberg's later work identifies five main business structures:

- **entrepreneurial** structure, in which the chief executive officer exercises a good deal of personal power
- **machine bureaucracy**, in which decision making is centralised and formal

- **divisionalised**, where semi-autonomous business units share a common administrative structure
- **professional bureaucracy**, which operates by relying on the skills and knowledge of highly trained employees
- **adhocracy**, involving flexible project teams working to develop innovative solutions to the problems facing the business.

Mintzberg continues to write extensively about the role of managers and the way in which they make decisions. His recent work has focused on the extent to which decision makers are able to identify small, but significant, changes in the organisation's environment and respond to the opportunities these present.

TOM PETERS

Born:	1942
Area of study:	People
Key text:	In Search of Excellence, Harper and Row, 1982 (co-author: Robert Waterman)

Major contribution to the study of business:

The work of Tom Peters is more likely to be found on the desk of a practising manager in the UK than that of any other business writer. His text *In Search of Excellence*, written with Bob Waterman, is the world's best-selling business book. Peters worked for the United States management consulting firm McKinsey, before leaving to become an author and leading speaker. He has become well known for his almost evangelical platform performances presented to groups of practising managers. Companies are prepared to pay large fees to hear his outspoken views of what brings business success.

In Search of Excellence identified 43 companies which had remained in the top half of their industry over a 20-year period. These 'excellent' organisations were then analysed in order to detect common features which generated success. Eight factors emerged:

- the use of small project teams
- elimination of bureaucracy
- the ability to listen to and learn from the customer
- support for individuals willing to innovate
- recognition of employees as the firm's core asset
- a clear outline of the organisation's mission
- tightly held common values but room for employees to act within them
- an ability to identify and concentrate on the core business.

The credibility of this work was dealt a heavy blow because within five years more than half of these companies had fallen from favour on Wall Street. Nevertheless, Peters' reputation was established by this book.

Tom Peters has produced a range of texts in the intervening period. These use case studies to illustrate his views on what represents good management practice. They are written in a way which communicates his evident enthusiasm for business subjects. The main theme of his later work is the need for rapid change in the new, increasingly competitive, business environment. He regards substantial reorganisation on a regular basis as the way in which customer loyalty can be 'captured' and maintained. He argues that organisation structures should be flat, with functional barriers broken down, and supervisors giving way to self-managed teams. This approach encourages task orientation, innovation and commitment, and focuses the minds of employees. The key to business success is to involve everyone within the firm in virtually everything. Peters believes there are no limits to the ability of individuals to contribute to business success.

Many of the ideas which Tom Peters presents are not original. But his ability to bring them to life for practising managers by using real examples, combined with his undoubted communication skills, mean he may be the most influential current management guru.

MICHAEL PORTER

Born:	1947
Area of study:	Objectives and strategy
Key text:	Competitive Advantage, *Free Press*, 1985

Major contribution to the study of business:

The work of Michael Porter on competitive advantage, for businesses and even for countries, has had a great impact on managers and politicians over the last 10 years. He is currently the most influential business academic. His work emerged at a key point in the development of United States industry. The growing success of Japan in penetrating export markets created a desire for a new understanding of the nature of competition. Porter offered a series of business tools which managers could employ to analyse their own company and its competitive environment. Then devise a strategy for success.

Porter developed a model called 'the five forces' to analyse the competitive space within which a business operates. This technique offers a means by which managers can identify opportunities and threats, and therefore potential profitability, in their industry. Its five key elements are the extent of rivalry between existing competitors, the likelihood of new market entrants, the bargaining power of both suppliers and buyers, and finally the danger of substitute products emerging. For a more detailed outline of how to employ this analytic tool, see Unit 85.

In order to understand the internal strengths of a business, Porter developed the concept of the 'value chain'. Each activity in a production and supply process is identified. This allows the identification of those actions which fail to add value for the organisation, leading to cost reductions when they are eliminated. Careful study by managers should help identify how specific activities can be performed better than by competitors, and as a result prove a source of advantage over them.

Porter suggests that the strengths of the business, represented by activities within the value chain, must be 'matched' to opportunities in the organisation's environment. Then a strategy can be built around cost leadership or product differentiation. These two generic strategies can be focused on a niche, or used for mass marketing purposes.

Porter's 'diamond' is a model seeking to explain 'the competitive advantage of nations' by applying the ideas found in his 'five forces' theory to countries rather than industries. A careful study of 10 national economies, including the UK, allowed him to build up an understanding of why some nations were able to grow and increase living standards, while others stagnated. The four key elements within this analysis are the structure, strategy and rivalry of firms in the nation's domestic economy, conditions of demand in the home market, availability and quality of factors of production and the interrelationships between supporting industries. One key factor in national success is the ability to build 'clusters' of related industries which serve each other.

Porter is currently Professor of General Management at Harvard Business School, but his work first gained national prominence as a result of his appointment to President Reagan's Commission of Industrial Competitiveness in the mid-1980s. He still works actively as a management consultant and continues to develop his extensive body of research work.

INTEGRATED PEOPLE IN ORGANISATIONS

45.1 People – an overview

INTRODUCTION

A common phrase uttered by managers in the modern business world is that 'people are our most valuable asset'. Twenty years or more ago, the opposite seemed to be true. Businesses appeared to run despite the best attempts of 'the workers' to take high wage increases in return for less and less work. The business world was characterised by an attitude of 'them and us'.

Since then, massive changes have taken place in a short period of time. They cover a wide range of topics connected to people in business organisations, such as:

- motivation
- communication
- labour relations
- job design
- workplace design.

People management is perhaps changing more rapidly than any other area of Business Studies. Old assumptions are quickly being overturned. Today's workers are developing different expectations in their working lives which need to be fulfilled if businesses are to operate effectively.

The implications of accepting the phrase 'people are our most valuable asset' as a basis for decisions are wide ranging. They can be costly to firms and threatening to managers and, perhaps, workers as well. The changing style of personnel management is one that goes to the very heart of any business and its corporate culture.

HOW ARE PEOPLE MANAGED IN BUSINESS ORGANISATIONS?

People in business organisations can be treated by managers on a variety of levels.

- At its simplest, there is the mechanistic function involved in administrating the working lives of all the firm's employees, such as payroll, contracts and so on.
- On a second level, the personnel department can be involved in the preparation of the workforce for

their jobs through induction, training and appraisal.
- On a higher level, the work of the personnel/HR department can be a key ingredient in the establishment of the culture of the whole organisation. Management styles, the organisation of the workplace and lines of communication can all fall within the range of work covered by this department.

Of course, the work of managing people must form a single part of the whole jigsaw that makes up the work of a business. Nevertheless, it can be argued that the way a business treats its workers sets the tone for all the activities in the business. Levels of service to customers, relations with suppliers, levels of worker efficiency and commitment can all be traced back to people management.

'A' GRADE PEOPLE IN ORGANISATIONS

The study of people in business organisations is made up of several distinct areas, each of which has its own body of theory and empirical evidence. Motivation, communication, employee relations and the internal organisation of the business are often treated as separate topics. Better students are able to go beyond these separate areas and develop arguments that follow key themes through each of the areas. A question on changing management styles may have implications for the motivation techniques used and therefore employee relations, which may in turn require different lines of communication, and so on. Adopting an approach such as this demonstrates overall understanding of the subject and a full grasp of its integrated nature.

A common distinction between 'A' grade writing and answers that attract lower grades lies in the approach undertaken to personnel issues. It is possible to argue for empowerment, job enrichment and so on because they seem to be the 'right' or 'nice' thing to do. Better answers will relate the relevant theory to more tangible benefits. The key effect of motivation, for example, will not be a happier workforce, but one that has a higher labour productivity as shown by concrete calculations.

'A' grade people in business organisations requires a grasp of big underlying issues such as those that follow.

These are areas of discussion for case study conclusions. They represent ways of evaluating the wider significance of the concepts covered in this area.

ISSUE 1   Has the management of people improved in recent years?

Most research suggests that it has not. The pace of organisational change has been compounded by frequent changes to personnel practices. Human resource management (HRM) was supposed to give personnel issues a bigger strategic voice. In fact HRM has often been a banner under which labour flexibility has become associated with insecurity and uncertainty.

A key feature of modern firms is the huge gulf between personnel approaches. Some firms are far-sightedly developing staff through extensive training and interesting initiatives in consultation. Other firms are creating atmospheres of fear and mistrust. A recent survey of 1,300 managers was run jointly by UMIST and the Institute of Management. It showed the negative view of recent changes held by many managers – especially those working in the public sector (see the table below).

What has been the effect of organisational change?

PERCENTAGE SAYING THAT:	ALL	PRIVATE SECTOR	PUBLIC SECTOR
Decision making is faster	29%	31%	25%
Morale has decreased	64%	53%	81%
Motivation has decreased	49%	39%	65%
Sense of job security has decreased	65%	52%	80%

ISSUE 2   Is Japanisation a passing fad?

The adoption of 'modern' personnel management techniques has followed a seemingly logical course. In the 1970s UK firms were losing out in competition with rivals from Japan. One reason identified for the better performance of Japanese firms was the production techniques used and the way in which workers formed an integral part of the production process. It seemed clear that kaizen groups, quality circles and the like were the way to compete in the international market.

How long will this trend be followed? For every firm that has successfully adopted these techniques there are examples of other firms that have tried and failed. Adding to the unease on these 'miracle' techniques is the growing economic crisis in Japan and its Far Eastern neighbours. Time will tell if the current push for these 'modern' management techniques will prove themselves as reliable tools, or if the management gurus will develop new ideas that will take centre stage in the future.

ISSUE 3   Are people the main assets of a business?

A simple answer to this must be 'yes'. Without people there would be no business. However, people on their own could not produce efficient productive units making highly complex technological products, so capital machinery can be seen as being equally important. The argument can follow, then, that all aspects of business are equally important.

This line of reasoning, however, neglects the crucial fact of personnel management. The work of the personnel department sets the tone for the whole culture of the organisation. A happy, content and committed workforce will be more productive than one in which workers feel oppressed and under-valued. On the sporting field and in armed conflicts, victory has often gone to the side that was more committed and unified in its aims than the one with the better individuals or better equipment.

In a competitive environment staff motivation and effectiveness can make the crucial difference between success and failure.

People in organisations

A. SHORT-ANSWER QUESTIONS

1 Give three factors that may influence the choice of location of a financial services organisation. *(3)*

2 Give two reasons why a manager might delegate authority to a subordinate. *(2)*

3 State two factors that might influence the effective span of control in a business organisation. *(2)*

4 Give two benefits to an organisation from employing a 'flatter' organisation structure. *(2)*

5 Give three examples of how a firm may set out to satisfy the lower level needs of its employees. *(3)*

6 Distinguish between job enlargement and job enrichment. *(3)*

7 Define the term 'decentralisation' as used in organisation theory. *(3)*

8 How is labour productivity calculated? *(2)*

9 Distinguish between formal and informal communication in a business. *(3)*

10 State three ways in which the use of information technology might aid the efficiency of a business organisation. *(3)*

11 State two indicators of low morale in a firm. *(2)*

12 State three reasons for dismissing an employee that are considered 'fair' in law. *(3)*

13 What courses of action are available to a trade union when wage negotiations break down? *(2)*

14 State three reasons in support of employee participation in the decision making of a business enterprise. *(3)*

15 Explain two benefits a firm might derive from its employees participating in quality circles. *(4)*

16 Give three symptoms of unsatisfactory recruitment procedures in a business enterprise. *(3)*

17 What factors might be taken into account when preparing a wages budget? *(2)*

18 Give four reasons why a firm might promote from within the existing workforce rather than appoint from outside. *(4)*

19 Give four examples of monetary payments that may be received by a manual worker in addition to the basic wage. *(4)*

20 List three reasons why a business enterprise might attach importance to a training programme for staff. *(3)*

B1 DATA RESPONSE

Modern Trade Unionism

In March 1998, British Vauxhall car workers were warned by the US owners (General Motors) that one or more of the factories faced closure as a result of a fall in demand for Vauxhall cars across Europe. Other General Motors plants on the continent such as Russelsheim in Germany and Antwerp in Belgium had been assured of their future. The British factories were said to be vulnerable because of overcapacity and low levels of productivity. The low productivity levels were made worse by the strength of the pound. This made British-produced goods more expensive abroad.

Vauxhall's trade unions responded to this threat in a cooperative manner. The Transport and General Workers Union spent weeks in negotiations with the management to arrive at a compromise deal to avert the closure of the Luton plant and the loss of 4,500 jobs. The deal comprised a three-year package with an initial pay rise of 2.5% (just below the rate of inflation) followed by rises in line with inflation for the next two years. In return, workers would adopt new work practices aimed at boosting productivity.

A week later, with workers still discussing the deal, Vauxhall's chairman and managing director, Nick Reilly, vowed to give up his salary for one year if the deal were accepted. He would forego his basic salary of £160,000 while eight directors would take a pay cut and 25 senior executives would have their pay frozen. Mr Reilly's gesture was designed to demonstrate to workers that the problems of the company were being shared by everyone involved. This might help break down 'them-and-us' barriers between management and workers.

However, workers remained sceptical. Mr Reilly was giving up his basic salary, but would still benefit from bonuses which would increase if productivity improved. The previous year he earned about £90,000 in bonuses, compared with an average assembly line wage of £17,000, including overtime. One worker said: 'He is president of five other companies – is he giving up those salaries too? No-one is particularly impressed by this offer. If he couldn't afford it, he wouldn't do it. All we know is that we earn so little that we couldn't afford to give up one penny.'

Source: Adapted from the *Independent*, April 1998

Questions (30 marks; 40 minutes)

1 Define the following terms:
 a overcapacity (3)
 b productivity. (3)
2 Consider how Vauxhall may have benefited from having the Transport and General Workers Union representing its workforce. (8)
3 What might be the consequences of Mr Reilly's gesture on industrial relations at Vauxhall? (6)
4 Discuss whether trade unions are needed in the current business and economic climate. (10)

B2 CASE STUDY

Modern Working Life

A recent study on the UK labour market, entitled 'Different Jobs, Different Lives', forecasts significant changes in the types of jobs available and the type of person needed to fill these posts. Traditional manufacturing jobs will shrink to 3 million by 2006. Growth will come from the 'creative professions' such as the music business, design or professional sport. It is thought that by 2001 there will be 4.5 million managers, 2.6 million professionals, such as doctors and lawyers, and another 1.9 million 'associate professionals', such as legal executives and computer programmers. These are the highest paid categories, with average earnings ranging up to £569 per week for a male manager. These occupations also demand the highest level of qualifications. Four-fifths of professionals and a third of managers and administrators have degrees.

At the other end of the scale, demand is expected to grow in some lower paid jobs as well. The report foresees 2.7 million people in occupations such as health care and catering. The number working in childcare is expected to rise significantly to half a million by 2006.

Such figures suggest that not only is working life changing, but also the structure of companies is changing too. For some time company chairpeople have said that 'people are the most important asset of a business' and that 'knowledge workers are the way forward'. Now organisational structures may be changing to match these trends.

Studies show that some firms are developing corporate structures based on people rather than physical assets. This involves the creation of a business without a recognisable centre. Instead, there is a network structure with a core in which the various elements are connected through internal and external alliances. Such an organisation has leaders throughout its operations who focus on themes such as people, values, strategy, customers and learning.

The function of the 'global core' as differentiated from the centre of an organisation is to create a sense of purpose, creating a context for growth. It sets the tone rather than dishing out orders, and aims to add value rather than overheads. The functions of the core are:

- identifying the organisation's strengths
- encouraging business units to build on those strengths
- providing strategic leadership
- minimising the cost of capital
- exercising control on behalf of the board and shareholders.

For this decentralised structure to work, a different kind of organisation must be developed. It must be flexible and capable of working effectively with the various units and outside organisations who are linked via strategic alliances.

Source: Adapted from the *Independent*, 16/4/98; the *Independent on Sunday*, 12/4/98

Questions (35 marks; 60 minutes)

1 Define the following terms:
 a labour market (3)
 b corporate structure (3)
 c decentralised structure. (3)
2 Explain the phrase 'people are the most important asset of the business'. (6)
3 a What are the implications for individual workers of the changes in corporate structure described here? (10)
 b How do these changes compare with Handy's theory of the shamrock organisation? (10)

C. ROLE PLAYS AND SIMULATIONS

Should Sierra close a plant – if so, which?

Appendix A – Briefing document

As Joint Personnel Directors:

> Sierra Foods plc has made a name for itself supplying own-brand pizzas to national supermarket chains. They operate three plants, two in Lancashire, one of which acts as company headquarters, and a third in South Wales.
>
> Recently the company has come under increasing pressure, particularly from international competitors, who are regularly introducing innovative product ideas at prices below those Sierra wishes to charge.
>
> A proposal has been made to rationalise production on two of the existing sites, closing a third.

1 Decide what you would recommend and why.
2 Prepare a presentation to explain your views.

Appendix B – Operational data for the three plants (averages for the last four years)

	Leyland (HQ)	Wigan	Pontypool
Labour productivity	22,500	23,000	18,913
Capacity usage	0.87	0.6	0.77
Annual output	£45m	£18.4	£28.37
Waste levels	2%	2.3%	3.1%

Appendix C – Market size and market share

	3 years ago	2 years ago	Last year	This year
Total market sales	£125m	£130m	£137m	£160m
Sierra total sales	19%	16%	16%	17%

Appendix D – Employee relations data (last four years)

	Leyland (HQ)	Wigan	Pontypool
Average working days lost due to industrial action	0	0	5
Absenteeism rate	4%	3%	6%
Labour turnover	14%	17%	28%

Appendix E – UK economic trends

	3 years ago	2 years ago	Last year	This year
GDP indexed (5 years ago = 100)	104	105	109	116
Unemployment	2.9m	2.7m	2.4m	2m
Inflation	2.5%	2.4%	2.7%	3.1%

D. INTEGRATED CASE STUDY

Changing Times

After 35 years as managing director of his family firm, Sir John Jackson was able to look back with some pride at his achievements. He and his family had built Jackson's Ales Ltd into one of the most highly regarded small brewers in the North of England.

The last decade, though, had not been kind to the business financially. The workforce had to be cut back, though fortunately through natural wastage rather than redundancy. Costs had to be cut at every opportunity. In a highly competitive market, customers had switched from premium priced beers to cheaper, mass market products.

Sir John and the other directors were following a policy of focusing on the higher priced end of the market, hoping to achieve high profit margins on limited sales. At the start of the 1990s the firm began to run into serious difficulties with an ever decreasing market share.

The workforce, many of whom had been with the business all their working lives, were becoming disheartened with future prospects. The loss of jobs and weakening performance of the firm were worrying signs. Though the excellent relations with the Jackson family meant the workers continued to trust Sir John's leadership.

In 1993 it was decided to employ a non-family member as a manager to control the day-to-day running of the business. The firm took on Sam Beckett, a business graduate. She had already developed an excellent reputation for herself as production manager with Whittingtons, one of the major mass market brewers.

Sam persuaded the family to reposition itself in the marketplace. While retaining the traditional Jackson's Ale as a premium product, she also wanted to launch Quantum Ale as a more mainstream product. The estimated sales meant there would have to be an increase in output from the firm's one brewery. Sam was confident the existing staff could make the necessary adjustments to meet the new production targets.

In particular, Sam was convinced output could be increased without adding to the firm's overheads. More efficient organisation within the workplace and an emphasis on getting the mix of ingredients right first time should lead to large increases in productivity.

By 1996, Sam had implemented the changes to her satisfaction. A small but significant foothold had been gained in the mass market by Quantum Ale. The firm had begun to take on workers again. The table shows how the output of the firm changed between 1991 to 1998, along with the number of workers employed by the firm.

Data for Jackson's Ales, 1991–1998

Year	Output ('000 gallons)	No. of workers
1991	37	37
1992	38	32
1993	33	32
1994	29	30
1995	35	32
1996	41	34
1997	43	36
1998	45	38

The workers in the factory, although wary at first, warmed to Sam over time. One worker, who had been with Jackson's for 30 years, was heard to remark:

'When she first came here, she seemed to be full of the latest jargon. Always wanted to change things just for the sake of it. She wasn't very popular when she tried to change things the Jacksons had always done. They would turn a blind eye to us leaving the shop floor for an occasional smoke, but she was very strict on that kind of thing. On the other hand, old Mr Jackson knew what he wanted and how he wanted it. He didn't take kindly to suggestions from the workers. Now Sam has these workgroup meetings where we can put forward our own ideas. I was really pleased when she changed the sampling process after I made a suggestion.'

Another worker who joined the business in 1996 from a rival firm was astonished with the attitude of the workers:

'When I first arrived, I was amazed at everyone's enthusiasm to get the product right. They all seemed to take it very personally if something went wrong with a particular batch.

And yet if something did go wrong, the manager would talk about it being a learning experience. Not like at the other place. You were for the high jump if you made a mistake there.'

Not everyone, though, was happy with the way things had gone. Most resistance came from Sam's fellow managers, some of whom felt marginalised by the changes. One said:

'She seems to be getting results, but for how long? You can't have a business being run from the shop floor without things going seriously wrong. She doesn't seem to want to make real decisions without consulting the workers first. It seems like the workers do all the thinking, and she goes along with what they propose. I mean, what is our job now that decisions are being made at the bottom of the hierarchy?'

Questions   (80 marks; 90 minutes)

1 Define the following terms:
   a natural wastage   (3)
   b productivity   (3)
2 How would you describe the motivation within the business:
   a before the changes   (8)
   b after the changes?   (8)
3 Calculate:
   a labour productivity for each of the years 1991–98 (6)
   b labour turnover rate for each of the years 1991–98. (6)
   c Draw a graph to show how these figures have changed over this period.   (6)
   d What do these figures indicate for the business?   (10)
4 Assess Sam's personnel management style.   (10)
5 What would you recommend she does next? Justify your recommendations.   (20)

OPERATIONS OBJECTIVES AND STRATEGY

46.1 Introduction

In any firm engaged in production, the management of its operations will be central to its level of success. The keys to success lie in achieving two things within the wider context of the business as a whole:

- quality
- flexibility.

In particular, as illustrated in Figure 46.1, the level of success the firm will have in achieving quality and flexibility will be determined by a range of other organisational factors:

- organisational objectives
- organisational strategies
- human resource management
- decision making strategies.

Figure 46.1 Factors affecting successful operations

46.2 Quality

The quality of a product is often defined as 'fitness for purpose'. In other words, the product does *not* have to be the best ever. In the market for high fashion clothing, many young people are happy to buy clothes that will *not* last for years. The purpose is to wear them two or three times, then replace them. So the key qualities are good design and relatively low cost manufacture.

If the firm is aiming to sell to the mass market, then the cost of production may be more important than producing the highest possible quality product. This assumes that there is a trade off between the quality of a product and the cost of producing it. This assumption, as illustrated in Figure 46.2, has been the traditional view in British firms for many years.

Figure 46.2 Cost v. quality – traditional view

This shows a positive relationship between quality and cost. As the quality of a product improves, the costs of production will also go up. It was believed that workers needed to spend more time producing each item to make them better, higher quality raw materials had to be used and more products would be rejected as higher standards were applied.

Recently, however, a different perspective has grown up. The researcher Crosby is credited with the phrase that 'quality is free'. By this he means that quality can be achieved without incurring any extra costs. Achieving accurate production first time, every time, will reduce the levels of wastage and will also increase the total output of the firm. There will be a **negative correlation** between costs and quality, in that as quality improves, the cost of producing each unit will fall. This is illustrated in Figure 46.3.

One of the key aims of operations management is to bring about this seemingly ideal situation. This would involve the firm in:

- training workers to get things right first time

- changing the **corporate culture** to one where workers accept that quality is their responsibility
- organising the workplace so that each individual worker has the opportunity to use his or her abilities.

Figure 46.3 Cost v. quality – modern view

The achievement of quality is also closely linked to the success of the firm's research and development function. If a firm is to keep ahead of competitors in the development of new products, it will need to spend time and money on the research and development of new technologies and new product innovations.

QUALITY AT 3M

3M, the American firm best known for products such as Post-it™ notes and Sellotape, takes a very serious view of quality issues. The company has taken 500 up-and-coming managers to work full-time on a range of quality improvement projects. In addition, each of its 28,000 employees is receiving a full week of quality training.

The company realises that quality is a massive, long term issue. The chief executive has spoken of a 10–15 year commitment to fully establish the sort of quality culture that he believes is necessary if the firm is to be able to meet the requirements of a real, workable TQM system.

Source: *The Financial Times*

Business IN

There is also a need for operations management to liaise closely with the firm's marketing function. By defining quality as fitness for purpose, there is a need for the firm to understand what that purpose will be. In short, product design and development in themselves are only useful if they fulfil consumer demand. The development of the Sony Walkman met a need from consumers to be able to listen to cassettes while on the move. Yet Sony's Betamax video recorders failed, because Sony failed to see that the key to success was the quantity of available software (pre-recorded videos) rather than the quality of the hardware.

46.3 Flexibility

In business, flexibility is usually taken to mean that both the firm and its workforce are willing and able to change from existing methods of working to new ones.

A COGENT USE OF FLEXIBILITY

Cogent is a financial firm located in the City. Its boss, Ian Barnard, has tried to tackle the 'long hours and macho culture' of other City firms by giving staff more time off and allowing some to work from home.

Barnard believes his staff have become more loyal, more motivated and work less overtime since the introduction of flexible working patterns. Productivity is up, and staff turnover is down.

Mr Barnard says that until he had children of his own the issue of flexible working had never occurred to him. However, while his staff now work a nine-day fortnight, he still works a 45 hour, 5 day week.

Source: *The Birmingham Post*

Business IN

Flexibility can be achieved by having a workforce that is not resistant to change and is also multi-skilled. Producing this state of affairs, however, is not always easy.

Factors affecting the flexibility of the firm:

- *Training*
- *Corporate culture*
- *Management style*
- *Society*

1 TRAINING

To produce a flexible workforce, each employee must be capable of undertaking different roles in the workplace. This means they can cover for absent colleagues, or move to different tasks to cater for changes in demand in the marketplace.

In the past, workers were apprenticed in a particular trade and used those skills throughout the rest of their working lives. Today, with technology changing rapidly, this approach is unlikely to work. The techniques and materials used will change and it may be that the task itself becomes outdated and no longer required. Many craftsmen have found their work being taken over by machines.

When this has happened in the past, it was normal for the workers with the outdated skills to be made redundant and a new set of workers brought in for the new task. It is now recognised that this is a wasteful and stressful way of operating. Being able to switch workers from one task to another internally is cheaper for the firm and much better for morale within the workforce.

2 CORPORATE CULTURE

Creating a flexible workforce depends on a suitable atmosphere being developed within the business. A firm based on a traditional 'them and us' approach will find a workforce that is reluctant to change. It will tend to see each person's job as fixed and will not want to take on additional roles. Workers will feel that if they take on these extra jobs they will be stepping into another person's area and taking work from them. This idea of **demarcation** has, in the past, been a source of much industrial conflict in British business.

Convincing the whole workforce that such rigid demarcation lines promote inefficiency is a major step to achieving flexibility. Flexibility becomes possible when workers feel their role is to contribute in any way possible so that the firm can produce a high quality product. Then they will be willing to learn and apply new skills and knowledge, and participate in decisions which lead to further change.

The ideal corporate culture is one which encourages and rewards workers who are willing and able to help the firm in any way necessary. This will encourage all employees to value the contributions of others in making their firm a better one.

3 MANAGEMENT STYLE

Managers who want to develop a flexible workforce must adopt an appropriate style. They must be open and communicate with their staff. Problems shared with the workforce may find unexpected solutions. Workers who feel valued and a part of the company will tend to contribute more in return.

This does not mean, however, that managers allow the workers to run the business. Managers must still manage. In particular, they must be responsible for achieving the overall objectives and strategy of the firm. Suggestions from the **shop-floor** should be welcomed, but only implemented if they are going to push the firm towards its objectives.

4 SOCIETY

Flexibility in the past has been hindered by the 'them and us' mentality of managers and workers alike. This led to the importance of the trade union movement in looking after the concerns of the workforce against the strength of management.

Today, the situation is more complex. Some firms and trade unions have worked hard to break down the barriers of status, terms and conditions and pay structure between managers and workers. Part of the management motivation may have been to weaken the influence of trade unions, by linking the needs of workers more clearly to the needs of the firm. In fact, though, many unions have encouraged the move to a more mature, cooperative approach to management–worker relations.

Unfortunately, many other companies have taken a different approach. They have tried to force flexibility onto their workers by threats of redundancies or factory closures. Aggressive, macho-management made a comeback in the 1980s and 1990s, sometimes accompanied by derecognition of trade unions. In the long run, the risk is that this will prolong the 'them and us' divide. Certainly there was evidence in 2001–2003 of a tougher position by trade unions, perhaps in response to more aggressive managements.

Factors influencing the achievement of quality and flexibility

To achieve the twin goals of quality and flexibility, there are a number of factors that have to be taken into account.

ORGANISATIONAL OBJECTIVES

The aims and objectives of the organisation will have a bearing on whether or not a firm attempts to achieve flexibility and quality. And whether such an attempt would be successful.

- Is the firm concerned with maximising its profits or is the owner happy with a **satisficing** level of profits? Profit maximisers may be more likely to make all the necessary changes to bring about as flexible a workforce as possible. They will also be constantly on the lookout for new product ideas to satisfy the changing demands of potential consumers. The satisficing firm, on the other hand, will tend to be content to allow matters to continue in the way they always have done, at least up to the point where survival becomes threatened.
- Does the firm wish to be the market leader, or is it better suited to imitating the products being established by other firms? Smaller firms who may only have a localised market may find their best strategy is to follow the trends and ideas of larger, national level firms. The independent brewers, for example, usually respond to demand after the larger firms in the industry have developed new ideas such as the draught-flow widget in beer cans.

ORGANISATIONAL STRATEGIES

The organisation's strategy is the medium- or long-term plan stating how the firm's objectives are going to be achieved. This plan will describe what is to be done, the finance necessary, the personnel required and the demands to be placed on production.

The exact composition of these strategies will determine the ability of the firm to achieve the twin aims of quality and flexibility.

- If the firm undertakes a SWOT analysis to examine its own strengths and weaknesses in relation to its opportunities and the threats it faces in the marketplace, then it may require production techniques and changes to take advantage of the opportunities available to it. Other firms may be more inward looking and will not be as responsive to external demands. The strategies they adopt are not as likely to involve the development of flexibility.
- Some firms will adopt a clear strategy for contingency planning, looking at how best they could respond to a variety of unfortunate events. Planning for contingencies implies that the firm has the ability to respond quickly and appropriately to changing circumstances. This implies that the firm is both flexible and able to produce a quality output even when this involves making rapid, short-term changes.

HUMAN RESOURCE MANAGEMENT

The workforce plays a central role in any attempt by a firm to achieve quality in its output, and it must be willing and able to change with the firm if the goal of flexibility in operations is to be realistic.

The workforce is usually one of the firm's most expensive assets, but unlike tools and machinery, once employed it can change and develop. In this sense it is the firm's most valuable asset.

Management style, motivation techniques and industrial relations all play a vital role in encouraging the workforce to move with the firm. For operations management, the keys are for workers to feel a sense of ownership to the firm and for workers to feel empowered within the organisation.

- **Ownership**

  In the past, many workers' relationships with the firm for which they worked was based only on pay. They went to work, did their job and took home a pay packet at the end of the week. More recently some managements have come to see workers as one of the main stakeholders in a business. Just like shareholders, customers, the local community and suppliers, the workers have a direct interest in the performance of the firm. This sense of ownership and involvement from workers, if it can be developed successfully, can lead to them making much greater efforts on behalf of the firm.

- **Empowerment**

  This is when staff are able to exercise some degree of power over their own working lives. The development of an empowered workforce depends greatly on the degree of trust between the workers and the managers who have traditionally held this power for themselves. Managers need to trust workers, appreciate their abilities and accept that they have the firm's best interests at heart. Then they are more likely to allow the workforce some real control over their working lives. Similarly, staff must trust that the managers are empowering them for the right reasons, such as to raise standards and develop their potential.

DECISION MAKING STRATEGIES

An important factor in the development of operations that are both high quality and flexible is the way in which decisions are actually made in a business. To a large part, this will be determined by the internal structure of the firm. A small, sole trader business is not likely to spend a great deal of time considering many different options before making a decision. The person involved will probably have neither the time nor expertise to do so. A large multinational firm, on the other hand, would be as methodical as possible about decision making. The approaches to decision making that could have an impact on the way the firm operates are:

- Is the decision making done on a scientific basis, or are decisions made more randomly? Scientific decision making tries to ensure that all decisions in the business are arrived at in a logical and methodical fashion. A typical system would be to set a target, gather relevant data, form a likely idea, test the idea in practical terms, review the outcome and then revisit the original aim to see what new direction ought to be taken. Random decision making will often be based on hunches or previous experience. Although the random decisions are much quicker to arrive at, they can be much more dangerous in a situation which is constantly changing. A response to an issue that was successful in the past may no longer be valid for the current situation.
- Are decisions usually based on quantitative data or qualitative issues? Quantitative data involves looking at any item that can be measured, often in money terms. Decisions that are based on quantitative data alone will tend to look for the cheapest alternative. Workers could be replaced by machines, or factories closed if their contribution to the firm's profits is not high enough. Such decisions will tend to remove many types of qualitative information from the decision making process. Qualitative data involves looking at people's behaviour, motivations and attitudes. It is only when such information is taken on board that workers will begin to feel valued by the firm. This is a major step forward in encouraging workers to be committed to the firm and to work with the firm for the achievement of its aims.

corporate culture – the prevailing attitudes and ways of behaving within a business.

demarcation – drawing a rigid dividing line between one job function and another.

negative correlation – when the change in one variable is associated with the opposite change in another, e.g. price up, demand down.

satisficing – being satisfied with a compromise between competing objectives.

shop-floor – where jobs are completed that have a direct impact on production or sales, e.g. the factory floor or the shop sales floor.

AS Level Exercises

A. REVISION QUESTIONS
(30 marks; 60 minutes)

Read the unit, then answer:

1 Outline the reasons why people believe:
 a improvements in quality will cost the firm more (3)
 b improvements in quality will pay for themselves. (3)
2 Give three ways in which a firm can attempt to improve quality. (3)
3 How can management style affect quality? (4)
4 Why may flexibility be important in modern, fast-moving markets? (3)
5 What is meant by 'flexible specialisation'? (3)
6 How might a policy of growth affect a firm's attitude to flexible specialisation? (3)
7 How might a firm which 'satisfices' approach its management of quality? (4)
8 Why must operations management always be closely associated with marketing? (4)

B. REVISION EXERCISES

B1 Data Response
Stevens Engineering produces equipment for the building trade. It is located away from major conurbations, having taken advantage of government grants to locate in a development zone in the north-west of England.

Stevens has a reputation as a market leader in the design and development of new products. The managing director, Derek Stevens, puts this success down to a strong belief in research and development. He said, 'No matter how the firm is doing at the moment, I would never cut back on research. It is only by getting new products and ideas out first that we can compete and survive in the long term. Cutting R&D would be short-sighted and foolish.'

Despite this, the finance director has shocked his fellow directors by suggesting that the R&D function should be contracted out to an independent supplier. Derek will take some convincing.

Questions *(30 marks; 35 minutes)*
1 What is meant by 'research and development'? (3)
2 How does R&D contribute to a firm's competitive position? (6)
3 To what extent do you believe that R&D contributes to the success of a firm such as this? (9)
4 Assess the advantages and disadvantages of Stevens Engineering being located away from centres of population. (6)
5 Write a short memo to Derek Stevens justifying the outsourcing of the R&D function. (6)

B2 Case Study

Early in 1998 the Mersey Docks and Harbour Company finally managed to settle a two-year strike which had involved over half its workforce and caused a great deal of ill-feeling in the local community.

However, by August of the same year, attitudes at Liverpool's docks had changed so much that it was widely reported that at least 70% of the workforce were now saving hard to buy shares in their employer. What had caused this change in attitude amongst the workforce and in the fortunes of the company?

Some key points were:

- the full agreement reached in settling the two-year dispute
- the company's investment of £50 million in new capital equipment
- productivity up 40% on the levels before the dispute
- profits at record levels, sales increasing in line with profits and the shareholders' dividends set at a record high.

Questions   (40 marks; 50 minutes)

1 Describe the ways in which the company may have attempted to change the attitudes of its workforce since the settlement.   (8)

2 Examine the advantages and disadvantages to workers of a major investment in capital equipment.   (10)

3 Explore the links between the internal culture of a company such as this and its market performance.   (12)

4 Assess the objectives the company may adopt in its current climate of optimism.   (10)

C. ESSAY QUESTIONS

1 '"Quality is free" may be fine in the long term, but it can be very expensive in the short term.' Evaluate this statement.

2 Assess the factors that determine a company's flexibility.

3 To what extent are a firm's objectives governed by external factors rather than internal desires?

ECONOMIES AND DISECONOMIES OF SCALE

DEFINITION

Economies of scale are factors which cause average unit costs to fall as the scale of output increases. Diseconomies of scale are factors causing average costs to rise as the scale of output increases.

47.1 Two ways firms can grow

- Internal growth occurs when a firm expands its own sales and output. Firms growing in this manner must invest in new machinery and usually take on extra labour too. Firms that are successful in achieving internal growth have to be competitive. Companies like Sony have grown rapidly by taking market share from their less efficient competitors.
- External growth is created by takeover and merger activity. In early 2003 the low-cost airline Ryanair bought smaller rival Buzz. The intention was to cut costs by pooling overheads (such as booking systems). Also Ryanair gained market share by acquiring the many routes Buzz had established to France and Italy.

The trend towards increased industrial concentration has been largely due to external growth. There are many reasons why firms may wish to grow by takeover or merger. One of the most significant is that many managers believe growth will create cost savings for their firms. They anticipate benefiting from economies of scale. Unfortunately, this is not always true. Many mergers and takeovers actually reduce efficiency. Any economies of scale prove to be outweighed by diseconomies. Research has shown consistently that, on average, takeovers and mergers fail to improve efficiency.

47.2 Economies of scale

When a firm grows there are some things it can do more efficiently. The group term given to these factors is 'economies of scale'. When firms experience economies of scale their unit costs fall. For example, a pottery which could produce 100 vases at £5 each produces 1,000 vases at £4.50 per unit. The total cost rises (from £500 to £4,500) but the cost per unit falls. Assuming the firm sells the vases for £6 each, the profit margin rises from £1 per vase to £1.50.

Economies of scale are, in effect, the benefits of being big. Therefore, for small firms, they represent a threat. If a large-scale producer of televisions can sell them for £99 and still make a profit, there may be no chance for the small guy.

There are five main economies of scale. These are discussed below.

BULK-BUYING ECONOMIES

As a firm grows larger it will have to order more raw materials and components. This is likely to mean an increase in the average order size the firm places with its suppliers. Large orders are more profitable to the supplier. Both the buyer and the potential suppliers are aware of this. Consequently, firms who can place large orders have significant market power. The larger the order the larger the opportunity cost of losing it. Therefore the supplier has a big incentive to offer a discount. Big multinational manufacturers like

THE $3,000 MILLION DISCOUNT

How much would you be willing to pay for a brand new 150-seater Airbus 319? Film stars such as John Travolta strip out the seats and furnish the interior luxuriously. The list price for an Airbus 319 is $50 million. Yet in October 2002 easyJet struck a deal to buy 120 of these aircraft at a 50% discount. Aircraft priced at $6,000 million were bought for just $3,000 million. This bulk buying benefit helped to justify easyJet's boldness in taking over the rival discount airline 'Go'. Together, the purchasing power of easyJet plus Go made it far easier to pressure the European makers of Airbus, and thereby benefit from purchasing economies of scale.

Business in

Volkswagen have been relentless in demanding larger discounts from their component suppliers. This has helped Volkswagen reduce its variable costs per car.

TECHNICAL ECONOMIES

When supplying a product or service there is usually more than one production method that could be used. As a firm grows it will usually have a greater desire and a greater ability to invest in new technology. Using more machinery and less labour will usually generate cost savings. Second, the new machinery may well be less wasteful. Reducing the quantity of raw materials being wasted will cut the firm's variable costs.

These cost savings may not be available to smaller firms. They may lack the financial resources required to purchase the machinery. Even if the firm did have the money it may still not invest. Technology only becomes viable to use if the firm has a long enough production run to spread out the fixed costs of the equipment. For example, a small company may wish to buy a new computer. As the firm is small it may end up using it for only two days a week. The total cost of the computer will be the same whether the firm uses it one day or five days per week. So the average cost of each job done will be high as the small firm is unable to make full use of its investment. **Capital investment** becomes more viable as a firm grows because capital costs per unit fall as usage rises.

MANAGERIAL ECONOMIES

When firms grow there is greater potential for managers to specialise in particular tasks. For instance, large firms will probably have enough specialised personnel work to warrant employing a full-time personnel specialist. In many small firms the owner has to make numerous decisions, some of which he or she may have little knowledge of, for example accounting. This means the quality of decision making in large firms could be better than in small firms. If fewer mistakes are made, large firms should gain a cost advantage.

FINANCIAL ECONOMIES

Many small firms find it difficult to obtain finance. Even if banks are willing to lend they will tend to charge very high rates of interest. This is because logic and experience shows that lending to small (especially new) firms is more risky. They are more likely to go into liquidation than large firms. There are two main reasons for this:

- Successful small firms grow into large firms. Consequently, large firms tend to have more established products and have experienced teams of managers.
- Small firms are often over-reliant on one product or one customer; larger firms' risks are more widely spread.

The result of all this is that large firms find it far easier to find potential lenders. Second, they also pay lower rates of interest.

MARKETING ECONOMIES

Every aspect of marketing is expensive. Probably the most expensive, though, is the salesforce. These are the people who visit wholesale and retail outlets to try to persuade them to stock the firm's goods. To cover the country, nothing less than six sales staff would be realistic. Yet that would cost a firm around £200,000 per year. For a small firm with sales of under £1 million a year, this would be a crippling cost. Larger firms can spread the costs over multi-million sales, cutting the costs per unit.

BUSINESS CONCENTRATION

In early 2003 a take-over battle began as each of the major supermarkets tried to buy Safeway.

But how important is scale? Does the biggest firm have such an advantage that others can never catch up? By no means. J&P Coats was once Britain's largest manufacturing company. Today it forms one small part of a medium-sized business. Looking at it the other way, today's monster companies include many that were small or did not even exist 30 years ago. These include Microsoft, Intel, Philip Morris (Marlboro) and Toyota.

It is not even true to say that large firms are taking a larger share of national output. The heyday of large firms was in the 1970s, as the table shows:

Percentage share of manufacturing output by the largest 100 manufacturers

	1918	1970	1990
US	2%	33%	33%
Japan	23%	22%	21%
Germany	17%	30%	23%
UK	17%	40%	36%

Source: Adapted from City University Business School Working Paper

The point is, therefore, that despite the apparent benefits from economies of scale, very large firms have no guarantee of permanent success. They often became the biggest due to mergers or takeovers, and can shrink again when managerial problems become overwhelming.

Size matters, but size is no guarantee of success.

In Business

47.3 Other benefits of size

Apart from achieving cost-reducing economies of scale there are some other benefits attached to size.

REDUCED RISK

If a firm grows by diversifying into new markets the firm will now be less dependent on one product. A recession might cause sales in one area of a business to fall. However, if the firm also manufactures products which sell strongly in recessions, the overall turnover of the organisation may change little. In recent years a high percentage of takeovers and mergers have involved firms operating in totally different industries. When Volvo bought out Procordia, a firm in the processed food business, Volvo was seeking a wider product base. This helps the company avoid the risk inherent in 'having all your eggs in one basket'.

INCREASED CAPACITY UTILISATION

Some firms may wish to grow in order to increase their **capacity utilisation**. Capacity utilisation measures the firm's current output as a percentage of the maximum the firm can produce. Increasing capacity utilisation will spread the fixed costs over more units of output. This lowers the total cost per unit.

47.4 Diseconomies of scale

When firms grow, costs rise. But why should costs per unit rise? This is because growth can also create diseconomies of scale. Diseconomies of scale are factors that tend to push unit costs up. Large organisations face three main types of diseconomy of scale.

POOR EMPLOYEE MOTIVATION

When firms grow, staff may have less personal contact with management. In large organisations there is often a sense of alienation. If staff believe that their efforts are going unnoticed a sense of despondency may spread. According to the motivation theorist Elton Mayo, employees enjoy working for managers who pay an interest in them as individuals. This is the so-called 'Hawthorne effect'. In large firms some managers may feel they do not have sufficient time for frequent informal chats with their staff. Professor Herzberg also believes that recognition for achievement is vital for employee motivation. If managers do not take this into account the likelihood is that staff motivation will fall. A falling level of work effort will increase the firm's costs. Poor motivation will make staff work less hard when they are actually at work. Absenteeism is also a consequence of poor motivation. This means that the firm may have to employ more staff to cover for the staff they expect to be absent on any given day. In both cases output per worker will fall. As a result, labour costs per unit will rise.

POOR COMMUNICATION

Communication can be a significant problem when a firm grows. First, effective communication is dependent on high levels of motivation. Communication is only effective if the person being communicated with is willing to listen. If growth has left the workforce with a feeling of alienation, communication can deteriorate alongside productivity. A second reason for poor communication in large organisations is that the methods chosen to communicate may be less effective. As a firm grows it may become necessary to use written forms of communication more frequently. Unlike verbal communication, written communication is less personal and therefore less motivating. Written messages are easier to ignore and provide less feedback. Relying too much on written forms of communication could result in an increase in the number of expensive mistakes being made.

POOR MANAGERIAL COORDINATION

In a small firm coordination is easy. The boss decides what the goals are, and who is doing what. As firms grow, it becomes harder for the person at the top to control and coordinate effectively. The leader who refuses to **delegate** 'drowns' under the weight of work. The leader who delegates finds (later) that manager A is heading in a slightly different direction from manager B. Regular meetings are arranged to try to keep everyone focused on the same goals through the same strategy. But not only are such meetings expensive, they are also rather ineffective. Coordination is effective and free in a small firm, expensive and hugely ineffective in large corporations.

47.5 Combining economies and diseconomies of scale

It is important to realise that growth normally creates both economies and diseconomies of scale. If growth creates more economies than diseconomies then unit costs will fall. On the other hand, if the growth creates more diseconomies, the opposite will happen (see Figure 47.1).

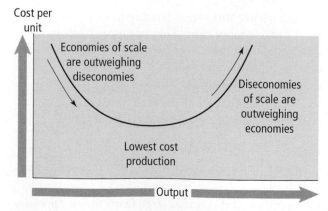

Figure 47.1 Production costs and production scale

Normally, when a firm is small, initial bouts of growth will create more economies of scale than diseconomies. So growth pushes average costs down.

WHAT CAN MANAGERS DO ABOUT DISECONOMIES OF SCALE?

Diseconomies of scale are to a certain extent inevitable. However, this does not mean that managers should just accept them. With careful planning, many diseconomies may be minimised or avoided completely. They key point is that diseconomies are more likely to arise either when growth is unplanned or when it is too rapid. When a firm embarks on a programme of growth it is vital that managers recognise the need to change and adapt.

DISECONOMIES OF SCALE	CORRECTIVE ACTION REQUIRED

Poor motivation	• Delegate decision making power
	• Job enrichment
	• Split the business up by using the following:
	  – profit/cost centres
	  – cell production

Poor communication	• Improve employee motivation as above • Send managers on attitudinal training courses • Create new communication structures such as works councils
Poor coordination	• Decentralise • Empowerment • Wider spans of control

Economies of scale is a concept used frequently by students in examinations. When using it to analyse a business situation, the following points should be considered:

- In most business circumstances, a rise in demand cuts average costs because of improved capacity utilisation. In other words, if a half-used factory gets a big order, unit costs fall because the fixed overheads are spread over more output. This is great, but should not be referred to as an economy of scale. It is simply an increase in capacity utilisation. The term 'economies of scale' refers to increases in the scale of operation, e.g. when a firm moves to new, bigger premises.
- The cost advantages from bulk buying can be considerable, but are often exaggerated. A medium sized builder can buy bricks at much the same cost per brick as a multinational construction company. It should also be remembered that materials and components form quite a low proportion of the total costs for many products. For cosmetics or pharmaceuticals, bought-in materials would usually cost less than one-tenth of the selling price of the product. So lively minds dreaming up new products will count for far more than minor savings from bulk buying.
- Traditionally, managers of growing or merging companies have tended to predict economies of scale with confidence, but to turn a blind eye to diseconomies. In the medium to long term, though, managerial problems of coping with huge organisations have tended to create more diseconomies than economies of scale.

47.6 Economies and diseconomies of scale
an evaluation

Three important issues should be considered:

- If diseconomies are all people problems, why can't they be better managed?

  Most diseconomies of scale are caused by an inability to manage people effectively. When firms grow managers must be willing to delegate power in an attempt to avoid the problems caused by alienation. Some types of manager might find it hard to accept the need for delegation. If the manager has strong status needs and has **Theory X** attitudes, he or she may find it difficult to cope.

  Enriching jobs and running training courses are expensive in the short term. These costs are also easy to quantify financially. The benefits of job enrichment and training are more long term. Second, they are harder to quantify financially. This means that it can be quite hard for the managers of a company to push through the changes required to minimise the damage created by diseconomies of scale. Public limited companies may find this a particular problem. Their shares can be bought freely and sold on the stock market. This means that considerable pressure is put on the managers to achieve consistently good financial results. The penalty for investing too much in any one year could be a falling share price and an increased risk of takeover.

- Do economies of scale make it impossible for small firms to survive?

  In highly competitive markets it is difficult for small firms to compete with large established businesses. Especially if they try to compete with them in the mass market. In this situation the small firm will lose out nine times out of ten. The small firm will not be able to achieve the same economies of scale. As a result, its prices will have to be higher to compensate for its higher costs.

  To a degree this view is correct. However, the fact that the majority of firms within the economy have less than 200 employees proves that small firms do find ways of surviving, despite the existence of economies of scale.

- The importance of being unimportant.

  Many small firms do not need economies of scale to survive. They rely upon the fact that they do not compete head on with their larger competitors. Small firms often produce a highly specialised product. These products are well differentiated. This means the small firm can charge higher prices. So even though they have higher costs their profit margins can be healthy. The larger firms in the industry are frequently not interested in launching their own specialist products. They believe there is more money to be made from the much larger mass market. By operating in these smaller so-called niche markets, many small firms not only survive but often prosper. By being small and by operating in tiny market segments they are not seen as a threat to the larger firms. As a consequence they are ignored because large firms see them as unimportant.

AS Level Exercises

A. REVISION QUESTIONS
(35 marks; 70 minutes)

Read the unit, then answer:

1 Identify three managerial motives for growth. *(3)*
2 Give three examples of managerial economies of scale. *(3)*
3 Explain why large companies are frequently able to command larger discounts from their suppliers than are smaller firms. *(4)*
4 Give three examples of managerial diseconomies of scale. *(3)*
5 Explain the likely consequences for a large firm of a failure to control and coordinate the business effectively. *(4)*
6 Many car manufacturers like Nissan are attempting to reduce the complexity of their designs by using fewer parts in different models. With reference to the concept of economies of scale, explain why this is happening. *(4)*
7 Give three reasons why employee morale can deteriorate as a consequence of growth? *(3)*
8 Give three examples of corrective measures that managers could decide to undertake in order to tackle these morale problems. *(3)*
9 Explain how economies of scale could give a firm a considerable marketing advantage. *(4)*
10 What is meant by 'the importance of being unimportant'? *(4)*

B. REVISION EXERCISES

B1 Data Response

Geoff Horsfield and his sister Alex are worried about whether they can compete effectively with their big local competitor, Bracewell plc. Alex believes that Bracewell's economies of scale mean that Horsfield Trading cannot compete head-on. Therefore she wants to switch the company's marketing approach away from the mass market towards smaller niches.

Geoff is not sure of this. He knows that Bracewell has a more up-to-date manufacturing technique, but has heard of inefficiencies in the warehousing and office staff. He doubts that Bracewell is as efficient as Alex supposes. Therefore he argues that Horsfield Trading can still compete in the mass market.

Fortunately the employment of an accountant from Bracewell plc has enabled direct comparisons to be made. These figures, shown below, should help Geoff and Alex decide on Horsfield's future strategy.

	Horsfield Trading Ltd	Bracewell plc
Capital investment	£240,000	£880,000
Factory employees	28	49
Other employees	7	21
Guarantee claims per 100 sales	1.2	2.1
Output per employee (units per day)	21	23

Questions   *(30 marks; 35 minutes)*

1 Calculate the capital investment per employee at each company. What do the figures tell you?   *(6)*
2 Outline the probable reasons for Alex's wish to aim at smaller market niches.   *(5)*
3 **a** What explanations may there be for the differences between the guarantee claims of each business?   *(8)*
  b What may be the short- and long-term effects of these differences?   *(6)*
4 Outline any other evidence in the case of diseconomies of scale at Bracewell plc.   *(5)*

B2 Case Study: Expanding European Airways

European Airways is a successful cut-price airline offering scheduled services to the major cities of Europe. The company's director, Daniel Addana, had always been keen on planes and flying. He had inherited a chain of hotels based in mainland Europe, but sold it to raise enough money to purchase his first aircraft.

His business plan came as a result of his experiences as a customer. On his travels around Europe Dan felt aggrieved about the high prices he was often asked to pay for what were relatively short journeys. He then struck upon the idea of setting up his own airline that would be able to undercut the established competi-

tion. Initially Dan targeted the London to Amsterdam route. By offering low fares Addana filled nearly every seat, so despite his low prices he made handsome profits. The key to the company's success has been its ability to achieve a high seat occupancy rate. In the airline industry load factors are crucial. Aircraft are expensive to purchase, they are also costly to run. Therefore to be efficient, every single seat must be filled in order to dilute these costs so that profits can be made from prices that are competitive.

The company has subsequently expanded and now has 10 Airbus A300s in the fleet.

Dan Addana believes that the company's winning formula can also be applied to a new destination. The only choice Addana has to make is which type of aircraft the company will buy to service the route. The finance director advises buying an A340. The A340 is much larger than the A300 and can carry 400 passengers rather than 255. However it does burn 15% more fuel per kilometre than the A300. Despite this apparent superior efficiency, Addana has two doubts about buying the A340. The first is that the A340 will only deliver its technical economies of scale if load factors remain high. Second, if the airline buys a new type of aircraft, economies of scale might be lost in maintenance, spare parts and training.

Questions   *(40 marks; 60 minutes)*

1 Using the above information, prove that economies of scale will be generated if the A340 is bought for the new route.   *(6)*
2 Using examples from the case study, distinguish between gains in efficiency created through high capacity utilisation and efficiency gains created though economies of scale.   *(12)*
3 Explain the logic behind Addana's second concern about buying the A340 over the A300.   *(6)*
4 What actions could Airbus Industrie take in order to minimise the loss of maintenance, spare parts and training for customers like European Airlines?   *(6)*
5 Identify and then evaluate the external threats that could affect the success of Addana's latest expansion plan.   *(10)*

C. ESSAY QUESTIONS

1 Small firms are often said to have better internal communications than larger organisations. Does this mean that growth will always create communication problems? If so what can be done about these difficulties?
2 MHK plc is a large manufacturer of semiconductors. Discuss the opportunities and problems it may face if it decides on a strategy of growth through centralising production.
3 Given the existence of economies of scale, how do small firms manage to survive?

B3 Case Study:

The Drugs Deal That Went Wrong

In 2000 Glaxo and SmithKline, two giants of the pharmaceutical industry merged. The goal was to create cost saving economies of scale that would hopefully boost profitability. City analysts claimed that the deal might create economies of scale worth as much as £1.8 billion. It was also hoped that the merger would create a dominant and innovative industry Goliath, that would be able to generate new products at a rate that the competition could not match.

Unfortunately, GlaxoSmithKline discovered that in business size matters but not in the way they had hoped. Bigger does not always equate to better because growth can create problems that, if not tackled, will push costs up. Like many companies before them, GlaxoSmithKline forgot that growth creates both economies and diseconomies of scale.

By 2002 these diseconomies began to emerge. Poor profitability, the loss of patents on top selling products and the loss of key skilled personnel led to a halving of the share price. The rumour on the stock market was that the new company was struggling to adjust to its new scale of operation. Overheads soared following the merger. A good example was the new Head Office which was so big that it required a permanent team of window cleaners. There were many corporate luxuries for the staff at Head Office. In addition to cafés and shops, staff had the pleasure of a river that ran through the middle of the site.

The growth created by the merger also led to a change in organisational culture. Prior to the merger both companies were known for their innovative and entrepreneurial approach. This culture began to wane in the new organisation, as the company became progressively more and more bureaucratic. For example, staff selection for crucial middle-management positions began to favour those with strong organisational skills over those possessing the qualities of vision and inspiration.

Growth also created co-ordination and control problems for the London-based management. Their centralised business empire now consisted of 104 manufacturing sites in 40 countries and a further 24 research and development centres in seven countries. With an organisation this large, attempts to monitor the performance of every division proved unsuccessful. Under-performing overseas divisions were not spotted fast enough; so corrective action was sometimes taken too late to prevent losses.

Questions
(25 marks; 35 minutes)

1 Define what is meant by the term 'diseconomies of scale'. *(2)*
2 Outline the diseconomies of scale that came about as a result of the GlaxoSmithKline merger. *(6)*
3 Growth through merger and takeover has become an increasingly common business objective in the past 15 years. Apart from the desire to achieve economies of scale can you explain why this might be so? *(7)*
4 Most business theorists believe that diseconomies of scale are not inevitable. Discuss the actions GlaxoSmithKline should have taken in order to minimise potential diseconomies of scale. *(10)*

CAPACITY UTILISATION

Capacity utilisation is the proportion of maximum possible output that is currently being used. A football stadium is at full capacity when all the seats are filled. A company producing 15,000 units a week when the factory is capable of 20,000 units has a capacity utilisation of 75%.

48.1 How is capacity utilisation measured?

Capacity utilisation is measured using the following formula;

$$\frac{\text{current output}}{\text{maximum possible output}} \times 100$$

What does capacity depend upon? The amount a firm can make is determined by the quantity of buildings, machinery and labour it has available. The level of output achieved when the firm is making full use of all the buildings, machinery and labour available is the maximum output. The firm is said to be working at full capacity, or 100% capacity utilisation.

For a service business the same logic applies. Though it is much harder to identify a precise figure. This is because it may take a different time to serve each customer. In a shop or a bank branch, demand may exceed capacity at certain times of the day. In which case queues will form. At other times the staff may have little to do. A service business wishing to keep cost competitive will measure demand at different times of the day and then schedule the staffing level to match the capacity utilisation.

Many of these service businesses are better able to cope with fluctuating demand by employing temporary or part-time staff. A glance at employment figures for the UK will show the growing importance of temporary and part-time jobs in the UK. These employees bring a far greater degree of flexibility to employers. Part-time hours can be increased or extra temporary staff can be employed to increase capacity easily. If demand falls, temporary staff can be laid off without redundancy payments or part-time staff can have their hours reduced, thus reducing capacity easily and cheaply. This flexibility is good for businesses, helping to reduce spare capacity. However the situation may not be as appealing for employees who have fewer rights than their full-time salaried predecessors.

48.2 Fixed costs and capacity

It is vital to understand clearly the relationship between fixed costs and capacity utilisation. Fixed costs are fixed in relation to output. This means that whether capacity utilisation is 50% or 100%, fixed costs will not change. The implication of this is clear. If a football club invests in a huge, expensive playing staff (whose salaries are a fixed cost) but matches are played to a half-empty stadium, the fixed costs will become a huge burden. This is because the very fact that fixed costs do not change *in total* as output changes means that they do change *per unit* of output/demand. A half-empty stadium means that the fixed costs per unit are double the level at maximum capacity. For example:

	FULL STADIUM 50,000 FANS	HALF EMPTY 25,000 FANS
Weekly salary bill (fixed costs)	£250,000	£250,000
Salary fixed cost per unit	£5 (£250,000/50,000)	£10 (£250,000/25,000)

When the stadium capacity utilisation is at 50%, then, £10 of the ticket price is needed for the players' wages alone. The many other fixed and variable costs of running a football club would be on top of this, of course.

The reason why capacity utilisation is so important is that it has an inverse (opposite) effect upon fixed costs per unit. In other words, when utilisation is high, fixed costs are spread over many units. This cuts the cost per unit. Which enables the producer either to cut prices to boost demand further, or to enjoy large profit margins. If utilisation is low, fixed costs per unit become punishingly high. As Disneyland Paris found when it opened up in 1992 and demand proved lower than expected.

The ideal level of capacity utilisation, therefore, is at or near 100%. This spreads fixed costs as thinly as possible, boosting profit margins. There are two key concerns about operating at maximum capacity for long, however. These are:

- the risk that rising demand could be met only by competitors, as you are already producing flat out
- the risk that you will never have the time to service machinery, change/improve production methods or train/retrain staff; this may prove costly in the long term, and may increase the chances of production breakdowns in the short term.

The production ideal, therefore, is a capacity utilisation of around 90%.

USING SPARE CAPACITY

JD Wetherspoon's, the pub group, announced plans in September 2002 to make use of spare capacity by opening their pubs earlier in the morning to serve breakfast. Pubs would open at around 10am and would serve breakfasts for around £3. Coffee would also be on offer at around 75p per cup.

The company would be using existing resources, so no increase in total capacity would be needed. The buildings were already in place – notably almost all in prime High Street locations. Each pub already offered food, so no extra investment in cooking facilities would be required. Staff turned up to work at 10am already, so increased staff costs would be minimal – the firm was simply seeking to use some of its spare capacity (in this case, time during which the pubs were closed), to generate extra revenue.

48.3 How to get towards full capacity

If a firm's capacity utilisation is an unsatisfactory 45%, how could it be increased to a more acceptable level of around 90%? There are two possible approaches.

1 Increase demand (in this case, double it!). Demand for existing products could be boosted by extra promotional spending, price cutting or – more fundamentally – devising a new strategy to reposition the products into growth sectors. If supermarket own-label products are flourishing, perhaps offer to produce under the Tesco or Sainsbury's banner. If doubling of sales is needed, it is unlikely that existing products will provide the whole answer. The other approach is to launch new products. This could be highly effective, but implies long-term planning and investment.

2 Cut capacity. If your current factory and labour force is capable of producing 10,000 units a week,

but there is only demand for 4,500, there will be a great temptation to cut capacity to 5,000. This might be done by cutting out the night shift, i.e. making those workers redundant. This would avoid the disruption and inflexibility caused by the alternative, which is to move to smaller premises. Moving will enable all fixed costs to be cut (rent, rates, salaries and so on), but may look silly if, six months later, demand has recovered to 6,000 units when your new factory capacity is only 5,000.

A key factor in deciding whether to cut capacity or boost demand is the underlying cause of the low utilisation. It may be the result of a known temporary demand shortfall, such as a seasonal low point in the toy business. Or it may be due to an economic recession which (on past experience) may hit demand for around 18–24 months. Either way, it might prove a mistake in the long run to cut capacity. Nevertheless, if a firm faces huge short-term losses from its excess fixed costs, it may have to forget the future and concentrate on short-term survival.

Figure 48.1 shows the proportion of UK business operating at full capacity over the five years from January 1993 to October 1998. The graph implies a strong correlation between the trade cycle and the number of firms with spare capacity. In times of recession, there are fewer firms operating at full capacity. As recovery begins more firms are able to get close to full capacity, until the economy enters a period of prosperity, when the majority of firms are operating at full capacity.

Source: CBI Industrial Trends Surveys

Figure 48.1 % of UK firms operating at full capacity (Jan 93–Oct 98)

48.4 Why and how to change capacity

Firms may find themselves with **excess capacity** if demand for their products slows down. Unless the reduction in demand is just a short-term glitch, a firm will seek to find ways to reduce its maximum capacity. This process is commonly called **rationalising**. It means reorganising in order to boost efficiency (though cynics call 'rationalising' a polite way of saying redundancies).

Clearly, if capacity is dependent on the amount of buildings, machinery and labour available to a firm, a change in capacity must mean a change in one or more of these resources. In the case of buildings, the firm may decide to sell off a factory or part of a factory if it feels it will not need that space in the future. Or the firm may decide to lease out factory space to other companies, on a short-term basis. This will enable it to get the extra space back if demand improves.

Machinery can be sold off second-hand or for scrap. In both cases, though, it is likely that the firm will be unable to gain the true financial value of the machinery when it is sold. A more flexible solution is to rent machinery rather than buy it outright in the first place. This would enable the firm to return machinery in times when capacity needs to be reduced.

Redundancy is the obvious answer for a firm whose workforce is too large. It is important to remember that making staff redundant is an expensive business for firms. Wherever possible, firms may look to reassign their employees to other roles or, if money allows, send staff on training programmes while they are not needed for production. Many firms with excess labour will cut down the length of time worked by employees, perhaps by shortening shifts. In October 2002 Jaguar put their X-type car workers at Halewood on a 4 day week to cut production levels.

RATIONALISING THE SKIES

Business IN

A process of rationalisation is always likely to follow a sudden fall in demand within an industry. Just such a demand shock followed the 11 September 2001 attacks, in the airline industry. In a market which already had too many seats for the passengers it was attracting, an estimated 10% fall in worldwide demand in the year following the attacks was the cue for a round of rationalisation.

Older aircraft were retired in order to cut running costs, whilst many firms followed the lead of Virgin Atlantic and put craft into a kind of hibernation in massive airliner parks, mothballed until demand picks up. Some companies, such as Swissair and Belgium's Sabena, found themselves unable to shed capacity fast enough and went bankrupt. Meanwhile, in America, airlines sought help through government loans and subsidies as a way of covering their costs in the hope that demand would recover. This course of action was all that was left as attempts to cut costs were met by determined trade union opposition within the US.

Recovery had begun by late 2002 with European carriers such as Lufthansa, BA and SAS beginning to emerge from the setback. However, American companies remained in dire straits, expecting several bankruptcies along with further capacity cutting by individual firms.

Source: Adapted from the *Guardian*

OVERCAPACITY IN CARS

Business IN

Jaguar and Land Rover, both owned by Ford, announced a programme of redundancies on 19 September 2002. Both firms appeared to have excess production capacity at their plants within the UK. They are both seeking voluntary redundancies among production staff as a way of reducing their cost base – reducing their fixed costs. These announcements came despite news that sales of both brands of car were healthy and production levels were not expected to fall as a result of the redundancies. Trade union representatives were not surprised by the announcements, suggesting that more could be in the pipeline. Jaguar will also be introducing a 4-day week for production personnel at their Halewood plant – a further indication of overcapacity in the car market.

48.5 Advantages and disadvantages of full capacity

ADVANTAGES

- If a firm is working at full capacity, its fixed costs per unit are at the lowest possible level. The firm is producing as many units as possible so fixed costs are spread as widely as they can be. The result is that the amount of fixed costs borne by each unit is at its lowest possible level.
- At full capacity, the firm is assumed to be using all its fixed assets as effectively as possible. Since fixed assets generate profit, profits should be high.
- A firm working at full capacity will be perceived as a successful firm. Full capacity utilisation implies that demand for the firm's products is healthy. This perception will have positive internal and external effects. Internally, workers will feel secure in their jobs and may well feel a certain pride in working for a successful organisation. Externally, customers and potential customers will feel that if the firm is working at full capacity, it must be manufacturing a good product.

- Firms working at full capacity may need to turn away potential customers. Even if the firm does not turn customers away, the prospect of a long wait for the firm's products may well lead to customers going elsewhere.
- Workers who are working at full capacity will have little, if any, time to relax and will need to work as hard as possible at all times. This may make some workers feel overworked.
- Managers may be subject to high stress levels if the firm is operating at full capacity. With no time available to make up for mistakes, it is vital that production planning is accurate and effective.
- If a firm is working at full capacity, its machinery is assumed to be working all the time. This means that there is no **down time** available when routine maintenance can be carried out. Without regular maintenance, most machinery is more likely to break down, causing a complete halt.

It follows, therefore, that firms which are enjoying high capacity utilisation should consider investing to boost their total production capacity. From the viewpoint of the economy as a whole, there can be economic growth and long-term increases in prosperity only if firms increase their capacity.

ISSUES FOR **analysis**

When developing an argument in answer to a case study or essay question, the following lines of analysis should be considered:

- The importance of considering the time frame of the question. Is spare capacity caused by a short-term fall in demand or is there a longer term downward trend? Only if the demand decline is a long-term trend should capacity be cut. It must be remembered, though, that it is always hard to be sure of these things. In the 1980s and early 1990s, falling football crowds meant that when clubs such as Manchester United and Newcastle rebuilt their stadiums, they cut the crowd capacity. Looking back it is easy to say they were wrong. At the time they made what seemed the right decision. So consider the timescale, but be careful of sounding too definite about the 'right' solution.
- The link between capacity utilisation, fixed costs per unit and profitability. If dealing with a question about how to improve profitability, increasing capacity utilisation could well be a valid solution. If profits are poor, be sure to ask what capacity utilisation is at present.
- Modern production theory praises systems such as just-in-time, **flexible specialisation** and lean production. Successful management of all three of these approaches is likely to mean capacity utilisation that is well below 100%. This is because all three approaches require flexible responses to customer requirements/orders. In turn, this requires spare capacity. How can any firm afford to operate deliberately at a low level of average capacity utilisation? By keeping fixed costs down and by charging relatively high prices for the products.

EXPANDING CAPACITY

IN Business

In the mid-1990s, Electro Furnace Products (EFP) was enjoying buoyant demand for its output of insulating materials for the heating elements in electric kettles and washing machines. After careful forecasts of future demand, the company took a big risk by investing £4.2 million to quadruple production capacity. From 4,000 tonnes per year, capacity reached 18,000 tonnes. Fortunately the expected sales increases came about, allowing EFP to operate at 80% of capacity. Its bold decision allowed export sales to rise 170% within three years. No wonder the company received the Queen's Award For Export Achievement in 1998.
Source: *The Financial Times*

48.6 Capacity utilisation
an evaluation

Most firms will aim to operate close to full capacity, but probably not at 100%. A small amount of spare capacity is accepted as necessary, bringing a certain degree of flexibility in case of need. In this way, sudden surges of demand can be coped with in the short run by increasing output, or down time can be used for maintenance. Spare capacity can be a good thing, particularly in small doses.

Firms operating close to full capacity are those who may be considering investing in new premises or machinery. This is often the scenario in which questions on investment appraisal are set. In addition to considering whether demand is stable in the long run, the firm must also consider the length of time between deciding to build extra capacity and when the extra capacity is available for use. Building new factories takes time as well as huge quantities of money. Can the firm afford to wait 18 months for its capacity to be expanded? Perhaps the firm would be better served subcontracting certain areas of its work to other companies, thus freeing capacity.

Capacity utilisation also raises the difficult issue of cutting capacity by **rationalisation** and, often, redundancy. This incorporates many issues of human resource management, motivation and social responsibilities. There are fewer more important tests of the skills and far-sightedness of senior managers.

When tackling case studies, it is important that you take a step back from any case study dealing with such a situation to consider the cause and the effect. Is **excess capacity** the problem or an indicator of another problem such as declining market share? By showing the broader picture in this way you can also show the skill of evaluation.

down time –any period when machinery is not being used in production. It is used for carrying out maintenance, so some down time for all machinery is necessary. However, too much down time indicates a low level of capacity utilisation.

excess capacity – when there is more capacity than justified by current demand, i.e. utilisation is low.

flexible specialisation – a production system based upon batches of goods aimed at many market niches, instead of mass production/mass market.

rationalisation – reorganising in order to increase efficiency. This often implies cutting capacity to increase the percentage utilisation.

AS Level Exercises

A. REVISION QUESTIONS
(25 marks; 50 minutes)

Read the unit, then answer:

1 What is meant by the phrase '100% capacity utilisation'? *(3)*

2 At what level of capacity utilisation will fixed costs per unit be lowest for any firm? Briefly explain your answer. *(4)*

3 What formula is used to calculate the capacity utilisation of a firm? *(2)*

4 How can a firm increase its capacity utilisation without increasing output? *(3)*

5 If a firm is currently selling 11,000 units per month and this represents a capacity utilisation of 55%, what is its maximum capacity? *(4)*

6 Use the following information to calculate profit per week at 50%, 75% and 100% capacity utilisation:

Maximum capacity	800 units per week
Variable cost per unit	£1,800
Total fixed cost per week	£1.5 million
Selling price	£4,300 *(9)*

B. REVISION EXERCISES

B1 Data Response
K Leonard and Co was founded 50 years ago. It has a successful history of manufacturing high quality bicycle chains which are supplied direct to retailers. In recent years, orders from retail customers have fallen, meaning that the firm is now only manufacturing and selling 12,000 chains per month.

The following cost information has been made available:

Materials cost per unit:	80p
Shop-floor worker's salary:	£10,000 p.a.
Salary paid to other staff:	£12,000 p.a.
Manager's salary:	£32,000 p.a.
Maximum capacity:	20,000 units per month
General overheads:	£40,000 p.m.
Current selling price:	£5.80
Number of managers currently employed:	3
Number of shop-floor staff currently employed:	10
Number of other staff currently employed:	4

The finance manager has called the other two managers to a meeting to discuss the firm's future. She puts forward two alternative courses of action:

● Make four shop-floor and two other staff redundant, thus cutting the firm's fixed costs, and reducing maximum capacity to 12,000 units per month.

● Sign a contract to supply a large bicycle manufacturer with a fixed quantity of 8,000 chains per month at £5.80 each for the next four years. Breaking the contract will lead to heavy financial penalties.

Questions *(30 marks; 35 minutes)*

1 What is the firm's current monthly profit? *(5)*

2 Calculate the monthly profit which would result from each of the two options. *(10)*

3 Explain the advantages and disadvantages of each option. *(10)*

4 State which of the two options you would choose and list any other information you would need before making the final decision. *(5)*

B2 Case Study

European car manufacturers still lag behind the US and Japan in the key matters of quality, productivity, profitability, matching production capacity to demand and producing cars with genuine worldwide appeal. However, most European motor bosses are united in their refusal to accept that sales are about to dive, or that they are doomed to be victims of overcapacity. A recent Economist Intelligence Unit (EIU) report suggested that Europe is carrying sufficient idle capacity to produce 3 million extra cars on top of the 13 million made in the previous year. Other estimates of overcapacity in Europe range from 1 million cars per year to 6 million. The EIU report recommends savage cost cutting based on factory closures and job losses.

Chrysler chairman, Bob Lutz, has been quoted as saying: 'You have to bite the bullet, the US car industry has been through a fundamental shake-up in recent years. It is hard but you have to shut down excess plants. Too many European factories have been built on the basis of production and jobs coming first, with the hope that you can find the customers for the cars later. But manufacturing must flow from demand.'

European car makers are operating in a flat market. They have struggled to break into other markets in the way their US and Japanese rivals have done. Some action is beginning to happen – Renault has just closed a factory in Belgium, amid political uproar over job losses. Renault's executive vice-president, Carlos Ghosen, told last week's *Financial Times* conference: 'It is true that there is overcapacity in Europe, but you have to know where your break-even point is. If it is near full capacity you are in trouble. But if you can make a profit, you can keep spare capacity for a rise in the market.'

Overall, most experts agree that manufacturers need to cut capacity in Europe, in addition to improving the way they match capacity to demand. Rover is currently suffering from chronic overcapacity for its larger cars but cannot meet demand for its MGF sports car.

Source: Adapted from an article by Joanna Walters published in *The Observer*, 14/9/97

Questions   *(40 marks; 60 minutes)*

1 Explain what is meant by the phrase 'estimates of overcapacity in Europe range from 1 million cars a year to 6 million'.   *(4)*
2 Why might car manufacturers be reluctant to reduce capacity by closing factories?   *(8)*
3 Explain why 'you are in trouble if your break-even point is near full capacity'.   *(6)*
4 Discuss the problem faced by Rover, with excess large-car capacity yet not enough production of MGF sports cars.   *(12)*
5 Assess the importance of the statement by Bob Lutz that 'manufacturing must flow from demand'.   *(10)*

TYPES OF PRODUCTION

DEFINITION

The type of production is the method by which goods and services are produced.

49.1 Introduction

Operations management is concerned with the transformation of inputs into outputs (see Figure 49.1). People, materials, machines, money and technology are all combined to produce goods and services. During this transformation process value is added to the materials. £10 worth of wood becomes a chair selling for £65. The aim of operations management is to ensure the efficiency of this process of adding value.

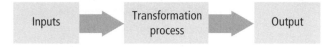

Figure 49.1 Transformation of inputs into outputs

There are many different types of production: restaurants producing meals; construction workers building a house; a manufacturing company producing aluminium cans. All of these are involved in one form of transformation process or another. Although there are many production methods they tend to be classified as job, batch, flow or lean production. Lean production is dealt with in Unit 50.

49.2 Job production

Job production occurs when firms produce items which meet the specific requirements of each customer. Every time you order a meal in a good restaurant, for example, it will be made just as you want it. Similarly, a tailor-made suit is designed to fit one particular customer rather than being bought 'off the peg' in a retail outlet. Major constructions such as Wembley Stadium are also one-off items which are designed and produced to meet a specific order.

Job production is very flexible in that each product is made to order. At the same time, it is often an expensive production process. Instead of setting up machines and letting them run for hours on end, producing hundreds or thousands of items, a firm involved in job production is producing a new item or offering a new service each time. Imagine you are a solicitor, for example. Each client's situation will be unique and you

THERE'S ONLY ONE WEMBLEY

After almost 7 years of political and financial problems it was finally announced in July 2002 that work was about to begin on the new Wembley stadium. The old stadium would be knocked down and a new one built with a capacity of 90,000. This would take about 3 years and is a good example of one-off job production.

The estimated costs associated with Wembley have spiralled from £185 million to more than £750 milion since it was first proposed, making it the most expensive stadium project in history, and putting it on a par with the ill-fated Millennium Dome. The last match was played at the old stadium in October 2000.

The costs include:
- £120 million of lottery money which was largely used to buy the site of the current derelict stadium.
- Construction costs of around £452 million, including £80 million to demolish the old stadium.
- £80 million for design, legal and financing fees.
- Developing the infrastructure and transport links around the new stadium.

in Business

The new Wembley stadium ©www.wembleystadium.com

will offer specific advice to that person. This provides a highly personalised service but is very labour intensive.

In manufacturing, job production requires highly skilled staff and a wide range of equipment because the firm must be able to adapt to different requests. Typically, the firm will have a series of machines which are grouped according to their function. By changing the route of any item from one type of machine to another, a unique product can be produced each time. Alternatively a skilled worker may carry out the job without any purpose-built tools. A potter, for example, can produce a specially shaped vase using only his or her hands and a potter's wheel.

The management of job production tends to be quite complex because each order is unique. Therefore the organisation of orders can become difficult to coordinate. However the level of motivation is usually quite high. This is because each job is different – providing employees with variety in their work. Employees also have a very direct input into the production process. They can see the result of their efforts because there is a usually a clear start and finish to a job. Today a worker starts to build a garden wall; by Friday the task is complete and the customer (and worker) satisfied.

49.3 Batch production

Batch production, by comparison, produces a group of items at one time. Each group undergoes one stage of the process before being moved on to the next stage. For example, when baking bread a batch of loaves will be prepared, then cooked and finally wrapped and dispatched. Similarly, a fish and chip shop is based around a batch process. A batch of chips or fish is prepared and then cooked ready for customers. When this is

Batch production © Bruce Peebles/Corbis

gone another batch is prepared. Alternatively imagine that you are running a printing company. You will set up the printing presses to print the pages of one particular book. These will be printed then glued together then moved on to be bound, trimmed and despatched. New printing plates will be placed on the presses and a new book produced in the same way.

The advantage of batch production is that more items are produced at any one time than in the job system. This allows the firm to spread its overheads and so reduce the unit costs. However, it is obviously less flexible than job production. Once a batch is in production it cannot easily be changed to produce something else. Switching from one to another takes time and involves a loss of output.

McJIT

In the late 1990s, McDonald's introduced a new 'made for you' system bringing just-in-time production techniques to the service industry. The system (which costs $25,000 to install) speeds up the time taken for a customer to receive his or her order. This helps McDonald's respond to the success of competitors, such as Burger King, which have stressed in their promotion that their customers can choose exactly what they want and how they want it cooked. In the past, McDonald's franchises cooked their food in batches ready for the busy periods. This meant that some of it sat around before being eaten and so lost some of its flavour. The 'made for you' system includes new technology and a re-engineering of the old process. It includes equipment which toasts buns in 10 seconds and ovens which keep burgers fresh for up to 20 minutes. Everything is designed to increase the speed of service and cut the maximum customer waiting time to 90 seconds.

Batch production can also lead to high stock levels as items wait to move on to the next stage of the process. This takes up space, involves an opportunity cost and creates the possibility of items deteriorating or being damaged.

49.4 Flow production

The third type of production is '**flow**' or 'mass' production. With this system an item moves from one stage of the process straight on to the next stage. Oil refining or bottling plants are both examples of a flow process. In a bottling plant, for example, the bottles move

Flow production © Richmond Foods

continuously from the cleansing operation to the actual bottling, to capping, labelling and despatch. The flow from one stage to the next is achieved either by conveyor belts or – in the case of liquids – by pipeline.

Flow production is highly capital intensive. It involves a high level of investment in modern machinery and computer-controlled equipment. The process produces a standardised product in high volumes, such as the Mars factory in Slough which produces three million Mars bars per day. The advantage of this type of process is that the high initial costs can be spread over thousands or millions of units. This generates technical and purchasing **economies of scale**. But to be profitable it relies on high and stable demand. Perfect for producing long-term big sellers such as Kit-Kat, Heinz baked beans or cars such as the Renault Megane.

A custom-built flow production line is difficult and expensive to alter. The system is efficient but inflexible. The firm must therefore be certain that the market will remain large enough to be profitable. The management of people on a flow process can also cause difficulties. Work is often repetitive and relatively unskilled. Staff have little direct input into the way the product is made. The process is also vulnerable to stoppages. Any problem at any stage will hold up the entire production process. Yet the machines need to be running to enable the firm to recoup the high level of initial investment.

49.5 Job, batch and flow

The different types of production can be analysed in terms of a product–process matrix (see Figure 49.2). If, for example, the product is a unique one-off item, then the most suitable production process is job production. If the product needs to be standardised and

MASS PRODUCING CHOC ICES

The production process starts by mixing a huge vat of vanilla ice-cream mixture. This is semi-frozen and then squeezed out of a rectangular pipe facing downwards towards a conveyor belt. A mechanical arm slices through the ice-cream mixture, so that slices drop onto the conveyor belt – three semi-frozen, white ice-cream bars per second. The conveyor then enters a refrigerated chamber where the ice-cream circulates slowly until, 15 minutes later, it is frozen rock hard. The conveyor emerges and deposits the bars onto another conveyor which takes each bar through two sheets of warm, liquid chocolate. The chocolate sticks instantly to the frozen bar, which then goes through a little chocolate bath to coat the underside.

After a brief spell in another refrigerated chamber, the conveyor takes the bars to an automated wrapping machine. Three wrapped choc ices per second are packed into cardboard outer boxes and put into cold store awaiting the refrigerated delivery vans. The whole process has taken no more than 45 minutes. No-one has touched the ice-cream. Only six operators are needed to produce more than 10,000 choc ices per hour.

Business IN

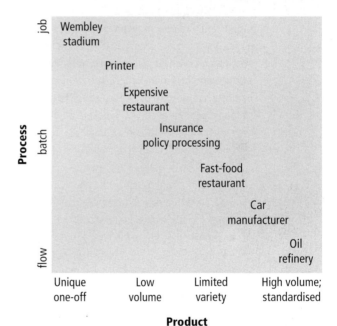

Figure 49.2 Product–process matrix

	JOB	BATCH	FLOW
Quantity of products:	One-off item	Group of products produced together	Large quantities
Variety of products:	Very flexible	Can vary from batch to batch	Not flexible

produced in large volumes, then the most appropriate production process would be flow production.

49.6 Technology

Developments in technology such as computer-aided design, computer-aided manufacture and the use of robots have allowed firms to design, develop and produce products more rapidly. They have also allowed companies to build greater variety into their production process. Car companies, for example, can now build several models of car based on the same basic features. Similarly, many personal stereos have few differences between them; by changing only certain features a firm is able to produce a wide range of 'different' models. These are mass produced products which look tailored to the needs of individuals.

MASS CUSTOMISATION

When Henry Ford launched the Model T Ford over 90 years ago customers were delighted with the low price made possible by mass production. The only problem was the lack of choice ('any colour as long as it's black'). As time has gone on customers have come to expect more and more variety, and producers in all sectors need to be as responsive as possible to customer needs. At the same time they must try to keep production as simple as possible to benefit from economies of scale.

The solution is 'mass customisation' whereby firms offer customers the ability to choose from a number of standardised parts. By combining these parts in different ways customers feel they are getting a tailor-made product, but the actual production process does not become too complex. Cars, washing machines, fridges and computers are all being produced in this way. One of the leaders in mass customisation is Dell Computers. Dell customers specify what features they want on their PC and pay upfront by credit card. The machine is then assembled and dispatched, usually arriving within 3 days. Dell PCs can be put together in about 4 minutes flat, with a further 90 minutes needed to load up the software. Most of the customisation comes from the software that is chosen. This formula has allowed Dell to grow by 20% a year in recent years, even as the PC industry as a whole has been growing by less than 10%.

When analysing the type of production process a firm should adopt, it is useful to consider the following points:

- The most appropriate type of production will depend on the nature of the market. If the firm wants to produce large volumes of standardised products it will move towards a flow process. If it wants unique tailor-made products it will need to adopt a job process.
- Many firms would like the cost advantages of low volumes combined with the ability to produce different products for different markets. Technology is giving firms more flexibility so they can produce various models from the same basic design and production process.
- Only large firms can afford the high capital outlay to set up automated or robot-operated production lines. But small firms are the only ones with the flexibility to design and produce the exact specifications wanted by the one-off customer.

49.7 Types of production
an evaluation

The differences between job, batch and flow production are becoming blurred. Companies such as Dell Computers, for example, can build the product you want in a few hours. Although a production line approach is used, it now has the flexibility to assemble slightly different versions of the same basic computer. In the past, job (and, to a lesser extent, batch) production has been the mainstay of the small firm. So, is the flexibility of modern robotic technology a threat to the future of the small firm? In some cases, yes. Though there will always be a need for the small-scale, highly skilled business which can produce the uniquely designed, tailor-made wedding dress, or Elton John's next swimming pool.

Crucially, flow production means mass production which means mass marketing. This will always struggle to add as much value as specialised, tailor-made, craft skills. Niche marketing implies batch production rather than flow. And the smallest niche of all is one-off production to meet one-off demand. Argos will always sell more rings than a specialist jewellers. But not everyone wants to buy the ring that everyone else buys.

Business
IN

assembly line – stage of production when different parts of a product are put together to produce the finished product. Usually involves high division of labour and conveyor belt.

automation – replacing workers with machines.

batch production – production process in which groups of items are produced together and move together from one stage of the process to the next.

economies of scale – lower unit costs achieved through expansion.

flow production – occurs when items are produced in a continuously moving process.

job production – one-off production; producing to order.

AS Level Exercises

A. REVISION QUESTIONS
(40 marks; 70 minutes)

Read the unit, then answer:

1 Distinguish between job, batch and flow production. *(5)*
2 Which type of production would be the most suitable for the following tasks? Briefly explain your answer.
   a Producing 500 pairs of Crystal Palace baby boots. *(2)*
   b Producing tins of baked beans for Sainsbury's own brand. *(2)*
   c Producing a yacht to Bill Gates' precise specifications. *(2)*
3 Why might the choice of production process involve a trade off between productivity and flexibility? *(4)*
4 Outline three factors which might influence the type of production process chosen by a firm. *(6)*
5 Read the In Business feature on 'Mass Producing Choc Ices'. Use the text to outline two advantages and two disadvantages of mass production. *(8)*
6 Explain the possible problems of switching from a job to a batch production process. *(5)*
7 Explain the potential advantages of using a flow production process. *(3)*
8 What marketing advantages might be gained from job production? *(3)*

B. REVISION EXERCISES

B1 Data Response

Better Factories

The organisation of the factory and the equipment it employs is a key component of the ability to compete. The successful manufacturer needs to take a number of specific actions including:

- Select the most effective processes, which match customer needs and give a competitive advantage. The manufacturing response must be to develop factories and processes which enable such products to be manufactured efficiently, in a way which is manageable, cost effective and not wasteful of resources.
- Create a flexible factory capable of responding to changing customer requirements, from fluctuations in volume and mix to the need to manufacture new products.
- Develop appropriate automation for the variety of products on offer and their associated life cycles. Factors to consider include whether automation could improve any aspects of the process which are vital to the cost/service/quality of the product; the flexibility/capital cost break-even points; how readily the equipment could be modified to enhance its flexibility; whether the required labour skills are readily available and will be in the future; and whether the automated process under consideration fits into the overall strategy and the overall factory control system.
- Create a reliable factory, using preventive maintenance, continuous improvements to reduce downtime, and softer aspects such as employee ownership of the process, empowerment, training and involvement in improvements.

Source: Adapted from Department of Trade and Industry report

Questions
(30 marks; 35 minutes)

1 What is meant by a 'flexible factory'? (3)
2 What is meant by 'preventive maintenance'? (3)
3 Outline the circumstances in which the best way to 'match customer needs' may be by using:
   a flow production
   b job production. (6)
4 Examine the ways in which the type of production process can provide a competitive advantage. (9)
5 Consider the advantages of greater automation in the production process. (9)

B2 Case Study

Shearers

Shearers Ltd is a producer of clothing based in the north-west. The firm has tended to produce relatively small batches of clothes, allowing it to change quickly according to market trends. However, the managing director is eager to expand quickly. Even though the company is still quite young its managers are hungry for growth and believe the way to do this is to attack the mass market. Until now its clothes designs have been ever-changing, aimed at a younger market and sold under the 'Energise' brand.

The company thinks it is possible to take this brand to a wider audience and produce on a much larger scale. It is considering a significant expansion of its production capabilities. For the numbers to add up the equipment must be used almost continuously and the firm will not be able to change its designs too frequently. The process of changing over to the new production equipment will be expensive and may involve other problems.

The costs involved are set out below.

	Energise	Future Production
Costs of changeover		£220,000
Materials costs per unit	£6.50	£6.20
Labour cost per unit	£5.80	£2.60
Overhead costs per unit	£6.20	£4.20

Questions
(30 marks; 40 minutes)

1 Explain two problems the firm might have experienced from using batch production. (4)
2 Analyse Shearers' estimates of its future compared with its existing production costs. (8)
3 Discuss whether Shearers should enter the mass market. (10)
4 If the firm did decide to go ahead and buy the new equipment, examine the problems it might incur during the changeover. (8)

C. ESSAY QUESTIONS

1 'Using flow production is no longer competitive, given the variety of consumers' tastes.' Discuss this view.
2 'The way in which a firm produces is a primary determinant of its success.' Discuss.
3 To what extent can the nature of a firm's production process differentiate its offerings from its competitors?

LEAN PRODUCTION

DEFINITION

Lean production is a philosophy that aims to produce more using less, by eliminating all forms of waste ('waste' being defined as anything that does not add value to the final product).

50.1 Introduction

The rise of the Japanese approach to production has been unstoppable in recent years. JIT (**just-in-time**) and quality circles have been widely written about, but the underlying philosophy has sometimes been overlooked. That total approach is now termed 'lean production'. It is based upon a combined focus by management and workers on minimising the use of the key business resources: materials, manpower, capital, floor space and time. Consequently, if it is implemented successfully, lean production will create the cost advantages that are associated with high levels of labour productivity, low stockholding and high utilisation of capacity. The components of lean production are:

- just-in-time (JIT)
- **total quality management** (TQM)
- time-based management.

TOYOTA AND THE ORIGINS OF LEAN PRODUCTION

In most industries, new ideas and methods tend to emerge during a period of crisis when old ideas no longer seem to work. The motor industry is no different. The inspiration came from Eiji Toyoda's three-month visit to Ford's Rouge plant in Detroit during 1950. Eiji's family had set up the Toyota Motor Company in 1937. Now, in Japan's situation of desperate shortages after the Second World War, he hoped to learn from Ford. On his return, Eiji reported that the mass production system at the Rouge plant was riddled with 'muda' (the Japanese term for wasted effort, materials and time). By analysing the weaknesses of mass production, Toyota was the first company to develop lean production.

Toyota realised that mass production could only be fully economic if identical products could be produced continuously. Yet Henry Ford's statement that 'they can have any colour they want ... as long as it's black' was no longer acceptable to customers. Mass production was also very wasteful, as poor quality production led to a high reject rate at the end of the production line.

Toyota's solution was to design machines that could be used for many different operations – flexible production. Mass producers took a whole day to change a stamping machine from producing one part to mak-

ing another. Toyota eventually reduced this time to just three minutes! And had so simplified the process that factory line workers could do it without any help from engineers. This carried with it the advantage of flexibility. If buying habits changed in the US, Ford could not react quickly, because each production line was dedicated to producing a particular product in a particular way. Toyota's multi-purpose machines could adapt quickly to a surge of demand for, for example, open-top cars or right-hand drive models.

By a process of continuous refinement, Toyota developed the approach to:

- maximise the input from staff
- focus attention upon the quality of supplies and production
- minimise wasted resources in stock through just-in-time.

By the 1990s, the company was able to turn the spotlight onto product development – to shorten the time between product conception and product launch.

50.2 The benefits of lean production

In the autumn of 1984, following US concerns that Japanese car makers were becoming too dominant, the Massachusetts Institute of Technology (MIT) undertook a five-year, $5 million study of the world car industry. It was to produce a new way of looking at production, a new buzzword and a best-selling book called *The Machine That Changed The World*. The study was a **benchmarking** exercise. It compared the new production techniques used mainly by the Japanese with the approach of US and European manufacturers. It aimed to measure the performance of car producers worldwide against a series of yardsticks such as production hours and quality defects per car. Early on in the process, the MIT researchers noticed fundamental differences between conventional mass producers such as Ford and the companies they came to term lean producers, such as Toyota.

As the table below illustrates, the study revealed that the lean producers led the way by minimising the assembly hours per car, the amount of stock held and the assembly defects per 100 cars. It was hoped that the findings of the study would show:

- exactly how far behind the mass producers were
- the reasons for the underperformance
- the ways in which improvements could be achieved.

Not only did this prove to be the case, but the book also became an international best-seller – to the surprise of all those involved.

General Motors Framingham assembly plant versus Toyota Takaoka assembly plant

	GM FRAMINGHAM	TOYOTA TAKAOKA
Gross assembly hours per car	40.7	18.0
Adjusted assembly hours per car	31.0	16.0
Assembly defects per 100 cars	130	45
Assembly space per car (sq ft)	8.1	4.8
Stocks of major components	2 weeks	2 hours

Source: *The Machine That Changed The World*, p81, Womack, Jones and Roos, Rawson Associates, 1990

The term 'lean production' was first coined by MIT researcher John Krafcik. He wrote that 'lean production is lean because it aims to use less of everything' compared with mass production. It is based upon a combined focus by management and workers on minimising the use of the key business resources: materials, manpower, capital, floor space and time.

TIME-BASED MANAGEMENT

Zara is a fashion retailing phenomenon built on an understanding of the importance of time. When, in 2002, Christian Dior featured a glamourous embroidered Afghan coat on the catwalk, Zara had its own version in its shops within a fortnight. It was able to design, manufacture and distribute the coat to its shops throughout Europe within just 14 days – and sell it for just £95. If a style doesn't succeed within a week, it is withdrawn. No style stays on the shop floor for more than four weeks. The immediate result is obvious. Fashion-and-price-conscious women flock to Zara. Less obviously, Zara benefits from a vital secondary factor. In Spain, Zara's home country, an average high-street clothes store expects its regular customers to visit three times a year. That goes up to 17 for Zara. As the stock is constantly changing, the store is constantly worth visiting. It took Zara's owner 40 years to build his business fortune from £18 in 1963 to £6 billion by 2002. Time well spent.

Lean production:

- Creates higher levels of labour productivity, therefore it uses less labour.
- Requires less stock, less factory space and less capital equipment than a mass producer of comparable size. The lean producer therefore has substantial cost advantages over the mass producer.
- Creates substantial marketing advantages. First, it results in far fewer defects, improving quality and reliability for the customer. Second, lean production requires half the engineering hours to develop a new product. This means the lean producer can develop a vast range of products a mass producer cannot afford to match.

50.3 The components of lean production

LEAN PEOPLE MANAGEMENT

Lean producers reject the waste of human talent involved in narrow, repetitive jobs. They believe in empowerment, teamworking and job enrichment. Problem solving is not just left to specialist engineers. Employees are trained in preventative maintenance, to spot when a fault is developing and correct it before the production line has to stop. If a problem does emerge on the line, they are trained to solve it without needing an engineer or a supervisor. Teams meet regularly to discuss ways in which their sections could be run more smoothly.

LEAN APPROACH TO QUALITY

In a mass production system, quality control is a specialised job that takes place at the end of the line. In a lean system, each team is responsible for checking the quality of its own work. If a fault is spotted, every worker has the power to stop the assembly line. This policy prevents errors being passed on, to be corrected only once the fault has been found at the end of the line. The lean approach, therefore, is self-checking at every production stage so that quality failures at the end (or with customers) become extremely rare.

The objective of lean production is to prevent the need for any reworking, in other words to achieve perfect quality first time. This requires a total focus upon quality throughout the organisation. Must quality improvements add to cost? A mass producer would say yes, because more modern machines, better materials and more quality inspectors all cost money. A lean producer, however, believes that good quality costs less. By solving problems at source there is less reworking and therefore a saving in materials and labour wastage. Traditionally it was considered that quality and productivity were opposites. Lean producers see high quality work as a way of boosting productivity.

Business

One way to achieve lean quality is *total quality management* (TQM). This attempts to achieve a culture of quality throughout the organisation. So that the primary objective of all employees is to achieve quality the first time around without the need for any reworking. To achieve total quality managers must 'make quality the number one, non-negotiable priority and actively seek and listen to the views of employees on how to improve quality' – Roger Trapp, *The Independent*.

LEAN DESIGN

As consumers become more demanding and technology advances, car design has become highly complex. This threatens to boost costs and development times. Lean producers combat this by simultaneous engineering. This means integrating the development functions so that separate design and engineering stages are tackled at the same time. This speeds up development times, which cuts costs and reduces the risk of early obsolescence. Whereas US and European car manufacturers take over 60 months (five years!) from conception to launch of a new car model, the Japanese take 40+ months. Crucial to lean design and development is the principle of empowerment. Consequently, team members feel a greater pressure to make the right decision because it is more likely to hold.

LEAN COMPONENT SUPPLY

The approach to component supply varies greatly from company to company. Mass producers tend to have rather distant relationships with suppliers, often based on minimising the delivery cost per unit. They may buy from several sources to keep up the competitive pressure. The supplier, in turn, may be secretive about costs and profit margins to prevent the buyer from pressing for still lower prices. Lean producers work in partnership with their suppliers or, more often, with a single supplier. They keep the supplier fully informed of new product developments, encouraging ideas and technical advice. This means that by the time the assembly line starts running, errors have been ironed out so there are very few running changes or failures. Both parties are also likely to share financial and sales information electronically. This encourages an atmosphere of trust and common purpose, and aids planning.

50.4 Just-in-time

Lean producers run with minimal buffer stocks, relying on daily or hourly deliveries from trusted suppliers. As there is no safety net, a faulty shipment of components could bring an entire factory to a halt. Mass producers rely on stockpiles, just in case. Lean producers insist on zero defects whereas mass producers are happy enough with a quality standard that is 'good enough'.

The just-in-time (JIT) system of manufacturing is perhaps the best known element of lean production. JIT aims to minimise the costs of holding unnecessary stocks of raw materials, components, work in progress and finished products. The principle that underpins JIT is that production should be 'pulled through' rather than 'pushed through'. This means that production should be for specific customer orders, so that the production cycle starts only once a customer has placed an order with the producer. Stocks are delivered only when they are needed so there are almost no buffer stocks held to guard against production or delivery problems. Consequently, this approach requires several deliveries of stock per day. Each consignment is sent directly to the production line for immediate use.

SUMMARY OF THE JUST-IN-TIME APPROACH

- No buffer stocks of any type are held.
- Production is to order.

LEAN PRODUCTION

PACE Inc. is an American company that makes soldering systems that are used to attach or remove computer chips from motherboards. In 2001 the company decided to change its production system in order to reduce unit costs.

The key was to change shop floor working practices. Prior to the changes one worker used to do just one job – such as cutting a piece of metal to a specific size – but now does several. That means instead of going down an assembly line, a product stays in one area, or cell, and is produced mainly by one person.

Additionally, PACE now makes a system only when a customer orders it, instead of stockpiling products on warehouse shelves. Workers are also encouraged to suggest changes and become more involved in the way operations flow.

As a result, the 135-person company has trimmed its stock holdings from about $6 million to an average of $1.7 million. 'Six million in cash was tied up in assets that were doing nothing,' said John Walter, PACE's vice president of manufacturing and engineering. 'Now that cash isn't tied up and is in the bank and can be used for new product development. It's excellent asset utilisation.'

Business
IN

- Stock is only ordered when it is needed, just in time.
- Zero defects are essential as no stock safety net exists.
- No 'spare' workers are employed.
- Staff are multi-skilled and are capable of filling in for absent colleagues.
- Used by lean producers.

- Stocks of raw materials, components, work in progress and finished products are held by the producer.
- Production is frequently stockpiled as manufacturers often seek economies of scale even at a time when sales are falling.
- Stock is ordered less frequently because the average order size tends to be large in order to take advantage of bulk-buying discounts.
- The incentive to achieve zero defects is less strong as stocks at every stage of production are held just in case of mistakes.
- Overmanning is common to cover for sick/absent workers.
- The system favoured by traditional mass producers.

The main advantage of 'pulled-through' production is that it eliminates waste.

- **Capital and interest waste**

  Holding stock creates both actual and opportunity costs. The actual costs are the costs of paying for somewhere to keep the stock. The opportunity cost is the interest that could have been received had the capital tied up in stock been available to invest elsewhere.

- **Defect waste**

  By holding very little stock firms no longer have a safety net. Consequently quality must improve – ideally to achieve zero defects. Firms must tackle quality problems at source, changing production methods or suppliers where necessary.

- **Overproduction waste**

  Mass producers set production levels on the basis of sales forecasts derived from quantitative market research findings. These forecasts may prove wrong. This can lead to heavy price discounting in order to clear surplus stock. By producing to order this wastage is avoidable.

50.5 Time-based management

Time-based management involves managing time in the same way most companies manage costs, quality or stock. Time-based manufacturers try to shorten rather than lengthen production runs in order to reduce costs and to increase levels of customer satis-

faction. To do this manufacturers invest in flexible capital – machines that can make more than one model. Training must also be seen as a priority because staff have to be multi-skilled. This enables the firm to produce a variety of models without a cost penalty. Something that mass producers using a high division of labour with inflexible capital thought impossible.

Time-based management creates four benefits:

1 By reducing lead and set-up times, productivity improves creating a cost advantage.
2 Shortening lead times cuts customer response times, increasing consumer satisfaction as customers receive their orders sooner.
3 Lower stockholding costs – short lead and set-up times make firms more responsive to changes in the market. Consequently there should be less need for long production runs and stockpiles of finished products. If demand does suddenly increase production can simply be quickly restarted.
4 An ability to offer the consumer a more varied product range without losing cost-reducing economies of scale. Time-based management therefore makes market segmentation a much cheaper strategy to operate.

Business IN — TIME-BASED MISMANAGEMENT

During the early 1990s, Boeing responded to a cutback in demand by moving to a lean production system. It was designed to cut stock levels, reduce production time and therefore boost cash flow and sales (shorter delivery times would win customers from the rival European producer, Airbus Industrie).

Then, in 1996, orders started moving ahead sharply. Boeing found it had to nearly treble its daily rate of production. Suppliers struggled to cope, leaving gaps which forced the whole production of a plane to be held up. Without a buffer stock, no supply meant no production. By October 1997, the situation had become so bad that Boeing decided to halt production for 20 days to allow stock levels to be rebuilt. Meanwhile, airlines such as British Airways were having to wait for new planes promised by a certain date. Boeing had to pay huge compensation claims as the company's time-based management strategy backfired.

- Lean production seeks to eliminate waste of all forms. By adopting lean techniques, firms should therefore become more efficient. By reducing waste, unit costs will be reduced. This makes it possible for lean producers to offer lower prices without any sacrifice of profit margin. Or to offer higher product specifications for the same price as rivals. Consequently, lean production techniques can have an impact on firms' marketing strategies.
- Lean new product development techniques are increasingly decisive in a highly competitive world where product life cycles are becoming shorter. In this environment reducing design lead times is vital. For a product to be considered innovative it must be launched quickly. If competitors beat you to it, your product will be seen as just another 'me too'.
- The attempt to achieve lean production can be expensive. Some firms have invested heavily in 'flexible' computer-aided manufacturing equipment. True lean production depends upon people rather than machines.

50.6 Lean production
an evaluation

Some of the arguments put forward above could be criticised for being too black and white (mass production – terrible; lean production – wonderful). The reality of business is often to do with shades of grey, with some lean producers having their own weaknesses. Some trends are unarguable, however. Since the start of the programme, the US arm of Ford has moved away from its traditional stance as an autocratic, mass producer. It has embraced lean production with considerable success. In Britain, Nissan, Honda and even Rolls Royce have all embraced lean production successfully.

However, in recent times lean production has been associated with rationalisation and redundancy. By definition lean production involves the elimination of waste. This waste could be overmanning. So by switching to a leaner system the consequence could be redundancies. Especially if the firm's leadership has **Theory X** attitudes. Lean production in this context becomes little more than a fig leaf that a ruthless manager may wish to hide behind when seeking to justify controversial staffing decisions.

KEY terms

benchmarking – comparing a firm's performance with best practice within the industry.

just-in-case – keeping buffer stocks of materials and components just in case something goes wrong.

just-in-time – producing with minimum stock levels so every process must be completed just in time for the process that follows.

Theory X – managerial attitudes based on the assumption that workers dislike work and responsibility – they only work for money.

total quality management – a passion for quality that starts at the top, then spreads throughout the organisation.

AS Level Exercises

A. REVISION QUESTIONS
(35 marks; 70 minutes)

Read the unit, then answer:

1 State the three components of lean production. (3)
2 Outline three problems of mass production. (3)
3 Distinguish between just-in-time and just-in-case. (4)
4 What advantages are there in using time-based management? (4)
5 Why is it important to reduce machine set-up times? (3)
6 What are the opportunity costs of holding too much stock? (4)
7 How can a cell production system contribute to a total quality management system? (4)
8 What is reworking and why does it add to costs? (5)
9 Why might it be important to be first to the market with a new product idea? (5)

B. REVISION EXERCISES

B1 Data Response

Flexibility Keeps Work Flowing for Pump Maker

One of the UK's biggest makers of specialist pumps has cut delivery times by two-thirds since beginning a flexible manufacturing project two years ago. Edwards High Vacuum is a world leader in high technology pumps used in the fabrication equipment required to make silicon chips. By bringing together production and office staff, the firm has succeeded in dramatically reducing lead times. Today it takes an average of only three weeks from receiving an order to turning out a sophisticated pump for the semiconductor industry. It previously took 10 weeks.

The key change was to bring production, sales and engineering staff closer together. Rather than working in isolation each department now works virtually alongside each other, separated only by a glass screen. The proximity helps to create a quick interchange of ideas. Something which is needed to help Edwards turn out its pumps with a lot of variation – each one matched to the precise customer requirement. The pumps sell for as much as £35,000 each.

Recently Edwards had an indication of how its flexible working system can lead to new orders. A Korean company asked if it

could have 10 pumps by the end of the month. Ms Anne Stanhope, the sales engineer who took the call, checked with her production colleague on the other side of screen before telling her customer that Edwards could fulfil the order.

Edwards has also managed to develop the concept of mass customisation. Each pump is made from about 1,000 parts which can be put together in an astonishing 33,000 different ways. The company also orders parts on a just-in-time basis from a group of about 20 suppliers.

Source: Adapted from *The Times*, 13/11/96

Questions *(30 marks, 35 minutes)*

1 Explain why flexibility is seen by Edwards High Vacuum as being essential given the fierce competition that exists in the market for semiconductor pumps. (6)
2 How did bringing sales and production staff closer together help the firm to become more flexible? (6)
3 Explain the term 'mass customisation'. Does offering variety always lead to higher costs? (8)
4 What problems did you think Edwards High Vacuum may have had when implementing its more flexible system of production? (6)
5 Why was it important for the Korean customer to know straight away that Edwards could fulfil its order? (4)

B2 Case Study

Time-based Management at Huttledorf Engineering

Huttledorf engineering was co-founded by Richard Fitzinger and Elisabeth Schmid in 1950. This Austrian company specialises in manufacturing braking systems for trains. The company is currently in a strong competitive position. Fitzinger and Schmid feel that continuous investment is crucial in their industry. Consequently they have always tried to plough back a high percentage of their profits into new capital equipment. They also believe in recruiting the best, even if this means paying their staff very well. Even with these strengths and an order book that is full for the next 18 months, both Fitzinger and Schmid are concerned about the future. In particular they are worried about low-price competition from Eastern Europe. Fitzinger and Schmid realise that in order to compete they must step up their efforts to improve productivity.

In a recent staff newsletter Schmid explained the situation to her staff in the following way:

'Competing in today's global marketplace requires us to keep moving forward as quickly and efficiently as possible. We must cut our costs if we are to survive. The easiest way to do this would be to make cutbacks. We do not propose to do this. Instead, we intend to reduce our costs by eliminating wastage. In particular we want to target 'track time'. This is the total time for a unit to go from raw materials to finished product. By finding ways of reducing track time we will be able to squeeze out more finished product from the same overheads, therefore our unit costs will fall.'

'At present the track time for our basic 385 model is 31 minutes 22 seconds. It breaks down as follows:

Time to load and unload sub-assemblies: 12 mins 25 secs
Time to clamp and unclamp parts: 2 mins 10 secs
Ram cutting: 12 mins 35 secs
Ram return time: 4 mins 12 secs.

Our objective is to reduce the track time of the 385 model by at least 20% within the next 12 months. We intend to implement the following strategy in order to achieve this objective:

- Cell production – at present we spend too much time on handling components. We already have the right equipment; the problem is that it's in the wrong location.
- Preventative maintenance and in-process inspection – at present we waste too much time fixing machinery that has gone wrong. We want this issue to be given Number One priority in future. We shall look for answers from the weekly quality circle discussion groups.
- Identifying new suppliers who will be more reliable.

These ideas will be discussed in next week's works council meeting before any final decisions are made.'

Questions
(50 marks; 60 minutes)

1 Explain why Huttledorf Engineering is attempting to reduce its 'track time'. *(6)*
2 How will a move towards cell production help the firm in terms of achieving its goal of a 20% time reduction? *(10)*
3 Consider how the staff at Huttledorf Engineering might benefit from Schmid's proposals. *(10)*
4 Many British firms prefer to employ temporary or part-time workers to 'do a job', rather than get involved in consultation exercises such as works councils or quality circles. Why may this be? *(12)*
5 In the context of this case study discuss whether all firms have to constantly adapt and change in order to survive. *(12)*

C. ESSAY QUESTIONS

1 Discuss the difficulties and dilemmas faced by managers who are considering a switch to lean methods of production.
2 In some companies, lean production is viewed as just being another in a long line of management fads. In others it is embraced with enthusiasm by the staff. Why may this be so?
3 Why do some firms seem far better than others in terms of their ability to successfully implement lean production techniques?
4 Discuss the benefits, and the possible disadvantages, of lean production methods being utilised by an aircraft manufacturer. How might the balance between the benefits and the possible disadvantages change in the long term?

KAIZEN (CONTINUOUS IMPROVEMENT)

DEFINITION

Kaizen is a Japanese term meaning continuous improvement. Staff at firms such as Toyota generate thousands of new ideas each year – each aimed at improving productivity or quality. Over time, these small steps forward add up to significant improvements in competitiveness.

51.1 Introduction

'If a man has not been seen for three days his friends should take a good look at him to see what changes have befallen him.'

This ancient Japanese saying seems to sum up **kaizen** quite nicely. Continuous improvement or 'kaizen' is a philosophy of ongoing improvement based around small changes involving everyone – managers and workers alike.

There are two key elements to kaizen:

- Most kaizen improvements are based around people and their ideas rather than investment in new technology.
- Each change on its own may be of little importance. However, if hundreds of small changes are made, the cumulative effects can be substantial.

An example of a kaizen improvement comes from Barclaycard. In processing billions of pounds of credit card transactions per year, a major problem is fraud. An employee suggested a way of analysing bogus calls to the company's authorisation department. This has saved Barclaycard over £100,000 a year. The precise method is secret, but it works by blocking the credit card numbers of callers trying to buy goods fraudulently. It can also trace the callers, resulting in the arrest of the fraudsters involved.

In the 1990s, continuous improvement became one of the main operations management strategies in Britain. A 1997 study by *IRS Employment Trends* found that 70% of private sector service businesses and 62% of manufacturers claimed to use kaizen. Nine-tenths of these firms had introduced this approach since 1990.

51.2 The components of the kaizen philosophy

Describing kaizen as just 'continuous improvement' is simplistic. To work effectively kaizen requires a commitment from management to establish a special, positive culture within their organisation. This culture must be communicated and accepted by all those working at the company. It must permeate the whole organisation. What are the characteristics of this culture or philosophy?

ONE EMPLOYEE, TWO JOBS

According to the Kaizen Institute the goal of any kaizen programme should be to convince all employees that they have two jobs to do – doing the job and then looking for ways of improving it. The kaizen culture is based on the belief that the production line worker is the real expert. The worker on the assembly line does the job day in day out. This means knowing more about the causes of problems and their solutions than the highly qualified engineer who sits in an office. The kaizen philosophy recognises the fact that any company's greatest resource is its staff. Good ideas can be shared. Arthur Anderson, for example, uses a computer network to spread information around its staff about best practices. Staff are encouraged to post any good ideas that they might have onto the network.

TEAMWORKING

To operate kaizen successfully employees cannot be allowed to work as isolated individuals. Teamworking is vital to the process of continuous improvement. These teams are composed of employees who work on the same section of the production line as a self-contained unit. Each team is often referred to as a 'cell'. The members of a cell are responsible for the quality of the work in their section. Over time the cell becomes expert about the processes within its section of the production line. Kaizen attempts to tap into this knowledge by organising each cell into a quality circle. The members of each cell meet regularly to discuss problems cropping up within their section. The circle then puts forward solutions and recommendations for the management to consider.

EMPOWERMENT

Empowerment is essential to any kaizen programme. Empowerment involves giving employees the right to make decisions that affect the quality of their working lives. Empowerment enables good shop-floor ideas to be implemented quickly.

Once the necessary kaizen apparatus is in place good ideas and the resulting improvements should keep coming. The number of suggestions made each month should improve over time once employees see the effects of their own solutions. At LucasVarity (motor components) there are over 125 different kaizen groups in their UK-based cable division. Over 2,000 kaizen suggestions are implemented each month and the rate of suggestions is still rising.

However, if quality circles and teamworking are to be truly effective employees must be given real decision making power. If good ideas are constantly being ignored by management they will eventually dry up as the employees become disillusioned with the whole process.

PERFORMANCE TARGETS

Setting performance targets and then monitoring achievement is also a key component of kaizen. A very simple device that supports this process is the 'level-up' chart. OKI, a Japanese-owned manufacturer of computer printers, uses daily performance targets as an integral part of its kaizen programme. At OKI each production cell is given daily quality targets. They are based on maximum defect rates. These targets are then displayed publicly on a large chart inside the factory. The chart is updated regularly to show each cell's performance in relation to its target. This is sometimes called the level-up chart.

Target setting and monitoring creates three benefits:

- If quality problems do occur it should be easier to trace the fault so that causes can be identified. Those involved at that particular stage of production can then put forward solutions to be discussed.
- Targets can be used to judge whether a kaizen change has been successful.
- Setting and then monitoring quantitative targets can enable benchmarking surveys to take place. (See Unit 52.)

Words of wisdom – kaizen

> 'Continuous improvement is better than delayed perfection.'
>
> *Mark Twain, famous American writer*

> 'If there's a way to do it better … find it.'
>
> *Thomas Edison, inventor*

> 'If you're not making progress all the time, you're slipping backwards.'
>
> *Sir John Harvey Jones, former chief of ICI*

> 'I believe that there is hardly a single operation in the making of our car that is the same as when we made our first car of the present model. That is why we make them so cheaply.'
>
> *Henry Ford, legendary car maker*

> 'Our company has, indeed, stumbled onto some of its new products. But never forget that you can only stumble if you're moving.'
>
> *Richard Carlton, former chief at American giant 3M*

> 'Be not afraid of going slowly; be only afraid of standing still.'
>
> *Chinese proverb*

Source: *The Ultimate Book of Business Quotations*, Stuart Crainer, Capstone Publishing, 1997

Business IN

REPEAT KAIZENS

An American engineering firm called FNGP experimented with a three-day Kaizen workshop in 1992. Factory workers were encouraged to suggest ways of improving productivity and product quality. The results were so impressive they held five more Kaizen events over the following three years. The results are shown in the table below.

Note that accident levels fell 92% over this period and the capital expenditure required to make the improvements amounted to less than $1,000.

Source: Adapted from *Lean Thinking* by J Womack and D Jones (1997). Reprinted with the permission of Pocket Books, a Division of Simon & Schuster

51.3 Potential problems of implementing a successful kaizen programme

CULTURE

In order for kaizen to really work, employees must be proud to contribute their ideas to the company. Japanese companies do not offer financial rewards in return for suggestions. Their attitude is that employees are told that kaizen is part of the company policy when they are recruited. For them employee commitment to kaizen is gained via genuine staff motivation rather than by financial bonuses. Creating the right organisational culture is therefore vital for success. Resistance can come from two quarters:

- Management resistance – managers with autocratic tendencies may be unwilling to pass decision making power down the hierarchy. Empowerment, de-layering, quality circles and other tools to promote industrial democracy can be seen as a threat to their own status and power.
- Employee resistance – a history of poor industrial relations and a climate of mistrust can create resistance to change among the staff. Employees may not view the delegation of power as a chance to do a more interesting job. Instead, the 'new empowerment programme' may be seen by the workforce as just the latest in a long line of cynical attempts to get more out of the staff for less. The result? Reluctant cooperation at best, but little in terms of real motivation.

TRAINING COSTS

Mistakes made by managers in the past can have severe long-term effects. Changing an organisation's culture is difficult as it involves changing attitudes. The training required to change attitudes tends to be expensive. It can also take a very long time to change attitudes. Consequently, the costs are likely to be great.

JUSTIFYING THE COST OF KAIZEN

The training cost and the opportunity cost of lost output is easy to quantify. It may be harder to identify and prove the financial benefits of a kaizen programme. Managers can quite easily produce financial

Results of FNGP kaizen experiment

	Feb 92	Apr 92	May 92	Nov 92	Jan 93	Jan 94	Aug 95
Number of staff	21	18	15	12	6	3	3
Units per worker	55	86	112	140	225	450	600
Total output	1,155	1,548	1,680	1,680	1,350	1,350	1,800
Space utilised (sq ft)	2,300	2,000	1,850	1,662	1,360	1,200	1,200

estimates of the benefits of capital investment. It is much harder to assess programmes designed to develop the stock of human capital within the company. Consequently, in firms dominated by the accountant it can be very difficult to win budgets for kaizen programmes.

51.4 Business process re-engineering: an alternative approach to kaizen improvement

Business process re-engineering (or BPR for short) was a fashionable 1990s' buzzword for something that is as old as the hills. Michael Hammer, author of *Re-engineering The Organisation* calls the approach 'rethinking and redesigning business processes to bring about sharp increases in performance'. According to the re-engineering approach, managers should not attempt to just tinker with existing systems in order to make marginal improvements. Instead, managers should seek genuine breakthroughs, usually through heavy programmes of capital expenditure. These breakthroughs are achieved by scrapping existing systems rather than modifying them. Many BPR programmes can thus be seen as revolutionary, whereas kaizen is evolutionary.

Managers (or management consultants) engaged in BPR programmes are encouraged to rethink everything. For those who believe in BPR, this system has a major advantage over kaizen. Their argument is that starting with a clean slate ensures managers will not be held back by tradition. According to BPR everything should be questioned. This is the way to make major breakthroughs.

This approach is very attractive to company bosses, especially new ones. They can sweep old traditions away and establish an entirely new approach. Fashioned in the image of the leader. Graham Souness did exactly this when he took over as manager of Liverpool Football Club. A number of superb players were sold off; new ones came, and the playing tactics changed dramatically. If it had worked he would have been the hero. It would have been the Souness team, not the Liverpool team. The re-engineering failed, however.

Figure 51.1 shows the effect kaizen has on productivity compared with BPR. Large-scale reorganisations take time to implement, especially if they are based on new machinery and plant. Consequently the firm using BPR may be constantly behind its kaizen competitors and never able to catch up, never mind overtake. The crucial point is that kaizen is all about continuous change. The problem faced by the BPR firm is that by the time the new plant and process are operational the plant may be already out of date. The cause being the changes made by the kaizen competitor in the interim period.

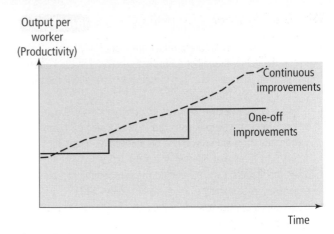

Figure 51.1

51.5 The limitations of kaizen

DIMINISHING RETURNS

Some managers argue that the improvements created through a kaizen programme will invariably fall as time goes on. The logic is that the organisation will seek ways of solving the most important problems first. So by implication the problems that remain will become progressively less important. If this is the case it might prove to be difficult to maintain staff enthusiasm. However, supporters of kaizen would reject this criticism on the grounds that there is no such thing as a perfect system. According to them, even the best system is capable of being improved. Cadbury Schweppes' chief executive John Sunderland was asked which management theory was the most overrated. He replied 'If it ain't broke don't fix it. Everything can be improved.' This is a perfect statement in favour of kaizen.

RADICAL SOLUTIONS

Sometimes radical solutions implemented quickly are necessary in order to tackle radical problems. Kaizen may not be appropriate in all situations. The solution might have to be more dramatic than yet another change to an old system. It may be time to throw out all of the old and replace it with something totally new. This is usually the case in industries facing radical changes brought on by a rapid surge in technology.

A perfect example is the Dutch electronics manufacturer Phillips. During the 1980s the company's product range aged. By the end of the decade the firm was in a real crisis. Both market share and profitability had sunk. Something radical needed to be done and quickly. The senior management at Phillips devised a company-wide BPR project which they called the Centurian programme. The objective of the programme was to re-engineer Phillips' new product development processes. The goal being to reduce design lead time so that Phillips' new products got onto the market first – before the competition. Without this rapid and fundamental rethink of the design process Phillips may not have been able to survive.

- Kaizen improvements to a product are more likely to be effective in the earlier stages of a product's life cycle. If the kaizen programme is started too late it may only slow down the rate of decline rather than reverse it.
- If BPR is to be effective, the restructuring process will need to be ongoing. If the firm pauses too long between each reorganisation, the programme will just be an exercise in catching up. This is why firms that have adopted the kaizen philosophy are often the leaders. Lagging behind the competition can be very expensive, as Sainsbury's discovered in 1999–2001.
- In the short run, the cash flow impacts of BPR can be severe. This is because of the reliance upon technology as the method for seeking major improvement. Struggling firms should therefore be aware of the dangers of BPR. The heavy programmes of capital expenditure required will create immediate outflows of cash. If the radical changes fail to work, the consequences may prove severe.

In the circumstances it is not surprising that those who are afraid of anything too radical choose kaizen over BPR. Kaizen is less threatening. This is because each improvement is relatively small in relation to a massive one-off BPR reorganisation. The attraction of kaizen may be that managers can pretend their firm is 'committed to excellence', yet use kaizen as an excuse to reject any idea that is too radical and which may rock the boat. In summary, when those with bureaucratic tendencies embrace kaizen the result can be very little in terms of meaningful change.

Are kaizen and BPR mutually exclusive? It is possible to use both approaches. Even in Japan kaizen is not used exclusively. The Japanese even have their own word for BPR. They call it 'kaikaku' which roughly translated means 'a radical redesign'. In practice, many Japanese firms use kaikaku as a source of a major breakthrough when one is required. They then follow this up with a kaizen programme in order to perfect and then adapt this new system to suit new conditions as they emerge.

51.6 Kaizen
an evaluation

Does the kaizen approach encourage bureaucracy? In the global market of the 21st century, managers have come to realise that an ability to adapt and change is vital if the firm is to survive. However, many managers and many businesses have great problems with change management. The main issue is that many individuals are frightened of the uncertainty that usually goes hand in hand with change. Some managers seek security, stability and predictability in their own working lives. So which method of change management should managers like this use, kaizen or BPR?

KEY terms

business culture – the attitudes prevailing within a business.

business process re-engineering (BPR) – redesigning key aspects of a business from scratch, often at the cost of job losses.

kaizen – continuous improvement.

suggestion scheme – a formal method of obtaining written employee suggestions about improvements in the workplace.

AS Level Exercises

A. REVISION QUESTIONS
(35 marks; 70 minutes)

Read the unit, then answer:

1 Give three reasons why kaizen improvements can prove to be cheaper than improvements gained via business process re-engineering. *(3)*
2 State three limitations of the kaizen philosophy. *(3)*
3 Explain why a re-engineering programme can lead to a deterioration in employee morale within the organisation being re-engineered. *(3)*
4 Why might some managers find it harder to implement kaizen than others? *(4)*
5 Give three reasons why it is vital to involve both management and shop-floor staff in any programme of continuous improvement. *(3)*
6 To be truly effective why must kaizen programmes be ongoing? *(3)*
7 Why is it important to set and monitor performance targets when attempting to operate kaizen? *(4)*
8 Explain how kaizen can help to create a better motivated workforce. *(4)*
9 Why might some managers believe that kaizen brings diminishing returns over time? *(4)*
10 Read the In Business headed 'Kaizen Stock Control'. What benefits may Acuson have gained from the improvements to the accuracy of its stock records? *(4)*

B. REVISION EXERCISES

B1 Data Response

Hail The Star

Julian Hails was once a star player in lower league football teams such as Southend. He believed in teamwork, in training and in continuous improvement. He joined Star Electronics as a sales manager, but became managing director after just three years – promoted over the head of the chairman's son, Richard Star. His enthusiasm was infectious, and his kaizen programme soon bore fruit. This was fortunate because a slump in Star's sector of the electronics market caused a decline in market size.

At the latest board meeting, Julian presented figures recording the impact of the company's kaizen programme. Young Richard Star took the opportunity to snipe at Julian's achievements, saying: 'So after this programme of continuous upheaval, I see our total costs per unit are higher than they were two years ago.'

	Two Years Ago	Last Year	This Year
Rejects per unit of output	7.8	6.8	6.2
Assembly time (minutes)	46	43	39
Stock value per unit of output	£145	£128	£111
Direct costs per unit	£42.50	£39	£36.50
Overhead costs per unit	£64	£67	£72

Questions *(30 marks; 35 minutes)*

1 Explain the links between 'teamwork' and 'continuous improvement'. *(4)*
2 Analyse the data provided above to evaluate the key successes of Julian's policies. *(12)*
3 Explain what Richard Star meant by his use of the term 'continuous upheaval'? *(6)*
4 What further information is needed to assess the validity of Richard Star's claim? *(8)*

B2 Case Study

Continuous Improvement at Dray Technologies

When Neryn Gaul took over an electrical cable business in 1992 he diagnosed that it was failing fast. 'On my first day here I was shocked by the poor working conditions the staff were expected to put up with. The walls were burnt black and the floor was so dirty your shoes stuck to it.' The previous manager, Mr Smith, had also left a management regime that was highly autocratic. Employees were not trusted or given any decision making power. The management accounts figures also made depressing reading. During Gaul's first month in charge, market share fell for the sixth consecutive month. Urgent action had to be taken to improve the situation.

Gaul's first step was to interview every member of staff to collect ideas and opinions on the causes of the firm's problems and what could be done about them. Gaul started by talking to the production manager, Mr Giles. Giles argued that the cause of the drop in sales was an inability to compete with cut-price competition from the Far East. In order to compete, Dray must find a way of cutting its unit labour costs. Giles' preferred method was to scrap the existing plant and purchase the latest computer-aided manufacturing equipment. 'By investing in this new equipment we will be able to lay off 50 staff and still manage to produce the same volume as we do today. This modernisation programme is essential. We can't pay the same wage rates as our competitors in the East. The only solution is to invest in the new technology that will allow us to improve our productivity by reducing the head count at the factory.' Gaul listened with interest to Giles' argument. However he did feel that this radical modernisation programme was highly risky. Dray's capital gearing was already 65% and due to the company's private limited status the only realistic way of raising the necessary finance would be more loan capital.

Gaul then began to interview the staff and a different picture emerged. The climate of fear created by Mr Smith had stifled innovation and change at Dray. Staff devoted all their energies into self defence and job preservation. No-one was keen to come up with new ideas on how to adapt existing systems to improve productivity because of concerns about the job losses that might follow. Consequently the result was stagnation. Now Gaul felt he had found the true cause of the firm's problems. Gaul decided to reject Giles' advice. Rather than relying on a massive one-off burst of capital expenditure Gaul decided to build the company's future around its staff instead. The next step would be far harder. How was he to set about changing the organisation's culture so that employee ideas would flow?

Questions   *(50 marks; 70 minutes)*

1 What were the probable reasons for the loss of market share suffered at Dray Technologies prior to Mr Gaul's takeover?   *(8)*

2 Using the arguments put forward by Mr Giles, explain how investment in new technology can enable firms to compete against firms operating from low-wage economies?   *(8)*

3 Identify and assess the drawbacks of Mr Giles' proposals.   *(10)*

4 How could a firm in the same position as Dray Technologies set about changing its organisational structure in order to encourage greater employee participation?   *(9)*

5 Using the text as a starting point, evaluate the merits of continuous improvement over business process re-engineering.   *(15)*

C. ESSAY QUESTIONS

1 Two years ago the management team at Lynx Engineering commissioned a benchmarking survey to assess its relative position within the marketplace. To their horror the managers discovered that they were lagging behind their competition in terms of both cost and product quality. In an attempt to rectify the situation a massive £2 million re-engineering programme was announced. Two years later things have still not improved. Assess what could have gone wrong. What should the company do next?

2 How might a firm set about improving its efficiency? What factors are likely to affect the success of any strategy designed to achieve this goal?

3 'It has been proven time and time again that in order to survive firms must be willing to initiate change successfully within their own organisations. Firms that are afraid of change will fail because those that are more adventurous will always leave them behind.' To what extent do you agree or disagree with this statement?

BENCHMARKING

Benchmarking is a management tool which helps companies improve their performance. It involves comparing aspects of business performance with those of other companies. The purpose is to identify the best achievements, for instance in terms of delivery reliability. The business will then change some or all of its practices in order to try to match the best company.

52.1 How did it develop?

Benchmarking arose from a recognition that profitability and growth come from improving performance. This is not just year on year improvement. It needs to be improvement compared with the best performers. Benchmarking developed during the 1980s when businesses in Europe and the USA faced strong competition from Japanese companies. They were losing their home markets to imported products. To survive they had to compete. This meant discovering why they were losing business. Two major issues were identified:

1 The Japanese companies produced better quality products. Customers received a more reliable product and a higher standard of service.
2 Japanese companies were more efficient at producing the product. This meant that prices could be kept lower. The improved **efficiency** meant that more finance was available for research and development. Existing products were updated more frequently and new innovative products were being brought to the market.

Having realised they were not as efficient as their Japanese competitors, some American and British companies started to look at what these competitors were doing. They began to incorporate some of the Japanese ways of doing things in order to try to catch up.

Benchmarking as a management tool started to be mentioned in 1980s. In 1985 none of the top 500 US companies were engaged in benchmarking. By 1990 over half of them were using the technique. In the UK the use of benchmarking continues to grow. The Confederation of British Industry (CBI) has a set of diagnostic and benchmarking tools that are available to both its members and non-members. PROBE stands for **PRO**moting **B**usiness **E**xcellence. It was designed by the CBI in conjunction with industry leaders and leading academics.

The Department of Trade and Industry (DTI) has published a guide to benchmarking aimed at small businesses.

BIG BUSINESS, BETTER BUSINESS

Type the word 'benchmarking' into your internet search engine and the number of results gives a good indication of the growth in interest in benchmarking. Not only are there a huge number of firms who will assist but there are also plenty of opportunities for businesses to join in benchmarking activities.

In the UK the Department of Trade and Industry (DTI) runs a scheme that encourages businesses to share information about their processes and to find partners for benchmarking (www.dti.gov.org).

The US web-based Benchmarking Exchange claims to have 44,000 members in 79 countries. Through this website members can share information and views and find other similar firms to benchmark against. They conduct a regular survey of the most popular benchmarking activities.

In September 2002 the top ten were:

1 Customer service/satisfaction
2 Information systems/technology
3 Employee Development/training
4 Process improvement
5 Call centres/help desks
6 Performance measurement /improvement
7 Employee recruiting/staffing
8 Manufacturing assembly
9 Human resources
10 Project management.

Although the list is continually changing it shows the range of activities that are being benchmarked as businesses attempt to improve performance.

(Top ten list from www.benchnet.com)

Business IN

INVENTION, INNOVATION AND DESIGN

DEFINITION

An invention occurs when a new product or process is created. Inventions will only earn money if they are put into practice, in other words innovation takes place.

Innovation means using a new idea in the marketplace or the workplace.

Design involves developing both the physical appearance and the internal workings of a product. Design is used by firms to ensure that their products are attractive and practical.

54.1 Introduction

At the heart of any business is the product it sells. That product is the key to success. **Invention, innovation** and design are the processes by which interesting, new or unique products enter markets. As illustrated by the business example below, inventions can increase the total value of a market, or can lead to the birth of totally new markets.

54.2 Invention

The very activity of inventing new products is somewhat hit and miss. Many new products have been invented by accident. The Post-it note was the result of the discovery of a seemingly useless glue, which wasn't very sticky. Sony's Walkman exists only because someone happened to see both a miniaturised tape player and a miniature set of headphones in two separate research labs at Sony on the same day. Fortunately, that someone was the chairman of the company, Akio Morita. Other products have been invented in order to fulfil a particular purpose, such as stairlifts for the elderly and disabled.

Invention is not limited to products. Production processes have been invented which lead to great

Business IN

INNOVATION UNDER WATER

For over 20 years, scuba divers were kept under water by the same type of 'open' oxygen system. They breathed in from their oxygen tank and breathed out through a tube that sent a stream of air bubbles to the surface. With the technology unchanged, suppliers' market shares were also stable. In recent years, however, closed 'Rebreather' systems have been developed and marketed.

Exhaled oxygen is recycled, enabling the diver to stay under water for two to three times as long. The system also avoids the streams of bubbles which might frighten away the fish or whales the diver is trying to observe.

Although the cost of around £2,500 is far more than open diving equipment, Rebreathers have sold well in places like Florida and the Bahamas. This new technology has added value, changed market shares and increased total spending within the market place.

TYPE OF INVENTION	DESCRIPTION	EXAMPLES
Product invention	Devising a new type or category of product, i.e. opening up a new market	• Video recorder • Digital radio • Alcoholic lemonade
Process invention	Devising a new way of producing or manufacturing (which may allow new products to be made, or improve the efficiency of making existing products)	• Spray painting • Soft ice coating (Wall's Solero) • Robotic welding

competitive advantages. The glass manufacturer Pilkington plc developed the float glass process. This enables higher quality, lower cost production and earned the firm significant sums in licensing revenues from foreign manufacturers.

Although many inventions come from company research programmes, there is still a place for the lone inventor. An individual may come up with an idea which can be produced and marketed under licence by a larger firm with greater facilities. Or the inventor may set up his or her own firm, if the product idea is good enough and enough capital can be raised. James Dyson, inventor of the cyclonic vacuum cleaner, had his idea rejected by many major manufacturers. So he set up his own business in 1993 in order to manufacture his revolutionary new cleaner. By 2002, the firm had grown so that it employed 600 staff, claimed a 50% share of the UK market and was estimated to be worth between £250 and £500 million.

Having come up with an invention, a vital step is to **patent** it. This means registering with the Patent Office that the new technical process is a genuine step forward from previous patents. If a patent is granted, no other firm has the legal right to use your new process for at least 20 years. This provides a long period in which the inventor enjoys exclusive rights to sell the new product/process. This allows the inventor to gain high rewards from selling at a high price due to the product's uniqueness. Dyson cleaners, for example, sell at more than twice the price of most other vacuum cleaners.

54.3 Innovation

As with invention, innovation can be based on products or processes. However, successful innovation requires business skill in addition to inventive talent. The inventive idea must be honed into a marketable product. Meanwhile the method of production must be developed and finance found. Successful innovation is vital for the long-term survival of a firm. Innovation allows the firm to update its product portfolio by replacing products at the end of their life cycle.

It is particularly important to continue to innovate in markets where competition is strong, product life cycles short and the rate of innovation is high. Computer manufacturers seek to launch a new innovation every few months, in an attempt to gain a competitive advantage over their rivals. In industries such as this, innovation is essential for survival. A computer firm selling three-year-old technology is unlikely to be able to add much value or sell high volumes.

Radical innovations such as the robot cleaner are rare. In most markets, the term 'innovation' means nothing so dramatic. In the salad cream market, the first squeezable bottle was called an innovation by Heinz. Breweries were equally thrilled to announce the first 'widget' canned beer. The reason is that in large,

A REPUTATION FOR INNOVATION

By the start of the 21st century, Dyson had a firmly established reputation as a manufacturer of genuinely innovative household cleaners. Not content to sit still, the firm sought to cement this reputation elsewhere in the household equipment market, with the launch of their CR01 2 drum washing machine. Complete with this unique selling point and Dyson's own, distinctive design style – purples, yellows and grey – the firm looked set to shake up another rather tired market.

However, trouble struck shortly after the launch of the new machine as rivals, along with the UK's *Which?* magazine, argued that Dyson's claims of faster, cheaper and cleaner performance weren't quite right. Sales of washing machines have been nowhere near as successful as the vacuum cleaners, but Dyson's image remains largely intact – sales of vacuum cleaners are still buoyant and the Dyson price premium justified by the innovative nature of their products remains as healthy as ever. Any further launches will certainly gain publicity as consumers expect more innovative household help.

Dyson vacuum cleaner © Dyson

established markets quite small product innovations can have a large impact on market share. Tetley's introduction of the round tea bag in the mid-1990s was a case in point. It provided the firm with its biggest step forward in market share for years.

The Sony PlayStation 2 © Sony

54.4 Design

The design of a product is not just about its appearance and shape. It is also about the product's function, quality and durability. Designers work to a design brief which tells them the criteria for looks, cost and quality. All must be considered in designing the finished product. Larger firms may have their own design teams on the payroll. Smaller firms may rely on design consultants to turn a product idea or requirement into a finished product.

A useful way to consider design is through the design mix. As Figure 54.1 indicates, every designer must consider three factors:

- Aesthetics – the look, feel, smell or taste, i.e. the appeal to the senses.
- Function – does it work? Is it reliable? Is it strong enough or light enough for the customer's purpose?

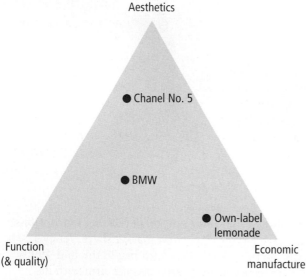

Figure 54.1 The design mix

- Economic manufacture – is the design simple enough for it to be made quickly and efficiently?

In some cases, all three factors will be of equal importance. In most, there will be a clear priority. As Figure 54.1 shows, with own-label lemonade, cheap production would be the overwhelming priority. Therefore cheap design using low-cost materials which are easy to manufacture. For BMW, design for function would be important, as would the car's appearance. Firms decide on their design priorities after careful market research to identify the purchasing motivations of existing and potential customers.

The design process is shown in Figure 54.2 on the next page.

54.5 Invention and innovation in business

INVENTION AND INNOVATION IN MARKETING

Many would argue that the most important element of the marketing mix is the product itself. Successful product development keeps a firm one step ahead of the competition. This usually means keeping one step ahead in pricing as well. Whether you are introducing a new drug such as Viagra or a new football management computer game, you have the opportunity to charge a premium price. Innovative new products are

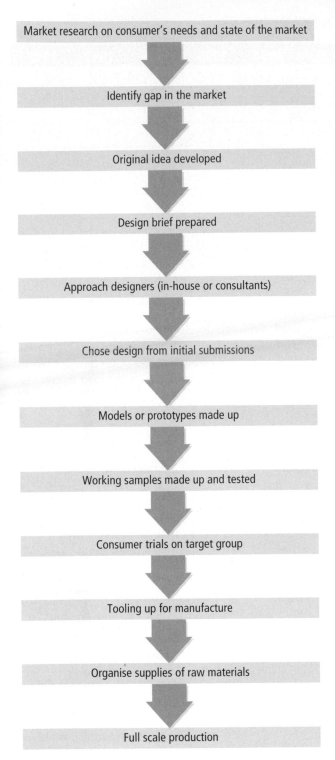

Market research on consumer's needs and state of the market

↓

Identify gap in the market

↓

Original idea developed

↓

Design brief prepared

↓

Approach designers (in-house or consultants)

↓

Chose design from initial submissions

↓

Models or prototypes made up

↓

Working samples made up and tested

↓

Consumer trials on target group

↓

Tooling up for manufacture

↓

Organise supplies of raw materials

↓

Full scale production

Figure 54.2 The design process

also very likely to get good distribution. Sainsbury's are very reluctant to find space on their shelves for just another ('me too') cola or toothpaste. But if the new product is truly innovative, the space will be found.

INVENTION AND INNOVATION IN FINANCE

Invention, innovation and design all require significant amounts of long-term investment. Innovation takes time, and that time is spent by highly paid researchers. The result is that firms who are unwilling to accept long payback periods are unlikely to be

innovators. Short-termist companies are far more likely to copy other firms' successes. In fact, much of the money spent by firms on invention and innovation provides no direct payback. Ideas are researched and developed before discovering that they will not succeed in the marketplace. The result is that innovation is something of a hit or miss process. There are no guaranteed rewards, but a possibility of a brand new, market-changing product. It is these successes which can radically alter the competitive conditions within a marketplace, allowing an innovative company to claim a dominant position.

INVENTION AND INNOVATION IN PEOPLE

Inventors are sometimes caricatured as 'mad scientists' working alone in laboratories with bubbling test tubes. This is far from the truth. For many years, firms have realised that teamworking provides many of the most successful innovations. As a result, research teams are encouraged to share their breakthroughs on a regular basis in the hope that the team can put their ideas together to create a successful product. These research teams are often created by taking specialists in various different fields of operation, from different departments within an organisation. This means that a team may consist of several scientists, an accountant, a production specialist and someone from the marketing department. This blend of expertise will enable the team to identify cost-effective, marketable new ideas which can be produced by the company, without the need for the new idea to be passed around the different departments within an organisation.

Many management gurus, such as Tom Peters, believe that in the future, innovation will be the responsibility of everyone within an organisation. In this way, the organisation can harness the creative power of an even wider range of specialists. In theory, this idea is excellent. The problems arise in the practical implementation of such a system.

INVENTION AND INNOVATION IN PRODUCTION

As previously mentioned, invention and innovation are not limited to finished products. New production processes can be invented or developed. These can lead to more efficient, cheaper or higher quality production. Furthermore, new products often need new machinery and processes to be developed for their manufacture. Design is also important in production. The process needs to be thought through clearly so that every machine and activity has a logical place in the production system.

54.6 Research and development

WHAT IS RESEARCH AND DEVELOPMENT?

Research and development (R&D) is scientific research and technical development. It is carried out

	1986	1989	1991	1993	1994	1995	1996	1997	1998
Pharmaceuticals	11.8	14.7	15.8	25.7	27.4	28.0	31.4	32.6	34.2
Aerospace	9.3	7.7	8.5	10.9	10.0	11.3	9.6	7.6	8.0
Electrical Machinery	5.4	4.4	3.9	5.6	3.6	3.5	4.1	3.8	4.0
Electronics	6.0	3.8	3.8	6.5	5.7	3.6	3.2	3.2	4.0
Motor Vehicles	2.5	2.2	2.5	2.8	2.5	2.5	3.0	3.0	2.9
Chemicals	2.3	2.7	2.9	3.1	2.6	2.5	2.4	2.7	2.8
Mechanical Engineering	1.1	1.4	1.1	1.9	2.0	1.6	1.5	1.5	1.6
Other Manufacturing	0.5	0.4	0.4	0.5	0.5	0.5	0.5	0.5	0.6

Association of the British Pharmaceutical Industry website 2002 (http://www.abpi.org.uk)

by companies in order to develop new products or improve existing products. Larger firms, particularly multinational companies, will tend to have separate research and development facilities. These will be staffed by highly trained scientists, usually working towards developing products to a specific brief.

Product oriented firms are likely to focus on areas of scientific expertise and push their researchers to produce the most technically advanced product possible. For market oriented firms, the research brief will be largely influenced by the needs of consumers and any gaps identified in the market.

As can be seen from the table above, some industries see particularly heavy R&D spending. One in particular is the pharmaceutical industry. Companies spend vast quantities of money, researching new drugs or cures for diseases.

54.7 Patents and copyrights

Inventions, innovations and designs can provide a competitive advantage. Firms will therefore be keen to ensure that their competitors cannot use the same new developments themselves. Intellectual property is a legal concept, which recognises the ownership of new ideas or designs. The major rights of intellectual property are described and briefly explained in the table below.

Fewer purchasing decisions are being made on price alone. Other important elements, particularly design, play a key part in determining a product's success. Within the UK market, as disposable incomes increase, consumers are willing to pay a premium price for well-designed, innovative products. Since British firms are unlikely to be able to compete globally on price alone, experts argue that Britain's future must lie in specialisation in innovation and good design. Evidence suggests that Britain has the expertise

required, although developments in education will govern future levels of technical expertise. The more pressing worry concerns the level of investment by British firms in R&D (see table on the next page).

The table provides worrying reading for those concerned about Britain's future competitiveness.

Patents	• A patent is the exclusive right to use an invention. • Patents can last for up to 20 years. • Patents are a commodity, which can be bought, sold, hired or licensed.
Registered designs	• Designs can be protected in two ways. • Design right gives a weak form of protection, but registered designs can only be used by the firm or individual holding the registration. • The registration can last for up to 25 years and, just like a patent, can be bought or sold.
Trade marks	• A trade mark allows a firm to differentiate itself, or its products, from its competitors. • Most trade marks are words or symbols, or a combination, but sounds and smells can be registered as trade marks. Registration of a trademark is denoted by the symbol ®.

World league on R&D

RANKING	COUNTRY	R&D/SALES RATIO
1	Denmark	15.1
2	Canada	10.8
3	Finland	8.9
4	Sweden	7.4
5	Switzerland	6.2
7	Japan	4.9
8	Germany	4.7
9	USA	4.3
12	UK	2.3

Business IN

INNOVATION – THE KEY TO NEW MARKETS FOR JCB

JCB, the famous manufacturer of construction vehicles, decided to diversify into the industrial handling market. This meant breaking into the market for forklift trucks, a fiercely competitive arena dominated by large, established firms. These rivals have a reputation for expertise within a market in which JCB had no experience. JCB knew it needed an innovative product to achieve a successful entry into this market.

So was born the Teletruk – a different type of forklift, designed using many components from JCB's existing product range, most notably the single telescopic arm on which the fork sits. Early sales levels suggest that the vehicle is selling better than originally planned and may be the key to allowing JCB to expand its operations by breaking into this new market.

ISSUES FOR **analysis**

- Invention should not be confused with innovation. The British have a proud record as inventors. Hovercraft, television, penicillin, Viagra and many more products were British inventions. In recent years, however, there has been less success in this country with innovation. The Japanese have been the great innovators in electronics, the Americans in computers and the Swiss in watches. British firms have failed to invest sufficiently to develop ranges of really innovative new products.

- Major innovation can completely change a firm's competitive environment. The market shares of leading companies may change little for years. Then an innovation comes along which changes everything. The firm that has not prepared for such change can be swept aside. This may happen to bookshops which do not establish a major presence on the Internet.

- Good management means looking ahead, not only to the next hill but the one after that. Anticipation makes change manageable. It may even ensure that your own firm becomes market leader due to far-sightedness of your own innovation. In turn, that would ensure high product differentiation and allow relatively high prices to be charged.

- Innovation can happen in management procedures, attitudes and styles. A management which is progressive and adventurous might well find that an empowered workforce is generating the new ideas that seemed lacking before. It would not be wise to assume that invention and innovation is all about scientists and engineering. It is about people.

54.8 Invention, innovation and design

an evaluation

The fundamental theme for evaluating any question involving invention and innovation are long- and short-term thinking. Invention and innovation are long-term activities. Companies whose objective is short-term profit maximisation are unlikely to spend heavily on innovation. However, a firm with objectives directly related to producing innovative products is likely to spend heavily on research. GlaxoSmithKline, Britain's highest spender on R&D (£2,555 million in 2001) is an excellent example.

Most British companies do not have a particularly impressive record in invention and innovation. The table on this page showing a comparison of international R&D spending places Britain outside the top ten. The conclusion must be that short-termism is a particular problem in Britain. An unhealthy focus on success in the short-term does not fit in with a commitment to expensive R&D, designed to ensure long-term growth. As a result, British firms have a tendency to please their shareholders with high dividend payments, rather than retaining profits for investment in R&D.

KEY terms

computer-aided design (CAD) – software which allows designers to simulate their designs on a computer in 3D. It is potentially cheaper than paper drawings, especially if different customers want slightly different product specifications.

innovation – bringing a profitable new product or process to life.

invention – drawing up a new way of making a product or process.

patent – registering a new technical process in order to enjoy monopoly rights to it for 20+ years.

research and development (R&D) – scientific research and technical development.

A Level Exercises

A. REVISION QUESTIONS

(40 marks; 70 minutes)

Read the unit, then answer:

1 Distinguish between innovation and invention. *(3)*
2 Why is it important to reduce the time taken to develop new ideas? *(4)*
3 Distinguish between product and process innovation. *(3)*
4 Why is it 'vital' to patent an invention? *(3)*
5 What marketing advantages does good design bring to a firm? *(4)*
6 Where, on Figure 54.1, might you plot:
   a Marks and Spencer jumpers *(3)*
   b a Ferrari? *(3)*
   Briefly explain your answers.
7 Why might product oriented firms produce more inventions than market oriented ones? *(4)*
8 How are the concepts of short-termism and innovation linked? *(4)*
9 Many businesses are concerned at the fall in the number of students taking science A levels. How might this affect firms in the long term? *(5)*
10 What effect would a lack of innovation have on a company's product portfolio? *(4)*

B. REVISION EXERCISES

B1 Data Response

How the UK Can Catch Up with Competition

Management guru Michael Porter has warned that the UK must take a number of vital steps if it is to improve its international competitiveness:

* more funds invested in higher education and research and development
* tougher competition rules
* a big reduction in tax.

Porter, who has just finished compiling a 'national innovation index', said that the UK's poor position in the index came as a shock to him. The index is based on a number of factors involved in innovation, including spending on R&D, spending on higher education and the protection of intellectual property. The UK was placed eighth in the index, ahead only of Italy out of the world's nine leading industrial nations. Despite the UK's history of successful innovation, the rate of innovation has declined markedly, leading to low national income per head, poor levels of productivity and a reduced potential for innovation.

Porter believes that the most important job for the UK's government is to boost investment in university education and developing human resources throughout the country. He warns that massive investment will be needed because of an investment shortfall in these areas over the last decade. Further to this, he said:

'Merger approval and the regulatory process is overly politicised. Too many competition-destroying mergers are occurring.'

His final advice was to suggest that capital gains tax should be halved in an attempt to boost investment in innovation whilst tax credit for research and development should be readily available.

Source: Adapted from *The Independent*, 11/12/98

Questions *(30 marks; 35 minutes)*

1 Why does Michael Porter suggest that 'tougher competition rules' are needed to encourage innovation in the UK? *(6)*
2 a What is 'short-termism'? *(2)*
   b How does the article illustrate the problems caused by short-termism in British business? *(6)*
3 Analyse the implications of the 'national innovation index' results on the UK's international competitiveness. *(8)*
4 Evaluate the importance of the role of governments in providing incentives for Research and Development. *(8)*

B2 Case Study

Mach 3 – At the Cutting Edge of Technology

Gillette's UK research and development facility is located just outside Reading. Men in white coats test revolutionary shaving technologies – all searching for the perfect shaving experience. From its position of UK market dominance (57% market share), which has been based on innovation, including the launch in 1971 of the world's first twin-bladed razor, Gillette is pushing forward the frontiers of shaving technology. The newest model to have been developed by Gillette is the Mach 3. The new product has been described as the 'Porsche of the shaving world', with its sleek design, based on the liquid metal bad guy of *Terminator 2*, and its hefty price tag of £4.99 for the handle and two cartridges. The Mach 3 was advertised in America as the 'billion dollar blade'. However, this was probably an underestimate of the costs incurred during the razor's seven-year development:

$750 million (£440 million) on building the production system for the razor

$300 million on the launch marketing

$200 per year on research and development.

Gillette expects to sell 1.2 billion units of the Mach 3 per year.

The testing regime for Gillette's new products involves a product evaluation group of more than 3,000 men throughout the UK who are supplied with Gillette products and provide feedback on the level of quality consistency, in addition to testing experimental products. Among these guinea pigs are the mysterious men who turn up at the research facility in Reading every morning – paid for the shaving risks they take there and performing the role of test pilots – sworn to secrecy on the new technology they are using.

The building, an old jam factory, is kitted out with the latest CAD technology. Research focuses on computer models of human skin – a substance which Gillette has found very tough to model accurately. However, their current modelling is the most accurate they have ever used and skin irritation is measured using the same laser technology as police radar guns. The jam factory was the birthplace of the Mach 3, a birth heralded by success in the long running attempt to add a third blade, without causing blood loss. With sales of the Mach 3 starting off at encouraging levels, the old jam factory appears to have turned out another winning idea.

Questions
(40 marks; 60 minutes)

1 Using examples from the text, suggest what marketing advantages arise from successful innovation. *(8)*

2 Describe the pre-launch testing methods used by Gillette and explain why these are so vital to success. *(9)*

3 Why might the research laboratories for a product as ordinary as a razor be shrouded in secrecy? *(6)*

4 Using examples from the Gillette story, explain why successful innovation requires input from all departments within a firm, not just the research and development department. *(12)*

5 Given the information in the text, how long will it take Gillette to recover the research, development and launch costs of the Mach 3, if running costs average out to £2.99 per unit. *(5)*

C. ESSAY QUESTIONS

1 To what extent does an innovative product guarantee success?

2 'Any business has two, and only two, basic functions. Marketing and innovation.' Discuss whether there is value in this statement by Peter Drucker.

3 'Luck is the most important factor in successful innovation.' Discuss the validity of this statement.

4 'Spending on research and development is wasted money since many firms find success through copying other firms' products.' Discuss this statement.

QUALITY MANAGEMENT

DEFINITION

Quality control is the maintenance of consistent levels of quality. Levels of quality are defined by product specifications and customer requirements.

Quality control prevents defects, controls costs and generates customer satisfaction.

55.1 What is quality?

Quality is very hard to define. W Edward Deming, the American quality guru, said that 'quality is defined by the customer'. The customer may define quality by insisting on certain specifications. Or by exercising choice in the market. Another definition of quality is 'fit for use'. Although hard to define, there is no doubt that customers are now very aware of quality. They use perceived quality as part of the buying decision. The importance of quality in that decision will depend on the choice available and the balance of power between the customer and the supplier.

Branded goods: are you paying for real, or perceived, quality?

In a competitive market where there is a range of goods available, quality is one of the ingredients in purchasing decisions. The customer will accept some trade-off between price and quality. There is, however, a minimum level of quality that is acceptable. The customer wants the product to work (be fit for use) regardless of the price. Below a minimum level customers will not buy the product. Above the minimum level of acceptable quality customers will expect to get more as they pay more.

When competition is fierce, businesses have to meet or exceed the quality offered by their competitors. The one hairdresser in a village can relate quality to customer satisfaction. If there are four competitors, though, quality may require customers to be delighted rather than satisfied.

A CLOSER SHAVE

In 2001 Gillette achieved a staggering 71.1% global market share in the razor market. Not even Coca-Cola, Levi's or McDonald's come close to this level of market dominance. By 1997 sales of its leading razor, the Sensor, were at maturity. The company spent $200 million dollars on research and development. The company objective was clear. It wanted a product that would expand the market for non-electric shaving but at higher prices. This required a product with considerable added value. The Mach3 was the result and was launched in April 1998. Since then it has captured 23% of the global market with worldwide sales totalling over $3 billion.

Although it took sales from the Sensor this was not a problem for the company as the Mach3's price premium ensured increased profitability. Gillette's assumption that customers would be prepared to pay a premium for higher quality has been proved correct.

The company is hoping that this will again prove to be true. It has now launched a new product: the Mach3Turbo. In March 2002 when launching an advertising campaign to support the new product, Peter K. Hoffman, President Grooming, said, 'With more than 60 million men around the world already shaving with Mach3, we are confident that this campaign will inspire many of them to trade up to the even better-performing Mach3Turbo, as well as introduce entirely new users to the razor's benefits.'

Business IN

Dell is a hugely successful computer manufacturer which sells directly to customers through the Internet or newspaper advertising. Its mission statement says:

'Customers must have a quality experience and be pleased not just satisfied.'

Gillette's Mach3 Turbo: better quality at a higher price ©Gillette

55.2 Quality defined by specifications

Where the customer is in a powerful position, quality is directly defined by the customer. Many firms lay down minimum standards for their suppliers. This in turn helps them to maintain their own quality standards. Large businesses such as supermarkets and chain stores are able to insist on quality standards. They have the buying power to force their suppliers to conform. For many years, Marks and Spencer has worked with suppliers to ensure that standards are met. Other large purchasers such as government departments and local authorities are also able to insist on high standards for supplies. As new roads and motorways are built, the surface is checked to ensure its quality. If the surface does not conform to the required standards the contractor will have to re-lay the area.

55.3 Quality defined by law

The law lays down minimum quality standards. This applies particularly to products where health or safety are involved. Food must be fresh and has to be handled with care, by trained staff. It is illegal to sell electrical equipment without a plug fitted.

There are also trading standards. These are often industry based. They set minimum standards for particular goods and services. Some trade associations offer guarantees for work done by members of their association. The National House Building Council offers purchasers a 10-year guarantee for work done by their members. Some industries have watchdogs. They ensure that minimum standards are met. OFWAT, the water industry regulator, has the task of ensuring that water quality is maintained.

Other firms, and in particular local and central government agencies, will insist that their suppliers have obtained BS 5750 or the international equivalent ISO 9000 (see below). This ensures that suppliers are operating within a quality framework.

ISO 9000 is an international standard for quality systems. It is a British standard that is recognised worldwide. It was previously known as BS 5750. Companies who are registered can display the BSI symbol. In order to register, companies have to document their business procedures, prepare a quality manual and assess their quality management systems. They are assessed by an independent assessor. After obtaining the award, businesses are visited at regular intervals to ensure compliance. It is necessary that everyone in the organisation follows the processes outlined in the quality manual.

Firms who have registered say that it has provided a range of benefits to the business. These include:

- *increased competitiveness*
- *increased customer satisfaction*
- *less waste*
- *cost savings*
- *fewer mistakes*
- *increased efficiency*
- *better motivated employees*
- *improved communications*
- *increased profits.*

For all customers, quality is about satisfying their expectations. Customers expect products to work and to be of a consistent standard. For many customers the issues are not limited to reliability. The customer will take into account the total buying experience. Customer service and after-sales service may be as important as the product itself. The inability to obtain spare parts is also a quality issue. The way the product is sold, even where it is sold, all contribute to the customers' feelings about the quality of the product.

Quality is a moving target. Quality that is acceptable today may not be in the future. Customer expectations of quality are constantly changing. As quality improves, customer demands also increase.

Quality:
- *is satisfying customer expectations*
- *applies to services as well as products*
- *involves the whole business process, not just the manufacturing of the product*
- *is always changing.*

B. REVISION EXERCISES

B1 Data Response

Trac Parts

Trac Parts is a major manufacturer of parts for farm and construction machinery. It has been operating from a new centralised warehouse for four years. This year the company applied for BS ISO 9000. It gained accreditation. The main reason for applying was that several large customers had indicated that they would only deal with BS ISO 9000 companies when negotiating new contracts. The warehouse manager has been pleasantly surprised by the operational performance figures since accreditation:

- orders completed on time up from 75% to 84%
- errors in completing orders reduced by 40%
- average time from order receipt to dispatch reduced by two days.

Questions   (25 marks; 30 minutes)

1 What is BS ISO 9000?   (3)
2 Why might a business want this accreditation?   (4)
3 Examine the benefits to Trac Parts of the performance improvements identified in the text.   (6)
4 In order to gain accreditation, the firm will have had to introduce procedures to ensure that levels of quality are maintained. Using the four stages of quality control (prevention, detection, correction and improvement) suggest actions it might have taken.   (12)

B2 Case Study

Tricolour

Tricolour is a French computer manufacturer. It has worries about falling sales. It believes it is losing sales to Japanese and American companies that have set up manufacturing facilities in Europe. It has also lost sales to other European competitors. An industry survey has produced data on industry levels of production defects. It has added its own figures and produced the chart shown below.

The firm realises that survival depends upon addressing the quality problems. It has decided to employ a quality manager, Celeste Dubois, to address the issues. Her first suggestion is to get together a group of workers from each department to discuss the problems and issues. Following a survey of the factory she has also suggested that the layout of the production facilities should be changed. This will be an expensive exercise and the management is reluctant to make the changes. The changes will require production to stop for a week and investment in new equipment. The firm's weak cash flow position makes it hard for

the board to accept new capital spending. The other area that Celeste has identified is a problem with one particular component. She has suggested that a new supplier should be found, or that she should work with the existing supplier to improve the quality of the component.

Questions   (40 marks; 50 minutes)

1 a What does the chart show?   (2)
  b What further data would help to make the bar chart more useful?   (4)
2 From the case study identify two reasons for the quality problems experienced by Tricolour.   (2)
3 What are the marketing implications for Tricolour of the data in the bar chart?   (8)
4 Outline the advantages Tricolour might get from the discussion group formed to discuss the quality problems.   (8)
5 How might Celeste convince the firm's management to change the layout of the production facilities? (6)
6 Once these changes have been made the firm needs to ensure that quality is maintained and improved. Discuss the implications for the firm of implementing a total quality management initiative.   (10)

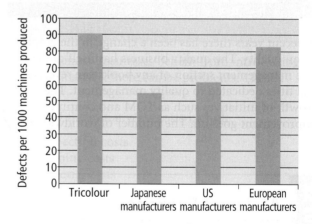

Manufacturing defects – producer comparisons

C. ESSAY QUESTIONS

1 'Quality control is about building quality in, not inspecting it out.' Discuss.
2 Consider whether quality management is solely a matter for the production department.
3 To what extent is quality a major competitive issue in service businesses?

STOCK CONTROL

DEFINITION

The management process that makes sure stock is ordered, delivered and handled in the best possible way. An efficient stock control system will balance the need to meet customer demand against the cost of holding stock.

56.1 Purchasing

Manufacturing businesses rely on stocks being bought in from other firms. These stocks can either be in the form of raw materials or components. These stocks are part of the inputs which manufacturing firms process into outputs.

The purchasing function acts as a service to the rest of the business. Its main objective is to meet the needs of those running the internal operations of the business. In a factory, inefficient purchasing may lead (in the extreme) to a shutdown if key materials or components have not turned up when needed. In a retail store, poor purchasing could mean empty shelves or an over-full stockroom. In order to avoid this, the purchasing function of a business will try to ensure that:

- a sufficient quantity of stocks is available at all times…
- …but not so much as to represent a waste of resources
- stocks are of the right quality
- stocks are available where they are needed in the factory
- the price paid for stocks is as competitive as possible
- good relations are built up with suppliers.

When purchasing stocks, a business must ask a range of questions about potential suppliers. The main two things that the buyer must be convinced of are that the supplier can meet its requirements on quality and on price.

- Quality can be checked through samples and/or a visit to the supplier's factory to inspect methods and conditions. If the supplier has achieved its BS 5750 certificate (or the European equivalent ISO 9000) it means it has an effective quality assurance system.
- The price may be negotiated, especially if the buyer is purchasing in bulk or is a regular customer. A lower price may be agreed, or longer credit periods established.

In addition, the buyer will have to consider other questions before deciding which supplier to use. This will include such things as:

- Will the supplier be consistent, supplying the quantity and quality needed on time, every time?

- Is the financial position of the firm sufficiently safe to guarantee, as far as possible, its future survival?
- If the needs of the buyer change, can the supplier change quickly to meet demand?
- Can the supplier expand if the buyer's demand grows?

In the past, firms tended to focus on short-term buying decisions based upon the lowest quoted price. Today's supplies might be from XZ Ltd; tomorrow's from PQ and Co. Companies such as Marks and Spencer and Toyota took a different approach. They aimed to form an effective and lasting partnership with suppliers. In that way both businesses benefit from the relationship. More and more British companies are following this lead.

The purchasing department will need to take a strategic decision on how best to operate. Key questions will be:

- Should the firm place large orders occasionally, or small orders frequently?
- Should the firm accept lower quality stocks at a lower cost?
- Should the firm rely on one supplier or use several?

56.2 Types of stock

Manufacturing firms hold three types of stock:

- Raw materials and components. These are the stocks the business has purchased from outside suppliers. They will be held by the firm until it is ready to process them into its finished output.
- Work in progress. At any given moment, a manufacturing firm will have some items which it has started to process, but which are incomplete. This may be because they are presently moving through the production process. It may be because the firm stores unfinished goods to give it some flexibility to meet consumer demand.
- Finished goods. Once a product is complete, the firm may keep possession of it for some time. This could be because they sell goods in large batches or no buyer has yet come in for the product. For producers of seasonal goods such as toys, most of the year's production may be building stock in preparation for the pre-Christmas sales rush. This process is known as producing for stock, or stockpiling.

As explained in Section 56.5, the firm's costs increase if it holds more stock. However, this needs to be set against the **opportunity cost** of keeping too little stock, such as not being able to meet customer demand. One theory is that a firm should try to keep as little stock as possible at all times. This system, known as just-in-time, is looked at in Section 56.7.

The firm must keep control of all the different types of stock to ensure it runs at peak efficiency.

56.3 Stock management

Stock management is the way a firm controls the stock within the business. If the purchasing function has been efficient, the business will receive the right quantity and quality of stock at the right time. However, once the stocks are inside the firm, they must be handled and used correctly. This is to make sure they are still in peak condition when the come to be used in the production process.

STOCK ROTATION

Wherever possible, a firm will want to use its oldest stock first. This will mean stocks do not deteriorate, go past their sell-by date or become obsolete. Stock can go obsolete if new specifications are used or if the product of which they were a part is no longer manufactured. By using a system of **stock rotation**, the firm will ensure that the risks of stock going out of date are minimised. Supermarkets, for example, should always put new stock at the back of the shelf to encourage shoppers to take the older stock first. The principle behind stock rotation is first-in-first-out (FIFO). This is to avoid a situation in which new stock is used first, leaving older stock to become unusable at the back of a shelf or a warehouse.

STOCK WASTAGE

This is the loss of stock in either a production or service process. Any wastage is a cost to the firm as it has paid for stock which it will not use.

In a manufacturing process, the main causes of stock wastage are:

- materials being wasted, such as scraps of cloth being thrown away as off-cuts from a dress maker; this can be minimised by careful planning – perhaps helped by computer-aided design (CAD) software
- the reworking of items that were not done correctly first time; good training and a highly motivated staff are the best ways to avoid this
- defective products that cannot be put right, which will often be sold off as seconds or damaged goods.

For a retailer, the main causes of stock wastage will be:

- products becoming damaged due to improper handling or storage

In massive warehouses like this, accurate stock management is crucial

- stealing from the shop, whether by customers or staff
- products such as food passing their sell-by dates.

In all of these cases, sound management and administrative techniques could reduce or even eliminate the problem of stock wastage. Any wastage is a cost to the firm, and procedures need to be set up to prevent such losses.

However, it is important that the cost of the processes set up is not more than the money being saved by them. Cost effective measures are needed to maximise the returns to the firm.

56.4 Stock control charts

One way in which a firm analyses its stock situation is by using stock control charts. These line graphs look at the level of stock in the firm over time. Managers will be able to see from these charts how stock levels have changed during the period, and will be able to note any unusual events with which they may need to be concerned.

A typical stock control graph is shown in Figure 56.1. On this chart there are four lines. These represent:

- Stock levels. This line shows how stock levels have changed over this time period. As the stock is used up, the level of stock gradually falls from left to right. When a delivery is made, however, the stock level leaps upwards in a vertical line. The greater the rise in the vertical line, the more stock has been delivered.
- Maximum stock level. This shows the most that the firm is either willing or able to hold in stock. It may reflect the physical size of the warehouse and be the maximum because no more can be taken in. It may

also, however, be set by management on the basis that:
- it is the most that be used by the production process
- it is the most that can be kept to ensure sell-by dates are not missed
- it is sufficient, given the time between deliveries and the rate of usage.

- Re-order level. This is a 'trigger' quantity. When stocks fall to this level a new order will be sent in to the supplier. The re-order level is reached some time before the delivery (shown by the vertical part of the stock level line). This is because the supplier will need some 'lead time' to process the order and make the delivery.
- Minimum stock level. This is also known as the **buffer stock.** The firm will want to keep a certain minimum level of stock for reasons of safety. It will have something to fall back on if an order does not arrive on time or if stock is used up particularly quickly, perhaps due to a sudden increase in demand.

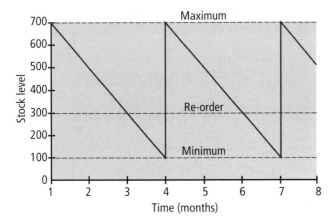

Figure 56.1 Stock control chart

Diagrams such as this, showing a neat and regular pattern to stockholding, will not happen in reality. Orders may arrive late and may not always be in the correct quantity. The rate of usage is unlikely to be constant. The slope of the stock level line may be steeper showing more stock being used than normal, or shallower showing a slower use of stock.

However, as a basis for analysing stock levels over time, stock control charts such as these give managers a clear picture of how things have changed, and shows them what questions need to be asked. For example, it may show that stocks are constantly arriving late. Managers would then know to ask if suppliers were taking longer than the agreed lead time. Or if orders were not being placed when the re-order level of stock was reached.

Figure 56.2 shows a more realistic stock control graph. It is based on actual sales of Nestlé Lion bars at a newsagent in south-west London over a three-month period.

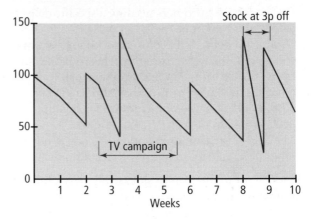

Figure 56.2 Weekly sales of Lion bars at one newsagent

56.3 The costs of stock

The initial cost of purchasing stock is only one of the costs associated with a firm's stockholding. A firm can hold too much stock or too little stock. Both cases will add to the costs of the firm.

Too much stock can lead to:

- Opportunity cost. Holding the firm's wealth in the form of stock prevents it using its capital in other ways, such as investing in new machinery or research and development on a new product. By missing out on such opportunities the firm may put itself at a disadvantage compared with competitors.
- Liquidity problems. Holding the firm's wealth as stock may cause problems if it proves slow moving. There may be insufficient cash to pay suppliers.
- Increased storage costs. As well as the physical space needed to hold the stock, there may be increases in associated costs such as labour within the warehouse, heating and lighting or refrigeration. Stocks need to be insured against fire and theft, the cost of which will increase as more stocks are held.
- Increased finance costs; if the capital needs to be borrowed, the cost of that capital (the interest rate) will be a significant added annual overhead
- Increased stock wastage. The more stocks that are held, the greater the risk of it going out of date or deteriorating in condition.

This does not, however, mean that the business is free to carry very low stocks. Unless it can confidently run just-in-time systems the firm may well face increased costs from holding too little stock as well. These could be:

- Workers and machines standing idle as there are not enough materials or components to allow the process to operate. This costs the business in lost output and wages being paid for no work. It could also cost the business at a later date if extra overtime is needed to make up for the production lost.

- Lost orders as customers needing a specific delivery date which cannot be met go elsewhere.
- Orders not being fulfilled on time leading to worsening relations with customers. This could lead to future orders being lost as customers turn to more reliable suppliers. The firm may also have to pay customers financial compensation for missing delivery dates.
- The loss of the firm's reputation and any goodwill it has been able to build up with its customers.

The total cost to the firm of stocks will therefore be a combination of these factors. As the level of stocks grows, the costs of holding that stock will increase, but the costs of not holding stock will decrease. The cost of holding stock will therefore look like Figure 56.3.

Figure 56.3 Cost of stockholding

For a firm, the optimum level of stock to hold will be where the total costs of holding stock are the lowest.

A further consideration to the quantity of stocks being held is how much stock to order at any one time. Large orders need only be made a few times to keep sufficient stock levels, whilst smaller orders will mean that they have to be placed more regularly. The arguments for both of these are shown below:

Advantages of many smaller orders:

- *Less storage space needed*
- *More flexible to changing needs*
- *Less stock wastage*

Advantages of few larger orders:

- *Economies from buying in bulk*
- *Avoids chance of running out of stock*
- *Prevents machines and workers standing idle*

56.6 IT and stock control

As computers become cheaper and more powerful they are being used more and more in business. The management of stock is a good example. Stock control is all about the efficient handling of information about current and required stocks. Information technology can handle large quantities of data quickly and easily. Therefore the use of IT can make the task of stock control both easier and more accurate.

Most businesses will hold records of their stock on large databases. Stock control systems exist that allow these databases to be updated instantaneously as stock leaves the warehouse or goes through the checkout. The systems that achieve this are bar-code scanners which read the details of the stock coming in or going out. This data can be transferred immediately to the warehouse computer system which can then keep an accurate, up-to-the-second picture of how much stock is held at any given time. The need to re-order stock can be identified by the system, and the order sent automatically from the warehouse IT system to the supplier's IT system. Such a system largely does away with the need for human involvement in the stock control process once the system and the rules by which it operates are set up.

Stock control systems such as these add to the ability of managers to analyse stock movements. It should make it possible for more accurate decisions to be made on what stock to hold and in what quantities.

STOCK CONTROL AT JAGUAR

When Jaguar began production of its new X-Type, it felt the need for a more tightly controlled stock management system to help increase efficiency, productivity and to meet consumer demand.

A particular area of concern was the availability of the welding tips used by robotic arms to seal the bodyshell. Thousands of such tips are used daily. Without them, car manufacture would slow down or even cease altogether. To prevent this happening, tips were usually overstocked – many more were held than were ever going to be needed.

Previously there had been no computerised tracking or controlled storage system in place. With the X-Type being produced, Jaguar felt the need to have a system to accurately manage and control stock levels, to allow production to be as cheap and efficient as possible.

It is believed that this new system has saved Jaguar up to £8,000 per year. In addition, staff have been given more responsibility for stock management, boosting their involvement and motivation.

Source: *The Engineer*

Supermarkets, for example, make much use of IT as the basis for decisions about stocks. Through electronic data interchange (EDI) links, manufacturers can even see the sales level of their products at supermarket checkouts. This enables them to anticipate the orders the supermarkets will soon be placing. Without such instant information, strategies such as just-in-time would be very difficult.

56.7 Just-in-time

Just-in-time (JIT) is a system of stock control that has become popular in UK firms over the last couple of decades. The basis of the system is that the costs of holding stock, as shown in Section 56.5, should be unacceptable to a firm, and so the level of stock held by the firm ought to be as small as possible. In other words, JIT is the attempt to operate with a zero buffer stock.

At the same time, a system must be developed so that the costs and risks of running out of stock are avoided by the firm.

A firm adopting the JIT system will attempt to do this by developing a close working relationship with suppliers. By involving suppliers closely with the business and by demonstrating the benefits to both the supplier and purchaser, it should be possible for both parties to work together for the common good.

The supplier will be required under the JIT system to make frequent deliveries to the purchaser as and when goods are needed. A delivery that arrives too early is as much a cost to the purchaser as a delivery arriving late. The purchaser will have to be certain that the deliveries will be made just-in-time for the goods to be used.

The advantages and disadvantages of a just-in-time system are shown below.

Advantages of using JIT:

- *Improves the firm's liquidity*
- *The costs of holding stocks are reduced*
- *Storage space can be converted to a more productive use*
- *Stock wastage and stock rotation become lesser issues for management*
- *Response time to changing demands are speeded up as new components can be ordered instantly*

Disadvantages of using JIT:

- *Any break in supply causes immediate problems for the purchaser*
- *The costs of processing orders may be increased*
- *The purchaser's reputation is placed in the hands of the external supplier*

Establishing a JIT system is not something that can or should be achieved overnight. The risks of running out of stock are too great. Figure 56.4 shows how a firm might set out to achieve a JIT system in a carefully planned way. The diagram shows five phases, after which the firm would intend to keep going with phases 6, 7 and thereafter, until it could get as close as possible to zero buffer stock. The five phases are as follows:

- Phase 1 – the firm orders 20,000 units of stock to arrive every 3rd week.
- Phase 2 – suppliers are asked to move to weekly deliveries, therefore only one-third of the quantity is ordered.
- Phase 3 – as phase 2 has proved successful, there is no longer any need for such a high buffer stock. Stock levels are allowed to fall to a new, lower level.
- Phase 4 – with phase 3 complete, the firm now moves to deliveries twice a week. Therefore the order level is halved.
- Phase 5 – the suppliers have proved reliable enough to allow the buffer to be cut again.

JUST-IN-TIME AT ASDA

The petrol 'strikes' of September 2000 brought home a fatal flaw of the JIT system. If something happens to delay even a few delivery trucks, the system can collapse like a row of dominoes.

In 1996–97, ASDA used 410 lorries to drive 45 million miles to make deliveries to its stores. But it has now discovered that if diesel fuel runs out for those trucks, every ASDA store closes in just a few days.

The growing dependence of the UK economy on a fragile logistical system has clearly given businesses a potential headache. For all the cost savings and efficiency gains of a JIT system, there exists a fatal weakness in that, in the space of a single week, a complete collapse can appear as a real possibility.

Source: *The Scotsman*

Business IN

Figure 56.4 Step-by-step progress towards JIT stock control

56.8 Kanban

One way to control the flow of stocks so that they are ready just in time for when they are needed is to use a Japanese system called Kanban. This is usually translated as 'sign board' or 'visible record'. Each item or load of stock has a data card – the Kanban – attached to it. This contains information such as the supplier's name and the area of the factory where it will be used.

At its simplest, the system uses two boxes of stock at any one time. When one box is emptied, it is taken to the component production area where more items will be made. The key to the system is having the empty box refilled and in position ready for use just in time for the second container being emptied. In this way there is a continuous flow of stock arriving where needed on the shop floor just in time for use.

As well as ensuring a constant flow of stock throughout the factory, the Kanban system can help in the empowerment and motivation of the workforce. The Kanban system allows employees to take responsibility for managing their own jobs. By sending the Kanban cards back to the component production area, the employee is taking on an important role in the management of material flow and therefore contributes to the management functions of ordering parts and stock control. Employees know that they must take responsibility for this process if it is to meet the crucial timings involved. Any hiccups in the re-ordering of parts could bring the factory to a standstill.

ISSUES FOR **analysis**

Among the key issues for analysis are:

- Stock is an important issue for some firms; a vital one for others. Greengrocers with small turnovers cannot survive, because slow-moving stock means poor quality fruit and vegetables. For many firms, poor stock control leads to increased theft, rising costs and a threat to survival.
- As with many aspects of management, there is no single answer to the question of how best to manage a firm's stock. Different sized firms in different industries will have widely different stock control needs. JIT may be ideal in one context but inappropriate elsewhere.
- The use of IT as a means of stock control has, until recently, been restricted mainly to large firms needing to control masses of stock in different locations. Whilst the applications are being made available in forms suitable for smaller firms now, it is questionable whether or not such firms are able to use the technology efficiently.
- How will the arrival of Internet marketing (home shopping) affect decisions by retailers about stock levels? Will they feel they have to make greater efforts to ensure they have exactly the right size/colour combination for every customer? In other words, increase the breadth and depth of their stock levels?

56.9 Stock control
an evaluation

Whilst the notion of just-in-time stock control has many attractive features, it is unclear to what extent such a system could realistically operate in the UK. The system relies on a constant flow of deliveries arriving at the right location at the right time. This implies that the country's roads, rail and communications must be capable of dealing with a much greater volume of industrial traffic than it has been designed for. An increasingly common feature of Japanese industrial life, where just-in-time has been in use for many years, is of massive congestion on roads around industrial centres, resulting in just-in-time often becoming just-too-late.

In addition, just-in-time requires close collaboration between purchasers and suppliers. The purchasing firm needs to bring the supplier into discussions on product development. Advice may be needed on components and materials as well as to gain the supplier's commitment to the new project. In the UK there is little past history of firms taking other firms into their confidence in this way. Such openness will require a massive shift in culture throughout industry. Changes in business culture, though, are becoming increasingly common and necessary. So perhaps the required changes will happen.

KEY terms

buffer stock – the desired minimum stock level held by a firm just in case something goes wrong.

opportunity cost – the cost of missing out on the next best alternative when making a decision (or when committing resources).

stockholding costs – the overheads resulting from the stock levels held by a firm.

stock rotation – the administrative and physical processes to ensure that older stock is used first.

AS Level Exercises

A. REVISION QUESTIONS
(35 marks; 70 minutes)

Read the unit, then answer:

1 Why might it be important to maintain good relationships with suppliers? *(3)*
2 State the three main categories of stock. *(3)*
3 What is meant by 'internal customers'? *(3)*
4 How would stock rotation help a firm manage its resources better? *(4)*
5 Sketch a typical stock control chart. *(6)*
6 State three costs associated with holding too much stock. *(3)*
7 Give three costs associated with running out of stock. *(3)*
8 What is meant by 'just-in-time' stock control? *(4)*
9 Explain the meaning of the phrase in the text that: 'The purchaser's reputation is placed in the hands of the external supplier.' *(3)*
10 Why is stock control of particular importance to a greengrocer? *(3)*

B. REVISION EXERCISES

B1 Activities
(35 marks; 40 minutes)

1 A firm sells 40,000 units a month. It receives monthly deliveries. Its maximum stock level is 50,000 and minimum (buffer) stock is 10,000. After two months (8 weeks) it decides to switch to weekly deliveries.
   a Sketch a 12-week stock control graph to illustrate this situation. Assume the firm starts the first week with 50,000 units of stock. *(10)*
   b What short-term problems might the firm face in switching to weekly deliveries? *(6)*
   c Consider the long-term benefits that may result from the change. *(9)*
2 Sketch a graph to show the impact upon stock levels of a downturn in demand for a product for which a company has a non-cancellable fixed order from its suppliers. Fully label the graph to explain *what* happens *when*. *(10)*

B2 Data Response
Ann Brennan established a bakery in Wigan in the early 1980s. Although the firm is profitable, Ann is considering the introduction of modern techniques to help the company develop. In particular she wishes to introduce information technology to improve communications between her five shops and the central bakery and to help her manage her stock of raw materials more effectively.

Stocks of raw materials at the business are currently purchased in response to usage. For example, the bakery uses on average 500 kilos of flour per week. The most Ann wishes to hold at any time is 2,000 kilos. She would be worried if the stock fell below 500 kilos. An order takes one week to arrive, so Ann always re-orders when her stock falls to 1,000 kilos.

Questions *(30 marks; 35 minutes)*
1 What is meant by the terms:
   a re-order level
   b buffer stock
   c lead time? *(6)*
2 a Draw a stock control graph for flour at Brennan's Bakery over a six-week period. *(6)*
   b Draw a second graph showing the situation if twice the normal amount of flour were used in the fourth week. *(6)*
3 How might information technology be used to improve communication between Ann's shops and between the bakery and its suppliers? *(6)*
4 Assess the effect of a 'stock-out' on Brennan's Bakery. *(6)*

B3 Case Study
A recent survey by accountancy firm KPMG painted a gloomy picture for British car component suppliers. Car manufacturers were dissatisfied with the service they were receiving. Their main concerns were:

Concern	% of Manufacturers Reporting Concern
Cost	100
Quality	68
On-time delivery	60

The report found that many suppliers had only survived by having historical relationships with manufacturers and by advantageous exchange rates rather than by adapting to new global markets.

However, the exchange rate is now much less favourable, and improvements in transport mean having local suppliers is less important than it once was. If component suppliers are to survive, they must quickly reassess and respond to the needs of their customers.

Source: West Midlands Automotive Supply Chain Development Study, KPMG

56.10 Workbook

Questions *(30 marks; 35 minutes)*

1 What is meant by historical relationships in this context? *(3)*
2 What is meant by an 'advantageous exchange rate'? *(4)*
3 Why might some firms be especially worried about 'on-time delivery'? *(5)*
4 Assess the impact external factors might have on suppliers. *(8)*
5 'Suppliers should consider themselves part of the firms they supply.' Evaluate this statement. *(10)*

B4 Case Study

After many years working for Toy Town, the well known chain of toy shops, Moira Gradwell had recently been appointed manager of the company's distribution system. Most of the company's toys were imported, either from the United States or the Far East.

One particular problem facing all toy retailers is the 'must-have' toy. It seems that almost every year one toy grabs the imagination of children across the country, demand soars and toy shop shelves quickly empty. New stock can take months to arrive, leaving children, parents and retailers all very frustrated. Recent examples of this have been Harry Potter Lego, Thunderbird Tracy Islands and Yo-yos.

Moira's key task is to ensure that Toy Town isn't caught out by the next craze.

Questions *(25 marks; 30 minutes)*

1 Normally, stock patterns for Toy Town are fairly regular, as shown in Figure 56.5.
From this chart, what is:
  a the normal re-order quantity *(2)*
  b the normal re-order level *(2)*
  c the normal time for an order to arrive *(2)*
  d the firm's minimum stock level *(2)*
  e the firm's maximum stock level? *(2)*
2 Sketch a chart to show what would happen if a toy suddenly became a 'craze'. *(5)*
3 Assess the steps Moira could take to ensure Toy Town doesn't face a 'stock-out' of the latest craze. *(10)*

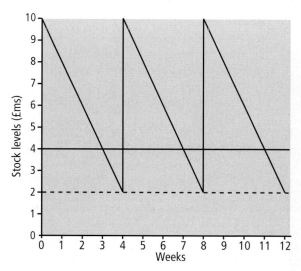

C. ESSAY QUESTIONS

1 'The use of information technology makes stock control an automatic function, requiring little input from human beings.' Assess this statement.
2 Evaluate whether a medium-sized retailer such as Next would be wise to move to just-in-time stock control.
3 Assess the view that with today's information technology, no firm ought to experience stock control problems.

UNIT 56 I STOCK CONTROL

INDUSTRIAL AND INTERNATIONAL LOCATION

DEFINITION

'Industrial location' is the geographic positioning of an operation in relation to its customers, resources and any other organisations it deals with.

'Location' is the general area selected for a particular site. Its choice is likely to involve a detailed process of analysing alternatives using business techniques such as break-even analysis and investment appraisal.

57.1 Making the location decision: business-based methods

Choice of location is one of the most important long-term decisions managers face. It is likely to be the single largest expenditure in establishing the business. In addition it is a decision which is costly to reverse once made.

The choice of location affects the costs of producing the organisation's goods or services, and also the revenue received from selling them. For example, lower costs may be achieved by a careful analysis of the transport implications of alternative sites. While higher revenues may be possible as a result of positioning closer to the customer. This is especially true of service businesses such as banks. The improved product offering due to the good location may add sufficient value to enable the firm to charge higher prices.

Buying and developing a site from which to operate is a form of investment, in the same way as purchasing any fixed asset. The decision may be more expensive and more complex, but the basic analytical tools used to assess the choices remain the same.

Two business techniques suitable for making the location decision are *break-even analysis* and *investment appraisal*. In both cases the potential revenues and costs associated with every site must be estimated.

Using break-even analysis requires identifying and estimating the fixed and variable costs associated with each potential site. These can be compared with the possible revenues. This will allow the calculation of how many units of output must be produced at each site to break even. And also to estimate the likely profit at each site, given the forecast revenues.

Investment appraisal techniques require consideration of the inflow and outflow of cash over time. Discounted cash flow calculations can be undertaken in order to estimate the net present value of the money flows associated with each site. The location yielding the greatest net return in present day money terms represents the optimum site. Though non-financial factors should also be considered.

57.2 Making the location decision: fixed costs associated with a location

Whether using break-even or investment appraisal analysis, the starting point would be a prediction of revenues and costs at different sites.

The **fixed costs** associated with a location are the 'lump sum' payments which will change with each different site, but which do not vary with the level of output produced once the operation is established at a particular place.

When selecting a location an organisation will consider the likely profitability of each site. This will come about through a combination of how high are the forecast revenues and how low are the expected fixed and **variable costs**. The fixed costs are determined by:

Site cost: The cost of land will vary across the different regions of the country. For example, a site in the City of London 'square mile' will cost many times more than one in the north of England. Rents per square foot might be £100 in the best locations but only £6 in the worst. However, the short-term gain which low land prices represent must be set against the long-term sales potential of a prime site.

Alongside the cost of land must be set the interest charges on loans taken out to finance the purchase and the cost of installing services such as water or electricity.

Availability and cost of management and other salaried staff: Management and other salaried staff represent a substantial fixed cost associated with location. Salaries may have to be higher in some areas of the country in order to attract and retain appropriate candidates for managerial positions. For example, the high cost of housing in the south-east of England makes it necessary to offer higher salaries. Where candidates for managerial positions are not available locally, the organisation will face the expense of training and developing individuals. This cost may exceed the high salaries which must be paid in other areas of the country where qualified managers are more widely available.

Regional incentives: The cost of establishing operations in a specific area may be reduced by local authority or central government grants. These payments are sums of money intended to induce firms to consider locating in a specific area in order to create new jobs and help reduce otherwise high levels of unemployment. They are unlikely to vary with output and so represent a means of reducing the fixed costs associated with a specific location.

Some parts of the UK suffering from unusually depressed economic conditions are identified as development areas by the Government. Selective regional assistance is offered to firms who choose to set up operations in these locations. The European Union is also increasingly providing financial assistance to those organisations willing to establish themselves in the poorest areas of its member countries.

57.3 Making the location decision: variable costs associated with a location

The average variable costs associated with a location are the payments made per unit of output produced. As production increases, total variable costs increase in proportion. The choice of location may influence the cost of producing each unit. The same amount of raw material may be more expensive in one location than another. With improvements in transport and communication, this factor is of less importance within Britain than it used to be. It is very significant internationally, though.

Distance to markets and the cost of reaching them: In the process of manufacture some products gain weight. These are said to be 'bulk increasing'. The final output is heavier or bulkier than the resources used in production. Examples include soft drinks, potato crisps and bread. It is sensible to locate the manufacture of these items close to the marketplace. This will minimise transport costs. In some industries moving the final product is impossible. These must locate at the market. For example, services such as shops, health care, or restaurants.

Locating a facility close to the final product market not only helps to minimise transport costs, it also maximises the potential for providing a high standard of customer service. For example, just-in-time delivery is only a realistic option if the distances which goods must be moved are relatively short. Location close to the market allows the business to develop a quick response to demand changes.

The cost of raw material sources and the distance they must be transported: In the process of manufacture some products lose weight. These are said to be 'bulk reducing'. The final output is lighter than the resources used in production. It is sensible to locate the manufacturer

---

BAILEY'S (NORTHERN) IRISH CREAM

In September 2002 Diageo plc, the drinks multinational, announced a £41 million investment in a state-of-the-art production plant for Bailey's Irish Cream Liqueur in Mallusk, Northern Ireland. It is part of Diageo's strategy for meeting its objective of doubling sales of Bailey's by 2005.

The Northern Ireland site complements the existing site in the Republic of Ireland. The data below helps to show why Mallusk was chosen. Diageo's managing director also highlighted that 'we will be recruiting highly motivated and flexible individuals with a relatively high technical skills base'. The new plant becomes operational in July 2003 and starts with a workforce of 50, which should build up to 93 members within 2 years.

One other contributory factor in the choice of Northern Ireland was government regional assistance worth £2,235 million towards the cost of the investment. This is expected to be recouped quite quickly due to the indirect benefits to local supply and service businesses.

	REPUBLIC OF IRELAND	NORTHERN IRELAND	GERMANY	US
Office rents (Capital city) per square foot	$52.74	$20.90	$43.36	$63.22
Index of manufacturing wage costs (US = 100)	77	68	116	100
Rate for 3 minute peak telephone call to France	0.83p	0.21p	0.27p	0.45p

of these items close to the source of raw materials, to minimise transport costs. For example, food processing plants are usually sited in farming areas.

Figure 57.1 Minimising the variable costs of transport

INDUSTRY CLUSTERING: CAR MANUFACTURE

The Japanese company Aisin Seiki, which is the world's fourth largest car parts producer, recently announced its decision to build a £5 million facility in Birmingham. This plant is the firm's first in Europe and will supply Toyota, Renault, Volvo and Nissan with oil and water pumps, generating £16 million pounds turnover each year.

Toyota is said to have been instrumental in this location decision. The largest Japanese car maker owns a 22% interest in Aisin Seiki and was keen to encourage the business to set up close to its own plant which is situated at Burnaston, near Derby.

A spokesman for Aisin Seiki confirmed that 'the West Midlands was chosen on account of its proximity to existing and potential customers, the ease of access into Europe from the region and its obvious qualities as a prime location for automotive suppliers'.

Source: Adapted from *The Financial Times*

The availability and cost of appropriately skilled labour: Employees paid on piece rate represent a variable cost of selecting a specific location. Wage rates may fluctuate between different regions depending on supply and demand in local labour markets. This issue is particularly important when comparing locations in different countries. It explains Nike's decision to manufacture trainers in China, Vietnam and Indonesia.

Firms seek locations where the local labour force has a good balance of skill, wage rate and attitude to work. The level of absenteeism and labour turnover in an area may be taken into account because of their implications for human resource costs. Finally, employers may be put off if a region has a history of poor industrial relations. This may suggest an unwillingness to adopt flexible work practices with the result that productivity improvements could be hard to achieve.

57.4 Making the location decision: potential revenue associated with a location

The potential revenue associated with a location reflects two variables:

- The extent to which a given site adds value to each unit of output, allowing an increase in selling price. In order to achieve this the area must differentiate the product from that of competitors in a manner which is attractive to the customer and for which they are willing to pay. For example, 'made in Devon' adds value to dairy products; 'made in Germany' is a valuable label for cars and other engineering products.
- Certain locations offer the opportunity to sell a greater quantity of output, such as London's Oxford Street.

Convenience for customers: If a business can offer its customers greater convenience than its competitors because of its location, then this may allow it to charge higher prices. A manufacturer may locate close to a major customer in order to communicate closely with them, so that their product needs can be precisely met. In retailing it explains why corner shops can survive despite higher prices than supermarkets. Location in a city or a shopping centre is convenient for those attracted by the wide range of shops and services on offer. Rents can be very high, but fully justified by the high sales turnover.

Suitability of land and climate: The geology and climate (humidity, temperature, atmospheric conditions) of a location can have a major impact on the quality an organisation can provide. Caribbean holiday resorts are able to charge high prices because of the hot weather and sandy beaches they offer tourists. French wine growers are able to use the climate and soil conditions of their country to command premium prices.

Image of the location: Certain locations are associated with a specific product or service and as a result an organisation which sets up within them can charge higher prices. For example, a doctor who has a surgery on Harley Street, or a bank with offices in the City of London.

The local economic and business climate: If a business is dependent on a local market then local economic conditions are important. A shop located in a town where a major industry closes will face a significant decline in its takings. Whereas location in a booming region such as the Thames Valley may allow the firm to increase its prices.

57.5 Making the location decision: qualitative considerations

A decision making technique such as investment appraisal must always be set in the context of non-financial, qualitative information. Factors of this type will have an important part to play in a location decision. Indeed, because it can be hard to forecast cost and revenue data with certainty, qualitative considerations can be the key ones.

Room for further expansion: When making a location decision firms should consider possible future developments, such as market growth. However desirable it might be to acquire additional land for future development, the extra fixed costs may not be affordable.

Safety requirements: Some production processes may create additional dangers for the local community. For example the operation of nuclear power stations. As a result it is desirable to select a remote location where these impacts can be minimised.

Environmental restrictions may also be important when selecting a site. They may prohibit the choice of a particular location completely. Local regulations of this kind may create additional fixed costs, such as the provision of equipment to reduce pollution.

Quality of life: Research shows that directors make location decisions on a mixture of financial and non-financial criteria. If they are going to work at the site in question, they cannot fail to consider the simple question – would I like to live there? The quality of local housing, schools, shops, sports clubs and transport system may all be influential.

Local infrastructure: The transport system in an area, such as air, road, rail, water and pipeline links, will influence the choice of location. For example, if a large proportion of output is exported, an appropriate site would be near a port or airport. However, this depends on the type of product and the cost, convenience and suitability of the different modes of transport.

57.6 Making the location decision: international location

MULTINATIONAL LOCATION STRATEGIES

A **multinational organisation** is a firm with a number of manufacturing or assembly plants spread around the world. Key decisions need to be made about the location of production facilities in order to balance cost minimisation with access to a wide range of national markets. Trading across international boundaries introduces a series of new location issues:

Location overseas to avoid trade barriers: It is still common for governments to 'protect' their domestic industries by erecting trade barriers to limit imports of foreign products. These may take the form of tariffs, quotas or non-tariff barriers. Multinational companies may select a particular location in order to avoid these restrictions. This is particularly true of trading blocks like the European Union. Within the Union, there are no import taxes or barriers. But outsiders have to pay a tax of at least 10%, and may have their access restricted. In this way the decision to locate in, for example, the UK gives a firm free access to the whole of the European Union. This has been important in encouraging investment in the UK by Japanese companies such as Nissan and Toyota.

Impact of exchange rate fluctuations: As a country's exchange rate changes in value, the competitiveness of a business located within its borders is influenced. For example, a rising pound will make UK exports more expensive, reducing their attractiveness to overseas consumers.

UNILEVER WARNS ON EURO

Recently the chairman of Unilever, Britain's biggest consumer business, warned that government dithering over the Euro would 'profoundly affect business decisions'. As a true multinational, with business throughout Europe, Unilever wants the certainty that the Euro brings to forecasts of revenues and costs. He argues that if it did not join 'Britain would float away from being a central part of Europe, which is its major market, and lose influence, investment, jobs and economic growth'.

These comments came only a few weeks after Peugeot Citroen said it would take into account British non-membership of the Euro when deciding whether to invest £100 million in its Coventry factory.

Business IN

A multinational company making a location decision must anticipate the long-term trend in currency movements and estimate the impact of these on profit margins. Firms such as Britain's TI Group carefully locate a number of production facilities in different countries. This acts as a form of protection against a large swing in a single currency, thus reducing their financial risk. For businesses operating in continental Europe, the single currency (the Euro) provides 100% protection against exchange rate changes. This is why many people worry about the risks to Britain of staying out of the Eurozone.

Political stability: The external environment within which a business operates changes constantly. The key issue is the degree of change. It is therefore sensible to locate in countries where shifts in government regulation of industry are gradual so that forward planning can be undertaken. This problem is highlighted when a country is so unstable that peace can not be relied upon. In some areas of the world this issue can be dominant in making a location decision.

Language barriers: Fundamental to business success is good communications. There are always barriers to communication, even if all staff speak the same language. Therefore multinational firms can be influenced by language in their choice of location. This has been a great help to Britain in recent years, as English is the most common second language in the world. So firms looking for a European Union location often choose Britain.

ISSUES FOR **analysis**

When considering an organisation's existing location, ask the question: Would the benefits of moving from this site exceed the costs? Many firms establish themselves in an area by accident. For example, the original owner happened to live there. Try to identify those operations which are suffering from 'industrial inertia'. This means their location is no longer the best available for the business, but the inconvenience of moving deters management from taking appropriate action. It often results from changes in the pattern of demand, or cost structure, to which managers fail to respond.

Selecting a new location demands a balance between quantitative information, such as the impact on costs and revenues, and qualitative factors, such as the provision of local housing for management. Look for situations in which this balance has not been preserved. The result may be either the domination of financial aspects, or too much concern about qualitative factors may have resulted in the selection of an unprofitable site.

A business which involves heavy capital costs, such as a chemical plant, will be dauntingly expensive to relocate. This is due to the size of investment which would be sacrificed when moving. Service businesses with high labour costs are much cheaper and easier to relocate. So there is little excuse for a manager of an unsuccessful restaurant staying in a poor location. Case study work on business location will always be strengthened by analysis of the cost structure of the business concerned.

57.7 Location

an evaluation

In the case of service businesses, location can be the difference between success or failure. It is vital that the financial implications of a location decision are estimated and analysed using an appropriate technique such as investment appraisal. New, small firms are often short of capital. Therefore they may focus too much on cost minimisation. But a cheap location can be a false economy if there are few customers nearby. Non-financial factors should influence the decision, but only if minimum financial criteria are met.

403

KEY terms

fixed costs of a location – the costs which change with each different site, but which do not vary with the level of output produced once the operation is established at a particular place.

infrastructure – the basic utilities which provide a network allowing businesses to operate within an area, such as road, rail and air links.

multinational organisation – a business which has its head office in a single country, but has operating facilities in other nations.

variable costs of a location – the choice of location may influence the cost of producing each unit of output produced. As a result, total variable costs will differ between alternative areas in which an operating facility may be placed.

A Level Exercises

A. REVISION QUESTIONS

(40 marks; 70 minutes)

1 Outline two business techniques which might be used to evaluate a potential industrial location. *(4)*

2 Identify the main fixed and variable costs associated with a potential industrial location. *(6)*

3 Explain two ways in which a location decision for a service business might differ from a decision about where to site a manufacturing firm. *(6)*

4 What factors might cause the revenue earned by a business to fluctuate between different potential industrial locations? *(4)*

5 Why might a computer manufacturing business choose to locate in 'Silicon Glen' – the region in Scotland where many other computer manufacturers are established already? *(4)*

6 To what extent should the selection of an industrial location depend upon non-numerate considerations? *(5)*

7 Indicate the main factors an organisation will consider when deciding in which country to place a new factory. *(5)*

8 Consider why a producer of chilled, ready-to-eat lasagnes might decide to relocate from Birmingham to Northern France. *(6)*

B. REVISION EXERCISES

B1 Data Response

In 1998 Nissan's Sunderland plant was judged Europe's most productive by the Economist Intelligence Unit for the second year running. It takes less than 18 hours to turn sheet metal into a finished vehicle.

Greenfield location is the key advantage enjoyed by Nissan and fellow Japanese car makers Toyota and Honda at their UK plants, says Professor Garel Rhys of Cardiff Business School. Such a site gave Nissan a clean sheet in terms of physical infrastructure, supplier relationships and working methods, as well as in recruitment of motivated, youthful personnel with no preconceptions about making cars.

By the standards of the north-east, Nissan employees are paid well; including shift allowance, a production worker averages £19,215 and supervisors £29,136. 'People in this area treasure a job,' says Craig Douglas, a production supervisor, 'The attitude is, stick in and keep it.'

Since its construction in 1984, £1.5 billion has been spent on the site, creating a highly automated plant laid out for maximum efficiency. Just-in-time deliveries arrive direct from component suppliers' plants to Nissan's shop-floor. Whereas the majority of components were imported from Japan in 1984, these days the great majority come from factories in the north-east or elsewhere in Britain.

The Nissan plant proved so successful that, in February 1999, the company announced 800 new jobs to add to the 4,500 employed in Sunderland already.

Source: *The Financial Times*, 24/11/98 and 4/2/99

Questions *(30 marks; 35 minutes)*

1 a Explain the meaning of the term 'greenfield site'. *(3)*

 b What might be the disadvantages of constructing a factory on a greenfield site? *(6)*

 c Despite these disadvantages, analyse why the Sunderland greenfield site proved so successful for Nissan? *(9)*

2 Discuss the pros and cons to the local community of Nissan's establishment in the north-east. *(12)*

B2 Case Study

A Location Decision: Savoury Spreads

Savoury Spreads had developed a new line of food dips which were proving immensely successful. So much so that the firm's management team was taken by surprise and had no strategic plan to cope with expansion. Sales in the first three months exceeded targets set by 43%. The main factory in Derby worked at full capacity in an effort to meet the growing number of orders.

Even more encouraging was the enquiry from a major supermarket chain about the possibility of Savoury Spreads producing a series of own-brand dips for the retailer. An emergency board meeting was held and the decision was made to build a second factory in order to allow the opportunity for growth to be taken as quickly as possible. Three sites were identified as potential locations and the firm's project director Martin Deepdale was asked to gather appropriate data and assess their relative merits.

Four weeks later Martin sat in his hotel room. For the last month he had been gathering information about the potential locations the Savoury Spreads board had asked him to consider. All three areas had suitable sites available and not surprisingly representatives from each of the local councils had been anxious to convince him of the merits of their own town. He was now in a position to complete the first draft of his report to the board. He condensed the key pieces of data onto a single sheet of A4 paper and sat down with his calculator.

Site cost
Estimated total rent and rates cost (cost per annum):

Altrincham	£222,000
Barnsley	£205,000
Chesterfield	£195,000

Raw material cost
The following are estimated unit costs at each location:

Altrincham	£0.49
Barnsley	£0.43
Chesterfield	£0.55

Transport cost
The following are estimated unit costs at each location:

	Material Delivery	Final Product Delivery
Altrincham	£0.15	£0.12
Barnsley	£0.18	£0.11
Chesterfield	£0.13	£0.17

Employee cost
The following are estimated unit costs in each area based on local piece work rates

Altrincham	£0.05
Barnsley	£0.06
Chesterfield	£0.04

The cost of those staff paid by salary is more difficult to estimate, but the approximate total at the Barnsley location will be £325,000, Altringham is likely to prove 6% more expensive, while Chesterfield might be as much as 4% cheaper.

Martin knew that dips carrying the Savoury Spreads brand name sold for £1.25 and that the anticipated output at the new factory would be 1,400,000 units in the first year. If the additional facility was used exclusively for the firm's own products it would allow the Derby plant to switch a portion of its capacity to fulfil the supermarket order. Having considered the data in front of him he plugged in his laptop computer and began to type up the report.

Questions *(50 marks; 70 minutes)*
1 Using the data at Martin's disposal, identify the fixed and variable costs associated with each site. *(4)*
2 Calculate the annual break-even quantity of dips for each of the three locations and recommend a choice to the Savoury Spreads board based on this analysis. *(13)*
3 Advise the management of Savoury Spreads about the extent to which you would regard this form of location analysis as reliable. *(10)*
4 Outline the further information about each location you would like to have at your disposal before making a final choice of site. *(8)*
5 Prepare Martin's draft report for the Savoury Spreads board based on the evidence available about each location. *(15)*

C. ESSAY QUESTIONS

1 Discuss the location factors most likely to provide a chocolate manufacturer with a competitive advantage.
2 Compare and contrast the key factors in siting a Burger King with the main criteria for locating a car factory.
3 To what extent could it be said that location decisions are especially important for firms operating on a just-in-time basis?

APPLICATIONS OF IT

DEFINITION

Information technology means the computer hardware and software used to handle, analyse and communicate business data. It is becoming common to refer to it as ICT: information and communications technology.

58.1 Introduction

Information technology (IT) applications in business are various and rapidly changing. Often, though, the changes are to processing speed and business jargon. The essential tasks remain the same. In recent years, the most important business IT innovation has been the emergence of the Internet. This will be covered relatively briefly, because the pace of change means that magazine articles will provide a more up-to-date understanding of the Internet's business potential.

To most managers, the key business applications are spreadsheets and databases. Both provide the opportunity to make significant improvements to the management of business information. Both have

implications for financial, marketing and personnel management.

58.2 Spreadsheets

Although the use of spreadsheets is widespread throughout firms, the major users are the finance and marketing departments.

FINANCE

The heart of modern financial management is the budget. Devised by line managers perhaps months before the start of a financial year, it is the driving force behind many business decisions. It sets out forecast revenues and costs, usually broken down in minute detail. Each month's actual performance is then recorded and compared with the budgeted figure to show any variances. This is the most widespread use of spreadsheets in business.

The process and importance of budgeting is covered in detail in Unit 27.

MARKETING

Although marketing management is assumed to be a creative job, much of the time is spent with figures. Are sales of Wotsits rising in the North-East? Or is it a statistical blip? A freakishly good couple of months? If they are really rising, why and what can we learn from this success? The ability to break down sales figures and interpret the findings is an important one.

Marketing managers need to be fully aware of market trends, competitors' sales, market segmentation, distribution figures and sales by brand, by region and by type of outlet. For all these, spreadsheets are invaluable for their ability to store, calculate and graph information.

58.3 Databases

A database is a store of information which can be rearranged and sorted in numerous ways. For example, if you had a database of all your friends, classmates and work colleagues, you might like to:

- sort them by birthday, so that you never missed the chance of a party invitation

406

FRIENDS REUNITED

After middle class, middle-aged people have stopped talking about house prices, they start on the subject of *Friends Reunited*. This website was inspired by Julie Pankhurst, who wanted to know how many of her old schoolfriends were now mums. Husband Steve and a friend Jason Porter produced a site, inviting people to register where they went to school and what they have done since. Anyone wanting to contact old friends then pays £5 for their email addresses.

Started in a North London bedroom in 2000, by 2003 *Friends Reunited* had more than 6 million people registered, making it one of Britain's biggest websites – with never a penny spent on publicity. With 15 people now employed in the business, the founders decided it had become too big for them to manage effectively, and they started looking around for a buyer. In January 2003 they were looking at offers valued at over £30 million. This represents a huge illustration of the potential of the internet, a great example of the power of word-of-mouth, and not a bad 3 years' work.

Adapted from the *Guardian*

Business IN

- sort them by activity, so that you could rustle up a football or hockey team when needed
- sort them by location, to give you a mailing list for organising a school reunion.

For businesses, the ability to store information on thousands, perhaps millions of customers is invaluable. In order to maximise the speed and flexibility of a database, every type of information needs to be held in a different 'field'. Field 1 may be the surname, Field 3 the address, Field 7 the age and so on. This enables the data to be sorted or picked out in different ways. If you have a new product aiming at over-40s, those aged 40 and over can be picked out and a mailing list produced in seconds.

To obtain this data, businesses use various approaches:

- asking customers to fill in their name and address when purchasing goods
- recording the information on product warranty cards
- supplying 'loyalty' cards such as Tesco's Clubcard
- buying databases from companies which specialise in gathering data.

After starting to build a database, firms are legally required to register their database with the Data Protection Registrar. The 1984 Data Protection Act gives people the right to see their personal file, for example one held by a bank on a customer's credit-worthiness.

FINANCIAL MANAGEMENT AND THE USE OF DATABASES

Successful day-to-day financial management is not about profit and loss accounts or balance sheets. The key is careful control of working capital. This boils down to two issues: stock control and credit control. Both affect not only the company's cash position, but also the customer. Customers want the freshest possible goods and the highest possible availability. This requires highly efficient stock control.

Stock control: Modern stock control systems are based upon laser scanning of bar-coded information. This ensures the computer knows the exact quantity of each product/size/colour that has come into the stockroom. In retail outlets, a laser scanning till is then used to record exactly what has been sold. This allows the store's computer to keep up-to-date records of current stocks of every item. This data can enable a buyer to decide how much extra to order, or an electronic link with the supplier can re-order automatically (see section on EDI below).

All this information will be held in the form of a database. This makes it easy for the firm to carry out an aged stock analysis. The computer provides a printout showing the stock in order of age. The next table shows a list of stock in a clothes shop, with the oldest first. It enables the manager to make informed decisions about what to do now and in the future. In this case:

- big price reductions seem called for on the first five items – they have been around too long
- there should be fewer orders in future for size 8 dresses.

GARMENT	RECEIVED (DAYS AGO)	NO. RECEIVED	IN STOCK TODAY
Green Fabrice dress, size 8	285	2	1
Blue Channelle dress, size 14	241	1	1
Red Channelle dress, size 8	241	2	2
Red Grigio jacket, size 10	235	4	2
Black Grigio dress, size 8	235	3	2
Black Fabrice dress, size 12	202	2	1
Blue Florentine suit, size 8	197	1	1

IT STRATEGY

Business

IN

In 2002 Unilever started an initiative called Supplier Managed Inventory. This provides selected suppliers with access to Unilever's computerised sales and stock information. The supplier can see when new supplies are needed and make sure they arrive on time. This saves Unilever from placing orders at all! In effect, the supplier acts when the reorder level has been reached, and delivers just in time before stock runs out. By 2004 the company expects 200 strategic suppliers to be working on this system, saving Unilever over £40 million in reduced staffing and administration costs. The IT link is achieved over the Internet, and therefore costs very little to set up.

Credit control: Even firms with tight stock control can be lax about controlling customer credit. The reason is simple. Every call to a customer about paying a bill is a potential argument and therefore loss of future business. Yet if a firm becomes known to be a soft touch, it may suffer ever-worsening payment delays. This will increase its debtors total at the cost of its cash balances.

As in the case of stock control, good database management can be a great help. The starting point is aged debtors analysis. This puts customer credit periods in order of age. It can also show you the recent payment record of each customer. This provides not only a tool for controlling credit, but also an aid to decision making if your firm needs to cut its debtors total. Instead of sending pleading or threatening letters to all your customers (risking loss of goodwill), you can focus solely upon persistent late payers.

The table below shows an aged debtors analysis. It can be used to send out letters automatically. A polite reminder on day 50 that payment is due in 10 days' time; a polite note on day 65 that payment is overdue; a stiff reminder on day 80 … and so on until threats of legal action. Individual initiatives can be taken as well. In this case the company may refuse to accept more orders from VW Harvey and Italian Clothing. Jesmond Ltd and Staton Couture look as though they need a quick, friendly phone call. These regular payers may just have made an administrative error.

MARKETING AND DATABASE MANAGEMENT

Mailing lists have existed for decades. American Express, Readers Digest and many others have built their business through well-targeted direct ('junk') mail. They achieved this through the use of large, expensive mainframe computers. Nowadays even the smallest firm can afford a computer and some database software. Customers can be sorted into regular, light and occasional users, and be sent an appropriate mailshot. Each letter can be personalised ('Dear Miss Hendrick') and therefore better suited to building a relationship with the customer. Or telephone sales staff can make direct contact to check on customer satisfaction and enquire whether any extra services are required.

The pursuit of an up-to-date, detailed database has reached its high point with supermarket loyalty cards. A Clubcard application form requires the customer to state details such as address, number of children, job and income. These details can be related to their lifestyle by recording what they buy and how much they spend. If Tesco then wants to promote wine costing more than £5 per bottle, it can invite to an in-store tasting all those who have spent over £4 on a bottle of wine over the past six months. Having an accurate

database minimises the waste and therefore the cost of such mailings. This makes them a more attractive proposition compared with other advertising media.

DATABASES AND PERSONNEL MANAGEMENT

The most important computer application in this area has long been payroll management. This calculates each employee's monthly basic pay, bonus, tax, national insurance and pension contributions. A more sophisticated approach is to link this with a job costing and budgeting programme from which the bonuses can be calculated.

There are also several performance indicators which personnel managers are likely to consider. These include labour turnover, absenteeism, quality defects and lateness. All can and should be analysed by department and over time, to identify any trends and take any necessary action.

THE JOBS INTRANET

The giant multinational Unilever employs over 200,000 people worldwide. One of the reasons people like working for such a giant is the career prospects. Every day there are promotion opportunities somewhere in the world. But how can an individual employee find out about them?

In January 2002 Unilever launched a new Open Jobs Posting intranet website. This advertises every management job and provides a search option so that staff can refine what they are looking for (R&D jobs, perhaps, or accounting ones). Within 3 months the site was receiving 35,000 hits per week. One successful user, Nick Allen, used it to apply for and achieve the post of chief financial officer for Unilever corporate ventures. He praises the site for enabling you to 'take responsibility for your own career'.

Aged debtors analysis

CUSTOMER	INVOICE TOTAL	ORDER NUMBER	AGE OF DEBT	PREVIOUS PAYMENT TIMES	
VW Harvey & Sons	£4,240.00	1438	143 days	128 days	104 days
Italian Clothing Ltd	£3,512.50	1442	127 days	145 days	130 days
J Jesmond Ltd	£537.80	1443	126 days	68 days	71 days
Italian Clothing Ltd	£6,342.25	1453	115 days	145 days	130 days
Kevin Fashions	£2,780.00	1459	104 days	86 days	105 days
Staton Couture plc	£8,489.90	1463	98 days	59 days	63 days
Average	£3,450.43		64 days	63 days	62.5 days

Other IT applications

ELECTRONIC DATA INTERCHANGE (EDI)

EDI is a permanent link between computers on different sites, enabling specified types of data to be exchanged. By establishing an EDI link firms can ensure that the latest information is available instantly to other branches of their business, or even to other businesses. For example, the Heinz link with Tesco enables Heinz to see how sales of soups are going this week. If chicken soup sales have pushed ahead 20% (perhaps because they were featured on a TV programme), production increases can be planned even before the Tesco head office phones through with a large order. This makes a just-in-time operation far more feasible.

Of course, Tesco does not want Heinz to have access to all its computer files, so the EDI link only covers specified data. Heinz might allow Tesco access to its stock levels and production plans in exchange for Tesco's daily sales data. This cooperation can help ensure that shelves are rarely empty.

Up until 2001 EDI was only affordable between large companies. Over 90% of large companies depended on it, but very few small firms. Then service providers started to provide low-cost Internet-based EDI. This gave smaller traders the opportunity to benefit from instant, two-way communications with suppliers or customers. Sainsbury's, for example, set up JSnet for its smaller suppliers.

ELECTRONIC POINT OF SALE (EPOS)

EPOS equipment is at the heart of data collection by retailers. Laser scanning systems gather data from bar codes which allows the computer to record exactly what has been bought and at what price. This forms the basis of the stock control system and also the recording of sales revenues. As with other aspects of IT, rapid falls in the cost of EPOS systems makes them increasingly affordable by small shops. Nowadays some supermarkets allow customers to scan their

Shop-and-go at Safeway: the Handiscan (© Safeway)

shopping for themselves. This 'shop and go' self-scanning system is based on a portable EPOS, and will work if shoppers prove trustworthy.

COMPUTER-AIDED DESIGN (CAD)

In most firms today, design means computer-aided design. Drawings are produced on screen, not by hand. The attractions are simple:

- CAD drawings can be altered without needing to start again
- CAD drawings can be stored on computer and changed easily to meet new customer specifications
- CAD software can show models in 3D and rotate them, so that the designer can look at every view and angle
- if linked with manufacturing resource planning software (MRP II), the design can automatically be fed in to form the basis of cost estimates and the ordering of supplies.

An important spin-off from the widespread use of CAD is that firms are better able to make design changes quickly and cheaply. That makes it more possible to produce to order, either by the job or in batches. This, in turn, helps firms achieve just-in-time production. Designing exactly what the customer wants and delivering it when it is wanted is the essence of JIT manufacture.

COMPUTER-AIDED MANUFACTURE (CAM)

In all but the smallest firms, it is hard to imagine any business that does not employ some computing power within its manufacturing process. CAM, though, has a more specific meaning. It is integrated software capable of supplying instructions to complete a production task through computer-managed machines. It does not imply total automation (doing away with production workers altogether) but it does suggest that a substantial proportion of the process is computer controlled.

KINGCUP MUSHROOMS, EDI AND THE WEB

Business **IN**

In 1998 a firm with only 30 employees became a pioneer of using EDI though the Internet. Kingcup Mushrooms installed a Windows PC and a Web browser to trade electronically with Tesco. The supermarket chain can place its orders and Kingcup can supply invoices through the Internet. Kingcup is also able to see Tesco's stock levels and to gauge instantly the impact of promotions.

If linked with CAD, a CAD/CAM production site should be quick, efficient and flexible. It should allow for what is known as flexible specialisation. This provides firms with the ability to meet precise customer requirements within a specialised area of production. For instance, a small bus company in Wales may want five coaches with seating for 5–11-year-old children. A good CAD/CAM system should be able to meet this customer request without difficulty.

MANUFACTURING RESOURCE PLANNING (MRP II)

MRP II is a sophisticated computer software package that models an entire production process. The model includes labour time and skills, requirements for materials and components, and it matches the need for machine time with the available capacity. It therefore enables managers to find out quickly whether an order can be fulfilled in the time available. And will help in the management and control of the order in practice.

Good managers will use their MRP II software to devise contingency plans to cover emergencies, and can use it to move successfully to just-in-time production control. As the service sector becomes ever more important, there is a trend to rename MRP II as ERP – enterprise resource planning.

THE INTERNET

The Internet is an electronic meeting place for ideas, information and people. It was created to spread academic information between universities. Since the creation of the World Wide Web, access to this information has been easier for ordinary computer users. The further development of the Web browser made it more possible for ordinary users to find what they wanted to know.

Although its origins are in providing information, businesses soon saw the potential for making money by accepting or placing advertisements on Web pages. From there, it was only a short step to selling goods directly over the Internet. This took off in 1995, when a method was found to take credit card payments without creating a security risk by sending a card number on the Internet.

The pace of growth in shopping on the Internet is breathtaking. In 1998, Dell Computers made headlines by announcing sales of $5 million per day via the Internet. In 2001, the daily sales figure was $50 million. When the Arcadia Group (Dorothy Perkins, Burtons, Top Shop and others) trialled online clothes shopping, critics expected failure. They argued that women enjoyed trying clothes on. In fact the trial Arcadia website enjoyed 2.7 million visitors per month – and 70% of online buyers were women.

For small firms the World Wide Web provides especially exciting possibilities. Setting up a site may cost a few thousand pounds, but that is trivial compared with the cost of establishing an overseas sales and distribution network. So exporting becomes much more affordable. This has great potential for firms offering a wide range of highly specialised goods. For example, a shop selling stamps or one selling spare parts for classic sports cars. Orders may start coming in from Tokyo or California.

ELECTRONIC MAIL (E-MAIL)

A major benefit of access to the Internet is its e-mail facility. This allows computer files to be sent instantly to whoever you want, wherever you want. The major benefit is that the exchange of letters becomes so quick and easy that letters become conversations.

- Sales executive A sends the week's orders to area manager B.
- Five minutes later A receives an e-mail query about why a regular customer's order is half the usual level.
- A replies that their biggest rival has been running a '2 for the price of 1' promotion.
- B says 'match it' … and so on.

58.5 Communications technology

Electronic data interchange and e-mail are examples of the instant communications available to modern businesses. These developments, together with the mobile phone, have enabled firms to question whether people need to work in conventional offices. Teleworking has become a possibility, either full-time or, more commonly, by staff working from home one or two days per week.

Teleworking means working at home, but with direct electronic links to the workplace. Reports completed at home are e-mailed to the office. Computer-aided designs can be sent via a direct ISDN link to the office. And so on.

The social and business philosopher Charles Handy refers to 'the empty raincoat'. He envisages companies which have an outer coat, but nothing visible inside. Many of the activities are contracted out, and most of the workforce is at home, working for the company. This is an extreme view, but as city centres become harder to get to during the rush hour, radical solutions may be needed. Already there are many management consultancies in London where staff have no office. If they want to come in to work, they phone in to book a desk for the day. This 'hot desking' cuts down on office overhead costs and discourages people from building their work lives around a comfortable private office.

Information and communications technology provides a series of tools which can be used to help businesses operate more effectively. As one of the fastest moving aspects of business it raises many issues for analysis. Among them are:

- Will electronic shopping mean shops are on the way out? The answer is no. But Internet shopping will put new competitive pressures on high streets and shopping centres. If this book could be ordered in minutes on the Internet and arrive in three days' time, would it make sense to go and look for it in a bookshop? It might not be in stock. Retailers are going to have to think very hard about whether they are offering the level of personal service to make a visit worthwhile.

- Management control – when directors discuss marketing or personnel issues, everyone has an opinion. Everyone feels they understand the implications of a request for a 30% increase in the advertising budget or a 5% pay rise. IT is different, however. Few directors understand current technologies, let alone future possibilities. This places IT managers in a strong position. Their request for an extra £500,000 of 'essential' equipment may be hard to turn down. Even though research shows that major British firms have regularly been disappointed that the promised benefits from IT developments have not happened. Firms are often driven more by fear of being left behind than confidence that investment in IT will be profitable.

- Speed of change – despite the above, some applications of IT have caused rapid changes at the workplace. Jobs in banking have been transformed by automatic ('hole-in-the-wall') cash dispensers. These have wiped out thousands of jobs for bank clerks. They have also led to the closure of hundreds of bank branches. This has cost many more jobs. These changes may be inevitable, but the speed of change put huge strains on bank staff. Managers were forced to make thousands of redundancies in an industry where job security had been particularly high. Firms need a sophisticated understanding of change management to be able to carry out such an upheaval with success.

58.6 Applications of IT
an evaluation

In the early 1990s Guinness thought change management was a technical question. When a change was needed, such as a new distribution system, it hired consultants whose main focus was to establish effective information and communications technology (ICT) links. Time after time it was disappointed by the results. Improvements only began when it realised that the key variable was not the technology but the people. Not only were results better if staff were consulted fully, but also the new systems were only successful if staff applied them with enthusiasm and confidence.

Technology is only a set of tools. It can form the basis of a major competitive advantage, as with Dell Computer's Internet sales. More often, though, the successful application of IT relies on good understanding of customer and staff needs and wants. This suggests that good management of information technology is no different from good management generally.

A Level Exercises

A. REVISION QUESTIONS
(45 marks; 70 minutes)

Read the unit, then answer:

1 How could a spreadsheet help a firm in constructing a cash flow forecast? *(3)*
2 A database could be used by an aircraft manufacturer such as Boeing to record the supplier and batch number of every part used on every aircraft. How might this information be used? *(3)*
3 State three benefits of good database management in achieving efficient stock control. *(3)*
4 Telephone surveys use a database of all the telephone numbers in Britain. A computer randomly generates and dials numbers for the interviewers. Outline one benefit and one drawback to such a system of sampling. *(4)*
5 Outline two possible benefits to the customer of the use of EDI by Kingcup Mushrooms (see In Business). *(4)*
6 Explain one benefit and one drawback to computer-aided manufacture (CAM). *(4)*
7 How significant might Internet retailing become for each of the following types of business?
    a A music shop specialising in 1960s classic pop and rock. *(2)*
    b A builders' merchant (selling bricks, cement, etc). *(2)*
    c A mail order clothing firm. *(2)*
8 1n early 1999 the American stock market was so excited about Internet companies that high share prices valued loss-making firms at billions of dollars. What factors might limit the potential of Internet retailing (e-commerce)? *(5)*
9 Read section 58.5. Outline two advantages and two drawbacks to firms of the pattern of work set out in this section. *(8)*
10 These days, information technology is sometimes called information and communications technology (ICT). From what you have read in this Unit, is that a sensible change of name? *(5)*

B. REVISION EXERCISES

B1 Data Response
The Computer-aided Puma

Car firms have long been seeking ways to reduce development times for new cars. Part of the answer, according to John Gardiner, Ford's manager for design and technology, lies in the use of computer-aided design (CAD). Ford took just 135 days to design the Puma sports car, the first car to be designed solely on a computer. It is also claimed that

CAD improves quality and safety. Indeed, computers can be used to simulate crash tests – a very expensive part of the design process. A crash test costs around £40,000, along with the cost of each prototype (£300,000). A computer crash test costs just £120 and can be completed in just 15 minutes.

Ford claims to have more computing power than any other car manufacturer – illustrated by the fact that a crash test would take 15 weeks to run on a home PC. However, CAD has some drawbacks. Many designers are still happier working with pencil and paper. A further danger, foreseen by journalist David Fox, is that faster lead times may 'lead to cars being produced as fashion items, which quickly become dated and lose their value more quickly'.

Source: The *Independent*, 14/10/97 and David Fox

Questions *(30 marks; 35 minutes)*
1 Explain the meaning of the term 'CAD'. *(2)*
2 Outline the business significance of reducing the development times for new cars. *(8)*
3 Consider the possible benefits to Ford's international competitiveness of having more computing power than any other car manufacturer. *(10)*
4 Discuss the strengths and weaknesses of the commentator's argument that CAD may 'lead to cars being produced as fashion items'. *(10)*

B2 Case Study
Aiming at the Web

It was in a Business Studies class that Jayesh and Sunil first talked about aims and objectives. Both agreed that their aim was 'to be rich'. Sunil had turned the aim into the objective of 'to make my first half million by the age of 25'. Yesterday, on his 26th birthday, Sunil had received a card from Jayesh saying: 'Made it?'

The real answer was no, but not far off. After university, Sunil used his CAD expertise to start up a business designing and selling upmarket, special occasion clothing for his local community in Tooting, South London. He tested out his designs on family and friends (on the computer screen) then downloaded the computer files to a factory in Calcutta, India. The garments could be hand-made to an excellent finish within two weeks and at very low costs per unit.

Within a year, Sunil's website was receiving orders from Southall, Leicester and even New York. Purchasers could click onto the design they wanted, choose from a range of colours and then feed in a series of precise measurements so that the clothes could be tailored to their precise specifications. Business boomed.

At first, Sunil was able to run the whole operation on his own. But after six months he needed to take on people to handle the packing and dispatch, the accounts and day-to-day e-mail conversations with the Calcutta factory. Later he recruited two designers to produce a wider range of clothing. They work from home, but have a direct EDI link with Sunil's office. Last year Sunil's business employed six people and had a turnover of just over £1 million. The profit of over £200,000 showed that even if the objective had not quite been realised, the aim certainly would.

Questions   *(60 marks; 70 minutes)*

1 Outline the key benefits Sunil has derived from information technology (IT) in establishing his business. *(12)*
2 Traditional businesses required large sums of capital to build factories and buy machinery. Sunil was able to start up with only a small investment. If this pattern becomes more widespread, what may it imply for the future of:
   a the competitiveness of markets *(8)*
   b the role of banks in business? *(8)*

3 Sunil's business almost conforms to Charles Handy's description of 'the empty raincoat', with an outer coat but little inside. What problems might this present if the business expands further? *(8)*
4 Over the coming years, Sunil anticipates a lot of competition as others copy his Internet retailing of Indian clothing. Consider the actions he might take to strengthen the market position of his own website. *(12)*
5 Discuss the importance of aims and objectives such as Sunil's in setting up a successful small business. *(12)*

C. ESSAY QUESTIONS

1 Information and communications technology (ICT) is reducing the need to meet people face to face. Discuss the implications of this for running a successful business.
2 For many years computer hardware and software has been sold on the promise that it will deliver a 'paperless office'. Yet paper sales are higher than ever. Why do you think it has proved so difficult for electronic communication to replace paper?
3 'Internet retailing will mean the death of the high street'. Discuss.

INTEGRATED OPERATIONS MANAGEMENT

59.1 Operations management – an overview

INTRODUCTION

All departments in an organisation tend to see themselves as the most important. Marketing people argue that without successful marketing even the greatest product in the world would fail. Those who work in personnel point out that without motivation, marketing and sales staff will achieve little.

Operations management can also claim a position of importance in the same way. Mercedes cars, Sony electronics and Boeing airplanes are not just well packaged. They are brilliantly conceived and developed, and superbly made. They are wonderful examples of the potential of top-class operations management.

These days there is a growing recognition of the need for productive efficiency. The globalisation of business has placed a great emphasis on the ability of firms to compete internationally. How is this done? Through the adoption of production techniques and ideas which set standards (benchmarking) and then make the best possible use of the available resources (lean production) to produce the best possible products (R&D, efficiency).

WHAT IS OPERATIONS MANAGEMENT?

Operations management is a very wide-ranging term. While the basis of operations management can be seen in the management of the production process, the phrase covers a much wider range of ideas. In particular, the term is applied equally to firms who provide a service as to those involved in production. The same sorts of questions need to be answered, such as:

- Where should the firm be located?
- How can the firm develop more innovative products and services?
- How can the firm become more efficient?

- How can the firm maintain control of its quality?
- How best can the firm control its stock?
- How best can the workforce be organised?

The management of operations ties in very closely to the management of people. The two functions will often be carried out by the same managers at the same time. Motivation of the workforce is tied up very closely with management style. This will show itself most directly through the way in which the workplace is organised and tasks are allocated.

'A' GRADE GRADE OPERATIONS MANAGEMENT

More than perhaps any other area of business, operations management is intertwined with the other areas of the syllabus. This is most obvious in the links between operations management and personnel management. A fundamental reason for altering production methods is to improve the motivation and productivity of labour. In a similar way, the design and development function of operations management must tie in closely with the results of market research and the firm's competitive position. Top grade writing will consider the broader impact of operations management rather than taking a narrow, one-dimensional view.

The implications of some of the ideas must also be considered with care. The notion of kaizen, for example, is readily accepted by most students but its wider implications are rarely considered. Continual improvement implies a high degree of uncertainty and a constant state of change. What will the effect be on a firm, its workers and managers of such uncertainty? An 'A' grade answer would be able to reconcile the contradiction between the problems caused by change and uncertainty and the benefits of a policy of kaizen.

'A' grade operations management requires a grasp of big underlying issues such as those that follow. These are areas of discussion for conclusions to answers or case studies. They represent ways of evaluating the wider significance of the concepts covered.

ISSUE 1 How important is operations management for international competitiveness?

A major reason for the growing importance of operations management is the need for firms to compete more effectively on an international stage. The start of the Euro on 1 January 2002 is the latest in a series of European developments that have forced firms such as Tesco and Kingfisher to look beyond Britain. Nor is it just a matter of looking to Europe. The 'shrinking' of the world through improvements in transport and communications have made many UK firms adopt a more international perspective.

While all areas of business need to be effective if a firm is to compete on the international stage, the foremost areas of concern revolve around the cost and quality of products. It is only by firms producing the best quality products at competitive costs that they stand a chance of winning a share of the international market. However, getting everything right internally is still not a guarantee of success. External factors such as high exchange rates can damage the competitiveness of the most efficient firms.

ISSUE 2 When does a fad become a trend?

The 'Japanisation' of UK businesses has become a widely established phenomenon in recent years. The idea of kaizen, quality circle groups and aiming for zero defects are now common in both business literature and the workplace. There are, however, detractors who feel that these ideas are either:

- a restatement of established ideas, or
- broad generalisations with little application to the real world.

They argue that these ideas are more for the benefit of business 'gurus' who can earn a good living selling books and giving lectures based on these 'new' ideas than for the benefit and development of businesses.

For evidence, they can point to many examples of businesses that have applied these ideas but shown no sign of significant improvement or have even gone into further decline.

'A' grade students realise that the newer developments in operations management are no miracle cure for businesses. There is no one solution that will raise every business to levels of international competitiveness. The real task for managers is to adapt the principles and culture to their own individual circumstances, and continue adapting them over time as those circumstances change. Good students analyse answers by weighing up the suitability of a management method to the circumstances of the company.

ISSUE 3 Operations management in the service sector

It is sometimes easy to think of operations management purely in terms of manufacturing firms. Clearly, though, the same issues apply to the service sector. If operations management is thought of as 'what, where, when and how' to produce, then service producers should have to answer these questions in the same way.

There will, of course, be some key differences. Service providers will have much more contact with the firm's final customers while goods manufacturers will have much more distant relations. In addition, services will often be very labour intensive while a lot of manufacturing firms today are highly automated. Perhaps the most important difference of all is in location. For services such as retailing, location is central to the marketing strategy of the business. For manufacturers, location is more likely to be a relatively minor factor.

A final difference will lie in the issue of stocks. Manufacturing firms will need to manage stocks of raw materials, work in progress and finished goods, even if they are using a just-in-time system that minimises the quantities of each held. Many service businesses, however, will have very little in the way of stocks. A firm of solicitors, for example, may keep a stock of stationery, but the output of the firm, its legal advice and work, will not appear as any sort of stock at all. Needless to say, the same does not apply to retailing, where stocks are a vital issue, nor catering, where stocks and work-in-progress are key elements in success.

Operations management

A. SHORT-ANSWER QUESTIONS

1 Give four factors that could influence a business decision about location. *(4)*
2 What is meant by an 'enterprise zone'? *(2)*
3 Give two reasons for foreign firms setting up plants in the UK. *(2)*
4 Give two consequences of industrial inertia. *(2)*
5 Name two internal diseconomies of scale. *(2)*
6 What is meant by batch production? *(2)*
7 What is meant by research and development? *(2)*
8 Give two ways a firm could increase its level of capacity utilisation. *(2)*
9 What is shown by the total float in a critical path analysis? *(2)*
10 List four difficulties a business may face when automating production. *(4)*
11 Give two advantages to a company of introducing a quality assurance system such as BS 5750? *(2)*
12 State two factors that would affect the minimum amount of stock held by a company. *(2)*
13 Why is an efficient stock control system important to a manufacturing business? *(2)*
14 State two pieces of information a manufacturer might require before choosing a new supplier of components. *(2)*
15 Explain one factor a firm should take into account when implementing a just-in-time (JIT) manufacturing system. *(2)*
16 Explain two benefits a firm might derive from its employees participating in quality circles. *(4)*
17 What is meant by a kaizen group? *(2)*
18 Explain why simultaneous engineering is important in developing a new product. *(2)*
19 What is meant by cell production? *(2)*
20 Define the term benchmarking. *(2)*

B1 DATA RESPONSE

Stocking for Seasonal Demand at Cadbury

For Cadbury, Easter is one of the busiest times of the year. It supplies around 350 million Easter eggs to almost 30,000 delivery points across the country. The sales value is over £250 million.

As a production problem, gearing up to meet such targets in a brief span of time requires timing and coordination. Marketing may create the demand but delivery and, before that, the purchase of stocks needs to be carefully planned. As with bonfire night for fireworks manufacturers, there is an externally set deadline that will not move to accommodate any problems an individual firm may face.

To put the supply problem into perspective, Cadbury will purchase 60,000 tonnes of cocoa from West Africa, 180,000,000 litres of milk from farms in the UK, mainly around Herefordshire, and 80,000 tonnes of sugar. In total, Cadbury spends £300 million a year on raw materials and an additional £200 million on gas, electricity, water and transport.

The profit that Cadbury makes from its operation will depend largely on how it manages its extended supply chain. Cadbury's manager of logistics (supply and transport), Andy Phythian, is responsible for running an almost military style operation to ensure the least possible wastage across the extended supply chain. He has conducted a five-year review of supplies to Cadbury with the stated aim of improving the level of service at a greater speed with less cost.

As an example of the improvements made following the five-year review, Cadbury reduced its packaging suppliers from 45 to 22. To encourage the remaining suppliers, it gave them three-year contracts to improve relationships and the quality of service. As a result, its packaging costs fell by 16%. In a similar way, the number of non-edible materials suppliers was halved from 3,000 to 1,500.

Cadbury's efforts to apply modern business practices to its purchasing and supply functions reflects a broad business trend. Businesses are forming partnerships with their suppliers to work together for the benefit of all.

Source: Adapted from the *Independent on Sunday*, 12/4/98

Questions *(25 marks; 35 minutes)*

1 a What is meant by the term 'supply chain'? *(2)*
  b Assess the reasons for the changes introduced by Cadbury in the management of its supply chain. *(6)*
2 Assuming that the Easter period accounts for one-fifth of all Cadbury's business, calculate the average added value for each egg sold. *(4)*
3 Taking the whole article into account, what is the evidence that Cadbury's needs 'timing and coordination' to meet its production targets? *(7)*
4 Outline the problems Cadbury's might face if it moved to just-in-time production methods? *(6)*

B2. CASE STUDY

Research and Development: The Key to Prosperity

High technology research and development (R&D) requires heavy financing. But money is not enough, as British Aerospace (BAe) is finding out. A project currently being undertaken by the Aerospace giant costing £45 million is being described by the former leader of the project as a 'shambles'. Yet this project is seen as vital to the future of both the company and the whole aerospace industry in the UK.

The case highlights the central importance of R&D to a firm's competitiveness. The BAe research project is aiming to develop a revolutionary all carbon-fibre wing for the Airbus family of aircraft. US rival Boeing is also working on similar composite wing technology. The benefits are that composite wings should cost less to make than metal wings. And because they are lighter, they substantially reduce running costs through lower fuel consumption. The first company to master the techniques required for mass production will have a head start in the world market.

Roger Redman, former project leader for BAe on its composite wing programme, is concerned that BAe's management has failed to set a clear shape or goal for the project. Outside consultants are also concerned that the project was not 'holistic'. In other words, the project appeared fragmented with the roles of different individuals being uncoordinated. While the company itself remained confident that the project would be successful, the implications of failure would be serious. Losing the £45 million investment would hurt. Trying to sell aircraft against superior technology from Boeing would hurt far more.

Source: Adapted from the *Independent*, 29/4/98, the *Independent on Sunday*, 3/5/98

Questions   (25 marks; 40 minutes)

1 What is meant by the following terms?
   a research and development   (3)
   b competitiveness   (3)
2 Outline why it is necessary for complex research projects to be 'holistic'.   (5)
3 Discuss the importance of R&D to the international competitiveness of a firm such as British Aerospace. (6)
4 'R&D is so risky that firms should severely restrict the amount they spend on it.' To what extent would you agree with this view?   (8)

C. ACTIVITY

Working in groups of three or four, you are to investigate local engineering, manufacturing or assembly firms. The aim is for each group to report on a different firm so that a range of experiences are recorded. This should provide insight into the extent to which production theory is actually put into practice.

Each group is to identify a suitable local firm and arrange a visit, preferably to be shown around the plant or, if this is not possible, to be able to put questions to the firm.

Possible areas for questions could be:

- Who are the customers? Who has the greater say in design and specifications – the firm or its customers?
- How is production organised (job, batch, flow or cell production)? How are relations between the sections of the shop-floor organised?
- What quality control procedures are in place? Who is responsible for quality control?
- How far has the firm incorporated new technology in its operations?
- Are workers involved in a variety of tasks in their working lives?
- How much involvement has the firm with research and development?
- How did the firm come to be located where it is? What is its history?
- What stock control procedures are in place?

Each group can feed back to the whole group through a short presentation, allowing an overall picture to be compiled of the state of local manufacturing firms.

D. ROLE PLAYS AND SIMULATIONS

You work in the operations management department of PB Bearings plc, an engineering company based in Durham. The department has recently acquired a new head, Doug Travis, who has been reviewing the firm's current position and planning for the future.

He summarises the position as follows: 'There has recently been a disappointing downward trend in the performance of the firm. Our competitive position has been further eroded by the entry of Deutsches Mechaniks.' This large multinational company is entering the UK market for the first time.

Doug has outlined three possible strategies to the board of directors:

- Option A – stay in the current factory with the existing level of technology
- Option B – stay in the current factory with investment into state-of-the-art technology
- Option C – move to a smaller, purpose-built factory unit with state-of-the-art technology.

Now he has asked for your views before he makes a recommendation to the directors about his preferred option. Using the following information, write a report, making a justified recommendation as to which option you think the firm should choose.

Appendix A – Sales data (£m), past, present and forecast future

Year	1	2	3*	4	5
Total UK sales	2.3	2.7	3.0	3.3	3.8
PB Bearings sales	0.5	0.6	0.6	0.65	0.7
Deutsches Mechaniks sales	–	–	–	0.5	0.75

* This year

Appendix B – Capacity utilisation

Current level of capacity utilisation at existing plant (option A)	68%
Current output as a % of new machinery capacity at existing plant (option B)	47%
Current output as a % of new plant capacity (option C)	60%

Appendix C – Research and development spending (as a % of sales), past present and future

Year	1	2	3*	4	5
PB Bearings	7%	6%	5%	6%	6%
Industry average	8%	8%	8%	10%	10%
Typical cost of developing a successful new product = £200,000					

* This year

Appendix D – Personnel data

Average travel to work:

	Old factory	New site
Distance	1.75 miles	2.5 miles
Time	25 mins	35 mins

No. of staff required at full capacity:

Current plant	150
New machinery	120
New location	160

Appendix E – Net costs of change

Net investment in new technology at existing plant	£5m
Net investment in new technology and new factory	£4m

E. INTEGRATED CASE STUDY

The Location Decision

Karen James knew she would have to make a decision soon. She faced a crucial moment with big repercussions for her future. In many ways, it was what she had hoped for ever since she set up her own business on leaving school seven years ago. But now the crunch had arrived, she felt the pressure of the choices she faced.

After achieving reasonable passes at A level in Art and Business Studies, Karen had begun producing and selling individualised pottery locally. Early success had allowed her to install a small kiln in her parents' spare bedroom and for a time she was able to keep up with demand. As her reputation spread, however, she struggled to cope with the workload.

Over time she bought a house of her own and converted the double garage into the main work area. The living room

became the office and the spare bedroom was used to store the finished products. Contracts with local shops allowed her to take on some part-time employees, and for a while she felt on top of the pressures of the business. It was then that Karen was approached by a regional supermarket chain, Asco. The Asco buyers wanted large-scale supplies for the chain of outlets. Knowing that she could not cope with the work, Karen had to turn down the chance, although she knew that such a decision carried a high opportunity cost.

Continued success over the next couple of years meant Karen was kept at full stretch. It became clear that the premises were becoming overrun. Karen began to look for purpose-built premises that would allow the firm to increase capacity, take on more staff and chase larger orders, like the one from Asco. Before starting to look for premises, Karen and her employees compiled a set of decision making criteria. After much searching, Karen found two potential sites that met the criteria. Both were within easy travelling distance of her present house, and had good general transport links. Importantly, both were big enough to allow flow production to take place instead of the job and batch methods used in the past.

After researching the two alternatives, Karen was able to produce the following estimates for the two sites. The unit of production is taken to be a full set of crockery.

	Site A	Site B
Fixed costs (per annum)	(£000)	(£000)
Rent and rates	2,480	4,200
Administration	7,320	9,000
Depreciation	3,800	3,800
Interest charges	2,400	3,000
Variable costs (per unit)	(£)	(£)
Raw materials	179	160
Direct labour	8	10
Delivery costs	19	10
Travel and expenses	20	8

The average selling price of a set of crockery is £250. When Karen began to work on the figures, she realised that her decision would have to take in more than just the numbers in front of her.

Questions (40 marks; 60 minutes)

1 Define the following terms:
   a opportunity cost (3)
   b capacity (2)
2 Calculate the break-even points for both these sites assuming that a full set of crockery is priced at £250. (8)
3 Consider the non-financial factors the firm could take into account when making this decision. (9)
4 Explain the meaning of the term 'flow production'. Analyse the possible effect on Karen's business of a move to a flow production system. (10)
5 Asco Supermarkets are very keen that quality standards should be high and consistent. How might Karen set out to ensure this once the scale of output has increased? (8)

EXTERNAL INFLUENCES AND MARKET FORCES

DEFINITION

External influences are factors outside a firm's control, such as changes in the economy or the law. Market forces are the influences of customer demand and producer decisions on supply upon price and customer satisfaction.

60.1 Introduction

The external environment of the business creates opportunities as well as threats. Successful businesses have to be flexible enough both to cope with the threats and to exploit the opportunities. By careful analysis of market trends they can plan ahead. Then external change can be treated as an opportunity. For example, in recent years, car owners have become more worried about car thefts. The figures are actually falling, but the fear of it is not. So BMW put particular effort into making their cars harder to steal.

Some businesses watch their markets, adapting their products to consumer preferences, and looking out for potential new possibilities. These firms are unlikely to face falling sales when consumers change their habits. These are aspects of change management – the process by which businesses adapt to external influences by planning and implementing new strategies and methods of working.

External influences can be divided into four categories:

● Demand – a whole range of influences arise from customer demand
● Inputs – many external influences have their impact on the business through its requirements for inputs
● Government – all businesses are affected by government policies; some very significantly
● Social factors – businesses are increasingly sensitive to ethical issues, including environmental considerations.

These categories of external influence are not watertight – they link together and sometimes overlap. Units 61–65 deal with these areas in more detail. This introductory unit focuses upon demand and the market mechanism. Both factors are crucial to an understanding of business economics.

60.2 Demand for the product

Some products sell for a long time. Cadbury's Dairy Milk chocolate has been around since 1905, in much the same form as it is sold now. Other products have a very short life. Some recordings by Atomic Kitten may have sold quite briefly and there may be some uncertainty as to their long-term prospects. An important factor in what happens to a particular product is the level of demand and how it changes over time.

Often changes occur simply because people's preferences change. This may be a matter of taste or fashion. No matter how they are promoted, Atomic Kitten's recordings may be selling well, or poorly or not at all by the time you are reading this. Consumer choices are often fickle and unpredictable.

For some products, incomes can be important. In the UK, over the long run, output usually rises by an average of around 2% per year. This is known as the long-term trend rate of economic growth. This means that real incomes and standards of living rise over time. (Real incomes are incomes measured in terms of their purchasing power, i.e. not influenced by inflation). As a result it may become possible to sell large volumes of products which few people could have afforded in the past. 700,000 Rolex watches, for example, are sold each year. In the early 1980s the figure was below 100,000. Considerable business opportunities can be created in this way, and businesses which can predict accurately how rising real incomes will affect them are in a good position to exploit these opportunities.

Competition is often of crucial importance in determining the level of demand for the product. Often, we find that we are choosing from a range of competing products. Many of them are quite good substitutes. A change in the price or marketing strategy of a competing substitute can be a very important external influence on the business concerned. In the extreme there may be a price war in which competing sellers keep on undercutting each other. They may find they are under pressure to set prices below their costs of production, at least temporarily.

These many and various influences on demand are an important part of the subject matter of Units 61 and 62.

THE BUSINESS CYCLE AND DEMAND

Economies as a whole are subject to a pattern of ups and downs in demand. Demand for all products taken together is known as *aggregate demand*. When aggregate demand is rising, the economy is enjoying a recovery. If this has gone on for a while, total output will be rising and the economy may be said to be booming. Economic growth will be higher than the long-run average, measured in percentage terms. The reverse, a downturn in aggregate demand is often called a recession and, if this is very prolonged, a depression or slump. During this time economic growth may be negative, meaning that output declines.

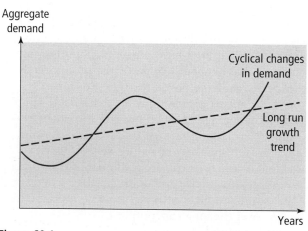

Figure 60.1

Some products are very vulnerable to **business cycle** fluctuations. When aggregate demand is falling, incomes will be falling and there will be some products which people feel they can do without. Between 1998 and 1999, for example, sales of Rolls Royce cars fell by 31% as the economy grew more slowly. The business which relies on sales of luxury items may experience serious problems unless it has other products for which demand is falling less or not at all. So recession can spell trouble for builders of yachts and swimming pools. Producers of biscuits may have little to worry about. When the recovery comes, however, it will be the yacht and swimming pool businesses which will experience increasing demand. The biscuit manufacturers may gain very little.

The nature and impact of the business cycle are looked at in more detail in Unit 62. Unemployment is invariably a feature of recession. Equally, accelerating inflation can be a consequence of prolonged, above average economic growth. These problems figure large in government thinking, and are often the reason for changes in a range of government policies. These are covered in Unit 67.

In the long run, most economies experience fairly steady economic growth. It is this which provides the rising standards of living which have been a feature of the past hundred years or so. This is examined in Unit 65.

DEMAND FROM ABROAD

If times are hard on the home market, international trade may provide a solution. The business may look for foreign markets and export. The level of demand abroad is an important external influence for any business which is able to export. There are some industries where exporting has always been important, such as cars and chemicals. But large numbers of firms need to be more enterprising to develop export markets.

FINDING NEW MARKETS

Americans don't like front-loading washing machines. What they want is a top-loader, a big one, with twice the average capacity of European machines. But Whirlpool wanted to break into the US market without having to design a special product for that market alone.

Front-loaders are generally more efficient than top-loaders in the use of energy and water. So Whirlpool used the 'platform' principle, which means using a single basic design for a wide range of different markets. This can be given small modifications to suit individual market expectations. In the planning stages, the engineers posed as market researchers, so they could get to talk with individual families in the US, finding out their preferences.

The company came up with a large front-loader. This meant that it could market the product as environmentally friendly *and* big enough for the US market. It went on sale in 2002. It's the Duet in the US and the Dreamspace in Europe. Asia next?

Of course an exporting business has to contend with business cycle fluctuations in other countries. This adds a degree of complexity to its trading position. But it may be able to compensate for low demand in one country by selling in another country which is in a recovery phase. This is a way of spreading risk. Sometimes recessions coincide in many countries of the world, but this is rare.

Where international trade is important as a source of business, governments' trade and exchange rate policies will be major external influences. The role of trade and the importance of competitiveness are looked at in Unit 63. In looking at these issues, the likely impact of European Monetary Union will be considered in detail.

60.3 How decisions affect the economy

A business which is about to take the decision to produce a new brand has to be reasonably confident it can make a profit. It must be able to cover all the costs of production, including the **capital** costs. In fact it will be hopeful of making a little more than that. The better the prospect of profit, the more ambitious its plans are likely to be. In economics, this decision is described as leading to an increase in supply.

If the business fails to cover its costs, and cannot see that the situation will change in the near future, it will decide to cut or even end production. There is no point in producing something which makes continuous losses. The outcome will be a decrease in supply.

Obviously the nature of this decision depends greatly on the price at which the product can be sold. Consumers' decisions will depend on the price too. No-one is going to buy the product if they can get an equally satisfactory one for a lower price.

THE PROFIT SIGNALLING MECHANISM

Many years ago economists tried to answer three questions:

- What will be produced?
- How will it be produced?
- For whom will it be produced?

They were trying to work out how society as a whole would use the resources available. Why would large quantities of some items be produced and only small quantities of others? What would be the best way to produce the things people want? Why do some people have the chance to enjoy many different consumer goods, while others have barely enough to keep themselves alive? These questions are all part of one big question: How are resources allocated?

When a business identifies a profitable opportunity, it decides to allocate more resources to that line of production. In order to produce more chrysanthemums, Ian Wade bought a piece of land adjoining his existing site, built another glasshouse, and took on two more people to help with the planting, picking and other tasks. The resources he needed to do this were land, labour and capital. Of course these resources were quite costly for him, but he reckoned the extra sales revenue he would get would be more than enough to make expansion worthwhile. The profit signalling mechanism was telling him that it would be worth increasing his output.

BLOOMING BUSINESS

Ian Wade grows and sells chrysanthemums, all year round. He has six big heated glasshouses with lights and blackout which can be used to fool the plants into thinking it is autumn even when it is actually winter or spring.

He sends some of the flowers to Covent Garden Market where they are sold on to florists. Others he sells direct to local florists and greengrocers. How does he decide what price to charge to local shops?

'You charge what you can get away with. You think what the florist will be able to charge the type of customers they will be getting, and offer a bit less. I'm confident that if I can continue to get £2 per bunch in local shops and £1.50 in the market, it will be worth putting up another glasshouse next year. It's a big investment but sales are rising and it should be profitable.'

ENTRY AND EXIT

When a new business starts up, it is entering the market. A business which is making losses will probably **exit** from the market. When businesses are free to enter and exit the market, it is described as a free market. That means that market forces are free to operate, drawing resources into particular lines of production where there is some demand for them. Equally, resources will be moving out of lines of production which no-one wants. In this way resources are free to move so that the pattern of output reflects consumer demand.

When resources are reallocated in this way, we think of the market as 'working'. Resources won't be wasted on valueless production. Consumers will reject low quality items offering poor value for money, and it simply won't be worthwhile for anyone to produce them. Instead they will buy the things which offer the best value. It will be hard for businesses to survive unless they can offer good value. The market will force them to be efficient, and if they can't be, they will make losses and exit from the market. Efficient producers will find they have opportunities to expand.

So when markets are working well, they help people to get what they want.

CONSUMER SOVEREIGNTY

Market forces work to produce a combination of products which match the pattern of consumer demand. Products people do not want will not be profitable and the businesses producing them will have to close down. This means that the ultimate decision takers in a free market economy are the consumers. Economists say, consumers have sovereignty. The customer is king.

In practice there is no economy in the world which is organised completely freely. Everywhere governments intervene to manage and control market forces. Sometimes one business can become so large that it can influence the market in such a way that consumers are not making completely free choices. The important factor in deciding whether consumers have the ultimate market power is whether there are many businesses competing in the market. Unit 61 looks in detail at how competition works in practice.

In this unit, markets are analysed on the assumption that most are reasonably competitive. This approach is very characteristic of how economics works. To get a good understanding of the relationships in the economy, it helps to assume that some of life's complicating factors do not exist. Later on, this assumption will be relaxed. Then the real world of business can be analysed in full.

ENDANGERED

Have you seen your milkman lately? Probably not, for they are an endangered species. What went wrong?

Most people can still get milk delivered, if they want it. The snag is that customers have been drifting away to the supermarkets. They compete on price. Families needing a lot of milk, who have cars, can pick up a two litre plastic bottle for a lot less than the milkman would charge for four pints in returnable bottles.

The dairies which deliver have been left trying to compete on convenience, offering quite a range of food products, drinks and even potting compost and wood chips for the garden. Still, their numbers are declining and seem likely to carry on down. The lure of milk delivered to your door is not enough to stop people from bringing cheap plastic cartons home next time they go to the supermarket.

60.4 How market forces work

SUPPLY

Businesses which can foresee potential profits have an incentive to increase production. The more profit they can make, the bigger the incentive. So the quantity businesses want to supply is related to the price which

can be charged. The higher the price, the greater the potential profit and the larger the quantity supplied. This relationship can be presented in the form of a graph or supply curve, as shown in Figure 60.2. If the price falls, businesses will reduce output and look around for other products which are more profitable.

Figure 60.2 Supply curve

DEMAND

When businesses identify a profitable opportunity they are observing the existence of potential demand for the product. Whether they can create this opportunity for themselves depends very much on the price at which they are proposing to sell the product. There is a very easily understood relationship between the quantity which consumers wish to buy and the price they will be charged. You have only to think of what happens during the January and July sales to appreciate the nature of this relationship. It can be presented in the form of a demand curve, as shown in Figure 60.3.

The price cuts in the January sales move the consumer down the demand curve. If the price is cut they become active potential buyers. For some products, a price cut means that they will buy larger quantities. More winter weekend mini-breaks are possible for many people if the price looks a good deal. The demand curve plots the relationship between price and quantity bought.

WHAT WILL THE PRICE BE?

Markets always have at least two players – a buyer and a seller. The price depends on the interaction between them. If you want to sell something such as a car, no matter how valuable you think it is, the price will depend on what the buyer is prepared to pay. However, the price on offer may be so low that you don't think it is worth selling. The deal will take place only if both buyer and seller can settle on an acceptable price.

Price
£s

8

6

4   7   Quantity
millions

Figure 60.3 Demand curve

This acceptable price is called the **equilibrium price**. This can be represented on a diagram as the intersection of the supply and the demand curve, as shown in Figure 60.4. The idea of an equilibrium price is important because at that price the amount which sellers wish to sell is equal to the amount which buyers wish to buy. There are no unsold stocks and no customers standing in a queue waiting for more deliveries. A market which has either unsold stocks or unsatisfied customers is in disequilibrium.

Many markets are in a state of constant change, moving from one equilibrium to another. Similarly, some markets are often in a state of disequilibrium. Analysing these changes is the subject of the next section.

Price
£s

Supply

Equilibrium
price

52

Demand

24   Quantity
000 units

Figure 60.4 Supply and demand in equilibrium

Situations of disequilibrium:

- Late in the day, supermarkets may mark some of their stock 'reduced to clear', as some items reach the end of their shelf life. They realise that they set the price a little above the equilibrium level for that item and they will have unsold stocks of perishable items if they do not reduce the price.
- Tickets for some sporting events are fewer in number than the people who would like to buy them. The equilibrium price is above the face value of the ticket.

60.5 Dynamic markets

Markets in disequilibrium usually have symptoms. Reasons will vary, but the evidence takes the form of **excess demand** or **excess supply**.

EXCESS DEMAND

You can sometimes *see* excess demand. Symptoms might include a long queue for tickets at the Wimbledon tennis championships. If there is a fixed supply of something which is popular, and for some reason the price does not go up, there will be rationing by queues or waiting lists, as with popular schools.

There have been times in recent years when the excess demand for flats and houses in central London has been visible in the estate agents' windows. They would put 'wanted' signs in the window, or if they had, say, three windows, put the same set of properties in each window.

Disequilibrium situations can persist for quite a while if people are slow to adjust their expectations or actions. Sellers may have reasons for not putting up prices. But over time, property prices have risen and that has meant less of a shortage of places for sale in London. Between mid-2001 and mid-2002 UK property prices rose 20.9%, on average. The estate agents' windows filled up again, indicating much less excess demand at the new prices. Equilibrium was gradually restored.

The existence of excess demand usually implies that there is a shortage of the productive capacity needed to satisfy demand. Unsatisfied demand will tend to drive up prices and increase the potential profits. In time, businesses have an incentive to come into the market and expand production so that the excess supply will usually disappear.

EXCESS SUPPLY

Unsold stocks of any product suggest that the price is above its equilibrium level. Not enough customers are being attracted to buy the product. At current prices, the quantity supplied exceeds the quantity demanded. Only a price cut will clear the market, and in the long run it may be necessary to cut production. A situation of excess supply is shown in Figure 60.5.
Something like this happened with beef after the BSE crisis. When people discovered that eating beef might cause the fatal disease CJD, demand for beef fell. Farmers were left with beef cattle they could not sell at current prices; an excess supply.

Price
£s

60

40

Price cut needed to boost
demand to match supply

Supply

Demand

Current
supply

Quantity

Figure 60.5 Excess supply

SUMMARY

Markets bring together buyers and sellers so that transactions can take place, allowing people to exchange what they have for what they want. Businesses have an incentive to produce in response to market demand. This means that consumers ultimately determine the pattern, or structure, of output.

Supply and demand (price theory) can be useful because:

• the impact of changes in demand and supply can be predicted

• different kinds of changes can be identified and classified according to their causes

• the theory can be used to analyse the relationships which determine prices and quantities.

Competition forces businesses to produce efficiently in order to survive. They need to be market oriented in their decision taking. Otherwise their costs will rise above the minimum necessary. This will reduce their profits.

60.6 Structural change

All the time, patterns of consumer demand are shifting and the structure of output changes in response. This means that resources are constantly being reallocated from one use to another. Sometimes this reallocation takes place within a business, as it diversifies its products. Reallocation also occurs as new businesses are set up and old ones close down. The land, labour and capital which is made redundant from a closing or shrinking business becomes available to one which is setting up or expanding. In the 1970s, high streets were full of shops. In the 1980s estate agents and building societies had taken over. In the 1990s these were taken over by restaurants and cafés and that process is continuing in the 2000s.

Technology also plays a big part in the process of structural change. The invention of a completely new *product* leads to structural changes as production facilities for that product are set up. Even more importantly, many lines of production benefit from new *process* technologies which lead both to cost reductions and quality improvements.

Looking at the structure of production nationally, we can identify a number of broad trends. Some changes take place swiftly as people respond to short-term changes. Other changes are part of very long-term trends.

As economies develop industrially, they move resources out of agriculture and into manufacturing. Later on in the process there is a shift towards services. All developed economies (broadly, North America, Japan, Australia and New Zealand and most of Europe) have shown a shift away from manufacturing and towards the production of services. So resources have tended to move into restaurants, hotels and holidays, hairdressers, leisure and financial services. Consumers often want to acquire a certain number of manufactured products, but once they have them, they spend more on services. A household's need to cook is satisfied by the possession of one cooker. As incomes rise further, people opt for more and more take-away food. So goods are more likely to reach market saturation than services.

The table below shows the changes in output by sector for the UK, with figures for Japan and India (a developing country with much lower income levels) for comparison.

When looking at the process of structural change, growing and declining industries can be identified. Declining industries are having to contract because demand for their products is either falling, or growing more slowly than the rest of the economy. The most obvious declining industry in recent years has been

The structure of production – % of gross domestic product

COUNTRY	AGRICULTURE		INDUSTRY		SERVICES	
	1980	2000	1980	2000	1980	2000
UK	2	1	43	25	55	74
Japan	4	2	42	36	54	62
India	38	27	26	27	36	46

Source: World Bank, World Development Report, 2002

coal mining. A combination of factors (some political) have led to a fall in demand for coal. Increasingly, power stations have switched to gas. Many mines have closed down and employment in the industry has dropped away to almost nothing. The number of butchers, fishmongers and bakers has declined in response to the relentless expansion of supermarkets.

An example of a growing industry is electronics. Chemicals have done well too. These are industries where technology has played a part in the story. Leisure, media and financial services have also grown robustly.

Coal mining has declined due to external factors
© Zen Icknow/CORBIS

60.7 Other kinds of markets

So far this unit has focused on markets for end products and services. Yet any resource which has a money value can be traded in a market. There are markets in the inputs to the production process – land, labour and capital, the three factors of production.

In the labour market, people seeking employment are selling their labour. Potential employers are buying it. The equilibrium price is the wage rate. It is possible to use the same principles of supply and demand and equilibrium price to analyse labour markets. If demand is high for computer analysts, their wage rate will rise.

Similarly, money markets are subject to market forces. Interest rates are the price which brings the funds available into line with the demand for loans. These markets are examined in more detail in later units. It will be important to be able to apply the understanding of markets gained in this unit.

ISSUES FOR **analysis**

When examining the impact on a firm of the external environment, there is an enormous range of different influences. The first issue for analysis is to select the most significant influences. These are some of the questions which address the issues:

- What kind of market will the business operate in?
- Will the necessary employees, with the skills required, be readily available?
- Is government policy likely to change demand for the product?
- Will inflation or exchange rate changes force the business into rethinking pricing policies?
- Are there important regulations which will constrain the business?
- Does the possibility of international trade lead to larger markets?
- Are technical changes going to alter cost structures or the nature of the competition?

KEY terms

business cycle – the fluctuations in demand and output which show a pattern of boom, recession, slump and recovery over a period of years, which affects the whole economy.

capital – the buildings, plant and machinery needed in the production process. These must be combined with land, labour and other inputs in order to create the final product.

competition – the process by which businesses act as rivals with one another in order to attract customers and increase sales.

consumer sovereignty – the process by which consumer choice signals to businesses what they should be producing.

entry – the process by which businesses may set up new lines of production where they think profitable opportunities exist.

equilibrium price – the price at which quantity demanded equals quantity supplied.

excess demand – a situation in which quantity demanded is greater than quantity supplied at current prices.

excess supply – a situation in which quantity supplied is greater than quantity demanded at current prices.

exit – the process by which businesses withdraw from markets where they are making disappointing profits.

macro-economic – a factor which affects the whole economy.

AS Level Exercises

A. REVISION QUESTIONS
(40 marks; 70 minutes)

Read the unit, then answer:

1 Outline three external influences upon a chocolate manufacturer such as Cadbury's. *(6)*
2 Give four examples of products for which sales are likely to rise as incomes rise. *(4)*
3 From your awareness of current events, outline the stage in the business cycle you believe the economy is in currently. *(4)*
4 What is the role of profit in business decisions? *(4)*
5 What is meant by the term 'allocation of resources'. *(3)*
6 Identify three major influences on the demand for Quality Street. *(4)*
7 What is meant by 'equilibrium price'? How is it determined? *(4)*
8 Give an example of a market in disequilibrium which you have observed personally, and explain why the disequilibrium situation occurred. *(4)*
9 Explain why the disequilibrium which you described in your answer to question 8 will or will not persist over time. *(4)*
10 What problems may arise in the process of structural change? *(3)*

B. REVISION EXERCISES

B1 Activities
1 Identify a local business which started up fairly recently. Gather as much information about it as you can. Write a report covering the following points:
   a Why did the business believe there was a potential market for its product?
   b What sort of competition did it face at the outset?
   c What impact did its entry to the market have on other businesses?
   d What future changes do you think may be important in determining the future of the business?

B3 Case Study

A market for business jets?
If you want an executive jet right now, you will be looking at a price of around US$3.5 million. Eclipse Aviation is building one that will cost $838,000. It's a six-seater that can fly 1,300 miles at around 400 mph and it had its first test flight in summer 2002. The low price reflects developments in the use of cheaper electronic systems and new welding techniques. Also, the price assumes that volume manufacturing will be possible – in other words, it has to sell in quantity (at least 1,000 a year) to keep the price down.

Will it make it? There are big risks associated with developing a new aircraft. To succeed, this project depends on the development of a new concept, the air

2 In the early 1990s trainers became hugely fashionable, then faded away. In 1998 yo-yos became the must-have item for 10–12-year-olds. Consider the market for a fashion item which you have recently observed in the process of rising and then falling demand.
   a Using supply and demand analysis describe what happened to price and quantity sold. *(15)*
   b Explain what you think will happen next. *(10)*

B2 Data Response
Output in three industries
Index: 1990 = 100

Year	Clothing & Footwear	Food, Drink & Tobacco	Electrical Investment Goods
1986	111	93	73
1987	112	96	78
1988	107	98	91
1989	103	98	101
1990	100	100	100
1991	89	98	99
1992	89	100	105
1993	88	100	116
1994	91	101	136
1995	89	103	151
1996	90	104	159
1997	85	108	172
1998	76	105	198

Source: ONS Monthly Digest of Statistics, Crown copyright, Jan 1999

Questions *(30 marks; 35 minutes)*
1 Choose a suitable way to show the above data on graph paper. Label your diagram carefully. *(10)*
2 Explain how the changes in output have differed in the three industries in the table. *(8)*
3 Analyse the changes in each industry and explain the trends. *(12)*

taxi. This will cash in on business executives' frustration with scheduled flights and people who need to fly to small airports. Eclipse has an initial order for 1,000 jets, destined for the air taxi service, with production scheduled to start in 2004. The current market for business jets is around 1,900 a year.

Questions *(25 marks; 30 minutes)*
1 List three possible reasons why this project might fail. *(6)*
2 To what extent do you think Eclipse is depending on new buyers emerging? What sort of market can it expect from businesses replacing an older executive jet? *(10)*
3 Describe what will happen if this aircraft does not sell in the required quantities. *(9)*

MARKETS AND COMPETITION

Competition occurs when people can choose from a range of similar products, selecting the ones which most closely fit their needs. It occurs when a number of sellers are rivals with each other. Or when many buyers are competing to obtain something which is scarce. It can occur in the labour and capital markets as well as the markets for goods and services.

61.1 Markets

As a general rule a market consists of many buyers and many sellers. You can easily see this in a street market. For each type of product sold, there may be five or six competing sellers. You wander around looking for bargains and find that all the traders are selling at roughly the same price! In fact they have to. If one trader sold at much lower prices all his or her stock would be gone in a short time, but at very low profit margins. Lower than if he or she had more patience and stood there all day. Similarly, a trader who charges more than others will sell little because potential customers will go to another stall.

The term 'market' is used broadly and includes anyone who might buy or sell the product wherever they happen to be. The famous London stock market used to be a building where traders met to buy and sell shares. Today shares are bought and sold over the telephone by people who may never meet each other.

Businesses spend a lot of time working out how to defeat the competition. To get themselves into a position where **market forces** create fewer problems. What are you doing right now? You are studying for qualifications which will give you skills that you hope will be scarce. The more skills you have, the more attractive you will be to employers. And the easier it will be to defeat the competition when it comes to landing that difficult first job. You are striving for a competitive advantage.

People in business are constantly trying to defeat the competition and sometimes they succeed. If they actually manage to create something that no-one else can produce, they will have a **monopoly**. They will be able to charge a much higher price. Their profits will soar.

MICROSOFT

Many people would say that Microsoft has a monopoly with its Windows operating system. Most computer users want it because it makes their system compatible with the rest of the world.

The US government's competition authorities certainly thought Microsoft was a monopoly, and that the company had abused its market power. The case against Microsoft spelt out how it had seriously damaged the much smaller competing software, Netscape, and the Java programming script. The courtroom arguments will run and run.

When Bill Gates took the witness stand in the US Court of Appeals, he said that without Windows in its current form, there would be a digital disaster. There would be widespread confusion amongst computer users, incompatible programs, failing software firms and a fall-off in the rate of innovation. He opposed the idea that customers should be able to choose rival companies' software to replace certain parts of the Windows system.

Buying and selling in the 'market'
© The Image Bank/Getty Images

61.2 Choices for all

Every choice has an **opportunity cost**. Therefore all the alternatives should be considered before making a business decision. Similarly, consumers make the most

Business

IN

of their spending power by thinking hard about the alternative uses of their money. This process ensures that a complacent producer will soon find customers are looking elsewhere. Competition is good for consumers.

The drive for profit which motivates many business decisions also has a very important implication. It means businesses will always be striving to defeat the competition. Direct competition is bad for business, because it forces prices down. So businesses strive for competitive advantage which makes them stand out from their rivals.

This tension between the needs of consumers and the needs of business points to many interesting issues. Governments try to promote competition because it forces businesses to be efficient. This keeps costs and prices down. Businesses can be less than thrilled by these efforts to promote competition.

In order to survive competition, many businesses make a major effort to cut costs and increase efficiency. This often leads to lower prices for consumers. In trying to increase long-term profits, businesses may spend large sums on research and development and find important new ways of implementing new technologies. These efforts may increase profits and may lead to lower prices for consumers.

These last two points are important reasons why in recent years market forces have come to be seen as a crucial element in an efficient, modern economy. Market forces have the power to make society better off. But they work in complicated ways and the outcome of the free play of market forces is not always what everyone wishes. How market forces work depends on the circumstances. Indeed, market forces do not always work. Governments can both encourage and discourage market forces. The reasons why they intervene in markets may be very varied.

61.3 Scale and competition

Some products need to be produced on a large scale to be cost effective. In other cases scale is unimportant. For example, small-scale production of cars works only if the car is to be marketed as a high status or specialist vehicle. The value added has to be high enough to justify the high price the producer will need to charge. Volume car producers need to produce 1–2 million cars per year to compete on world markets. Only then do **economies of scale** allow production costs to be low enough to compete.

Businesses which encounter severe diseconomies of scale will tend to flourish using relatively small-scale production methods. In some sectors, small- and large-scale operations coexist quite comfortably. In the hotel sector, small guest houses and huge hotel chains both flourish. This pattern is common in the service sector.

61.4 The degree of competition in the market

It can be useful to look at the range of competitive situations which occur. This is illustrated in Figure 61.1. At one extreme is the situation of the stalls on market day. There are many sellers, each aware that people can shop at the neighbouring stall. Very similar products are on offer. Prices are set just high enough to cover costs and make a reasonable profit.

This is known as **perfect competition**. It defines the perfect market, where market forces ensure that the only successful seller is the one who offers customers what they want. In this situation:

- production is efficient (i.e. lowest cost) because only the most efficient businesses can survive the competition
- consumers are free to choose the combination of products they most want, subject to the constraint of their income
- prices are kept low and quality kept high by the forces of competition.

Perfect competition has a set of essential features (see the table below). They give us a yardstick with which we can measure deviations from the state of perfect competition (i.e. market imperfections). All other competitive situations are categorised as imperfect competition.

Perfect competition	Monopolistic competition	Oligopoly	Monopoly
● homogenous product	● differentiated product	● differentiated product	● no substitutes
● free entry	● free entry	● barriers to entry	● barriers to entry
● many sellers	● many sellers	● few sellers	● single seller
● price takers	● price takers	● price makers	● price makers
		● interdependence	

Figure 61.1 The spectrum of competition

The essential features of perfect competition

FEATURES	WHAT THEY MEAN IN PRACTICE
Homogeneous products	It is impossible to distinguish one seller's product from that of another
Free entry and exit	It is easy for new businesses to set up production and compete with existing sellers
Large numbers of buyers and sellers	The buyer has access to a large range of sellers
Full information is obtainable	Buyers can easily find out where the product is being sold most cheaply

At the other extreme of the spectrum of competition there is monopoly, the single seller. This too is rare, though individual railway companies have a monopoly on particular routes. Virgin, for instance, has a monopoly on the busy London - Manchester route and most travellers condemn the poor service and high prices.

Two market categories come in between the extreme cases of monopoly and perfect competition: **monopolistic competition** and **oligopoly**. Monopolistic competition occurs when there are many sellers, but each has a differentiated product. So it is possible to distinguish the different brands. An example of this would be in football club shirts. The shirts compete with each other in a way, but not fully. Product differentiation is achieved through the club name and the product design.

Oligopoly is competition between the few. For example, 90% of chocolate sales in Britain come from Mars, Cadbury's and Nestlé. Branding is very important and businesses will copy and counter each other's marketing strategies all the time. Defeating the competition is everything. Prices may be well above average costs, and sometimes oligopolists will avoid competing on price so that all of them achieve high profit margins. Then non-price competition through advertising and promotions becomes very important.

For this situation to persist, there must be **barriers to entry**. These may arise because high minimum efficient scale means that entry cannot be achieved through small-scale production. The amount of capital needed to set up a large, competitive business may be prohibitive. In markets such as for chocolate, however, the underlying strength of the brand names is as important as any other feature.

These categories help clarify the nature of competition in different situations. Competition between oligopolists is quite different from all other competitive situations. Some of the time they may collude, quietly collaborating with each other. Where possible the government will try to control this type of behav-

iour through the Office of Fair Trading and the Competition Commission. If one firm is suffering loss of market share, it may shake the market up in its attempt to restore its position. In such circumstances, price wars may break out. This occurred in the newspaper business in 2002, with the *Mirror* losing out to ferocious price competition by the *Sun*.

61.5 Competition and profit

The profitability of a firm depends, in part, on the nature of the market. It is useful to use the idea of price takers and price makers. Price takers have to set the price close to that of competing products, otherwise they will have low sales. So they look at the market and consider what price will be competitive. Or in other words, what the market will bear. Price takers are found in situations which resemble perfect competition. They are also found among the smaller companies in an oligopolistic market.

Price makers, by contrast, are able to decide prices. They are products or services with the market power to set the price which others will follow. Heinz can do this in the salad cream market. British Airways can do the same on routes such as to Australia or South Africa. There are few satisfactory substitutes for their product so they can choose the price which will give them a commanding market position. This will not always be the highest price they might charge. It may be a price which is very profitable, but not so high as to encourage new entrants to the market. New entrants would create a more competitive market, which is the last thing the price maker wants. This kind of situation is very characteristic of an oligopoly.

To the extent that businesses succeed in increasing their market power, they will be more insulated from competition. That makes them able to make more

BANKS AND SMALL BUSINESSES

'The report from the Competition Commission is crystal clear – competition in the market for banking services to small and medium sized enterprises (SMEs) is not working properly.

'As a result, SMEs in England and Wales are being overcharged. We cannot allow small businesses to continue paying a higher price for banking services than is right. SMEs are a vital part of our economy, employing over half the workforce. It is essential that they have a proper choice of banking services, supplied at competitive prices.'

Patricia Hewitt, Secretary of State for Trade and Industry.

Business

IN

profit by increasing prices. But complacency may set in. Weak competitive pressure may result in less efficiency and less focus on the customer. There is evidence that this happened with the banks' small business accounts in recent years.

61.6 Unfair competition

There is a very fine line between fair and unfair competition. Successive governments have attempted to draw that line in order to distinguish legal from illegal behaviour.

Where oligopolists avoid competing on price, there may be tacit agreement. This means that they all charge rather similar prices which are above the minimum needed to cover costs. This is not in itself illegal, although it may still be investigated by the Office of Fair Trading if a complaint has been lodged.

Market sharing agreements are definitely illegal. Businesses which agree to carve up the market by operating in different geographical areas are indulging in a restrictive practice. Cartels are usually found to be illegal – they allow producers to agree upon a way of limiting competition between them. They may decide to restrict supply so as to force up the price. There are many other ways in which businesses may try to avoid having to compete on a level playing field.

Unfair competition is never good for the consumer. It can limit the possibilities for businesses too. So governments in all developed countries have competition policies. These are examined in more detail in Unit 67.

Air pollution by this factory could be indicative of market failure
© W. Cody/Corbis

61.7 Market failure

Market failure occurs where market forces lead to the production of more or less of a product than consumers require, given the costs of production in terms of real resources. It is best explained with a range of examples. Pollution is an indication of market failure. There is a cost to society which is not being paid fully by the producer. And therefore not being passed on to the consumers of the polluting product. Ideally all the costs of production, including those created by the pollution, should be covered by the price to the consumer. Then less of the polluting product would be bought because the price would be higher. Similarly, markets fail when there is a monopoly. Monopolists usually produce less, and charge higher prices, than would be the case in a competitive market.

Market failure often involves an element of unfair competition. Some people argue that it is unfair that rail users usually have to pay the full cost of their travel, which is clean and safe and creates no external costs for society. The railways compete with road transport. Road building is funded through the tax system, so motorists only have to cover the marginal cost of their own vehicle and fuel. Road travel creates considerable environmental costs. Effectively the polluting product is subsidised while the rail system is not.

The fact that markets *can* fail to allocate resources effectively means that government action may be needed. In the old communist economies of Eastern Europe, the government made all the economic decisions. Government officials decided on the number of chocolate bars to be produced, the number of staff who should work on the railways and so on. The Western reliance upon the free market to determine these issues has proved far more effective. Yet there is still an important role for government to step in when markets fail. Pollution can be controlled by laws and regulations, poverty wages can be avoided by setting a legal minimum wage, and traffic congestion could be reduced by massive investment in public transport.

ISSUES FOR **analysis**

Studying market systems provides numerous possibilities for analysis of business situations:

- Business cases can be considered in relation to the underlying market structure. Is the XYZ Company in an oligopolistic market? If so, that will need to be reflected in its actions and strategies.
- Business strategies can be analysed in terms of their impact on the competition. The outcome can then be examined from the point of view of both consumers and producers.
- In most markets, competition is fierce, but not as direct as in perfect competition. This is why product and marketing innovations are so vital for most firms. Standing still is rarely an option.

- Market failure points not only to the occasional need for government intervention, but also to the important potential role for pressure groups. Groups such as Greenpeace can draw public attention to the downside of business activity. This can force firms to change their ways or, if not, alerts politicians to the need for tighter regulation.

61.8 Markets and competition
an evaluation

Business Studies focuses largely on what an individual firm can and should do in a given situation. Management decisions are considered in terms of their effectiveness at achieving the company's objectives. It is often implied that top quality management makes a big difference in the strategies and performance of firms.

This unit has used economic analysis to show that the wider market structure may be at least as important an influence. A superb young manager working in an oligopoly may end up making the same, cautious decision as would anyone else. A 'let's not rock the boat' decision to avoid a radical new strategy. After all, if you are one of three firms each with a 30% market share, why risk shaking things up?

This acts as a useful counterpoint to the view put forward by so many top company directors: that their personal qualities are so vital as to justify huge salary and bonus packages. If competition between the few is usually quite straightforward, perhaps it is not that hard to be the chairman of Bird's Eye Walls or Heinz. It may be much more demanding to run a smaller firm in a market where competition is fiercer.

KEY terms

economies of scale – a fall in average total costs due to an increase in the scale of a firm's operation.

market forces – the pressure exerted on the price of a product by customer demand and the willingness of producers to supply. Growing demand will push prices up. Growing supply will tend to flood the market and drive prices down.

monopolistic competition – occurs when there are many sellers in the market but each has a slightly differentiated product.

monopoly – a single seller in the market.

oligopoly – a small group of sellers competing with one another, most commonly by means of non-price competition.

opportunity cost – the cost of missing out on the alternatives when making a decision.

perfect competition – where many sellers compete with each other to sell a homogeneous product.

barriers to entry – obstacles which prevent new businesses from entering a particular market.

WORKBOOK | 61.9

AS Level Exercises

A. REVISION QUESTIONS
(40 marks; 70 minutes)

Read the unit, then answer:

1 Describe two ways in which businesses compete with one another. *(4)*
2 In your view, what kinds of competition does McDonald's face at the moment? *(4)*
3 Briefly explain whether each of the following markets is perfectly competitive, monopolistically competitive, an oligopoly or a monopoly:
  a the UK market for chocolate bars
  b the UK market for cars
  c the wholesale market for potatoes
  d the market for Premiership tickets in Manchester. *(8)*
4 What are the key features of an oligopoly? *(3)*

5 What is meant by the term 'barriers to entry'? *(3)*
6 What impact do barriers to entry have on
  a producers
  b consumers? *(4)*
7 Identify three ways in which a business may achieve a competitive advantage. *(3)*
8 What is meant by 'unfair competition'? *(3)*
9 What is market failure? *(2)*
10 Decide whether each of the following is an example of market failure or unfair competition:
  a three firms agreeing to control output to push up prices
  b acid rain in Scotland caused by polluting power stations in the Midlands
  c firms poaching experienced staff from rivals instead of training their own.
  Briefly explain your reasoning. *(6)*

B. REVISION EXERCISES

B1 Investigation

Write a report analysing the competitive position of a business in your area, or one which you have studied. Cover the following points:

- How competitive is the market?
- In what category would you place it, e.g. monopolistic competition?
- How does the business cope with the competition? What is its competitive advantage?
- What would happen to the business if competition increased?

B2 Data Response

De Beers, which sells uncut diamonds, is one company which has managed to exert considerable control over the market since the late nineteenth century. It has ways of influencing the world supply and pricing of diamonds.

De Beers Cuts Diamond Deal to Seal Cartel

De Beers, the giant South African diamond cartel, has signed an agreement with Russia's biggest diamond producer giving the Russian company a role in regulating the world market and confirming the Russian diamond-cutting industry's rights.

The deal, which comes after months of wrangling, represents a significant concession by the South Africans. Under the agreement, De Beers will buy a minimum of £340 million worth of diamonds a year from the Russian company – 40% of its output. The bulk of the rest will be sold within the Commonwealth of Independent States (Russia and its neighbouring countries). The Russian company gains equal rights on the regulation of the volume, assortment and pricing of its exports. The agreement also gives the Russian diamond cutting and polishing industry preemptive rights in the selection of uncut gems. Some Russian cutting plants will be invited to London diamond sales organised by De Beers.

It was not clear yesterday what assurances De Beers had received from the Russian company on measures to stabilise the once chaotic supply of Russian diamonds. And to prevent frequently substantial 'leakages' onto the world market. In the past this had forced De Beers to buy increasing quantities of diamonds on second-hand markets in Antwerp and Tel Aviv to maintain price regulation.

De Beers emphasised that it was in the interests of both sides to keep to an agreement that it was sure would contribute to the stability of the market.

Source: Adapted from *The Times*, 22/10/97

Questions *(30 marks; 35 minutes)*

1 Why would it be in De Beers' and the Russian company's interests to regulate the export of diamonds? *(8)*
2 What impact may this deal have on consumer buyers of diamonds? *(8)*
3 De Beers tries to keep up the world price of diamonds not only by controlling supply but also by extensive advertising in magazines worldwide. Analyse the company's reasoning using supply and demand theory. *(6)*
4 Ought this kind of deal to be prevented? If so, by whom? *(8)*

B3 Data Response

Antony Buck and Robert Calcraft were running a market research business but what they really wanted was to have their own products and sell them. They set up REN, which is Swedish for 'clean'. They manufacture and sell a range of pricey natural skin care products. This looks like a product area with barriers to entry due to the need for heavy advertising to create a market. Not so, says Mr. Buck, 'It's an unusual market, in that it's not so much driven by advertising as by public relations. Beauty journalists, celebrities, people who write about it'. The two had already had some experience of marketing cosmetics. Already they have two London shops, a growing Internet sales department and supply deals with department stores.

Questions *(30 minutes; 25 marks)*

1 Give reasons for the success of this business. *(4)*
2 What type of market is this? Explain the extent of competition within it. *(7)*
3 How might competitors react to the arrival of a new business in their midst? *(7)*
4 What opportunities and what threats might the business face in the future? *(7)*

C. ESSAY QUESTIONS

1 Why are most washing products produced by one of two large firms, while the construction business is made up of a huge variety of large, small and medium-sized businesses?
2 'The companies which *sustain* monopolistic market shares do so, paradoxically, by acting as if they were beset by formidable competitors on every side.'

Robert Heller.

Why may a monopoly business lose its strong position unless it adopts the approach recommended by Robert Heller?

DEMAND AND THE BUSINESS CYCLE

DEFINITION
Over time, most businesses experience a sequence of changes in the level of demand for their products. This sequence is called the business cycle. Demand will grow for a period of years, peaking in a boom phase. This is followed by a downturn in which business conditions become difficult and demand slackens. For a time, demand may grow very slowly, be static, or actually decline. Eventually, demand picks up and most businesses begin to recover. Some businesses are affected by the business cycle very much more than others.

62.1 Cyclical changes

The business cycle is easily observed. Do you know where the UK economy is in the business cycle right now? In the newspapers you will see words such as **recovery**, **recession**, **boom**, skill shortages and so on. These indicate that there are trends in the economy which affect not just one business but all of them. This unit is about how these movements can be recognised as they happen, how the pattern of events can be used to aid understanding, and how businesses are affected.

Figure 62.1 shows the annual growth rate of GDP at constant prices for the years 1988–2002. GDP stands for gross domestic product. It means the value of all output from the economy for the year. It is one of the standard measures of the size of the economy, used all over the world to provide information. It is very useful for making comparisons over time. It is given here in constant prices. This is important – it means that the figures have been 'deflated' to remove the effects of inflation. So it can be used as a measure of **real income** for the year. Real income tells us the actual value of what we produce, year by year. Money values can be misleading because some of the change they show reflects price changes.

Figure 62.1 shows that the UK has experienced some very rapid growth. The peak reached in 1988 was far above the average. That was the year in which the economy was in a massive boom. The next year growth slowed dramatically as the economy moved into recession. By 1991, output and sales were actually falling. Yet the recovery, when it came in 1992, again led to high rates of growth up until 1998. Then the economy began to slow a little. Output grew every year but by less, especially in 2001.

The business cycle consists of a sequence in which a recession is followed by recovery which leads into a boom. After a period of boom conditions there will be a downturn leading to recession. This is usually characterised as a period of slower growth or stagnation. It can be followed immediately by a period of recovery.

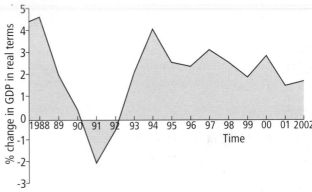

Source: Annual Abstract of Statistics, Crown copyright 2002

Figure 62.1 Economic growth, 1988–2002

Or persist to the point where incomes and output are actually falling, in which case there is a depression or **slump**. These are the terms used to describe the phases of the business cycle.

In recent years the UK has felt slump threatening but the data shows that it did not actually happen. It is not easy to predict what will happen in the economy. This can mean businesses are caught out by events. They try to study the trends and evaluate the likely consequences

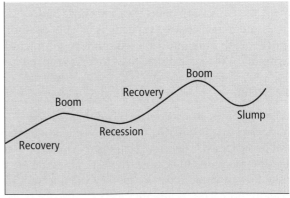

Figure 62.2 The business cycle

for themselves. They always hope that the Government will be able to smooth out the fluctuations in demand. Changes in economic policy can have important effects. But governments also find economic forecasting difficult and quite often predict wrongly. Sometimes they add to uncertainty rather than reduce it.

62.2 The phases of the business cycle

It used to be thought that the business cycle consisted of a sequence of events which would recur at fairly regular intervals, usually taking about nine years. If this were ever true, it certainly does not provide an accurate picture now. For a while after World War Two it seemed possible that government policies would keep the economy growing smoothly. But in 1974 and 1981 severe recessions occurred. The slump which occurred in 1990–1992, clearly visible in Figure 62.1, was also quite severe. Although growth has been fairly steady in recent years, recession could become a problem still.

RECESSION

In a recession, you will probably observe the following:

- businesses complaining of falling demand
- cuts in output
- rising unemployment
- few job opportunities
- gloomy expectations
- low levels of capacity utilisation
- falling levels of **investment**
- many businesses making losses
- some businesses closing down.

A recession starts with falling sales. At first, the business tries to keep things going, making extra marketing effort. It will be intensely conscious of increased competition; customers may seem very price sensitive. If the situation continues, cuts in output and employment follow. Though most businesses keep their 'key' workers – people with skills which are hard to replace when times improve. Few businesses implement the expansion plans they may have had. Investment in increased capacity is usually postponed. Indeed, with much under-used capital equipment the temptation is to cut rather than increase capacity.

RECOVERY

When it comes, recovery is usually rather halting. Businesses are unsure that the improvement in demand will be sustained. Their expectations remain depressed and they continue to be unenthusiastic about taking the risk of investment. In particular, they will not want to take on more labour until they are sure that the recovery is real. Unemployment is likely to stay high. Lack of business confidence can become a self-fulfilling prophecy.

Recovery phases can last a long time. So long as there is spare capacity in the economy, output can increase quite sharply. Initially, businesses use their under-utilised capital equipment to increase output. When they are running at full capacity, they put expansion plans in motion, investing in new buildings, plant and machinery.

THE BOOM

As the recovery turns into a boom, various features emerge:

- as investment increases, equipment suppliers have difficulty supplying all customers
- most businesses are working flat out
- many businesses experience shortages of skilled labour
- in order to attract the people they need, businesses bid against each other so that wages begin to rise faster than inflation
- prices are increased
- high levels of demand mean that higher prices have little effect on the growth of sales
- inflation, i.e. a general rise in the level of prices, increases.

When a recovery turns into a boom it 'overheats'. The economy is growing at too fast a rate to be sustainable in the medium term. The reason is that growth requires resources. At any given time there is a limit to the quantity of resources available. So long as there are unemployed people who have the skills required by employers, businesses can go on hiring. Once all those people have jobs, the only way a business can hire more people is to poach them from each other. This requires an incentive, usually higher wages. Even that may not attract enough people with scarce skills. It may be necessary to pay *more* and wait for staff to undergo the necessary training. That takes time. Employers want people *now*.

Economists call this a supply constraint; businesses call it a bottleneck. There are others. If capital equipment producers are working flat out, orders for labour-saving equipment will go on the order books, but won't be produced for some time. This is called having a full order book. It is highly profitable for the supplier but indicates a shortage of capacity.

Full capacity output in the economy is the maximum production level possible when all resources are working flat out. The closer the economy gets to full capacity output, the greater the supply constraints. Therefore costs tend to rise. As costs rise, inflation accelerates. Then governments (and businesses) start to worry about the unpredictable consequences of high and rising inflation. They usually respond by raising interest rates.

DOWNTURN

The rising costs associated with a boom will, in time, discourage continuing growth. They have a tendency to reduce profitability and the attractiveness of further investment. But usually government anticipates the need to damp down the economy. Rising interest rates put people off spending. Consumers who have to pay more for their mortgages spend less on consumer goods. Businesses which borrow to finance investment find their calculations less favourable when they have to pay higher interest charges.

The result is that demand for all sorts of products will fall. This has a cumulative effect on the economy. It has a big impact on construction. Higher mortgage rates mean lower demand for housing. Builders find that the houses they are working on are less profitable than they had hoped. So they cut back their plans and let some of their employees go. These people have difficulty finding a new employer and may have to rely on unemployment benefit. The cut in their incomes means less spending on luxuries. Businesses such as theme parks and restaurants face a drop in demand. Incomes fall there too.

In this way, the impact of higher interest rates is felt in lower levels of demand all through the economy. Once demand starts to fall, reduced real incomes cause demand to fall further. Some sectors will be affected less than others. Cadbury's feels a recession less than

most, because chocolate consumption is largely unaffected. Sales of **consumer durables** such as cars and carpets may fall sharply. As will luxuries such as malt whisky or Chanel No 5.

Producers of investment goods are affected the most. Plans to invest can be postponed. Figure 62.3 shows the volatility of consumption spending. Household incomes are protected somewhat by benefits. Also many people draw on past savings when they become unemployed. This helps to stabilise their spending over time.

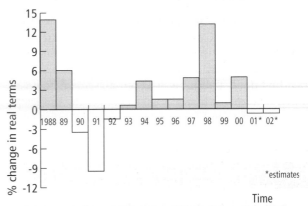

Source: Annual Abstract of Statistics, ONS, Crown copyright 2002

Figure 62.3 Investment spending, 1988–2002

62.3 The role of investment

Experience shows that investment fluctuates far more than consumption. This can have a major effect on the business cycle. Supposing the economy has been weak, leading to a fall in interest rates. Some people in business become a little more optimistic and make some positive investment decisions. The increase in spending produces rising incomes for some. Their increased spending generates a further increase in incomes. Aggregate demand continues to rise and business expectations improve further.

The reverse process occurs at the end of a boom. Rising costs coupled with rising interest rates depress business expectations. Investment starts to drop away as it becomes less profitable. The result is a cumulative fall in incomes and a slowing down of aggregate demand. If the process continues, incomes and output will fall.

STOCKS AND THE BUSINESS CYCLE

Investment in stocks of inputs or finished goods can also be an important factor in the cycle. When demand is rising, businesses will meet it partly by selling stocks. This is a signal to them that they should increase output. Similarly the early signs of recession may include rising stock levels as buyers spend less.

A decision to hold lower levels of stocks can mean that output will fall sharply for a while. This is known as **destocking**. The resulting fall in incomes is likely to affect aggregate demand. If it is widespread enough it will affect the whole economy. The converse is true too: if firms increase their stock levels there will be a rise in output, incomes and employment, which will stimulate the economy.

Although stocks are important in the analysis of real world events, their significance as determinants of the business cycle has been reduced by just-in-time production. If the policy is to minimise stocks at all times, changes in the level of stockholding will have little impact.

CONSUMER DURABLES

Figure 62.4 shows that car sales are very sensitive to changes in income over the course of the business cycle. Changes in spending on consumer durables affect the economy in the same way that investment spending does. This is because purchases can be post poned or brought forward. Like changes in stocks, changes in demand for durables can explain the nature of business fluctuations.

62.4 How businesses are affected

It has already been pointed out that business fluctuations have a very variable impact on the individual firm. Producers of pickled onions may hardly notice the difference. People may even want to buy *more* of them when incomes fall, to spice up some cheaper food items. Toothpaste producers will probably notice no change at all. Producers of machinery for manufacturing – machine toolmakers – may be so badly affected that they cannot survive a recession.

Figure 62.5 shows how many business failed during the early 1990s. The data is for net registrations. So a positive figure indicates more new businesses setting up

than business failures. During 1991, business start-ups just about balanced business failures, but in the next two years vast numbers of businesses closed down as the recession created increasingly difficult conditions. Often it is during recessions that businesses address

Source: Regional Trends, ONS, Crown copyright and ONS Website

Figure 62.5 Business registrations and deregistrations

their weaknesses. If they survive the recession they may emerge stronger and better able to compete. They may use improved human resource management strategies, new technologies, or more efficient approaches to organisation generally. They may try to predict the start of a recession to be ready for it when it comes.

One way to survive recession is to diversify the product range so that the business is not too dependent for its profits on items which are likely to experience wide variations in demand over the course of the cycle. This can be a good strategy for suppliers of consumer goods but may be of little help to a supplier of specialist steels. Falling investment will mean a sharp decrease in demand for steel. A steel company would need to make sufficient profits during economic upturns to survive the difficult times. Shareholders should come to expect wide variations in profits over time.

Source: Society of Motor Manufacturers and Traders Ltd

Figure 62.4 New car registrations in the UK

TV, TOYS AND PENSIONS

Even when the economy is performing well, some businesses will get to the end of the road. But then, in favourable trading conditions, others will be expanding. On one weekend in 2002, Equitable Life, the pensions and insurance company, was in desperate trouble while HIT Entertainment, the animators behind *Bob the Builder*, reported increased profits.

Lengthening life expectancy was putting pressure on all pension funds. Promises about pensions made decades ago to contributors are now hard to keep; they have to be paid for so many years. Falling share prices added to the woe, increasing as profit forecasts worsened and confidence declined. It looked as though at least one pension fund could become insolvent (i.e. have insufficient funds to meet its obligations).

A disaster scenario of this sort does not mean that all businesses are in trouble. HIT (founded to help create the *Muppets*) had bought the rights to *Thomas the Tank Engine* and *Barney the Dinosaur*, and had sold *Rubbadubbers* to the BBC and some European TV stations.

ISSUES FOR analysis

Many business decisions are affected in some way by the business cycle. In considering business strategies, therefore, always consider the effect of trading conditions in the economy as a whole.

Particular points to consider:

- Is the product one which is significantly affected by the business cycle? Some products are much less vulnerable than others.
- Are sales forecasts or budgets likely to be disrupted by an impending recession?
- If the economy is entering a boom phase, might there be some difficulty in recruiting skilled labour?
- Could higher interest rates raise the cost of investment?
- Is the balance sheet strong enough to cope with a sharp recession? Is liquidity high enough and gearing low enough?
- If recession is imminent, ought the business to consider diversifying into products less prone to falling demand?

62.5 Demand and the business cycle
an evaluation

The problem with the business cycle is similar to the difficulty in using the concept of the product life cycle.

In both cases, you can only draw the graph *after* the event. In other words, neither is easy to predict. The past does not necessarily tell you about the future. Therefore it is not easy to decide how significant its impact is likely to be in any given situation. Some businesses survive recessions with little difficulty, while others are pushed to the limits or collapse altogether.

However, difficult conditions can force businesses to address their weaknesses. In this way they may emerge from recession leaner and more competitive. Managements may tackle organisational problems they should have solved a long time ago. The early 1990s' recession saw a wave of 'de-layering', as companies removed entire layers of management from top-heavy, bureaucratic companies. Such cutbacks inevitably cause short-term difficulties but can have beneficial effects in the long term.

The existence of a rather unpredictable business cycle justifies the use of contingency planning by all firms. Today's successes should not lead to complacency but to careful thought about tomorrow's possible dangers. Similarly, during a recession a wise firm starts to think about consumer tastes in the next boom.

KEY terms

boom – a time of rapid economic growth, above the level which can be sustained in the long run, during which large numbers of businesses experience buoyant trading conditions.

consumer durables – the household equivalent of fixed assets, i.e. products used over many years such as cars, fridges and carpets.

destocking – running down stocks in response to a fall in demand

investment – spending today which will generate income in the future.

real income – the value of spending power for the population as a whole, or the value of output produced by the economy as a whole, with the effects of inflation removed.

recession – a period in which demand is growing more slowly than before, so that large numbers of businesses find they are selling less than they expected to.

recovery – a period of economic growth starting from a depressed situation in which the economy moves towards its full capacity, maximum possible output.

slump – a time of falling output and real incomes, accompanied by rising unemployment and gloomy business expectations.

AS Level Exercises

A. REVISION QUESTIONS

(30 marks; 60 minutes)

Read the unit, then answer:

1 Briefly describe each of the four phases of the business cycle. *(4)*
2 How are fluctuations in output measured? *(2)*
3 What problems are likely to arise during a boom? *(3)*
4 Why does investment fluctuate more than consumption? *(4)*
5 How can changes in stock levels affect the business cycle? *(3)*
6 Outline two ways a firm may benefit from a recession. *(4)*
7 Why is a recession difficult to predict? *(4)*
8 Explain three ways in which a firm might react to a recession. *(6)*

B. REVISION EXERCISES

B1 Data Response

Interest Rate Cuts 'Needed to Avoid Recession'

The Bank of England should continue cutting interest rates to ward off the threat of recession, according to two of Britain's leading independent economic forecasting groups. Oxford Economic Forecasting and the London Business School believe the economy is likely to avoid recession narrowly next year, but with the risks clearly on the downside.

The groups predict the economy will expand by 0.9% in 1999. They argue that there are several factors that could nonetheless push the economy into recession: for example weaker-than-expected world demand, aggressive destocking and higher saving.

Meanwhile inflation is expected to undershoot the government's 2.5% target, reaching a trough just below 2% in the middle of next year.

Source: *The Financial Times*, 24/11/98

Questions *(30 marks; 35 minutes)*

1 Explain how cutting interest rates might help 'ward off the threat of recession'. *(6)*
2 The UK economy grows, on average, by about 2.5% per year. What are the implications for firms of the economy growing at only 0.9%? *(8)*

3 a Explain the meaning of the term 'destocking'. *(2)*
   b Why might some firms undertake 'aggressive destocking'? *(7)*
4 Outline why inflation might be expected to 'undershoot' its target during an economic slowdown. *(7)*

B2 Data Response

Labour shortage worst for 25 years

The threat of a shortage of unskilled labour is at its most extreme for 25 years, according to a report yesterday that will raise fears that the jobs market is overheating.

The number of manufacturers warning that recruitment difficulties could hit their businesses has hit levels not seen since 1974 – higher, even, than the boom of 1989, the last time the survey recorded major unskilled labour shortages.

The Confederation of British Industry (CBI), the employers' organisation, said firms were worried that shortages of semi- and unskilled labour would hit output in the next four months.

The most recent detailed unemployment figures show that the number of people claiming benefit in parts of the south-east has fallen as low as 1%. On this measure, Newbury in Berkshire and Crawley in West Sussex have unemployment rates of 1.1%. But towns in the industrial areas of northern England suffer high jobless rates. Hartlepool has 11.5% and Liverpool 8.7%.

The CBI found businesses were almost as worried about shortage of manual workers as they were about difficulty in recruiting skilled employees.

Source: The *Independent*, 28/7/99

Questions *(30 marks; 35 minutes)*

1 What is indicated by the data about the position of the UK economy with respect to the business cycle in late 1999? *(2)*
2 What are the options open to businesses that want to expand but have difficulty recruiting skilled labour? *(3)*
3 What options are available when unskilled labour is hard to recruit? *(3)*
4 Why are there big differences in the availablity of labour between different regions within the UK? *(8)*
5 What consequences for the economy as a whole would you expect as a result of labour shortages becoming a problem? *(14)*

A Level Exercises

A. REVISION QUESTIONS
(30 marks; 60 minutes)

Read the unit, then answer:

1 What financial and marketing strategies might a firm adopt to prevent recession from being a threat to its survival? *(4)*
2 What are the major influences on the level of investment? *(3)*
3 Describe the conditions likely to confront a manufacturer of washing machines during a recession. *(4)*
4 What types of business are most likely to be able to survive a recession? *(4)*
5 What role do consumer and business expectations play in the business cycle? *(4)*
6 How would an increase in the general level of investment affect a truck manufacturer? *(4)*
7 What corporate strategies might a car producer adopt to minimise the impact of the business cycle? *(4)*
8 How is the business cycle likely to affect the decisions of people engaged in human resources management? *(3)*

B. REVISION EXERCISES

B1 Data Response
The construction industry is particularly vulnerable to the fluctuations of the business cycle. The table below shows the value of new housing orders obtained for the industry.

Value of new private sector housing orders obtained by contractors (£m)

1988	7893	1995	4905
1989	6497	1996	5416
1990	4855	1997	6253
1991	4552	1998	5997
1992	4016	1999	5901
1993	4874	2000	6085
1994	5721	2001	6525

Source: ONS Monthly Digest of Statistics, ONS Website

Questions *(30 marks; 35 minutes)*

1 What are the two largest percentage changes in orders from year to year shown in the data? *(4)*
2 To what extent would these changes be predictable? *(5)*
3 Explain why construction business is so closely tied to the progress of the business cycle. *(6)*
4 How may construction businesses react to changes such as those provided in the data? *(9)*
5 Outline two strategies a construction company could adopt to maximise its chances of surviving the next time there is a slump as severe as 1990. *(6)*

C. ESSAY QUESTIONS

1 Under what circumstances might company directors keep open a loss-making factory?
2 What difficulties would boom conditions create for a company designing computer systems for a manufacturing industry?
3 What human resource management strategies might help a business to survive recession?

INTERNATIONAL TRADE, EXCHANGE RATES AND COMPETITIVENESS

DEFINITION

Trade refers to the process of buying and selling goods and services. This makes it possible for people to specialise in the type of production they do best. They concentrate on producing items in which they have a competitive advantage. Then they exchange these for other products they need or want. When goods and services are exchanged by people in different countries, international trade takes place. In order to engage in international trade, a business must offer good value and attractive products; it must be competitive.

63.1 International trade

For some businesses, the market consists of a group of buyers who are close at hand. For other businesses the market could be anywhere in the world. In between there are large numbers of businesses which have some export markets. The Covent Garden Soup Company exports its cartons of soup to France. Because it has a perishable product it probably cannot extend its markets too far beyond this. Many businesses share this pattern of primary dependence on one market, with some sales overseas. This is a way of enlarging the market without becoming heavily dependent on overseas sales.

Many businesses face competition from imports. Growers of lettuces in the UK face strong competition from Dutch growers. The price at which they can sell their lettuces in UK markets will be limited by the price of the competition.

Figure 63.1 shows how the UK earns export revenue. Within these categories machinery, vehicles and chemicals are the important items. In practice, huge numbers of UK firms are involved in exports, sometimes of seemingly improbable items. Chemicals and cars are important UK exports, as are North Sea oil, Scotch whisky and marmalade.

Remember that the data in Figure 63.1 cover goods only; there are also significant exports of services. For instance, Americans wanting to travel on a Virgin Atlantic flight. 40% of Virgin Atlantic's customers originate outside the UK. The American pays dollars in the New York travel agent, but Virgin must be paid pounds. So the travel agent exchanges the dollars for pounds in order to pay the fare. This is known as an *invisible export*. Invisible because the product is a service, an export because it earns foreign currency.

International trade greatly increases the number of businesses competing with one another for most

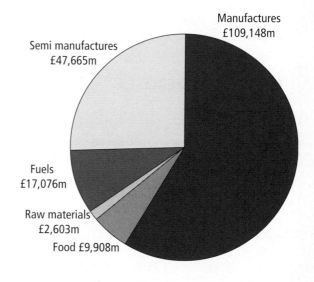

Source: Monthly Digest 2002, ONS

Figure 63.1 UK exports of goods by category, 2000

products. It almost always leads to prices being lower than they would be without trade. This creates a very satisfactory situation for consumers because they have more choice and pay lower prices. This increases their spending power and, in turn, their standard of living.

Businesses which are involved in international trade have to cope with some uncertainties. Deliveries take longer and cost more. They may be subject to unforeseen delays. Even more importantly, at least one party to the deal will be making payments in foreign currency. Floating exchange rates can make the real value of payments unpredictable.

THE SHIFTING PATTERN OF TRADE

The pattern of trade – the quantities and the products traded and the markets to which they go – does not stand still. It shifts continuously for all sorts of reasons:

- new businesses set up and develop their export markets
- new technologies open up previously impossible export and import markets
- businesses which are constantly striving to improve their competitive performance acquire advantages they did not previously have
- changes in exchange rates alter the prices at which goods and services can be sold abroad.

Export marketing is often a matter of extending market orientation to an unfamiliar market. The nature of that market and the particular requirements of customers there must be studied carefully. All aspects of marketing must be adapted to fit the circumstances. The impact of new technologies will be discussed in a later unit. Striving for competitive advantage involves good decision making in production and human resource management. Exchange rate changes present problems, and these must be studied in some detail.

Business IN

MANUFACTURING OR SERVICES?

Traditionally, the UK has exported both goods and services. Exports of manufactures grew strongly in the 1990s. Now services are gaining an edge. Exports of financial products, technical services (e.g. in engineering) and computing services are significant, as are royalties. These are mostly payments for licences to use technologies for which there are intellectual property rights. (They also include books, TV programmes, films and so on.)

In 1996, 25% of total exports consisted of services. In 2001, the figure had risen to 28.7%. Over the same period, total exports grew by 20% in real terms. This represents a significant source of market growth.

63.2 Exchange rates

The exchange rate is the value of a currency measured in how much foreign currency it can buy. In 1980 a pound could buy 525 Japanese yen. By 1995 the pound had fallen to only 135 yen. In 2002 it was again touching 140 yen, after some fluctuations. Clearly, exchange rates vary. They may be stable for a while, but then enter a period of instability in which they rise or fall sharply. In the long term the exchange rate is determined by the pattern of international trade – supply and demand for imports and exports. In the short term, however, speculation can cause wide variations in a currency's value.

This speculation can be based upon:

- expectations about the future level of interest rates
- expectations about a country's future trade performance
- political uncertainties.

AN INTERNATIONAL MARKET

Cars are sold in a global market. On the whole, sales of UK car exports held up quite well in the late 1990s. However, the strong pound became a real problem for UK manufacturers after it jumped upwards in 1996. Still, in 2001 63% of total UK car production was exported.

Source: Society of Motor Manufacturers and Traders

Ford is one of the big players in the world car market. Tucked inside it is the Premier Auto Group (PAG) which includes Jaguar, Land Rover, Aston Martin and Volvo. It is seen as Ford's luxury car arm. In 2002, of these, only Volvo was making any money.

Jaguar, based in the West Midlands, expanded sales dramatically, with growth running at around 50% in 2002. Of its output of 57,000 cars, 68% was exported and 48% went to the potentially lucrative US market. Despite this, it looked likely to lose £500 million for the year.

Ford lost altogether US$5.4 billion in 2001. There was pressure on PAG from Bill Ford, the group CEO, to cut costs. A new CEO was appointed with instructions to make PAG contribute one third of Ford's total profit within five years. Somehow Jaguar had to try to maintain its style and cutting-edge technology, while also creating big-time profits. It would help a lot if the pound went down. Jaguar could either keep the same foreign currency prices, and get a bigger profit margin on each car sold, or it could cut the price and go for a bigger market share. Meantime, the high pound created a cut-throat market.

Figure 63.2 shows how the **sterling index** has fluctuated since 1988. The business uncertainties implied by these variations have encouraged many companies to press for Britain to join the single European currency. This pressure increased after the successful launch of Euro notes and coins in January 2002.

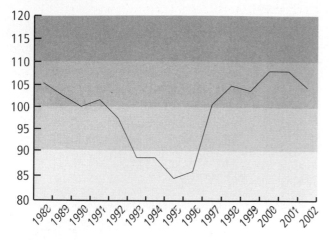

Figure 63.2 Sterling exchange rate index (1990 = 100) (Source: Eurostat, © European Communities, 2002

63.3 The impact of exchange rate changes

Businesses which are exporting and importing on a regular basis find fluctuations in exchange rates a source of considerable uncertainty. This can be enough to stop them from developing export markets. It is not too much of a problem for exporters if the exchange rate falls because the effect is to increase competitiveness. But if the exchange rate rises, the loss of competitiveness erodes profit margins. This makes exporting unattractive. The resulting loss of markets can be very painful. Look back at Figure 63.2. Notice the rise in the value of the pound in 1996. Prices set in pounds rise sharply in foreign currency terms when the exchange rate rises.

The reverse effect can be expected for importers. If the exchange rate rises, the price they have to pay in pounds for the goods they import will fall. They can either cut prices in pounds or maintain prices and increase their margins. If they cut prices sales revenue may rise. What exactly are the effects on companies of changing exchange rates? The table below provides a step-by-step guide.

Overall, an **appreciation** of the exchange rate leads to a loss of competitiveness, while a **depreciation** leads to a gain in competitiveness. The unstable nature of floating exchange rates creates difficulties for businesses. So governments have made repeated attempts to fix their currency values in terms of other currencies. Some peg the value of their currency to the US$. The European Exchange Rate Mechanism limited the extent to which member currencies could diverge from one another. European Monetary Union goes one step further by creating a single currency, the Euro, for member countries. These policies will be discussed later.

The effect on firms of changes in the value of the pound – a step-by-step guide:

1 The effect upon exports of a falling pound

The external value of the pound is measured by what it will buy. If it once bought $2 but now only buys $1.60, it has fallen by 20%.

Pound down means fewer $s per pound. So UK exporters don't need to charge as many dollars per pounds' worth of exports. For example, if a £200 coat is exported to the US:

- *At $2 to the pound the coat must be priced at $400 to get a UK revenue of £200.*
- *At $1.60 to the pound you only have to charge $320. So a 20% fall in the pound improves UK export competitiveness by 20%.*

Summary: A devaluation of the pound makes our exports more competitive; this boosts UK export sales, as foreign buyers switch to cheaper UK goods.

2 The effect upon imports of a falling pound

When £1 = $2 a US company selling Superman comics in Britain for £1 will receive $2 per unit. If the pound falls to $1.60, then each £1 comic generates only $1.60 in US revenue.

So a falling pound hits the revenue of those importing goods into the UK. As their revenues are hit, importers are likely to push up their UK prices (e.g. to £1.25 so that the dollar revenues are £1.25 × 1.60 = $2).

Summary: Devaluation pushes import prices up, which reduces their competitiveness. So import levels should fall. However, the increased import prices include food and fuel. So they can be expected to push the inflation rate up.

3 Effect of rising pound upon exports

If £1 rises to equal $2.40, exporters may have to increase their overseas prices.

The £200 coat must now be priced at $480 if the exporter wants to go on receiving £200 per export. This will cut demand. The % fall in sales will be determined by the price elasticity of the product. The price increase will cause a sharp fall in sales for a highly price elastic product.

If UK firms choose to hold their export prices constant, each dollar they charge will translate back into fewer pounds, so exporting firms' profit margins will suffer.

The $400 coat will now only provide $400/$2.4 = £166.6 of revenue.

Summary: Pound up means export prices up and therefore export volumes down.

4 The effect on imports of a high pound

If the pound rises, importers will find that each pound they receive will be worth more of their local currency. Therefore their profit margins increase. This encourages them to increase their marketing effort in the UK, as selling here is so profitable. If they choose to do so, they could afford to cut their pound prices. If import prices are cut, UK firms will enjoy lower costs on imported materials and components. But they will suffer fiercer competition from importers of rival products.

Summary: Pound up means imports up, with foreign firms increasing their share of our market (at the expense of our firms/jobs).

CHINA TAKING A POUNDING

It's a long time since life was easy in the Potteries. All the big china and pottery producers in Stoke-on-Trent have had problems. Royal Doulton had a major restructuring. Wedgwood brought in big name designers. Some long-established firms closed down. The basic problem was labour-intensive production facing intensive competition from countries with cheaper labour, and the strong pound.

Churchill China was in trouble in 1990, and had a visit from BBC's 'troubleshooter', John Harvey-Jones. He advised investing more and delegating more and it seemed to work. By 1996, the company was exporting 60% of sales, mostly to European markets. Then in 1997 the pound rose and stayed high. For a while, Churchill was able to rely on its hotel and restaurant customers, who valued its reliability. Then, the company began to lose money again and decided to go up-market.

New designs continued the very English style of the traditional Churchill product. Stephen Roper, the third generation chair of this family business, said that, along with the 'Made in England' stamp on the bottom, this would help them to compete in this market.

No one in the china business ever thinks you can just stand still. Continental Europe, where Churchill was successful in the past, has been dogged by slow economic growth. Survival generally requires action.

IN Business

63.4 The implications for business strategies

Businesses are under pressure to buy their inputs from the cheapest source. They will also try to expand their markets wherever possible. Many businesses have become increasingly involved in overseas markets. They may be buying imported inputs, or selling their products abroad. In time they may need to set up subsidiaries overseas, either for manufacturing or distribution or both. At that point they become multinational enterprises (sometimes also termed transnationals). Some companies are operating in so many countries that they should be seen as global companies selling global products. A good example is Coca-Cola.

The process by which this has taken place has come to be known generally as globalisation. It has been greatly aided over the years by the development of cheaper and easier means of transport and communication. Transport costs are now insignificant for many products. Unless the ratio of bulk to value is very high, they are unlikely to give local producers a telling advantage in the market.

Business thinkers sometimes say 'think globally, act locally'. This is really just a reminder that a market oriented attitude demands that each individual market be understood and catered for. For most products this approach is important. The product must be suited to the needs of the market, and the marketing strategies must be in tune with the culture of that market.

Some companies hardly need to bother; Coca-Cola is one example, Starbucks another. Actually they are rather special cases. They are selling an image of the American way of life. Adaptation to local markets is unnecessary. It is the image that is in demand. These two are exceptions. For most companies it is essential to understand the market they are selling into. And adapt both product and marketing accordingly.

SELLING CHINESE UNDERWEAR

Marketing consultants in Hong Kong are keen to help Chinese manufacturers to market their products. They tell stories of mistakes which have been made. One Chinese manufacturer of men's underwear wanted to sell to Western markets. It decided it would be good to name its range after a flower. They rummaged around the dictionary and decided to call it the Pansy range. They found it simply would not sell in Europe. If only they had sought advice from marketing people in Hong Kong.

IN Business

63.5 What determines international competitiveness?

Businesses compete on a number of fronts. Price competitiveness is extremely important for some products. For others, non-price competition may be more important. In general, businesses seek to improve their competitiveness in order to secure a larger market.

The decisions involved here are internal to the business and involve aspects of production, marketing and human resource management. They revolve around two issues:

- How can efficiency and productivity (output per person employed) be increased?
- How can the business create new areas of demand for the product?

However, competitiveness may be affected by the business environment. Exchange rate changes may make them more or less competitive. Rising input prices will push managers to consider raising prices. A general rise in prices – inflation – will affect competitiveness too. A change in the rules of the World Trade Organisation (WTO) may mean that import duties change. All of these factors are external to the business and involve deciding the most effective reaction.

REACTING TO EXCHANGE RATE CHANGES

The business which competes with imports and finds the exchange rate rising is under added pressure to improve its efficiency. It may consider increasing investment in labour-saving machinery and reducing the workforce. It may introduce new technologies and new organisational strategies. It will increase its marketing efforts. The fight will be on just to *maintain* competitiveness. Sometimes governments have allowed the exchange rate to rise in the attempt to force businesses to increase their competitiveness.

The business which is exporting when the exchange rate falls has a bonus. The value in pounds of its product will rise if the foreign currency price stays the same. It has a choice. It could leave prices the same and accept a higher profit margin. Or it could cut the price in the hope of higher sales. The best strategy will depend on the price elasticity of demand for its product. A high elasticity – greater than 1 – will mean that a price cut will bring a disproportionately large increase in sales.

Similarly, the exporter which has to contend with a rising exchange rate must decide how higher prices in foreign currency will affect sales. If they will tend to fall because foreign buyers will switch to competing substitutes whose price has remained the same, it may be better to accept lower profit margins. Staying competitive when the exchange rate is rising is very difficult. Most big businesses want a stable, and low, exchange rate if export markets are important to them. Staying competitive is further complicated for the business which imports inputs as well as exporting the final product. Deciding a strategy means thinking through all the angles.

In 2003, after several years of the pound being high against the Euro, Volkswagen decided to reduce its car prices in Britain. To avoid any dent to its image, it advertised its 'surprising' prices very subtly.

There are many issues for analysis regarding the effects on business of changing exchange rates and changing patterns of international trade. They include:

- Existing trade patterns give clues as to profitable opportunities for the future in markets abroad, and their likely growth potential.
- The advent of the Euro is likely to accelerate the trend towards international trade. Small and medium-sized firms could avoid exporting in the past. In future, they are likely to be hit by more imports. This may force them to fight harder for export sales.
- A decision to enter certain export markets will be affected by the likely exchange rate risk. Within the Eurozone, other member countries will have a great advantage over outsiders.
- No firm should allow itself to be overly reliant upon one foreign currency. If 50% of a British firm's sales go to one foreign country, a rise in the value of the pound could be crippling.

63.6 International trade
an evaluation

For many businesses, selling abroad is absolutely essential. It is the only way they can expand their markets. However, there are always more uncertainties in export markets. Market change, exchange rate changes and changes in the rules of world trade can all create problems.

Special efforts must be made to ensure that good market knowledge is obtained in foreign markets. Cultural differences can have a big impact and an understanding of these is often necessary. Careful evaluation of the risks associated with uncertainty may be needed.

International markets are usually more competitive than those where the business focuses on local markets. This is partly because there are more companies competing. The result is that exporting companies are usually among the most progressive. They refuse to accept low quality standards or poor management. This makes them livelier (though less secure) places to work.

KEY terms

appreciation – a rise in the exchange rate such that prices of imports fall and prices of exports in foreign currency rise.

depreciation – a fall in the exchange rate such that prices of imports rise and prices of exports in foreign currency fall.

sterling – a widely used term meaning the British pound.

sterling index – an index of the value of the pound compared with other currencies.

AS Level Exercises

A. REVISION QUESTIONS
(30 marks; 60 minutes)

Read the unit, then answer:

1 Give three examples of services that are important in international trade. *(3)*
2 Identify three sources of business uncertainty for exporting firms. *(3)*
3 Why may market orientation be especially important for an exporter? *(3)*
4 How are importers to the UK affected by depreciation in the value of the pound? *(3)*
5 What will happen to exporters' profits if the exchange rate falls? Explain your answer. *(4)*
6 Briefly outline how each of the following exporters to America might respond to a sharp rise in the value of the pound against the dollar:
  a Rolls Royce
  b EIDOS (producers of games software such as *Tomb Raider*)
  c British Steel, selling sheet steel for making car body panels. *(6)*
7 What is likely to happen to consumer demand if import prices rise? *(2)*
8 Outline one type of business that would suffer severely and one type that would benefit greatly from a high pound. *(6)*

B. REVISION EXERCISES

B1 Data Response

> Exports of manufacturers from the UK depend heavily on being fully competitive on world markets. Between early 1996 and early 1998 the pound rose steadily on the foreign exchange markets, threatening competitiveness. The table below gives the change in the value of the pound against the US dollar and the Deutschmark.
>
> | | US$ | DM |
> |---|---|---|
> | 1996 Quarter 1 | 1.53 | 2.26 |
> | 1998 Quarter 1 | 1.66 | 2.98 |
>
> **Source:** NIER, 1998

Questions *(30 marks; 35 minutes)*
1 Using cars as an example, calculate:
  a the price of a £12,000 car in both currencies at the beginning of 1996 *(4)*
  b the price of the same £12,000 car in both currencies at the start of 1998 *(4)*

c the percentage change in each currency over the two-year period. *(4)*
2 What would you expect to happen to sales of UK cars in the US and in Germany as a result of this appreciation? *(5)*
3 How would your answer to question 2 be affected by the knowledge that a British producer of sports cars believes the price elasticity of its products is approximately 0.5?(*(5)*
4 What impact would the rise in the pound have generally on UK car producers' sales turnover and profits? Explain your answer. *(8)*

B2 Data Response

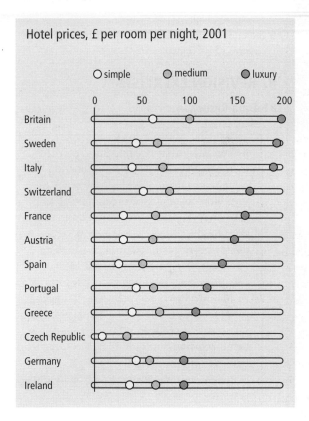

Hotel prices, £ per room per night, 2001

○ simple ◐ medium ● luxury

0 50 100 150 200

Britain
Sweden
Italy
Switzerland
France
Austria
Spain
Portugal
Greece
Czech Republic
Germany
Ireland

Source: The *Which?* Hotel Guide 2002

Questions *(30 marks; 35 minutes)*
1 How does the tourist trade affect exports and imports? *(4)*
2 Give three reasons that might explain why London hotel prices are exceptionally high. *(6)*
3 To what extent are London hotel prices likely to affect the level of tourism in the UK? *(4)*
4 What types of UK businesses are likely to be affected by the high price of London hotels? *(8)*
5 What might be done to make accommodation costs more competitive? *(8)*

A Level Exercises

A. REVISION QUESTIONS

(25 marks; 50 minutes)

Read the unit, then answer:

1 How can companies maintain competitiveness in the face of a high exchange rate? *(4)*
2 What impact would you expect a high exchange rate to have on employment? *(4)*
3 Which types of companies would be most likely to survive a period when the pound is high? *(4)*
4 How do businesses cope with unstable exchange rates? *(3)*
5 Outline two possible strategies for a UK pottery exporter which has suffered severely from past periods when the pound was high. *(6)*
6 State four factors that affect the international competitiveness of UK firms. *(4)*

B. REVISION EXERCISES

B1 Data Response

> Britain's engineering companies recorded their biggest monthly fall in production for more than a decade in May. Yesterday's figures show that engineering output fell by 2.3% in May. This was the biggest monthly drop for over 10 years. Engineering is one of the sectors of manufacturing most reliant upon exports. Output of textiles, leather, chemicals, metals and plastics all fell too.
>
> Manufacturers generally were struggling to cope with the effects of a strong pound. There was a seasonally adjusted 1.1% fall in manufacturing output in May, according to figures from the Office for National Statistics. This was the biggest drop in four years.
>
> Despite this gloom among producers, the Confederation of British Industry reported healthy growth in the services sector. As a result, economists were predicting that the Chancellor would increase base rates over the coming months.
>
> Source: Adapted from *The Financial Times*, the *Guardian* and *The Times*, 8/7/97

Questions *(30 marks; 35 minutes)*

1 Explain why the 'biggest monthly fall in production for more than a decade' may be due to 'the effects of a strong pound'. *(5)*
2 Assess why the high pound may have hit the engineering sector harder than manufacturing as a whole. *(5)*
3 What is meant by the terms:
   a seasonally adjusted *(3)*
   b base rates. *(3)*
4 What effect might an increase in base (interest) rates have on the value of the pound? *(3)*
5 Outline two possible benefits to British firms of 'a strong pound'. *(6)*
6 Why might the service sector be prosperous even when the pound is high? *(5)*

C. ESSAY QUESTIONS

1 Assess the impact of a sharp fall in the pound against the dollar upon Wedgwood – a world famous UK producer of china that exports more than a quarter of all its output to America.
2 Consider the advantages and disadvantages of a sharp rise in the pound upon different UK businesses.
3 Discuss the possible effects upon British manufacturing firms of a decision to join the European single currency (the Euro).

INFLATION AND UNEMPLOYMENT

DEFINITION

Inflation is a general rise in prices across a wide range of goods and services. Inflation is a loss in the purchasing power of money.

Unemployment occurs when people who are available to work cannot find jobs.

64.1 Does inflation matter?

The simplest way to understand inflation is to see it as rising prices. This is true, but it leads to an unfortunate consequence. A price increase usually causes demand to fall. Therefore it seems logical to assume that rising inflation causes lower consumer spending – and therefore leads to recession. This is a misunderstanding. At a time of 5% inflation, not only prices are rising by 5% but also wages. So people can pay for their 5% higher shopping bill with their 5% extra income. **Aggregate demand** need not be changed.

Inflation is easiest to understand as rising prices, but *best* understood as a fall in the value of money. In other words, a pound is not worth as much as it used to be.

So does inflation matter? If people can pay the 5% higher prices with their 5% higher salaries, who loses? At these relatively low levels, no-one loses much at all. The fear of inflation is largely the fear of hyper-inflation. For example, inflation in Germany in 1923 was over 1,000,000%. In Russia it was over 2,500% between 1990 and 1996. At these high levels, families can find their life savings becoming worthless within months.

64.2 Measuring inflation

Over the years inflation has been very variable. You can see the dramatic changes in British inflation in Figure 64.1. This shows the annual rate of inflation, i.e. the percentage change in prices generally each year. During the 1970s and 1980s the rate of inflation fluctuated very considerably. It became apparent that inflation could also be very unpredictable. This makes it hard for businesses to forecast trends and make plans. An investment appraisal, for example, becomes much more uncertain if the inflation outlook is unclear.

In recent years inflation has not been a problem and there are fears that deflation, generally falling prices, may be more of a threat.

The figures on which Figure 64.1 is based are the outcome of a lengthy process of measurement from which the **retail price index** (RPI) is constructed. An **index** number is one which shows a time series using a base year which is given the figure 100. The table on the next page shows the RPI (inflation) figures as a series based on 1995 prices equalling 100.

Source: Eurostat (© European Communities, 2002)

Figure 64.1 UK inflation rate

The Office of National Statistics (ONS) is responsible for compiling the RPI. It is based on a vast amount of data. Prices are collected for a wide range of goods and services in different places and types of retail outlet. These prices are then weighted according to their relative importance in people's budgets. So an increase in the price of cars will have a bigger impact on the index than an increase in the price of potatoes. The data upon which these weightings are based comes from the Family Expenditure Survey, which records the expenditures of 7,000 households. These are representative of all types of household and all regions. In this way price changes are expressed as a weighted average which measures reasonably accurately the impact of inflation on consumers generally.

Retail price index, UK, 1992–2002 (1995 = 100)

YEAR	RPI
1992	92.9
1993	94.4
1994	96.7
1995	100.0
1996	102.4
1997	105.6
1998	109.3
1999	111.0
2000	114.2
2001	116.3
2002	118.1

Source: National Institute Economic Review, Crown copyright 2002

Expressing price changes in index numbers makes it easier to compare values over the years. At the time of writing the base year is 1995. Each figure after 1995 shows the percentage increase in prices compared with 1995. It does *not* show the percentage increase in prices year by year – that requires an additional calculation of each year's change as a percentage of the previous year's value.

Of course, prices are changing all the time and some go down. Think about air fares, or electronic products. Other products encounter price falls because demand is diminishing. These changes are included in the RPI because it is an average figure for the change in prices generally.

64.3 How inflation develops

Unit 62 discusses the business cycle. It shows how an upswing and then a boom might trigger an acceleration in the rate of inflation. During a boom, demand is growing faster than the capacity of businesses to satisfy it. This situation is sometimes called **excess demand**. It happens when the most crucial resources needed to expand output are becoming scarce because of recent rapid growth in output.

When the economy is growing strongly, employers look for people with the scarce skills needed to help them expand. In time, the shortage of skills becomes a supply constraint. Employers are then likely to try to attract employees with higher pay. As pay is increased, costs rise and businesses seek to recover these through higher prices.

At first this process is very gradual. It causes little alarm. If consumer spending is growing, it may be possible to raise prices without losing customers. But by degrees price increases become more numerous and begin to show up in a rising rate of inflation. As people observe the increase in the inflation rate, they build rising prices into their expectations.

OVERHEATING

At some point in the upswing of the business cycle, a point is reached at which the economy is nearing its full capacity output. The result is that aggregate demand from all sources is growing faster than aggregate supply. This is known as excess demand; another term used to describe it is **overheating**. If it persists, inflation will accelerate as competition to obtain the available supplies intensifies.

This situation can be described as demand–pull inflation. Prices rise because people and businesses are trying to spend more. But the goods and services needed to satisfy demand cannot, in the short run, be produced. Another possible consequence of this is that imports will rise.

EXPECTATIONS

At this point in the explanation of how inflation develops, it is important to think about how wages and prices are determined. Businesses can raise prices provided they are confident that customers will still buy the product. If they have sufficient spending power, they will. So whether they can or not depends on the extent to which earnings are rising to match inflation. In other words, prices can rise provided they are matched by rising earnings.

How can employees make sure that their earnings rise? One way, of course, is to ensure that they have the scarce skills that employers need. Another is to join a strong trade union and negotiate pay increases by means of collective bargaining. Recent research shows that union members in the UK still earn, on average, about 11% more than non-union members.

During the period 1970–1990, any increase in inflation quickly got built into the expectations of wage negotiators. It was extremely difficult for employers to avoid paying an increase in real wages every year. It was expected that in money terms pay would always increase by more than the rate of inflation. Anything else would be unacceptable. So earnings tended to rise at the existing rate of inflation plus a little more.

The result can be a **wage–price spiral**. Wages rise to cover expected inflation. Costs rise, so prices are increased and inflation continues. This kind of inflation is sometimes called **cost–push inflation**, because it can continue even when there is no excess demand in the economy. In order to reduce inflation in this situation, some way must be found to reduce expectations of inflation. This will be looked at in more detail in Unit 65.

One way in which inflation may be given a twist upwards is through an exchange rate change. When the currency depreciates, imports get dearer and exports become cheaper. The increase in import prices will feed through into the RPI. This includes prices of imported consumer goods. The index also records price increases by British producers suffering higher costs of imported materials. A rising exchange rate will have the opposite effect. For that reason a strong exchange rate can be part of government policy to reduce inflation.

64.4 The impact of inflation on business

As already observed, when inflation is high it is also hard to predict. Forecasting expected sales revenue can be made very difficult. This is partly because of the price changes and partly because the presence of inflation makes it likely that the government will make changes to its economic policy.

When prices are changing quickly, businesses have more difficulty in keeping track of competitors' pricing strategies.

Deflation – when prices are falling on average – could be part of a real problem for businesses. When demand is stagnant or growing slowly, price competition is apt to be very keen. There may be price wars and it may be hard to guess what the competition is going to do next. In Japan, low levels of consumer spending have actually caused deflation. The Bank of Japan does not seem to know how to get the economy moving again.

64.5 The effects of government policy

When overheating occurs, governments feel threatened by rising inflation and a worsening balance of payments. Too many imports are sucked in by the spending boom. The usual government response is to tighten economic policy to dampen down demand. Taxes might be increased or interest rates pushed up. In 1997 and early 1998 the Bank of England increased interest rates to try to slow down a consumer spending boom. They did this again in 2000.

FITNESS FIRST

When incomes are growing, health clubs do very well. A little inflation is not a problem for them. Fitness First has 700,000 members at its network of clubs in the UK, Europe, Asia and Australia. While the economy looked strong, it opened many new clubs in the UK, only to find that they were not filling up very fast. The kind of people it was aiming for as members were finding that their incomes were at best growing rather slowly. Some were being made redundant as the economy slowed in 2001.

With overcapacity in the health club market generally, a price war seemed all too likely. Profits were falling and it was clear that some competition on price would be inevitable.

When economic policy changes such as this occur, the economy does not respond immediately. Consumers used to high spending during a boom are reluctant to cut back. Firms have investment plans which may take months or years to complete. It is normal for a time lag to occur. The Bank of England usually anticipates a time lag of eighteen months or two years.

For firms, therefore, it is important to be aware of the possibility of changing government policy, but wrong to assume that demand will change straight away. So there should, therefore, be time to carry through strategies such as cutting stocks or carrying out a zero budgeting exercise.

Ways Businesses Benefit from High Inflation	Problems for Business from High Inflation
Highly geared firms benefit from the cut in the real value of their loan repayments	Cash flow is squeezed by the rising cost of new materials and equipment
Balance sheets look stronger as rising property and stock values boost reserves	Forecasting is subject to greater uncertainty, which makes firms look for higher forecast rates of return
Smaller firms benefit from the reducing importance of brand names; they can compete on price/service	Owners of big brand names may struggle, as greater consumer price consciousness makes customers more price sensitive. This cuts the value added by brand names
It is easier to increase the price of your own product when prices are rising generally. So cost increases can be passed on to the consumer	Staff become much more wage conscious as inflation poses a threat to real living standards; therefore industrial disputes and labour turnover tend to rise

64.6 Unemployment

Figure 64.2 shows what has happened to the percentage of the labour force which is unemployed in the UK. These figures show dramatic changes which had a marked effect on many people's lives. They are total figures and disguise the fact that unemployment is actually most serious within certain well-defined groups of people. The young, older people, men who previously worked in manufacturing, unskilled people and ethnic minorities are the groups most affected.

Source: ONS, Monthly Digest of Statistics, Crown copyright 2002

Figure 64.2 UK unemployment

The real face of unemployment: outside a Job Centre in London (© Michael Ann Mullen/Format)

TYPES OF UNEMPLOYMENT

There are many reasons why a person may become and then remain unemployed. Quite often it is difficult to separate the reasons when looking at an individual case. Sometimes an employee will lose a job for one reason but fail to find alternative employment for quite other reasons. Having said this, three broad categories of unemployment can be identified.

1 Cyclical unemployment:

- **Cyclical unemployment** occurs when firms cut back on staff during the recession phase of the business cycle. During recession and slump or depression conditions, unemployment typically rises sharply. It will fall again as the economy recovers.
- When the economy is depressed, the main impact on incomes is born by those who lose their jobs. Those who remain employed typically manage to maintain real incomes most of the time.
- Counter-inflation policies which work by reducing the level of aggregate demand will necessarily tend to reduce the demand for labour and so create unemployment.

2 Frictional unemployment:

- **Frictional unemployment** occurs temporarily when people are between jobs. There are always some people who have left one job and are in the process of finding another. It has increased over the years because labour turnover has risen.
- Frictional unemployment can be reduced by developing improved flows of information about jobs available. It can also be affected by the level of income people have when their employment ceases. Redundancy payments give people time to look around for a job which suits them, rather than simply taking the first available job.

3 Structural unemployment:

In 2000, the UK economy was booming. Unemployment was falling. Yet even then, 5.5% of the workforce was unemployed. How could this be, when employers were desperate to find people?

Unemployment which persists even when the economy is at its full capacity output is either frictional or structural in origin. It is definitely not cyclical. Yet when employers have many vacancies, frictional unemployment is not likely to be significant because people can find jobs easily. So the main problem has to be **structural unemployment**.

To understand structural unemployment, it is necessary to look at the rather complex problems which lie beneath it. There are four important factors to be considered:

- As shown in the following table, there has been a major shift away from manufacturing jobs to the service sector; skilled metal-workers do not take easily to switching to working at B&Q.
- Changing technologies have caused employers to look for a different range of skills.
- Efforts to stay competitive can lead to the installation of labour-saving equipment.
- New technologies sometimes require more capital and less labour.

Demand for individual products changes for many reasons. However, in modern economies certain broad trends can be observed. Changes in tastes and fashions affect demand. Rising incomes bring some products within reach which previously had been unaffordable. An imported substitute which is newly available can reduce demand for the domestic product.

Supply changes too. For example, new technologies affect both products and processes. Some items become cheaper, and then demand for competing substitutes will fall. These changes are summarised in Figure 64.3.

These changes entail the expansion of some businesses while others contract. Also, they entail changes in the mix of skills required by businesses. As the pace of changes gathers speed, the rate at which people are made redundant from businesses which no longer need them increases. More people are looking around for new employers. Changes in patterns of employment can be seen in the table below. It shows the long-term trend away from employment in agriculture and manufacturing and towards employment in the service sector.

Employment by sector, Great Britain (000s)

	1979	2000
Agriculture	359	335
Manufacturing	7,113	4,162
Services	13,239	18,621
Total employment	22,639	24,314

Source: Crown copyright, ONS Annual Abstract, 1985 and 2001

IMMOBILITIES

Two awkward factors get in the way of the process of movement from one job to another and so worsen structural unemployment. One is occupational immobility. This is when the skills people have are not the ones which employers are currently seeking. The solution to this is to retrain. But there are all sorts of problems. The person concerned must have the aptitude, must know that retraining is possible and must be aware of the existence of jobs in the relevant field. Funds must be available from either the government or the individual to pay for retraining. For all these reasons, occupational immobilities have been very persistent in recent years.

The other awkward factor is known as geographical immobility. This is defined as a situation in which the unemployed person is unable (or unwilling) to move to a place where jobs are available. It is easy to see how this arises. House prices are higher in areas where jobs are available than in areas of high unemployment. Most owner-occupiers can't afford to move. If they are renting a council house, they will not qualify for one in an area of employment opportunity. When this situation is combined with the decline of a localised industry such as shipbuilding, high levels of structural unemployment can persist for decades.

THE OUTLOOK

Structural unemployment does decline eventually, as people have time to adjust to economic change. However, the process can take a long time. Many people who are unemployed for long periods become 'discouraged workers'. They lose their skills and their work habit, and become steadily less attractive to employers. Attempts to arrest this process by retraining have been only partially successful, perhaps because too little finance was available to do the job properly. Structural unemployment remains one of the major economic problems of the times. It is very acute in other European countries and remains a problem in the UK.

Possible government policies to deal with structural unemployment will be considered in Unit 67.

ISSUES FOR **analysis**

Inflation, or the threat of it, dominated economic policy making for many years. Governments tend to be very afraid of it. However, the long-term social effects of high unemployment are also very problematic. Inflation presents a range of issues for each individual decision taker.

Figure 64.3 Trends and changes

- Higher rates of inflation are also usually more variable rates of inflation, so an accelerating rate of inflation may be creating an unpredictable situation. Both governments and businesses may find it more difficult to forecast accurately.
- Despite this, many businesses grow and prosper at times of inflation. For much of the past decade the problem for Japan has been deflation. In other words, economic depression leading to falls in average prices. This is very damaging to consumer and business confidence.
- Rising inflation may mean that governments want to reduce demand in the economy; policy measures such as higher taxes or higher interest rates will hit sales for many businesses.
- Different kinds of unemployment have different implications and it can be important to have a good understanding of the underlying causes of unemployment at any given time.
- Cynical though it sounds, many businesses benefit from moderately high unemployment. Workers are focused on job security, not on pay rises. Staff generally are more willing to accept change in methods and organisation.
- If unemployment is largely structural, the people who are seeking work may not be in the places where employers are creating jobs, or may not have the skills which happen to be required. In these circumstances it may be important to be able to retrain.

64.7 Inflation and unemployment
an evaluation

In the past low inflation rates have been associated with high unemployment. This is what happens when the economy is in recession. The reverse is also true. This can mean that governments have to perform a balancing act. From 2000 to 2002, there was a happy balance of low inflation and fairly low unemployment too. For businesses, the difficulty is that the attempt by government to achieve a happy balance means that economic policy changes regularly. This was clear in 2000, when the interest rate was raised to 6%, but was falling again by the end of the year.

For individual firms, the problems caused by rising inflation or rising unemployment should be manageable. The most important thing is to have a well-diversified range of products selling into a wide range of markets. Then shortfalls in demand in one area can be cancelled out by successes elsewhere. A good example of this is Whitbread, whose low-priced Travel Inn hotels did well in 2002/03 at a time when luxury hotels were struggling.

KEY terms

aggregate demand – the total of all demand for goods and services throughout the economy.

cost–push inflation – when rising business costs force firms to increase prices in order to protect their profit margins.

cyclical unemployment – unemployment which results from a level of demand which is insufficient to buy all of current output

deflation – when the average price level is falling, i.e. negative inflation

excess demand – a level of demand which is greater, at current prices, than the capacity of the economy to supply goods and services

frictional unemployment – unemployment which occurs as people who have left one job seek out another. By definition, it covers only those unemployed for whom there is a job available once it can be found

index – a series of data which uses a base year with a value of 100 and expresses the data for all other years in relation to that base year

overheating – the phase in the business cycle in which demand is growing faster than the capacity of the economy to meet it by producing goods and services

retail price index – the data series used to measure the rate of inflation. It is a weighted average of the prices of all items commonly bought by consumers

structural unemployment – unemployment which occurs because the structure of the economy is changing, with some areas of production growing and others declining, while those people made redundant are unable to move to other areas of the economy because of immobilities

wage–price spiral – a sequence in which prices rise because of increased costs, which causes a rise in the rate of inflation, which in turn creates expectations of further inflation and increased wage demands leading to higher pay settlements.

AS Level Exercises

A. REVISION QUESTIONS
(25 marks; 50 minutes)

Read the unit, then answer:

1 Why is inflation generally regarded as being undesirable?
(3)

2 How is inflation measured? *(2)*

3 In what way is inflation connected with the business cycle? *(4)*

4 Why are expectations important in the inflation process? *(4)*

5 Outline two advantages inflation can have for a business. *(4)*

6 What is structural unemployment? *(3)*

7 How is it possible for employers to have difficulty in recruiting, even when there are large numbers of unemployed? *(4)*

8 What happens to unemployment in a recession? *(1)*

B. REVISION EXERCISES

B1 Data Response
Every three months, the Confederation of British Industry asks a sample of companies whether they expect that their output will be constrained over the coming four months by skill shortages. A rising percentage of positive answers indicates that skill shortages are on the increase. The data below shows half-yearly figures for expected skill shortages, average earnings increases and the rate of inflation for the year to that point. It covers the period 1994–97 when output was growing strongly (as shown in the last column). In looking at the connections between the figures, it is important to remember that there may be some time lags between cause and effect.

Questions   *(35 marks; 40 minutes)*

1 At what point did the level of expectation of skill shortages increase significantly? *(1)*

2 Explain when the UK economy was operating close to full capacity. *(4)*

3 What impact did this have on the rate of growth of average earnings? *(3)*

4 Is there a connection between earnings growth and the rate of inflation? *(3)*

5 From the figures, why do you think the Bank of England decided to increase interest rates in mid-1997? *(6)*

6 From your library, find out what has happened to the rate of growth of output and the rate of inflation since mid-1997. Present both series of data as lines on a graph. *(10)*

7 Try to predict what will happen in the economy over the next year. Forecast the rate of output growth (GDP) and the rate of inflation (RPI) in six months' time. Give a brief explanation of your reasoning. *(8)*

Skill shortages, earnings and inflation

Half-year		Expected Skill Shortages (%)	Yearly Growth in Average Earnings (%)	Inflation at Annual Rate (%)	Output Growth Since 12 Months Ago (%)
1994:	I	7	2.8	2.6	4.9
	II	10	3.3	2.6	3.4
1995:	I	11	3.6	3.4	1.6
	II	10	4.1	3.2	2.1
1996:	I	9	3.5	2.3	2.4
	II	11	3.0	2.6	3.4
1997:	I	11	4.5	2.7	3.6
	II	17	5.0	3.6	3.7

Source: *National Institute Economic Review*, 1998/1

B2 Case Study

The Mobile Video-phone

Claire built her business from nothing. It started with a small, independent mobile phone shop in Taunton. By the time the national chains such as Carphone Warehouse and The Link started up, Claire had already made a great deal of money. On a business trip to Taiwan (she liked to cut out the middle-man) she saw her first mobile video-phone. And fell in love with it. Immediately she commissioned her own version, made with a royal blue plastic outer shell and branded *Claron*.

Within six months, the Claron video-phone had sales of over 500,000 in the UK. At an average price of £80, that came to an astounding £40 million. Claire built up her organisation hugely, with a sales force and a large administrative staff.

Then, just as Claire was starting to feel the effects of tougher competition, the economic environment became tougher. Two years of consumer spending boom had led to rising inflation. This was causing difficulties with staff, who were pushing for pay rises of around 10%. Several were urging others to join a trade union. Shocked into action by the widespread evidence of inflationary pressures, the government decided to raise interest rates sharply. This was to discourage consumers and firms from spending so much on consumable or investment goods.

Faced with this difficult marketplace, Claire could not decide what to do. Unfortunately others chose to cut prices to boost their market share. This had little effect at first, but after a month sales of the Claron started to slip. A radical new strategy was needed, or else it would be essential to cut Claron's price. Claire would have to make a decision – and very soon.

Questions   (40 marks; 60 minutes)

1 Explain why Claire had such a success with the Claron.   (6)
2 How might a consumer spending boom lead to rising inflation?   (6)
3 If Claire does not make any changes, consider the possible effects upon her business of the market conditions outlined in the text.   (12)
4 a Outline two new strategies Claire might consider, given her circumstances.   (6)
   b Which of the two should she adopt? Make a fully justified recommendation.   (10)

B3 Case Study

Employment puzzles

For nearly 1,000 workers at Black and Decker's Spennymoor plant in the north-east, the news that they had been dreading came last week. The American-owned firm is moving production to the Czech Republic, where labour costs are lower.

John Bridge, Chairman of One NorthEast, the development agency, says that many more 'high volume, low value' manufacturing jobs will be moved offshore. The Engineering Employers' Federation (EEF) predicts 150,000 job losses this year.

There was also bad news for 850 workers at Prudential's Reading call centre, with the announcement that their work is being relocated to Mumbai to take advantage of India's lower labour costs and greater availability of skilled workers.

Digby Jones, director-general of the CBI, says Britain is in danger of 'sleepwalking into decline' as a result of increased labour market regulation and an erosion of low-tax advantages. An EEF survey of members shows that many are planning job cuts as a direct result of the national insurance rises next April.

Other job losses last week included more than 300 at Birds Eye in Grimsby and Hull, and more than 200 at Enterprise Jewellers in Bridgnorth. Unions are predicting another 10,000 job losses at Royal Mail.

There are puzzles about our employment market. While job losses continue, the unemployment count is at a 27-year low. The latest data suggests that growth is continuing even though manufacturing is struggling.

Source: *The Sunday Times*, 6/10/02

Questions   (30 marks; 35 minutes)

1 What kinds of jobs were being cut at the time when the passage was written?   (4)
2 List the four main reasons for job cuts, explaining the importance of each.   (10)
3 To what extent could these changes be related to the business cycle?   (6)
4 Evaluate the extent to which these job cuts matter at a time when employment is growing for the economy as a whole.   (10)

MACRO-ECONOMIC POLICY

DEFINITION
Macro-economic policy is the government's attempt to influence the level of demand in the economy as a whole. It works primarily through the impact of interest rates and government tax and expenditure changes.

65.1 The problems

Macro-economic policies affect everyone. Taxes may rise, interest rates may fall, motorways may or may not be built. These changes affect individuals and businesses alike. Although macro-economic policies are not the only ones available to governments, they tend to be a preoccupation.

As explained in Unit 62, the economy goes through fluctuations in business activity which are generally known as the business cycle. The four major variables which are affected are the rate of economic growth, the rate of inflation, the level of unemployment and the balance of payments.

Most governments in developed countries would be pleased if:

- GDP is growing at 2% or a little more
- inflation is at or below 2.5%
- unemployment is not causing serious distress to the electorate
- the deficit on the **current account** of the balance of payments can be covered easily by funds coming from overseas investors.

In the past it has been rare for all these conditions to hold true. In the UK since 1996, we have been getting closer. At the beginning of that period, unemployment was still high at 8% but it did fall after that.

The table at the top of the next page shows the changes in the four macro-economic areas in recent years.

The problem of managing the business cycle is the degree of **trade-off** between the four objectives of government policy. In a boom, GDP and employment are both growing. But inflation is accelerating and the generally high level of demand may suck in imports. During a recession, inflation will usually slow down and exports will rise as businesses seek foreign markets. But growth will be sluggish and unemployment will rise, perhaps quickly.

The choice of macro-economic policies depends a good deal on the priorities of the government of the day. Traditionally, Conservative governments have given high priority to controlling inflation and have been comfortable with a relatively high rate of unemployment. Labour governments have been less inclined to adopt fierce counter-inflation policies and have tried to keep unemployment down. However, during the last ten years all European governments have been concerned to keep inflation down, irrespective of their politics.

Keeping inflation down means in practice that the level of demand in the economy, in money terms, must not grow faster than its productive capacity. The level of demand in the economy as a whole can be influenced by **monetary policy**. This works mainly through changes in interest rates. **Fiscal policy** can also be used. It comes into play when changes are made in taxes and government expenditures. The government may also have a view on the 'correct' exchange rate. If so, their economic policies will reflect this.

In 1997, major changes were made to the way macro-economic policy is decided. Within a few weeks of coming to power, the new Labour Chancellor of the Exchequer announced a radical change. Until then, the Bank of England had worked in partnership with the Treasury over interest rates. The Chancellor, Gordon Brown, decided to make the Bank of England wholly responsible for the conduct of monetary policy. Although the Bank was not made fully independent of the government, the decision making was to be undertaken by the **monetary policy committee**. This meets each month to decide whether any changes in interest rates are needed. The objective was to make the control of inflation independent of political issues. The committee of experts is appointed by the government. It examines the evidence and decides on an appropriate interest rate. The target rate of inflation was set at 2.5%.

This change means that the government is no longer wholly in control of macro-economic policy. It makes all decisions relating to fiscal policy, the control of tax and expenditure measures. But it is no longer in command of monetary and interest rate policy.

Year	GDP Growth (%)	Unemployment (%) (Claimant)	Inflation (Excl. Mortgage Interest)	Balance of Payments as % of GDP
1989	2.2	6.3	7.8	−4.3
1990	0.4	5.8	9.5	−3.4
1991	−2.0	8.1	5.9	−1.4
1992	−0.5	9.8	3.7	−1.7
1993	2.1	10.4	1.6	−1.6
1994	3.9	9.4	2.5	−0.2
1995	2.5	8.3	3.4	−0.5
1996	1.8	7.5	2.5	−0.3
1997	3.4	5.4	3.5	0.2
1998	3.0	4.6	2.0	0.4
1999	2.2	4.1	1.6	−2.2
2000	3.1	3.6	1.5	−2.0
2001	1.7	3.2	0.4	−2.1
2002	1.8	3.1	1.6	−1.8

65.2 How the macro-economy works

Demand in the economy comes from a variety of sources. Consumers, businesses and the government all contribute, as do foreign buyers of British exports.

When demand is growing strongly, businesses and individuals prosper and standards of living can rise in real terms. Unemployment falls and the economy is generally regarded as performing well. Businesses can afford to expand, buying more capital equipment and perhaps innovating in terms of both products and production methods. This is the attractive scenario which governments hope to see around election time.

If this situation persists for a while it may even help to raise the long-term trend rate of growth. The rate of growth of GDP in any one year is determined by two factors:

- changes in output brought about by the business cycle
- growth which reflects the long-term increase in capital (both physical and human) and the benefits of new technologies. In Britain, this long-run growth rate has been about 2.2% per year.

It is the latter kind of growth which holds the potential to give many people in society a better life. Governments obviously welcome signs that this kind of growth is taking place.

Growth can be encouraged by allowing demand to increase. Keeping interest rates down and reducing taxes will both have this effect. Low interest rates encourage investment and tax cuts give people more spending power.

GROWING TOO FAST

The catch is that when demand is growing fast, the economy may be approaching its full capacity output. At this point, businesses will find difficulty in recruiting staff with the types of skill they require in order to expand. Wages will be bid upwards, costs will rise and inflation will tend to accelerate.

With ample demand in the domestic economy, businesses have little incentive to look for export markets. Usually, a high level of consumer demand is associated with a high level of demand for imports. So if demand is growing fast, imports tend to rise and exports to fall. The result will usually be an increasing **trade deficit**. Imports will exceed exports by a growing margin.

DEALING WITH A BOOM

When symptoms of overheating start to appear, it is clear that the growth of GDP is too fast. Governments, faced with accelerating inflation and rising imports, will want to reduce the rate at which demand is growing. They will focus upon ways of reducing consumer and government spending. In fact they will probably find that reduced spending in these areas will also seriously discourage investment spending. Governments are less pleased about this as lower investment may reduce productivity and perhaps also competitiveness.

Reducing the level of demand to cut inflationary pressures can be done in three ways:

- Interest rates can be increased – this will make it expensive for businesses and individuals to borrow. Businesses will invest less. Individuals will consume less, especially if they have mortgages. Cutting investment and consumption will reduce the level of demand in the economy.
- Taxes can be increased – this will reduce purchasing power and consumption generally.
- Government expenditure can be cut.

A combination of measures is possible. However, all these measures take time; people take a while to adjust to the changes. This means it is important for the government and the Bank of England to act quickly once they are sure that inflation is becoming a problem.

DEALING WITH DECLINE

When the economy is growing it is tempting for the government to do nothing. So **contractionary policies** of the sort described above may be implemented rather late, after inflation has become a problem. The policies needed to stop inflation from rising may throw the economy into recession. Falling demand will cause businesses to cut production. They will make people redundant and their incomes will then fall. They will spend less, which will cause demand to fall further in a downward spiral. Before long, the prob-lem of inflation will give way to unemployment and slow or non-existent economic growth. Weak demand elsewhere in the world can also contribute to recession. Declining demand in export markets can be just as serious for exporters as it would be on the domestic market. Competition becomes more intense and profit margins are shaved in attempts to keep prices low. Sales may grow more slowly or they may actually decline. Then businesses may postpone or abandon plans to invest in new capacity.

65.3 The policies: changing interest rates

Figure 65.1 shows that there is an inverse relationship between interest rates and growth in GDP. It is not straightforward; other factors are important at different times and there are time lags. Still, it is clear that the peak in interest rates in 1989–90 was followed by falling output in 1991. Equally, the graph shows that recovery was associated with falling interest rates.

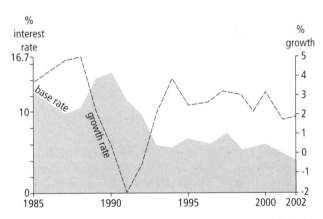

Source: ONS, Monthly Digest of Statistics, Crown copyright 2002

Figure 65.1 GDP growth and base rates

At the same time, it is easy to see that the use of interest rates to control the economy has caused recessions to be very deep. Is it possible to use interest rates to head off inflation before price increases get too large? Could the interest rate changes be small enough not to disrupt businesses and cause serious unemployment?

This question has no simple answer but we can look at the recent experience. Monetary policy is now determined by the monetary policy committee of the Bank of England. At its monthly meetings it examines the evidence and decides whether changes should be made to base rate. This is the rate which determines the interest charges for borrowing from the banks. Business borrowers usually have to pay 3–5% above base rate. In other words, during most of 2002, businesses were charged 7.00–9.00% per year on their bank loans.

LUXURIES SUFFER

Declining demand has hit UK producers of luxury items hard. Troubles began early on in 2001. Then the terrorist attacks of September 11 brought a big fall in the number of tourists, who can normally be relied on to go shopping. When the tourists came back, they turned out to be different ones, with rather lower incomes and spending plans.

Among the suffering companies are Dawson International, the cashmere company; Chester Barrie, Savile Row tailors; Hardy Amies; and even Fortnum and Mason. Staff pay there has been frozen and after all of 300 years, it is for the first time opening on Sunday. Delivering groceries to the Queen is not quite enough. Meantime, Pringle, the Scottish producer of classic knitwear, has managed well; having given itself a complete makeover, it is poised to expand as soon as demand improves.

Figure 65.2 summarises the impact which rising interest rates can have. The process can be reversed when interest rates fall. The problem is the human cost of a large increase in interest rates. It may be very effective in cooling down the economy, but it also causes reduced real incomes. People may experience serious hardship and personal distress, especially those who lose their jobs.

Interest rates have an additional dimension. They have a significant impact on the exchange rate, which in turn affects inflation. When interest rates are high, capital from abroad flows into the country in order to take advantage of the attractive rates which can be obtained on bank deposits. These capital flows increase demand for the currency and tend to push up its price, i.e. the exchange rate. As exchange rates rise, export prices rise and exporters lose competitiveness. Export sales will tend to fall off as buyers turn to cheaper substitutes. The resulting fall in demand for exports creates downward pressure on output and employment in Britain. It is a major factor in the way interest rates affect the economy.

During 2002 base rate was unusually low (at 4%) compared to the previous two decades. There were widespread forecasts of recession, especially for the US and for the rest of the EU. After the rather slow growth of 2001, the Monetary Policy Committee wanted to provide a stimulus, especially for the troubled manufacturing sector. Low levels of investment suggested that businesses badly needed the relief of cheap borrowing.

Base rate changes, Feb 2000 – Feb 2003

Feb 2000 – Jan 2001	6.00%
Feb – Mar 2001	5.75%
Apr – July 2001	5.50%
Aug 2001	5.00%
Sept 2001	4.75%
Oct 2001	4.50%
Nov 2001 – Jan 2003	4.00%
Feb 2003	3.75%

Source: Bank of England

65.4 Using fiscal policy

Tax and expenditure changes can be a very effective way of influencing demand. A tax increase effectively reduces the spending power of the taxpayers. It can be used selectively, to target particular groups of people or types of spending. The table below shows how different policy objectives can be achieved through different types of tax change.

There are two main categories of tax:

- **Direct taxes**

   These are taxes on incomes. Households pay income tax and National Insurance. Businesses pay corporation tax. Direct taxes are usually levied pro-

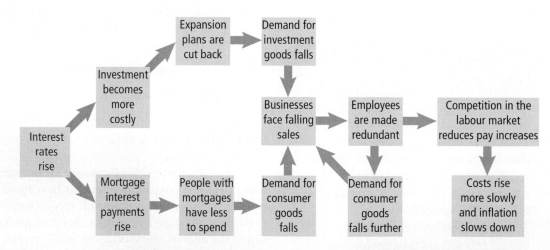

Figure 65.2 The impact of rising interest rates

OBJECTIVE OF GOVERNMENT POLICY	TAX CHANGE
• Increase incentives to start up businesses	• Cut corporation tax for small firms
• Cut consumer spending	• Increase in VAT
• Increase the rate of business recycling	• Increase the tax on dumping waste materials ('landfill')
• Reduce smoking	• Increase the duty on cigarettes
• Redistribute wealth to the less well off	• Increase higher rate income tax; cut the starting rate

portionately, so the more income/profit you have, the more tax you pay. Indeed, there may be a higher tax rate to pay if your earnings are high. At the time of writing, small firms pay 20% of their pre-tax profit in corporation tax. Large firms pay 30%.

- **Indirect taxes**

  These are taxes on spending. The most widespread is VAT, i.e. value-added tax. With almost every product and service you buy, the supplier must pay 17.5% VAT to the government. Other products have further taxes. Petrol, cigarettes and alcoholic drink all have heavy tax 'duties' imposed upon them by the Chancellor of the Exchequer. The combination of duties plus VAT means that over half of the revenue generated by these products goes to the government.

In recent years, fiscal policy has been used to encourage businesses and individuals to change their behaviour. It has been less important as a way of changing the economy in the short term. This has led governments to rely heavily on interest rates as their tool of macro-economic policy.

Fiscal policy could in theory be used in the future to control the level of demand in the economy. It remains to be seen whether it will be.

65.5 How businesses react to macro-economic policies

During 1997, the UK economy was growing fast. Inflation was accelerating (though still quite low). The new Chancellor believed the rate of economic growth could not be sustained. The economy was overheating. Interest rates were raised several times.

Increasing interest rates causes businesses to be hit in two ways. First they find that the cost of borrowing has risen. If they have been trying to expand it is quite likely that they will have large loans. Their cash flow will immediately be hit by the larger interest payments. Second, they find that their sales are down. People who have borrowed to finance consumption spending, e.g. on a car, and people who have mortgages, have less spending money after their interest payments are made. They will have to cut back consumption.

For both these reasons, many businesses will find they are accumulating stocks of unsold goods. Lower sales revenue may force them to borrow more from the bank, just when borrowing has become more expensive. They may try to dispose of unsold goods by cutting prices, which is very good for inflation but not nearly so good for profits.

A decision to cut production is likely at this point. This may mean redundancies. People who lose their jobs will usually have to cut consumption, and so there is a circular quality to this process. Once

demand falls, or just grows more slowly, the process is likely to be cumulative. The rate of economic growth will fall, perhaps GDP will actually go into decline.

Climbing out of this situation can be difficult. The level of investment depends to a large extent on business expectations and once they become gloomy, positive decisions to expand seem very risky. For some businesses expectations were gloomy in 2001/2002, leading to cutbacks in investment spending.

Investment fell by 5% in 2001 and 13% in 2002 in the UK manufacturing sector. This implies a real reduction in productive capacity. By the time you read this you may be able to assess the impact of the downturn.

ARE ALL BUSINESSES AFFECTED IN THE SAME WAY?

Macro-economic policy affects businesses in many different ways. Some are almost 'recession-proof'. All have to cope with higher interest rates, but some will have borrowed much more than others. Equally, many businesses survive easily because they are producing things which people go on buying even when their incomes fall.

Which businesses are most likely to have borrowed heavily? The ones which experienced the biggest boom in sales may have the most ambitious expansion plans. They are the ones producing things people want to buy more of when their incomes are high and rising. Makers of cars or yachts, hotels and restaurants might all do well in a boom. But just as demand rises with incomes, it also falls when incomes fall.

A good way to analyse the impact of difficult economic conditions is to consider the income elasticity of demand for the product. Income elasticity of demand is defined as:

$$\frac{\% \text{ change in quantity demanded}}{\% \text{ change in income}}$$

SUPERPLANTS

Superplants leases pot plants to UK businesses who want their reception areas to look attractive, or to decorate exhibition stands or conference platforms. But when many businesses began to experience falling demand, and started looking for ways to cut costs, many of their plants had to be composted. Expectations of reduced profits made their customers very wary of any expenses that could be avoided.

Could Superplants be helped by a cut in interest rates? This would reduce the cost of bank loans for many businesses. It might well lead to some recovery in demand for services to business.

IN Business

Income elasticity is high if it is greater than 1. If, for example, demand for yachts goes up by 10% when incomes are rising by 5% in real terms, the income elasticity of demand is 2.

Many everyday products have an income elasticity of demand which is less than 1. Sometimes very much less. Do you use less toothpaste when you are hard up? Provided you manage to avoid becoming homeless, the answer is probably no. It follows that toothpaste manufacturers can weather an increase in interest rates and a slow down in the economy fairly easily. In recent years the service sector has experienced fewer problems than has the manufacturing sector. It relies less on exports and has benefited from buoyant consumer demand within the UK.

MONETARY POLICY AND THE EXCHANGE RATE

Interest rates can affect the exchange rate. If they are high, the exchange rate may rise. This will affect international competitiveness.

Business IN

OAG

OAG produces airline timetables for travel agents. This involves collating a mammoth quantity of information from a total of 850 airlines. The products include an Executive Flight Guide at £119 and the full Flight Guide, at £500. The company used to be part of the Reed publishing empire but was bought out by a venture capital company.

On the face of it, any business involved with flying should have been in trouble, especially after the terrorist attacks of 11 September 2001. In fact OAG broke even. Careful attention to the techniques used in the data gathering side of the business, and to the needs of advertisers, brought major benefits. A market-oriented approach made all the difference.

Businesses which find themselves uncompetitive because of a high exchange rate are under pressure. If they can implement cost-cutting measures they will survive. If, however, they have already done all that can be done to reduce costs, the outlook is less rosy. They may contract operations or go out of business.

Many businesses put a good deal of effort into planning for difficult times. Others get caught out. Yet others may be little affected by the problem. It remains the case that most businesses would like to see stability in economic conditions over time. That way they would be able to make plans and set budgets with confidence. Politicians often promise stability. It remains the primary macro-economic goal.

65.6 The Budget

Governments generally set their Budget in March. All taxes are subject to possible changes. The Budget provides an opportunity not only to take an overview of the macro-economy, but also to make changes to the incentive structures created by different taxes. The Chancellor has many objectives to consider at Budget time:

- reviewing the macro-economy
- influencing overall spending power through taxes
- redistributing income among various groups within society
- raising specific taxes in line with inflation
- reviewing public sector borrowing
- changing benefits, so reducing the poverty trap and encouraging people to work
- taxing polluting fuels so as to discourage their use
- improving the accounting processes with which small businesses must comply
- changing the regulations governing different types of savings accounts.

65.7 Policies for growth

Economic growth occurs when there is a sustained increase in overall output within an economy. This provides the increase in real income which is the basis of rising standards of living within that society. Economic growth is measured by the rate of rise in the gross domestic product.

Governments have usually been in favour of economic growth because higher standards of living appeal to most voters. In the decades immediately following World War Two it was sometimes possible for governments to encourage growth by having an expansionary fiscal and monetary policy. However in time it became clear that this risked increasing inflation. The policy went out of fashion, although it is still the case that demand can be increased if there are unemployed resources which could be set to work.

If it is impossible to increase demand then other ways have to be found to promote growth. In recent years most governments have been strongly in favour of encouraging markets to work efficiently. This helps in two ways:

- it ensures that the goods and services produced meet consumer demand as effectively as possible
- if markets are genuinely competitive, prices will be kept down. This forces businesses to keep costs down.

Growth policy is often broadly defined as including any policy which can help to increase output. Because demand is not usually used to promote growth, these policies have become collectively known as **supply-side policies**. Obvious examples include measures to improve education and training, to increase competition and to create incentives.

Most supply-side policies can be characterised as micro-economic policies because they involve particular parts of the economy rather than the economy as a whole. Their underlying objective is to make markets work in ways which optimise the level of output.

INVESTMENT IN INFRASTRUCTURE

Economic growth can often be helped along by government provision of **infrastructure**. This includes transport and communications systems and the provision of essential services. In the past, investment in infrastructure came almost entirely from the government as the utilities were nationalised, i.e. belonged to the government. Most have now been privatised, but the government still retains substantial influence through its transport policy and the planning laws. For example, spending on improvements to the A55 brought a series of economically isolated North Wales communities within an hour's drive of the M6. This means that they are effectively connected to the national motorway network. The potential for job creation in areas of high unemployment can be enhanced in this way. The rapid growth of the M4 corridor provides another example.

PROMOTING STABILITY

One way of fostering growth is to provide a stable environment for business. This means, in effect, reducing the likelihood and the depth of recessions. Unfortunately, measures to combat inflation helped to deepen rather than reduce the serious recessions of the early 1980s and early 1990s. At the time of writing, it is not clear whether it will be possible to avoid recession in the future. Ask yourself the question, has the government been successful in pursuing stable, sustainable growth? If not, why?

PROMOTING TRADE

The link between trade and growth can create opportunities for governments. Policies which make trade easier can lead to larger markets and possibilities of expansion. In recent years governments have sought to open up their markets to each other. The World Trade Organisation helps member countries to reduce trade barriers. The European single market aims to create a large area within which there are no barriers at all. The growth possibilities which this offers form a large part of the rationale for creating the single market. There are also huge opportunities in the Far East, especially China.

65.8 Growth across the world

For many businesses, the rate of economic growth in important export markets is critical to their success. Mature economies, such as that of the UK, tend to grow relatively slowly. Developing countries grow in

BUILDING MARKETS

One company dominates the world of ice-cream – Unilever. With brands such as Wall's Magnum selling over £1 billion of ice-cream per year, it is the world's biggest and most profitable producer. Why, then, would it want to invest in a market where Magnum is a luxury even when priced at 15p, and where ice-cream consumption per head is less than 100th of that of America? In 'the most competitive ice-cream market in the world,' according to Duncan Garood, Wall's general manager.

The reason is that China may be a very poor country, but its population of 1,300 million is greater than America, Japan and all the European countries put together. And with its rapid rate of economic growth, China will be a major market in the future. Ice-cream sales have been growing at over 10% per year in the last decade.

Unilever's strategy is to build up its refrigerator/distribution network and offer a wide range of product lines from those costing only a few pence to 'luxury' lines such as Magnum. Advertising and promotional spending does little more than add to trading losses at the moment. The future prize, however, may be a large share of a massive market. At this stage in the product life cycle for ice-cream in China, heavy cash investment makes business sense. As long as the firm's sights are set on the future and its pockets are deep.

Ice-cream market size – in 1998 and in 20 years' time

	Population (m)	Consumption per head p.a. (litres)	Market size by volume (m litres)
USA 1998	260	21.0	5,460
China 1998	1,300	0.2	260
USA 2018	280	22.0	6,160
China 2018	1,500	1.35	2,025

Source: Adapted from trade estimates based on 10% growth per year in China

Business IN

different ways. The successful ones (mainly in Asia) tend to grow very fast for a number of years, until they achieve a fairly high standard of living. Then the growth rate slows. Some of this growth results from high levels of investment.

Other developing countries experience slower economic growth and correspondingly modest improvements in their standard of living. Yet others, mainly but not exclusively in Africa, have actually experienced a decline in output, in some cases because of war or AIDS. Some of them have chronic debt problems which impoverish their people but have not yet been solved by international action. Still, some multinationals, such as Unilever, are active in almost all markets.

In 1997–99, economic growth was interrupted in many countries by the Asian financial crisis. This was serious at the time. One contributing cause of it was a loss of confidence brought about by large numbers of bad debts which threatened the stability of the banks. The resulting exchange rate panics created considerable instability and a major disruption of the pattern of economic growth. This had serious consequences for UK businesses with significant markets in Asia. With the rise in the value of the pound, some manufacturers experienced very difficult trading conditions. This was one crisis that blew over quite quickly, but some exporters did not recover their markets.

GDP growth data is suspect in some countries. Not all governments have effective mechanisms for collecting data and many people are sceptical. Still, the figures below give an idea of the possibilities in some economies. Potential export markets have to be researched carefully, wherever they are, before decisions are taken but the data provides a starting point for secondary research.

Growth rates in Asia

	AVERAGE ANNUAL GROWTH, 1990–2000 (%)	INVESTMENT (% OF GDP)
China	10.3	38
India	6.0	25
Indonesia	4.2	18
Japan	1.3	26
South Korea	5.7	31
Thailand	4.2	22

Source: World Bank, World Development Report 2002

ISSUES FOR **analysis**

The four main objectives of macro-economic policy are low inflation, low unemployment, steady economic growth and a reasonable balance between imports and exports. However, there are a number of reasons why it can be difficult for governments to achieve all these objectives at the same time. In particular, difficult trading conditions may affect many businesses and it may be hard for the Government to increase confidence.

- As in any trade-off situation, the government may have to accept that its policies have a high cost.
- If the economy is allowed to grow too fast, inflation may accelerate and then the government will try to reduce demand, using fiscal or monetary policies or both.
- Reducing demand will bring falling sales and redundancies.
- Unemployment will increase, though probably only after a time lag.
- It may be very difficult to get the economy growing again after a period of recession, because businesses may lack confidence and be unwilling to invest until they are sure demand is growing.
- The Budget provides an opportunity to review economic performance and to change fiscal policies where they are likely to have beneficial effects.
- In thinking about the effect of macro-economic policies, it should always be remembered that they will work with a time lag.

65.9 Macro-economic policy
an evaluation

The world is becoming more and more integrated. This means all countries are increasingly dependent on markets in other countries. It makes it very important that governments collaborate in formulating their economic policies. So the Budget is not quite as important as it used to be. Some decisions will be taken elsewhere, in central banks, in the EU and in inter-governmental meetings. In this way, many countries have been able to participate in the general increase in real incomes worldwide. Collaboration is needed if countries are to avoid passing economic instability on to each other.

For the individual firm, the lessons from the past are clear. It is very risky to be highly geared, because government policy might change at any time, pushing up interest rates. It is also risky to be too dependent on government spending. Construction companies should look for private clients; not just rely on government contracts for building hospitals or repairing roads. The Chancellor's next Budget may cut back government spending.

The important effects of government economic policy upon business explains why so many organisations try to influence government decisions. They do this by lobbying the media and government. If an employers' organisation managed to persuade the Chancellor to spend more on public transport, it would be a real achievement.

contractionary policies – fiscal and monetary policies which tend to reduce aggregate demand and therefore cause output to fall or grow more slowly.

current account – that part of the balance of payments account which covers exports and imports. The figures include visible and invisible exports and imports; that is to say both goods and services.

fiscal policy – measures which involve changes in taxation or government spending.

infrastructure – the network of transport, communication and other essential services upon which businesses depend.

monetary policy – measures which involve changes in interest rates.

monetary policy committee – the Bank of England committee which oversees monetary policy. It meets monthly to decide whether changes in interest rates are required.

supply-side policies – measures which increase quantities supplied through encouraging markets to work more efficiently. They may apply not only to product markets but also to the labour and capital markets.

trade deficit – a situation in which imports are greater than exports.

trade-off – when the achievement of one desirable outcome is only possible at the expense of another.

WORKBOOK I 65.10

AS Level Exercises

A. REVISION QUESTIONS
(35 marks; 70 minutes)

Read the unit, then answer:

1 State three economic objectives a government might pursue. *(3)*
2 Explain the meaning of the term 'fiscal policy'. *(3)*
3 Explain the meaning of the phrase: '…long-run growth rate has been about 2.5% per year'. *(4)*
4 Identify three policy measures a government could take to reduce demand in the economy. *(3)*
5 Outline the possible effect upon a supermarket chain such as Tesco of a cut in government expenditure. *(4)*
6 Explain how a change in interest rates might affect businesses. *(6)*
7 Distinguish between direct and indirect taxation. *(3)*
8 Outline two changes in business activity that could be achieved by a change in fiscal policy. *(4)*
9 Give three examples of firms whose demand levels would be affected little by recession. *(3)*
10 What would be the likely effect on the exchange rate of an increase in interest rates? *(2)*

B. REVISION EXERCISES

B1 Investigations

1 Make a flow chart which starts with an increase in interest rates. Show the sequence of events, starting with an individual business, and showing how the impact of the change can fan out into the economy as a whole.
2 Explain the objectives of macro-economic policy. What have been the government's priorities during the time you have been studying Business?
3 When trading conditions get difficult, it is often the case that the worst hit businesses are those which have problems anyway. During 1998, UK microchip manufacturers found themselves in difficulties. The US company National Semiconductor made 600 employees redundant and announced plans to sell its remaining plant in central Scotland. The company was affected by a range of trends: the exchange rate was high, competition from overseas was stiff and high interest rates became a problem too.

    Select a business in your own local area and consider the ways its fortunes have changed over time. Has it been affected by interest rate changes or fiscal policy? Are other economic factors causing it difficulties or creating opportunities?

A Level Exercises

A. REVISION QUESTIONS
(35 marks; 70 minutes)

Read the unit, then answer:

1 How fast can the economy grow without inflation accelerating? *(3)*

2 Which businesses are most likely to be greatly affected by a rise in interest rates? *(4)*

3 How important are time lags in macro-economic policy? *(3)*

4 Outline the likely effect of a sharp rise in interest rates upon:
   a a small house-building firm *(3)*
   b McDonald's *(3)*
   c Rolls Royce Motors, which exports more than 50% of its output *(3)*
   d a young, rapidly growing mobile phone retail chain. *(3)*

5 What impact are contractionary economic policies likely to have on businesses? *(4)*

6 Why is Budget Day important? *(3)*

7 Given the uncertainty for businesses about the future progress of the economy, outline two strategic decisions that would be wise for every firm to consider. *(6)*

B. REVISION EXERCISES

B1 Investigation
Gather annual data for the period between 1996 and the present covering the UK and EU economic growth rates, levels of investment, volume of exports and interest rates. Compare the data with that provided in this unit and then answer the following questions.

1 To what extent have growth rates diverged from the long-term trend rate?

2 What reasons can you give for any changes?

3 How have individual businesses been affected by the changes? Choose a service sector business other than retailing, a manufacturer of consumer goods and a manufacturer of intermediate goods (i.e. a product which sells to industry).

4 What changes have taken place in the structure of employment in your area? Have any major employers closed down or contracted? What alternative opportunities have opened up?

B2 Data Response
In June 1998, the Bank of England raised interest rates to 7.5%. Between October 1998 and February 1999 it reduced them progressively to 5.5%. Between June and October, a number of manufacturing businesses announced redundancies and some decided upon plant closures.
The table below shows how interest rates were changed during 1988–89, when accelerating inflation was becoming a problem.

Jan 1988	9.0
April 1988	8.5
July 1988	11.6
Oct 1988	12.7
Jan 1989	13.0
April 1989	14.0
July 1989	14.0
Oct 1989	15.0
Jan 1990	15.0
April 1990	15.0
July 1990	15.0
Oct 1990	14.0
Jan 1991	13.5
April 1991	11.9
July 1991	10.9
Oct 1991	10.5

Source: *National Institute Economic Review*

Questions *(20 marks; 30 minutes)*

1 How does the interest rate policy followed in 1998 compare with that followed during and after the late 1980s' period when the economy was booming? *(5)*

2 What impact did the high interest rates of the 1989–91 period have on the economy? (Use the figures on page 456 to help you.) *(5)*

3 Why may it have taken so long for the economy to pull out of recession during the 1990s? *(5)*

4 To what extent was the period 1997–99 comparable with the period 1987–88? *(5)*

C. ESSAY QUESTIONS

1 If faced with rising inflation, the government might apply a severely contractionary economic policy. What might that involve and what might be the effects upon a business of your choosing?

2 Tony Blair's Labour government has been keen to listen to business leaders. What macro-economic policies might business leaders consider ideal? Consider how they might work in practice.

3 To what extent have government policies helped promote economic growth in recent years?

B3 Case Study

Changing output in a two-speed economy

% CHANGES	MANU-FACTURING	PUBLIC SECTOR	DISTRI-BUTION	BUSINESS SERVICES	CONSTRUCTION	OIL	REST	TOTAL
1999	0.3	1.9	2.8	4.7	0.8	4.4	2.9	2.2
2000	2.8	1.9	2.2	4.6	1.8	−1.3	5.6	3.1
2001	−2.3	2.4	2.2	5.4	3.6	−4.9	1.6	1.7
2002 (est.)	−2.7	1.8	3.0	3.5	5.8	−0.2	3.2	1.9

Source: National Institute Economic Review, 2002

Sage

Sage is the UK's biggest supplier of software for small businesses. When there was a lot of doom and gloom around because of weak demand for manufactures, Sage was busy with restructuring its operations in the US. The idea was to unite all of its products in a single brand, 'Best Software'. Paul Walker, the chief executive, launched the strategy in Boston. 'These changes will allow the Best brand to stand out. This in one way deals with the amount of noise that Microsoft gets in the market place, which is a bit of a nonsense really because if you look at revenues compared to Great Plains (Microsoft's subsidiary), we are one of the biggest players in the market', he said.

By 2002, the US was taking more than half of Sage's output. Walker went on, 'We now have a structure that will allow us to be more acquisitive and invest in new products. There are a number of opportunities we are looking at'. Despite the downturn in the IT market, Sage expects organic growth because it can sell new products to its loyal customer base.

Questions   *(35 marks; 45 minutes)*

1 To what extent have different sectors in the UK economy experienced different levels of demand? *(6)*
2 Discuss the reasons for the differences. *(8)*
3 Describe the range of opportunities that Sage has identified for possible future growth. *(6)*
4 Analyse the reasons for Sage's confidence in the future. *(8)*
5 To what extent is this confidence justified? What possible threats could Sage face? *(7)*

BUSINESS AND THE EUROPEAN UNION

DEFINITION

The EU is the 'new' regional European bloc formed following the final ratification by the then 12 members of the European Community of the Maastricht Treaty in November 1993. This treaty provides for closer unification of the economic, social and political systems of the member states.

66.1 The origins of the European Union

A vision of a new Europe began to emerge at the conclusion of World War Two in 1945. The objective was to unite the economies of Europe and thereby overcome long-established national rivalries.

The origins of the European Union (EU) lie in the creation of the European Coal and Steel Community (ECSC) in 1952. The original members who signed the Treaty of Paris were Belgium, Holland, Luxembourg, Italy and France. West Germany later became a member. The UK participated in the negotiations but refused to join.

In 1957 the six members agreed to form a common market in which no trade barriers would be allowed between member states. The Treaty of Rome established the European Economic Community (EEC). The six members of the EEC enjoyed exceptionally high economic growth. This encouraged Britain to join this **free trade** area in 1973, along with Ireland and Denmark.

In December 1991 Europe took a major step forward when the Maastricht Treaty of European Union was signed by all the member states. It took effect on 1 November 1993. This treaty created the European Union with the aim of even greater unity between member states. Many viewed the treaty as a move towards close political ties within a federal Europe – a United States of Europe. The treaty foresaw the introduction of monetary union and a single European currency by 1999. At the time there were many who doubted that this would ever happen. Its arrival, on time, on 1 January 1999 was a remarkable political achievement. The Maastricht Treaty also envisaged common policies on industrial and social affairs as well as defence, education and health. It was designed to push the pace of European unity forwards more quickly.

Figure 66.1 summarises the growth of membership of the EU since 1957. A number of other nations, and especially those in eastern Europe, have expressed interest in joining the EU. The EU is on the brink of admitting ten new members, many of them in 2004.

Source: 'Institutions of the EU', Office for Official Publications of the European Communities

Figure 66.1 The growth of the EU (Source: 'Institutions of the European Community', Office for Official Publications of the European Communities, © European Communities, 1995)

THE EVOLUTION OF THE EUROPEAN UNION

The EU has moved from establishing a free trade area to a point at which monetary and economic union is being enacted, and political union – according to some commentators – is just around the corner.

1 Creating a free trade area: This occurs when a group of countries abolish barriers to trade – most commonly tariffs and quotas. The European states began this process in the late 1950s, meaning that businesses could export and import more easily.

2 Establishing a customs union: This often occurs simultaneously with the abolition of trade barriers. A customs union merely requires the imposition of a common external tariff against goods and services from outside the area. The EU operates such a tariff, offering benefits to businesses within the area and encouraging non-European businesses to establish factories within Europe. Honda at Swindon and Nissan at Sunderland are high profile examples of this policy.

3 The formation of a common market: This stage in the process of creating a Union brings together a free trade area and a common external tariff with the free movement of all factors of production across national boundaries. An agreement between member states of the then European Community in 1986 committed the countries to the creation of a 'single market' by the end of 1992.

4 Economic union: By late 1992 the EU had removed most of the remaining barriers to the free movement of goods, services and factors of production. However, a genuinely single market cannot be established whilst the exchange rates of the currencies of the member states fluctuate. This is a major difference between domestic trade and trade within the EU. This economic union requires a single currency and coordinated fiscal and monetary policies.

5 Political union: Many supporters of greater European integration perceive the final stage as the establishment of a federal Europe similar in structure to the United States of America. Important powers would then lie solely with the European Parliament with national governments having limited powers.

FUTURE MEMBERSHIP

Many countries outside the European Union are very keen to become members. The Treaty of Nice in December 2000 committed the EU to substantial expansion and outlined the changes to the Union's institutions that would be essential to accommodate this increase in membership.

Ten countries have been given membership of the EU as part of what European politicians have heralded as 'an historic expansion'. Those joining in 2004 are: Cyprus, the Czech Republic, Estonia, Hungary, Latvia, Lithuania, Malta, Poland, Slovakia and Slovenia. This expansion will increase the population of the EU by over 20%, but will add much less to its GNP.

Low wage rates in countries such as Hungary and Poland will make these new EU members fierce competitors for jobs. They will, however, provide a rich market opportunity for many EU businesses. We shall return to this topic later in the unit.

At some future date other countries may become members. Romania and Bulgaria are expected to become members before 2008, but Turkey seems destined to remain in the cold for the foreseeable future. Controversially, in spite of repeated requests for membership, Turkey is considered to be 'not ready'.

66.2 The institutions of the Community

The EU is managed by its institutions. Currently, these are as follows.

THE EUROPEAN COMMISSION

This is based mainly in Brussels and, to a lesser extent, in Luxembourg. It proposes EU policy and legislation which is then passed on to the Council of Ministers. The Commission also executes the decisions taken by the Council of Ministers.

The Commission has 20 members – two each from France, Germany, Italy, Spain and the UK and one from each of the remaining states. All the Commissioners are obliged to act independently of national interest and to act only in the interests of the EU.

A meeting of the European Commission (© Associated Press)

THE COUNCIL OF MINISTERS

This is the Union's decision making body. It agrees or adopts legislation on the basis of proposals from the Commission. It is, in effect, the Cabinet of the EU. Each member state acts as President of the Council for six months. Meetings are held each April, June and October and one minister from each state attends meetings.

Twice yearly, heads of government meet in what is known as the European Council. This sets broad guidelines for future action by the Union.

THE EUROPEAN PARLIAMENT

The European Parliament meets in Strasbourg in Eastern France. It has 626 members (members of the European Parliament, or MEPs) of whom 87 are from the UK. MEPs are elected by proportional representation for a fixed period of five years.

The Parliament's opinion is needed on proposals before the Council can adopt them. It is a supervisory body with the power to approve and dismiss the **European Commission**. The Parliament votes on the Commission's programmes and monitors day-to-day management of European policies. In spite of this, the Parliament currently has little authority or power.

TYPES OF EU LEGISLATION

The Council and the Commission can impose their will upon the Union by means of:

- Regulations – these have binding legal effect without confirmation by the member countries' parliaments. These regulations have primacy over national law if any conflict arises.
- Directives – these require member states to introduce legislation in their national parliaments to enact certain EU decisions. If the member does not introduce the directive the Commission may refer the matter to the Court of Justice as a last resort.
- Recommendations and opinions – these have no binding force but express the view of the issuing institution.

66.3 The single market

Over recent years there have been a number of issues within the European Union which have had, and will continue to have, significant implications for businesses. The changing nature of the European Union offers opportunities and constraints for all types of businesses.

One such key issue is that of the single market. The original vision of the European Union was of a market in which goods, services, people and money could move freely. This was to be achieved by opening up borders and implementing common economic policies. By the late 1970s it was apparent that this aim had not been achieved and a programme was devised to create a genuinely single market. Over 300 measures comprised the reforms necessary to create the single market. Key elements of this have been:

- the creation of common technical standards for EU products, meaning one product can be designed to sell throughout the EU
- the harmonisation of taxation, for example aligning VAT and excise duties, ending tax advantages resulting from location in a particular EU member state
- the free movement of people – citizens are allowed to travel, reside, study and work wherever they wish in the European Union
- a reduction in the number of customs posts and the paperwork necessary for trade within the EU
- the free movement of capital making it possible to invest money anywhere in the Union

- ending duty-free sales within the EU from 1999.

The introduction of the single market is a conscious attempt to remove remaining barriers to trade within the European Union. It is by no means complete, but the impact of the changes should not be underestimated. European firms are now selling to a market which comprises over 360 million people – larger than the markets of Japan and the USA added together. This constitutes a major opportunity for all European firms. At the same time, it will bring ever fiercer competition.

The new, larger market will allow businesses to produce and operate on a larger scale. This may offer the advantages of economies of scale. Firms will also have the opportunity to become more highly specialised as they operate within the enlarged market. This increase in scale may continue to be fuelled by mergers and joint ventures between national companies to establish European conglomerates. Belief in the benefits of scale in this enlarged market can be seen in:

- the purchase of the French insurance company Victoire for £1.5 billion by the UK's Commercial Union
- the decision by Toyota, the Japanese car manufacturer, to increase its production in the UK from 170,000 to 220,000 vehicles a year. Over 80% of the cars made in Toyota's Burnaston factory are exported to other EU countries. This move will allow the company to utilise the capacity at its Burnaston factory more fully.

Small and medium-sized companies have experienced fierce competition as a result of the enlargement and restructuring of their particular markets. Even those companies which trade principally in their own national markets have commented on increasing competition within these markets.

One of the principal changes resulting from the move to a single market in Europe was the creation of common technical standards. Products which meet the new technical requirements devised by the EU carry the 'CE' mark which means they may be sold throughout the Union. Many European firms have had to revise the safety aspects of their products to meet the relevant CE standards.

The move to a **single European market** has also involved attempts to harmonise taxes and duties. The intention is that, for example, the rate of VAT levied in member states should be broadly the same. The same is true of the rate of excise duties on products such as alcohol and tobacco. Since 1993 the total tax on cigarettes has had to be at least 57% of the retail price in all EU states. This will have significance for companies who sell throughout the EU in terms of their pricing policies and marketing.

Finally, there have been a number of reforms intended to ease trading within the EU. The paperwork necessary has been simplified and customs posts removed (except in Britain).

66.4 European Monetary Union (EMU)

By the late 1970s it was apparent that trade within Europe would be helped by some form of linking of exchange rates. Businesses could gain confidence from knowing that earnings from export sales were unlikely to alter due to fluctuations in exchange rates. From this idea the concept of the EMU was born with two principal elements:

- the European currency unit (ecu) – a common currency to be used for transactions throughout the Union
- the Exchange Rate Mechanism (ERM) which links domestic currencies to the ecu and to each other.

The heart of the EMU was the Exchange Rate Mechanism but is now the single currency – the Euro. Within the Exchange Rate Mechanism each currency had an exchange rate against the ecu. The aim was to restrict currencies to fluctuations of no more than 2.25%. In 1992 the ERM failed when the UK, Italian and Spanish governments were unable to support their currencies and withdrew from the mechanism. The ERM was replaced by the single currency (the Euro) on 1 January 1999.

At this time the exchange rates of the participating currencies (excluding Britain) were locked together. Transactions between banks are in the new currency – the Euro. On 1 January 2002, Euro notes and coins were issued to the retail sector, and the old notes and coins of the participating national currencies were withdrawn on 30 June 2002.

66.5 Business and European Monetary Union

The implications of joining the EMU for British businesses are both positive and negative. A single currency and a common European monetary policy would make trading easier and cheaper. Costs of raw materials from other EU states would not vary, allowing more accurate financial forecasting. Earnings from exports would not be subject to variations in exchange rates. Businesses would no longer need to pay commission when exchanging pounds sterling for Euros. Estimates are that this alone would save firms about 0.5% of their total costs.

Businesses and final consumers would find comparisons between the prices of products from various European producers simpler. A single currency and common interest and inflation rates would encourage firms to operate in a wider market bringing benefits such as economies of scale. Firms are more likely to seek out new markets if trading is eased through the introduction of a single currency. Equally, new, and improved, sources of supply might become viable

once exchange rate fluctuations are no longer relevant.

Investment from the rest of the world is likely to increase as a result of a move to a single currency since it will result in a large market in which trade is simple and relatively cheap. The UK is fortunate to have been the major recipient of direct investment from the rest of the world. This has lead, for example, to the establishment of the Nissan plant near Sunderland and Honda's factory in Swindon. By locating in the UK, non-EU producers can operate within the EU's common external tariff.

Businesses that handle large amounts of cash are likely to be the most seriously affected by the transition to the Euro. One-off transition costs include changes to cash tills, vending machines, menus and advertising literature and accounting systems. Retailers' own estimates of the costs associated with the introduction of a single currency vary considerably. Tesco estimates

Euro notes (© Associated Press)

NISSAN WARNING OVER EURO

The president and chief executive of Nissan, Carlos Ghosn, has warned that the future of the company's Sunderland factory could depend upon whether the UK adopts the euro. Mr Ghosn said that the company was concerned that its costs were denoted in pounds whilst its sales revenue was earned in euros. This makes the company highly vulnerable to changes in exchange rates.

Nissan recently invested £235 million in its Sunderland factory to secure future production of the Micra. However, Carlos Ghosn hinted that any future decisions about investment in the UK would depend heavily upon whether the UK is using the euro and any exchange rate risk being eliminated.

costs at £40 million. It is important to emphasise, though, that these are one-off costs and are therefore not very significant.

Since more than 50% of the UK's overseas trade is conducted outside the EU there are many firms who will have to meet the costs of converting their systems to dual prices and then to the Euro. These firms will not, however, benefit from the reduced costs of exchanging currencies.

66.6 The Social Chapter

This is an element of the Maastricht Treaty signed by the 12 members of the Union in 1992. The intention of the Social Chapter is to harmonise working conditions throughout the Union. This ensures that all EU workers are guaranteed the following basic rights:

- the right to join a trade union
- the right to take industrial action
- the right to be consulted and informed about company plans
- the right to equal treatment for men and women
- the right to a minimum wage and a maximum working week of 48 hours
- the right to a minimum of four weeks paid holiday per year

In addition, the Chapter contains provisions relating to redundancies and it also seeks to encourage employee participation and consultation.

In 1993 the UK took the decision to opt out of the Social Chapter, fearing that it would impose extra costs on UK businesses. The current Labour government has reversed this decision and has signed the Social Chapter.

66.7 Opportunities in Eastern Europe

The fall of the communist governments in Eastern Europe in 1989 and 1990 has had major implications for businesses in the remainder of Europe. The absorption of the former East Germany into the Union offered opportunities as a significant new market became accessible. The attempts of many of the former communist states to adopt capitalism is reflected in their interest in becoming members of the EU.

The East European countries have a combined population in excess of 100 million and a wide range of resources attractive to Western firms. Above all else, the countries represent fresh new markets for companies facing saturated markets in Western Europe. Companies operating in mature markets such as those for chocolate or detergent can see huge potential for whoever can establish their brand name first.

Already, Central and East European nations purchase over half their imports from the Union and this percentage has risen steadily throughout the 1990s. In 2000 they took over 16% of EU exports. These parts of Europe offer vast opportunities and EU businesses have sought to take advantage of them in a number of ways.

1 Joint ventures: The joint ventures are based on EU firms contributing cash, machinery and management skills, whilst their eastern neighbours provide land, buildings and labour. The benefits to the EU firms from such deals are apparent. They gain a cheap source of production as wages and rents are lower than in the West. Controls on production (for example, in relation to pollution) may also be less stringent, further reducing costs of production. At the same time they gain access to a relatively untapped market. Many UK companies, including Taylor Woodrow, British Gas, United Biscuits and Morgan Grenfell, have negotiated deals with companies in Central and Eastern Europe.

2 Technical cooperation: Many agreements have been reached between EU businesses and firms from the East to allow some co-production, short of a formal joint venture. Such agreements might encompass joint assembly of products or the creation of an assembly plant in Central or Eastern Europe near to potential markets. This reduces production costs for Western producers whilst offering Eastern firms technical expertise. Volvos are assembled in Hungary as part of this type of agreement and Renault allows its cars to be assembled in Hungary under licence.

3 Selling expertise: Many producers in Central and Eastern Europe are eager to purchase Western technol-

The Social Chapter – the balance sheet

For	Against
• Workers may be better motivated, improving efficiency and productivity	• It will raise labour costs by possibly reducing working hours and increasing pay rates
• Industrial relations may improve as a result of increased participation and consultation	• Higher labour costs may make it more difficult for EU firms to compete against, say, Asian producers
• If all EU countries sign the Social Chapter, then none will be placed at a disadvantage	• Not all EU firms are starting from the same base; some countries have a tradition of shorter working weeks and higher pay

ogy and expertise. Often this know-how is in the form of licences to produce particular products, usually well-known brands. Coca-Cola has granted a licence to allow manufacture in Bulgaria. For the soft drinks giant this is a cheap way to expand its market.

THE DIFFICULTIES AND DANGERS OF TRADING WITH THE EAST

The East represents a huge opportunity for EU businesses, but a number of potential pitfalls exist.

- The markets in the East are not wealthy ones. The average income in Eastern Europe is approximately one-third of that in the EU. This means Eastern consumers have relatively little income to spend on the products of EU firms.
- The political systems of many Central and Eastern European states are still immature. They are, as yet, unused to democracy and can behave in unpredictable ways. The prolonged war in the former Yugoslavia highlights the difficulties inherent in trading in an unstable region.
- Bureaucracy still exists as a hangover from communist regimes. This can mean delays in receiving permission for new buildings or to employ local people. Corruption still exists in some countries resulting in obstacles to trade unless officials receive payment.

66.8 Developing a European strategy

Trading throughout Europe involves businesses in a dilemma: there are benefits to be derived from producing on a larger scale, yet the market is differentiated and fragmented. Firms have responded to this in a variety of ways, developing new strategies to respond to the challenge of Europe.

The starting point for many firms is to analyse the environment in which they operate, perhaps through SWOT analysis. This can help the company in determining its current position in the market and assist the senior managers in establishing their new European objectives. The managers then determine the changes that are necessary to achieve the agreed objectives.

The sort of questions posed for firms by the opening up of the European market are enormous. They include:

- Where do we produce?
- From where do we purchase our raw materials?
- What new markets exist?
- Do we use a common marketing strategy throughout Europe (pan-European marketing) or treat each region as a separate market sector?
- Can we offer production licences to overseas producers?

Business IN

PILKINGTON GLASS AND THE EUROPEAN MARKET

Pilkington Glass is based in Lancashire and manufactures a range of glass products which it sells internationally. Overcapacity in the world market and the opening up of Europe has forced the company to rethink its strategy. This new strategy contains a number of features:

The company aims to produce a narrower range of products targeted at the enlarged European market. In this way the company expects to benefit from economies of scale in production.

The company appreciates the importance of staying close to its markets. Because of its inability to split production onto a number of sites for economic reasons, Pilkington has elected to establish sales and marketing agencies throughout the EU. This has allowed it to monitor customer needs and ensure they are met.

Aggressive moves by European competitors have meant that Pilkington has concentrated on competing effectively in domestic markets. This has meant focusing on products in which it has a competitive advantage.

- Should we engage in a joint venture with other producers?
- Should we merge or take over other producers?
- Will our existing organisational structure be appropriate for trading throughout Europe?

The strategy adopted by any single company will vary according to the circumstances of that company. The strategy will be influenced by:

- the company's objectives
- the current trading position of the company
- the resources available to the company
- the abilities and beliefs of the senior managers.

A key element in success is the ability of companies to achieve economies of scale whilst meeting the individual demands of the specialist sub-markets which comprise the European market. It is important that managers have access to all the information they require to make the correct decisions. Information technology can play an important part in this respect. Finally, there is no single recipe for success in the European market, but flexible and forward-thinking management is necessary; if not on its own a guarantee of success.

The European Union is a fruitful area for examiners. Analytical answers are more likely to result if you:

- ensure that your answer is integrated – that is, you consider production and personnel, marketing and finance as well as the external environment
- explore the consequences of European marketing decisions – for example, the need to retrain employees in language skills
- examine the type of firm in question – large multinationals are more likely to be affected by the European dimension, but may have more difficulty in responding due to rigid organisational structures.

66.9 Business and the EU
an evaluation

Responding to the challenges posed by the European Union is high on the agenda of many firms at board level. Changes in technical regulations come hand in hand with increased competition and structural changes such as the single market and the single currency. The enlargement of the EU in 2004 presents a major strategic opportunity.

A key element in any management strategy to deal with the European dimension is one of balance. It is important to balance efforts in maintaining the home market with the natural desire to make inroads into the market in continental Europe. It is also vital to balance the benefits resulting from scale economies with the need to meet what can be diverse demands from various parts of the European market. A product or service which is successful in the Netherlands may not sell in Italy or Greece.

It could be argued that the message from this is: managers should concentrate on developing systems which allow the business to respond to the various

facets of the European market. These systems should also permit the maximum degree of integration in production and marketing and encourage flexible management.

KEY terms

European Commission – the Commission has 20 members representing all EU member states. It proposes policy and legislation and executes any decisions taken by the Council of Ministers.

European Monetary Union (EMU) – this will result in all member states using a common currency – the Euro. It will also entail the adoption of common monetary policies (for example, a European rate of interest).

Euro – this is the currency of the European Union. It was launched in 1999 and twelve EU states adopted it as their national currency from 2002.

Eurozone – this is the term given to the twelve EU member states that have adopted the euro in place of their former national currencies. The countries are Austria, Belgium, Finland, France, Germany, Greece, Ireland, Italy, Luxembourg, the Netherlands, Portugal and Spain.

free trade – the ability to export without restriction or unfair taxation.

the single European market – the agreement between the EU member states that the trading differences between countries were to be eliminated so that businesses could treat the whole of the Community as their home market. This became effective on 1 January 1993.

A Level Exercises

A. REVISION QUESTIONS
(40 marks; 70 minutes)

Read the unit, then answer:

1 State two ways in which a UK company could cooperate with firms in Central and Eastern Europe to exploit their local markets. *(2)*
2 Outline three benefits which EU firms might derive from developing into the eastern European markets. *(6)*
3 List three industries which might benefit from increasing their links with Central and Eastern Europe. *(3)*

4 Why should firms exercise caution when expanding into the markets of Central and Eastern Europe? *(5)*
5 How do the European Commission and the Council of Ministers work together in the government of the EU? *(3)*
6 State three ways in which full implementation of the single market may pose a threat to a medium-sized UK-based manufacturer. *(3)*
7 What advantages may producers have gained as a result of the implementation of common technical standards throughout the EU? *(3)*

8 Why do many managers of businesses favour the introduction of the Euro, when much of the population of the UK opposes it? *(4)*

9 Explain why introducing the Euro as a common currency could prove to be a very painful experience for European businesses. *(4)*

10 Why might the introduction of the Social Chapter not, in fact, increase business costs? *(3)*

11 Outline two difficulties a firm might experience in operating successfully throughout the EU. *(4)*

B. REVISION EXERCISES

B1 Data Response

> January 4 1999 was the first day for trading in Euros. Many British companies treated it as an irritation. Yet another currency that had to be dealt with. Nokia, the electronics company from Finland, switched smoothly from trading in 12 European currencies to just one – the Euro. Suppliers had been warned long before that the company wished to convert immediately to Euro trading. After all, it would put an end to currency exchange costs, currency exchange exposure and administration time and cost.
>
> One of the hardest things to put right had been computer accounting software. Careful planning, however, made sure that the problems had been ironed out in 1998. A senior financial manager at Nokia said he regarded the Euro as a commercial advantage. The cost of adjusting to the single currency would be vastly outweighed by the prospective financial benefits.

Questions *(30 marks; 35 minutes)*

1 Explain the meaning of the terms:
 a currency exchange costs *(3)*
 b currency exchange exposure. *(3)*

2 Nokia planned ahead to ensure a smooth change to the Euro. What would you consider the keys to effective planning ahead? *(6)*

3 What might have been the costs to Nokia of 'adjusting to the single currency'? *(6)*

4 Discuss the possible financial benefits of the Euro to a Europe-wide firm such as Nokia. *(12)*

B2 Case Study

LineMaster

LineMaster is a small firm (25 employees) located in Surrey producing line marking equipment used by sports organisations to mark pitches and courts. In the late1980s and early 1990s the company experienced trading difficulties. Falling sales and profits led to a review of the situation.

Research showed that the company was projecting an unfocused image and was offering products and after-sales service below the standard required by customers. In consequence, the company severely pruned its product range. This allowed its limited resources to be concentrated on fewer market segments.

The company invested heavily in its niche products and responded effectively to the challenges posed by the single European market. From mid-1998 it was assuring all its European customers that it would be willing to invoice in Euros from the start of 1999. Its strengthening European presence allowed it to extend its niche strategy to the USA as well as the countries of the EU.

Managing director Graham Thorpe looks to the future with confidence. 'We are a forward-thinking European company operating in a highly specialist market. LineMaster has reaped significant benefits from operating throughout the EU. We look forward to Britain joining the single currency.'

Questions *(40 marks; 60 minutes)*

1 Why might it have been important that LineMaster assured its European customers that it would invoice in Euros from 1 January 1999? *(6)*

2 Assess the benefits to a small manufacturing company of '…operating throughout the EU'. *(12)*

3 Why might LineMaster look forward to Britain joining the Euro? *(10)*

4 Discuss the issues LineMaster should consider when devising its European strategy for the next 10 years. *(12)*

C. ESSAY QUESTIONS

1 'The single European market created more opportunities than threats for UK businesses.' To what extent do you agree with this view?

2 Discuss the advantages and disadvantages of British membership of the Euro for a UK supermarket retailer operating throughout the EU.

3 The managing director of a large manufacturing firm commented: 'The Social Chapter is irrelevant – any well-managed UK business would already meet all the relevant criteria.' Discuss the reasoning which might lie behind such a statement.

GOVERNMENT POLICIES AFFECTING BUSINESS

DEFINITION

Governments seek to control the business environment in order to meet a range of objectives. These include stability and predictability, health and safety, equity and fairness, the promotion of international trade and the efficient use of resources.

67.1 An overview

Governments vary considerably in their approach to policies which affect business. However, some aspects of policy command such widespread support that most of the time we don't even think about them. The legal framework which ensures that debts are paid, for example, is taken for granted. Yet it is absolutely crucial to the efficient functioning of business. People who are considering going into business have to be sure that they can get the money they are owed. Otherwise the risks would be so great that they would be deterred from starting up.

Similarly, the legal requirements on businesses to provide accounts ensure that there are ways of finding out something of the way the business has been running. This can provide vital reassurance for shareholders, suppliers and employees. These and other basic features of Western market economies ensure a degree of predictability in business. This is important to people who must plan for the future in an uncertain world.

There are other areas of policy which involve constant responses to change. Macro-economic policy must be continuously reviewed and adapted in the light of circumstances. In addition, policy may vary depending on which political party is in power. There are a number of contentious issues affecting the relationship between government and business.

This unit addresses the policy areas shown in Figure 67.1 on the next page. Each policy area has difficult open questions to which the answers change over time. Aspects of education, training and employment policy are subject to constant changes. Similarly the various aspects of business taxation policy are adjusted at each year's Budget. A very important aspect of government policy involves the area of business **regulation**, competition policy and **deregulation**. Finally, trade policy evolves continuously as international conditions develop over time. As these changes take place, current concerns shift and public debate creates new priorities.

67.2 The labour market and unemployment

Businesses want a ready supply of suitably qualified recruits. People want to be able to find work when they are without a job. Governments want to be able to show that unemployment has fallen. In addition, governments regulate the ways people are treated at work so as to ensure that the conditions of work are fair. Some of these regulations are embodied in the Social Chapter of the Maastricht Agreement which set up the EU single market. This ensures employees are treated similarly all over the EU.

Unit 64 explains that the most persistent form of unemployment is structural. It arises because of long-term changes in the structure of production due to the growth of some industries and the decline of others. It persists because people are often immobile. They may be occupationally immobile because they lack the skills employers are demanding. Businesses experience the problem as a limited supply of suitably qualified recruits.

The problem is not simple but it can be tackled through the provision of education and training. Improved general education makes people more flexible and better able to adapt to new demands in the workplace. Training and retraining can be adapted to meet specific needs. The difficulty is that both education and training are expensive. Neither government nor employers are especially keen to provide additional funds. There are also some open questions about the effectiveness of particular training programmes. However, an increase in the level of communication between businesses and colleges, through the Learnings and Skills Councils, has probably been a step in the right direction. Setting up the Investors In People scheme, whereby employers are encouraged to provide regular training for employees, probably also helps.

One way in which governments can reduce unemployment is by creating **incentives** to work. When it came to power in 1997, the Labour government was determined to tackle youth unemployment. Early in

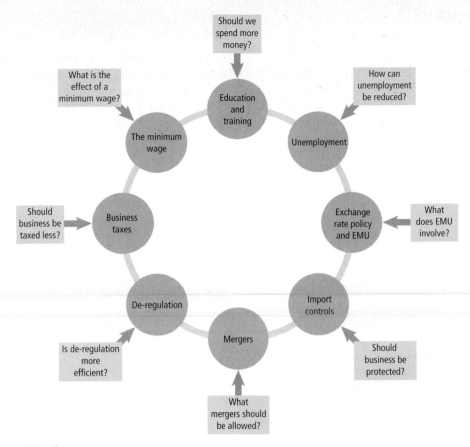

Figure 67.1 Policies which affect business

1998 it introduced the New Deal. According to the policy, all 18–24-year-olds who have been out of work for more than six months risk losing benefits unless they:

- take a subsidised job in the private or the public sector
- work in the voluntary sector or on an environmental programme, or
- enter full-time education or training which will last at least six months.

This provides a substantial incentive to get back into the labour market.

MEASURES WHICH INCREASE LABOUR MARKET FLEXIBILITY

Employers usually welcome any change which tends to make it easier for them to hire and fire employees. This makes them hesitate less before taking on more people. Increased use of part-time and short-term contracts has had this effect. Government policies which may have contributed to increased flexibility in the labour market include making benefits harder to obtain and reducing the power of trade unions to oppose redundancies.

Policies to reduce unemployment can also include improving flows of information about vacancies and the provision of inducements for people looking to become self-employed. The latter can be helpful in getting small businesses started.

NEW DEAL

Under the rules of the New Deal, the employer gets £60 per week for six months for each person taken on. Strict rules prevent the employer from sacking other workers to make way for New Deal recruits. The New Deal is widely believed to have been a success. Essential elements in the process include close mentoring and travel subsidies at the beginning. Private sector employment specialists are paid to ensure that people actually stay in their work placements. However, although almost 400,000 have found jobs, these were undoubtedly the easier ones to employ.

There is plenty of evidence to show that employers are normally unwilling to take on people who have been unemployed for more than six months, because they believe them to have lost their work habits and skills. This programme aims to clear that logjam by helping young people back into work and providing inducements for employers.

Business IN

NATIONALISATION AND PRIVATISATION

When a whole industry is taken into public ownership it usually becomes a monopoly. As explained in Unit 61, monopolies face little pressure to stay efficient and may allow their costs to rise more than if they faced strong competition. Their losses are carried by the government and ultimately by the taxpayer. Some nationalised industries such as British Airways and BT were reasonably profitable. Others, which were perhaps less market oriented in their approach, such as British Coal, British Steel and British Rail, lost large sums over the years.

As the losses mounted in the public sector, political pressure grew to return the nationalised industries to private ownership. A wave of **privatisations** took place during the 1980s and 1990s. Many shares were bought by people who would not in the past have considered investing in this way, thus broadening the ownership base of industry generally.

Privatisation has a variety of meanings, from contracting out street cleaning within a local authority to the sale of government-owned assets. It is as much a way of thinking as a closely defined programme. However, the majority of people, when they talk of privatisation, tend to mean the high profile transfers of nationalised industries into public limited companies. Examples include the sale of British Telecom (BT) or the break-up and sale of the former British Rail to form a number of operating companies such as Virgin Rail and GNER.

Arguments in favour of privatisation and the critics' responses are shown in the table below.

When the discipline created by real competition is absent, privatised monopolies can exercise serious market power. They can use this to charge high prices for a poor service. Anticipating this problem, the government set up watchdogs when it privatised utilities such as British Gas and others. These regulators include OFWAT for water and OFGEM for gas and electricity. These bodies have substantial powers to require the companies to cut or maintain existing prices. They can also set performance standards and, where relevant, can make it possible for new entrants to the market to get started.

PART-PRIVATISATION

A significant part of 'New Labour' thinking has been focused on finding a new, half-way measure between nationalisation and privatisation. What has been known as part-privatisation has focused especially on the **Private Finance Initiative**, the PFI. This has encouraged private firms to bid for contracts in which they would be paid a fee for a service, but might not end up owning the assets of the business concerned. In theory, the private sector provides the management skills and takes on some of the risks, while the state sets out the rules within which the jobs are done. By 2003 many new hospitals had been commissioned in this way, as had the part-privatisation of the London Underground.

DEREGULATION

When an industry is heavily regulated, the regulations themselves can stifle competition. Two areas of importance where deregulation occurred were the financial sector and buses. Controls were common in the financial sector because it had always been seen that the public needed to be protected from possible bank failures and from fraudulent investment advice. Buses were tightly controlled because in the 1930s, cut-throat competition had led to safety problems on the roads.

The deregulation of financial services was an extremely complex process. It encouraged building societies to turn themselves into banks, which increased competition. Whether this has improved customer service or reduced prices is a matter for

Arguments For Privatisation	Critics' Response
• As has been proved in the former communist countries, the state is not a good decider of how to distribute factors of production. The bureaucratic processes involved with decision making prevent efficiency gains which come about through the market mechanism.	• Many state-run enterprises operate in areas where people have a basic right to enjoy the good or service without effective rationing by price. Examples include water, gas and rail travel.
• Many state-owned companies were monopolies which exploited the public. Privatisation introduced competition, such as Mercury and Orange competing with BT.	• Many nationalised industries were natural monopolies meaning that there was room for only one producer in the market. The creation of privatised monopolies has allowed the water companies and others to exploit customers more than ever before.
• Industrial relations and productivity should improve as workers recognise that there is no state support if the company fails. Managers will also have greater responsibilities for ensuring continuity of production.	• Industrial relations have improved in terms of days lost in strikes, but that is true of the whole economy. This may have more to do with legislation or unemployment than anything else. Accusations of greed against some privatised industry bosses may have soured underlying industrial relations in companies such as British Gas.

debate. Deregulating the buses has led to more frequent services in some areas but not in others. For a variety of reasons, fares have risen and the numbers using buses has fallen.

COMPETITION POLICY

The Office of Fair Trading (OFT) oversees the government's competition policy. There are two broad strands to its work. One is to prevent restrictive practices, i.e. any agreement between firms which restricts competition between them. Examples include market sharing pricing agreements. The other strand operates through the work of the Competition Commission. This investigates the likely impact of mergers. The Director General of Fair Trading can refer mergers to the CC if he or she believes they may be against the public interest.

The Office of Fair Trading also becomes involved when there is evidence of unfair competition between firms. Common types of unfair competition include:

- Cartels – agreements between 'rivals' to restrict supply and therefore control or increase prices.
- Full-line forcing – when a major supplier forces retailers to stock a full range of its products, instead of picking strong-selling brands from several suppliers. Wall's has been accused of this practice in the ice-cream market.
- Predatory pricing – deliberately selling below cost on one product or in one area, to drive a financially weaker competitor out of business.

67.5 More trade or less?

For 50 years governments have been working on ways of making international trade easier. There have been two broad areas of action:

- setting up regional groupings within which trade would be free, such as the European Union (EU)
- reducing import controls by international agreement.

The EU has become progressively more important as its provisions have reached further and further into trading arrangements. Its most basic principle is the free movement of people, capital and goods. No tariffs (import duties) are levied on goods crossing borders within the EU. Equally, no government may impose quotas which might restrict imports of goods from other member countries. This has made trade within the EU much easier and encouraged a big increase in trade between member countries.

Encouraging international trade can help to increase economic growth. It is for this reason that governments have tried to reduce import controls. Figure 67.3 shows how trade and growth are linked. It is easy to see that businesses with strong export markets will be keen to keep trade restrictions to a minimum.

ISSUES FOR **analysis**

The impact of government policies on business in recent years can be analysed by examining the different ways in which they help markets become more efficient:

- In the labour market there has been considerable emphasis on giving people an incentive to work.
- Other measures have been designed to increase the flexibility of the labour market.
- A minimum wage has been introduced to try to make sure that everyone is paid a living wage.
- Nationalised industries have been privatised in order to open them up to the discipline of market forces.
- Many privatised industries have regulatory bodies so that they are prevented from using their market power in ways which are against the public interest.
- Competition policy is designed to prevent mergers and takeovers which have the potential to create monopoly powers.
- Trade negotiations have aimed to create free markets for the exchange of imports and exports.

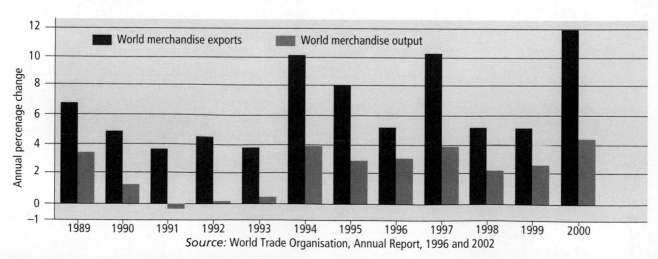

Source: World Trade Organisation, Annual Report, 1996 and 2002

Figure 67.3 Growth in the volume of world merchandise exports and merchandise output, 1985–2000 (annual percentage change)

A CARTEL

In February 2000, the OFT announced that there was evidence of a major price-fixing cartel operated by twelve Volvo dealers in eight counties in southern England. They had agreed to restrict the discounts available to commercial customers. They also agreed to sell only at the recommended retail price to retail customers. The cartel lasted from 1994 to 1996.

John Bridgeman, the then Director General of Fair Trading, said, 'This cartel operated in secret for some time. It is impossible to say what effect it had on prices and to what extent consumers lost out ... I warn companies still involved in cartels like this that they will not get off so lightly in future.'

This announcement was made just before the Competition Act 1998 came into force. This gave the OFT stronger powers and allowed fines of 10% of turnover for each year of infringement. It also permitted the OFT to stage dawn raids to collect the evidence required for proof. Prison sentences are in the offing.

omy has given way to privatisation. Some industries are regulated because they have the potential to exploit the customer. Other industries are deregulated because it is thought they would work more efficiently with less interference. On the whole, governments now are less directly involved in the day-to-day decisions within the economy, but more involved in creating regulations which constrain business decisions.

The focus of policy change has now shifted towards measures which can reduce unemployment and measures that make international trade freer.

67.6 Government policies
an evaluation

Government policies affecting business have undergone substantial changes as attitudes have changed over time. Public ownership of key sectors of the econ-

KEY terms

corporation tax – tax levied on profits made by businesses.

deregulation – a process by which government controls on an industry are reduced.

incentive – a money benefit which arises from pursuing a particular course of action.

nationalisation – occurs when the government takes over the ownership of a whole industry.

private finance initiative (PFI) – the use of private sector capital to invest in public sector infrastructure.

privatisation – occurs when a nationalised industry is put back into private hands by selling its shares to the public.

regulation – the process by which governments require businesses to act in the public interest.

A Level Exercises

A. REVISION QUESTIONS
(40 marks: 70 minutes)

Read the unit, then answer:

1 Why do businesses sometimes have difficulty in recruiting the employees they need? *(3)*

2 Outline one advantage and one disadvantage to business of the government's New Deal. *(4)*

3 How may employers react to the legal requirement to pay a minimum wage? *(3)*

4 In what ways may the level of corporation tax affect UK businesses? *(4)*

5 Identify three reasons why governments in the 1980s and 1990s privatised much of the UK's public enterprise. *(3)*

6 Outline two functions of a regulator, such as the water industry's OFWAT. *(4)*

7 What is the purpose of deregulation? *(3)*

8 What attitude does the government take towards proposed mergers? *(4)*

9 Outline one disadvantage to the consumer of each of the following practices:
   a cartels *(3)*
   b full-line forcing *(3)*
   c predatory pricing. *(3)*

10 How do governments influence the level of international trade? *(3)*

B.1 REVISION EXERCISES

B1 Exercises

1 For some people, the minimum wage will increase their likely earnings and may give them an incentive to work rather than stay on benefits. If this is the case, analyse the effects on businesses and the economy as a whole of the introduction of the minimum wage.

2 If governments reduce import duties, what happens to the prices paid by consumers? What then happens to consumers' real incomes? What would you expect to be the overall effect on the economy of reducing trade restrictions?

3 About 60% of UK exports already go to Europe. How might this level of trade be affected by a government decision to withdraw from the European Union free trade area?

B2 Role Play

Late in 1998, the UK government proposed a £2 billion per year energy tax on business. The objective was to give businesses an incentive to use less fuel and so reduce greenhouse gas emissions. This was thought to be a cost-effective way of tackling the problem. Carbon taxes have been found to be effective in reducing emissions in other EU countries.

The government planned to offset the effects of introducing this new tax on business by reducing other taxes. The Confederation of British Industry (CBI) reacted immediately. In its view, the proposed tax would damage UK competitiveness.

You are part of a team which will put the CBI view to the government. Construct your argument as to why the proposed tax might be damaging to UK businesses. Remember that the government has obligations under international agreements to reduce greenhouse gas emissions.

B3 Data Response

Bus Companies Accused of Price Rigging

> The Office of Fair Trading said yesterday that it had exposed a cartel operated by Stagecoach and 12 other bus companies to rig the price of contracts to operate school buses.

> John Bridgeman, Director General of Fair Trading, said representatives of the companies met secretly in a hotel and agreed on minimum prices at which they would tender to supply school bus services to Kingston Upon Hull city council. He said the bus companies also agreed which routes each operator would bid for.
>
> The alleged agreement came to light after the council complained to the OFT's cartels taskforce. The OFT has applied to the restrictive practices court for orders preventing the companies from acting on the alleged agreement, or any similar agreements not notified under the Restrictive Trade Practices Act.
>
> Pat Edwards, the OFT's legal director, said the tenders would have resulted in higher costs to the council and to local council taxpayers. 'Cartels destroy competition and can have very serious effects,' she said.
>
> Source: *The Financial Times*, 20/11/98

Questions *(30 marks; 35 minutes)*

1 a Explain the meaning of the term 'cartel'. *(2)*
  b Explain what 'very serious side effects' might be expected from allowing cartels freedom to operate. *(8)*

2 In this case the companies were alleged to have met at a hotel to agree minimum prices. How would you expect firms to make their pricing decisions in a free market? *(6)*

3 Cartels are one example of unfair competition. Outline two others. *(6)*

4 The government is bringing in a new, tougher Competition Act in March 2000. It will allow cartel offenders to be fined up to 10% of their sales turnover. Consider how likely it is that this will prevent cartels, such as the school bus one, in future. *(8)*

C. ESSAY QUESTIONS

1 'In the modern world, workers must move to wherever the jobs are.' How realistic is this proposition and what social consequences might it have?

2 Consider whether the privatisation of the railways has been of benefit to the public.

BUSINESS AND THE LAW

Laws are established by Acts of Parliament and by previous judgements made in courts. Businesses must work within the law to maintain their reputation and to avoid legal penalties.

68.1 Introduction

The government (and now the European Union) plays a major role in shaping the environment in which businesses operate. It does this by creating and implementing legislation which affects business. This unit considers the scope and impact of the key aspects of business legislation. It focuses upon the ways laws enhance or constrain business activity.

Almost all areas of business activity are affected by the law. These include marketing, production, financial activities, the employment of people and the establishment of the business itself. This unit looks at the relevant legislation in outline, then spends longer on the purpose of the legislation and its effects on firms.

68.2 Types of law

The sources of law which impact upon UK businesses are numerous, and are discussed below.

ACTS OF PARLIAMENT

Throughout its period in office, each government passes a series of Acts through Parliament. These generally reflect the policies set out in its election manifesto. Legislation arising in this way is termed statute law. Recent examples of statute law include the Employment Act, 2002 (see In Business below).

COMMON LAW (JUDICIAL PRECEDENT)

Despite the Acts passed by Parliament, much business legislation is the result of the decisions of judges. Legal decisions today may depend on the precedent set by a judge 40 years ago. Common law may involve the interpretation of a new statute or a decision when a new circumstance arises. Judicial precedent can only be set by the House of Lords, the Court of Appeal and the High Court.

EUROPEAN UNION LAW

The UK joined the European Union on 1 January 1973. Since then the UK has been subject to EU legislation.

This is of particular importance to businesses since many of the EU's objectives are economic. The EU has passed laws affecting free competition between businesses, the free movement of labour and capital and conditions faced by employees. The **Social Chapter**, to which the UK became a signatory in 1997, extends EU legislation to health and safety, working conditions, collective bargaining and the right to strike.

IN Business

WORKERS' RIGHTS UPDATED

The Department of Trade & Industry has developed a new piece of workplace legislation designed to bring employment rights of British workers into line with their European counterparts. The DTI claims that the new law (the Employment Act, 2002) represents a compromise offering workers added protection without imposing many extra costs on employers.

The new measures increase paid maternity leave from 18 to 26 weeks and allow employees to have a further 26 weeks' unpaid leave. At the same time the Act grants fathers 2 weeks paid paternity leave following the birth of a child. Many businesses, especially small ones, will be compensated by the government for additional costs arising from this legislation.

Much EU law is derived from the treaties which established the European Union. The legislation which originates from Brussels is applicable throughout the EU and overrides much of the law passed by national parliaments.

68.3 Health and safety legislation

Health and safety is the regulation of the working practices of organisations so as to discourage dangerous practices. It usually focuses upon the avoidance of accidents rather than the active promotion of good health.

The main legislation in Britain is the Health and Safety at Work Act of 1974. This was supplemented by extra regulations which came into effect on 1 January 1996. These set out new minimum standards to which employers must maintain the workplace and the working environment.

The Health and Safety at Work Act 1974 imposes on employers the duty 'to ensure, so far as is reasonably practicable, the health, safety and welfare at work' of all staff. 'Reasonably practicable' means that it is accepted that the risks of hazard can be weighed against the cost of prevention. The main provisions of the Health and Safety at Work Act are:

- firms must provide all necessary safety equipment and clothing free of charge
- employers must provide a safe working environment
- an obligation is placed upon employees to observe safety rules
- all firms with five or more employees must have a written safety policy on display
- union-appointed safety representatives have the right to investigate and inspect the workplace and the causes of any accidents.

Health and safety imposes significant constraints upon businesses. Businesses incur substantial additional costs of production. Firms have to appoint safety representatives who become non-productive personnel for at least part of their time at work. Further costs are involved in providing a safe working environment, for example guards for machinery and protective equipment and clothes for operatives.

Health and safety legislation does, however, provide advantages as well. A secure and safe working environment can provide a sound basis for building a motivated, participative workforce. Firms are also keen to improve their health and safety records (see the In Business article above). A good reputation for providing a safe working environment is likely to assist businesses in recruiting high calibre employees.

HEALTH AND SAFETY AT WORK: THE EUROPEAN POSITION

The main European legislation dealing with health and safety relate to the following issues:

- pregnant workers
- working hours
- manual handling, especially heavy weights
- VDU equipment.

Health and safety matters in Europe are decided by the majority voting system, unlike employment matters which require unanimity. The UK can therefore not block health and safety directives.

68.4 Employment protection

There exists a wide body of legislation and judicial decisions relating to employment. Such labour law has two main forms. These are individual and **collective labour law**.

INDIVIDUAL LABOUR LAW

This body of law relates to the rights and obligations of individual employees. Over the last 30 years the amount of individual labour law has increased considerably. The increasing influence of the European Union has been a major factor behind this trend. Some of the major Acts in this area include:

- Equal Pay Act 1970 – this Act states that both sexes should be treated equally with regard to employment. Thus a woman employed in the same job as a man must have the same pay and conditions. This legislation has been strengthened by European Union law, most notably the 1975 Equal Pay Directive.
- Sex Discrimination Act 1975 – in the employment field this Act's main purpose is to outlaw discriminatory practices relating to recruitment, promotion, dismissal and access to benefits, facilities or services. It is not directly concerned with

CONSTRUCTION WORKERS AT RISK

The Health & Safety Executive (HSE) has identified construction as one of the most dangerous industries in Britain. Construction workers are six times more likely to be killed than any other employees. In the last 10 years nearly 900 construction workers and over 50 members of the public were killed as a consequence of construction work. The HSE report announced that the construction industry accounts for over 32% of all employment-related deaths. The industry suffered 79 fatal accidents in the year March 2001–March 2002.

During an inspection of 223 construction sites in London in 2002 the HSE:

- ordered improvements to working practices at 110 sites
- stopped work on four sites because of the extent of danger to employees.

The construction industry has agreed a voluntary target to improve health and safety within the industry. This includes a planned reduction in fatal accidents and serious injuries of 66% by 2009.

IN Business

discrimination in the matter of pay. The Equal Opportunities Commission was established to enforce the legislation.

- Race Relations Act 1976 – this Act makes it unlawful to discriminate in relation to employment, against men or women on the grounds of sex, marital status, colour, race, nationality or ethnic or national origins. These provisions apply to the recruitment of employees and to the way they are treated once employed. This legislation is enforced by the Commission for Racial Equality.
- Disability Discrimination Act 1995 – the main employment-related provisions of the 1995 Act are:
  - to make it unlawful for an employer to treat a disabled person less favourably than others
  - to require employers to make reasonable adjustments to working conditions and environment to help overcome the practical effects of disability.

COLLECTIVE LABOUR LAW

These laws relate to the activities of trade unions and the operation of industrial relations. Traditionally, in the UK, legislation has not played a large part in industrial relations.

Throughout the 1980s the Conservative governments passed a series of laws which restricted the power of trade unions. This legislation gave employers the opportunity to sue trade unions for loss of earnings. As a consequence there was a significant increase in the involvement of the law in industrial relations.

The main elements of recent legislation include:

- Employment Act 1980 – the first of five Employment Acts passed by Mrs Thatcher's Conservative governments. The Act repealed the existing procedures for trade union recognition, thereby enabling firms to refuse to negotiate with unions. It also restricted picketing to employees' 'own place of work'.
- Employment Act 1982 – this Act further tightened the 1980 rules. It placed further restrictions on lawful industrial action by redefining a 'lawful dispute' and made unions liable for damages of up to £250,000. It also made the dismissal of strikers easier.
- Trade Union Act 1984 – this piece of legislation allowed employers to sue trade unions if a strike was authorised without a secret ballot of the membership.
- Trade Union Reform and Employment Rights Act 1993 – a law that critics said was designed to weaken trade unions, though the government declared its aims were to increase the rights of individual employees and trade union members, and to improve competitiveness. The Act required unions to provide employers with at least seven days' notice of official industrial action. It created a new 'citizen's right' to restrain unlawfully organised

industrial action (making it easier to stop unofficial strikes). Finally, it abolished the remaining wages councils and their statutory minimum pay rates.

Business IN

POSTAL WORKERS HAVE CHANGE OF HEART

In August 2002 over 2,000 postal workers in Glasgow engaged in a 24-hour walk out following a dispute over changes in job roles. About 75 junior Royal Mail employees were deemed to be surplus to requirements for sorting mail and offered other employment by the Royal Mail at similar rates of pay. However, the Glasgow postal workers were unhappy at this move and workers at 9 of the city's 33 sorting centres stopped work. This action delayed an estimated half a million items of post.

The industrial action occurred despite the Royal Mail agreeing the changes with the postal workers' union – the Union of Communication Workers. The action was unofficial and the workers had not conducted a strike ballot as required by the Trade Union Act, 1984. The Union, fearing the possibility of legal action by the Royal Mail, called for its members to return to work. After a workers' meeting the employees changed their minds and called off the strike.

68.5 Consumer protection legislation

Consumer protection describes various laws designed to protect consumers from unfair and unscrupulous business practices. Some of the legislation deals with consumer safety. Other laws attempt to protect the consumer from exploitation by strong or unethical firms.

Over the last decade or two consumers have become more sophisticated and informed purchasers. This trend was encouraged by the popularity of consumer organisations such as the Consumers' Association and its publication *Which?*. There has been a parallel growth in consumer television programmes such as *Watchdog* which has helped to highlight consumer issues. This has led to more calls for protection for consumers – often in the form of legislation. This trend, sometimes referred to as **consumerism**, has also served to make producers more aware of, and responsive to, the views of the consumer lobby.

In the UK, the Fair Trading Act of 1973 enables the **Office of Fair Trading** to:

- continuously review consumer affairs in general
- deal with trading practices which may unfairly affect consumers' interests
- take action against persistent offenders against existing legislation
- negotiate self-regulatory codes of practice to raise trading standards.

The major Acts comprising consumer legislation include the following:

- Sale of Goods Act 1893 and 1979 – the 1979 Act lays down the contractual arrangements implied by the purchase of an item. It specifies that goods must be of 'merchantable quality', i.e. fit for the purpose for which they were purchased.
- Weights and Measures Acts 1963 and 1985 – legislation making it illegal to sell goods below their stated weight or volume, together with an enforcement procedure through trading standards officers and the Office of Fair Trading. The 1985 Act allows metric measures to be used.
- Trade Descriptions Act 1968 – this prohibits false or misleading descriptions of a product's contents, effects or price. This affects packaging, advertising and promotional material. It is one of the key pieces of consumer protection legislation.
- Food Safety Act 1990 – this is a wide-ranging law which strengthens and updates consumer protection in the food sector. This brought food sources, and by implication farmers and growers, specifically under food safety legislation for the first time. It made it an offence to sell food which is not of the 'nature or substance or quality' demanded by the purchaser.

THE IMPACT OF CONSUMER PROTECTION LEGISLATION

All firms supplying goods and services are affected by this legislation. The effects can take a number of forms:

1 Ensuring customer satisfaction: Consumerism has resulted in a new culture amongst those purchasing goods and services. Consumers are ready to complain if products are defective in any way. In order to maintain the business's image and standing and to avoid consumers resorting to the law, businesses regularly establish customer services departments. These are intended to rectify problems before they become serious. Similarly, firms might attempt to meet customer needs through the use of market research as part of a market oriented approach.

2 Increased emphasis upon quality control: Firms are nowadays more vulnerable to prosecution for supplying products which are unsuitable or damaged. Consumer safety and weights and measures legislation can be used against businesses who supply unsafe goods or do not supply the stated quantity, for example.

3 Increases in production costs: This is a consequence for firms of most business-related legislation. Food safety legislation, for example, means that those in the catering industry have to meet strict hygiene standards and offer staff appropriate training. Both factors result in increased costs for businesses.

68.6 Competition legislation

Competition legislation covers a number of aspects of business activity including mergers and takeovers, monopolies and **restrictive practices**. Competition legislation is a weapon deployed by government with the intention of promoting greater competition within markets. The aim of this aspect of government policy is enhanced consumer welfare with the cheapest possible supply. Governments aim to achieve a 'fair' price for the consumer and 'fair' profits for producers.

For many years UK governments have adopted a flexible approach to competition policy and the associated legislation. Unlike some governments, they have not determined that all anti-competitive practices (such as monopolies) are harmful and should be abolished. Rather they have argued that cases should be investigated and judged on their individual merit. The key criterion remains: is the practice against the public interest? This approach recognises that there may be benefits to be derived from mergers and from very large-scale production, particularly in international markets. It also acknowledges that there are disadvantages which may outweigh the benefits.

This approach has led to investigations into various business activities. The organisation created to carry out this work is the **Competition Commission**.

THE COMPETITION COMMISSION

The Competition Commission is a government-financed organisation whose function is to oversee proposed mergers and to check that where monopolies do exist, they are not against the public interest. The Commission was established by the Competition Act 1998, although it had existed as the Monopolies Commission since 1948. As a general rule, any merger which is likely to lead to a 25% or greater market dominance will be investigated by the Commission. It will also look into existing cases of the apparent abuse of **monopoly** power. The Commission itself cannot take legal action. It can only advise the Office of Fair Trading that action is necessary.

KEY ELEMENTS OF COMPETITION LEGISLATION

The Office of Fair Trading plays a key role in enforcing the government's competition policy. It has the power to investigate trading activities and to order investigations where it suspects that markets are not being operated in the 'public interest'.

The Fair Trading Act 1973: This set up the Office of Fair Trading, the government agency responsible for providing ministers with advice on legislation and action with regard to monopolies, mergers and restrictive practices. The Act granted the OFT the power to recommend which merger or monopoly situations should be investigated by the Competition Commission.

A preliminary investigation by the Competition Commission into the mobile phone industry has concluded that customers are overcharged.

One of the most controversial issues is high mobile termination charges. These are fees that mobile phone operators charge to rival companies for connecting calls to their networks. Inevitably the mobile phone companies pass these charges on to the consumer. The Competition Commission is contemplating limiting these charges, but a decision is not expected until 2003. Any restrictions on prices would be likely to affect all four British mobile network operators: Orange, Vodafone, T-Mobile and mmO2.

Restrictive Practices Acts 1956, 1968 and 1976: These comprise a body of legislation to control restrictive trade practices between rival suppliers. Restrictive trade practices are active interferences by producers into the free working of markets. This reduces competition and is therefore likely to lead to higher consumer prices and lower standards of customer service.

Examples of restrictive practices are market sharing and price fixing.

- A market-sharing agreement occurs when a number of firms in an industry agree to allow each a profitable part of the total market. Generally this is illegal as it means that price competition is being suspended (forcing consumers to pay excessive prices). A market-sharing agreement is only likely if supply is dominated by a small number of firms, and if it is hard for new competitors to enter the market. A commonly used term for market-sharing is a 'cartel'.

- Price fixing takes place when manufacturers instruct retailers as to the prices at which they may sell their products. Manufacturers may refuse to supply retailers who fail to follow their instructions. This prevents free competition between retailers resulting in higher prices for consumers. There have been allegations in recent years that manufacturers of household electrical equipment have engaged in covert price fixing.

The Restrictive Practices Acts make restrictive practices illegal unless specifically exempted by the Office of Fair Trading. This might occur after an investigation by the Restrictive Practices Court. The Restrictive Practices Court operates the reverse of the usual legal practice; practices are deemed to be illegal unless the business concerned can prove otherwise.

Competition Act 1980: The 1980 Act allowed anti-competitive practices such as the refusal to supply to be investigated by the Competition Commission.

Competition Act 1998: This Act strengthens competition policy in two areas. The first aspect reinforces legislation against anti-competitive practices and cartels. (A cartel is the name given to a group of producers who make an agreement to limit output in order to keep prices high). The second element strengthens penalties against the abuse of a dominant market position. Firms engaging in such anti-competitive practices will face huge fines – up to 10% of turnover.

68.7 European Union competition policy

The are distinct differences between UK and EU competition policy. There have, for many years, been calls for a reform of UK competition legislation to bring it in line with that operated by the European Union. As with most areas of business legislation EU law has primacy if a dispute exists over which code of law should be applied in any given circumstances.

A comparison of UK and EU competition policy

	UK POLICY	EU POLICY
Restrictive agreements	Dealt with by the Office of Fair Trading and possibly the Restrictive Practices Court. No fines for first offenders	Investigated by the EU under Article 85. Offenders may be fined up to 10% of worldwide turnover
Abuses of monopoly power	Dealt with by the Office of Fair Trading and the Competition Commission. No fines for offenders	Investigated by the EU under Article 86. Offenders may be fined up to 10% of worldwide turnover
Mergers	Investigated by the Office of Fair Trading and the Monopolies and Mergers Commission. Secretary of State for Trade and Industry plays a key role	Investigated by the EU's Merger Task Force. Political influence may determine which mergers are permitted

EU policy towards restrictive practices concentrates on the *effects* of the restrictive agreement, whereas UK policy considers the *nature* of the agreement. A restrictive practice would be deemed illegal in the UK just because it contains certain terms and conditions. The EU would carefully assess the effect on the marketplace and would only declare it illegal if the agreement adversely affected consumers.

The abuse of monopoly power is dealt with severely by EU legislation. Large fines are levied on firms who compete unfairly, for example by pricing below cost. Critics have said that the EU's approach contains uncertainties. Only the dominant firm in the industry is considered to be acting illegally when setting its prices below production costs. In some cases it can be difficult to decide whether a firm is, in fact, dominant. The UK's approach is more pragmatic, judging the impact of each monopoly situation in terms of the criterion of public interest. In turn this is criticised for being weak and ineffective.

ISSUES FOR **analysis**

It is important when considering legislation relating to businesses not to get too bogged down in the detail of the Acts. A level Business Studies does not require an in-depth knowledge of the law but rather a clear understanding of its nature, scope and effects. You will not need to have detailed knowledge of the legislation such as that creating a minimum wage. However, you may be required to explain the possible consequences of the introduction of this legislation. You may also be asked to present arguments in favour of and against the policy. It is important to appreciate that there are two aspects to business legislation: it may constrain some aspects of business activity, but it can enhance it in other ways.

You could argue that the legislation discussed in this unit merely serves to constrain the activities of businesses. To some extent this is a valid argument. Small firms, particularly, may find the burden of legislation a struggle. It may damage their competitiveness within the world market. Legal controls increase the proportion of non-productive personnel (for example, health and safety officers) to ensure compliance with the relevant legislation. This increases costs which will be passed on to the consumer in the form of higher prices.

On the other hand, if a workforce feels well looked after and protected it is likely to be more productive. The workforce may also be more responsive to new techniques and ideas. Abraham Maslow (an American psychologist) would argue that this is because the workers' security needs have been met. This may result in improved industrial relations eliminating many of the costs associated with disputes.

One of the themes running through this unit has been that the impact of legislation has good and bad effects upon most businesses. Evaluation in the context of business legislation could centre upon assessing how the law may affect particular groups or types of businesses.

It could be argued that multinational businesses are less affected by business legislation. A prime argument is that strict legislation which forces up costs (such as the imposition of a generous minimum wage) will result in the business moving to other locations. Large businesses employ specialist lawyers who can advise on ways to minimise the impact of legislation. Furthermore, major businesses have considerable political influence and can lobby even the most independent of governments to change their policies. In 2002 small business in the UK lobbied the government to end the tax imposed on energy purchases. The government is considering changing the law in response to the activities of this lobby group.

Equally it is possible to put the case that large businesses are more affected by this kind of legislation. Much competition legislation is aimed at large firms. They are more likely to enjoy (and abuse?) monopoly power or to engage in mergers which are against the consumers' interest. They have reputations which they guard jealously. Large firms do not want to be prosecuted for infringing consumer protection legislation for fear of the consequent adverse impact upon sales. For example, between 1998 and 2003 there was fierce criticism (from the government and consumer bodies) of the financial services industry over advice given in relation to private pensions. Many firms in the financial services industry will have been embarrassed by this publicity and it is likely that their sales have suffered.

collective labour law – laws which relate to the activities of trade unions and the operation of industrial relations.

Competition Commission – a government-financed organisation whose function is to oversee proposed mergers and to check that where monopolies do exist, they are not against the public interest.

consumerism – an approach that places the interests of the consumer at the heart of discussions about business decisions or activities. This could be contrasted with trade unionism, which places the interests of workers first.

EU directives – the general term given to legislation enacted by the European Union.

monopoly – in theory, this is a single producer within a market, in practice it rarely exists because most products have close substitutes and because nowadays markets are international.

Office of Fair Trading (OFT) – the government body set up to ensure that firms are complying with the Fair Trading Act 1973.

restrictive practice – active interference by producers into the free working of markets. This reduces competition and is therefore likely to lead to higher consumer prices.

Social Chapter – a set of statutory and non-statutory measures designed to harmonise social legislation within the EU, alongside economic measures.

AS Level Exercises

A. REVISION QUESTIONS

(35 marks; 75 minutes)

Read the unit, then answer:

1 State three areas of business activity which may be affected by business legislation. (3)
2 Explain the term 'delegated legislation'. (3)
3 Why might a business follow a code of practice which has no legal authority but is, in fact, voluntary? (3)
4 State two provisions of the Health and Safety at Work Act, 1974. (2)
5 Outline one advantage to businesses of the Health and Safety at Work Act 1974. (3)
6 Give three examples of unfair dismissal under current employment protection legislation. (3)
7 Explain the term 'consumerism'. (3)
8 Outline the function of the Office of Fair Trading. (3)
9 Outline what the UK government and the EU hope to achieve through the operation of their competition policies. (4)
10 State two reasons why the authorities wish to outlaw restrictive practices. (2)
11 What is a cartel? Why might a cartel be against the public interest? (4)
12 State two differences between UK and EU competition policy. (2)

B. REVISION EXERCISES

B1 Data Response

A Week In Court

This is a week in the court life of West Yorkshire trading standards officers. Thousands of inspections are made each year, but prosecutions are only undertaken if traders are found to be seriously flouting the law.

Monday – Wakefield
This morning the bench hear four separate cases of goods vehicle overloading. All the defendants were caught out on the same day at a local weighbridge. Today everyone pleads guilty and the fines range from £150 to £1,200.

Tuesday – Bradford
A tour operator has advertised a holiday as 'exclusively for adults' and a couple booked on the strength of this statement. In fact the hotel was full of families with small children. The company pleaded guilty and was fined £1,450.

Wednesday – Huddersfield

Two off-licence owners are attending court, one for selling fireworks to a 15-year-old boy and the other for selling cigarettes to a 13-year-old girl. They are found guilty and fined £200 and £150 respectively.

Thursday – Halifax

A publican is pleading not guilty to selling short-measure beer to an undercover officer. After the evidence is heard the publican is found guilty and fined £300 plus (substantial) costs.

Friday – Leeds

A prosecution is taken out against a retailer selling goods described as 'Russian Vodka'. The bottles are found to contain diluted methylated spirits. The retailer is found guilty and fined £500 plus substantial costs.

Source: *Trading Standards Update*, Winter 1998, West Yorkshire Trading Standards Service

Questions *(30 marks; 35 minutes)*

1 Outline the benefits of the work of trading standards officers in implementing laws affecting:
   a consumers *(6)*
   b the general public. *(6)*
2 Firms worry about the cost of meeting rules and regulations, but how may responsible business owners benefit from legislation being enforced as in the cases above? *(10)*
3 The law also tries to protect consumers from anti-competitive practices such as price fixing between 'rival' firms. Why may this be beneficial to the firms concerned in the long run? *(8)*

B2 Stimulus Question

Car Dealers Exposed in Price-fixing Investigation

Volvo, the Scandinavian motor manufacturer, was accused yesterday of 'price fixing' under European law by discouraging dealers from offering customers discounts. In a further example of the influence of consumerism, an undercover researcher from *Which?* magazine posed as an interested buyer at 12 Volvo dealerships. The researcher could only get a 'very small' discount on a car worth £16,675.

Some dealers allegedly went further, telling the researcher that Volvo told them not to offer discounts. According to this month's *Which?* report, one dealer in Farnham told the researcher that the car maker 'would rap the knuckles' of dealers caught discounting.

In a statement, the company said it did not engage in restrictive practices and that it did not '...restrict in any way the price at which dealers may sell cars'. The motor vehicle industry is an oligopoly with a few large manufacturers supplying the market. In spite of this, research revealed a significant variation in practices amongst dealers. Ford, for example, offered 'substantial discounts of up to £1,000'.

Despite reports such as this there is a strong lobby which contends that European firms face legislative controls which are too strict. Some employers have argued that they are placed at a disadvantage when trading in world markets because of the tight legislative control they face in their home market.

Source: Adapted from the *Independent*, 8/1/98

Questions *(30 marks; 35 minutes)*

1 Explain the meaning of the following terms:
   a price fixing
   b oligopoly. *(4)*
2 Outline two benefits a firm may enjoy as a result of engaging in restrictive practices. *(6)*
3 Consider the factors which have led to the rise of 'consumerism' in recent years. *(8)*
4 Discuss the view that European firms are hampered from competing effectively in world markets because of '...the tight legislative controls they face in their home market'. *(12)*

C. ESSAY QUESTIONS

1 Some business leaders suggest that scrapping legal constraints upon firms would significantly improve Britain's international competitiveness. Discuss this view.
2 Economists such as Milton Friedman believe people should be free to choose what to sell and what to buy. Others believe regulation is needed to save the consumer from unscrupulous traders. Discuss these views and draw your own conclusions.

STAKEHOLDING

DEFINITION

A stakeholder is an individual or group which has an effect on and is affected by an organisation.

69.1 Introduction

All firms are affected by the environment in which they operate. For example, the managers of an organisation come into contact on a daily basis with suppliers, customers, the local community and employees. Each of these groups has an impact on the firm's success and at the same time is likely to be affected by any change in its activities. If, for example, the managers decide to expand the business, this may lead to:

- overtime for employees
- more orders for suppliers
- a wider range of products for consumers
- more traffic for the local community.

Groups such as suppliers, employees and the community are known as the firm's **stakeholder** groups because of their close links with the organisation. A stakeholder group both has an effect on and is affected by the decisions of the firm. Each stakeholder group will have its own objectives. The managers of a firm must decide on the extent to which they should change their behaviour to meet these objectives. Some

managers believe it is very important to focus on the needs of stakeholder groups. Others believe that a company's sole duty is to its **shareholders**.

The traditional view of an organisation is known as the 'shareholder concept'. Under this view managers are responsible solely to the owners of the organisation – the shareholders. The logic is clear: the shareholders employ managers to run the company on their behalf. So everything the managers do should be in the direct interests of shareholders. The managers should not take the needs or objectives of any other group into consideration. If the owners want short-run profit, for example, this is what the managers should provide. If the owners want expansion then this is what the managers should aim for. According to this view, the only consideration managers should have when making any decision is to meet their owners' objectives. Generally, this means maximising **shareholder value**, e.g. increasing the share price.

The alternative view places emphasis on the need to meet the objectives of a wider group. This has led to the growth of 'the stakeholder concept' as opposed to 'the shareholder concept'. The stakeholder approach suggests that managers should take into account their responsibilities to other groups, not just to the owners, when making decisions. The belief is that a firm can benefit significantly from cooperating with its stakeholder groups and incorporating their needs into the decision making process. Examples include:

- improving the working life of employees through more challenging work, better pay and greater responsibilities so that the firm benefits from a more motivated and committed workforce
- giving something back to the community to ensure greater cooperation from local inhabitants whenever the firm needs their help, for example when seeking planning permission for expansion
- treating suppliers with respect and involving them in its plans so that the firm builds up a long-term relationship. This should lead to better quality supplies and a better all-round service. If, for example, your supplier has limited availability of an item, it is more likely you would still get supplied because of the way you have treated the supplier in the past.

The stakeholder approach is, therefore, based on an inclusive view in which the various groups which the firm affects are included in its decision making rather than ignored. This, it is argued, can lead to significant advantages for the firm.

RAILTRACK

In 2002 the government ensured that Railtrack, the company that controlled the UK's railway lines, was taken over by a not-for-profit organisation called Network Rail. Various disasters on the railways such as Hatfield in 2000 had led to upgrading of the rail system which ultimately Railtrack could not afford to pay for. Also, many people felt that Railtrack had been so actively pursuing profit that safety standards had suffered, thereby endangering the lives of passengers. With a not-for-profit organisation running the railways, this conflict should not exist. The Board of Members for the new company includes stakeholders such as the train operating companies, passengers, train drivers and unions. Critics, however, question whether a not-for-profit organisation will have any incentive to be efficient.

Business IN

STAKEHOLDERS: ENRON

In 2001 Enron, a huge American energy company, was discovered to have been falsifying its accounts. Senior executives of both Enron and Andersen, its auditors, were taken to court because they had lied about the company's financial position. The fall out from the Enron scandal was enormous. People became wary of investing in companies because they felt the accounts departments could not be trusted (especially when another giant, WorldCom, was found to have been falsifying its accounts as well); as a result share prices fell significantly.

At the heart of this scandal was the enormous pressure on managers at both Enron and Andersen to deliver ever better results for their bosses and owners. At Enron managers who were able to produce improved growth figures each year received tremendous bonuses and rapid promotion; at Andersen the Enron account was extremely important and they were terrified of losing it. The desire for personal rewards meant that the needs of other stakeholder groups were ignored. Enron shareholders were misled only to discover, once the scandal broke, that their shares were worthless.

69.2 What are the gains of the stakeholding approach?

There are numerous gains which might result from the stakeholding approach. For example, existing employees might be more willing to stay with the firm. It may also attract people to work for the organisation. Employees are increasingly concerned about the ethical behaviour of the organisation they work for. Firms which put the shareholders above all else may deter some people from applying or accepting a job there. The stakeholder approach is also increasingly popular with investors. There are a growing number of financial institutions which specifically seek to invest in organisations which follow the stakeholder approach in the belief that it will lead to long-term rewards. A firm can also gain from better relations with the community, suppliers and distributors and more favourable media coverage. By working with other groups rather than against them a firm is also less likely to be targeted by a **pressure group**.

While this approach may seem attractive in theory there are a number of problems in practice. First, the owners may insist that the managers serve their interests and no-one else's. Many shareholders of public limited companies, for example, demand short-term rewards and may take some convincing that the firm should be paying attention to the needs of other groups. After all, it is their money which is invested in the business. Second, the managers may not be able to meet all their potential responsibilities to these various groups and may have to make some decisions regarding priorities. They may also have to decide between what they regard as their obligations to society and what is commercially viable.

Interestingly, society's view of the responsibilities of business seems to grow each year. This means we are expecting firms to take a much broader view of their activities than in the past. At one stage, for example, we would not have expected firms to be responsible for the political activities of the governments in the countries where they operate. However, the criticism of Shell in the late 1990s for failing to influence the Nigerian government over its human rights policy highlights that firms are now being held responsible for the actions of others, not just themselves. Similarly, Nike was heavily criticised for the behaviour of suppliers which employed child labour. Even though Nike was not directly responsible for this, pressure group activity forced the company to take action to prevent this occurring again.

GREGGS THE BAKERS

In 1964 Ian Gregg reluctantly took over the family bakery shop in Newcastle when his father died. In 2003 he is retiring from the business, though he remains the biggest shareholder. In those years, he has built Greggs into Britain's biggest chain of bakery outlets, with more than 1,000 stores and sales of nearly £400 million a year.

To help fund the huge expansion, Greggs was floated onto the stock market in 1984. In the following 20 years the share price rose by more than 2,000%. Yet Ian Gregg makes it clear that he sees shareholders as the third most important stakeholder behind employees and customers. This, he says, reflects the values and sense of responsibility that underpin the business. Of the future, he is sure that, 'We will not seek to maximise shareholder value in the short term. We take a lot of flak about it.' He can point to the past profit and share price growth to show that there are long term benefits from such an approach. And he points to the company's plan for £1 billion annual sales by 2010 to show that there is no lack of ambition.

Source: Adapted from *The Financial Times*

69.3 Is the stakeholder concept really new?

In recent years people have come to expect more from business organisations. In the past they were just expected to provide good quality goods. Now many consumers want to know exactly how the goods are produced, what the company does for the environment and how it treats its employees. Stories about the use of child labour, the sale of goods to a military regime or the pollution of the environment can all be very damaging to firms. The fact that consumers and investors are becoming more demanding and have set higher ethical and social standards for organisations means that more firms have chosen to adopt the stakeholder approach. However, there are a number of companies such as the John Lewis Partnership which pioneered this approach long before the term 'stakeholder' was even thought of. Many of the origins of this approach go back to the paternalistic style of companies such as Rowntree and Cadbury in the nineteenth century. These family companies were the major employers in an area and built a reputation for treating customers, employees and suppliers with great respect.

69.4 Can a firm satisfy all stakeholder groups?

According to the shareholder concept a firm's responsibilities to other groups directly conflicts with its responsibilities to shareholders. If the firm tried to help the local community, for example, this would take funds away from the shareholders. Similarly, more rewards for the owners would mean less resources for employees. In the shareholder view all these different groups are competing for a fixed set of rewards. If one group has a larger slice of the profits this leaves less for others.

Under the stakeholder approach, however, it is believed that all groups can benefit at the same time. By working with its various stakeholder groups the firm can generate more profit. Imagine, for example, that more rewards are given to employees out of profits. In the short run this may reduce rewards for the shareholder. But in the long run it may generate more rewards for everyone. Better quality work can lead to improved customer loyalty and therefore less marketing expenditure to achieve the same level of sales. Similarly, by building up better relations with suppliers the firm can produce better quality goods leading to more orders and more business for both parties.

STAKEHOLDERS: BAT

In July 2002 British American Tobacco (BAT) launched its first corporate social responsibility report. Unfortunately many stakeholders who had been asked to contribute to the report refused to take part. BAT's chairman said, 'You demonstrate a willingness to be responsible and to get a better understanding of what other parties want of you, but when it comes to the opportunity to talk they refuse because they'd rather shout from the sidelines than play a constructive role'. Groups that refused to take part included Action on Smoking and Health which said, 'It is quite possible and likely that well-meaning engagement with BAT will strengthen a public relations exercise, lend credibility to worthless and damaging initiatives, and work against public health and sustainable development'.

In BAT's report the chairman directly asked the question which has puzzled many an observer, 'Can a business be socially responsible if its core product can harm people?'

BAT's chairman firmly believes the answer is yes, saying, 'Our products pose risks to health, and if a business is managing such products, we believe it is all the more important that it does so responsibly. We acknowledge the significant responsibilities that go with our business, and we are working hard to demonstrate that we are carrying them out ... We do not see Corporate Social Responsibility as about 'PR spin' or window dressing. It is about ensuring best practice in all aspects of our business conduct. We are committed to working to build trust, to listening and responding, and to balancing contrasting stakeholder expectations with each other and with our proper commercial goals.'

Martin Broughton, Chairman, British American Tobacco plc, *The Financial Times*, July 2002

ISSUES FOR **analysis**

When answering a case study or essay question it might be useful to consider the following points:

● An increasing number of firms claim to be adopting the stakeholder approach. They recognise their responsibilities to groups other than the shareholders and are taking their views into account when making decisions.

● It should be remembered, though, that the claims made by firms may largely be for public relations reasons. Companies should be judged on what they do, not what they say.

● Even firms which genuinely mean to change will find many managers stuck in the previous culture of profit/shareholder first. Changing to a stakeholder culture will take years.

● The stakeholder approach can lead to many benefits for organisations, such as attracting new customers, attracting and keeping employees and building a strong long-term corporate image. However, the firm may not be able to fulfil the objectives of all groups. Meeting the needs of one group may conflict with the needs of others.

- The stakeholder approach may prove to be a fad. When the profits of firms fall, for example, they sometimes decide that short-term profit is much more important than obligations to other groups. So a sharp recession would be likely to make every business more profit/shareholder focused.

However, it may not be possible to meet the needs of all interest groups. Firms must decide on the extent to which they take stakeholders into account. Given their limited resources and other obligations, managers must decide on their priorities. In difficult times it may well be that the need for short-term profit overcomes the demands of various stakeholder groups. It would be naïve to ignore the fact that TV consumer programmes such as BBC's *Watchdog* keep exposing business malpractice. Even if progress is being made in general, there are still many firms which persist in seeing short-term profit as the sole business objective.

69.5 Stakeholding
an evaluation

In recent years there has been much greater interest in the idea that firms should pay attention to their **social responsibilities**. Increasingly firms are being asked to consider and justify their actions towards a wide range of groups rather than just their shareholders. Managers are expected to take into account the interests and opinions of numerous internal and external groups before they make a decision. This social responsibility often makes good business sense. If you ignore your stakeholder groups you are vulnerable to pressure group action and may well lose employees and investors. If, however, you build your social responsibility into your marketing this can create new customers and save you money through activities such as recycling.

KEY terms

pressure group – a group of people with a common interest who try to further that interest, e.g. Greenpeace.

shareholder – an owner of a company.

shareholder value – the 1990s' term widely used by company chairmen and chairwomen which means little more than the attempt to maximise the company's share price.

social responsibilities – duties towards stakeholder groups which the firm may or may not accept.

stakeholder – an individual or group which affects and is affected by an organisation.

AS Level Exercises

A. REVISION QUESTIONS
(20 marks; 45 minutes)

Read the unit, then answer.

1 What is meant by a 'stakeholder'? (2)
2 Distinguish between the 'shareholder concept' and the 'stakeholder' concept. (3)
3 Some people believe that an increasing number of firms are now trying to meet their social responsibilities. Explain why this might be the case. (3)
4 Outline two responsibilities a firm may have to :
   a its employees (4)
   b its customers (4)
   c the local community. (4)

B. REVISION EXERCISES

B1 Data Response

Shell's Business Principles

Shell is one the first UK companies to produce a statement of its business principles. The company recognises five areas of responsibility. These are:

- To shareholders – to protect shareholders' investment, and provide an acceptable return.
- To customers – to win and maintain customers by developing and providing products and services which offer value in terms of price, quality, safety and environmental impact.

- To employees – to respect the human rights of their employees, to provide their employees with good and safe conditions of work, and good and competitive terms and conditions of service, to promote the development and best use of human talent and equal opportunity employment and to encourage the involvement of employees in the planning and direction for their work, and in the application of these principles within their company.
- To those with whom they do business – to seek mutually beneficial relationships with contractors, suppliers and in joint ventures.
- To society – to conduct business as responsible corporate members of society, to observe the laws of countries in which they operate, to express support for fundamental human rights in line with the legitimate role of business and to give proper regard to health, safety and the environment consistent with their commitment to contribute to sustainable development.

Source: Adapted from *Shell Statement of General Business Principles*

Questions *(30 marks; 35 minutes)*
1 How is Shell making use of the 'stakeholder' concept? *(4)*
2 Why might Shell have published a statement of its business principles? *(8)*
3 Consider the possible implications for Shell of producing a statement of business principles. *(8)*
4 Discuss whether the responsibilities identified by Shell may conflict with each other. *(10)*

B2 Case Study

Sandler plc produces a range of paints which are sold in the major DIY stores in the UK under the brand name Lifestyles. The company has had a very successful few years and expects demand to be much higher than capacity in the next few years. The company has considered two options:

- extending capacity at the existing site, or
- moving to a new purpose-built factory 60 miles away.

Although the second option is more expensive initially, building a completely new factory is estimated to be more profitable in the long run.

The problem is that the chosen site is close to an area of natural beauty and the firm is concerned that protesters might object to it building there. Also, the closure of the existing factory at Headington will lead to serious job losses in the area. The company has been based at Headington for over 50 years and has worked well with the community. Telling the workforce and local authorities will not be easy. On the other hand it will be creating jobs at the new location, which is an area of high unemployment, whereas Headington is booming at the moment.

Questions *(40 marks; 60 minutes)*
1 Identify four stakeholder groups which may be affected if Sandler closes the Headington factory. Explain briefly how each would be affected. *(8)*
2 Should Sandler plc close the Headington factory? Fully justify your answer. *(12)*
3 If the firm decides to close the Headington factory should it tell the employees immediately or wait until nearer the time? Explain your reasoning. *(10)*
4 Outline the difficulties Sandler might face with stakeholders other than the workforce if the decision is taken to move to the new site. *(10)*

A Level Exercises

A. REVISION QUESTIONS
(25 marks; 50 minutes)

Read the unit, then answer:

1 Explain why a firm may increase its profits by meeting its shareholder responsibilities. *(4)*
2 Explain why a firm's profit may fall by meeting its stakeholder responsibilities. *(4)*
3 Consider whether firms are more or less likely to accept their responsibilities to stakeholder groups in the future. *(4)*

4 The chairman of Dixons Stores Group rejects the idea of stakeholding. He believes a company's duty is purely to its shareholders. Outline two points in favour and two points against this opinion. *(8)*
5 What factors are likely to determine whether a firm accepts its responsibilities to a particular stakeholder group? *(5)*

B. REVISION EXERCISES

B1 Data Response

Stakeholders v Shareholders

In a recent poll, 72% of UK business leaders said shareholders were served best if the company concentrated on customers, suppliers and other stakeholders. Only 17% thought focusing on shareholders was the only way to succeed. This represents a marked change from five years ago, when the stakeholding idea was widely ignored.

However, not everyone agrees with the stakeholder view. According to two UK writers, Shiv Mathur and Alfred Kenyon: '[The stakeholder view] mistakes the essential nature of a business. A business is not a moral agent at all. It is an investment project…Its raison d'etre is financial.'

Others believe the stakeholder and shareholder views do not necessarily conflict with each other. For example, the US consultant James Knight writes:

'Managing a company for value requires delivering maximum return to the investors while balancing the interests of the other important constituents, including customers and employees. Companies that consistently deliver value for investors have learned this lesson.'

Source: Adapted from *The Financial Times*

Questions   (30 marks; 35 minutes)

1 Distinguish between shareholders and stakeholders. (4)
2 Analyse the possible reasons for the growth in popularity of the stakeholder view in recent years. (8)
3 Examine the factors which might influence whether a firm adopts the stakeholder or the shareholder approach. (8)
4 Discuss the view that the interests of shareholders and stakeholders necessarily conflict. (10)

B2 Case Study

Andrew Morton liked his job in the finance department of Mancy's department store but was not always very happy about the way the company treated its suppliers. 'Pay them as late as you can,' his boss said, 'ignore the first invoice and the second and only even think about paying when they threaten to bring in the lawyers.' Andrew could see the logic for this; the later they paid the supplier the more time they had the money in the bank themselves earning them interest. 'Remember it's the shareholders who employ us, not the suppliers,' his boss always said. 'The more we make for them the more secure our jobs are.'

Although there was logic in this Andrew knew that many of the suppliers had cash flow problems – particularly the smaller ones – and Mancy's policies caused real hardship. In some cases it had cost people their livelihoods. Andrew also knew of some firms which had collapsed because Mancy's had persuaded them to increase their capacity to be able to produce the quantities Mancy's needed only to be dropped at the last minute for another cheaper supplier. 'Business is war. Only the ruthless survive, not the generous. Businesses succeed through competition not cooperation. Stop worrying about others and focus on our profits. Without profits we are the ones who will go out of business.'

Questions   (40 marks; 60 minutes)

1 Is Mancy's right to delay payment to its suppliers for as long as it can? (8)
2 Analyse the factors which might make Mancy's managers accept more responsibilities to their stakeholders in future. (12)
3 'Businesses succeed through competition not cooperation.' Critically assess this view. (12)
4 Would Mancy's approach to its suppliers be acceptable if Mancy's was itself suffering from financial difficulties? (8)

C. ESSAY QUESTIONS

1 'Meeting the objectives of different stakeholder groups may be desirable but it is rarely profitable.' Discuss.
2 Consider whether the objectives of the different stakeholder groups necessarily conflict.
3 'A manager's responsibility should be to the shareholders alone.' Critically assess this view.

BUSINESS ETHICS

DEFINITION

Ethics are the moral principles that should underpin decision making. A decision made on ethical grounds might reject the most profitable solution in favour of one of greater benefit to society as well as the firm.

70.1 What are business ethics?

Ethics can be defined as a code of behaviour considered morally correct. Our individual ethics are shaped by a number of factors including the values and behaviour of our parents or guardians, those of our religion, our peers and the society in which we live and work.

Business ethics can provide moral guidelines for the conduct of business affairs. This is based on some assertion of what is right and what is wrong. An ethical decision means doing what is morally right. It is not a matter of scientifically calculating costs, benefit and profit. Most actions and activities in the business world have an ethical dimension. This has been highlighted recently in relation to whole industries (such as cigarettes) and to businesses which use cheap labour in less developed countries.

Two major influences shape the moral behaviour of businesses. First, an organisation is comprised of individuals. All of these have their own moral codes, their own values and principles. Naturally they bring these to bear on the decisions that they have to make as a part of their working lives. Second, businesses have cultures that shape corporate ethical standards. These two factors combine to determine the behaviour of businesses in a variety of circumstances having an ethical dimension.

The extract below illustrates a situation in which the corporate culture may well be dominant. Texas Instruments prepares its employees to take ethical decisions at all levels within the organisation. If unsure, employees are urged to seek advice from their line manager rather than make a decision that may be unethical.

70.2 Business ethics and business objectives

A useful starting point may be to consider business objectives in relation to ethical behaviour. We can pose the question: Why do businesses exist? For many businesses the answer would be 'to make the maximum profit possible in order to satisfy the owners of the business'.

Some notable academics support this view. Milton Friedman, a famous American economist, holds the view that all businesses should use the resources available to them as efficiently as possible. Friedman argues that making the highest possible profit creates the maximum possible wealth to the benefit of the whole society.

Friedman's view, however, ignores the fact that many individuals and groups have an interest in each and every business – the stakeholders. We could argue that to meet the demands of stakeholders means that a business has to take morally correct decisions. The following scenarios illustrate circumstances in which maximising profits conflicts with the interests of stakeholders.

Scenario 1:

Tobacco companies have responded to declining sales in the Western world by increasing production and sales in Asia and Latin America. Consumers in these countries are less knowledgeable about the dangers of smoking and more likely to purchase potentially harmful products.

Ethics is the Cornerstone of TI

Our reputation at TI depends upon all of the decisions we make and all the actions we take personally each day. Our values define how we will evaluate our decisions and actions ... and how we will conduct our business. We are working in a difficult and demanding, ever-changing business environment. Together we are building a work environment on the foundation of integrity, innovation and commitment. Together we are moving our company into a new century ... one good decision at a time. We are prepared to make the tough decisions or take the critical actions ... and do it right. Our high standards have rewarded us with an enviable reputation in today's marketplace ... a reputation of integrity, honesty and trustworthiness. That strong ethical reputation is a vital asset ... and each of us shares a personal responsibility to protect, to preserve and to enhance it. Our reputation is a strong but silent partner in all business relationships. By understanding and applying the values presented on the following pages, each of us can say to ourselves and to others, 'TI is a good company, and one reason is that I am a part of it'.

Know what is right. Value what is right. Do what is right.

Source: Texas Instruments website, October 2002

TOBACCO INDUSTRY SEEKS TO AVOID BAN

In March 2003, after a 30-year battle, cigarette advertising was finally banned in Britain. But the head of a cancer charity criticised the British tobacco industry right up to that point, for continually seeking ways to get round the legislation.

Allegedly the tobacco industry planned to use direct mail to communicate with households to encourage smokers to purchase tobacco products or to switch brands. Professor Gerard Hastings, of Cancer Research UK, said the tobacco industry lobbied government to exempt direct mail from any new legislation.

Unsurprisingly, the UK tobacco industry opposes the legislation. It believes that cigarette advertising raises no ethical questions because adults can make their own minds up about smoking.

Scenario 2:

Should a company seek to minimise its production costs to provide the greatest possible return to its shareholders or should it consider the wider community, particularly the less well-off members of that community? The In Business section below focuses on the activities of Monsanto, a biotechnology company. Following a merger in 1998 Monsanto is one of the largest corporations in the world and wields immense power.

MONSANTO GUILTY OF POLLUTING RIVER

A decision by a court in Alabama in the United States in 2002 proved that the law has a long memory as well as a long arm. The court found bio-technology company Monsanto guilty of dumping many thousands of tons of chemicals into rivers near the town of Anniston during the period 1935–1971. The company only halted production of PCBs after complaints from many different groups.

The court's verdict means that Monsanto is likely to be sued by many local residents who claim that the company's actions in discharging polychlorinated biphenyls into the water system have resulted in severe illnesses including cancer.

70.3 Encouraging ethical behaviour

A number high profile accidents in the late 1980s led to calls for businesses to act in more socially responsible ways and to put moral considerations before profits. Incidents such as the disastrous fire on the North Sea oil rig Piper Alpha in 1988 prompted demands for greater ethical accountability. The pressures on UK businesses increased as a series of investigations exposed fraudulent activities at a number of high profile companies, including the Bank of Commerce and Credit International and Guinness.

This move towards changing corporate cultures was strengthened as a result of the report of the Cadbury Committee in 1992. One of the recommendations of the Committee was to reinforce the role of non-executive directors. It was hoped that these independent directors would encourage a more ethical culture in corporate decision making. Non-executive directors do not take an active role in the management of the company and are well placed to control unethical practices.

Changing corporate cultures is not easy to achieve even when external pressures are encouraging such change. Texas Instruments (profiled earlier) took the view that ethical behaviour began at the grassroots of the company. Its management contended that for a business to behave ethically all of its employees must behave ethically. The quote below highlights one of the ways in which the management team at Texas Instruments endeavours to create an ethical culture within the business.

> 'Is the action legal?
> Does it comply with our values?
> If you do it, will you feel bad?
> How will it look in the newspaper?
> If you know it's wrong, don't do it.
> If you are not sure, ask.
> Keep asking until you get an answer.'
>
> **Source: Texas Instruments website, March 1998**

Texas Instruments issues this advice to all employees on a business card.

By attempting to ensure that all staff within the organisation behave in an agreed ethical manner, companies seek to avoid the potential conflict of ethics and delegation. In organisations where the culture of ethical behaviour does not extend beyond senior (and perhaps middle) managers, delegation brings risks. Delegation in such circumstances may result in junior staff taking decisions which may be regarded as immoral or unethical.

Other companies have operated on ethical principles since their inception. The Body Shop International is recognised as operating in a socially responsible and ethical manner and uses this as a major element of its marketing. That ethical behaviour is firmly rooted in

The Body Shop is indicated by this extract from its mission statement:

> 'To meaningfully contribute to local, national and international communities in which we trade, by adopting a code of conduct which ensures care, honesty, fairness and respect.'

70.4 Ethical codes of practice

As a response to consumer expectations and competitive pressures, businesses have introduced **ethical codes** of practice. These are intended to improve the behaviour and image of a business. The extract below highlights the extent to which UK businesses have appreciated the importance of being seen to behave ethically. Furthermore, the very existence of the Institute of Business Ethics is evidence of the growing importance of this aspect of business behaviour.

The Institute of Business Ethics

The aims of the Institute are to emphasise the essentially ethical nature of wealth creation, to encourage the highest standards of behaviour by companies, to publicise the best ethical practices and to demonstrate that business ethics involve positive initiatives as well as constraints.

*A Report on a Survey on Corporate Codes of Conduct
By Simon Webley and Martin Le Jeune
Executive Summary*

Every three years the IBE surveys larger companies known to have codes of ethics/conduct/business principles. The research asks about the use they make of these codes and their views about current business ethics issues. The main findings of the latest survey were as follows:

In 2001 (compared to 1998) more larger companies:
- *provide a code of ethics for their employees*
- *provide procedures for asking questions in a confidential manner*
- *include conforming with the code in employment contracts*
- *show interest in ethical/social audits*
- *use their codes to 'give staff guidance' rather than for 'enhancing reputation'*
- *use the intranet to deliver ethics awareness and training.*

But fewer:
- *are training staff in business ethics*
- *are reporting on ethics in Annual Reports*
- *have a process for revision of their code.*

An ethical code of practice is a document setting out the way a business believes its employees should respond to situations that challenge their integrity or social responsibility.

The precise focus of the code will depend on the business concerned. Banks may concentrate on honesty, and chemical firms on pollution control. It has proved difficult to produce meaningful, comprehensive codes. The National Westminster Bank, for example, took two years to produce its 10-page document. The typical code might include sections on:

- personal integrity – in dealings with suppliers and in handling the firm's resources
- corporate integrity – such as forbidding collusion with competitors and forbidding predatory pricing
- **environmental responsibility** – highlighting a duty to minimise pollution emissions and maximise recycling
- social responsibility – to provide products of genuine value that are promoted with honesty and dignity.

A common feature of ethical codes of practice is that companies publicise them. This is because they believe that being seen to behave ethically is an important element of the marketing strategy of many businesses.

Critics of ethical codes believe them to be public relations exercises rather than genuine attempts to change business behaviour. What is not in doubt is that the proof of their effectiveness can only be measured by how firms actually behave, not by what they write or say.

Public outcry in the wake of the Piper Alpha disaster forced companies to reassess their ethical codes of practice (© Associated Press)

70.5 Pressure groups and ethics

The activities of **pressure groups** affect all types of businesses and most aspects of their behaviour. Most of the high profile pressure groups are multi-cause and operate internationally. Greenpeace is one of the best known pressure groups and lobbies businesses to restrict behaviour which might adversely affect the environment. Other single-cause pressure groups exist to control the activities of businesses in one particular sphere of operations.

- Action on Smoking and Health (ASH) is an international organisation established to oppose the production and smoking of tobacco. It publicises actions of tobacco companies that may be considered to be unethical. ASH frequently focuses on the long-term effects of tobacco on the consumers of the product.
- Compassion in World Farming is a UK-based pressure group campaigning specifically for an end to the factory farming of animals. The group engages in political lobbying and high profile publicity campaigns in an attempt to end the suffering endured by many farm animals.

PRESSURE GROUP TARGETS McDONALD'S

McDonald's, the multinational fast food chain, is facing calls to introduce common animal welfare standards in all its operations worldwide. The company currently operates high welfare standards in the United States and Britain, but operates lower standards in the other 119 countries in which it trades.

An American pressure group People for the Ethical Treatment of Animals (PETA) has organised a resolution at McDonald's 2002 Annual General Meeting. The resolution, which is opposed by McDonald's Board, requires the burger chain to operate the highest animal welfare standards throughout the world.

Business IN

If public opinion and pressure group activities force firms to take the publicity impact of their decisions into account, this may change the decisions made. This would not mean, however, that the firm was becoming more ethically minded. An ethical decision means doing what is morally right; it is not a matter of scientifically calculating costs and benefits.

70.6 The ethical balance sheet

ADVANTAGES OF ETHICAL BEHAVIOUR

Companies receive many benefits from behaving, or being seen to behave, in an ethical manner. These are discussed below.

Marketing advantages: Many modern consumers expect to purchase goods and services from organisations that operate in ways that they consider morally correct. Some consumers are unwilling to buy products from businesses that behave in any other way. This trend has been accelerated by the rise of consumerism. This has meant that consumers have become increasingly well informed and are prepared to think carefully before spending their money.

Some companies have developed their ethical behaviour into a unique selling point (USP). They base their marketing campaigns on these perceived differences. An example of a high profile company adopting this strategy is The Body Shop International.

A key point is that not only does the company seek to support relatively poor communities in the less developed world, but it publicises these actions. By creating a caring image through its marketing The Body Shop hopes to gain increased sales.

Companies also gain considerable public relations advantages from ethical behaviour. Once again this can help enhance the image of the business with positive implications for sales and profits.

In 2002 the Co-operative Bank announced a 12% increase in pre-tax profits to £107.5 million whilst

STARBUCKS TO SELL 'ETHICAL' COFFEE

In 2002 the Starbucks coffee chain took the decision to sell Fairtrade coffee in the UK. Farmers who grow Fairtrade coffee work in co-operatives and operate high environmental and ethical standards. This ensures that the communities who grow the coffee beans receive fair rewards.

The Fairtrade Foundation said the move would provide excellent publicity for its coffee, benefiting the environment and the coffee communities in the producer nations, even though the amount sold would be small. Due to global overproduction, the price of coffee beans dropped about 70% last year, causing severe economic and social hardship in coffee growing countries.

Starbucks, which buys about 1% of the global coffee crop, will promote its latest addition to its product range strongly.

Business IN

confirming the maintenance of its ethical principles. The bank's chief executive, Martyn Pedelty, commented that the ethical position adopted by the company had attracted many customers from the wealthy A, B and C1 social groups. These customers held large, and profitable, balances with the bank.

Positive effects on the workforce: Firms who adopt ethical practices may experience benefits in relation to their workforce. They may expect to recruit staff who are better qualified and motivated. Employees can be expected to respond positively to working for a business with a positive ethical image and this can lead to greater competition for employment with such companies. A recent survey revealed that 75% of The Body Shop's UK employees were 'proud' to work for the company. Equally, employees may be less likely to leave employment because of dissatisfaction with their job. All of these factors can help to reduce the employment costs incurred by the business.

Creating an ethical culture within a business can also improve employee motivation. This may be part of a wider policy towards employee empowerment.

DISADVANTAGES OF ETHICAL BEHAVIOUR

Inevitably, a number of disadvantages can result from businesses adopting ethical policies.

Reduced profitability: It is likely that any business adopting an ethical policy will face higher costs. It may also be that the company has to turn down the opportunity to invest in projects offering potentially high returns. Exploiting cheap labour in less developed countries may be immoral but it can be very profitable. Equally, The Body Shop International's commitment to purchasing its supplies from sustainable sources means that it incurs higher costs than if it purchased raw materials without regard to the environment.

Businesses adopting an ethical policy may also incur additional costs in training their staff to behave ethically in their decision making. Similarly, adapting production processes to protect the environment may result in increased costs of production.

It is possible to argue that, depending on the nature of the business and its market, profits may not be reduced as a consequence of adopting an ethical policy. A premium price may be possible, or new niche markets may be uncovered by a business marketing itself as ethical.

Conflict with existing policies: Introducing an ethical policy can create internal divisions within the business. A business with a tradition of delegation and empowerment might experience problems introducing an ethical policy. Staff may perceive the implementation as autocratic and a move towards centralisation. They could argue that such a concept conflicts with the philosophy of delegation. As a consequence they may resist the policy.

A company may also experience difficulty in spreading the message in a company which is decentralised. Even if employees view an ethical policy favourably, it may be difficult to implement it into everyday activities. Almost certainly considerable training will be required.

70.7 Ethical behaviour – future developments

It has been suggested that most of the interest in business ethics and its development has been in universities and colleges. However, there is evidence available to suggest that ethical awareness is becoming more firmly rooted in business practice. A number of arguments can be set out to support the view that ethics will be of increasing importance to businesses throughout the world.

The adoption of ethical practices: By 1998 over half the major businesses in the UK had implemented an ethical code of practice. The equivalent figure for 1988 was 18%. Over 30% of chairmen or chief executives see ethical practices and behaviour as their responsibility. Although everyone in a business needs to conform to an ethical code of practice, it is only senior managers who have the power to bring about the necessary changes in corporate culture.

The commercial success of high profile 'ethical' companies: Companies that are seen to have high ethical standards have enjoyed considerable commercial success over recent years. The Co-operative is well known for its ethical stance and has enjoyed rising profits since the mid 1990s. Similarly, Mitsubishi has benefited financially from its highly publicised decision to use sustainable resources in its factories.

A new ethical business was launched in October 2002 amid much publicity. The 'not-for-profit' Charity Bank will provide cheap loans to charities with no access to mainstream lending facilities. Investors in the new Bank will receive a flat rate of interest of 2% and will use any surpluses to support charities. The launch of The Charity Bank builds upon the commercial success of other ethical businesses.

Public expectations: The success of the 'ethical' companies mentioned above is evidence that the public respond favourably to a positive ethical stance. Consumers are likely to become better informed and better educated about products, processes and companies. They will demand products and services that do not pollute, exploit, harm or waste. Successful companies will need to respond positively to the demands of the 'new' consumer.

Cynics might well argue that many businesses may adopt so-called ethical practices simply to project a good public image. Such organisations would produce an ethical code of practice and derive positive publicity from a small number of 'token' ethical actions whilst their underlying business culture remained unchanged. Such businesses, it is argued, would not alter the way in which the majority of their employees behaved, and decisions would continue to be taken with profits (rather than morals) in mind.

This may be a realistic scenario for a number of businesses. But it is also a dangerous strategy in a society where increasing numbers of people have access to information. Certainly the media would be looking to publicise any breaches in a business's ethical code of practice. Being revealed as hypocritical is always a difficult position to defend.

Among the key issues for analysis are:

- What is the underlying intent? If a decision has been made on the basis of profit, it is not truly ethical. An ethical decision is made on the basis of what is morally correct.
- What are the circumstances? A profit-focused decision which might be considered questionable in good times, might be justifiable when times are hard. For example, a firm threatened with closure would be more justified in spending the minimum possible on pollution controls.
- What are the trade-offs? In many cases the key ethical question is profit versus morality. In others, though, the trade-offs are more complex. Making a coal mine close to 100% safe for the workers would be so expensive as to make the mine uneconomic – thereby costing the miners their jobs.

70.8 Business ethics
an evaluation

Evaluation involves making some sort of informed judgement. Businesses are required to make a judgement about the benefits of ethical behaviour. Their key question may well be whether ethics are profitable or not.

In this unit, convincing arguments have been put together as to why this might be the case. For example, ethical behaviour can give a clear competitive advantage on which marketing activities can be based. However, disadvantages may lurk behind an ethical approach. The policy can be the cause of conflict and may be expected to reduce profits.

Operating an ethical policy gives a USP if none of your competitors has taken the plunge. Being first may result in gaining market share before others catch up. In these circumstances an ethical code may enhance profitability. It can also be an attractive option in a market where businesses and products are virtually indistinguishable. In these circumstances a USP can be most valuable.

Ethical policies may add to profits if additional costs are relatively small. Thus for a financial institution to adopt an ethical policy may be less costly than that for a chemical manufacturer. Clearly companies need to weigh increased costs against the marketing (and revenue) benefits which might result.

Ethical policies are more likely to be profitable if consumers are informed and concerned about ethical issues. It may be that businesses can develop new niche markets as a result of an ethical stance.

KEY terms

business culture – the culture of an organisation is the (perhaps unwritten) code that affects the attitudes, decision making and management style of its staff.

environmental responsibility – this involves businesses choosing to adopt processes and procedures which minimise harmful effects on the environment. For example, placing filters on coal-fired power stations to reduce emissions.

ethical code – document setting out the way a company believes its employees should respond to situations that challenge their integrity or social responsibility.

ethical investment – a stock market investment based on a restricted list of firms that are seen as ethically sound.

pressure groups – groups of people with common interests who act together to further that interest.

stakeholder interests – stakeholders are groups such as shareholders and consumers who have a direct interest in a business. These interests frequently cause conflict, for example shareholders may want higher profits whilst consumers want environmentally friendly products, which are more costly.

voluntary codes of practice – these are methods of working recommended by appropriate committees and approved by the government. They have no legal authority. For example, much advertising is controlled by voluntary codes of practice.

AS Level Exercises

A. REVISION QUESTIONS
(25 marks; 60 minutes)

Read the unit, then answer:

1 Define the term 'business ethics'. *(3)*
2 State two factors that may shape the moral behaviour of businesses. *(2)*
3 Outline one circumstance in which a company might face an ethical dilemma. *(4)*
4 Explain the difference between a business behaving legally and a business behaving ethically. *(4)*
5 Why might decisions made upon the basis of a moral code (ethics) conflict with profit? *(4)*
6 Look at each of the following business actions and decide whether they were motivated by ethical considerations. Briefly explain your reasoning each time.
   a An advertising agency refusing to accept business from cigarette producers. *(2)*
   b A private hospital refusing to accept an ill elderly person whose only income is the state pension. *(2)*
   c A small baker refusing to accept supplies of genetically modified flour. *(2)*
   d A small baker refusing to deliver to a restaurant known locally as a racist employer. *(2)*

B. REVISION EXERCISES

B1 Stimulus Questions

BAe in Export Drive for Controversial Jet

British Aerospace is looking for overseas orders worth over £2.5 billion for the Hawk trainer fighter. This aircraft is at the centre of the controversy over exports to Indonesia. John Weston, managing director of the company's military business division, said that the export business was worth £20 billion and created a large number of jobs in the UK.

The company, Britain's biggest exporter, has been in close contact with the government over its decision to introduce a more ethical approach to military business overseas, but has no plans to change tactics.

He said: 'We have always had an ethical guidelines policy from government to government. We take them very seriously.' Mr Weston said the group is waiting to assess the impact of the latest initiative taken by Robin Cook, the foreign secretary. He added: 'We are not rushing to make any amendments to our business plan for sales overseas.'

The company has discussions with the Indonesian government about new business

but is conscious of competition. Indonesia is in the market for surface-to-air missiles that could be supplied by Matra BAe, the joint French venture.

So far BAe has supplied Indonesia with 60 Hawk aircraft and starts delivery of the final batch of 14 this year. The Hawk has won considerable business around the world, and BAe is involved in 14 marketing campaigns to attract new business.

Questions *(30 marks; 35 minutes)*

1 Explain the term '…a more ethical approach…'. *(3)*
2 Explain the ethical dilemma that British Aerospace might face in exporting fighter aircraft to a less developed nation. *(6)*
3 British Aerospace presents itself as a very moral company. Analyse the factors that might shape a moral business culture. *(9)*
4 Some business analysts have observed that the government's ethical policy will make firms such as British Aerospace less profitable. Discuss whether this is likely to be true. *(12)*

B2 Stimulus Questions

Turning Iceland Green

In 2001 the managing director of the Iceland Group, Malcolm Walker, resigned. Walker had established a reputation as one of the UK's greenest entrepreneurs and introduced an ethical code to the company. Walker built the Iceland Group from a roadside stall into a chain of 760 supermarkets. For many years the company was successful in the highly competitive supermarket field and enjoyed rising sales.

The success of Iceland was based upon the increasing numbers of UK homes with a freezer. The company's stores sold predominantly frozen products, initially own brand, later other brands.

Iceland first established its ethical credentials by refusing to sell tobacco products because of their potential to damage consumers' health. It was the first national food store to ban genetically modified products from own-label produce, much to the delight of environmental pressure groups. In 1999 the firm banned artificial colours and flavours from own-brand foods. And in 2000 the company bought 40% of the world's organic vegetable crop to become UK supermarket leader in the pesticide-free field.

In 2001 Iceland suffered a slump in the sales of organic food and blamed its poor trading record on this. Malcolm Walker's downfall was sealed by his controversial sale of his shares in Iceland five weeks before the company announced a slump in profits.

Source: Adapted from www.news.bbc.co.uk. 31/1/01

Questions *(25 marks; 30 minutes)*

1 What is meant by the following terms:
  a 'ethical code'
  b 'pressure groups'? *(4)*
2 Explain one way in which the Iceland Group might encourage its staff to behave in an ethical manner *(4)*
3 Analyse two reasons why the Iceland Group may have chosen to adopt an ethical stance. *(8)*
4 Discuss whether Malcolm Walker's resignation suggests that ethical supermarkets are not viable in the long-term. *(9)*

A Level Exercises

A. REVISION QUESTIONS

(25 marks; 45 minutes)

Read the unit, then answer:

1 Explain how the report of the Cadbury Committee in 1992 encouraged businesses to behave more ethically. *(5)*
2 Why might a policy of delegation make it more difficult for a business to behave ethically? *(4)*
3 Give two reasons why a business might introduce an ethical code of practice. *(2)*
4 Why might a business agree to abide by a voluntary code of practice, when the code has no legal authority? *(4)*
5 Outline the positive effects the adoption of an ethical policy may have on a business's workforce. *(4)*
6 Explain three steps that are important when introducing an ethical code of conduct. *(6)*

B. REVISION EXERCISES

B1 Case Study

Vivien's Bank Under Fire

Vivien's appointment as chief executive was front page news. She was the first woman to lead one of Britain's Big Four banks. Her predecessor, Malcolm Stanton, had been fired due to the bank's poor profit performance. The board made it clear to Vivien that a significant profit improvement was needed within 18 months.

Vivien's approach to management was broadly Theory Y. She trusted that people would give their best as long as the goals were clear. The manager of the bank's overseas section was delighted to be told there would no longer be a monthly review of performance. In future, an annual meeting with Vivien would be sufficient. The target of a 40% profit increase was more of a shock, but after discussion Vivien relaxed it to 33%.

At the half-year stage, Vivien was delighted to see that overseas profits were up by more than 30%. Her delegation programme had worked. The first sign that anything was going wrong came from an article in

Private Eye magazine. Its headline 'Vivien's Bank Under Fire!' was followed by an article suggesting that the bank was the main financier of the arms trade in war-torn Central America. Within a fortnight the national papers had dredged up more scandal. The bank was accused of involvement with an environmental disaster in Brazil and a corruption case in the Far East.

Interviewed on the BBC's *Today* programme, Vivien defended herself by assuring the audience that 'Neither I nor any board member has any knowledge of any of these cases. I have put in hand a thorough inquiry that will look into every aspect of these rumours. This bank has an ethical code that we take very seriously. I am confident that these stories will prove to be just that. Stories.'

Questions *(50 marks; 60 minutes)*

1 Outline the business benefits Vivien would have been expecting to gain from her policy of delegation. *(10)*
2 Why might her approach to delegation have created a situation in which unethical practices were adopted by the overseas section of the bank? *(12)*
3 Consider why the bank's ethical code may have been ineffective in this case. *(12)*
4 Business ethics are strongly influenced by the culture of the workplace.
  a What is meant by the term 'culture'? *(4)*
  b Discuss the approaches Vivien might take to influence the ethical culture of the bank in future. *(12)*

C. ESSAY QUESTIONS

1 'A modern, democratically-led company with an empowered workforce would be the type of organisation that would be expected to operate an ethical policy'. To what extent do you agree with this statement.
2 Discuss the view that few businesses take truly moral decisions and that most implement ethical policies to gain a competitive advantage.

BUSINESS AND ENVIRONMENTAL ISSUES

DEFINITION

Environmental issues are those relating to pollution, global warming, sustainable development and other elements of the 'green' agenda. Businesses today are making more effort to measure and publicise their performance through environmental audits.

71.1 Introduction

This is not a unit on the environment. You do not need a scientific understanding of the processes involved in global warming or acid rain. This unit outlines the ways in which environmental issues act as an external constraint on the operation of business. Successful businesses need to consider the effects of their activities on the environment, whether positive or negative.

Many companies, especially large public limited companies, already have environmental policies. These are designed to minimise any damage their activities may cause to the environment. These policies usually cover production issues, but may be used as a positive aspect in the companies' marketing activities. There is little doubt that the importance of the environment as an issue for businesses has grown over the last 20 years. However, environmental legislation is imperfect in the UK and throughout the EU. Relatively few firms seem to take their responsibility to the environment very seriously.

71.2 The environmental issues affecting business

POLLUTION

As societies become wealthier, consumers start to think less about money and more about their quality of life. Factory smoke becomes unacceptable, as does the inconvenience and pollution caused by traffic jams. Voters put pressure on government to pass stronger laws. Firms find that 'fish die in river pollution disaster' is front page news. So most try to prevent bad publicity by looking carefully at their noise, air and water emissions. Some firms even go so far as to pursue zero emissions.

RECYCLING

From Brazilian rainforests to South African gold mines, the extraction of natural resources is expensive and often damaging environmentally. Higher levels of **recycling** can reduce the need to extract more raw materials.

It also reduces the amount of waste material that needs to be dumped or incinerated. Firms today are proud to display the recycling logo that tells the customer the firm is trying to minimise its use of primary materials.

SUSTAINABLE DEVELOPMENT

Key building blocks of modern life include oil, coal and wood. If modern economies use these commodities excessively there must be a threat that, in the long term, the resources will be depleted. This has already happened with fish stocks in the North Sea. Firms such as The Body Shop pride themselves on their care at ensuring that they plan for the replacement of any materials they use. For example, if they need 10 trees to turn into paper bags, they will plant 10 saplings to ensure that The Body Shop is not damaging the country's environmental future.

GLOBAL WARMING

Excessive production of carbon dioxide is believed to be a primary cause of global warming. This largely comes from burning fossil fuels such as coal and oil in order to produce electricity. Firms able to help counter global warming could expect excellent publicity.

71.3 International environmental standards

In 1992, hundreds of world leaders and thousands of environmentalists gathered in Rio de Janeiro for what became known as the Earth Summit. After two weeks of heavy negotiations, the conference adopted a document known as Agenda 21. Agenda 21 is a summary of the actions the countries at the conference proposed to take in order to ensure protection of the environment in the future. It included targets covering factors such as emissions from factories and recycling materials. Agenda 21 also suggested ways in which less developed countries could continue their economic development without damaging their environments. This is known as sustainable development.

In the same way that quality standards exist to certify excellence in quality control, there are similar certifications to highlight good environmental practice. The International Standards Organisation (ISO) has an environmental certification (ISO14001) which is mainly applicable to manufacturing industry.

71.4 Environmental auditing

An **environmental audit** is an independent check on the pollution emission levels, wastage levels and recycling practices of a firm. If firms carried out environmental audits annually, they may be more willing to invest in methods of improving their environmental practices. The Body Shop, ICI and IBM have all been publishing annual environmental audits for a number of years, however, there is no legal obligation to do so. As a result, firms who perform poorly in this area are unlikely to publish the results of any audit. An EU proposal of the early 1990s proposed compulsory environmental auditing in certain key industries. This proposal was watered down as a result of pressure from industrialists and environmental audits remain voluntary.

71.5 The environment and marketing

There are a number of environmental issues which may have a bearing on marketing decisions taken by firms. A number of firms have emerged which are prepared to actively use environmental friendliness as a marketing tool. A good reputation can act as a positive encouragement to certain consumers to choose one brand over another. So firms have spent time and money building up a 'green' image as an integral part of their marketing strategy. Examples include the Co-operative Bank and Asda Stores.

If a firm is successful in its image creation, a number of advantages may follow. In addition to increased sales and possibly stronger brand loyalty, a 'green' firm may well be in a position to charge a price premium for its products. Many different products, from shampoos to banks, trade on the environment as a unique selling point. Many analysts suggest that this trend may continue until a 'green' image is no longer unique, but a requirement for all products.

A positive image in relation to the environment can help a firm's marketing activities. It is important to remember, however, that there is an opposite – and often much stronger – reaction to those who damage the environment. Bad publicity for firms who cause damage to the environment can result in significant marketing problems. One example is the oil company Shell, which began to lose revenues of up to £5 million per day as a result of a Greenpeace-led customer boycott. The boycott was protesting against the disposal of the oil platform Brent Spar by dumping it in the Atlantic Ocean. Firms must therefore be very wary of creating bad environmental publicity.

ARE SHOPPERS REALLY GREEN?

Philips expected high sales from its first eco-friendly light bulb, as it used 75% less energy than other bulbs. In fact sales were very poor. So the firm redesigned the bulb, making it look more conventional, and changed the name from Earthlight to Marathon. At its relaunch in 2002, the emphasis was on longer lasting rather than environmentally friendly. Sales took off immediately. Green shoppers are growing in number, but they still represent a small niche of younger, more affluent buyers.

71.6 The environment and finance

Although perhaps hard to see immediately, environmental issues can have serious impacts on a firm's financial activities. Firms may find it easier to gain

FORD'S ENVIRONMENTAL FARM

Ford seem to be trying to take their environmental responsibilities seriously as they announced plans to convert space at their Dagenham site, freed by the closure of the car assembly plant, into London's first Wind Farm. The decision to stop car assembly operations at Dagenham had undoubtedly harmed Ford's corporate image in the UK. This despite the announcement of their continued presence at Dagenham, which safeguards 5,000 jobs in an engine plant, destined to supply a new generation of diesel engines for Ford Europe.

Three giant wind turbines will provide power for the engine plant and one will also feature a viewing platform, from which visitors will be able to enjoy an excellent view up the River Thames into London. Whatever their motives for the decision to use wind power, the benefits to Ford are clear, in terms of ensuring that their image is enhanced through a move towards 'clean' energy sources.

The deeper question as yet unanswered relates to the fact that Ford's product – cars – is the world's major environmental polluter. Environmentalists would prefer to see solid progress on the development of cars powered by 'clean' energy sources.

Source: Adapted from the *Independent*, 25/9/02

Business

IN

finance if they are able to point to a solid record of enhancing rather than damaging the environment. There are now a number of banks, most notably the Co-operative Bank, which will not invest in firms with a proven reputation for damaging the environment.

A further financial issue surrounds the traditional investment appraisal techniques. Many environmentalists argue that these techniques are inadequate when appraising investments since they fail to adequately take into account the effects that the investment may have on the environment. Environmentalists urge firms to allow for the full social costs of a decision, whereas accountants traditionally consider only the internal costs to the business.

A solution would be to use full-cost accounting. This measures all costs, rather than just the obvious ones such as materials and equipment. Other, less obvious, costs may arise from an investment, such as waste disposal costs and costs involved in safely scrapping machinery after its useful life. Full-cost accounting ensures that all these costs are included in investment appraisal calculations.

Even if full-cost accounting is used, criticisms of standard investment appraisal techniques still exist. These criticisms are particularly evident when considering investments in equipment or machinery which may be hazardous to the environment at the end of its useful life. An extreme, but helpful, example may be a nuclear power station.

Example:

Initial investment	= £100 million
Annual net cash flow (excluding materials disposal costs)	= £15 million
Cost of disposing of hazardous materials per year	= £5 million
Real annual net cash flow	= £10 million
Payback	= 10 years
Average rate of return	= 8%
Cost of safely decommissioning the entire power station at the end of its 50-year useful life	= £200 million

So payback looks relatively attractive for such a large project. However, calculation of payback completely ignores any costs incurred at the end of the project's life, after payback has been achieved. The ARR of 8% is halved to just 4% if we include the decommissioning costs in the calculation.

71.7 The environment and people

The implications of increased awareness of the importance of the environment on people management are mainly in terms of changing attitudes. An organisation which is keen to improve its overall environmental reputation and performance will need the commitment of its staff. This commitment can only come about as a result of good communication and training.

However, even more general than process-based training is attitudinal training. If an organisation is to be environmentally friendly, staff will need to behave in a way that is consistent with this. They will require training which makes clear what activities damage the environment and how the damage can be limited or halted. As with any training programme, costs are likely to be high, whilst payback will be hard to measure. Attitudinal training, such as that required to improve a firm's environmental awareness, is designed more to change the culture of the organisation than to lead to specific cost reductions or increases in revenue. It is perhaps this absence of clear, financial benefits which goes furthest towards explaining the limited degree to which business in general has responded to the environmental challenge.

One side-effect of a commitment to the environment is the possibility of an improvement in the quality of job applicants. High quality applicants may be attracted by a firm whose reputation fits in with their own personal opinions.

A further knock-on effect is the possibility of improved motivation. Anita Roddick, formerly chief executive of The Body Shop, believes her company's environmental campaigning helped to motivate staff. It gave them a clear sense of purpose, a 'mission'. It enabled them to tie in their working activities with campaigning activities which they had previously done outside the workplace.

71.8 The environment and production

There are three stages of production in which environmental issues may have an important effect. These are illustrated in Figure 71.1 (overleaf).

The materials used to manufacture a product may be finite or replenishable. Materials such as oil or coal, once used up, cannot be replaced. These are materials of which the Earth has a limited supply. Other materials may be replaceable, such as wood. If trees are planted to replace those which are cut down, the supply of wood can continue indefinitely. In some circumstances, firms may be able to choose whether to use finite or renewable resources to manufacture their products. Often the finite resource may be cheaper. The firm must then face a straight choice – cheap or environmentally sound.

The processes used to manufacture products may be more or less harmful to the environment. The key issue here is energy. Some processes require more energy than others and energy is a problem. The main sources of energy generation on Earth are oil and coal – both finite resources. Furthermore, burning coal and oil to generate energy gives off harmful emissions, which damage the environment. There are more environmentally friendly energy sources, such as solar energy, but energy generated in this way tends to be more expensive. Again, firms are faced with the same choice – cheap or environmentally friendly.

Probably the most obvious environmental choices faced by a firm involve waste and by-products generated by its production process. These will need to be disposed of in some way. Gases may be released from large chimneys into the environment, while liquid waste may be pumped into rivers. Solid waste is likely to be taken away and buried somewhere in what is known as a landfill site. All of these methods of disposal are harmful to the environment.

A firm's natural inclination would be to use the cheapest method to dispose of its waste. Governments may tax or fine firms which pollute the environment. In many cases, though, it may be cheaper to the firm to pay the fines and continue polluting, than to find a better way to dispose of the waste. The real test of a firm's environmental priorities is whether it is willing to do more than the lowest cost option. Firms which

POLLUTION DISAPPEARING

The latest results of pressure group Friends of the Earth's Factory Watch survey show that UK manufacturers are reducing pollution. The period 1998–2000 saw a 40% fall in the amount of carcinogenic substances being released by UK factories. However, worryingly for those living in certain areas, the top 10 polluting factories in the UK now account for 70% of the UK's carcinogenic pollution.

Releases of recognised carcinogens, 1998–2000

RANK, 2000		1998 (TONNES)	1999	2000	% CHANGE, (1998–2000)
1	Ineos Chlor Runcorn	3233	3324	2531	−22
2	Associated Octel Ellesmere Port	4159	2234	1358	−67
3	Glaxo Ulverston	1072	847	622	−42
4	Carpenter Glossop	422	426	451	+7
5	Ineos Chlor Teesside	518	264	408	−21
6	Acordis Acetate Lancaster	299	295	306	+2
7	Recticel Manufacturing Alfreton	316	298	262	−17
8	BASF N Tees	164	181	201	+22
9	Vitafoam Middleton	285	205	195	−32
10	Esso Petroleum Fawley	197	177	185	−6
Top 10 total		10,665	8,251	6,519	
National total		15,181	11,920	9,608	−37

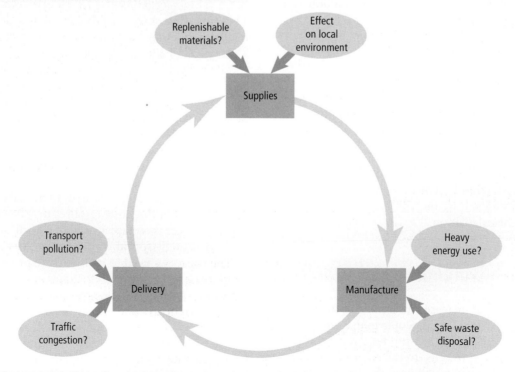

Figure 71.1 Environmental effects of production

publish an environmental audit want to be able to show progress each year on measures such as pollution emissions. Therefore they are likely to invest in systems to achieve more than the minimum standards.

Many firms continue to do the absolute minimum, however. This is forgivable for firms struggling to survive. But there are many wealthy businesses which simply prefer to boost profit instead of protecting the environment.

There tends to be one main area for analysis when considering the effects of the environment on the decisions of firms. That is cost-benefit analysis. This means weighing up the financial and social costs and benefits of an action. If the benefits outweigh the costs, the firm should go ahead with the decision. If not, then it should go for another option. The specific relevance of this technique to the environment is the importance that firms place on environmental costs and benefits. Certain companies may place little value on the effects a decision may have on the environment. Other organisations may treat environmental costs and benefits as having the same importance as financial ones.

The key issue in analysing questions on this subject is to be sure to consider both costs and benefits. In many cases a particular course of action which may have environmental benefits may also have other social costs, such as unemployment. Is it right to make 200 workers redundant because the factory they work in is polluting the environment? It is important not to ignore one side of the argument in favour of another.

71.9 Environmental issues
an evaluation

Judgement can often be shown by looking for the underlying cause of a problem. In this context, the root cause of the environmental problems faced or caused by business. Although production activities may damage the environment, the bulk of environmental harm is actually caused by the consumption of products. Many firms are actually quite good at producing in an environmentally friendly way. However, their products may cause more harm to the environment when they have been consumed. This may be the result of the need to dispose of the consumed product or its packaging, or because the product is designed to be used only once, thus encouraging further consumption and therefore production.

Many environmentalists believe that the most important step which business and consumers need to take is to move away from the so-called 'disposable society'. This is where products are used once and then thrown away. There may be a need to return to a more traditional situation where products are designed to last for a long time, in order to avoid the need to replace them frequently. This, however, might threaten to reduce levels of production and presumably profit. This is therefore unlikely to happen as a result of decisions taken by businesses. Perhaps the only way is for consumers to make it clear to firms that they care about the environment. Therefore they will base their purchasing decisions on a firm's environmental record, not just product image and price.

KEY terms

environmental audit – an independent check on the pollution emission levels, wastage levels and recycling practices of a firm.

environmental policy – a written statement of a firm's approach to dealing with the environmental disturbance or hazards it may face or create.

opportunity cost – the cost of missing out on the next best alternative, when making a decision.

recycling – dismantling and/or sorting products so that they can be collected and reused. This reduces the need for fresh raw materials to be used.

A Level Exercises

A. REVISION QUESTIONS
(20 marks; 40 minutes)

Read the unit, then answer:

1 What aspects of a firm's activities will be covered by an environmental policy? (3)
2 What is meant by the term 'sustainable development'? (3)
3 What marketing advantages may come from an 'environmentally friendly' image? (4)
4 'Environmentally friendly' firms may find various aspects of people management easier as a result of their image. Why might this be so? (4)
5 How can recycling lead to cost reductions? (4)
6 Why would longer lasting products cause less harm to the environment? (2)

B. REVISION EXERCISES

B1 Data Response: Factory in a League of its Own

Top 20 polluting factories

Albright and Wilson UK Ltd **67,490**

Glaxochem Ltd **813,400**

ICI Ltd (N Tees) **575,000**

ICI Ltd (Wilton) **361,412**

Courtaulds Chemicals **353,600**

Hodgson Chemicals Ltd **89,760**

BASF PLC **47,563**

Zeneca Ltd **39,000**

Zeneca Ltd **39,000**

Synthomer Ltd **95,000**

European Vinyls Corp **761,430**

ICI Ltd (Hillhouse) **85,050**

Dow Chemical Co Ltd **117,601**

ICI Ltd (Runcorn) **2,150,499**

Recticel Manufacturing **233,400**

Associated Octel Co Ltd **5,339,997**

Shell UK Ltd **37,041**

Montell Ltd **87,400**

Ciba Geigy PLC **50,160**

Rhone-Poulenc Rorer Ltd **56,702**

The Associated Octel plant at Ellesmere Port, Merseyside, tops Friends of the Earth's list of polluting factories in Britain. It is a factory manufacturing tertraethyl lead, the petrol additive that is now being phased out in Europe because of health risks, but is still in use in many countries, especially in the developing world.

According to Friends of the Earth's analysis, in 1996 – the last year for which figures are available – this one site alone emitted nearly half the total of potentially cancer-causing chemicals discharged by large British factories. The pressure group says that, according to the government's Environment Agency, the factory emitted a 'terrifying' 5,339 tons of recognised carcinogens.

The company said yesterday: 'The claim is false. The company's emissions standards are subject to rigorous supervision by the Environment Agency. All the processes on site are covered by licences issued by the Environment Agency and the company operates in compliance with those licences.'

The company added: 'Friends of the Earth should have made it clear that the concentrations of the substances emitted are so low as to present no health hazard either to the workforce or the local population, based on standards set by the Health and Safety Commission.'

'Technical improvements and other changes will mean that emissions in 1999 will fall to less than half their 1996 levels,' the company said. Source: The *Independent,* 8/2/99 and Michael McCarthy

Questions *(30 marks; 35 minutes)*

1 Explain two reasons why products which carry health risks which are being phased out in Europe may still remain popular in developing countries. *(6)*

2 Firms releasing certain types of pollution must apply for a licence from the Environment Agency to gain permission to operate with these emissions. Outline the pros and cons of this system of controlling emissions. *(6)*

3 Associated Octel claims that the emissions are not hazardous to health. Even if this is so, they may still cause environmental damage. Analyse the possibly conflicting aims of the following groups of stakeholders in this case: the local community, employees and the business itself. *(12)*

4 Upon what grounds could a firm justify to its shareholders expensive technical improvements designed to lower emissions? *(6)*

B2 Case Study

War of the World

Big business secured a victory in the opening battles of today's climate control talks, despite pleas from certain quarters, such as the ambassador from Samoa, who said: 'Let not the many be sacrificed for the few. There would be moral repugnance in that.'

Such anguished calls from developing nations for action on global warming were elbowed out by the oil, coal and motor industries. It seems that some new kind of world war is now being fought, with whole blocs of nations lining up against one another. European Union members are progressive in their outlook, but line up against their traditional North American rivals. Oil-producing developing countries line up in opposition to their developing brothers.

Within this mess of conflicting sides, two clear points of view emerge – those that think global warming is a dire problem that threatens to wipe out the planet given time and those who don't. A big problem to the outsider is who to believe. The United Nations' best estimates suggest that global warming will, at some point in the not too distant future, sweep through global economies, laying waste to them – after all, who can do good business in a world whose thermometer is 'up the spout'.

One industry that seems to be particularly worried is the insurance industry. Munich Re, the largest reinsurer in the world, states in its latest annual report that 'the

possible losses caused by extreme natural catastrophes in one of the world's major metropolises or industrial centres could be so great as to cause the collapse of entire countries' economic systems.'

There are some positive signs, from perhaps unexpected quarters. BP has announced that solar energy has a big future in the battle against global warming. Meanwhile representatives of Enron, the USA's biggest gas company, and Daimler Benz offered support to the campaign for emissions control. Thirteen major US firms, including Mitsubushi America and Nike, took out a newspaper advert last week encouraging President Clinton to support the emissions control movement. However, the advert appeared in response to one which urged Clinton to do nothing, supported by 130 US companies.

The battles are going on around tables in diplomatic circles. The results of the battles vary and the outcome of the war on global warming is still a long way off.

Source: *The Guardian*, 12/11/97

Questions *(30 marks; 45 minutes)*

1 Explain why most oil companies are lobbying against moves to impose emissions control targets. *(4)*

2 Explain the sentence in the text 'who can do good business in a world whose thermometer is "up the spout"'. *(4)*

3 Discuss the possible implications of global warming for a confectionery producer such as Mars. *(12)*

4 How does the issue of emissions control link with the concept of short-termism? *(10)*

C. ESSAY QUESTIONS

1 The environment will only be safe from the harm caused by business when consumers change their attitudes to consumption and recycling. Do you agree?

2 A chemical manufacturer which sells only to other businesses has a terrible pollution record. In what ways might stakeholders ensure that the record is improved?

3 A major multinational has developed an everlasting lightbulb.
   a What are the environmental implications of such a product?
   b The firm has refused to release the product, having patented the design. Why might this be so?

PRESSURE GROUPS

DEFINITION

A pressure group is an organisation formed by people with a shared goal who put pressure on the public, governments and businesses with a view to achieving that goal.

72.1 Introduction

The definition above encompasses a wide range of different organisations. Not only 'traditional' pressure groups such as Greenpeace, but also trade associations such as the National Farmers' Union. The bulk of this unit deals with groups which try to change the actions of businesses. By contrast, trade associations work to promote the interests of their business members.

Examples of pressure groups and their main areas of activity

NAME	AREA OF ACTIVITY
Greenpeace	Environment
Friends of the Earth	Environment
Surfers Against Sewage	Beach pollution
Trade unions	Employee rights
Confederation of British Industry (CBI)	Employers' interests
Consumers' Association	Consumer protection
Worldwide Fund for Nature	Animal protection
Jubilee 2000	Debt forgiveness in less developed countries
Chambers of Commerce	Local business interests
Amnesty International	Human rights

Pressure group activity is an important issue in Business Studies because of the effect it can have on a company's strategy or image. For example, Nestlé was pushing hard to develop sales of baby milk powder in less developed countries. Many pressure groups criticised Nestlé for marketing a product that can become a dangerous chemical cocktail if mixed in unhygienic conditions. Pressure groups organised a worldwide consumer boycott against Nestlé products. Similar consumer action has hit Shell and Barclays Bank at other times.

In order to achieve their aims, pressure groups have three main targets:

- pressuring a company to change its policies

- imposing change by encouraging new laws to be passed by parliament
- encouraging the public to change its approach to consumption or disposal/pollution.

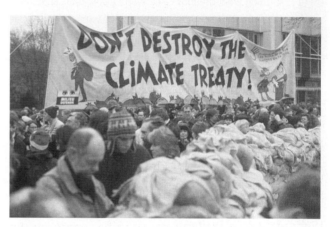

Putting pressure on government ©Jennifer Bates/Friends of the Earth

72.2 How pressure groups work

Pressure group activity aimed at achieving changes in the law has two general areas of focus. First, the pressure group will attempt to persuade the government ministers who make the laws and the Members of Parliament who vote them in. This process, of trying to influence those in power, is known as **lobbying**.

There is a second important way pressure groups attempt to achieve changes in the law. If a pressure group can successfully sway public opinion to its side, the pressure from the public and the media may be enough to convince the government of the need for change. The process of convincing the public to believe in the pressure group's cause is likely to follow two paths:

1 Pressure groups attempt to use the news media to report their story in a favourable light. This use of public relations (PR) as a form of marketing is common. The backbone of any PR strategy is a stream of **press releases**. Pressure group press releases may take the form of a warning that some form of demonstration or direct action is going to take place. This is how the evening news is able, for example, to feature a group of Greenpeace protestors delivering mock containers of nuclear waste to

the gates of Downing Street. Reporters and TV cameras will have been forewarned by a press release to turn up at a particular time. Some people feel this kind of manipulation of the media is not right. However, it does allow even relatively small pressure groups significant amounts of media exposure.

2 Pressure groups also provide statistics to back up the cause for which they are campaigning. Sympathetic journalists then write about this data as if they had found it out for themselves.

72.3 Pressure groups as stakeholders

The job of a business pressure group is to become accepted as a stakeholder. Where a pressure group is seeking changes in the objectives or strategy of a business, it must convince the firm of its claim to be a valid stakeholder. In order for this to happen, the pressure group must persuade the business that it represents the views of people affected by the actions of the business. For example, a trade union may represent the interests of workers and the Consumers' Association may be accepted as the representative of

customers. Businesses are unlikely to accept a new stakeholder easily. Instead they will use a range of tactics to disprove the notion that the pressure group is a valid stakeholder. The winner of this battle is likely to win the underlying argument.

A business may be able to convince its other stakeholders that the pressure group has no right to be considered when making corporate decisions. Then it will be able to operate without undue concern about the pressure group's activities. However, where a pressure group has succeeded in gaining acceptance as a stakeholder, it is in the firm's self-interest to listen to its views. This is because a disgruntled stakeholder could damage a firm's image sufficiently to cause significant harm to its trading results. On the other hand, where the pressure group is not perceived to be a stakeholder, the firm's image is unlikely to be directly affected by the actions of the pressure group. Secure in this knowledge, the firm is therefore safe to pursue its strategy.

72.4 How pressure groups affect businesses

CHANGING CONSUMER BEHAVIOUR

Some pressure groups campaign for consumers to change their behaviour. For example, environmental groups are keen to promote the sale of reusable products. The implications of this fact for a manufacturer of disposable nappies will be different from those for a manufacturer of cotton ones! It goes without saying that it is vital that firms keep a close watch on behavioural trends within their market. This is even more important when a pressure group is actively campaigning for change within a certain market. The change need not be viewed as a threat; some firms may see it as an opportunity.

CHANGES IN THE LAW

Where a pressure group succeeds in its campaign for a change in the law, firms may find that they are required by law to alter their operations in some way. This may mean, in the case of a chemical firm for example, the need to fit pollution filters to its factory in order to reduce emissions which are harmful to the environment.

RISING COSTS

The example of the pollution filters given above illustrates one way in which the activities of a pressure group may force a firm's costs to increase. Other cost increases may result from battling against pressure groups, perhaps by running advertisements that dispute claims made by pressure groups about the firm's activities.

REPUTATION AND IMAGE

The image which a firm seeks to convey to its customers may be harmed as a result of pressure group actions. This is especially so in cases where a pressure group is campaigning directly against one particular firm. The result may well be a decline in sales.

72.5 | What businesses can do

POSITIVE RESPONSE

In certain circumstances companies may agree with pressure groups and actually institute the changes which pressure groups are demanding. This decision could be motivated by genuine ethical beliefs, by a desire to protect the image of the company, or simply as a result of the desire to avoid the costs which may be incurred in doing battle with a pressure group. Often, a compromise will be reached, following negotiations between the company in question and representatives of the pressure group.

PUBLIC RELATIONS

A common way in which firms deal with the actions of pressure groups is to launch their own PR campaign, aimed at discrediting or countering the claims of the pressure group. Although this course of action

costs money and probably takes some time, it means that a firm is able to use its financial and marketing muscle in order to compete with the pressure group. Often, the resources which firms have available to them will be sufficient to defeat the pressure group.

TRADE ASSOCIATIONS

A trade association is an organisation set up to represent the interests of all firms within an industry. Trade associations often lobby parliament on behalf of their industry and usually have significant access to the ears of politicians. Although this action tends to happen behind the scenes, away from the glare of media attention, it is often the most effective way to ensure that a pressure group, campaigning for changes in the law, is defeated.

PRESSURE OR PR?

Are pressure groups all they appear? In April 2002 the founders of Ben & Jerry's ice cream (Ben Cohen and Jerry Greenfield) launched an international campaign against global warming. Ben and Jerry urged people to press the government for change, blaming global warming on 'unbridled capitalism run amok'. The launch of the 'One Sweet Whirled' campaign received positive press coverage.

Yet in fact Ben & Jerry were representing the new owners of their company. The Anglo-Dutch multinational Unilever had bought the business for $326 million and were launching a new ice cream brand called 'One Sweet Whirled'!

72.6 | What factors determine a pressure group's success?

FINANCE

A well-financed pressure group is more likely to be able to achieve success than one with few funds. Finance helps with both marketing and organisational issues. Well-funded pressure groups will be able to stage publicity-grabbing events more regularly and on a larger scale. This helps the public relations activities of the group.

The bigger pressure groups such as Friends of the Earth run marketing campaigns in just the same way as any large business. They commission market research companies to help them identify the right target audience for their particular cause. They may then run expensive advertising, such as Friends of the Earth's poster campaign on acid rain. Another form of marketing made available by increased finance is the use of direct mail shots to raise awareness and attract new members.

PUBLIC SYMPATHY

The ideal position for a pressure group is to be campaigning for changes which the general public

---

SAS BATTLES RESULT IN A STRING OF SUCCESSES

Surfers Against Sewage was set up in May 1990 to campaign for clean beaches around the UK. Since its formation, through PR events and lobbying, SAS has made its voice heard in a number of important places.

It has been invited to give evidence to the House of Lords Select Committee on bathing water, the European Parliament and Commission, the Chartered Institute of Water and Environmental Management and the Monopolies and Mergers Commission. It has also supported a number of legal cases, brought against water companies charged with polluting beaches.

SAS has campaigned for water companies to fully treat all marine sewage discharges. This policy has been adopted by Welsh Water, with another water company expected to follow soon.

Through a range of different activities, Surfers Against Sewage has significantly affected the operations of many of the UK's water companies. This has been achieved in a remarkably short space of time.

Source: Adapted from SAS website

IN Business

support. If the pressure group has the backing of the public, the pressure it brings to bear on politicians will be much more severe. The pressure group will tend to act as a *focus* for public support, rather than battling to achieve it. Theoretically, politicians should respond to the wishes of those who elected them and change should follow.

Pressure groups campaigning for causes which the public either disagree with or, more likely, don't know or care about, face a much tougher task. They have to raise the public's level of awareness before persuading them of their case. This is likely to take a long time and may require high risk or 'gimmicks' to achieve the high level of media coverage needed to get the message through.

ACCESS TO POLITICIANS

Accepting the fact that the key objective of many pressure groups is to force changes in the law, it is the law makers they must seek to influence. This means that access to politicians enhances the chances of success for pressure groups. Concern has been expressed over the extent to which certain pressure groups can influence politicians. Many trade associations have 'friends in high places' and various instances of unethical practice have come to light. Some of the most notable have involved the tobacco industry and sales of arms and weapons to foreign countries, sanctioned by the government.

GLOBAL CLIMATE COALITION

The Global Climate Coalition is a pressure group based in Washington DC. It has a tiny staff but represents the interests of thousands of small to medium-sized American firms along with a number of giant American oil and power companies, including Exxon Mobil (Esso in the UK). As a result of this backing, the organisation is immensely powerful, having access to millions of dollars of funding. Furthermore, the group has extensive connections throughout the US government – a government headed by former oil man, George W Bush, whose election campaign received massive backing from America's oil industry.

It was no surprise, then, to see the President satisfy the demands of the Global Climate Coalition by withdrawing US support for the United Nations Convention on Climate control, which had reached agreement on worldwide reductions in greenhouse gasses. The Global Climate Coalition proves that you don't need to be well known or supported by the public to get what you want – it succeeds through its wealth and connections.

Business IN

ACCESS TO MEDIA

Since much pressure group activity involves using the media as a mouthpiece via public relations exercises, good access to the media plays a crucial part in a pressure group's success. Some pressure groups seem to have great success in attracting media attention, whether due to who they know, what they do or what they say. However it is achieved, media coverage amounts to free advertising for the pressure group concerned – vital to its success, given limited marketing budgets.

REPUTATION

The reputation of a pressure group is likely to determine how seriously the public, media or politicians actually listen to its message. Credibility is vital to pressure groups. The scientific data they provide to back up their arguments will only be accepted as reliable if their reputation is good. More broadly, pressure groups with a reputation for caring passionately about their causes are more likely to attract public support.

GREENPEACE

Greenpeace managed to hit the front pages in September 2002, with the attempt to publicise the return of 5 tons of plutonium and uranium mixed oxide (nuclear waste) to British Nuclear Fuel's Sellafield site. A flotilla of boats representing Greenpeace and other environmental groups tracked the ship carrying the waste. The ship had been afloat for over 3 years – unable to find a country willing to accept its cargo. Stunts such as these have characterised Greenpeace's operations. Camera-friendly actions make for great images to be plastered on newspaper front pages whilst raising the image of the pressure group. This reminds the public of the cause and highlights particular issues.

Greenpeace's ability to use the media remains strong, whilst direct action (with the associated press coverage) continues to play an important role in the group's operations.

Business IN

Protesting against war with Iraq, outside Westminster, London, March 2003 (© Greenpeace)

Should businesses agree to the demands of pressure groups? Each particular situation is different and the decisions which businesses come to will depend on the particular scenario. The kinds of issues which will need analysis are:

- How powerful is the group? A small company is likely to be unwilling to go into battle with a large pressure group. On the other hand, where the business being threatened is a huge multinational, it is likely to have significantly more financial, marketing and human resources to deploy than a pressure group, and is therefore less likely to concede.
- How will the demands of the group affect the business's activities? If only small, relatively inexpensive changes are required to meet the demands of the pressure group, a business is more likely to meet those demands. Indeed, if appropriately handled, it could turn the situation into a positive public relations exercise with which to boost the firm's image. However, some pressure groups demand changes which could put the future of a whole industry in jeopardy. In these cases, the firms involved will be expected to fight hard to protect their interests.
- A further issue concerns the importance of public opinion. Firms which do not sell their goods or services to the general public may feel they need not worry too much about damage to their reputation caused by adverse publicity generated by pressure groups. Arms suppliers will not find sales adversely affected by public outcry at home, unless that public outcry is strong enough to lead to direct government intervention.

72.7 Pressure groups
an evaluation

It is extremely important, when answering questions on pressure groups, to remember to keep the focus on business. Your most important priority is to understand how businesses are affected by pressure groups. All too often, Business Studies answers related to pressure groups fail to mention business at all!

Having said this, pressure group activity is becoming very important. Increasingly, governments are being bombarded with demands from single-issue groups who have the backing of public opinion. As a result, pressure groups are becoming more powerful. However, to counter this, some people argue that the power of governments to be able to bow to public opinion through the action of pressure groups is diminishing as huge multinational corporations continue to grow. In global terms it is possible that environmental groups should be more concerned with getting companies to agree to targets for controlling pollution, rather than convincing individual governments.

KEY terms

lobbying – putting your viewpoint across directly to a person in a position of power and influence.

press release – a statement issued to the media in the hope of gaining favourable editorial publicity.

72.8 Workbook

A Level Exercises

A. REVISION QUESTIONS
(30 marks; 60 minutes)

Read the unit, then answer:

1 What are the key factors that determine the success of a pressure group? (4)
2 a What is meant by 'lobbying'? (2)
  b Why might a firm lobby the government? (3)
3 How can pressure groups use the traditional marketing mix? (4)
4 In what ways could pressure group activities cause a business' costs to rise? (3)
5 How does a trade association differ from a pressure group? (2)
6 In what ways can a pressure group damage a company's sales figures? (3)
7 How can pressure groups use market research to improve their position? (3)

8 Briefly outline a campaign run recently by a pressure group attempting to change a decision or an action taken by a firm. (6)

B. REVISION EXERCISES

B1 Data Response

Local Residents Object to Supermarket Plans

> Local Tory councillors who have been conducting a survey into local feelings about a proposed new Waitrose supermarket development say that opposition to the plan is growing. One of the councillors, Eric Shaw, said 'we have had a tremendous response to the survey and so far only around a dozen

people said they back the scheme.' He went on to explain that over 100 people are against the plan, along with the local Residents' Association.

The major concerns expressed by the Residents' Association are:

- the likely loss of trade for other local businesses
- the environmental impact of the development
- more noise and disturbance in the village
- more traffic leading to congestion problems in the area.

Residents just three miles away in Selsdon are meeting tonight to discuss how to coordinate opposition to a plan by Sainsbury's to redevelop the site of the local library and halls. Sainsbury's plan involves building a supermarket on the original site of the library and also building a new library, community hall and day centre.

Source: Adapted from *The Croydon Advertiser*, 22/1/99

Questions   *(30 marks; 35 minutes)*

1 Outline a strategy that Waitrose could pursue in dealing with opposition to its plans.   *(6)*
2 Why might the results of the survey be misleading?   *(8)*
3 Many new supermarkets are built with deals such as that being offered by Sainsbury's. Outline the implications of such a deal on the firm's investment appraisal calculations.   *(6)*
4 Evaluate the effects of the local pressure group activity discussed in the article on the image of the supermarket chains.   *(10)*

C. ESSAY QUESTIONS

1 In what way do the challenges facing the management of a pressure group differ from those facing the management of a business?
2 The role of pressure groups is vital in ensuring that firms behave in an ethical manner. Discuss.
3 Powerful trade associations can exert a great influence over the way a market works. This fact means that trade associations may be working against the public's best interests and their powers should be controlled. To what extent would you agree with this proposition?

B2 Case Study

A Trade Association Leak

A leak from the Society of Motor Manufacturers and Traders (SMMT) to the pressure group Friends of the Earth, revealed yesterday that the motor industry is planning a £12 million public relations campaign aimed at damaging the government's transport policies. Fears that the government is seeking to discourage car use have prompted the five-year campaign which will be aimed at schoolchildren as well as more traditionally influential groups in the media and politics. More specifically, the campaign plans to use schools TV programmes, campaign weeks, conferences, direct mailshots and a £10 million advertising campaign to promote the message that the industry is working hard to meet its environmental responsibilities.

The leaked document indicated that the industry would shift its arguments away from scientific arguments (which did not help Shell in its efforts to dispose of the Brent Spar oil platform) towards emphasising the positive role of cars in providing mobility and independence.

A representative of Friends of the Earth said that the document shows that the motor industry is not only cynical but immoral. The SMMT responded by confirming that the 'internal discussion document' was nothing to be embarrassed about.

'The industry has been conducting a PR campaign since 1902, informing people about the real benefits of modern technology.'

The SMMT repeated their commitment to work with the government on the goal of reducing the environmental impact of motor vehicles.

Source: Adapted from *The Independent*, 20/8/98

Questions   *(40 marks; 50 minutes)*

1 a What is a trade association?   *(2)*
   b How does the case study illustrate the role of trade associations?   *(5)*
2 The SMMT has, in the past, proven itself to be a highly influential organisation. Explain why this might be so.   *(6)*
3 To what extent does the text illustrate the similarity of marketing strategies for businesses and pressure groups?   *(8)*
4 Examine the implications of the SMMT's proposals for UK car manufacturers.   *(9)*
5 In your opinion, is the SMMT justified in conducting the proposed campaign? (Be sure to consider both sides of the argument.)   *(10)*

TECHNOLOGICAL CHANGE

DEFINITION
Technological change involves developments both in terms of what is being produced by a firm, and how it is being made.

73.1 Introduction

Technology is changing at an extremely fast rate. New products and new processes are being developed all the time. In markets such as computers and mobile phones hundreds of new products are being launched every month. Almost the minute you buy the latest CD player, PC, mobile phone or fax machine you know it is about to be outdated! Firms face similar problems. If you visit a business and ask about its equipment you will inevitably find that the last piece of machinery it bought is already less efficient than the newest model on the market, which is probably available at a much lower price. Whatever you buy, whatever technology you use, the chances are someone somewhere is working on an improved version.

This rate of change seems to be getting ever faster. Product development times are getting quicker and, consequently, more products are getting to the market in less time. The result is that the typical product life cycle is getting shorter. Naturally this creates serious problems for firms. With more and more products being developed the chances of any one product succeeding is reduced. Even if it does succeed its life cycle is likely to be relatively short. Given the ever-higher quality demanded by customers firms are having to spend more on developing products but have less time to recoup their investment.

One of the main reasons for the rapid growth of technology is technology itself. The development of **computer-aided design** (CAD) and **computer-aided manufacture** (CAM) has enabled even faster development of other products and processes. Technology feeds off itself and generates even more ideas and innovations. This rapid rate of change creates both threats and opportunities for firms. The threats are clear. Firms which do not adopt competitive technology will:

- struggle to keep their unit costs down
- be unable to provide goods or services of sufficient quality relative to their competitors.

Imagine if you were still trying to sell typewriters in the UK against the latest Personal Computer, for example.

Technology can certainly make life a great deal easier for firms. Just think of how slow it would be to

Business in

COMPUTER AIDED DESIGN

When Peter Fenn started Fenn Tool Ltd in 1982 it had 3 employees, was based in an old church hall and imported quality machine tools from Switzerland and Austria. It sold them to UK customers at competitive prices. Over time the business grew, moving into larger premises, taking on more staff and opening an office in Ireland. A few years ago the company realised there was a market for specialist cutting and grinding tools, especially in the aerospace and telecommunications industry. The typical waiting time to get these produced and imported into the UK was 6 to 10 weeks. This meant customers were kept waiting and so lost valuable production time.

After much discussion and worrying about the risks involved, Fenn Tool decided to spend £250,000 on a computer-aided design package linked to a computer-aided manufacturing system. This used up much of the firm's available capital, but cut customer lead times to just 48 hours from order to finished product. With its new equipment Fenn Tool has complete flexibility of design, and tools can be made in a variety of metals and finishes that will do the job more efficiently than a standard drill or cutter. The company has since bought a second machine and has been awarded the Parcel Force Worldwide Small Business of the Year and the prestigious Manufacturing Industry Achievement Award.

work out all of a large company's accounts by hand instead of using a computer spreadsheet. If one company avoids the latest technology while its rivals adopt it, it is likely to suffer real problems with competitiveness. The rivals may be able to offer lower prices or substantially better or faster service standards.

73.2 Problems of introducing new technology

Unfortunately, because of the costs, it is not always possible for a firm to acquire the technology it wants. New technology can represent a significant investment for a firm and cannot always be undertaken as and when the managers feel like it. This is particularly true when technology is changing at such a rate that any investment may be out of date very rapidly. The difficulty is knowing when to buy. Buy too late and you may well have lost the competitive advantage – your rivals will already be producing better quality, more cost-competitive work. Buy too early and you may find yourself committed to technology which is no longer relevant. Consumers who invested in Betamax videos, for example, found they were soon replaced by the present day VHS system.

Technology also creates problems within the firm. First, the managers must consider how it links up with what they have already. It is all too easy to buy one piece of equipment only to find it is not compatible with other parts of your production process. It is surprising how many firms have various elements of technology which do not match up. For example, a retailer may have scanning equipment which cannot feed information through to the manufacturer. Or some parts of the organisation may be on a computer network while others are not. Within factories you often find 'islands of **automation**'. Parts of the process are automated while others are not.

Second, technological change can create industrial relations problems. In some cases new technology may mean some employees lose their jobs. This often happens with relatively routine jobs such as repetitively cutting, pressing or moving items. In other cases people will still keep their jobs but will have to retrain or learn new skills to be able to use the technology successfully. This in itself may cause friction. Some employees will no doubt welcome the opportunity to use technology and regard retraining as a challenge. Others may be worried about their ability to cope. Imagine that you are very good at using one particular type of software, for example, and someone asks you to learn a new way of doing things. You may wonder what the point of changing is and you may be worried that you will not be able to cope quite so well with the new system. In this situation people will need reassuring. They will need to understand why the new technology is being introduced, and be trained and supported during the whole process of adjustment.

There will always be some people who object to change because they like things the way they are. There will also be some who object because they will actually be worse off. For example, they may have to transfer to a department headed by someone they dislike. In many cases, however, people object to change because they are scared by it or do not understand why it is needed. The management of technological change, therefore, needs careful handling. The process must be done at the right pace and employees must be involved wherever possible.

Resistance to change will come from:

- people who do not understand why it is necessary
- people who will be worse off (e.g. they no longer have the right skills)
- people who are worried about its effects, possibly unnecessarily
- people who disagree with it – they understand it, but are convinced it is a bad idea.

Firms must also consider the costs involved in training employees to be able to use new technology. These costs will include the direct costs of on-the-job or off-the-job training as well as the opportunity cost of the output lost while they are learning new skills. The firms also run the risk of training staff in the latest technology, only to have them leave for better paid jobs elsewhere.

Business IN

ROBOTS

The purchase of robots in the UK continues to increase as more firms automate their production processes. The number of robots has risen, particularly in the automotive and engineering sectors. These areas were hit by the strength of the pound increasing the pressure on them to become more efficient. In 2001 around 2,000 robots were purchased in the UK; 75% of these were purchased in the automotive industry. By contrast, numbers bought in the plastics and rubber industries fell as production in these areas has been switched to lower cost locations overseas. In total the UK robot population is around 13,500. This is well behind Germany and Japan which have a much longer tradition of automation.

73.3 Benefits from introducing new technology

Technological change can provide enormous opportunities for firms. There is a tendency to think of technology as something which leads to mass unemployment. In fact it is an aid to us all. Imagine what life would be like without televisions, phones, videos, cashpoints, CDs or credit cards, for example. Similarly, technology makes working life considerably easier. Routine jobs can be replaced, work can generally be speeded up and problem solving made easier. Just think what it would be like solving some of your business problems without a calculator.

Technology also creates new markets. Telephone banking, computer games, e-mail, CD-ROMs, DVDs and Eurostar are all relatively recent developments which we now take for granted. These markets create huge opportunities for firms that are able to exploit them and for people with skills that are in demand.

INTERNET USAGE

One of the most significant technological developments in recent years is the Internet. The use of the Internet is revolutionising the way firms communicate and the way they do business. The opportunities continue to grow as more people access the Internet. In the UK, for example, the number of regular home web users increased from just over 11 million to 16.5 million in 2002. The total number of people in the UK with Internet connections rose to around 30 million – around half the population. Globally, there are now 241 million active home web users.

As with any change, technological developments create potential gains and potential threats. Whether a particular firm wins or loses depends on its ability to predict this change and its ability to react. In the 1980s the American computer giant IBM provided a classic example of the dangers in failing to keep close to the market. It failed to anticipate the switch away from large mainframe computers to smaller desktop models and home computers. This meant it was very late to enter the home computer market and missed the chance to dominate it as an early entrant. By the time IBM appreciated the potential of the personal computer market it faced intense competition and had lost 'first mover' advantage. As technological change continues, firms must monitor their environments closely, look for the opportunities and protect themselves against the threats.

ISSUES FOR **analysis**

When answering questions about new technology, bear in mind the following:

- Technology creates both opportunities and threats. It both destroys and creates new markets; it can provide a firm with a competitive advantage or make its product or service obsolete.
- The introduction of technology needs to be carefully managed. Managers have to consider issues such as the compatibility of the new technology with existing equipment, the financial implications and how best to introduce it.
- New technology can place additional stress on employees who might be worried about their ability to cope with the change.

73.4 Technological change
an evaluation

Whether new technology provides an opportunity or a threat for an organisation depends on the technology itself, the resources of the firm and the management's attitude to change. Used effectively new technology can reduce costs, increase flexibility and speed up the firm's response time. In all areas of the firm, from marketing to operations, technology can provide increased productivity, reduced wastage and better quality goods and services.

However, it may not always be possible for a firm to adopt the most appropriate technology (perhaps because it does not have the necessary finance). Even if it does, the firm needs to ensure that the change is managed effectively. People are often suspicious or worried by new technology and managers must think carefully about the speed of the change and the method of introduction.

Organisations must also monitor the technology of their competitors. If they fail to keep up they may find they cannot match their competitors' quality standards. However, they may be limited by their ability to afford the technology. Typically, managers will be faced with an almost constant flow of demands for new technology from employees. Nearly everyone can think of some machine or gadget they would like in an ideal world. Managers must decide on priorities, given their limited resources, and also look for the gains that can be achieved with existing equipment. As the **kaizen** approach shows, success sometimes comes from gradual improvements rather than dramatic technological change.

KEY terms

automation – occurs when jobs which were previously done by people are now done by machines.

computer-aided design – software that provides 3D plans and designs for new products or processes.

computer-aided manufacture – a production process planned and controlled by a computer program. When linked with computer-aided design, CAD/CAM can be a highly efficient, fast and cheap way to produce small quantities of a wide range of products.

kaizen – an approach, originating from Japan, which aims to achieve continuous improvement in business.

robot – a programmable machine that handles tasks automatically.

AS Level Exercises

A. REVISION QUESTIONS

(35 marks; 60 minutes)

Read the unit, then answer:

1 What is meant by the term 'technology'? *(3)*
2 Explain how technology can improve a firm's performance. *(4)*
3 What benefits might a firm derive from linking CAD to CAM? *(3)*
4 Examine three possible problems of introducing new technology. *(6)*
5 Explain how technological change has helped in the following areas;
   a retailing *(3)*
   b stock control *(3)*
   c car production. *(3)*
6 Outline two factors that might explain why there are so few robots in the UK. *(4)*
7 Why may technology be an important factor in a firm's international competitiveness? *(3)*
8 How may staff benefit from the introduction of new technology? *(3)*

B. REVISION EXERCISES

B1 Data Response

Tyre Technology

A technical revolution is happening in the world tyre industry which should lead to better and cheaper products. For much of its history, tyre making has been multi-stage and highly labour intensive. Automation has been gradual involving activities such as automatic cutting and feeding of materials. Now new technology is being introduced which will cut the labour input, increase productivity and provide a much greater degree of flexibility. Where commercially viable production meant continuous output of thousands of a single size and type of tyre it is now becoming possible to get a profit on a batch of just a few hundred.

The developments by the leading companies (the top six control more than 70% of the world market) is extremely worrying for the dozens of smaller players which lack the financial and technical resource to make their own developments. The new systems developed independently by the firms concerned are heavily computerised. Michelin's system is said to need half the workforce and one-tenth of the usual production space with a capital cost of $15 million per 500,000 of annual capacity. One perceived disadvantage is that it needs new and dedicated facilities. The introduction has tended to be gradual to minimise the social and employment disruptions associated with the process.

Source: Adapted from *The Financial Times*

Questions *(30 marks; 35 minutes)*

1 Explain the meaning of the terms:
   a automation *(2)*
   b batch. *(2)*
2 Outline the factors involved when deciding whether to adopt new technology. *(7)*
3 Analyse the potential 'social and employment disruptions' associated with the new technology. *(9)*
4 'Without the latest technology firms cannot hope to compete effectively.' Critically assess this view. *(10)*

B2 Case Study

Brooks

Last Monday the management of Brooks plc announced the purchase of new equipment which would radically improve productivity levels. The investment would lead to some job losses, the management explained, but there was no doubt it was in the best interests of the company as a whole. Employees had not been consulted because management felt they had more than enough information to make the decision. Consultation would simply slow up the process. In the long run the new equipment should increase the firm's competitiveness and the purchase was an expensive necessity. Working practices would, of course, have to be altered and employees would certainly have to learn new skills. The managers promised to provide the necessary training although they could not guarantee everyone a job if they could not adapt successfully.

Following the announcement the employees were furious and considered taking industrial action. Hearing the rumours of possible strikes the management admitted that it might not have handled the issue in the best way possible but would not reconsider the decision.

Questions *(40 marks; 60 minutes)*

1 What factors may have made the management of Brooks plc decide to invest in new technology? *(8)*
2 Do you think the employees at Brooks plc would be justified in taking industrial action? Explain your answer. *(10)*
3 Analyse the factors which the managers at Brooks plc might have taken into account before acquiring the new equipment. *(10)*
4 The management of Brooks plc admitted it may not have handled the issue in the best possible way. In your opinion, how should the managers have handled it? Justify your answer. *(12)*

C. ESSAY QUESTIONS

1 'Technology is something to be feared rather than welcomed.' Consider this view.
2 To what extent should a firm make introducing new technology a priority?
3 'The key to better performance is better management not more technology.' Critically assess this view.

INTEGRATED EXTERNAL ISSUES

74.1 | External influences – an overview

INTRODUCTION

The external environment of the business affects all its decisions. When answering questions about production or finance or marketing decisions, the context will be all-important in determining whether a particular business decision is appropriate. Have interest rates just risen sharply? Is there ferocious competition from the Far East? Is a change in the law going to open up new opportunities?

A good example of the importance of the external context is the impact of the business cycle. It is clear that many business decisions will be different depending on whether the economy is booming or depressed. No less important is careful analysis of the strengths and strategies of a firm's main competitors. This will provide important information which should be fed into the decision making process.

WHAT ARE EXTERNAL INFLUENCES?

External influences create both opportunities and constraints for the business. They stem from various sources, including economic, social, technological, legal and political factors. Different firms will be affected by different factors, but all will be subject to economic change.

Economics as a subject can help considerably to lead to an understanding of the external environment of the business. It is useful to be able to divide external economic influences into two groups. Macro-economic influences involve the whole economy and affect all businesses. Micro-economic influences affect specific sectors of the economy and may or may not be important for individual business decisions.

- Macro-economic influences include long-term growth rates, the business cycle, inflation and unemployment, macro-economic policies and international trade policy.
- Micro-economic influences include individual markets and government policies affecting the labour market or particular industries. Another important

part of the background for any business is the process of technological change. This will affect the inputs available to the business and the competition which it faces. The need to adapt to change is a factor of growing importance for many decision takers.

Social opportunities and constraints reflect the pressure on businesses to acknowledge responsibility for the well-being of different stakeholder groups. They include ethical and environmental considerations and lead businesses to change the way they do things for reasons other than those related to straightforward profit making.

'A' GRADE EXTERNAL ISSUES

The external environment of the business involves all those issues which are currently important in the world in which the business operates.

One strategy might be to keep in mind a checklist of the main external issues. Then when tackling any major question on business decisions, ask: are any of these factors relevant to this decision? The most important factors are:

- What kind of market is the business operating in?
- How stiff is the competition from other businesses?
- Is the business cycle going to have an important impact in this situation?
- Will the government's macro-economic policies influence the outcome of this decision?
- What opportunities might arise in overseas markets?
- Does economic growth provide opportunities which did not previously exist?
- Do the European Union or the World Trade Organisation have regulations which will affect the decision by creating threats or opportunities?
- Will changes in government micro-economic policy be important to this decision?
- Should ethical considerations dictate changes in the way decisions are made?
- Are stakeholders and pressure groups influencing decisions in ways which should be taken into account?
- Is technological change opening up opportunities which should not be ignored?

Often it will not be necessary to write about any of these questions in detail. What is required is to select the relevant questions for the case in hand, then develop an answer based upon the internal objectives and issues facing the business.

In addition to the above, four issues are especially worth looking at before facing an examination.

ISSUE 1   When is the state of the economy most important to business?

Businesses want demand to grow in a steady and predictable fashion. Then all businesses can grow or at least continue producing and the pressures of competition are not too intense. When incomes start to fall because the economy is in recession, some businesses will be relatively unaffected. Suppliers of toothpaste may have quite an easy time but suppliers of luxury yachts, for example, may not survive if the recession persists. The construction industry typically faces great difficulties because fewer people have incomes sufficiently high to buy houses and fewer businesses are investing in new buildings. In general, most businesses will face reduced profits. The early 1990s' recession provided ample evidence of the problems.

ISSUE 2   How big an influence should government have on business decisions?

Businesses want governments to keep the economy stable. So they tend to oppose big increases in government spending. Many people in business resent taxation of their personal gains and therefore oppose increased tax rates. So many business organisations support the view that reduced government intervention is desirable.

However, much government intervention is about ensuring fair treatment. In this, the welfare of consumers (who are also voters) can be very important. Most businesses dislike competition policies which constrain their activities. But competition can be very important in keeping prices down for consumers. In the long run, competition ensures that businesses produce efficiently and consider the needs of all their stakeholders.

ISSUE 3   How important are ethical issues in business today?

Ethical issues have become increasingly widely publicised, but it is harder to say whether they have become more important. Many businesses have shown over the years that their own sense of social responsibility can ensure good decision taking, regardless of external pressures. Businesses which have pioneered customer service strategies or environmental friendliness have often believed in their approaches as being representative of good practice. However, while 'cowboy' businesses remain there will continue to be an assortment of legal and pressure group constraints upon business activity. Therefore ethical questions will remain central to the study of business.

ISSUE 4   Should the UK join the Euro Area?

Joining the Euro Area would have a number of advantages for UK businesses. It would mean that they would be protected from exchange rate risk when buying or selling from other Euro Area countries. As this includes most of the EU members, the advantage would be significant. Alongside the UK, only Sweden and Denmark still have their own currencies and Sweden may decide to opt in too. Reducing risks means that forecasting future revenues is easier and more certain. Firms would be less vulnerable to a rise in the pound which formerly made them less competitive. They could make investment plans with greater confidence.

The major drawback is that the European Central Bank (ECB) makes monetary policy for the Euro Area as a whole. It would be likely that at a time when the UK economy could benefit from a change in interest rates, the needs of the Euro Area might be different from those of the UK. The one-size-fits-all interest rate may not be the best for the individual economy.

It is impossible to tell in advance how the ECB monetary policy would work for the UK. The rather slow growth rates in the Eurozone are not very reassuring while the work of the Monetary Policy Committee of the Bank of England is generally well regarded. Probably, the decision will be taken on political grounds.

External issues

A. SHORT-ANSWER QUESTIONS

1 How would an increase in incomes affect the following?
 a cauliflower producers
 b hairdressers
 c insurance advisers
 d building workers *(8)*

2 What effect might a fall in oil prices have on the British economy? *(3)*

3 What would happen to the price of burgers if McDonald's took over Burger King? *(3)*

4 How might an increase in interest rates affect a retail chain such as Woolworth's? *(3)*

5 How might tax cuts affect the following?
 a car owners
 b car manufacturers
 c road builders
 d petrol companies *(8)*

6 If the pound rose on the foreign exchange markets, what would happen to the price of scotch whisky in Japan? *(3)*

7 If economic growth slows down during recession, how would car producers react? *(2)*

8 During a period of high unemployment, large numbers of people may be forced to accept jobs at lower wage rates than they had previously. How would this affect employers? *(2)*

9 How has EU harmonisation affected businesses? *(3)*

10 What consequences might political uncertainty in Japan have for UK businesses? *(2)*

11 How would UK businesses be affected by a reduction in import duties by a number of Far East countries? *(2)*

12 List three measures which have resulted from UK adoption of the Social Chapter of the Treaty of Maastricht. *(3)*

13 Give two reasons why UK businesses opposed the adoption of the Social Chapter. *(2)*

14 Give three specific examples of environmentally friendly changes made by individual UK businesses. *(3)*

15 Give two examples of pressure groups which have brought about change in the way UK businesses operate. *(2)*

16 Explain the impact which improved telecommunications might have on the activities of a UK shoe manufacturer. *(4)*

17 Provide three examples of ways in which the UK government might encourage small businesses. *(3)*

18 Give two reasons why monetary policy is now in the hands of the monetary policy committee of the Bank of England, rather than the Chancellor of the Exchequer. *(2)*

19 Explain why many businesses are strongly in favour of European Monetary Union. *(4)*

20 State three possible effects upon firms of the invention of cheap, efficient industrial robots. *(3)*

B. DATA RESPONSE QUESTIONS

1 It is 1998. Your are working in the accounts department of a business producing commercial refrigerators with glass doors. They sell to pubs and restaurants and are used to both store and display drinks. Roughly half of production is exported and, of the exports, 40% is sold to EU buyers and 50% to Asian countries, principally Malaysia and Thailand.

 Your employer is seriously considering a major expansion of capacity and has asked a team, including yourself, to assess the feasibility of the project. You are rather disturbed to find that all the discussion seems to be about production and marketing aspects of the decision. You decide to present the following information to the next planning meeting. The government's target for inflation is 2.5% and for earnings growth, 4.25%.

Annual GDP growth, quarter 1 (%), 1998

UK	3.0
France	3.4
Germany	3.8
Italy	2.5
Malaysia	−1.8
Thailand	0.4

UK data (Source: *The Economist*, 25/6/98)

Inflation (May)	4.2%
Earnings increase (March)	5.2%
Interest rate (Bank of England base rate, December)	6.25%
Exchange rate (trade weighted index, June)	106.9

Questions *(20 marks; 30 minutes)*

a How will you explain the relevance of the information you are providing? *(8)*

b What will your argument be as to how the information should be used in making the final decision? *(12)*

2 Study the figures below (adapted from the *Guardian*, 17/4/98):

Export sales, percentage balance reporting sales increase

Exchange rate index

1990	112.0
1991	113.0
1992	108.7
1993	99.7
1994	100.0
1995	95.1
1996	96.7
1997	112.7
1998	106.9

Source: National Institute Economic Review, May 1998

Questions   (30 marks; 35 minutes)

a For what reasons might the exchange rate have been changing during the 1990s?   (6)

b How has the exchange rate affected exports of manufacturers and services?   (6)

c Why might services have been less severely affected than manufacturers?   (6)

d What impact would you expect these trends to have on the UK economy overall?   (12)

C. ROLE PLAYS AND SIMULATIONS

The Future of the Burger

On the basis of the evidence which follows, can McDonald's and Burger King's expansion programmes succeed in Britain?

Appendix A

McDonald's had 830 restaurants in the UK at the beginning of 1998. It planned to add a further 100 during 1998 and the same again in 1999. Burger King had 445 restaurants in the UK at the beginning of 1998 and planned a further 55 outlets during 1998.

Appendix B

Wages in McDonald,s were raised in January 1998 from £3.25 to £3.50 an hour. In May 1998 the minimum wage in the UK was set at £3.60. McDonald's says its average rates of pay are above the minimum wage. However, prices may have to rise to recoup increased costs.

Appendix C

Burger King cut the price of its Whopper to gain market share. It claims that its Big King, which has two burgers and two slices of cheese, has increased its sales substantially in the US. Also in the US, McDonald's is facing a saturated market and has had to resort to new product developments such as the Chilli McDonald's and the McRibs, in an attempt to maintain its market share. It has also abandoned batch cooking and now makes burgers to order.

Appendix D

Other kinds of fast-food outlets are gaining ground. Pret a Manger and other chains are offering healthy and interesting menus.

The so-called McLibel case which ended in 1996 demonstrated that some members of the public have considerable doubts about McDonald's environmental stance. The 'McLibel Two' were able to defend themselves against McDonald's by showing that there were doubts about how environmentally friendly their packaging and purchasing policies actually were.

Appendix E

Burger King promises a continuous programme of new products. It says it has doubled its R&D budget. McDonald's has exploited its partnership with Disney to create added attractions for customers.

D. INTEGRATED CASE STUDIES

Making a Living

George Wheeler was a potter. He spent long years at art college and emerged with skills and artistic flair which made him well equipped to make a living. He had one other major advantage. His mother had inherited some money and was prepared to invest in his business.

George was able to rent an old mill in a small town on the edge of the Lake District. He was well placed to attract tourists and he set about creating a viable business. He developed his own personal style. His mugs, plates and vases were distinctive yet very suitable for everyday use. The future looked bright. He was able to invest in the equipment he needed easily enough and within three months his showroom was stocked and ready to open.

Plenty of people came to look round the showroom. Unfortunately many left without making a purchase. Even though George had accepted a small mark-up, hand-made pottery seemed expensive in comparison with the mass produced product. People enjoyed looking but did not always buy.

At the end of six months, George knew he had to rethink. He had covered his input costs and the rent on the building but he had a pitiful sum left to live on. He decided that he would stock a large range of gifts alongside his hand-made pots, and see if that would increase turnover.

The strategy worked quite well. The mark-up on the glasses and ornaments he bought in was larger. It was depressing to think that so many people preferred mass produced products to his own, but he made a living and still spent most of his time doing what he wanted to do, creating individual pots.

The crunch came after about five years. The 1998/9 recession brought an end to the real income growth which had helped George at the start. Sales in early 1999 were 18% down on the previous year. George realised that he would have a hard time paying back his loans. They were not large but it became clear that his business was barely profitable.

An old friend came to visit. He had stayed on in the art college where George had trained as a teacher. There was a vacancy there for a potter. George's design skills had developed while he worked and he agreed to apply for the job. He realised it would pay more than the profit he had been making in the pottery. Within three months he sold off the stock and closed down for good.

Questions
(30 marks; 40 minutes)

1 What reasons did George have for thinking his business would be viable when he made his plans? *(5)*
2 Why did the business deteriorate under recession conditions? *(6)*
3 George never went bankrupt. Why then did he close down the business? *(5)*
4 In general, what types of products are vulnerable to recession? *(5)*
5 Could a business such as this survive in the long run? Give reasons for your conclusion. *(9)*

Healthy Clarks doubles profits

Clarks signalled a change in strategy as the UK's largest shoe retailer yesterday, as the privately run company unveiled a doubling of pre-tax profits.

Peter Bolliger, who took over as chief executive 2 months ago said, 'I will not be pursuing acquisitions. I believe in growing the Clarks brand organically, particularly outside the UK and Europe'.

In the 6 months to 31 July pre-tax profits more than doubled to £34.1 million on turnover of £440 million.

Mr Bolliger said there was no pressure from shareholders, who include 400 former employees and members of the Clarks family, to list the company on the stock market. He said expansion would be funded from cash flow and the company had no need to raise capital.

Mr Bolliger worked for Mohamed Al Fayed as managing director of Harrods, the luxury retailer, before joining Clarks as head of UK operations in 1994. He took over after the surprise departure of Tim Parker, now chief executive of Kwik-Fit, the auto services group.

Mr Parker oversaw a radical overhaul of Clarks during his tenure, increasing outsourcing, moving production overseas and promoting an aggressive expansion policy in the US. Under his tenure, several thousand workers at factories in and around Clarks' home town of Street, Somerset, lost their jobs. Having made a pre-tax loss of £409,000 in 1996, Clarks has since increased its turnover and profits each year.

Exceptionals of £1.5 million included a £3.5 million profit on the sale of a factory in Weston-super-Mare and £2 million of costs associated with redundancies. Mr. Bolliger said there would be more restructuring costs.

Source: *Financial Times*, 8/10/02.

Questions
(45 marks; 60 minutes)

1 Why did Clarks greatly increase outsourcing? *(6)*
2 What consequences did this have and why? *(6)*
3 Clarks developed a number of new technologies for use in shoe production. To what extent did these improve the company's competitive position? *(7)*
4 What actions will be required for Clarks to reach its objective of 'growing the brand'? *(8)*
5 Evaluate the risks that are being taken in adopting this strategy. *(8)*
6 Analyse the effect that the business environment has had on Clarks' strategy since it was put in place. *(10)*

BUSINESS START-UPS

DEFINITION

An 'entrepreneur' is prepared to take risks in order to exploit a business opportunity. This term is often used to describe a person starting their own venture, perhaps for the first time. A new firm operating in the marketplace for the first time is known as a 'business start-up'.

75.1 Personal characteristics

What kind of person is willing to take the risk of starting a business? What are the qualities needed for success? It is difficult to generalise, as each case must be viewed on its own merits. A great deal of academic research has been carried out to try and find out who makes a good entrepreneur.

HARD WORKING

Successful entrepreneurs usually demonstrate high levels of energy. Research conducted with 40 successful business leaders concluded that many 'don't know how to stop working, they always seem restless, work 15–18-hour days, take few holidays, … and report great reserves of psychic/physical energy'.

STRONG MOTIVATION TO SUCCEED

Evidence from research suggests that entrepreneurs tend to demonstrate a driving ambition to succeed. Many measure their success by the extent to which they satisfy their inner sense of achievement. David McClelland identified three traits of individuals with a high need for achievement. He considered them to be strongly connected with entrepreneurial success:

- a willingness to take personal responsibility for finding solutions to problems
- a desire to set moderate achievement goals and take calculated risks
- the need for concrete feedback on performance.

McClelland also identified the need for power as a possible source of the successful business leader's ambition. However, evidence suggests that entrepreneurs with a great need for power perform less well when starting their own business than those with a moderate need. The latter group are able to adopt a more democratic style of management and delegate decision making as the business grows.

Many people who start their own business do so to gain some control over their own working lives. This is more likely to reflect a desire for independence than for power over others. Motivation of this kind is particularly strong for members of minority groups who feel they may not rise to the top in large organisations because of discrimination.

THE ABILITY TO INNOVATE

Research also shows that successful entrepreneurs are likely to be **innovative** and creative. The ability to develop new ideas for products or services, or think of new ways of satisfying customer needs, gives these individuals a head start in the marketplace when they set up their business.

The kind of person most likely to be successful in starting a business is an innovative and creative thinker. It is more important to be hard working than to be highly intelligent. Ambition to achieve and the desire for power and control are also key factors. Successful entrepreneurs are prepared to take the risks, and put in the time and effort, to make their business a winner.

75.2 Identifying an opportunity

It is estimated that one in three business start-ups fail in the first three years of operation. In contrast, this figure falls to one in six amongst those small firms which seek advice and then carefully plan their development. A common feature of those start-ups that

---

THE AMAZING AMAZON

Business start-ups rarely come bigger than the story of Jeff Bezos and Amazon. In 1994 Jeff, aged 30, quit his well paid job in finance, borrowed $300,000 and set up the world's first internet bookshop. By 1997 the shares were quoted on the New York stock market and Amazon.com had already become well known worldwide. Amazon's unique selling point was that it was the easiest way to buy a book – easier than going into town to a bookshop, and easier to use than other on-line book stores. When the internet stock market boom pushed Amazon shares to $115 in 2000, Jeff Bezos was one of the richest men in the world. By November 2002 the shares had slipped, but his holdings were still worth over $1,000 million.

Business IN

METHOD	STRENGTH	WEAKNESS
Identifying a business suited to your personal qualities and skills	Should be personally satisfying ,if successful	May overemphasise personal needs rather than market needs
Analysing market gaps in your local area	Based on the customer, which should increase chances of success	The gaps may be due to lack of demand, or – if successful – rivals may be attracted in soon after
Innovative thinking based upon strong knowledge of the market	Good combination of market knowledge and product differentiation	Unless the market potential is too small to attract bigger competitors, major rivals will soon arrive
Acquiring a franchise in a business with proven success elsewhere	Relatively low risk start-up, so easier to get bank loans	You must look beyond the franchisor's claims; careful research is still essential

struggle to survive is lack of initial market research. Many people assume they know about the customers within a market and therefore that they do not need research.

Before conducting background research, it is necessary to decide upon a specific market in which the business will operate. Some people find this decision very simple. A person made redundant with long experience of a particular market sector will already have the knowledge and personal contacts needed to build a business. But is there necessarily a gap in the market?

75.3 Small budget research and marketing

The first stage for a business start-up when conducting small budget market research is to look at what potential competitors are doing. Business directories like

Yellow Pages are useful for identifying these. What are they offering and where? By marking local competitors on a map, it may become clear that one area is under-served by kebab shops, off-licences, or whatever.

Market mapping can also be used in a non-geographical way (see Figure 75.1). It provides an analytical tool to judge the market segments each business is covering. This may provide insight into which areas of the market are not being covered by any product offering at present. This will lead naturally into the second phase of the research process which is to build up a clear understanding of the customer-base.

Secondary sources, such as local census data, can give an indication of likely customer profiles (age, income, etc.). Primary research is also important. Small firms cannot afford to launch statistically significant investigations into the nature of the customer-base, particularly when it is geographically spread. However, a lot can be learned from listening to what individuals and small groups of customers have

Figure 75.1

to say about the products and services available on the market. This approach is particularly useful for identifying potential market segments. As people express their ideas they will tend to polarise into different groups.

One key principle of successful business start-up is to decide who the firm will serve. A specific set of customers must be targeted. Only then will a small business be able to position itself in the market against its competitors. Market segmentation is a particularly useful technique for a start-up business with a limited marketing budget. General leaflet drops can be replaced with targeted campaigns concentrating on a specific housing estate or set of streets. Or a general advertisement in a local newspaper can give way to a carefully focused special offer aimed at attracting a particular group of customers. When resources are limited the key is to target directly those most likely to purchase.

Some potential advertising media which are ideal for business start-ups are given in the table below.

Advertising media suitable for business start-ups

MEDIUM	ADVANTAGES FOR A SMALL FIRM
Local newspapers	• Relatively low cost • High penetration of local market
Trade/hobby magazines	• Well-defined, enthusiastic readership • Low cost targeting of a market segment
Business directories, e.g. Yellow Pages	• Reference guide for local services • Users often want to make an immediate purchase
Public relations (PR), i.e. obtaining free editorial coverage in suitable media	• Not only free but also editorial coverage has more credibility than advertising

For most business start-ups the most important marketing aim will be to create satisfied customers. This will generate repeat purchases and develop a customer-base as the message of your success passes from person to person, via word of mouth.

75.4 Identifying a profitable product or service

Over the last 30 years, eight out of every ten new products launched have been a failure. Why do so many new products fail? Many customers do not like change. It is simply easier not to go to the trouble of learning how to use a new product, or to take the risk of trying out a new service. So a small firm with an innovative idea must help the consumer see how to use it – and

IN THE SOUP

In 1990 two young entrepreneurs saw a gap in the market for premium-priced 'fresh soup'. Unusual recipes, top quality ingredients and packaging in fresh milk cartons rather than tins were all fundamental to the success of the New Covent Garden Soup Company. Sales went wonderfully well, and in 1997 a small publicly quoted company, S Daniels, bought the soup business for £22 million. By 2000, S Daniels was making profits of £5 million a year on a turnover of over £50 million, but according to chief executive Cyril Freedman this was still not enough to impress the stock market. Therefore, when the business needed to raise more capital, it was easier to allow a Singapore-based firm to buy into the business. In 2002 the Singapore investors bought the whole of the S Daniels business for just £23 million. The soup company had been swallowed up.

therefore see the benefit of the spending involved. A start-up business will find it difficult to overcome consumer resistance on a limited marketing budget.

Even if a product or service has immediate attractions, problems may remain. Few businesses are built on one-off purchases. Most require the steady income that comes from repeat business. It may be possible to create a situation in which this occurs. In the case of the New Covent Garden Soup Company (above), the strategy was to offer inventive new flavours and outstanding quality. Coupled with product variety (a 'soup of the month') it ensured regular purchasing and steady cash flow throughout the year. High quality also generated invaluable word of mouth advertising.

The majority of start-up businesses select an existing item and find a new innovative approach to providing it, which allows value to be added. To succeed, the entrepreneur needs a complete understanding of who the customers are and what they want. Careful market research is therefore the secret to identifying a profitable product or service.

75.5 Protecting a profitable product or service

A patent gives the holder the right to be the sole user of a production process, or the only manufacturer of a particular product. The Copyright, Designs and Patents Act of 1988 provides this protection for a 20-year period after registration. In order to register an invention, a set of drawings must be lodged with the

OPPORTUNITY FOR ADDING VALUE: THE CASE OF THE FLYING SUITS

A small business start-up can be built around identifying a new way of adding value to an existing product or service.

Richard Branson found that business travellers on Virgin's flights to Hong Kong wanted to buy a new suit while there, but had no time to do so. An in-flight tailoring service was introduced which allowed individuals to be measured and their details sent by fax to a Hong Kong factory. The garment was manufactured and delivered to the airport for the customer's return flight.

A new business opportunity opened up for a Hong Kong tailor, and Virgin's business travellers appreciated the customer service.

Patent Office which shows that the product, or process, has original features. The inventor must state that these ideas are his or her own and have not been copied from another source. The work of authors, composers and artists is also legally protected against others copying it. However, in this case there is no requirement to register the copyright.

The holder of a patent has a potentially valuable asset which can be used to protect, or develop, a position in the marketplace. However, it is up to the individual to enforce the patent if he or she believes it is being infringed. This must be done through legal action, which is time-consuming and expensive.

Large organisations may be prepared to acquire smaller businesses if they hold an important patent. Given the expense of a product launch, many small businesses choose to sell patent rights rather than carry the financial burden themselves. A start-up business with a new product idea would be well advised to protect its main asset by patenting it.

75.6 The practical problems of business start-up

FINANCE

Business start-ups face a problem in raising sufficient finance to establish themselves. New undertakings have no past track record by which their future potential can be judged. This means that any investor is taking a very high risk if they choose to supply finance. As a consequence lenders will charge high interest rates, if they are willing to lend at all. In fact many small firms are funded by loans from friends and relatives.

To avoid high interest charges, many individuals save, sell personal possessions, or mortgage their house to raise start-up finance. Another source is a lump sum resulting from redundancy or early retirement.

Estimating the cost of equipment or production facilities can be done with a degree of accuracy. In contrast, it is more difficult to judge the quantity of money required for working capital. Careful planning of cash flow is required to determine the finance required at start-up. It is important not to begin trading with too little capital, but it is equally sensible not to borrow more than is necessary. Cash lying unused in the business carries a high opportunity cost.

A potential lender, such as a bank, will wish to see the entrepreneur putting a substantial sum of his or her own money at risk in the business. This will ensure that the owner makes every effort to try and make the firm a success. In addition, some form of **security** will be required so that if the loan can not be repaid an asset of the borrower becomes the property of the lender. This will often be the premises of the business.

Banks provide approximately 60% of external finance for small business start-ups. The two most frequently employed forms of bank financing are:

- Loan capital – a commitment by the bank to provide a sum of money to the business for a defined period of time. A typical bank loan lasts for 2–3 years and is used to buy fixed assets.
- Overdrafts – these allow a firm to borrow up to an agreed maximum sum without a stated time limit. This is the most flexible form of borrowing and is therefore highly suitable for financing day-to-day working capital needs.

In recent years there has been a shift in the balance between these two forms of finance away from overdrafts towards loans. Banks claim that bank lending is increasingly based on the borrower's business plan, rather than on the security which can be offered. This approach has been developed in answer to the criticism that banks were not prepared to take the risks required to help foster new business formation in the UK. There remain, however, many commentators who believe banks are far too keen to avoid risks with small firms.

To help overcome the reluctance by banks to take risks with business start-ups, the **Loan Guarantee Scheme** was set up by the government. It promises a bank making a loan that if the business fails to repay, up to 80% will be provided by the government. This allows banks to support business start-ups which may otherwise be regarded as too risky. The government charges an interest rate premium of 1.5–2.5% of the annual value of the loan, which is paid by the borrower.

Other sources of finance exist for business start-ups in addition to banks:

- The **venture capital** industry exists to provide capital to small or medium-sized firms. In practice it has been criticised for its reluctance to provide 'seed corn' (start-up) investment, which represents only 4% of its total lending. Venture capitalists prefer to finance expansion by already established firms because this represents a lower risk. Few are willing to invest much less than £250,000.

- Business angels are people who have enough personal finance to fund start-ups which attract their interest. The capital they offer complements the formal venture capital industry because they provide money at an earlier stage in the firm's development. Evidence suggests that loans of £50,000 or less are involved, and that many individuals like to have some role in the business they are investing in.

BUSINESS ANGELS FUND A FRESHER FUTURE

Fresh Approach is a business start-up based around an innovative new idea which allows fresh fruit and vegetables to be preserved for long periods of time. The technique employed is a type of packaging that uses high levels of gas to keep food fresh. This approach is the opposite of existing technology which removes oxygen to preserve the product.

The founders of the business are two food scientists, Alan English and Nigel Parker. The potential is great, given that the freshly prepared food market is worth £250 million each year and is currently growing at 15–25% per annum. Despite the profit potential this represents, raising financial backing for their venture proved far from easy.

Alan and Nigel approached a number of venture capitalists. None were prepared to take the risk of investing in the project, even though the pair were willing to use £100,000 of their own money. The Co-op Bank did feel able to match their contribution with a loan of the same amount, but this still left a large financial gap. As a result, the start-up was only possible because of the support of business angels. The further £80,000 capital required was raised by cash injections of between £2,000 and £30,000 by 32 different individual investors.

A shareholder's agreement has been drawn up which gives English and Parker 15% of the company each and sets target growth rates which the organisation must aim to achieve. The projected sales of the business are £1 million in the first year of operation with initial profits expected within nine months of start-up.

LOCATION

A key consideration when selecting premises is the need to keep fixed costs to a minimum. When finance is limited, reducing the output required to break even makes the survival of the business more likely. As a result it may be appropriate in the first instance to operate from the owner's home, if this is practical. However, the difficulties this may create should not be underestimated. For example, it may be hard to escape the pressure of running the business.

If business premises are to be acquired, decisions are needed about size and location. This will involve an evaluation of the likely revenue generated compared with the purchase and running costs. In this context it is worth recalling an old retail saying that 'the three most important things in retail are location, location and location'. The same point holds good for most service businesses. So new firms are torn between the desire to keep costs down (poor location) and maximise revenue (costly location).

A more detailed analysis of business location can be found in Unit 57.

BUILDING A CUSTOMER-BASE

The best and least expensive form of advertising available to a business start-up is word-of-mouth recommendation. The long-term strength of the business will depend on building a customer-base prepared to return to purchase products again and again. In order to achieve this, customers must be satisfied with the service they are offered by the business. There are a number of factors to consider when trying to build up customer loyalty:

- Provide a basic service that is efficient and meets the standards expected by the customer. For example, the business must ensure product availability.
- Develop an after-sales service. For example, deal effectively with consumer complaints, treating them as an opportunity to learn about how to improve customer service.
- Take every chance to understand more about the customer-base. For example, observe purchasing patterns at varying times of the day and week.
- Ensure positive contact between customers and staff to create a pleasant experience for the consumer each time they come into contact with the business.

The future success of any business start-up will be determined to a large extent by its ability to develop a group of satisfied customers.

CASH FLOW

Research evidence suggests that approximately 70% of small business failure occurs because of poor cash flow management. Firms which are profitable find it impossible to continue trading because they are unable to meet their current debts. Often cash is tied up in stocks which can not be used immediately to pay bills.

It is therefore vital that even a profitable business, which has orders allowing it to work at full capacity, keeps enough cash available within the firm to ensure it does not run out of working capital. In order to do so, it is wise for business start-ups to prepare a **cash flow forecast** as part of the initial business plan. This will allow overdraft facilities to be arranged should a need for additional cash be identified at some future point in the firm's development. For a more detailed analysis of the role of cash flow forecasting in planning start-up business finance, see Unit 18.

Among the key lines of analysis are:

- Has the entrepreneur the drive, the personality and the vision to succeed at the start? If so, has the same person the leadership skills, the trusting nature and the human relations skills to manage growth effectively? At its simplest, most successful entrepreneurs are brilliant but arrogant workaholics. Those same qualities can become problems for a leader of a growing organisation.
- Apart from the abilities of the leader, the next most important issue is market knowledge. Can a real consumer desire be identified and met in an innovative way? Analysis should concentrate on identifying this group of customers and then considering the most cost effective means of communicating with them.
- Has the business plan been made prudently or is it window dressed to encourage financiers to put their money in? The founder should remember that his or her own money is as much at risk as that of any other shareholder (and more so than the banks, who will have insisted on security for any loans). Enthusiasm and optimism are vital qualities for entrepreneurs; but the optimism must not become blind.

FLIKABALL

Leon and Vaughn Gingell were in the pub one Wednesday night when a business idea struck them. 'Why can't we put a football player in a marble?' They visualised a new craze. Instead of collecting stickers in an album, young children would collect Premiership marbles. Sold in packs of 3, there would be 240 to collect – 12 for each Premiership club. They could play with them, swop them, talk about them – all the hallmarks of a kids' craze.

The brothers spent some time trying to interest someone in their idea, but existing marble manufacturers simply said it was impossible. Eventually, though, a clever manufacturer managed to produce two marble halves that could have a tiny Alan Shearer photo put in the middle. The halves were then fixed together. Hey presto, a 'Flikaball'. Appearances on children's TV shows led Merlin Toys to sign a deal. Merlin bought the concept, paying the Gingells a small initial fee and a percentage of the sales turnover. If 'Flikaball' was able to sell the 14 million units forecast by Merlin Toys, the brothers would be rich.

It took 18 months to perfect the production method and the marketing, but finally the product was launched in Spring 1997. Despite Alan Shearer's help in launching the product and an expensive TV advertising campaign, Flikaball did not really take off. Children bought one or two packs (at 75p each), but saw no need to keep collecting. The actual sales of 4 million units left Merlin Toys with a hole in its annual sales turnover, and Leon and Vaughn with a very small payout.

Business IN

75.7 Business start-ups
an evaluation

Establishing a new business is risky. The potential for failure can be reduced by appropriate planning, but never completely removed. It is clear that initial market research, and the thorough monitoring of financial performance, are vital factors which make success more likely.

Within a short space of time, though, a growing business will rely increasingly on the effective management of its staff. This can be an acute problem for the founder whose personal objectives were not only to make money but also to be the boss. Staff who were there from day one will probably accept the founder's obsession with his or her own 'child'. New employees will be more inclined to treat the business as much the same as others, and may find it hard to fit in.

It is important to realise, therefore, that although initial success or failure may depend on financial and marketing issues, the management of people will soon become an issue. For any entrepreneur to be a master of all these aspects of business is a tall order indeed. Which is doubtless why most new businesses are financial disappointments.

At the end of the day the extent to which a start-up has been successful must be judged by the individual, or group of people, who took the risk of creating the business in the first place. Only they can know if their personal objectives have been achieved.

cash flow forecast – an estimate of the firm's cash inflows and outflows over the coming months.

innovative – describes a product or service that brings something new to the marketplace.

Loan Guarantee Scheme – government-funded insurance for banks against bad debts by small firms.

market mapping – analysing how existing products are rated in relation to customer preferences to identify whether any gaps exist in the market.

security – assets that can be used as collateral by a lender, i.e. can be sold for cash if the borrower fails to keep up the repayments.

venture capital – risk capital put into small to medium-sized businesses, usually as a mixture of loan and share capital.

AS Level Exercises

A. REVISION QUESTIONS

(30 marks; 60 minutes)

Read the unit, then answer:

1 Outline the personal qualities which academic research suggests successful entrepreneurs demonstrate. *(4)*
2 Why is innovativeness a valuable quality in an entrepreneur? *(3)*
3 Outline two ways market mapping might help when considering starting a new business. *(4)*
4 Explain the role of primary information sources in 'small budget' market research. *(4)*
5 Why might a small builder decide to advertise only in a directory such as *Yellow Pages*? *(4)*
6 Why do 'patents' represent a strategic asset to a business? *(4)*
7 What are the most common sources of finance open to a small business? *(4)*
8 Explain the role of 'business angels'. *(3)*

B. REVISION EXERCISES

B1 Data Response

> A visit to an away game at Old Trafford proved the spur to Claire and Jon. They visited Roosters Rotisserie, a successful restaurant/café based around spit-roasted chicken. They enjoyed a good value meal and while Jon observed the cooking process in the open kitchen behind the service counter, Claire watched with interest the steady stream of take-away customers. Claire's mental arithmetic told her that the outlet had taken £200 in the half hour they had been there. Her guess was that weekly takings might be around £8,000 and the gross profit margins around 60%. So on their return journey to London, they talked about setting up Rotisserie de Paris in Fulham.
>
> Within three days Jon had contacted suppliers about the costs of equipment: the five-spit, 30 bird spit-roasters costing £6,500 each; the extractor fans to keep the restaurant cool; the fixtures and fittings and much else. He estimated that £80,000 would be needed as an equipment budget. At the same time, Claire looked for a suitable location. On the third day she found a superb spot. A café had just closed down on the Fulham Road. It was a large site and planning permission would not be needed. The cost quoted by the estate agent was scary (£25,000 for a 10-year lease and then £60,000 per year) but Claire was convinced it was the right area.
>
> Within a week they had arranged £200,000 finance from friends and family (all borrowed at an annual interest rate of 10%), had bought the lease and had hired an architect, a designer and builders to remodel the outlet as a Rotisserie de Paris on a budget of £50,000. While work proceeded, Claire interviewed and hired eight staff while Jon visited suppliers and drew up the menus and prices. Within six weeks the restaurant was ready and Claire and Jon had a great (but expensive) weekend inviting friends to visit for free, just to give the staff some practice.
>
> The following Thursday's opening day proved a huge success. It seemed that Rotisserie de Paris was a winner.

Questions *(40 marks; 60 minutes)*

1 What proportion of Jon and Claire's capital was invested in start-up costs, and therefore how much was left for working capital? *(6)*

2 Jon and Claire were lucky enough to obtain finance from their own contacts.

  a How else might they have set about raising the £200,000 they needed? *(8)*

  b What constraints would have been placed upon Jon and Claire by each method you suggest? *(8)*

3 If sales in the first year proved to be £400,000 and the fixed overheads of running the restaurant proved to be £80,000 on top of the annual lease payment, what profit would have been made? *(6)*

4 Claire and Jon's business start-up went very smoothly. They naturally assume that they are brilliant entrepreneurs. Another possibility is that they were lucky. Which of the two views do you take and why? *(12)*

B2 Case Study

Read the In Business 'Flikaball' in the unit, then answer the questions.

Questions *(40 marks; 60 minutes)*

1 How well do the Gingell brothers fit into McClelland's theory about the motivations of entrepreneurs? *(9)*

2 Examine three types of market research you believe Merlin should have undertaken before launching Flikaball. *(9)*

3 **a** If the deal between Merlin and the Gingells had the following royalty structure, what sum would they have earned in the first year if the sales target had been met?

0–5 million	0%
5–10 million	5%
10+ million	8%

  NB If 6 million sold, 5 million at 0%, 1 million at 5%. *(6)*

  b Why would Merlin Toys have negotiated a royalty structure such as this? *(6)*

4 After the disappointment of the 1997/8 sales of Flikaball, Merlin Toys had to decide whether it was worth trying again. Analyse the appropriateness of the marketing of Flikaball to help decide whether Merlin should try again in the future. *(10)*

C. ESSAY QUESTIONS

1 An American business leader once defined an entrepreneur as a risk taker who would rather be a spectacular failure than a dismal success. Discuss.

2 Consider the factors most likely to lead to success when starting a new hairdressers.

BUSINESS ORGANISATIONS

DEFINITION

Business organisations are the different legal forms a business can adopt. The key distinction is that some provide the owners with limited liability for any debts the business incurs. Other forms of business organisation have unlimited liability.

76.1 Sole traders

A **sole trader** is an individual who owns and operates his or her own business. Although there may be one or two employees, this person makes the final decisions about the running of the business. A sole trader is the only one who benefits financially from success, but must face the burden of any failure. In the eyes of the law the individual and the business are the same. This means that the owner has **unlimited liability** for any debts that result from running the firm. If a sole trader cannot pay his or her bills, the courts can allow their personal assets to be seized by creditors in order to meet outstanding debts. For example, the family home or car may be sold. If insufficient funds can be raised in this way the person will be declared bankrupt.

Despite the financial dangers involved, the sole trader is the most common form of legal structure adopted by UK business. In some areas of the economy this kind of business dominates. Particularly where the finance required to run the business is small and customers demand a personal service. Examples include trades such as builders and plumbers, and many independent shopkeepers.

There are no formal rules to follow when establishing a sole trader, or administrative costs to pay. Complete confidentiality can be maintained because accounts are not published. As a result many business start-ups adopt this structure. Sole traders will usually be small organisations in which the owner is able to make rapid decisions giving the benefit of total control. They are also likely to create close contacts with customers and get to know employees on a personal basis. The result is the ability to respond quickly to changes in the competitive environment. This may allow survival even when faced with competition from much larger organisations able to charge lower prices.

The main disadvantages facing a sole trader are the limited sources of finance available, long hours of work involved (including the difficulty of taking a holiday) and concern with respect to running the business during periods of ill health.

76.2 Partnerships

The principal difference between a sole trader and a partnership is the number of owners. The key advantages and disadvantages which derive from multiple ownership are as follows:

ADVANTAGES

- Additional skills – a new partner may have abilities which the sole trader does not possess. These can help to strengthen the business, perhaps allowing new products or services to be offered, or improving the quality of existing provision.
- More capital – a number of people together can inject more finance into the business than one person alone.
- Expansion – with the new skills, increased labour and greater capital a partner brings, the business will have an increased potential for future growth.

The primary reasons for taking on a partner are the need to put more money into the business, or to share the responsibility of running the firm.

DISADVANTAGES

- Sharing profit – the financial benefits derived from running the business will have to be divided up between the partners according to the partnership agreement made on formation. This can easily lead to disagreements about 'fair' distribution of workload and profits.
- Loss of control – multiple ownership means that no individual can force an action on the business; decision making must be shared.
- Unlimited liability – it is one thing to be unlimitedly liable for your own mistakes (a sole trader); far more worrying, surely, to have unlimited liability for the mistakes of your partners. This problem hit many investors in the Lloyds insurance market in the 1990s. Certain partnerships (called syndicates) lost millions of pounds from huge insurance claims. Some investors lost their life savings.

76.3 Incorporation

The process of **incorporation** creates a separate legal identity for the organisation. In the eyes of the law the owners of the business and the company itself are now two different things. The business can take legal action against others and have legal action taken against it. This means that each owner will now have the benefit of **limited liability**. Their investment in the business will be represented by shares. The money which they have used to purchase these is the only finance they will lose if the business is unable to meet its debts. If a firm is declared insolvent, all the assets of the business will be sold off to raise money to repay the creditors. If that is insufficient, the creditors lose out. Unlimited liability sounds unfairly weighted towards the shareholders, but it encourages individuals to put forward capital because the financial risk is limited to the amount they invest.

In order to gain separate legal status a company must be registered with the **Registrar of Companies**. Two key documents must be completed:

- The Memorandum of Association which governs the relationship between the company and the outside world. This includes the company name, the object of the company (often recorded simply as 'as the owners see fit'), limitation of liability and the size of the authorised share capital.
- The Articles of Association which outline the internal management of the company. This includes the rights of shareholders, the role of directors and frequency of shareholder meetings.

The key advantages and disadvantages which result from forming a company limited by the issue of shares are as follows:

ADVANTAGES

- Shareholders experience the benefits of limited liability.
- Companies have a separate legal identity.
- A limited company is able to gain access to a wider range of borrowing opportunities. This makes funding the growth of the business potentially easier.

DISADVANTAGES

- Limited companies must make financial information available publicly at Companies' House. Small firms are not required to make full disclosure of their company accounts, so this requirement is not too onerous.
- By law, company accounts must be audited. This adds to the administrative costs of the business.
- Limited companies must conform with extensive formalities, such as holding the annual general meeting of shareholders and publishing annual returns.

Business **IN**

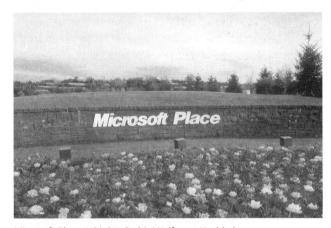

Microsoft Place, USA (© Corbis/Wolfgang Kaehler)

76.4 Private and public companies

Two types of company can be formed – private limited companies and public limited companies.

PRIVATE LIMITED COMPANIES

The shares of a private limited company cannot be bought and sold without the agreement of the other directors. This means the company cannot be listed on the stock market. As a result it is possible to maintain close control over the way the business is run. This form of business is often run by a family or small group of friends and may pursue objectives other than pure profit maximisation. Share capital may not exceed £50,000 and 'Ltd' must be stated after the company name. This warns those dealing with the business that the firm is relatively small and has limited liability. By implication, therefore, its cheques are not as secure as ones from an unlimited liability business. This is why some petrol stations have notices saying 'no company cheques allowed'.

Business IN

PIETRO'S BUSINESS

After 10 years working as a chef at a prestigious restaurant in Wimbledon, Pietro Pontone knew it was time to start his own restaurant. It would be a friendly, local restaurant aiming to provide authentic cooking 'as if you were in an Italian restaurant in the 1920s'. Called La Nonna (the grandmother) it would be located in an impressive corner site near the town centre. Pietro and his partner invested more than £500,000 in buying the site, paying for building work and equipment, and making the restaurant look just right. It was due to open in November 2002.

But what would be the ideal form of business organisation? None of the capital was borrowed, so there was no immediate threat of unpaid debts. Therefore it was not essential to form a limited company. Yet after careful consideration Pietro decided that the risks of running up debts with suppliers during quieter seasons of the year made it sensible to get the protection of limited liability. A private limited company was formed.

PUBLIC LIMITED COMPANIES

The shares of public limited companies can be floated and then traded on the stock market. Any member of the general public can therefore become an owner of these organisations. The memorandum of association must state clearly that the business is a public company and it must be registered as such. The term 'plc' must appear after its name.

The principal differences between private and public limited companies are:

- A public company can raise capital from the general public, while a private limited company is prohibited from doing so.
- The minimum capital requirement of a public company is £50,000. There is no minimum for a private limited company.

- Public limited companies must publish far more detailed accounts than private limited companies.

The key advantages and disadvantages which result from forming a public limited company with a Stock Exchange listing rather than a private limited company are as follows:

Advantages:
- A listed company will find it easier to raise finance than a private limited company.
- Public limited companies will be regarded by lenders as representing a lower risk investment than private limited companies. They are therefore likely to benefit from smaller interest charges on any loans obtained.
- Suppliers are likely to offer listed companies more attractive credit facilities. This is because they will be thought less likely to default on payments than private limited companies.
- The standing of the organisation in its own markets, both with customers and suppliers, may be enhanced by a Stock Exchange listing.

Business IN

GOING PUBLIC: IT'S RAINING CASH!

In January 1998 a former fishfinger salesman became one of Britain's richest men. By selling off a quarter of his 96% stake in the clothing retailer Monsoon, 48-year-old Peter Simon made £87 million. After his early days as a Birds Eye sales rep, Peter Simon's business career started by borrowing £1,000 to set up a stall selling shaggy Afghan coats in London's Portobello Road. Three years later, in 1973, he opened his first Monsoon shop (he was born in Sri Lanka during a monsoon – hence the name). By 1997, his empire had grown to 103 Monsoons and 179 Accessorize shops. Sales of £108 million in the year generated pre-tax profits of £25.4 million. All this growth had been achieved without taking on outside loans or shareholders.

So why go public at all? Simon's answer was that 'as a private company it was hard to come up with schemes to incentivise our senior staff'. Having the company's shares quoted on the stock market made share options and share-save schemes far easier to implement. For Simon's family, there was also the reassurance that the £87 million could be diversified into other forms of secure investment.

By 2002 Monsoon's sales had risen to £204 million and profits were at a record high.

Disadvantages:

- The cost of floating a business on the Stock Exchange is high. Some of the outlay is fixed and therefore falls heavily on small issues. This makes gaining a listing more cost effective as the size of the company increases.
- A public limited company must keep a wide range of people informed about its financial performance. As a result it will face greater administrative costs than a private limited company and more sensitive data will be available to the public and competitors.
- The extent to which any one individual, or group, can maintain control of an organisation is severely limited by the sale of its shares on the Stock Exchange. For example, a family may find their influence on a business diminished when a listing is obtained. In turn, this means that publicly quoted companies are always vulnerable to a takeover bid. This may affect the decisions taken by directors. For example, they may be more inclined to cut back on staffing during a recession, whereas a private firm would want to hold on to experienced staff for when the economy starts to recover.
- Stock market investors place a great emphasis on the short-term financial performance of the business in order to maintain dividends and share price, rather than other long-term objectives. This was the reason Richard Branson gave when he took the unusual step of withdrawing his Virgin empire from the stock market in the early 1990s. Private limited companies do not face the same immediate pressure for short-term profit maximisation.

76.5 Divorce of ownership and control

Shareholders are the owners of public limited companies, but they do not make decisions on a day-to-day basis. Many will have little detailed knowledge of the firm's operation. Through the mechanism of the annual general meeting, they appoint a board of directors who are entrusted to represent their interests and manage the organisation on their behalf. However, the AGM is often not well attended and even when it is, large institutional investors may dominate voting.

So shareholders are the owners, but they have no effective control over the day-to-day decisions made by directors. Once the ownership and control of the company are divorced it can no longer be certain that the decision takers (i.e. the managers) will always act in a way consistent with the interests of the owners (i.e. the shareholders). Managers may select a strategic approach based on improving their own careers or bank balances. For example, evidence suggests that over half of takeovers fail to achieve the objectives set for them. This may reflect the fact that a decision to acquire a business is taken in order to benefit management in some way, rather than shareholders.

76.6 Other forms of business organisation

MUTUALITY

Building societies and mutual life assurance businesses are non-profit making organisations. They have no shareholders and no owners. They exist solely for the best interests of members, i.e. customers. In the 1990s this became regarded as an old-fashioned, inefficient structure. It was suggested that without a clear owner, such organisations were inevitably run by the staff for the staff. And therefore that they were inefficient and bureaucratic. In fact, there is no evidence that former building societies such as Abbey National have become more efficient since becoming public limited companies.

COOPERATIVES

Whether worker owned or customer owned (such as the retail Co-op), cooperatives have the potential to offer a more united cause for the workforce than the profit of shareholders. Unfortunately, the retail Co-op has been in decline for many years, partly due to its unclear objectives. Is it a social service or a profit-making retailer? Worker cooperatives have become tainted with failures of the past. Often the problems lay in disagreements between management and the workforce – problems that the cooperative structure was supposed to avoid.

On a brighter note, retail Co-ops showed their first positive business move for years when they bid over £100 million to buy the Alldays group of convenience stores in 2002. Furthermore, the Co-op Bank's stance as 'the ethical bank' has brought it success.

NOT-FOR-PROFIT ORGANISATIONS

Many important organisations within the business world have charitable status. These include pressure groups such as Greenpeace and Friends of the Earth. They also include conventional charities such as Oxfam and Save The Children Fund. Charitable status ensures that those who fund the charity are not liable for any debts. It also provides significant tax benefits.

ISSUES FOR **analysis**

When analysing which type of organisation is the most suitable for a business, consider:

- The financial risks involved. Manufacturing businesses require heavy investment in plant and equipment before anything is available for sale. Therefore a great deal of capital is put at risk. This suggests limited liability is essential. Some service businesses such as tax advisors or dry cleaners require relatively little capital outlay. If the owner intends to finance the start-up without any borrowings, there is no need to seek limited liability.

- The image you wish to portray. Although cautious businesses may refuse company cheques, most people think 'M Staton Ltd' sounds more established and professional than 'Mervin Staton'. In the same vein, a small software production company called TIB Ltd thought of changing its name to TIB plc. It rightly thought it sounded bigger and more impressive. What's in a name? Ask Coca-Cola.
- An organisation considering a move to public company status and a stock market listing has far bigger issues to consider. It must weigh the benefits to be gained, particularly in terms of raising additional finance, against the costs incurred and the loss of control. Many business questions can be analysed fruitfully by considering short- versus long-term issues. Private (family) versus public (stock market investor) ownership is a classic case in point.

76.7 Business organisations
an evaluation

Business organisation is a dry, technical subject. It does contain some important business themes, however. Three are particularly valuable sources of evaluative comment:

- The existence of limited liability has had huge effects on business. Some have been unarguably beneficial. How could firms become really big if the owners felt threatened by equally big debts? Limited liability helps firms take reasonable business risks. It also, however, gives scope for dubious business practices. Start a firm, live a great lifestyle, then go into liquidation leaving the customers/creditors out of pocket. Then start again. All too often this is the story told by programmes such as the BBC's *Watchdog*. Companies Acts try to make this harder to do, but it still happens. Such unethical behaviour is why government intervention to protect the consumer can always be justified.
- Bill Gates and Richard Branson are worth billions of dollars. How can such wealth be justified? The answer lies in the risks involved in business. For every Richard Branson there are hundreds of thousands of small entrepreneurs who sink their life savings into a business, only to lose them. Sadly, there are thousands every year who end up personally bankrupt. In other words, in a business world in which risk is ever present, rewards for success should be accepted.
- Short-termism is a curse for effective business decision making. There is no proof that a Stock Exchange listing leads to short-termism, only the suspicion that in many cases it does. Of course, massive companies such as Unilever, Nestlé and Shell are likely to be above the pressures for short-term performance. In many other cases, though, there is a strong suspicion that directors focus too much on the short-term share price. Their worries about shareholder pressures or takeover bids may distract managers from the long-term business building of companies such as Sony, Mercedes and Toyota.

KEY terms

incorporation – establishing a business as a separate legal entity from its owners, and therefore allowing at to have limited liability.

limited liability – owners are not liable for the debts of the business; they can lose no more than the sum they invested.

Registrar of Companies – the government department which can allow firms to become incorporated. Located at Companies' House, where articles of association, memorandums of association and the annual accounts of limited companies are available for public scrutiny.

sole trader – a one-person business with unlimited liability.

unlimited liability – owners are liable for any debts incurred by the business, even if it requires them to sell all their assets and possessions and become personally bankrupt.

AS Level Exercises

A. REVISION QUESTIONS

(30 marks; 60 minutes)

Read the unit, then answer:

1 Explain two types of business that should *not* start up as a sole trader. (4)

2 Why might the proprietors of a business choose to apply for incorporation? (4)

3 Explain the business implications of limited liability. (5)

4 State two features that distinguish a private limited company from a plc. (2)

5 Outline two reasons why a growing company might choose *not* to become a plc. (4)

6 What is meant by the phrase 'divorce of ownership and control'? (3)

7 Why might mutual organisations such as building societies serve customers better than companies such as the high street banks? (4)

8 Why may retail Co-ops fail to serve their customers any better than companies such as Tesco? (4)

B. REVISION EXERCISES

B1 Data Response

Planet Organic, the UK's only organic supermarket, has set an ambitious expansion plan for the next 10 years. Founder director Renee Elliott said financial restructuring within the next few months would pave the way for a nationwide chain. Established in 1995, the company's 13 investors are largely Elliott's family and friends. She is examining a number of options for refinancing the business including raising venture capital. Thirteen investors she describes as 'a bit unwieldy'.

'We will be consolidating over the next nine months then moving into an aggressive expansion programme,' Elliott said. 'I would like another 30 to 40 shops nationwide and I think that's achievable.'

The principles behind a Planet store are about offering shoppers an environmentally friendly and healthier alternative to the usual supermarket. 'Our goal is to change food retailing in the UK. We'd like to see people eating food that sustains them and the environment.'

The recent spate of food scares and ongoing concerns about genetically modified (GM) foods have boosted Planet's fortunes. The store received its first serious upturn in

February 1996 when the BSE crisis broke. Elliott said there had been a noticeable boost over the last fortnight as the GM debate raged. She does not think it's a passing fad.

Source: Adapted from *The Grocer*, 27/2/99

Questions *(30 marks; 35 minutes)*

1 **a** What type of business organisation is Planet Organic? (2)

b Why do you think that? (5)

2 Outline the ways in which Renee Elliott may be finding 13 investors 'a bit unwieldy'. (7)

3 If Elliott had not been able to finance her start-up through family and friends, explain three other ways she might have obtained the capital. (6)

4 Discuss how successful you believe Planet Organic is likely to be in the future. (10)

B2 Case Study

Business Start-up Proposal: 'Flavours of the Sea'

Midshire Bank small business advisor Nicole James picked up the file marked 'Flavours of the Sea'. It was 15 minutes before her meeting with Andrew Ellis, just enough time to refresh her memory about his start-up proposal.

Midshire Bank Business Proposal Form

In order to be considered for our 'Acorn' small business loan scheme please complete each of the questions below:

What will your business be called?
'Flavours of the Sea'

What product or service will it offer to customers?
The business will offer seafood buffets delivered to the customer's door. The intention is to sell our product to people holding dinner parties, wedding receptions or other special occasions. This is a catering service with a difference because our dishes will use fresh seafood products from the North Shields docks.

What quantities will be produced and what price do you propose to charge?
In the first few months it is anticipated that two to three orders will be filled each week, with most of the work being at weekends.

The fact that the meals are unusual should allow quite high prices to be charged, on average a buffet for 20 people should bring in about £300.

How much competition do you expect your business to face?

In this region there are quite a few catering firms offering buffets of various types, the biggest is the Whitestone Hotel Group. We could not compete with this kind of 'mass' service on price, but we wouldn't want to. The *Yellow Pages* lists no catering business like ours.

How will you make potential customers aware of your product or service?

The intention would be to advertise in the local paper at first, featuring primarily the dinner party element of the service. As we make a success of things, reputation should grow quite rapidly. Recommendation from past customers should be a very effective form of promotion.

Who will work in the business?

There are two of us. I am Andrew Ellis, an ex-shop manager, with experience in running a small branch (four full-time staff) of a national electrical goods chain. I was made redundant five months ago when the company cut back and closed quite a number of its regional stores. I have always loved cooking and finished second in a regional heat of the BBC Master Chef programme two years ago. My partner John King has been employed in a number of local hotels and restaurants as an assistant chef, including recently at The Harbour where fish dishes are a major speciality.

What premises and equipment will be needed?

We intend to work from my home at first. The kitchen is large and the basic facilities are adequate. It is possible that a number of smaller items will be needed, such as storage boxes to keep the food in good condition when we transport it. The only real large expenditure will be on a van. Our first contact with the customer will be as we pull up their driveway, so we must not give the wrong impression. A smart, well-decorated vehicle carrying the business logo (A swordfish and lobster interlinked) is vital. The local dealer says £10,000 should be enough to cover this.

What is the likely cash flow position in the first four months of operation?

Again these are estimates. (We have assumed that the van is bought on hire purchase). We will have to pay for our fish on the day we buy it, but we do not anticipate customers settling their bills for approximately four weeks.

	May	June	July	August
Opening balance	7,000	5,100	5,810	6,520
Total in	0	2,160	2,160	2,160
Money out:				
Food	720	720	720	720
Advertising	150	150	150	150
Van	880	430	430	430
Admin.	150	150	150	150
Total out	1,900	1,450	1,450	1,450
Cash flow	(1,900)	710	710	710
Closing balance	5,100	5,810	6,520	7,230

How much money do you propose to put into the business yourself?

I intend to put the £2,000 which remains from my redundancy payment into the business. This sum may be enough to start Flavours of the Sea, but as you can see from the cash flow forecast above it would leave the firm with very little margin for error in the first few months of operations.

How much do you wish to borrow from the Midshire Bank?

We are applying for a £5,000 loan over two years. If this is not possible then an overdraft facility of £2,000 would be appreciated.

Questions   *(50 marks; 70 minutes)*

1 a Does the start-up proposal provide sufficient indication that the market for seafood buffets has been adequately researched?   *(6)*

  b What further information about the potential market would you advise Andrew Ellis to gather to support his application for a loan?   *(6)*

2 Having identified the potential competitors of Flavours of the Sea, how might Andrew analyse its relative strength in the marketplace?   *(6)*

3 How realistic do you think Andrew's decision to work from home is? What advantages and disadvantages will result from making this choice? *(10)*

4 How useful do you regard the Flavours of the Sea cash flow forecast to the running of the business?   *(10)*

5 Would you advise Nicole to grant Andrew Ellis the loan, the overdraft facility, or neither?   *(12)*

BUSINESS PLANNING

DEFINITION
A business plan is a document designed to provide sufficient information about a new or existing business to convince financial backers to invest in the business.

Every business, whether new or established, large or small, needs a plan for the future. In the case of large, established companies planning will be done by strategists or consultants. In small firms and new business start-ups, the owner of the business is likely to be both manager and planner. This unit is primarily concerned with the small business start-up and the vital role that the business plan has to play in attempting to ensure the success of these enterprises.

77.1 Purposes of a business plan

To clarify the idea: The process involved in creating a business plan means that the **entrepreneur** has to ask a number of key questions about their idea. This should ensure that before starting up, the business idea has been considered with care.

To gain finance: The plan will often be used as a means of showing potential investors or lenders why the business will succeed. Banks insist on seeing a business plan before any loan or overdraft is granted. Private shareholders might invest because they believe in the entrepreneur. Professional providers of **venture capital** will demand evidence of careful planning.

To monitor progress over time: The business plan can be used as a working document for the owner. Regular checks, particularly against the objectives and the financial forecasts included in the plan, can act as a useful indicator of how well the business is doing. This can be the start of an ongoing monitoring process to help the owner run an efficient organisation in the future.

77.2 What's in a business plan?

The contents of a business plan will vary tremendously, depending upon the type of business, the expertise of the entrepreneur, who the plan is aimed at and how much time is spent researching the plan. However, the sections outlined below will be found in most business plans.

INTRODUCTION

The plan starts with a brief summary of what the business will do, where it will be done and why the entrepreneur has decided to set up this business. This section will provide little detail, but is designed to give the reader of the plan an overall impression of the business idea.

PERSONAL INFORMATION

A curriculum vitae (CV) of each owner will be included, focused particularly on any previous experience, in this line of business, in previous business start-ups or in management generally. Also included may be personal details of other key staff within the business. The owner(s) may wish to make a statement of their own personal objectives in order to show the reader of the plan how committed they are and exactly what they hope to gain from the enterprise.

OBJECTIVES

The business plan should provide a clear statement of the objectives the firm is aiming to achieve. These objectives should be quantifiable targets. In other words, it should be possible to measure whether or not the objective has been achieved within the timescale allowed for that target. In some cases, the objectives will be split into short, medium and long term. Short-term objectives will cover the first year of trading, perhaps stating that the business aims to break even in its first year of trading. Medium-term objectives will cover anything from two to five years in the future and may be less specific than the short-term objectives. They will often relate to the size of the business, specifically how the business may grow. Examples could include increase sales turnover by 20% per year for the first five years, or open up a second outlet within five years. Long-term objectives will be even less specific. Planning for the long-term future is far harder than planning in the short term. Examples may include diversification into other markets, products or regions.

MARKETING PLAN

The reader of the plan will want to know why this business idea should succeed in the marketplace. What will make this product/service stand out? What will be its unique selling point (USP)? And how will this USP be communicated to potential customers? Practical details such as pricing and promotion will be judged by how well they fit in with this strategy. Is enough money being budgeted to communicate the USP successfully?

Apart from the 'product', the aspect of the marketing mix potential investors will look at with greatest care is 'place'. In other words, how, where and at what cost is distribution to be achieved? Someone may have found a way to make better breakfast cereals than Kelloggs. How will Tesco and Sainsbury's be persuaded to stock them, though?

The marketing plan may be structured around the four Ps, but it is important to remember that a small firm's marketing strategy is very different from that of a large firm. The topic of small business marketing is covered in Unit 75.

Pricing the product will often be based on breaking even. As a result, cost based methods, particularly mark-up pricing, will be used. However, small businesses must also consider the market within which they are operating – since they are likely to be price takers. An awareness of competitors' prices is vital and the small business must strike the right balance between covering costs and undercutting competitors in an attempt to gain market share. Often firms will begin by practising a form of penetration pricing in the first few months of trading. This is to build up a customer base, in other words gain a foothold in the market.

The single most important feature of the marketing plan, though, will be the sales forecast. This is, after all, not only the key marketing question. It is also the key financial issue. The revenue must be high enough to cover the costs. So the research and care put into the sales forecast will be checked with particular care by potential investors.

Overall, the marketing plan should aim to answer questions such as the following, taken from NatWest Bank's *Business Start-Up Guide*:

- What is the market size and potential? Is the market growing or getting smaller?
- Who are your customers? What are their needs?
- Who are the major competitors? What are their prices, strengths and weaknesses?
- What is your expected turnover in the first year?
- Why do you think you can achieve your expected turnover?
- Has your product or service been market tested?
- What marketing and sales methods will you use? What are the costs involved?

If the marketing plan is able to provide satisfactory answers to these questions, it is likely that any potential provider of finance will be satisfied that the business idea is sound. They will now be interested in seeing the production plan and financial information.

THE BUSINESS PLAN

Business IN

Chris and Becky Barnard risked everything on opening a restaurant in the country. Their sales projections had convinced the bank to provide a £40,000 overdraft (on top of a £110,000 mortgage on the property). They decided on the upmarket name Avins Bridge Restaurant and set their price at £17 a head for a three-course meal. The restaurant opened in the summer 1997.

Although the evening trade proved reasonable, the shock for them was that lunchtimes were dead. By February 1998 the situation was very worrying. With an average of just 16 meals a day, the business was operating well below break-even. Drastic action was needed. A special offer of a free dessert proved, if anything, that their middle-aged, affluent customers were not price sensitive. It did nothing for sales. So the Barnards decided to push prices up – and to cut costs by running the restaurant without any outside staff.

Although the restaurant is still struggling, the hope is to build up a summer daytime trade with more snacky food served in the garden. They have also started advertising in the local press. Chris and Becky have learned the hard way that good-looking figures on a business plan count for nothing when the business gets going.

Source: *Caterer & Hotelkeeper*

PRODUCTION PLAN

The production plan is the section of the business plan which explains how the business will create the goods or services it intends to sell (see the table at the top of the next page). To be considered – staffing levels, knowledge and qualifications required and stocks of certain items (particularly relevant in a shop).

It is this section of the plan which is most flexible in format, depending upon the type of business being planned. Whatever type of business, the production plan must demonstrate that the entrepreneur has carefully thought through the exact details of how the business will run. In other words, the day-to-day, practical details of the activities involved.

FINANCIAL INFORMATION

This, the heart of the business plan, will include a projected balance sheet for the end of the first year's trading, a projected profit and loss account for the

Details required in a production plan

FOR A MANUFACTURING BUSINESS	FOR A SERVICE BUSINESS
The production process which will be used	How customers are to be serviced: personally? Or with automated systems such as voicemail and the Internet?
The materials needed to produce the product	The staff levels needed (and their training)
The labour and machinery required for production	The equipment required for information and communications technology; and the target stock levels
Details of production capacity and lead times from order to delivery	The planned customer service times

first year and a cash flow forecast for the first six to twelve months. Also found in this section may be a break-even analysis. This will show either the number of units the business needs to sell, or the sales turnover needed, to cover the overheads. A statement of financial requirements will also be included, usually showing a prospective lender how much money is required and how that money will be spent.

CALCULATING BREAK-EVEN REVENUE

For many businesses, traditional break-even analysis is impractical. This is because they may sell a range of different products at a range of prices. If this is the case, it is still possible to use break-even analysis to calculate the level of turnover required to break even. In order to calculate the break-even revenue, it is necessary to know the firm's overheads and to have an estimation of their average gross profit margin. With this information, the following formula can be used to calculate break-even sales revenue:

$$\frac{\text{fixed overheads}}{\text{average gross profit margin}} \times 100$$

If the firm is able to achieve this level of sales, and its gross profit margin does not fall below the average level, it will break even.

Example:
Bell's Dried Fruits sells a range of dried fruit and nut products. Its average gross profit margin on each product is 50%. It has monthly overheads of £12,000. Therefore its break-even revenue is:

$$\frac{£12,000}{50} \times 100 = 240 \times 100$$

$$= £24,000$$

COLLATERAL

However impressive the sales, cash flow and profit forecasts, banks are unwilling to lend money to finance business plans without **collateral**. This means security, in other words securing the loan against assets which can be sold to repay any debts. A bank lending £20,000 may require £25,000 of property

assets as security. If the business has these assets, there is no problem. Often, though, a new small firm has few assets. It rents property rather than buying it. If the business has no assets to use as collateral, the entrepreneur may have to offer personal assets as security, such as his or her house. In which case business failure may be a financial disaster for the family concerned.

All business plans directed at borrowing capital require a statement of assets of the business and the assets of the individuals concerned.

ISSUES FOR **analysis**

Analysing a business plan should involve the following issues:

- Is the idea a sensible one for starting a business? Perhaps the product itself is not attractive or the service being offered will not be wanted.
- Is the actual production of the product or service feasible? Perhaps the entrepreneur has overestimated how much his or her employees will be able to produce in a given time, or the employees may not be suitably skilled to do the job required.
- Is the financial side of the plan realistic? Any financial plan will be based on assumptions. This is particularly important for a new business start-up, with no track record upon which to base forecasts. It is important to consider whether or not the assumptions made in drawing up the forecasts are valid.
- What is the level of risk? Given the high rate of business failures amongst small business start-ups, any new business is at risk of failure. Some will close soon after opening and this will usually mean a substantial loss for the entrepreneur. Although a business plan is created as an attempt to reduce the risks involved, it does not eliminate risk.

77.3 Business planning
an evaluation

Business planning questions lend themselves to offering opportunities for demonstrating evaluation. Two important themes to consider are:

1 One of the key themes to evaluation is the ability to be able to gauge appropriateness. When considering business plans, the appropriateness of each section must be considered. For example, should a business plan for a small plumber contain details of his planned television advertising campaign? Surely local newspapers or the *Yellow Pages* are more appropriate for advertising this type of business? Not only will this be more cost effective in reaching local consumers, it is also more appropriate in the context of the promotional budget for a small firm.

2 A second evaluative theme in business planning is an awareness of reality. Roughly 90% of small businesses cease trading within five years of starting up. Rates of business failure are high and those with detailed business plans can also fail. These failures may be the result of changes in tastes or fashions, unexpected competition, bad luck or a whole host of other, often external, constraints. Another important reminder of reality is that many small business start-ups are financed by redundancy payments or inheritances. So no additional finance is required. In these cases, it is highly likely that no formal business plan will exist. Entrepreneurs are, however, likely to have skill or expertise in their particular field. An electrician starting up as a sole trader may not know what a sole trader is, but does know how to re-wire a house. In reality, when you hire an electrician you would prefer them to have a detailed knowledge of electrical matters than business matters.

KEY terms

collateral – the assets needed as security on a bank loan.

entrepreneur – a person who is prepared to take business opportunities, often in the context of starting up a new business.

venture capital – risk capital put into a small to medium-sized business, usually as a mix of equity and loan capital.

544

UNIT 77 | BUSINESS PLANNING

77.4 Workbook

AS Level Exercises

A. REVISION QUESTIONS
(35 marks; 50 minutes)

Read the unit, then answer:

1 State the three main uses of a business plan. *(3)*

2 In what circumstances is a business likely to start up with no plan? *(2)*

3 Read the list of seven key questions from NatWest's *Business Start-Up Guide*. Which three do you consider the most important? Explain why. *(6)*

4 If a firm has a pricing policy of adding a 100% mark-up onto variable cost and has monthly fixed costs of £50,000, how much does it need to sell to break even? *(4)*

5 Explain why break-even analysis plays such an important role in assessing the validity of a new business idea. *(6)*

6 Why are banks so keen to have collateral on their loans to small firms? *(2)*

7 What benefits might there be to the economy of a relaxation by banks on their policy of insisting upon collateral before financing a businesses start-up? *(6)*

8 State and explain three reasons why a good business plan is no guarantee of success. *(6)*

B. REVISION EXERCISES

B1 Data Response

Fresh from college, Bhrijesh Patel used the money received in an inheritance to start up a sports shop in his local high street. He spent three months contacting suppliers in order to get a clear idea of the costs involved. He discovered that his £30,000 was sufficient to pay a year's rent on the shop, redecorate the shop just the way he wanted, buy the stock he needed and provide a small amount of working capital. His was the only sports shop on the local high street.

By the end of the first week, he was happy that so many people had come into the shop, but disappointed at the level of sales. Particularly weak were sales of branded trainers. As the weeks passed, the pattern continued. So Bhrijesh drew up a simple questionnaire for people entering the shop, but not buying. Within a week, he had identified his problem. Although he had no direct competition in the local high street, the large shopping centre just out of town had three sports shops. These shops sold little equipment or specialist clothing. They were mainly selling fashion items – particularly trainers – for up to 20% less than Bhrijesh.

Having discovered this, Bhrijesh dropped the prices on

the trainers he had in stock in order to prepare for a change in strategy. He spent the next few months developing a range of stock to differentiate his shop from those of his competitors. He repositioned his shop as a specialist, selling clothing and equipment that his fashion-conscious competitors did not stock.

The change of strategy worked. The shop gained a large number of regular customers and managed to survive its difficult first few years of trading.

Questions   (30 marks; 35 minutes)

1 Examine the weaknesses in Bhrijesh's approach to starting up his business.   (6)
2 Despite some weaknesses, a strength was that he did not stick rigidly to a plan that was not working.
   a Why may some small business proprietors do this?   (4)
   b What would be the likely consequences?   (4)
3 A common mistake made by those who are starting their first business is to underestimate their working capital needs. What are the implications of this?   (8)
4 Nowadays Bhrijesh produces an updated business plan every year. What benefits is he likely to gain from it?   (8)

B2 Case Study

Suzie Jones left college determined to make a success of the business idea that had occurred to her while travelling in the Middle East the previous summer. Along with many other young people of various nationalities, Suzie had spent her summer working on a Kibbutz in Israel, picking fruit by day and partying at night.

Suzie felt sure that this sort of summer job would be perfect for many students who wanted to spend summer in the sun, but needed to work to pay for their trip. She would form a private limited company called Summer Sun and run it from home to keep overheads low.

The service she proposed to offer was a choice of packages, covering one-, two-, three- and six-month trips. Customers would pay enough to cover the cost of their flight and a 25% mark-up to cover Suzie's overheads. Customers would then work on the Kibbutz where food and accommodation were provided, along with a small amount of 'pocket money' for entertainment.

Having travelled back to Israel and built up a collection of contacts at various Kibbutz sites, she felt that

she could cope with a maximum of 500 customers at any one time. Initial market research indicated that Suzie had no competition within a local market which included three large FE colleges and many school sixth forms. She felt confident that with the right marketing, her idea could be a great success.

The business plan she drew up included the following sections:

- an outline of her idea
- a marketing plan
- a production section detailing her plans to reserve blocks of seats on a number of flights to Israel for a 10% booking deposit. Seats would need to be booked in January of each year in order to achieve the greatest cost savings. Suzie would carry out market research in December to help her judge roughly how many seats to book each year and when customers would be most likely to travel.
- a financial plan detailing the expected costs and revenues of the business. This would detail the £3,000 overheads per year and provide information on the direct costs per customer, which would differ depending upon their length of stay and date of departure.

Questions   (30 marks; 40 minutes)

1 In what ways does the case study reflect the importance of cash flow to new firms?   (4)
2 How would you advise Suzie to set about marketing her firm?   (8)
3 Using examples, suggest how a business plan can aid the survival of new firms in the first few months of existence.   (8)
4 Suzie decided to form a private limited company. Explain why this was ideal in her situation.   (6)
5 What is Suzie's break-even revenue?   (4)

C. ESSAY QUESTIONS

1 'I only did the plan to get the finance from the bank. Lots of it is guesswork so I can't see the point myself.' Try to persuade this business proprietor about the value of a business plan.
2 Discuss whether the time and cost of devising a thoroughly researched business plan can ever be worthwhile.

HANDLING RAPID GROWTH

DEFINITION

'Rapid' growth is hard to define. For firms in the computer business such as Microsoft, a growth rate of 25% a year would seem slow. Whereas for Marks and Spencer it would be unmanageably fast. Rapid growth implies a sustained, substantial increase in sales turnover, sufficient to affect the managerial structure of the business.

78.1 Introduction

Growth is a common business objective. When a new market is opening up, it can be crucial to become the dominant supplier. Microsoft Windows dominated, then competitors fell by the wayside. VHS video recorders became the leading format, then Sony's Betamax system fell away. The dot com boom of 2000-2001 was driven by the desire by firms such as Lastminute.com to grow large enough to dominate online travel bookings. There can be no doubt, then,

1400 Smith Street

Enron – mishandling rapid growth (© Greg Smith/CORBIS SABA)

that certain business circumstances make rapid growth essential.

For many other firms, growth may not be essential but certainly seems desirable. Which company chairperson would not like to stand up at the AGM and announce a 20% sales and market share increase? The reality is, though, that rapid growth is extremely difficult to manage. The same chairperson might stand up the following year and sheepishly announce a profit downturn.

The problems of growth are threefold:

- financial – especially the effects upon cash flow and gearing
- managerial – notably problems of coordination and control
- operational – especially the difficulty of boosting supply in line with demand.

The problems arise as a result of various internal and external causes of growth. The internal ones (such as a change in objectives) should at least be planned for. External causes of growth may be unexpected, though. This makes them far harder to manage. The following table sets out some possible internal and external causes of growth.

Business IN ENRON

During the 1990s the American firm Enron grew from a small Texan company to become the world's biggest energy supplier. Between 1996 and 2000 sales revenues grew by more than 600%. This frantic growth was seen by the stockmarket as a huge tribute to Enron's innovative, dynamic leadership. Shares shot ahead by over 1,400% between 1990 and 2000. In January 2001 the share price of $85 meant the company had a stock market value of $60,000 million. Yet by December 2001 the shares were worthless.

Enron collapsed in 2001 because it became clear that the financial strains of extremely rapid growth had been covered up by highly questionable accounting. To achieve the growth, huge bonuses had been given to 'successes' and the sack given to 'failures'. This atmosphere of fear and greed had led staff to accept increasingly doubtful business practices. Meanwhile, cash flow was struggling to keep up with the firm's debts and declining profits.

The Enron case shows all three of the 'problems of growth' mentioned in the text.

INTERNAL CAUSES	EXTERNAL CAUSES
• New growth objectives set by management • Decision to open up new export markets • Reorganisation makes increased output possible	• Rising consumer demand/ the product becomes fashionable • Economic boom benefits a luxury product • Closure/fire/strike hits competitor, boosting your sales • New laws favour your product, e.g. new safety laws boost sales of first-aid kits

78.2 Business effects of forecast rapid growth

In certain circumstances managers can anticipate a period of rapid growth. This may be temporary (such as the effect of a change in the law) or may seem likely to be permanent, such as the growth in demand for computer games software. The most successful firms will be those that devise a plan that is detailed enough to help in a practical way, but flexible enough to allow for the differences between forecasts and reality.

When rapid growth has been forecast, firms can:

• compare the sales estimate with the available production capacity
• budget for any necessary increases in capacity and staffing

CASH EATEN BY SLUG

In October 2002 SFI, owner of the Slug and Lettuce and Bar Med pub chains, cancelled its dividend and admitted that it was struggling to pay its creditors. SFI shares collapsed to 25p. They had already fallen by 80% since September – the month before the cash flow problems emerged.

Andrew Latham, chief executive, 'admitted that rapid expansion had allowed too little room for error' (*The Financial Times*). SFI had opened 46 new outlets in its 2001/2002 financial year and another 8 in the first quarter of 2002/2003. This had put too great a strain on working capital, forcing it to become heavily overdrawn. Now SFI would need to sell off part of its operations to put more secure finance in place. It was a classic case of overtrading.

IN Business

• produce a cash flow forecast to anticipate any short-term financing shortfall
• discuss how to raise any extra capital needed.

Timescales remain important, though. The forecast may cover the next three months, but increasing capacity may involve building a factory extension which will take eight months. In which case there may be five months of excess demand to cope with (perhaps by subcontracting).

Smooth though all this sounds, there remains a lot of scope for error. The starting point is the increased workload on staff. Extra sales may put pressure on the accounting system, the warehouse manager and the delivery drivers. With everyone being kept busy, occasional things can start to go wrong. Invoices are sent out a little later, unpaid bills are not chased as quickly and stock deliveries are not checked as carefully. Suddenly the cash flow position worsens and costs start to rise. A strong, effective manager could retrieve this, but many are weak and woolly. Once they start to go wrong, plans are hard to sort out.

78.3 Management reorganisation during growth

PROBLEM OF ADJUSTMENT FROM BOSS TO LEADER/MANAGER

The typical creator of a successful new business is lively, energetic, creative, often impatient and always a risk taker. Such a person will have a strong personality, and quite possibly an autocratic though charismatic leadership style. When the business started, their own speed of decision making, attention to detail and hard work were fundamental to the firm's success.

With success comes a problem. How to cope with the additional workload. At first the boss works ever harder; then he or she takes on more junior staff. Then comes the crunch. Is he or she willing to appoint a senior manager with real decision making power? Or will a weak manager be appointed who always has to check decisions with the boss?

Staff will always find it hard to accept a new manager because everyone will know that it is really the boss's business. It is said that 10 years after Walt Disney died, managers were still rejecting ideas on the basis that 'Walt wouldn't have done it that way'. How much harder if the founder is still there: Richard Branson at Virgin, Bill Gates at Microsoft or Tim Waterstone at Waterstone's bookshops.

The boss must make the break, however. No longer should they attend every key meeting or demand regular reports on day-to-day matters. Delegation is necessary. In other words, authority should be passed down the hierarchy to middle managers without interference from above. And instead of looking for the next great opportunity the boss may have to focus on getting the right management structure to ensure a smooth running business.

Even if the founder of the company *is* able to adjust to managing a large organisation, there remains the problem of motivation. Will the new staff be as 'hungry' as the small team that built the business? Usually the answer is no. The drinks giant Diageo thinks it has a solution, though. Diageo is the giant result of the 1997 merger of Guinness and Grand Metropolitan. It is a business with annual sales of over £17,000 million, including Smirnoff, Baileys, Guinness and Burger King. To keep staff hungry, the chief executive gives managers a 'HAT' – a 'hairy audacious target'. In other words, a bold, challenging goal. Achieving these HATs will give each manager the chance to make huge bonuses. In 1998 Diageo set itself the goal of doubling the value of the business by the end of 2002 – and achieved it. The chief executive believes HATs can stretch 'our people's imaginations to achieve these aggressive targets'. It remains to be seen whether this approach works, but it shows the lengths to which large firms may have to go to achieve the growth they seek.

CHANGE IN MANAGEMENT STRUCTURE/HIERARCHY

As a business grows, the management structure has not only to grow but also to change. New layers of management may be needed and completely new departments may be founded, such as personnel or public relations. And all the time, as the business grows, new staff are being recruited, inducted and trained. So there is constant change in personnel and their responsibilities. This can be disconcerting for customers and suppliers. Strong relationships are hard to build, making customer loyalty tough to achieve.

Even more important, though, is the internal effect of these personnel changes. With new staff appearing frequently and managerial changes occurring regularly, team spirit may be hard to achieve. Junior and middle managers may spend too much of their time looking upwards to the promotion prospects instead of concentrating on their own departments. The potential for inefficiency or even chaos is clear. Too many new staff may mean too many mistakes. If customer relations are relatively weak, the result could easily be loss of business.

These unpleasant possibilities can largely be set aside if a good example is set from the top. If the founder of the business continues to be involved – especially on customer service – all may still be well. The leader needs to make sure staff keep sight of the qualities that brought the business its success in the first place. If new management structures threaten to create communications barriers, the leader should set an example by visiting staff, chatting to them and acting on their advice. The leader must fight against being cut off from the grassroots – the staff and the customers.

RISK OF LOSS OF DIRECTION AND CONTROL

Each year, Templeton College Oxford produces data on what it calls the *Fast Track 100*. These are the fastest growing 100 small companies in Britain. A recent survey showed that the average growth rate of these firms was:

- sales turnover: +93% per year
- employees: +75% per year

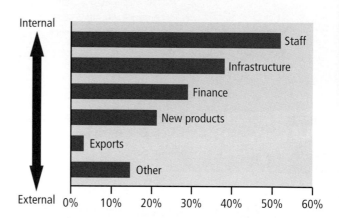

Figure 78.1 Key challenges (Source: *Fast Track 100*, Templeton College)

The typical *Fast Track 100* firm had gone from 25 staff to 136 staff in the past three years. No wonder, then, that rapidly growing small firms can struggle to cope. The same survey showed that the key challenges faced by these companies were staff and infrastructure. As Figure 78.1 shows, the problems tend to be internal to the business, not external.

Faced with major challenges in managing the staff, the structure and the support infrastructure of the business (such as IT systems), there is a serious risk of losing focus. The successful small firms are those that keep sight of strengths that can maintain the level of innovation and competitive advantage. The survey showed the dominant growth strategy was to focus on customer service and meeting customer needs. Next most important was to focus on the company's own staff. Also important was to keep developing quality products and services. Figure 78.2 shows the findings in more detail.

The entrepreneurs who get swamped by the success of the business are those whose firms will fail to sustain their growth. They may become sidetracked by the attractions of expense account living. Or – the other extreme – become so excited by their own success that they start opening up several different businesses. They assume that their golden touch will ensure success in whatever they do. Instead, just as their core business becomes harder to handle, they are looking at a different venture altogether. Problems may then hit from several directions at once.

The key message is, therefore: focus on what you are good at.

Figure 78.2 Growth types (Source: *Fast Track 100*, Templeton College)

78.4 Problems of transition in size

FROM PRIVATE TO PUBLIC

At certain points in a firm's life there are critical decisions regarding growth. Few are more fundamental than the decision to 'go public'. A private limited company is a family business, often dominated by the shareholdings of one person – probably the founder. Although its accounts must be published, it is still able to maintain a substantial veil over its activities. Its private status minimises the pressures upon the management. A year of poor trading may disappoint the family, but there is no publicly quoted share price to embarrass or to threaten the firm with a hostile takeover. This protection from outside pressures enables private companies to take a long-term view of what they want to achieve and how. The Virgin Group floated onto the stock market in the 1980s, but within four years Richard Branson took it back into private ownership. He blamed the short-term horizons of stock market investors which he thought would damage his business in the long term.

Switching from private to public company status is not, in itself, a difficult or expensive process. The big

change comes when a firm floats its shares onto the stock market. Only public companies are allowed to do this. From the protected world of the private company, the firm will enter the glare of public scrutiny. Before floating, the firm must issue a *prospectus* which sets out every detail of the firm's business, its financial record, its expectations and its key personnel. Newspapers and analysts will scrutinise this fully, and carry on writing about the firm when every set of financial results comes out.

The purpose of going public is usually to achieve a substantial increase in share capital. This can enable a highly geared private firm to achieve a more balanced capital structure, as shown in the table below.

Cutting gearing by going public

SHARPS LTD (BEFORE GOING PUBLIC)		**SHARPS PLC (AFTER RAISING £4M ON THE STOCK MARKET)**	
Loan capital	£4m	Loan capital	£4m
Share capital	£1m	Share capital	£5m
Reserves	£3m	Reserves	£3m
Capital employed	**£8m**	**Capital employed**	**£12m**
Gearing level:	50%	Gearing level:	33%

In the case of Sharps plc, the addition of 50% more capital (from £8 million to £12 million) will give a huge opportunity for major expansion. Indeed, if the management act slowly, the purchasers of the £4 million extra shares may get restless. So the managers will be inclined to make a big move. Perhaps they will make a takeover bid. Or perhaps a diversification, by launching a new product range. Either way, the risks

— EASYJET

EasyJet floated onto the stock market in September 2000. £600 million was raised by selling 25% of the company's shares, leaving control in the hands of the founder, Stelios Haji-Ioannou.

This helped finance incredibly rapid growth. Between November 2000 and June 2002, passenger numbers doubled. Then easyJet's purchase of the rival airline Go, helped double numbers again between June and August 2002. The purchase of Go was financed in part by issuing more shares on the London stock market.

The rapid growth led to strains showing through in August 2002, with easyJet forced to cut flights in order to stop pilots from working beyond their legally allowable maximum number of hours. A new staff roster was criticised by the pilots' union Balpa, with a union official claiming that 'Among a lot of low cost airline pilots there is a quiet concern that they are being overstretched and that safety could suffer'. This was implicitly accepted by easyJet's operations director who wrote to pilots saying 'the current situation cannot continue'. He also admitted that the group's rapid expansion had stretched the airline to its limits.

Nevertheless, chief executive Martin Webster insisted that safety was not being compromised, with customers simply being inconvenienced 'at the margin'. When easyJet announced one of the world's biggest-ever orders for new aircraft, in October 2002, it was clear that the stock market listing had helped easyJet navigate through a difficult growth period.

are substantial. Does this business have the expertise to succeed with either approach? What it needs is the confidence to keep focused upon what the management is good at. But the public pressure to make a big step forward may encourage the management to take a step too far.

NATIONAL TO INTERNATIONAL

Most new businesses deal with local customers in their early months or years. Slowly they build up the customer contacts and the transport and distribution networks to operate nationally. Dealing with London customers may seem quite strange for a firm with its roots in Manchester, but adjustments can be made quite easily.

The next step is likely to be much harder. Many firms have struggled when building up a business overseas. In retailing, the list is endless: Tesco in France; Sainsbury's, Sock Shop, Tie Rack and Laura Ashley in America; and Marks & Spencer struggled so much overseas that in 2000 it closed all its branches outside Britain.

There are several underlying problems. These include:

- the assumption that a 'winning formula' in Britain will necessarily travel abroad
- insufficient understanding of the local market – from customer habits and attitudes through to the best locations for a retail store or for product distribution
- problems of control – if the decision is made to delegate full authority to a local managing director.

These difficulties are compounded by the view of many managers that sales success only occurs once a 'critical mass' has been achieved. Sometimes this is true. America's first serious attempt at building a national soccer league was based around the star-studded New York Cosmos, featuring football greats such as Pele and Beckenbauer. But who would they play, week by week? Football had not (and still has not) reached its critical mass as a spectator sport in America. So, when the first Sock Shop proved unsuccessful in America, the temptation was to say 'well, perhaps we need a bigger store with a wider range' or 'it's only when there's a Sock Shop at every station and airport that people will start taking them seriously'. Unfortunately, investing good money after bad is a very expensive approach. It nearly proved fatal for Sock Shop and Laura Ashley.

RETRENCHMENT

Just as big steps forward can lead to problems, so can steps backward. Yet few firms will keep growing without the occasional sharp setback. Retrenchment means cutting back. This may be through a general reduction in staffing, or perhaps only a halt on recruitment. Most often, though, it will imply a rationalisation in which there are significant changes to the organisational structure and/or to the capacity level of the business.

In 2002 there were major worldwide rationalisations by giants such as Ford, Gap, Siemens and NEC. On a smaller scale, British Steel and Dr Marten's also cut back. In all cases, the key factor is to ensure that retrenchment does not cause lasting damage to morale, relationships and trust. Therefore it is vital to be honest, open, fair and as generous as possible to anyone who is losing a job.

When forced to cut back, firms have many options. These are described in the table at the bottom of the page.

When tackling questions about rapid growth, the following lines of analysis are helpful:

- Is the growth planned (internal) or unplanned (external)?
- Is the business leader's management style capable of changing as the business develops?
- Is there scope for containing the growth? For example, can some contracts be turned down without threatening the future health of the business? If so, this may be wise.
- Does the firm have the financial resources to cope with the growing needs for capital?
- How well does the firm cope with growth shocks, such as a stock market flotation? Can the management keep focused upon the strategy and the strengths of the business.
- Would managers who have handled growth well be equally good at handling retrenchment? Only if they have and deserve the trust of the staff.

WARNING SIGNS OF COLLAPSE

Business consultant John Argenti says there are three phases in corporate collapse. The first involves gaps and imbalances appearing in a company's management, often because of rapid growth. In this phase, processes of monitoring fall apart, so managers start to lose touch with what is really happening within the business. In the second phase these defects lead managers to make wrong decisions. The final phase sees cracks appearing openly, such as rising staff turnover and signs of cash flow problems, e.g. late payment of bills.

Thirty years ago Argenti developed a way of measuring the risk of corporate collapse, which he called the A-score. As the table on page 552 shows, it is a mixture of leadership and managerial factors, plus financial measures. Argenti says it succeeds in predicting nine out of ten corporate crises.

Business IN

78.5 Handling rapid growth
an evaluation

One of the hardest judgements to make about growth is when a rapid rate becomes excessive. Can firms cope with growth rates of over 50%, year after year? The *Fast Track 100* survey suggests that the answer is yes. A recent winner enjoyed turnover growth from £1 million to £26.4 million in three years. Such dramatic success is possible, but only if the management is well focused

TYPE OF RETRENCHMENT	ADVANTAGES	DISADVANTAGES
Freezing recruitment and/or offering voluntary redundancy	• Not threatening; should not cause problems of job insecurity • Viewed by staff as fair	• No chance to reshape the business • Good people are always leaving, so they need to be replaced
De-layering, i.e. removing a whole management layer	• Should not affect direct operations (such as staff on the shop-floor) • May empower/enrich remaining jobs	• May over-intensify the work of other managers, causing stress • Risk of losing a generation of managers • Loss of promotion prospects for those who remain
Closing a division, a factory or a number of loss-making outlets	• Sharp reduction in fixed overhead costs will reduce break-even point • Capacity utilisation may rise in the firm's other factories	• Once closed, the capacity is unlikely to be available for the next economic upturn • Lose many good staff
Making targeted cutbacks and redundancies in divisions throughout the business	• Can reshape the business to meet the future, e.g. no cutbacks among IT staff • By keeping good staff, their average quality level may rise	• Huge problems of perceived fairness (unless there is a high degree of trust) • Job security may be hit ('will it be me next?')

and flexible. Many companies are dragged under by their failure to cope with success.

Why does rapid growth matter? Britain has for many years been one of Europe's leading economies for small business start-ups. Too often, though, they are part hobby and part self-employment. Rapid growth matters because job creation and economic growth depend upon small firms building up into medium or large businesses. Fifteen years ago, the American equivalent of the *Fast Track 100* identified unknown companies such as Microsoft, Oracle and Domino's Pizza. These are the growth stories that make a difference. All show that rapid growth can be managed. But all the managers would agree that it is never easy.

A-SCORES – IS THE COMPANY A OK?

To calculate the A score, mark each criterion out of the total shown. Do not use half marks. If in doubt, score zero. Argenti's total scores are in the second column. In the third are the editor's estimates of Enron's position during 1999–2001. Enron collapsed in early 2002.

DEFECTS	Total	Enron
Autocratic leadership	8	8
Combined chairman and chief executive	4	0
Passive board	2	2
Unbalanced skills	2	0
Weak finance director	2	0
Poor management depth	1	0
No budgetary control	3	1
No cash-flow plans	3	0
No costing system	3	3
Poor response to change (ageing product, plant, directors etc)	15	0
MISTAKES		
High gearing	15	12
Overtrading (expansion under-financed)	15	8
Big project (overwhelming the rest of the business)	15	2
SYMPTOMS		
Financial signs	4	4
Creative accounting	4	4
Non-financial signs (e.g. staff turnover)	3	1
Terminal signs	1	0
OVERALL TOTAL	100	45
Pass mark	25	25

Stable companies score well under 25. Those at risk of insolvency score between 35 and 70.

A Level Exercises

A. REVISION QUESTIONS
(50 marks; 70 minutes)

Read the unit, then answer:

1 Explain why rapid growth can cause problems for a company's:
   a cash flow *(2)*
   b management control. *(2)*
2 Distinguish between internal and external causes of growth, using examples. *(5)*
3 Why might there be a problem in adjusting from 'boss' to 'leader/manager'? *(4)*
4 How might large firms benefit from setting staff 'Hairy Audacious Targets'? *(3)*
5 Examine the bar chart headed 'Key Challenges'. Outline two important conclusions. *(6)*
6 Identify three problems for a fast-growing firm caused by changes in the management structure. *(3)*
7 Outline two strengths and two potential weaknesses of stock market flotation for a rapidly growing business. *(8)*
8 Explain the possible problems (and benefits) to a small computer software firm of changing status from private to public limited company. *(4)*
9 **a** Explain the meaning of the term 'retrenchment'. *(3)*
   b Outline two suitable methods of retrenchment for an airline that is losing market share. *(4)*
10 From your knowledge of current business events, identify two firms that have recently enjoyed very rapid growth. Analyse the likely causes of the growth in both cases. *(6)*

B. REVISION EXERCISES

B1 Data Response

Diseconomies at The Body Shop
The Body Shop was a huge 1980s' success story. It shot up from a single shop in Brighton to a multinational empire. Founder Anita Roddick was convinced that bulk buying and mass production would push costs down and profit margins up. By 1998, however, it was clear that things were not going according to plan. As the *Sunday Times* commented: 'As it has mushroomed from a company with 70 employees to an international retail group with more than 5,000, some of the arteries have clogged up.'

The directors had come to realise that it had become difficult to bring new ideas into their shops quickly. One pointed out that 'we are now in 47 countries with 19 languages … you have a pretty complicated business'. Problems had arisen of communication and coordination – but especially of motivation. When small, Anita Roddick had been able to inspire staff to care passionately about The Body Shop's mission to spread a message of social concern. Now the business was big and a little fat.

Questions
(30 marks; 35 minutes)

1 Outline the ways in which a firm's arteries might be expected to clog up when its staff level has 'mushroomed' from 70 staff to 5,000. *(10)*
2 Examine the issues in the case study that indicate problems with diseconomies of scale. *(6)*
3 The Body Shop grew at a rate of nearly 100% per year during the 1980s, yet it never hit any serious cash flow or financing difficulties. What might be the reasons for this? *(6)*
4 One of The Body Shop's recent problems has been the weak performance of several of its overseas subsidiaries. How might the management tackle this problem? *(8)*

B2 Data Response

Heinz Tries to Squeeze More out of the Ketchup Bottle

There are few better known brand names than HJ Heinz. Yet it is wrong to assume that well-known names always grow. The difficulty for Heinz has been transferring its success in bottled and canned foods to the faster growing chilled and frozen-food sectors. A 1997 retrenchment led to 20 plant closures, 2,500 job cuts and $200 million of savings per year. Even that was insufficient, however, and in 1999 a new plan was announced.

The 1999 plan (called Operation Excel) would cost $900 million and cost the jobs of 10% of the 40,000 staff worldwide. Three strategies lie at the heart of the programme:

- selling off the 30-year-old Weight Watchers business
- reorganising the group along product lines rather than geographically (making pan-European marketing easier to accomplish)
- increasing the marketing budget from 9% to 10% of the $9,000 million annual sales.

To its credit, Heinz is not content to cut back and cut back. It wants to transfer resources to marketing, in order to get sales moving again. As evidence of the potential of this approach, the company boasted that extra marketing spending in America on its mature Heinz ketchup products had boosted sales by 24% in January 1999. This will be little consolation to the 4,000 staff who will lose their jobs in 1999, but will reassure the remaining staff that management has a strategy for rebuilding the business.

Source: Adapted from *The Financial Times*, 19/2/99

C. ESSAY QUESTIONS

1 Dell Computers has grown at a rate of 50% per year for nearly a decade. Outline the problems this might cause. What might be the most effective way for management to tackle them?

2 Charlie is a hugely successful hairdresser's in York. A wealthy client has offered to invest £500,000 to finance the establishment of Charlie outlets in Leeds and Harrogate. Discuss whether the proprietor should accept the offer or not.

Questions *(30 marks; 35 minutes)*

1 Use the text and the graphs below to explain why Heinz is carrying out a retrenchment programme. *(8)*

2 Outline two alternative approaches management might take to achieve the staff reduction by 4,000. Which of the two would you recommend and why? *(12)*

3 a By how much is Heinz increasing its marketing spending (in $s)? *(2)*

 b To what extent could this decision be expected to overcome the impact upon morale of the staff cutbacks? *(8)*

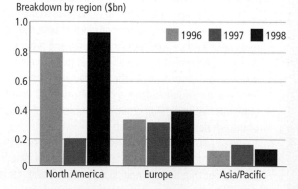

Source: Adapted from Datastream/ICV; company

MULTINATIONALS

DEFINITION

A multinational is a firm which has its headquarters in one country and branches, manufacturing or assembly plants in others. In other words it is not just an exporter. It has business operations in several countries.

79.1 Introduction

Some multinationals are giants. The table below compares the turnover of several large multinationals with the total output of various entire countries.

Comparative size of selected multinational companies and national economies

COMPANY/COUNTRY	TURNOVER/GDP (US$BN)
USA	9810
Japan	4765
Germany	1866
UK	1427
General Motors	176.6
Saudi Arabia	173
Denmark	163
Ford	162.6
ExxonMobil	160.9
Indonesia	153
DaimlerChryslerAG	151
Wal-Mart Stores	137.6
Mitsubushi Corp	127.3
Finland	121
Toyota Motor Corp	119.7
General Electric	111.6
Royal Dutch/Shell Group	105.4
Ireland	95

Source: UNCTAD World Investment Report 2001

Multinationals will tend to have their headquarters in Europe, the USA or Japan. Their other branches or factories may also be located in highly developed economies. However, many multinationals build and run production facilities in **less developed nations**, especially in South America or Asia.

79.2 Advantages of operating in several countries

NEARNESS TO LOCAL MARKETS

Many multinational expansions are driven by the desire to produce close to the market. Local production facilities will result in lower transport costs and probably more competitive prices. Multinationals may also set up local production facilities in order to avoid import tariffs or taxes. Producing in the country for which the products are required means that no products are being imported. The multinational is able to avoid any import restrictions imposed by the host country. During the 1970s and 1980s, Japanese firms built car plants in the USA in order to break into the world's largest car market and to avoid import restrictions. During the 1980s and 1990s, these same firms set up plants within the European Union, in order to take advantage of the free trade area in Europe.

Among other benefits from local production are:

- It is far easier to tailor products to local customer preferences if senior managers live locally and therefore learn to understand local customs.
- In the long term it may be possible to become thought of as a local company. Many in Britain assume Ford and Vauxhall to be British rather than American, which may make them more inclined to 'buy British'.

LOW LABOUR COSTS

Many multinationals shift production facilities to less economically developed countries where wage rates are low. Mass producers are able to set up production facilities in these countries and employ unskilled or semi-skilled workers to produce their products. If firms can reduce the labour cost per unit, they can either afford to drop prices, or they can keep price unchanged and accept a higher profit per unit – a pleasant choice to make! This practice is now very common, as any trip to a high street will show.

TESCO THE MULTINATIONAL

Tesco is the one UK supermarket chain to have pursued a strategy of multinational expansion. In 1997, the company began its overseas expansion in Eastern Europe, Ireland and South-East Asia. After 5 years of difficult performance, the strategy appears to be succeeding as Tesco announced 2002 profits in 8 of its 10 overseas operations.

Rather than use takeovers to break into local markets, Tesco used its own brand to grow organically by opening new stores as and when opportunities arose. The company now claims to be the leading chain in 5 of its 10 overseas markets. By 2002, profits of £59 million were being generated on overseas sales of £2.3 billion. Further profit growth is expected as the group's expansion continues and begins to benefit from trading in markets with margins that are traditionally higher than those generated in the UK.

The next targets being considered by the retailer are Turkey and the biggest prize of all – China.

GOVERNMENT INCENTIVES

Governments of host countries are usually keen to attract multinationals. In order to do this, governments are prepared to offer a range of incentives to encourage multinationals to choose their country rather than any other. Among the methods for attracting this inward investment are reduced or zero tax rates, subsidies and reduced rate loans. The British government has been relatively successful at attracting foreign investors such as Nissan, Bosch, Intel and IBM.

LOW TAXES

This may attract inward investment, as firms seek to find countries where their profits will be taxed at a lower rate than in their home country. This fact is used by many governments as a deliberate incentive to encourage investment by multinationals.

The existence of different tax rates in different countries allows multinationals to practice **transfer pricing**. This is a practice used by multinationals to boost their profits by taking advantage of different tax levels in their countries of operation. It involves declaring high profits in countries where tax rates are low and only declaring minimal profits in high tax countries.

The legality of transfer pricing tends to vary from country to country. As a result, it is difficult to clamp down on this practice, which many feel to be unfair. Local, probably smaller, British companies have to pay the full 30% tax. So it is hard for them to compete with multinationals.

79.3 Benefits of multinationals to host countries

1 Foreign currency – many of the world's less economically developed countries owe millions of dollars to international banks as a result of loans issued, mainly in the 1970s. The interest payments on these loans are huge and many countries are unable to meet these, let alone repay their debts. As a result, these countries are desperate to earn foreign currency from multinationals, which can be used to keep up their interest payments.

2 Jobs – new factories should mean jobs for local workers. Not only directly (i.e. jobs in the factory), but also from service jobs such as shopkeeping that stem from the extra cash in the local economy. Also, local suppliers of materials and components will benefit.

3 Skills – local workers employed by multinationals are likely to receive training. This will equip them with skills which they may be able to pass on to other locals or use for local businesses in the future.

4 Improved **infrastructure** – particularly in less developed countries, the multinational may be unhappy with existing transport and communication links. They may pay to improve local roads and railway lines which will help them to move their goods. Other improvements to the local infrastructure may come in the shape of a hospital for use by the factory staff and local community or a school for training locals.

5 Technology trickle-down – new technology introduced to a country may 'trickle down' to local businesses, enabling them to produce goods and use techniques which were previously unavailable in that country.

6 Management expertise – multinationals will usually start new factories using their own managers from elsewhere in the world. However, once the factory is up and running, local staff may be trained in managerial positions. These local staff may be able to use the knowledge gained in other businesses once they have left the firm. A good example of this was the way in which Nissan and Honda introduced Japanese management techniques in their Sunderland and Swindon factories respectively. Those same techniques spread quickly throughout Britain and are used, in one form or another, in many larger UK businesses today.

79.4 Problems experienced by multinationals

Communication problems can arise between local workers and foreign managers. Not only may workers be unable to follow instructions due to the language barrier, but also it may be difficult to build the team spirit required for successful motivation.

The second cause of communication difficulties may be geographical. A multinational with its headquarters in one country and various distant outposts will need to have communication channels in place to enable effective messages to get through to distant countries. With modern advances in telecommunications, this problem is lessening. Many companies now operate multinational **intranets**, as well as online computer links. It is important to remember, though, that the richest form of communication is a face-to-face chat. Video conferencing is supposed to provide that possibility, but users find it rather impersonal.

Another problem which is particularly acute in less economically developed countries is the lack of a suitably skilled workforce. New factories may require trained machine operators – a position which may be unheard of in certain areas. Even though most countries' workforces will have skills suited to the local economy, retraining will often be required. Multinationals will need to provide this training, often not simply for specific jobs, but often educating locals

BRITISH JOBS AT THE MERCY OF THE MULTINATIONALS

On 21 March 2002, the last car manufactured at the General Motors car plant in Luton rolled off the production line, signalling the end of a century of production at the site. This happened just weeks after Ford finally closed its UK plant at Dagenham. Reaction to the closures criticised both the firms and the UK government. Trade unions argued that, since UK labour laws are less restrictive than in most other EU countries, multinationals needing to shed excess capacity in Europe will look to close their UK plants first. Has Britain become the victim of exploitation from powerful multinationals simply looking to take advantage of government incentives and weak labour laws? Or is the real reason – as argued by the employers – that the British government has put too many financial and regulatory burdens onto firms operating in Britain?

Source: Adapted from the *Guardian*

in the company's culture and objectives. Clearly, effective training may be made harder by language problems.

79.5 Problems multinationals bring to host countries

Many multinationals that set up production facilities in less economically developed countries are accused of operating sub-standard, outdated safety precautions. Often, safety regulations in these countries are not as tough as those in developed countries. As a result, multinationals can use older equipment and machinery, which is perhaps not so safe as that used in other parts of the world. The result may be higher levels of accidents and injuries. Since plants in less developed countries are far from the press and **pressure groups** in the multinationals' home countries, these problems may not be addressed.

An example of this occurred in 1985 in Bhopal, India. Poor safety precautions at Union Carbide's chemical plant were blamed for the deaths of many thousands of nearby residents when toxic gas escaped from the plant. It is interesting to note that despite short-term damage to the firm's reputation and share price, no long-term ill effects were felt by the multinational. It closed the factory and left. Local residents are still suffering the physical and psychological after effects.

If the multinational is operating in direct competition with local firms, it is possible that the local economy may be adversely affected. Multinationals have tremendous power and may be able to use this to force local competitors out of the market. Rupert Murdoch's TV empire has often been accused of exactly this, by using its huge spending power to buy up the rights to the most important sports or other popular programmes. Local business closures will result in local job losses. This would be especially damaging if the multinational's profits were sent back to its home country, rather than reinvested in the local economy.

Many multinationals set up production or mining facilities in less developed countries for the sole purpose of extracting valuable raw materials. The majority of the Earth's remaining **natural resources** are to be found in less developed countries. It is to these places that many multinationals are attracted, in order to secure their supply of all important materials. Although the resources mined are irreplaceable, many less developed countries are happy to allow multinationals to exploit their resources in return for the benefits provided. In the short term, both sides are content, but once resources have dried up the multinational can move on, whilst the host country is left richer but without resources.

The prevalence of Coca-Cola logos in many less economically developed parts of the world symbolise the concern that traditional, local cultures are being wiped out by the spread of multinational products. Some suggest that traditions should be preserved, untainted by imported cultures. This whole issue is a difficult one. The Coca-Cola Corporation is not forcing anyone to drink Coke. Multinationals argue that everyone has the freedom to choose.

ISSUES FOR **analysis**

The issue of exploitation is one which is relevant in many questions on multinationals. Particularly in a situation where a multinational is operating in less economically developed countries. Local workers may be paid very low wage rates. But are these rates low in comparison to the local standard of living? Early British and American economic growth was associated with very low wages and awful working conditions. If pressure groups are too effective at policing employment practices, perhaps the jobs will go anyway. Is that necessarily a good thing? The balance between fair trade and exploitation is a fine one. Whatever your opinion on any particular situation, you can be sure that there are two sides to the argument which need developing.

Workers in different cultures may be motivated by different things. A study by motivation researcher Don Elizur carried out in various parts of the world discovered that money is the major motivator in some countries whilst in other countries it was less important. Other factors such as good relations with co-workers and recognition for achievement were much more important than pay. This means that firms may need to use different management techniques in different countries in order to build a motivated workforce. Clearly, this research can be related directly to Maslow's hierachy of needs.

79.6 Multinationals
an evaluation

When considering the motives behind a host country's decision to encourage multinational investment, it is important to consider the government's objectives. Many governments in less economically developed countries are desperate for foreign currency to repay loans. They may be prepared to accept the damage to the environment and depletion of natural resources which may result from the activities of the multinational. Various campaigns are underway to encourage Western banks and governments to write off the debts of less developed countries which they may never be able to repay. If this gesture were made, local governments could make decisions about multinationals purely on the merits of the case.

In evaluation of questions on this topic it is important to remember who is in a position of power. Multinationals are huge organisations, as seen earlier in the unit – often larger, in terms of income, than whole countries. The resources available to these companies, both financial and managerial, give them great advantages in any kind of negotiation. For a prospective host seeking inward investment from a multinational, this power can be overwhelming. The incentives offered to multinationals will need to be sufficiently attractive to stop the multinational from choosing to invest elsewhere in the world. Despite all the possible negatives, most countries in the world are keen to experience the benefits brought by multinationals. Russia welcomed McDonald's just as China welcomed Unilever. The critics of multinationals may be overstating their case.

infrastructure – the economic fabric of the country, such as roads, railways, water and energy supplies.

intranet – an internal Internet, in other words computers which can be linked by telephone anywhere in the world, but only company employees have access.

less developed nations – countries with low wage levels and standards of living due to their lack of economic development.

natural resources – raw materials which can be grown, mined, extracted or caught, such as wheat, gold, oil or fish.

pressure groups – organisations formed to achieve a specific goal by lobbying government or by creating publicity favourable to their cause.

transfer pricing – a way multinationals can minimise their worldwide tax liabilities by transfering their profits from high-tax to low-tax countries.

AS Level Exercises

A. REVISION QUESTIONS
(30 marks; 60 minutes)

Read the unit, then answer:

1 a State four advantages of operating in several countries. *(4)*

  b Which of the four would be the most important for each of the following businesses? Explain your reasoning:
    i Rolls Royce Motors, if its management decided to open a factory overseas. *(3)*
    ii Cadbury's, if it wanted to open a factory in the Far East. *(3)*
    iii EIDOS, the British software firm behind Tomb Raider, considering setting up a software development site overseas. *(3)*

2 State five problems of operating in several countries. *(5)*

3 What is transfer pricing? *(3)*

4 How might a multinational seek to overcome language barriers experienced in internal communication? *(4)*

5 Outline the advantages of producing in the country in which you are selling. *(5)*

B. REVISION EXERCISES

B1 Data Response
In late 1997, Daewoo, the Korean multinational, launched a new car – the Leganza. It represents Daewoo's attempt to break into the 'upper-mid' saloon car market, providing a different set of attractions to those previously offered by the company to its European customers. Since it entered the UK market in the early 1990s, Daewoo's market share has grown considerably, mainly at the cheaper end of the market. The company has achieved success by offering efficient yet uninspiring cars with an innovative marketing strategy, based on a no-frills approach characterised by simple, flat rate prices and supermarket style showrooms. This was backed up by an advertising campaign using straplines such as:

'Daewoo – the biggest car manufacturer you've never heard of.'

In reality, most people are likely to own something produced by Daewoo. In addition to cars, its name is used as a brand for a wide range of different products, such as televisions and tape recorders. Furthermore it produces many different products under licence for other well-known brands – trainers for Nike and mobile phones for Nokia.

Daewoo is a truly multinational company, producing a wide range of different products in different countries. This fact is illustrated by the Leganza – a truly global product, which was road tested in countries as far apart as Canada, Sweden, Russia, Ecuador, Germany, Oman and the UK.

Questions *(30 marks; 35 minutes)*

1 Explain the term 'diversification'. *(3)*

2 One of the toughest jobs facing a multinational like Daewoo is breaking into a market whose culture is vastly different to their home market.
  a Why is this so hard to do? *(5)*
  b What methods are available to multinationals seeking to overcome these problems? *(6)*

3 Most of Daewoo's cars sold in Europe are manufactured in its factories in Poland and Hungary. Outline three advantages it may gain from this. *(6)*

4 In the late 1990s, the financial crisis which hit the Far East threatened Daewoo's success. Consider why it was in a better position to face the crisis than many of its local rivals in Korea. *(10)*

A Level Exercises

B2 Case Study

Brickell Group plc manufactures a wide range of electrical goods throughout the world. With production facilities in 18 different countries, it is a true multinational.

One of the firm's products, a food processor, is the current focus of much management attention. The food processor has sold fairly well in its standardised form throughout the developed world. Complex components are manufactured in Indonesia, while the shell and attachments of the processor are made in Hungary. Both plants ship their output to Brickell's new high-tech assembly plant in the Philippines.

The assembly process has been dogged by problems since the plant opened six months ago. Production engineers have tracked the problem to the processor shells they receive, which have been varying too much in size. The high-tech machinery is unable to cope with the inconsistent sizes.

A further issue of concern to the firm's accountants is how to achieve the highest possible profit for the firm from the food processors. The following table gives certain cost information on the food processors.

Country	Costs Incurred	Local Tax Rate
Indonesia	£5	25%
Hungary	£10	30%
Philippines	£20	10%

The firm sells the product for a factory gate price of £45 to distributors in all its markets, where average tax rates are 40%. The accountants at head office are trying to decide how much profit to declare in each location. They have a fair degree of flexibility, as long as the price charged by each plant covers the cost incurred there and the overall prices add up to less than the £45 customer selling price.

Questions *(50 marks; 60 minutes)*

1 Explain the business significance of the terms:
   a plc
   b standardised. *(10)*
2 How does the text illustrate the economies and diseconomies of scale experienced by many multinationals? *(10)*
3 Bearing in mind local tax rates, how would you maximise Brickell's overall post-tax profit per unit on the food processors? *(10)*
4 a Outline how and why Brickell uses transfer pricing. *(12)*
   b Is transfer pricing ethical? *(8)*

C. ESSAY QUESTIONS

1 A Japanese electrical goods manufacturer is considering building a new plant in France to serve the European market. Discuss the factors that may influence this decision.
2 Some industries are dominated by multinational organisations, while others see little or no multinational activity. What might be the reasons for this state of affairs?
3 The major problem associated with multinationals is the difficulty of coordinating the firm's activities. Discuss the steps that may be taken to improve organisational effectiveness for a multinational.

CHANGES IN OWNERSHIP

DEFINITION

Changes in business ownership are mainly due to mergers and takeovers. These can be known collectively as corporate integration. Mergers occur when two companies' directors and shareholders agree to come together under one board of directors. Takeovers occur when one firm buys a majority of the shares in another and therefore has full management control.

80.1 Introduction

Every time a company's shares are bought or sold on the Stock Exchange, there is a change in the ownership of that company. However, the significant changes occur when a majority of shares is bought by an individual or company. Any individual or organisation which owns 51% of a company's shares has effective control over that company. Any vote at the company's **annual general meeting** can be won with 51% of votes. To successfully take over a company, a firm must therefore acquire 51% of shares. Even without a majority of shares, a substantial stakeholding can bring effective control. This requires the major shareholder to persuade other shareholders to vote with him or her on major issues.

80.2 Why do firms merge with or take over other companies?

GROWTH

The fastest way for any firm to achieve significant growth is to merge with, or take over, another company. The motives behind the objective of growth may be based on any of the reasons outlined below. However, as a basic motive behind mergers and takeovers, growth is the overriding factor.

Cost savings are often used as a primary argument for **corporate integration**. It is suggested that **economies of scale** will arise from operating on a larger scale. If two businesses merge, output will increase. As a result, they are more likely to benefit from economies of scale, such as cheaper bulk purchasing of supplies.

DIVERSIFICATION

This means entering different markets in order to reduce dependence upon current products and customers. Diversification is a way of reducing the risk faced by a company. Selling a range of different products to different groups of consumers will mean that if any one product fails, sales of the other products should keep the business healthy. The simplest way to diversify is to merge with or take over another company. This saves time and money spent developing new products for markets in which the firm may have no expertise.

GO GOES TO EASYJET

The summer of 2002 saw the coming together of 2 of the 3 major players in the European low-cost airline market. EasyJet announced a merger deal with Go – the low-cost airline originally set up by British Airways. EasyJet – renowned for its bright orange aircraft and its larger-than-life founder, Stelios – will now be Europe's largest low-cost airline, taking over the position previously occupied by Ryanair.

The merger was generally welcomed by city analysts who accepted the logic in Easyjet eliminating a competitor. The deal would not be hampered by the problems of duplication many such deals face, as the two airlines shared very few routes before the deal. Instead, the merger sees the company able to cover a much greater proportion of European short-haul routes than had been possible before.

Job losses were not expected. Any cost savings from the deal were expected to come from the blending of the two firms' administrative and maintenance operations – saving money on equipment rather than people. Indeed, this merger is clearly motivated by the desire to remove a competitor rather than by any attempts to boost profitability through direct cost savings.

Business in

MARKET POWER

When two competitors in the same market merge, the combined business will have an increased level of power in the market. It may be possible that this increased power can be used to reduce the overall competitiveness within the market. If prices can be increased a little, then margins will increase and the market will become more profitable.

ASSET STRIPPING

This is the process of buying another company and then selling its assets in order to generate short-term cash flows. This is an unpopular process which can be used by large firms to increase their asset base and liquidity. Asset stripping is most likely where the target company's shares are undervalued. The asset stripper may believe the value of the firm's assets is greater than the purchase price of its shares. In which case it will be able to make a capital gain by buying the company and selling off its assets.

80.3 Types of business integration

There are four main types of merger or takeover (see Figure 80.1).

Figure 80.1 Vertical and horizontal integration

VERTICAL INTEGRATION

Vertical integration occurs when one firm takes over or merges with another at a different stage in the production process, but within the same industry.

Backward vertical integration occurs when a firm buys out a supplier. An example is the purchase of diamond mines in southern Africa by diamond dealer De Beers. The key benefit of a backward vertical takeover is security of supply.

Forward vertical integration means buying out a customer, such as brewery Whitbread's purchase of restaurant chain Beefeater. This guarantees outlets for your products.

The table on the following page explains the major advantages and disadvantages of backward and forward vertical integration for three important stakeholders: the company (and its shareholders), the workforce and the customers.

ASK BOOTS

In 1989, Boots decided to diversify. It stepped into the fast-growing DIY market by buying Ward White, the owner of the Payless chain of 91 stores. Payless sales had doubled in two years, profits had quadrupled. Boots would be able to use its financial muscle to help Payless expand. What could go wrong?

Then came a dramatic downturn in the demand for new housing, due to high interest rates. This pulled down the demand for DIY goods. The stage was set for a vicious price war. With Payless struggling, Boots came up with a bright idea: merge Payless (4th in the market) with WH Smith's Do It All chain (3rd in the market). This would create a strong rival for the market-leading B&Q and Texas chains. Unfortunately, putting together two weak businesses does not necessarily make one strong one. 'The merger was a disaster,' said Richard Perks of Verdict Research. The consumer was not sure what to expect in a Payless/Do It All store, so they stopped coming. The combined group's market share halved from 6.7% in 1990 to 3.4% in 1997.

In 1996 WH Smith had the sense to pull out, leaving Boots to try to clear up the mess. In the year to March 1997 a £6.7 million loss was made. With Boots in full control, 1998 saw an improvement to a £2.5 million profit. Yet, with B&Q making a 1998 profit of £161 million, Boots decided enough was enough. It would sell the Do It All business, despite having to write off the £400 million it had spent trying to make the business a success. No-one should ever assume that takeovers are easy. Ask Boots.

By late 2002, Boots had recovered sufficiently to think of more acquisitive activity. Having built up a pot of around £1 billion, the company was rumoured to be considering buying brands in the coughs, colds and pain relief sectors. The company seemed to have learnt from the DIY disaster to stick closer to home, in areas in which it has a strong record, reputation and expertise.

IN **Business**

	BACKWARD VERTICAL INTEGRATION	FORWARD VERTICAL INTEGRATION
Advantages to the company	• Closer links with suppliers aid new product development and give more control over the quality, quantity and timing of supplies • Absorbing the suppliers' profit margins may cut supply costs	• Control of competition in own retail outlets; prominent display of own brands • Firm put in direct contact with end users/consumers
Disadvantages to the company	• Supplier division may become complacent if there is no need to compete for customers • Costs might rise, therefore, and delivery and quality become slack	• Consumers may resent the dominance of one firm's products in retail outlets, causing sales to decline • Worries about image may obstruct the outlet, e.g. Levi Stores rarely offer discounted prices
Advantages to the workforce	• Secure customer for the suppliers may increase job security • Larger scale of the combined organisation may lead to enhanced benefits such as pension or career opportunities	• Increased control over the market may increase job security • Designers can now influence not only how the products look, but also how they are displayed
Disadvantages to the workforce	• Becoming part of a large firm may affect the sense of team morale built up at the supplier • Job losses may result from attempts to cut out duplication of support roles such as in personnel and accounting	• Staff in retail outlets may find themselves deskilled. Owner may dictate exactly what products to stock and how to display them. This would be demotivating
Advantages to the consumer	• Better coordination between company and supplier may lead to more innovative new product ideas • Ownership of the whole supply process may make the business more conscious of product and service quality	• With luxury products, customers like to see perfect displays and be served by expert staff, e.g. at perfume counters in department stores • Prices may fall if a large retail margin is absorbed by the supplier
Disadvantages to the consumer	• The firm's control over one supplier may in fact reduce the variety of goods available • Supplier complacency may lead to rising costs, passed on to customers as higher prices	• Increased power within the market could lead to price rises • If the outlet only supplies the parent company's products, consumer choice will be hit, as in brewery-owned clubs or pubs

HORIZONTAL INTEGRATION

Horizontal integration occurs when one firm buys out another in the same industry at the same stage of the supply chain, for example the 1998 merger between car manufacturers Daimler Benz and Chrysler. In effect, this means buying a competitor. In the UK, if the market share of the combined companies is greater than 25%, the Competition Commission is likely to investigate before the integration will be allowed.

Of the four types of takeover, the most common by far is horizontal integration with a competitor. Typical examples include:

• EasyJet taking over Go – a major rival
• The merger of Halifax and Bank of Scotland to form HBOS

• The merger between Glaxo Wellcome and SmithKline Beecham to form the world's largest drug company
• Coca-Cola taking over Orangina, a distinctive product with very strong distribution in France.

For the purchaser, there are three major attractions:

1 huge scope for cost cutting by eliminating duplication of sales force, distribution and marketing overheads and by improved capacity utilisation
2 opportunities for major economies of scale
3 reduction in competition should enable prices to be pushed up.

Of course, no purchaser states publicly that the plan is to push prices up. But if you owned four consecutive motorway service stations covering over 190 km of driving, would you not be tempted to charge a bit more?

As horizontal mergers have particular implications for competition, they are likely to be looked at by the Office of Fair Trading. If there is believed to be a threat to competition, the Competition Commission will be asked to investigate. The Competition Commission has the power to recommend that the Office of Fair Trading refuse to allow the integration, or to recommend changes before it can go through. For example, if Unilever (which produces Wall's ice-cream and much else) made a bid for Mars, the Competition Commission would probably let the takeover through, on the condition that the Mars ice-cream business was sold off.

CONGLOMERATE INTEGRATION

Conglomerate integration occurs when one firm buys out another with no clear connection to its own line of business. An example was the purchase of Tussaud's Limited, the company which runs Madame Tussaud's waxworks, by media company Pearson, the owner of the *Financial Times*. Conglomerate integration is likely to be prompted by the desire to diversify, but may be for purely financial motives such as asset stripping. Although the achievement of successful diversification helps to spread risk, research shows that conglomerate mergers are the ones least likely to succeed. This is largely because the managers of the purchasing company have, by definition, little knowledge of the marketplace of the company that has been bought. Why should a company specialising in air travel and music (Virgin) be good at running trains or a cosmetics business (Virgin Vie)?

80.4 Demergers

There has been growing scepticism about the benefits of mergers and takeovers. This has resulted in a growing trend in the past few years towards the **demerger**. This occurs when a company is split into two or more parts, either by selling off separate divisions or by floating them separately on the Stock Exchange. Demergers are often the result of unsuccessful takeovers. Once a firm has seen that the economies of scale it expected are not happening, it will seek to sell off the business it originally bought.

Another common situation leading to demergers is the desire of a company to reduce interest payments in times of economic downturn. Since many takeovers are financed heavily by borrowed capital, selling off recently acquired businesses will generate cash to pay back those loans.

Some firms, however, may simply decide to concentrate on core activities due to a change in their overall strategy. This might be caused by a change in economic circumstances or just because a new chief executive has been appointed. Having identified the core activities they will sell off others, even if they are profitable.

80.5 Management buy-outs

A **management buy-out** occurs when the management team of a company buys the company that it runs. The three most common situations in which management buy-outs occur are:

- The directors of a large firm decide to sell off a small section of the business. This may be done to raise cash, to get rid of a non-profitable section or to refocus the business on other areas.
- The owners of a family business may decide to sell their firm in order to pursue other interests or to retire. Instead of submitting their employees to unknown new owners, they may decide to offer the business to the existing management team.
- If a company runs out of cash it is taken over by a receiver whose job is to keep the firm going if possible. One way to raise money to pay off creditors and to keep the firm trading is to sell a part of the firm to the management team.

HOW DOES IT HAPPEN?

It is rare to find managers with enough cash to buy the firm. Usually, each member of the management team will be required to put in a substantial amount of his or her own money and this will be added to by a venture capitalist. The venture capitalist will provide finance, partly in return for a shareholding in the business and partly in the form of loans. This way, the managers will receive interest on their loan and, if the business is successful, they will receive dividends and possibly benefit from the firm being floated on the Stock Exchange.

DO THEY WORK?

Management buy-outs often lead to great success. Previously failing businesses can be turned round or profitable businesses can find increased profitability as a result of the change in ownership. The fundamental reason behind the success is the extra motivation of the management team. It is now personally responsible for the success or failure of the company it actually owns. Other, more specific advantages of management buy-outs include:

- Clear objectives – since managers no longer have to worry about what head office has to say, the firm can work towards its own objectives, providing a clearer sense of purpose for all employees.
- No need to make contributions towards paying head office overheads – this can lead to higher net profit margins.
- Decentralisation – the independent business no longer has to obtain approval for decisions from a distant head office. Therefore the speed and effectiveness of decision making will increase.
- Share ownership – employees may have been offered share ownership as part of the management buy-out. In this case, they are likely to be more motivated in their work.

Among the better-known management buy-out successes are Premier Brands (which makes Famous Names chocolate liqueurs, Cadbury's biscuits and drinking chocolate) and Denby Pottery.

PROBLEMS?

Not all management buy-outs are successful. When an unprofitable business has been sold to its management, the problems may be insurmountable. Management buy-outs can overcome unprofitability caused by a lack of motivation or by excessive contributions to head office overheads. However, if the business was unprofitable because its market had disappeared, there is little that can be done to overcome this problem. In cases such as these, the buy-out is likely to end in failure, meaning personal losses for the managers and a loss for the venture capitalist. It is also important to bear in mind that management buy-outs are usually saddled with a high level of gearing. Therefore they are vulnerable to changes in interest rates.

Among the better-known buy-outs that struggled are Magnet & Southern and MFI.

A POT OF GOLD?

Many management buy-outs last for less than 10 years. Some of these will fail, but some will be successful. So much so that the management can float the company on the Stock Exchange or sell its shares in a takeover. In these cases, the rewards received by the managers are usually substantial. When the management buy-out takes place, managers can only afford to invest tens of thousands of pounds. In return for this they receive an substantial shareholding in the company. If they cash in this shareholding by floating on the Stock Exchange, they will probably receive a sum measured in hundreds of thousands, if not millions, of pounds. Management buy-outs have created many millionaires.

It has been suggested that there is an ethical problem with management buy-outs. The rewards for a successful buy-out are substantial. They are, however, usually only available to the management. The consequences of failure are shared amongst the whole workforce. Employees may see their jobs disappear, jobs which may have been safer if the business had remained a part of a larger group of companies. The problem is that the downside is shared; the benefits may only be shared by a few. However, those involved in management buy-outs argue, with some justification, that they have taken the risk with their own capital, and should therefore be entitled to the rewards of success. In cases such as Denby, employees would have lost their jobs anyway if the management had not stepped in.

- The key theme for analysis when considering any question on mergers and takeovers is the identification of advantages and disadvantages. These are outlined briefly above, for each type of transaction. It is important to consider which advantages and disadvantages are likely to be relevant in the particular situation being considered. For example, a sugar producer which buys a soft drink manufacturer will not have any significant degree of control over the way its products are sold by retailers. In this case, one of the most significant advantages of forward integration disappears.

- Never forget that a merger or takeover will bring disadvantages as well as advantages. Research in America and Britain has shown consistently that the majority of takeovers fail to improve business performance. This is largely because managers anticipate the economies of scale from integration. However they overlook the diseconomies from problems such as communication and coordination.

- Another important analytical theme is the differing effects upon different stakeholder groups. Many questions will offer marks for analysing the effects on consumers, or the workforce, rather than simply focusing on the effects on the firm as a whole.

ARCADIA

Arcadia plc was a group of UK High Street clothing retailers, formed over many years as a result of a series of mergers and takeovers. In the summer of 2002, Philip Green, the owner of BHS, launched a successful takeover bid for Arcadia, worth some £770 million.

What is significant is that as a result of the takeover, Arcadia's stores became part of a private limited company. Private ownership means that there is no short-term pressure to ensure a buoyant share price. This means that dividends can be postponed if major investment is necessary. Even more fundamentally, it could give the firm a clearer sense of purpose. The sole aim now will be to do what Philip Green wants done. No longer will separate groups of private and institutional shareholders need to be kept happy.

IN Business

Synergy is a word commonly used when explaining why mergers or takeovers occur. It means that combining the two businesses will produce one enterprise which is more powerful and efficient than the two firms put together. Synergy occurs when the whole is greater than the sum of the parts, i.e. when 2 + 2 = 5. Synergies are anticipated in takeovers largely because the combined businesses will be in a better position to take advantage of economies of scale. However, what managers underestimate is the fact that a larger business is more likely to be affected by diseconomies of scale.

A further explanation for the problems firms may encounter after a merger or takeover is resistance to change. It has been suggested that it is human nature to oppose change. Certainly any significant change within a business is likely to disturb many of the employees. They naturally feel concerned that their jobs may be in danger, or they may be worried that the nature of their job will change. Although hard to identify, the effect of change on most firms is unsettling, at least in the short term.

The other key issue raised in this unit is that of diversification. Traditionally, diversification was perceived as a good thing. Recent management theorists such as Tom Peters and Bob Waterman have raised serious doubts. In many cases, raising sufficient cash to finance a takeover puts a serious strain on the financial position of the whole business. Meanwhile, the management of the original company may know little about the industry within which the new business operates. This means that those making major strategic decisions may be doing so from a position of ignorance. The advice in recent years has been to 'stick to the knitting', in other words, concentrate on doing what you do best. This does not mean that diversification cannot occur. It does, however, suggest that firms should attempt partial diversification. In other words, look for targets in industries which are related to their own. Whitbread's diversification into leisure and health clubs is a good example of this.

KEY terms

annual general meeting – the once yearly meeting at which shareholders have the opportunity to question the chairperson and to vote new directors to the board.

corporate integration – bringing together two or more companies to form one larger one.

demerger – this occurs when a firm is split into two or more different companies.

economies of scale – the factors that cause average costs to be lower in large-scale operations than small ones.

management buy-in (MBI) – this occurs when a group of managers from outside the business buy out the shareholders, thus gaining ownership and control. Management buy-ins are less common than management buy-outs.

management buy-out (MBO) – a specialised form of takeover where the managers of a business buy out the shareholders, thereby buying ownership and control of the firm.

synergy – this occurs when the whole is greater than the sum of the parts (2 + 2 = 5). It is often the reason given for mergers or takeovers occurring.

A Level Exercises

A. REVISION QUESTIONS

(20 marks; 50 minutes)

Read the unit, then answer:

1 What is horizontal integration? (2)
2 For what reasons might a manufacturer take over one of its suppliers? (4)
3 How might a management buy-out be financed? (2)
4 Why might a firm decide to carry out a demerger? (3)
5 Why are management buy-outs so often successful? (3)
6 Why might diversification be a bad idea for a growing firm? (3)
7 Explain the meaning of the word 'synergy'. (3)

B. REVISION EXERCISES

B1 Data Response

The chart opposite shows the effects of a number of recent mergers on the value of shares in the new combined company. Those mergers described as 'value enhancing' are those where the total stockmarket value of the newly merged business has grown, relative to the combined value of the two separate companies.

The chart is the result of research by US investment bankers JP Morgan. Their research discovered that the most successful mergers were those that combined firms of roughly the same size. Takeovers and mergers between companies of differing sizes are less likely to be successful. Their research suggests that over two-thirds of 'mergers of equals' added shareholder value, whilst a still impressive 56% of all merger and takeover deals added shareholder value. Given the wave of merger activity which characterised the latter part of the 1990s, this research provides much needed justification for this frenzy of activity.

Other findings from the research indicated that:

- Cross-border deals within the EU were least likely to be beneficial to shareholders.
- Most successful deals are those with a clear strategic purpose.
- Many unsuccessful deals are characterised by little specific information being made available at the time of the deal and a general unwillingness of managements to release any details of the proposed new arrangements following the deal.
- The introduction of the European single currency suggests that the largest firms in Europe will become the centre of attention with medium-sized firms, typically national market leaders, being overlooked by investors.

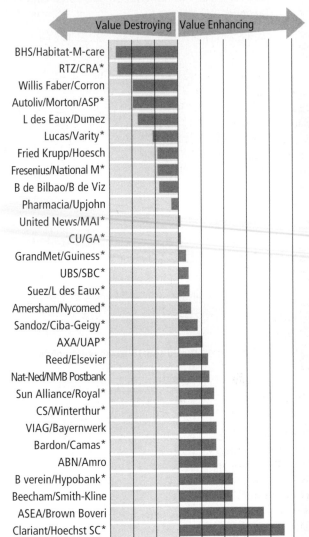

*Less than three years' data
Source: JP Morgan: European mergers-of-equals, July 10, 1998

Questions
(30 marks; 35 minutes)

1 How is total stock market value measured? (4)
2 Discuss the validity of the final statement, about mergers after the single currency. (10)
3 Use examples to illustrate what a 'clear strategic purpose' might be. (7)
4 Using a recently announced merger deal as an example, comment upon the likelihood of success, using the data from the article as your guide. (9)

B2 Case Study

Ford Aims For The Top With $6.5bn Volvo Cars Takeover

On the 28 January 1999, Ford announced its £4 billion takeover of the car division Volvo. The deal will increase Ford's market share in the global car market to 14% and may well lead to further mergers and takeovers in the market. Jacques Nasser, Ford Chief Executive, said that the group aimed to produce around 700,000 luxury vehicles next year, ultimately seeking to reach an output of 1,000,000. This output will be made up from Ford's stable of luxury marques – Jaguar, Lincoln and now Volvo. Mr Nasser also suggested that Ford were still looking to make further acquisitions.

Ford is rumoured to have been in talks with Nissan and BMW (owner of the Rover and Rolls-Royce brands). Fiat has been interested in purchasing the Volvo group, however, they were not interested in buying Volvo's car division separately. Leif Johannson, Volvo's Chief Executive, said that Volvo's relatively small volumes meant that it lacked the kind of resources needed to fund the development of future models, invest in new technology or support its dealer network.

Ford's chairman, Bill Ford, justified the deal by saying that he expected increased sales and economies of scale in purchasing, engineering, platform design and distribution. Ford indicated that there would be no plant closures as a result of the deal.

Jacques Nasser also suggested that there was 'huge potential' for the Volvo brand. The product range could be expanded and a global presence achieved. This is based upon the fact that 60% of Volvo's sales are made in Europe and there is virtually no overlap between Ford models and the Volvo range. Nasser also pledged that Volvo would continue to be managed from Gothenburg and research and development activity would continue to be based in Sweden. He added that 'Ford would respect and build on the traditional strengths of the Volvo brand – safety, care for the environment and family-oriented design'.

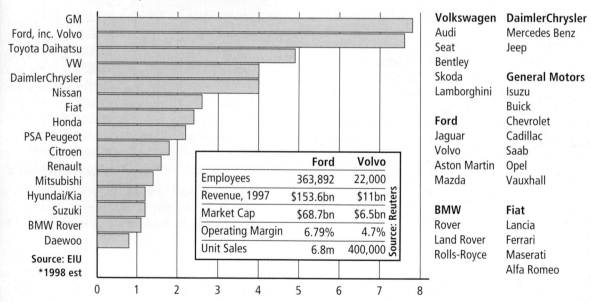

World top 15 car makers, millions*

Source: EIU
*1998 est

	Ford	Volvo
Employees	363,892	22,000
Revenue, 1997	$153.6bn	$11bn
Market Cap	$68.7bn	$6.5bn
Operating Margin	6.79%	4.7%
Unit Sales	6.8m	400,000

Source: Reuters

Volkswagen	DaimlerChrysler
Audi	Mercedes Benz
Seat	Jeep
Bentley	
Skoda	**General Motors**
Lamborghini	Isuzu
	Buick
Ford	Chevrolet
Jaguar	Cadillac
Volvo	Saab
Aston Martin	Opel
Mazda	Vauxhall
BMW	**Fiat**
Rover	Lancia
Land Rover	Ferrari
Rolls-Royce	Maserati
	Alfa Romeo

Questions   (40 marks; 60 minutes)

1 a How would you classify this deal in terms of forwards, backwards or horizontal integration? Explain your answer.   (2)
  b What might Ford hope to gain from its purchase of Volvo cars?   (8)
2 a Using the figures in the table, calculate the average revenue per car received by Ford and Volvo in 1997. (4)
  b Suggest possible explanations for the difference.   (6)
3 Evaluate how Volvo employees may feel about the takeover.   (10)
4 The article speaks about 'no overlap' between the two firms' product ranges. What does this mean and what are the advantages and disadvantages of this to Ford?   (10)

C. ESSAY QUESTIONS

1 Discuss the people management problems that may arise within a firm which has been taken over.
2 'The high level of takeover activity in the UK leads to short-termism'. Explain why this is so and discuss the implications for UK firms.
3 Synergy is often quoted as the reason for mergers and takeovers.
  a What is synergy?
  b To what extent is synergy a myth?

CORPORATE AIMS, MISSION AND GOALS

81.1 Corporate aims and goals

Winning teams share a collective view of what it means to be successful in the long term. For a sports team the aim is simple, to finish first. Establishing aims for an organisation is more difficult. Yet it is equally important if sustained success is to be achieved. Corporate aims help build team spirit, encouraging commitment to the organisation and cooperation within it.

One of the stated aims of the McDonald's fast-food chain is to provide 'friendly service in a relaxed, safe, and consistent restaurant environment'. The success of the organisation depends upon turning this aim into practice. In order for this to be achieved employees must understand and share the aim. When a customer enters a McDonald's restaurant anywhere in the world they know what to expect. The organisation has the ability to reproduce the same 'relaxed, safe and consistent' atmosphere with different staff, in different locations. This has built the company's reputation. This corporate aim is effective because it recognises what lies at the heart of the organisation's success.

Many businesses do not write down their aims or even spend time trying to define them. This is particularly true of small organisations where employees know each other and understand their shared purpose. Staff in a small firm may work together to achieve a common vision with a commitment that may not exist in a large firm which sets out its aims in writing.

Whether stated or unstated, corporate aims act as a basis upon which to form goals or objectives for the organisation. These are the intermediate targets which must be achieved if the aims are to be realised. The success or failure of each individual decision within the firm can be judged by the extent to which it meets the business objectives. This allows the delegation of authority within the organisation, while at the same time maintaining coordination.

81.2 Turning corporate aims into a mission statement

A mission statement is an attempt to put corporate aims into words. The London night club *The Ministry of Sound* states as its mission the desire to build 'a global entertainment business based on a strong aspirational brand, respected for its creativity and quality'. Employees are more likely to be motivated by a mission statement of this kind, which identifies positive characteristics such as 'creativity and quality', rather than by the desire to maximise profit.

To develop a strong mission statement it is necessary to link each of the four elements of the mission model so they reinforce each other (see Figure 81.1).

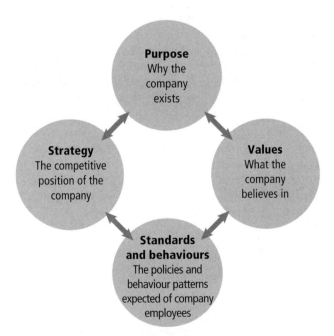

Figure 81.1 The mission model (After Campbell, Devine and Young, 1990)

Mission statements which attempt to establish purpose:

- *The Body Shop – 'Tirelessly work to narrow the gap between principle and practice, whilst making fun, passion and care part of our daily lives'*

- *Coca-Cola – 'Our mission is to get more people to drink Coke than water'*

- *Pret A Manger – 'Our mission is to sell handmade extremely fresh food …'*

- *Unilever – 'Raise the quality of life'*

- *James Dyson – 'Long-term business success based on newly invented, innovatively designed products'*

- *Conservative Party – 'Our mission is to create the greatest volunteer party in the Western democratic world'*

81.3 Purpose

The purpose outlined in the mission statement should be the ultimate reason for the organisation's existence. It provides employees with a justification for their work.

It is likely that a mission statement will identify one or several **stakeholders** in whose interests the business is said to be run. Stakeholders in a business are individuals or groups who have an interest in, and are affected by, the way in which the organisation is operated.

An organisation's mission statement should establish which stakeholder needs will be identified and considered when strategic policy is developed. In order to motivate employees, firms may choose to consider a range of stakeholders rather than emphasising only shareholder value. However, balancing the interests of stakeholders may be made more difficult because the aims of some of these groups may conflict. For example, a new production technique may increase profits to shareholders but pollute the local environment to the disadvantage of the community. Alternatively, efficiency savings which cut costs may allow consumer price cuts but cause job losses for employees. The impact of the mission statement will tend to be most forceful when the purpose identified for the organisation rises above the needs of one single group and recognises a number of stakeholder interests.

81.4 Values

The values of an organisation reflect the most commonly held beliefs and assumptions among employees. In any workplace there will be an accepted view of 'the way we do things around here'. This unwritten code is called the culture of the business. It will influence people's attitudes, their approach to management and how they make decisions.

Business IN

— MEETING STAKEHOLDER NEEDS AT HEATHROW AIRPORT

The mission statement of Heathrow Airport clearly identifies the local community as a stakeholder in its business. The airport says that one of its aims is to be 'a good neighbour, recognising the needs of the community and the environment'.

The airport has appointed a management team with an annual budget of £4.5 million specifically to deal with environmental issues. A range of environmental targets have been established. The local community receives an annual written report, with an account of the progress towards meeting these goals.

An example of this mission statement in practice is the approach adopted towards noise control. The airport has a nine-point action plan to deal with noise pollution. In the period the programme has been in place, £200,000 has been raised to finance local community projects by fining aircraft which break the noise regulations. In addition, 7,000 local homes have been fitted with noise insulation.

This programme of action to improve the local environment shows how a commitment made in a mission statement can be put into practice.

An organisation's mission statement provides an opportunity to shape this **business culture**. The challenge is to develop a set of values which employees can feel proud of. It should also motivate them to work towards the organisation's objectives. This may be difficult to achieve, particularly in large companies where each different department of the firm may have its own culture. In this case there may be no dominant corporate culture.

THE SOURCES OF BUSINESS CULTURE

If a mission statement is to influence business culture then it must impact on the sources which shape it. These include:

- Company routines – the way everyday decisions and tasks are undertaken.
- Formal controls – the rules and procedures which govern employee actions.
- Organisation structure – the way management is organised both vertically (e.g. by function) and horizontally (i.e. layers of hierarchy).

- Power structure – the interrelationships between the individuals or groups who take decisions about how the organisation's resources will be used.
- Symbols – the emblems which represent the organisation's culture, such as the form of language used, or signs of status like pay or size and location of office.
- Rituals and myths – the patterns of behaviour which have become formalised in the everyday life of the organisation and the stories which are told of the organisation's past.

ATTITUDES AND BUSINESS CULTURE

When an organisation develops its mission statement, its business culture is likely to be influential. A company with a hard-nosed, results oriented culture such as Dixons (electrical stores) will focus on shareholders, not stakeholders. For The Body Shop, the softer, less profit-focused culture will lead to a more socially based mission statement. When analysing business culture for the purposes of developing a mission statement, it is useful to consider the organisation's approach to a series of key issues.

Attitude towards risk when making decisions: In some firms risk taking is encouraged. Failure is tolerated in order that large gains can be achieved on those projects which succeed. The emphasis will be on maximising the possible return on each investment, rather than minimising potential losses. This type of culture might be described as 'entrepreneurial' and is often associated with new businesses in the early years of their development.

The opposite approach is to discourage risk taking within the organisation. A cautious, or 'risk averse', business culture will penalise a manager who introduces an unsuccessful project. Individuals in organisations of this type will fear failure and seek to reduce the possibility of it occurring. Exciting projects will be turned down because they involve an element of uncertainty. As businesses mature, they may develop in this way and become excessively bureaucratic. They move towards a culture of caution.

Maximise the benefits of potential success	Minimise the potential costs of failure
Entrepreneurial business culture	Cautious business culture

Direction of movement as business matures

Figure 81.2 Business culture and decision making

Business IN

571

UNIT 81 | CORPORATE AIMS, MISSION AND GOALS

Attitude towards reward distribution within the organisation: In some businesses a careful line is drawn between management and workforce. Each group is seen as competing with the other for a share of the value a company adds to its resources. The shop floor employees pressure management for higher wages and better working conditions. Managers seek to keep wages down in order to control costs. A 'them and us' business culture develops in which the difference in pay between the most senior managers in the organisation and the rest of the employees becomes very large. The high earners are sometimes described as 'fat cats'. Their income is seen to be the result of the hard work of others. However, these individuals argue that in order to attract top managerial talent a high salary must be paid. Therefore their income is justified. As a business matures and becomes more bureaucratic the division between those in senior positions and the rest of the employees is likely to grow larger.

In contrast, many organisations try to remove the barriers between management and shop-floor workers. These businesses put great emphasis on teamwork and see equal treatment of all employees as a way of encouraging this. The difference in payment between those at the top of the organisation and those at the bottom is monitored and not allowed to grow beyond justifiable limits. All employees share common facilities, such as canteens and may even wear similar uniforms. Small businesses may not generate enough income for this divide to be a major issue and managers are likely to know every member of the

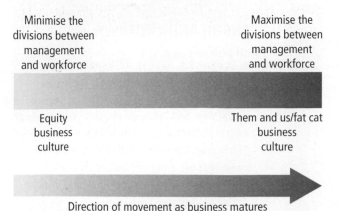

Minimise the divisions between management and workforce

Maximise the divisions between management and workforce

Equity business culture

Them and us/fat cat business culture

Direction of movement as business matures

Figure 81.3 Business culture and reward distribution

workforce personally. A business culture based on 'equity' is more likely in small firms. However, some large companies may deliberately try to develop a culture of this type. An example is the Nissan plant at Sunderland.

TYPES OF BUSINESS CULTURE

In his book *Gods of Management*, Charles Handy developed four ways of classifying business culture. These can be used to provide a more formal analysis of an organisation's values when developing its mission statement.

Power cultures: Power cultures are found in organisations in which there is one, or a small group of, power holders. Pleasing the boss can become the driving force behind the daily actions of staff. There are likely to be few rules or procedures and most communication will be by personal contact. This encourages flexibility amongst employees. Decision making is not limited by any code of practice. This can result in questionable, perhaps unethical, actions being taken in the attempt to please the boss.

Role cultures: Role cultures are found in established organisations which have developed a lot of formal rules as they have grown. Power depends on the position an individual holds in the business, rather than the qualities of the person themselves. All employees are expected to conform to rules and procedures and promotion follows a predictable pattern. This culture is bureaucratic, cautious and focused on the avoidance of mistakes. It may be appropriate when the competitive environment is stable, for example in industries with long product life cycles. However, if the pace of change becomes more rapid, staff will struggle to adapt to new market conditions.

Power

Power flows down from the top of the organisation

Figure 81.4 Role culture

Task cultures: Task cultures have no single power source. Senior managers allocate projects to teams of employees made up of representatives from different functional departments. Each group is formed for the purpose of a single undertaking and is then disbanded. Power within the team lies in the expertise of each individual and is not dependent on status or role. This culture can be effective in dealing with rapidly changing competitive environments because it is flexible, for example in markets with short product life cycles. However, project teams may develop their own objectives independent of the firm.

Person cultures: Person cultures are developed when individuals with similar training and background form groups to enhance their expertise and share knowledge. This type of culture is most often found within functional departments of large complex organisations, or amongst professionals such as lawyers or accountants.

One of the principal reasons for introducing a mission statement is the desire to provide a common purpose amongst employees. This should be more important than individual or departmental needs. If this can be achieved, a strong corporate culture will be developed which matches both the purpose established for the organisation and its strategic approach.

81.5 Behaviour standards

Many mission statements fail to achieve any impact on company performance. This is because they do not provide a clear signal as to how the purpose, values and strategy should guide employee actions. A mission statement is of no value if it does not affect staff actions and decisions.

IBM's mission statement establishes that all managers should operate an 'open door policy'. This means every employee can raise an important issue with management, at any time. The responsibility is placed on individuals to decide when a problem is important enough to demand the time of a senior manager. It encourages open communication and should mean difficulties are identified before they develop into a crisis. In this case the mission statement establishes a process which reflects the values the organisation wishes to promote.

One criticism often made of mission statements is that they contain a set of idealistic values which are only intended to promote the company with the public. They have no meaning in practice. They are part of a public relations strategy. This view has arisen because of the failure of many mission statements to show how the fine ideals are to be put into practice. The missing link is to identify the standards of behaviour expected from employees which symbolise the purpose, strategy and values of the organisation. Without this fourth element of the mission model in place, the other three elements will have little effect.

81.6 Developing a mission statement

A mission statement should be more than a simple description of managerial values or strategy. To develop a successful one, it is necessary to involve employees and perhaps other stakeholder groups. By extending participation beyond management the resulting document is more likely to be accepted by the workforce and affect day-to-day behaviour.

If all staff are involved in preparing (and agree with the outcome of) a mission statement focusing upon the business culture, the result will be a statement of shared values. This can provide agreement about what the business stands for and is trying to achieve. For example, in a clothing retailer, is the purpose to maximise sales, or to serve the customer in the best way possible? The issues involved can be looked at by considering how the firm would like staff to answer the following question:

'If a woman tries on, and appears to like, a dress which looks ill-fitting at the back, should you step in to point this out?'

If the business culture is strong, all staff should (in theory) answer in the same way. The sales-driven staff, perhaps operating in a business with a power culture, might all say no. The risk of losing the sale would be too great. In another business with a longer term focus on the customer, staff should say yes. And do so in practice. Note that this is not necessarily a bad business move. Today a customer may go home having spent nothing. Confident in the honesty of the staff, surely she will be back, and perhaps will tell others.

In addition to discussing values, staff may also be invited to discuss the strategy itself. If the finished document concentrates on strategy, the result will be employees working together to develop a plan for the future in which they share ownership. The strongest mission statements will develop a balance between strategy and values.

81.7 Content of a mission statement

The length and content of a mission statement can vary considerably. Many companies publish a one page summary or even try to capture the meaning of the statement in a single phrase. Other firms prepare extensive documents considering the purpose, strategy and values of the organisation in detail. It is important the statement should be memorable if it is to affect the behaviour of individuals throughout the company. This suggests that to be effective it should be brief.

The results of a research survey of 135 mission statements is presented below. It provides some indication of the content included by organisations.

Content of mission statements

		INCLUDED	NOT INCLUDED
1	Financial objectives	54%	46%
2	Non-financial objectives	92%	8%
3	Values and beliefs	71%	29%
4	Definition of success	65%	35%
5	Number one priority	95%	5%
6	Specific product definition	75%	25%
7	Specific market definition	67%	33%
8	Basis of competition	89%	11%
9	Number of stakeholders mentioned:	0	10%
		1	39%
		2	15%
		3	24%
		>3	12%
10	Four most commonly named stakeholders: customer employees shareholders community		

Sources: Adapted from Baetz and Bart. Reprinted from *The Journal of Long Range Planning*, Volume 29, Number 4, 'Developing mission statements which work', pp 526–533, 1996, with permission of Elsevier Science.

81.8 Criticisms of mission statements

The most widespread criticism of the idea of expressing corporate aims in the form of a mission statement is that it has no purpose other than to gain publicity. It is common for quite different firms to have what appear to be very similar mission statements. This suggests that the time and effort which goes into preparing these documents could be used more effectively elsewhere in the business.

Even when the statement sets out the organisation's purpose, strategy and values, many firms fail to overcome the difficulties involved in implementing these ideas. This may be due to failure to consider how they

Figure 81.5 Four types of mission (After Baetz and Bart, 1996)

are put into practice. Or because managers only pay lip service to value statements. In practice, they may only praise actions which help to meet sales or profit targets. Mission statements are also much harder to develop in a diversified organisation which competes in a range of unrelated markets.

Research suggests that as many as 86% of organisations now have a mission statement. The number which actually affect the way the business is run is substantially smaller.

In order to analyse the aims of an organisation there are a number of key issues which should be considered. These include:

- Are employees aware of what the organisation is trying to achieve? Is it necessary to write down these aims? Or is an understanding of the purpose of the business embedded so deeply in individuals that it influences their actions without them realising?
- Can the aims which have been established realistically be achieved?
- To what extent have employees, and perhaps other stakeholders, been involved in establishing the organisation's aims?
- Are the aims of the organisation reflected in its culture? For example, what is the underlying attitude towards risk taking, sharing information and evenly distributing rewards in the firm?
- To what extent do the goals which have been set reflect the common aim of the business and therefore act to coordinate the action of all employees?
- Are the aims of the organisation formally written down in a mission statement? If they are, to what extent are values promoted which will help to motivate individuals in their work?

The aims of an organisation need not be formally written down to be effective. The most important fact is that employees know what the business is striving to achieve and share this vision. In successful firms the workforce will often understand instinctively the direction in which the organisation is moving and their own role within it. In which case it is not necessary to formally state aims in a mission statement.

The culture of the business is really the key factor at work. If the organisation's formal aims are in conflict with how people behave and the values that underlie their actions, then they will have no genuine impact. Stating what the business is trying to achieve is only of value if it influences the culture of the organisation. This is true if the aims are written down formally as a mission statement, or if they are not.

Developing a clear aim for the organisation is only the first step in moving the business forward. A set of goals must be created which guide the actions of employees step by step. Aims cannot therefore be viewed in isolation, it is also necessary to consider the objectives and strategic policy of the business before evaluating their impact on competitive success.

business culture – the culture of a business is a set of rules, usually unwritten, which govern the way employees behave. These are not formal procedures, but a set of practices which grow up over time and represent 'the way we do things around here'.

person culture – an organisation in which employees with similar training and background form groups to enhance their expertise and share knowledge. This culture is often associated with professionals such as doctors.

power culture – an organisation in which one person, or a small group, make all the decisions and control access to key resources. Decision making will be quick allowing a swift response to changing market conditions.

role culture – an organisation with well-defined, formal rules governing employee actions. Each job in the business will have certain powers associated with it regardless of the ability of the individual undertaking it at a particular point in time.

stakeholders – groups with a direct interest in the way an organisation is performing and the action it takes. Examples include the firm's employees, shareholders, customers, suppliers and the local community.

task culture – an organisation in which power is based upon the knowledge and skills which an individual demonstrates. The job title which an employee holds is less important than the contribution he or she can make to achieving a specific objective.

A Level Exercises

A. REVISION QUESTIONS
(30 marks; 60 minutes)

Read the unit, then answer:

1 Why might a formal statement of aims be unnecessary in a small business with a limited number of employees? *(3)*

2 **a** Explain the link between aims and goals. *(3)*
   b How do they combine to act in a way which allows authority to be delegated in a large organisation? *(4)*

3 **a** What is the purpose of a mission statement? *(3)*
   b Identify the four elements which make up the 'mission model'. *(4)*

4 How may the interests of the different stakeholders in a business conflict? *(3)*

5 **a** Outline two types of business culture. *(4)*
   b Give an example of an organisation which might be expected to fall into either category. *(2)*

6 Why are mission statements often criticised for being ineffective in practice? *(4)*

B. REVISION QUESTIONS

B1 Data Response
In 1994, a 30-year-old New Yorker called Jeff Bezos read about the Internet. He moved to California and in a year had set up an Internet bookshop. When orders came in, he packed and posted the books from his garage. By February 1999 he employed 1,600 people and his shares were worth $2,500 million. Jeff Bezos is the founder and 40% shareholder in Amazon.com, the world's biggest Internet bookshop.

What are the aims that helped guide him to become one of the first Internet billionaires? His workforce mission is to 'Change the world in an important and fundamental way. Our motto is: Work hard, have fun, make history.'

The aim in relation to customers is to '…provide the best customer experience… That means we have to have the biggest selection! The easiest to use website! The lowest prices! And the best purchase decision information!'

Asked about his huge wealth, Bezos replied: 'I don't think it matters much. The biggest change is that I don't have to look at menu prices any more.'

Questions *(30 marks; 35 minutes)*

1 Distinguish between aims and mission with reference to this case. *(6)*

2 Do you consider that Mr Bezos was successful because of his aims, or that his success allowed him to adopt such aims? Explain your answer. *(10)*

3 What evidence is there in the text that business people are not only motivated by money. *(6)*

4 Outline four factors that might lead to a change in Amazon.com's aims in future. *(8)*

B2 Case Study

Creating a Sense of Mission at Hartson

Christine had a feeling she was saying the wrong thing even as she opened her mouth, but she was tired of hearing the same old phrase repeated over and over again. 'Everybody knows what our mission statement is. If you go down on the shop-floor now and stop anyone they will tell you … *"We put the customer first in everything we do – Hartson the last word in top quality machine tools across the world"*. But does anybody actually take any notice of it? I don't think it has any impact at all on the way people act.'

Hillary, the managing director, smiled. 'I think you have probably been here for such a long time now that you just take our business culture for granted. You know the pride most of our workforce take in fulfilling their roles in the company. Our mission statement reminds them of what we are trying to achieve in a simple and effective way. I like the phrase; it shows we know what business we are operating in, and that we aim to compete by differentiating our product. Every employee can take real satisfaction in thinking they work for a British business, that makes high quality products, and wants everyone around the world to know about it.'

Christine responded: 'When we spent all that time developing a mission statement we intended a lot more by the phrase *"we put the customer first"*. We had just introduced TQM and everybody on the line was meant to see themselves as the customer of the previous workstation. Our whole operation was going to consist of a chain of internal producers and consumers providing instant feedback to each other in order to maximise quality. Nobody thinks that is what the mission statement is about now. The shop-floor workers and supervisors still regard quality as an issue of sorting out defects and making sure they don't reach the customer, rather than ensuring there are no mistakes in the first place. The mission statement has not helped us get any closer to achieving our main aim of maximising profits by differentiating our product based on high quality.'

Hillary looked disapprovingly: 'Christine, surely you know a mission statement is vital to any successful business nowadays.'

Questions   *(40 marks; 60 minutes)*

1 Analyse Hartson's mission statement, considering the extent to which it fulfils each of the four requirements which are set out by the 'mission model'.   *(8)*
2 What extra information would you advise the Hartson managers to gather if they wish to find out the degree to which employee behaviour has been influenced by the mission statement?   *(6)*
3 To what extent does the Hartson mission statement reflect the organisation's principal aim?   *(8)*
4 Suggest a sequence of objectives which the management of Hartson might set in order to achieve the aim of maximising profits by differentiating products based on high quality.   *(8)*
5 Evaluate Christine's argument that mission statements are ineffective in achieving business aims. *(10)*

C. ESSAY QUESTIONS

1 If a newly appointed chief executive officer announced on appointment a determination to 'change the culture of the organisation', what effects might this have, and how might this process be undertaken?
2 'Ultimately the businesses that win are those where all the people have the same aim and give freely in their commitment to it.'

John Harvey-Jones, former Chairman of ICI

How might a business leader achieve this?

CORPORATE OBJECTIVES AND STRATEGY

DEFINITION

Corporate objectives are the goals that the whole organisation is trying to achieve. The corporate aims, which are often set out in a mission statement, form the basis upon which these targets are developed.

Corporate strategy is the organisation's plan of action which, when implemented, will lead to the achievement of the corporate objectives. Strategy cannot therefore be considered before the firm's goals are clearly established.

82.1 Corporate objectives

The larger the group, the more difficult it is to coordinate its actions towards a common goal. When a business is small its manager has personal contact with every employee. The long-term direction of the firm will be communicated clearly from day to day. Motivating the workforce to act together will be an easier task than in a large company. Objectives will be understood informally rather than written down.

As the firm grows the job of coordinating the actions of every employee becomes harder. A mission statement may be needed to provide a shared vision of the company's future. This may be needed to motivate the workforce. It is also the basis for developing **corporate objectives**. These represent the goals of the whole enterprise. These can take any form, but a number of targets are widely adopted:

Maximising the amount of profit earned by the organisation: This is usually regarded as the primary objective of any business in the private sector. In practice, profit maximisation is usually the principal target only when the firm's survival is threatened in the *short run*. It will govern decision making until the point at which the financial health of the organisation is restored. In the *long run*, if a business is functioning efficiently and healthily, alternative objectives will be of more importance such as growth or diversifi-cation.

In large public limited companies the owners of the firm (the shareholders) are not the decision makers (the management). A board of directors is elected to run the company on behalf of the shareholders. This group may develop aims for the business which recognise a wider group of stakeholders than just owners. As a result, the firm may not set profit maximisation as its key goal, even in the short run.

Maximising shareholder wealth: This is increasingly presented by the board of directors of large companies as the modern equivalent of profit maximisation. Share prices reflect the present value of the dividends the company is expected to pay out in the future. As a

GOING FOR GROWTH

Most small firms try to avoid tackling big firms head on. Yet James Lambert, boss of Richmond Foods, wants to take on and beat Unilever, a business 1,000 times its size. Unilever is a multinational giant, with a dominant share of the UK ice cream market (it owns Wall's and Ben & Jerry's).

Richmond Foods owns the small brand 'Treats', and makes organic ice cream for Marks & Spencer. In October 2001, it paid £10 million to buy the loss-making Nestlé ice cream business. This included brands such as Fab, Zoom and Mivvi, plus the Nestlé confectionery ice cream brands, e.g. Rolo, Fruit Pastilles and Smarties. Now Richmond Foods has concentrated production at its home factory in Richmond, Yorkshire. This has become the biggest ice cream factory in Europe. With economies of scale and the indirect support of Nestlé's substantial advertising budgets for Smarties and other chocolate brands, Richmond hopes to compete with Unilever. Of course, with its financial muscle, Unilever could push Richmond out of business through unfair competition such as predatory pricing, but James Lambert is confident that this will not happen. His is a very bold strategy based upon a clear objective of growth.

result this objective means taking actions which maximise the price of the organisation's shares on the stock market.

Growth in the size of the firm: The managers of a business may choose to take decisions with the objective of making the organisation larger. The motivation behind this goal could be the natural desire to see the business achieve its full potential. It may also help defend the firm from hostile takeover bids. If your firm is the biggest, who could be big enough to take you over?

Diversification to spread risk: In other words, to reduce dependence on one product or market. Such as Cadbury's developing soft drinks (Schweppes and 7-Up) to provide sales success in hot weather to counteract the fall in chocolate sales. In this way the long-term survival prospects of the business are improved. A firm may also diversify if it has a key product in the decline phase of the product life cycle; for example, cigarette manufacturers. Diversification will allow movement into 'growth' markets.

Focus on core capabilities: An increasing number of managers identify the key strengths which lie within their organisation, such as talent for innovation. Then focus the resources of the firm on developing the skills into profitable products.

Increasing market standing: If a business has a good reputation with its suppliers, distributors and customers then this will make it easier to launch new products.

In order to be effective, corporate objectives must be measurable. A target which is directional but with no given value, such as 'increasing market share', will not have the desired impact on employee motivation. A goal of 'boosting market share from 6% to 9%' provides a specific figure for individuals to work towards. However, the objective must be achievable. Otherwise it becomes demoralising. It is also important to provide a timescale within which the goal must be attained.

82.2 Business strategy

The managers of a business should develop a medium- to long-term plan about how to achieve the objectives they have established. This is the organisation's corporate strategy. It sets out the actions that will be taken in order to achieve the goals. And the implications for the firm's human, financial and production resources. The key to success when forming a strategy of this kind is relating the firm's strengths to the opportunities which exist in the marketplace.

Figure 82.2 Strategy formation

Adapted from *Shareholder Value* by Richard Barfield, published in *Accountancy*, October 1991

Figure 82.1 Maximising shareholder wealth

This analysis can take place at each level of the business, allowing a series of strategies to be formed in order to achieve the goals already established.

- Corporate strategy deals with the major issues such as what industry, or industries, the business should compete in, in order to achieve corporate objectives. Managers must identify industries where the long-term profit prospects are likely to be favourable. In 2002, for example, Diageo decided to pull out of the fast food business by selling its Burger King subsidiary.
- Business unit (or divisional) strategy should address the issue of how the organisation will compete in the industry selected by corporate strategy. This will involve selecting a position in the marketplace to distinguish the firm from its competitors.
- Functional (or department) strategy is developed in order to identify how best to succeed in the market position identified in the divisional strategy.

such as Bailey's. Its success would not be helped by trying to run the Number 2 fast food chain. So Burger King had to go. The sale was completed in 2003.

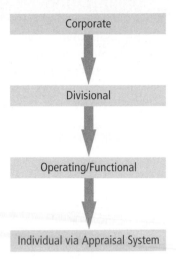

Figure 82.3 Hierarchy of strategy

Figure 82.4 Strategic fit

IN Business

JAGUAR

In 1989 Ford bought Jaguar cars for $2.5 billion. This looked foolish during the following 4 years, as Jaguar made huge losses. By the late 1990s, though, Jaguar was at the heart of Ford's luxury car division, alongside other brands such as Volvo, Land Rover and Aston Martin. Ford's senior management set their luxury car division the objective of contributing a third of Ford's worldwide profits by 2005. It was a huge blow, therefore, to have to admit in 2002 that Jaguar would make an operating loss for the year of $500 million. The causes were disappointing sales of the X-type range launched in 2001, plus production delays to the Jaguar XJ, intended to be the company's flagship model. By autumn 2002, it was starting to look as if the 2005 objective was being undermined by a weak strategy.

If targets are established for individual employees, it is quite possible that a personal strategy for achieving these goals may be established as part of the company's appraisal process.

Just as the objectives of the organisation cascade down to the lowest levels of the business ensuring consistent planning, so too do strategies. This is to establish coordinated action. If a strategy is to achieve the objectives set, it must match the firm's strengths to its competitive environment. Diageo decided that its strength was in running international drinks brands

82.3 Understanding the organisation's strengths: core capabilities

As a company develops over time its employees acquire knowledge and skills. This 'organisational learning' represents what the firm as a whole is good at doing, or its **core capabilities**. The key products or services produced by the business will reflect these strengths. Viagra, the anti-impotence drug developed by Pfizer, represents the company's innovative abilities as a result of its research and development programme and scientific expertise.

Core capabilities need not be limited to a particular market. Marks and Spencer's move into financial services was based on a reputation for reliability and quality. This had built up over many years by its operation in the clothing and food markets. Corporate strategy can be shaped by identifying new opportunities to apply the existing strengths of the organisation.

82.4 Forming corporate strategy to fit the competitive environment of the organisation

Michael Porter in his book *Competitive Advantage: Creating and Sustaining Superior Performance* develops a method by which an organisation can analyse the competitive environment within which it operates in order to create strategic policy.

Figure 82.5 The five forces framework (After Porter, 1985)

Porter suggests that firms need to analyse five factors within an industry in order to understand its nature. This will help managers understand how fierce or how favourable the competitive environment is. Each of the 'five forces' provide information which can be used to help devise an appropriate **business strategy**.

THREAT OF NEW COMPETITORS ENTERING THE MARKET

New firms entering a market increase the level of competition in the industry. This may result in prices and potential profit being forced down. If barriers exist which stop new firms entering, businesses which are already operating in the industry are more secure. Wall's dominance of the UK ice-cream market (over 50% of branded sales) has put it in this comfortable position.

Porter suggests a number of potential strategies are available in order to create obstacles aimed at stopping additional businesses entering an industry:

- Invest heavily in capital equipment in order to make it very expensive for firms considering entering the industry to compete on an equal footing.
- Promote products intensively to create established brand names which will make the potential advertising costs prohibitive for firms wishing to enter the market.
- Make it difficult for new firms to find retail outlets willing to sell their products by taking action designed to gain control of distribution channels.
- Patent both products and operating processes, to stop market entrants copying them and therefore avoiding research and development costs.

THE POWER OF BUYERS

Buyers will clearly wish prices in the industry to be as low as possible. The more powerful this group is, the lower profit in the industry is likely to be. For example, UK biscuit manufacturers receive nearly 50% of their buying orders from just three companies: Tesco, Sainsbury's and Asda. The buyers at these three retailers have huge power over the biscuit suppliers.

A number of potential strategies are available to firms in order to reduce the power of buyers in the marketplace:

- Open up or acquire retail outlets in order to gain control of the sale of the firm's output to the customer (forward vertical integration).
- Make it expensive for the buyer to switch to the output of a competitor. Many people have spent time learning how to use Microsoft's Windows computer software. The cost of moving to a new company's products would not just be financial, but would include the effort required to master a new system. The buyer is therefore in a weaker position in this market.

THE POWER OF SUPPLIERS

Suppliers will charge as much as they can for the resources they offer to the industry. If they have substantial market power, their high prices will hit the industry's profits. A number of potential strategies are available to firms in order to reduce the power of suppliers in the marketplace:

- Acquire a supplying firm in order to control the availability of raw materials to the business (backward vertical integration).
- Encourage the development of new suppliers by buying from multiple sources. The greater the number of businesses prepared to provide raw materials, the less reliant it is necessary to be on any one of them.
- Minimise the quantity of information suppliers have about the industry. For example, if suppliers find it difficult to establish the price of final products in the market they provide inputs for, they will have limited ability to influence that industry. This strategy is in conflict with the growing desire of organisations to build 'supply chains' which encourage close relationships with other firms.

THE THREAT OF SUBSTITUTE PRODUCTS

If direct substitutes exist for the output of an industry, consumers have the option of buying an alternative good. In this case the industry will be forced to maintain lower prices in order to minimise the risk of buyers switching. This will reduce the profitability of the industry. For example, if cable television could provide a viable alternative to satellite, BSkyB would have to cut its monthly rental charges.

Mars ice-cream satisfies a range of ice-cream needs © Mars

Two potential strategies are available to firms in order to reduce the threat of substitute products emerging:

- Undertake research and development activity to identify substitute products with the intention of patenting them before a competitor can do so. If a new close substitute does emerge manufactured by another organisation, consider buying this business to secure its patent rights.
- If a substitute product is made available for sale, use spoiling tactics. Firms may cut their prices or run huge promotions to try to prevent the competitor becoming established. For, if a new product fails to achieve good distribution levels, customers cannot buy it easily and may not get into the habit of buying it regularly.

RIVALRY BETWEEN ESTABLISHED COMPETITORS IN THE INDUSTRY

The more intense the rivalry between existing firms within the industry, the more likely that prices are forced down by competitive pressure. A number of potential strategies are available to firms in order to reduce the amount of rivalry between established competitors in the marketplace:

- Develop a differentiated product. A strong brand image encourages customers to perceive a product or service to be superior to the competition. This reduces the day-to-day threat to sales caused by competitor actions such as price promotions or TV advertising.
- Restrict output in the industry, perhaps by forming some form of 'cartel' agreement with competitors. In order to do this firms must control a large proportion of the products produced, and they must agree on levels of production. This strategy may not be legal under the conditions of the 1973 Fair Trading Act. Furthermore, it is certainly not ethical. Nevertheless, prestigious firms such as ICI have been caught and fined for cartel operations in the recent past. So there is no doubt that such activities take place.

- Acquire competitors. This strategy is also subject to the legal requirements of the 1973 Fair Trading Act. Any takeover giving a business in excess of a 25% market share may be subject to investigation by the Competition Commission.

When analysing a firm's approach to establishing corporate objectives and developing strategic policy to achieve these goals, it is useful to consider the following points:

- Are the objectives of the business precisely defined? And are they understood and supported by staff?
- Is the outcome of each objective measurable so that it will be clear when it has been achieved?
- Does each objective have a target date for completion in order to ensure action?
- Are the organisation's objectives focused excessively on short-run profit maximisation at the expense of the long-term development of the business?
- Do the managers of the business clearly understand its strengths and weaknesses?
- Have opportunities in the competitive environment been identified?
- Does the strategic policy of the organisation 'match' the firm's strengths to opportunities in the competitive environment?
- Finally, and most importantly, do the strategies match the objectives?

82.5 Corporate objectives and strategy
an evaluation

In many organisations, particularly small businesses, the idea of stating objectives and developing strategy to achieve them may seem unnecessary. Some managers may claim their firm has no explicit strategy or planning process and yet is very successful.

The first issue here is the existence of strategy. Every organisation has a strategy. It may not be written down, or even clearly defined, but by observing the behaviour of the business over time a pattern will emerge in the actions which are taken. This pattern reflects the strategy adopted by the firm's management. Strategy in many businesses reflects a slow development towards a position in the market which is never formally identified, but is reached through a process of intuitive decisions. Managers shape the organisation's strengths to fit the competitive environment based on their knowledge and experience of that market.

A second issue is whether careful strategic planning can ever be as helpful in practice as in theory. It will always be difficult for managers or consultants to capture a complete picture of the current competitive environment. Especially in a global economy where change is occurring very quickly. Even harder, of course, is to anticipate how any market will look in one, five or ten years' time. The transformation of industries may be so rapid that assessment using a model such as Porter's five forces becomes almost impossible.

A Level Exercises

A. REVISION QUESTIONS

(35 marks; 70 minutes)

Read the unit, then answer:

1 a List four potential corporate objectives. (4)

  b Consider the extent to which each is focused on the short or long run. (4)

2 Explain why it might be more appropriate for a public limited company to set an objective of maximising shareholder wealth than annual profit. (5)

3 a What is a corporate strategy? (3)

  b Identify the factors an organisation might consider when forming strategy. (4)

4 Outline how strategies formed at different levels of the business might interlink to form a hierarchy. (4)

5 a What are an organisation's 'core capabilities'?

  b Suggest two likely core capabilities of:

    i Wall's ice-cream

    ii Orange

    iii Tesco. (6)

6 List the five factors Porter suggests determine an industry's competitive environment. (5)

B1 Data Response

Wrapping It Up

In December 1993 Olivia Manduca struggled to find something glamorous to wear over her wedding dress. She made a satin and velvet stole which friends thought stunning. So she went into business. She produced half a dozen and persuaded Harrods to stock them. 1994's sales turnover of £50,000 persuaded her to form a limited company called Wonderful Wraps. She also found a factory in London's East End which has been making the wraps ever since.

By 1998 turnover reached £150,000 and net profit margins were over 50%. Making the business a lot more than a hobby. Olivia had started her business with an investment of just £500 and had never needed to borrow a penny. She was starting to face her first big decision. Whether to expand further or to keep Wonderful Wraps small.

Questions *(30 marks; 35 minutes)*

1 a Outline three possible business objectives that Olivia may have had from the start. (6)

  b From the text, which do you think was her main objective? Explain your reasoning. (5)

2 a In 1998 alone, what percentage return was Olivia receiving on her £500 investment? (4)

  b Can such returns ever be justified? (6)

3 Discuss the factors Olivia should take into account in deciding 'whether to expand further or to keep Wonderful Wraps small'? (9)

B2 Case Study

Forming Strategic Policy at Ember Fuels plc

Nichola, the chief executive of Ember Fuels plc, stood to address her management team. Her intention was to explain the strategic thinking behind the takeover bid for Farlow Construction. She wanted to make sure everyone was in possession of all the key information. The actions of this group would be vital to the success of the bid over the next few weeks.

'The proposed purchase of Farlow will cost us approximately £76 million. We are trying to address a number of weaknesses in our own business by making the purchase.

First, a range of our products are at their mature stage and may be moving into decline. This is beginning to dent our trading performance. Our cash flow is also uneven because our coal sales are so seasonal.

Second, we do not have much experience in strategic planning and acquisition. We need to improve in this area if we are to carry out our plan to move into new markets using takeovers.'

A little later in her presentation Nichola turned her attention to the benefits that Farlow could offer Ember Fuels if the acquisition was to take place:

'…As far as new products are concerned Farlow have developed Element, a world-leading brand in waterproofing and lining, used, for example, on the inside of tunnels. It is in great demand already in the mining industry. In addition, the DIY market may be a potential source of substantial sales in the future…

…Farlow acquired a waste disposal business three years ago. This division of the firm specialises in asbestos removal and cleaning industrial boilers and chemical plants. There is great potential in combining our quarrying work with this part of Farlow's business.

Together these two areas of operation could become a real "star" in our product portfolio…

…The management expertise at Farlow is also an important factor behind our offer. Their senior executives have a lot of experience of strategic planning and organising takeover bids. This could be very valuable to us in the future, given our long-term aim to diversify'.

As Nichola finished her presentation she felt exhilarated. At last the strategy she had wanted was beginning to take shape.

Questions   (40 marks; 60 minutes)

1 Outline the key difficulties which face Ember Fuels plc.   (6)
2 Analyse the takeover of Farlow Construction and evaluate the extent to which this takeover strategy helps to overcome the main weaknesses of the business.   (10)
3 Examine the obstacles that might reduce the benefits to Ember Fuels from the takeover.   (8)
4 a Examine why Ember Fuels may wish to pursue the objectives of growth and diversification by takeover.   (8)
   b Evaluate the extent to which this approach conflicts with the idea of a business concentrating on its 'core capabilities'.   (8)

C. ESSAY QUESTIONS

1 Consider the issues which might determine whether or not an organisation chooses to adopt objectives and strategic policy with a short- or long-term focus.
2 The management expert Peter Drucker believes that it is a mistake for a business to focus upon a single objective. To what extent do you support him in this view?

DECISION TREES

DEFINITION

Decision trees are diagrams that set out all the options available when making a decision plus the outcomes that might result by chance.

83.1 Introduction

Decision trees provide a logical process for decision making. The decision problem can be set out in the form of a diagram, like a tree on its side. It can take into account the occasions when a decision can be taken and the occasions when chance will determine the outcome. Chance can be estimated by assigning **probability**. While the estimate of the probability may only be a guess, at least probability is quantitative and gives the decision process a scientific quality.

The kinds of problems which are suited to decision tree analysis are those where a sequence of events or options has to be followed in conditions of uncertainty. The decision whether or not to launch a new product, enter a new market, build a new factory, hire or buy machinery, for example, are all cases where decision tree analysis is appropriate. It would also be possible to use investment appraisal. The advantage of a decision tree is that it allows for uncertainty/chance. This makes it a better model of the reality of an uncertain business world.

Invest in a robot welder

Retrain existing staff

*Do nothing

*Note that 'do nothing' is an option for every business decision.

Figure 83.1

Robot proves effective from start

0.8

Robot proves unreliable

0.2

Figure 83.2

83.2 Step-by-step approach to decision tree analysis

STEP 1: THE BASICS

- The tree is a diagram setting out the key features of a decision making problem.
- The tree is shown lying on its side, roots on the left, branches on the right.
- The decision problem is set out from left to right with events laid out in the sequence in which they occur.
- The branches consist of:
  - a decision to be made (see Figure 83.1)
  - chance events or alternatives beyond the decision maker's control (see Figure 83.2).
- Note carefully that a square means a decision and a circle means a chance event, i.e. one of two or more events *may* follow. Therefore:
  - there must be a probability attaching to each of the chance events/alternatives

- these probabilities must add up to 1 as one of them must happen. In Figure 83.2, the decision maker has allowed for an 80% (0.8) chance that the robot will work well and a 20% (0.2) chance that it will prove unreliable. These figures could be arrived at from experience with robots in the past.
- At any square, the decision maker has the power to choose which branch to take, but at the circles chance takes over. You can choose whether or not to invest in a robot. But there is a chance that the robot may prove unreliable. The full tree so far is shown in Figure 83.3.
- The decision maker will choose which branch provides the better or best value.
- If buying costs a net cash outflow of £1,000 per year while hiring costs £800, it is better to hire (see Figure 83.4).

Note that the branch *not* taken is crossed out, as shown in Figure 83.5.

Figure 83.3

Figure 83.4

Figure 83.5

STEP 2: DRAWING A DECISION TREE

- Bantox plc must decide whether to launch a new product (see Figure 83.6).

Figure 83.6

- Research suggests a 70% chance of success in a new product launch. This would be shown as a probability of 0.7 (see Figure 83.7).

Figure 83.7

Note that, because probabilities must add up to 1, the implied chance of failure is 0.3.

- To make a decision based on the above tree, estimates are needed of the financial costs and returns. In this case, let's assume:
  - the new product launch will cost £10 million
  - a new product success will generate £15 million of positive net cash flows
  - a new product failure will generate only £3 million
  - no launch means no movements in net cash.

The full decision tree now looks like Figure 83.8.

Figure 83.8

STEP 3: MAKING CALCULATIONS

At each probability circle, a calculation is required of the average outcome, given the probabilities involved. If a launch costing £10 million will generate either £15 million or £3 million, what will be the average result, if the same circumstances happened several times over? Sometimes the firm would get £15 million and sometimes £3 million. Usually, to work out an average, you would add the numbers and divide by 2, i.e:

$$\frac{£15m + £3m}{2} = £9m$$

That assumes, though, that there is an equal chance of £15 million and £3 million. In fact, the probabilities are not 50/50, they are 70/30. There is a 70% chance of £15 million. So the correct (weighted) average outcome is:

£15m × 0.7 = £10.5m
£3m × 0.3 = £0.9m
total £11.4m

In decision trees, the **expected values** at probability circles are always calculated by weighted averages.

- Calculations on decision trees are carried out from right to left, i.e. working backwards through the tree, making calculations at each probability circle.
- In the case of Bantox, only one calculation is needed. If there are several circles, it is helpful to number them, and show your weighted average calculations clearly (see Figure 83.9).

STEP 4: SHOWING YOUR DECISIONS

Having calculated the expected value (weighted average) at each probability circle, a rational decision can be made. As Figure 83.9 shows, launching the new product will, on average, turn £10 million into £11.4 million, i.e. generate a profit of £1.4 million. Therefore it is preferable to not launch. The decision to launch is indicated by crossing out the 'don't launch' option.

Figure 83.9

83.3 Summary of key points

A decision tree is a diagrammatic presentation of a problem involving decisions (squares) and chance events (circles).

1 The problem is laid out from left to right. Decisions are shown as squares, chance events as circles.
2 Each chance event has a probability estimated for it. The probabilities must add up to 1 since one of them *must* happen.
3 Two money values are shown:
   - the cost of the decision (shown as a negative number, i.e. in brackets)
   - the benefit or cost of a specific outcome occurring. These are shown at the end of each branch of the tree.
4 Working from right to left, the decision maker calculates the expected value at each circle. These values are calculated by multiplying the money value by the probability, then adding the results.
5 Still working from right to left, the decision maker decides at each square which branches to cross off, leaving only the better or best alternative open.

83.4 Advantages and disadvantages of decision trees

ADVANTAGES OF DECISION TREES

- Decision trees set out problems clearly and encourage a logical approach. The discipline of setting out the problem in a decision tree requires logical thinking and can also generate new ideas and approaches.
- Decision trees encourage a quantitative approach and force assessments of the chances and implications of success and failure.
- Decision trees not only show the average expected values for each decision but also set the probability of a specific outcome occurring.
- Decision trees are most useful when similar scenarios have occurred before so that good estimates for probabilities and predicted **actual values** exist.
- Decision trees are most useful in tactical or routine decisions rather than strategic decisions.

DISADVANTAGES OF DECISION TREES

- It may be difficult to get meaningful data, especially for estimated probabilities and of success or failure.
- Decision trees are less useful in the case of completely new problems or one-off strategic problems.
- It can be relatively easy for a manager seeking to prove a case to manipulate the data. A biased approach to the estimated probabilities or values could 'prove' the pre-desired result rather than the logically determined outcome.

- Decision trees do not take into account the variability of the business environment.
- Decision trees might divert managers from the need to take account of qualitative as well as quantitative information when making a decision.

Decision trees raise many issues of value when analysing business problems:

- The importance of allowing for uncertainty. The most common technique for business decision making is investment appraisal. This is based upon a forecast of future cash flows from which the payback period and profitability of the investment can be assessed. The great weakness with this approach is that it is based on a cash flow forecast. In reality, every decision can result in a range of possible outcomes, not just one. By focusing firms on uncertainty, decision trees can help ensure that managers make more carefully considered decisions.
- The importance of looking at alternatives. Although it is important to be single-minded – to have clear goals – too many managers adopt a strategy without fully considering the alternatives. They perhaps choose the approach that worked last time, or the one adopted by their competitors. Decision trees encourage careful consideration of the alternatives available before a decision is made.
- All quantitative methods can be biased, consciously or unconsciously. Optimism is often a virtue, but it may lead to exaggerated sales figures or excessively high probabilities for success. This does not mean quantitative methods should be rejected. Only that it is sensible to ask who provided the figures and assess whether they had any reason to want a particular outcome. Cynicism about decision trees is out of place; scepticism is wholly valid.

83.5 Decision making
an evaluation

Small firms run by one person benefit from clear, speedy decision making. The entrepreneur knows the customers, knows the competition and the staff. Therefore he or she can make effective decisions quickly, with no need to justify them to others. Some may prove faulty, but the quick responses of a small firm should ensure that damage is limited. The business will stand or fall on the hunches and judgements of the boss.

In large firms, the same rules do not apply. A successful career path at a company such as Mars or Unilever often depends upon avoiding mistakes. Therefore it is important to be able to justify why a decision was made. Even if it proves wrong, that should not matter as long as the method for making the decision was thorough and analytic. After all, if four out of five new products prove a failure, what would be the reason for firing a manager who has just launched a flop?

It can be a matter for regret that methods such as decision trees are used to 'protect the back' of decision makers. In other words, they may not be valued for themselves, only for their value as a protector. Often, though, the process of trying to protect themselves encourages managers to think hard about their decision making methods. Those who use decision trees positively may find an improvement in their record of success, and help the big firms to compete with the faster moving small firms.

KEY terms

actual values – although known as 'actual values' or 'payoffs', these are the forecasts of the net cash flow which result from following a sequence of decisions and chance events through a decision tree. They should always be shown at the ends of the branches of the tree.

decision tree node – a point in a decision tree. A square is used where a decision is needed; a circle where there are possible paths or chance events that are out of the decision maker's control.

expected values – these are the forecast actual values adjusted by the probability of their occurrence. Although called 'expected', they are not the actual cash flows which result. Expected equals actual × probability.

probability – the likelihood of something occurring. This can be expressed as a numerical value, which can be a percentage e.g. 50% chance, a fraction e.g. 1/2 or a decimal e.g. 0.5. The probability of something certain is 100% or 1. The probability of something impossible is zero. So probabilities range from 1 to zero.

A2 Level Exercises

REVISION QUESTIONS
(30 marks; 60 minutes)

Read the unit, then answer:

1 When drawing a decision tree, what symbol is used to show:

  a when a decision must be made

  b when chance takes over? *(2)*

2 If the probability of the successful launch of a new product is estimated to be 0.72, the probability of a failed launch must be 0.28. Explain why. *(3)*

3 State whether each of the following is a decision or a chance event:

  a choosing between three different new product options

  b a new product succeeding or failing in the marketplace

  c good weather on the day of the open air concert

  d whether to advertise or to cut the price. *(4)*

4 Explain the difference between an expected value and an actual value. *(3)*

5 State three advantages and three potential pitfalls of using decision trees. *(6)*

6 Explain the circumstances when decision trees are least useful. *(4)*

7 If the chance of achieving £200,000 is 0.2 and the chance of £20,000 is 0.8, what is the expected value of a decision? *(4)*

8 Explain how decision trees might help managers assess the best decision by 'what if?' analysis. *(4)*

B. REVISION EXERCISES

B1 Practice Exercise
Look at the tree diagram below. Calculate the expected values at nodes 1–4 and state your decisions at decision points A–C. Indicate your decisions on the tree diagram.

B2 Data Response
Denham Potteries has a capital spending budget of £100,000. The production manager has put in a bid for £100,000 for a new tunnel kiln. The marketing manager has countered with a proposal to spend £80,000 on launching a new product. This new product is in line with the firm's objective of diversifying, but may be rather risky given the firm's past record of only one success for every five new products.

Ken Coton, the marketing manager, has provided a handy table of figures to summarise the information.

Outcome	Probability	Actual Value (surplus over next 5 years)
New product		
Big success	0.1	£900,000
Modest success	0.1	£500,000
Failure	0.8	£30,000
Tunnel kiln		
Success	0.8	£200,000
Failure	0.2	£60,000

Questions *(25 marks; 30 minutes)*

1 Draw a fully labelled decision tree to set out the options. *(10)*

2 What decision should the firm make on purely numerate grounds? *(3)*

3 Outline the qualitative factors the board should take into account before making the decision. *(12)*

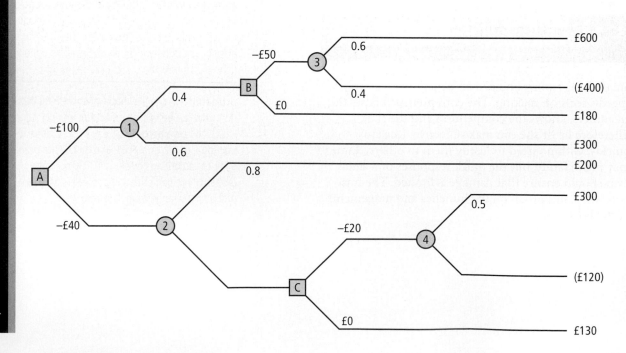

B3 Practice Exercise

Mansfield Town FC is considering buying a South American centre forward. The club knows statistics show that only one in four overseas forwards succeeds in the lower divisions. But things are desperate. The player's contract will cost £500,000 and, if successful, could increase home attendances sufficiently to be worth £1.2 million over the three-year contract. Even if the player is unsuccessful, attendances should rise by £200,000.

Questions   (20 marks; 15 minutes)

1 Draw the decision tree and label it carefully.   (12)
2 On the basis of the tree, what decision should the club take?   (4)
3 Outline two reasons why the club might decide to proceed.   (4)

B4 Case Study

The research and development department in Gregson plc has just invented a new higher quality version of the product sold by a rival business, Winder plc. The product is code named 'Copycat'. At present Gregson lacks the technology to manufacture the product itself. After further research, it decides there are three immediate choices:

1 buy the technology to manufacture the product itself
2 sell all rights to Winder
3 sell all rights on a royalty basis to a third company.

The marketing department believes that Copycat, as it stands, has a 50% chance of success, with no further development.

However, the research and development department in Gregson believes it could improve Copycat still further by some design enhancements. However, it only wants to do so if Copycat had already succeeded and if choice 2 above had not been taken. After design enhancement, the chance of a successful launch is estimated to be 60%.

The forecast actual values are shown in the table below.

Questions   (30 marks; 35 minutes)

1 Prepare a decision tree to illustrate this situation, showing branches, probabilities, and actual values.   (8)
2 Calculate the expected values.   (6)
3 Explain the optimal decision strategy based on these calculations.   (8)
4 State and explain two other factors which Gregson might take into account before making the final choice of decision strategy.   (8)

Decision Outcome	Manufacture	Sell all Rights to Winder(£000s)	Sell on a Royalty Basis to a Third Company
Fails before design enhancement	−262.5	15	7.5
Succeeds after design enhancement	375	–	300
Succeeds but no design enhancement	150	15	82.5
Fails after design enhancement	−412.5	–	−142.5

STRATEGIC ANALYSIS

DEFINITION

Strategic analysis is the process of examining the factors within the organisation which will have an impact on its long-term success, and comparing these with the conditions identified in the firm's competitive environment.

84.1 What is strategy?

In order to achieve a goal, it is necessary to develop a plan of action. For example, a timetable to guide examination revision and success. Organisations also have objectives to achieve. This process requires an outline of the steps that will be taken to reach a given target. A plan of this kind is called a strategy.

84.2 A model for conducting a strategic analysis

In order to form a strategic plan it is necessary to gather information about the business and its marketplace. This will come from two sources:

- internal sources of information, such as the company's prices, costs and efficiency levels
- external data from organisations like the government and trade associations.

The planning should be undertaken regularly and involve the department managers closest to the key issues. It should not be a crisis measure, or else hasty decisions may be made.

The process of strategic analysis involves an *internal audit* to appraise the strengths and weaknesses of the firm. And an **external audit** to evaluate the threats and opportunities in the company's competitive environment (see Figure 84.1).

84.3 External audit

An external audit should investigate three key areas of the competitive environment facing an organisation:

1. The general business and economic conditions which exist within each of the countries which the firm serves.
2. The conditions within each specific market to which the business sells.
3. The nature of the competition in each market segment targeted by the organisation.

BUSINESS AND ECONOMIC CONDITIONS

To analyse the business and economic conditions a firm faces, 'PEST-G' analysis is helpful.

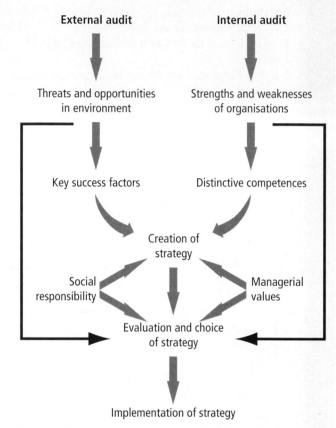

Figure 84.1 Model guiding strategic analysis (After Mintzberg, 1990)

PEST-G analysis:

- **P for Political**

  Government policy can have a major impact on the operation of a business. For example, laws on competitive practices will influence the number of firms operating in an industry and therefore the strength of competition. Health and safety legislation will affect work practices and production costs. Marketing tactics will be limited by consumer legislation. It is important to study the political environment within which business operates, particularly in countries where governments are unstable and therefore investment risks are high.

- **E for Economic**

  Economic factors will influence the future potential profit of a business. The level of consumer demand is a key variable affecting the quantity of sales and the price at which output can be sold. Interest rates will determine the cost of finance to the company.

BMW AND MERCEDES: SHARED OBJECTIVES BUT DIFFERENT STRATEGIES

The German giants BMW and Mercedes built their reputations on large, luxury cars. However, strategic market analysis in the early 1990s pointed both companies towards younger buyers of smaller cars. The average age of a Mercedes owner was 60, while BMW drivers were in their 40s.

The objective of long-term growth pointed both companies towards the small car market, but they chose very different strategies. Mercedes decided to develop two new small cars: the family-focused A-class, and the young, town-y Smart car. Both had huge teething troubles before and during their launch in the late 1990s; however, both became great successes. Given that only 1 in 6 new products succeeds in the marketplace, a strike rate of 2 out of 2 is very impressive.

BMW's approach was different. It chose to buy Rover Cars in late 1994 for £800 million. This doubled BMW's capacity, and enabled it to develop small cars without risking diluting the BMW brand. The BMW move proved a disaster. Hundreds of millions were invested in improving Rover productivity and quality, but the sharp rise in the value of the £ in 1996 meant it was impossible to make profits from the cars. After five very costly years, BMW in effect paid to get Rover taken off its hands. The only part it kept was the Mini brand, which was re-launched very successfully in 2001. The Mini's success has not been sufficient, however, to hide the failure of BMW's strategy compared with that of Mercedes.

Final profits will be taxed by the government. The economic cycle of recession and recovery is an important influence on the opportunities and threats to the organisation.

- **S for Social**

Consumers reflect changes in lifestyles over time. This means businesses must observe shifts in the characteristics and habits of the population. Especially where these influence segments of the existing market. For example, as the UK population ages, new opportunities open up such as holidays aimed specifically at older people. Demographic variations may also represent a threat to companies. For example, a fall in the birth rate would jeopardise the competitive position of Mothercare.

- **T for Technology**

An external audit must monitor developments in technology. These can affect the production methods employed by the organisation, or the products/services offered for sale. A new manufacturing technique might make existing production too expensive for the business to remain profitable. A product may become obsolete because new technology has developed a more effective substitute. However, changes in technology also offer opportunities, such as the potential to break into new markets by producing a new, radically different, product offering.

PRODUCT REPOSITIONING: LUCOZADE

In the 1970s Lucozade was regarded by consumers as a glucose drink to be given to people who were not feeling well. Its slogan was 'Lucozade aids recovery'. The packaging and pricing reflected this. A premium price was charged for a large glass bottle wrapped in cellophane. Distribution was largely through chemists. This established an image radically different from that adopted by other soft drinks.

In the 1980s changes in consumer lifestyles led to a growth in health consciousness and particularly personal fitness. Lucozade was radically repositioned in the market. Advertising was used to promote the product as an energy-giving sports drink. A series of nationally known personalities, such as John Barnes, the England football player, appeared in Lucozade commercials. The packaging of the product was changed to conventional soft drink cans and much smaller bottles. These were designed to be consumed as a single drink during or after sport rather than stored away for repeated use. General retailers were encouraged to stock the relaunched product alongside other canned soft drinks.

Lucozade is now firmly established as an energy-giving soft drink for health conscious consumers. This offers the potential for a greater sales volume than the original target segment of those recovering from illness. It is this kind of dramatic revival of a product's sales potential which reflects the benefits which can result from a careful analysis of the market environment.

- **G for Green issues**

  Consumers and governments are becoming increasingly aware of the impact of business upon the environment. Organisations must now monitor their actions and consider their environmental implications. For example, Shell met with substantial opposition to its plan to sink a disused oil rig in the Atlantic Ocean. An issue of this kind can influence the corporate image of an organisation. The resulting publicity may damage the effectiveness of the firm's promotional activities.

THE MARKET ENVIRONMENT

An external audit should consider each of the major markets in which the firm competes. Key factors of importance are:

- Market size – measured by value and volume of sales.
- Market growth – measured by the percentage change in the value and volume of sales.

THE BIGGEST BUSINESS GAMBLE EVER?

The mobile phone business has been a phenomenal money-spinner. In Britain, each of the four licensed operators (Vodafone, Orange, Cellnet/MmO2 and One-2-One/T-Mobile) made fortunes out of the first and second generations of phones and networks. By 2000, all the talk was of third generation (3G) mobile phones with ready Internet access plus video links. When the governments of Europe put the network licences up for auction, a total of $100,000 million (yes, $100 billion) was bid by the major phone companies. It was perhaps the biggest strategic gamble of all time on new technology.

By 2002, the 3G phones were expected to have swept all others away. Yet by November 2002, Nokia was still only in the testing stage, and the market was being attracted to camera phones based on 2G technology. Future mobile users had been expected to order their shopping on-line, while on the train back from work (a 3G application). Instead, the evidence was that low-tech text messaging was far more important to users than fancy extras. The strategy had turned into a gamble. For Vodafone alone, the gamble involved £13.5 billion. Commentators were suggesting that this huge sum might never be recouped.

IN Business

- Market trends – such as the position of the product in its life cycle.
- Market share of each manufacturer – based on product type and brand name.
- New products introduced to the market – not just those items which compete directly with the company's output, but also complementary and substitute goods.
- Product positioning – a process widely adopted by marketers is to 'map' consumer impressions of the goods available for purchase, based on the most important benefits the product offers consumers. This method allows managers the opportunity to analyse the potential for changes in strategic approach towards a particular brand.

THE COMPETITIVE ENVIRONMENT

The final phase of the external audit concentrates on the organisation's direct competitors (see Figure 84.2).

Market coverage = C+D+E
Market share = D+E
Earned market share = D/(D+E)
Win ratio = D/(C+D)

Figure 84.2 Audit of the competitive environment (K. Ohmae, 1983)

- Identify who they are and how they conduct their business.
- Determine their approximate size in terms of sales value and volume.
- Assess their production capabilities, including the maximum volume of output of which they are capable and the extent to which machinery is currently being utilised.
- Use their published annual accounts to assess their financial strength.

- Consider the extent to which the organisation has diversified into a range of different product types and is involved in trading across international markets.
- Investigate the channels of distribution which they use.
- Judge their market standing with consumers and the extent to which each item in the product range contributes to their reputation.

The information gathered in the audit of competitors should be used to assess the likely objectives and strategies that the firm may adopt in the future.

SHARING INFORMATION WITH COMPETITORS: BEST PRACTICE BENCHMARKING

An audit which aims to gather information about competitors in the same industry is difficult to conduct. Many firms make very few facts about themselves public, except when required to by law. Best practice benchmarking breaks with the idea of keeping material secret. Companies form alliances in order to share knowledge about how to conduct their business as efficiently as possible. The purpose of the approach is to gain an understanding of how to undertake specific processes in the most efficient way possible. By copying best practice in each area of the business a company which is second best at each activity can become the best company overall.

84.4 Internal audit

An **internal audit** is a way of compiling a list of a firm's main strengths and weaknesses. Robert Townsend, former chairman of Avis Car Rental, said the first thing he did when taking charge was to 'go and talk to all 1,000 employees and find out what they do. And what stops them being the best in the world at what they do.' Today, internal audits are more likely to be carried out by a **management consultant**.

An organisation undertaking an internal audit must seek to identify the strengths and weaknesses of the firm *relative to its competitors*. A business may have modern, highly efficient machinery, but if every other company in the industry has access to similar technology then this is not a strength.

Managers should be objective in assessing their own departments. An internal audit will be of little use if it is the result of over-optimistic analysis. Fortunately, it should be possible to base much of the evidence on facts (such as product costs) rather than estimates.

An internal audit should analyse financial data such as cost trends, actual performance against budget estimates and the profit in relation to capital employed. Much of the relevant data will already have been produced by management accountants to guide decision making within the firm.

In addition to financial information, marketing, human resource and operations strategies must be considered in detail. In each case direct comparisons with competitors can be made as a result of the knowledge gathered in the external audit, or via benchmarking.

The following table gives examples of internal auditing in practice:

DEPARTMENT BEING AUDITED	CRITERIA FOR AUDITING
Human resources	Labour turnover, employee satisfaction surveys, absenteeism, skills audit
Marketing	Sales trends for each of the firm's products, advertising spending per product, size and skills of sales force
Operations management	Trends in defect rate (production quality), productivity, lead time, stock turnover
Financial management	Production costs, analyses of sales and cost variances, audits of profitability of past capital investments (did the appraisal of cash flow data prove accurate?)

84.5 Presenting the strategic analysis: SWOT diagrams

A large quantity of information will result from the external and internal audit. These facts must be organised into a format which allows them to be understood by managers in order to aid their decision making. A SWOT (Strengths, Weaknesses, Opportunities and Threats) diagram is the most widely adopted method used for presentation purposes (see Figure 84.3).

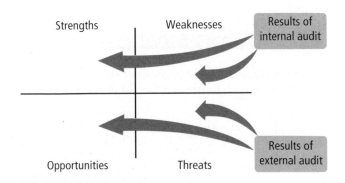

Figure 84.3 SWOT diagram

The results of the internal audit are divided into two groups:

- factors which are positive relative to competitors are recorded as strengths
- factors which are negative relative to competitors are recorded as weaknesses.

The results of the external audit are also divided into two groups:

- factors in the external environment which have the potential to bring benefits to the organisation are recorded as opportunities
- factors in the external environment which have the potential to cause a negative effect on the organisation are recorded as threats.

The SWOT diagram should focus on the relevant key factors in each case. A brief outline highlighting the reasons for good or bad performance should accompany the diagram. In order to be effective it must be relevant to those managers using it and creative in its interpretation of the internal and external audit data.

ISSUES FOR **analysis**

In order to consider the approach adopted towards strategic analysis by an organisation there are a number of key issues which should be reviewed. These include:

- Do the managers of the business undertake a regular planning exercise, including an internal and external audit?
- If an external audit has been completed, has sufficient attention been paid to the business and economic environment, market conditions and the nature of competition?
- Has the firm used best practice benchmarking in order to establish an external measure of success and the most efficient way to conduct specific operations?
- If an internal audit has been completed, is the resulting assessment of the organisation's strengths and weaknesses realistic and placed in the context of the competition faced?
- Have managers of the business developed a SWOT analysis of the firm's position? If so, to what extent are its findings used to shape a strategy for achieving the long-term aims and objectives of the organisation?

84.6 Strategic analysis
an evaluation

All successful organisations conduct strategic analysis. This does *not* have to mean a formal process.

The owner of a small business may monitor competitors' prices, or recognise a particular employee's skills, without any conscious decision to study strengths, weaknesses, opportunities or threats in detail. The formal process set out in this unit is a large firm's way of trying to match the market knowledge and instincts of a successful small trader. Strategic policy which emerges as a pattern in action over time can be highly effective.

The key issue here is the size of the firm. The larger the organisation, the more likely it is that formal strategic analysis will be required in order to establish and maintain competitive advantage. This is because coordination of employee action becomes increasingly complex as a business grows. The process of preparing a SWOT diagram provides a focus to strategic analysis. There is always a risk, however, that a formal planning process can come to seem an annual ritual – more boring paperwork. In the long term, strategic analysis will only keep being successful if all staff are made fully aware of its effects upon decision making. The process of **SWOT analysis** is not enough. Its findings and consequences must be communicated effectively to staff.

KEY terms

external audit – the process of analysing the business and economic environment, market conditions and the nature of competition facing an organisation. The results can inform a SWOT analysis by highlighting the firm's opportunities and threats.

internal audit – the process of analysing the organisation and effectiveness of each business department and activity. The results can inform a SWOT analysis by highlighting the firm's strengths and weaknesses.

management consultant – independent advisors brought in to analyse a problem and recommend solutions in an objective way.

SWOT analysis – a four-box summary of the results of internal and external auditing. Strengths and weaknesses represent the internal position of the business today. Opportunities and threats represent the external position of the business which will influence its future development.

A Level Exercises

A. REVISION QUESTIONS
(45 marks; 70 minutes)

Read the unit, then answer:

1 Identify the two sources of information gathered for the purposes of strategic analysis and give examples of each. (6)

2 a Consider Figure 84.1; is a large or a small business more likely to adopt this formal approach to strategic analysis? Why? (4)

 b Explain who should conduct a strategic analysis and why it should be undertaken regularly. (3)

3 What is the purpose of:

 a an internal audit (3)

 b an external audit? (3)

4 Outline the purpose of the three main elements of an external audit and provide an example of the kind of analysis which takes place in each. (6)

5 What is 'best-practice benchmarking'? Why might competitors choose to share information in this way? (6)

6 a How are the results of the internal and external audit used to prepare a SWOT diagram? (5)

 b What is the purpose of this analytical technique? (4)

7 How can strategic analysis be employed by managers in order to help achieve the organisation's aims and objectives? (5)

B. REVISION EXERCISES

B1 Case Study

Analysing the Strategic Position of ULV

ULV is a British manufacturer of motor components. It supplies major car makers in the UK and abroad. Every six months senior managers hold a key meeting. They review the firm's present position in the light of immediate planning targets and its longer term strategic position. The following are extracts from the most recent of these discussions:

Stephen Cross (Finance Director):
'Let's start with the good news. We are going to meet our objective of increasing return on capital employed by 2% this year. We should be able to pay a higher interim dividend to shareholders. If we are still thinking about expansion I believe we have the potential to raise additional capital. We are very lucky to have access to the kind of financial expertise available in the City of London. On the other hand, we have to be alert to the threat of takeover. Actions are sometimes necessary to protect our independence in the short term, even if it means sacrificing future growth.'

Lisa Taylor (Marketing Director):
'The expansion of the European Union is very promising for us. The potential of trading, without barriers, in some of the Eastern European economies is very exciting. There is no reason we can't develop our two main product lines to become familiar to customer firms right across Europe. That would allow us to enjoy economies of scale and establish a position in the market as cost leaders. However, the low labour costs of the Eastern European manufacturers make them very serious competitors. In addition the slow down in the Asian economies is concerning. Not just because it might lead to world recession, but because we have built up a good reputation with our customers in that part of the world and as a result it is a growing source of demand.'

Peter Collins (Operations Director):
'It's a shame we closed down the Birmingham plant. I know the 1991 recession hit us hard, but we sometimes find ourselves turning away orders now because our capacity is so limited. The Long Eaton facility is still in need of new machinery and I am concerned about some of our equipment getting out of date. We need to look more closely at modernising our operations before any thoughts of expansion.'

Brian Shaw (Human Resource Director):
'I am concerned that the reintroduction of a minimum wage and other new European laws might cause us problems and eat into our competitive advantage. At least our training programme is taking effect and we are starting to reach a position where we can work in a more flexible way. As you know for a long time we have had a real shortage of skilled staff, particularly with appropriate computing knowledge, but the recruitment drive has been successful and the new employee share scheme has helped cut down labour turnover and improve motivation significantly.'

Questions *(40 marks; 60 minutes)*

1 Analyse the extracts from ULV's planning meeting to indicate those factors which would have been identified in an external business audit. (6)

2 Analyse the extracts from ULV's planning meeting to indicate those factors which would have been identified in an internal business audit. (6)

3 Prepare a SWOT diagram based on the analysis presented in your answers to questions 1 and 2. (16)

4 Identify and evaluate potential strategic policy options available to ULV by using the SWOT diagram prepared in your answer to question 3. (12)

C. ESSAY QUESTION

Many successful organisations do not undertake formal strategic analysis. Consider the issues which might make the preparation of a SWOT diagram worthwhile and discuss how it could be used to shape a firm's strategic policy.

STRATEGIC PLANNING

85.1 Planning a strategic direction

The strategic planning process is undertaken by an organisation's senior managers. The first decision which they face is: 'In which **strategic direction** should we move the business?' There are two methods of gaining advantage over competitors in an industry:

- Reducing the *cost* of producing goods or services. This allows competitive prices to be charged, or greater profits to be earned.
- Making the good or service brought to the market appear different from those of competitors. This is known as creating *product differentiation*. It allows a higher price to be charged because customers believe the product to be unique in some way.

If a business tries to achieve both of these methods of competing at one time, it is likely to fail. You cannot be Rolls Royce and Volkswagen simultaneously.

THE STRATEGIC MATRIX

Between 1993 and 2002 there were many phases of price war between the main national newspapers. The motives were to increase market share and to halt a slide in overall newspaper readership. The first shots were fired by Rupert Murdoch's papers, the *Sun* and *The Times*.

The *Sun* was able to cut its price because it was the lowest cost producer among the tabloid papers. Sales of the *Mirror* and the *Express* suffered badly. The *Mail*, however, was unaffected. Its more female, more middle-class readership was not interested in the *Sun* at any price.

Among the broadsheet papers, the *Guardian* managed to survive equally well. The price cut on *The Times* doubled sales, but the losers were the Independent and the *Express* – not the more distinctive *Guardian*.

Business IN

Once a choice has been made between cost leadership and product differentiation, the scope of the market in which the firm will operate must be considered. The firm may adopt one of two possibilities:

- To compete in a mass market. The potential profit to be gained from securing a strategic position in a large market is clearly high. However, establishing and maintaining a substantial market share will be difficult.
- To concentrate on a specific group of consumers, or a market segment. The potential financial gains from this approach are likely to be smaller, but establishing and maintaining market share should be easier.

In his book *Competitive Advantage: Creating and Sustaining Superior Performance*, Michael Porter presents these two sets of decisions in the form of a matrix. This provides four cells each containing a possible strategic direction which managers can choose for their organisation (see Figure 85.1). Porter believes that the safest place to be is at one of the corners of the matrix. For example, the lowest cost producer will always be able to compete. So will the business with the most distinctive (differentiated) products. The dangerous competitive position is to be neither low cost nor differentiated.

		COMPETITIVE ADVANTAGE	
		Low cost	Differentiation
COMPETITIVE SCOPE	**Broad target**	Cost leadership	Differentiation
	Narrow target	Cost focus	Focused differentiation

Figure 85.1 Strategy matrix (Porter, 1985)

The process of strategic planning can be helped by mapping out the method of competition which other firms have selected (see Figure 85.2).

Along the bottom of the map the productivity of each business is measured. This reflects the efficiency with which the firm turns inputs (e.g. raw materials) into output (i.e. finished goods). The greater the efficiency of the business the lower the unit cost. As a result, a firm with high productivity will have a cost advantage over its competitors.

Figure 85.2 A strategic direction map (*Strategic Marketing Planning*, M. McDonald, 1992)

The vertical axis of the map shows an organisation's ability to add value to its inputs. A firm which has a well known brand name can charge a higher price for its output. This means that it can add more value than its competitors. The ability to add value therefore reflects the potential to develop a strategy of differentiation.

The shaded circle in the centre of the map shows the 'middle ground' in which neither cost leadership nor differentiation have been achieved. A firm in this position would face high costs as it tries unsuccessfully to differentiate its products. While at the same time its price is driven down because brand image is weak. Porter warns that very few firms can adopt both positions at once, as McDonald's does.

85.2 Identifying a strategic gap

Having established the strategic direction the organisation will adopt, the senior managers must next set the boundaries within which middle and junior management will take day-to-day decisions. A series of integrated actions must be set out. These will have the purpose of moving the organisation forward in the identified strategic direction. This plan will be introduced over a period of time known as a **planning horizon**. This will commonly be between one and three years, but may vary depending on the stability of the organisation's competitive environment. The greater the stability, the longer the planning horizon will be.

Strategic planning is only necessary because firms operate in a changing environment. If this was not the case then a single strategy, once designed, would bring success to the business on a permanent basis. However, changes in key variables such as technology, consumer tastes and communications make planning strategy increasingly important. The pace of change is intensifying, creating shorter product life cycles and encouraging increased competition. It is change which creates the **strategic gap** which must be closed by the second phase of the planning process.

TRAINER WARS

In 1987, Reebok was the dominant supplier of sports footwear to America. It had a 30% share – far in excess of the Number 2, Nike. Then, as the market size exploded in the early 1990s, Reebok found it increasingly difficult to compete. Nike kept hitting home with the smarter moves. With Michael Jordan and Tiger Woods, it was Nike who tied up the biggest star names. And Nike who proved one step ahead in new product development. By 1996 Nike was spending almost $1,000 million a year on marketing. Reebok could only afford $400 million, but even this was insufficient to prevent a slide in market share. Between 1994 and 1996, Reebok's market share fell from 21% to under 16% of the US market. Nike, meanwhile, jumped from 30% to 43%.

In early 1998 Reebok announced a change in strategy. No longer would it attempt to compete in the fashion-oriented youth market dominated by Nike marketing. Reebok would aim more at the adult market, accepting that lower market share would not matter as long as costs fell sharply enough.

Reebok was raising the white flag in the trainer wars. In Europe, it would be Adidas that would keep Nike on its toes.

McDONALD'S PLOTS STRATEGIC PLAN

McDonald's has succeeded in a strategic plan to achieve both cost *and* value leadership (see Figure 85.3). First the company identified the change in lifestyles which encouraged more people to use fast-food restaurants. Through careful promotion a brand image was created allowing differentiation of its products when compared with competitors. This added value, enabling higher prices to be charged. The profits helped fund large advertising campaigns which generated high sales. This allowed the business to benefit from economies of scale. Efficient techniques were devised in order to bring down costs while maintaining a differentiated product. Armed with this twin benefit of cost and value leadership, McDonald's moved ahead to become one of the world's most valuable brand names.

ADDED VALUE

Figure 85.3

Figure 85.5 A strategic gap

Organisations which seek to achieve objectives such as the maximisation of long-term profits will set themselves financial targets. These will be influenced by shareholders' expectations and the personal and business ambitions of the company directors. These expectations will determine the *financial objectives* of the organisation over the forthcoming planning period.

In order that a forecast can be made of the likely *actual* financial performance of the organisation over the interval of the planning horizon, an audit of the firm's present position should be completed. This will include an analysis of the firm's market position, manpower levels, financial situation and **capacity utilisation**.

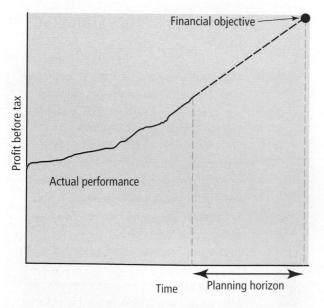

Figure 85.4 Financial objectives

The difference between the profit objective and the forecast performance of the business is known as a strategic gap (see Figure 85.5).

85.3 Closing a strategic gap

Once a strategic gap has been identified it is necessary to devise a series of strategies to close it.

It may be possible to achieve this to some extent by performing existing operations more efficiently, in order to reduce costs and boost profit. However, this is unlikely to solve the whole problem. Only careful strategic planning can develop the means by which the organisation can increase its effectiveness in order to meet its financial objective.

Strategic analysis will have provided a knowledge of the existing opportunities in the firm's environment and the key strengths, or core capabilities, of the organisation. Strategies must be designed to match what the firm is good at doing, to the potential possibilities available in the marketplace.

In 1993 the Castrol motor oil company appointed a new chief executive officer, Tim Stevenson. He identified a strategic gap facing the organisation. This was caused by a decline in market share in North America and Europe. The competition in these areas had grown but the market size was quite static because the number of cars and motorcycles in use was relatively stable. There was little prospect for sales growth.

Stevenson developed a plan to close the strategic gap created by Castrol's weak performance in its established Western markets. He identified the company's key strength was its ability to use promotion and sponsorship to build the image that 'Castrol means success'.

Castrol decided to use this expertise to develop new markets for its existing products. Asia was the region selected because it offered the attraction of rapidly expanding car and motorbike sales and therefore increasing demand for oil.

The firm's senior managers developed a set of objectives for Castrol in which 'a key plank' was to

Castrol in Asia: the key to closing the strategic gap (© Castrol International)

'grow our business in Asia Pacific very substantially'. The **strategic plan** to achieve this goal depended on 'making sure that we maximise our presence there'. So instead of spreading marketing activity thinly over many countries, Castrol would spend heavily in one country at a time.

Vietnam was chosen as the first location. The heavy expenditure worked, and Vietnam has become a significant market for Castrol products. To consolidate this success in Asia, Castrol moved managers based in Britain out to set up an Asian headquarters in Hong Kong.

The same approach was then launched in India. Stevenson observed that 'We did it in exactly the way we've done it in Vietnam: by blanketing the market with Castrol imagery and driving the business forward. You go to the remotest parts of India, and you see walls that are plastered with the Castrol logo and the Castrol colours.'

The experience of Castrol International reflects the kind of strategic planning which is necessary in a global economy. As the conditions in one market become less favourable, creating a strategic gap, it is necessary to develop strategies based on the company's strengths in order to build up new sources of demand. This involves careful planning of resource allocation within the firm and even building alliances outside the organisation.

Senior management must provide clear guidelines to shape middle and junior management decision making so that it is consistent with corporate objectives and strategy. In Castrol's case this involved high short-term expenditure to establish a brand name and moving human resources to be closer to the new market. Castrol was willing to risk the cost which was incurred by this strategy in order to meet the company's long-term objective of continued growth.

85.4 Contingency planning

A strategic plan should outline the critical assumptions which have been made about the future

competitive environment. If the success of the project depends on these judgements a 'fallback' position, or contingency plan, should be developed in case they prove wrong. As part of the planning process, 'what if?' questions should be asked. For example, Castrol might ask how the company should respond if one of its main competitors chooses to target the same Asian country.

Contingency planning allows the firm to consider what action it will take if particular opportunities or threats emerge as a strategy is implemented. Contingency planning is covered in more detail in Unit 86.

Strategic planning demands that the series of actions which the organisation intends to take are integrated. For example, the policy for human resources must match that for production capacity, or new technology. If a firm buys new machinery to expand output, it must have its manpower plan in place. If new skills are required to use the equipment then training must be provided or new staff recruited. The planning process must ensure that every implication of the strategy is considered. Each action in the plan must be matched to overall corporate strategy, in order that the organisation achieves its objectives.

When faced with the need to close a strategic gap, one approach to analysing the problem is to consider the extent to which new markets can be found for existing products, as Castrol has done. An alternative approach is to develop new products for the existing market or even diversify into a new industry. Whichever option is chosen, the organisation must analyse whether it is better to develop the resources to put the strategy into operation internally, or to acquire access to them externally.

85.5 Strategic planning
an evaluation

Many successful businesses do not have a formal strategic planning process. This does not mean that the issues raised here are not relevant to these organisations. The same problems must be dealt with when strategy emerges over time, as when it is planned more systematically. The advantage of explicitly setting aside time for strategic planning is that managers' minds are concentrated on the key questions facing the firm in the future. Then the actions decided upon can be more closely integrated.

Very few organisations will state publicly: 'We face a strategic gap.' However, as the Castrol case study shows, senior managers do identify that their firm's financial performance is disappointing and look for ways to solve this problem. The issue is not the terminology used, but that the concept helps us to understand the actions many managers take.

As the pace of change accelerates in many markets it is becoming increasingly difficult to plan long-term strategy. This highlights the need for a range of alternative approaches to be considered. The increasing complexity of global markets encourages firms to work together, by forming **strategic alliances** to the benefit of both parties. If strategic planning is to be a useful business tool in the future, it must be employed in a flexible way, responding to the changing external influences on the organisation.

A Level Exercises

A. REVISION QUESTIONS

(35 marks; 60 minutes)

Read the unit, then answer:

1 **a** Outline two methods of gaining competitive advantage. *(4)*
   b Explain why an organisation which tries to achieve both at once may be likely to fail. *(4)*
2 Draw a strategic direction map to illustrate the nature of competition in an industry of your choice. (For example, mobile phones, football, pop music or air travel?) *(6)*
3 **a** What is meant by the term 'planning horizon'? *(2)*
   b How long do you think the planning horizons are for:
      i a bridge construction engineer
      ii a Premiership football manager
      iii the directors of Microsoft?
   Briefly explain your reasoning. *(6)*
4 Explain why an organisation may face a 'strategic gap'. *(4)*
5 Identify four alternative actions which are available to a firm wishing to close a 'strategic gap'. *(4)*
6 What is contingency planning? Why might a business choose to undertake this process? *(5)*

B. REVISION EXERCISES

B. Case Study

Strategic Direction at United Chemicals

Christopher Gregson sat down to consider tomorrow's board meeting, his first in charge of the ageing industrial giant, United Chemicals. He had known what a difficult job he was taking on when he agreed to join the company two months ago, but the financial position was far worse than he expected. He looked down again at the key financial data in front of him (see the table on the next page).

The decline of the company had been dramatic. Established in the 1920s the business had dominated the UK market for years. The industry came to believe it took its customers for granted. Christopher already sensed the culture of the organisation reflected the feeling that it was not necessary to seek business, or take risks to develop new products or markets. At times, senior managers seemed arrogant and complacent. The

Summary of latest financial data – United Chemicals plc

	Industrials	Chemicals	Consumer	Total
Sales this year	£560m	£1,120m	£340m	£2,020m
Sales five years ago	£490m	£1,030m	£260m	£1,780m
Change	+£70m	+£90m	+£80m	+£240m
Return on capital	8.7%	10.1%	16.4%	10.6%
Acid test ratio				1.1
Gearing				45%

organisation structure of the business had remained the same for decades, with 12 divisions concentrated on specific product types like 'organic chemicals' and 'industrial explosives'. Although they often had customers in common, communication between each was rare and joint projects appeared 'unthinkable'.

United produced two quite different forms of product. Their industrial goods were made in bulk. Christopher recognised these immediately as 'commodities'. Chemicals such as alkalis and chlorine were manufactured, both in the UK and Western Europe, and sold for use in the production process of other goods. Price, above all else, was the key in these markets. Unfortunately the competitive environment facing United in these markets was not encouraging. Across the world the major manufacturers faced falling demand and overcapacity. Christopher shook his head sadly again. How could United still charge prices as much as 5% to 15% above competitors with plant lying idle and immense fixed costs to cover?

The consumer product market was a different ball game entirely. Here United produced paints and solvents with brand names instantly recognisable to every high street customer. The thought of managing such well-known products as Stick It and Cover All had been one of the great attractions for Christopher in taking on his new post. The potential for adding value in these markets seemed immense. Yet United's prices still only exceeded competitors by the same kind of margins employed in the bulk chemical market. These product types demanded a high level of expenditure on both promotion and research. United did support a large product development budget but it was soon obvious to Christopher that much of this spending was on complex scientific research rather than finding out what customers actually wanted to buy. The performance of United products in some foreign markets was disappointing. Christopher had already asked the pointed question: 'How can the US market achieve 20% market growth over five years while our market share in Australasia and the Far East has actually shrunk by 2% over the same period?'

As Christopher looked out of his office window at the vast chemical plant below he knew that tomor-

row's meeting was going to be crucial for the future of the once great company he now managed. He asked himself the same question again which had been bothering him for weeks: How am I going to convince people that change is vital? If we don't restructure and establish a strategic direction now, our business has no future.

Questions *(50 marks; 75 minutes)*

1 Provide evidence to show whether the approach currently adopted by United Chemicals is product or market oriented. *(8)*

2 a Use strategic direction diagrams to show the most suitable approach to competing in:
   i the bulk chemical market
   ii the consumer product market. *(8)*
  b Explain what is shown by each of your diagrams. *(6)*

3 How might the organisation be restructured to reflect the contrast between these two quite different markets? *(8)*

4 An Australian chemical company, with established presence in Far East markets, is currently experiencing difficulties and could provide a possible method of United Chemicals strengthening its performance in this area of the world. Consider whether you would advise Christopher to recommend takeover of this business. *(10)*

5 Analyse the alternative strategic approaches that Christopher might recommend to his board of directors and select a suitable course of action to improve the long-term performance of the business. *(10)*

C. ESSAY QUESTIONS

1 As part of the strategic planning process, Deverill Engineering plc has identified a strategic gap. Consider why this may have occurred and discuss what alternative actions might be taken in order to close it.

2 Michael Porter suggests that successful firms must choose between cost leadership and differentiation. By implication, being a little bit of both is a difficult and dangerous strategy. To what extent do you support Porter's theory?

CRISIS MANAGEMENT

86.1 What is a crisis?

A crisis is any event that threatens the well-being or survival of a brand or a whole firm. This is, necessarily, a broad definition. Crises can come in many guises, but most have one thing in common – they are unexpected. Crisis management is the term used to describe the efforts firms make to deal with crises as they arise. Crisis management is very closely linked to **contingency planning**. In other words, planning for unexpected, often unwelcome events.

86.2 Different forms of crises

Crises are unpredictable, therefore it is impossible to list every type of crisis which may arise. There are, however, a number of fairly common types of crisis which firms may face:

- Hostile takeover bids – when a predator company launches a hostile takeover bid, the defending company must try to convince its shareholders not to sell their shares. Failure will mean the bidder wins the battle. A takeover battle is a true battle for survival.
- Environmental disasters – leakage or spillage of dangerous substances can cause a crisis. This is even more intense when local communities and the environment are affected. There are many examples of this kind of crisis. Each has the potential to cause serious damage to the reputation of the company concerned.
- Faulty or dangerous products – these crises hit the headlines if a manufacturer's product is found to be unsafe – as in the Mercedes A Class car in 1997 (see In Business overleaf). They can be very expensive to put right, but no matter how much money is spent, the effect on the company's image may linger.
- Strikes by the workforce – although uncommon, strikes such as the action taken by cabin crew at British Airways in 1997 can undermine customer confidence and loyalty.
- Major customers withdrawing their orders – firms who rely on a few major customers for a large proportion of their sales can be plunged into crisis if one customer goes elsewhere. This is especially likely to be true for small firms who supply components to large manufacturers.

- Physical destruction – this might be due to a natural disaster, such as the earthquake which destroyed the Japanese city of Kobe in 1995, or to terrorist activity. The latter may be targeted directly at the firm, such as animal rights activists damaging research laboratories. Or the firm may be an indirect target, as with the businesses affected by the terrorist action on 11 September 2001.

86.3 Contingency planning

The most effective crisis management is undoubtedly based on contingency planning. If a firm is prepared, it should be in a better position to manage any crisis that occurs. Contingency planning for crises can be shown as a five-stage process:

1 recognise the need for contingency planning
2 catalogue as many crisis scenarios as possible
3 search for ways to prevent each crisis
4 formulate plans for dealing with each crisis
5 simulate crises and the operation of each plan – practice makes perfect!

No firm will be prepared for a crisis without recognising the need to plan. In many firms, this first stage will not occur, perhaps as a result of short-sightedness. Or perhaps due to ignorance of the need for planning.

The second stage – cataloguing as many crisis scenarios as possible, involves much pessimistic imagination. What are the possibilities which may place the firm under threat in the future? This stage should be all-inclusive, considering as many crisis situations as possible. The approach required is sometimes called 'what if?' analysis. What if glass were found in our baby food product? What if our main supplier went into liquidation? And so on.

There is no doubt that prevention is better than cure, so firms should first aim to pursue strategies which will avoid each crisis. For example, extra quality checks could be made, or supply contracts split between two or more companies.

Once possible crises have been identified, the firm can begin to make plans for dealing with each one. These plans will be based on the resources needed and how they will be used in dealing with the crisis. The resources considered will be human, financial and physical. This stage of the process will be dealt with in greater detail later in this unit.

With plans in place, the firm can now begin to simulate its response to each type of crisis. These simulations may be computer-based, or they can be actual exercises. The purpose of these exercises is to check for any weaknesses in the plan and to familiarise staff with the procedures in the event of a crisis. Any weaknesses in the plans identified by the simulation should be addressed and changes made to the plan. In this way, successful contingency planning should be an ongoing process, with plans being updated and revised continually as circumstances change.

CONTINGENCY PLANNING – IT WORKS

Travel Company Thomas Cook proved the value of contingency planning following a tragic coach crash on one of their holidays to South Africa. The crash, which left 28 dead, could have led to massive damage to the firm's reputation and could potentially have hit sales hard. Thomas Cook's response to the crisis was straight from the crisis management textbook.

An Incident Control team gathered within 20 minutes of the news reaching the UK. A Relative Response Hotline was opened for worried families and seats were block-booked on flights to South Africa later in the day for relatives of the deceased who wanted to travel to the accident site. Trauma counsellors and company representatives were also on site within 24 hours.

The company had issued a worldwide press release within 2 hours of the crash and kept supplying information freely to the press through their General Manager – who was essentially the focus of the crisis management effort.

Only 7 people cancelled their holidays to South Africa as a result of the accident. For Thomas Cook, preparation for crisis led to a thoroughly professional and effective response.

Source: www.regesterlarkin.com – website of crisis management consultancy

86.4 Management of the actual crisis

Crises have effects on the marketing, finances, operations and personnel aspects of business.

Successful **public relations** will often form a vital part in the management of a crisis. Often, it is the firm's image which is under threat. This means the firm needs to communicate to its consumers, directly and clearly. This communication may take the form of a wave of informative advertising, designed to get a clear message across. This can be an expensive solution, since the advertising will undoubtedly be required to reach as many consumers as possible as quickly as possible. Alternatively, traditional public relations

THE MERCEDES A CLASS

Problems can also occur with the actual design of the product itself. Weaknesses in the design of a new product may mean that the product fails to meet safety standards. This was the case with the Mercedes A Class. The A Class was the first small car Mercedes had ever made. It won praise from the motoring press and appeared to be experiencing a successful launch, until photographs emerged from a test in Sweden called the moose test. The test aims to simulate the manoeuvres required to avoid a moose which wanders onto the road and involves swerving the car at speeds of around 30 mph. The photograph, published around the world, showed a battered Mercedes which had rolled over when attempting the moose test.

Customer confidence was shattered and Mercedes had a serious crisis on its hands. Immediately, it announced withdrawal and recalls of all A Class cars sold and produced. Designers were sent off to redesign the chassis to overcome the problem shown by the test. It took months, but the A Class was relaunched, with a modified design, a design which would pass the moose test.

Mercedes demonstrated the importance of acting swiftly, clearly and in the manner consumers would expect of a firm with a reputation for safety. Although the firm's image was dented in the short term, the long-term status of the brand was not seriously damaged by the crisis, whilst Mercedes was able to go ahead with a second attempt to break into the small car market. All of this was the result of good, clear communication, communication which made its handling of the crisis highly effective.

methods, such as press releases and press conferences, can be used. These involve few costs, but leave the message in the hands of the journalists. So it is vital that the firm manages its press releases and press conferences as cleverly and openly as possible.

FINANCE

There is little doubt as to the key financial aspect of crisis management – cash. Most crisis management situations will require immediate cash expenditures. Whether these are on advertising campaigns, environmental clean-up operations or fighting a hostile takeover bid, the firm will need to have a healthy cash situation. Logically this implies that liquidity is key. A firm with a healthy acid test ratio will be better prepared to deal with a crisis. However, high liquidity is not good for business. It means resources tied up in working capital, not earning the returns which may be available from other uses. A possible answer is the prior negotiation of an overdraft facility. To be used only in emergencies as a short-term source of cash. Whatever the firm decides to do, its contingency planning should face up to the possible need for quick cash.

OPERATIONS

The production of goods or services can be the cause of many crises. A contamination scare such as when benzine was found in Perrier water can seriously damage a firm's image. So can the failure to provide proper customer service. In 2003 the London Underground let down customers and businesses by its slowness in re-opening the Central Line after a derailment. The line took two months to open.

Risks with suppliers were highlighted when a massive earthquake hit the Japanese city of Kobe in 1995. Mitsubushi car plants ground to a halt as the factories of several of their suppliers were devastated by earthquake damage. Mitsubushi's just-in-time production system, based on having few suppliers, was in no position to cope. With the low stock levels required by just-in-time production, supplies of components ran out within minutes rather than days and the whole production system was halted. This key weakness of modern just-in-time systems is only highlighted when there is a crisis. It is, however, another important factor for consideration in the contingency planning process.

PERSONNEL

Leadership: There is no doubt as to the most effective style of leadership in a crisis. Authoritarian leaders are able to issue instructions and make decisions immediately, with the speed required in a crisis. The leader should be backed up by a well-trained support staff of experts in a range of relevant fields. Their role should be advisory so that the leader can seek their advice

when required. In this way, not only is decision making speeded up, but also there is a minimal risk of coordination problems. Mixed messages coming from a firm during a crisis will make communication ineffective and confusing. With a single, authoritarian decision maker in charge, a firm is in the best position to deal rapidly and effectively with the crisis.

Communication: Both internal and external communication are vital in a crisis. Many observers recommend setting up a control centre which can handle both internal and external communication in a crisis. This control centre should be staffed by senior managers and public relations experts. The managers will be able to ensure effective internal communication. The public relations staff will be those best able to deal with press or public enquiries. This system will only work if everyone within the control centre is clearly briefed as to the exact nature of the crisis and the firm's response to the situation. Firms should have clear chains of command in place and the communication channels which accompany them. These communication channels should be as direct as possible, eliminating the need to communicate through intermediaries.

The actual physical systems of communication need to be considered too. The communications centre should be ready to go into operation at a moment's notice, whilst those staff allocated to the crisis management team must be available whenever a crisis strikes. For this reason, detailed lists of contact phone numbers and possibly electronic pager numbers should be available for all relevant staff. There should also be back-up staff, fully trained, ready to step in if members of the crisis team are abroad or ill. The control centre itself should have dedicated telephone, fax and Internet lines in place. Some of these lines can be used to handle enquiries from the public or the press. Others should be reserved for internal communication only. If these steps are taken, communication – a vital aspect of good crisis management – should be effective.

Key aspects of good crisis management

Aspect of Business	Requirement for Good Crisis Management
Internal communication	Direct, open, rapid
External communication (public relations)	Informative, truthful, controlled
Leadership style	Directive, even authoritarian
Production	Plan for contingencies (especially if using JIT)
Finance	Cash position always kept strong enough to cope

WORLD TRADE CENTRE – A NEW KIND OF CRISIS

ESpeed is one of the major suppliers of network communication services for electronic financial trading. ESpeed is a subsidiary of Cantor Fitzgerald, the firm that lost 657 employees in the World Trade Centre on 11 September 2001. Everyone in their New York offices at the time was killed – this was a crisis beyond all previous crises.

Amazingly, eSpeed was back and operational on the US markets again within 3 days of the disaster. This was the result of a number of factors, identified by Cantor Fitzgerald's London CEO Lee Amaitis as including:

- Dedicated staff in eSpeed's London offices working 20-hour days, staying at their office continually and reprogramming the networks required for trading.
- A strong infrastructure of technical services – all New York systems were backed up at one of the other two eSpeed offices in London and New Jersey.
- A strong financial position – allowing money to be spent on assets that needed to be hired in the short term.
- Spare office space in New Jersey – allowing US operations to shift to a single location, aiding coordination.
- Dedicated people – staff willing to go further than anyone could have expected to try to help the company.

Perhaps linked to the dedication of the staff was the announcement from Cantor's Chairman, Howard Lutnick, that a quarter of the firm's profits would go to the families of staff lost in the disaster. Remaining staff were given a clear way in which they could help the families of the friends they had lost, by working for the company's success.

ESpeed recovered to turn in a profit within a year of the attacks. This was due to effective contingency planning, flexibility and good management.

Among the key issues for analysis are:

- The cost of prevention versus the cost of the event. Having identified potential crises, firms can decide whether to spend money on prevention, or gamble on avoiding them. In the context of a business case study, arguments can be developed for and against either option. A decision can then be reached on which argument is the stronger in the business context.
- The need for a scientific approach to contingency planning. Analysis in business is often carried out through a combination of written and numerical work. In the case of contingency planning, firms can use a quite simple method of numerical analysis. This can be used to help decide how much it is worth spending to plan a response to different crisis situations. Firms will multiply the probability of a particular crisis occurring by the expected financial damage it will cause. Consider two possibilities. A firm considers there is a 5% chance of a crisis which would cost it £2 million in lost revenue, and a 1% chance of a crisis which will cost £100 million.

$$5\% \times £2m = £100,000$$
$$1\% \times £100m = £1,000,000$$

Therefore the firm should allocate 10 times as much money and time to prepare for the second crisis.

- Contingency planning is a key test of whether a firm is looking to its long-term future. Spending £1 million now may save £100 million in the long run. This may ensure the long-term survival of the company.
- Analysing a crisis situation and making a choice between alternative courses of action. An examination may present a number of possible responses to a particular crisis. The student must pick out the advantages and disadvantages of each course of action. These would depend upon the financial and other circumstances of the firm. Full consideration should be given to the guidelines to crisis management detailed above when assessing a particular method. A final judgement should always be made as to the best way of dealing with the crisis. See the evaluation section below for help with this.

86.5 Crisis management
an evaluation

It is important to remember that what has been described in this unit is a theoretical account of successful crisis management. The reality is never so simple. Crises are unpredictable and it is important to consider that no matter how well a firm has planned for a crisis, things will go wrong. By their nature, crises present a whole range of unexpected difficulties and firms will aim to emerge from crises as best they can. This means, therefore, that crisis management is basically a damage limitation exercise. Once the crisis has occurred, the firm has been damaged in some way. The goal must be to get through the crisis with as little harm as possible to the firm's reputation and operations.

This leads on to another, more positive result of crises. Although crises are damaging in the short term, they can present opportunities for firms. A firm may suffer a crisis as a result of a factor outside its control. If it does all it can to minimise the effect on its customers, its reputation may actually be enhanced. Firms that take a positive, long-term attitude to crisis management may find opportunities arising from crises.

Building on the notion of a long-term approach is the generally accepted fact that in a crisis, the truth is better than a lie. Lies may help to deflect the effects of a crisis in the short term. In the long run, the truth usually comes out, damaging the reputation of the firm, perhaps more than the original crisis. For this reason, open and truthful communication should be the order of the day. Although the truth may not be what the public want to hear in the short run, con-

sumers can be unforgiving if they find they have been lied to.

A final evaluative comment is that although it is generally only large firms which practice the kind of contingency planning outlined in this unit, all firms may face crises. Even small firms may find themselves in a position of needing to take swift action to ensure survival. It is up to those firms to apply, if possible, the key aspects of crisis management, albeit on a smaller scale.

KEY terms

contingency planning – preparing for unwanted or unlikely possibilities. Contingency planning allows the firm to ask 'what if?' questions, testing out alternative responses in a modelled situation, often on computer.

public relations (PR) – the process of obtaining favourable publicity via the editorial columns of press media, or in television/radio broadcasts.

scenario planning – considering alternative visions of how the future may look. This is similar to contingency planning, but implies looking for opportunities as well as threats.

A Level Exercises

A. REVISION QUESTIONS
(30 marks; 60 minutes)

Read the unit, then answer:

1 Give three examples of recent crises, other than those mentioned in the unit. *(3)*
2 Give three reasons why firms might ignore the need for contingency planning. *(3)*
3 Briefly explain why a consultative management style is unlikely to be effective in a crisis. *(2)*
4 Why might a clear organisational chart be a useful tool in crisis management? *(3)*
5 What costs are likely to result in the production of a large batch of faulty cars which need to be recalled? *(4)*
6 What are the likely effects of contingency planning on the motivation of staff? *(3)*
7 Why might lean producers suffer more than other firms in a crisis? *(3)*
8 Outline the likely effects on the firm of each of the following crises:
   a Several serious food poisoning incidents at a leading fast-food chain. *(3)*
   b A computer virus which forces a high street bank to close down its entire computer network for a month. *(3)*
   c The unexpected death of the charismatic owner and leader of a diversified consumer goods company. *(3)*

B. REVISION EXERCISES

B1 Data Response
Crisis at Sellafield, But Don't Panic

On the edge of the lake district, at Sellafield in Cumbria, British Nuclear Fuels' (BNFL) reprocessing plant sits beside a huge lagoon, home to around 650 tonnes of used nuclear fuel. The fuel rods are waiting for reprocessing – a system which splits the used fuel into waste and plutonium. The latter can be reused in generating nuclear energy.

Last week, Jurgen Tritten, Germany's new Environment Minister, urged BNFL to stop reprocessing the fuel rods. He informed them that Germany, its second biggest foreign customer, would immediately stop sending waste to BNFL, thus removing a vital source of business for the firm. Given BNFL's allegedly precarious financial position (analysts have suggested that it has been losing money regularly for many years) the loss of such a major customer could be fatal.

Fortunately, BNFL was able to get intervention at the highest level, from Britain's Secretary for Trade and Industry, Stephen Byers. He informed the German government that Britain would immediately return all the used fuel from Germany currently stored here. Since Germany has no facilities to store used fuel and no reprocessing facilities, this move forced the German government to climb down.

Despite this close escape, a large crisis looms in the long term for BNFL's reprocessing plant. The problem is that reprocessing nuclear fuel is not economically viable. The world has plenty of reprocessed materials already and new deposits of uranium, the primary nuclear fuel, are being found throughout the world. Uranium is therefore much cheaper than plutonium. It is also better environmentally, since the reprocessing adds to the volume of nuclear waste materials.

Japan, BNFL's largest single customer, is likely to stop using its services soon. Even Britain's nuclear fuel industry is likely to phase out its use of reprocessing in the near future. What will be left for the plant to do if no-one needs fuel reprocessed?

Questions *(25 marks; 30 minutes)*

1 Explain why reliance on a few large customers leaves a firm open to crises. *(6)*
2 To what extent does BNFL appear to have used contingency planning in this example? *(6)*
3 How might BNFL set about the process of contingency planning in the next few years? *(6)*
4 For what reasons might BNFL be expected to be particularly good at crisis management? *(7)*

B2 Case Study

Crashing Into Crisis

On 3 September 1998, Swiss Air flight 111 crashed into the sea off the eastern coast of North America, shortly after leaving New York. All on board were killed.

Two years earlier, in 1996, TWA flight 800 crashed into the sea off the eastern coast of North America shortly after leaving New York. All on board were killed.

These two tragic air disasters share many similarities, yet the effects of the crashes on the two airlines involved were vastly different.

TWA was accused of incompetence and insensitivity in responding to the needs of victims' families. The company refused to publish passenger lists until they were sure of exactly who was actually on the flight and had contacted the families of all the victims. This process took nearly a full day. Freephone helplines set up to answer relatives' questions were often left unanswered whilst relatives also claimed that TWA paid insufficient attention to their travel and accommodation needs. Quickly, politicians and the media began to criticise TWA's handling of the crisis.

Swiss Air, on the other hand, in the days that followed the crash, became perceived as the airline that could do no wrong. Flight lists were published within hours, working freephone hotlines were set up and hundreds of crisis counsellors arrived in New York within 24 hours of the disaster. In the hours after the crash, Swiss Air made sure that families of victims were kept fully informed of the latest developments and offered the families $20,000 each to cover their immediate expenses. Although it seems strange to suggest, Swiss Air's reputation may even have benefited from the disaster rather than suffering the terrible blow that TWA's received.

There are a number of reasons that explain why the two firms handled their crises differently. The Swiss Air crash happened after US legislation forced airlines to produce contingency plans covering passenger lists, freephone numbers, the return of personal effects and how to help families with travel and personal needs.

Swiss Air has an arrangement with Delta Airlines (the 3rd biggest US carrier) which amounts to a partnership in the US. Delta treated the crash as if one of its own planes had gone down and therefore added their own resources to the crisis management effort. TWA was on its own and as luck would have it, had just parted company with two senior executives. Meanwhile, at the time of the crash, their chief executive was in the UK on business.

TWA's problems were intensified by the suspicion that terrorist actions might have brought the aircraft down. Government agencies took control of the situation from TWA and barred relatives from visiting the crash site.

Questions *(40 marks; 50 minutes)*

1 Suggest why the following caused particular problems for TWA in its management of the crisis:
  a loss of two senior executives
  b chief executive being out of the country
  c terrorist action being suspected. *(12)*
2 What key factors can you identify to explain Swiss Air's good crisis management? *(8)*
3 Using examples from this case study and other industries, explain how governments might help to ensure effective crisis management. *(8)*
4 How does the case illustrate the importance of the following aspects of preparing for a crisis:
  a high available liquidity
  b contingency planning
  c good external communication? *(12)*

C. ESSAY QUESTIONS

1 Effective contingency planning can be very expensive to firms and provides no guarantee of crisis survival. If this is the case, why do so many firms spend thousands of pounds on contingency planning?
2 'The most important factor in crisis management is communication.' Discuss.
3 Crisis management and contingency planning are recognised as an important aspect in the management of large companies. Discuss why they might be equally important to small firms and explain how crisis management may differ within small firms.

INTEGRATED OBJECTIVES AND STRATEGY

Objectives and strategy

A. AS LEVEL REVISION QUESTIONS
(30 marks; 30 minutes)

1 Identify three possible aims for a small, family-run bakery. *(3)*
2 Distinguish between aims and objectives. *(3)*
3 Suggest two reasons why many firms have mission statements. *(2)*
4 What is meant by the term 'venture capital'? *(3)*
5 Outline two problems that might be encountered when starting a business. *(4)*
6 List two documents which must be submitted when applying to incorporate a company. *(2)*
7 Explain why a firm might obtain a patent. *(4)*
8 State three groups to which a business has some responsibility. *(3)*
9 What is meant by the term SWOT analysis? *(2)*
10 How might a firm set about determining its opportunities and threats? *(4)*

B. AS LEVEL REVISION EXERCISES

B1 Data Response

The Management Buyout

Streamer plc annual accounts
Profit and loss account, year-end 31 March

	This Year (000s)	Last Year (000s)
Turnover	£91,178	£92,846
Cost of sales	£61,969	£63,542
Gross profit	a	a
Selling & distribution costs	£14,814	£15,365
Administrative expenses	£9,006	£9,568
Interest	b	b
Operating profit	£3,136	£2,027
Taxation	£791	£581
Dividends	£684	–
Retained profit	c	c

Balance sheet as at 31 March

	This Year (000s)	Last Year (000s)
Intangible assets	1,560	1,672
Tangible assets	593	546
Stocks	24,553	29,392
Debtors	22,982	21,645
Cash	8,338	1,070
Creditors (falling due within one year)	37,000	33,793
Net current assets	w	w
Assets employed	x	x
Loans	158	581
Share capital	28,655	28,655
Reserves	y	y
Capital employed	z	z

Questions *(30 marks; 35 minutes)*

1 Look at the above accounts and fill in the gaps (a–c and w–z). *(7)*
2 If you were managers of Streamer plc, considering a management buyout, what is the maximum price you would consider offering the shareholders of the business, to buy them out? Explain your logic. *(9)*
3 Outline two ways you might finance the buyout. *(4)*
4 The managers have met to discuss their approach if they succeed with an offer. Their new objective will be to 'grow the business by 50% over the next three years and then re-float onto the stock market'. Consider the possible effects of this objective upon the performance of Streamer. *(10)*

C. A LEVEL REVISION QUESTIONS

(40 marks; 40 minutes)

1 What is goodwill? Why might a business be prepared to pay for goodwill? (4)

2 What is meant by the term 'stakeholders'? Give three examples of stakeholders. (5)

3 Distinguish between horizontal and vertical integration. (3)

4 Identify two ways profits might increase as a result of backward integration. (2)

5 Give two reasons why multinational firms might not be welcome in a country. (2)

6 Outline two economies of scale a multinational firm might be able to benefit from. (4)

7 Explain two reasons a business might be run more efficiently after a management buyout. (4)

8 Outline two factors that might constrain a firm pursuing the objective of growth. (4)

9 In what circumstances might a mission statement be ineffective. (4)

10 Identify three possible problems for a small firm that is growing rapidly. (3)

11 Research shows consistently that most takeovers fail to generate economic benefits. Why, then, may so many takeover bids continue to be made? (3)

12 What problems may arise for a firm that has just been floated onto the stock market? (2)

D. A LEVEL REVISION EXERCISES

D1 Case Study

AEB Summer 1997 Paper 2
Read the case study and answer all the questions which follow.

High IQ

Imran Qureshi had been lucky to get his A Levels. On three occasions he was nearly asked to leave the college because of his lack of commitment. He always said he was 'completing contracts', but not many of the staff believed that. Eventually, he achieved three modest pass grades in Art, Graphical Communications and Business Studies.

In fact, Imran *had* been completing contracts. His mother was an accountant and, realising his mastery of computer programming, had come to rely on her son's ability to tailor software to the needs of individual businesses. Just two weeks before his first A Level examination, Imran was still working on a job worth £2,000.

The six months after leaving college proved very profitable for Imran. He earned over £18,000. Yet he was becoming restless working on similar problems with similar software. Bored, he used all his savings to buy a £15,000 computer with £6,000 of software — state-of-the-art equipment capable of the animation

wizardry of the film Jurassic Park. For several months Imran barely moved from his bedroom as he mastered the system's design and animation techniques. Eventually, he could turn static logos into people, give them adventures and then transform them back onto a soft drink's can or sweet wrapper.

Armed with his expertise and a laptop computer, Imran visited a number of advertising agencies in Central London. Impressed with the quality and creativity of his work, orders started coming in. A five-second sequence here, to liven up an ice-cream commercial, a fifteen-second cartoon there, as part of a trailer for a TV programme. As few others in London had the equipment or the expertise for this work, Imran found himself able to charge ever-higher fees. Yet the work kept flooding in. From his bedroom Imran generated £45,000 in eight months.

Snowed under by work, feeling the need to work closer to his clients and in desperate need of staff, Imran found a studio in Wardour Street – the centre of commercial TV and film production in London. The four-year lease cost £20,000; more worrying was the £24,000 annual rent. To give himself some protection from these financial commitments, Imran formed a company, IQ Ltd. He took on a secretary/bookkeeper/credit controller and brought in two computer programming friends to cope with the work. After paying for a new £20,000 computer workstation, Imran's capital was nearly used up.

Although his clients were delighted to see the professionalism of his London studio, Imran hit problems from the start. Instead of working flat out every day, his friends wanted to stop and chat, go out for lunch and enjoy a normal working life. Despite their computer skills, both programmers needed a lot of training, advice and support on the computer animation software. Imran gave this grudgingly. Business Studies theory ensured that he knew the importance of training, but time and money pressures made him very reluctant to 'waste' time in this way. The atmosphere in the studio became very strained.

From an early stage, Imran took care to maintain a rolling, six-month cash flow forecast. This helped him through the move to the studio and always impressed his bank manager. In March 1996, however, just three months after the move, Imran was hit hard by the liquidation of a major advertising agency client. It owed IQ Ltd £28,000. Fortunately the bank was very helpful, allowing Imran a temporary overdraft facility.

With his company struggling, in June 1996 came a much more pleasant shock. At the advertising industry's annual award ceremony Imran won one gold and one silver medal for his computer animation work on two television commercials. In the following week he received over sixty calls from advertisers, directors and producers – including three from New York and one from Los Angeles!

The most exiting was the latter – a proposal from an independent producer of children's television programmes for a series of computer animated shows based on the Snoopy cartoon character. The producer offered Imran the choice of either being paid a flat fee for the work, or taking a small percentage of the show's earnings. The Los Angeles producer explained:

'Imran, it's like this. You take £5,000 per show or 8% of the gross takings. If it's bought by one of our national TV networks we'll gross £100,000 per show in fees and repeats. And Snoopy's big worldwide, so we might decide to spend some money selling the show to TV stations abroad. The selling costs will be £40,000 per show, but the rewards can be very high. You'll get 8% of the revenue, after allowing for the selling costs. That's in addition to the US income, of course.'

Within ten minutes of the call ending, Imran received a fax setting out the options on a decision tree (see Appendix).

Whichever method of payment he chose, if he accepted the Los Angeles order he would need to increase his production capacity still further. Would he be able to cope? Before rushing in, Imran decided to draw up a business plan to identify the likely consequences of accepting the Los Angeles order.

Questions *(50 marks; 90 minutes)*

1 With reference to the text, explain the business significance of the following terms.
   a Ltd *(4)*
   b production capacity. *(4)*

2 Many successful entrepreneurs admit that luck played an important part in their rise. To what extend has Imran's success been due to this cause? *(10)*

3 If Imran decides to accept the Los Angeles order, would you recommend the lump-sum deal or the 8% royalty? Use the Appendix and any calculations you find helpful to support your answer. *(12)*

4 a Consider the main areas Imran should cover within his business plan. *(8)*
   b Taking the whole case into account, do you consider that Imran should accept the Los Angeles order or not? Justify your answer. *(12)*

Appendix: Decision tree showing potential revenues from the Los Angeles order

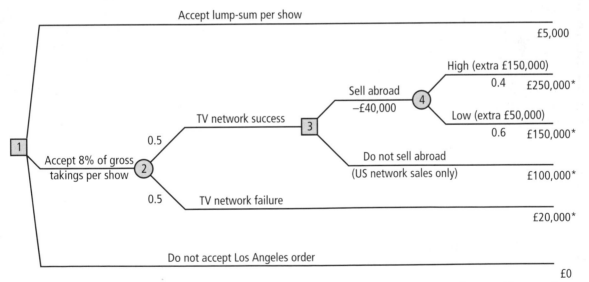

D2 Numerical Report
AEB Summer 1998 Paper 3

Section A
Answer this question. You should spend up to 50 minutes on this section.

1 Total for this question: 25 marks

Making Dough
The Grayton Bakery owns three shops, each selling bread, sandwiches and cakes. Each shop is supplied daily from the bakery itself, which is in the heart of Grayton. The family owners have recently appointed a new managing director. He is critical of the 'poor profit record' of the business. He often points to the shops' 6% profit margin as an example of past managerial weakness.

The Chairman Grayton's Board has asked you, as a local management consultant, to write a report analysing the strengths and weaknesses of the business and 'to recommend a strategy for the 21st Century'. (2 marks are included for appropriate report format.)

Appendices

Appendix A	Contribution Statement per Shop (£000s)
Appendix B	Shop Efficiency Data
Appendix C	Workforce Performance Data per Shop
Appendix D	Sales Growth per Shop (Indexed)
Appendix E	Sales Profile (1997 by value)

Appendix A – Contribution statement per shop (£000s)

	Darton Road	Beamish Avenue	The Grange
Sales turnover	165	145	220
Contribution	42	18	62
Allocated overheads	30	30	30
Profit per shop	12	(12)	32

Appendix B – Shop efficiency data

	Darton Road	Beamish Avenue	The Grange
Sales per employee (£000s)	27.5	29	34
Sales per square foot (£)	360	330	410
Stock wastage (£000s)	8	14	11

Appendix C – Workforce performance data per shop

	Darton Road	Beamish Avenue	The Grange
Staff (full-time equivalent)	6	5	6.5
Staff employed in last year	8	14	7
Labour turnover	33%	180%	8%
Absence rate	4%	11%	2%

Appendix D – Sales growth per shop (indexed: 1990 = 100)

Year	Darton Road	Beamish Avenue	The Grange
1993	118	114	122
1994	123	117	134
1995	127	120	143
1996	133	123	146
1997	138	127	150

Appendix E – Sales profile (1997 by value)

	Darton Road	Beamish Avenue	The Grange
Bread	44%	52%	36%
Sandwiches	18%	22%	24%
Cakes	38%	26%	40%

Section B

Answer one question from this section.

2 The Plastics Division of Horlock Engineering plc has made losses in two of the last four years. Now Horlock has suggested a management buyout of the Division at a price of £26 million.

Consider the issue which might determine whether or not the management decides to buy the Division.

(25 marks)

3 Shortly after being appointed, the new Chief Executive announced her determination to 'change the culture of the organisation'. Discuss the effect this might have.

(25 marks)

4 A sharp recession sends some firms into receivership, while others emerge stronger than ever. Discuss the factors which may determine the effect of a sharp recession upon a firm.

(25 marks)

5 'At their best, UK companies are as good as any in the world. But there is a long grey tail of poorly performing small and medium-sized companies.'

Source: John Neill, Group Chief Executive, the Unipart Group (The Guardian) 21 December 1996

Consider the factors which might enable this 'long grey tail' to improve its performance over the coming years.

(25 marks)

TACKLING EXAMINATION PAPERS

DEFINITION

Levels of response mark scheme – a way of marking answers based upon different academic skills rather than the quantity of knowledge shown.

Time allocation – the amount of time available to each element of an examination paper. This is calculated by dividing the minutes available by the total marks on offer.

Analyse – to break a topic down into its component parts. This should help to identify the causes and effects of the issue. It is important, when analysing, to follow a line of argument.

Evaluate – this vital term means to weigh up evidence in order to reach a judgement.

Many examiners have been heard to comment: 'The candidate had a pretty good knowledge of the subject, but was not well prepared for the examination'. Knowing your subject matter is not enough. You have to prepare carefully for examinations by practising the skills you need on a regular basis.

88.1 Methods of assessment

Students taking A level Business Studies are likely to encounter a variety of methods of assessment. The precise composition will depend upon the syllabus followed. The main methods include:

1. DATA RESPONSE QUESTIONS

These are series of questions relating to stimulus material in the form of graphs, charts, pictures or prose. Some, or all, of the questions will be based upon this information. However, you will be required to apply your subject knowledge and demonstrate your examination skills.

2. NUMERICAL REPORTS

Numerical reports test your understanding of a broad range of data in numerical and graphical forms. You are normally required to analyse the data to arrive at a decision. This type of paper focuses upon the skills of analysis and evaluation, as this type of assessent calls for the ability to develop and justify arguments.

3. ESSAYS

Essays test your ability to present a logical case and to appreciate that there are usually two sides to an argument. Essays will place heavy emphasis on the skills of analysis, evaluation and synthesis. Essays are considered more fully in Unit 89.

4. CASE STUDIES

A case study places you within a business scenario and invites an analysis of the situation. You will be required to offer solutions to problems and to propose business actions in a variety of circumstances. Commonly, case studies are employed to integrate the assessment of the various elements of Business Studies. To find out more about case studies you should read Unit 90.

5. PROJECTS

These entail a personal investigation into a business situation. They involve a structured approach with clear objectives and place heavy emphasis on collecting data. Projects are covered in detail in Unit 92.

88.2 Examination hints

BEFORE THE EXAMINATION

In spite of the increasing need for examination skills, it is important to revise thoroughly for examinations. The strategy adopted for revision is a matter of personal preference. However, there are a number of steps you should take:

- plan your time carefully – you should work to a revision timetable
- ensure that you have covered the entire syllabus – check your class notes against the exam board's syllabus and repair any gaps
- organise your notes into the sections covered by the various examinations to assist your preparation
- devise a system for working through your notes – perhaps by writing revision notes
- make extensive use of past papers in your revision and ask your teacher or lecturer for copies of the mark schemes

- practise writing answers to past papers working within the actual time limits of the examination
- focus your revision on topics which have not been tested for some time as these are more likely to come up in the forthcoming examination.

DURING THE EXAMINATION

There is a trend in Business Studies (and other subjects) towards shorter examinations. This places more pressure upon students to make effective use of the limited time available. Any errors in examination technique are highlighted as there is little time for recovery. Some key principles include:

- It is vital to read the question paper carefully and to ensure that you do exactly what is required of you. It is also important to read case studies, stimulus materials, charts and figures carefully as well as the associated questions. You must resist the desire to start writing as soon as possible – remember, it is quality that matters, not quantity.
- Plan your answers. Even for answers worth just a few marks, a little planning can avoid irrelevance and maximise your mark scoring potential. Too many examination candidates begin writing whilst still thinking about their answers. This results in fairly meaningless opening sentences and a tendency to repeat the wording of the question. For longer responses it is worth writing out a very brief plan at the top of your answer and adding to it as ideas occur to you.

- Timing is an important aspect of any examination. You should calculate how much time is available for each mark on the paper. Thus, if an examination lasts for 90 minutes and is worth 80 marks, the calculation might be as shown below:

ALLOCATING TIME WITHIN EXAMINATIONS

Time available:	90 minutes
Reading time:	10 minutes
Time for writing answers:	80 minutes
Marks available:	80
Minutes available per mark:	1

- Ensure that you answer the correct number of questions. It will limit your performance severely if you answer fewer questions than required. It is important to read the wording on the paper, but you should be familiar with the format of the examination before you sit it.
- Layout is important. Numerical responses are often poorly presented and this can make marking very difficult. You should lay out work clearly, spacing it out and showing workings. Key figures within answers (for example, total sales income, gross profit, etc.) should be labelled to assist the examiner. If the question calls for a graph, then as a matter of routine this should be titled, and all lines, as well as both the axes, should be labelled.

HOW TO WRITE AN ESSAY

Some people believe that essays require a plan. Others favour spider diagrams. In fact, there is no evidence on exam papers that essay plans lead to better essays. Good essays are far more likely to come from practice.

So what are the skills that need practice? The single most important one is the ability to build an argument. Take this exam essay title:

'A crisis has led to a dramatic loss of confidence among the customers of a medium-sized company. Consider the effects this may have on the organisation and how it may respond.'

Many answers to a title such as this will include six, seven, perhaps twelve points. As a result, each point will be developed through no more than four or five lines of writing. In effect, a point will be made and then given a sentence or two of development. This approach can never develop the depth of analysis required for essay success. A far more successful approach is to tackle only two or three themes (not points), then develop each one into a lengthy (perhaps half-page) paragraph. Acquiring the skill of writing developed prose proves equally important in case study work as well.

Having completed your analysis of key themes to answer the question, it is time to write a fully reasoned conclusion. This should be focused upon the question, making judgements on the issues you have analysed. A conclusion is usually worth about one-third of the marks for an essay, so it is worth devoting plenty of time to it. Certainly no less than ten minutes.

To help you write a good essay, here are ten golden rules you should follow.

1. THERE IS NO SUCH THING AS AN ESSAY ABOUT A TOPIC

An essay is a response to a specific title. At A level, the title is usually worded so that it cannot be answered by repeating paragraphs from your notes. Hence there is no such thing as 'the communications essay', because every answer should depend upon the title, not the topic. A past exam essay question read *'When selling a good, price is the single most important factor. Evaluate this statement.'* This popular question was widely misinterpreted and yielded low marks to candidates. The reason was that few students focused upon the words 'single most important'. They chose, instead, to consider price in relation to the remainder of the marketing mix. Therefore they failed to weigh up the market, economic or corporate factors that could lead price to become the single most important factor (or not, as the case may be).

2. THERE IS NO SUCH THING AS A ONE-SIDED ESSAY

If the title asks you to consider that 'change is inevitable' (as on a past exam question), do not fall into the trap of assuming that the examiner just wants you to prove it. If there was only one side to an answer, the question would not be worth asking. The only questions A level examiners set are ones which can provoke differing viewpoints. Therefore, after developing a strong argument in one direction, write 'On the other hand, it could be argued that …' so that you assess the opposite viewpoint.

3. ALL ESSAYS HAVE THE SAME ANSWER

With few exceptions, A level essay questions can be answered in two words: 'It depends'. Put another way, the cause or solution to a business problem or opportunity usually depends upon a series of factors, such as the company's objectives and the internal and external constraints it faces. Often, then, your main task in planning the essay is to consider what the answer depends upon.

4. ESSAYS NEED A STRUCTURE

When marking essays it is awful to feel you have no idea where the answer is leading. Some structure is needed. If you do not jot down a plan, at least tackle an essay which asks you to 'Discuss the factors …' by stating that 'There are three main factors …'. A useful trick is to leave the number blank until you have finished the essay – by which time you will have found out how many factors you think there are!

5. MOST CANDIDATES HAVE FORGOTTEN THE TITLE BY THE SECOND PAGE

As set out in points 1 and 2, the key to a good answer is the wording of the title. Discipline yourself to refer back to the question regularly – probably at the end of every paragraph.

6. EVERY PARAGRAPH SHOULD ANSWER THE QUESTION SET

A good paragraph is one which answers a specific aspect of the question in enough depth to impress the reader. Read over one or two of your essays and ask yourself whether *every* paragraph is directed at the question set. You will probably find that several are sidetracks or simple repetition of your notes/a text-book. In an exam, such paragraphs gain virtually no marks. The examiner is only interested in material that answers the precise wording of the question.

7. CONTENT

Good marks come from the breadth of your knowledge and the clarity of understanding you have shown. Generally, if you *analyse* the question with care you will pick up most of the content marks in passing. For example in the essay mentioned in point 2, analysis of the circumstances in which price might not be the most important factor would have led to discussion of distribution, promotion and the product itself. There was no need for a paragraph of description of the marketing mix.

8. ANALYSIS

How well can you apply yourself to the question set? Can you break the material down in a way that helps reveal the issues involved? Can you think your way into the context outlined by the question? For example, an investment appraisal question set in the context of a stable market such as chocolate should read differently to one set in a frantic market such as for computer games software. Can you use relevant concepts to explore the causes and effects? Analysis means using business concepts to answer the question with precision and depth.

9. EVALUATION – THE KEY TO HIGH ESSAY MARKS

Evaluation means judgement. For good marks you need to:

- show the ability to examine arguments critically, and to highlight differing opinions
- distinguish between fact, well-supported argument and opinion
- weigh up the strength of different factors or arguments, in order to show which you believe to be the most important and why
- show how the topic fits into wider business, social, political or economic issues.

10. PLAY THE GAME

Examiners love to read business concepts and terminology used appropriately. They hate streetwise language ('They're all on the fiddle') and any implication that the issues are simple ('It is obvious that …'). Keep your work concise, business-like and relevant, making sure that you leave long enough to write a thoughtful conclusion.

TACKLING AQA CASE STUDY PAPERS

90.1 Exam technique for all AQA case studies

Good case study answers combine a firm grasp of the case material with the ability to apply business concepts and theory to the questions set.

1. THE CASE MATERIAL

Writing an exam case study takes a great deal of time. Care is taken over the plot, the characters, the external context and over the underlying business themes. Weak answers reveal little grasp of even the most obvious parts of the text. Good candidates show a thoughtful approach to the key issues and characters. They appear not only to have read the material a couple of times, but also to have sat back for a moment or two to reflect upon it.

2. BUSINESS CONCEPTS

The job of every exam is to test the candidate's grasp of the concepts and content of the syllabus. Therefore, when reading a case study, it can be very helpful to note in the margin the business concepts hinted at in the text. When the case says 'they came up with a radical new design', your note in the margin might read 'value added' or 'price inelastic'. Then, when answering questions, there is a greater likelihood that your answer will be rooted in the theory of the subject.

3. THE QUESTIONS

The third crucial variable in exam success is the questions themselves. Mastering the precise wording of the questions is important for all exams, but with case studies there are other issues relating to the questions. The biggest is that a student may answer question 2a using material they later realise would have been more appropriate for answering question 3. Case study questions are much easier to answer if *all* the questions have been read at the start.

Taking all of the above points together, it is possible to come up with ground rules for how to tackle a case study exam. When you open the exam paper, follow this method:

1 Skim-read the text.
2 Briefly analyse any numerical material contained, perhaps, in an appendix. The reason for doing this now is that you have to understand the business fully before you can tackle the first question. If market share figures show a declining picture, you would need to know this to answer a question on marketing, finance, people or operations management.
3 Reflect for a moment on case material, then jot down the objectives of the featured business. Most business decisions are made with company objectives in mind. A candidate who has not thought about the firm's objectives is in a weak position to give a mature answer.
4 Read *all* the questions.
5 Re-read the case, jotting down relevant concepts in the margin of the exam paper.

Taking 10-15 minutes to digest and think about the material at the start of a 90-minute case study exam is time well spent. Top marks go to those who understand the business and its problems, have thought about how they relate to the theory of the subject, and make sure they answer the precise wording of each question.

90.2 Exam technique for the AS level AQA case study

This case study paper covers two sections of the AS syllabus: Units 2 and 3. The business case will focus upon the personnel and operations issues faced by a firm that also needs to think hard about strategy in the face of important external, e.g. economic, opportunities or threats. Top candidates will be those who can write lengthy, analytic answers to the questions posed. Such answers will require a good grasp of the syllabus material plus a great deal of practice at case studies for homework or in the lead-up to the examinations.

Among the most common question styles will be:

● Short-answer questions of fact, such as definitions.
● Questions asking for an outline or an explanation of subject matter. This will test the ability to show

detailed knowledge and understanding of syllabus material.

- Analytic questions, asking for the application, examination or analysis of an issue in the context of the case material.
- Evaluative questions, which look for judgements to be made, often by weighing one series of factors against another. These would be provoked by phrases such as 'make a fully justified recommendation …' or 'discuss' or even 'evaluate'. These questions carry 15 marks, and all have a mark allocation of:

    Knowledge 3marks
    Application 3 marks
    Analysis 4 marks
    Evaluation 5 marks.

90.3 Exam technique for the decision making paper

The decision making paper has to examine the A2 syllabus content of Marketing, Finance, People and Operations. In addition it will include a substantial numerical question. The style of the paper will be similar to a case study, but with rather more additional numerical or graphical material than is common. The text and numerical material will all concern one particular business decision, such as whether the XYZ Company should invest £80,000 in new equipment. The 80 marks available on the question paper are split equally between the four subject areas mentioned earlier. So there will be 20 marks of questions on Marketing, 20 on Finance, 20 on People and 20 on Operations.

The decision making paper awards especially high marks for those with good skills of application and analysis. Therefore a full mastery of the material will be invaluable. Timing is exceptionally tight on this paper, so great care must be taken to stick to the principle of a mark a mintue.

90.4 Exam technique for the A level synoptic case study (Unit 6)

This exam paper has two roles. It has to assess the A level subject content from External Influences and Objectives and Strategy. In addition it must provide synoptic assessment. This means testing whether candidates have an integrated understanding of the subject as a whole. A synoptic question might ask a student to assess the business opportunities open to the XYZ Company in the coming years. This contrasts with narrower questions on marketing or other departmental aspects of a business.

In this case study, the skill of evaluation generates the highest marks. Therefore exam candidates will benefit greatly from writing full conclusions which weigh up the arguments they have made in their answers. This skill, plus a broad view of business as a whole, should help achieve good marks on this paper.

SUCCESS AT OCR BUSINESS STUDIES

91.1 The new OCR modular examinations

September 2000 sees a new OCR (Cambridge) syllabus for those following an AS or a 2-year A level course. The AS consists of 3 units of examination; the A level has 6 units, which include the 3 AS units.

The AS examined units comprise:

1 An unseen case study on Businesses, Their Objectives and Environment
2 A data response paper on Business Decisions
3 A pre-issued case study on Business Behaviour.

The A level includes the above three, plus:

4 An unseen case study chosen from one of four subject options (Marketing, Accounting and Finance, People in Organisations and Operations Management)
5 A project, or the new option of a Business Thematic Enquiry examined by an unseen case study
6 A pre-issued case study on Business Strategy. This paper tests whether the subject of Business is understood in an integrated way.

Unseen case studies are covered in Unit 90 and the project in Unit 92. This unit concentrates largely on pre-issued case studies and the Business Thematic Enquiry, special OCR features. It is essential to obtain a syllabus from OCR, together with specimen papers.

When the case material arrives, tackle it systematically. The cases are written to test the syllabus, so have a copy to hand. Go through the text looking for the main syllabus areas. For example, in a Marketing case, there might be a reference to cutting price to beat competition. This immediately suggests revision of price elasticity of demand and a study of the role of price in the marketing mix, among other areas. If the competitive environment has become more hostile, then this raises questions of strategy or planning to face new circumstances. By its nature, marketing is an all-embracing activity and issues of overall strategy, planning and evaluation should arise. Pre-issue does not limit the scope for study but helps to focus it.

It is important to check if the syllabus contains a quantitative element, for example, investment appraisal or sales forecasting. There is no need to fear quantitative questions as the emphasis will be on understanding and analysis rather than calculation. The use, suitability and limitations of a technique in a context are important.

New information can be introduced in the questions but only in a limited way. For example, if depreciation of a fixed asset is being considered, the method or rate of depreciation might be given in the question paper only. Further assumptions about the context might be given in the question papers.

The cases are generally written as contemporaneous so any useful up-to-date background knowledge of the economy, the EU or the market is sensible: credit could be given for this.

91.2 Pre-issued case studies

Pre-issued case studies allow tutors and students to focus on specifically relevant material before the examination, when candidates see the questions for the first time.

The case-material will touch on all, or virtually all, syllabus areas and so it is not possible to ignore the 'harder' or less interesting parts of the subject. The best advice to teachers and students is to cover the whole syllabus, explore the case study thoroughly, and to avoid question-spotting.

91.3 Levels of response

Examiners award marks using a 'levels of response' marking strategy. This has replaced the traditional approach of rewarding basic points made and the development of those points. The net effect of the change is to reward the depth of an answer rather than the breadth.

The four levels of response correspond to the level of skill used in the answer. At the end of each statement is an example of the marks that might be awarded out of 12.

LEVEL 1

Level 1 is a response based on knowledge only, unrelated to the context, simply rehearsing pre-learnt material. Suppose a candidate answers a question about the marketing of a specific business by writing a long answer explaining the marketing mix, its content, its advantages and disadvantages etc. However 'good' or 'comprehensive' this answer may be, this is a Level 1 answer because it is unconnected with the context of the question set. It would typically receive 1–3 marks out of 12.

LEVEL 2

Level 2 responses are characterised by explanation and understanding rather than pure regurgitation of knowledge. Also, there is reference to the case material so that application to the context is effected. At Level 2 answers tend to be explanatory or descriptive, rather than exploring causes or setting out the links in a chain of argument or logic. They might receive 4–6 marks out of 12.

LEVEL 3

At Level 3 candidates show strong grasp of the concepts and theoretical underpinnings of the subject and demonstrate a chain of logic and analysis. An example would be an analysis of the effects of a rise in interest rates on a firm. For example: 'Investment plans are affected by an increase in the cost of capital. Marketing decisions are altered as a rise in interest rates affects aggregate demand and hence the market for its products via the income elasticity of demand. Employment plans change given the possible downturn in demand and the derived effects on the demand for labour.' Analytic answers receive 7–9 marks out of 12.

LEVEL 4

A Level 4 response is evaluative showing not only a command of analysis but also an ability to reach a judgement using the analysis and weighting it. For example, a question may be about the best time to launch a new product. There might be several arguments for and several against, based on different analyses or approaches. The evaluative answer discriminates or weights these different examples of analysis and comes to reasoned judgement. It is not necessary for the examiner to agree with the judgement reached to award Level 4 marks, merely to recognise that evaluation has taken place. Level 4 answers are likely to receive 10–12 out of 12.

Finally, by way of reassurance, Level 4 responses are relatively rare and Level 3 not as common as examiners would wish. A strong performance at A Level can be achieved by consistently achieving a high Level 2 with some Level 3 or 4.

91.4 The project and the alternative business thematic enquiry

The project will continue to be a problem solving exercise of 4,000 to 6,000 words. The alternative, a business thematic enquiry, will be an unseen case study examination based upon research into a topic provided by the Board at the start of the academic year. For example, the topic for the year might be the fashion industry. Candidates would be advised to collect all the primary and secondary data they can on the industry during the year. Useful activities would include:

- visits to manufacturers and retailers
- using the *Monthly Digest of Statistics* (ONS) to assess the level of import penetration
- collecting newspaper cuttings on the industry
- watching out for relevant TV business programmes on the industry
- visiting a good business library to find out market intelligence reports such as Mintel, Retail Business or Key Notes

The marking criteria for the project and the business thematic enquiry are the same. They differ slightly from the former OCR research assignment. The following guidelines will help.

CRITERION	MARKS
Skill with which the problem has been explained in context	5
Skill with which appropriate and realistic objectives have been set and used	10
Evidence of appropriate research methods	10
Evidence of appropriate primary and secondary research	10
Evidence of understanding and use of appropriate business studies knowledge	15
Selectivity, analysis and synthesis	15
Evaluation, recommendation or strategy development	15
Presentation: e.g. titles, paragraphing, tables, glossary, labelling, sources etc.	5
Written communication skills	5
Total	90

To sum up, the OCR syllabus has a variety of forms of assessment, each of which requires careful study. The Workbook sections in this book provide invaluable preparation for data response and case study examinations. Nevertheless it is still essential to obtain past (or specimen) exam papers from your tutor or from the exam board.

THE A LEVEL PROJECT

92.1 Introduction

Most A level Business Studies projects are based on problem solving or decision making. They are rooted in contacts made with an existing business. After visits and discussion, a medium- to long-term problem or opportunity is identified which the student researches and makes recommendations upon.

There is no doubt that planning is the single most important aspect of project work. It is vital to know from the start what you are aiming to do with your coursework and how you are going to achieve it.

Your planning should include:

- titles
- preliminary research
- action plans.

TITLES

At the initial planning stage it is usually helpful to think through several possible titles that you may be able to use for your project. Have your titles checked by your teacher, who may be able to suggest:

- which titles appear manageable
- which are over-ambitious
- which lend themselves to scoring well in the criteria outlined in the mark scheme.

PRELIMINARY RESEARCH

After selecting your working title, undertake some preliminary research. You may wish to use financial information from a particular firm, only to find out that it will not release the necessary information to you. This might force a rethink on your title. On the other hand, you may find, in talking to a manager, that there is an ideal problem that could be looked at, about which you were unaware. This time you can change your title for the better, having a clear idea of what you will be looking for.

ACTION PLANS

Your action plan should include the following elements:

- Primary research – identify the sources you will use, agree dates for interviewing relevant people, etc.
- Secondary research – identify your sources. Will you need to book resources from the local library? What data will you ideally like to find?

- Process and analyse your data. What numerical techniques are you going to use? How are you going to split the report up into sensible sections?
- Write your first draft report. Let several people read it and comment on it, such as your teacher, parents and the people about whose business you are writing. They may all be able to make helpful suggestions that could improve the content, layout and writing style of the report.
- Rewrite the report as appropriate, perhaps including new data or changing the order of the material included.
- Produce a finished version for final submission.

92.2 Data collection

Data collection is the main element that distinguishes coursework from the other activities you undertake on an A level course. Your coursework needs to be about what is going on in the real world, not what is being written about in a textbook.

The main techniques for collecting data that you may use are as follows.

PRIMARY

Interviews – although often time consuming, if you are well-prepared with appropriate questions you will usually be able to gather a lot of information that will be of direct use in answering your question.

SECONDARY

Government statistics can usually be accepted as accurate, but be careful that the information you obtain actually reflects the questions you are asking. Most coursework is based on local firms, so be wary of drawing conclusions from national data. There are many useful publications that carry information on a staggering range of issues. These vary in scope from the product reports of 'Which?' magazine to detailed market research reports from firms such as Mintel. The Internet has, of course, led to the availability of an overwhelming quantity of data.

At the stage of data collection, you will gather more information than you will eventually use in your report. One of the key skills you will need later on is the ability to edit your material so that what remains is central to the topic being discussed. However, you will need to check that you have sufficient relevant information as you go along – a mass of data will often obscure the purpose of the research and send you down interesting chains of ideas that bear no relation to the topic being discussed.

92.3 Analysis

Once you have collected your data and removed everything that does *not* help to answer your project title, you must begin to analyse your data.

In this context, analysis means breaking data down into its component parts, finding out cause and effect and determining which aspects of your study are interrelated. You could introduce relevant business theories here and show how your data corresponds to commonly accepted 'textbook' arguments.

The A level course contains several analytical tools which could be of use to you in analysing your research findings. These include written techniques, such as:

- SWOT analyses (Strengths, Weaknesses, Opportunities, Threats)
- PEST analyses (Political, Economic, Social, Technological)
- product life cycles
- Boston Matrix.

and numerical techniques, such as:

- investment appraisal
- break-even analysis
- critical path analysis
- decision trees
- variance analysis
- averages
- correlation.

To score highly on analysis you will need to use both written and numerate techniques in a detailed and appropriate way.

92.4 Answer your question

At the end of a long piece of work such as this, students can fail to state an answer or conclusion that relates to their initial title or question.

Clearly, examiners are looking for the ability to draw appropriate conclusions from the material gathered, together with accepted business theory. However, there is more to evaluation than a simple yes or no answer or a judgement that ABC Co is better at a certain aspect of its business than XYZ Co.

You also need to include your judgements on the reliability of the data you have collected, the soundness of the data collection techniques you used and your techniques for analysis.

Most importantly, you need to go beyond the basic question you have been investigating and show an awareness of the overall situation of the firm and its circumstances. Are there any underlying themes that have emerged from your research that have a clear impact on the issue you are discussing?

92.5 Structure of the report

In writing up your final report you need to use a clear structure that helps you put your case clearly and which guides the reader through your thoughts to your final conclusions. Your report may contain the following sections:

1 Title
2 Contents page
3 Sub-objectives
4 Background
5 Methodology
6 Analysis
7 Evaluation
8 Summary of the report
9 Bibliography
10 Appendices.

92.6 Write up the report

Although everyone has a different writing style, there are several points that can help you to produce a final piece of work that is of a high quality and maximises the rewards for all the hard work you have put in.

- If possible, wordprocess your piece. This makes for a clearer and neater presentation which will immediately give the reader a favourable impression. On a more practical level, it will make the job of rewriting your report much more manageable.
- Use sub-headings whenever possible. This helps to break up your report into more manageable chunks. It is also a useful idea to keep each section relatively short, although there must of course be scope for depth of analysis and evaluation.
- In writing up your report, you must always remember that whilst you have an overall picture of the situation from your own knowledge and research, the reader may never have heard of the firm before or have a great knowledge of the local area. Everything that goes into your final report ought to be fully explained and contextualised.
- Reread the report yourself, and allow someone else to read through it as well. You need to look out for clumsy phraseology which blurs the meaning of your writing, and you can still be looking to remove any issues that are not central to your argument. Remember that the word count of 3,000 words is only a target figure, and you will not be penalised directly for writing more or less than this.

HOW TO REVISE FOR BUSINESS EXAMS

Studies have shown that good revision can add as much as two grades to a student's result at A level. The aim of this unit is to help you to appreciate what makes up a quality revision programme.

93.1 Aims and objectives

A good revision programme will be aimed at achieving specific targets that will maximise your chances of success in the exam. How should these targets be set?

The basis for setting revision targets can be found in two places:

- the syllabus
- past papers.

THE SYLLABUS

The content of the course will be outlined in some detail. Since the questions in the exam will be based closely on this document, you must ensure that you have sufficient knowledge of each area.

The specification will tell you what skills the examiner will be looking for. As well as basic factual recall as appropriate to the case being discussed, there will be a range of other skills you must demonstrate if you are to score highly. An example is given below.

Definitions of higher academic qualities:

Analysis (breaking down)
- *Identification of cause, effect and interrelationships.*
- *The appropriate use of theory or business cases/practice to investigate the question set.*
- *Breaking the material down to show underlying causes or problems.*
- *Use of appropriate techniques to analyse data.*

Synthesis (bringing together)
- *Building the points/themes within the answer into a connected whole.*
- *Logical sequencing of argument.*
- *Clarity through summarising an argument.*

Evaluation (judgement)
- *Judgement shown in weighing up the relative importance of different points or sides of an argument, in order to reach a conclusion.*
- *Informed comment on the reliability of evidence.*
- *Distinguishing between fact and opinion.*
- *Judgement of the wider issues and implications.*
- *Conclusions drawn from the evidence presented.*
- *Selectivity – ensuring material is all relevant to the question.*

Source: AQA A Level Business Studies Mark Scheme

Knowing what skills the examiner is looking for will help you produce better quality answers in an exam. However, these are skills and like all skills they can only be developed through practice.

PAST PAPERS

Previous exam papers are also very important in helping you to prepare for your exam. They will show you exactly what sort of questions you will face and the number of marks available. They will also give you a feel for the type of words used in the question. It goes without saying that exam questions must be read carefully. However, there will be key words used in the questions that tell you how to answer them. There is, for example, a great difference in the expected answers for the following two questions:

1 Outline Maslow's motivation theory.
2 Evaluate Maslow's motivation theory.

Unless you know what is expected from these two questions, you are unlikely to know how much detail is required or how your answer ought to be structured.

93.2 Resources

The following list contains items which will be of enormous value in preparing for an exam. They should all be familiar to you before you begin revising, and should have played a constant part of your studies throughout the course.

1 class notes
2 a copy of the specfication
3 past exam papers and mark schemes
4 a revision plan
5 newspapers/cuttings files
6 a good textbook
7 access to your teacher
8 other students.

Class notes: Since these are the product of your work and a record of your activities, they will form a vital part of your understanding of the subject. Hopefully they will contain past work you have done on exam-style questions and model answers that will help prepare you for the exam.

A copy of the specification: The specification tells you several important things:

- what knowledge you could be tested on
- what skills the examiner will be looking for
- how the marks will be allocated
- what you will be expected to do in each exam paper you will sit.

Past exam papers and mark schemes: By working from past papers you will develop a feel for the type of question you will be asked and the sorts of responses you will be expected to give.

A revision plan: As described in the previous section. It will help keep you on target to achieve everything that you need to cover before the exam.

Newspapers/cuttings files: Since Business Studies is a real-life subject, the ability to bring in relevant examples will boost your answers and their grades.

A good textbook: One that will help clarify any points that you are still unsure about.

Access to your teacher: To be able to receive help and advice, to quell sudden panics and to help review your progress by marking work done and suggesting ways to improve your performance.

Other students: To help discuss points and clarify ideas.

93.3 Learning the language of the subject

Clear definitions of business terms are essential for exam success. They count for much more than the odd two-mark question here or there. In June 2002, many students who tackled an AQA paper 6 question on 'Ethics' knew the term too vaguely to be able to construct a valid answer.

There are many possible sources of good definitions of business terms. In this book, key terms have been given clear and concise definitions. The defini-

tions should be written without using the word in question.

> *Revising business definitions:*
> - *Definition cards*
> - *Past papers*
> - *Crosswords/word games*
> - *Brainteasers*

It is important, then, that you can produce high quality definitions in an exam. This can only be done through learning and practice. Possible ways to achieve this are as follows.

DEFINITION CARDS

Take a pack of index cards or postcards, or similar-sized pieces of thick paper. On each, write each term or phrase that you can find in the specification document. Remember to include things like motivation theories where a clear definition/description can give an excellent overview. It is extremely unlikely that you will be asked to know a precise definition for any term that is not specifically in the syllabus.

On the back of each card write an appropriate definition. This could come from your class notes, a textbook or a dictionary such as *The Complete A–Z Business Studies Handbook* 4th edition, Lines, Marcousé and Martin, Hodder and Stoughton 2003. Make sure that the definition you write is:

- concise
- clear
- does not use the word being defined in the definition.

Learn them by continual repetition. Put a tick or cross on each card to show whether or not you came up with an acceptable effort. Over time, you should see the number of ticks growing.

Shuffle the cards occasionally so that you are not being given clues to some definitions because of the words or phrases preceding them.

Try the exercise backwards by looking at the definitions and applying the correct word or phrase.

PAST PAPERS

By using as many past papers as possible you can find out exactly what type of definition questions are asked. More importantly, you can see how many marks are available for them, which will tell you exactly how much detail you need to go into in your answer.

If possible, get hold of examiners' mark schemes. These will again give you a clear idea of what is being looked for from your answer.

You will be able to find many examples of 'word games' in magazines such as *Business Review* (Philip Allan, Market Place, Deddington, OX15 OSE). By completing these you are developing your business vocabulary and linking words with their meanings.

For a fuller, alphabetical source of exercises such as these, Ian Marcousé's *A-Z Business Studies Workbook* is very helpful. It contains literally thousands of questions - all with answers in the back of the book.

93.4 Numbers

All business courses contain aspects of number work which can be specifically tested in exams. It must be remembered, however, that there are two clear aspects to numbers:

1 calculation
2 interpretation.

The calculation aspects of business courses are one area where practice is by far the best advice. Each numerical element has its own techniques that you will be expected to be able to demonstrate. The techniques can be learnt, and by working through many examples they can become second nature. Even if mathematics is not your strong point, the calculations ought not to cause problems to an A level student. Something that at first sight appears complex, such as decision trees, requires only simple techniques such as multiplying fractions, adding and subtraction. Going through the workbook sections of this book will be invaluable. Ask your teacher for a photocopy of the answers available in the Teachers Guide.

Once calculated, all business numbers need to be used. It is all very well to calculate the accounting ratios, but if the numbers are then unused the exercise has been wasted. You must attempt to follow each calculation by stating what the numbers are saying and their implications for the business.

93.5 General tips for revision

1 start early
2 know the purpose of your revision
3 work more on weaker areas
4 use past papers as far as is possible
5 keep a clear perspective.

And finally, do no more revision on the night before the exam – it won't help and can only cause you anxiety. Eat well and get a good night's sleep. This way you will be in good physical shape to perform your best in the exam.

MARKING BUSINESS STUDIES PAPERS

If you understand how AS and A level papers in Business Studies are marked then it will be easier for you to obtain high marks.

94.1 Levels of response marking

Almost all Business Studies papers are now marked using levels of response marking schemes. This type of marking scheme operates through the application of a number of descriptors against which your work is assessed. The levels of response are based on assessment objectives such as analysis and evaluation.

The most important thing to understand about levels of response marking is that it rewards quality and depth. It penalises those who write a large quantity of brief, simple points. Full paragraphs that develop a theme will always do better, therefore, than lists of bullet points. The reason is simple. Examiners want to award good grades to those who can write thoughtfully about the subject.

Questions that are only worth up to four marks are unlikely to require more than subject knowledge. They might merely require the appropriate knowledge to be stated or perhaps expressed in the form of explanation. However, questions with higher mark allocations inevitably require application as well as analytic and evaluative writing.

A question worth 10 marks might be assessed using the levels of response set out in the table opposite.

As you can see simply basing your argument on your subject knowledge will severely restrict the number of marks available to you. In this case you may only receive two marks out of the ten available. To gain full marks it is essential to:

- relate your answers to the scenario
- develop your arguments
- offer some judgement in the form of evaluation.

Not all questions require all these skills. It is important that you learn to recognize the skills that each question requires of you.

The example shown on the following page is based on a part of a recent examination set by AQA. You will note that the verb in the question (**discuss**) highlights clearly what was required of candidates sitting this

LEVEL	CONTENT 2 MARKS	APPLICATION 2 MARKS	ANALYSIS 3 MARKS	EVALUATION 3 MARKS
2	**2 marks** Candidate offers two or more relevant arguments.	**2 marks** Candidate applies knowledge effectively to scenario.	**3–2 marks** Good analysis of argument.	**3–2 marks** Sound judgement shown in answers and conclusions.
1	**1 mark** Candidate offers single relevant argument.	**1 mark** Candidate attempts to apply knowledge to scenario.	**1 mark** Limited analysis of argument.	**1 mark** Some judgement shown in response.
0	**0 marks** No relevant content present.	**0 marks** No discernible attempt to apply knowledge	**0 marks** No analysis present.	**0 marks** No evaluation present.

examination. If you answered this question without writing evaluatively, then the maximum mark you could achieve would be 10 out of 15. Similarly, failure to apply your knowledge to the scenario of the question (in this case a firm of tailors) or to use relevant theory to develop analytical arguments, would limit the mark you might achieve.

If you simply wrote a list of points stating whether or not health and safety laws constrain any businesses, you would only receive marks under the 'content' heading; thus three is the maximum mark you would achieve. If however, you related your answer to the circumstances of 'Fitz' then the marks under the heading application could be awarded to you. In the same way the use of analysis and evaluation makes marks in these categories available. You should appreciate that to have good subject knowledge is not enough. You should be able to use that information effectively to demonstrate that you have the necessary examination skills.

The same principles apply to case study and essay writing. Analysis and evaluation are the key skills for exam success. This is why this book has sections within every unit headed 'Issues for Analysis' and 'An evaluation'. When preparing a revision programme, these sections are invaluable. They act as both a summary of the key themes within each unit and as a pointer to the issues most likely to generate the lines of argument for answering the longer, tougher questions.

The key points to remember about exam marking, then, are:

- Markers admire well-developed argument, as long as it is relevant to the question set.
- Bullet point lists generate only knowledge marks – the lowest level of response.
- Arguments should ideally be developed using the theory of the subject …
- … and then be weighed up, in order to show the ability to evaluate (judge) the appropriate answer to the question set.

QUESTION FROM JUNE 2003 EXAMINATION

'Many commentators suggest that employment and health and safety laws are a constraint that damages business competitiveness. Discuss whether this could be said to apply to the case of Fitz.'

Possible answers include:

Case for such laws

- As in this case, managers can act unfeelingly towards staff, and ignore the potential long-term damage to morale and trust caused by short-term fixes; legislation may save them from themselves.
- The same case was made against legislation to ban child chimney sweeps in nineteenth-century Britain, but social improvements are an essential part of economic progress. Society cannot be held back to the level of the world's worst standards.
- Highly interventionist countries such as Sweden and Germany are at least as successful as Britain.

Case against such laws

- Given the acute competitiveness problem of the textile industry, UK legislation may make life too easy for Far East, low-cost producers.
- Followers of a laissez-faire approach emphasise that laws are often ineffective and that 'red tape' can dissuade potential entrepreneurs from taking the plunge … but there is no evidence of this in the case of Fitz.
- The Fitz case shows that people do not lie down and let themselves be exploited. If people are unhappy with the working conditions they can leave; the resignation of five staff was the catalyst for change, not the laws.

Source: AQA Marking Scheme, Unit Three, Summer 2002

LEVEL	CONTENT 3 MARKS	APPLICATION 3 MARKS	ANALYSIS 4 MARKS	EVALUATION 5 MARKS
3				**5 marks** Judgement shown in weighing up the impact of legislation on the competitiveness of "Fitz", giving clear conclusions.
2	**3 marks** At least one point explaining about legislation, showing understanding.	**3 marks** Point or points made are applied in detail to the case.	**4–3 marks** Analysis of the question set using relevant theory.	**4–3 marks** Judgement shown in weighing up the impact of legislation.
1	**2–1 marks** One or more relevant points made about legislation.	**2–1 marks** Point or points made are applied to the case.	**2–1 marks** One or two points applied in a limited way to analyse the question set.	**2–1 marks** Some judgement shown in text or conclusions.
0	**0 marks** No relevant content present.	**0 marks** No relevant points applied to the case.	**0 marks** No analysis of the question set.	**0 marks** No judgement shown in text or conclusion.

RESEARCHING FOR HOMEWORK

Homework is training for exams. In a Business Studies exam you are required to demonstrate a range of skills which need to be learnt and practised. You need to pick up skills of analysis, argument and evaluation. Your teacher will tell you what is involved in each skill, but you need to practise these skills in order to master them in time for your exams. Although there will be opportunities to practise in class, the majority of your training will need to take place outside the classroom.

The ideas that follow present a basic structure designed to help you produce better homework throughout your Business Studies A level.

95.1 Reading around the subject

The key skills of successful Business Studies are analysis and evaluation. In order to demonstrate these skills you need to have an awareness of the reality of the business world. In order to place an argument or answer into context, you should understand what really happens in business. Unless you have worked in business for several years, it is hard to gain this understanding. You need to find a way to simulate the experience.

Newspapers provide a daily set of real life case studies, covering a broad spectrum of topic areas. The *Financial Times* is undoubtedly the richest source of business stories, however the other broadsheets have useful business pages. One useful way to use the business pages of newspapers is to build up a scrapbook. If you cut out one newspaper article per day and write a brief explanation of its relevance to the theory you have studied in class, you should have a comprehensive set of up-to-date case study examples by the time you need to revise for your final exams.

Magazines can be used in a very similar way. *Business Review* magazine is published four times per year and should be available at your school or college – if not, ask your teacher about it. The magazine is specifically tailored for A level Business Studies students and provides a range of different articles related to various areas on the syllabus. In addition, it provides guidance on exam technique, coursework and revision. In addition, trade magazines such as *The*

Grocer provide a valuable insight into the way in which a particular industry works.

Watching television is another way to understand more about business. The main evening news on most days will include a business-related story. BBC1's early morning *Business Breakfast* is a useful way to start the day, BBC2 series such as *Back to the Floor* and *Trouble at the Top* provide useful business insight.

95.2 How to do a case study homework

You should follow a simple pattern when attempting a case study that you have been set for homework. The pattern is shown below:

1 Read the case study the evening it is set.
2 Look up the key terms in the library.
3 Plan your answers to the questions.
4 Check with your teacher that you are thinking along the right lines.
5 Write up full answers to the questions.
6 Read your answers carefully to ensure that they make sense and they answer the questions.

READ THE CASE STUDY

You must read the case study as early as possible. This will allow you to start planning what research needs to be done.

LOOK UP KEY TERMS

You should identify the key terms included in the questions and also try to work out what business concepts are relevant to the case study. Once this is done, you should look up these terms and concepts in a range of different sources.

PLAN YOUR ANSWERS

Make a few brief notes on each question, identifying the key ideas around which you will construct your final answer. At this stage, you do not need to explain fully, but do try to develop your ideas, linking one concept to another when trying to develop an argument.

You should try to get your teacher to have a quick look through your answers at this stage. Your teacher will then be able to tell you if you are working in the right direction or if you have misunderstood the question. If this is the case, your teacher should be able to provide you with some other ideas which you can then go away and research.

WRITE UP FULL ANSWERS

You should try to do this in one go – keep your thoughts focused on the case study in order to ensure that all of your answers are relevant. The most important part of writing out full answers is to check that you are doing what the question asks for. If the question wants you to analyse something, this will usually involve attempting to construct a logical argument, based on a sequence of small steps. Be sure not to miss out any steps that you have taken in building up your argument. This way your arguments will be easy to follow and reliable. If you are asked to evaluate your arguments, you should seek to conclude your answer with some form of judgement, perhaps suggesting which choice a firm should make or which factors are the *most* important when making a decision.

EDIT YOUR ANSWERS

After you have written your answers, try to read them again, perhaps the next day. You should seek to check that you have actually answered each question set – is your work really focused on the question? You may well find that you have begun to talk about irrelevant issues – cut these out of your answer to improve it. You should also try to make sure that your work is easy to read, logically set out and well thought through. Above all, make sure that you have done as good a job as possible.

If at all possible, you will gain significant advantages from using a word processor to produce your homework. Wordprocessed work is always easier to read for teachers and better laid out by students, but these are not the main advantages of wordprocessing your work. A word processor makes editing your work much easier. As you will discover, the key to producing successful homeworks is to reflect upon your first draft and improve upon your initial ideas. Without a word processor, this will often mean writing out an entire essay all over again – a waste of your valuable time.

95.3 Producing better essays for homework

1 Research key terms in the title.
2 Decide what concepts the answer will need to include.
3 Check with your teacher to ensure you are working along the right lines.
4 Read up on those concepts in a range of books.
5 Find some examples to illustrate your answer.
6 Sit down and write your answer to the question in one go.
7 Edit your answer.

95.4 Summary of main lessons to be learnt

TIME

It is age-old advice, but incredibly important – make sure you don't leave it until the last minute. If you are going to get the most out of homeworks, you should follow the steps outlined above. These take time, particularly when you need to check things with your teacher. You must therefore look at homework on the day it is set – then you can work out a series of mini-deadlines to help you work through each stage of the process.

ANSWER THE QUESTION

As with exam papers, the key to earning good marks is to answer the question you have been asked. Make sure that what you have written is relevant to the particular task and that you have actually answered a question, rather than simply writing down everything you know about a concept.

USE A RANGE OF SOURCES

Different books will have slightly different explanations of different topics. It is important that you try to read a range of different explanations before stopping your research. In this way you are likely to develop a broader understanding of the topic being researched.

AS EXAM REVISION FOR BUSINESS STUDIES

AS examinations are aimed to be 'at a level to be expected half way through an A level course'. In other words, about half way between GCSE standard and A level standard. They focus on the skills of Knowledge and Application, though also require some Analysis and Evaluation. It is therefore helpful to make good use of the final sections of each Unit of this book, entitled Issues for Analysis and An Evaluation.

A very valuable supplement to this book is the *Complete A-Z Business Studies Handbook* 4th Edition, by Lines, Marcousé and Martin, published by Hodder & Stoughton, ISBN 0 340 87263 2.

If you are studying this subject at evening classes or as a self-study student, you will find it helpful to obtain the accompanying Teacher's Book. It contains detailed mark schemes to show how best to tackle the Workbook questions, and is obtainable from good bookshops or from Amazon.co.uk; published by Hodder & Stoughton, ISBN 0 340 81113 7.

96.1 AQA

DATA RESPONSE UNIT 1

For revision, read through a Unit, then immediately go through the Revision Questions in the Workbook section, referring back to the text when necessary. Make sure to revise the Key Terms listed, then consider the Revision Exercises.

Examination Unit 1 of the AQA scheme is a data response paper. It has a running time of 60 minutes and contains two questions, both out of 25 marks. At the end of every Unit of this textbook is a Workbook section that includes data response questions. The style, level and timing of these data response questions is a good indication of the actual AS level exams. Do take care to note, though, that some Workbooks contain both AS and A2 questions. Needless to say, make sure you choose the AS ones.

For daily revision of approximately 90 minutes:
1 Read a Unit and answer the Revision Questions
2 Learn the Key Terms
3 Do one AS level data response question

In the case of the Examination Unit 1, this revision programme will require 20 days. In addition allow two days for going back over the chapters of the book, re-reading the short sections called Issues for Analysis and An Evaluation. At the same time, check your recall of the Key Terms.

The key subject content for AS level is in the following Units:

Examination Unit 1 AS Marketing and Finance
- Marketing: 1, 2, 3, 4, 5, 6, 7, 9, 10, 11, 13
- Finance: 14, 15, 16, 17.1 to 17.4, 18, 19.1 to 19.4, 20, 27, 28.1 to 28.2

EXAMINATION UNITS 2 AND 3

Whereas a data response paper focuses on knowledge, understanding and application, case studies have a tighter focus on analysis and evaluation. This makes it important to write longer, deeper answers focusing upon one or two key themes, rather than broad answers that make many points. Naturally, the sections called Issues for Analysis and An Evaluation become even more important than for the first paper.

Recommended revision approach:

1 Read each Unit at a time, briefly answering the Revision Questions
2 Learn the Key Terms
3 Tackle one AS level data response question
4 Try the following case studies:
   - The Mobile Video Phone, page 454
   - Brooks, page 520
   - Integrated Case Study, page 524
   - Case Study, page 545

The key subject content for AS level is in the following Units:

Examination Unit 2 AS People and Operations
- People: 30, 31, 32, 33, 35, 36, 40, 45
- Operations management: 46, 47, 48, 49, 50, 51, 52, 55, 56, 59

Examination Unit 3 AS External Influences, Objectives and Strategy
- External Influences: 60, 61, 62, 63, 64, 68, 70, 73, 74
- Objectives and Strategy: 69, 75, 76, 77, 81

96.2 OCR

EXAMINATION UNIT 1 BUSINESSES, THEIR OBJECTIVES AND ENVIRONMENT

This 60-minute exam consists of pre-issued questions based upon a case study. In fact the material will often be drawn from newspaper articles, therefore the exam is very similar to a data response paper. It is therefore wise to use the data response questions as well as the case studies that come at the end of each Unit of this book.

For AS revision, the following Units are recommended:

- Nature, Classification and Objectives of Business: 75, 76, 77, 69, 78, 81, 82
- External Influences: 60, 61, 62, 63, 64, 65.1–65.4, 68, 70, 73, 74

For revision, read through a Unit, then immediately go through the Revision Questions in the Workbook section, referring back to the text when necessary. Make sure to revise the Key Terms listed, then consider the Revision Exercises. For the OCR Examination Unit 1 it will be helpful to tackle a mixture of data response and case study questions. The following are recommended especially:

- Data Response B2 on page 432
- Data Response B1 on page 438
- Data Response B1 on page 445
- The Mobile Video-phone, page 454
- Brooks, page 520
- Integrated Case Study, page 524
- Data Response B1 on page 533
- Data Response B1 on page 539
- Case Study, page 545
- Data Response B1 on page 575
- Data Response B1 on page 582

For daily revision of approximately 90 minutes:

1 Read a Unit and answer the Revision Questions
2 Learn the Key Terms
3 Do one AS level data response or case study exercise

EXAMINATION UNIT 2 BUSINESS IN ACTION

This 45-minute exam consists of one compulsory data response question based upon unseen material. The stimulus material is likely to be drawn from newspaper articles or devised by the examiners to test numerical aspects of the subject. Comparable questions are included at the end of each Unit of this book.

For AS revision, the following Units are recommended:

- Marketing: 1, 2, 3, 4, 5, 9.1–9.6, 10, 13
- Finance and Accounting: 14, 15, 16, 18, 21.1–21.4, 22.1–22.3, 24.1–24.3, 26.1–26.4 (payback and ARR only), 27

- People: 30, 31, 32, 33, 35, 36, 40, 45
- Operations Management: 46, 47, 48, 49, 50, 52, 55, 56, 59

When revising, particular care should be taken over numerate topics such as price elasticity, cash flow, investment appraisal (pay-back and ARR) and break-even analysis. These are likely to be tested quite regularly within this exam. Make a particular effort to practise:

- Price elasticity: Revision questions A1–10 and B1 on page 63
- Cash flow: Revision Exercise B1 on page 126
- Investment appraisal: Revision Questions A1–10 and Revision Exercise B1 Question 1
- Break-even: Revision Exercises B1 and B2 on page 113

Leading up to the exam, for daily revision of approximately 90 minutes:

1 Read a Unit and answer the Revision Questions
2 Learn the Key Terms
3 Do one AS level data response exercise

EXAMINATION UNIT 3 BUSINESS BEHAVIOUR

This 75-minute exam consists of four compulsory questions based upon a pre-issued case study. The subject content combines the above Examination Units 1 and 2. Therefore the only extra work involved is to look carefully at the pre-released case material and to prepare for the particular demands of case study technique. Read Unit 91 of this book for guidance from a senior OCR examiner.

In addition to the revision suggestions for Exams 1 and 2 (above) it would be helpful to tackle the following case studies from this book:

- Page 93: Integrated (Marketing) Case Study
- Page 224: B2 Case Study
- Page 241: B2 Case Study 'Toshiba Changing Course'
- Page 335: B2 Case Study 'Expanding European Airways'
- Page 342: B2 Case Study
- Page 390: B2 Case Study 'Tricolour'

96.3 Edexcel

EXAMINATION UNIT 1 BUSINESS STRUCTURES, OBJECTIVES AND EXTERNAL INFLUENCES

All three examination units will be based upon a comon pre-issued case study. This 60-minute examination consists of three compulsory questions. For revision, read through one of the Units of this book, then immediately go through the Revision Questions in the Workbook section, referring back to the text when necessary. Make sure to revise the Key Terms listed, then consider the Revision Exercises. The style, level and timing of the data response questions is a good indication of the actual AS level exams. Do take care to note, though, that some Workbooks contain both AS and A2 questions. Needless to say, make sure you choose the AS ones.

For daily revision of approximately 90 minutes:

1 Read a Unit and answer the Revision Questions
2 Learn the Key Terms
3 Do one AS level data response question

In addition, allow two days for going back over the chapters of the book, re-reading the short sections called Issues for Analysis and An Evaluation. At the same time, check your recall of the Key Terms.

The key subject content for AS level Exam Unit 1 is in the following Units:

- External Factors: 9, 61, 62, 63, 64, 67, 68, 69, 75, 76, 81, 82
- Internal Factors: 31, 32, 33, 34, 35, 37, 45

EXAMINATION UNIT 2 MARKETING AND PRODUCTION

This Unit is examined by 60 minutes of questions based on pre-seen material. Case studies have a focus on analysis and evaluation. This makes it important to write relatively long answers focusing upon one or two key themes, rather than broad answers that make many points. The textbook sections called Issues for Analysis and An Evaluation become especially important.

Recommended revision approach:

1 Read each Unit at a time, briefly answering the Revision Questions

2 Learn the Key Terms
3 Tackle one AS level data response question
4 Try the following case studies:
- Case Study B2, page 20
- Integrated Case Study, page 93
- Case Study B2 page 335
- Case Study B2, page 388

The key subject content for AS level Exam Unit 2 is in the following Units:

- Marketing: 1, 2, 3, 4, 5, 6, 7, 9, 10, 11, 13
- Operations management: 46, 47, 48, 49, 55, 56

EXAMINATION UNIT 3 FINANCIAL MANAGEMENT

This Unit is examined by 60 minutes of questions based upon pre-seen case material. This exam will place especial importance upon business calculations, particularly break-even analysis and ratio analysis.

Recommended revision approach:

1 Read each Unit at a time, briefly answering the Revision Questions
2 Learn the Key Terms
3 Tackle one AS level data response question

The key subject content for AS level Exam Unit 3 is in the following Units:

- Finance and Accounting : 14, 15, 16, 17, 18, 19, 20, 21, 22, 23, 24, 25, 27, 29

633

INDEX

Minimum wages have been part of Labour party policy for some time. The objective is to prevent employers from paying wages which can provide only a very low standard of living. The drawback to a minimum wage from the employer's point of view is that it raises costs and may lead to rising prices and loss of competitiveness. Also, by making the cost of employing labour higher, it gives employers an incentive to reduce the number of jobs. However, most developed countries have a legal minimum wage because lower wage rates are considered unacceptable.

THE MINIMUM WAGE

The national minimum wage (NMW) was introduced in 1999. It was set at £4.20 in October 2002. The rate for 18–21 year olds was set at £3.60. To start with, the impact on both jobs and wages was rather uncertain. In London, wages were already so much above the national average that only 1.8% of adults benefited. In other regions it was more significant. In north-east England and Wales, the benefit was greater: 8.7% and 7.6% respectively.

The view from the Confederation of British Industry was that the NMW had been set low and that its impact on job creation was 'contained'. Adair Turner, the then CBI Director-General said 'Some sectors have encountered specific problems. These range from pubs and corner shops to homes for the elderly'.

Of the people who gained from the NMW, 70% were women. The New Earnings Survey for 2001, produced by the Office for National Statistics, found that 10% of women manual workers were still paid less than £4 per hour. They would be likely to benefit from rises in the NMW.

The occupations where earnings increased the most were in hairdressing, hospitality, cleaning and security. Waitresses on average received 9% more in wages. There was also some impact in clothing and textiles.

Despite regular increases, the NMW is still quite low by international standards. The Council of Europe's 'decency threshold' in 2002 was just under £8 an hour.

IN Business

67.3 Taxing business

Business profits are taxed in the same way as income is taxed. These are direct taxes, designed to raise revenue and help pay for the services which governments provide. **Corporation tax** is set at a standard rate of 30p in the pound, with a 20p rate for small businesses. In addition to corporation tax, businesses pay the uniform business rate to their local authority. This is based on the value of the property owned by the business.

In recent years corporation tax rates have been reduced in order to make life easier for businesses. Complex regulations govern the way investment spending can be written off for tax purposes and in practice these have a big impact on the amounts actually paid. Figure 67.2 shows how the share of corporation tax in total direct tax revenue has varied. Recession can affect the amount paid, as well as the percentage rate set by government.

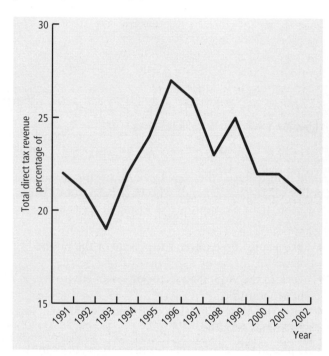

Figure 67.3 Corporation taxes (Source: Inland Revenue website)

67.4 Regulate, control or allow?

As economies develop, governments tend to make more and more rules about how businesses must operate. These rules taken together are collectively known as regulation. Some aspects of regulation are not controversial. The regulation of food industries to ensure their products are safe to eat is an example. However, regulation can restrict competition. Equally, it can be used to prevent monopolies from exploiting their market power. So regulation and competition policy are closely related. Competition policy itself is used to prevent monopoly power from developing through mergers and other business strategies.